Preface

The 1976 edition of the *Handbook of Industrial and Organizational Psychology* contained only a single chapter having anything to do with cross-cultural issues. In fact, it was titled *Cross-cultural Issues in Industrial and Organizational Psychology,* and its authors were Gerald Barrett and Bernard Bass. Their chapter discussed four substantive areas chosen because they were not likely to be sensitive to cross-cultural effects: motivation and attitudes, management and supervision, assessment, and training.

In planning the structure of this second edition of the *Handbook,* Dunnette naively decided once again to include just a single chapter about cross-cultural issues. Harry Triandis was asked to author such a chapter, and he quickly agreed to do so. In retrospect, it seems that he just as quickly wrote the chapter because his finished chapter was in our editorial offices within a few months—well before the deadline that had been suggested, and, in fact, even before final arrangements had been completed with our publisher, Consulting Psychologists Press (CPP).

By the time a publishing agreement had been developed with CPP, it became apparent that the second edition would be published in several volumes instead of only one. This coincided with our recognition of what should have been obvious much earlier: The world had become a far different place during the last decade of the twentieth century than it had been twenty years earlier at the time the first edition of the *Handbook* had been developed. Triandis' chapter, written for this second edition, describes the pace of change, the globalization of industrial and organizational psychology, and the interdependencies of the countries and peoples of the world. Obviously, a single chapter could not properly represent nor sufficiently elaborate the implications of the facts recognized so clearly in the Triandis chapter.

Our publishers accepted our proposal to develop a fourth volume of the current *Handbook* so that proper representation could be given to industrial and organizational psychology as seen by authors from several other countries. Equally important, if not more so, was Triandis' willingness to step in as a senior editor of this fourth volume.

Accordingly, this fourth volume contains chapters written by authors from Australia, France, Germany, Hong Kong, India, Israel (two), Japan (two), the Netherlands, the People's Republic of China, Spain, and the United Kingdom.

Our letters to authors requesting chapters from them emphasized that we did not want to constrain them in any way according to their choice of subject matter. Instead, we asked that they choose subjects according to their own areas of interest, expertise, or research activities. We were rewarded with chapters representing a broad range of content. Taken together, these chapters from authors throughout the world represent a wealth of information about research and practice of industrial and organizational psychology in countries outside the United States.

Below, we provide a short listing and a few comments about each of the chapters in this volume.

- Raymond Katzell was asked several years ago to provide an overview and discussion of the chapters contained in the first three volumes of this second edition of the *Handbook*. He has done far more than this in chapter 1 of this volume. He discusses meta-trends in industrial and organizational psychology and places the content of these 41 chapters in the context of those trends.

- In chapter 2, Triandis introduces the field of cross-cultural industrial and organizational psychology in the context of changes in the international economy.

- Lévy-Leboyer, in chapter 3, surveys methods employed by the industrial countries of Europe in assessing and selecting personnel.

- In chapter 4, Hesketh and Bochner discuss the impact of the accelerated pace of technological change and increased intercultural interaction on the nature of training and development required in an increasingly global economy.

- Ronen, in chapter 5, presents a theoretical integration of factors that are more motivating to different groups of employees working in different cultures.

- Frese and Zapf, in chapter 6, state that a most important contribution in Germany has been action theory, and they argue convincingly that action theory is *the* important theory for understanding work behavior in industrial and organizational psychology.

- In chapter 7, Thierry and Meijman discuss the importance of aspects of time (e.g., work scheduling, flextime, shiftwork, etc.) in relation to employees' responses to work and to work outcomes (e.g., accidents, productivity, turnover, etc.).

- Graen and Wakabayashi, in chapter 8, discuss the cross-cultural findings related to the development of reciprocal bonds of harmony, obligation, and trust between two or more persons in an organization.

They summarize considerable empirical support for Graen's theory of leadership making.

- Forteza and Prieto, in chapter 9, and Warr, in chapter 10, discuss issues related to aging and work. Forteza and Prieto examine life cycles and labor cycles of employees and their effects on psychological functioning. Warr reviews stereotypes about the elderly and stresses that both declines and gains in job performance occur over the span of a person's work life. For example, increases in efficiency with age are not uncommon in jobs involving knowledge-based judgments where there is little time pressure. In contrast, declines may be expected with age in jobs that are continuous and involve paced data processing.

- In chapter 11, Erez argues that cross-cultural industrial and organizational psychology needs to bring culture into its important models. She contrasts self-derived needs with group-derived needs and examines implications for work behavior of these differing types of needs.

- Kashima and Callan, in chapter 12, examine the Japanese work group by contrasting the family metaphor of the Japanese organization with the machine metaphor of Western organization.

- In chapter 13, Redding, Norman, and Schlander argue that the *organization* has different meanings in every culture and that this results in variations across cultures in the nature of individuals' attachments to organizations. They suggest implications of these differences in meanings for theories of organization, leadership, and motivation.

- Wang, in chapter 14, examines the role of culture in economic reform and industrial and organizational psychology in China. In so doing, he describes the close collaboration between psychologists and practitioners (such as managers and government officials) in applying theories of industrial and organizational psychology to economic reform.

- In chapter 15, Sinha describes and discusses the effects of a culture that is collectivist, emphasizing hierarchy and personalized relationships. Sinha also presents his own theory of leadership and describes its usefulnesss in India.

- In the final chapter of this volume, Triandis, Kurowski, and Gelfand examine cultural variations within the United States. They present a theoretical model that is useful in describing the complexities of relationships between a number of relevant constructs. The model can also be used to emphasize several ways in which interpersonal relationships across cultures may be improved.

As has been true of contributors to the first three volumes, the level of scholarship shown by all contributors to volume 4 has been superb. Each author obviously devoted serious and extended effort to the task of organizing new ideas and communicating them effectively. The hundreds of industrial and organizational psychologists who have joined our ranks over the last two decades, as well as the next several generations of entering students of industrial and organizational psychology and organizational behavior, will profit from what is in this volume and in the previous three volumes of this second edition of the *Handbook*.

As with the previous two volumes, Kim Downing has provided indispensable assistance. She handles a major portion of the correspondence with authors of these chapters and with a vast number of other authors and publishers during the process of obtaining required permissions. She most certainly deserves a medal of honor for diligence and perspicacity. Kim tackled problems as they appeared and solved them quickly and efficiently. As with the first three volumes, our editorial activities were eased considerably by her quickness, her persistence, and on occasion, her friendly audacity when called upon to exercise it.

We have been gratified that we have had the opportunity to work with Consulting Psychologists Press as our publisher. We appreciate the helpfulness of Bob Most, John Black,* and, in particular, CPP's president and CEO, Lorin Letendre, for their support and enthusiasm in choosing this project as a major vehicle for their expansion into publishing state-of-the-art contributions in industrial and organizational psychology.

A special advantage in working with Consulting Psychologists Press has been the privilege of working with the director of their book division, Lee Langhammer Law, and associate editor, Kathleen Hummel. Lee managed the editing and production of volumes 1 and 2. Kathy and Lee worked together on volume 3, and Kathy has been largely responsible for shepherding all aspects of editing and seeing the present volume through to successful completion. Both Lee and Kathy carried these activities through with wisdom and patience. They have been more helpful to us and to our contributing authors than we could have imagined when we first undertook this enterprise many years ago.

The so-called incidental expenses involved in a project of this magnitude can grow far beyond what one would ever reasonably estimate. Hundreds of phone calls, thousands of pages of copying costs, and a seemingly endless stream of letters and packages requiring substantial amounts of postage, air express fees, and other special delivery charges accumulated over the days, weeks, months, and years. These costs have been borne by grants made to the project by Personnel Decisions Research Institute and by the Department of Psychology of the University of Illinois in Urbana/Champaign. It is fair to say that the financial feasibility of this undertaking would be difficult to justify purely on the basis of sound

---

* It is with great sadness that we report that John Black died on June 3, 1993. He founded CPP in 1956 and served as its president, CEO, and Chairman until his death.

business reasoning. The generosity of PDRI's Board of Trustees and of the Illinois Psychology Department is deeply appreciated for their willingness to grant facilities and funds to help in handling the substantial incidental expenses accumulated over the lifetime of this effort.

HARRY C. TRIANDIS
MARVIN D. DUNNETTE
LEAETTA M. HOUGH
St. Paul, Minnesota
July 1993

Meta-trends in Industrial and Organizational Psychology

Ray Katzell, the Dean of industrial and organization psychology, was asked to evaluate the achievements of the field during the past 20 years by reviewing the first three volumes of the *Handbook*. He makes suggestions about the subjects that we need to concentrate on in the future in order to provide more depth and scope to industrial and organizational psychology.

He points out that while it is true that our conceptions, theories, and methods that have developed during the last 20 years allow us to cope better with the complexities of our subject matter, the world keeps changing, and so must industrial and organizational psychology. And complexities, such as diversity and the international dimension, must also be mastered.

He is happy to see that what we have learned contributes substantially to the economic effectiveness of work organizations and to the quality of employee work life, and contributes also to the scientific knowledge of human nature in general. He presents several meta-trends that counterbalance the forces that make for fragmentation and overspecialization. The field is maturing, but it is still true that what we don't know exceeds what we do know. That makes the *Handbook* a springboard for the new generation of industrial and organizational psychologists so that they can take off and explore new horizons.

—THE EDITORS

CHAPTER 1

Contemporary Meta-trends in Industrial and Organizational Psychology

Raymond A. Katzell
New York University

This chapter is a sort of epilogue to the first three volumes of the Handbook.
*It identifies and discusses 12 themes or trends, each of which emerged in multiple
chapters of those volumes. They were chosen because, by linking individual
chapters, they might have an integrative function—one that may serve to bind
diverse parts of industrial and organizational psychology into larger unities that
share common interests and concerns. It was also my hope that they might shed
light on the directions in which the field is moving. Because these themes go
beyond the boundaries of individual chapters, the term* meta-trend *was coined
to differentiate them from those discussed by the authors of the individual
chapters.*

*Forced by the realities of time and space to discuss a limited number of
meta-trends, I selected 12 that seemed to me to be particularly important to the
science and practice of industrial and organizational psychology and that, in
addition, were of current and growing interest to the field. (Personal predilection
also undoubtedly played a part, as did closure provided by the round number of
a dozen.) The final list comprises the following: "Time Is of the Essence"; "The
Whole Is More Than the Sum of Its Parts"; "Systems Concepts, Models, and
Theories"; "Cybernetics in Industrial and Organizational Psychology"; "The
Cognitive Perspective"; "Multiple Levels"; "The Revival of Personality";
"Groups at Work"; "Attending to Work Force Diversity"; "Nontraditional
Outcomes"; "Muddles in Methodology"; and "Enter Technology."*

I came away from my reading deeply impressed by evidence of the maturing of industrial and organizational psychology. Much knowledge has been generated that has contributed to science and practice. There is evidence, too, of growing wisdom and compassion and of striving to do even better. The viability of the 12 meta-trends, and of others that were not discussed, points to the existence of centripetal forces that help counter those making for overspecialization and fragmentation.

Because the first three volumes of the Handbook *were based largely on the work of American industrial and organizational psychologists, the picture reported in this epilogue necessarily has the same focus. Hopefully, the remaining chapters in the present volume will help broaden that view.*

Introduction

WHEN THE *HANDBOOK* editors invited me to write an epilogue chapter to the first three volumes, I accepted with a mixture of trepidation and arousal: trepidation because of the scope and difficulty of the assignment, arousal because of the well-known effect of challenging goals. The editors left to me the matter of providing goal clarity.

My initial thought was to discuss the various contributions in historical perspective, but I soon realized that to do so would require adding still another volume to the *Handbook*. (Anyone interested in my less ambitious historical views is invited to read the article by Katzell and Austin, 1992, on the development of industrial and organizational psychology in the United States.) An alternative possibility was to write something like a chapter in the *Annual Review of Psychology*, in this instance, reviewing the 41 chapters and 2,076 pages (exclusive of indexes and credits). On second thought, that struck me as rather useless. For one thing, unlike the scattered sources surveyed in an *Annual Review* chapter, the *Handbook* is all in one place—or three, anyway. Furthermore, a person interested in an overview of the *Handbook* contents can read the chapter abstracts and concluding summaries, together with the editor's integrating introductions to the various sections.

It seemed to me that perhaps what might make a useful epilogue is something overarching, something that would tie the parts of the books together, that cannot be learned by considering the chapters singly or by section. In that vein, it struck me that the chapter authors had already identified issues, trends, and themes that run through their respective subjects. What remained to be done was to identify trends and topics that emerged in a number of subjects and that could provide a kind of integration to diverse chapters. With the editors' concurrence, that's what I set forth as the agenda for this chapter. I have coined the word *meta-trends* for these overarching themes, since they go beyond those observed in the individual chapters—the prefix, *meta,* meaning beyond (not mega-trend, *pace* John Naisbitt, although some of the trends may indeed turn out to be mega).

There are, of course, many themes that transcend individual chapters. Since practical considerations required me to be selective, I set certain criteria for my choices. First, the trends must be important to science and practice of industrial and organizational psychology (if it's important to one, it's bound sooner or later to be important to the other). For a trend to meet that criterion, it had to impress me as advancing the field by an appreciable increment, or at least promising to do so.

A second criterion is that the trend must be recent, or at least on an upward trajectory. Since, by definition, trends must have a history, I decided to mention their early roots. But the emphasis is on recent and emerging developments with future implications.

Finally and in retrospect, I must confess that I probably opted to discuss some trends and not others based on my personal apperceptive mass (there's history for you), or if you prefer, cognitive schema. So if you can think of a trend that seems to meet the first two criteria but is not discussed, attribute that to the third criterion plus limitations of space and time.

The final list of meta-trends numbers an even dozen. It includes, in no particular order:

- "Time Is of the Essence," or the developmental perspective in industrial and organizational psychology
- "The Whole Is More Than the Sum of Its Parts," or the use of complex models and theories
- "Systems Concepts, Models, and Theories"
- "Cybernetics in Industrial and Organizational Psychology"
- "The Cognitive Perspective"
- "Multiple Levels"
- "The Revival of Personality"
- "Groups at Work"
- "Attending to Work Force Diversity"
- "Nontraditional Outcomes"
- "Muddles in Methodology"
- "Enter Technology"

Although my analysis of each of those meta-trends draws heavily on the trends in theory, research, and practice discussed in various of the *Handbook* chapters, I inevitably found it useful to refer to other literature, too.

The meta-trends will be discussed in the order listed above, followed by an overview.

Time Is of the Essence

Most psychologists, including those of the industrial and organizational variety, act as if the phenomena they are dealing with can be understood in the time frame of the present. Relatively little attention is given to the extent to which those phenomena may differ with time.

Yet historical data may illuminate the present, and in turn can help us cope with the future.

Perhaps responding to a warning by Ghiselli (1974) about the "impermanence of facts," industrial and organizational psychologists are increasingly attending to questions of how things got the way they are and of why and how things change or persist over time. In short, time has become increasingly a matter of interest, either as an independent or a moderator variable. We will illustrate that meta-trend by discussing the dynamic nature of criteria, historical determinants of attitudes and motivation, seeing workers in developmental terms, and changes in group behavior over time.

Dynamic Criteria

One of the earliest statements regarding the phenomenon of dynamic criteria in industrial and organizational psychology was expressed by Ghiselli (1956), who noted that aspects of job performance might change as people become more experienced in their work. As a consequence, the predictability of a criterion reflecting a particular aspect of job performance would be subject to change as time went on.

Updates of this notion are found in the reviews by Ackerman and Humphreys (1990) and by Weiss (1990), in volume 1 of this *Handbook*, of the extensive later literature dealing with the predictive strength of cognitive ability and task-specific tests for criteria of performance at different stages of learning. It appears that the importance of cognitive factors diminishes with practice on tasks amenable to greater automaticity of task performance. There is also evidence indicating that the validity of task-specific tests may correspondingly increase (Fleishman, 1972). In effect, early task performance seems to be more dependent on general learning ability, whereas later performance may depend more on task-specific skills with practice of such tasks.

A study by Helmreich, Sawin, and Carlsrud (1986), involving quite different tests and work from the foregoing, is also supportive of the dynamic criterion concept. They found that none of the tests of three aspects of achievement motivation predicted the performance of airline reservation agents after three months on the job, whereas two of them had significant correlations with performance criteria after six months.

In this example as well as the previous one, retrospective explanations seem to make sense. In the case of the reservation agents, the findings could be due to the possibility that motivational factors were unimportant relative to cognitive ones at the early stage, but not after the jobs had been learned. The early salience of cognitive factors was similarly exhibited in studies of psychomotor and intellectual tasks. The dominant role of cognitive ability during the stage of learning a task or job, and the greater relevance of other factors thereafter, has been captured in a two-stage dynamic model by Murphy (1989). Adler and Weiss (1988) have similarly presented evidence that personality factors become more important relative to cognitive ones after early stages of employment.

Barrett, Caldwell, and Alexander (1985) reviewed a number of previous studies bearing on the issue of dynamic criteria and concluded that the supportive findings could be attributed mostly to artifacts. However, their interpretation was challenged by Austin, Humphreys, and Hulin (1989), who felt that the findings of those studies may constitute a simplex with validity coefficients decreasing

over time. Ackerman (1989) questioned the ubiquity of decay over time of ability measures and argued that validity can be maintained and, in some instances, even increased over time. But a recent meta-analysis of a large number of studies has further supported the simplex hypothesis; the average within-study correlation between the size of a validity coefficient and the time at which performance is measured was found to equal −.80 (Hulin, Henry, & Noon, 1990).[1] Decay over time of the predictive validity of biodata has also been noted in a set of studies discussed by Mumford and Stokes (1992).

In addition to differences in psychological requirements discussed above, there are several possible explanations for this kind of effect: As time goes on, people may change; they may employ different task strategies; the nature of the work may change; different standards of performance may be applied; and/or different resources may become available. This suggests an additional research agenda—understanding the factors that account for changes in predictors and criteria over time (cf. Ackerman & Humphreys, 1990). In addition to explaining the foregoing effects, that research would clarify how workers and work change with time, a subject of interest in itself.

The possibility of change in the ingredients of a criterion over time is, of course, relevant to inquiries into the relationships between performance and independent variables other than predictors. An example illustrating its relevance to evaluation of training is provided by Hand, Richards, and Slocum (1973). Those investigators found no change in behavior three months after completion of a human relations training program, but changes did become manifest 18 months after training. As suggested in the chapter by Hellervik, Hazucha, and Schneider (1992) in volume 3 of this *Handbook*, complex criterion behaviors may require posttraining practice before they become manifest. Again, however, such explanations are hypotheses subject to empirical inquiry into why criteria are dynamic.

Persistence and Change in Motivated Behavior

Both the cognitive and environmental emphases in contemporary psychology are reflected in a tendency to envision workers' motivation and attitudes episodically, that is, as determined by essentially proximal, here-and-now conditions: perceptions of instrumentality and expectancy, goals and intentions, incentives and rewards, leader and peer behavior, and so forth. However, there is growing awareness that such phenomena are also shaped by more distal factors in the person's history. For example, Weiss and Ilgen (1985) made a plausible case for routinization as a basis for much of the behavior people exhibit in their work. Naylor, Pritchard, and Ilgen (1980) proposed a dispositional determinant of effort expenditure in work. Similarly, Katzell and Thompson (1990) suggested that people bring to their proximal work situations habitual attitudes and action dispositions resulting from previous reinforcement.

Motivational tendencies that operate continuously over relatively long periods of time are a central feature of the motivation theory of Atkinson and Birch (1970, 1974); behavior at any given time is viewed as a consequence of the relative dominance of various of those tendencies, depending on the operation of instigating and inhibiting forces. In this view, again we see the emphasis on motivational dynamics that can be understood only in a relatively long-term perspective. Fichman (1988) applied this perspective with some success in predicting absenteeism and attendance among coal miners.

Evidence of a considerable degree of consistency of behavior and attitudes in different work settings at different points in time (e.g. Staw, Bell, & Clausen, 1986; Staw & Ross, 1985; Stogdill, Shartle, Scott, Coon, & Jaynes,

1956) supports the contention that enduring habits and dispositions of people affect their responses to work situations in addition to proximal conditions. There is even evidence of biological influences on such phenomena (Arvey, Bouchard, Segal, & Abraham, 1989). In her *Handbook* chapter, Kanfer (1990, vol. 1) persuasively set forth the need to consider distal as well as proximal factors in understanding motivation. All this suggests the potential usefulness of measuring those proclivities, of understanding their etiology, and of devising ways of managing counterproductive tendencies.

The Developmental Perspective

The preceding treatments of time viewed it as a moderator of relationships or as a perspective through which to examine the persistence or change in certain motivational processes. In this section, we will consider attention being devoted to evolution of work-related behavior over relatively long periods of time: in particular, intraindividual change and stability, the patterning of life history events, and career development.

Changes in Personal Characteristics. The growing attention to the extent to which changes in specific characteristics occur over time was nicely illustrated in the *Handbook* chapter by Hellervik, Hazucha, and Schneider (1992, vol. 3). On the basis of their review of a number of studies, they concluded that measures of personality and interest generally are quite stable over time, although there are substantial individual differences in that regard.

Howard and Bray (1988) similarly reported consistency in personality measures of AT&T managers over a 20-year period, when stability was defined in terms of test-retest correlations. However, they also found significant mean changes, including increasing needs for achievement, aggression, and autonomy, and decreasing needs for advancement, affiliation, deference, and abasement. Interpersonal skills also declined over the eight-year period in which it was studied, probably because of lower motivation to be interpersonally effective. Longitudinal data analyzed by Andrisani and Nestel (1976) indicated that occupational success induces greater internality in a measure of locus of control.

Howard and Bray (1988) found that cognitive ability improved during the first 8 years of their study, but pretty much leveled off over the final 12 years. However, there was some continuing improvement in the verbal component that was counterbalanced by a decline in the quantitative area. It should be noted that their subjects were still middle-aged at year 20. Numerous other studies have reported some decline in various aspects of intellectual functioning in later life (Botwinick, 1977; Schaie, 1982). To what extent that represents a decrement in ability versus a decrement in performance is unclear (Datan, Rodeheaver, & Hughes, 1987). Performance depends not only on ability but on motivation, energy, response speed, task strategy, and so forth.

Whether the decrement is one of ability or performance is not a trivial issue to psychologists concerned with organizational behavior, for the work force will increasingly be populated with older people. If the problem is one of intellectual ability, the operative strategy would have to be primarily one of matching people and jobs, at least until there is clearer evidence that training or medication can overcome it. On the other hand, if the issue relates to other aspects of performance, it would seem feasible to devise techniques for dealing with declining motivation, less efficient task strategies, or other psychological problems; even physical deficiencies might be overcome by interventions such as changes in equipment, job redesign, or shorter work schedules.

Life History Patterns. With relatively few exceptions (Owens, 1976), life history data have historically been treated in industrial and organizational psychology in a radically empirical fashion. Usually, large numbers of biodata items were screened for their correlations with criteria of interest and assembled into an empirically keyed questionnaire with little attention to their construct representation. Among the more recent trends, informed by a theoretical perspective, has been the identification of patterns of biographical events that show continuity over considerable periods of the individuals' lives. These patterns are not necessarily defined by invariant items, but rather by underlying themes that extend over time. An example is the identification of a theme of accomplishment in biographical data used for selecting professionals (Hough, 1984).

Extending the work of Owens and Schoenfeldt (1979), Mumford and Stokes (1992, vol. 3) in their *Handbook* chapter showed that biodata can define typologies of people sharing similar life history patterns, such as "unconventional overachieving leaders" or "enterprising intellectuals." It has been shown that the degree to which a person's job is congruent with his or her earlier developmental history is related to job satisfaction, job involvement, and job level. In short, a job can be viewed as an extension of a person's history of finding certain kinds of experiences and activities rewarding or not: To the extent that their work is consistent with a coherent history of rewarding activities and events, people are likely to find it a source of satisfaction and achievement. Schoenfeldt (1974) employed this concept in developing a system for matching people and jobs on the basis of biodata. There are recent indications that people who have not had coherent evolution of their life histories may be less likely to be as affected by their jobs (Mumford & Stokes, 1992).

Career Development. The significance of earlier life history for adjustment and performance in one's job evidently deserves more attention than it is receiving as a basis for personnel assessment. In addition, it has implications for career development. As we will observe in the section on nontraditional outcomes, that topic has only recently attracted industrial and organizational psychologists. As organizations become more volatile as a result of technological, economic, political, social, and corporate changes, the world of work is changing apace: Old careers are disappearing, new ones are emerging, and changes in the careers of individuals are occurring earlier, more frequently, and more radically (Cornish, 1988). Responding to this scenario, the Society for Industrial and Organizational Psychology (SIOP) elected to devote the initial volume in its "Frontiers" series to the topic of career development in organizations (Hall & Associates, 1986).

As noted there, career development issues embroil both the individual, in career planning, and the employing organization, in career management. Both sets of concerns converge on the target of making career change as effective and smooth a transition as possible. In turn, this implies that each career stage should evolve from previous career successes, in much the same way as is more broadly represented in the coherent life history patterns described above. This is a challenging assignment. Success in dealing with it will result in important benefits to individuals, organizations, and society. There is still much to be learned about the patterns and continuities that optimize career development and about the technology of using that information in career planning and management.

Another approach to dealing with life history patterns is to examine different stages in people's lives. This was the method employed by Levinson and Associates (1978). One of the aspects of life that they examined in their sample of men was that of occupation. The investigators observed that "at best, [a man's] occupation permits the fulfillment of basic values and goals. At worst, a man's work life over the years

is oppressing and corruptive, and contributes to a growing alienation from self, work and society"(p. 45). Occupational behavior typically assumes certain patterns at different stages in life. In a man's twenties, he is typically a novice who is immersed in forming an occupation; that involves not only choosing but also exploring, developing skills, and acquiring credentials. By his early thirties and into his forties, his central concerns are likely to involve advancement in status, income, and occupation, in keeping with the general metaphor of a ladder that characterizes this "settling down" phase. Likewise, different career concerns dominate other stages of life.

Sheehy (1976) discerned developmental stages in the working lives of women, too, but they tend to be more variable since the place of work differs according to the more general pattern of women's lives—for example, whether or when they accord higher priority to family or career.

The Time Dimension in Groups

Early conceptions of group formation and behavior typically viewed groups as passing through certain fixed stages, summarized by Tuckman (1965) as forming, storming, norming, and performing. But more recent formulations (Gersick, 1988; McGrath, 1991) view groups as responsive to varying task and time demands, and therefore as not following given sequences of behavior. Gersick (1989) developed and tested a model that suggests that a group's attention to time demands and pacing facilitate its progress in creative projects. Over a period of years, the creativity and performance of problem-solving groups may decline, partly as a result of decreased communication among members (Katz, 1982). These and other time-related issues reviewed in the *Handbook* chapter by Guzzo and Shea (1992) indicate that temporal factors play a significant role in the development and performance of groups. However, as relatively

FIGURE 1

Original Model of Goal Setting and Related Variables

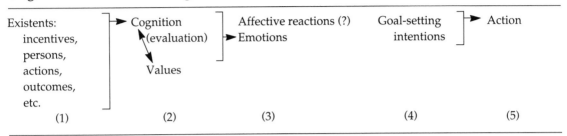

Existents: incentives, persons, actions, outcomes, etc.	Cognition (evaluation) Values	Affective reactions (?) Emotions	Goal-setting intentions	Action
(1)	(2)	(3)	(4)	(5)

little research has yet been done on them, the subject is one ripe for further elaboration.

Summary

The temporal meta-trend summarized in this section literally as well as figuratively adds an important dimension to industrial and organizational psychology. Paying more attention to consistencies and changes over time contributes to a better understanding of various subjects of interest, and thereby to more effective ways of dealing with them. In the examples discussed here, the time factor elucidates variations in predictor-criterion relationships, the etiology of work attitudes and motivation, and developmental patterns of personal characteristics and occupational behavior that are relevant to various concerns of human resource management. They confirm the arguments advanced by McGrath and Kelly (1986), who devoted an entire book to the importance of considering temporal factors in conceptual, substantive, and methodological matters.

The fact that many psychological variables, be they independent or dependent in research or practice, are being found to be moderated with the passage of time indicates the importance of considering the temporal dimension in our inquiries. This calls for the increasing use of designs in which difference over time is a dimension in such diverse topics as motivation (Kanfer, 1990), stress (Kahn & Byosiere, 1992), and group behavior (McGrath, 1991), to name but a few.

The Whole Is More Than the Sum of Its Parts

The meta-trend suggested by this caption refers not to the core principle of Gestalt psychology, which was the origin of the statement, but rather to the growing prevalence of more complex theories and models in industrial and organizational psychology. There seem to be two driving forces behind that development. One is that empirical research has identified additional variables that contribute to the understanding of the target subject. In addition to that inductive source of theory complexity, there appears to be what can be termed a deductive approach. Given the existence of alternative theories, each of which is shown to account for only a modest amount of the variance in the target phenomenon, some theorists have deduced that several of them can be combined into a more veridical conception. Examples of each kind of development will be offered in the following pages.

FIGURE 2

Revised Model of Goal Setting and Related Variables

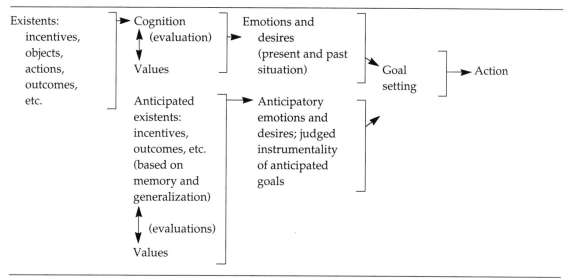

From "Studies of the Relationship Between Satisfaction, Goal-setting, and Performance" by E. A. Locke, N. Cartledge, and C. S. Knerr, 1970, *Organizational Behavior and Human Performance, 5*, p. 158. Copyright 1970 by Academic Press. Reprinted by permission.

The Inductive Approach

The well-known work on goal setting by Locke and his associates (cf. Locke & Latham, 1990a) illustrates how a model, originally relatively simple, is elaborated as well as refined on the basis of subsequent research. In an early version, it was portrayed as shown in Figure 1 (Locke, Cartledge, & Knerr, 1970).

That model was based partly on prior research and partly on earlier theory. Basically, it was organized as a causal sequence of consciousness, cognition, evaluation, and affective reactions to evaluation paralleled by the regulation of action via adoption of goals and intentions.

Additional research soon suggested that, rather than being parallel consequences of evaluation, affective states (degree of satisfaction/dissatisfaction) induce anticipated rewards and outcomes, which in turn lead to the affect anticipated through future actions, producing an intention to act so as to attain a valued goal, followed by action in accordance with that intention. The revised model is portrayed in Figure 2 (Locke, Cartledge, & Knerr, 1970).

Later research, much of it summarized by Austin and Bobko (1985), attempted to illuminate the processes underlying goal-setting effects and to identify moderating conditions, thereby contributing to further development of the theory by incremental steps. Extensions of the theory now include the role of feedback or knowledge of results and the importance of choice and commitment to the goal. The current version of the goal-setting model of Locke and Latham (1990b) is shown in Figure 3. The extent to which it has evolved inductively from the earlier models is apparent when the figures are compared.

The construct of goal commitment has become increasingly salient, prompting Locke, Latham, and Erez (1988) to suggest a number of factors that affect it. Hollenbeck

FIGURE 3

Late Model of Goal Setting and Related Variables

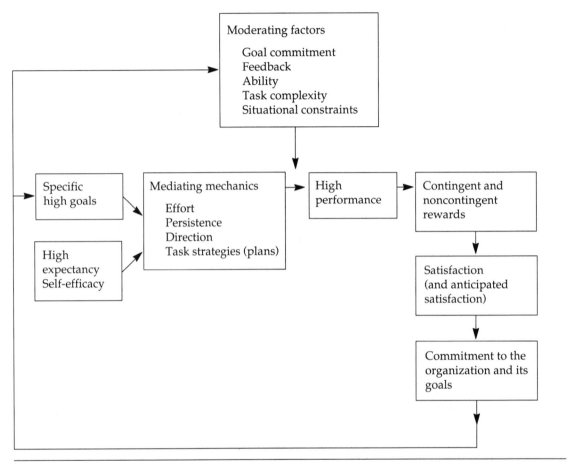

and Klein (1987) proposed a model of how various situational and personal factors, much like those identified by Locke et al. (1988), affect goal commitment and thereby performance. The Hollenbeck-Klein model, which was developed inductively out of prior research by many investigators, is described in the *Handbook* (Kanfer, 1990, vol. 1). Presumably it could be integrated with the model shown in Figure 3 to create an even more comprehensive model of goal setting.

On a practical level, this line of theorizing has led to the practice of setting attractive, specific, and difficult goals, accompanied by feedback of results; various techniques for managing those features have been described by Locke and Latham (1984).

FIGURE 4

Original Model of Work Adjustment

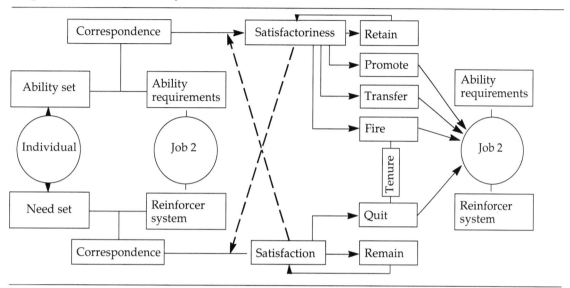

From *A Theory of Work Adjustment: Minnesota Studies in Vocational Rehabilitation, XV* by R. V. Dawis, G. W. England, and L. H. Lofquist, 1964, Minneapolis: University of Minnesota.

A second noteworthy example of the inductive approach to developing integrative theories is the theory of work adjustment described by Dawis and Lofquist (1984). In that book, the authors pointed out that disparate literatures on the subject had appeared over the years, leading them and their colleagues to sense the need for "an integrating theory" (p. 54). The theory appeared in its first version in 1964 (Dawis, England, & Lofquist). It is diagrammed in Figure 4.

The theory evolved further out of the extensive research of the Work Adjustment Project at the University of Minnesota over a period of approximately three decades.

When later described from a systems standpoint, the current version of the theory is depicted in Figure 5, which may be verbalized as follows:

The individual (I) is located in the upper left-hand corner and the work environment (E) is located in the lower right-hand corner. *I* comes to work with a set of needs and evaluates these against a set of expected reinforcers. If these reinforcers equal or exceed the needs, *I* feels satisfaction (SN) and proceeds to behave in the manner that *I* feels is expected (work behavior). *I*'s work behavior consists mainly of task performance, which is then evaluated by *E* against the task requirements. If *I*'s task performance meets or exceeds task requirements, *I* is considered satisfactory, or as having achieved satisfactoriness (SS). This, in turn, results in organizational behavior that produces the reinforcement necessary to meet *I*'s needs. *I* now can evaluate the actual reinforcers against needs and should continue to be satisfied and satisfactory until significant changes take place....

FIGURE 5

Systems Model of Work Adjustment

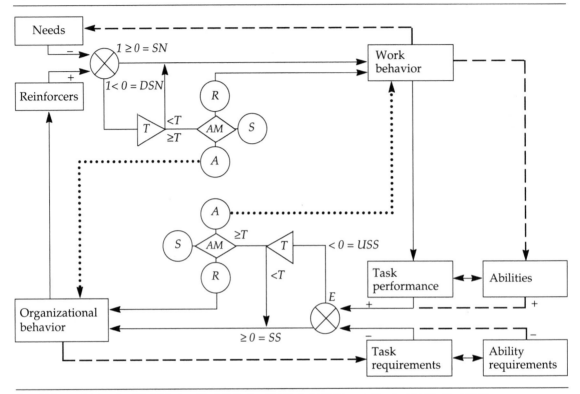

From "A Note on the Dynamics of Work Adjustment" by R. V. Dawis and L. H. Lofquist, 1978, *Journal of Vocational Behavior, 12,* pp. 76–79. Copyright 1978 byAcademic Press. Reprinted by permission.

When *I* evaluates reinforcers as not meeting needs, *I* feels dissatisfaction (DSN). If DSN rises above *I*'s threshold (T), *I* will move to seek a better adjustment. *I* may use either or both of two adjustment modes (AM): *I* may accommodate to *E* by using a reactive mode (R) of adjustment, or *I* may act to change *E* by using an active mode (A). If these adjustments result in a tolerable level of dissatisfaction, *I*'s work behavior will be directed toward meeting *E*'s task requirements. If not, *I* will leave the work situation and separation (S) will occur.

When *E* evaluates *I*'s task performance as not meeting task requirements, *I* will be considered unsatisfactory (USS). If USS exceeds *E*'s threshold (T), *E* will move to make the appropriate adjustments. *E* may accommodate *I* by being reactive (R), or *E* may take steps to effect a change in *I* by being active (A). If neither of these modes of adjustment by *E* achieves the desired effect, *E* will effect the separation (S) of *I* from the specific work situation . . . .(Dawis & Lofquist, 1984, pp. 65–66)

Much research related to the theory has already been done, including instrument development, the prediction of satisfaction and satisfactoriness, and the relationship between the two. The theory and its instrumentation have seen practical use in career counseling, vocational counseling, and personal counseling. Although not derived specifically from the theory, there have been many practical applications of parts of it in industry, such as the prediction of turnover from job satisfaction and the matching of ability with job requirements to predict performance. As yet, however, derivations from the total system have not been applied in work organizations, although it manifestly has potential utility.

Additional comprehensive models and theories in the area of industrial and organizational psychology that have been developed inductively include the contingency theories of leadership of Fiedler (Fiedler, 1967, 1978; Fiedler & Garcia, 1987) and of Vroom (Vroom & Jago, 1988; Vroom & Yetton, 1973); Vroom's (1964) expectancy-instrumentality-valence theory of motivation (Campbell & Pritchard, 1976; Mitchell, 1974; Porter & Lawler, 1968); job characteristics theory (Arnold & House, 1980; Hackman & Oldham, 1976, 1980); various theories of mental ability of which Guilford's (1967) theory of intelligence is the most comprehensive example; item response theory in psychological measurement (Drasgow & Hulin, 1990); models of determinants of ratings of job performance (Borman, White, Pulakos, & Oppler, 1991), and Jacoby's consumer motivation model (Jacoby, 1976; Jacoby, Hoyer, & Brief, 1992).

The Deductive Approach

This approach can be illustrated by models developed in two somewhat different fields of industrial and organizational psychology and discussed in volume 1 of the *Handbook*, namely, performance prediction and work motivation. The model of performance prediction was presented by J. P. Campbell (1990a) and is depicted there on page 707. It is reproduced here as Figure 6. Campbell did not cite all of the specific research or theorizing that provided the elements for the model, but it was obviously deduced from much that has been done before. For example, Campbell referred to the writings of Anderson (1985) and of Kanfer and Ackerman (1989) regarding declarative knowledge and procedural knowledge, and to the traditional representations that constitute his three ingredients of motivation.

Campbell noted that the precise functional form of the equation $PC = f\ (DK, PKS, M)$ is unknown and perhaps unknowable. He suggested, instead, that its utility lies more in identifying the possible determinants of a performance problem. This implies a research agenda of defining the relationships, in a particular job, between the predictor elements and each of the several components of performance, such as task proficiency and exerting effort. Further, it suggests the need to ascertain what variables, practices, or conditions positively or negatively affect each of the predictor elements. The practical application of this general approach was demonstrated in the mammoth Army selection and classification project described in a monograph introduced by Campbell (1990b).

Campbell's model is an example of what Kanfer (1990), in her chapter in volume 1 of this *Handbook*, called a new paradigm approach, that is, one that uses concepts and theories from different fields of psychology. Among the other examples that she cited was her work with Ackerman, which links ability, motivation, and task characteristics. The model postulates performance to be a function of the person's cognitive ability and the proportion of total ability that he or she is motivated to allocate to the task; tasks are held to differ in their allocation requirements. Kanfer (1990) cited prior conceptualizations that were combined in the model, including information processing and resource functions.

FIGURE 6

Model of Determinants of Job Performance

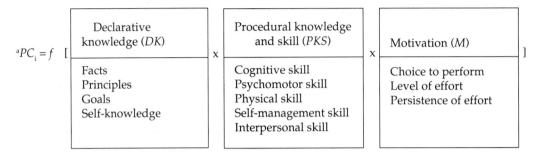

$i = 1,2\ldots k$ performance components

Predictors of Performance Determinants[b]

DK = f [(ability, personality, interests), (education, training, experience), (aptitude-treatment interactions)]

PKS = f [(ability, personality, interests), (education, training, practice, experience), (aptitude-treatment interactions)]

M = f [Whatever independent variables are stipulated by your favorite motivation theory]

Note: This entire schema can be repeated for educational performance, training performance, and laboratory task performance.

[a]Obviously, performance differences can also be produced by situational effects such as the quality of equipment, degree of staff support, or nature of the working conditions. For purposes of this model of performance, these conditionals are assumed to be held constant (experimentally, statistically, or judgmentally).

[b]Individual differences, learning, and motivational manipulations can only influence performance by increasing declarative knowledge, procedural knowledge and skill, or the three choices.

From "Modeling the Performance Prediction Problem in Industrial and Organizational Psychology" by J. P. Campbell in Volume 1 of this *Handbook,* p. 707.

Another example of a deductive model is the model of work motivation proposed by myself and Donna Thompson (Katzell & Thompson, 1990) and described by Kanfer (1990) as an amalgamation model. This model, too, can be summarized by a figure (Kanfer, 1990, vol. 1) reproduced here as Figure 7. The figure is a path diagram that hypothesizes causal relationships among the constituent elements. The elements and their relationships were explicitly derived from previous theories and research, each of which the authors believed to have demonstrated appreciable but limited ability to explain motivated work performance. The model endeavors to integrate those theories so that they are complementary, in the hope that their combination can better account for a given aspect of performance, such as quantity of work done or quitting the job.

FIGURE 7

Model of Work Attitudes, Motivation, and Performance

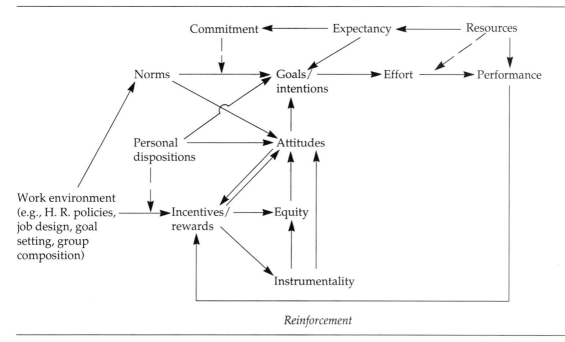

From "An Integrative Model of Work Attitudes, Motivation, and Performance" by R. A. Katzell and D. E. Thompson. In *Human Performance, Volume 3* (p. 71), 1990, Hillsdale, NJ: Lawrence Erlbaum Associates. Copyright 1990 by Lawrence Erlbaum Associates. Reprinted by permission.

The model is too complex to be explained verbally in detail here (the interested reader is referred to the article by Katzell & Thompson, 1990). In general, though, it hypothesizes that the level of a particular kind of job performance is indirectly caused by various *human resource policies and practices*. The influence of these policies and practices is mediated by certain motivationally relevant reactions of the individual, such as perceptions of *intrinsic and extrinsic reward* levels, which are moderated by the person's *values* and needs. The effects of the intrinsic and extrinsic reward levels in turn depend on how those rewards are seen to be administered, that is, *equity* and *instrumentality*. The foregoing perceptions affect the person's *attitudes* (satisfaction, involvement), which help determine his or her performance *intentions*. The latter are also shaped by the *norms* or goals set by management and peers. Those intentions get translated into *effort*, which, along with the personal and technical *resources* of the worker, determine behavior and *performance*. Resources also affect *expectancy* that effort will lead to performance, thereby influencing the worker's *commitment* to the norms. The *reinforcement* received from performance teaches the worker about the rewarding properties of the work situation and also induces habitual attitudes, performance intentions, and level of effort.

From this thumbnail sketch, the reader can discern the contributions of various theoretical positions, including need theory, reward/incentive theory, expectancy-instrumentality theory, goal-setting theory, attitude theory, self-efficacy theory, norm theory, and so forth, which by deduction were built into the model.

In addition to suggesting that parts of the model could profit from further research to strengthen the evidence on which those parts were based, Katzell and Thompson (1990) proposed that the model as a whole, since it is presented as a path diagram, is subject to empirical testing by path-analytic methods. They themselves conducted LISREL analyses, using measures of most of the constructs in field settings, with results supporting a moderate level of fit of the model to the intercorrelations. One of those studies was reported by Katzell, Thompson, and Guzzo (1992). However, since the correlations were typically rather low, the total causal effect on performance was still modest. This suggests additional agenda, namely, improving the reliability and construct validity of the measures employed.

The practical utility of this model is similar to the diagnostic function that was suggested by Campbell (1990a) for his model. Low readings on one or more of the motivational mediators would indicate priorities for action to improve performance. Moreover, since the Katzell-Thompson model stipulates human resource practices as exogenous or input variables, it provides action levers for improvement.

Additional examples of theories or models in industrial and organizational psychology that recently have been built largely by deduction from more circumscribed theories and empirical findings include the general theory of behavior in organizations of Naylor, Pritchard, and Ilgen (1980), the model of organizational adaptation and withdrawal of Hulin, Roznowski, and Hachiya (1985), which was discussed in Hulin's (1991, vol. 1) *Handbook* chapter, the multiple linkage model of leadership described by Yukl (1989) and summarized in his *Handbook* chapter with Van Fleet (Yukl & Van Fleet, 1992, vol. 3), and the model of conflict in organizations described by Thomas in the *Handbook* (1992, vol. 3).

Combinations of Induction and Deduction

The distinction that we have made between inductive and deductive approaches to developing comprehensive models and theories is in reality overdrawn. All of the examples cited above were derived by using both processes. Indeed, models of each type often make use of the same elements that were used in building models of the other type, for example, goal setting, commitment, expectancy, instrumentality, choice, measurement theory, and so forth. However, some models were more heavily dependent on one or the other of the two processes of reasoning, and it is on that basis that they were distinguished here. The dichotomy was employed more as a convenience in presentation than as an issue of theory.

Probably the most extensive integrative theory/model in industrial and organizational psychology is the one of behavior in organizations by Katz and Kahn (1966, 1978). Its development involved both induction and deduction in nearly equal measures. Since it took them an entire book to describe and document their theory, it defies brief summarization here. However, as their approach is basically an open systems model, we will discuss it further in the next section.

Summary

Before leaving this section, it is fair to ask whether the meta-trend of building integrative models and theories has served to advance the field. The issue is complicated by the fact that integration is really a continuum; thus, arguments have been advanced for the value of "middle range" theories (cf. Landy & Becker, 1987). Nearly a decade ago, Miner (1984) published a review of major theories in the field of organizational behavior that indicated that only a minority of them could be rated highly with respect either to their scientific or their practical value. A later paper by Webster and Starbuck (1988) concluded that theory in the field had not progressed very far. However, neither paper examined more integrative theories in relation to more limited ones, although the Webster and Starbuck (1988) critique, which was largely methodological, presumably would apply equally to both types.

In any event, both of those reviews essentially were seen through the eyes of the beholders. Objective evaluations would involve comparing integrative and limited theories with respect to the proportion of variance they explain in their targeted phenomena. Limited data exist that suggest that at least some of the more integrative theories predict behavior better than their limited elements do; an example is the better prediction of task performance by the extended goal-setting model versus its simpler antecedents.

However, as Kanfer (1990) has pointed out, integrative models are often aimed more at explaining what is going on in behavior than in predicting specific outcomes. For example, as mentioned above, Campbell (1990a) stated that the principal utility of his model was in diagnosis of performance problems rather than prediction of performance. Nevertheless, empirical research guided in part by the conceptualizations underlying the model found that various components of performance were predicted rather well; for example, across nine different army jobs, the mean multiple R was .65 between 11 cognitive ability scores and criteria of technical proficiency, and was .69 for criteria of general soldiering proficiency (McHenry, Hough, Toquam, Hanson, & Ashworth, 1990). Those validation results were, of course, superior to those usually found in studies of personnel selection (cf. Lubinski & Dawis, 1992), but that is neither specifically a test of the Campbell model nor a comparison with more limited models applied to the same jobs.

An analytical approach to dealing with the agenda of testing integrative models is to cast them in the form of causal models that can be tested by structural equation methods. Katzell, Thompson, and Guzzo (1992) did that with a modified version of the Katzell and Thompson

(1990) integrative model discussed above and reported that their data fit the unadjusted model "moderately well." Also, Locke and Latham (1990b) called attention to the convergence in both theory and data between their work, developed mainly inductively from experimental data, and that of Katzell and Thompson, developed independently mainly by deduction and tested with correlational survey data. That convergence lends credibility to both formulations.

Reviewing theory and research on job satisfaction, its components, and its correlates, Guion (1992) espoused the integrative approaches of Katzell, Thompson, and Guzzo (1992) and of Dawis and Lofquist (1984) as models for future work, preferable to narrower approaches to the subject. Additional instances can be cited where integrative models explained the behavior in question (e.g., Kanfer & Ackerman, 1989; Vroom & Jago, 1988). The various findings summarized above speak to the scientific and practical utility of such multivariate formulations of work behavior, and are supportive of the meta-trend discussed here.

Systems Concepts, Models, and Theories

Like any comprehensive view of natural phenomena, what came to be called open systems theory, or more simply systems theory, had many precursors. However, its emergence in the consciousness of the natural and social sciences can be attributed to Ludwig von Bertalanffy's (1950) seminal paper. He characterized a *system* essentially as an organized complex of interacting components that serve to maintain its integrity in an external environment. In a 1962 publication, he identified other intellectual contributions to the development of general systems theory, including cybernetics, information theory, game theory, decision theory, topology, and factor analysis, terms and concepts that are no doubt familiar to the industrial and organizational psychologist. J. G. Miller (1955) applied systems conceptions to psychology and other behavioral sciences. Rapoport and Horwath (1959) discussed a similar set of underpinnings in a systems approach to organization theory, as did Berrien (1976) in the first edition of the *Handbook*.

An early application of systems theory in industrial and organizational psychology was the sociotechnical view espoused by members of the Tavistock Institute (Emery & Trist, 1960; Miller & Rice, 1967; Trist & Bamforth, 1951). This view put special emphasis on the mutual interdependencies of the technical features of the task system and the human properties of the workers, and on the relationship of the total system and each of its parts to their respective environments. More recent evolutions and applications from that view have focused on the design of jobs and the work of teams so as to optimize the technological and social subsystems (e.g., Rousseau, 1977; Susman, 1976).

Daniel Katz and Robert Kahn (1966) were largely responsible for bringing this mode of thinking more specifically to the broad field of industrial and organizational psychology. In their book, *The Social Psychology of Organizations* (1966, 1978), they enumerated the properties of open systems as follows:

> These include the importation of energy from the environment, the throughput or transformation of the imported energy into some product form that is characteristic of the system, the exporting of that product into the environment, and the reenergizing of the system from sources in the environment.
>
> Open systems also share the characteristics of negative entropy, feedback, homeostasis, differentiation, coordination and equifinality. The law of negative entropy

states that systems survive and maintain their characteristic internal order only as long as they import from the environment more energy than they expend in the process of transformation and exportation. The feedback principle has to do with information input, which is a special kind of energic importation, a kind of signal to the system about environmental conditions and about the functioning of the system in relation to its environment. The feedback of such information enables the system to correct for its own malfunctioning or for changes in the environment, and thus to maintain a steady state or homeostasis. This is a dynamic rather than a static balance, however. Open systems are not at rest but tend toward differentiation and elaboration, both because of subsystem dynamics and because of the relationship between growth and survival. Finally, open systems are characterized by the principle of equifinality, which asserts that systems can reach the same final state from different initial conditions and by different paths of development. (1978, pp. 33–34)

Katz and Kahn went on to note that systems contain subsystems that enable them to thrive. Their outline of the formal subsystems of organizations is reproduced in Table 1. Subsystems I, II, IV, and V are domains in which industrial and organizational psychologists are active and in which their work is represented by various chapters in the *Handbook*. Subsystem III is perhaps less familiar, but even that is represented by *Handbook* chapters dealing with recruitment (Rynes, 1991, vol. 2), consumers (Jacoby, Hoyer, & Brief, 1992, vol. 3), and organization-environment relations (Davis & Powell, 1992, vol. 3).

In sum, the field of industrial and organizational psychology and the work of its members can be represented as improving the operation

TABLE 1

Formal Subsystem of Organizations: Their Functions, Dynamics, and Mechanisms

Subsystem Structure	Function	Dynamic	Mechanisms
I. Production: primary processes	Task accomplishment: energy transformation within organization	Proficiency	Division of labor: setting up of job specification and standards
II. Maintenance of working structure	Mediating between task demands and human needs to keep structure in operation	Maintenance of steady state	Formalization of activities into standard legitimized procedures: setting up of system rewards; socialization of new members
III. Boundary systems			
A. Production-supportive: procurement of materials and manpower and product disposal	Transactional exchanges at system boundaries	Specifically focused manipulation of organizational environment	Acquiring control of sources of supply; creation of image
B. Institutional system	Obtaining social support and legitimation	Societal manipulation and integration	Contributing to community, influencing other social structure
IV. Adaptive	Intelligence, research and development; planning	Pressure for change	Making recommendations for change to management
V. Managerial	Resolving conflicts between hierarchical levels	Control	Use of sanctions of authority
	Coordinating and directing functional substructures	Compromise vs. integration	Alternative concessions; setting up machinery for adjudication
	Coordinating external requirements and organizational resources and needs	Long-term survival; optimization, better use of resources, development of increased capabilities	Increasing volume of business; adding functions; controlling environment through absorbing it or changing it; restructuring

From *The Social Psychology of Organizations* (2nd ed., p. 84) by D. Katz and R. Kahn, 1978, New York: Wiley. Copyright © 1978 by Wiley. Reprinted by permission.

FIGURE 8

Model of Person-Machine System

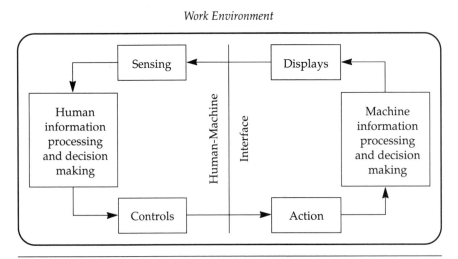

From "Human Factors in the Work Place" by W. C. Howell in Volume 2 of this *Handbook*, p. 214.

of the subsystems that comprise viable organizational systems that are effective in attaining their respective goals. Moreover, in a contemporary meta-trend, many models and theories in the field are now being cast in the form of systems, each forming part of the broader organizational open system described by Katz and Kahn (1966, 1978). That is true, for example, of the integrative theories of work adjustment (Dawis & Lofquist, 1984), of goal setting (Locke & Latham, 1990a), and of work motivation (Katzell & Thompson, 1990) described in the previous section.

Another example, this one from quite a different area of the field, was provided by Howell (1991, vol. 2) in his *Handbook* chapter on human factors in the workplace. There he wrote "the nature of modern human factors thinking and practice centers around the system concept...that human and machine constitute interacting components, or *subsystems*, of a goal-oriented entity referred to as

the *human-machine system*" (p. 213). In simplified form, that model is sketched in Figure 8.

A word of caution is in order. It is not enough for a model to be represented by boxes connected by arrows to be considered a systems model. The systems features described by Katz and Kahn (1978) and summarized above need to be prominent in it. Those features are incorporated in Howell's (1991) discussion of the human factors model and in the others cited earlier.

Systems thinking has penetrated the field not only in the form of its comprehensive models but also in that one or another of its elements have influenced many more limited conceptions. Notions of interacting parts, of feedback, of interchange with the environment, of input-throughput-output transformations, of dynamic equilibrium, and of equifinality have become part of our intellectual vocabulary. As is discussed in the following section, a recent importation has been the use of cybernetic control theory in explaining motivation. For example, Campion and Lord (1982) have explained the fact that specific goals induce better performance than general goals because the former provide information that is more helpful in reducing the discrepancy between a goal and performance; and Lord and Hanges (1987) have suggested that the behavior of others serves to feed back information that a person may use in self-regulation.

Another influence of systems theory consists of the growing use of its concept of equifinality, that is, that systems afford multiple channels for accomplishing a given end. That idea is specifically cited by Katzell and Thompson (1990) as an application of their model of work motivation; they suggest, for example, that perceptions of inequity that may be found to be due largely to an organization's promotion policies may be more easily and quickly counteracted by improving the compensation system. Another example is provided by the views of Kerr and Jermier (1978) and Howell, Bowen, Dorfman, Kerr, and Podsakoff (1990), who embodied the notion of equifinality in their proposition that such factors as task design, employee competence, and organizational policies and practices can substitute for leadership, thereby helping to remedy problems attributable to the latter. Even more recently, McGrath (1991) has espoused the concept of equifinality as superior to that of process losses in explaining the performance of work groups.

On a more general level, systems thinking is present in the incorporation of transformation or mediating processes in models and in research designs. The older paradigm often consisted of two variables: predictors and criteria, stimuli and responses, treatments and outcomes. Familiar examples included selection studies, training programs, and job satisfaction-performance conceptions. Prompted by less-than-satisfactory results of that approach, a meta-trend has evolved that introduces mediating variables that intervene between

independent and dependent variables, transforming inputs into outputs. For example, the personnel selection model of J. P. Campbell (1990a), discussed in the preceding section, incorporates performance determinants, that is, declarative knowledge, procedural knowledge, and motivation, as intervening between independent variables (e.g., test scores, motivational manipulations, training) and performance. The Katzell and Thompson (1990) motivation model holds the effect of greater job satisfaction on performance to be mediated by the acceptance of higher goals, which in turn lead to greater effort that generates better performance, provided resources are adequate. As a further example, mediating processes have been more prominently featured in models and research on group performance ever since Hackman and Morris (1975) concluded that group effectiveness is best viewed in an input-process-output framework; their mediating constructs comprised interaction patterns, communication, interpersonal relations, and the like. Guzzo and Shea's (1992, vol. 3) *Handbook* chapter discussed a number of recent models, research designs, and application strategies that derive from that conception.

Summary

Open systems concepts have been influencing theories and models of varying scope and diverse content in industrial and organizational psychology. These in turn have often led to changes in research strategies and to new applications that, in aggregate, have been contributing significantly to the science and practice of the field.

Cybernetics in Industrial and Organizational Psychology

Following the seminal work of Norbert Wiener (1948), the term *cybernetics* entered popular as well as technical vocabularies. The

Random House Dictionary (1966) defines the term in part as "the study of human control functions" (p. 259). The popularity of the term has waned, but control concepts and theory gradually have permeated psychology, including, more recently, industrial and organizational psychology. Indeed Ganster and Fusilier (1989) have gone so far as to say that the idea of personal control in one form or another underlies much of the thinking in industrial and organizational psychology. The use of control notions goes even beyond personal control, being applied also at levels both more micro and macro than that. In fact, the number of levels and range of phenomena to which control concepts have been applied are so wide that there is reason to doubt that the term has the same meaning in its various applications.

Nevertheless, there is a common thread. The word *cybernetics* is derived from the Greek, meaning "to steer." In all instances, control likewise refers to the processes by which some form of thought or action is steered or directed. At all levels, there is interest in such parameters as the province of control, its locus or distribution, how it is accomplished, and what the consequences are. Also, they all share at least some of the elements of control theory (Carver & Scheier, 1982; Wiener, 1948), which involves comparing a sensed input (e.g., performance data) against a standard (e.g., a goal) and communicating (feedback) any discrepancy to an agent that (or who) activates the system so as to reduce the discrepancy.

Before saying prematurely that we are here dealing with a unitary construct, or contrarily concluding that its unity is more apparent than real, it may be of interest to review various ways in which the concept of control has been entering into industrial and organizational psychology. In doing so, it may be helpful to organize our overview under rubrics corresponding to levels of analysis: individuals, jobs, groups, and organizations. In our discussion, we shall not try to differentiate the verb and noun *control* from other terms used as its close synonyms, such as influence; all refer to steering.

Individual Level

In individual psychology, control concepts have been applied to learning, to cognition, to motivation, and to personality. The essence of learning is, of course, modification of thought or behavior as a consequence of experience. In industrial and organizational psychology, the field of training (Goldstein, 1991) is concerned with the programming of experience so as to induce certain desired changes in employees, actually a form of control. Operant conditioning is a virtual archetype of such control, and indeed Skinner has been castigated by some for the possible Machiavellian implications of his methods. Behavior modeling is a training method that aims to shape behavior via self-regulation or self-control (Decker & Nathan, 1985).

In the realm of individual motivation, notions of control are employed in a variety of ways. One is as a species of motive. For example, as Kanfer (1990, vol. 1) pointed out in her *Handbook* chapter on motivation, achievement motivation involves a dimension of mastery or control, and intrinsic motivation is partly a result of the person's belief that he or she is in control. Self-regulation approaches to motivation emphasize the processes that guide the allocation of effort involved in goal attainment. Fundamental to goal-setting theory and practices is the idea that action is controlled by goals. Control theory has more recently been explicitly applied to clarify the relationships among task complexity, performance, and goal choices, using such concepts as cognitive scripts (Klein, 1989) and speed of feedback (Lord & Hanges, 1987). Hyland (1988) has suggested that several theories of motivation, including those of Locke and Deci, can be integrated in a control model, as has Klein (1989).

Control concepts have long been features in various classic formulations of individual personality, such as Freud's construct of aggression/dominance and Murray's need categories of dominance and abasement. They persist in more modern form, such as the power and achievement elements of leader personality (McClelland & Boyatzis, 1982), and the dominance-submission personality dimension in interpersonal relations (Wiggins, 1979). Cummings and Cooper (1979) proposed a cybernetic framework for understanding occupational stress; in a test of that conception, Frome and McFarlin (1989) found that blue collar workers whose work exposed them to chronic, uncontrollable stressors showed stronger symptoms of strain, which were even greater in people inclined to be more self-conscious. Another personality characteristic, locus of control, has also been found to be associated with experienced role stress (Jackson & Schuler, 1985), probably because people whose locus of control is more external are prone to be more sensitive to environmental conditions; in a tie to motivation, research has also shown externals to have lower expectancies regarding the linkages of effort, performance, and reward. Persons whose perceived locus of control is more internal than external are more prone to be successful at work (Andrisani & Nestel, 1976). A person's experience with his or her ability to control what happens teaches the person to develop a depressed, passive personality or, conversely, an optimistic disposition, which in turn can affect job performance, phenomena respectively called *learned helplessness* and *learned optimism* (Seligman, 1975, 1990).

The *Handbook* chapter by Lord and Maher (1991a, vol. 2) described several ways in which control is used in cognitive theory. For example, it appears that conscious control has a smaller role in guiding strategic decisions than is usually assumed, as illustrated by a study by Dutton and Jackson (1987) showing that cognitive categorizations of situations as threats or opportunities influence the nature of decisions. In a different application, Athey

and McIntyre (1987) have suggested that greater use of controlled information processing, which requires relatively high levels of attention and thought, may help offset errors in rating due to more automatic, less controlled processing of information.

Job Level

In their *Handbook* chapter, Ilgen and Hollenbeck (1991, vol. 2) identified three general orientations toward describing jobs: those of human factors psychologists, job analysts, and motivationally focused psychologists. Each, as we shall see, deals with the concept of control, although in rather different ways.

We have already noted the prototypic model of personal-machine systems described by Howell (1991, vol. 2) in his *Handbook* chapter on human factors; it is diagrammed in Figure 8. Information processing and decision making by humans and by machines are key elements in the control and effectiveness of performance of those systems. Howell (1991) pointed out that control theory is one of the conceptualizations of the role of the humans. When systems are largely under direct manual control, the person is viewed as a servomechanism operating to control errors by correcting deviations from a standard. Semiautomated systems involve supervisory control in which the person monitors and adjusts as necessary the largely autonomous, computer-controlled machine components.

As noted in Harvey's (1991, vol. 2) *Handbook* chapter on job analysis, control is a common task element in jobs even when the machine component is minimal. For example, clerks may control certain aspects of paperwork and executives may exercise control over investment decisions. Standard systems of job analysis, such as those of McCormick, Jeanneret, and Meacham (1972) and of Fine and Wiley (1971), accordingly include control among their task elements. Ilgen and Hollenbeck (1991) have suggested that informal emergent task elements exist in addition to the established ones in order to enact the job in a particular situation; these also would seem to have control implications, especially insofar as they entail role definitions by the incumbents and by those with whom they interact.

Psychologists interested in motivational effects of jobs have been concerned with the degree of autonomy that the incumbents have in their work, that is, the extent to which they are free of control by rules, by other people, or by mechanical or physical features of the job. Hackman and Oldham (1976), for instance, hypothesized that people who have substantial freedom and discretion in scheduling their work and how it is to be done are likely to experience personal responsibility for work outcomes and, therefore, to perform better and be more satisfied. Increasing control over one's job is also recommended as a way of reducing job-related stress (Kahn & Byosiere, 1992).

Group Level

We have seen how conceptions of control enter into explaining individual behavior and the nature of jobs. In this section, we will consider control as an aspect of the face-to-face relations between workers in dyads and in groups.

In his classic chapter entitled "Influence, Leadership, Control," Cartwright (1965) viewed influence as a special instance of causality, that is, the change in a person's behavior resulting from the actions of another, such as a leader. He organized his review in terms of properties of the agent, 0, who exerts influence or control; properties of the person, P, subjected to that influence; methods employed for exerting influence or power; and relationships between the two parties. We will consider here some of the newer developments in that line of work.

Graen and Scandura (1987) have proposed a model of leader-member dyads that aims to describe how the latter's work role evolves. In the initial phase, the two parties attempt to explore each other's expectations, motives, and potential resources. The second phase involves solidifying the employee's role by negotiation, persuasion, and reinforcement. The final phase, which may not always develop, consists of routinization and internalization of role behavior. It is in the second phase that control processes are especially operative, as each party in the dyad attempts to get the other to understand and accept their respective roles. Control flows in both directions, although not necessarily symmetrically. In the third phase, external control is largely replaced by self-control.

In their *Handbook* chapter on leadership, Yukl and Van Fleet (1992, vol. 3) reviewed recent research concerned with explaining leader effectiveness in terms of the amount and source of the leader's power to control and how it is exercised. For example, it appears that more effective leaders rely on a combination of power sources: referent and expert power are needed to supplement position power. Attention is being given also to the tactics by which managers attempt to influence others; the most effective tactics for securing commitment appear to include rational persuasion, consultation, and inspirational appeals, whereas pressure, coalition formation, and legitimation tactics are among the least effective (although they may obtain compliance). Another way in which supervisors can control the behavior of their subordinates is by use of operant techniques (Komaki, 1986). For example, Komaki, Berwick, and Scott (1978) showed that supervisors could improve the safety-related behavior of their subordinates by commenting favorably when they observed them acting in prescribed ways.

Traditionally, the effects of power have been considered in terms of the target person. Lord Acton, however, reversed the process when he observed that "power corrupts, and absolute power corrupts absolutely." It was Kipnis (1976) who called the attention of industrial and organizational psychologists to how power can affect the powerholders. Research has revealed that the successful exercise of control over others is likely to change the powerholders' views of themselves and of those whom they influence; for example, the former are likely to see themselves as more worthy than the latter.

The attribution of one's power to one's greater worth is only one example of how attribution theory has informed leadership phenomena. Subordinates may also be prone to make attributions, such as when they infer that leaders known to be effective have greater personal power. Indeed, Hollander and Offermann (1990) have observed that "today, the emphasis has shifted from traits to follower attributions of leaders that make followers respond affirmatively or otherwise"(p. 180).

Hollander and Offermann (1990) also noted that there has been some shift of emphasis from the power of leaders to the empowerment of subordinates. The idea of sharing power by authorizing subordinates to participate in decisions was, of course, a prime principle of the human relations movement. A recent review of the research literature by Schweiger and Leana (1986) confirmed the proposition advanced early by Katzell (1962) by concluding that the effects of participation on performance do depend strongly on situational moderators. However, the delegation of power to actually make decisions is a newer idea and is closer to the construct of empowerment, that is, the redistribution of power (Leana, 1987). We have already encountered empowerment of the individual worker in the form of autonomy in the design of the job. We now see it extended to the redistribution of control between group leaders and their subordinates; indeed, autonomy is now specified as one of the features of effective work teams (Sundstrom, DeMeuse, & Futrell, 1990).

Leana (1987) and Hollander and Offermann (1990) viewed delegation as typically involving decision making by individual subordinates rather than by groups; conceived that way, it seems to be related to the concept of autonomy in individual jobs. However, other authors (cf. Goodman, Devadas, & Hughson, 1988; Pearce & Ravlin, 1987) referred to "self-regulating work groups," "self-managing teams," or "autonomous work groups" as having control over their work and division of labor, where control means that the group has the authority and responsibility to initiate what have traditionally been management activities; in effect, certain management functions are assigned to the group. In either case, we are dealing with the redistribution of control over the work of individuals or groups, with relatively less being exercised by their leaders and supervisors.

The role of control in groups is not limited to leader-member relations. Hackman's (1992, vol. 3) *Handbook* chapter was devoted to explaining how groups influence and control the beliefs, attitudes, and actions of their individual members. He described five mechanisms by which that occurs: (a) the group context (e.g., the attributes of group members, the group task, the physical setting) provides ambient stimuli that shape individuals' responses; (b) groups enhance or depress arousal of the individuals; (c) groups reinforce the behavior of their members by applying rewards and punishments in a discretionary way; (d) groups affect members' behavior by influencing beliefs and attitudes that underlie it, especially the valences attached to various outcomes and expectancies regarding behavior-outcome linkages; and (e) groups define and enforce norms regarding appropriate and inappropriate behavior. In their *Handbook* chapter, Guzzo and Shea (1992, vol. 3) emphasized group goals as further influences on members' attitudes and behavior.

Organization Level

In his comprehensive chapter on organizational control in the 1976 *Handbook,* Lawler conceived of organizational control as the system employed to ensure that planned activities produce the desired results and used the analogy of the thermostat, a staple of literature on cybernetics. He noted a number of respects in which control systems can have adverse effects on the organization's members, such as lack of commitment to goals set by others, inadequacies in information feedback, and inequities in relating rewards to performance. He noted that employee participation in the control system can counter such dysfunctional consequences, but that its applicability may be constrained by various contextual circumstances, including personalities of the members and whether they have the expertise to make good decisions. Later, Dachler and Wilpert (1978) pointed out that issues of participation and its boundaries can be fruitfully considered in terms of control.

In the years since then, some of the hesitancy about the wider distribution of control in organizations has subsided. Participation and empowerment have increasingly become not just a matter of democratic leadership, but characteristics of organization-wide management systems. The autonomy of work groups and teams has been a cardinal principle of sociotechnical systems design, as pointed out in the *Handbook* chapter by Guzzo and Shea (1992, vol. 3). Even more recently, the concept has spread to self-managed work teams (Goodman, Devadas, & Hughson, 1988) and to employee involvement programs (Banas, 1988; Lawler, 1982), often with positive effects on attitudes and performance.

That this kind of thinking about organizational control is going beyond industrial and organizational psychology is illustrated by a recent article in the *New York Times* (Holusha, 1992). The article reported the shift in views of J. F. Welsh, Jr., chairman of the General Electric Company, characterized as formerly exemplifying the "relentless executive." He is quoted now as saying that managers must have "the self-confidence to empower others.... Trust and respect between workers and managers is essential. [Managers must be] open to ideas from anywhere..." (p. D-1). Welsh related how teams

of hourly workers in one of the G.E. plants operate efficiently and without supervision $20 million in new machinery that they specified, tested, and approved for purchase. The basic idea, which Welsh says he developed over the past few years by studying other companies and testing the idea at G.E., is to eliminate bureaucracy by encouraging communication outside traditional channels and involving factory employees in workplace decisions.

To the extent that the kind of thinking expressed by Welsh permeates his company, it will affect the attitudes and performance of its members in ways that go beyond its substantive focus on autonomy. By helping to create mutual trust, shared belief in company and group effectiveness, and clear company values, top executives can build a corporate culture that also affects group and individual attitudes and performance (Sundstrom, DeMeuse, & Futrell, 1990). The organization, of course, controls the attitudes and behavior of its members in many additional ways, including via training programs, the reward system, resources provided, physical working arrangements, and, as emphasized in sociotechnical theory, the technical system of production. In his *Handbook* chapter, Weiss (1990, vol. 1) described how organizations shape the behavior of their members by socialization and by operant procedures. Kerr and Slocum (1981) listed various other mechanisms whereby organizations control employee behavior.

Summary

We have seen that the use of cybernetic or control concepts has become a meta-trend in industrial and organizational psychology, infusing theory, research, and practice in a variety of domains: individual, job, group, and organization. Aspects of control are being employed as independent variables (as in leader-subordinate relations), as mediating variables (as in linkages between stimulus persons and how they are rated), as moderators (as when a person's locus of control is found to affect responses to role stressors), as dependent variables (as products of organizational designs), and as complexes of the foregoing.

Are we dealing with a congeries of variables having in common only semantic similarity, or is there really an underlying unity? Probably some of both. Certainly, the self-monitoring that an individual performs in pursuing a goal has little operational resemblance to the budget control system of an organization. Yet they are functionally analogous, that is, they each provide an agent with feedback regarding the extent to which the system (person or organization) may be off target, thereby furnishing cues for remedial action.

In all of the levels we have discussed, the control system contains standards or desirable conditions, sensors that detect the system's performance relative to the standard as well as detecting ambient circumstances that may affect its attainment, feedback of information regarding the foregoing, a mechanism for evaluating the feedback, effectors that respond to that evaluation by changing or maintaining the performance, communication channels connecting the foregoing, and energy that enables them to operate. Of course, unlike thermostats, complex systems have more than one goal and control processes pertaining to each that may be more or less salient at a given time. Moreover, human systems, including organizations, have the capacity to modify one or more elements through experience, a central tenet of organizational development (cf. Porras & Robertson, 1992, vol. 3). The goal-oriented behavior of a person features all of those elements, as does (analogously) the mission-oriented behavior of a firm, or the production of a work group. Even personality characteristics of an individual can be fitted to that paradigm: Aggressiveness enters into the definition of desired outcomes, as well as governing energy available for pursuing them; locus of control relates to the weight given to ambient signals, and so on.

In short, the cybernetic paradigm appears to be useful in understanding a wide range of concerns of the industrial and organizational psychologist. As we try better to understand a system at whatever level, or to intervene in order to ameliorate its performance, looking into control-relevant aspects may be a good way to begin.

The Cognitive Perspective

The field of industrial and organizational psychology never bought into the radical behaviorism that exiled mind and consciousness beyond the pale of scientific psychology. Mental constructs were central in topics of concern from the very outset of the field, including intelligence, rating, learning, and attitudes (Katzell & Austin, 1992). However, like most other psychologists, the industrial and organizational variety did not probe very deeply into the mechanisms and processes that underlay those constructs. That scrutiny awaited the so-called cognitive revolution that became prominent in psychology during approximately the last twenty-five years and has more recently been developing as a meta-trend in the industrial and organizational field. The escalation of interest in this approach is illustrated by the survey of industrial and organizational literature reported by Lord and Maher (1989); they found 18 articles in 1977 in which cognitive processes were central, 27 in 1982, and 56 in 1986, an increase of more than threefold in ten years, proportionately greater than that of all industrial and organizational literature.

The cognitive approach is concerned with how people receive, interpret, store, retrieve, evaluate, and act upon information. Research on such matters typically involves obtaining detailed information about the processes people employ in performing various tasks. That information can be obtained from sources such as verbal protocols, behavior manifested in search for information or in choices among options, and measures of time or accuracy of responses. As can be deduced from the methods of inquiry, not all cognitive processes are regarded as necessarily represented in consciousness; some are inferred from behavior. Evidence that much information processing occurs with little or no conscious attention (Lord & Maher, 1991a) raises questions about the heavy reliance that industrial and organizational psychologists place on self-report and perceptual measures.

One can organize an overview of how cognitive approaches are being employed in industrial and organizational psychology either by cognitive theories or by industrial and organizational substantive foci. For our purpose, I have chosen the latter framework. Furthermore, I will not burden this summary with specific reference to numerous illustrative studies, but will refer the reader desiring more detail to the reviews recently published by Ilgen and Klein (1989), Koopman and Pool (1990), Lord and Maher (1989, 1991a), Stevenson, Busemeyer, and Naylor (1990), and Taylor (1992). Many examples can also be found throughout other chapters in this *Handbook*. Following are brief descriptions of how cognitive treatments are being applied in several substantive areas of industrial and organizational psychology.

Problem Solving and Decision Making

Work on these two related topics has generally been addressed to describing how individuals go about performing such activities. Examples include how problems are recognized and what phases people pass through once they identify a problem, how people make judgments about cues from which they draw inferences and make predictions, rational versus normative models governing decisions, cybernetic aspects of successive decisions, and how decisions are affected by contingent conditions such as time pressure, degree of uncertainty, or the nature of the problem. It turns out that people generally don't utilize the most efficient strategy. For example, in categorization tasks such as making hiring decisions, they are inclined to employ a probabilistic rather than optimizing strategy; in making decisions under risk, they are inclined to employ a faulty utility model, and so on.

Although potentially useful in improving the judgments and decisions that individuals make, this line of research has yet to produce a technology that can be employed for such ends. Teaching decision makers how to develop and use prediction models, such as utility analysis described in the *Handbook* chapter by Boudreau (1991, vol. 2), would undoubtedly help.

A rather different stream of theory and research concerns decision-making patterns in organizations. For example, Taylor (1992, vol. 3), in this *Handbook*, described eight types of strategic decision-making models, such as bureaucratic, strategic planning, contingency, and so forth. Other studies have found relations between decision-making patterns and organizational characteristics such as complexity and centralization, and with properties of the organizational environment, such as stability or turbulence. Although individuals' cognitive processes are involved in group and organizational decisions, the intersections between those different levels remain unexplored (cf. Taylor, 1992).

In describing how management teams deal with strategy formulation, some authors have identified group processes very much like those that cognitive psychologists ascribe to information processing by individuals (cf. Jackson, 1992). This line of research has also been mainly descriptive rather than normative, and has yet to produce many research-based guidelines for improving the process of making decisions or dealing with planning.

Related to the topic of decisions in organizations is the earlier topic of problem solving and decision making by small groups. That work examined, for example, communication and interaction patterns among group members when confronted with a problem, as well as the effects of moderating factors, like the nature of the task and member heterogeneity, on group processes and outcomes. After a period of relative stagnation (cf. Steiner, 1986), there has been a resurgence of interest in small groups, including their decision-making processes (Guzzo, 1986; Levine & Moreland, 1990). Topics of recent interest include the decision rules for combining members' preferences, transitions in member preferences, and the extent to which group members share information. The subject was examined in the *Handbook* chapter by Guzzo and Shea (1992, vol. 3).

The practical implications of the earlier work on group problem solving were discussed by Hoffman (1979). A more recent example is afforded by Bentel and Jackson (1989), who studied the innovativeness of problem solutions of top management teams in banks, hypothesizing that team composition would be a significant factor. That hypothesis was derived from previous research, mainly in the laboratory, showing that team composition can affect problem identification, solution generation, and solution implementation. Their data, drawn from 199 banks, showed that more innovative banks were managed by teams whose members were more educated and more diverse with respect to functional areas of expertise. The role of team composition was especially salient where top management had more control over decisions.

Performance Appraisal

In none of the domains of traditional industrial psychology has the cognitive approach been employed more extensively than in this one. That is amply illustrated in the *Handbook* chapter by Borman (1991, vol. 2).

One of the most comprehensive cognitive models of the appraisal process was proposed by DeNisi, Cafferty, and Meglino (1984). It is diagramed in Figure 9. As can be seen, it features many of the basic elements of information processing, including perceiving, encoding, storing, retrieving, interpreting, evaluating, and deciding. Other models, and research based on them, emphasize other cognitive processes such as categorization (including the formation of schemata), stereotype and prototype usage, and implicit theories of raters.

Research based on these cognitive notions has examined the effects on rating accuracy of distribution of attention, memory distortion, prior expectations, intervening experience with the ratee, and cues employed by the raters. Although such research has illuminated how raters make judgments, it thus far has contributed relatively little to improving the accuracy and utility of performance ratings in field settings (cf. Guion, 1991). One of the exceptions was the conclusion drawn by Landy, Zedeck, and Cleveland (1983) that appraisals can be improved by having one person observe and record performance information that is then evaluated by another.

Leadership

Two of the major theories of leadership have in recent updates placed emphasis on cognition. The normative model of Vroom and Jago (1988) prescribed how leaders should decide to act in view of the circumstances in which they and their groups find themselves. Fiedler and Garcia (1987) extended Fiedler's contingency theory to include the leader's cognitive resources. However, as pointed out by Ilgen and Klein (1989), neither of those theories closely examines the nature of the cognitive processes involved.

More specifically cognitive approaches to the study of leadership include attributions based on performance cues and behavior, and use of implicit theory and prototypes as explanations of emergence of leaders. In the laboratory, Cronshaw and Lord (1987) demonstrated the applicability of a model of leadership perception that incorporates the standard cognitive processes of encoding, storing, and

FIGURE 9

Model of Performance Rating

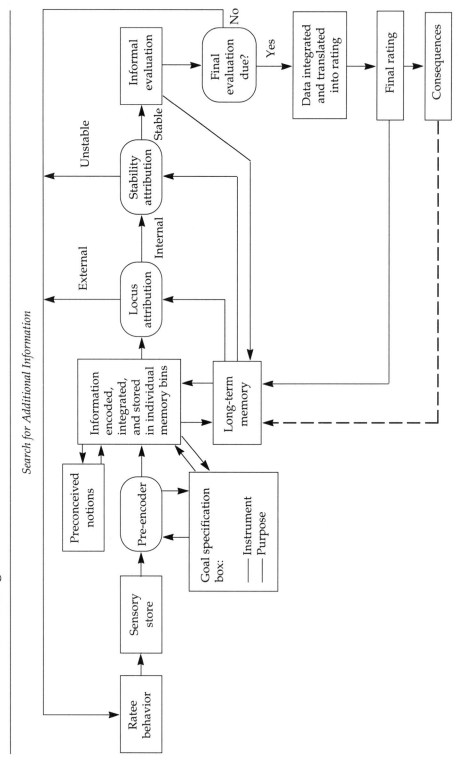

Search for Additional Information

From "A Cognitive View of the Appraisal Process: A Model and Research Propositions" by A. S. De Nisi, T. P. Cafferty, and B. M. Meglino, 1984, *Organizational Behavior and Human Performance, 33,* p. 363. Copyright 1984 by Academic Press, Inc. Adapted by permission.

retrieving information about the leader's behavior. Lord and Maher (1991b) more recently described how a number of aspects of leadership can be viewed in terms of leadership perception. Yukl and Van Fleet (1992, vol. 3), in their *Handbook* chapter, noted the growing use of cognitive concepts in work on leadership. However, it is not yet clear how much micro-level cognitive concepts will contribute to the improvement of leadership.

Human Factors

In his *Handbook* chapter on this subject, Howell (1991, vol. 2) stated that "as in much of psychology, the emphasis has shifted from the behaviorist to the cognitive paradigm" (p. 215). The schematic representation of the man-machine system that he presented on page 214 and that is reproduced here as Figure 8 portrays the centrality of cognitive processes. Also noteworthy is the inclusion of information processing and decision making by machines, notably computers. Computer models of human cognition have also stimulated the field of artificial intelligence, which examines ways in which machines can take over cognitive functions traditionally carried out by humans in performing tasks. A leading example is the SOAR computer program that seeks to model the entire domain of cognition, including perception, memory, learning, language, and reasoning (Newell, 1990). Function allocation between people and machines is accordingly a key element in developing "advanced technology" in office and factory operations, a topic that we will examine further later on.

Consumer Behavior

The chapter by Jacoby, Hoyer, and Brief (1992, vol. 3) in this *Handbook* illustrates how the cognitive approach has come to dominate this field since the time of the corresponding chapter in the first edition (Jacoby, 1976). Present areas of concern include problem recognition by the consumer, internal information search and retrieval from memory, search for additional information, integration of information, decision making, and evaluation of decision outcomes by the consumer. Cognitive processes, such as expectancies and evaluation, are also prominent in theories of consumer motivation. The chapter's authors underscored the similarities between the cognitive and motivational models of consumer behavior and those of organizational behavior.

Summary

In addition to the industrial and organizational topics discussed above, cognitive concepts are increasingly prominent in other areas of the field, as shown in the *Handbook* chapters on mental measurement (Ackerman & Humphreys, 1990, vol. 1), training (Goldstein, 1991, vol. 2), organizational commitment (Hulin, 1991, vol. 2), motivation (Kanfer, 1990, vol. 1), job choice (Rynes, 1991, vol. 2), and learning (Weiss, 1990, vol. 1). This is not to say that the same cognitive constructs are employed in all those subjects. Even within the topic of decision making, the micro-level processes that are central to the analysis of judgment and decision making by individuals are not much represented in descriptions of group or organizational decision patterns, nor do they overlap very much with those processes that seem most useful to the understanding of motivation, leadership, and other topics central to the organizational domain of industrial and organizational psychology.

This suggests that *cognition* may be being used as a catchall term for many constructs and processes that don't even share the common thread of conscious representation. Its contemporary usage seems to be pretty much synonymous with a panoply of mediating processes that intervene between stimuli and responses and that involve acquisition, transformation, transmission, or use of information.

It is worth noting that several authorities have written caveats concerning the use of cognitive approaches in industrial and organizational psychology. For instance, Lubinski and Dawis (1992, vol. 3), in their *Handbook* chapter, expressed reservations about whether information processing measures of ability offer anything beyond what conventional psychometric methods provide. Thomas (1992, vol. 3), in his *Handbook* chapter, decried the focus on cognitive and rational processes in approaches to conflict and its resolution compared to the relative disregard of emotional factors. As was earlier stated, reservations have been voiced about the value of cognitive approaches in improving performance ratings (Guion, 1991). Ilgen and Klein (1989) have suggested that the cognitive literature has done little more than demonstrate the applicability of cognitive concepts to organizational behavior, but thus far has not substantially advanced either theory or practice in the field.

Since one test of good theory is its power to improve practice, it must be admitted that the value of cognitive approaches in the practice of industrial and organizational psychology is yet to be well documented beyond certain limited domains such as person-machine systems. A core problem is that theory and research on cognition focus on mediating variables, whereas practice typically is concerned with independent variables, that is, interventions. As Herbert Simon (1992) pointed out, cognitive science offers a new means of explaining behavior, thereby abetting its prediction. But bridging cognitive science and industrial and organizational practice will require relating organizational and worker-related independent variables to cognitive mediators, and the latter to relevant dependent variables. That agenda is worth further attention.

Multiple Levels

The early focus of industrial psychology was what Scott and Clothier (1923) called "the worker in his work unit." The traditional topics of the field dealt mainly with the individual: selection, training, job analysis, fatigue, and the immediate physical work environment. Stimulated by the Hawthorne studies and the work of Kurt Lewin, the attention of the field was expanded in the 1930s to include the work group (cf. Katzell & Austin, 1992). Constructs and variables at the organizational level remained largely the province of management theorists and sociologists until after World War II, when they became the concern of industrial and organizational psychologists, including Argyris (1957), Likert (1961), and McGregor (1960). Some even examined international and intercultural factors, reviewed by Barrett and Bass (1976) in the first edition of the *Handbook*.

More recently, those kinds of issues have crystallized into what are called levels of analysis, of which we can discern the following: individual, dyad, group, department, organization, social/economic environment, and national location. These levels can be arranged along a dimension of embeddedness, from individual (embedded in all the other levels) to national (which comprises all of the others).

The broad terms micro and macro (for microscopic and macroscopic) have also been applied to levels, although their boundaries are not altogether clear. Staw (1984) equated macro with organization theory, stated that it deals with questions of organization design, structure, and socioeconomic contexts, and identified its roots as being in the disciplines of sociology, political science, and economics. O'Reilly (1991) accepted that characterization, adding that macro researchers are usually interested in broad theories and descriptive research not aimed at applications. Both Staw and O'Reilly identified the micro level more closely with psychology, and as being principally concerned with individual attitudes and behavior. Both also included at the micro level studies of the relations between organizations and their individual members. Cappelli and Sherer (1991) basically went along with those categorizations, but proposed in addition a third level, called *meso*; the meso level was defined as addressing relations between socioeconomic environments and individuals, thereby completing the chain linking environments, organizations, and individuals.[2]

What constitutes a significant meta-trend is, of course, not merely the definition of the various levels. Rather, there are three somewhat related concerns pertaining to levels that are receiving contemporary attention. They are (a) the identification and operationalization of constructs pertinent to a given level, (b) specification of the level(s) at which it is appropriate to measure a construct, and (c) establishing relationships among variables at different levels.

Definition of Constructs

Concerns with identification and measurement of constructs at the level of the individual and the job are virtually coextensive with the life of industrial and organizational psychology. Much progress has been made in dealing with concepts and measures of ability, personality, interests, motivation, work-related attitudes, job analysis, job design, and so forth. Despite decades of attention, however, there still remain questions and uncertainties, as is clearly illustrated by various chapters in the *Handbook*. But compared to the state of the art of 50 years ago, one would have to say that current efforts at this level are more often in the nature of fine-tuning than basic discovery. That is even more apparent when one compares the state of the art at the level of the individual with those at levels of the group, organization, and society.

At the level of the work group, industrial and organizational psychology is far from agreement regarding the constructs of interest. Only recently, for example, has the significance of the dyadic relationship between leader and subordinate been examined (Graen & Scandura, 1987), and even here many of the operative constructs have yet to be elaborated and measured. Unlike our understanding of what makes for the effective individual (appropriate KSAs, high performance goals, adequate resources, etc.), the ingredients of group effectiveness are still being explored, let alone measured (cf. Guzzo & Shea, 1992).

In keeping with the assertions cited earlier to the effect that the macro level is more the domain of the sociologist, political scientist, and economist (and one might add management specialist and industrial engineer), industrial and organizational psychologists have historically avoided trying to define and measure constructs characterizing organizations, let alone societies or economies. I am not referring to aggregated perceptions that members have of, say, their organization's climate (Rousseau, 1988) or its control structure (Tannenbaum, Kavcic, Rosner, Vianello, & Wieser, 1974). Nor do I refer to specific organizational or environmental variables that are fairly easily identified and operationalized, such as the organization's recruitment system or national location. Rather, I refer to more holistic macro constructs such as labor market or productivity or organizational environment. For example, the multiple meanings and complexities of various constructs have been described in the literature: of the productivity construct by Mahoney (1988), of the culture construct in the volume by Frost, Moore, Louis, Lundberg, and Martin (1985), and of the organizational environment in the first (Starbuck, 1976) and second (Davis & Powell, 1992, vol. 3) editions of the *Handbook*. Most industrial and organizational psychologists would do well to approach such macroscopic topics with trepidation and humility in their research and practice, unless they work in collaboration with relevant specialists or otherwise obtain the requisite expertise. It is no accident, for example, that the authors of, and most of the references in, the *Handbook* chapter on organization-environment relations are not psychologists (Davis & Powell, 1992, vol. 3). Another example was furnished by Burke (1992); discovering that his work as a psychological consultant was requiring him to deal with broader management problems, he found it necessary to educate himself in areas beyond those covered by his training.[3]

Levels of Analysis

A relatively recent development in the field is attention to the level at which it is appropriate to study and measure a particular construct (Dansereau & Alutto, 1990; Rousseau, 1985). A related issue concerns how to determine whether a construct may be studied at more than one level at a time. In discussing this development, I will follow closely part of its treatment by Dansereau and Alutto (1990) vis à vis the topic of climate in organizations.

The single-level focus concerns whether or not the phenomenon exists at a certain level, such as individual, group, or organization. In dealing with this issue, one can ask whether, at a given level, it is appropriate to consider the units (e.g., groups) as undifferentiated *wholes* that differ from one another in terms of the variable of interest. Alternatively, should the units be viewed as composed of heterogeneous *parts,* with all units being heterogeneous in the same way? In analytical terms, the "wholes" condition amounts to finding intergroup differences in the subject variable but virtually no variance attributable to differences among individuals constituting each group; whereas in the "parts" instance, individual differences show similiar patterns in each group, and there are no appreciable intergroup differences. If statistical tests show the latter to be the case, the phenomenon should be measured and analyzed at the individual (or more embedded) level, whereas it should be studied at the group (or more comprehensive) level if the former is demonstrated. An implication of this line of statistical reasoning is that data obtained at a more embedded or lower level of analysis should be aggregated to represent a construct at a more comprehensive level only if statistical analysis shows that the variable clearly exists at that higher level. A method called WABA

(within-and-between-analysis) permits testing a data set to determine whether it corresponds to the "wholes" or "parts" (or neither) condition (Dansereau, Alutto, & Yammarino, 1984). Kenny and LaVoie (1985) described an ANOVA approach to dealing with this issue.

The statistical test may reject both of the above patterns, indicating that the phenomenon is attributable to some extent to both the lower and the comprehensive levels of analysis. Investigators differ in their views of dealing with this kind of finding. James, Joyce, and Slocum (1988) adopted a cross-level view of organizational climate and believed that it can be regarded as a property of both individuals and organizations, whereas Glick (1985) argued that it is proper to pursue it solely as an organizational construct.

Later conceptual and analytic developments include multiple-level analysis, which permits examination of various combinations of different facets of the focal construct, for example, climate, at different levels. This procedure serves to identify the level appropriate to each of the several aspects of the construct under investigation. It may help reconcile the aforementioned different positions regarding more than one locus of climate because some elements of climate may be found to exist at one level and other elements at another. Another recent development, multiple-relationship analysis, allows for all of those analyses under different conditions, including moderating and temporal considerations. Dansereau, Alutto, and Yammartino (1984) have described these more complex methods.

Issues pertaining to levels of analysis not only have important implications for theory and research but have implications for practice as well. Identifying the level(s) at which variable(s) of interest exist can help the practitioner design interventions aimed at the appropriate level. If, for example, intention to quit were found to be essentially an organization-level phenomenon (rather than group or individual level), efforts to curb turnover would be more usefully addressed to organizational policies (e.g., compensation) than to micro-level practices such as supervision or selection.

Inter-level Relations

We have already encountered in this section one aspect of this subject, namely, the identification of a construct at different levels of analysis, called a cross-level formulation by Dansereau and Alutto (1990). Rousseau (1985) referred to this kind of inquiry as composition research. By way of illustration, James, Joyce, and Slocum (1988) averred that organizational climate is a matter of individual perception as well as a representation of organizational properties. Elsewhere in this chapter, I suggest the similarity between the concept of self-efficacy belief or self-confidence (an individual-level variable) and that of potency of the group. Only further research can show whether we are dealing in such instances with the same construct at different levels, or whether there are really different constructs that happen to sound alike. That research would entail the inclusion of one or more independent or criterion variables in addition to measures of the focal variables in what amounts to a construct validation strategy. The multiple-variable and multiple-relationship methods would be applicable to such problems, as would customary construct validation techniques.

Of course, interest in the levels at which constructs operate is only one facet of the more general subject of inter-level relationships. Increasingly, attention has been turning to relationships among variables at different levels, called cross-level research by Rousseau (1985). As observed by Katzell and Austin (1992), the interface between I and 0 began receiving increasing attention in the 1960s, and has become a mainstream interest. In the sections of this chapter dealing with cybernetics and with groups, we note how organizations and groups affect their individual members. A reverse

example is furnished by the reference to ingroup and outgroup identification by individuals as a factor in intergroup relations. We also referred to studies of national and cultural influences on individuals reviewed by Barrett and Bass (1976). A more recent example is Hofstede's (1980) extensive study of work-related values of people in 40 different countries, concluding that there are significant differences in organization members, organization management, and even how organizations are conceptualized and studied. In another example, Rosenstein (1985) reported that managers in Japanese and Scandinavian organizations were more prone to be promoted because of cooperative behavior than was the case in other countries studied. Numerous additional examples will be found in the present volume.

Another kind of inter-level concern is with the moderating effect of one level on relations between variables associated with other levels. Thus Ronen (1986) reviewed the international factors that impinge on the effectiveness of human resource management practices. Turnage (1990) has pointed out that different job designs and supervisor-subordinate relations are needed in high technology firms than in traditional settings. Those are but examples of many contingencies that one level may impose on effects at other levels, and which are increasingly the subject of attention from industrial and organizational psychologists.

Whereas, as previously mentioned, the effects of variables at higher levels (e.g., organizations) on lower levels (e.g., individuals) have been the usual subjects of study, we find that attention is lately being given to the reverse process. Leadership is now often considered not in terms of the traditional top-down, one-on-one model, but as a reciprocal, even systemic, relationship (Hollander & Offermann, 1990; Yukl & Van Fleet, 1992). Characteristics of departmental leaders, including their tenure and autonomy, were found to affect the size and structure of their departments

(Meyer, 1978). Schneider (1987) has advanced the thesis that "people make the place," that is, that through processes of attraction, selection, and attrition, organization members shape the organizations to which they belong.

Summary

We see, therefore, that in various ways industrial and organizational psychology is attending not only to the individual workers and leaders who have historically been their focus, and not only to groups to whom they later attended, but to organizational and even social environments. Inter-level constructs, relationships, and moderators are becoming increasingly subjects of interest. This meta-trend is consistent with the open systems thinking that we discuss elsewhere in this chapter: The person, the group, the various hierarchical and lateral components, the organization, and the socioeconomic and cultural environments are envisioned in interconnected, reciprocal, and dynamic terms.

The Revival of Personality

R. T. Hogan's (1991, vol. 2) *Handbook* chapter succinctly summarizes the rise, fall, and revival of personality as a construct in the firmament of psychology. The renewed attention to personality constructs and measures is the meta-trend discussed in this section. For some time following publication of Mischel's (1968) influential book, it became "politically correct" for psychologists to challenge the unity and even the validity of the notion of "personality," principally on the grounds of apparent inconsistency of social behavior in different situations. A further argument was based on the low correlations often found between personality measures and behavior, as revealed, for example, by the meta-analysis reported by Schmitt, Gooding, Noe, and Kirsch (1984). Most industrial and

organizational psychologists probably never did quite adopt that stance. For example, personality measures continued to be featured in personnel assessment. But some felt reservations in the face of such findings (cf. Guion & Gottier, 1965).

Later research on personality measurement provided fresh reasons for rehabilitating the construct and its measures. The rehabilitation of the construct of personality for industrial and organizational psychology was cogently advanced by Weiss and Adler (1984) and by Adler and Weiss (1988), who pointed out that the concept of coherence or equivalence of behavior across situations is more pertinent than consistency of specific behaviors when behavioral requirements might differ.

Personality theory and personality measurement are similarly experiencing renewed vigor throughout the entire field of psychology, as witnessed by publication of the massive *Handbook of Personality: Theory and Research* (Pervin, 1990). Cervone (1991) noted that current thinking about personality can be divided into two broad approaches, which he labeled "social-cognitive" and "trait/dispositional." Those approaches are represented also in the work of industrial and organizational psychologists.

Trait/Dispositional Approach

The notion that a person tends to behave with some consistency in a variety of circumstances is as old as humankind. Each such behavioral disposition is called a *trait*. Gordon Allport (1937) wrote that a trait serves to render different stimuli functionally equivalent, thereby accounting for behavioral consistency across certain situations.

Attempts to classify traits go back at least as far as the four "humors" of medieval times. In modern psychology, this agenda was cogently undertaken by the Allport brothers in 1921, who also suggested ways in which traits could be measured (Allport & Allport, 1921). More recent taxonomies were proposed on the basis of factor analyses of personality measures. For example, Cattell (1950) concluded that personality questionnaires yield some 11 tolerably well-defined factors, such as Emotional Stability and Surgency. Tupes and Christal (1961) identified five higher-order constructs that are tapped by personality ratings and scales, namely, Surgency, Agreeableness, Dependability, Emotional Stability, and Culture; under various names, these have become known as the "Big Five" (Digman, 1990).

Hough (1992) has described a program of research that included relating personality scales to performance criteria, and that led to a taxonomy of nine factors. Four were pretty much the same as those identified by Tupes and Christal (1961); under slightly different names, they are Dependability, Agreeableness, Adjustment, and Intellectance (the latter two corresponding approximately to the earlier Emotional Stability and Culture, respectively). Surgency was decomposed into three factors: Affiliation, Potency, and Achievement (which also contains elements of the earlier Dependability). Two new factors were added, Locus of Control and Rugged Individualism (similar to what is called Masculinity in some scales), for a total of nine.

It is significant that scales measuring those nine constructs were found to differ in their average correlations with various criteria of job performance. For example, Achievement and Locus of Control had the highest average correlations (.19) with ratings of overall performance, whereas Intellectance correlated only .01 with that criterion. Conversely, Intellectance correlated .16 with technical proficiency, but Achievement and Locus of Control had negligible correlations with that criterion.

The utility of decomposing one of the global traits into more specific measures was also shown by the study of airline reservation agents by Helmreich, Sawin, and Carlsrud (1986) reported in our section on the time factor. They differentiated Achievement into measures of inclination to perform well, to master new challenges, and to do better than others. The first two of these correlated significantly with performance after six months on the job, but the third did not.

Based partly on such findings, Guion (1991) has suggested that a desirable alternative to measuring global personality traits is to measure narrowly focused characteristics that correspond to specific work requirements. He cited as an example the Service Orientation scale (Hogan, Hogan, & Busch, 1984) for jobs involving provision of service. An earlier example was provided by Ghiselli (1971), who devised a personality inventory that contained a Supervisory Ability scale developed on strictly empirical grounds; that scale was found to have an average correlation of .55 with rated performance in four samples of executives, higher than that of any of the other 12 more abstract traits measured by the inventory.

The issue of the breadth of the constructs has arisen also in conjunction with the study of leader and manager personalities. After a period of disenchantment with the trait approach to determining effectiveness, here too personality has enjoyed some revival. Yukl and Van Fleet (1992) have noted that the recent progress may be due partly to the abandonment of abstract, general traits in favor of more specific traits that can be related to behaviors required for effective leadership in given situations. Among the latter are such traits as high energy level and tolerance for stress, both presumably helpful in coping with the pressures and conflicting demands of many managerial jobs. A recent volume reporting a conference on the measurement of leadership attests to the diversity of personality constructs and measures that have applicability to this subject (Clark & Clark, 1990).

Research has not yet clarified the relative merits of using broad versus specific personality constructs. It may turn out that each approach has advantages for different purposes, for they both have been found useful. In this vein, Funder (1991) has asserted that global traits are more useful for purposes of explanation, but that narrow traits are better for purposes of prediction.

For purposes of prediction, not only is the scope of the personality predictor important, but also, as we have already seen in the report by Hough (1992), is the specific nature of the criterion. Her report also serves as a reminder that the relationship even between a given personality trait and a particular criterion is not invariant, but that it can vary with the job. For example, Achievement correlated .18 on average with job proficiency in samples of managers and executives, but −.24 in a sample of health care workers; Agreeableness had a criterion correlation of .19 in the latter sample, but only .07 among the managers and executives.

Additional evidence along those lines was provided by a meta-analysis by Barrick and Mount (1991) of the validity of measures of the "Big Five" for different criteria and different jobs. Only Conscientiousness (Dependability) showed consistent relationships with the three types of criteria (job proficiency, training proficiency, and career data such as turnover and status changes) in all five job families (professionals, police, managers, sales, and skilled/semiskilled). Measures of the other four traits were valid only for certain criteria and/or only in certain kinds of jobs.

The aforementioned research by Helmreich, Sawin, and Carlsrud (1986) reminds us of still another parameter: the stage of work experience at which the criterion is measured, considered also in our section on temporal factors. None of the three facets of Achievement that were measured in that study predicted job performance after three months, but two of them did after six months of experience on the job. Adler and Weiss (1988) have pointed out that, in general, personality factors become increasingly important after the worker has mastered the cognitive challenges of the early stages of job experience.

Pattern/Theme Approach

A species of the social-cognitive approach that is especially relevant to industrial and organizational psychology describes personality in terms of holistic patterns of behavior rather than segmental traits. These patterns or themes are viewed as expressions of cognitive structures (comprising values, attributions, judgments, etc.) by which people assign meaning to and deal with their worlds. In everyday parlance, for example, we speak of "go-getters," "yuppies," "born losers," and the like.

One of the manifestations of this approach in industrial and organizational psychology is the theory-guided study of life histories by means of biographical data, discussed in the *Handbook* chapter by Mumford and Stokes (1992, vol. 3) and summarized in our section on the temporal meta-trend. In the present section, we wish merely to note that biographical data may constitute themes or patterns that show continuity during substantial periods of a person's life. The existence of such themes is indicative of consistency of the decisions that a person makes when confronted with opportunities for choice—decisions shaped by the aforementioned cognitive structures that define the person's personality and that may be relevant to occupational behavior. Thus Schoenfeldt (1974) found it possible to match people and jobs on the basis of biodata. Another example is the theme of accomplishment that Hough (1984) identified and was able to use successfully in selecting professionals for employment.

Another application of the concept of personality as a cognitive structure may be found in the AT&T Management Progress Study reported by Howard and Bray (1988). Among the experimental measures used to predict the career progress of managers were interviews intended to gauge their involvement with nine life themes. The degree to which the managers projected future involvement with certain themes in their lives was predictive of their organizational rank 20 years later. Involvement with themes relating to service, occupation, finances, and self-development were especially propitious, whereas involvement with familial themes, both marital and parental, was associated with relative lack of progress. Miner (1978) has reviewed research showing that another cognitive-social structure related to success of managers is motivation for the managerial role.

Cervone (1991) observed that the trait/dispositional and social-cognitive approaches have pursued separate paths. The fact that, as we have seen, each contributes to the understanding and prediction of occupational performance suggests a functional convergence that has yet to be explored. A useful start would be to correlate and integrate data obtained by both approaches. For example, Howard and Bray (1988) made use of both approaches in their prediction of management progress. More work along this interface would seem to be worth doing.

Applications of Personality

To this point, our discussion of personality has focused on its conceptualization, measurement, and use in predicting job-relevant criteria. The concept and its measurement have also been applied otherwise in industrial and organizational psychology. In our section on nontraditional outcomes, we shall encounter personality as a dependent variable, that is, changes in personality with time and work experience.

In addition to its aforementioned use as an independent or predictor variable and as a dependent or outcome variable, personality has been employed in industrial and organizational psychology as a moderator of the relationships between other variables. Self-esteem has been prominently invoked in this way. Korman (1977) summarized empirical research supporting his view that people with high self-esteem will experience satisfaction with task success, whereas those with low self-esteem will not—a prediction that is consistent with attribution theory. He has also shown that people with high self-esteem, as compared to those with low self-esteem, are more likely to choose vocations that accord with their self-rated abilities (Korman, 1967). Self-esteem, via its effect on expectancy of success and therefore on commitment to attain high goals, has been held to moderate the relationship between goal-levels and performance (Katzell & Thompson, 1990). Growth need strength and locus of control are two more personality constructs that have been shown to act as moderators, the former of the relationship between job scope and satisfaction, and the latter of the relationship between stress and strain.

Summary

Personality has reemerged as a useful construct in explaining and predicting behavior when its use is guided by theory rather than by supposition (Adler & Weiss, 1988; Furnham, 1992; R. T. Hogan, 1991). As an independent variable, it can predict with a fair degree of accuracy various aspects of occupational behavior. Further, as reported by Tett, Jackson, and Rothstein (1991), validity is likely to be higher when the personality measures are chosen on the basis of systematic job analyses or hypothesis testing rather than ad hoc exploration. Personality measures are therefore good candidates for the advice voiced in the *Handbook* chapter by Lubinski and Dawis (1992, vol. 3): Concluding that the validity ceiling for ability tests seems to be about .50, they suggested adding measures of other kinds of attributes to improve prediction. The pertinence of this advice was supported by the recent study by Day and Silverman (1989) showing that the addition of personality to ability measures improved the prediction of accountants' performance. Personality measures are especially likely to be predictive of criteria taken after incumbents have learned their jobs and in jobs that are relatively unstructured.

Personality measures are also important dependent variables as industrial and organizational psychology endeavors to learn more about how work affects people as human beings and not just as hired hands. As moderator variables, they can help industrial and organizational psychologists to understand better the contingencies that affect the relationships between independent and dependent variables.

The sanguine conclusions just voiced need to be tempered by recognizing that the use of personality measures is beset with a number of pitfalls (cf. Adler & Weiss, 1988; Hollenbeck & Whitener, 1988), to some of which we have alluded and of which the researcher and the practitioner need to be mindful of if they are to avoid mistakes of the past.

Groups at Work

Interest in groups was ignited about 60 years ago by the Hawthorne studies and by the creative work of Kurt Lewin (Katzell & Austin, 1992). It continued to flourish for a couple of decades after World War II, in part because of the human relations movement. Levine and Moreland (1990), citing Steiner (1974, 1986), observed that interest in small groups by psychologists waned thereafter, but that industrial and organizational psychologists have now picked up the torch. That is the meta-trend under discussion in this section.

Three foci of contemporary interest will be discussed: the effect of the group on its individual members, relations among groups, and the group as a productive entity. As the last of them has received the greatest attention from industrial and organizational psychologists, we will reserve our discussion of it until last.

The Group's Effect on Individual Members

In the earlier section on cybernetics, we noted that the thoughts and actions of individuals are subject to considerable control by the groups to which they belong. We cited Hackman's (1992) incisive analysis of the mechanisms by which that is done: the ambient stimuli generated by the group context, the effects of groups on arousal, the use of discretionary stimuli to reinforce group members, the group's ability to shape members' beliefs and attitudes that underlie motivated action, and the structuring of norms of behavior. That analysis, based on extensive research, documented the prescient point made by Viteles in 1932, that "the individual is always acting under group conditions" (p. 619), which therefore can affect attitudes and performance for better or for worse.

Although the performance of groups is generally superior to that of the average of its individual members, it is often less than that of the best individual performer in tasks that can be done by individuals (Hill, 1982). That is partly a consequence of process losses in group work due to problems of coordinating and motivating the individual members (Steiner, 1972). The motivational problem, evidenced in what has been called "social loafing" (Latane, Williams, & Harkins, 1979), is exacerbated when the individual loses identity, control, and importance in the group task, effects that are likely to be more serious the larger the group and the less intrinsically arousing the work is. Other possible sources of reduced individual motivation in groups are the "free rider" and "sucker" effects (Kerr, 1983; Kerr & Bruun, 1983). Although most of that research has been conducted in the laboratory, the findings have manifest implications for the management of groups in organizations.

Among the recent foci of interest is that of decision making by groups. The "groupthink" phenomenon refers to pressure put on group members to reach consensus, which may result in poor decisions (Janis, 1982). A related problem is the tendency for decisions made by group consensus to be more risky than those made by the individual members, as well as the tendency of individual members' views to become more extreme after group discussion than they were before (Isenberg, 1986). Group decision making in organizational settings was examined in a conference led by Guzzo (1982). Other aspects of the subject were noted in our sections on cybernetics and cognition.

The group's influence on the individual is often positive as well as negative. Working in the mere presence of others, as is often the case, has been shown to increase the individual's arousal and performance (Guerin, 1986). Groups can also help members learn effective skills and role behavior by supplying models (Manz & Sims, 1986). Groups can affect their members' performance and satisfaction by furnishing cues that shape their perceptions of organizational practices such as job enrichment (White & Mitchell, 1979). Employees' turnover is likewise determined in part by their observation of turnover behavior on the part of co-workers (Krackhardt & Porter, 1986).

The illustrative studies cited above not only demonstrate the effects that groups can have on their individual members but illuminate as well the processes that account for those effects. The industrial and organizational field is therefore now in a better position to create conditions that generate positive and avoid negative consequences of group membership.

Intergroup Relations

Analysis of relations between work groups has lagged behind the study of the internal dynamics of groups. The earliest systematic studies of intergroup relations in industry included the study by Trist and Bamforth (1951) of relations between teams of coal miners under two different systems of mining coal and Whyte's (1948) report on conflict between waitresses and cooks in restaurants. Both studies showed that antagonistic and cooperative behavior of workers could be explained by various sociopsychological factors. More recently, it has been noted that interpersonal relations are also heavily influenced by membership in different groups (Alderfer, 1987; Tajfel, 1982).

Recent reviews of theory and research by Alderfer (1987) and by Guzzo and Shea (1992) identified the sociopsychological dynamics of cooperative and antagonistic intergroup relations. Prominent among these factors is comparative power. For example, conflict is more likely to occur between groups when there are relatively gross differences in power between them, partly because groups of people who have little power seek to protect and promote the interests of their members against the frustrations and threats posed by the more powerful groups. Coalition formation by members of minority groups, to be discussed in our section on work force diversity, can be understood in these terms.

Group identification has been cited as another factor shaping intergroup relations (Tajfel, 1982). People tend to value and support the groups with which they identify (*ingroups*) and to disparage and oppose other groups with which they interact (*outgroups*). In an organization, group identities can be formed either on an organizational basis (e.g., work units, functional specialties) or nonorganizational basis (e.g., gender, ethnicity). The potential for conflict among such groups depends on the importance that people attach to their membership in them, ambiguity in their domains of responsibility, the scarcity of available resources, whether reward systems foster competition, and the extent to which the production system creates potential for frustration or interference between interdependent groups.

Organizations are able to a considerable extent to manage circumstances in ways that can promote harmony among groups. They include clear allocations of responsibility, equitable reward practices and resource allocation, designing production systems on sound sociotechnical principles, and recognizing the functions of groups having nonorganizational origins, for instance, by practices noted in our section on work force diversity.

The bottom-line implications of intergroup relations in organizations have been the subject of little systematic attention, probably because they seem so self-evident. Support for that belief was found in the coal mine study mentioned above; in the work system that generated more intergroup friction, absences were more than twice as frequent, productivity was lower, and jurisdictional disputes were more common (Trist & Bamforth, 1951). However, to extrapolate from what we know about their motivating effects on individuals, it would be a mistake to assume that conflict and competition are always disadvantageous. Where groups are not highly interdependent (e.g., teams in a sports league or decentralized divisions of a firm), properly channeled competition or even conflict may stimulate greater effort.

Work Group Performance

Sundstrom, DeMeuse, and Futrell (1990) reported that a number of authorities have recently been emphasizing the key role of work groups or teams in modern systems of management. Peters (1988), for example, recommended that organizations organize every function into largely self-managing teams of between 10 and 30 members. However, even when that is done, the question remains as to how to facilitate their effective performance. We will here summarize some of the recent work on that subject.

Group Composition. It seems plausible to assume that the degree to which groups are composed of either psychologically similar or heterogeneous people will affect the group's performance. Indeed, laboratory research shows that such factors do affect group dynamics, such as patterns of interaction and attraction (cf. Shaw, 1981). However, recent reviews of the relatively few studies relating those factors to group effectiveness do not reveal a clear or consistent picture (Guzzo & Shea, 1992; Jackson, 1992). This may be because different kinds of tasks place different demands on the group's makeup. For example, heterogeneity

in members' personalities typically facilitates performance in tasks emphasizing group problem solving and creativity, but not consistently when the task mainly involves performance using available knowledge and skills. Also, the variables in terms of which heterogeneity and homogeneity are defined are likely to make a difference. So, for example, although, as just noted, the personality mix of members is not found to be consistently associated with routine task performance, heterogeneity of members' abilities does usually contribute to performance. However, even here Tziner and Eden (1985) found that interdependent military crews composed of all higher-ability or all lower-ability people were respectively more effective or less effective than would be predicted from individual members' abilities; in short, the effect of homogeneity in ability may be greater than the sum of its parts, at least in this kind of task. Clearly, there is still much to be learned about this subject.

If turnover is considered as the measure of performance, the evidence is that it is generally lower in groups that are homogeneous with respect to attitudes and to demographic characteristics. Unlike the studies of problem solving and task performance, most of which were done in the laboratory, a considerable amount of the evidence on turnover comes from the field. Schneider (1987) has proposed an attraction-selection-attrition model of organizational membership based on members' interactions, the attrition term reflecting the well-documented propensity for people who don't fit in with their peers to be prone to leave the group.

Whereas Schneider's (1987) model focused on the interpersonal effects of similarity/dissimilarity of group members, Pfeffer (1983) suggested that the organization's demography shapes the attitudes and behavior of its members. Here, the perspective shifts from the interactions among members to the attitudes, norms, and behavior patterns that derive from the demographic makeup of the organization and that in turn are disseminated as features of organizational life. Among these are factors that help explain effectiveness, turnover, and other outcomes of interest.

Organizational Context. In addition to its demography, other elements of organizational context that affect group performance are the aggregate of management policies and practices, which include group mission and goals, task design and technology, autonomy, performance feedback, rewards, physical environment, and resources. Sundstrom, DeMeuse, and Futtrell (1990) viewed factors like those as impinging on the group's differentiation as a unit within the organization and on its external coordination with other entities both within and outside the organization (e.g., customers). In the remainder of this section, we will examine the roles of various of those factors in determining group effectiveness.

Group goals, that is, goals that members have for the group, appear to operate in the same way that individual goals do, that is, the presence of clear, specific, challenging goals, is associated with superior performance (Shaw, 1981; Shea & Guzzo, 1987). Feedback regarding performance relative to goal attainment would also be desirable when valid measures of performance can be developed (e.g., Pritchard, Jones, Roth, Stuebing, & Ekeberg, 1988). Member participation in setting group goals has been found to have positive effects (Pearson, 1987). An additional factor in the group situation is the degree of agreement among members regarding the goals. In organizations, it is also important to clarify the missions of various teams in relation to one another (Pearce & Ravlin, 1987).

Sundstrom, DeMeuse, and Futtrell (1990) summarized a number of the facets of task design and technology that have been shown to affect work group performance. Basically, what seems to be required is an optimal fit among task, technology, social arrangements, and personal requirements, much in the tradition of

sociotechnical theory. For example, performance is likely to be superior when groups produce whole products, work on jobs having wide rather than limited scope, and are of small size compatible with work requirements.

Goodman (1986) found that technology, equipment, and physical working conditions were even more important to group productivity than the differences in social arrangements that he had studied in a coal mine. That finding is consistent with the important roles played by situational facilitators and constraints (Peters & O'Connor, 1980; Schoorman & Schneider, 1988). Similarly, the physical ecology or layout of the work environment can affect communication and coordination within and between groups, and hence their performance (Sundstrom & Altman, 1989).

One of the important dimensions of team task design is the degree of autonomy accorded the team, as discussed in our section on cybernetics. The allocation of greater control and self-regulation to work groups is a popular trend (Pasmore, Francis, Haldeman, & Shani, 1982). Studies of sociotechnical systems, which typically involve optimizing autonomy for groups, generally have positive effects on productivity and on certain attitudes as well (Goodman, Devadas, & Hughson, 1988; Guzzo, Jette, & Katzell, 1985).

In their *Handbook* chapter, Guzzo and Shea (1992, vol. 3) emphasized the importance of outcome interdependence to group effectiveness. They meant by that term the extent to which the number and importance of positive and negative consequences to its members derive from the group's performance. They viewed outcome interdependence as positively related to effectiveness when task interdependence is high, but not when it is low. That conclusion is consistent with the one reached by Katzell, Yankelovich, and others (1975) from their review of earlier research on financial incentives. Social psychologists have become interested in the effects of differential allocation of outcomes among group members

(Levine & Moreland, 1990), but that issue has thus far not surfaced in industrial and organizational psychology.

Guzzo and Shea (1992) proposed as an additional contributor to performance the collective belief of a group's members that it can be effective, termed *potency*. The authors believed that potency has a beneficial motivational effect on group performance; this is not unlike self-efficacy belief on the individual level (Bandura, 1982).

Sundstrom, DeMeuse, and Futrell (1990) listed organizational culture, that is, an organization's collective values and norms, among the factors in team effectiveness, and suggested that it may be a stronger factor in teams that are less clearly defined as work units. However, as recently indicated in a scientifically oriented volume on organizational climate and culture (Schneider, 1990), the meaning and causal significance of those constructs are still rather murky, and their ties to group performance seem to be tenuous and indirect.

Team Development.   Team development refers to a set of techniques intended to improve the functioning among members of a team. They include improved interpersonal relations, goal setting, role and norm clarification, process consultation, and task-related problem solving. One assumption underlying these programs is that by improving group dynamics, they will help improve group effectiveness. Recent reviews of evaluative studies show that the assumption is supported in no more than half the cases (see Guzzo & Shea, 1992, for a summary of those reviews). Programs addressed to task-related issues, such as problem solving and role negotiation, seem somewhat more likely to improve group effectiveness than those emphasizing social relations, although the latter often do have positive effects on the socioemotional aspects of group life. The findings are in keeping with much of the research summarized in this section

showing that contextual, structural, and technological features are key influences on group effectiveness.

Leadership.   Leadership and its related construct, supervision, are usually treated as topics separate from that of group performance. In reality, though, leader-member relations are a characteristic of groups and, as is well known, can have significant effects on the group's performance. From the meta-trend standpoint of this section, what is especially noteworthy is that, after a somewhat stagnant period, the topic has resurfaced with renewed vigor and new ideas (cf. Clark & Clark, 1990; Hollander & Offermann, 1990; Yukl, 1989; Yukl & Van Fleet, 1992). Among the newer developments are the distinctions among transactional, charismatic, and transformational leadership patterns, the importance of followership as well as leadership, the evolution of roles and relationships over time and, as discussed in our section on cybernetics, changes in the nature and distribution of power. Although the effects of these newer developments on group performance and effectiveness have yet to be mapped in detail, the potentiality is there. More progress could be made in linking leader-member relations to group effectiveness if the processes mediating the two were better understood. Yukl's (1989) multiple linkage model is a promising framework for this, but he, too, calls for more research in order to specify and test the relationships involved.

Models of Group Performance.   The same situation exists to a greater or lesser degree with all of the more general models of work group performance. A number of these mediating processes have been described by Goodman, Ravlin, and Argote (1986) and by Guzzo and Shea (1992). But like the Yukl (1989) model, even Hackman's (1987) model of group performance, probably the most comprehensive one on the subject, is rather general when it comes to specifying parameters that determine relationships. Nevertheless, until further research permits greater specificity, models like those of Yukl (1989) and Hackman (1987) serve a valuable heuristic function for both science and practice in their respective domains. The trend to develop and test such models (cf. Hackman, 1990) is therefore highly laudable.

In sum, the meta-trend discussed here is the increasing emphasis being given to group-level phenomena as factors in many of the concerns of industrial and organizational psychologists, including productivity, turnover, decision making, job satisfaction, and conflict.

Attending to Work Force Diversity

One of the products of testing the mental ability of American soldiers in World War I was the comparison of different racial and ethnic groups. The finding of mean differences among those groups was, however, given scant attention by industrial and organizational psychologists, as was also true of later research comparing men and women (Anastasi, 1958). There were some rare exceptions, such as the work at Minnesota discussed by Paterson (1957) and a study by Gordon (1953) reporting on the applicability of the cutting score on a qualifying test to white, black, and female air force personnel. However, as late as 1966, Porter could observe that industrial and organizational psychologists by and large were ignoring the social, political, and practical implications of those findings. The passage of the Civil Rights Act in 1964 changed that. As is well known, Title VII of that act prohibited employment practices that discriminate against certain protected groups, unless justified by business necessity. That legislation prompted research into the matter, early examples being the research of Kirkpatrick, Ewen, Barrett, and Katzell (1968), Lopez (1966), and Tenopyr (1967). The focus of most of that early work was on possible differences in validity and fairness of selection tests among different ethnic groups, principally whites, blacks, and Hispanics.

However, the ethos of the period's civil rights movement called for more than avoidance of unfair discrimination. More positive, proactive approaches, collectively termed *affirmative action*, were urged to facilitate successful entry of disadvantaged groups into the work force. An executive order by President Lyndon Johnson in 1965 virtually mandated such efforts on the part of sizeable firms having contracts with the federal government.

By the beginning of the following decade, industrial and organizational psychologists began extending increased attention to issues of employment discrimination and affirmative action to women as well (e.g., M. E. Katzell & Byham, 1972). The context for that development included, in addition to the civil rights movement, a revision of the traditional roles and careers of women as a feature of "women's liberation."

Two factors will operate to create a work force that will have proportionately more older workers than has been traditional. One is the extension of the civil rights movement to legislation that forbids discrimination in employment on the basis of age and, with certain rare exceptions, outlaws mandatory retirement. Another is the projected future reduction in the number of younger workers entering the labor market (Offermann & Gowing, 1990), a deficit that will have to be made up by employing a larger number of older people.

An additional source of work force diversification is immigration, which expanded in recent years as a consequence of the liberalization of the immigration laws of the United States. It has been estimated that the United States now accepts more than 750,000 legal immigrants and refugees each year. In addition, an untold number of illegal immigrants enter this country.

As a consequence of those developments, the composition of the American work force is undergoing a marked change from the native-born, relatively young, white male that traditionally dominated it. By the year 2000, the work force is expected to comprise approximately equal numbers of women and men. During the decade of the 1990s, only 58 percent of the new entrants to the labor market are expected to consist of native-born whites; the remaining 42 percent will be about equally divided between immigrants and native minorities, mainly Afro-American and Hispanic-American (Johnston & Packer, 1987).

Those developments are creating a work force that is diverse not only biologically but psychologically as well. Differences in race, ethnicity, age, sex, and nationality may be accompanied by differences in values, aptitudes, education, training, and social perceptions.

In response to the manifest implications of those trends for their province of concern, industrial and organizational psychologists have extended the range of their agenda to deal with issues beyond the initial focus on validity and fairness of selection techniques (cf. Glickman, 1982). The contemporary involvement is betokened by the decision of SIOP to publish as the second volume in its Professional Practice Series a book entitled *Diversity in the Workplace* (Jackson & Associates, 1992). Additional evidence of this meta-trend can be discerned in recent reviews of the topics of women at work (Gutek, Laurie, & Stromberg, 1986); career management for women and minorities (Morrison & Von Glinow, 1990); aging workers (Davis, Matthews, & Wong, 1991; Rhodes, 1983; Stagner, 1985); facilitating the promotion of minorities (Morrison, 1992; Thompson & DiTomaso, 1988); and the effects of diversity in work groups (Jackson, 1991). We will review below some of the main strands of interest. These will be grouped under four rubrics. We have already alluded to the earliest of them: fair employment practices. To that will be added what R. R. Thomas (1992) labeled affirmative action, understanding diversity, and managing diversity.

Fair Employment

We refer here to efforts to ensure that members of various demographic groups have equal opportunity and receive equal treatment in employment. *Handbook* chapters by Ackerman and Humphreys (1990, vol. 1) and Guion (1991, vol. 2) treat various aspects of this topic. The overall strategy is essentially a negative one, viz., avoidance of discrimination. That agenda is complicated by the fact that groups may differ on the average in values, abilities, and job-related skills. For example, whites typically have higher mean scores on cognitive tests than blacks, most men are physically stronger than most women, there are many male-female differences in vocational interests, proportionately more whites and Asians complete higher education than do blacks and Hispanics, aging is usually accompanied by changes in certain physical and mental abilities, and so on.

Given such differences, a crucial question is to what extent they are related to bona fide occupational qualifications. Initially, attention was devoted to investigating whether measures of those variables, principally employment test scores, were equally valid for and predictive of job performance of members of different ethnic groups. That was the thrust of guidelines promulgated by various federal and state agencies established to enforce equal employment opportunities (Byham & Spitzer, 1971). The consensus that has emerged from numerous investigations of such issues is that, although there are instances when selection procedures operate differentially in different ethnic groups, by and large they do not discriminate unfairly, that is, differences in performance on selection measures are usually paralleled by differences in job performance (Hartigan & Wigdor, 1989).

Compared to the attention given to those issues as they relate to different ethnic groups, there has been relatively little attention to how they pertain to other demographic breakdowns.

In general, industrial and organizational psychologists seem to be disposed to accept the findings of ethnicity-focused research as applicable to other demographically diverse subgroups as well. In this vein, a recent analysis of the issue of age in relation to employment for public safety jobs concluded that mental and physical tests would furnish better bases for hiring and retention than would chronological age (Landy & Associates, 1992). However, that is not to gainsay the need for more research on the equitability for employment of psychological assessment procedures in various of those other demographic subgroups; there is evidence, for example, that cognitive ability tests underpredict the scholastic performance of females and that age decrements shown in tests of memory and other cognitive functions are not necessarily paralleled by decrements in competence in work and other activities.

A concern related to the foregoing interest in test validity and fairness has been the extent to which validity is situation-specific, as has been assumed by government guidelines. Guion (1991) reflected the current consensus regarding tests of general cognitive ability in stating that "meta-analyses (specifically, validity generalization studies) of validity coefficients show that they are far more generalizable than previously supposed" (p. 332). However, he noted that validity generalization methodology is not without its critics (cf. Rubin, 1988). Also, there is reason to believe that a battery of more specific aptitude tests may exceed the validity of a test of general cognitive ability in some situations (cf. Linn, 1986). Moreover, Guion (1991) argued against the use of personality measures without research that shows their validity for specific purposes, a position consistent with evidence considered in our section on the revival of personality. The specificity of psychomotor tests is also well established, as indicated in the *Handbook* chapter by J. C. Hogan (1991, vol. 2). In short, although it appears that the validity of

well-developed tests of general cognitive functioning generalizes to many jobs requiring that kind of ability, batteries of more specific ability tests may be more valid in certain situations, and the broad generalization of validity of most other kinds of tests is open to question.

In addition to fairness in hiring, other fair employment issues concern creating job choices and promotional opportunities (cf. Gutek, Laurie, & Stromberg, 1986; Thompson & DiTomaso, 1988), and equitable compensation (Gerhart & Milkovich, 1992).

Despite the progress made by industrial and organizational psychologists in coping with the issues of fair employment, the aforementioned mean differences among demographic groups in various job-relevant characteristics pose a persistent problem. In their *Handbook* chapter, Gerhart and Milkovich (1992, vol. 3) described the problems encountered in attempting to adjust differences in compensation levels for group differences in pay determinants such as education, work experience, and occupations. As pointed out by Gottfredson (1992), adverse impact is the rule, not the exception, when hiring and promotion procedures are job-related and when they predict job performance equally well for all groups involved. She noted that attempts to circumvent that predicament by such practices as race norming or reducing standards across the board are likely to have negative consequences on productivity and/or the attitudes of victims of reverse discrimination. There also is evidence that preferential treatment can diminish the self-concept of its purported beneficiaries (Heilman, Block, & Lucas, 1992; Heilman, Simon, & Repper, 1987). In addition, there are obvious ethical and legal problems in those remedies as indicated, for example, by the banning of employment quotas by the Civil Rights Act of 1991.

Advocates of diversification dispute the inevitability of those forebodings. And even if they were to be realized, those advocates feel that the social, political, and moral benefits of proportional demographic representation in a diversified work force outweigh the possible negative effects.

A position that aims to balance the pros and cons of strict meritocracy versus proportional demographic diversification accepts the possible disadvantages of the latter as a relatively short-term cost worth incurring on the road to the longer-term benefits of the former. That strategy seeks eventually to create a work force that is demographically diverse, highly effective, and psychologically well, within the framework of social and political justice. But to approach this utopian goal, it recognizes the need to go beyond fair employment and equal opportunity. Those are the aims of the other three strategies mentioned earlier, that is, affirmative action, understanding and appreciating diversity, and managing diversity. Descriptions of case examples of them may be found in Jackson and Associates (1992) and in Thompson and DiTomaso (1988).

Affirmative Action

In its initial form, this strategy was viewed as integral with providing equal employment opportunity; it emphasized facilitating entry of members of protected groups into the work force by such measures as setting employment goals, active recruitment, providing transportation, and the like. In some instances, adjustments were made in employment standards, such as race norming of tests. Viewed more broadly, it has come to refer to efforts not only to recruit and hire members of those demographic groups but to assimilate them into the work force (R. R. Thomas, 1992).

Measures undertaken to accomplish those ends include, in addition to making special efforts to recruit members of the target groups, formulating and communicating affirmative action as official company policy and planning, setting employment and promotion goals and timetables to be met, establishing training programs designed to prepare members of disadvantaged groups for employment, assigning mentors to assist transition to organizational life, allocating responsibility for affirmative action to managers and to affirmative action officers, and incorporating affirmative action results among factors in the appraisal and compensation of managers.

Appreciating Diversity

The emphasis in equal employment and affirmative action is on new policies and practices that will help create a diversified work force. Changes in the attitudes and behavior on the part of both the traditional and new incumbents are hoped for as by-products. There are, however, programs and practices that have the accomplishment of such changes as their principal objectives. The underlying premise is that diversification of the work force is likely to have negative consequences if its diverse members do not mesh their values, habits, and social perceptions—in short, if they fail to understand and appreciate their differences.

Whereas equal opportunity and affirmative action programs are focused at the institutional level, those targeting mutual understanding and respect are necessarily aimed at individuals and their groups. They typically consist of some form of organizational and group development program, starting again with the formulation of a corporate policy promoting work force diversification. In keeping with general principles of organizational development (Porras & Robertson, 1992), these programs usually involve diagnosis of the state of intergroup relations employing a survey of present perceptions and feelings, followed by lectures, discussions, and exercises designed to create awareness of extant problems, commitment to overcoming them, and practice in actions chosen as avenues to improved relations. Ideally, there is an effort to gather data evaluating progress in overcoming the problems identified in the diagnosis, followed by feedback to and further consideration by program participants.

Another kind of intervention, often used to supplement the OD-type program, is the formation of caucus groups comprising members of newer demographic cadres, for example, blacks or women. These caucuses, in addition to providing mutual support, serve as vehicles for identifying needs and problems that can be brought to the attention of the majority group in order to further their understanding of the former's predicament. Still another type of intervention consists of the formation of work groups or task forces that are composed of members of diverse demographic groups, based on the belief that by working together, people will learn to understand and appreciate one another despite their differences. Again, the principal efforts have been addressed to ethnic diversity, but more recently they have been extended to diversity in gender, clashes of corporate culture resulting from mergers, and even to understanding and appreciating individual differences irrespective of demography.

Managing Diversity

The term *strategic initiatives* has been applied to this fourth category of programs because they comprise "corporate responses to diversity that are intentionally planned, targeted against business objectives, long-term oriented, *and* involve the entire organization" (Jackson & Associates, 1992, p. 197). This kind of change is, therefore, aimed at the overall corporate culture and management system, changing and adjusting it as required to enable its people to be successful by tapping their potential.

An illustration of this approach was afforded by the American Express Company. Recognizing that its travel services clerical staff not only was composed mostly of women but that increasingly they were younger, were partners in dual-career marriages, and had dependent children, the company revised its human resource management policies by instituting such measures as flexible work schedules, more family and sick leave, sabbatical leaves for personal reasons, and improved benefits for part-time employees (Morrison & Herlihy, 1992).

Other exemplars have devised quite different approaches, but they all illustrate the theme stated at the outset of this section. To do so, they typically generate initiatives that are relevant to their special circumstances instead of adopting a universal pattern, often tolerating by necessity a certain amount of trial and error.

The four general approaches described here for dealing with the increasing work force diversity differ in their amenability to precise research and evaluation roughly in the order in which they were listed: affording equal employment, taking affirmative action, enhancing understanding, and managing diversity. In that order, too, they represent the spectrum from industrial and organizational science to industrial and organizational practice. But even though the rigorous scientist may be impatient with the inability of the people at American Express, for example, to specify exactly which independent variables were responsible for which observed outcomes, let alone what the mediating processes were, the practitioners were nonetheless applying their scientific backgrounds: Survey techniques were employed to identify needs and gauge progress, use was made of prior research on flexible work schedules and dual career families, and psychological knowledge guided much of their overall approach.

Throughout this set of strategies for dealing with work force diversity, we have a number of examples of how industrial and organizational science can be applied in and validated by industrial and organizational practice. Nor is the street altogether one-way; grappling with practical applications, industrial and organizational practitioners have contributed to our understanding of Spearman's g, clarified the nature of stereotypes and indicated how they can be changed, added information about demographic group similarities and differences, and in a number of ways have both expanded scientific knowledge and identified needs for further research and development.

Basic Industrial and Organizational Research

The subject meta-trend is further illustrated by numerous studies that did not address the problems of work force diversity of specific organizations but rather were stimulated by an awareness that the existence of such problems poses a relevant topic for psychological inquiry. I employ the term *basic* for such research in contradistinction to *applied* research, although perhaps the less familiar label *applicable* would be more appropriate since it is concerned with discoveries that may eventually be applied to dealing with specific practical problems. Some examples include analyses of aggregated investigations of the validity of selection tests in different ethnic groups with the objective of learning whether ethnicity moderates validity (e.g., Katzell & Dyer, 1977; Schmidt, Berner, & Hunter, 1973), research on how the basis of stereotypes of the suitability of females for certain kinds of employment can be changed (e.g., Heilman, 1984), studies of the effects of demographic diversity in teams (e.g., Jackson, 1991), studies of possible bias in rater evaluations of demographically similar and dissimilar ratees (e.g., Sackett & DuBois, 1991), assessment of the impact of preferential treatment on the self-concept of the presumed beneficiaries (e.g., Heilman, Simon, & Repper, 1992), and studies of age-related differences in work attitudes and behavior (e.g., Rhodes, 1983). Research of this sort contributes to both science and practice.

The prospects are for a work force that will be increasingly diverse in terms of psychological characteristics. In addition to the demographic changes that are under way, recent federal legislation extends equal employment requirements to the disabled as well

(Youngstrom, 1992). As we have seen, industrial and organizational psychologists have become active in examining the consequences of those developments in both their research and their practice. Dealing with work force diversity has become a meta-trend that still has a long way to go.

Nontraditional Outcomes

In their 1983 paper, Katzell and Guzzo categorized the performance outcomes that were studied in 207 field experiments as comprising production (including quantity and/or quality), withdrawal (including turnover and absenteeism), disruptions (an infrequent catch-all comprising such diverse phenomena as accidents, strikes, and pilferage), and attitudes (job satisfaction and its relatives). Those rubrics embrace the dependent variables that, with relatively uncommon exceptions, have been the traditional concerns of industrial and organizational psychology. That is because they reflect bottom-line organizational values either directly or, as in the case of work-related attitudes, mainly because of their putative correlations with one or another of those having economic repercussions.

In this section, however, we will take note of a meta-trend that makes those bottom-line outcomes subordinate to, and even irrelevant to, the lives of organizations' members as human beings. In their place are outcomes that focus on organization members as people rather than only as workers. To the extent that these nontraditional outcomes have bottom-line implications, they are at best remote and indirect. That kind of concern is, of course, by no means new. In the last century, social theorists such as Emile Durkheim, Karl Marx, and Robert Owen criticized what they viewed as the harmful effects of conventional work systems on workers. Leaping ahead to our century, humanistic industrial and organizational psychologists such as Argyris (1957) and McGregor (1960) also pointed to ways in which they believed traditional organizational policies and practices were dysfunctional in meeting the needs of mature personalities. At about the same time, Kornhauser (1965), too, was marching to a different drummer when he investigated the mental health of automobile workers and found that it was indeed related to their work; workers who had more rewarding jobs, both intrinsically and extrinsically, were likely to exhibit better mental health than those in less rewarding jobs, even after controlling for a number of background variables.

Concern with the quality of work life burgeoned in the following decade. A landmark was publication of a report entitled *Work in America* (Special Task Force, 1973), which emphasized the importance of considering what it called the human results of work as well as traditional economic results. In the same year, a volume appeared that addressed the measurement of quality of work, adding a number of outcome variables to the traditional economic ones (Biderman & Drury, 1973). Another of the several influential works of the period was the *Quality of Working Life* by Davis, Cherns, and Associates (1975).

Those developments were reflections of what Daniel Bell (1973) called the postindustrial society, characterized among other things by a shift in emphasis from economic to social concerns. What started as a trickle has by now swelled to a stream, although it is still small relative to that comprising economic outcomes. In this section, we will review various of the nontraditional criteria that characterize that stream.

Stress, Strain, and Burnout

Stress and strain are among the nontraditional subjects that have received the greatest attention from industrial and organizational psychologists. *Stress* refers to the environmental forces that impinge on the worker to create strain. Stress is also viewed as a cause of burnout, which is often a consequence of prolonged strain. *Strain* may be assessed by physiological (e.g., pulse rate), medical (e.g., heart attacks), or subjective (e.g., feelings) measures. We have employed here the classical distinction between stress and strain, although stress is often employed as synonymous with strain.

Kahn (1981) described a causal model that has guided a program of research on this subject at the University of Michigan. The model holds that objective stressors (such as work overload), as experienced by the person, cause strains of the aforementioned kinds. Those effects are moderated by enduring properties of the person (e.g., flexibility) and the nature of the social environment (e.g., supportiveness). Ironson (1992) described a similar model, extended it to show links to health, and reviewed research evidence that generally supports both her model and Kahn's.

Burnout refers to feelings of emotional exhaustion associated with prolonged strain, plus two modes of coping with it—namely, depersonalization of people as sources of stress and learned helplessness that results in reduced accomplishment (cf. Lee & Ashforth, 1990).

Attention has recently been turning to stress management interventions as ways of reducing strain and burnout. Ivancevich, Matteson, Freedman, and Phillips (1990) reviewed the recent field studies and found that most of them focused on helping the individual to deal with stress by such methods as relaxation or cognitive modification. A few were aimed at changing the objective environment by such means as increasing participation and job redesign. Positive effects were often reported on one or more measures of strain, but there were no evaluations of long-term effects on health.

Health and Fitness

Physical and mental health items were included in the national survey of quality of employment conducted by the University of

Michigan (Quinn & Shepard, 1974) and served to portray how the nature and frequency of health problems varied with the type of employment. House (1976) further proposed that objective data on mortality and morbidity could serve as criteria of quality of employment. Indicating the growing emphasis on such outcomes, Gebhardt and Crump (1990) reported an exponential increase in industrial programs addressed to promoting fitness and health. These programs are capable of description at three general levels: (a) those concerned with increasing employee interest and motivation to engage in health improvement efforts; (b) those concerned with exercise, diet, and lifestyle changes; and (c) those concerned with steps intended to extend and maintain the results of the preceding, for example, by enrolling employees in continuing activities or by providing improved health-building facilities. Various of these programs were described by Matteson and Ivancevich (1988).

Few of the industrial programs and studies reviewed by Gebhardt and Crump (1990) were conducted by psychologists or reported in psychological media. This is in spite of the fact that health psychology has become a lively specialty (cf. Krantz, Grunberg, & Baum, 1985; Rodin & Salovey, 1989), even to the extent of being represented by a division of APA. Industrial and organizational psychologists are now pointing out ways in which their field can contribute to health and fitness outcomes (Ilgen, 1990; Terborg, 1986). They include consideration of health-related factors in programs of selection, training, ergonomics, and design of jobs and work settings. On the process level, industrial and organizational psychologists can help facilitate adoption of and participation in health programs and can help design, conduct, and evaluate such programs. The last, of course, includes participating in the definition and operationalization of criteria of program effectiveness.

After the few faltering early beginnings, industrial and organizational psychologists are at last becoming active in this area (e.g., Glasgow & Terborg, 1988). This is only the start of what is likely to become an important trend.

The Worker's Persona

There recently have appeared several studies sharing an agenda that was formerly absent from industrial and organizational psychological research. These studies examined the effects of work on people—not just transitory *state* variables such as job satisfaction or strain, but enduring *trait* variables that characterize the human persona.

We have already encountered one of those studies, the Howard and Bray (1988) report on AT&T managers over a 20-year period. It was cited to illustrate the developmental perspective in the meta-trend that takes account of time. Instances of stability and change in personal characteristics were reported, some of which were mentioned illustratively in that section of this chapter. Of interest in the present section is their use of personal characteristics as dependent variables, including measures of cognitive ability, motivation, and personality. Independent variables hypothesized as responsible for the effects included culture change, differences in generations, aging cum experience, and a mixture of such factors. Although the results of those analyses were not unequivocal, there was evidence that differences between older and younger generations were responsible for the latter's lesser identification with management, increased nonconformity, and reduced dominance; culture shift was deemed likely to be responsible for declining deference to authority, need for approval, and certain aspects of masculinity; and aging appeared to account for diminished cognitive ability as well as several changes in motivation (e.g., lower need for achievement) and personality (e.g., greater resistance to stress).

Howard and Bray (1988) suggested that a considerable number of their findings have practical implications for the management of managers. For example, since the overall motivation to exert leadership was found to be lower in the younger generation of managers, companies may no longer be able to count as heavily on those internalized motives to drive performance.

Another noteworthy study reporting changes in personal characteristics of workers as outcomes was published by Kohn and Schooler (1983), with the collaboration of several of their associates at the National Institute of Mental Health. Among other things, they were interested in the effects on cognitive and personality characteristics of job conditions, especially degree of self-direction or autonomy and level of substantive complexity. Data were collected by structured interviews on a broad sample of men employed in various cities in the United States; 687 men were interviewed in 1964 and again 10 years later. Scale scores were derived from responses to questions about both the job and the self. Causal modeling was used to analyze the longitudinal data. Among the numerous findings of interest here were that jobs that provided relatively high levels of complexity and self-direction increased the men's ideational flexibility and self-directed versus conformist orientation to self and to society; feelings of distress were more prominent in men who had occupied jobs lower in those feature. Of interest, too, was the discovery of reciprocal personality-to-job effects; apparently many men either modified their jobs or moved to other jobs that were relevant to their personal qualities.

A monograph by Mortimer, Lorence, and Kumka (1986) reported a set of developmental studies that in aggregate also support the conclusion that psychologically enriched jobs have positive effects on personality, as do opportunities for social interaction on the job. Job features like promotions (Andrisani & Nestel, 1976) and wrestling successfully with tough problems (Brousseau, 1984) have been found to lead to higher internal locus of control.

Findings like these, together with those mentioned earlier regarding effects on mental health, have important implications for design of jobs and work and for company programs of personal and career development (cf. Morrison & Hock, 1986), in addition to their humanitarian value.

Careers

Until about 20 years ago, concern with careers lay more in the province of fields like education, vocational guidance, and occupational sociology than in industrial and organizational psychology. Only recently has the subject engaged the interest of industrial and organizational psychologists (Boerlijst, 1984). As pointed out in our section on the temporal meta-trend, the field of career development embraces a spectrum of activities that range from an organizational focus, called career management, to an employee focus, called career planning. Reviews of research and theory dealing with careers from personal and organizational perspectives have been published by Driver (1988) and Hall and Associates (1986).

Although the outcomes of career management seem likely to have traditional economic implications (cf. Campbell & Moses, 1986), those outcomes are likely to be rather remote in career planning for the individual. In this latter connection, organizations may provide employees with such things as occupational information, self-directed workbooks and cassettes, and even the services of counselors to assist them in laying out career paths that may in some cases actually result in the employee's decision to leave the organization. It would be optimistic to assume that career planning is optimally beneficial from the organization's economic standpoint. The continuing vitality of career development in organizations is indicated by the publication in 1991 of a volume on that subject edited by Morrison and Adams; it shows that the scope of the subject is even expanding, for example, by including the linkage between career development and corporate strategic planning.

Even more recent than those career development activities is the interest that industrial and organizational psychologists are exhibiting in entrepreneurship, that is, careers that involve taking risks to start new business ventures by assembling the capital, labor, and other resources needed to convert an idea into reality. Hisrich (1990) reviewed the work that is being done on this subject. Thus far, it mainly focuses on characteristics of entrepreneurs, including personality, personal history, and education, as well as on their role models and support systems.

Comparisons of female and male entrepreneurs have shown more similarities than differences, the latter including evidence that the women are more prone to be motivated by needs for independence and achievement, whereas the men are more often motivated by desire for control; entrepreneurs of both sexes are typically energetic and independent, but the men are on average more self-confident and less flexible. The two sexes also differ in the kinds of businesses that they are likely to start: Men are more likely to initiate manufacturing, construction, and high-tech firms, whereas women more often start service-related businesses. The interest of industrial and organizational psychologists here again seems to be prompted more by humanistic than economic considerations.

Work and Leisure

Super (1986) regarded paid employment or occupation as only one of several careers that people may enact simultaneously or successively in their lives. Other examples include student, homemaker, community service volunteer, retiree, leisurite, and so forth. In this view, leisure and work are not separate enclaves but may have interacting or complementary roles in a person's life. Underscoring that notion is a study of British blue collar workers that found that many viewed their jobs mainly as means of earning enough money to enjoy their nonwork lives (Goldthorpe, Lockwood, Bechhofer, & Platt, 1969). But leisure may not only serve to compensate for unsatisfying work; Super (1940) found that avocational interests may also be extensions of one's work, as in the proverbial busdriver's holiday. Leisure may also be a substitute for work for the unemployed or retired person. Super (1986) suggested that either or both may serve the function of self-realization.

Kabanoff (1980) reviewed research on work-leisure relationships and found some support for each of three conceptions of their relationship: compensatory, spillover, and independence. A study aimed at comparing the validity of the different models of work-leisure relationships was performed by Kabanoff and O'Brien (1980). They compared the work and leisure activities of 1,383 Australians in terms of 5 task attributes characterizing each of the two types of activity. Neither the compensation, spillover, nor independence models adequately explained the obtained patterns of relationships between those variables or their relationships to various personal and occupational characteristics. Apparently, more sophisticated models are needed to account for the complexities.

Although the systematic study of leisure has more typically been the province of sociologists (e.g., Parker & Smith, 1976) and social psychologists (e.g., Neulinger, 1974), it is not divorced from the interests of industrial and organizational psychologists (Super, 1986). The results of the Kabanoff and O'Brien (1980) study point to an important industrial and organizational agenda: clarifying how and why leisure and work are or are not related. Some additional topics suggested by Mankin (1978) as relevant to industrial and organizational psychology are presented on the next page.

- Industrial recreation programs are a type of company benefit that may contribute to employee physical and mental fitness, job satisfaction, organizational commitment, and stress reduction, thereby relating to some of the other outcomes discussed in this section.

- The optimum structure of alternative work schedules may depend in part on how well they fit leisure as well as family needs of employees.

- The development of avocational interests and activities for preretirees may facilitate their transition and adjustment to retirement (see also Smith, Kendall, & Hulin, 1969).

- Avocational counseling may be a useful supplement to career counseling, discussed above.

- With the prospect that, in a postindustrial society, people may have more discretionary time as workers and retirees, industrial and organizational psychologists can apply their knowledge and skills (selection, training, counseling, work design, etc.) to meeting society's need to create more suitable and rewarding leisure activities for its citizens (see also Dunnette, 1973; Super, 1986). It is noteworthy in this connection that about half the workers surveyed nationally indicated that, if they worked fewer hours, they would choose to spend more of the extra time in leisure activities; also, almost half the workers surveyed said that the most important things that happen to them involve leisure (Quinn & Staines, 1979).

The murmurings of industrial and organizational psychology's interest in the subject of leisure, as reflected in references cited above, may well grow louder in the future.

Work and Family

In the aforementioned national survey, an even larger percentage of workers, about 95 percent, said that the most important things that happen to them involve their families (Quinn & Staines, 1979). Given that picture, it is curious that interest in the relationships between work and family life started even later than interest in work-leisure relations. However, the former has recently accelerated at a much greater pace.

An article by Zedeck and Mosier (1990) summarized the literature on work and family, noted the diversity of variables that have been used to study each of the two, and described five models that have been proposed for explaining why and how they should be related. Those models, like some dealing with work-leisure relations, include spillover or generalization between what happens at work and at home; compensation for shortcomings in one domain by what happens in the other; segmentation or independence between the two domains; conflict between the domains, implying that success in one domain requires sacrifice in the other; and the instrumental view that holds that one domain serves as a means of obtaining valued outcomes in the other. Research provides some evidence in support of each model and refutes none, as was the case with research on models of work-leisure relationships reviewed by Kabanoff (1980). Here, too, research is needed to clarify how and when these or different models may explain the phenomena.

Zedeck and Mosier (1990) also described several family-responsive policies and practices that organizations have instituted, including parental leaves, child and dependent care, alternative work schedules, telecommuting between home and work, and family-related assistance programs. Although hard evidence is sparse regarding the effects of those programs, employees generally like them.

Those and related topics were covered in greater depth in the SIOP-sponsored volume entitled *Work, Families, and Organizations* (Zedeck, 1992). The volume also contained discussions of the work-family interface as a moderator of the effects of work stress, the extension of the previously discussed AT&T follow-up study to include managers' family-related outcomes, the plight of dual-career managers, effects of family-related programs on employee commitment, the home as a workplace, family businesses, and work-family relations in Israel and in the United Kingdom. Space limitations preclude expatiation here of those numerous and diverse subjects, but it is apparent that issues of work-family relations offer fertile soil for industrial and organizational science and practice.

Work and Life

The foregoing discussions in this section show that work impinges significantly on various aspects of the person's life beyond the workplace. If a person is free of strain, physically and mentally fit, has a rewarding family life, is making progress on a suitable career path, and, in addition, has a job that he or she is performing successfully and with satisfaction, that person is likely to be living a happy, fulfilling life off the job. The reverse also may be true: The quality of one's life in general can rub off on a person's work life. About 30 years ago, industrial and organizational psychologists and others began to look into these interesting possibilities by undertaking research aimed at specifying the connections between work and nonwork and formulating theories to account for the findings.

Although industrial and organizational psychologists were by then quite adept at defining and measuring various facets of work life, including working conditions, attitudes, and performance, there remained the need to do something similar with nonwork in order to examine the relations between the two realms.

The early study by Brayfield, Wells, and Strate (1957) employed questionnaire measures to compare satisfaction with work and with life in a sample of office workers. Among men, correlations between scores in the two domains ranged between .20 and .68, depending on the facet of satisfaction being measured. There were no significant correlations among women, which the investigators surmised might be due to lower job level and/or to the possibility that work was less important to the women (remember, this was the mid-fifties).

As pointed out by Payton-Miyazaki and Brayfield (1978), assessment of the quality both of work and of nonwork needs to include variables in addition to perceptions and subjective feelings of well-being; the latter are a necessary but not a sufficient index of quality, which they suggested should also include measures of opportunity and of behavior.[4] That approach had been anticipated in the work domain by Merrihue and Katzell (1955), who devised an index of the quality of employment comprising measures of turnover, absenteeism, dispensary visits, benefit plan participation, grievances, disciplinary actions, and work stoppages. Various other suggestions were made in a later volume edited by Biderman and Drury (1973), including properties of the physical and social work environments, congruence between individual and organizational goals, and employee morbidity data.

Near, Rice, and Hunt (1980) and Zanders (1984) have reviewed similar efforts devoted to assessing the quality of life. In addition to measures of work quality, these typically include indicators of health, longevity, leisure time activities, social activities, family life, and physical and social environments. Both perceptual and objective measures have been employed, as also is the case with assessments of work quality.

The general picture from research comparing quality of work and nonwork is that, on average, the two are moderately and positively correlated, whether measured perceptually or objectively (Near, Rice, & Hunt, 1980; Rice, Near, & Hunt, 1980). The extensive and intensive interview studies of psychological well-being conducted by the National Opinion Research Center (Bradburn, 1969) indicated that the relationships may be complicated. For one thing, it was learned that positive and negative feelings about one's well-being are rather independent dimensions. Moreover, certain aspects of work (e.g., promotions and chances for advancement) are more strongly associated with positive affect toward life, whereas other aspects (e.g., job satisfaction and feeling adequate in one's work) are associated (inversely) more with negative affect toward life. Taken together with the aforementioned findings of Brayfield, Wells, and Strate (1957) and of some of the other research reviewed by Morf (1989), Near, Rice, and Hunt (1980), and Rice, Near, and Hunt (1980), the evidence is that the relationships between the qualities of life and work vary with the aspects of each that are measured as well as certain moderators such as the sex and job status of the subjects. Furthermore, the mediators of the relationships are not well understood.

The models that have been proposed to explain the relationships between work and life include the same five that were stated above for explaining work-family relationships, plus an integrative or identity model that holds that the two are so closly fused that they cannot be uncoupled, and a consequence model that postulates the two being affected by some common third factor such as personality or illness.

Research has attempted to clarify the ties between quality of work and nonwork. For example, a causal-correlational analysis by Orpen (1978) indicated that job satisfaction is more likely to be causative of nonwork satisfaction (combining leisure and life in general) than the reverse. On the other hand, Crosby (1984) interpreted the results of her survey of Newton, Massachusetts, residents to mean that the best predictor of positive job attitudes is a full life outside of work. Howard's (1992) data from AT&T managers indicated that work satisfaction affects life satisfaction directly, and also indirectly through its influence on family satisfaction, which also affects life satisfaction; all three are also subject to influence by the person's general affective tone. Again, we find here a challenging subject for future research.

Summary

Interest on the part of industrial and organizational psychologists appears to have been waning in the past few years on the relations among quality of work, leisure, and life in general. The simultaneous escalation of interest in work and the family may have drained time and attention from the earlier topics, all of which obviously remain in a state of unclarity if not confusion. Because all four panels of quality constructs—work, leisure, family, and life—have been found to be interconnected, it would be strategic to continue to attend to all of them. That was the approach taken by the conference reported under the title *Management of Work and Personal Life* (Lee & Kanungo, 1984), which considered them to be all parts of the person's life space. The other outcomes considered in this section can also be accommodated in that framework. Appropriateness of careers, states of fitness and health, degree of stress, and effects on the persona are all likely to be somehow tied to quality of work life, leisure, family life, and life in general.

The contemporary interest in and importance of nontraditional outcomes of work is signified by such instances as the following:

- The recent publication by APA of monographs entitled *Stress and Well-Being at Work* (Quick, Murphy, & Hurrell, 1992) and *Work and Well-Being: An Agenda for the 1990s* (Keita & Sauter, 1992)

- The naming of psychology and work as the presidential theme of the APA centennial convention in 1992

- The 1990 conference on occupational stress and wellness jointly sponsored by APA and the National Institute of Occupational Safety and Health

- The inclusion of measurements of personal discipline and physical fitness among criteria of soldier performance (McHenry et al., 1990)

- The inclusion of such outcomes of work as self-respect and family relations in the agenda of the human capital initiative currently being organized under the leadership of the American Psychological Society (National Behavioral Science Research Agenda Committee, 1992)

Further exploration of the various nontraditional outcomes obviously affords an enormous agenda for scientific inquiries and practical applications on the part of industrial and organizational psychologists.

Muddles in Methodology

Not long ago, there was general consensus about the appropriate way to do research in industrial and organizational psychology. The model was essentially that of the natural sciences, involving hypothesis formulation, selection of a suitable sample of subjects, observation or measurement of the relevant variables with techniques of demonstrated reliability and validity, control of possible sources of error, testing outcomes for statistical significance, and so on; these operations were to be performed by, or at least controlled by, the scientist responsible for the research. Increasingly, those sacraments are being questioned

regarding their propriety for much if not all of industrial and organizational psychology. That is the meta-trend to be considered in this section.

In his chapter in this *Handbook*, Campbell (1990a) called attention to "a relatively strong theme in the literature on what's wrong with organizational behavioral science research. It is the distinction between 'traditional' and 'alternative' research methods..." (vol. 1, p. 53). Alternative methods often feature case studies, small samples, qualitative data, shared responsibility with clients and subjects, and, in general, preference for in vivo veridicality for in vitro precision. The issue is also considered in one form or another in the *Handbook* chapters by McCall and Bobko (1990, vol. 1) and by Sackett and Larson (1990, vol. 1). In addition, that dichotomy has been discussed in several recent compendia, including Lawler et al. (1985), Fiske and Schweder (1986), Nicholson and Wall (1982) and Van Maanen, Dabbs, and Faulkner (1982).

Other methodological issues, some related to that dichotomy and others not, have also been joined. A number of them have been discussed in other chapters in the two editions of the *Handbook* (Argyris, 1976; Bouchard, 1976; Fromkin & Streufert, 1976; McCall & Bobko, 1990; Sackett & Larson, 1990) as well as elsewhere (e.g., Dipboye, 1990; Lawler et al., 1985; Locke, 1986; Nicholson & Wall, 1982; Weick, 1965). All ultimately reduce to questions of how well the research methods cope with the potential threats to one or more of the four aspects of validity described in the *Handbook* chapter by Cook, Campbell, and Peracchio (1990, vol. 1), that is, construct, internal, external, and statistical conclusion validity. (Unfortunately, the discussions have not always been couched in those terms.)

The issues do not all lend themselves to be sorted neatly into the traditional versus alternative dichotomy. That is because some issues may be associated with both of them, and others may arise irrespective of the dichotomy. Also, since neither category is altogether homogeneous with respect to specific methods, an issue that pertains to some of them may not pertain to others. We will therefore consider the issues separately, indicating their relevance to the dichotomy where warranted. In essence, we will summarize some of the principal criticisms that are being voiced, a number of which were noted in Dunnette's (1984) survey of prominent industrial and organizational psychologists.

Irrelevance to Practice

Traditional scientifically oriented industrial and organizational research has been faulted for irrelevance to the industrial and organizational practitioner. One reason is that the subject matter of much of that research is chosen on the basis of interest in theory rather than concern with "real world" problems. Another is that the research may fail to deal with action levers that practitioners can operate to alleviate their problems. That difficulty is particularly prevalent in research on intervening processes such as cognitions, expectancies, and attributions. The aphorism that there is nothing so practical as a good theory has a hollow ring in what some have alleged is the absence of good theories that bear on many of the practitioner's problems. Although scientific research may some day develop such theories, practitioners ask what's to be done in the meantime. Disenchanted practitioners can also point to evidence that much of the significant scientific research in industrial and organizational psychology had its origins in practical problems (Campbell, Daft, & Hulin, 1982).

Irrelevance to Theory

The counterpart of the above is the accusation that much applied research, addressed to solving problems of particular organizations, makes negligible contributions to theory. Apart from its failure to cope with sources of invalidity, to be considered below, the ad hoc, one-shot character that is typical of that work produces findings that create a kaleidoscopic rather than a coherent picture that is the essence of science. Countering that criticism is the argument that it is up to the theorist to impose order on scattered data, which is far better than having few data, and that it is the role of theory-driven research to fill interstices. However, in something of a plague on both houses, the survey of published research by Sackett and Larson (1990, vol. 1) in this *Handbook* found that most of it is neither problem-driven nor theory-driven, but rather consists of relatively minor extensions of previous literature.

Trivial Research

The "add-on" or "coupling" nature of most research reported by Sackett and Larson (1990) may underlie the allegation that too much industrial and organizational research is trivial. Another implicated factor may be the tendency for research to be neither theory-driven nor problem-driven but technique-driven. It is believed that many theoretical and practical problems are researched not so much because they are significant to their respective domains as because some fashionable technique can be applied to them, for example, factor analysis, quality circles, or what have you. Important problems are bypassed because they are difficult to study, while minor ones are researched because they are amenable to ready-made techniques. "Safe" research that can be done quickly with publishable results may be motivated in part by personal reasons (such as obtaining promotions or academic tenure), since rewards are often based more on the quantity than on the significance of the work.

Lack of Validity

Research is often faulted because it fails to deal adequately with one or more of the four threats to validity described in this *Handbook* by Cook, Campbell, and Peracchio (1990, vol. 1). Field studies and experiments, especially those conducted by methods "alternative" to those of traditional industrial and organizational science, usually suffer from various threats to internal validity that result in questionable conclusions about what really causes the observed phenomena. Because their statistical power is often low, there is a high probability that some real effects can be missed. Their external validity is restricted by the special and limited nature of the situation(s) under study. Even their vaunted construct validity, based on their performance in "real-life" situations, is limited by the fact that ostensibly similar measures in two companies may tap rather different constructs; for example, in Company A, high ratings of managers may depend principally on interpersonal relations, whereas they may depend more on operating results in Company B.

Traditional scientific investigations are also subject to various sources of invalidity. Rigorous experiments and quasi experiments conducted in field settings are often subject to the same problems of external and construct validity as above. Although they usually do a better job of controlling some threats to internal validity, such as by using control groups and obtaining pre- and postmeasures, their intrusive nature can introduce other forms of bias. Correlational field studies typically contain the additional threat to internal validity of ambiguity of cause and effect, although the validity of their conclusions on statistical grounds is usually adequate.

Laboratory experiments, which now constitute about half of those reported in leading industrial and organizational journals (Sackett & Larson, 1990), also usually show sufficient statistical validity. Their internal validity is likely to be higher than any of the other methodologies, owing to their amenability to greater control and precise measurement. However, insofar as their manipulations are aimed at capturing constructs that obtain in field settings, for example, supervision or commitment, they are susceptible to grave doubts. Although there is evidence that certain laboratory findings parallel those obtained in field settings (Locke, 1986), there remain strong reservations concerning their overall limitations in representing significant contingent and contextual conditions, as well as long-term effects.

Insider Versus Outsider

In traditional scientific methodology, the researcher defines the problem, imposes the research design on the setting, owns the results, and shares them with the interested public. The researcher essentially remains outside the setting, treating it as an object of interest much as a biologist might do with a specimen under study. In field studies, there is somewhat more identification with the target setting than in the laboratory, if for no other reason than that it may be necessary in order to obtain cooperation, but the researcher still remains largely outside its boundaries.

This model is being questioned, and sometimes rejected. One argument is that it is inappropriate for problem-driven research, for the problem is that of the investigator rather than that of the client. Moreover, in assuming the typical arm's-length, objective attitude, the researcher may fail to understand crucial meanings underlying what is being measured; this may reduce the construct validity of the investigation as well as its problem-solving utility. A telling example of that problem is Bowers' (1973) criticism that laboratory research, by imposing situations on the subjects, makes it appear that behavior is more a response to situations than an expression of the subjects' personalities. Furthermore, that arm's length posture is prone to be associated with the investigation of relatively few variables, resulting in violence to the inherent complexity of the target phenomenon; the shortcoming is said to be compounded by the superficiality with which even those variables are usually studied, for example, by means of questionnaires or rating scales. Furthermore, when research findings are viewed as the property of the researcher rather than as being jointly owned by the client, the latter is prevented from using them to learn and to improve. That not only diminishes the problem-solving contribution of the work, but less obviously its potential scientific value as well, for changes made on the basis of the research could serve as the subjects of further research.

The alternatives to the traditional approach to studying organizational behavior were extensively discussed in the conference reported by Lawler et al. (1985). Although the points varied somewhat in particulars, a common theme was that research should be a joint enterprise of the researcher and client; indeed, the boundaries between the two became faint, as did the distinction between research and practice. As a consequence, or at least a by-product, the advantages claimed for this approach include that it is more apt to address the client's real problems, be tuned specifically to his, hers, or its situation, study the client more comprehensively as well as penetratingly, involve the client in design and interpretation of the study, and, by overcoming or at least diminishing some of the previously noted shortcomings of the traditional scientific methodology, make more of a contribution to both science and practice.

The focus of the Lawler et al. (1985) report was research on and consultation with organizations at a macro level, but it has much in common with the general idiographic approach to knowledge. On the individual level, the issue of idiographic methodology has been raised historically in terms of actuarial versus clinical prediction. It has more recently emerged in work with small groups (Hackman, 1990; Guzzo & Shea, 1992).

Traditional industrial and organizational research is nomothetic rather than idiographic. An example of a more nomothetic approach to studying and working with organizations was described by Seashore, Lawler, Mirvis, and Cammann (1983). It is unlikely that the superiority of idiographic versus nomothetic methodology will be settled any time soon, if ever, as it has long been debated in the annals of the philosophy of science. Of course, the practice of industrial and organizational psychology is and often has been idiographic, for example, in organizational development and individual assessment. But its growing representation in industrial and organizational research constitutes a recent meta-trend.

Discovery

Traditional industrial and organizational scientific methodology has been questioned on grounds other than validity, contribution, and practicality. It is also seen as responsible in part for the trivial, unimaginative quality of much of what is going on in the field, as well as for what is not going on but should be. This criticism was eloquently voiced in the *Handbook* chapter by McCall and Bobko (1990, vol. 1). Conceding that traditional methodology is appropriate for verification of hypotheses, they argued that its premature application is likely to hinder discovery of new ideas and problems. They suggested, instead, some sort of foreplay that postpones the strictures of psychometric precision, experimental control, and representative sampling. Experimental tinkering, thinking in terms of metaphors rather than scientific theories, willingness to employ diverse and unusual methods, and reaching beyond single disciplinary boundaries were mentioned as ways of facilitating discovery and innovation. Note, however, that this is not so much an argument against traditional scientific methodology as it is for using mind-stretching antecedents or accompaniments to it. Truth still awaits verification.

Order Out of Chaos

The bifurcation in industrial and organizational psychology between traditional and alternative approaches resembles a controversy in the field of ecology reported by Gleick (1987). Some ecologists, believing in an orderly world, expected populations to be regulated and steady, but with exceptions. Others believed that populations fluctuate erratically, again with exceptions. The former espoused traditional deterministic models and methods, whereas the latter argued that the subject required an approach that accommodates idiosyncrasy and uniqueness. The disagreement has a familiar ring.

The biologist, Robert May, had been exposed to the recent work of mathematicians and scientists who were trying to cope with deterministic disorder, a technical field now called *chaos*. He pointed out that this line of thought could resolve the controversy: Deterministic models can indeed produce what looks like random behavior, but the model must have a fine structure that accommodates the appearance of noise when one looks at any piece of the system's behavior. In other words, both disputants were partly right and partly wrong.

The approach to science called chaos, well explained in Gleick's (1987) book, is applicable to systems that are characterized by measurement error, nonlinearity, interaction, turbulence, feedback, perturbations, and change. It has been applied in biology, physics, chemistry, geology, and economics. Since the aforementioned properties aptly describe much of the subject matter of industrial and organizational psychology, the vision of chaos may likewise open a route that can integrate the traditional and alternative modes of thinking and research in industrial and organizational psychology.

The several sources of discomfort, if not disenchantment, with traditional scientific methodology should be weighed against the evidence that relatively rigorous interventions in field settings, using techniques and concepts usually based on earlier industrial and organizational research in the field and laboratory, generally have favorable effects on performance criteria (Guzzo, Jette, & Katzell, 1985). We must have been doing something right. On the other hand, experimenting with some of the modifications that are being voiced may result in methodologies that may usefully supplement, even if they don't altogether replace, the more traditional methodology. That hypothesis will, of course, also require empirical testing.

Enter Technology

The subject of technology had hardly any place in industrial and organizational psychology in the United States prior to the last decade. Unlike the present edition of the *Handbook*, the first edition (Dunnette, 1976) did not even list the word in its index. However, the subject in actuality did enter into the first edition's chapter on organizational structure and climate (Payne & Pugh, 1976). It is no happenstance that the authors of that chapter are British, for that nation's industrial and organizational psychologists were pioneers in bringing technology into focus among psychologists in the English-speaking nations.

The engine behind that interest can be attributed to the sociotechnical approach, which was discussed in our section on systems. The nub of that approach is to regard work organizations as open systems comprising interacting technical and human subsystems. The practical agenda is to integrate and harmonize those subsystems. Katz and Kahn (1966) helped popularize the concept among American industrial and organizational psychologists, and early research applications here were made by

Rousseau (1977) and Susman (1970). Enter technology into the firmament of U.S. industrial and organizational psychology. Because technology ramifies into many other topics of concern to contemporary industrial and organizational psychology, its growing salience is a noteworthy meta-trend.

Some 10 years ago, psychology's interest in technology was massively stimulated by the explosive growth of so-called advanced or high technology in the workplace, a development that has been likened to a 20th century industrial revolution. High technology (HT) has two principal facets: computer control of operations and telecommunication among people and machines. Various species of each are being used in both offices and factories, as well as in more specialized organizations such as hospitals and libraries.

Within the past 10 years, a number of books, reports, and articles have been published on the subject of HT and its implications for work organizations and their members. However, owing to the recency of most of that work and the complexity of the multifaceted subject, the present state of knowledge may be characterized more as a hodgepodge of facts and concepts than as a coherent nomology. Given that situation, I believe that I can best serve the purposes of this chapter by summarizing what seem to be some of the more interesting and useful concepts and findings pertinent to industrial and organizational psychology, together with a list of bibliographical references that describe them and that the reader desiring more detailed information may consult.

A nonexhaustive list of bibliographical references includes Brotherton (1988); Davis and Associates (1986); Goodman, Sproull, and Associates (1990); Hulin and Roznowski (1985); Majchrzak (1988); National Academy of Sciences (1986); Office of Technology Assessment (1984, 1985); Turnage (1990); Wall, Clegg, and Kemp (1987); Wall, Corbett, Clegg, Jackson, and Martin (1990a); and Wall and Davids (1992).

The bibliographies of those publications contain numerous additional references to literature of the subject. The majority of empirical reports consist of case studies, although some nomothetic research is appearing (e.g., Jackson & Wall, 1991; Majchrzak & Cotton, 1988; Wall, Corbett, Martin, Clegg, & Jackson, 1990b). Majchrzak (1988) has appended a list of empirical studies. An overview follows of the picture that appears to be emerging from the literature in the field.

Defining High Technology

We may define any technology as a system comprising physical and intellectual processes used to transform inputs into usable outputs (Hulin & Roznowski, 1985). Its components include equipment, materials, money, physical environments, and programs, which can be patterned in various ways. The configuration of those components in advanced technologies, compared to traditional forms, produces events that are both more stochastic and abstract (Weick, 1990). They are stochastic, or unpredictable, because their human operators often do not fully understand the technology and its cause-and-effect linkages. This in turn is due to the abstract nature of those technologies; because connections and controls are typically effected by electronic rather than mechanical or manual means, their operations are largely unobservable. Those properties obviously place different demands on the human operators and maintenance personnel and on organizational and managerial strategies than are the case with traditional technologies.

I have employed the plural form of the word—*technologies*—because in fact there are several different forms and components of HT, just as is true of traditional ones. For example, the forms of advanced manufacturing technology (AMT) include computer-aided manufacturing (CAM), computer-aided design (CAD), computer-aided engineering (CAE), and industrial robotics (IR), that is, computer controlled manipulations and machining (cf. Hattrup & Kozlowski, in press). Susman (1990) considered as additional elements of AMT such advanced manufacturing practices as just-in-time inventory management and total quality control. As mentioned earlier, advanced telecommunications (e.g., teleconferencing and networks of computer terminals) represent additional new technologies that are especially applicable to office operations (cf. Office of Technology Assessment, 1985).

In its review of AMT, the Office of Technology Assessment (1984) commented that "the main stumbling blocks in the near future are not technical, but rather are the barriers of cost, organization of the factory, availability of appropriate skills and social effects of these technologies" (p. 94). As the human issues are the ones of most immediate relevance to industrial and organizational psychology (cf. Frese, Ulich, & Dzida, 1987), it is to them that we turn next. Specifically, we will consider four themes: effects of HT on jobs, effects on human outcomes, theoretical issues, and implementation issues.

Effects on Jobs

Based on more or less formal job analyses and observations, as well as inferences from HT literature, it has been inferred that HT has significant effects on the content of jobs. Among these effects are increased attention to detail, pattern recognition, and reasoning (Weick, 1990); more planning and problem solving and greater task interdependence (Susman, 1990); either less or more autonomy (Susman, 1990); more time spent in monitoring and less in production tasks, as well as less responsibility (Turnage, 1990); de-skilling and reduced job scope, for example, less variety, challenge, and so forth (Argote & Goodman, 1986; Goodman, Griffith, & Fenner, 1990; Turnage, 1990); more stressors, including attentional demands and costly potential errors, as well as constraints on social interaction (Wall & Davids,

1992); and some physical dislocations and ergonomic problems (Sundstrom, 1986; Turnage, 1990).

Empirical research has supported some of the foregoing inferences and has failed to support others. For example, Argote, Goodman, and Schkade (1983) studied consequences of the use of robotics in a factory machining operation and observed that the operators' job essentially changed from manually performing the operation to monitoring it; operators reported that the changed job was less fatiguing, required higher skills, imposed greater responsibility, reduced social interaction, and afforded more recognition. The Office of Technology Assessment (1984) reported that the use of welding robots in the automobile industry likewise reduced the physical demands on the operators. Buchanan and Boddy (1983) found that the introduction of computer controls in a biscuit manufacturing plant had diverse effects on two operating jobs: The more highly skilled doughmaker job was de-skilled, whereas certain tasks were added to the oven operator's job; discretion to monitor and control the process was retained; and rapid feedback on performance was provided. De-skilling was also observed in the case study by Blumberg and Gerwin (1984), but not in that by Wall, Clegg, Davies, Remp, and Mueller (1987). Majchrzak and Cotton (1988) reported a longitudinal study of change from mass production to computer automated batch production that altered the jobs of unskilled assembly workers by reducing the amount of human labor in the assembly, reducing the predictability of the production process, reducing personal control, increasing interaction and coordination with maintenance workers and supervisors, creating longer work cycles, and providing more opportunity for informal communication; most of the job changes were perceived as such by the workers, but there were no significant changes in scores of the five core dimensions of the *Job Diagnostic Survey*. A field experiment has shown that it is possible to successfully redesign the jobs of operators in an AMT setup so as to give them broader responsibilities and greater control over operating processes and problems (Wall et al., 1990b).

This somewhat inconsistent picture of how jobs are affected by HT should create an expectation that its effects on various outcomes will also lack consistency. That is our next subject.

Effects on Outcomes

We will organize this analysis by the type of outcome under consideration.

Job Satisfaction/Affect. That such outcomes are related to technology was demonstrated by Rousseau (1977), who found that feelings of satisfaction and alienation were more negative among workers in long-linked technology than in mediating and intensive technologies. The robotics study by Argote et al. (1983) found that the workers felt positively about the experienced reduction in fatigue and the increased skill requirement, responsibility, and recognition. Wall et al. (1990b) found that the redesigned AMT jobs that afforded greater worker control and responsibility resulted in greater intrinsic job satisfaction than in jobs where those job elements were allocated more to specialists; however, extrinsic job satisfaction did not differ significantly. Also related to intrinsic job satisfaction was the increase in job challenge and interest expressed by the bakery oven operators whose job had been enlarged, and the greater boredom and apathy of the de-skilled doughmakers (Buchanan & Boddy, 1983). However, among assembly workers whose jobs were changed by a shift from mass to automated production, there was a statistically significant decrease in organizational commitment, while neither extrinsic job satisfaction nor perceived quality of life changed significantly (Majchrzak & Cotton, 1988). In general, these findings accord with previous studies of the determinants of worker attitudes.

Stress and Strain. Turnage (1990) reported evidence of stress-related symptoms such as anxiety, tension, sleeplessness, and physical problems among office workers using visual display terminals, although she cautioned that the evidence is not altogether persuasive. She also discussed the potentially stressful effects of computer monitoring of work, but cited the suggestion of Smith (1988) to the effect that it is distressing to workers when used for evaluating them but not when used for providing them with nonevaluative feedback. Turnage (1990) further noted the pace of change and the information explosion as potential sources of strain on knowledge-workers in HT settings. Some support for this possibility was found in the survey of AMT by the Office of Technology Assessment (1984), which reported that repair supervisors experienced greater stress after the introduction of robots, apparently because of pressures involved in maintaining the complicated system. In AMT situations, Argote et al. (1983) reported that operators in a robotic cell experienced greater stress, but Wall et al. (1990b) found that machine operators given greater control and responsibility reported significantly less job pressure and no appreciable difference in general strain. Again, further empirical verification is needed of these potential sources of strain, especially with respect to the conditions affecting their occurrence or absence.

Performance. Wall et al. (1990b) found that AMT machine operators given greater control and responsibility had less total downtime (an important aspect of performance in AMT), although the smaller number of incidents was not statistically significant; that suggests that the operators may have been able to diagnose and remedy problems more quickly. The effects were stronger in systems that were less predictable. A study by Jackson and Wall (1991) did find fewer production delays resulting from greater worker control, but not less downtime per incident, implying that in this situation the improved downtime performance could be attributed to a more proactive, preventive role on the part of the operators. A survey of experience with teleworking, that is., doing white collar work by telecommunications at locations away from the office, suggests increased productivity, due in part to the ability of the workers to control their schedules (Office of Technology Assessment, 1985).

The difficulty of assessing performance outcomes in complex systemwide HT is illustrated by a case study of a sociotechnical approach to the employment of computer-aided design technology (Taylor, Gustafson, & Carter, 1986). Although the study demonstrated the feasibility and utility of the new system, an outside analyst concluded that the multiplicity of changes over time, including product changes, made it unfair to compare its performance with that of the earlier system. It underscores the salience of the point made by Argote and Goodman (1986) of the need for multiple criteria, including productivity, product quality, manufacturing flexibility, downtime, and employee motivation and well-being. That may help explain the rarity of performance evaluations of HT, with the consequent inability to draw firm conclusions.

Quality of Work Life. Goodman, Griffith, and Fenner (1990) suggested that the new technology movement may often conflict with the quality of life movement because the former may allow workers to perform with little involvement, shift control from operators to technical experts, reduce the variety and challenge of jobs, and prevent the use of semiautonomous work groups in view of the high need for coordination. Susman (1990), a leading figure in the QWL movement, also raised this spectre, but believed that it could be averted by selecting and training workers who are capable of preventing and solving problems, including sources of possible adverse effects on QWL, and by

encouraging and rewarding such proactivity on their parts.

Our review of the few studies reporting effects of HT on outcomes related to QWL showed mixed results. It seems reasonable to suppose that those effects depend on the specific kinds of job changes and whether they are made in accord with the joint optimization principle central to sociotechnical theory.

Employment. The most drastic potential effect of HT is on the number of jobs. Optimists suggest that emerging new industries and growth of existing ones should create more jobs. Pessimists note that technological displacement will shrink the need for workers. Each of those scenarios may be correct in part. There certainly have been instances of technological displacement of workers in individual organizations. Certain kinds of jobs, for example, low-skill manual and clerical work, are especially prone to be eliminated. Reduction in layers of management has also occurred. However, the need increases for various kinds of specialists, such as computer engineers and programmers. On a national scale, the overall consequences of HT on jobs have yet to be determined, although some observers have suggested that the current relatively high level of unemployment may be due in part to technological displacement.

We have seen from the foregoing that the effects of HT on jobs and on outcomes are far from clear. In part that is due to the few data points that are available from which we can draw conclusions. The problem of few studies is exacerbated by the fact that HT is not a monolithic intervention and has been employed in a variety of work settings involving workers with different characteristics in a variety of jobs. An additional problem is that what little empirical research has been done has been mainly adventitious rather than theory-driven. Hence the kaleidoscopic picture that currently exists. In the following section, we will review attempts to make sense out of that picture, that is, preliminary stabs at theory development.

Issue of Theory. Hulin and Roznowski (1985) suggested a sociotechnical framework dealing with the relationships between organizational technologies and their members' responses. They hypothesized that technology influences the organization's structural features (control system, communication networks, etc.) and task characteristics of incumbents' jobs; both of these, in turn, affect the workers. Reciprocal effects were also posited. Admittedly scattered empirical support for those views was cited. To move from the framework of Hulin and Roznowski (1985) to a theory would require, of course, further specification of the constructs contained under each of their broad rubrics.

For example, what are the psychologically meaningful dimensions of technology, and how can they be measured? Davis and Taylor (1975) noted that the conceptualizations of technology are typically rather gross, involving such broad dimensions as automation and mechanization, and stated that progress in understanding relations between technology and psychosocial phenomena is handicapped by that situation. A three-category taxonomy devised by Thompson (1967) is often cited; it classified technologies as long-linked, mediating, or intensive, which is rather coarse for these purposes. Conceptualization and measurement of more specific organizational properties is further along and comprises such dimensions as routinization, standardization, mechanization, complexity, and departmentalization (cf. Price & Mueller, 1986). It would seem that technologies could also be defined in terms of such dimensions, and indeed Price and Mueller (1986) proposed that measures of those five specific characteristics be used for that purpose. Sociotechnical theorists would certainly add autonomy (Susman, 1990) and control over variance (Cherns, 1976) to that list of technological properties. In the HT area, a taxonomy of phenotypes was noted earlier, for example, CAM, IR, and so on (Hattrup & Kozlowski, in press).

A theory would also need to postulate how technological properties get transformed into workers' reactions, that is, what mediates between the two panels of variables, extending the approach of Hulin and Roznowski (1985). Since technology changes job content, its effects on the five core motivating properties of jobs (skill variety, task identity, task significance, autonomy, and feedback from the job; Hackman & Oldham, 1976) have been employed by Rousseau (1977), Majchrzak and Cotton (1988), and Slocum and Sims (1983). Noting similarities between job design and sociotechnical theory regarding effects of technology on workers, Rousseau (1977) added from the latter feedback from agents, dealing with others and learning. Stressors such as work overload, role ambiguity, and work pressure have also been employed as mediators between technology and behavior. Also invoked have been the concepts of use of discretion and of predictability of system performance (Rousseau, 1977) and of job control (Wall & Davids, 1992). Sociotechnical theorists (e.g., Miller & Rice, 1967; Susman, 1976) have emphasized the effects of technology on group and social relations of workers; those mediational processes are of the kinds discussed in the *Handbook* chapters on groups by Guzzo and Shea (1992, vol. 3) and Hackman (1992, vol. 3).

Kipnis (1991) has listed a number of other ways in which technology may affect people, including reducing physical and mental effort, reducing social interaction, changing interpersonal perceptions and relationships, increasing or decreasing self-esteem and cognitive competence, and shifting power relationships. Based on her HT case studies, Zuboff (1988) also concluded that power relationships among hierarchical levels are changed in what she called "the informated organization"; in addition, she noted that because HT work is largely invisible, it calls for greater reliance on intrinsic

FIGURE 10

A Preliminary Model of the Effects of Technology

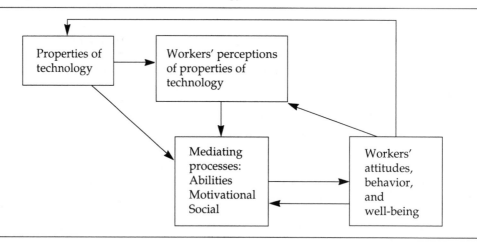

Note: Environmental and psychological factors moderate various of these effects.

motivation and imposes more and wider responsibility on workers.

There is manifestly no lack of interesting hypotheses regarding the processes that mediate worker responses to HT. Conceivably different processes are salient under different technological and organizational arrangements. However, this entire subject has yet to be systematically investigated.

Another relevant literature is found in the field of human factors (cf. Howell, 1991). It is here that attention has been given to effects of technology on human cognitive, sensory, and motor processes and abilities largely ignored in the organizational literature. In part, that is due to the human factors focus on the machine-operator interface and on the operation of relatively small subsystems. As Howell (1991) pointed out in his discussion of office automation, it is in this kind of realm where the interaction of the person-machine subsystem with the larger system becomes critical. Nevertheless, the mediating roles of cognitive, sensory, and motor processes and abilities merit more

attention, in addition to psychosocial ones, than is usually given them by organizational psychologists and theorists.

A general model linking technology and workers' performance and attitudes is suggested in Figure 10. (The reverse arrow from worker attitudes and behavior captures the sociotechnical principle of joint optimization by adjusting technology in the light of psychosocial consequences.) However, the development of this gross model into a theory would require specification of the constructs contained in each of the boxes. Contextual moderators would also eventually have to be added.

Empirical evidence testing the model would require ways of measuring the hypothesized variables. Although some progress has been made along those lines (e.g., Majchrzak & Cotton, 1988; Price & Mueller, 1986; Rousseau, 1977), there remains the need for considerable further development in measuring dimensions of technology as well as some of the relevant mediating variables.

Implementation Issues. Another domain in which industrial and organizational psychology can contribute to technology has to do with facilitating technological change. This agenda can be subdivided into adopting new technology and effectiveness of implementation.

Based on his review of extensive literature on the subject, most of it based on case studies and/or managerial experience, Davis (1986) concluded that the adoption of technological innovations is more likely in organizations that stress technological sophistication, have structures that permit decentralized decision making, have high proportions of managers and technical personnel who are professionally active, and have managers who are receptive to new ideas and change. The inclusion of technology in the organization's strategic planning also seems to be important.

Jelinek and Goldhar (1986) stated that strategies and tactics of implementing HT are not the same as those suitable for old technologies. That is because HT is more complex, entails protracted and incremental processes of decision and implementation, and requires greater flexibility. Their counsel therefore included taking account of those features in managing the change as well as involving all levels and all departments of the organization in considering and implementing the changes, taking an incremental approach based on learning, considering marketing implications, and building the necessary support capabilities. Turnage (1990) summarized similar suggestions made by other authors. The potential contributions of OD technology (Porras & Robertson, 1992) to the implementation process are manifest.

Hattrup and Kozlowski (in press) performed a quantitative analysis of the relations of various process and context factors on the effectiveness of AMT implementation. Those variables were measured by questionnaire responses from 369 individuals who had experience with AMT in a number of organizations. Results indicated that type of AMT technology, organization context (e.g., prior AMT experience, support for technical updating), and social and human resource (HR) factors (e.g., management's technical and HR knowledge, receptivity of operating personnel) were all interrelated. The social and HR processes were found to have a direct relationship with the perceived effectiveness of AMT implementation, thereby supporting the widespread view that effective implementation is heavily dependent on proper management of the human element. Adverse effects of negative HR factors were mitigated by the provision of updating support, a finding consistent with the counsel of Jelinek and Goldhar (1986).

The importance of the human dimension of HT, and indeed all technological development, points to another important way in which industrial and organizational psychology can help implementation of HT in the work force. Turnage (1990) reminded us that effective implementation involves application of HR management techniques to the development of a work force able and motivated to perform effectively in HT work environments. There are obvious implications for personnel selection, training, appraisal, job design, supervision, reward systems, career development, and indeed all the HR programs to which psychologists are capable of contributing. Books by Kleingartner and Anderson (1987) and Majchrzak (1988) described those kinds of needs in HT settings. However, most of the prescriptions in the HT field are based on case experience and extrapolations from what is known in other settings; more evidence based on systematic research is sorely needed.

Summary

There are still relatively few rigorous empirical studies of the technology-people interface. This underscores the importance of the suggestion by Wall and Davids (1992) that the subject would benefit from more involvement of industrial and organizational psychologists. The foggy state of our present knowledge about technology-worker relations will not clear up until we have more and better data on variables chosen on the basis of theoretically relevant hypotheses. The foregoing review pointed out a number of needs that could profitably be addressed.

The matter is not made simpler, but it is made more challenging in light of a thesis advanced by Davis and Taylor (1975). Their review of the earlier empirical literature suggested that similar technologies may be associated with markedly different psychosocial systems. From that they inferred that the effects of technology on workers must depend heavily on the psychological assumptions of the designers of technical systems. The variable effects of AMT that we have found in the later literature do not refute that inference. If it is in fact correct, industrial and organizational psychologists have an important and challenging role to play in designing AMT systems in ways that are optimally congenial to the performance and well-being of the people who staff them.

Summary

As a sort of epilogue to the first three volumes of the *Handbook* (Dunnette & Hough, 1990, 1991, 1992), I undertook to identify certain themes or trends that impressed me as noteworthy in contemporary industrial and organizational psychology. Trends were selected for discussion because they each related to several subfields of industrial and organizational psychology, thereby serving to tie various of the *Handbook* chapters with each other as well as with other recent literature. The term *meta-trends* was employed to connote that transcendent quality.

Twelve meta-trends were identified and discussed, although it should be recognized that they do not exhaust the list of possibilities. They happen to be those that especially caught my attention and that I could discuss within the limits of space and time at my disposal. These meta-trends may be summarized as follows.

"Time Is of the Essence" takes note of the increasing use of a dynamic perspective in industrial and organizational psychology. Examples that are discussed are variations in the predictability of performance criteria at different stages of work experience, temporal factors in work motivation and attitudes, changes in workers' personal characteristics, patterns of life histories, career development, and the relevance of time to understanding group behavior. It is concluded that taking account of time figuratively as well as literally adds a dimension to the understanding of those subjects.

"The Whole Is More Than the Sum of Its Parts" deals with the growing prevalence of more complex theories and models in industrial and organizational psychology. Two sources of that meta-trend are identified: (a) an increase in the number of variables revealed by empirical research as relevant to a subject, and (b) evidence that existing limited theories seem each to account for different fractions of the variance in the phenomena of interest. Building larger theories or models out of the first set of circumstances is based mostly on induction, whereas deduction is the main process involved in combining limited theories. Whether these more comprehensive views work better than earlier approaches remains to be seen, but the promise is there.

"Systems Concepts, Models, and Theories" notes that our conceptions, whether involving relatively simple or complex models, are increasingly phrased in terms of open systems. Examples that are discussed are organizations as open systems, man-machine systems, and the incorporation in various models of systems elements such as feedback, equifinality, and transformation or mediating processes.

"Cybernetics in Industrial and Organizational Psychology" discusses how control theory

is being employed in cognition, motivation, learn-ing, personality, stress, person-machine systems, job design, leadership, group design, and organiza-tional theory. The ubiquity of its application leads to the question of whether the construct or only the word is truly applicable in all these ways, but control does seem to be a use-ful way to think about a number of issues, both theoretical and practical.

"The Cognitive Perspective" deals with another conception that is permeating the field: Cognitive constructs are being used to study problem solving, decision making, performance appraisal, leadership, human factors, consumer behavior, and other sub-jects of interest to industrial and organizational psychologists. The cognitive perspective helps to explain many of the observations. A caveat is that, like control, cognition may be being used as a catch-all term for diverse constructs, some of which have little in common other than they involve information processing. The practicality of the approach could be enhanced by relating cognitive processes to the kinds of variables that are manipulable in work situations.

"Multiple Levels" is in part concerned with the question of whether constructs like control or infor-mation processing are really the same when applied to entities at different levels of complexity, for ex-ample, individuals, groups, or organizations. That kind of question is not only being raised, but techniques for answering it are being devised. Even more fundamental is the identification and definition of constructs relevant to under-standing phenomena at any given level, for example, organizational culture. Also of cur-rent interest is the examination and analysis of relationships between variables that pertain to different levels, for example, organizational technologies and individual performance. Ap-proaches to dealing with those kinds of impor-tant issues are discussed in this section of the chapter.

"The Revival of Personality" notes that concepts and measures of personality are being employed with greater frequency and confidence, after a period when their utility and validity were in doubt. A major reason for the revival is the mounting empirical evidence of their value when used in a manner consistent with theory, rather than in the shotgun manner that characterized much of the earlier work. Note is taken of two approaches to concept-ualizing and measuring personality: traits and themes.

"Groups at Work" also takes note of a revival, in this case the importance of the work group as a level of analysis and application in industrial and organizational psychology. Foci of contemporary attention are the group's effects on its mem-bers, intergroup relations, and work group effectiveness.

"Attending to Work Force Diversity" deals with other kinds of groups of increasing interest in industrial and organizational psychology, such as demographic and ethnic groupings. Whereas the American work force was once composed largely of relatively young white males, it is now being composed of increasing numbers of older workers, women, and members of racial and ethnic minorities. As these recent arrivals often have different average levels and kinds of ability, education, experience, mo-tivation, attitudes, and needs, their absorption into the work force poses various problems and challenges. They include standards for se-lection, training needs, career opportunities, and intergroup relations. In this section, vari-ous measures being undertaken to deal with those and related issues are examined.

"Nontraditional Outcomes" explores criteria that are irrelevant to, or at best only indirectly related to, such economically relevant outcomes as productivity, turnover, and overall performance, which traditionally have been employed by industrial and organizational psychologists. These include stress and strain, burnout, health and fitness, the worker's personal leisure, careers, the family, and quality of life. These interests are probably driven by both internal

and external forces that are generating stronger humanistic values.

"Muddles in Methodology" takes cognizance of growing restiveness with traditional research methods in the field. Alternative proposals include idiographic studies, small samples, qualitative data, shared responsibility with clients and subjects, and real-life immersion. There are calls for more research that is congenial to discovery as contrasted with confirmation, and research that is simultaneously useful to both theory and practice. This metatrend is treated here with sympathy, but with the reminder that the success of our field has been generated mostly by research in the more traditional scientific mode.

"Enter Technology" brings industrial and organizational psychology into the 20th century industrial revolution wrought by high technology (HT). Effects of technology on work and workers are discussed, but the current state of knowledge is described as kaleidoscopic because of the complexity of the subject and the relatively few rigorous studies that have been performed. Also discussed are issues of human resource management and implementation of technological change. It is concluded that the subject is in crying need of attention by industrial and organizational psychologists.

As I look back at what I wrote in this chapter, as well as what I read in the first three *Handbook* volumes and elsewhere, I come away with several general conclusions:

- We now know more, and about more subjects, than ever before; industrial and organizational psychology has grown in both depth and scope.

- Both our conceptions and our methods have developed in ways that enable us to cope better with the complexities of our subject matter.

- There is increased attention to development of more sophisticated theories in order to better organize the growing accumulation of facts and to explain and predict occupational behavior.

- What we have learned contributes substantially to the economic effectiveness of our work organizations and the quality of work life of their employees.

- Much of what we have learned contributes also to scientific knowledge of human nature in general. As observed by Katzell and Austin (1992), the world's understanding of such subjects as aptitudes, interests, motivation, fatigue, stress, group dynamics, leadership, ethnic and gender differences, and decision making, among others, would be impoverished were it not for the work of industrial and organizational psychologists. Those contributions have been effected by verification and extension in the workplace of scientific principles and theories developed elsewhere, by discoveries that were by-products of applied research aimed at solving specific practical problems, and by programs of basic research motivated by potential applicability to workplace problems.

- In addition to its involvement with managerial concerns, the field is increasingly dealing with issues that concern workers as human beings and not only as beneficiaries of more productive enterprises.

- The 12 meta-trends I chose to discuss by no means exhaust the list of those that are noteworthy. Additional examples include the roles of facilitators and inhibitors; the use of multiple measures involving multiple methods, as in construct measurement and in assessment centers; applications of social learning both as an explanatory process and a practical technique; attention to biological as well as learned dispositions as factors in behavior; meta-analysis and validity generalization; and utility analysis.

- Also of interest are examples of developments holding promise for becoming meta-trends that have somehow failed to take wing. These include quasi-experimental research designs; mathematical models and conceptualizations, for example, of group behavior; psychologically meaningful taxonomies of technology and organizations, or, more generally, of situations; computer simulation of complex systems as tools of research and practice; and applications of the theory of chaos to organizational behavior. Are those and other possible candidates for becoming integrative meta-trends being overlooked or rejected, or are they still percolating? Our recent history suggests that, as the field matures, we can expect additional integration in the form of meta-trends.

- The emergence of numerous meta-trends is a development that serves to counterbalance the forces that make for fragmentation and overspecialization. It may be evidence of the field's maturation.

- As this and other chapters in the *Handbook* have made clear, what we don't know still exceeds what we do know. The challenges and opportunities that lie ahead are both enormous and exhilarating. Go to it!

I wish to express appreciation for the assistance of a number of colleagues, notably, James Austin, Susan Jackson, and Donna Thompson; Mildred Katzell deserves a special vote of thanks.

Notes

1 Barrett, Alexander, and Doverspike (1992) subsequently argued that few of the studies reviewed by Hulin et al. (1990) were the kind of principal interest to industrial and organizational psychologists, that is, field studies of predictor-criterion pairs; they also pointed out that some field studies showed stable or even increasing validity over time.

2 Like Molière's character who was astonished to learn that he had been speaking prose all his life, I didn't realize that my colleagues and I had done meso-level research more than 30 years ago (Katzell, Barrett, & Parker, 1961). Studying different plants of a company, we found that employee job satisfaction was related to sociocultural differences in plant settings.

3 Mankin (1978) argued provocatively that industrial and organizational psychologists should even be addressing societal policy issues relating to quality of life in general, as such issues become increasingly salient in postindustrial society. Having espoused a more proactive stance by industrial and organizational psychologists (cf. Katzell, 1989; Katzell & Austin, 1992), I'm hardly in a position to disagree. However, my caveat still stands.

4 Bradburn (1969) reported correspondences between subjective reports of psychological well-being and other indicators, thereby lending credence to construct validity of the subjective approach. An index composed of objective indicators of quality of employment (Merrihue & Katzell, 1955) was found likewise to correspond to attitude survey data (Katzell, 1958).

References

Ackerman, P. L. (1989). Within-task intercorrelations of skilled performance: Implications for predicting individual differences? (A comment on Henry & Hulin, 1987). *Journal of Applied Psychology, 74*, 360–364.

Ackerman, P. L., & Humphreys, L. G. (1990). Individual differences theory in industrial and organizational psychology. In M. D. Dunnette & L. M. Hough (Eds.), *Handbook of industrial and organizational psychology* (2nd ed., vol. 1, pp. 223–282). Palo Alto, CA: Consulting Psychologists Press.

Adler, S., & Weiss, H. M. (1988). Recent developments in the study of personality and organizational behavior. In C. L. Cooper & I. Robertson (Eds.), *International review of industrial and organizational psychology* (vol. 3, pp. 307–330). Chichester, UK: Wiley.

Alderfer, C. P. (1987). An intergroup perspective on group dynamics. In J. W. Lorsch (Ed.), *Handbook of organizational behavior* (pp. 190–222). Englewood Cliffs, NJ: Prentice-Hall.

Allport, F. H., & Allport, G. W. (1921). Personality traits: Their classification and measurement. *Journal of Abnormal and Social Psychology, 16*, 6–40.

Allport, G. W. (1937). *Personality.* New York: Holt.

Anastasi, A. (1958). *Differential psychology* (3rd ed.). New York: Macmillan.

Anderson, J. R. (1985). *Cognitive psychology and its implications* (2nd ed.). New York: Freeman.

Andrisani, P. J., & Nestel, G. (1976). Internal-external control as contributor to and outcome of work experience. *Journal of Applied Psychology, 61*, 156–165.

Argote, L., & Goodman, P. S. (1986). The organizational implications of robotics. In D. D. Davis and Associates, *Managing technological innovation* (pp. 127–153). San Francisco: Jossey-Bass.

Argote, L., Goodman, P. S., & Schkade, D. (1983). The human side of robotics: How workers react to a robot. *Sloan Management Review, 24* (3), 31–41.

Argyris, C. (1957). *Personality and organization.* New York: Harper.

Argyris, C. (1976). Problems and new directions for industrial psychology. In M. D. Dunnete (Ed.), *Handbook of industrial and organizational psychology* (pp. 151–184). Chicago: Rand McNally.

Arnold, H. J., & House, R. J. (1980). Methodological and substantive extensions to the job characteristics model of motivation. *Organizational Behavior and Human Performance, 25*, 161–183.

Arvey, R. D., Bouchard, T. J., Jr., Segal, N. L., & Abraham, L. M.(1989). Job satisfaction: Environmental and genetic components. *Journal of Applied Psychology, 74*, 187–192.

Athey, T. R., & McIntyre, R. M. (1987). Effect of rater training on rater accuracy: Levels of processing theory and social facilitation theory perspectives. *Journal of Applied Psychology, 72*, 567–572.

Atkinson, J. W., & Birch, D. (1970). *The dynamics of action.* New York: Wiley.

Atkinson, J. W., & Birch, D. (1974). The dynamics of achievement-oriented activity. In J. W. Atkinson & J. O. Raynor (Eds.), *Motivation and achievement.* Washington, DC: Winston.

Austin, J. T., & Bobko, P. (1985). Goal setting theory: Unexplored areas and future research needs. *Journal of Occupational Psychology, 58*, 289–308.

Austin, J. T., Humphreys, L. G., & Hulin, C. L. (1989). Another view of dynamic criteria: A critical reanalysis of Barrett, Caldwell, and Alexander. *Personnel Psychology, 42*, 583–597.

Banas, P. A. (1988). Employee involvement: A sustained labor/management initiative at the Ford Motor Company. In J. P. Campbell & R. J. Campbell (Eds.), *Productivity in organizations* (pp. 388–416). San Francisco: Jossey-Bass.

Bandura, A. (1982). Self-efficacy mechanism in human agency. *American Psychologist, 32*, 122–147.

Barrett, G. V., Alexander, R. A., & Doverspike, D. (1992). The implications for personnel selection of apparent declines in predictive validities over time: A critique of Hulin, Henry, and Noon. *Personnel Psychology, 45*, 601–617.

Barrett, G. V., & Bass, B. M. (1976). Cross-cultural issues in industrial and organizational psychology. In M. D. Dunnette (Ed.), *Handbook of industrial and organizational psychology* (pp. 1639–1686). Chicago: Rand McNally.

Barrett, G. V., Caldwell, M. S., & Alexander, R. A. (1985). The concept of dynamic criteria: A critical reanalysis. *Personnel Psychology, 38*, 41–56.

Barrick, M. R., & Mount, M. K. (1991). The Big Five personality dimensions and job performance: A meta-analysis. *Personnel Psychology, 44*, 1–26.

Bell, D. (1973). *The coming of post-industrial society.* New York: Basic Books.

Bentel, K. A., & Jackson, S. E. (1989). Top management and innovations in banking: Does the composition of the top team make a difference? *Strategic Management Journal, 10,* 107–124.

Berrien, F. K. (1976). A general systems approach to organizations. In M. D. Dunnette (Ed.), *Handbook of industrial and organizational psychology* (pp. 41–62). Chicago: Rand McNally.

Biderman, A. D., & Drury, T. F. (Eds.). (1973). *Measuring work quality for social reporting.* New York: Halstead.

Blumberg, M., & Gerwin, D. (1984). Coping with advanced manufacturing technology. *Journal of Occupational Behaviour, 5,* 287–314.

Boerlijst, J. G. (1984). Career development and career guidance. In P. J. Drenth, H. Thierry, P. J. Willeims, & C. J. de Wolff (Eds.), *Handbook of work and organizational psychology* (Vol. 1, pp. 313–343). Chichester, UK: Wiley.

Borman, W. C. (1991). Job behavior, performance, and effectiveness. In M. D. Dunnette & L. M. Hough (Eds.), *Handbook of industrial and organizational psychology* (2nd ed., vol. 2, pp. 271–326). Palo Alto, CA: Consulting Psychologists Press.

Borman, W. C., White, C. A., Pulakos, E. D., & Oppler, S. H. (1991). Models of supervisory job performance ratings. *Journal of Applied Psychology, 76,* 863–872.

Botwinick, J. (1977). *Aging and behavior* (2nd ed.). New York: Springer.

Bouchard, T. J., Jr. (1976). Field research methods: Interviewing, questionnaires, participant observation, systematic observation, unobtrusive measures. In M. D. Dunnette (Ed.), *Handbook of industrial and organizational psychology* (pp. 363–413). Chicago: Rand McNally.

Boudreau, J. W. (1991). Utility analysis for decisions in human resource management. In M. D. Dunnette & L. M. Hough (Eds.), *Handbook of industrial and organizational psychology* (2nd ed., vol. 2, pp. 621–745). Palo Alto, CA: Consulting Psychologists Press.

Bowers, K. S. (1973). Situationism in psychology: An analysis and critique. *Psychological Review, 80,* 307–336.

Bradburn, N. (1969). The *structure of psychological well-being.* Chicago: Aldine.

Brayfield, A. W., Wells, R. V., & Strate, M. W. (1957). The interrelationships among measures of job satisfaction and general satisfaction. *Journal of Applied Psychology, 41,* 210–215.

Brotherton, C. (Ed.). (1988). Technological change and innovation. *Journal of Occupational Psychology, 61.*

Brousseau, K. R. (1984). Job–person dynamics and career development. In K. M. Rowland & G. R. Ferris (Eds.), *Research in personnel and human resource management* (Vol. 2, pp. 125–154). Greenwich, CT: JAI Press.

Buchanan, D. F., & Boddy, D. (1983). Advanced technology and the quality of working life: The effects of computerized controls on biscuit-making operators. *Journal of Occupational Psychology, 56,* 109–119.

Burke, W. W. (1992, August). *The changing world of organizational change.* Paper presented at the 100th convention of the American Psychological Association, Washington, DC.

Byham, W. C., & Spitzer, M. E. (1971). *The law and personnel testing.* New York: American Management Association.

Campbell, J. P. (1990a). Modeling the performance prediction problem in industrial and organizational psychology. In M. D. Dunnette & L. M. Hough (Eds.), *Handbook of industrial and organizational psychology* (2nd ed., vol. 1, pp. 687–732). Palo Alto, CA: Consulting Psychologists Press.

Campbell, J. P. (1990b). An overview of the army selection and classification project (Project A) [Special issue]. *Personnel Psychology, 43,* 231–239.

Campbell, J. P., Daft, R. L., & Hulin, C. L. (1982). *What to study: Generating and developing research questions.* Beverly Hills, CA: Sage.

Campbell, J. P., & Pritchard, R. D. (1976). Motivation theory in industrial and organizational psychology. In M. D. Dunnette (Ed.), *Handbook of industrial and organizational psychology* (pp. 63–130). Chicago: Rand McNally.

Campbell, R. J., & Moses, J. L. (1986). Careers from an organizational perspective. In D. T. Hall and Associates, *Career development in organizations* (pp. 274–309). San Francisco: Jossey-Bass.

Campion, M. A., & Lord, R. G. (1982). A control systems conceptualization of the goal-setting and changing process. *Organizational Behavior and Human Performance, 30,* 265–287.

Cappelli, P., & Sherer, P. D. (1991). The missing role of context in OB: The need for a meso-level approach. In L. L. Cummings & B. M. Staw (Eds.), *Research in organizational behavior* (Vol. 13, pp. 55–110). Greenwich, CT: JAI Press.

Cartwright, D. (1965). Influence, leadership, control. In J. G. March (Ed.), *Handbook of organizations* (pp. 1–47). Chicago: Rand McNally.

Carver, C. S., & Scheier, M. F. (1982). Control theory: A useful conceptual framework for personality-social, clinical, and health psychology. *Psychological Bulletin, 92,* 111–135.

Cattell, R. B. (1950). *Personality.* New York: McGraw-Hill.

Cervone, D. (1991). Feature review: The two disciplines of personality psychology. *Psychological Science, 2,* 371–377.

Cherns, A. B. (1976). Principles of sociotechnical systems design. *Human Relations, 29,* 783–792.

Clark, K. W., & Clark, M. D. (Eds.). (1990). *Measures of leadership.* West Orange, NJ: Leadership Library of America.

Cook, T. D., Campbell, D. R., & Perracchio, L. (1990). Quasi experimentation. In M. D. Dunnette & L. M. Hough (Eds.), *Handbook of industrial and organizational psychology* (2nd ed., vol. 1, pp. 491–576). Palo Alto, CA: Consulting Psychologists Press.

Cornish, E. (1988). *Careers tomorrow: The outlook for work in a changing world.* Bethesda, MD: World Future Society.

Cronshaw, S. F., & Lord, R. G. (1987). Effects of categorization, attribution, and encoding processes on leadership perceptions. *Journal of Applied Psychology, 72,* 97–106.

Crosby, F. (1984). Job satisfaction and domestic life. In M. D. Lee & R. N. Kanungo (Eds.), *Managing work and personal life* (pp. 41–62). New York: Praeger.

Cummings, T. G., & Cooper, C. L. (1979). A cybernetic framework for studying occupational stress. *Human Relations, 32,* 395–418.

Dachler, H. P., & Wilpert, B. (1978). Conceptual dimensions and boundaries of participation in organizations. *Administrative Science Quarterly, 23,* 1–39.

Dansereau, F., & Alutto, J. A. (1990). Level of analysis issues in climate and culture research. In B. Schneider (Ed.), *Organizational climate and culture* (pp. 193–236). San Francisco: Jossey-Bass.

Dansereau, F., Alutto, J. A., & Yammarino, F. (1984). *Theory testing in organizational behavior.* Englewood Cliffs, NJ: Prentice-Hall.

Datan, N., Rodeheaver, D., & Hughes, F. (1987). Adult development and aging. *Annual Review of Psychology, 38,* 153–180.

Davis, D. D. (1986). Technological innovation and organizational change. In D. D. Davis & Associates, *Managing technological innovation* (pp. 1–22). San Francisco: Jossey-Bass.

Davis, D. D., & Associates (1986). *Managing technological innovation.* San Francisco: Jossey-Bass.

Davis, D. R., Matthews, G., & Wong, C. S., Jr. (1991). Aging and work. In C. L. Cooper & I. T. Robertson (Eds.), *International review of industrial and organizational psychology* (Vol. 6, pp. 149–211). Chichester, UK: Wiley.

Davis, G. F., & Powell, W. W. (1992). Organization-environment relations. In M. D. Dunnette & L. M. Hough (Eds.), *Handbook of industrial and organizational psychology* (2nd ed., vol. 3, pp. 315–375). Palo Alto, CA: Consulting Psychologists Press.

Davis, L. E., Cherns, A. B., & Associates (1975). *The quality of working life* (2 vols.). New York: Free Press.

Davis, L. E., & Taylor, J. C. (1975). Technology effects on job, work, and organizational structure: A contingency view. In L. E. Davis & A. B. Cherns (Eds.), *The quality of working life* (Vol. 1, pp. 220–241). New York: Free Press.

Davis, L. E., & Taylor, J. C. (1976). Technology, organization, and job structure. In R. Dubin (Ed.), *Handbook of work, organization, and society* (pp. 379–419). Chicago: Rand McNally.

Dawis, R. V., England, G. W., & Lofquist, L. H. (1964). *A theory of work adjustment: Minnesota Studies in Vocational Rehabilitation, XV.* Minneapolis: University of Minnesota.

Dawis, R. V., & Lofquist, L. H. (1978). A note on the dynamics of work adjustment. *Journal of Vocational Behavior, 12,* 76–79.

Dawis, R. V., & Lofquist, L. H. (1984). *A psychological theory of work adjustment.* Minneapolis: University of Minnesota Press.

Day, D. C., & Silverman, S. B. (1989). Personality and job performance: Evidence of incremental validity. *Personnel Psychology, 42,* 25–36.

Decker, P. J., & Nathan, B. R. (1985). *Behavior modeling training: Principles and applications.* New York: Praeger.

DeNisi, A. S., Cafferty, T. P., & Meglino, B. M. (1984). A cognitive view of the performance appraisal process: A model and research proposition. *Organizational Behavior and Human Performance, 33,* 360–396.

Digman, J. M. (1990). Personality structure: Emergence of the five-factor model. *Annual Review of Psychology, 41,* 417–440.

Dipboye, R. L. (1990). Laboratory vs. field research in industrial and organizational psychology. In C. L. Cooper & I. T. Robertson (Eds.), *International review of industrial and organizational psychology* (Vol. 5, pp. 1–34). New York: Wiley.

Drasgow, F., & Hulin, C. L. (1990). Item response theory. In M. D. Dunnette & L. M. Hough (Eds.), *Handbook of industrial and organizational psychology* (2nd ed., vol. 1, pp. 577–636). Palo Alto, CA: Consulting Psychologists Press.

Driver, M. J. (1988). Careers: A review of personal and organizational research. In C. L. Cooper & I. T. Robertson (Eds.), *International review of industrial and organizational psychology* (Vol. 3, pp. 245–278). New York: Wiley.

Dunnette, M. D. (1973). *Work and nonwork in the year 2001.* Monterey, CA: Brooks/Cole.

Dunnette, M. D. (Ed.). (1976). *Handbook of industrial and organizational psychology.* Chicago: Rand McNally.

Dunnette, M. D. (1984, August). *Industrial and organizational psychology in the 80s: Fads, fashions, and folderol revisited.* Invited address at the 92nd annual convention of the American Psychological Association, Toronto.

Dunnette, M. D., & Hough, L. M. (Eds.) (1990–1992). *Handbook of industrial and organizational psychology* (2nd ed., vols. 1–3). Palo Alto, CA: Consulting Psychologists Press.

Dutton, J. E., & Jackson, S. E. (1987). Categorizing strategic issues: Links to organizational action. *Academy of Management Review, 12,* 76–90.

Emery, F. E., & Trist, E. L. (1960). Sociotechnical systems. In C. E. Churchman & M. Verhulst (Eds.), *Management science, models, and techniques* (Vol. 2, pp. 83–97). New York: Pergamon.

Fichman, M. (1988). Motivational consequences of absence and attendance: Proportional hazard estimation of a dynamic motivation model. *Journal of Applied Psychology, 73,* 119–134.

Fiedler, F. E. (1967). *A theory of leadership effectiveness.* New York: McGraw-Hill.

Fiedler, F. E. (1978). The contingency model and the dynamics of the leadership process. In L. Berkowitz (Ed.), *Advances in experimental social psychology* (Vol. 11). New York: Academic Press.

Fiedler, F. E., & Garcia, J. E. (1987). *New approaches to leadership: Cognitive resources and organizational performance.* New York: Wiley.

Fine, S. E., & Wiley, W. W. (1971). *An introduction to functional job analysis.* Washington, DC: Upjohn Institute for Employment Research.

Fiske, D. W., & Schweder, R. A. (Eds.) (1986). *Metatheory in social science.* Chicago: University of Chicago Press.

Fleishman, E. A. (1972). On the relation between abilities, learning, and human performance. *American Psychologist, 27,* 1017–1032.

Frese, M., Ulich, E., & Dzida, W. (Eds.). (1987). *Psychosocial issues of human-computer interactions.* New York: Elsevier Science.

Frome, M. R., & McFarlin, D. B. (1989). Chronic occupational stressors, self-focused attention, and well-being: Testing a cybernetic model. *Journal of Applied Psychology, 74,* 876–883.

Fromkin, H. L., & Streufert, S. (1976). Laboratory experimentation. In M. D. Dunnette (Ed.), *Handbook of industrial and organizational psychology* (pp. 415–465). Chicago: Rand McNally.

Frost, P. J., Moore, L. F., Louis, M. R., Lundberg, C. C., & Martin, J. (1985). *Organizational culture.* Newbury Park, CA: Sage.

Funder, D. C. (1991). Global traits: A neo-Allportian approach to personality. *Psychological Science, 2,* 31–39.

Furnham, A. (1992). *Personality at work.* New York: Routledge.

Ganster, D. C., & Fusilier, M. R. (1989). Control in the workplace. In C. L. Cooper & I. T. Robertson (Eds.), *International review of industrial and organizational psychology* (Vol. 4, pp. 235–280). Chichester, UK: Wiley.

Gebhardt, D. L., & Crump, C. E. (1990). Employee fitness and wellness programs in the workplace. *American Psychologist, 45,* 262–272.

Gerhart, B., & Milkovich, G. T. (1992). Employee compensation: Research and practice. In M. D. Dunnette & L. M. Hough (Eds.), *Handbook of industrial and organizational psychology* (2nd ed., vol. 3, pp. 481–569). Palo Alto, CA: Consulting Psychologists Press.

Gersick, C. J. G. (1988). Time and transition in work teams: Toward a new model of group development. *Academy of Management Journal, 31,* 9–41.

Gersick, C. J. G. (1989). Marking time: Predictable transitions in task groups. *Academy of Management Journal, 32,* 274-309.

Ghiselli, E. E. (1956). Dimensional problems of criteria. *Journal of Applied Psychology, 40,* 1–4.

Ghiselli, E. E. (1971). *Explorations in managerial talent.* Pacific Palisades, CA: Goodyear.

Ghiselli, E. E. (1974). Some perspectives for industrial psychology. *American Psychologist, 29,* 80–87.

Glasgow, R. E., & Terborg, J. R. (1988). Occupational health promotion programs to reduce cardiovascular risk. *Journal of Consulting and Clinical Psychology, 56,* 365–373.

Gleick, J. (1987). *Chaos: Making a new science.* New York: Viking Penguin.

Glick, W. (1985). Conceptualizing and measuring organizational and psychological climate. *Academy of Management Review, 10,* 601–616.

Glickman, A. S. (Ed.). (1982). *The changing composition of the work force.* New York: Plenum.

Goldstein, I. L. (1991). Training in work organizations. In M. D. Dunnette & L. M. Hough (Eds.), *Handbook of industrial and organizational psychology* (2nd ed., vol. 2, pp. 507–619). Palo Alto, CA: Consulting Psychologists Press.

Goldthorpe, J. H., Lockwood, D., Bechhofer, D., & Platt, J. (1969). *The affluent worker in the class structure.* Cambridge, UK: Cambridge University Press.

Goodman, P. S. (1986). The impact of task and technology on group performance. In P. S. Goodman (Ed.), *Designing effective work groups* (pp. 120–167). San Francisco: Jossey-Bass.

Goodman, P. S., Devadas, R., & Hughson, T. L. G. (1988). Groups and productivity: Analyzing the effectiveness of self-managing teams. In J. P. Campbell & R. J. Campbell (Eds.), *Productivity in organizations* (pp. 295–327). San Francisco: Jossey-Bass.

Goodman, P. S., Griffith, T. L., & Fenner, D. B. (1990). Understanding technology and the individual in an organizational context. In P. S. Goodman, L. S. Sproull, & Associates, *Technology and organizations* (pp. 45–86). San Francisco: Jossey-Bass.

Goodman, P. S., Ravlin, E. C., & Argote, L. (1986). Current thinking about groups. In P. S. Goodman (Ed.), *Designing effective work groups* (pp. 1–33). San Francisco: Jossey-Bass.

Goodman, P. S., Sproull, L. S., & Associates. (1990). *Technology and organizations.* San Francisco: Jossey-Bass.

Gordon, M. A. (1953). *A study in the applicability of the same minimum qualifying scores for technical schools to white males, WAF, and Negro males* (Tech. Rep. No. 53–54). San Antonio, TX: Human Resources Research Center, Lackland Air Force Base.

Gottfredson, L. S. (1992). Dilemmas in developing diversity programs. In S. E. Jackson & Associates, *Diversity in the workplace* (pp. 279–305). New York: Guilford.

Graen, G. B., & Scandura, T. A. (1987). Toward a psychology of dyadic organizing. In L. L. Cummings & B. M. Staw (Eds.), *Research in organizational behavior* (Vol. 9, pp. 175–208). Greenwich, CT: JAI Press.

Guerin, B. (1986). Mere presence effects in humans: A review. *Journal of Experimental Social Psychology, 22,* 38–77.

Guilford, J. P. (1967). *The nature of human intelligence.* New York: McGraw-Hill.

Guion, R. M. (1991). Personnel assessment, selection, and placement. In M. D. Dunnette & L. M. Hough (Eds.), *Handbook of industrial and organizational psychology* (2nd ed., vol. 2, pp. 327–397). Palo Alto, CA: Consulting Psychologists Press.

Guion, R. M. (1992). Agenda for research and action. In C. J. Cranny, P. C. Smith, & E. F. Stone (Eds.), *Job satisfaction* (pp. 257–281). New York: Lexington.

Guion, R. M., & Gottier, R. F. (1965). Validity of personality measures in personnel selection. *Personnel Psychology, 18,* 135–164.

Gutek, B., Laurie, L., & Stromberg, A. (1986). Women at work. In C. L. Cooper & I. T. Robertson (Eds.), *International review of industrial and organizational psychology* (Vol. 1, pp. 217–234). New York: Wiley.

Guzzo, R. A. (Ed.). (1982). *Improving group decision making in organizations.* New York: Academic Press.

Guzzo, R. A. (1986). Group decision making and group effectiveness in organizations. In P. S. Goodman (Ed.), *Designing effective work groups* (pp. 34–71). San Francisco: Jossey-Bass.

Guzzo, R. A., Jette, R. D., & Katzell, R. A. (1985). The effects of psychologically based intervention programs on worker productivity: A meta-analysis. *Personnel Psychology, 38,* 275–292.

Guzzo, R. A., & Shea, G. P. (1992). Group performance and intergroup relations in organizations. In M. D. Dunnette & L. M. Hough (Eds.), *Handbook of industrial and organizational psychology* (2nd ed., vol. 3, pp. 269–313). Palo Alto, CA: Consulting Psychologists Press.

Hackman, J. R. (1987). The design of work teams. In J. W. Lorsch (Ed.), *Handbook of organizational behavior* (pp. 315–342). Englewood Cliffs, NJ: Prentice-Hall.

Hackman, J. R. (Ed.). (1990). *Groups that work (and those that don't): Creating conditions for effective teamwork.* San Francisco: Jossey-Bass.

Hackman, J. R. (1992). Group influences on individuals in organizations. In M. D. Dunnette & L. M. Hough (Eds.), *Handbook of industrial and organizational psychology* (2nd ed., vol. 3, pp. 199–267). Palo Alto, CA: Consulting Psychologists Press.

Hackman, J. R., & Morris, C. G. (1975). Group tasks, group interaction process, and group performance effectiveness: A review and proposed integration. In L. Berkowitz (Ed.), *Advances in experimental social psychology* (Vol. 8). New York: Academic Press.

Hackman, J. R., & Oldham, G. R. (1976). Motivation through the design of work: Test of a theory. *Organizational Behavior and Human Performance, 16,* 250–279.

Hackman, J. R., & Oldham, G. R. (1980). *Work redesign.* Reading, MA: Addison-Wesley.

Hall, D. T., & Associates (1986). *Career development in organizations.* San Francisco: Jossey-Bass.

Hand, H. H., Richards, M. D., & Slocum, J. W., Jr. (1973). Organizational climate and the effectiveness of a human relations training program. *Academy of Management Journal, 16,* 185–195.

Hartigan, J. A., & Wigdor, A. K. (Eds.). (1989). *Fairness in employment testing.* Washington, DC: National Academy Press.

Harvey, R. J. (1991). Job analysis. In M. D. Dunnette & L. M. Hough (Eds.), *Handbook of industrial and organizational psychology* (2nd ed., vol. 2, pp. 71–164). Palo Alto, CA: Consulting Psychologists Press.

Hattrup, K., & Kozlowski, S. W. J. (in press). An across-organization analysis of the implementation of advanced manufacturing technologies. *Journal of High Technology Management Research.*

Heilman, M. E. (1984). Information as a deterrent against sex discrimination: The effects of applicant sex and information type on preliminary employment decisions. *Organizational Behavior and Human Performance, 33,* 174–186.

Heilman, M. E., Block, C. J., & Lucas, J. A. (1992). Presumed incompetent? Stigmatization and affirmative action efforts. *Journal of Applied Psychology, 77,* 536–544.

Heilman, M. E., Simon, M. C., & Repper, D. P. (1987). Intentionally favored, unintentionally harmed? Impact of sex-biased preferential treatment on self-perceptions and self-evaluations. *Journal of Applied Psychology, 72,* 62–68.

Hellervik, L. W., Hazucha, J. F., & Schneider, R. J. (1992). Behavior change: Models, methods, and a review of the evidence. In M. D. Dunnette & L. M. Hough (Eds.), *Handbook of industrial and organizational psychology* (2nd ed., vol. 3, pp. 823–895). Palo Alto, CA: Consulting Psychologists Press.

Helmreich, R. L., Sawin, L. L., & Carlsrud, A. L. (1986). The honeymoon effect in job performance: Temporal increases in predictive power of achievement motivation. *Journal of Applied Psychology, 71,* 185–188.

Hill, M. (1982). Group versus individual performance: Are $N + I$ heads better than one? *Psychological Bulletin, 91,* 517–539.

Hisrich, R. D. (1990). Entrepreneurship/intrapreneurship. *American Psychologist, 45,* 209–222.

Hoffman, L. R. (1979). Applying experimental research on group problem solving to organizations. *Journal of Applied Behavioral Science, 15,* 375–391.

Hofstede, G. (1980). *Culture's consequences: International differences in work-related values.* Beverly Hills, CA: Sage.

Hogan, J., Hogan, R., & Busch, C. M. (1984). How to measure service orientation. *Journal of Applied Psychology, 69,* 167–173.

Hogan, J. C. (1991). Physical abilities. In M. D. Dunnette & L. M. Hough (Eds.), *Handbook of industrial and organizational psychology* (2nd ed., vol. 2, pp. 753–832). Palo Alto, CA: Consulting Psychologists Press.

Hogan, R. T. (1991). Personality and personality measurement. In M. D. Dunnette & L. M. Hough (Eds.), *Handbook of industrial and organizational psychology* (2nd ed., vol. 2, pp. 873–919). Palo Alto, CA: Consulting Psychologists Press.

Hollander, E. P., & Offermann, L. R. (1990). Power and leadership in organizations. *American Psychologist, 45,* 179–189.

Hollenbeck, J. R., & Klein, H. J. (1987). Goal commitment and the goal-setting process: Problems, prospects, and proposals for future research. *Journal of Applied Psychology, 72,* 212–220.

Hollenbeck, J. R., & Whitener, E. M. (1988). Reclaiming personality traits for personnel selection: Self-esteem as an illustrative case. *Journal of Management, 14,* 81–91.

Holusha, J. (1992, March 4). A call for kinder gentler managers at G. E. *New York Times,* D–1f.

Hough, L. M. (1984). Development and evaluation of the "accomplishment record" method of selecting and promoting professionals. *Journal of Applied Psychology, 69,* 135–146.

Hough, L. M. (1992). The "Big Five" personality variables—construct confusion: Description versus prediction. *Human Performance, 5,* 139–155.

House, J. S. (1976). Using health criteria as indicators of the quality of employment. In A. D. Biderman & T. F. Drury (Eds.), *Measuring work quality for social reporting* (pp. 63–88). New York: Halstead.

Howard, A. (1992). Work and family crossroads spanning the career. In S. Zedeck (Ed.), *Work, families, and organizations* (pp. 70–137). San Francisco: Jossey-Bass.

Howard, A. & Bray, D. W. (1988). *Managerial lives in transition.* New York: Guilford.

Howell, W. C. (1991). Human factors in the workplace. In M. D. Dunnette & L. M. Hough (Eds.), *Handbook of industrial and organizational psychology* (2nd ed., vol. 2, pp. 209–269). Palo Alto, CA: Consulting Psychologists Press.

Howell, J. P., Bowen, D. E., Dorfman, P. W., Kerr, S., & Podsakoff, P. M. (1990). Substitutes for leadership: Effective alternatives to ineffective leadership. *Organizational Dynamics, 19,* 21–38.

Hulin, C. L. (1991). Adaptation, persistence, and commitment in organizations. In M. D. Dunnette & L. M. Hough (Eds.), *Handbook of industrial and organizational psychology* (2nd ed., vol. 2, pp. 445–505). Palo Alto, CA: Consulting Psychologists Press.

Hulin, C. L., Henry, R. A., & Noon, S. L. (1990). Adding a dimension: Time as a factor in the generalizability of predictive relationships. *Psychological Bulletin, 107,* 328–340.

Hulin, C. L., & Roznowski, M. (1985). Organizational technologies: Effects on organizations' characteristics and individuals' responses. In L.

L. Cummings & B. M. Staw (Eds.), *Research in organizational behavior* (Vol. 7). Greenwich, CT: JAI Press.

Hulin, C. L., Roznowski, M., & Hachiya, D. (1985). Alternative opportunities and withdrawal decisions: Empirical and theoretical discrepancies and an integration. *Psychological Bulletin, 97,* 233–250.

Hyland, M. E. (1988). Motivational control theory: An integrative framework. *Journal of Personality and Social Psychology, 55,* 642–651.

Ilgen, D. R. (1990). Health issues at work: Opportunities for industrial/organizational psychology. *American Psychologist, 45,* 273–283.

Ilgen, D. R., & Hollenbeck, J. R. (1991). The structure of work: Job design and roles. In M. D. Dunnette & L. M. Hough (Eds.), *Handbook of industrial and organizational psychology* (2nd ed., vol. 2, pp. 165–208). Palo Alto, CA: Consulting Psychologists Press.

Ilgen, D. R., & Klein, H. J. (1989). Organizational behavior. *Annual Review of Psychology, 40,* 327–352.

Ironson, G. (1992). Work, job stress, and health. In S. Zedeck (Ed.), *Work, families, and organizations* (pp. 33–69). San Francisco: Jossey-Bass.

Isenberg, D. J. (1986). Group polarization: A critical review and meta-analysis. *Journal of Personality and Social Psychology, 50,* 1141–1151.

Ivancevich, J. M., Matteson, M. E., Freedman, S. M., & Phillips, J. S. (1990). Worksite stress management interventions. *American Psychologist, 45,* 252–261.

Jackson, P. R., & Wall, T. D. (1991). How does operator control enhance performance of advanced manufacturing technology? *Ergonomics, 34,* 1301–1311.

Jackson, S. E. (1991). Team composition in organizational settings: Issues in managing an increasingly diverse work force. In S. Worchel, W. Wood, & J. A. Simpson (Eds.), *Group process and productivity* (pp. 138–173). Newbury Park, CA: Sage.

Jackson, S. E. (1992). Consequences of group composition for the interpersonal dynamics of strategic issue processing. In P. Shrivasta, A. Huff, & J. Dutton (Eds.), *Advances in strategic management* (Vol. 8, pp. 345–382). Greenwich, CT: JAI Press.

Jackson, S. E., & Associates. (1992). *Diversity in the workplace.* New York: Guilford.

Jackson, S. E., & Schuler, R. S. (1985). A meta-analysis and conceptual critique of research on role ambiguity and role conflict in work settings. *Organizational Behavior and Human Decision Processes, 36,* 16–78.

Jacoby, J. (1976). Consumer and industrial psychology: Prospects for theory corroboration and mutual contribution. In M. D. Dunnette (Ed.), *Handbook of industrial and organizational psychology* (pp. 1031–1061). Chicago: Rand McNally.

Jacoby, J., Hoyer, W., & Brief, A. (1992). Consumer psychology. In M. D. Dunnette & L. M. Hough (Eds.), *Handbook of industrial and organizational psychology* (2nd ed., vol. 3, pp. 377–441). Palo Alto, CA: Consulting Psychologists Press.

James, L. R., Joyce, W. E., & Slocum, J. W. (1988). Comment: Organizations do not cognize. *Academy of Management Review, 13,* 129–132.

Janis, I. L. (1982). *Groupthink* (2nd ed.). Boston: Houghton Mifflin.

Jelinek, M., & Goldhar, J. D. (1986). Maximizing strategic opportunities in implementing advanced manufacturing systems. In D. D. Davis and Associates, *Managing technological innovation* (pp. 220–238). San Francisco: Jossey-Bass.

Johnston, W. B., & Packer, A. E. (1987). *Workforce 2000: Work and workers for the 21st century.* Indianapolis: Hudson Institute.

Kabanoff, B. (1980). Work and non-work: A review of models, methods, and findings. *Psychological Bulletin, 88,* 60–77.

Kabanoff, B., & O'Brien, G. E. (1980). Work and leisure: A task attributes analysis. *Journal of Applied Psychology, 65,* 596–609.

Kahn, R. L. (1981). *Work and health.* New York: Wiley.

Kahn, R. L., & Byosiere, P. (1992). Stress in organizations. In M. D. Dunnette & L. M. Hough (Eds.), *Handbook of industrial and organizational psychology* (2nd ed., vol. 3, pp. 571–650). Palo Alto, CA: Consulting Psychologists Press.

Kanfer, R. (1990). Motivation theory in industrial psychology. In M. D. Dunnette & L. M. Hough (Eds.), *Handbook of industrial and organizational psychology* (2nd ed., vol. 1, pp. 75–170). Palo Alto, CA: Consulting Psychologists Press.

Kanfer, R., & Ackerman, P. L. (1989). Motivation and cognitive abilities: An integrative/aptitude-treatment interaction approach to skill acquisition. *Journal of Applied Psychology, 74,* 657–690.

Katz, D., & Kahn, R. L. (1966). *The social psychology of organizations.* New York: Wiley.

Katz, D., & Kahn, R. L. (1978). *The social psychology of organizations* (2nd ed.). New York: Wiley.

Katz, R. (1982). Effects of group longevity on project communication and performance. *Administrative Science Quarterly, 27,* 81–104.

Katzell, M. E., & Byham, W. C. (1972). *Women in the work force: Confrontation with change.* New York: Behavioral Publications.

Katzell, R. A. (1958). *Research on objective indicators of employee motivation.* Paper presented at Psychology Department colloquium, New York University, New York.

Katzell, R. A. (1962). Contrasting systems of work organization. *American Psychologist, 17,* 102–108.

Katzell, R. A. (1989, August). *Boos and bravos: Some comments on contemporary I/O psychology.* Paper presented at the 97th annual convention of the American Psychological Association, New Orleans. Audiotape available from Sound Images, Inc., Box 460519, Aurora, CO, 80015.

Katzell, R. A., & Austin, J. T. (1992). From then to now: The development of industrial-organizational psychology in the U.S.A. *Journal of Applied Psychology.*

Katzell, R. A., Barrett, R. S., & Parker, T. C. (1961). Job satisfaction, job performance, and situational characteristics. *Journal of Applied Psychology, 45,* 65–72.

Katzell, R. A., & Dyer, F. J. (1977). Differential validity revived. *Journal of Applied Psychology, 62,* 137–145.

Katzell, R. A., & Guzzo, R. A. (1983). Psychological approaches to productivity improvement. *American Psychologist, 38,* 468–472.

Katzell, R. A., & Thompson, D. E. (1990). An integrative model of work attitudes, motivation, and performance. *Human Performance, 3,* 63–85.

Katzell, R. A., Thompson, D. E., & Guzzo, R. A. (1992). How job satisfaction and job performance are and are not linked. In C. J. Cranny, P. C. Smith, & E. F. Stone (Eds.), *Job satisfaction* (pp. 195–218). New York: Lexington.

Katzell, R. A., Yankelovich, D., & others. (1975). *Work, productivity, and job satisfaction.* New York: The Psychological Corporation.

Keita, G. P., & Sauter, S. L. (Eds.). (1992). *Work and well-being: An agenda for the 1990's.* Hyattsville, MD: American Psychological Association.

Kenny, D., & LaVoie, L. (1985). Separating individual and group effects. *Journal of Personality and Social Psychology, 48*, 339–348.

Kerr, N. L. (1983). Motivation losses in task-peforming groups: A social dilemma analysis. *Journal of Personality and Social Psychology, 45*, 819–828.

Kerr, N. L., & Bruun, S. E. (1983). Dispensability of member effort and group motivation losses: Free-rider effects. *Journal of Personality and Social Psychology, 44*, 78–94.

Kerr, S., & Jermier, J. M. (1978). Substitutes for leadership: Their meaning and measurement. *Organizational Behavior and Human Performance, 22*, 375–403.

Kerr, S., & Slocum, J. W., Jr. (1981). Controlling the performance of people in organizations. In P. C. Nystrom & W. H. Starbuck (Eds.), *Handbook of organizational design* (pp. 116–134). New York: Oxford University Press.

Kipnis, D. (1976). *The powerholders*. Chicago: University of Chicago Press.

Kipnis, D. (1991). The technological perspective. *Psychological Science, 2*, 62–69.

Kirkpatrick, J. J., Ewen, R. B., Barrett, R. S., & Katzell, R. A. (1968). *Testing and fair employment: Fairness and validity of personnel tests for different ethnic groups*. New York: New York University.

Klein, H. J. (1989). An integrated control theory model of work motivation. *Academy of Management Review, 14*, 150–172.

Kleingartner, A., & Anderson, C. S. (1987). *Human resource management in high technology firms*. Lexington, MA: Lexington Books.

Kohn, M. L., & Schooler, C. (1983). *Work and personality: An inquiry into the impact of social stratification*. Norwood, NJ: Ablex.

Komaki, J. (1986).Toward effective supervision: An operant analysis and comparison of managers at work. *Journal of Applied Psychology, 71*, 270–279.

Komaki, J., Berwick, K. D., & Scott, L. R. (1978). A behavioral approach to occupational safety: Pinpointing and reinforcing safe performance in a food manufacturing plant. *Journal of Applied Psychology, 63*, 434–445.

Koopman, P. L., & Pool, J. (1990). Decision making in organizations. In C. L. Cooper & I. T. Robertson (Eds.), *International review of industrial and organizational psychology* (Vol. 5, pp. 101–148). New York: Wiley.

Korman, A. K. (1967). Self-esteem as a moderator of the relationship between self-perceived abilities and vocational choice. *Journal of Applied Psychology, 51*, 65–67.

Korman, A. K. (1977). *Organizational behavior*. Englewood Cliffs, NJ: Prentice-Hall.

Kornhauser, A. W. (1965). *Mental health of the industrial worker*. New York: Wiley.

Krackhardt, D., & Porter, L. W. (1986). The snowball effect: Turnover embedded in communication networks. *Journal of Applied Psychology, 71*, 50–55.

Krantz, D. S., Grunberg, N. E., & Baum, A. (1985). Health psychology. *Annual Review of Psychology, 36*, 349–383.

Landy, F. J., & Associates (1992). *Alternatives to chronological age in determining standards of suitability for public safety jobs: Executive summary*. University Park, PA: Center for Applied Behavioral Science, Pennsylvania State University.

Landy, F. J., & Becker, W. S. (1987). Motivation theory reconsidered. In L. L. Cummings & B. M. Staw (Eds.), *Research in organizational behavior* (Vol. 9, pp. 1–38). Greenwich, CT: JAI Press.

Landy, F. J., Zedeck, S., & Cleveland, J. (1983). *Performance measurement and theory*. Hillsdale, NJ: Erlbaum.

Latane, B., Williams, K., & Harkins, S. (1979). Many hands make light work: The causes and consequences of social loafing. *Journal of Personality and Social Psychology, 37*, 822–832.

Lawler, E. E., III. (1976). Control systems in organizations. In M. D. Dunnette (Ed.), *Handbook of industrial and organizational psychology* (pp. 1247–1292). Chicago: Rand McNally.

Lawler, E. E., III. (1982). Increasing worker involvement to enhance organizational effectiveness. In P. S. Goodman (Ed.), *Change in organizatons: New perspectives on theory, research, and practice*. San Francisco: Jossey-Bass.

Lawler, E. E., III, Mohrman, A. M., Jr., et al. (1985). *Doing research that is useful for theory and practice*. San Francisco: Jossey-Bass.

Leana, C. R. (1987). Power relinquishment versus powersharing: Theoretical clarification and empirical comparison of delegation and participation. *Journal of Applied Psychology, 72*, 228–233.

Lee, M. D., & Kanungo, R. N. (Eds.). (1984). *Management of work and personal life*. New York: Praeger.

Lee, R. T., & Ashforth, B. E. (1990). On the meaning of Maslach's three dimensions of burnout. *Journal of Applied Psychology, 75,* 743–747.

Levine, J. M., & Moreland, R. L. (1990). Progress in small group research. *Annual Review of Psychology, 41,* 585–634.

Levinson, D. J., & Associates. (1978). *The seasons of a man's life*. New York: Knopf.

Likert, R. (1961). *New patterns of management*. New York: McGraw-Hill.

Linn, R. L. (1986). Comments on the *g* factor in employment testing. *Journal of Vocational Behavior, 29,* 438–444.

Locke, E. A. (Ed.). (1986). *Generalizing from laboratory to field settings*. Lexington, MA: Heath.

Locke, E. A., Cartledge, N., & Knerr, C. S. (1970). Studies of the relationship between satisfaction, goal-setting, and performance. *Organizational Behavior and Human Performance, 5,* 135–158.

Locke, E. A., & Latham, G. P. (1984). *Goal setting: A motivational technique that works*. Englewood Cliffs, NJ: Prentice-Hall.

Locke, E. A., & Latham, G. P. (1990a). *A theory of goal setting and task performance*. Englewood Cliffs, NJ: Prentice-Hall.

Locke, E. A., & Latham, G. P. (1990b). Work motivation and satisfaction: Light at the end of the tunnel. *Psychological Science, 1,* 240–246.

Locke, E. A., Latham, G. P., & Erez, M. (1988). The determinants of goal commitment. *Academy of Management Review, 13,* 23–39.

Lopez, F. M., Jr. (1966). Current problems in test performance of job applicants: I. *Personnel Psychology, 19,* 10–18.

Lord, R. G., & Hanges, P. J. (1987). A control systems model of organizational motivation: Theoretical development and applied implications. *Behavioral Science, 32,* 161-178.

Lord, R. G., & Maher, K. J. (1989). Cognitive processes in industrial and organizational psychology. In C. L. Cooper & I. T. Robertson (Eds.), *International review of industrial and organizational psychology* (Vol. 4). New York: Wiley.

Lord, R. G., & Maher, K. J. (1991a). Cognitive theory in industrial and organizational psychology. In M. D. Dunnette & L. M. Hough (Eds.), *Handbook of industrial and organizational psychology* (2nd ed., vol. 2, pp. 1–62). Palo Alto, CA: Consulting Psychologists Press.

Lord, R. G., & Maher, K. J. (1991b). *Leadership and information processing*. New York: Unwin Hyman Academic.

Lubinski, D., & Dawis, R. V. (1992). Aptitudes, skills, and proficiencies. In M. D. Dunnette & L. M. Hough (Eds.), *Handbook of industrial and organizational psychology* (2nd ed., vol. 3, pp. 1–60). Palo Alto, CA: Consulting Psychologists Press.

Mahoney, T. A. (1988). Productivity defined: The relativity of efficiency, effectiveness, and change. In J. P. Campbell, R. J. Campbell, & Associates, *Productivity in organizations* (pp. 13–39). San Francisco: Jossey-Bass.

Majchrzak, A. (1988). *The human side of factory automation*. San Francisco: Jossey-Bass.

Majchrzak, A., & Cotton, J. (1988). A longitudinal study of adjustment to technological change: From mass to computer-automated batch production. *Journal of Occupational Psychology, 61,* 43–66.

Mankin, D. (1978). *Toward a post-industrial psychology*. New York: Wiley.

Manz, C. C., & Sims, H. P. (1986). Beyond imitation: Complex behavioral and affective linkages resulting from exposure to leadership training models. *Journal of Applied Psychology, 71,* 571–578.

Matteson, M. T., & Ivancevich, J. M. (1988). Health promotion at work. In C. L. Cooper & I. T. Robertson (Eds.), *International review of industrial and organizational psychology* (Vol. 6, pp. 279–300). New York: Wiley.

McCall, M. W., Jr., & Bobko, P. (1990). Research methods in the service of discovery. In M. D. Dunnette & L. M. Hough (Eds.), *Handbook of industrial and organizational psychology* (Vol. 1, pp. 381–418). Palo Alto, CA: Consulting Psychologists Press.

McClelland, D. C., & Boyatzis, R. E. (1982). Leadership motive pattern and long term success in management. *Journal of Applied Psychology, 61,* 737–743.

McCormick, E. J., Jeanneret, P. R., & Meacham, R. C. (1972). A study of job characteristics and job dimensions as based on the Position Analysis Questionnaire (PAC). *Journal of Applied Psychology, 56,* 347–367.

McGrath, J. E. (1991). Time, interaction, and performance (TIP): A theory of groups. *Small Group Research, 22,* 147–174.

McGrath, J. E., & Kelly, J. R. (1986). *Time and human interaction.* New York: Guilford.

McGregor, D. (1960). *The human side of enterprise.* New York: McGraw-Hill.

McHenry, J. J., Hough, L. M., Toquam, J. I, Hanson, M. A., & Ashworth, S. (1990). Project A validity results: The relationship between predictor and criterion domains. *Personnel Psychology, 43,* 335–354.

Merrihue, W. V., & Katzell, R. A. (1955). ERI—Yardstick of employee relations. *Harvard Business Review, 33* (6), 91–99.

Meyer, J. W. (1978). Strategies for further research: Varieties of environmental variation. In M. W. Meyer and Associates, *Environments and organizations* (pp. 352–368). San Francisco: Jossey-Bass.

Miller, E. G., & Rice, A. K. (1967). *Systems of organization.* London: Tavistock.

Miller, J. G. (1955). Toward a general theory for the behavioral sciences. *American Psychologist, 10,* 513–531.

Miner, J. B. (1978). Twenty years of research on role motivation theory of managerial effectiveness. *Personnel Psychology, 31,* 739–760.

Miner, J. B. (1984). The validity and usefulness of theories in an emerging organizational science. *Academy of Management Review, 9,* 296–306.

Mischel, W. (1968). *Personality and assessment.* New York: Wiley.

Mitchell, T. R. (1974). Expectancy models of job satisfaction, occupational preference and effort: A theoretical, methodological, and empirical approach. *Psychological Bulletin, 81,* 1053–1077.

Morf, M. (1989). *The work/life dichotomy.* Westport, CT: Quorum.

Morrison, A. M. (1992). *The new leaders.* San Francisco: Jossey-Bass.

Morrison, A. M., & Von Glinow, M. A. (1990). Women and minorities in management. *American Psychologist, 45,* 200–208.

Morrison, E. W. , & Herlihy, J. M. (1992). Becoming the best place to work: Managing diversity at American Express Travel Related Services. In S. E. Jackson & Associates, *Diversity in the workplace* (pp. 203–226). New York: Guilford.

Morrison, R. F., & Adams, J. (Eds.). (1991). *Contemporary career development issues.* Hillsdale, NJ: Erlbaum.

Morrison, R. F., & Hock, R. R. (1986). Career building: Learning from cumulative work experience. In D. T. Hall & Associates, *Career development in organizations* (pp. 235–273). San Francisco: Jossey-Bass .

Mortimer, J. T., Lorence, J., & Kumka, D. S. (1986). *Work, family, and personality: Transition to adulthood.* Norwood, NJ: Ablex.

Mumford, M. D., & Stokes, G. S. (1992). Developmental determinants of individual action: Theory and practice in applying background measures. In M. D. Dunnette & L. M. Hough (Eds.), *Handbook of industrial and organizational psychology* (2nd ed., vol. 3, pp. 61–138). Palo Alto, CA: Consulting Psychologists Press.

Murphy, K. R. (1989). Is the relationship between cognitive ability and job performance stable over time? *Human Performance, 2,* 183–200.

National Academy of Sciences. (1986). *Human resource practices for implementing advanced manufacturing technology.* Washington, DC: National Academy Press.

National Behavioral Science Research Agenda Committee. (1992, February). Human capital initiative [Special issue]. APS Observer.

Naylor, J. C., Pritchard, R. D., & Ilgen, D. R. (1980). *A theory of behavior in organizations.* New York: Academic Press.

Near, J. P., Rice, R. W., & Hunt, R. G. (1980). The relationship between work and nonwork domains: A review of empirical research. *Academy of Management Review, 5,* 415–429.

Neulinger, J. (1974). *The psychology of leisure.* Springfield, IL: Thomas.

Newell, A. (1990). *Unified theories of cognition.* Cambridge, MA: Harvard University Press.

Nicholson, N., & Wall, T. D. (Eds.). (1982). *The theory and practice of organizational psychology.* London: Academic Press.

Offermann, L. R., & Gowing, M. K. (1990). Organizations of the future: Changes and challenges. *American Psychologist, 45,* 95–108.

Office of Technology Assessment. (1984). *Computerized manufacturing automation: Employment, education and the workplace.* Washington, DC: Author.

Office of Technology Assessment. (1985). *Automation of American offices, 1985–2000*. Washington, DC: Author.

O'Reilly, C. A., III. (1991). Organizational behavior: Where we've been, where we're going. *Annual Review of Psychology, 42,* 427–458.

Orpen, C. (1978). Work and non-work satisfaction: A causal-correlational analysis. *Journal of Applied Psychology, 63,* 530–552.

Owens, W. A. (1976). Background data. In M. D. Dunnette (Ed.), *Handbook of industrial and organizational psychology* (pp. 609–644). Chicago: Rand McNally.

Owens, W. A., & Schoenfeldt, L. F. (1979). Toward a classification of persons. *Journal of Applied Psychology, 64,* 569–607.

Parker, S. R., & Smith, M. A. (1976). Work and leisure. In R. Dubin (Ed.), *Handbook of work, organization, and society* (pp. 37–64). Chicago: Rand McNally.

Pasmore, W., Francis, C., Haldeman, J., & Shani, A. (1982). Sociotechnical systems: A North American reflection on empirical studies of the seventies. *Human Relations, 35,* 1179–1204.

Paterson, D. G. (1957). The conservation of human talent. *American Psychologist, 12,* 134–144.

Payne, R., & Pugh, D. S. (1976). Organizational structure and climate. In M. D. Dunnette (Ed.), *Handbook of industrial and organizational psychology* (pp. 1125–1173). Chicago: Rand McNally.

Payton-Miyazaki, M., & Brayfield, A. H. (1978). The good job and the good life: Relation of characteristics of employment to general well-being. In A. D. Biderman & T. F. Drury (Eds.), *Measuring work quality for social reporting* (pp. 125–150). New York: Halstead.

Pearce, J. A., & Ravlin, E. C. (1987). The design and activation of self-regulating work groups. *Human Relations, 40,* 751-782.

Pearson, C. A. L. (1987). Participative goal setting as a strategy for improving performance and job satisfaction: A longitudinal evaluation with railway track maintenance gangs. *Human Relations, 40,* 473–488.

Pervin, L. A. (1990). *Handbook of personality: Theory and research.* New York: Guilford.

Peters, L. H., & O'Connor, E. J. (1980). Situational constraints and work outcomes: The influences of a frequently overlooked construct. *Academy of Management Review, 3,* 712–721.

Peters, T. J. (1988). *Thriving on chaos.* New York: Knopf.

Pfeffer, J. (1983). Organizational demography. In L. L. Cummings & B. M. Staw (Eds.), *Research in organizational behavior* (Vol. 5, pp. 299–357). Greenwich, CT: JAI Press.

Porras, J. I., & Robertson, P. J. (1992). Organizational development: Theory, practice, and research. In M. D. Dunnette & L. M. Hough (Eds.), *Handbook of industrial and organizational psychology* (2nd ed., vol. 3, pp. 719–822). Palo Alto, CA: Consulting Psychologists Press.

Porter, L. W. (1966). Personnel management. *Annual Review of Psychology, 17,* 395–422.

Porter, L. W., & Lawler, E. E., III. (1968). *Managerial attitudes and performance.* Homewood, IL: Irwin-Dorsey.

Price, J. L., & Mueller, C. W. (1986). *Handbook of organizational measurement.* Marshfield, MA: Pitman.

Pritchard, R. D., Jones, S. D., Roth, P. L., Stuebing, K. K., & Ekeberg, S. E. (1988). Effects of group feedback, goal setting, and incentives on organizational productivity. *Journal of Applied Psychology, 73,* 337-358.

Quick, J. C., Murphy, L. R., & Hurrell, J. J. (Eds.). (1992). *Stress and well-being at work: Assessments and interventions for occupational mental health.* Hyattsville, MD: American Psychological Association.

Quinn, R. E., & Shepard, L. J. (1974). *The 1972–73 quality of employment survey.* Ann Arbor, MI: Survey Research Center, University of Michigan.

Quinn, R. E., & Staines, G. L. (1979). *The 1977 quality of employment survey.* Ann Arbor, MI: Survey Research Center, University of Michigan.

Random House Dictionary. (1966). New York: Random House.

Rapoport, A. & Horwath, W. J. (1959). Thoughts on organization theory. *General Systems, 4,* 87–91.

Rhodes, S. R. (1983). Age-related differences in work attitudes and behavior: A review and conceptual analysis. *Psychological Bulletin, 93,* 328–367.

Rice, R. W., Near, J. P., & Hunt, R. G. (1980). The job satisfaction/life satisfaction relationship: A review of empirical research. *Basic and Applied Social Psychology, 1,* 37–64.

Rodin, J., & Salovey, P. (1989). Health psychology. *Annual Review of Psychology, 40,* 533–579.

Ronen, S. (1986). *Comparative and international management.* New York: Wiley.

Rosenstein, E. (1985). Cooperativeness and advancement of managers: An international perspective. *Human Relations, 38,* 1–21.

Rousseau, D. M. (1977). Technological differences in job characteristics, employee satisfaction, and motivation: A synthesis of job design research and sociotechnical systems theory. *Organizational Behavior and Human Performance, 19,* 18–42.

Rousseau, D. M. (1985). Issues of level in organizational research: Multilevel and cross-level perspectives. In L. L. Cummings & B. M. Staw (Eds.), *Research in organizational behavior* (pp. 1–38). Greenwich, CT: JAI Press.

Rousseau, D. M. (1988). The construction of climate in organizational research. In C. L. Cooper & I. T. Robertson (Eds.), *International review of industrial and organizational psychology* (Vol. 3). New York: Wiley.

Rubin, D. B. (1988). Discussion. In R. Wainer & H. I. Braun (Eds.), *Test validity* (pp. 241–256). Hillsdale, NJ: Erlbaum.

Rynes, S. L. (1991). Recruitment, job choice, and post-hire consequences: A call for new research directions. In M. D. Dunnette & L. M. Hough (Eds.), *Handbook of industrial and organizational psychology* (2nd ed., vol. 2, pp. 399–444). Palo Alto, CA: Consulting Psychologists Press.

Sackett, P. R., & DuBois, C. L. Z. (1991). Rater-ratee race effects on performance evaluation: Challenging meta-analysis conclusions. *Journal of Applied Psychology, 76,* 873–877.

Sackett, P. R., & Larson, J. R., Jr. (1990). Research strategies and tactics in industrial and organizational psycholgy. In M. D. Dunnette & L. M. Hough (Eds.), *Handbook of industrial and organizational psychology* (2nd ed., vol. 1, pp. 419–489). Palo Alto, CA: Consulting Psychologists Press.

Schaie, K. W. (Ed.). (1982). *Longitudinal studies of adult psychological development.* New York: Guilford.

Schmidt, F. L., Berner, J. G., & Hunter, J. E. (1973). Racial differences in validity of employment tests. Reality or illusion? *Journal of Applied Psychology, 58,* 5–9.

Schmitt, N., Gooding, R. Z., Noe, R. A., & Kirsch. M. (1984). Meta-analysis of validity studies published between 1964 and 1982 and the investigation of study characteristics. *Personnel Psychology, 37,* 407–422.

Schneider, B. (1987). People make the place. *Personnel Psychology, 40,* 437–454.

Schneider, B. (Ed.). (1990). *Organization climate and culture.* San Francisco: Jossey-Bass.

Schoenfeldt, L. F. (1974). Utilization of manpower: Development and evaluation of an assessment-classification model of matching individuals with jobs. *Journal of Applied Psychology, 59,* 583–595.

Schoorman, F. D., & Schneider, B. (Eds.). (1988). *Facilitating work effectiveness.* Lexington, MA: Lexington.

Schweiger, D. M., & Leana, C. R. (1986). Participation in decision making. In E. A. Locke (Ed.), *Generalizing from laboratory to field settings* (pp. 147-166). Lexington, MA: Heath.

Scott, W. D., & Clothier, R. C. (1923). *Personnel management.* Chicago: Shaw.

Seashore, S. E., Lawler, E. E., III, Mirvis, P. H., & Cammann, C. (Eds.). (1983). *Assessing organizational change.* New York: Wiley-Interscience.

Seligman, M. E. P. (1975). *Helplessness: Depression, development, and death.* San Francisco: Freeman.

Seligman, M. E. P. (1990). *Learned optimism.* New York: Knopf.

Shaw, M. E. (1981). *Group dynamics* (3rd ed.). New York: McGraw-Hill.

Shea, G. P., & Guzzo, R. A. (1987). Group effectiveness. What really matters? *Sloan Management Review, 28* (3), 25–31.

Sheehy, G. (1976). *Passages: Predictable crises of adult life.* New York: Dutton.

Simon, H. A. (1992). What is an "explanation" of behavior? *Psychological Science, 3,* 150–161.

Slocum, J., & Sims, H. (1983). A typology for integrating technology, organization, and job design. *Human Relations, 33,* 193–212.

Smith, M. J. (1988). Electronic performance monitoring at the workplace: Part of a new industrial revolution. *Human Factors Society Bulletin, 31* (2), 1–3.

Smith, P. C., Kendall, L. M., & Hulin, C. L. (1969). *The measurement of satisfaction in work and retirement.* Chicago: Rand McNally.

Special Task Force to the Secretary of Health, Education, and Welfare. (1973). *Work in America.* Cambridge, MA: MIT Press.

Stagner, R. (1985). Aging in industry. In J. E. Birren & K. W. Schaie (Eds.), *Handbook of the psychology of aging* (2nd ed.). New York: Van Nostrand Reinhold.

Starbuck, W. F. (1976). Organizations and their environments. In M. D. Dunnette (Ed.), *Handbook of industrial and organizational psychology* (pp. 1069–1124). Chicago: Rand McNally.

Staw, B. M. (1984). Organizational behavior: A review and reformulation of the field's outcome variables. *Annual Review of Psychology, 35,* 627–666.

Staw, B. M., Bell, N. E., & Clausen, J. A. (1986). The dispositional approach to job attitudes. *Administrative Science Quarterly, 31,* 56–77.

Staw, B. M., & Ross, J. (1985). Stability in the midst of change: A dispositional approach to job attitudes. *Journal of Applied Psychology, 70,* 469–480.

Steiner, I. D. (1972). *Group process and productivity.* New York: Academic Press.

Steiner, I. D. (1974). What ever happened to the group in social psychology? *Journal of Experimental Social Psychology, 10,* 94-108.

Steiner, I. D. (1986). Paradigms and groups. *Advances in Experimental Social Psychology, 19,* 251–289.

Stevenson, M. K., Busemeyer, J. R., & Naylor, J. C. (1990). Judgment and decision-making theory. In M. D. Dunnette & L. M. Hough (Eds.), *Handbook of industrial and organizational psychology* (2nd ed., vol. 1, pp. 283–374). Palo Alto, CA: Consulting Psychologists Press.

Stogdill, R. M., Shartle, C. L., Scott, E. L., Coon, A. E., & Jaynes, W. E. (1956). *A predictive study of administrative work patterns.* Columbus: Bureau of Business Research, Ohio State University.

Sundstrom, E. (1986). *Work places.* New York: Cambridge University Press.

Sundstrom, E., & Altman, I. (1989). Physical environments and work group effectiveness. In L. L. Cummings & B. M. Staw (Eds.), *Research in organizational behavior* (Vol. 16, pp. 175–209). Greenwich, CT: JAI Press.

Sundstrom, E., DeMeuse, K. P., & Futrell, D. (1990). Work teams: Applications and effectiveness. *American Psychologist, 45,* 120–133.

Super, D. (1940). *Avocational interest patterns.* Stanford, CA: Stanford University Press.

Super, D. E. (1986). Life career roles: Self-realization in work and leisure. In D. T. Hall & Associates, *Career development in organizations* (pp. 95–119). San Francisco: Jossey-Bass.

Susman, G. I. (1970). The impact of automation on work group autonomy and task specialization. *Human Relations, 23,* 567-577.

Susman, G. I. (1976). *Autonomy at work.* New York: Praeger.

Susman, G. I. (1990). Work groups: Autonomy, technology, and choice. In P. S. Goodman, L. S. Sproull, & Associates, *Technology and organizations* (pp. 87-108). San Francisco: Jossey-Bass.

Tajfel, H. (1982). Social psychology of intergroup relations. *Annual Review of Psychology, 33,* 1–40.

Tannenbaum, A. S., Kavcic, B., Rosner, M., Vianello, M., & Wieser, G. (1974). *Hierarchy in organizations.* San Francisco: Jossey-Bass.

Taylor, J. C., Gustafson, P. W., & Carter, W. S. (1986). Integrating the social and technical systems of organizations. In D. D. Davis & Associates, *Managing technological innovation* (pp. 154–186). San Francisco: Jossey-Bass.

Taylor, R. N. (1992). Strategic decision making. In M. D. Dunnette & L. M. Hough (Eds.), *Handbook of industrial and organizational psychology* (2nd ed., vol. 3, pp. 961–1007). Palo Alto, CA: Consulting Psychologists Press.

Tenopyr, M. L. (1967, September). *Race and socioeconomic status as moderators in predicting machine-shop training success.* Paper presented at the annual convention of the American Psychological Association, Washington, DC.

Terborg, J. R. (1986). Health promotion at the worksite: A research challenge for personnel and human resource management. In K. M. Rowland & G. R. Ferris (Eds.), *Research in personnel and human resource management* (Vol. 4, pp. 225–268). Greenwich, CT: JAI Press.

Tett, R. P., Jackson, D. N., & Rothstein, M. (1991). Personality measures as predictors of job performance: A meta-analytic review. *Personnel Psychology, 44,* 703–742.

Thomas, K. W. (1992). Conflict and negotiation processes in organizations. In M. D. Dunnette & L. M. Hough (Eds.), *Handbook of industrial and organizational psychology* (2nd ed., vol. 3, pp. 651–717). Palo Alto, CA: Consulting Psychologists Press.

Thomas, R. R., Jr. (1992). Managing diversity: A conceptual framework. In S. E. Jackson & Associates, *Diversity in the workplace* (pp. 306–318). New York: Guilford.

Thompson, D. E., & DiTomaso, N. (Eds.). (1988). *Insuring minority success in corporate management.* New York: Plenum.

Thompson, J. D. (1967). *Organizations in action.* New York: McGraw-Hill.

Trist, E. L., & Bamforth, K. W. (1951). Some social and psychological consequences of the long-wall method of coal-getting. *Human Relations, 4*, 3–38.

Tuckman, B. W. (1965). Developmental sequence in small groups. *Psychological Bulletin, 63*, 384–399.

Tupes, E. C., & Christal, R. E. (1961). *Recurrent personality factors based on trait ratings* (ASD-TR-61-57). Lackland Air Force Base, TX: Personnel Laboratory Aeronautical Systems Division.

Turnage, J. J. (1990). The challenge of the new work place technology for psychology. *American Psychologist, 45*, 171–178.

Tziner, A., & Eden, D. (1985). Effects of crew composition on crew performance: Does the whole equal the sum of its parts? *Journal of Applied Psychology, 70*, 85–93.

Van Maanen, J., Dabbs, J. M., Jr., & Faulkner, R. R. (1982). *Varieties of qualitative research.* Beverly Hills, CA: Sage.

Viteles, M. S. (1932). *Industrial psychology.* New York: Norton.

von Bertalanffy, L. (1950). The theory of open systems in physics and biology. *Science, 111*, 23–28.

von Bertalanffy, L. (1962). General system theory—A critical review. *General Systems, 7*, 1–20.

Vroom, V. H. (1964). *Work and motivation.* New York: Wiley.

Vroom, V. H., & Jago, A. G. (1988). *The new leadership: Managing participation in organizations.* Englewood Cliffs, NJ: Prentice-Hall.

Vroom, V. H., & Yetton, P. W. (1973). *Leadership and decision making.* Pittsburgh: University of Pittsburgh Press.

Wall, T. D., Clegg, C. W., Davies, R. T., Kemp, N. J., & Mueller, W. S. (1987). Advanced manufacturing technology and work simplification: An empirical study. *Journal of Occupational Behavior, 8*, 233–250.

Wall, T. D., Clegg, C. W., & Kemp, N. J. (Eds.). (1987). *The human side of advanced manufacturing technology.* Chichester, UK: Wiley.

Wall, T. D., Corbett, J. M., Clegg, C. W., Jackson, P. R., & Martin, R. (1990a). Advanced manufacturing technology and work groups: Towards a theoretical framework. *Journal of Organizational Behavior, 11*, 201–219.

Wall, T. D., Corbett, J. M., Martin, R., Clegg, C. W., & Jackson, P. R. (1990b). Advanced manufacturing technology, work design and performance: A change study. *Journal of Applied Psychology, 75*, 691–697.

Wall, T. D., & Davids, K. (1992). Shopfloor work organization and advanced manufacturing technology. In C. L. Cooper & I. T. Robertson (Eds.), *International review of industrial and organizational psychology* (Vol. 7, pp. 361-398). Chichester, UK: Wiley.

Webster, J., & Starbuck, W. H. (1988). Theory building in industrial and organizational psychology. In C. L. Cooper & I. T. Robertson (Eds.), *International review of industrial and organizational psychology* (Vol. 3, pp. 93–138). New York: Wiley.

Weick, K. E. (1965). Laboratory experimentation with organizations. In J. G. March (Ed.), *Handbook of organizations.* Chicago: Rand McNally.

Weick, K. E. (1990). Technology as equivoque: Sensemaking in new technologies. In P. S. Goodman, L. S. Sproull, & Associates. *Technology and organizations* (pp. 1–44). San Francisco: Jossey-Bass.

Weiss, H. M. (1990). Learning theory and industrial and organizational psychology. In M. D. Dunnette & L. M. Hough (Eds.), *Handbook of industrial and organizational psychology* (2nd ed., vol. 1, pp. 171–222). Palo Alto, CA: Consulting Psychologists Press.

Weiss, H. M., & Adler, S. (1984). Personality and organizational behavior. In B. M. Staw & L. L. Cummings (Eds.), *Research in organizational behavior* (Vol. 6, pp. 1–50). Greenwich, CT: JAI Press.

Weiss, H. M., & Ilgen, D. R. (1985). Routinized behavior in organizations. *Journal of Behavioral Economics, 14*, 57–67.

White, S. E., & Mitchell, T. R. (1979). Job enrichment versus social cues: A comparison and competitive test. *Journal of Applied Psychology, 64*, 1–9.

Whyte, W. F. (1948). *Human relations in the restaurant industry.* New York: McGraw-Hill.

Wiener, N. (1948). *Cybernetics: Control and communication in the animal and machine.* Cambridge, MA: MIT Press.

Wiggins, J. S. (1979). A psychological taxonomy of trait-descriptive terms: The interpersonal domain. *Journal of Personality and Social Psychology, 37,* 395–412.

Youngstrom, N. (1992, July). ADA is super-advocate for those with disabilities. *APA Monitor,* p. 26.

Yukl, G. A. (1989). *Leadership in organizations* (2nd ed.). Englewood Cliffs, NJ: Prentice-Hall.

Yukl, G. A., & Van Fleet, D. D. (1992). Theory and research on leadership in organizations. In M. D. Dunnette & L. M. Hough (Eds.), *Handbook of industrial and organizational psychology* (2nd ed., vol. 3, pp. 147–197). Palo Alto, CA: Consulting Psychologists Press.

Zanders, H. (1984). Social indicators. In P. J. D. Drenth, H. Thierry, P. J. Willeims, & C. J. de Wolff (Eds.), *Handbook of work and organizational psychology* (Vol. 2, pp. 1101–1119). Chichester, UK: Wiley.

Zedeck, S. (Ed.). (1992). *Work, families, and organizations.* San Francisco: Jossey-Bass.

Zedeck, S., & Mosier, K. L. (1990). Work in the family and employing organization. *American Psychologist, 45,* 240–251.

Zuboff, S. (1988). *In the age of the smart machine: The future of work and power.* New York: Basic Books.

Overview of Volume 4

One of the meta-trends mentioned by Katzell is the emphasis on diversity. He also notes that most of what he said was based on American data, and the rest of this volume should move to a broader perspective. Indeed, the main focus of this volume is international and examines how to deal with diversity.

We dedicated this volume to Morris Viteles. Viteles, more than anyone, was instrumental in defining and publicizing industrial and organizational psychology through the years of its adolescence. He did this through his books, which provided encyclopaedic statements about industrial and organizational psychology. He served as one of the early presidents of the International Association of Applied Psychology and thereby promoted industrial and organizational psychology on an international scale.

Most of industrial and organizational psychology is a product of the industrial countries, yet 70 percent or more of humans live in developing countries, aspiring to become industrial. A science cannot be bounded by geography. It would be ridiculous to have a physics that applies only to the earth; it is just as absurd to have an industrial and organizational psychology that applies only to the industrial countries. Work is a universal activity. We must understand work behavior no matter where it occurs.

Most of the writers of the first three volumes of the *Handbook* used data that was predominantly from the United States. Yet other industrial countries face similar problems and deal with them in both similar and different ways. It is important to find out both the similarities and the differences in the way other industrial countries deal with industrial and organizational psychology. Chapters 2 through 10 examine industrial and organizational psychology from the perspective of some of the other industrial countries.

From the perspective of the whole population of the world, the contrast between the industrial and the developing countries is of special interest. A myriad of cultural differences can be identified, but one stands out in a number of theoretical treatments about different kinds of societies. It is the difference between individualistic countries, such as those found in North America and Europe, and collectivist countries that are found in the rest of the world (Hofstede, 1980, 1991; Hsu, 1983; Triandis, 1988, 1990).

This contrast can be found in Durkheim (1949), who in the 19th century distinguished between societies that depend on *similarity* (mechanical solidarity) rather than *negotiated interdependence* (organic solidarity) to provide adequate interpersonal functioning. The former pattern reflects collectivism and the latter individualism. Other treatments of this contrast can be found in Toennies' (1957) *Gemeinschaft und Gesellschaft,* Parson and Shils' (1951) collectivity and self-emphasis, Kluckhohn and Strodtbeck's (1961) collaterality and individualism, Bakan's (1966) community and agency, Weber's (1947) and Inkeles and Smith's (1974) traditionalism-modernity, Fiske's (1992) communal sharing and market pricing, and Markus and Kitayama's (1991) interdependent and independent self.

This contrast is profound because the very assumptions about the unit of analysis in theory and method are different in these two perspectives. The individualists have no doubt that the individual should be the unit of analysis; the collectivists have no doubt that the group, or the collective, should be the unit of analysis. Furthermore, the individualists emphasize processes internal to individuals, such as abilities, attitudes, cognitions, decisions, errors, interests, memories, motivation, fatigue, stress, and so forth as *the* important determinants of industrial and organizational phenomena; while the collectivists emphasize dyadic interactions, group identity, norms, roles, shared values, social structure, intergroup conflict, and so forth as the crucial determinants of industrial and organizational phenomena. Of course, each pays some lip service to the variables of the other camp, but the individualists are not uncomfortable when the group variables are given little emphasis, and the collectivists find many of the individual variables of "trivial importance."

Taking this difference in world view seriously, we present in chapters 2 through 10 statements about industrial and organizational psychology written by authors from individualistic cultures, and in chapters 11 through 15 statements about industial and organizational psychology written mostly by authors from collectivist cultures. Chapter 11 provides a bridge between the two sections by presenting a model that incorporates individualism and collectivism as well as other dimensions of cultural variation as parameters of industrial and organizational theories, and by showing that the choice of research topics is greatly influenced by the culture of the researcher. But collectivism is not absent in industrial countries. In fact, significant minorities, such as Asian-Americans and Hispanic-Americans, are collectivists. Thus, in Chapter 16, we return to the United States to examine diversity and again discuss collectivism.

—The Editors

References

Bakan, D. (1966). *The duality of human existence.* Chicago: Rand McNally.

Durkheim, E. (1949). *The division of labor in society.* Glencoe, IL: Free Press.

Fiske, A. P. (1992). The four elementary forms of sociality: Framework for a unified theory of social relations. *Psychological Review, 99, 689–723.*

Hofstede, G. (1980). *Culture's consequences.* Beverly Hills, CA: Sage.

Hofstede, G. (1991). *Cultures and organizations.* London: McGraw-Hill.

Hsu, F. L. (1983). *Rugged individualism reconsidered.* Knoxville: University of Tennessee Press.

Inkeles, A., & Smith, D. H. (1974). *Becoming modern.* Cambridge, MA: Harvard University Press.

Kluckhohn, F., & Strodtbeck, F. (1961). *Variations in value orientations.* Evanston, IL: Row Peterson.

Markus, H., & Kitayama, S. (1991). Culture and self: Implications for cognition, emotion and motivation. *Psychological Review, 98,* 224–253.

Parson, T., & Shils, E. A. (1951). *Toward a general theory of action.* Cambridge, MA: Harvard University Press.

Toennies, F. (1957). *Community and society.* East Lansing: Michigan State University Press.

Triandis, H. C. (1988). Collectivism and individualism: A reconceptualization of a basic concept in cross-cultural psychology. In G. K. Verma and C. Bagley (Eds.), *Personality, attitudes, and cognitions* (pp. 60–96). London: Macmillan.

Triandis, H. C. (1990). Cross-cultural studies of individualism and collectivism. In J. Berman (Ed.), *Nebraska symposium on motivation, 1989* (pp. 41–133). Lincoln: University of Nebraska Press.

Weber, M. (1947). *The theory of social and economic organisation.* Glencoe, IL: Free Press.

Industrial and Organizational Psychology in Individualistic Cultures

Triandis' introduction in chapter 2 to the field of cross-cultural industrial and organizational psychology examines the demographically driven shifts in emphases and changes in the international economy that have increased the importance of culture as a variable in understanding industrial and organizational psychology phenomena. The changes of the environment of industrial and organizational psychology presses for the incorporation of culture into its theories and methods.

Triandis provides definitions of culture and a model for relating cultural variables to behavior, examines methodological difficulties in cross-cultural research, and explores the influence of culture on perception, cognition, norms, needs, attitudes, motives, and values as well as individual behavior and group and organizational phenomena.

Levy-Leboyer, in chapter 3, surveys the methods employed by the industrial countries of Europe in assessing and selecting personnel. She criticizes the weak link between research and application, the past overdependence on translations of American instruments, and the use of nonvalid selection techniques by personnel officers who are not psychologists in many of the countries of Europe. For example, in one of her tables, we find the results of a survey showing 93 percent of French enterprises depended on graphology for their selection. This can be understood when we note that many of those who do the selecting have law degrees, or other nonpsychological training, and look for the least expensive method of selection, such as "Send me a letter in your own handwriting."

She also shows that selection methods reflect in part the economic and sociopolitical realities of the country. In the United States, the fact that the population is quite diverse and there is great concern about the fairness of selection procedures have generated much on the validity and fairness of selection methods; in Europe, because of the high unemployment rates in some countries, even invalid methods give the appearance that something is done by the personnel department, and very small selection ratios are possible. Thus, even methods with relatively low validity may still possess some degree of utility.

Of special interest is European research on the social process of selection and on the effects of assessment on the assessees. The emphasis is on helping employees manage their own careers by providing them with information from assessments. New instruments are being developed that can enable employees to keep track of fruitful experiences and use the information when they make critical decisions.

Assessment is not only used for the organization but also for the individuals involved. Examples of current European research include studies of assessees' satisfaction with methods of selection, the use of biodata to predict future success, the degree of control felt by applicants during different types of interviews, the way feedback on the results of the testing may have changed the applicant's self-concept, and the assessee's attitude toward the assessment process.

Chapter 4, by Hesketh and Bochner, examines training and career development and brings an Australian perspective to the analysis of industrial and organizational phenomena. The authors are especially emphatic that the accelerated pace of technological change and intercultural contact will require new ways of thinking about training and careers. Training is shifting from trainer-centered to trainee-centered. Career planning is of central importance in designing training. Trainees have to be responsible for the kind of training that will be given, taking into account the changing conditions of the workplace.

The authors provide an excellent discussion of cognitive science applications to training, examine the effects of aging on training, focus on training for new technologies, and then turn to culture training.

Employees who were effective in their home countries are not necessarily effective overseas. This raises issues about how to select and train employees who are called upon to work abroad. Most American corporations invest little in this type of training, though their Far Eastern competitors invest a great deal. The result is that failure rates of American expatriates are often as high as 50 percent; obviously, this is not only detrimental to American competitiveness, but it also makes penetration of foreign markets difficult and reduces the self-esteem of employees who fail. The authors stress the importance of ensuring that trainees make attributions that are reasonably consonant with attributions made by host nationals when they form conclusions about the behavior of host nationals. This can be accomplished with culture assimilator training. However, just one type of training is not sufficient. Training that includes experience with members of the host culture and the development of social skills appropriate for the host culture must be included.

After selection and training we turn, in chapter 5, to motivation. Ronen presents a theoretical integration of the empirical work he has been doing in different, primarily industrial, cultures concerning the factors that are most motivating to different groups of employees. He identifies four clusters of importance of work outcomes, formed by two underlying facets: individualism-collectivism and materialism-nonmaterialism.

The collective/materialist quadrant includes *monetary security, benefits,* and *physical conditions of work.* The collective/nonmaterialist quadrant encompasses *relationships with managers and co-workers.* The individualist/nonmaterialist quadrant takes in *challenge, autonomy, skill, contribution,* and *training.* The individualist/materialist quadrant comprises *advancement, recognition,* and *promotion.* These empirically determined quadrants are shown to correspond to Maslow's, Alderfer's, Herzberg's, and McClelland's conceptualizations, thus accounting, in one theoretical integration, for the typologies of all the major theorists. Furthermore, they appear more or less as stated in the smallest space analyses of the motivational data from both individualist and collectivist cultures.

Germany has had a long tradition as a source of psychological theories. After an eclipse due to the Hitler era, psychology is coming back strong, and its most prominent contribution is action theory. Frese and Zapf, in chapter 6, argue that this is *the* important theory for industrial and organizational psychology. In short, they propose to establish a theory of work behavior based on the concept of action. "Action is goal-oriented behavior that is organized in specific ways by goals, information integration, plans, and feedback and can be regulated consciously or via routines."

The theory is applied to specific industrial and organizational phenomena: Why do people make errors? How can people manage errors? What is the relationship of work and personality? How does a superworker emerge who is competent, efficient, uses long-term strategies, understands work tasks, and organizes things well? It turns out that action theory suggests training strategies for the development of superworkers. Finally, how is work to be designed from an action-theoretical viewpoint?

Thierry and Meijman, in chapter 7, deal with time and the workplace. How much one works, when, and using what rhythms, and how work is divided across time (part-time, shift, overtime, flextime, temporary work, and other such arrangements) have implications for job satisfaction, accidents, health, turnover, absenteeism, and productivity. The chapter traces the complex links between time, work, and such outcomes.

For example, those who have irregular working hours are more likely to complain about noise, monotony, lack of learning opportunities, heavy work, lack of visitation, sweating, vibration, and accidents. Accidents are generally more likely at 2 A.M. and 2 P.M., though, depending on the shift during which one is working, there may be maxima at other times as well.

Moving from the individual to the dyadic level, Graen and Wakabayashi, in chapter 8, discuss the development of reciprocal bonds of harmony, obligation, and trust between two or more people in an organization. The perspective has been well developed for the United States, but here it is also found to be applicable to Japanese corporations manufacturing in the United Sates. Cross-cultural leadership making is necessary before the Japanese transplants can match the effectiveness of their home plants.

Graen's theory of leadership making is outlined and shown to have received considerable empirical support. Then it is applied to the situation of the Japanese transplants in the United States and shown to account for leadership making in that setting as well, though a number of culture-specific insights must be presented to really understand this process. For example, the underdeveloped sense of obligation of domestic managers to their company and their co-workers is a shock to their Japanese superiors and peers. American managers have difficulties (a) subordinating their personal needs to the needs of their team, (b) accepting all top management directives, and (c) accepting the lack of perks provided by their positions. Thus, Americans feel their traditional individualism challenged, and Japanese feel their traditional teamwork challenged. The authors advocate the creation of a third culture for leadership making. Each party must understand the conceptual tools of the other party. Joint training of a Japanese-American dyad suggests the assignment of tasks that require interacting as opposed to coacting. A third culture may develop by training that involves comparative problem solving. The authors show how role finding, making, and implementing can be shaped to produce bicultural professionals and a third culture through cross-cultural leadership making. Each partner has a culturally derived "tool kit" that must be learned by the other partner.

Demographic trends indicate that the population of all industrial countries is aging. Thus, one of the new frontiers of industrial and organizational psychology will be gerontological industrial and organizational psychology. Two perspectives on gerontological psychology, one from Spain and the other from the United Kingdom, by Forteza and Prieto in chapter 9 and Warr in chapter 10, respectively, complete this segment of the *Handbook.*

Forteza and Prieto examine the life cycles and labor cycles of employees and their effects on psychological functioning. They deal extensively with the methodological issues of gerontological research and draw implications of these cycles for public and corporate policies.

Older workers face stereotypes and prejudice that are not always justified. Some of the decisions about older people may be justified because the evidence shows that older people take longer to identify and interpret information that is presented in an incomplete and disorganized way, encounter difficulties when identifying concealed and disguised elements in a complex visual structure, have a tendency to be rigid in their perceptions even though new information suggests that their views should be modified, and need more time to process information and to carry out appropriate motor tasks. But for many jobs these attributes are irrelevant. Gerontological psychologists must advise the old and their employers concerning what is known about these processes so as to increase the validity of the way the old are perceived.

Forteza and Prieto review what is known about the relationship of aging and training as well as job satisfaction. They also deal with retirement, examining its meaning, factors that facilitate and improve psychological health during retirement, and the role of hobbies and leisure time.

Warr, in chapter 10, reviews the influences of work characteristics on aging itself and the impact of aging on work behavior and attitudes. He, like Forteza and Prieto, reviews the stereotypes about the old. He stresses that both declines and gains in job performance occur during aging and identifies four kinds of job categories that will show either deterioration or improvements in performance with age: Type A is exemplified by knowledge-based judgments with no time pressure, where a positive relationship can be expected with age; type B is represented by a job that is relatively undemanding for which we can expect no relationship with age; type C is typified by skilled manual work, where capacities might be exceeded but performance is enhanced by experience, and thus, again, no relationship is to be expected; and, finally, type D is exemplified by continuous, paced data processing, where basic capacities are likely to be exceeded, and performance does not improve with experience, in which case we can expect a negative relationship of performance and age. He also identifies laboratory tasks that can be used to assess jobs and thus decide whether they belong in one or another of these four categories.

In some British industries, after age 45 men were likely to move to easier work or to leave the industry altogether. Jobs with high demands of a perceptual kind are especially likely to be left by those over 50. Yet the unemployment rates for older members of the labor force are relatively low. Warr traces the possible explanations for this apparent paradox.

The civilian labor force participation rates are quite different in developing and industrialized countries. For example, 30 to 69 percent of men over age 65 and 5 to 19 percent of women are likely to be working in developing countries, but only 3 to 8 percent of the men and 1 to 2 percent of the women are likely to be working in the European industrialized countries.

—THE EDITORS

CHAPTER 2

Cross-cultural Industrial and Organizational Psychology

Harry C. Triandis
University of Illinois

In this chapter the need to consider the influence of culture on industrial and organizational processes is emphasized in view of the increased cultural diversity of industrial and organizational environments. The chapter examines the theoretical and methodological problems in defining and measuring culture and studying its effects on industrial and organizational processes as well as the influence of culture on perception, cognition, norms, needs, attitudes, motives, and values. Applications of these findings to the selection of personnel, the behavior of groups, organizational cultures, managerial behavior, job design, organizatioal development, and the resolution of conflict, such as in the case of international negotiations, are reviewed. The chapter ends with a discussion of research gaps indicating needed directions for future research.

Introduction

DEMOGRAPHIC TRENDS INDICATE that by the year 2000 no less than one-third of the new workers in the United States will be black and Hispanic. At the same time, the global market will continue developing and will be highly competitive. New products will be produced at tremendously rapid rates. Multinational corporations that can divide the costs of research and development by one billion potential customers—instead of by one quarter of a billion, as the United States is now doing—will have a tremendous advantage in that competitive market. Competing in this changing marketplace requires global marketing and an understanding of the needs of customers in both developed and rapidly developing parts of the world. Thus, industrial and organizational psychology will need to become more globally oriented.

In the competition to contribute to the development of cross-cultural industrial and organizational psychology, the United States finds itself at a disadvantage. For historical and fundamental reasons, psychology is still parochial in the United States. First, the country's history has implicitly, if not explicitly, supported a melting pot view of society—meaning that people who speak foreign languages and are greatly familiar with other cultures are considered deviant. Second, those who do show interests in other cultures are in the minority because, almost invariably, such people have had a foreign language and/or cultural experience during their formative years, and the vastness of the North American continent does not allow for many such experiences. Unlike Europe, where traveling a very short distance allows one to experience another language or culture, or Japan, where the global isolation of the country and its limited resources have emphasized interest in other cultures and foreign trade, the United States has been very comfortable with a decidedly inward focus. Third, much of psychology is based on studies of undergraduate college students or populations that can be found in one's environment. It is expensive and complex for researchers in the United States to find samples of other cultures. This does not put the United States in a position to successfully compete in the publish-or-perish world of higher education.

Thus, psychologists in Europe and Japan are likely to have an advantage in the next phase of the development of industrial and organizational psychology, which will require a global perspective. Whether the United States—with its current advantage in the field of psychology that can be traced in part back to Hitler, who sent the best German psychologists to this country—can maintain its lead in this field will depend on whether a change in fundamental attitudes occurs. There needs to be a shift away from research samples based on convenience and a shift toward acceptance of pluralism in the workplace, with all its attendant complications. Furthermore, cross-cultural research is methodologically much more difficult to do, but if progress is to be made in this field, more researchers will have to be willing to face that challenge.

The neglect of this field has resulted in an underdeveloped theory of the way culture influences social and organizational behavior. Furthermore, the little that is known about this topic is not widely known by psychologists. In other fields, such as in the science of international communication, there is a greater development of cross-cultural theory and a much greater appreciation of the efforts made by those people who have contributed such theoretical developments. For example, Gudykunst and Ting-Toomey (1988) have developed a theory of interpersonal communication that is directly relevant to understanding how culture affects social behavior. It is based on roughly 800 empirical studies, most of which are unknown to industrial and organizational psychologists. In this chapter I will try to provide an introduction to this research area.

As Adler (1983b) has indicated, the direct foreign investment of American corporations, the income from such investments, and other indices of economic trends are tripling or quadrupling every 10 years. No less than one-third of the profits of American multinationals now comes from overseas. The Japanese and Europeans are investing in the United States. At the same time, the United States trade balance has shifted from positive to negative, requiring increased efforts to sell American products abroad. Thus, in all countries, exporters are concerned with reaching foreign customers. To sell a product, a corporation needs to understand its customers. The social, cultural, and psychological factors that dominate buying decisions must be considered equally with economic factors.

As Japanese and Europeans buy American corporations, they need to train their managers to deal effectively with American workers. These trends are not limited to the United States. Japanese management operates in many countries of Asia, and European and Australian management operates worldwide. Plans call for joint ventures that will require various combinations of American, European, Japanese, and Russian business cooperation. The effectiveness of intercultural teams will depend on our understanding of how to select, train, and guide the individuals who will work in such teams.

Northwestern Europe and North America have been the centers of industrial development; more than 90 percent of the studies in industrial and organizational psychology have used data from these regions of the world. However, demographically speaking, such samples represent no greater than 15 percent of the world's population. Furthermore, it is a part of the world that highly values individualism. Individualism is a characteristic value structure of the European and, even more so, North American traditions. It is a philosophy that assumes that individuals have the right to "do their own thing," regardless of the needs or goals of family members, co-workers, fellow citizens, and other collectives, provided that what individuals do does not hurt others. As a result, contemporary psychological theories underestimate the importance of groups, cultures, and other human-made entities outside of the individual. While such an underestimation may not be a crucial distortion when individualistic cultures are considered, it most certainly is an important distortion when behavior is being considered in collectivist cultures. The areas of study also tend to focus more on events that occur *within* the individual (e.g., attitudes and cognitions) rather than on events that occur *between* individuals (e.g., interactions and negotiations) or between social aggregates and individuals (e.g., the influence of culture on social behavior).

A Major Dimension of Cultural Differences: Individualism and Collectivism

While most psychology reflects individualistic values and points of view, the majority of people in the world (at least 70%) are socialized in collectivist cultures. Thus, the contrast between individualism and collectivism must be understood if psychology is to become a universal science. Individualistic and collectivist themes coexist in all people, but the probability that they will be sampled differs with culture (Triandis, 1989, 1990). In northwestern Europe and North America north of the Rio Grande, the probability of sampling individualistic themes is very high; collectivist themes, on the other hand, are sampled most frequently in East Asia. In between, the probabilities are mixed, with a gradient of more individualism in Europe and less in Asia, Latin America, and Africa. Other factors should also be considered. In all societies, the upper classes are more individualistic than other societal classes; men are more individualistic than women, and those who live in large, complex cities are more individualistic than those who live in simple, rural environments (Daab, 1991).

A major antecedent of individualism is affluence. However, cultural complexity, social and geographic mobility, and exposure to the mass media are also important factors. A major antecedent of collectivism is cultural homogeneity. In addition, high population density and professions or occupations that require interdependence (the difference between performing work that cannot be accomplished by one person, such as digging an irrigation canal, and highly individualistic activities, such as writing a book) increase the probability of collectivism.

Collectivists use groups as the unit of analysis of social relationships. Individualists use individuals. In collectivistic cultures, the self is defined in ingroup terms (e.g., I am an employee of General Motors) rather than as an independent entity, detached from groups. The goals of ingroups take precedence over individual goals in collectivist cultures. Collectivist cultures are characterized by attitudes that favor interdependence, norms that favor embeddedness in the ingroup, and values that favor security, obedience, duty, ingroup harmony, ingroup hierarchy, and personalized relationships. Individualistic cultures are characterized by attitudes that favor independence, norms that favor independence from ingroups, and values that favor pleasure, achievement, competition, freedom, autonomy, exchange, and fairness. Collectivists have few ingroups, but are strongly linked to them; individualists have many ingroups and pick and choose them according to what maximizes their pleasure. Social behavior varies greatly, depending on whether collectivist or individualist themes have been sampled (see Triandis, 1990, for a review; Triandis, McCusker, & Hui, 1990, provide some empirical tests).

The relevance of the individualism-collectivism continuum for understanding differences in work values is illustrated in a study by Meindl, Hunt, and Lee (1989). They obtained the work values of young executives from the People's Republic of China, Korea, Taiwan, Hong Kong, and the United States. China was found to be the most collectivist culture and the United States the most individualistic. It should be noted, however, that the largest cultural difference in this study was between China, which is characterized by extreme collectivism, and the other countries. Collectivism was characterized by lower values on achievement, society, co-workers, esteem, feedback, independence, growth, and ability, as well as higher values on benefits, security, pay, recognition, and working conditions.

The applications of psychology to organizational behavior suffer as a result of an individualistic bias. Ilgen (1985) pointed out that

while organizational psychology is attempting to improve the operations of organizations, individualistic biases reduce the effectiveness of such efforts. Such biases can be traced to the reward systems of organizations. Furthermore, many of the research strategies of organizational psychologists relegate the variance due to group membership to the error term. As a result, group membership is often not investigated. For example, performance appraisals assume that most of the variance in role performance can be attributed to individuals; no consideration is given to situational and group membership sources of variance. As a result, Ilgen argues that "performance appraisal systems, with their strong individualistic orientation, may often limit the effectiveness of work groups structured in a team fashion" (p. 18). The underutilization of group incentive systems such as profit sharing by American industries is another example of individualistic bias. The overutilization of individual goals and individual rewards reflects the same bias. Losses of group creativity that result from individualistic group members refusing to accept the other people's good ideas have not been investigated sufficiently.

Our understanding of the differences between the United States and Japan in attitudes and work behaviors can improve if we use individualism-collectivism constructs. The Japanese treat the corporation as if it were a family: Jobs are assigned to groups, not individuals; ingroup harmony is valued most; emphasis is placed on virtuous action that benefits the group rather than on individual attitudes or opinions; and saving the other person's face is an important value. The chapter by Kashima and Callan in this volume discusses these matters in more detail.

As England (1983) has argued, the major lesson we must learn from the Japanese is how to make organizations consistent with cultures. Taking the highly individualistic American or European management systems, for example, and applying them to cultures that are low on individualism becomes problematic. Furthermore, even *within* individualistic cultures there are individuals who are more or less idiocentric—that is, they place their personal goals above the goals of their ingroups. Those who are allocentric—who give more weight to the goals of their ingroups than to their own personal goals—may be particularly effective in teams. While procedures for identifying allocentric or idiocentric tendencies do exist (Triandis, Leung, Villareal, & Clack, 1985), they have not been tested in team situations.

Individualism is associated with achievement and competition, while collectivism is associated with loyalty and cooperation. Cox, Lobel, and McLeod (1991) assembled groups of Asian, Hispanic, and black Americans and assumed that they would be more collectivist and therefore more cooperative when compared with Anglo-Americans. A Prisoner's Dilemma task was used to test the hypothesis, which was supported. The authors suggest that the greater cooperativeness of minorities is an asset when organizational success depends on cooperation.

The most rapidly growing economies in the world—Japan, Hong Kong, South Korea, Singapore, and Taiwan—have collectivist cultures. Their gross national products are increasing at much faster rates than Europe and North America. Their success can be attributed to their good educational systems, their high levels of motivation, a less confrontational labor-management climate, and their taking seriously the views of American industrial and organizational specialists. As Japanolist Robert Cole (1980) has pointed out, the Japanese sent many delegations to the United States to determine the causes of American productivity. During those visits, they met with American academics, such as Likert, and were told about such things as participative management and an organizational emphasis on cooperation and communication. Since they did not understand English proficiently, they were left with the impression that what they learned about was what actually took place in American industry. Such miscommunication was fortunate for them. They tried the ideas that American social scientists were unable to sell to American industry, and the ideas worked—only too well.

Cultural Universals and Specifics

This example demonstrates the operation of universals (*etics*) in organizational psychology. However, we must also remember that many phenomena have culture-specific (*emic*) aspects. What works in one culture does not necessarily work in another. Participation was an idea that could be adapted to Japanese cultural conditions. It just so happened that the Japanese already had the concept of the *ie* ("household") as the unit of work organization that included non-kin as well as kin. Also, Japanese culture emphasizes a subordinate's dependence on a superordinate (expressed in the cultural construct of *amae*; see Doi, 1971, 1973); it also values interdependence, harmony, duty, and moral obligations and uses shame as a major mechanism of social control. Under such circumstances, the manager can set the agenda and the worker will follow it. When work assignments are given to groups and extensive consultations and decisions are made by consensus, it is natural for groups to participate. In a culture with a high level of uncertainty avoidance (Hofstede, 1980a), the stability of employment offered by the oligopolistic Japanese firms to the best 30 percent of their employees could not help but prove highly motivating.

Cole (1971) saw a parallel between the Japanese system of group decision making and the Japanese family, "where the father, as head of the household, holds decision power, but in practice consults extensively with the rest of the family to determine their wishes" (pp. 186–187). In short, there was an excellent match between the social science prescription for participation and the country's cultural realities.

In other cultures the same prescription has not worked well. For example, in Latin America, where power distance (perceiving great differences between those who have power and those who do not) is high (Hofstede, 1980a), participation has not been a successful technique (Marrow, Bowers, & Seashore, 1967).

One of the generalizations that can be made after reading the six-volume *Handbook of Cross-cultural Psychology* (Triandis, 1980–1981) is that almost every phenomenon has both universal and culture-specific aspects. It is the task of cross-cultural organizational psychology to sort out the universal from the culture-specific in the case of behaviors in organizations (Tannenbaum, 1980).

In analyzing culture-behavior data, it is helpful to conceptualize *individuals* as belonging to different cultures, groups, organizations, and so on; *situations* as evoking different kinds of *behavior*; and a variety of constructs (such as habits, attitudes, and values) as linking consistencies in situations with consistencies in behavior. If individuals are grouped according to culture so that the within-group variance on the constructs of interest is smaller than the between-groups variance, then culture has a useful role as an explanatory variable.

When linking situations to behavior, we need to distinguish *process* from *content*. Processes usually are similar across cultural groups. Content is often different. For example, the learning process is the same in Japan and the United States, but the content within the two countries is different. Haruki, Shigehisa, Nedate, Wajima, and Ogawa (1984) showed that reinforcement is equally effective in the United States and Japan when subjects are rewarded for correct performance. They also learn, to some extent, when correct performance is followed by the experimenter rewarding him or herself. But the Japanese learn significantly more (about 50% more items) in the latter condition than do Americans. The *process* (correct response followed by a signal) is the same; the *content* (correct response leading to the experimenter receiving a reward) has a

different value in the two cultures. It is more motivating for the collectivist Japanese than it is for the individualistic Americans (Triandis, 1988).

The major contribution that culture makes in clarifying the relationships between situations and behaviors is in the *weights* given to the specific features of the situation, specific intervening constructs (e.g., values), or specific elements of a process. We can identify *cultural syndromes* that distinguish one culture from another. Cultural syndromes are patterns of beliefs, attitudes, norms, values, and a characteristic self-concept associated with a language-culture region. Individuals sample the elements of a cultural syndrome in the same way to the extent that they have been exposed to similar schedules of reinforcement (i.e., similar ecologies, histories, and social class experiences). Such a sampling of the elements of a syndrome results in characteristic ways of perceiving events, processing information, weighing information, and deciding what to do. The reinforced actions become habits, and widely shared habits are customs. As ecologies change, and as people are exposed to alternative cultural syndromes, the sampling of cultural elements becomes more idiosyncratic. Then culture makes an increasingly smaller contribution to the prediction of individual behavior.

This last point suggests that cultural factors will be more important when dealing with rank-and-file employees than with top managers, who are more likely to be jet-setters. However, even top managers in some cultures (e.g., Japan) are profoundly influenced by their culture. The major contribution of cross-cultural studies has been the development of theoretical constructs (such as the cultural syndromes) and the link of such constructs to organizational politics, procedures, or specific behaviors. Most of this work has been in the form of "Do not assume that what works in the United States will work in X" with relatively little contribution of the "This works in X" variety. In addition, major contributions have been methodological (Triandis & Berry, 1980). In this case, not only can we warn against the use of some methods in other contexts, but we can also suggest methods that work better when we collect data cross-culturally.

The emphasis on the study of the universal versus the culture-specific is found in all cross-cultural psychology. As Berry, Poortinga, Segall, and Dasen (1992) put it, "One of the goals of cross-cultural psychology is the eventual development of a *universal* psychology that incorporates all indigenous (including Western) psychologies" (p. 384). In industrial and organizational work, Child (1981) and Child and Tayeb (1983) have argued that technology, market, geographic diversification, large-scale production, and close interdependence with other organizations impose a logic of rational administration that requires managers to act in similar ways, regardless of culture. At the same time, however, many of these factors are influenced by culture, so that it is difficult to separate what is cultural from other influences. Much of the variance of managerial behavior may reflect "contingency factors," such as technology and markets, yet an examination of British and Japanese factories by Dore (1973) could not dispense with the concept of culture. An examination of British and French plants (Gallie, 1978) and French, British, and West German manufacturing units (Maurice, Sorge, & Warner, 1980) convinced Child (1981) that culture had to be considered in a complete analysis of managerial behavior. Thus, a full understanding of behavior requires the consideration of three perspectives: (a) contingency factors, (b) political factors (capitalism vs. socialism), and (c) culture. In each case, norms and values moderate the influence of the links between the contingency and political factors on the one hand and behavior on the other.

Overview of Chapter

This chapter will first examine the meaning of the term *culture*. Such an examination will have both theoretical and methodological significance, since many of the observations of phenomena occurring in different cultures are invalid because of methodological artifacts. Next, some of the major dimensions of cultural differences will be examined. These will deal with the impact of culture on the individual, the task, the group, and the organization. Intergroup relations will also be examined in light of cultural differences.

Within each of these topics, we will examine relevant applications. For example, when examining the impact of cultural variables on individuals, we will examine the values of managers, their achievement motivation, selection for overseas assignments, training for overseas assignments, evaluation of the success of overseas employees, and the development of reward systems for employees from different cultures.

Since the topic is vast, we will attempt to limit it by eliminating some subtopics for which good reviews are available. The history of the field has been covered by Barrett and Bass (1976, pp. 1640–1641) and Tannenbaum (1980, pp. 282–284). The issue of cultural influences in ability and their implications is central to ability testing in general and is covered in other sections of this *Handbook* or in prior good reviews (Irvine & Berry, 1983; Irvine & Carroll, 1980).

Previous Reviews

This chapter is, in a sense, a continuation of the Barrett and Bass (1976) chapter in the previous edition of this *Handbook*. It focuses specifically on the last 20 years of cross-cultural research on organizations. Other broad reviews have been published by Bhagat and McQuaid (1982), Drenth (1985), and Ronen and Kumar (1986). Ronen (1986) has written a comprehensive text, with excellent coverage of the literature on managing multinationals, which has major components relevant to international industrial and organizational psychology. A number of special journal issues (Adler, 1982; Negandhi, 1983) and books (Adler, 1986) have examined aspects of the topic. Especially notable is the work of Joynt and Warner (1985), which has theoretical and methodological chapters about cross-cultural research on organizations, the diversity of conceptions of management, management in the third world, and country-specific chapters about management systems. Blum (1981) argues that culture determines the form of industrial relations systems and the typical behavior found in labor-management relationships. Bean (1985) surveys national differences in the operation of trade unions, the organization of employers, collective bargaining, the settlement of industrial conflict, the role of the state in such activities, and the extent to which workers participate. Bean's book also has a chapter on industrial relations in developing countries. England, Negandhi, and Wilpert (1979) examine organizational functioning in a cross-cultural perspective, with special emphasis on the question of whether culture or other factors account for most of the variance in organizational phenomena. Several edited volumes (e.g., Berkman & Vernon, 1979; Lammers & Hickson, 1979; Webber, 1969) include relevant material. There are many volumes that speak more to the business professional than to the psychologist (e.g., Robinson, 1978; Vernon & Wells, 1981; Weinshall, 1977). Finally, there are reviews that touch on cultural (e.g., Berry et al., 1992; Segall, 1986; Segall, Dasen, Berry, & Poortinga, 1990) or organizational issues (e.g., Drenth, Thierry, Willems, & DeWolff, 1984) rather broadly.

Culture: Theoretical and Methodological Issues

Definition of Culture

Many reviewers of studies linking culture to psychological phenomena have commented that further advances in this area require a rigorous analysis and operationalization of the concept of culture (e.g., Jahoda, 1980; Roberts, 1970). Careless utilization of the concept, for instance, refers to the sharing of language, nationality, race, religion, and so on. But this will not help advance our understanding of the way culture affects organizational behavior.

Arguments about the definition of culture have had a long tradition in anthropology (Kroeber & Kluckhohn, 1952) and continue today (Shweder & LeVine, 1984). Definitions vary from the very inclusive (e.g., "culture is the human-made part of the environment"; Herskovits, 1955) to the highly focused ("culture is a shared meaning system"; Shweder & LeVine, 1984). Skinner (1953) saw culture as a set of schedules of reinforcement; Hofstede (1980a) saw it as a program that controls behavior in the same way that a computer program controls a computer. Hofstede (1991) called it "the software of the mind." Schein (1985) stressed that "unstated assumptions" are at the core of culture. Some theorists have tried to distinguish culture from social system (Rohner, 1984), and some have suggested that we do without the construct altogether (Segall, 1984); Jahoda has criticized both of these positions (1984).

Psychologists find the analogy, "Culture is to society what memory is to individuals," especially helpful because it focuses on the idea that what worked in the past is shared and transmitted to new generations and is culture. Of course, what worked in the past may no longer be useful; dysfunctional elements are important aspects of any culture.

Some theorists propose that culture is in people's heads, and some that it is in the head of the investigator. In other words, some theorists believe that one can study individuals to learn about culture, while others believe that the scientist must "construct" culture by using a broad set of inputs (history, observations, etc.). Triandis et al. (1984) found that individual models of social behavior could be analyzed and related to each other; evidence showed that people who lived in Hong Kong had different models of social behavior than people who lived in Mexico City. There was, however, significant similarity among such models, and the *within*-culture similarity did not account for much variance. Moreover, in order to understand the patterns of similarity, one needed much information not available in the models of social behavior, suggesting that much of our understanding of culture is in the mind of the investigator, in the form of multiple pieces of information fitting a complex schema. In short, both points of view are supported by this study.

For the purposes of this chapter, *culture* will be defined as the human-made part of the environment. It has both objective elements— tools, roads, and appliances—and subjective elements—categories, associations, beliefs, attitudes, norms, roles, and values. Subjective culture (Triandis, 1972) has elements that predict social behavior (Triandis, 1977a, 1980). It is further useful to use three criteria when identifying one culture as being different from another: language, time, and place. Culture emerges through social interaction and is transmitted through child-rearing patterns, or via cultural diffusion, through the mass media or travel. It requires interaction to be transmitted, so people must share a language, live in the same time period, and be geographically contiguous. This does *not* exclude people of different historical periods or continents (e.g., Australia, North America) from sharing many important elements of subjective culture. Historical factors (e.g., common migration from Britain) can create such similarities, as can ecological similarities (an unexplored vast continent in Australia and the United States).

The distinction between culture and personality has also resulted in theoretical controversy. D'Andrade (see Shweder & LeVine, 1984) objects to both the position that (a) attitudes and values that are shared by people who speak the same language are "culture" and those not shared are "personality," and that

(b) what the individual has to know to behave appropriately is culture and what is not necessary for good adaptation to the environment is personality. D'Andrade would instead place items of human learning in the culture or personality categories, depending on how they are placed within a system of relationships and processes. In the study of culture, these relationships involve adaptation to the environment; in the study of personality, these relationships involve consistency with the individual's motivational system. Thus, culture and personality are viewed as open systems that are linked together, with some elements belonging to both systems. From these considerations, D'Andrade argues that culture involves (a) knowledge (what is, what goes with what), (b) conceptual structures that create the central reality of a people, or the constructed reality of a group, and (c) institutions, such as the family, the market, the farm, and the church. Hence the definition—*culture* consists of "learned systems of meaning, communicated by means of natural language and other symbol systems, having representational, directive and affective functions, and capable of creating cultural entities and particular senses of reality" (Shweder & LeVine, 1984, p. 116). A more complete discussion of the meanings of culture can be found in Triandis, Kurowski, and Gelfand in this volume.

The distinctions proposed by D'Andrade seem reasonable but are difficult to operationalize. Yet we need some procedure that will help us decide what we will call culture and how we will distinguish it from what we will call personality. Triandis, Bontempo, Leung, and Hui (1990) have used groups of three individuals from the same language/ time/place group (in Illinois and Hong Kong) and presented them with what might be considered an element of either culture or personality—in this case, *values*. They timed the interval between presentation of the stimulus (the value) and the point at which the small group reached consensus that the value was important or unimportant. There was a clear, systematic relationship between latency and values consensus. In the case of some values, almost all of the three-person groups arrived at consensus in less than 6 seconds. In the case of other values, the groups disagreed and took time to discuss the elements, often not reaching consensus in 60 seconds. Since culture requires *sharing*, long response times imply that the element is *not* cultural. Thus, it is possible to distinguish what is cultural from what is subject to individual differences (personality). For example, "persistence" was an extremely high value in Hong Kong (100% of the triads agreed it was important in a mean time of 2.1 seconds); "to be able to take advantage of opportunities" was a very high value in Illinois (100% agreement; mean time of 4.2 seconds). "To be content, happy, feel enjoyment" was a clearer cultural value in Illinois (100% agreement; mean time of 4.1 seconds) than in Hong Kong (77% agreement; mean time of 15.2 seconds). But "to have a high monthly income that allows me to live just the way I want to live" was considered unimportant by half the triads in both cultures, so approval of this idea must be traced to personality.

This is one methodology for distinguishing the cultural from the individually psychological. There are two others. The second is to identify a variety of very different groups within a language/time/place/community and see if one can obtain the same results when measuring a variable. If differences such as social class, age, race, and sex do not emerge when appropriate probes are made, our certainty that we are dealing with a cultural rather than a sociological construct increases. Further, if the individual differences in these measurements are very small, our certainty that we are dealing with a cultural rather than a psychological construct increases. A good illustration of the advantages of multiple groups tested within a culture was provided by England and Harpaz (1983).

The third approach (Triandis, Kashima, Shimada, & Villareal, 1986) for distinguishing the cultural from the individually psychological requires the identification of individuals who differ in their level of acculturation. Suppose, for example, one studies Hispanics and non-Hispanics in the United States and has a way of identifying three levels of acculturation (e.g., length of stay in the United States). Further, let us consider measurements on some variable, such as an attitude. *If* the Hispanic samples show increasing convergence with the non-Hispanic samples as a function of their level of acculturation, then these data increase our confidence that a particular variable (in our example the attitude) is a cultural rather than a sociological or an individual differences variable.

It is also important to distinguish *core* and *peripheral* values (Lachman, 1983). Core values are formed during childhood socialization, while peripheral values are formed in later life. Core values are very difficult to change. If an organization's values are consistent with a person's core values, the person will feel especially well adapted to that organization, while inconsistency is likely to lead to the person leaving the organization, if such an option is available. Organizational socialization can change the peripheral but not the core values.

It is possible, then, to identify cultural variables and to separate them from sociological/demographic and individual difference variables. The task is not simple, however, and many of the one-shot, single-method studies are subject to criticism, since they may not be measuring a cultural variable. We will return to this point in the methodology section of this chapter.

Given the very rich and broad definition of culture employed here, there are a myriad of dimensions that can distinguish cultures. We need to examine dimensions that are particularly important to organizational psychologists. This will be done in the applications section of this chapter.

A Model for Relating
Cultural Variables to Behavior

It is possible to link cultural variables to behavior. A model of social behavior described more fully elsewhere (Triandis, 1977a, 1980) has received considerable empirical confirmation. In an oversimplified way, the model states that the probability of an act is a function of *habits* and *behavioral intentions*, moderated by *facilitating conditions*. The elements of subjective culture enter the model in many places. How the behavior itself is defined, or what is associated with the behavior, has implications for the form and content of the various components.

Behavioral intentions are self-instructions to do something. They are a function of three components. The first is called *social* and includes norms, roles, the person's self-concept, and interpersonal agreements; the second is called *affect* and includes the emotions that arise at the thought of the action; and the third is called *consequences* and is the usual subjective utility notion, operationalized as the sum of the products of the probability of each consequence times the value of the consequence. In collectivist cultures (Hofstede, 1980a) the social component plays a greater role and hence has a larger weight (see Davidson et al., 1976). In individualistic cultures, where hedonism is respectable, the weight for the affect component is larger.

Finally, the facilitating conditions component includes factors that are not under the control of the individual—for example, physiological states such as arousal, ability and task difficulty, and the geography of the behavioral environment. For example, whether a worker carries out a task depends not only on the worker's behavioral intentions (self-instructions to do the task) but also on facilitating conditions. Is the worker sufficiently (but not too highly) aroused? Does the worker have sufficient ability for the task's level of difficulty? Is the geographic environment optimal (e.g., supplies are in place, tools work as required)?

Many investigators did not control for facilitating conditions and thus were unable to obtain relationships between norms, roles, and values or attitudes on the one hand and behavior on the other.

Two major ways culture influences behavior are traceable to a person's habits and subjective utility components. Skinner (1953) is correct when he says that culturally determined contingencies of reinforcement shape behavior. For example, paralinguistic behaviors, such as the distances and orientations between the bodies of two interacting individuals, the frequency of looking at another person in the eyes, the loudness of one's voice, and the frequency of touching, are largely automatic behaviors, under habitual control. For novel behaviors, subjective utilities based on conscious processes are important; these depend on the fundamental values of the culture.

The model suggests that behavior is shaped by cultural factors in a very indirect way. Culture provides the "base rate," and accidents of the individual's history modify the behavior around that base rate. This argument is consistent with Draguns' (1980) view that psychopathology consists of an exaggeration or caricature of the existing cultural pattern.

In our review of how culture influences organizational behavior, the general pattern will be that culture enters those situations where interpersonal relationships are not constrained by technology or other contingent factors. For example, in the area of *attitudes* toward the job, culture plays a substantial role (Maguire & Kroliczak, 1983). Stockard and Dougherty (1983) compared the subjective cultures of women and men in an isolated Greek village and in two settings in Oregon. They concluded that both within- and between-culture sex differences in subjective culture are much greater for topics reflecting "group life" (social relationships) than for topics more constrained by the ecology. For example, if we examine *productivity*, much of the variance depends on the quality of the machines being used, and culture plays a small role. If we examine *job satisfaction*, on the other hand, much depends on expectations of the rewards that one is to receive on the job. Such expectations depend on the level of adaptation about how much one normally receives and equity considerations, and are often normative. Thus, culture has a considerable influence. Kiggundu, Jorgensen, and Hafsi (1983) make a similar point concerning the fit between Western-based theories and data obtained in developing countries. While such theories have Western biases, when they deal with the technical core of organizational behavior (e.g., technology) they show a good fit with the data; but when they focus on organizational relationships, they do not fit the data very well.

For any phenomenon, we can study within-culture variance in relation to between-cultures variance. In most studies where this was done (e.g., Minturn & Lambert, 1964), the within-culture variance is larger than the between-cultures variance. The between-cultures variance can be traced to differences in the ecology (physical conditions and schedules of reinforcement found in a particular environment). Specifically, that study found that 95 percent of the variance in the amount of responsibility training given by mothers to their children was within-culture and only 5 percent was between-cultures. But on aggression training, the picture was quite different. The substantial amount of between-cultures variance was traceable to whether the children interacted primarily with their kin or with non-kin. When they interacted with their kin, they were trained to control their aggression; when they interacted with non-kin, there was less aggression training. One can trace this difference to patterns of economic interdependence with kin that do not exist in the case of non-kin, so that the reinforcements used in training to control aggression are much greater when children interact with kin.

Methodological Issues in Cross-cultural Research

Cross-cultural research is difficult and full of methodological pitfalls that exceed those encountered in single-culture research. When we test the generality of a psychological law and find that it applies to other cultures, the difficulties are no greater than the ones experienced in single-culture research. But when we are showing a cultural difference, the difficulties are immense. There are so many *rival hypotheses* that must be checked and "controlled" that unless we are able to devote substantial resources to testing them, we should probably not even attempt to show such a difference.

This pessimistic assessment is not very different from Roberts and Boyacigiller's (1984). They set up eight criteria for what makes "good" cross-cultural organizational research and examined five major studies according to them—and found all of them wanting. Even the very best studies in the field are subject to severe criticism. Hakel (1981) noted the difficulties of such research, yet argued that it is important to do such research well. The difficulty, however, varies with the type of research being done (Adler, 1983a). Some very sophisticated new methodologies are now available (see Diaz-Guerrero, 1985), and with substantial resources it is possible to do good research.

Hui and Triandis (1985) examined several methods of comparing cultural data and found that each method makes some untested assumptions. No single method is adequate; a multimethod approach requiring a substantial research effort is needed. Unless major resources are used, a study is not likely to escape criticism.

Space limitations do not allow us to undertake a detailed exposition of methodology here, which can be found elsewhere (Lonner & Berry, 1986; Triandis, 1972, 1983; Triandis & Berry, 1980). However, the main points are as follows: Research is a social process. The way researchers present themselves to their subjects, the selection of stimuli (e.g., items), response continua, instructions, procedures, and social relationships that occur during the investigation can all affect the data. All of these are rival hypotheses when attempts are made to establish a cultural difference.

Problems of establishing equivalence of measurement across culture have been reviewed by Berry (1980a). A number of important advances have been made, such as the use of the Jöreskog simultaneous factor analysis approach (see Drasgow & Kanfer, 1985, for an example) to establish equivalence. However, the problem with rival hypotheses remains, since measurement nonequivalence is only one of many rival hypotheses. Depending on the culture, the research problem, and the situation, it may be most appropriate to use unobtrusive, nonreactive methods, such as participant observation or structured methods. When one knows a great deal about the cultures being considered, structured methods can provide reliability and tests of assumptions that are not possible with less structured methods. On the other hand, depth is greater in unstructured methodologies, which allow for extensive probing guided by answers given by the subjects. The problem here is also that many of the structured methods may be inappropriate (e.g., subjects are unfamiliar with the activity) in a particular culture. Furthermore, many relationships involving culture require the simultaneous consideration of numerous contextual variables, and it may not be possible to measure all of them with structured methods, though an observer may be able to observe them and conceptually integrate them.

Adapting a set of procedures, instruments, or items to reflect a culture-specific (emic) point of view requires extensive knowledge of local cultures. At the same time, one needs to use procedures and instruments that will provide sufficient similarity across cultures to allow for the differences to be embedded in the similarities (Campbell, 1964). For comparisons, one needs universal, culture-general (etic) instruments and items. (See Berry, 1980a, for a discussion of these terms.) Methodologies have been developed that utilize an etic theoretical framework and emic operationalizations of the variables (see Malpass, 1977; Triandis, 1972). Triandis (1992) shows how Thurstone scaling can be used to construct emic and etically equivalent measures.

If unobtrusive methods are needed, a number of them, such as the *lost letter technique,* are available (Bochner, 1980), in addition to participant observations. A good study also needs to define the unit of analysis clearly. The definition of culture as consisting of individuals who share a common language, time, and place could lead to an excessive and inaccurate number of cultures. We should not assume that nation, race, religion, or other natural aggregates of individuals necessarily constitute a culture until we have evidence that the individuals share points of view, unstated assumptions, meanings, or other elements of subjective culture. Thus, when we use the term "nation" as a substitute for "culture," we should keep in mind that this is only a preliminary step in this process.

Furthermore, we will understand the culture-organizational behavior relationships we wish to study much better if we have a number of cultures that are high and low on some cultural attribute (e.g., individualism). Ideally, those cultures high on the attribute should be in different parts of the world than those low on the attribute, so they will be truly independent cultures (to avoid the so-called *Galton's problem,* i.e., spuriously high correlations due to diffusion of cultural elements). On the other hand, for some purposes, comparisons of very similar cultures that differ on a single attribute can be revealing (e.g., Norway and Sweden have markedly different suicide rates).

When culture is the unit of analysis, the study is called *ecological;* when the individual is the unit of analysis, it is called *psychological.* Ecological and psychological studies sometimes produce different results. It is important to keep them distinct.

Artifacts are numerous. For example, one of the problems with surveys that use the Likert format is that cultures differ in their *response sets* (Hui & Triandis, 1989; Triandis, 1972). Specifically, East Asian cultures, such as the Japanese, tend to use the middle of the scale (point 3 on a 5-point scale) more frequently than do other samples. Stening and Everett (1984) used a 7-point scale and examined the response patterns of managers and found that 18 percent of the Japanese and 17 percent of the Hong Kong managers used the scale's midpoint. By contrast, 12 percent of the Filipino and 10 percent of the Thai managers used that response. Consistent with this finding, the Thai and Filipino, as well as the Indonesian and Malay, managers used positions 1 and 7 more frequently than the Japanese. The U.S. sample was intermediate. Keep in mind that these data are based on thousands of observations made in each culture, so that even small differences in percentages can suggest rival hypotheses that need to be investigated.

Luthans, McCaul, and Dodd (1985) reported that the "organizational commitment" of Korean and Japanese employees was *less* than that of U.S. employees, a finding which they described as surprising. But the rival hypothesis that the Japanese and Koreans use the point 3 response, no matter what the content of the question, was not explored.

There are a number of ways one can deal with this problem. For example, if one has a large and *heterogeneous* questionnaire, of *n* items, one can convert the scores of *each* subject to z-scores. There is no reason to expect differences in the cultural means for a heterogeneous questionnaire. Then, having eliminated the response set, one can compare the cultures. Leung and Bond (1989) have described standardization procedures necessary for factor analyses with data from many cultures.

Just to complicate things further, there is evidence that bilinguals will give more extreme answers in English than in their native language (Bennett, 1977a), will give more socially desirable answers in English (Marin, Triandis, Betancourt, & Kashima, 1983), and will show either ethnic affirmation (emphasizing their local values) or accommodation (moving in the direction of the culture whose language they are using), depending on the nationality of the person administering the questionnaire (Bond & Cheung, 1984). There are also cultural differences on whether it is appropriate to deceive a questioner (in some cultures one *must* lie to an outsider), and on whether one should give an "intelligent" or "dumb" answer (Glick, 1968).

In short, it is obvious that a monomethod approach that does not allow checks of *convergence* across methods is essentially meaningless. Ideally, one wants to have convergence across rather different methods, but resources may not be available at this stage of industrial and organizational psychology's development.

The optimal methods for organizational scientists have been debated for some time. Whyte (1984) presents a very reasonable and balanced account of this process. It tends to support the participant observer methodologies more than the surveys, but uses both. Others have emphasized a cognitive orientation (e.g., Smircich, 1983), the use of subjective, ideographic "insider" methodologies (e.g., Morey & Luthans, 1984), or the use of ethnoscientific methods (e.g., Gregory, 1983). It is probable that the debate should not be about *which method* is used, but about *which combination of many methods* is desirable. The problem is that we have a limited amount of time and funds and face many limitations concerning the use of subjects' time. Thus, arriving at an optimal methodology is not simply a scientific problem, it is also a problem that concerns funding, ethics (Warwick, 1980), and a study's theoretical importance.

One final point about methodology concerns sampling. It is obvious that representative samples of the cultures are the ideal, but, as mentioned earlier, resources may not allow for that. Once we sample systematically, we have many problems of equivalence. What does it mean to compare managers in a country where there are few managers with managers in a country where there are many managers? How is social class implicated? The suggestion made earlier about obtaining multiple samples by sex, social class, and so on, can solve part but not all of these problems.

Sampling the items (stimuli) to be presented as well as the response continua should receive the same attention as the sampling of the subjects. We do want to tap representatively the dimensions we are interested in and allow scenarios, situations, and stimuli to be culturally sensitive. Similarly, we want to use responses that are more or less natural in the culture and are representative of the responses made by people in everyday life.

Sampling of cultures is also important. We need to have samples that include cultures that are similar as well as different on several dimensions. For example, if we have two dimensions—X and Y—we want to have as a minimum two cultures in each of the cells of the factorial design created by high/low X and high/low Y. Ideally, these eight cultures will each supply one-eighth of the items of the questionnaire to reflect culture-specific operationalizations of X and Y. Some items may be quite similar, thus allowing us to find etic dimensions. Some "marker items" that are acceptable to all collaborators of the cross-cultural project should also be included.

Another issue of considerable importance is the ethical acceptability of the methodology (Tapp, Kelman, Triandis, Wrightsman, & Coelho, 1974; Warwick, 1980). It is desirable to establish ethical standards acceptable to all

concerned parties (subjects, researchers, the public, and government officials) before deciding on a particular methodology. Good methodology should be ethical. It would, for example, be unethical to bother the subjects in a study or the readers of a journal with a worthless study. Arranging an international collaboration is complex and difficult. Some experts in this kind of work (e.g., Drenth & Wilpert, 1980) have suggested that a contract be developed that spells out the rights and responsibilities of each member of the research team.

These difficulties clearly point to two conclusions: (a) Studies that do not have a relationship to a theoretical framework of some sort (Malpass, 1977) are likely to be of little value, and (b) studies that simply tell us that the subjects in culture A do X and that those in Culture B do Y are also meaningless. We need to know something about the *dimensions* that distinguish cultures A and B. Such dimensions constitute cultural syndromes, mentioned earlier, and will be presented later in this chapter.

In summary, no single research method is perfect. Each method has certain advantages and disadvantages. Multimethod approaches are highly desirable and are essential if one is to eliminate enough of the rival hypotheses to establish the existence of a cultural difference. Furthermore, even after the cultural difference has been established, it should fit with other observations made from previous investigations, or by other investigators, to provide sufficient evidence that the difference is not due to an artifact.

Culture and Perception/Cognition

Languages differ in the ways they allow people to categorize experience. That is, discriminably different stimuli are responded to as if they are equivalent (categorization) in every culture, but the categories are not identical. The cognitive links among categories and the way categories are organized into larger cognitive structures (e.g., schemata, value structures) also differ from culture to culture (for a review, see Triandis, 1964). As far as we know, people in all cultures use the same cognitive processes (e.g., categorization, association via contact, association via contiguity in time, association via similarity, and organization into levels of abstraction), but the content of categories, schemata, and values is different. For example, in all cultures, the category "good supervisor" is associated with the category "considerate." But what it means to be considerate differs from culture to culture. Smith and Peterson (1988, p. 110) report that a supervisor who talks to his or her colleagues about a subordinate's personal difficulties when the person is absent was viewed as inconsiderate in Britain and the United States and as considerate in Hong Kong and Japan. Individualists value "clearing the air," and confrontation within the ingroup is possible; collectivists, in contrast, are concerned with saving face, and thus the direct criticism of a subordinate is thought to be inconsiderate, while the indirect criticism (which allows a mediator to communicate the supervisor's criticism to the subordinate) is thought to be considerate.

Information is selected according to what is considered important in a culture. Thus, some cultures emphasize what a person does, while others emphasize who the person is. Person attributes that are differentially salient or important include ingroup or outgroup membership, sex, age, race, religion, tribe, nationality, ideology, or status. Collectivist cultures tend to emphasize the difference between ingroups and outgroups more than individualistic cultures (Chan, 1991; Triandis, 1972, 1990); sex is emphasized in cultures high on the "masculinity" dimension of Hofstede's (1980a) analysis of values; and status is emphasized in cultures high on the "power distance" dimension (Hofstede, 1980a). Race is important in cultures where race-linked norms are salient (e.g., South Africa); age is most important in traditional cultures (e.g., India); religion is important in many cultures in Africa and Asia; nationality is important in the Arab-Israeli conflict. A more detailed discussion of such differentiations and their consequences can be found in Triandis (1967, 1984a). Of special significance are cultural variations in the degree of utilization of (a) associations versus logical structures and (b) coherent-unitary cognitive frameworks versus differentiated-specific frameworks.

In *associative* cultures (Glenn, 1981), people use their own associations among categories when they communicate and assume that their listeners use the same associations. For example, if a person says, "The boss wants you to do that," the assumption is that the listener will also understand that if the task *isn't* done, then the individual will be fired, lose pension benefits, or be punished in some other way. In *abstractive* cultures, people tend to be much more explicit. They tend to define their terms and state the implications more fully. Thus, associative cultures depend a great deal on the *context* of the communication (Cohen, 1991). Much of what is communicated is not explicitly in the message but must be detected from the context—the associations. It is generally believed that context is used much more in Japan than in the United States, and more in the United States than in Switzerland, Germany, and other parts of central Europe. Bharati (1983) attributed Hitler's popularity in India during World War II to the use of the Indian sacred symbol, the swastika, and to Hitler's not eating beef. Whether this observation is correct need not concern us; it provides a good example of associative thinking.

Attribution theory has become the dominant theory in Western social psychology because Westerners value Aristotelian logic (if something is X, then it cannot be non-X), and depend a great deal on attributions to give meaning to social behavior. But some cultures do not use this logic. Bharati (1985) tells that "meat-eating vegetarians" can be found in

India, where attributions tend to be situational (Miller, 1984), such as "in the market he is intelligent, at home dumb." In the East it is said that "the opposite of a great truth is also true."

It should be stated emphatically that associative thinking is *not* inferior to abstractive thinking; it is just different. Poets make good use of associative thinking, and there are circumstances when such thinking is very efficient. For example, when a leader shouts "Fire!", signaling a complex sequence of activities, the communication is very efficient. Generally, associative cultures are characterized by frequent face-to-face communication among individuals who share a large body of information, while abstractive cultures are characterized by communication in the mass media or in places where people have different cultural backgrounds and thus do not share much information outside of their ingroups. Some writers (e.g., Gudykynst) see no difference between collectivist and context cultures.

Cognition and behavior in associative cultures are often *diffuse*. That is, if a person acts in a specific way (e.g., is helpful), the appropriate response (e.g., reciprocation) is often in a different mode (e.g., giving a gift) at a different time. This is a very sophisticated way of responding, but it requires one to keep previous behaviors in mind. In abstractive cultures social behavior tends to have the character of a direct exchange (e.g., when one person helps another, the recipient says, "Thank you"). Such exchanges tend to be more of the tit-for-tat variety, specific-specific. However, such specificity is also related to cognitive differentiation, so that in the West one can criticize a person's work without rejecting the person (Foa & Chemers, 1967). In associative cultures, it is difficult to criticize, since it is inevitably seen as equivalent to a rejection of the person.

Associative cultures also tend to have many individuals who score as field-dependent on Witkin's (1967) measures. Managers from cultures that are economically more developed are field-independent (Gruenfeld &

MacEachron, 1975). However, the parallelism among these various constructs (association, emphasis on context, diffusion, and field dependence) should not be interpreted to mean that they are identical. The Japanese emphasize context in their communication, but are very high in field independence. It appears that field independence is, in part, acquired in school and is confounded with ability (Widiger, Knudson, & Rorer, 1980). While evidence does not favor Witkin's measures as indicators of cognitive style in complex, highly literate societies, the measures do seem useful in simple societies (Boldt, 1978). It is only in preliterate societies, such as those studied by Berry (1979), that field dependence-independence can be a useful variable.

Redding (1980) provides a broad review of cognition as an aspect of culture and focuses in particular on how differences in cognition are likely to affect management processes. He uses the Bougon, Weick, and Binkhorst (1977) perspective on cognition in organizations, which focuses on the kinds of cognitive links that are perceived by organizational members, and discusses the way the concepts of causation and probability are utilized by Chinese and Western people and the implication such differences have for planning, organizing, and controlling.

Individuals presented with probabilistic problems—for example, being shown 100 cards, 30 of which are red and 70 of which are green, and asked to estimate the probability of drawing a red card—tend to overestimate the accuracy of their performance. For example, when the actual hit rate of respondents is about 65 percent, they estimate it to be about 90 percent. This phenomenon appears to be stronger in East Asian populations than it is in Western samples. Wright et al. (1978) presented data showing that several Chinese samples who had hit rates of about 50 percent estimated their hit rate to be about 90 percent, while Western samples estimated their hit rate at 90 percent when the actual rate was only 65 percent.

Phillips (1982) presents a "generation theory" to account for this phenomenon. It contrasts the probabilistic thinking widely used in the West with the fatalistic thinking frequently found in the East. He posits a learned predisposition to adopt a causal or fatalistic structure in tasks involving uncertainty among the Chinese and argues that fatalistic structures are more often used in the East than in the West. When the Chinese are given a problem, Phillips finds that they impose a fatalistic structure that determines their probability estimates (see also Yates, Zhu, Ronis, Wang, Shinotsuka, & Toda, 1989).

Attributions.   Several studies have found cultural differences in the attributions (beliefs about the causes of behavior) made by samples from different cultures. Some of these may reflect differences along the individualism-collectivism syndrome. For example, Chandler, Shama, Wolf, and Planchard (1981) examined the attributions for success and failure made by samples from India, Japan, South Africa, the United States, and Yugoslavia. They found many similarities, although the Japanese tended to use effort and luck more frequently than the other samples to explain success in affiliation. Kashima and Triandis (1986) found a Japanese sample that used luck and an American sample that used ability (attention, memory) to explain success. Explanations of promotions and demotions provided by U.S. and Indian college students in a study by Smith and Whitehead (1984) were also different. The students from the U.S. utilized ability and effort (internal factors), while the Indian students utilized matrimony, influence of friends, and corruption (external factors) more frequently than the other sample.

Intelligence.   The concept of intelligence is, in part, a reflection of cultural values. In traditional Africa, for instance, to be intelligent means to know how to behave correctly, so that good judgment, social competence, caution, and prudence are aspects of intelligence. Only

African elites converge with the Western view of intelligence, which has connotations of being quick, sharp, and correct. The higher their level of education, the more frequently Africans use this Western construct. (For a review, see Price-Williams, 1985, p. 1006.)

Cognitive Frames.   Another major contrast exists between cultures that emphasize coherent unitary frameworks for information processing, such as a religious system or Marxism, and those that utilize differentiated-specific frameworks, which tend to be pragmatic. The *ideologists* begin with the broad framework and sample facts only if they fit the framework (Glenn, 1981), while the *pragmatists* consider only those facts that are useful. Emphasis on spirits or ideology often contrasts with mechanistic interpretations of events. Even among very sophisticated samples in Africa one can find the coexistence of scientific and spiritual explanations of events (Jahoda, 1969). Reliance on astrology when making business decisions is very widespread in South and East Asia.

Communication.   The dimensions mentioned earlier result in different kinds of communication patterns (Triandis & Albert, 1987). In addition to the culture-general dimensions of associative-abstractive and ideological-pragmatic, there are numerous culture-specific contrasts. For example, Okabe (1983) contrasted Japanese and U.S. communication patterns, suggesting that there are differences in both process and content. Differences in process—such as synthesis-intuition versus analysis, concern with what was agreed versus what was said, reaching for consensus versus voting to resolve differences of opinion, and emphasis on *how* things are said versus *what* is said—characterized the Japanese and U.S. views, respectively. Differences in content included saying "we," "maybe," "perhaps," and "slightly" (in Japan) versus "I-you" or the use of superlatives, such as "terrific" (in the

U.S.), climatic argument presentation versus anticlimatic, and the use of well-tried expressions versus new expressions.

Japanese communication patterns have been studied more fully than those in other countries. For example, there are papers on the frequency of compliments exchanged in Japan and the United States (Barlund & Araki, 1984), the accuracy of decoding emotional states in the two cultures (see Sweeney, Cottle, & Kobayashi, 1980), the distance between the bodies of those holding a conversation (Sussman & Rosenfeld, 1982), and other topics. Texts on cross-cultural communication often contrast the United States and Japan (Kim & Gudykunst, 1988). Peterson and Shimada (1978) provide an interesting discussion of sources of management problems in Japanese-American joint ventures.

Culture and Norms

Much of the literature on cultural differences examines differences in conceptions of correct behavior in specific situations. Shweder, Mahapatra, and Miller (1990), for instance, compared adults from India and the United States responding to 39 scenarios and asked if the action taken in the particular situation was wrong. They obtained markedly different responses from the two samples. For instance, "The day after his father's death, the eldest son cut his hair and ate chicken" was seen as wrong by all subjects in the Indian sample and none in the American sample. Consider this incident: "A boy played hookey from school. The teacher told the boy's father and the father warned the boy not to do it again. But the boy did it again and the father beat him with a cane." The father's action was seen as wrong by 90 percent of the Americans, but only 9 percent of the Indians thought so.

The severity of the group's sanction for deviation is a function of (a) the degree of deviation and (b) the relevance of the norm (Mudd, 1968). Cultures apparently differ in the

extent to which particular norms are considered relevant. Thus, for instance, though all cultures recognize the concept of equity, the norm is not equally relevant. When replicating classic equity studies in Brazil, Rodrigues (1982) found that equity theory has severe limitations in that country: Tornblom, Jonsson, and Foa (1985) found that in Sweden equality is preferred over need, which was preferred over equity in the allocation of the resources included in Foa's model, while Americans preferred equity over equality. Leung and Bond (1984) found that in collectivist cultures equity or equality is preferred, depending on whether one is interacting with an ingroup or an outgroup member: When dealing with outgroups (people the subject will not meet again), the Chinese chose equity even more often than the Americans. But when dealing with ingroup members, equality was preferred. Ratings of the attractiveness of an allocator who used either equity or equality showed that the collectivist Chinese were more attracted to an allocator who used the equality norm within the ingroup; they regarded such a person as being more fair than did the Americans. Chinese subjects followed the equity norm when the other person was (a) an outgroup member or when (b) their own input was low and the other person was an ingroup member. They used the equality norm when the other person was an ingroup member and their own input was high. In addition to equality being a preferred norm over equity in collectivist cultures, there are many cases when need is emphasized more than equity (Berman, Murphy-Berman, & Singh, 1985; Triandis, Leung, Villareal, & Clack, 1985). In short, people in collectivist cultures try to distribute resources so that ingroup solidarity can be maintained, and tend to "bend backwards" to be fair to ingroup members.

Satisfaction with a reward received depends not only on perceived equity but also on the expected (preferred) level of the reward. Tannenbaum and Kuleck (1978) plotted job satisfaction versus the difference between preferred and perceived reward received in data from Austria, Italy, Israel, the United States, and Yugoslavia. All cultures gave inverted U-relationships. In short, people expressed that if they got more than what they expected, they would be satisfied; if they got what they expected, they would be very satisfied; and they would be quite dissatisfied if they got less than they expected, regardless of nationality. The curves did differ somewhat according to the type of reward being given and the country. For example, receiving less authority or influence than was preferred was rather devastating in an Israeli kibbutz but not nearly as important in Yugoslavia. It is possible, however, that some of these differences reflect measurement artifacts.

Expectations are determined by the level of adaptation (Helson, 1964). Social situations that occur frequently in a culture shift the neutral point for judging what is to be expected in the direction of these most frequent situations.

Moral judgments apparently follow Kohlberg's developmental sequence (see Snarey, 1985, for a review), but the more advanced stages that emphasize individual rights and universal ethical principles appear to be absent from folk cultures. Certain values, such as communal equality, collective happiness, the Buddhist conceptions of purity, sanctity, and chastity, the Chinese conception of filial piety, and the Indian form of moral reasoning about nonviolence are absent from the Kohlberg scoring manual (Ma, 1988), reflecting a Western bias in the conceptualization of moral development.

Culture and Motives

In his theory of the dependability of motives, Klineberg (1954) used three criteria of dependability: (a) Does the behavior have a physiological basis? (b) Is the behavior universal? and (c) Do lower animals, as well as humans, exhibit the behavior? Motives meeting all three criteria are defined as highly

dependable; those that do not meet any of the criteria are defined as undependable. Throughout much of his book, Klineberg analyzes motives according to their dependability using ethnographic information. According to his analysis, very few motives are dependable. In Maslow's (1943) hierarchy, the dependable motives are basic. If they are satisfied, higher order motives that are not dependable may emerge.

The cross-cultural evidence (Aram & Piraino, 1978; Hofstede, 1983b; Nevis 1983) suggests that humans are more pliable than Maslow would have us believe and are capable of shifting the importance of the less dependable motives. Self-actualization is an ideal of individualistic cultures; service to the ingroup is the ideal of collectivist cultures and is also the highest motive. Such service may at times be parochial but often contributes to the survival of the ingroup.

Culture and Attitudes

Beliefs probabilistically link an object or construct to other constructs. Constructs have affective aspects, often acquired through classical conditioning. Thus, *attitudes* emerge as "ideas charged with affect predisposing action" (Triandis, 1971). Attitudes, then, have a cognitive, affective, and behavioral component (Breckler, 1984).

Culture and Values

Attitude objects and values differ in their level of abstraction. At low levels of specificity (e.g., attitude toward a job), they may include beliefs (e.g., the job is hot), affect (I like the job), and behavioral intentions (self-instructions to do something, e.g., do more of that work). At higher levels of abstraction, there are *values* (i.e., abstract conceptions of the desirable) that have a strong affective component (e.g., equality is good), and while there may be many goals and behavioral intentions consistent with them, they do not necessarily predispose particular actions. Rokeach (1973) has discussed the nature and function of values; Kluckhohn and Strodtbeck (1961) have provided a broad cross-cultural framework of *value orientations*. Schwartz and Bilsky (1987) supplied a cross-cultural test of a universal structure of values.

Schwartz (1992, in press) coordinated a project that required 200-plus teachers and 200-plus "others" (mostly students, in some cases workers or representative samples of adults) to respond to a 56-item values questionnaire by rating the extent these values are "guidelines in my life." Least-space analyses indicated that the same structure of values occurred in every culture. Ecological and psychological analyses of the data were reasonably parallel. Collectivist values, such as respect for tradition, elders, and security, contrasted with individualist values such as pleasure, a variable life, and an exciting life. Collectivist values were found in Estonia, Malaysia, and other Southeast Asian samples; the most individualistic samples were found in Europe.

Komin (1990) studied about 2,500 Thai workers and an equal number of managers and found task achievement to be inhibited by social relationships among managers but not among workers. Thus, caution should be exercised when extrapolating from middle class samples to lower class samples.

The prediction of behavior from such cognitive structures is stronger when the structure is specific (e.g., do this particular job) than when it is abstract (e.g., work). However, specific cognitive structures predict only those behaviors that are directly linked to them. While we may enjoy trying to predict whether a particular person will do a specific job, we cannot use that information to predict the behavior of another person or the behavior of the first person toward another job. In the case of widely shared values, prediction is less strong, but each value links to a large number

of different behaviors. Thus, whether we research attitudes or values depends on what we are trying to accomplish: predicting one behavior well or predicting many behaviors less well.

Corresponding to values are *motives*, and here they are conceived as "representations of a future goal state that is desired" (Kagan, 1972, p. 54). McClelland (1980) has distinguished *operant* measures from *respondent* ones. According to this conception, motives are operant and values are respondent measures. Operant measures are obtained when the experimenter presents a minimal stimulus and the subject makes many responses (e.g., to a TAT card), while respondent measures are obtained from questionnaires. McClelland presents evidence that motives *drive, direct,* and *select* behavior, and that operant measures discriminate well on all three aspects of motivation, while respondent measures do not.

Using ecological correlations, where the N is the number of countries, Hofstede (1980a, p. 187) reports a multiple correlation of .74 predicting McClelland's need for achievement measures in children's readers from the particular country's average uncertainty avoidance and masculinity scores, obtained from Hofstede's survey of the values of employees of a multinational corporation. Low uncertainty avoidance and high masculinity scores correspond to high need for achievement. In other words, in cultures where people have values that favor risk-taking and assertiveness, children have achievement fantasies.

A theoretical controversy has developed concerning McClelland's conceptualization of need for achievement, which is thought by many to be strongly influenced by Western culture and values (e.g., Kornadt, Eckensberger, & Emmingaus, 1980; Maehr, 1974). Yet, as Kornadt et al. conclude, there is reason to believe that there are universal aspects to the conceptualization of need achievement. Specifically, the arousal of this motive depends on uncertainty in attaining standards of excellence with respect to some performance, affective reactions to success and failure when these standards are reached or not reached, and feelings of responsibility for reaching the goal or standard. Thus, a basic *structure* of motive arousal may be universal. However, the contents of the standards vary by culture, so that in some cultures, as in Japan, achievement may be mixed with high affiliation, while in other cultures it may be mixed with low affiliation.

Hulin and Triandis (1981) emphasized the importance of *frames of reference* in motive arousal. Such frames develop as a result of social comparisons, expectations that depend on the level of adaptation for similar situations and norms such as equity, and habits of thought that reflect previous reinforcements. Job satisfaction is a function of the discrepancy between such frames and obtained outcomes. The greater this discrepancy, the lower the person's job satisfaction. For example, in wealthy communities one expects to receive a higher salary; when one's inputs (e.g., education) are high, one expects a high salary; when one has received a high salary in the past, one expects a high salary in the future. Thus, one may expect less satisfaction in wealthy cultures than in rapidly developing cultures. The same argument can be made about any reward.

Again, the *structure of relationships* between frames of reference, obtained outcomes, and satisfaction is likely to be universal, but the *content* is likely to be culture-specific. In relationships between beliefs and attitudes, attitudes and behavioral intentions, and behavioral intentions and behavior, the relationships will also be universal but the content will be culture-specific (Davidson & Thomson, 1980).

There is evidence that interactions exist among the constructs just discussed. For example, Feather (1985) shows that the attributions that people make (i.e., beliefs) are related to their attitudes and values. Beliefs about the causes of unemployment in young people were found to be related to general conservatism and to ratings of importance on the *RokeachValues Survey* (Rokeach, 1983).

There are also interesting demographic and country correlates. For instance, in a study using representative samples ($N=12,463$) from 10 European nations, Stoetzel (1983) distinguished between *traditional* values (honesty and good manners) and *innovative* values (tolerance of others, self-control, and independence) and found an age-linked trend, with traditional values emphasized among the older samples and those with lower incomes, and innovative values preferred by the younger samples and those with higher incomes. He found that job satisfaction was high when the people sampled also said that they had "interesting work" or "challenging work" or work in which one can "show initiative"; smaller correlations were found between "satisfaction with co-workers" and "respect acquired on the job" and job satisfaction. Those who were more highly educated and had higher-status jobs were also more satisfied. These relationships were consistently found in all countries. However, there were also some differences. For example, financial satisfaction was related to the age of maximum income, which is high (around age 40) in the Netherlands and Denmark and low (around age 27) in Spain and Italy. Willingness to go back to work on Mondays was highest in Denmark and the Netherlands and lowest in Spain and France.

Another determinant of values is the size of the social organization. For example, England and Lee (1973) found that among Americans, Japanese, and Koreans, regardless of culture, managers in large organizations were more concerned with profit maximization, efficiency, productivity, and organizational growth than managers in small organizations.

Managerial Thinking

Beginning with the Haire, Ghiselli, and Porter (1966) study of managerial thinking, a voluminous literature on managerial attitudes and values has developed. Much of the emphasis has been on establishing relationships between attributes of the culture (e.g., language, religion, and geography) and managerial attitudes (e.g., Ronen, 1982, 1986; Ronen & Kumar, 1986). However, this literature has not provided much insight into the determinants of these attitudes. It is not particularly informative to learn that the Arab countries are similar to each other and that the Latin American countries are more similar to each other than are the Arabs to the Latin Americans. Too much of this literature is merely descriptive and tells us only that in culture area X managers have values A, B, and C, and that in culture area Z they have values L, M, and N. This does not tell us much about the nature of culture or the link of culture to values or attitudes.

Furthermore, the method chosen to show convergence in values or attitudes partly determines the results. Griffeth, Hom, DeNisi, and Kirchner (1985) have shown that the different methods of clustering countries result in different clusters, and there is very little convergence across analyses. Many studies also employ the *Rokeach Values Survey* with rankings, although evidence suggests that reliability is low when this is done. When response sets are corrected, ratings are to be preferred (Ng, 1982). There are numerous studies showing similar relationships (e.g., that job involvement is higher among top managers than it is at the bottom of the organizational hierarchy; Gomez-Mejia, 1984; Stoetzel, 1983) or that job satisfaction increases with age and tenure in an organization (e.g., Maguire & Kroliczak, 1983), and this is true regardless of country. Complaints about the use of Western models in non-Western environments abound (e.g., Kanungo, 1982), but few alternatives have been offered as a substitute.

Whitely and England (1980) used England's *Personal Values Questionnaire* (66 goals and ideas) with managers in the United States, Japan, Korea, India, and Australia. They categorized managers as pragmatists if they emphasized success and as moralists if they emphasized being right. They found numerous differences between countries in the judgments the managers made. Unfortunately, without a theory of culture, detailed findings about cultural differences are not useful.

The kind of social organization and position of the group in the economic structure will also influence values. Feldman, Sam, MacDonald, and Bechtel (1980) examined the work outcome preferences and evaluations of New Zealand, European, Maori, and Samoan samples. They found greater emphasis among the two non-European samples on collectivist outcomes (e.g., work with your relatives, being able to help friends and relatives get jobs at your company, little objection to following strict rules at work), while the European sample emphasized individualistic outcomes (e.g., boss lets you do your own work without constant supervision). Given the lower position of the non-European samples in the economic ladder and their greater tendency toward collectivism, it is not surprising that they also emphasized "being able to contribute money to your family" more than the European sample. Hui (1990) has found that collectivist samples are less satisfied in their jobs than individualist samples. It may be that collectivists expect more from the jobs, and thus there is greater discrepancy between expectations and reality.

Traditional values can either inhibit or facilitate the economic advancement of a group. For example, in some African tribes, such as the Fulbe, slaves traditionally perform the manual labor. These societies are unable to participate in modern economies that would require average citizens to do manual labor. Other tribes, such as the Temne, do not associate manual labor with loss of dignity and thus can participate in modern economies (Dawson, 1963).

Hofstede on Values

Most of the studies cited above used little theory, but Hofstede's (1980a) work has provided a genuine advance. Based on data from more than 60 countries (from IBM employees), the analyses have included data from either 40 or 53 countries at different stages of their reporting (Hofstede, 1982c, 1991). From 116,000 questionnaires completed by respondents matched by occupation, age, and sex at different time periods, four dimensions of cultural variation in values were identified. These dimensions can be studied in detail (e.g., see review by Triandis, 1990) and begin providing a theory of culture.

Hofstede's four dimensions are power distance, uncertainty avoidance, individualism, and masculinity. His 1991 book suggests a fifth dimension (truth vs. virtue). *Power distance* refers to the extent that members of a culture accept inequality and whether they perceive much distance between those with power (e.g., top management) and those with little power (e.g., rank-and-file workers). Hofstede found top power-distance countries to be the Philippines, Mexico, and Venezuela; the bottom power-distance countries were Austria, Israel, and Denmark. Hofstede offers numerous child-rearing, environmental, and historical antecedents. For example, in high-power-distance countries parents emphasize obedience, there tends to be a tropical climate, early legislation restricting the power of rulers was not developed, and inheritance is divided. In low-power-distance countries there is less emphasis on obedience, climate tends to be moderately cold, early legislation restricting the power of rulers was developed, and there tends to be a one-son inheritance. Hofstede also found several interesting consequences: In high-power-distance countries managers are more satisfied with a directive or persuasive superior, while in low-power-distance countries managers are more satisfied with a participative superior.

The major strength of Hofstede's work is that it relates the values identified among IBM employees to numerous other studies (thus obtaining some convergent validity), as well as to each value's antecedents and consequences. There is convergence between this value study and other value studies (e.g., Triandis, 1972) that utilized a different methodology. Granted, much of the work on antecedents and consequents is correlational and may not hold up to replication. But at least we now have a set of specific hypotheses for further testing (Hofstede, 1980a, 1982b). We need to test many hypotheses to discover which features of the ecology determine which aspects of the subjective culture of human groups (Triandis, 1972) and the relationships between subjective culture and social, managerial, or organizational behaviors. This kind of research is more likely to be productive when it focuses on specific dimensions of cultural variation, such as those uncovered by Hofstede, than when global variables such as "culture" or "country" are employed.

Uncertainty avoidance is reflected in an emphasis on ritual behavior, rules, and stable employment. It is found in cultures that report high levels of stress and is negatively correlated with need achievement in children's readers. High-uncertainty-avoidance countries also tend to be more ideological and less pragmatic than low-uncertainty-avoidance countries. The highest scores in uncertainty-avoidance were obtained in Greece, Portugal, Belgium, and Japan; the lowest were obtained in Singapore, Denmark, Sweden, and Hong Kong. The United States is low on this dimension. Though Hofstede does not provide hypotheses about antecedents, it seems plausible that historical factors such as invasions from neighbors or ecological factors such as relative soil infertility may have resulted in high levels of anxiety which then shaped the value. Cultural homogeneity may also be an antecedent. The consequences of this dimension—for example, the idea that managers should be selected because of their seniority—are quite interesting. Consequences such as emphasis on loyalty to the firm are also notable.

Hofstede's third dimension, *individualism*, reflects the extent that people emphasize personal or group goals. If they live in nuclear families that allow them to "do their own thing," individualism flourishes; if, however, they live with extended families or tribes that control their behavior, collectivism is more likely. The essence of collectivism, according to Triandis' (1988, 1990) review of the literature, is giving preference to ingroup over individual goals.

Triandis, McCusker, and Hui (1990) reported multimethod probes of the constructs of individualism and collectivism. They showed that attitudes, self-concepts, values, and differences in the perception of the relationship between social distance and expected appropriate behavior distinguish collectivist from individualistic cultures.

Hofstede found a .82 correlation between individualism and gross national product (GNP) per capita. The analysis was based on 1970 GNP per capita data, but recomputation with 1980 data yields a similar result (.71). The most individualistic countries are the United States and the other English-speaking countries. The most collectivist countries are Venezuela, Colombia, and Pakistan. Moderately cold climate, nuclear families, modern agriculture, and a tradition of individualist thinking appear to be relevant antecedents of individualism, while tropical climate, traditional agriculture, extended or tribal families, and a historical tradition of collectivist thinking and action in the country appear to be antecedents of collectivism. The consequents are quite interesting. For example, in the individualistic countries, more importance is placed on having freedom and challenge in jobs, and managers rate autonomy very highly; they choose pleasure, affection, and security as life goals. In contrast, in the collectivist countries, there is greater emphasis on training in jobs, on

conformity and orderliness, and on duty, expertise, and prestige as life goals.

Lévy-Leboyer (1984) documents major cultural shifts in the developed countries, such as France. At the turn of the century, people worked about 30 percent of their lives; now they work about 10 percent, yet the quality of work seems to be getting lower, productivity is stagnating, absenteeism is increasing, and people are desiring more leisure time. Lévy-Leboyer detects a cultural change toward putting forth the least possible effort in work, and toward consumerism, leisure, and the rejection of hard work. The only people who work hard seem to be some professionals and athletes or sportsmen whose activity is not defined as work. Manual labor brings prestige only if it is done outside of the work environment. In short, work has lost its central value. Lévy-Leboyer attributes part of this shift to extreme individualism. People no longer value service to the community, the work group, or the family. The clash between the professional workaholics and the rest of the population is perhaps additionally demotivating workers, since they must justify their emphasis on leisure in comparison with the other cultural group.

Masculinity, Hofstede's fourth dimension, is found in societies that differentiate very strongly by sex, while femininity is characteristic of cultures where sex differentiation is minimal. Feminine cultures emphasize quality of life more than job advancement and give more of their GNP to the third world. Hofstede found that the most masculine countries were Japan, Austria, and Venezuela, and the most feminine were Sweden, Norway, and the Netherlands. The centrality of work in a person's life is greater in the masculine cultures than it is in the feminine cultures. The antecedents are unclear, but perhaps the length of time that sex differentiation was not especially functional may be relevant. In Scandinavia and the Netherlands, industrialization, emphasis on commerce, and emphasis on influence through peaceful (economic) rather than forceful means have prevailed for at least the past 200 years. In contrast, being the center of great empires (e.g., in World War II Japan, Austria-Hungary, and Bolivar's New Spain) may have been relevant to shaping high masculinity in some countries. The high-masculinity countries are characterized by people who prefer having a higher salary over working shorter hours and who emphasize achievement; in low-masculinity cultures people prefer shorter working hours to having a higher salary, and they work to live rather than live to work. Leveling—that is, not trying to stand out—is a widely observed form of social behavior in low-masculinity countries.

One of the most valuable aspects of Hofstede's work is that he has drawn conclusions from these dimensions concerning managerial practices. For example, Hofstede (1982a, 1983a) has related his four dimensions to the validity of economic theories based on the following:

- Self-interest (less valid in high-power-distance, low-individualistic countries)

- The validity of psychological theories based on self-actualization (less valid in low-individualistic countries)

- The nature of the employer-employee relationship (calculative in highly individualistic countries, moral in low-individualistic countries)

- The priority of the task or the relationship (task more than relationship in highly individualistic countries)

- The role of the family in the work situation (nepotism is okay in low-individualistic countries)

- The importance of harmony (more important in low individualistic countries)

- The acceptability of paternalistic management (in high-power-distance countries)

- The acceptance of status differences (in high-power-distance countries)

- The respect for the old (in high-power-distance countries)

- The presence of channels for the handling of grievances (found only in low-power-distance countries)

- The feasibility of management by objectives, the managerial grid, system Y, theory Z managements (which do not work well in high-power-distance countries)

- The use of an appraisal system (requires low-power-distance, highly individualistic cultures)

- The need for formal rules (in high-masculinity countries)

- Types of planning (more popular to plan in low-uncertainty-avoidance countries)

- The meaning of time (more important in high-uncertainty-avoidance countries)

- The expression of emotion (tolerated under certain conditions in high-uncertainty-avoidance countries)

- Less tolerance for deviance in high-uncertainty-avoidance countries

- Emphasis on competitiveness, equity, and sympathy for the strong (in high-masculinity countries) and on solidarity, equality, sympathy for weak (in low-masculinity countries)

He has discussed

- Achievement motivation versus relationship motivation (achievement is high in high-masculinity, low-uncertainty-avoidance countries)

- The acceptability of machismo-style management (in high-power-distance and high-masculinity cultures)

- The rigidity of sex role job differentiation in high-masculinity cultures)

- The implications of such differences for management development (Hofstede, 1983a)

The Utility of Hofstede's Framework

Based on his results, Hofstede (1980b) has called for revision of current theories of motivation, leadership, and organization, as well as the current conceptions of the generality of the quality of life values (Hofstede, 1984, 1991).

Perhaps what is even more important is that Hofstede has provided a set of benchmarks against which other studies can be organized conceptually. For example, Bond (1988) has developed a *Chinese Values Scale*, which consists of 40 items (Chinese Cultural Connection, 1987). In a study of 22 cultures, he found that Taiwan, Hong Kong, South Korea, and Japan rated high on Confucian values. Factor analysis suggested clusters of values such as Confucianism. Confucianism predicts rapid increases in GNP per capita during the 1965 to 1984 period (Bond, 1988).

Working in Zimbabwe, Munro (1984) found, through second-order factor analysis, a factor that looks very much like individualism-collectivism. One pole includes freedom for self, being able to do what you like, not having to plan, doing your job, and living your life as you want and not as other people want you to; the other pole emphasized a comfortable life, conformity to convention, keeping busy, knowing what you are doing, and doing work that is important to others. In this setting, the subjects gave higher ratings to the collectivist items than they did for the individualist ones.

Individualism and masculinity appear relevant to economic development. Both the correlations of GNP with individualism and the rapid increases in standard of living among the masculine countries suggest this. Fyans,

Salili, Maehr, and Desai (1983) identified populations in which achievement is highly valued (Iran, Afghanistan, West Germany, and among whites in the United States) and countries where it is not so highly valued (India, Romania, Poland, Sweden, and among blacks in the United States). Using Osgood's Atlas data (Osgood, May, & Miron, 1975), they identified meaning links between achievement and other concepts in "high evaluation of achievement countries" which did not occur in the "low evaluation of achievement" groups.

Numerous empirical studies begin to make sense when the Hofstede framework is utilized. For example, the findings in Bass and Burger (1979) can now be interpreted. When we see that 33 percent of the Latin American and 20 percent of the Indian managers rank prestige as most important, while only 2 percent of the Japanese and 3 percent of the Scandinavian managers do so, we can explain these observations by reference to the differences on the power-distance dimension. When we see that 46 percent of the Japanese consider duty a top value while only 7 percent of the Germans do, or that 2 percent of the Japanese but 29 percent of the British managers emphasize pleasure, we can look at the difference in individualism in the countries for an explanation.

England (1984) has reported the greater centrality of work in Japan than in the United States. Wilpert and Quintanilla (1984) and the MOW International Research Team (1986) have reported that work is more important and more central to life in Japan, followed by Yugoslavia, Israel, the United States, Belgium, the Netherlands, Germany, and Britain. It is possible to use Hofstede's (1980a) data to determine which of his dimensions might be reflected in such findings. It is easy to do rank-order correlations, and when it is done, we see a rho of .72 ($p < .05$) for the uncertainty avoidance dimension, suggesting that work is most central in the high-uncertainty-avoidance countries. Perhaps valuing work is a way to avoid anxiety (recall that anxiety is high in the high-uncertainty-avoidance countries).

The MOW International Research Team project (1986) was a major undertaking. The eight-country study utilized specific target groups (e.g., the unemployed) as well as representative samples and used a multi-method approach. Work was found to be most central in Japan, where 71 percent of the respondents gave it either the top or the second highest place of importance. It was less central in the United States, where only 47 percent of the sample gave it so much weight, and it was even less central in Germany and Britain, 45 and 43 percent, respectively.

Professionals were shown to consider work more central than rank-and-file workers, students, or temporary workers, in that order. Older subjects considered work more central than younger samples, and men emphasized work more than women. For those under age 20, the difference between countries is insignificant, but the Japanese most notably become quite concerned with work when they are between the ages of 20 and 29.

The MOW team split work centrality into identification with work, involvement and commitment to work, and choice of work as a major mode of self-expression. They examined societal norms relevant to work (e.g., is one entitled to a job?), the rights and obligations of people, the valued outcomes of work, work goals, and rewards associated with work. Some interesting cultural differences were found (e.g., there is no religious or societal service function of work in Yugoslavia), but little attempt was made to relate such findings to other studies (e.g., Hofstede, 1980a).

Thus, while some fascinating data are presented by the MOW team, they are not placed in the kind of theoretical framework that will help us test hypotheses with additional studies. For example, the definitions of work differs by country. For example, Germany and Japan use "concrete definitions" (e.g., to get money); in Belgium and Israel the definition is "societal" (e.g., to contribute to society); in Japan and Yugoslavia it is characterized by an emphasis on "duty" (e.g., you have to do it); and in Germany and the United States there is relatively more emphasis on "burden" (e.g., work is strenuous). But the reasons for these differences remain unexplained.

Thus, the MOW team has provided their readers with a rich menu of data, but they leave them to digest the findings on their own. The readers may not be equipped to do so, since they are unlikely to be intimately familiar with all eight of the cultures in the study. Perhaps this will be done in forthcoming publications. There is one example, however, where this has already been done. In explaining some of the Japanese findings of the project, Misumi (1982) points out that Japanese workers change jobs within a company very frequently and therefore identify with the company rather than with a specific job. Such explanations, linking events in the environment to the findings of the project, are needed and will, it is hoped, be provided more often in the future.

Maehr and Braskamp (1986) examined the personal incentives used by 575 U.S. and 467 Japanese managers responding to their inventory. They found that the U.S. managers emphasized affiliation, recognition, and social concern more often than the Japanese, who emphasized financial incentives, the task, and excellence. The U.S. managers also emphasized self-reliance more often than did the Japanese. The total pattern suggests the differences in individualism (self-reliance) and masculinity (excellence, task, and financial) that the Hofstede analysis suggests. Superficially, this characterization does not agree with the American emphasis on affiliation, recognition, and social concern, which may appear as collectivist themes. However, as Triandis' (1988, 1990) discussion of collectivism-individualism points out, the collectivist has a stable ingroup, within which he or she is recognized. The individualist has to work hard to be accepted by a variety of ingroups, and social recognition has to be gained almost daily. Affiliation and recognition are more important issues for the individualist, and social concern is more likely to emerge as an incentive when one has to gain acceptance by many ingroups. The few versus many ingroups dimension is a key attribute to the collectivist-individualist contrast (Triandis, 1988). Individualists form their own ingroups, conform in order to be accepted by ingroups, stay with an ingroup as long as it serves their purposes, and drop it for another ingroup when a better opportunity arises elsewhere. A similar point can be made when interpreting the finding that the frequency of compliments is higher in the United States than in Japan. In collectivist cultures, one may not have to work as hard to get into ingroups (one is already a member) or to stay in them as one may have to in individualist cultures. Compliments presumably facilitate social relationships and are more needed by the individualist, who has to enter many diverse ingroups, than by the collectivist, who is secure in his or her ingroups. It is this kind of deeper understanding of Hofstede's dimensions that needs to be developed in future research, and then many of the inconsistencies in the data will become clear. Reviews of the broad literature on individualism (Triandis, 1990) and power distance are available. We need similar reviews for uncertainty avoidance and masculinity.

As we integrate the literature around the Hofstede dimensions, we should begin to understand the dimensions themselves better. For example, the greater collectivism in Ghana than exists in the United States and England may be a factor in the greater frequency and higher value of social interaction in Ghana than in the other two cultures (Earley, 1984). Social loafing is not as important a phenomenon among collectivist Chinese as it is in the West (Earley, 1989).

Bond, Wan, Leung, and Giacalone (1985) presented a study that sheds some light into the meaning of collectivism and power distance. They found that a high-status ingroup member can insult a low-status ingroup member with relative impunity in a collectivist, high-power-distance culture, such as Hong Kong, but not in the United States, which is low in collectivism and moderately low in power distance.

A more profound understanding of the masculinity dimension may explain why in all countries investigated thus far (the United States, Mexico, Japan, Yugoslavia, Turkey, and Thailand) those with internal locus of control are more job-involved than those with external locus of control, and this relationship is stronger for men than it is for women (Reitz & Jewell, 1979).

The framework provided by Hofstede's dimensions allow us to understand, also, the findings of many studies that by themselves did not fit into a broader pattern, such as the emphasis on individualism among American managers and the Japanese emphasis on social values, identified by Howard, Shudo, and Umeshima (1983); the weaker endorsement of the protestant work ethic (duty) by contemporary British respondents relative to Malay, Indian, and Chinese samples found by Furnham and Muhiudeen (1984); the more autocratic (high-power-distance) values of Nigerian relative to South African managers reported by Orpen (1982); the more collectivist French Canadian relative to English Canadian managerial attitudes reported by Kanungo and Wright (1983); and differences in risk-taking attitudes among Indian, American, and Japanese managers reported by Orpen (1983a).

The fact that values influence a wide range of behaviors seems widely accepted. The volume by Dlugos and Weiermair (1981) contains nearly 40 papers concerned with the influence of values on social and political system variables, the employment relationship, industrial relations, and industrial democracy. It seems plausible that in cultures where human nature is assumed to be basically good, there will be more theory Y type organizations; in cultures where human nature is assumed to be basically evil, there will be more theory X organizations. In cultures where mastery over nature is considered desirable, there will be more innovation; in cultures where the future is an important value, there will be more planning; and management by objectives seems consistent with an emphasis on the future. In cultures with a doing orientation, leaders high in initiation of structure should be more acceptable; in cultures emphasizing a being orientation, leaders high in consideration ought to be particularly welcome. In individualistic, low-power-distance cultures, there ought to be less differentiation in wage structures (e.g., Sweden and Iceland) than there is in collectivist, high-power-distance cultures (e.g., Peru). Thus, the Kluckhohn-Strodtbeck (1961), Hofstede (1980a), and Schwartz (1992, in press) frameworks can be used as theories for predictions of numerous attributes of organizational or managerial behaviors.

Such frameworks need further development. One direction for such development is the intensive study of cultural syndromes, such as individualism-collectivism. We need to use multimethod approaches, with observations, responses to attitude and value items, reactions to scenarios describing a variety of social situations, responses in experimental settings (e.g, Chan, 1991), and the like, converging to define each of several cultural syndromes. Then we need to examine the antecedents of each syndrome. Finally, we need to learn what the consequences of each syndrome are. For example, Triandis (1990) has reviewed studies indicating that there is convergence among (a) observations of behavior (e.g., people engage in more activities with others in collectivist cultures than they do in individualistic ones), (b) responses to attitude items, (c) responses to value items, (d) responses to scenarios in which people place a higher

priority on group goals than individual ones, (e) self-descriptions, and (f) perceptions of the appropriateness of behavior in specific situations (Triandis, McCusker, & Hui, 1990). Thus, it can be concluded that collectivism is a cultural syndrome and that in collectivist cultures, relative to individualistic cultures, there is:

- Priority given to the goals of ingroups (determined through common fate) rather than to personal goals

- A sharp difference in the behavior of individuals, depending on whether they are interacting with ingroup or non–ingroup members

- More regulation of social behavior by norms than by personal attitudes

- More emphasis on hierarchy

- A higher probability of definition of the self in terms of group memberships (e.g., I am Chinese)

- Emphasis on family integrity, security, obedience, and conformity to ingroups

As we deepen our understanding of each cultural syndrome, we will develop a theory of culture that can be used to conceptually integrate diverse findings.

It is not clear that the particular theoretical frameworks developed thus far are optimal. An exploration of broader frameworks by Triandis (1982, 1984a) suggests that, in addition to the Kluckhohn-Strodtbeck and Hofstede dimensions, several others are worthy of detailed study. About 20 such dimensions have been discussed in the literature, but little has been done to determine their convergent and discriminant validity. Many of the behaviors that appear to be value-determined may be influenced by more than one dimension. For example, it is not clear that an emphasis on equity rather than equality is due to the masculinity-femininity dimension, as suggested by Hofstede (1980a), or to the individualism-collectivism dimension, as suggested by Leung and Bond (1984), or to *both* dimensions. However, the general theoretical stance of using dimensions of cultural variation, and using dimensions of value-difference, in particular, to classify empirical findings, and utilizing such dimensions as parameters of organizational theories (Triandis, 1982) seems desirable. In other words, our theories eventually will say: "In cultures where value dimension V_1 is high, management type M_1 is likely to be effective; but where V_1 is low, M_{10} will be effective." Of course, we are a long way from such a level of specificity. However, keeping this objective in mind provides us with a clear research program.

Moreover, in the future, research ought to move beyond static structural perspectives, such as those provided by Hofstede, to dynamic perspectives that examine how norms, roles, self-concepts, and values are negotiated in each environment (e.g., Stryker & Statham, 1985). It should move away from models that deal with aggregates of individuals to models that utilize idiographic analyses (e.g., Triandis et al., 1984; Zavalloni, 1980). Finally, it should move away from techniques that utilize limited data sets to techniques that can depend on broad data sets obtained from representative samples of the population (e.g., Heise, 1979).

In addition, to the extent that we understand that values are correlated with *unstated* assumptions that influence a broad range of behaviors, ranging from the construction of the constitutions of various states (Massimini & Calegari, 1979) to setting speed limits (Hofstede, 1982b) for our highways, we will be able to reach a deeper understanding of the way culture affects behavior.

Also, as we decipher the relationships between culture-person-occupation and behavior, including their complex interactions, we will be able to make major advances in both health psychology and occupational psychology. A good example in this area is the work of Arsenault and Dolan (1983) and Dolan and

Arsenault (1984). They have developed a typology of personality types based on consideration of the Rotter internal–external control dimension and the Type A personality dimension. They related this personality typology both to ethnicity (English vs. French Canadian) and to reactions to extrinsic and intrinsic job stress. Extrinsic job stress resulted from underutilization of skills, career ambiguity, pay inequity, and role conflict. Intrinsic job stress was due to risky decisions, physical risks, job overload, or excessively difficult tasks. They found that English Canadians in Quebec hospitals were more sensitive to extrinsic job stress and French Canadians were more sensitive to intrinsic job stress. Intrinsic job stress was found to reduce absenteeism but did not relate to perceived performance; extrinsic job stress increased absenteeism and was found to reduce performance. These relationships seem parallel to Wanous' (1974) findings that extrinsic job satisfaction is linked to high performance and that performance results in intrinsic job satisfaction. The main point is this: If we study the interactions of culture and personality with behavior, we will gain a deeper understanding of culture.

Applications

Selecting and Training Personnel for Work in Other Cultures

The tremendous expansion of multinational corporations (Adler, 1983b) and the migration of millions of workers from the third world to the developed part of the world (Ekstrand, 1980) have created culturally heterogeneous work forces. Within pluralistic societies the integration of the organization is a significant problem (Fromkin & Sherwood, 1974; Jackson, 1992). As a result, a great body of literature has developed around the process of cross-cultural adaptation (Brislin, 1981; Brislin & Pedersen, 1976; Landis & Brislin, 1983).

Corporations are concerned with the possibility of having their executives fail in other cultures. Culture shock (Furnham & Bochner, 1986; Oberg, 1958) affects about half of executives who work in another culture and most of their spouses. Failure to complete an assignment in another culture costs companies as much as $500,000 per executive, as it does in Japan, where costs are very high.

When selecting employees for overseas assignments, corporations naturally base their decisions on the employee's previous behavior, performance, and accomplishments. The employee who is competent at home is expected to be competent abroad. This assumption, however, has come under question by Adler and Graham (1986). They found that "we do not behave identically with foreigners as with our own people" (p. 20). The behaviors were obtained in a negotiation involving Francophone and Anglophone Canadians. Since this is the only study that compares within-culture (Anglo-Anglo or Franco-Franco) with between-culture (Anglo-Franco) behavior, we do not know how far these results generalize. But they are important, since they suggest that the assumption that people who are effective in interpersonal relations at the home office will be effective abroad may be wrong.

The related problems of selecting employees for overseas work and the premature returns of employees assigned to work overseas has been reviewed by Brislin (1981), Kealey and Ruben (1983), and Mendenhall and Oddou (1985). Failure rates range from 25 to 40 percent, mostly due to inadequate selection and training. Mendenhall and Oddou conclude that four dimensions are important in employee selection and training: self-orientation, other orientation, accurate perceptions, and cultural toughness.

Self-orientation.   This refers to the expatriate's ability to substitute reinforcements provided in the new culture (e.g., exciting new foods) for those lost when the move occurred. Also, the

ability to reduce stress and technical competence are important in enabling expatriates to have a positive self-orientation and thus to be able to remain in the situation until the job assignment is completed.

Other Orientation.   Included here is the ability to develop friendships, language skills that allow interaction with host nationals, a positive attitude toward the host culture, and a desire to relate to it.

Accurate Perceptions.   One of the problems people experience when they interact with members of other cultures is that the attributions they make for their behavior are not the same as the attributions the host nationals make for their own behavior (Triandis, 1975, 1977a). The creation of nonisomorphic attributions results in misunderstandings that can be avoided if people are properly trained before they enter a new culture. Obviously, we cannot expect a visitor and host to make the same attributions. But if the visitor makes attributions concerning the behavior of the host that are fairly similar to the attributions that the host makes about his or her own behavior, then there is similar meaning given to the behavior of the host. Furthermore, being nonjudgmental, having a high tolerance for ambiguity (Nishida, 1985), and using broad categories (Detweiler, 1980) when thinking about events have all been found to be desirable characteristics of expatriates.

Black and Mendenhall (1990) have reviewed several studies concerned with the effectiveness of cross-cultural training. They concluded that such training is effective and can prevent the estimated $2 billion in losses that U.S. corporations suffer every year because they provide only about 15 percent of their expatriate managers with cross-country training. Many German companies have high failure rates. In contrast, Koreans and Japanese corporations take cross-cultural training very seriously. In some cases employees spend a full year studying a foreign language and culture at their companies' expense, while the employees receive $50,000 plus living expenses for working abroad (Anonymous, 1991).

Cultural Toughness. The more authoritarian the expatriate, the more distance he or she is likely to experience from members of the host culture (O'Driscoll & Feather, 1983). Elaborate stereotypes about nationals of other countries are common (e.g., Stening, Everett, & Longton, 1981), and the more derogatory such stereotypes are, the greater the distance between the two. The use of occupation rather than ethnicity in stereotyping (Feldman, MacDonald, & Sam, 1980) can be very helpful, and cross-cultural training that cultivates this tendency can be productive. Clearly, distance between host nationals and expatriates is likely to make the expatriate's adjustment difficult and increase the probability of their premature return home.

When selecting people to work abroad, it is desirable to validate measures of tolerance for ambiguity (Budner, 1962), a positive self-concept (Stephan & Rosenfeld, 1978), empathy (Taft, 1977), and task orientation (Ruben & Kealey, 1979). Brislin (1981, pp. 40–71) and Kealey and Ruben (1983, pp. 155–175) provide a more complete discussion.

Tung (1982) did a comparative analysis of the selection and training procedures of American, European, and Japanese multinationals. His report summarizes the characteristics that multinationals consider important in selecting managers for assignments abroad. The selection processes used by each firm in the study were assessed by two raters. The more rigorous the process, the lower was the failure rate. When numerous psychological tests were used to assess a candidate's ability, adaptability to new environments, and motivation for work abroad, there was an improvement in results.

However, the report says little about cross-cultural training.

While much attention has been given to the problems executives experience in other cultures, much less attention has focused on the experiences of workers and on the problems of reentry shock (Sussman, 1985). There is, however, some work along these lines (e.g., Leo-Dupont, 1985). Interested readers should also consult Ekstrand (1980).

Broad reviews of cross-cultural training (e.g., Brislin & Pedersen, 1976; Triandis, 1977a, 1977b) have suggested that there are four kinds of training: self-insight, attribution training, behavioral training, and experiential training.

Self-insight. This training attempts to provide trainees with a sense of how culture influences behavior by helping them realize that much social behavior can be traced to culture. Such an awareness will enable trainees to better understand what causes the behavior of host nationals. One approach to such training, used to train Americans who will work abroad, was developed by Stewart, Danielian, and Foster (1969). It involves the training of a "counter-American," who behaves in opposition to the way an American is likely to behave. The trainee interacts with the counter-American for several days, and discussions, as well as the viewing of the videotapes of their interactions, allow the trainee to understand how culture influences behavior. More specifically, trainees learn that they carry a certain amount of "cultural baggage" with them when they travel abroad, which reflects their own culture. Wallin (1979) has identified such themes as individualism (satisfaction and pride in one's own accomplishments), dominance over nature, viewpoints that derive from having a culture with abundant resources, an emphasis on youth and informality, egalitarian values, and an emphasis on work and material gain. Understanding that people from other cultures do not necessarily agree with these assumptions can lead to improved relationships with host nationals.

Attribution Training. Learning to make attributions similar to those made by people from a host culture can be achieved through so-called *culture assimilators* (Fiedler, Mitchell, & Triandis, 1971). Work with these training materials has been further developed in recent years. Triandis (1977b, 1984a) has proposed a number of different approaches to constructing such materials. Intranational applications are also available (e.g., Landis, Hope, & Day, 1984). The topic has been well reviewed by Albert (1983), who also provides a list of the available assimilators.

Behavioral Training. David (1972) has described how training can be used to substitute lost reinforcements with new reinforcements that are available in the host culture, to desensitize the trainee from noxious stimuli, and to control anxiety.

Experiential Training. Trifonovitch (1973) has described an approach that depends on the trainee having extensive experience with members of the host culture prior to traveling there.

Recent work on the cognitive psychology of intergroup relations (e.g., Stephan, 1985) suggests additional strategies for cross-cultural training. One strong finding is that in the West, outgroups are perceived as more homogeneous than ingroups. Thus, training that emphasizes the heterogeneity of outgroup members should reduce prejudice. In contrast, collectivist countries view heterogeneity negatively, so such training should not be attempted in these countries. Similarly, training that emphasizes the personal attributes of outgroup members should prove helpful for the trainees from individualistic cultures. Laboratory studies reported by Miller, Brewer, and Edwards (1985)

suggest that such an approach to training should prove beneficial. Training that emphasizes positive attributes of the outgroup, similarities between the outgroup and ingroup, and external rather than internal attributions to explain undesirable outgroup behaviors (Amir & Ben-Ari, 1985) has also proven useful.

Triandis (1977b) has outlined several research projects that are necessary to understand the effectiveness of such training. Unfortunately, with the exception of the culture assimilator, very few of these methods have been evaluated. There are many unanswered questions. Among them, what combination of methods is likely to be optimal? One study (Landis, Brislin, & Hulgus, 1985) suggests that culture assimilator training followed by experiential learning is quite effective, while training in the reverse order is not. The authors argue that when new attributions are learned, they should be practiced; experiential learning first leads to anxiety, which may block the learning of new attributions. This well-designed experiment (with random assignment to five training conditions, in a modified Solomon design) needs to be replicated in field settings.

Additional combinations of training methods also need to be tested. Can general training (nonspecific to a culture) be helpful? Brislin, Cushner, Cherrie, and Yong (1986) have developed a general culture assimilator, and current evaluations of this training (Cushner, 1989) are promising. When should the training be given— for example, before or after an employee arrives at the host culture? Who should conduct the training? Should all the trainers be from the host culture, or would a mixture of trainers from the two cultures be better? How should the trainees be selected? How do attributes of the trainees interact with the training?

Training aimed at understanding intercultural communication (e.g., Gudykunst & Kim, 1984; Gudykunst, Stewart, & Ting-Toomey, 1985) and training directed at better understanding the role of body language in such communication (Kudoh & Matsumoto, 1985), as well as the role of paralinguistic behaviors in intercultural adjustment (e.g., Wolfgang, 1979), needs to be examined both as a substitute for and as a complement of more cognitive kinds of training, such as the culture assimilator. If both kinds of training are needed, what is the best order for presentation? A plethora of questions and very few answers still characterize the literature on selection and training of personnel for work in other cultures.

The record on the evaluation of cross-cultural training is poor. Few studies have been published, and most of those published focus on culture assimilator training (Albert, 1983). Random assignment of subjects to training and placebo training conditions is rare. The criteria used include judgments by host nationals about the effectiveness of the trainee's behavior in their culture, self-judgments of effectiveness by the trainee, reports on feelings about the host culture, and task effectiveness. Rarely do such studies use objective criteria, such as the percentage of trained versus untrained employees who returned to their home country before completing their assignment.

Summary. A large number of techniques for cross-cultural training have been proposed. However, we know too little about how much such training is needed, how these techniques should be combined, how different people may profit from each of the techniques, who should conduct the training, and so on. The evaluation of training is expensive, and there have been few good studies done in this area. Much more needs to be done along these lines in the coming years.

Cultural Influences on Groups

In reviewing cross-cultural studies of small groups, Mann (1980) notes that much of the work examines the scope and intensity of conformity to group norms and cooperation with group members. Conformity in the Asch (1956) paradigm has been found in all cultures studied. Rates of conformity are roughly one-third, as in the original study, except for some African data in which conformity was about 50 percent and some German data where it was about 20 percent. Anticonformity, the tendency to go against the group even when it is correct, has been found among the Japanese. Conformity is especially high in subsistence agricultural societies and in societies where there are very strong sanctions for deviance. Collectivist cultures (e.g., the Japanese, the kibbutz) do not show especially high levels of conformity in the Asch paradigm. Keep in mind that collectivists conform to ingroups, and in the Asch paradigm the confederates are outgroup members.

Mann (1980) reports that research on cooperation and competition shows that rural samples in many countries are more cooperative than urban samples. Among children, there appears to be greater cooperation in cultures that have little caste or class structure. Collectivists are generally more cooperative than individualists.

Group decisions often function for members as sources of commitment. There are studies showing cultural differences in the extent to which participatory forms of leadership and communication are preferred (e.g., Misumi, 1972). The Misumi studies indicated that authoritarian-led groups of boys were more highly motivated and produced the best products. However, Misumi and Nakano (1960) found that this effect occurs only when the task being examined is difficult. With simple tasks, a democratic leader is more effective. Thus, there remains the possibility that both culture and level of task difficulty may cause the more authoritarian leader to be more effective than the democratic. Such a result is also consistent with Fiedler's (1978) reasoning, since when a task is very difficult, the leadership situation is especially difficult (the leader has little or no situational control), and a low-LPC leader is more effective in such a situation. For a relatively simple task, the leader has some situational control, but in a laboratory setting leader-member relations are only moderately good, and in such mixed situations a high-LPC leader will be more effective.

Misumi's (1985) book is one of the most important in the area of cross-cultural studies of leadership (Smith, Peterson, Misumi, & Sugiman, 1990). It utilizes the concepts of *P* (production or performance emphasis), and *M* (maintenance emphasis), and operationalizes leadership patterns primarily on the basis of ratings by subordinates. However, a different set of questionnaire items is used with each set of subordinates from industry, government, schools (students), families (children), or sports groups. The research was carried out in both laboratory and field settings. Both manipulations of *P* and *M* emphasis in laboratories and structural equations methodology for causal analysis in field settings were used.

The findings (Misumi & Peterson, 1985; Misumi & Seki, 1971) are surprisingly consistent across settings and methods: The leadership pattern that emphasizes both *P* and *M* is superior to the one that emphasizes much *P* and little *m* (*Pm*) or the other combinations (*pM* and *pm*). Evidence suggests that the interaction between *P* and *M* is responsible for the positive results. That is, the meaning of *P* changes in the presence of *M: P* is seen as "pressure for production" when *m* is used, but *P* becomes emphasis on "planning" when *M* is used.

It is remarkable that the rank order of the four leadership patterns (*PM* best, *Pm, pM, pm* least good) remains the same across a wide range of criteria. The criteria have included productivity, accidents, morale, job satisfaction, satisfaction with the company, satisfaction with co-workers, accuracy of communication, high production norms, reminiscence scores in lab experiments, success in problem solving, and the winning of games. Small variations in the best rank order have been found: for instance, the best teachers are *PM*, next come the *P*, next the *M*, while the least good

are the *pm*. Among high need for achievement subjects, the *PM > P* or *M > pm* rank order is evident, but among those low in need for achievement, the *P > PM* or *pm > M* rank order was found.

The consistency of these findings with the theoretical ideas of Bales (e.g., Bales & Slater, 1955) and Blake and Mouton (1964) suggests that this is a theory of considerable cross-cultural generality, though the specifics are probably valid only in Japan. While the *P* and *M* constructs at an abstract-theoretical level may be the same as the distinctions of Bales or Blake, one must emphasize an important difference: Misumi operationalizes *P* and *M* differently in each setting—for example, teachers and miners. Thus, he is more culture-specific (emic), and this allows him to tell us what specific behaviors are seen as *P* or *M* in specific settings. Smith and Peterson (1988, pp. 107–111) elaborated on this point.

The generality of the *P* and *M* factors can be seen in a study by Smith, Misumi, Tayeb, Peterson, and Bond (1989). Data from Britain, the United States, Hong Kong, and Japan showed, via factor analysis, that there were *P* and *M* factors in all four cultures. However, the correlations of these factors with specific items showed cultural differences.

Another indigenous leadership theory was provided by Sinha (1980, 1984, 1986). Sinha presents evidence that in India the best leader is nurturant *and* task oriented. Furthermore, while participative leadership can be effective in India, in order for it to be effective it must be preceded by a period in which the leader is nurturant and task oriented (*NT*). In an experiment in which subjects were randomly assigned to different orders of *NT* and participatory (*P*) leadership, the *NT, P* sequence treatment was superior to the *NT, NT* sequence, the *P, NT* sequence, or the *P, P* sequence.

The effectiveness of the *NT* leader, who does resemble Misumi's *PM* leader, and Ayman and Chemers' (1983) "benevolent autocrat," which is very effective in Iran, suggests that in collectivist, high-power-distant cultures, participative management may not be effective until subordinates learn to expect it. Expectations about participation are more likely to occur in individualistic, low-power-distance cultures. Yet even illiterate peasants in Peru have been trained to use participation (Dobyns, Doughty, & Lasswell, 1971). Thus, participative management appears to be a potentially universally effective management style, *provided* subordinates have the knowledge that they should use it and are given sufficient training.

In cultures where conformity to group norms is widely accepted, such as in Mexico, models of leadership behavior such as Fiedler's may not predict organizational variables, like job satisfaction, except perhaps for that subset of subjects who are deviants from the general cultural pattern of conformity. This was demonstrated in the studies of Ayman and Chemers (1986, 1991). Using the Snyder (1974) self-monitoring scale, they found that the match of LPC and leader situation is related to job satisfaction, but that this relationship did not hold for high self-monitors (who are sensitive to group norms), while it did hold for low self-monitors. Low self-monitors are internally directed, so they pay less attention to group norms and hence are free to show the usual relationships between LPC and other variables.

This is an important point because it shows that in collectivist cultures one may not be able to predict the leader behavior–group effectiveness relationships found in individualist cultures. Only the subset of culture members who behave similarly to individualists show the expected relationships.

Also worth noting is the fact that many of the tasks used in the laboratory do not have a different social significance in individualist versus collectivist cultures. For example, the broad research program on *social loafing* carried out by Latané (e.g., Harkins, Latané, & Williams, 1980) shows that for tasks such as hand clapping or shouting, the more group members

there are, the smaller the contribution of each member to the total group output. The phenomenon has been identified in Japan, Taiwan, India, Thailand, and the United States. However, when Gabrenya, Wang, and Latané (1985) changed the task to make it culturally significant for the subjects in Taiwan, the phenomenon did not appear. These authors hypothesized that Americans, coming from an individualistic culture, will demonstrate social loafing, while Taiwan Chinese, coming from a collectivist culture, will not when the task is socially significant. Consistent with this hypothesis, the Americans evidenced social loafing, performing less effectively in pairs than when alone; the Chinese evidenced social striving, performing better in pairs than when alone. Similar results were obtained by Earley (1989).

Thus, it is not surprising that in most of the studies concerning the effects of culture on group behavior, no important cultural effects have been found. For example, Anderson (1983) found that cultural heterogeneity had no effect on managerial effectiveness, satisfaction, or leader-member relations. Misumi (1981), using Japanese data, reports that group decisions reduce accident rates. Such a result might have been expected from Western samples as well.

Similarly, a reading of contemporary Soviet social psychology (Strickland, 1984) shows little that is different from the social psychology of the West. Of course, the terminology is different, but behind the unfamiliar jargon one finds the same old variables, working more or less the same old way. For instance, while Petrovskii (1984) contrasts the "stereometric analysis of the collective" in the former Soviet Union with the "planimetric analysis of the small group" by Homans in the United States and deals with the "degree of mediation of interpersonal relations by the group" and "the degree of development of the group according to social progress," careful reading shows that the former is the old group cohesiveness variable, and the latter is the consistency of group/organizational/societal goals. The relationships, reported with different names, turn out to be the same ones found in the West. If one learns to translate, instead of "directive," "collegial" and "passive nonintervention" leadership styles (Zhurvalev & Shorokhova), one could just as easily use the old Lewinian "authoritarian, democratic, and laissez-faire" leadership styles!

On the other hand, when we examine data from groups in cultures that are more distant from Europe and America, such as India, Japan, or Africa, we do find some differences. Certainly, competition is much greater in individualistic cultures, and it is bound to have some effects on group harmony or leader-member relations (Elleson, 1983).

Bennett (1977b) found that the relationship of LPC and effectiveness is much the same among Filipino and American managers, but when the same study was done with Hong Kong Chinese managers, the relationship was different. The high-LPC managers were more effective among the Chinese in situations where the low-LPC managers were expected to be effective. Bennett (1977b) argues that the difference is due to the fact that the Filipino managers are more Americanized than the Hong Kong managers. Furthermore, the meaning of *consideration* may depend on the cultural context.

Though such differences are obtained, one is impressed by the extent to which questionnaires, such as the *Leader Behavior Description Questionnaire* or the *Job Description Index*, do turn out to be useable in other cultures (Ayman & Chemers, 1983). When some differences are reported, the effects are often minuscule. For example, in a study by Rosenstein (1985), all correlations involving culture were smaller than .33; out of 120 coefficients, only 8 were at $p < .05$, which might have been expected by chance, and the only saving grace is that all coefficients are in the hypothesized direction.

Some more or less weak effects have been obtained. Thus, in collectivist cultures, leader social support appears to be more important than it is in individualist cultures (e.g., Bennett, 1977b; Orpen, 1982). In high-power-distance cultures, leaders may be effective even if they are not participatory (Kanungo, 1980). Hofstede (1980b) is probably correct in hypothesizing that leadership relationships will be different in high- and low-power-distance cultures.

Summary. Leadership and group behavior seem to be rather similar across culture. However, there are shifts in emphasis. For example, while in general leaders who are high on both production and maintenance are better than leaders who are characterized by different combinations of these attributes, in some cultures or subcultures a different profile is optimal. The behaviors that define *production* or *maintenance* differ across cultures. So, while the laws of group behavior, at a high level of abstraction, are the same, at the specific level of "What do I need to do to be viewed as considerate?" the leader must acquire different kinds of information.

Organizational Cultures

The fact that groups and organizations have cultures or climates has been acknowledged since Lewin, Lippitt, and White's (1939) research on social climates (authoritarian, democratic, and laissez-faire). The early work utilized primarily the concept of climate and survey instruments. The current work uses the concept of culture and qualitative methodology. Schneider (1985) points out that culture is now on the ascendance and climate is less popular. The popularity of the culture concept is evident from the fact that entire issues of *Administrative Science Quarterly* and *Organizational Dynamics* have been devoted to organizational cultures, and several books on this construct have been published (Deal & Kennedy, 1982; Frost, Moore, Louis, Lundberg, & Martin, 1985c; Kilmann, 1984; and Schein, 1985). The Peters and Waterman (1982) volume has been on the best-seller list, as have other popular works in this area. National magazines (*Business Week*, October1984; *Fortune*, October 1983) have discussed corporate culture.

Is the new emphasis on culture rather than climate just another fad? Perhaps, but culture is a more profound and richer construct. It deals with unstated assumptions, values, norms, meanings, myths, symbols, rituals, philosophies of life, heroes, war stories, and more. With such a rich construct, qualitative methods are appropriate. However, when such methods are used, problems of reliability and validity become severe. It may be comforting to researchers that none of their statements can be disconfirmed by data or by failures of replication, but that is hardly what science is about! Too much of what is published in this area is impressionistic, descriptive, or what might be called "fun." In fact, the Frost et al. volume begins with the statement: "Several spirit birds were flying together, returning from an extensive trip to investigate the cultures of human organizations." It then goes on to talk about a raven, an owl, a wren, an eagle, a stork, a pelican, and a phoenix. The piece is fun to read, but what exactly does it contribute to our understanding?

Much of the discussion in such books and the related articles is purely conceptual. For instance, Morgan and Smircich (1980) discuss such matters as "reality as a concrete structure" and "humans as responding mechanisms" (typical of behaviorism), and "reality as a concrete process" and "humans as adaptive mechanisms" (which is typical of open systems theory). Obviously, at that level of abstraction only qualitative methods are feasible. Smircich (1983) examines cultural and organizational theories at a similarly high level of abstraction. It is a stimulating discussion, but little that is empirically testable can be extracted from it.

The fascination of management with such abstractions is understandable. When making policy that will affect a myriad of persons, the psychological level of analysis is hardly relevant. Methodologically poor studies, such as Peters and Waterman's (1982), are easy to read (they are full of anecdotes), and one feels good after reading them. The validity of the wisdom they impart is an issue that many managers would rather not address. Yet Carroll's (1983) critique of the book is well taken: Attributes that are found in the successful companies may also be present in the unsuccessful. The study has no control groups. There is no theory linking many of the attributes to success. The attributes are presented as if they are valid regardless of the technology, market position, or time period. There is no investigation about whether the findings hold true in other cultural settings. Sampling of both the companies and the episodes described in the anecdotes is biased and subject to regression artifacts.

This does not mean that one should reject most of the book. There are many points (e.g., the importance of a sense of control) that can be supported by solid research done by others (e.g., Langer, 1983). It is exactly this sorting of anecdote from solid finding that remains to be done in the area of organizational cultures.

The implied negative comments just made about qualitative methodologies should not be taken as rejection of these methodologies. On the contrary, as Triandis (1972, 1983) has repeatedly advocated, the use of qualitative methods is essential in the *early* phases of a research project. There are situations in which such methods provide useful data, but the problem is that many researchers stop there. The more quantitative methods should be used also to test, confirm, and refine hypotheses. The importance of multimethod approaches needs to be emphasized. Whyte (1984) and Fiske and Shweder (1986) have commented soundly about the need to combine many methods.

The methodological argument that data obtained and analyzed at one level (individual, group, organizational, or cultural) have to be examined in the context of data obtained at the higher levels (Schneider, 1985) is sound. Schneider argues that "individually based motivation studies of performance or turnover on the one hand, or group-based studies of group output on the other hand, cannot be expected to yield strong findings because the unit of analysis being studied is embedded in, *and affected by,* at least the next level of analysis" (p. 597, italics in the original). By "affected by," Schneider does not mean moderated, but rather directly changed, as a function of variables at the organizational or cultural levels. Of course, this does not preclude their moderation by cultural variables that function as parameters of the relationships (Triandis, 1982).

The literature is rich with examples of differences in values, rituals, reward systems, myths, and the like. But studies of an organization's heroes, stories, and scripts (Martin, 1982), or rites and ceremonials (e.g., Trice & Beyer, 1984), or issues of cultural conflict within the same corporation (e.g., Martin & Siehl, 1983), or problems of transfer of the culture from one unit of the corporation to another unit (e.g., Jaeger, 1983) have usually been discussed with little reference to national cultures.

Hofstede (1984) discussed the meaning of "quality of life" in different cultures. He argued that in collectivist cultures prestige is especially important as an aspect of a good job and quality of life, while in individualist cultures recognition for what one has done is more important; in collectivist cultures work arrangements should allow individuals to save face, avoid shame, and emphasize harmony, while in individualist cultures the avoidance of guilt would be more valued; in collectivist cultures serving a larger collective (e.g., the country) and in individualist serving the self would be important elements of the quality of life. In cultures high in power distance, the benevolent patriarch is the ideal leader, while people in cultures low in that attribute value the consultative leader. Humanizing the work means different things, depending on the culture's position on Hofstede's masculinity dimension. In the United States it means job enlargement,

while in Sweden it means forming groups that complete the job. Hofstede (1991) presents a large empirical study of organizational cultures in the Netherlands and Denmark.

These are interesting hypotheses that require testing. At an even higher level of abstraction are discussions about the way national and organizational cultures must be made consistent (Nath, 1992). A plausible argument is that the managerial system should be consistent with the country's cultural values (England, 1983; Erez, 1992). Lincoln, Hanada, and Olson (1981) find that matching the employee's culture and the organizational culture results in job satisfaction. For instance, the Japanese approve of paternalism more than Americans in Japanese-owned firms. They found that the greater the hierarchical differentiation, the more satisfied the Japanese employees are, but the fact that the reverse is true for American employees seems worth noting. Japanese organizational structures and Japanese value orientations increase the probability that quality circles will be successful (Ferris & Wagner, 1985). Misumi (1984) provides an excellent discussion of Japanese organizational decision making. In it he shows how during the *sake* party subordinates can criticize their superior, how the *ringi* system of decision making is consistent with values of the early Meiji era, and how "this Japanese version of participatory management is so deeply rooted in Japan's tradition that it is in itself part of Japanese culture" (p. 535).

Schneider (1988) provides a good review of the difficulties of fitting an existing corporate culture in with a specific national culture. She indicates that the acceptance and implementation of human resource practices, such as career planning, appraisal and compensation systems, and selection and socialization, depends on the relationship that exists between corporate and national cultures.

Some of the elements of the Japanese management system were advocated by American social scientists for years (e.g., Likert, 1961; Likert & Likert, 1976) and have been used for a long time by American companies that Ouchi called Type Z. Ouchi and Jaeger (1978) contrasted the ideal types of Americans (Type A) and Japanese (Type J) with Type Z companies. According to Ouchi and Jaeger, the contrasting attributes for Types A and J are short-term versus lifetime employment, individual versus consensual decision making, individual versus collective responsibility, rapid versus slow evaluation and promotion, explicit vesus implicit and formalized versus informal control, specialized versus nonspecialized career paths, and segmented versus holistic concern for the employee by the organization. The Type Z companies are those American companies that use long-term employment, consensual decision making, individual responsibility, slow evaluation and promotion, implicit, informal control with explicit, formalized measures, moderately specialized career paths, and holistic concerns. Thus, Type Z is a combination of individualistic values and highly collective, nonindividual patterns of interaction. It "simultaneously satisfies old norms of independence and present needs for affiliation" (p. 311). Thus, Ouchi and Jaeger argue that Type Z is a successful American adaptation of an organizational culture to the national culture.

There is a need for much more research on the similarities and differences between national cultures and organizational cultures. The hypothesis of the need for a fit between the two is plausible. What we need now is more well-designed studies to test it.

Cooke and Rousseau (1988) provided a promising methodology for the study of American organizational cultures. It is the *Organizational Culture Inventory*, a 120-item questionnaire that identifies 12 management styles. It has a circumplex structure that is very similar to the structure reported by Schwartz (1992) for the values of teachers and students in several countries. Some of these styles may be found in other cultures. An examination of the extent these styles are consistent with national subjective cultures,

and whether such consistency leads to greater organizational effectiveness, seems worth attempting.

Summary. The construct *organizational culture* has gained popularity in recent years. A major hypothesis is that organizational cultures must be consistent with national cultures in order for the organization to function well. However, rigorous tests of this hypothesis are not yet available.

Management in Different Countries

It is apparent from the previous discussion that management philosophies and practices vary from organization to organization. However, there are some common elements in managerial behaviors across organizations within the same country. It is reasonable to conclude, from the prior discussion, that culture contributes some variance to managerial behaviors. A good review of cross-national management research can be found in Peng, Peterson, and Shyi (1991).

Many writers in the management area have discussed (a) defining goals, (b) planning, (c) selecting people, (d) controlling the organization, (e) training people, and (f) motivating people as being among the major functions of management. Schein (1985) states that managers basically "manage the organizational culture." In other words, they influence the inputs and throughputs (Katz & Kahn, 1978) to obtain the most desirable outputs. Managing the organizational culture, of course, means ensuring that goals are set and that values and norms are shaped.

From our discussion in the previous section we can extrapolate that each distinct culture may have a distinct management style and that what occurs in one culture may not necessarily occur in others. For example, Shuter (1984) reports that in Sweden this behavior is tolerated, though not approved. Swedes generally avoid criticizing others, so even though they may not like what they see, they are not apt to say anything. This kind of behavior, while tolerated in Sweden, is strictly inappropriate in high power-distance countries, and even in relatively low power-distance countries like the United States.

Sinha (1977) reviewed more than 300 publications concerning industrial and organizational psychology and management in India published between 1971 and 1976. While the topics parallel those found in the West, there are also findings unique to India. For example, leadership in Indian communities is determined by religion, caste, and class much more than it is in the West, yet in the case of Indian cooperatives, education and landholdings are more important determinants of leadership than caste or religion. Such a finding is consistent with Inkeles and Smith's (1974) point that cooperatives are modern organizations in India, and shows that while Western findings may be generally valid, they need to be qualified or modified when they are applied to specific cultures.

Sinha (1977) makes the notable observation that Indian researchers are more interested in job satisfaction than they are in productivity (see also Erez, this volume). Is this a result of placing a greater value on how one feels about a job than on getting things done, which is characteristic of a culture in which thinking and feeling are more important than doing, or is it simply a reflection of the relative difficulty associated with doing these kinds of studies? Sinha's review challenges many of the assumptions made by Western developmental theorists about factors that lead to economic development (Sinha, 1984). For example, he criticizes the Triandis (1984b) model of economic development as too dependent on McClelland's individualistic assumptions. Sinha points out that under limited resource conditions, such as those that prevail in India, individualistic striving for excellence becomes counterproductive competition, monopolizing, and hoarding of resources, and interferes with the optimal allocation and use of available resources. He reviews a number of experiments that support this point, arguing that in collectivist cultures effectiveness depends on getting the collective to change. "The logical corollary for man is to *grow with* the social group and collectives, rather than to strive for personal excellence which might alienate him from the persons around him" (Sinha, 1984, p. 173, italics in original).

Such analyses tell us why management styles that work well in the West might be ineffective in some cultures. A similar point is made by Negandhi (1984), who argues that in the developed world one usually finds lower power distance, and individualistic values stress mastery over nature and basic human goodness, which is different from the cultural attributes found in the third world. When studying the management styles in American subsidiaries and local firms in third world countries, Negandhi found many differences, though he ends his analysis by supporting the convergence hypothesis (that technology has its own logic and that those using the same technology behave similarly).

The higher power distance of the third world is reflected in such management practices as lower levels of delegation, centralization of decision making, secrecy and hoarding of information, and anti-union attitudes. Collectivism is reflected in ingroup recruitment, little evaluation of managers, promotion according to seniority, and a view of competition as unfair and destructive. The "subjugation to nature" value orientation is reflected in an acceptance of shortages of skilled employees. The wide use of centralized management techniques reflects prevailing assumptions about human nature. Negandhi (1984) finds that the contrast between American subsidiaries and locally owned firms is sharpest in the area where rationality as opposed to social criteria is used (e.g., "Does the employee produce?" vs. "Is the employee a good person?"). The greater use of (a) planning, (b) goal setting, (c) techniques that optimize plant capacity, (d) payment based on objective criteria, and

(e) emphasis on research are examples of the emphases of the American subsidiaries that are not found as often in the local firms.

The view that convergence is occurring seems supported by some studies (e.g., Form, 1979) and by the Japanese shift toward Western assumptions. Perhaps no change is going to be more radical in Japan than the adoption of the equal pay for equal work law, which came into effect in 1986. It reflects change in a society that holds the highest rating on Hofstede's masculinity dimension (differentiation by sex). Nevertheless, one should not overestimate the degree of Japanese sexism. As Lebra (1984) shows, there are numerous Japanese professional women and managers who seem to be accepted as managers. Lebra does not provide specific numbers for women managers, but 5 percent of corporate presidents in Japan are women (Iwao, 1993). The role takes over and determines the way others relate to them. Similarly, Adler (1987) finds that Western women can be successful in Asia because they are seen as *gaijin* (foreigners) and not primarily as women.

In most societies management tends to have its own characteristic attributes, but there is also tremendous variability. An excellent description of Indian management was provided by Khandwalla (1983). Based on data from 75 Indian organizations, he identified three Indian management style dimensions:

- *Modernity* (e.g., the use of the latest sophisticated equipment, an emphasis on innovation) versus *traditional style* (e.g., resisting innovations, relying on personal contacts for hiring)

- *Tenderness* (e.g., strong commitment to community welfare, avoiding competition) versus *toughness* (e.g., efficiency, pragmatism)

- *Mutuality* (e.g., emphasis on family-type relations, paternalism) versus *individualism* (e.g., contractual obligations with employees, emphasis on high-pressure selling tactics)

Khandwalla found some Indian firms in each of the cells defined by high, medium, and low levels of these three dimensions. He concluded that there is a great deal of diversity in management style and that one should not make sweeping generalizations about the Indian management style. No doubt, the within-culture variance exceeds the between-culture variance.

Collectivism is found in all the rapidly growing economies of the Far East: Hong Kong, Japan, South Korea, Singapore, and Taiwan. However, there are many kinds of collectivism (Hui, 1984; Triandis, 1990), and the kinds found in China and Japan are not identical. Also, the size of organizations is very different, with organizations in Hong Kong and Singapore tending toward family ownership and being smaller sized than the largest third of the Japanese enterprises. Also, when we discuss Japanese-style management we must remember that we are focusing on the third of the organizations that are in the international market. The vast majority of Japanese enterprises are still "mom and pop" stores.

The spectacular economic achievements of the Far East in the last quarter century cannot be due to chance. The exact causes of the "economic miracle," however, are difficult to identify. In any case, the data are clear. Each of the rapidly growing economies of the Far East has already surpassed some of the European countries in GNP per capita. For instance, Hong Kong is now ahead of Greece and other European Common Market countries. The exact cause of this success remains unclear. Ting Chau (1983) provides a very interesting, culturally sensitive analysis of both similarities and differences between the five economies. Similarities are traceable to Confucianism, which, though not a religion in the Western sense, is a way of life that has a great influence on values. Important common elements are the emphasis on familism and ingroup harmony, which may be a factor in both the extraordinarily low rates of labor unrest and paternalistic management practices; the emphasis on *Li*, which is the idea that to conduct oneself according to norms and the rule of propriety in itself gives one prestige and moral status; the emphasis on profit being justified only if one gives a quality product to the society; and the emphasis on interdependence.

The latter norm reflects the *Wu Lun* ("Five Cardinal Relations"), which focus on specific dyadic relations and emphasize *reciprocity*. For example, the sovereign must be benevolent and the subjects loyal; fathers must show affection, and sons must show filial piety. It is this reciprocity that is transferred to the work relationship. The corporation is paternal and the worker is filial. The worker sacrifices self-interest for the benefit of the group. Managerial practices, such as collective decision making and responsibility, and emphasis on group harmony and on "face as a collective property" (King & Bond, 1983) can be seen within the context of collectivism.

Diversity emerges on the other Hofstede dimensions. For example, Japan and Hong Kong are masculine, while Singapore and Taiwan are feminine. Ting Chau (1983) explores the implications of such differences in detail. For example, she indicates that the attitudes of Hong Kong managements toward the environment deemphasize pollution control, while in Singapore it is greatly emphasized.

Redding and Ng (1983) have explored the incompatibility of Western styles of management with the value of saving face, and Lindsay and Dempsey (1983) have explored the difficulties associated with using Western conceptions of management training in China. In China, until recently, individuals were expected to subordinate personal needs and wishes to group, organizational, and state interests. They were not supposed to develop their personal talents unless they served the group. Rewards were given to teams (e.g., farm brigades) and thus reached individuals indirectly. Teams were led by those who met two criteria: (a) They were recommended by their teammates based on open discussions, and (b) they were judged

by those in the hierarchy to be likely to act in the best interest of the state, organization, department, or team (Blake & Mouton, 1979).

Such an orientation is fundamentally different from the individualism found in the West. The management practices of the West are inevitably reflections of individualism and are thus often inappropriate for the East. Redding and Wong (1986) have reviewed the organizational behavior of the overseas Chinese. They tend to have small but successful enterprises that are not likely to become multinationals. They describe these people's "utilitarianistic familism" (p. 274); their tendency to work in small, family-owned companies; their greater (when compared to the West) levels of centralization and lower levels of specialization and standardization; their "didactic" leadership style (p. 278); their reluctance to share information with subordinates; their paternalism; their use of multiple standards for dealing with people; their emphasis on social rather than ego needs; and their loyalty, interpersonal sensitivies, materialism, and hard work. Some of the comments made about them are negative: superiors condescending to subordinates, public humiliation of subordinates, exploitation of relatives, and the conflict behind the facade of harmony. The authors try to determine how the complex pattern just described has resulted in the phenomenal increases in the standard of living of these Chinese communities. In contrast, Ronen (1986) summarizes studies that discuss organizational structures appropriate for multinational corporations.

Japanese Management

The literature on Japanese management is extensive (see Smith, 1984). Clarke (1992) provides an excellent summary of the literature. Keys and Miller (1984) provide a review in which they identify three underlying factors characteristic of Japanese management: long-term planning, career employment, and collective responsibility. The first is reflected in the use of longer periods of time to manage;[1] diligent implementation of plans, discipline, and order in work; sufficient time to implement concepts and systems; development of an integrated organizational philosophy; implicit rather than explicit control systems requiring extensive socialization but promoting internal behavioral controls; articulation of a company philosophy (which requires time to develop); and extensive investment in employee training and development (which also takes time, but results in employees being motivated by the organizational culture). Lifetime employment is also part of the articulated company philosophy and is consistent with extensive employee training, since the investment in such training is less likely to be lost. It is related to reduced employee turnover but requires extensive socialization of employees and a high degree of loyalty. It is also linked to nonspecialized career paths and the development of corporate unions. Finally, collective responsibility is seen as related to an emphasis on teamwork, cooperation, consensus decision making, participative management, trust and interdependence, and the use of quality circles.

Cole (1980) provides an excellent discussion of quality circles. He explains how during the 1940s and 1950s the American occupation authorities brought American experts on quality control (such as Deming and Juran) to teach the subject so that Japanese products, which had a poor reputation for quality, could be improved. The Japanese adapted these ideas to their culture, which happened to have many features compatible with them, and took advantage of the highly educated population and the mathematical training of their high school graduates (Stevenson, Lee, & Stigler, 1986) to make every worker a manager. As a result, they require fewer inspectors and have low rejection rates. Quality control is taught to all workers—including, for example, accountants and purchasing agents. Participation in quality circles brings prestige and allows

workers to act as professionals (e.g., going to conferences where workers explain their latest quality innovations and present papers on the subject). While monetary rewards for innovations are small, the prestige and the bonus that one gets from profitable companies are highly significant. Cole gives specific examples of quality changes and how they were instituted.

In evaluating the effects of quality circles, Cole points to the enthusiasm of Japanese management but is skeptical of some claims. A significant minority of Japanese workers seem to feel that quality circles are coercive. Nevertheless, those workers who dislike the system usually quit, and those who stay find it challenging. Bonuses paid to workers of profitable companies are enormous and remind one of Lincoln Electric of Cleveland, Ohio. In that company (see J. F. Lincoln, 1951), too, worker motivation is enormous, and cost reductions are not the only outcome of good management: Safety and industrial relations problems are kept at a minimum.

Japanese success seems related to collectivism and may be inspired by Confucian ethics. Collectivists commit themselves to ingroups for a long time, and it takes time to change ingroups, join ingroups, or change ingroup–outgroup perspectives. One is likely to see the ingroup in the context of several decades, and hence one is able to wait for the results of ingroup policies, even if it takes years for such results to materialize. Thus, managers are allowed to work on long-term plans. Collective responsibility, of course, is at the heart of collectivism.

The collectivism found in corporations reflects the collectivism of the national culture. Sakamoto (1975) reviewed the surveys that were conducted in Japan from 1953 to 1973 and found a persistence of collectivist themes. Karsh (1984) relates the Japanese management system to both historical and cultural antecedents. He examines the work group as a source of identity and personnel policies (such as pay determined largely by seniority, slow promotions, retirement at age 55, and paternalism) in the context of Japanese collectivism. He shows that while status is never ignored, it is submerged in the family metaphor. He discusses the varieties of Japanese workers (white collar vs. blue collar, regular, midterm, temporary, and outside), and the fact that lifetime employment is given only to the regular workers who constitute less than a third of the work force.[2] He describes the extensive training provided to employees and the fact that wages are viewed as company support for the sustenance of employees and their families rather than as a reward for services rendered. He describes the emphasis on obligation, duty, and loyalty, which leads to conforming behavior. Finally, he suggests that creativity and originality are discouraged, since risk-taking is not socially sanctioned.

Karsh emphasizes that the Japanese work ethic stresses how one's conduct may affect others. It is common for firms to sponsor retreats and weekends at spas during which members of work units live and relax with their supervisors and their families. The mix of monetary and nonmonetary rewards is weighted toward the latter in Japan (Leibenstein, 1984). The paternalism of Japanese firms often results in their spending more per employee on nonpayroll benefits than do American firms. This is also the case for Japanese firms operating in the United States (Pascale, 1978). While there is some evidence of convergence between Japan and the United States (Pascale & Maguire, 1980), there is also evidence that the greater the Japanese presence in joint ventures, the more elements of Japanese management style can be found in the organizational cultures of such ventures (Lincoln, Olson, & Hanada, 1978).

A survey of 911 Japanese and 450 U.S. managers from about 30 companies in each of the two countries conducted by the Japan Productivity Center (Baba, Hanaoka, Hara, & Thompson, 1984) confirmed that Japanese managers use a longer time perspective on personnel matters. They emphasize training, long-term employment, and seniority. Japanese collectivism emerges from answers to such questions as this: "Which do you consider more important when subordinates change sections or are promoted—the section's needs or the future of the subordinate concerned?" The predominant Japanese answer was the section's needs, while the predominant American answer was the future of the subordinate. Similarly, the Japanese put greater emphasis on the section's goals than on the individual's work load; the Americans emphasized the reverse pattern. Responsibility was seen as appropriately given to the group by the Japanese and to the individual by the Americans.

The Japanese answered a number of questions in a more authoritarian manner. For example, they used "will order" rather than "will suggest," but felt more integrated into the company and more willing to decide without checking with top management in the case of an emergency.

The attributions for success and failure were also different for managers from the two countries. The Japanese linked success and failure to effort and emphasized employee motivation; enthusiasm, interdependence, and harmony were also seen as sources of success. The Americans emphasized employee abilities, and though they were willing to delegate more, they were also more willing than the Japanese to discharge those found to be incompetent. Salary was seen as a function of "job importance" by the Japanese and of "results" by the Americans. The Japanese emphasized the setting of high goals, the consideration of all circumstances before punishing for a mistake, socialization of new workers, and staying with the same company as an ideal to a greater extent than did the Americans.

While such management surveys suggest that greatly different patterns of managerial attitudes exist in Japan and the United States, laboratory work in general shows very few cultural differences. Misumi (1978) has edited a volume of reviews of social psychology in Japan, which reports few cultural differences. Much of the research is inspired by American paradigms and finds support for them. A wide range of American findings was replicated in Japan. For example, support has been found for Norman's factor structure in person perception (p. 633) and Fiedler's contingency model of leadership (p. 655).

According to Nakane (1978), when examining Japan, the unit of analysis should not be the individual but the group. This group of coworkers is linked with their leader by a set of interdependent obligations. The leader gives love and care; the subordinates feel *amae* (Doi, 1971, 1973) toward the leader. *Amae* refers to dependence on the other. The boss responds by "taking care of the worker." The Japanese leader, by showing love, care, and paternalism, inspires and motivates subordinates to work hard, be cooperative, and sacrifice themselves for the good of the group.

The Japanese management system, taking advantage of elements of Japanese culture, basically results in workers feeling obligated to work hard to repay their benevolent supervisor, and it results in their receiving pressure from their fellow workers to work hard if they do not work hard. Thus, since job assignments are given to a group, and people have been trained to respond to group needs, the group also exerts a force toward productivity. In short, both an internal force, from the subordinate-supervisor relationship, and an external force from the group to the individual relationship, operate on the worker.

One can make the case that a parallel motivational pattern occurs in the Lincoln plan (Lincoln, 1951). In that case profits generated by the combined action of the company's employees are distributed each year. Since the profit sharing is often equivalent to a year's salary (e.g., in 1985 the average bonus was $17,381), workers are highly motivated. There is again both an internal force—if I work hard I will get a larger share of the profit—and an external force—those who do not work hard enough are pressured by their fellow workers to do so, because it is only when everyone works hard that the profits will be maximal. In short, the Japanese motivation system has a parallel in the United States.

Erez (1992) demonstrated that the Japanese interpersonal communication system is shaped by Japanese cultural values. This congruence intensifies the smooth flow of communication, which results in better consensus and commitment to shared values and greater levels of shared knowledge and information. She argues that such sharing enhances productivity and innovation.

Summary. This section on the Japanese management system illustrates the point that management systems must take culture into account. While there are some universal attributes of management systems, culture can both moderate and be a direct influence on the effectiveness of a managerial system.

Erez (1986) provides a good illustration of this point. She worked with first-level supervisors from three Israeli organizations that have different organizational cultures—private, public, and kibbutz. Her assumption, supported by data, was that the collectivism of the kibbutz would be greater than the collectivism of public or private organizations, and hence participative management would be most effective in the kibbutz. In a 3 x 3 design, the three types of supervisors were assigned to three experimental conditions—participative, delegative, and assigned. In the participative condition, the supervisors were allowed to set production goals in discussion with the researcher. As predicted, the performance of the kibbutz supervisors was best in the participatory condition and the least effective in the assigned condition; conversely, the performance of the supervisors from the private sector was excellent in the assigned condition and not very good in the participative condition. The public sector supervisors exhibited their best performance in the delegative condition but were also very good in the participatory and the least good in the assigned condition. Thus, the congruence of management system and culture was shown in this experiment to be a critical factor in obtaining the best performance.

Any motivational system is likely to have limitations. The Japanese motivational system works well in Japan. Yoshino (1976) has discussed its disadvantages for multinational organizations. The *ringi* system of consultation (see Misumi, 1984, for an excellent description) is difficult to operate with a heterogeneous work force. It assumes a fair amount of similarity in viewpoint, which is achieved through socialization. But socialization will homogenize attitudes only if the starting attitudes of workers are not too diverse.

The Japanese system overworks the competent and lets the incompetent do little. It does not use formal controls, but rather depends on the workers' internalization of the company culture, which is more difficult to achieve with a heterogeneous work force. Yoshino points out the difficulty of dealing with distance when the Japanese management system is so dependent on face-to-face communication. It is also difficult for the manager to be evaluated by supervisors who are thousands of miles away. Thus, Japanese managers resent being given work assignments abroad. In short, while the system works well in Japan, as a management system it has severe limitations for other cultures, and even for the Japanese multinationals themselves.

In summary, there is considerable literature linking management patterns to national setting. However, much skepticism about this literature seems justified, since one can find much within-national boundaries variability, and there is a suspicion that the within-culture variance may be greater than the between-cultures variance.

Employee Control of the Organization

The sense of control over one's environment is a major factor in motivation. Those who feel in control are likely to be satisfied with their lives, while those who do not feel in control are often depressed (Langer, 1983). Some people need to control their environment so much that in some laboratory experiments subjects preferred situations that were excruciatingly noisy but that they could control over situations that provided rewards but which they could not control (Thomson, 1983). Participation in decisions that affect one's outcomes is one way to increase control.

A good deal of evidence supports the effectiveness of participative management in U.S. contexts (Lawler, 1986). Marrow, Bowers, and Seashore (1967) provide a detailed analysis of the effects of shifting management practice from a traditional to a participatory style. However, even they caution against making rapid changes in cultures where high power distance is traditional (p. 70). The experience of the Harwood Company in Puerto Rico is one example of the consequences of shifting management styles too rapidly. As soon as management began using participatory methods, many of the Puerto Rican workers quit their jobs. Exit interviews with the employees determined that the problem concerned the workers' perception of the level of competence of management. "If they have to ask how to run this plant, they can't be that good," was the theme found in many of the exit interviews. The workers were quitting so that they could join "better managed" companies!

In addition to the expectations of the workers, there is also the issue of skills. Americans may learn participation in school or community organizations. In high-power-distance cultures, this may not be the case. Therefore, in high-power-distance cultures, change should be introduced gradually, intentionally, and self-consciously—that is, workers must be indoctrinated in the philosophy of participatory management.

Even in cultures where most people are illiterate, participatory management can be used if it is properly controlled. In the famous Peruvian experiment of anthropologist Alan Holmberg (see Dobyns et al., 1971), the introduction of participatory methods over a period of five years resulted in a complete transformation of the culture. Illiterate peasants learned to operate their own school, hotel, and industries; productivity increased tenfold, markets were opened, and some of. their workers' children went on to attend American universitites.

There is a large body of literature on national differences in participation. Some of these differences are the result of legal requirements. Prescribed (de jure) participation ranges from "no regulation" to "information must be given to the group," and "obligatory consultation" to "group has the final say." De facto participation concerns the perception by people that they are actually participating and making decisions (Wilpert, 1984). The Industrial Democracy in Europe (IDE, 1981) study of 134 firms in 12 European countries found a strong link between de jure and de facto participation. In addition to de jure participation, unionization and the extent to which employees have been representatives also predicted de facto participation. Unionization rates varied widely, from almost 100 percent in Scandinavia to about 25 percent in France. Employee experience with representativeness also varied, from about 45 percent in Yugoslavia to less than 10 percent in Belgium. The IDE (1981) volume provides a rich set of descriptive statistics. Cordova (1982) also examined national variation and concluded that there is a trend toward increased participation. Several national case studies can be found in Wilpert and Sorge (1984), while theoretical issues are

covered by Crouch and Heller (1983). Stern and McCarthy (1986) continue that series of volumes and include an evaluation of accomplishments made in this area.

Several papers review the effectiveness of participation. Specifically, the history of the studies of worker participation is well discussed by Whyte (1983). Cultural differences seem linked to differences in power distance. Forms of ownership, including the use of cooperatives, are also discussed. Schuster (1983) reviewed the effectiveness of the Scanlon plan, and Strauss (1982) provides the most extensive and useful review of studies of participation.

Tannenbaum and Rozgonyi (1986) explored the theoretical links between participation, control, and motivation. They showed that workers have a greater sense of control when they participate, but that the control of managers is *not* reduced as a result. In all economic systems hierarchy has demotivating effects, since the people at the top have more control and those at the bottom have less control and hence those at the bottom feel less satisfied with work participation (Tannenbaum, 1986).

Summary. The overall review of these writings indicates that participation is due to a multiplicity of factors. Culture is one of many relevant variables. Since so many variables determine this phenomenon, the amount of variance controlled by culture is limited.

Job Design in a Cross-cultural Perspective

The Hackman and Oldham (1980) theory of job design, which essentially argues that the more variety, task identity, and feedback that a job provides the greater will be the worker's satisfaction, has produced a large volume of research and criticism (Roberts & Glick, 1981). Support for that model has been obtained in Western countries (e.g., Karoly, 1982) and the Far East (Birnbaum, Farh, & Wong, 1986).

However, the link between the job attributes discussed earlier and job satisfaction has been found only in Westernized samples in South Africa (Orpen, 1983b). Earlier, Orpen (1976) reported that the level of job satisfaction of Western subgroups increased significantly as their jobs became larger or more enlarged, but this relationship was not obtained among the other South African groups. Shamir and Drory (1981) made a similar observation about Israeli subgroups. Morishima and Minami (1983) speculated that the model would also not work as well in collectivist cultures, where motivation is likely to be a function of *task interdependence* and opportunity to satisfy affiliation needs.

A more general way to think about task design is to think of the level of skills attained by a worker (X) and the demands made by the job (Y). When there is a match between X and Y, there is satisfaction; when the match is high, there is also a positive mood (Csikszentmihalyi, 1985), while when X is high and Y is low or when X is low and Y is high, there is a negative mood. When the job's demands are greater than a worker's skills, the worker experiences anxiety; when a worker's skills are greater than the job's demands, the worker experiences boredom. The more educated a population is, the higher its level of skills, and hence the greater the level of job demands needed to create balance. The lack of interesting work for large segments of the population of industrial countries is a common problem in the former Soviet Union, Europe, and the United States (Phillips & Benson, 1983). It is an inevitable consequence of having an educated work force that is forced to do uninteresting, unchallenging work—work that does not satisfy the values of workers.

In addition to the skill-challenge match, differences in values will make jobs more or less attractive to workers. Taking the Hofstede (1980a) typology seriously, we concur with Morishima and Minami (1983) that in collectivist cultures one would need to consider worker interdependence and opportunity for affiliation somewhat more than in the West when designing jobs. In cultures high in uncertainty avoidance, jobs that provide role ambiguity should be especially unwelcome, an observation that agrees with Shamir and Drory's (1981) data.

Summary.   When designing jobs, it is important to consider several kinds of matches: The *skills* of the worker must match the *challenge* of the job; the *needs* of the worker must match the *values* of the culture that can be satisfied by the job.

Organizational Development in a Cross-cultural Perspective

Reviews of organizational development (e.g., Faucheux, Amado, & Laurent, 1982) have generally focused on changing organizational cultures. However, this view disagrees with the more common view that the goal of organizational development should be defined by consensus of the participants making the change. In heterogeneous organizations, either view may create problems. If the culture is imposed, for instance, there will be objections from most people; if the culture is to be generated by consensus, the minority viewpoint may not have sufficient influence. Jaeger (1986) argues that organizational development in the United States is based on the assumption that the culture will be low in power distance, uncertainty avoidance, and masculinity (in the Hofstede, 1980, dimensions) and medium in individualism. Those countries that have very different value profiles (e.g., Japan, Greece, Brazil, and Mexico) require different kinds of organizational development interventions than the ones used in the United States. Reviews of the cross-cultural literature on social change (e.g., Berry, 1980b) have focused mostly on changes in tribal or national cultures. There is an obvious parallel between these two sets of studies. One can examine change at the level of individuals (e.g., changes in attitudes, beliefs, or individual values) or at the level of organizations (changes in unstated assumptions, norms, and organizational values) or at the level of cultures (changes in social patterns, institutions, laws, and changes in subjective culture).

Berry (1980b) has outlined a theoretical framework for such work. In it the antecedents of change are contact between an "external" and an "internal" culture or between "outsiders" and "insiders." The external culture could be another organization or tribe or culture; the outsiders could be agents of change (e.g., technical advisers), or consultants or members of the same multinational corporation from another unit (e.g., headquarters). Changes in the sociocultural level will have effects at the individual level, and vice versa. As a consequence of the contact, various processes will occur that will result in both cultural and psychological change. This is a rich and complex framework, and it is not surprising that very few of the relationships it proposes have actually been researched so far. Berry's chapter reviews the few studies that provide data on these relationships.

The complexity of the work required to study organizational development across cultures is well described by Zeira and Adler (1980). They outline a cube of data where one facet consists of the viewpoints of the parent culture (e.g., the multinational may be American, Dutch, or Japanese) and the host culture on various environmental factors such as social, political, economic, or technological issues. The second facet consists of human components, such as whether the contact is in host-country organizations, in settings where there are mostly host nationals or expatriate managers, or at the company's headquarters. The third facet borrows the attributes of the environment presented by Katz and Kahn (1978): stability-turbulence, diversity-homogeneity, clusterings-randomness, and

scarcity-munificence. The argument is that organizational development and change that do not consider these factors may fail. For example, what happens in a company's headquarters will depend in part on, for example, who from the host country is there, what particular social or economic factors are involved in the change, and what kind of environment is framing the change. In a stable environment one kind of change will work, while in a turbulent environment another kind of change may be more desirable; when the environment has much diversity or randomness or is characterized by scarcity, one kind of change will be better than at times when the other poles of the environmental attributes are influencing the organization.

This viewpoint calls for organizational development that is culture-specific. For example, Tainio and Santalainen (1984) found that an American organizational development program used in Finland did not produce results that were as strong and lasting as a Finnish organizational development program.

Summary.   It appears safe to say that an organizational development program should be consistent with the subjective culture of the group or organization being changed (Preston, 1987).

Organizational Conflict in a Cross-cultural Perspective

When individuals or units of an organization belong to different cultures, there is a great likelihood that conflict will occur. The units may have different responsibilities (e.g., engineers vs. marketing experts), different statuses (e.g., labor vs. management), different positions in the organization (e.g., headquarters vs. subsidiary), or may belong to different organizations (e.g., partners in joint ventures, customers, and suppliers).

There are some general findings about intergroup conflict that apply regardless of culture. For instance, minimal cues are needed to form groups that oppose each other, and as soon as this occurs people see the outgroup members in an unfavorable light, while they see their ingroup members in favorable terms. Furthermore, the difference between ingroup and outgroup tends to be exaggerated, and ingroups tend to be favored. Ingroup products are evaluated favorably even when there is objective evidence that suggests the contrary. Many other distortions in perception and attribution occur that favor the ingroup (Worchel & Austin, 1986). People join ingroups that enhance their positive identity. The sharp contrast between "us" and "them" increases when there is intensive conflict, a history of conflict, strong attachment to the ingroup, anonymity of group membership, and no possibility of moving from ingroup to outgroup. The conflict, of course, is stronger when groups have something real to divide, but it can occur without such a factor.

Conflict is more intense when individuals distrust the outgroup; distrust can be due to lack of knowledge of the outgroup or a lack of predictability of the outgroup's behavior. Certain personalities (e.g., ethnocentric, cognitively simple) are especially prone to conflict.

Discrepancies in subjective culture make such conflict more acute, as do stereotypes. Reductions in conflict can be obtained when ingroups and outgroups come into contact under particular conditions, such as when they have superordinate goals, when the contact is sanctioned by authorities, and when they adopt a win/win problem-solving perspective—that is, when the conflict is seen as a joint problem that must be solved through creative solutions (Worchel & Austin, 1986).

The outcome of conflict can include agreements, the imposition of bureaucratic controls, or the development of a new culture that controls one or both of the parties involved in the conflict. Jaeger (1986) has described how multinationals control their subsidiaries through either bureaucratic or cultural controls. American firms with a Type Z organization have some elements that are similar to the methods used by Japanese firms. Such firms tend to use cultural control. The data supported the existence of such patterns. The use of more paperwork by the bureaucratic control firms (e.g., 42 pages per month of reports from the subsidiary, 2,100 pages of manuals) contrasts with the use of less paper by the Type Z firms (27 pages of reports, 780 pages of manuals), who, it should be noted, spent three times as much money on travel and making informal contacts. The culture of subsidiaries and headquarters was more similar in the Type Z than in the other firms. Similarity extended to the type of buildings used and the signs posted in the parking lots. The bureaucratic firms allowed considerable cultural divergence from the headquarter's pattern, while the firms using cultural control did not.

It is difficult to evaluate the bureaucratic versus cultural control of an organization. The bureaucratic control firm is more likely to experience major conflict between headquarters and its subsidiary and to lack smooth operation *within* the multinational; the cultural control firm is more likely to have problems relating to its environment abroad and lack good adjustment with local conditions. The costs of the Type Z organization are also higher.

It is doubtful that it will be possible to develop generalizations about specific cultural patterns and their relationship to optimal conflict resolution techniques. It is more likely that one will be able to identify some general patterns (e.g., that bargaining conducted by representatives leads to more rigid bargaining behavior than bargaining conducted by individuals who represent themselves, Davis & Triandis, 1970; Holmes, Ellard, & Lamm, 1985) and a large number of culture-specific patterns (e.g., that Japanese managers generally trust Americans who request mutual referral for the resolution of disputes rather than Americans who propose binding arbitration). However, there are complications described by Sullivan, Peterson, Kameda, and Shimeda (1981), and Peterson and Shimada (1978). The study of Weiss and Stripp (1985) describes the kinds of things Americans should be aware of when they negotiate with the Chinese, French, Japanese, Mexicans, Nigerians, and Saudis. Cohen (1991) provides a detailed analysis of the communication patterns of collectivist and individualistic cultures. Friday (1989) contrasts the discussion behavior of German and American managers.

From the theory of collectivism-individualism, it is possible to make some predictions concerning negotiation behavior. These are generally supported by accounts of the negotiation styles of Russians and Americans (Glenn, 1981). Collectivists see more differences between ingroups and outgroups than do individualists (Chan, 1991; Triandis, 1972). Hence, conflict is seen as natural, and compromise is rejected. One may have to agree to the outgroup's demands, under pressure, but one must not agree on all issues. So compromise means accepting the outgroup's position on some issues. To take a position in between is generally rejected by collectivists (except in the case of top bosses, who can do so), while it makes a lot of sense to individualists.

Furthermore, collectivists have very clear ideas about ends. The supreme value is the survival of the ingroup, and any means is acceptable as long as it ensures such survival. So the collectivist focuses on *ends* (what is best for the collective), while the individualist is concerned with both *means* (how do I look when I act his way?) and *ends*. The sharp ingroup–outgroup contrast trains the collectivist to the negotiations by stating what is nonnegotiable. By contrast, the individualist looks for common ground and begins the negotiation by examining areas of agreement. Negotiation is greatly facilitated if there is no

audience to whom one must display one's devotion to the ingroup's interests, and this is especially important for collectivists. Information is used as a weapon, and thus it is not communicated by collectivists to the outgroup, even when it is likely to help resolve the conflict. Collectivists do not consider it a virtue to put themselves into other people's shoes; individualists are more likely to see this as a virtue. If the ingroup rejects a position, the negotiator will do so, especially among collectivists. Correspondence between feelings and beliefs and deeds is a virtue for individualists, but not for collectivists, who are mostly concerned with the deed: "As long as you do what is right, I do not care whether you like what you are doing or not."

The situation that frames the bargaining may be a more potent source of the variance than the culture, as suggested by Harnett and Cummings (1980). They used a bargaining game, with both student and manager samples from several countries, and attempted to clarify the determinants of bargaining behavior. The national differences were minor and did not show sufficient consistency with prior research to inspire confidence in their replicability. But the study showed that structural variables (e.g., the number of participants in the bargaining), individual differences (e.g., trusting the other side), and strategic variables (e.g., differences in opening bids) affected bargaining behavior more or less the same way in all cultures.

Summary.   As in other areas of cross-cultural industrial and organizational psychology, the major focus in the conflict area has been in distinguishing what is universal from what is culture-specific. There is a large body of literature being developed on universal and culture-specific forms of conflict. In general, it seems that conflict is more likely to occur in cross-cultural situations, and while the methods of reducing such conflict (e.g., use of superordinate goals) appear universal, there are many culture-specific strategies that need to be examined in separate studies.

Psychological Factors Affecting Economic Development

One of the more visible theories in the area of psychological factors in economic development was provided by McClelland (1961). McClelland's theory has generated a great deal of both empirical research and criticism. Serious doubts have been expressed about its applicability to Asian cultures (e.g., see Berry's, 1980b, review of the work of de Vos and Finison, as well as Maehr's work as represented in Maehr & Braskamp, 1986). While there is some consensus that universal motivational processes exist that can be traced to the common humanity of individuals across cultures (Kornadt, Eckensberger, & Emmingaus 1980), the varieties of achievement patterns around the world do not all fit McClelland's theory. For example, LeVine (1966) has examined African tribes that show two distinct patterns of achievement: tribes where one achieves status by working for a person with status, and tribes where one achieves status through outstanding performance in an occupational role. The former status structure encourages people to be obedient, servile, compliant, and to defer to authority; the latter encourages people to be industrious, independent, and daring. One is likely to find more achievement in the latter status than in the former. In other words, one needs to examine the local cultural features in order to understand achievement in particular societies. To the extent that this is so, McClelland's theory is limited.

A review of psychological work on economic development can be found in Triandis (1984b). A set of chapters examining the link between values and economic development was published by Sinha and Kao (1988). For example, Bond reports in that book that cultures that emphasize ordering relationships by status, thrift, persistence, and having a sense of shame and deemphasize personal steadiness are found predominantly in the Far East and have had the most rapid economic development in the past quarter century. The shift from collectivism to individualism appears linked to development, but it is unclear whether development is an antecedent or a consequence of this change. Circular causation seems more probable. Many of the papers in this book explore how cultural values that are considered important might be preserved during development; some are also concerned with the dysfunctional aspects of development, such as high crime and divorce rates.

Summary. Industrial and organizational psychologists have made some minor contributions to understanding the psychological factors that affect development. Given the vastness of the subject, this is one area that deserves more emphasis in the future than it has received in the past.

Research Gaps and Conclusions

The nearly 400 references in this chapter to other works may suggest that we know a lot about the way culture affects organizational behavior, but this would be an illusion. Our ideas are still quite vague. We still do not have a widely accepted definition of culture. We do not have a good way of sorting out (a) what is psychological from what is cultural, (b) what is universal from what is culture specific, or (c) what is specific to one case from what is a general pattern.

Much more needs to be done to examine how people and cultural variables affect management systems or job designs. We know that we need different management systems and different job designs, but we do not know how adaptable various management systems are to changing cultural conditions. Some exciting new experiments, such as the Japanese management style used with American workers at the Toyota-General Motors plant in Fremont, California, may result in new integrations of the best aspects of each system (Holden, 1986). There have been suggestions that American plants should adopt Japanese management methods (Minabe, 1986) in order to increase their international competitiveness. However, we do not know which aspects of these methods fit which types of organizations and work forces. Black, Mendenhall, and Oddou (1991) have proposed numerous hypotheses concerning international adjustment that should be tested.

Much of the work in this area is fragmented and does not fit into any clear conceptual framework. When a conceptual framework is provided, as was done when variables such as those supplied by Hofstede were used, there is still not enough research available to allow us to reach a profound understanding of these variables.

As more and more of the products of our industries and organizations compete in the world market, there will be an evolution toward a global economic and sociopolitical system. Issues of resource allocation, economic development of the third world, the maintenance of harmonious relationships among different national and ethnic groups, and the avoidance of culture shock when people move from one part of the globe to another will become even more acute than they are today. Psychologists will play a role in all these areas.

To play such a role, psychologists must become more involved in theoretical issues: For example, what is the impact of culture on attitudes, the self-concept, and values? How are elements of subjective culture, such as values, linked to social behavior? How are negotiations between people from two diverse cultures affected by their differences in subjective culture?

Psychologists must be more willing to use multimethod strategies, since any method is likely to interact with cultural differences in the meaning of the method. Finally, psychologists must be willing to explore some politically sensitive topics. For example, why is it that when upper-middle-class groups are forced to migrate (e.g., the Cuban and the Vietnamese migrations to the United States during the 1960s and 1970s, respectively) they do so well economically, while when people from other socioeconomic classes (e.g., the Mexican migrants of the 1960s) migrate they adapt with so much difficulty? The so-called boat people (Caplan, Whitmore, & Choy, 1989) arrived in the United States unable to speak English, but many of their children are already achieving better academic success in American schools than native-born American children. Are values, lifestyles, or norms the most important variables in accounting for such differences in adaptation rates? When people are subjected to unpleasant life events (e.g., unemployment), some recover while others do not, and this seems in part related to how well their culture is integrated. But there are undoubtedly other factors that can be considered. There is much more that we can learn.

These developments will enrich industrial and organizational psychology by bringing perspectives from other cultures to bear on our understanding of events in the industrialized world, and vice versa. So far, cross-cultural psychology has not had much influence on the shaping of psychology in North America and Europe, but in the future this situation may change. It will no longer be acceptable to have theories with severe limitations, in that they can be applied only under very restricted cultural conditions. Variables that reflect cultural variations will become parameters of our theories, which will then be much more general.

Cultural change will become an important topic as we develop the capability to monitor it in all its manifestations. The applications of these developments to practical problems—such as how to integrate immigrants from the less developed into the more developed parts of the world, and how to improve the acculturation and adjustment of such migrants, how to change organizational cultures to accommodate the new immigrants, and how work is to be redefined and new roles are to emerge—and a better understanding of the relationships between technological and cultural change will be among the many benefits of this development.

This chapter has avoided discussions of ethical issues. But perhaps this final paragraph needs to briefly address them. How do we deal with clashes of values? How do we deal, for example, with the economically successful cultures of Europe and North America modifying those of the third world in innumerable encounters? When the cultures of developed and underdeveloped countries come into contact, the cultures of less developed countries are modified or eliminated. The reward systems of such cultures are modified because often the symbols of success of the introduced culture are irrelevant in the culture that is in danger of disappearing. In the New Hebrides, for example, people's status used to depend on the number of pigs with curving tusks that they owned. Contact with the West made this distinction irrelevant, destroying one of the basic supports of that culture. How can we help cultures survive without depriving them of modern inventions, medicine, and the like? Do cultures have the right to survive just as much as people do?

I am grateful to Rabi Bhagat, Jack Feldman, and John Spangenberg for critical comments on an earlier draft.

Notes

1   Doktor (1983, 1990) finds that 44% of Japanese managers engage in tasks that take more than one hour to do, but only 10% of American managers do so; in contrast, 14% of the Japanese but 49% of the Americans engage in tasks that take less than 9 minutes to complete; incidentally, Korean managers are similar to the Japanese and Chinese managers are similar to Americans on this dimension.

2   Incidentally, while the *nenko* (lifetime employment) system is widely celebrated among students of Japanese management, the evidence is that tenure of 15 years or longer is actually more common in the United States than in Japan (Taira, 1982)! However, this is in part due to the different retirement ages in the two countries (65 in the United States vs. 55 in Japan).

References

Adler, N. J. (1982). Cross-cultural management [Special issue]. *International Studies of Management and Organization, 12.*

Adler, N. J. (1983a). A typology of management studies involving culture. *Journal of International Business Studies, 14,* 29–47.

Adler, N. J. (1983b). Cross-cultural management research: The ostrich and the trend. *Academy of Management Review, 8,* 226–232.

Adler, N. J. (1986). *International dimensions of organizational behavior.* Boston: Kent.

Adler, N. J. (1987). Pacific basin managers: A Gaijin, not a woman. *Human Resource Management, 26,* 169–191.

Adler, N. J., & Graham, J. L. (1986) *Cross-cultural interaction: The international comparison fallacy.* Unpublished manuscript.

Albert, R. (1983). The intercultural sensitizer or culture assimilator: A cognitive approach. In D. Landis & R. Brislin (Eds.), *Handbook of intercultural training* (Vol. 2, pp. 186–217). New York: Pergamon.

Amir, Y., & Ben-Ari, R. (1985). International tourism, ethnic contact and attitude change. *Journal of Social Issues, 41,* 105–116.

Anderson, L. R. (1983). Management of the mixed-cultural work group. *Organizational Behavior and Human Performance, 31,* 303–330.

Anonymous (1991). Taking the cultural blinkers off. *Business Korea, 9,* 44–45.

Aram, J., & Piraino, T. (1978). The hierarchy of needs theory: An evaluation in Chile. *Interamerican Journal of Psychology, 12,* 179–188.

Arsenault, A., & Dolan, S. (1983). The role of personality, occupation and organization in understanding the relationship between job stress, performance and absenteeism. *Journal of Occupational Psychology, 56,* 227–240.

Asch, S. (1956). Studies of independence and conformity: A minority of one against a unanimous majority [Special issue]. *Psychological Monographs, 70*(9), No. 416.

Ayman, R., & Chemers, M. M. (1983). Relationship of supervisory behavior ratings to work group effectiveness and subordinate satisfaction among Iranian managers. *Journal of Applied Psychology, 68,* 338–341.

Ayman, R., & Chemers, M. (1986, July). *The emic/etic approach to leadership orientation and job satisfaction of Mexican managers.* Paper presented at the meeting of the International Association of Applied Psychology, Jerusalem.

Ayman, R., & Chemers, M. M. (1991). The effect of leadership match on subordinate satisfaction in Mexican organizations: Some moderating influences of self-monitoring. *Applied Psychology: An International Review, 40,* 299–314.

Baba, M., Hanaoka, M., Hara, H., & Thompson, R. (1984). *Managerial behavior in Japan and the USA.* Tokyo: Japan Productivity Center.

Bales, R. F., & Slater, P. E. (1955). Role differentiation in small decision-making groups. In T. Parsons & R. F. Bales (Eds.), *Family, socialization, and interaction process.* Glencoe, IL: Free Press.

Barlund, D. C., & Araki, S. (1985). Intercultural encounters. The management of compliments by Japanese and Americans. *Journal of Cross-Cultural Psychology, 16,* 9–26.

Barrett, G. V., & Bass, B. M. (1976). Cross-cultural issues in industrial and organizational psychology. In M. D. Dunnette (Ed.), *Handbook of industrial and organizational psychology* (pp. 1639–1686). Chicago: Rand McNally.

Bass, B. M., & Burger, P. C. (1979). *Assessment of managers: An international comparison.* New York: Free Press.

Bean, R. (1985). *Comparative industrial relations: An introduction to cross-national perspectives.* London: Croom & Helm.

Bennett, M. (1977a). Response characteristics of bilingual managers to organizational questionnaires. *Personnel Psychology, 30,* 29–36.

Bennett, M. (1977b). Testing management theories cross-culturally. *Journal of Applied Psychology, 62,* 578–581.

Berkman, H. W., & Vernon, I. R. (Eds.). (1979). *Contemporary perspectives in international business.* Chicago: Rand McNally.

Berman, J. J., Murphy-Berman, V., & Singh, P. (1985). Cross-cultural similarities and differences in perceptions of fairness. *Journal of Cross-Cultural Psychology, 16,* 55–67.

Berry, J. W. (1979). A cultural ecology of social behavior. In L. Berkowitz (Ed.), *Advances in experimental social psychology* (Vol. 12). New York: Academic Press.

Berry, J. W. (1980a). Introduction to methodology. In H. C. Triandis & J. W. Berry (Eds.), *Handbook of cross-cultural psychology* (Vol. 2). Boston: Allyn & Bacon.

Berry, J. W. (1980b). Social and cultural change. In H. C. Triandis & R. W. Brislin (Eds.), *Handbook of cross-cultural psychology.* Boston: Allyn & Bacon.

Berry, J. W., Poortinga, Y., Segall, M., & Dasen, P. (1992). *Cross-cultural psychology.* New York: Cambridge Press.

Bhagat, R. S., & McQuaid, S. J. (1982). Role of subjective culture in organizations: A review and directions for future research. *Journal of Applied Psychology Monograph, 67,* 653–685.

Bharati, A. (1983). India: South Asian perspective on aggression. In A. P. Goldstein & M. H. Segall (Eds.), *Aggression in global perspective* (pp. 237–260). New York: Pergamon.

Bharati, A. (1985). The self in Hindu thought and action. In A. J. Marsella, G. deVos, & F. L. K. Hsu (Eds.), *Culture and self.* New York: Tavistoa Publications.

Birnbaum, P. H., Farh, J., & Wong, G. Y. Y. (1986). The job characteristics model in Hong Kong. *Journal of Applied Psychology, 71,* 598–605.

Black, J. S., & Mendenhall, M. (1990). Cross-cultural training effectiveness: A review and theoretical framework for future research. *Academy of Management Review, 15,* 113–136.

Black, J. S., Mendenhall, M., & Oddou, G. (1991). Toward a comprehensive model of international adjustment: An integration of multiple theoretical perspectives. *Academy of Management Review, 16,* 291–317.

Blake, R. R., & Mouton, J. S. (1964). *The managerial grid.* Houston: Gulf.

Blake, R. R., & Mouton, J. S. (1979). Motivating human productivity in the People's Republic of

China. *Group and Organizational Studies, 4,* 159–169.

Blum, A. A. (1981). *International handbook of industrial relations: Contemporary developments and research.* London: Aldwych.

Bochner, S. (1980). Unobtrusive methods in cross-cultural experimentation. In H. C. Triandis & J. W. Berry (Eds.), *Handbook of cross-cultural psychology* (Vol. 2, pp. 319–388). Boston: Allyn & Bacon.

Boldt, E. D. (1978). Structural tightness and cross-cultural research. *Journal of Cross-Cultural Psychology, 9,* 151–165.

Bond, M. (1988). Invitation to a wedding: Chinese values and global economic growth. In P. Sinha & H. Kao (Eds.), *Social values and development* (pp. 197–209). New Delhi, India: Sage.

Bond, M. H., & Cheung, M. (1984). Experimenter language choice and ethnic affirmation by Chinese trilinguals in Hong Kong. *International Journal of Intercultural Relations, 8,* 347–356.

Bond, M. H., Wan, K., Leung, K., & Giacalone, R. A. (1985). How are responses to verbal insult related to cultural collectivism and power distance? *Journal of Cross-Cultural Psychology, 16,* 111–127.

Bougon, M., Weick, K., & Binkhorst, D. (1977). Cognition in organizations: An analysis of the Utrecht jazz orchestra. *Administrative Science Quarterly, 22,* 606–639.

Breckler, S. J. (1984). Empirical validation of affect, behavior, and cognition as distinct components of attitude. *Journal of Personality and Social Psychology, 47,* 1191–1205.

Brislin, R. W. (1981). *Cross-cultural encounters.* New York: Pergamon.

Brislin, R. W., Cushner, K., Cherrie, C., & Yong, M. (1986). *Intercultural interactions: A practical guide.* Beverly Hills, CA: Sage.

Brislin, R. W., & Pedersen, P. (1976). *Cross-cultural orientation programs.* New York: Gardner Press.

Budner, S. (1962). Intolerance of ambiguity as a personality variable. *Journal of Personality, 30,* 29–50.

Campbell, D. T. (1964). Distinguishing differences of perception from failures of communication in cross-cultural studies. In F. S. C. Northrop & H. H. Livingston (Eds.), *Cross-cultural understanding: Epistemology in anthropology.* New York: Harper & Row.

Caplan, N., Whitmore, J. K., & Choy, M. H. (1989). *The boat people and achievement in America: A study of family life, hard work, and cultural values.* Ann Arbor, MI: University of Michigan Press.

Carroll, D. T. (1983, November–December). A disappointing search for excellence. *Harvard Business Review,* 78–88.

Chan, K. S. D. (1991). *Effects of concession pattern, relationship between negotiators, and culture on negotiation.* Unpublished master's thesis, Department of Psychology, University of Illinois, Urbana.

Chandler, T. A., Shama, D. D., Wolf, F. M., & Planchard, S. K. (1981). Multiattributional causality for social affiliation across five cross-national samples. *Journal of Psychology, 107,* 219–229.

Child, J. (1981). Culture, contingency and capitalism in the cross-national study of organizations. *Research in Organizational Behavior, 3,* 303–356.

Child, J., & Tayeb, M. (1983). Theoretical perspectives in cross-national organizational research. *International Studies of Management and Organization, 12,* 23–70.

Chinese Cultural Connection. (1987). Chinese values and the search for culture-free dimensions of culture. *Journal of Cross-Cultural Psychology, 18,* 143–164.

Clarke, C. H. (1992). Communicating benefits to a culturally diverse employee population. *Employee Benefits Journal, 17,* 26–31.

Cohen, R. (1991). *Negotiating across cultures.* Washington, DC: United States Institute of Peace Press.

Cole, R. E. (1971). *Japanese blue collar: The changing tradition.* Berkeley, CA: University of California Press.

Cole, R. E. (1980). *Work, mobility, and participation: A comparative study of American and Japanese industry.* Berkeley, CA: University of California Press.

Cooke, R. A., & Rousseau, D. M. (1988). Behavioral norms and expectations: A quantitative approach to the assessment of organizational culture. *Group and Organizational Studies, 13,* 245–274.

Cordova, E. (1982). Workers' participation in decisions within enterprises: Recent trends and problems. *International Labour Review, 121,* 125–140.

Cox, T. H., Lobel, S. A., & McLeod, P. L. (1991). Effects of ethnic group cultural differences on cooperative and competitive behavior on a group task. *Academy of Management Journal, 34,* 827–847.

Crouch, C., & Heller, F. A. (1983). *Organizational democracy & political processes.* New York: Wiley.

Csikszentmihalyi, M. (1985). *Measurement of enjoyment in everyday life.* Paper presented at the meeting of the Society for Experimental Social Psychology, Evanston, IL.

Cushner, K. (1989). Assessing the impact of a culture general assimilator. *International Journal of Intercultural Relations, 13,* 125–146.

Daab, W. Z. (1991, July). *Changing perspectives on individualism.* Paper presented at the meeting of the International Society of Political Psychology, Helsinki.

David, K. (1972). Intercultural adjustment and applications of reinforcement theory to problems of "culture shock." *Trends, 4,* 1–64.

Davidson, A. R., Jaccard, J. J., Triandis, H. C., Morales, M. L., & Diaz-Guerrero, R. (1976). Cross-cultural model testing: Toward a solution of the etic-emic dilemma. *International Journal of Psychology, 11,* 1–13.

Davidson, A. R., & Thomson, E. (1980). Cross-cultural studies of attitudes and beliefs. In H. C. Triandis & R. W. Brislin (Eds.), *Handbook of cross-cultural psychology* (Vol. 5). Boston: Allyn & Bacon.

Davis, E. E., & Triandis, H. C. (1970). An experimental study of white–black negotiations. *Journal of Applied Social Psychology, 1,* 240–262.

Dawson, J. L. M. (1963). Traditional values and work efficiency in a West African mine labor force. *Occupational Psychology, 37,* 209–218.

Deal, T. E., & Kennedy, A. A. (1982). *Corporate cultures.* Reading, MA: Addison-Wesley.

Detweiler, R. (1980). The categorization of the actions of people from another culture: A conceptual analysis and behavioral outcome. *International Journal of Intercultural Relations, 4,* 275–293.

Diaz-Guerrero, R. (1985). *Cross-cultural and national studies in social psychology.* Amsterdam: North Holland Publishing.

Dlugos, G., & Weiermair, K. (Eds.). (1981). *Management under differing value systems.* Berlin: Walter de Gruyer.

Dobyns, J., Doughty, P., & Lasswell, H. (1971). *Peasant, power and applied social change: Vicos as a model.* Beverly Hills, CA: Sage.

Doi, L. T. (1971). *Amae no kozo* (Yoshi Kashima, Trans.). Tokyo: Kobunsha.

Doi, L. T. (1973). *The anatomy of dependence.* Tokyo: Kodansha International.

Doktor, R. (1983). Culture and management of time: A comparison of Japanese and American top management practice. *Asia Pacific Journal of Management, 1,* 65–70.

Doktor, R. H. (1990). Asian and American CEOs: A comparative study. *Organizational Dynamics, 18,* 46–56.

Dolan, S., & Arsenault, A. (1984). Job demands, related cognitions, and psychosomatic ailments. In R. Schwarzer (Ed.), *The self in anxiety, stress, and depression* (pp. 265–282). New York: Elsevier.

Dore, R. (1973). *British factory-Japanese factory.* London: Allen & Unwin.

Draguns, J. G. (1980). Psychological disorders of clinical severity. In H. C. Triandis & J. G. Draguns (Eds.), *Handbook of cross-cultural psychology* (Vol. 6). Boston: Allyn & Bacon.

Drasgow, F., & Kanfer, R. (1985). Equivalence of psychological measurement in heterogeneous populations. *Journal of Applied Psychology,* 662–680.

Drenth, P. J. D. (1985). Cross-cultural organizational psychology: Challenges and limitations. In P. Joynt & M. Warner (Eds.), *Managing in different cultures.* Amsterdam: Universitetsforlaget, A.S.

Drenth, P. J. D., Thierry, H., Willems, P. J. K., & deWolff, C. J. (1984). *Handbook of work and organizational psychology* (Vols. 1, 2). New York: Wiley.

Drenth, P. J., & Wilpert, B. (1980). The role of "good contracts" in cross-cultural research. *International Review of Applied Psychology, 29,* 293–305.

Earley, P. C. (1984). Social interaction: The frequency of use and evaluation in the U. S., England, and

Ghana. *Journal of Cross-Cultural Psychology, 15,* 477–485.

Earley, P. C. (1989). Social loafing and collectionism: A comparison of the U.S. and the PRC. *Administrative Science Quarterly, 34,* 565–581.

Ekstrand, L. H. (1980). Bilingualism and biculturalism [Special issue]. *International Review of Applied Psychology, 29,* (1, 2).

Elleson, V. J. (1983). Competition: A cultural imperative? *Personnel and Guidance Journal, 62,* 195–198.

England, G. W. (1983). Japanese and American management: Theory Z and beyond. *Journal of International Business Studies, 14,* 131–141.

England, G. W. (1984, August). *Work centrality in Japan and the USA.* Paper presented at the annual meeting of the Academy of Management, Boston.

England, G. W., & Harpaz, I. (1983). Some methodological and analytical considerations in cross-national comparative research. *Journal of International Business Studies, 14,* 49–59.

England, G. W., & Lee, R. (1973). Organizational size as an influence on perceived organizational goals: A comparative study among American, Japanese and Korean managers. *Organizational Behavior and Human Performance, 9,* 48–58.

England, G. W., Negandhi, A. R., & Wilpert, B. (1979). *Organizational functioning in cross-cultural perspective.* Kent, UK: Comparative Administration Institute.

Erez, M. (1986). The congruence of goal-setting strategies with sociocultural values and its effects on performance. *Journal of Management, 12,* 83–90.

Erez, M. (1992). Interpersonal communication systems in organizations and their relationships to cultural values, productivity, and innovation. *Applied Psychology: An International Review, 41,* 43–64.

Faucheux, C., Amado, G., & Laurent, A. (1982). Organizational development and change. *Annual Review of Psychology, 33,* 343–370.

Feather, N. T. (1985). Attitudes, values and attributions: Explanations of unemployment. *Journal of Personality and Social Psychology, 48,* 876–889.

Feldman, J. M., Sam, I. A., MacDonald, F., & Bechtel, G. G. (1980). Work outcome preference and evaluation in three ethnic groups. *Journal of Cross-Cultural Psychology, 11,* 444–468.

Feldman, J., MacDonald, F., & Sam, I. A. (1980). Stereotype attribution in two ethnic groups. *International Journal of Intercultural Relations, 4,* 185–202.

Ferris, G. R., & Wagner, J. A. (1985). Quality circles in the United States: A conceptual reevaluation. *Journal of Applied Behavioral Science, 21,* 155–167.

Fiedler, F. E. (1978). The contingency model and the dynamics of the leadership process. In L. Berkowitz (Ed.), *Advances in experimental social psychology.* New York: Academic Press.

Fiedler, F. E., Mitchell, T. R., & Triandis, H. C. (1971). The culture assimilator: An approach to cross-cultural training. *Journal of Applied Psychology, 55,* 95–102.

Fiske, D. W., & Shweder, R. A. (1986). *Metatheory in social science.* Chicago: University of Chicago Press.

Foa, U., & Chemers, M. (1967). The significance of role behavior differentiation for cross-cultural interaction training. *International Journal of Psychology, 2,* 45–48.

Form, W. (1979). Comparative industrial sociology and the convergence hypothesis. *Annual Review of Sociology, 5,* 1–25.

Friday, R. A. (1989). Contrasts in discussion behaviors of German and American managers. *Intercultural Journal of Intercultural Relations, 13,* 429–446.

Fromkin, H. L., & Sherwood, J. J. (1974). *Integrating the organization.* New York: Free Press.

Frost, P. J., Moore, L. F., Louis, M. R., Lundberg, C. C., & Martin, J. (1985). *Organizational culture.* Beverly Hills, CA: Sage.

Furnham, A., & Bochner, S. (1986). *Culture shock.* London: Methuen.

Furnham, A., & Muhiudeen, C. (1984). The Protestant work ethic in Britain and Malaysia. *Journal of Social Psychology, 122,* 157–161.

Fyans, L. J., Salili, F., Maehr, M. L., & Desai, K. A. (1983). A cross-cultural exploration into the meaning of achievement. *Journal of Personality and Social Psychology, 44,* 1000–1013.

Gabrenya, W. K., Wang, Y., & Latané, B. (1985). Social loafing on an optimizing task. *Journal of Cross-Cultural Psychology, 16,* 223–242.

Gallie, D. (1978). *In search of the new working class: Automation and social integration within the capitalist enterprise.* Cambridge, UK: Cambridge University Press.

Glenn, E. (1981). *Man and mankind: Conflicts and communications between cultures.* Norwood, NJ: Ablex.

Glick, J. (1968, August). *Cognitive style among the Kpelle.* Paper presented at the annual meeting of the American Educational Research Association, Chicago.

Gomez-Mejia, L. R. (1984). Effect of occupation on task related, contextual and job involvement orientation: A cross-cultural perspective. *Academy of Management Journal, 27,* 706–720.

Gregory, K. L. (1983). Native-view paradigms: Multiple-cultures and culture conflicts in organizations. *Administrative Science Quarterly, 28,* 359–376.

Griffeth, R. W., Hom, P. W., DeNisi, A. S., & Kirchner, W. K. (1985). A comparison of different methods of clustering countries on the basis of employee attitudes. *Human Relations, 38,* 813–840.

Gruenfeld, L. W., & MacEachron, A. E. (1975). A cross-cultural study of cognitive style among managers and technicians. *International Journal of Psychology, 10,* 27–55.

Gudykunst, W. B., & Kim, Y. Y. (1984). *Communicating with strangers.* Reading, MA: Addison-Wesley.

Gudykunst, W. B., Stewart, L. P., & Ting-Toomey, S. (1985). *Communication culture and organizational effectiveness.* Beverly Hills, CA: Sage.

Gudykunst, W. B., & Ting-Toomey, S. (1988). *Culture and interpersonal communication.* Newbury Park, CA: Sage.

Hackman, J. R., & Oldham, G. R. (1980). *Work redesign.* Reading, MA: Addison-Wesley.

Haire, M., Ghiselli, E. E., & Porter, L. W. (1966). *Managerial thinking: An international study.* New York: Wiley.

Hakel, M. D. (1981). Challenges of diversity: An American view of work psychology in Europe. In C. DeWolff, S. Shimmin, & M. de Montmollin (Eds.), *Conflicts and contradictions: Work psychologists in Europe.* London: Academic Press.

Harkins, S. G., Latané, B., & Williams, K. (1980). Social loafing: Allocating effort or taking it easy? *Journal of Experimental Social Psychology, 16,* 457–465.

Harnett, D. L., & Cummings, L. L. (1980). *Bargaining behavior: An international study.* Houston: Dame.

Haruki, T., Shigehisa, R., Nedate, K., Wajima, M., & Ogawa, R. (1984). Effects of alien reinforcement and its combined type on learning behavior and efficiency in relation to personality. *International Journal of Psychology, 19,* 527–545.

Heise, D. R. (1979). *Understanding events.* Cambridge, UK: Cambridge University Press.

Helson, H. (1964). *Adaptation-level theory.* New York: Harper & Row.

Herskovits, M. J. (1955). *Cultural anthropology.* New York: Knopf.

Hofstede, G. (1980a). *Culture's consequences.* Beverly Hills, CA: Sage.

Hofstede, G. (1980b). Motivation, leadership and organization: Do American theories apply abroad? *Organizational Dynamics,* 42–63.

Hofstede, G. (1982a). *Cultural pitfalls for Dutch expatriates in Indonesia.* Deventer/Jakarta: TG International Management Consultants.

Hofstede, G. (1982b). Energy and human nature. *Indian Psychologist, 1,* 1–9.

Hofstede, G. (1982c). *Dimensions of national cultures in fifty countries and three regions.* Paper presented at International Congress of Cross-Cultural Psychology, Aberdeen, UK.

Hofstede, G. (1982d, July). *The interaction between national and organizational value systems.* Paper presented at the International Congress of Applied Psychology, Edinburgh.

Hofstede, G. (1983a, July). *Culture and management development.* Paper presented to UNDP/ILO Interregional Project, Geneva.

Hofstede, G. (1983b). The cultural relativity of organizational practices and theories. *Journal of International Business Studies, 14,* 75–89.

Hofstede, G. (1984). The cultural relativity of the quality of life concept. *Academy of Management Review, 9,* 389–398.

Hofstede, G. (1991). *Cultures and organizations.* London: McGraw-Hill.

Holden, C. (1986). New Toyota-GM plant is U.S. model for Japanese management. *Science, 233,* 273–277.

Holmes, J. G., Ellard, J. H., & Lamm, H. (1985). Boundary roles and intergroup conflict. In S. Worchel & W. G. Austin (Eds.), *Psychology of intergroup relations* (pp. 343–363). Chicago: Nelson-Hall.

Howard, A., Shudo, K., & Umeshima, M. (1983). Motivation and values among Japanese and American managers. *Personnel Psychology, 36,* 883–898.

Hui, C. C. (1984). *Individualism-collectivism: Theory, measurement and its relation to reward allocation.* Doctoral dissertation, Department of Psychology, University of Illinois, Urbana.

Hui, C. C. (1990). Work attitudes, leadership styles, and managerial behaviors in different cultures. In R. Brislin (Ed.), *Applied cross-cultural psychology* (pp. 186–208). Newbury Park, CA: Sage.

Hui, C. C., & Triandis, H. C. (1985). Measurement in cross-cultural psychology. *Journal of Cross-Cultural Psychology, 16,* 131–152.

Hui, C. C., & Triandis, H. C. (1989). Effects of culture and response format on extreme response style. *Journal of Cross-Cultural Psychology, 20,* 296–309.

Hulin, C. L., & Triandis, H. C. (1981). Meanings of work in different organizational environments. In P. C. Nystrom & W. H. Starbuck (Eds.),*Handbook of organizational design* (pp. 336–357). Oxford, UK: Oxford University Press.

IDE (Industrial Democracy in Europe—International Research Group). (1981). *Industrial democracy in Europe.* London: Oxford Press.

Ilgen, D. R. (1985, October). *Small groups in an individualistic world.* Paper presented at a symposium at Texas Tech University, Lubbock.

Inkeles, A., & Smith, D. H. (1974). *Becoming modern.* Cambridge, MA: Harvard Press.

Irvine, S. H., & Berry, J. W. (1983). *Human assessment and cultural factors.* New York: Plenum.

Irvine, S. H., & Carroll, W. K. (1980). Testing and assessment across cultures. In H. C. Triandis & J. W. Berry, (Eds.), *Handbook of cross-cultural psychology* (Vol. 2, pp. 181–243). Boston: Allyn & Bacon.

Iwao, S. (1993). *Japanese woman: Traditional image and changing reality.* New York: Free Press.

Jackson, S. E., and Associates. (1992). *Diversity in the workplace: Human resources initiatives.* New York: Guilford Press.

Jaeger, A. (1983). The transfer of organizational culture overseas: An approach to control in the multinational corporation. *Journal of International Business Studies, 14,* 91–114.

Jaeger, A. M. (1986). Organizational development and national culture: Where's the fit? *Academy of Management Review, 11,* 178–190.

Jahoda, G. (1969). *The psychology of superstition.* London: Allen Lane.

Jahoda, G. (1980). Theoretical and systematic approaches in cross-cultural psychology. In H. C. Triandis & W. W. Lambert (Eds.), *Handbook of cross-cultural psychology* (Vol. 1). Boston: Allyn & Bacon.

Jahoda, G. (1984). Do we need a concept of culture? *Journal of Cross-Cultural Psychology, 15,* 139–151.

Joynt, P., & Warner, M. (1985). *Managing in different cultures.* Amsterdam: Universitetforlaget.

Kagan, J. (1972). Motives and development. *Journal of Personality and Social Psychology, 22,* 51–66.

Kanungo, R. N. (1980). *Biculturalism and management.* Toronto: Butterworths.

Kanungo, R. N. (1982). Work alienation and the quality of work life: A cross-cultural perspective. *Indian Psychologist, 1,* 61–69.

Kanungo, R. N., & Wright, R. W. (1983). A cross-cultural comparative study of managerial job attitudes. *Journal of International Business Studies, 14,* 115–129.

Karoly, V. (1982). The control experiment of an industrial psychological model. *Magyar Pszichologiai Szemle, 39,* 383–403.

Karsh, B. (1984). Human resource management in Japanese large scale industry. *Journal of Industrial Relations, 26,* 226–245.

Kashima, Y., & Triandis, H. C. (1986). The self-serving bias in attributions as a coping strategy: A cross-cultural study. *Journal of Cross-cultural Psychology, 17,* 225–248.

Katz, D., & Kahn, R. L. (1978). *The social psychology of organizations* (2nd ed.). New York: Wiley.

Kealey, D. J., & Ruben, B. D. (1983). Cross-cultural personnel selection criteria, issues and methods. In D. Landis & R. Brislin (Eds.), *Handbook of intercultural training* (Vol. 1, pp. 155–175). New York: Pergamon.

Keys, J. B., & Miller, T. R. (1984). The Japanese management theory jungle. *Academy of Management Review, 9,* 342–353.

Khandwalla, P. N. (1983). The architecture of Indian top management. *Indian Management, 22,* 11–17.

Kiggundu, M. N., Jorgensen, J. J., & Hafsi, T. (1983). Administrative theory and practice in developing countries: A synthesis. *Administrative Science Quarterly, 28,* 66–84.

Kilmann, R. H. (1984). *Beyond the quick fix: Managing five tracks to organizational success.* San Francisco: Jossey-Bass.

Kim, Y. Y., & Gudykunst, W. B. (1988). *Theories of intercultural communication.* Beverly Hills, CA: Sage.

King, A. Y. C., & Bond, M. (1983, March). *The Confucian paradigm of men: A sociological view.* Paper presented at the conference on Chinese Culture and Mental Health at East-West Center, Honolulu.

Klineberg, O. (1954). *Social psychology.* New York: Holt.

Kluckhohn, F., & Strodtbeck, F. (1961). *Variations in value orientations.* Westport, CT: Greenwood Press.

Komin, S. (1990). Culture and work-related values in Thai organizations. *International Journal of Psychology, 25,* 681–704.

Kornadt, H. J., Eckensberger, L.H., & Emmingaus, W. B. (1980). Cross-cultural research on motivation and its contribution to a general theory of motivation. In H. C. Triandis & W. W. Lonner (Eds.), *Handbook of cross-cultural psychology* (Vol. 3). Boston: Allyn & Bacon.

Kroeber, A. L., & Kluckhohn, C. (1952). *Culture: A critical review of concepts and definitions* (Vol. 47, No. 1). Cambridge, MA: Peabody Museum.

Kudoh, T., & Matsumoto, D. (1985). Cross-cultural examination of the semantic dimensions of body postures. *Journal of Personality and Social Psychology, 48,* 1440–1446.

Lachman, R. (1983). Modernity change of core and periphery values of factory workers. *Human Relations, 36,* 563–580.

Lammers, C. T., & Hickson, D. J. (1979). *Organizations alike and unlike.* London: Routledge and Kegan Paul.

Landis, D., & Brislin, R. W. (1983). *Handbook of intercultural training: Vol. 1. Issues in theory and design; Vol. 2. Issues in training methodology; Vol. 3. Area studies in intercultural training.* New York: Pergamon.

Landis, D., Brislin, R. W., & Hulgus, J. F. (1985). Attributional training versus contact in acculturative learning: A laboratory study. *Journal of Applied Social Psychology, 15,* 466–482.

Landis, D., Hope, R. O., & Day, H. R. (1984). Training for desegregation in the military. In N. Miller & M. Brewer (Eds.), *Groups in contact* (pp. 257–278). New York: Academic Press.

Langer, E. J. (1983). *The psychology of control.* Beverly Hills, CA: Sage.

Lawler, E. E. (1986). *High involvement management.* San Francisco: Jossey-Bass.

Lebra, T. S. (1984). *Japanese women: Constraints and fulfillment.* Honolulu: University of Hawaii Press.

Leibenstein, H. (1984). *The Japanese company: An X-efficiency analysis.* Colloquium. College of Commerce, University of Illinois, Urbana.

Leo-Dupont, E. (1985). La formation et l'adaptation de stagiaires Algeriens. *Psychologie et Psychometrie, 6,* 5–66.

Leung, K., & Bond, M. (1984). The impact of cultural collectivism on reward allocation. *Journal of Personality and Social Psychology, 47,* 793–804.

Leung, K., & Bond, M. (1989). On the empirical identification of dimension for cross-cultural comparisons. *Journal of Cross-Cultural Psychology, 20,* 133–151.

LeVine, R. (1966). *Dreams and deeds: Achievement motivation in Nigeria.* Chicago: University of Chicago Press.

Levy-Leboyer, C. (1984). *La crise des motivations.* Paris: Presses Universitaires de France.

Lewin, K., Lippitt, R., & White, R. K. (1939). Patterns of aggressive behavior in experimentally created social climates. *Journal of Social Psychology, 10,* 271–299.

Likert, R. (1961). *New patterns of management.* New York: McGraw-Hill.

Likert, R., & Likert, J. G. (1976). *New ways of managing conflict.* New York: McGraw-Hill.

Lincoln, J. F. (1951). *Incentive management.* Cleveland, OH: Lincoln Electric.

Lincoln, J. R., Hanada, M. R., & Olson, J. (1981). Cultural orientation and individual reactions to organizations: A study of employees of Japanese armed forces. *Administrative Science Quarterly, 26,* 93–115.

Lincoln, J. R., Olson, J., & Hanada, M. (1978). Cultural effects on organizational structure: The case of Japanese firms in the United States. *American Sociological Review, 43,* 829–847.

Lindsay, C. P., & Dempsey, B. L. (1983). The painfully learned lessons about working in China: The insights of two American behavioral scientists. *Journal of Applied Behavioral Science, 19,* 265–276.

Lonner, W., & Berry, J. (1986). *Field methods in cross-cultural research.* Beverly Hills, CA: Sage.

Luthans, F., McCaul, H. S., & Dodd, N. G. (1985). Organizational commitment: A comparison of American, Japanese and Korean employees. *Academy Management Journal, 28,* 213–219.

Ma, H. K. (1988). Objective moral judgment in Hong Kong, Mainland China, and England. *Journal of Cross-Cultural Psychology, 19,* 78–95.

Maehr, M. L. (1974). Culture and achievement motivation. *American Psychologist, 29,* 887–896.

Maehr, M. L., & Braskamp, L. A. (1986). *The motivation factor: A theory of personal investment.* Lexington, MA: Lexington Press.

Maguire, M. A., & Kroliczak, A. (1983). Attitudes of Japanese and American workers: Convergence or diversity. *Sociological Quarterly, 24,* 107–122.

Malpass, R. S. (1977). Theory and method in cross-cultural psychology. *American Psychologist, 32,* 1069–1079.

Mann, L. (1980). Cross-cultural studies of small groups. In H. C. Triandis & R. W. Brislin (Eds.), *Handbook of cross-cultural psychology* (Vol. 5). Boston: Allyn & Bacon.

Marin, G., Triandis, H.C., Betancourt, H., & Kashima, Y. (1983). Ethnic affirmation versus social desirability: Explaining discrepancies in bilinguals' responses to a questionnaire. *Journal of Cross-Cultural Psychology, 14,* 173–186.

Marrow, A. J., Bowers, D. G., & Seashore, S. E. (1967). *Management by participation.* New York: Harper & Row.

Martin, J. (1982). Stories and scripts in organizational settings. In A. H. Hastorf & A. M. Isen (Eds.), *Cognitive social psychology* (pp. 255–306). New York: Elsevier.

Martin, J., & Siehl, C. (1983). Organizational culture and counterculture: An uneasy symbiosis. *Organizational Dynamics, 12,* 52–64.

Maslow, A. H. (1943). A theory of human motivation. *Psychological Review, 50,* 370–396.

Massimini, F., & Calegari, P. (1979). *Il contesto normativo sociale.* Milano: Angeli.

Maurice, M., Sorge, A., & Warner, M. (1980). Societal difference in organizing manufacturing units: A comparison of France, West Germany and Great Britain. *Organizational Studies, 1,* 59–86.

McClelland, D. C. (1961). *The achieving society.* Princeton, NJ: Van Nostrand.

McClelland, D. C. (1980). Motive dispositions: The merits of operant and respondent measures. In

L. Wheeler (Ed.), *Review of Personality and Social Psychology, 1,* 10–41.

Meindle, J. R., Hunt, R. G., & Lee, W. (1989). Individualism-collectivism and work values: Data from the United States, China, Taiwan, Korea and Hong Kong. *Research in Personnel and Human Resources Management,* Suppl. 1, 59–77.

Mendenhall, M., & Oddon, G. (1985). The dimensions of expatriate acculturation: A review. *Academy of Management Review, 10,* 39–47.

Miller, J. G. (1984). Culture and the development of everyday social explanation. *Journal of Personality and Social Psychology, 46,* 961–978.

Miller, N., Brewer, M. B., & Edwards, K. (1985). Cooperative interaction in desegregated settings: A laboratory analogue. *Journal of Social Issues, 41(3),* 63–80.

Minabe, S. (1986). Japanese competitiveness and Japanese management. *Science, 233,* 301–304.

Minturn, L., & Lambert, W. W. (1964). *Mothers of six cultures.* New York: Wiley.

Misumi, J. (1972). *Group dynamics in Japan.* Fukuoka, Japan: Faculty of Education, Kyushu University.

Misumi, J. (1978). *Social psychology in Japan.* Beverly Hills, CA: Sage.

Misumi, J. (1981). Action research on group decision making and organizational development. In H. Hiebsch, H. Brandstatter, & H. H. Kelley (Eds.), *Social psychology.* Berlin: VEB Deutscher Verlag der Wissenschaft.

Misumi, J. (1982). *Meaning of working life: An international comparison.* Paper presented at the International Congress of Applied Psychology, Edinburgh.

Misumi, J. (1984). Decision-making in Japanese groups and organizations. In B. Wilpert & A. Sorge (Eds.), *International perspectives on organizational democracy.* New York: Wiley.

Misumi, J. (1985). *The behavioral science of leadership. An interdisciplinary Japanese research program.* Ann Arbor, MI: University of Michigan Press.

Misumi, J., & Nakano, S. (1960). A cross-cultural study of the effect of democratic, authoritarian, and laissez-faire atmosphere in children's groups. *Japanese Journal of Educational Social Psychology, 1,* 10–22, 119–135.

Misumi, J., & Peterson, M. F. (1985). The performance-maintenance (PM) theory of leadership: Review of a Japanese research program. *Administrative Science Quarterly, 30,* 198–223.

Misumi, J., & Seki, F. (1971). Effects of achievement motivation on the effectiveness of leadership patterns. *Administrative Science Quarterly, 16,* 51–59.

Morey, N. C., & Luthans, F. (1984). An emic perspective and ethno-science methods for organizational research. *Academy of Management Review, 9,* 27–36.

Morishima, M., & Minami, T. (1983). Task interdependence and internal motivation: Application of job characteristics model to "collectivist" cultures. *Tetsugaku, 77,* 133–147.

Morgan, G., & Smircich, L. (1980). The case for qualitative research. *Academy of Management Review, 5,* 491–500.

MOW International Research Team (1986). *The meaning of working: An international perspective.* New York: Academic Press.

Mudd, S. A. (1968). Group sanction severity as a function of degree of behavior deviation and relevance of norm. *Journal of Personality and Social Psychology, 8,* 258–260.

Munro, D. (1984). A free-format value inventory: explorations with Zimbabwean student teachers. *South African Journal of Psychology, 15,* 33–41.

Nakane, C. (1978). *Tate shakai no rikigaku* (Yoshi Kashima, Trans.). Tokyo: Kodansha.

Nath, R. (1992). Impact of societal and organizational cultures of worker commitment. In R. N. Kenungo (Ed.), *Human resource management in developing countries* (pp. 294-316). Montreal: McGill University of Faculty of Management.

Negandhi, A. R. (1983). Cross-cultural management research: Trend and future directions. *Journal of International Business Studies, 14,* 17–28.

Negandhi, A. R. (1984). Management in the third world. *Advances in International Comparative Management, 1,* 123–154.

Nevis, E. C. (1983). Using an American perspective in understanding another culture: Towards a hierarchy of needs for the People's Republic of China. *Journal of Applied Behavioral Science, 19,* 249–264.

Ng, S. H. (1982). Choosing between ranking and rating procedures for the comparison of values across cultures. *European Journal of Social Psychology, 12,* 169–172.

Nishida, H. (1985). Japanese intercultural communication competence and cross-cultural adjustment. *International Journal of Intercultural Relations, 9,* 247–269.

Oberg, K. (1958). *Culture shock and the problem of adjustment to new cultural environments.* Washington, DC: Department of State, Foreign Service Institute.

O'Driscoll, M., & Feather, N. (1983). Perception of value congruence and interethnic behavioral intentions. *International Journal of Intercultural Relations, 7,* 239–252.

Okabe, R. (1983). Cultural assumptions of east and west: Japan and the United States. In W. B. Gudyhkunst (Ed.), *Intercultural communications theory: Current perspectives.* Beverly Hills, CA: Sage.

Orpen, C. (1976). Job enlargement, individual differences, and worker responses: A test with black workers in South Africa. *Journal of Cross-Cultural Psychology, 7,* 473–480.

Orpen, C. (1982). The effect of social support on reactions to role ambiguity and conflict: A study among white and black clerks in South Africa. *Journal of Cross-Cultural Psychology, 13,* 375–384.

Orpen, C. (1983a). Risk-taking attitudes among Indian, United States and Japanese managers. *Journal of Social Psychology, 120,* 283–284.

Orpen, C. (1983b). Westernization as a moderator of the effect of job attributes on employee satisfaction and performance. *Humanita: Journal of Research in the Human Sciences, 9,* 275–279.

Osgood, C. E., May, W., & Miron, M. (1975). *Cross-cultural universals of affective meaning.* Urbana, IL: University of Illinois Press.

Ouchi, W. G., & Jaeger, A. M. (1978). Type Z organization: Stability in the midst of mobility. *Academy of Management Review, 5,* 305–314.

Pareek, U. (1968). A motivational paradigm of development. *Journal of Social Issues, 2,* 115–124.

Pascale, R. T. (1978). Personnel practices and employee attitudes: A study of Japanese- and American-managed firms in the U.S. *Human Relations, 31,* 597–615.

Pascale, R. T., & Maguire, M. A. (1980). Comparison of selected work factors in Japan and the United States. *Human Relations, 33,* 433–455.

Peng, T. K., Peterson, M. F., & Shyi, Y. (1991). Quantitative methods in cross-national management research: Trends and equivalence issues. *Journal of Organizational Behavior, 12,* 87–107.

Peters, T. J., & Waterman, R. H. (1982). *In search of excellence.* New York: Harper & Row.

Peterson, R. B., & Shimada, J. Y. (1978). Sources of management problems in Japanese-American joint ventures. *Academy of Management Review, 3,* 796–804.

Petrovskii, A. V. (1984). The theory of activity mediation in interpersonal relations. In L. Strickland (Ed.), *Directions in Soviet social psychology* (pp. 99–112). New York: Springer.

Phillips, J. C., & Benson, J. E. (1983). Some aspects of job satisfaction in the Soviet Union. *Personnel Psychology, 36,* 633–646.

Phillips, L. D. (1982). Generation theory. In L. McAlister (Ed.), *Choice models for buyer behavior* (pp. 113–140). Greenwich, CT: JAI.

Preston, J. C. (1987). Cultural blinders: Take off before attempting international organizational development. *Organizational Development Journal, 5,* 50–56.

Price-Williams, D. R. (1985). Cultural psychology. In G. Lindzey & E. Aronson (Eds.), *Handbook of social psychology* (pp. 993-1037). New York: Random House.

Redding, S. G. (1980). Cognition as an aspect of culture and its relation to management processes: An exploratory view of the Chinese case. *Journal of Management Studies, 17,* 127–148.

Redding, S. G., & Ng, M. (1983). The role of "face" in the organizational perceptions of Chinese managers. *International Studies of Management and Organization, 13,* 92–123.

Redding, G., & Wong, G. Y. Y. (1986). The psychology of Chinese organizational behavior. In M. Bond (Ed.), *The psychology of Chinese people* (pp. 267–295). Hong Kong: Oxford University Press.

Reitz, J. H., & Jewell, L. N. (1979). Sex, locus of control, and job involvement: A six country investigation. *Academy of Management Journal, 22,* 72–80.

Roberts, K. H. (1970). On looking at an elephant: An evaluation of cross-cultural research related to organizations. *Psychological Bulletin, 74,* 327–350.

Roberts, K. H., & Boyacigiller, N. A. (1984). Cross-national organizational research: The grasp of the blind men. *Research in Organizational Behavior, 6,* 423–475.

Roberts, K. H., & Glick, W. (1981). The job characteristics approach to task design: A critical review. *Journal of Applied Psychology, 66,* 193–217.

Robinson, R. D., (1978). *International business management: A guide to decision making.* Hinsdale, IL: Dryden Press.

Rodrigues, A. (1982). Replication: A neglected type of research in social psychology. *Interamerican Journal of Psychology, 16,* 91–109.

Rohner, R. P. (1984). Toward a conception of culture for cross-cultural psychology. *Journal of Cross-Cultural Psychology, 15,* 111–138.

Rokeach, M. (1973). *The nature of human values.* New York: Free Press.

Rokeach, M. (1983). *The Rokeach Values Survey.* Palo Alto, CA: Consulting Psychologists Press.

Ronen, S. (1982). *Clustering countries on attitudinal dimensions: A review and synthesis.* Paper presented at the Twentieth International Congress of Applied Psychology, Edinburgh.

Ronen, S. (1986). *Comparative and multinational management.* New York: Wiley.

Ronen, S., & Kumar, R. (1986). Comparative management: A developmental perspective. In B. M. Bass, P. Weissenberg, & F. Heller (Eds.), *Handbook of cross-cultural organizational psychology.* Beverly Hills, CA: Sage.

Rosenstein, E. (1985). Cooperativeness and advancement of managers: An international perspective. *Human Relations, 38,* 1–22.

Ruben, B. D., & Kealey, D. J. (1979). Behavioral assessment of communication competency and the prediction of cross-cultural adaptation. *International Journal of Intercultural Relations, 3,* 15–47.

Sakamoto, Y. (1975). *A study of Japanese national character.* Tokyo: Research Committee on the Study of the Japanese National Character.

Schein, E. H. (1985). *Organizational culture and leadership.* San Francisco: Jossey-Bass.

Schneider, B. (1985). Organizational behavior. *Annual Review of Psychology, 36,* 573–611.

Schneider, S. C. (1988). National vs. corporate culture: Implications for human resource management. *Human Resource Management, 27,* 231–246.

Schuster, M. (1983). Forty years of Scanlan Plan research. In C. Crouch & F. A. Heller (Eds.), *Organizational democracy & political processes* (pp. 53–72). New York: Wiley.

Schwartz, S. (1992). Universals in the content and structure of values: Theoretical advances and empirical tests in 20 countries. In M. Zanna (Ed.), *Advances in experimental social psychology* (Vol. 25). New York: Academic Press.

Schwartz, S. (in press). Cultural dimensions of values: Toward an understanding of national differences. In U. Kim, H. C. Triandis, & G. Yoon (Eds.), *Individualism and collectivism: Theoretical and methodological perspectives.* Newbury Park, CA: Sage.

Schwartz, S., & Bilsky, W. (1987). Toward a universal psychological structure of human values. *Journal of Personality and Social Psychology, 53,* 550–562.

Segall, M. H. (1984). More than we need to know about culture but are afraid not to ask. *Journal of Cross-Cultural Psychology, 15,* 153–162.

Segall, M. H. (1986). Culture and behavior: Psychology in global perspective. *Annual Review of Psychology, 37,* 523–564.

Segall, M. H., Dasen, P. D., Berry, J. W., & Poortinga, Y. H. (1990). *Human behavior in global perspective.* New York: Pergamon Press.

Shamir, B., & Drory, A. (1981). A study of cross-cultural differences in work attitudes among three Israeli prison employees. *Journal of Occupational Behavior, 2,* 267–282.

Shuter, R. (1984, September 2). Know the local rules of the game. *The New York Times,* Business Section.

Shweder, R. A., & LeVine, R. A. (1984). *Culture theory: Essays on mind, self and emotion.* New York: Cambridge University Press.

Shweder, R. A., Mahapatra, M., & Miller, J. G. (1990). Culture and moral development. In J. W. Stigler, R. A. Shweder, & G. Herdt (Eds.), *Cultural psychology* (pp. 130–204). New York: Cambridge University Press.

Sinha, J. B. P. (1977). *Organizational dynamics.* Bombay, India: Popular Prakashan.

Sinha, J. B. P. (1980). *The nurturant task leader.* New Delhi, India: Concept.

Sinha, J. B. P. (1984). A model of effective leadership styles in India. *International Studies of Management and Organization, 14,* 86–98.

Sinha, J. B. P. (1986, July). *Concepts and controversies in Indian organizational psychology.* Paper presented at the meetings of the International Association of Applied Psychology, Jerusalem.

Sinha, D., & Kao, H. (1988). *Social values and development: Asian perspectives.* North Delhi, India: Sage.

Skinner, B. F. (1953). *Science and human behavior.* New York: Macmillan.

Smircich, L. (1983). Concepts of culture in organizational analysis. *Administrative Science Quarterly, 28,* 339–358.

Smith, P. B. (1984). The effectiveness of Japanese styles of management: A review and critique. *Journal of Occupational Psychology, 57,* 121–136.

Smith, P. B., Misumi, J., Tayeb, M., Peterson, M., & Bond, M. (1989). On the generality of leadership style measures across cultures. *Journal of Cross-Cultural Psychology, 62,* 97–109.

Smith, P. B., & Peterson, M. F. (1988). *Leadership organization and culture.* Newbury Park, CA: Sage.

Smith, P. B., Peterson, M. F., Misumi, J., & Sugiman, T. (1990). Cross-cultural tests of pm theory: East meets west. *Japanese Journal of Experimental Social Psychology, 29,* 53–63.

Smith, S. H., & Whitehead, G. T. (1984). Attributions for promotion and demotion in the U. S. and India. *Journal of Social Psychology, 124,* 27–34.

Snarey, J. R. (1985). Cross-cultural universality of social-moral development: A critical review of Kohlbergian research. *Psychological Bulletin, 97,* 202–232.

Snyder, M. (1974). Self-monitoring of expressive behavior. *Journal of personality and social psychology, 30,* 526–537.

Stening, B. W., & Everett, J. E. (1984). Response styles in a cross-cultural managerial study. *Journal of Social Psychology, 122,* 151–156.

Stening, B. W., Everett, J. E., & Longton, P. A. (1981). Mutual perception of managerial performance and style in multinational subsidiaries. *Journal of Occupational Psychology, 54,* 255–263.

Stephan, W. G. (1985). Intergroup relations. In G. Lindzey & E. Aronson (Eds.), *Handbook of social psychology.* New York: Random House.

Stephan, W. G., & Rosenfeld, D. (1978). Effects of desegregation on racial attitudes. *Journal of Personality and Social Psychology, 36,* 795–804.

Stern, R. N., & McCarthy, S. (Eds.). (1986). *The organizational practice of democracy.* New York: Wiley.

Stevenson, H. W., Lee, S., & Stigler, J. W. (1986). Mathematics achievement of Chinese, Japanese, and American children. *Science, 231,* 693–699.

Stewart, E., Danielian, J., & Foster, R. (1969). *Simulating intercultural communication through role playing* (HUMRRO Report No. 69–7).

Stockard, J., & Dougherty, M. (1983). Variations in subjective culture: A comparison of females and males in three settings. *Sex Roles, 9,* 953–974.

Stoetzel, J. (1983). *Les valeurs du temps present: Une enquete.* Paris: Presses Universitaires de France.

Strauss, G. (1982). Worker participation in management: An international perspective. In B. Shaw & L. L. Cummings (Eds.), *Research in organizational behavior* (Vol. 4). Greenwich, CT: JAI Press.

Strickland, L. H. (Ed.). (1984). *Directions in Soviet social psychology.* New York: Springer

Stryker, S., & Statham, A. (1985). Symbolic interaction and role theory. In G. Lindzey & E. Aronson (Eds.), *Handbook of social psychology* (pp. 311–377). New York: Random House,

Sullivan, J., Peterson, R. B., Kameda, N., & Shimeda, J. (1981). The relationship between conflict resolution approaches and trust: A cross-cultural study. *Academy of Management Journal, 24,* 803–815.

Sussman, N. M. (1985, July–August). From gaijin to one of the gang: Going back home after an overseas assignment. *The Journal of the American Chamber of Commerce in Japan.*

Sussman, N. M., & Rosenfeld, H. M. (1982). Influence of culture, language and sex on conversational distance. *Journal of Personality and Social Psychology, 42,* 66–74.

Sweeney, M. A., Cottle, W., & Kobayashi, M. J. (1980). Nonverbal communication: A cross-cultural comparison of American and Japanese counseling students. *Journal of Counseling Psychology, 27,* 150–156.

Taft, R. (1977). Coping with unfamiliar cultures. In N. Warren (Ed.), *Studies in cross-cultural psychology.* London: Academic Press.

Tainio, R., & Santalainen, T. (1984). Some evidence for the cultural relativity of organizational development programs. *Journal of Applied Behavioral Sciences, 20,* 95–111.

Taira, K. (1982). *Employment adjustment in Japanese industry.* Colloquium. University of Illinois, Urbana.

Tannenbaum, A. S. (1980). Organizational psychology. In H. C. Triandis & R. W. Brislin (Eds.), *Handbook of cross-cultural psychology* (Vol. 5). Boston: Allyn & Bacon.

Tannenbaum, A. S. (1986). Controversies about control and democracy in organizations. In R. N. Stern & McCarthy (Eds.), *The organizational practice of democracy* (pp. 279–305). New York: Wiley.

Tannenbaum, A. S., & Kuleck, W. J. (1978). The effect on organization members of discrepancy between perceived and preferred rewards implicit in work. *Human Relations, 31,* 809–822.

Tannenbaum, A. S., & Rozgonyi, T. (1986). *Authority and reward in organizations: An international research.* Ann Arbor, MI: Institute of Social Research.

Tapp, J. L., Kelman, H. C., Triandis, H. C., Wrightsman, L., & Coelho, G. (1974). Continuing concerns in cross-cultural ethics: A report. *International Journal of Psychology, 9,* 231–249.

Thomson, W. J. (1983). Effects of control on choice of reward or punishment. *Bulletin of the Psychonomic Society, 21,* 462–464.

Ting Chau, T. (1983). The applicability of theory Z to Hong Kong and other East Asian countries. *The Hong Kong Manager,* August 15–24.

Tornblom, K. Y., Jonsson, D., & Foa, U. G. (1985). Nationality resource class, and preferences among three allocation rules: Sweden vs. USA. *International Journal of Intercultural Relations, 9,* 51–77.

Triandis, H. C. (1964). Cultural influences upon cognitive processes. In L. Berkowitz (Ed.), *Advances in experimental social psychology* (pp. 2–48). New York: Academic Press.

Triandis, H. C. (1967). Toward an analysis of the components of interpersonal attitudes. In C. Sherif & M. Sherif (Eds.), *Attitudes, ego-involvement and change* (pp. 227-270). New York: Wiley.

Triandis, H. C. (1971). *Attitude and attitude change.* New York: Wiley.

Triandis, H. C. (1972). *The analysis of subjective culture.* New York: Wiley.

Triandis, H. C. (1975). Culture training, cognitive complexity and interpersonal attitudes. In R. Brislin, S. Bochner, & W. Lonner (Eds.), *Cross-cultural perspectives on learning.* Beverly Hills, CA: Sage.

Triandis, H. C. (1977a). *Interpersonal behavior.* Monterey, CA: Brooks/Cole.

Triandis, H. C. (1977b). Theoretical framework for evaluation of cross-cultural training effectiveness. *International Journal of Intercultural Relations, 1,* 19–46.

Triandis, H. C. (1978). Some universals of social behavior. *Personality and Social Psychology Bulletin, 4,* 1–16.

Triandis, H. C. (1980). Values, attitudes and interpersonal behavior. In H. E. Howe, Jr. & M. M. Page (Eds.), *Nebraska symposium on motivation, 1979.* Lincoln, NE: University of Nebraska Press.

Triandis, H. C. (1980–1981). *Handbook of cross-cultural psychology.* Boston: Allyn & Bacon.

Triandis, H. C. (1982). Dimensions of intercultural variation as parameters of organizational theories. *International Studies of Management and Organization, 12,* 139–169.

Triandis, H. C. (1983). Essentials of studying cultures. In D. Landis & R. W. Brislin (Eds.), *Handbook of intercultural training* (Vol. l, pp. 82–117). New York: Pergamon.

Triandis, H. C. (1984a). A theoretical framework for the more efficient construction of culture assimilators. *International Journal of Intercultural Relations, 8,* 301–330.

Triandis, H. C. (1984b). Toward a psychological theory of economic growth. *International Journal of Psychology, 19,* 79–96.

Triandis, H. C. (1988). Collectivism vs. individualism: A reconceptualization of a basic concept in cross-cultural social psychology. In G. K. Verma & C. Bagrey (Eds.), *Cross-cultural studies of personality, attitudes and cognition:* London: Macmillan.

Triandis, H. C. (1989). The self and social behavior in differing cultural contexts. *Psychological Review, 96,* 506–520.

Triandis, H. C. (1990). Cross-cultural studies of individualism and collectivism. In J. Berman (Ed.), *Nebraska Symposium on Motivation, 1989,* (pp. 41–133). Lincoln, NE: University of Nebraska Press.

Triandis, H. C. (1992). Cross-cultural research in social psychology. In D. Granberg & G. Sarup (Eds.), *Social judgment and intergroup relations: Essays in honor of Muzafer Sherf* (pp. 229-244). New York: Springer.

Triandis, H. C., & Albert, R. (1987). Cross-cultural perspectives. In F. M. Joblin, L. L. Putnam, K. H. Roberts, & L. W. Porter (Eds.), *Handbook of organizational communication* (pp. 264–295). Beverly Hills, CA: Sage.

Triandis, H. C., & Berry, J. W. (1980). *Handbook of cross-cultural psychology: Methodology* (Vol. 2). Boston: Allyn & Bacon.

Triandis, H. C., Bontempo, R., Leung, K., & Hui, C. H. (1990). A method for determining cultural, demographic, and personal constructs. *Journal of Cross-Cultural Psychology, 21,* 302–318.

Triandis, H. C., Hui, C. H., Albert, R. D., Leung, S., Lisansky, J., Diaz-Loving, R., Marin, G., Betancourt, H., & Loyola-Cintron, L. (1984). Individual models of social behavior. *Journal of Personality and Social Psychology, 46,* 1389–1404.

Triandis, H. C., Kashima, Y., Shimada, E., & Villareal, M. (1986). Acculturation indices as a means of confirming cultural differences. *International Journal of Psychology, 21,* 43–70.

Triandis, H. C., Leung, K., Villareal, M., & Clack, F. (1985). Allocentric vs. idiocentric tendencies: Convergent and discriminant validation. *Journal of Research in Personality, 19,* 395–415.

Triandis, H. C., McCusker, C., & Hui, C. (1990). Multimethod probes of individualism and collectivism. *Journal of Personality and Social Psychology, 59,* 1006–1020.

Trice, H. M., & Beyer, J. M. (1984). Studying organizational cultures through rites and ceremonials. *Academy of Management Review, 9,* 653–669.

Trifonovitch, G. (1973). On cross-cultural orientation techniques. *Topics in Culture Learning, 1,* 38–47.

Tung, R. L. (1982). Selection and training procedures of U.S., European and Japanese multinationals. *California Management Review, 25,* 57–71.

Vernon, I. R., & Wells, L. T. (1981). *Manager in the international economy.* Englewood Cliffs, NJ: Prentice-Hall.

Wallin, T. O. (1979). The international executive's baggage: Cultural values of the American frontier. In H. W. Berkman & I. R. Vernon (Eds.), *Contemporary perspectives in international business* (pp. 122–134). Chicago: Rand McNally.

Wanous, J. P. (1974). A causal-correlational analysis of the job satisfaction and performance relationship. *Journal of Applied Psychology, 59,* 139–144.

Warwick, D. P. (1980). The politics and ethics of cross-cultural research. In H. C. Triandis & W. W. Lambert (Eds.), *Handbook of cross-cultural psychology* (Vol. 1, pp. 319-372). Boston: Allyn & Bacon.

Webber, R. (Ed.). (1969). *Culture and management.* Homewood, IL: Irwin.

Weinshall, T. (Ed.). (1977). *Culture and management.* Middlesex, UK: Penguin.

Weiss, S. E., & Stripp, W. (1985). *Negotiating with foreign business persons: An introduction for Americans with propositions on six cultures* (Working Paper No. 1). New York: New York University Faculty of Business Administration.

Whitely, W., & England, G. W. (1980). Variability in common dimensions of managerial values due to value orientation and country difference. *Personal Psychology, 33,* 77–89.

Whyte, W. F. (1983). Worker participation: International and historical perspectives. *Journal of Applied Behavioral Science, 19,* 395–407.

Whyte, W. F. (1984). *Learning from the field.* Beverly Hills, CA: Sage.

Widiger, T. A., Knudson, R. M., & Rorer, L. G. (1980). Convergent and discriminant validity of measures of cognitive styles and abilities. *Journal of Personality and Social Psychology, 39,* 116–129.

Wilpert, B. (1984). Participation in organizations: Evidence from international comparative research. *International Social Science Journal, 36,* 355–366.

Wilpert, B., & Quintanilla, S. A. R. (1984). *Work-related values of the young: Findings from an eight-year national comparison.* Report prepared for UNESCO. Berlin: Technical University.

Wilpert, B., & Sorge, A. (1984). *International perspectives on organizational democracy.* New York: Wiley.

Witkin, H. A. (1967). A cognitive style approach to cross-cultural research. *International Journal of Psychology, 2,* 233–250.

Wolfgang, A. (1979). *Nonverbal behavior: Applications and cultural implications.* New York: Academic Press.

Worchel, S., & Austin, W. G. (1986). *Psychology of intergroup relations.* Chicago, IL: Nelson Hall.

Wright, G. N., Phillips, L. D., Whalley, P. C., Choo, C. T. G., Ng, K. O., Tan, I., & Wisuda, A. (1978). Cultural differences in probabilistic thinking. *Journal of Cross-Cultural Psychology, 9,* 285–299.

Yates, J. F., Zhu, Y., Ronis, D. L., Wang, D. F., Shinotsuka, H., & Toda, M. (1989). Probability judgment accuracy: China, Japan, and the United States. *Organizational Behavior and Human Decision Processes, 43,* 145–171.

Yoshino, M. Y. (1976). *Japan's multinational enterprises.* Cambridge, MA: Harvard University Press.

Zavalloni, M. (1980). Values. In H. C. Triandis & R. W. Brislin (Eds.), *Handbook of cross-cultural psychology* (Vol. 5, pp. 73–120). Boston: Allyn & Bacon.

Zeira, Y., & Adler, S. (1980). International organizational development: Goals, problems and challenges. *Group and Organizational Studies, 5,* 295–309.

Zhurvalev, A. L., & Shorokhova, E. V. (1984). Social psychological problems of managing the collective. In L. Strickland (Ed.), *Directions in Soviet social psychology* (pp. 133–148). New York: Springer.

CHAPTER 3

Selection and Assessment in Europe

C. Lévy-Leboyer
Université René Descartes, Paris

In order to give a picture of assessment and selection practices in Europe, this chapter adopts three approaches. In the first section, the history of differential psychology applied to work is reviewed, stressing the differences among the various European countries and between Eastern and Western Europe. A second section describes 13 surveys of the instruments most frequently used for selection in six countries, as well as some information from other countries. Common trends and specific features concerning the instruments used as well as the philosophy of selection and the weak relationship between research and application are emphasized. A third section presents a picture of research on selection and assessment and stresses specific European achievement, that is, a strong interest in the social process involved in selection. In addition, the differences between Europe and the United States are examined and explained by the greater diversity of the work force in the United States and the higher rate of unemployment in Europe.

A CHAPTER ON selection and assessment in Europe presupposes that this type of psychological activity is somewhat dependent on the geographical and sociological environment—in other words, that there are differences between selection and assessment in Europe and the United States. Furthermore, it assumes that these differences or, rather, the specific developments of selection and assessment in Europe, are worthy of description and comment for an audience of U.S. psychologists.

Why would we need a specific treatment of selection and assessment in Europe when we already have in this *Handbook* (vol. 2, pp. 327–398) a full chapter on "Personnel Selection, Assessment, and Placement" by Robert Guion, an expert on this matter? Certainly, because European activity in this field is not widely known in the United States: In Guion's nine-page reference list to his chapter, there are only two references to the work of European psychologists.

Thus, this chapter on selection and assessment in Europe will make available to U.S. psychologists the state of the art in that field in Europe. This approach follows the trend of the chapter on "Personnel Selection," written jointly by a U.S. psychologist, N. Schmitt, and a British psychologist, I. Robertson, for the *Annual Review of Psychology* (1990). They clearly express their wish to "identify contributions by authors outside the United States," but actually quote fewer than 10 European publications (5% of their references), most of which are from the United Kingdom. This shows how difficult it is to keep track of research and activities when they are done by practitioners, are not published in journals, or are written in languages other than English. Moreover, the development of selection activities and assessment tools has been very different in Western and Eastern European countries, so that a complete and coherent picture of this activity is almost impossible to achieve.

This chapter will also examine the differences between selection and assessment practices on the two sides of the Atlantic, with the intention of explaining them by examining the history of that area of applied psychology, the differences in the diversity of the work forces, the legal aspects of employment, the conditions of the countries' economies (e.g., the unemployment rates), the dominant societal values, and even the political environment.

The chapter is divided into three parts: The first section will be devoted to a brief examination of the history of selection and assessment, the second will draw a picture of the main instruments used for personnel assessment and selection, and the third will review research activities developed in Europe, with special emphasis on those that seem to be more developed in Europe than elsewhere.

A Look at the Past

The development of work psychology was slower in Europe than it was in the United States, but one should not forget that it all started here. True, Wundt, who founded the first laboratory of experimental psychology in Leipzig, is said to have been opposed to the overhasty application of experimental psychology to real-life decisions. But two of his students, Scott and Münsterberg, went to the United States and became the founding fathers of industrial psychology. Binet, who can be said to have been the first researcher to develop assessment methods for predicting future behavior, did not need to leave his own country; but his work was better received and used more widely in the United States than it was in France.

Early Years

The development of assessment methods in Europe occurred in four stages: (1) an interest in methods of assessing the intellectual development of mentally retarded children; (2) the application of the same instruments to developmentally normal children; (3) the use of these methods for vocational guidance; and (4) the development of military and industrial applications. In Europe, as in the United States, the First World War gave a strong impetus to the application of Binet's ideas to the selection and placement of adults. The postwar period was marked by the increased use of these methods in industry and the creation of "laboratories of industrial psychology" in several organizations (e.g., in the French railways, the Paris transportation system, Peugeot plants, the Swiss watch industry, Herstal metal works in Belgium, Pirelli in Milano, the national mining industry, and Philips in the Netherlands) and by the development of research centers such as the English Institute of Industrial Psychology, created by Myers in London, the Paris Institut de Psychologie, created by Piéron, and the Psychotechnical Laboratory of the free University of Amsterdam. That period witnessed the birth of the International Association of Applied Psychology (IAAP) in Europe, which had a wide range of interests, but whose dominant activity was the field of assessment. IAAP was founded in 1921 by a small group of psychologists, including Piéron and Claparède. They first met in Geneva to discuss "innate and acquired aptitudes."

However, in the 1930s, there was a marked decline of interest in Europe for the application of individual assessment. The mere idea of individual differences went against the dominant political philosophy of the Nazi regime and was opposed in the Communist countries. In Western Europe, the development of selection methods was slowed down by the economic crisis that preceded World War II and by the war itself. In the 1970s, it was interrupted by a change of attitudes. The 1968 Movement, a student uprising for democratization of universities that started in Europe, was especially influential in this change. For instance, in Sweden (personal communication, B. Marsden) after 1968, there was a growing suspicion of selection. Unions expressed their hostility toward testing, so that research on assessment tools stopped, and the application of assessment was limited to high-risk positions like pilots.

In short, the research on assessment methods, which began in Europe, was more or less abandoned there, while it continued to develop at a steady pace in the U.S. This explains why, for a long time, there were few activities worthy of interest for U.S. psychologists. Indeed, most of the techniques commonly used in the United Kingdom, the Netherlands, France, or Spain were straight translations of U.S. methods. This is still true today. A European test publisher's catalog consists primarily of U.S. instruments (e.g., those by Cattell, Strong, Kuder, Thurstone, Guilford, etc.). New ideas and approaches, such as assessment centers, utility estimations, validity generalization, critical incident techniques, situational interviews, biodata, the big five in personality, and so on, were and still are borrowed from the United States.

Recent Developments

The last decade has seen a revival of interest and activity in this field. Specific trends are given a strong emphasis, such as the analysis of the psychological process of selection, democratization (paying attention to the needs of applicants) through interactive procedures, and the use of feedback to the assessees. Several handbooks have been published in this field recently in the Netherlands, France, and England (Drenth & Sitjsma; Drenth, Thierry, Wilhelms, & de Wolff, 1984; Herriot et al., 1989; Lévy-Leboyer & Sperandio, 1987); also, several books focused on selection and assessment (Cook, 1988; Lévy-Leboyer, 1991a, 1991b; Smith & Robertson, 1986; Smith & Robertson, 1989). The European Network of Organizational Psychologists (ENOP), an informal group of work psychology academics founded about 15 years ago by B. Wilpert, Ch. de Wolff, and myself, has seen its activity increase every year and now extends its influence to Eastern Europe. Its 1988 annual meeting took place in Hungary, and the main topic at the most recent meeting examined the psychological issues raised by the adoption of a market economy in Eastern Europe. During the same period in most Western European countries, one detects a growing emphasis on the methods of selection and assessment as well as on the training of work psychologists. ENOP undertook a survey of the curricula of European Universities in order to facilitate student exchanges organized under a European Economic Community (EEC) program. French-speaking work psychologists now meet regularly, and several English-speaking meetings specially devoted to selection and assessment have been organized by English and German work psychologists.

Present Situation

This review of the history of psychology applied to selection and assessment helps explain the renewal of interest among U.S. psychologists concerning the European activities in this field. Work psychology, born in Europe, lost its ground after the Second World War and during the subsequent 40 years. Most of European work psychology was fed by U.S. research, models, and tools. But during the last decade, European work psychology has entered a new phase of development and should therefore be increasingly able to bring new ideas, theoretical contributions, models, and instruments to the field.

U.S. observers may find current trends in European work psychology difficult to follow. In the United States, new ideas, methods, and scientific results are quickly disseminated so that the level of knowledge and professional behavior is fairly uniform. The existence of strong and very large national organizations such as the American Psychological Association (APA) and the Society for Industrial and Organizational Psychology (SIOP), the frequent national meetings, and the availability of training for practitioners result in a quick and extensive circulation of new developments. Thus, there are relatively few differences among the various geographical regions of the country.

The situation is very different in Europe. It is marked by a strong diversity. Let us consider a few examples. In some countries, like the United Kingdom and the Netherlands and, to a certain extent, all the northern countries of Europe, the influence of published research from the United States has never stopped, even during the bleak postwar period. This is because for the British, publications were in their own language, and the works were in a second language for most of the people in the other countries. In contrast, in Eastern Europe, selection, assessment, and the study of individual differences was stopped for philosophical and political reasons. For instance, managers were selected on the basis of their membership in the Communist Party.

But the situation was diverse, even within this part of Europe. In a personal communication, B. Sverko (1991) described the situation in Croatia. After 1952, although the Communist Party retained a strong influence in the selection of key personnel, some freedom in recruitment and selection was given to companies. The largest companies therefore developed personnel departments and employed psychologists. In a 1977 survey, Sverko examined the activities of 47 psychologists employed in Croatian industries and noted that their main activities were the assessment of abilities and the selection of new workers. The survey was repeated in 1982 and in 1990 with the same results. In their work, industrial psychologists used tests of intellectual abilities, interviews, and personality inventories, as well as psychomotor and achievement tests. Some of these tests were adapted from the United States (Raven matrices, DAT battery, Dominos, etc.), others were devised locally. But the situation was somewhat different in Hungary (E. Dienes, personal communication, 1991). Between 1945 and 1960, work psychology disappeared from the university curriculum. In the 1960s, some industries created departments of applied psychology but lacked adequate methods for the assessment of employees for jobs. In order to improve this situation, the government created a Coordination Council of Work Psychology under the auspices of the Ministry of Labor in 1981. During the last ten years, this body has been active on different tasks: creating or adapting tests, helping with research taking place in various industries, training psychologists working in industry, and publishing a review of published literature.

A book on work psychology in Europe was published in Poland in 1980, partly in English and partly in Polish, with texts borrowed from Western European publications (Zamek-Gliszczynska, 1980). Research on the selection of professional drivers, which stopped after the last World War, was started again in Czechoslovakia, and the psychological laboratory of Karlovy University has been reopened.

When looking at the recent development of work psychology in Eastern Europe, one must stress several facts. First, there is a need for assessment tools and the adaptation of tests developed elsewhere. Second, there is a revival of interest on work values and motivation. Psychologists are assisting the transition within the workplace from passive obedience to creativity and initiative, and from fear of punishment to positive incentives. There is also a renewed interest in the study of careers. From the point of view of assessment, there is a focus on the possibility of predicting who will be able to adapt to a new economic environment and who will shift from authoritarian values and low self-esteem to a participative, achievement-oriented, entrepreneurial culture.

The historical evolution of this field was nearly the same in Spain, with a revival that started earlier and is now amazingly strong (Prieto, Blasco, & Quintanilla, 1991). An early phase was marked by the translation into Spanish of Münsterberg's book on industrial psychology. While leaving Germany to live in the United States, Münsterberg gave a copy of his book, which was written in German, to his Spanish colleagues. Thus, the Spanish translation appeared at the same time as the U.S. edition. The period that followed was very productive in terms of academic activity, with the creation of a special curriculum in the Madrid Complutense University and the

development of many selection and assessment programs, especially in the field of transportation and accident prevention. But the civil war in Spain stopped all such activity, and most Spanish psychologists left their country. A second phase started in 1960, with a strong focus on research and application of tests adapted from the United States. During this period, a new concept called *ecological validity* was developed in Spain. This concept suggests that assessment methods should assess an individual's ability to acquire new skills as well as measure current abilities. A third phase started with the beginning of a new democratic era, which also saw the deterioration of the country's economic situation. The economic crisis stimulated the development of new roles for Spanish psychologists. Departments of psychology were created quickly in public organizations because psychological tests were systematically included in the recruitment process for public jobs. The concern for the scientific quality of these tests stimulated the development of university curricula on selection and assessment in 10 different universities.

This strong development is not a common feature for southern Europe. In Italy, for instance, the use of tests for selection is limited by the country's laws on workers' rights (Shimmin, 1989), so that research and application focuses on guidance. In France, the 1968 movement was against the very idea of assessment and scoring individual differences. Grades for school children were replaced by qualitative scoring. Even though traditional grading was quickly reinstated because parents and pupils asked for it, the movement contributed to a sterilization of research in the field of psychological measurement. Meanwhile, because personnel decisions have to be made every day in organizations, test publishers have translated instruments that were developed in the United States and have sold them successfully. But the lack of academic research has benefitted charlatans, since buyers did not require proof of the validity of these instruments.

It is impossible, therefore, to give a homogeneous picture of European activities in the field of selection and assessment. Any European sketch will be a patchwork of local developments, with blank spots where information is missing.

Two methods were used to find the information used in this chapter. First, data banks were searched for references. Second, a letter was addressed to all ENOP members asking for information, reprints, and references. Several contacts, especially with work psychologists from Eastern Europe, helped gather more information, particularly on selection and assessment activities. A summary of these findings will be presented next.

Selection and Assessment Instruments

The general impression one gets from the accumulated material is that there is a discrepancy between the daily activity in the organizations and the research that was behind this activity. Of course, this is not equally true for all the countries in Europe. Moreover, it is fairly difficult to gather comparable information from different countries. However, some recent data exist. Two special issues and several papers (Antalovits, Roe, & Spaltro, 1988; Bruchon-Schweitzer & Ferrieux, 1991; Lévy-Leboyer, 1991b; Poortinga et al., 1982; Schuler, Frier, & Kauffmann, 1991; Tyler & Miller, 1986; Wieby, Altink, Roe, & Greuter, 1991) were devoted recently to selection and recruitment in Europe. But no two questionnaires or interview guides were identical. Furthermore, systematic surveys do not exist in many countries, and we had to limit ourselves to data from 13 surveys dealing with only six countries: Belgium, England, France, Germany, the Netherlands, and Norway. In addition, we include a systematic comparison of management selection in France and in England (Shackleton & Newell, 1991).

Survey Method

Each of these surveys used a different method (mailed questionnaire, telephone interview, direct interview) and a different method of rating the use of the various possible instruments. Some questions offered only two possible answers—"yes we use this" or "no, we don't." Others were much more refined and offered several possibilities, such as "never," "occasionally," "often," and "always"; or "always used," "used for more than half of the applicants," "used for half of them," "used for less than half of them," and "never used." Some of them limited their questions to the selection of managers. Samples were also different in size and in composition: They were mostly large organizations or a blend of organizations and consultants. But all the surveys had the same general aim: to gather information on the methods used for assessment and selection. In an effort to draw comparable figures for different countries, we transformed all the data so that they reflected equivalent information: the percentage of people saying that they use this method always, very often, or often. One must therefore see the data in the two tables in this chapter as indicating trends rather than giving precise information.

Four surveys cover the methods used to select managers in the United Kingdom, France, and Germany. They are presented in Table 1. The earliest one was done by Robertson and Makin (1986). They received 108 responses from a sample of 304 organizations drawn from the Times 1,000 (the UK equivalent to the Fortune 500). The survey concentrated specifically on interviews, references, psychological tests, biodata, and assessment centers, as well as graphology and astrology. To examine differences in practice, Shackleton and Newell (1991) later used the same type of sample and the same survey questions as Robertson and Makin. Moreover, an analogous sample was drawn

TABLE 1

Methods Used in Management Selection

	Survey			
Method	Robertson & Makin [a] (1984; United Kingdom) N = 108	Shackleton & Newell [a] (1990; United Kingdom) N = 73	Shackleton & Newell [a] (1990; France) N = 52	Schuler [b] (1991; Germany) N = 88
Interviews	88	92	94	57
References	81	88	41	54
Vitae, application forms	—	98	97	93
Simulations, simulation tests	—	—	—	7
Personality questionnaires	12	37	36	6
Cognitive and aptitude tests	8	42	23	1
Assessment centers	7	25	9	10
Biodata	3	8	4	10
Graphology	1	1	49	1
Astrology	0	0	0	—

[a]Figures in these studies represent the percentage of respondents who say they use the method.
[b]Figures in this study represent the percentage of respondents who say they use the method for half or more of the selections.
— indicates the question was not used in the survey.
Dates indicate when the survey was conducted, not published.

from "les 200 premières du groupe *Les Echos*" (the 200 largest companies according to *Les Echos* magazine) and the survey used the same questionnaire, which was translated into French. The results enabled us to compare French and British selection policies. It is interesting to note that the French respondents say they always have more than one interview with candidates. Yet one third of the British respondents say that they are satisfied with only one interview.

Schuler (1991) carried out the same type of survey in Germany and asked the same questions for different categories of personnel. Only the data dealing with managers are presented in Table 1. Although questions were asked separately for different types of interviews—for external and internal recruitment and for three levels of management (lower, middle, and upper)—few differences appear, so that the table provides the mean answers for the three groups of managers, for the two types of selection, and for the various types of interviews. However, one must note that half of Schuler's interviews were structured, which does not seem to be the case in the United Kingdom or France. This shows that in Germany research results influence selection practices more rapidly. The last two surveys in the table were organized by the test publishing group SHL in the United Kingdom and France.

This data enables us to emphasize common trends and national differences. Use of interviews and analysis of vitae and/or of application forms are dominant everywhere; references are widely used in the United Kingdom, but less so in Germany, and even less so in France, perhaps because the French are more reluctant to give reliable written assessments about people who have worked with them. Tests are used very differently in the various countries. The differences between the use of tests in Germany on the one hand, and in France and the United Kingdom on the other hand, are striking. Last, but not least, only France seems to use graphology on a large

scale, even though the low validity of this approach is well known. Two reasons are given for the popularity of graphology in France: It is easily accepted by the applicants, and it is inexpensive—one does not need to see an applicant, a handwritten letter of application is sufficient.

Survey Results

Results presented in Table 2 deal with surveys done in different European countries for all levels of employment. The Bruchon-Schweitzer survey (Bruchon-Schweitzer & Ferrieux, 1991; Bruchon-Schweitzer & Lievens, 1991) in France covers a good sample of 42 organizations and 20 consulting firms, with a balanced breakdown between the various sectors of the economy. The survey was done by a psychologist using a directive interview with the head of the human resources department or consulting firm. About one-half of the people interviewed who are in charge of assessment and selection departments have no psychological training; they are qualified in the fields of law, economics, business, or engineering. About one-fourth of the departments surveyed in large organizations had no psychologists. It is therefore not so surprising that graphology was used by nearly all the people surveyed, in spite of its now well-established lack of validity. Other invalid techniques (such as *numérologie, astrologie, hémato-psychologie,* and *morpho-psychologie*) were used by 15 percent of the respondents. The same survey asked respondents to list the tests they used. Two different categories were identified: aptitude and cognitive tests, most of which were old French-made tests such as those developed some 30 years ago by Bonnardel, and personality tests originally written in English (Cattell's *16 Personality Factors Test* and the *Guilford-Zimmerman Temperament Survey*) or recent additions of some new French-made questionnaires. However, one of the interesting features of this survey is the factorial

TABLE 2

Methods Used in Selection for All Levels of Employment

Survey

Method	Bruchon-Schweitzer (1989; France) N = 102	Smith (1990; United Kingdom) N = 40	Beavan & Fryatt (1987; United Kingdom) N = 293	Schuler (1990; Germany) N = 88	Abramsen (1990; Norway) N = 61	Lievens (1989; Belgium) N = 89	de Witte et al. (1991; Flanders) N = 53	Mabey SHL (1989; United Kingdom) N = 300	SHE (1992; France) N = 48
Interviews	99	100	95	37	93	100	98	100	90
References	—	—	78	9	—	73	59	—	—
Vitae, application forms	—	—	91	90	—	91	—	—	86
Situational tests, work samples	7	—	32	16	—	51	37	37	8
Personality questionnaires	35	10	9	6	16	42	63	47	39
Cognitive & aptitude tests	31	5	5	15	25	71	74	66	31
Projective techniques	12	—	—	—	—	42	6	—	6
Assessment centers	—	10	—	9	3	31	—	—	9
Biodata	—	3	—	6	1	—	—	—	6
Graphology	93	2	5	6	2	36	7	3	46
Other methods*	15	0	—	—	1	2	—	—	—

Note: Figures represent the percentage of respondents who say they use the method.

— Indicates the question was not used in the survey.

* Other methods include astrology and morphopsychology.

Dates indicate when the survey was conducted, not published.

analysis the authors performed on the survey results. It shows the role of the consultants' level of training on their practices. Two types of assessment processes were opposed: the first with assessors, trained as psychologists, who actively looked for reliable and valid methods and do their own research in order to improve their instruments; the second with non-psychologists who relied mainly on unstructured interviews without validation of their decisions.

Two other surveys (Beavan & Fryatt, 1988; Smith, 1991) completed recently in the United Kingdom showed very similar results. Here again, one can observe the dominant role of the interviews, the slow development of promising methods like biodata and assessment centers, and a much less frequent use of personality tests than we observe in France. Roughly the same pattern emerges from a survey done in Norway with the same questionnaire. The author, a Norwegian student studying in Manchester, England, reports the same pattern, except for a much more frequent use of personality questionnaires in Norway (cited in Smith, 1991). In both cases, the size of the organization is an important factor: Roughly speaking, the larger the organization, the more frequently tests are used. One can explain this general trend by the fact that large organizations can afford to place assessment specialists on their permanent staff.

Table 2 includes the part of Schuler's (1991) results dealing with nonmanagers. It gives a very different picture, with low use of interviews, high dependence on vitae and application forms, and about 10 percent of the sample using tests. Commenting on these results, Schuler remarked that psychological tests are rarely used for the selection of apprentices, and that graphology, formerly widely used in Germany, has now been almost entirely eliminated. Both remarks show, again, the good communication of research results to the field in Germany and stress the importance that this country gives to work experience and achievement in career management.

The two surveys from Belgium were done on two different samples in the same part of the country (Bruchon-Schweitzer & Lievens, 1991; de Witte, Van Laere, & Vervaecke, 1992). The former mentions a weak representation of the French-speaking organizations in their sample, while the survey done by de Witte and colleagues is limited to Flanders. In spite of some differences in the figures, which may be due to the way questions were written, the whole picture is rather coherent. Again we can see the frequent use of interviews; indeed, de Witte et al. state that 20 percent of the organizations surveyed use only an interview for the selection of their managers and 40 percent do the same for the selection of their sales staff. References are frequently used, as are various types of tests and personality questionnaires. The Dutch Committe for Testing Affairs (Visser, Vliet-Muider, Van Evers, & Laak, 1982) evaluated the reliability and validity of the most often used personality questionnaires (translated versions of Cattell's *16 Personality Factors Test* and the *Guilford-Zimmerman Temperament Survey*) and determined that they are inadequate; unfortunately, this has not stopped their use.

The last two surveys cited in Table 2 (one published by Mabey, 1989, and the other still unpublished) have been carried out by SHL, a consultant group in the United Kingdom, and SHE, its French subsidiary. Both give results that are consistent with the French and British data, except for graphology in France, which SHE indicates is used by only 46 percent of the respondents, in contrast to the 93 percent reported by Bruchon-Schweitzer (Bruchon-Schweitzer & Ferrieux, 1991; Bruchon-Schweitzer & Lievens, 1991). This difference may be explained by a recent change in attitudes among French consultants and also by the method used to obtain the data: interviews in the earlier study, a mailed questionnaire in the more recent one.

Although we did not find a recent survey from the Netherlands, we are able to mention the results of a survey done in 1982 by Greuter and Roe, which found that interviews were used most frequently (94%), followed by application forms (57%) and psychological tests (66% in the large organizations, 24% in those with fewer than 100 employees). In the last two decades, there has been a growing use of assessment centers: In 1990, 30 percent of the organizations surveyed by Altink, Roe, and Greuter (1991) expected to use assessment centers in the next few years.

Prieto et al. (1991), although they did not carry out a survey similar to those described above, gave an account of the selection and assessment methods used in Spain: intelligence and aptitude tests (many computer assisted), personality questionnaires and interest tests (most of them adapted from the United States), situation tests, and a very general use of interviews. The authors stressed the fact that the interview is not used for selection, but is seen rather as a social situation that provides an opportunity to discuss the applicant's aspirations and self-image, as well as his or her perception of different work positions (Blasco, 1987). References are often given by the applicants but rarely taken into account, and assessment centers are not yet in use.

Common Trends

If we look back at all these survey results, there are obvious common trends, such as the importance of interviews in the selection process and the care taken to check and analyze application forms and/or vitae. But we are amazed by the differences among countries. References are widely used, except in the case of France. The use of situational tests and of assessment centers is developing more rapidly in the United Kingdom, Germany, and the Netherlands than it is in France or Belgium. On the other hand, personality tests, as well as cognitive and aptitude tests, are more often used in France and Belgium than in Germany or the United Kingdom.

One of the interesting points, which is mentioned in all the documents, is the fact that not only are the methods used different for different categories of personnel (which is to

be expected), but they also vary according to the size of the organization. Roughly speaking, there are three different patterns in all the countries. Large organizations have a personnel department with, in most cases, at least one qualified psychologist. Small organizations usually have one person who has no training in psychology in charge of personnel management. Some consultant firms have psychologists on their staff, while others do not; in most cases, their value comes from their specialized knowledge of a small segment of the market, rather than from their competence in using specific assessment instruments. Thus, one should expect large organizations to be more careful in their choice and diversity of selection methods.

Another feature, repeatedly found in the papers describing selection and assessment processes, is the lack of influence of work psychology research on the applications of psychology to personnel assessment. Very few organizations collect data on criteria and check the predictive validity of the instruments. Moreover, the various authors of the surveys described above mention the managers' tendency to focus on "nebulous psychological traits" rather than on objectively described behaviors. Selection practices seem to be based more on clinical intuition than on scientific evidence and are seen as an art rather than as a science (de Witte et al., 1992; Roe, 1989). This is one of the arguments used by some test publishers who offer training in testing to nonpsychologists who, after certification, are authorized to administer the tests they received training on.

Differences Between the U.S. and European Approach

These remarks lead to the central topic of this chapter: differences between the American and the European approach to selection and assessment. In the United States, in the last decades, selection practices have been strongly influenced by lawsuits requiring proof of the validity of the decisions that were made based on test results, so that work psychologists in the United States have concentrated on legitimizing their selection procedures by showing non-discrimination. European work psychologists were (and still are) much more concerned than U.S. psychologists with the need to protect applicants by defending their privacy; they see selection as a participative process, where both the applicants and the organization must have their interests represented. In Europe, public action is focused on limiting an organization's right to access an applicant's privacy. This concern is obvious in several official reports (Hessel Commissie, 1977; Lyon-Caen, 1991), the first of which is provokingly entitled "An Applicant Is Also a [Human Being]" and the second "Public Freedom and Employment."

These differences in the philosophy of selection are far reaching. As a matter of fact, the meaning of *selection* is different in Europe and the United States. The European view of selection is not limited to the classical model of prediction, that is, the value of the assessment process being limited to its capacity to identify future work behavior. Instead, the total management of the selection process is emphasized "as a decision making negotiation between employer and applicant, with costs and benefits, taking account of the societal context of selection, such as legal regulations, and labour market conditions" (Roe, 1989, p. 127). This does not mean that the capacity of selection tools to collect information that will enable people to make the best possible decisions is ignored; but it means that two types of validity are taken into account: (a) the classical predictive and content validities and (b) what Schuler (1993) calls *social validity*. With the same orientation in mind, British work psychologists developed research on the effects that assessment and the selection process had on applicants. This means a shift from a focus on what is good for the organization to a focus on what is good for both the individual *and* the organization. A very recent development

along these same lines was a new law enacted by the French government that makes it compulsory for all the organizations to give free time (the equivalent of 24 work hours, or 3 work days) to all employees who wish to have a *bilan de compétences*, that is, an assessment of their skills and abilities (Aubret, Aubret, & Damiani, 1990; Aubret & Blanchard, 1991; Lévy-Leboyer, 1993). Moreover, the assessment results will be given to the assessees only, and they will have the right to ask for such a diagnosis every five years. The goal of this process is explicitly stated in the text of the law as "helping employees to be the managers of their own careers."

Research in Selection and Assessment

These last comments suggest the direction of research activities in the field of selection and assessment in Europe. In the first part, some examples are given of research that is being done on topics that could be dealt with the same way in the United States. In the second part, a summary is given of research orientations specific to European countries, primarily research on the social process of selection and the effects of assessment on the assessees themselves.

Claimed Research

Meta-analysis and the validity generalization hypothesis are central issues in assessment methodology. In a technically sophisticated booklet (Jansen, Roe, Vijn, & Algera, 1986), a team of four psychologists from the Netherlands discussed the methodological problems raised by the validity generalization approach. Although they acknowledge the important progress brought about by meta-analysis, they raise several issues: the fact that the procedure used has been employed over a much wider range than permitted by the classical psychometric model; the lack of attention to the deductive phase of deriving the validity value to be expected in further study; the loose classification of tests, jobs, and criteria; and the fact that the validity generalization model is not Bayesian in character.

Another important issue deals with the methodological problems involved in the development of computer-assisted testing. In an original paper, Schoonman (1989) described a project in which he administered computerized tests and examined response time as a personality characteristic, thus measuring impulsivity and cognitive style. Afterward, he explored ways of using response time in a predictive fashion. Next, Monte Carlo simulations were carried out in order to learn about the influence of pretests and the importance of the stopping criterion. Items were then rejected or accepted according to the Rasch model, and the adaptive testing was tried out in a real-life setting.

Notable published research has included the creation and validation of an automated system for pilot selection (Bartram, 1987); a critical analysis of ipsative personality tests (Johnson, Wood, & Blinkhorn, 1988); a contribution to the debate between the measurement of psychological dimensions or of the achievement in specific exercises at assessment centers, and the practical implications in the design and uses of these approaches (Robertson, Gratton, & Sharpley, 1987); attempts to improve the validity of an assessment center in a military environment (Jones, Herriot, Long, & Drakeley, 1991); and research on the reliability, validity, and use of a *development center*, which is a modification of the classical assessment centers designed to identify employee potential within an organization (Kerr & Davenport, 1989). Research also includes the validation of specific tools, such as work samples (Robertson & Kandola, 1982), drivers' selection (Bakalar, Kobliha, & Slikar, 1980), trainability tests, which assess how well an applicant can learn a new skill (Downs,

1985; Robertson & Downs, 1989), and situational interviews (Roberston & Makin, 1986; Schuler, 1989; Schuler & Funcke, 1989). Reviews of work have been provided on the selection of specific groups: university graduates (Herriot, 1984), army officers (Jones & Harrison, 1982), and police officers (Brier; cited in Smith, 1987).

In fact, it is impossible to trace all the applied research efforts dealing with the construction and study of the psychometric properties of old and new instruments, mainly because most of this literature is limited to mimeographed reports having a restricted circulation and often written in languages other than the most common European languages. Thus, the picture given in this chapter is biased in favor of the publications written in English, German, and French. What seems obvious when one looks at the various reports of activity, however, is the fact that at first, research focused on adapting instruments developed in the United States to different languages and cultures; in the last decade, the development of locally conceived instruments has dominated the research.

A good example of this evolution can be found in the activities of the Department Assessment Unit of the Finnish Institute of Occupational Health Psychology (personal communication, Kirjonen & Niiatmo, 1991). Since 1951, this institution has performed more than 100,000 individual assessments for a wide array of positions. In the beginning, they used translations and adaptations of U.S. measures. Over the last 20 years or so, they have constructed their own Finnish personality inventory, tests of cognitive ability, and psychomotor apparatus, as well as their own program of assessment centers. Research on the qualities and validities of these methods is systematically conducted, but published only in Finnish. And, interestingly enough, a new need is now emerging: selection tools for people with international jobs such as diplomats and commercial and technical people working abroad.

European-specific Research

All these examples belong to classic research that could take place in any part of the world. Before focusing on research trends more specific to the European setting, however, one should note the nature of the research done in the field of job analysis and criterion-related validity. Some instruments have been created or developed, primarily in the United Kingdom, such as the *Work Profiling System* (WPS; Saville, Nyfield, Sik, & Hackston, 1990) and the *Kelly Repertory Grid* for job analysis (Smith & Robertson, 1989). In fact, although mention is made by all the theoretical texts of the utility of job analysis as a way to develop an understanding of the job requirements and a list of reliable criteria against which predictive validity can be assessed, the whole model is rarely applied. In the majority of cases where there is a follow-up to the selection procedures, the assessment focuses on the global quality of the decisions, not on the relevance of specific tools in relation to job analysis requirements (Schuler & Guldin, 1990).

Several reasons may explain the lack of research on selection instruments. First, we are well aware, because of the validity generalizability theory, that a minimum number of subjects is needed for any validation results to earn an adequate amount of confidence. Second, there are many available applicants for most of the advertised job vacancies, forcing organizations to have a two-stage selection procedure, the first of which is low cost. Third, there is almost no reaction from the applicants and no legal system making it compulsory to prove that the selection system is objective and well grounded, although a law addressing this issue is being prepared in France. Instead, personality questionnaires are the only assessment measures that applicants object to, perceiving them as non–job-related and an invasion of their privacy. They usually do not question the relevance of other tests used in assessment or the predictive validity of interviews (even nonstructured ones) or (in France and Belgium) the reliability and validity of handwriting analysis.

A last explanation for the frequent absence of validation against job analysis results is the increasingly frequent use of assessment methods that are not linked to a selection decision. Redundancies and downsizing in large organizations and the growing number of unemployed workers from all levels of the work force stimulated the development of assessment tools aimed at helping the unemployed find new jobs or receive retraining. Outplacement usually begins with an evaluation of an individual's possibilities in order to help the unemployed in their job search. For those with a limited education who acquired most of their skills on the job, assessment is mainly aimed at a description of their acquired capacities.

Moreover, for careers that are becoming more and more complex, the growing gap between the existing human resources and the skills needed for particular jobs requires several different phases of adult training and is changing relationships between employers and employees. Employed people have to take more and more initiative in the management of their own careers. In order to allow them to do that, various actions are taken to help them identify their skills and handicaps, their acquired capacities, and their aptitudes. New instruments are being developed for that purpose, for instance, the so-called occupational wallet in Spain, which enables employees to keep track of their experiences and summarize them when faced with critical decisions.

Assessment is no longer seen as an operation devoted to gathering information for the organization's hiring decisions. It is seen as a social process involving both the organization and the individual. These developments create new needs that should stimulate research oriented toward the content validity of the instruments used for this type of assessment.

This new concern has stimulated research on selection and assessment as a social process, especially in Germany and the United Kingdom. Here are some examples: In several students' theses directed by Schuler (1993) and quoted in his paper on social validity, applicants were asked to rate their satisfaction with different methods of selection. Work samples and aptitude tests were described as relevant, informative, and respectful of their privacy, which is not the case for personality questionnaires and interest tests. Other research work described in Schuler's paper deals with the acceptability of biodata, the feeling of control during different types of interviews, and information on the way test items are processed and test results are used. Furthermore, Schuler points to the need to know more about the way feedback from results modifies an assessee's self-concept and attitude toward the assessment process. We already know that one of the advantages of assessment centers is that they provide social comparisons as well as systematic feedback. As soon as all assessments are seen as services to both individuals and organizations, these aspects will become central to the choice of assessment instruments and to the way they are introduced to applicants.

Another line of research in this same area deals with the analysis of interaction between clients and assessors during selection (Herriot, 1989a, 1989b). The selection process is seen as including several successive phases during which applicants gain information about the organization, about the job being offered, and about themselves and their self-efficacy in comparison to what will be expected of them. The role played by the self-concept as a determinant of individual behavior during the selection process and the role of the assessment and feedback on modification of the self-concept are now research and application priorities.

Concluding Remarks

This broad view of developments in selection and assessment methods in Europe enables us to examine why differences exist between the United States and Europe. In fact, one should also consider the differences among European countries. Employment for men ranges from 79 percent in Belgium to 88 percent in Portugal, and for women it ranges from 34 percent in the Netherlands to 79 percent in Sweden. In comparison, employment for men in the United States is 87 percent, while for women it is 64 percent. Unemployment ranges from 9 percent in Portugal to 30 percent in Spain. Part-time work is not equally common everywhere: It ranges from 4 percent of the work force in the Netherlands to 16 percent in Sweden.

There are two differences between the European countries and the United States that should be taken into account. On one hand, unemployment is much less of a recent phenomenon and much higher in most European countries than it is in the United States. On the other hand, the diversity of the work force is much greater in the United States than in most European countries. Unemployment and diversity are features that have important consequences on the way selection is done; they also influence the needs and attitudes of the people involved in selection.

Where the diversity of the work force and the existence of multiple minority groups are high, an emphasis is placed on a nondiscrimination policy. Hence, the need develops for employers to be able to prove that no applicant was excluded from a job because he or she belongs to a minority group, that is, for employers to prove that all personnel decisions are based on relevant information.

In the case of Europe, where unemployment is an acute problem, the focus is on assessment processes that can help people either find a new niche in the job market or become oriented toward retraining. From the legal point of view, applicants need to be protected because they may accept invalid selection devices. From an organization's point of view, the challenge is to deal with the great number of applicants without losing the best ones or spending too much time and money assessing them.

The importance of diversity in one case, and of unemployment in the other, may be seen as the main factors explaining the differences between selection and assessment practices in Europe and the United States. One should note that these differences could disappear as the opening of borders between European countries creates more diversity of the work force and the changing economic situation gives new potential roles to work psychologists in the United States.

I wish to thank the colleagues who sent or gave me useful information on what was and is taking place in their countries: J. Aubret (France), Z. Bures (Czechoslovakia), M. Bruchon-Schweitzer (France), G. de Cock (Belgium), E. Dienes (Hungary), M. Döbrzynski (Poland), G. Johansson (Sweden), T. Keenan (UK), J. Kirjonen (Finland), B. Mardberg (Sweden), P. Niiatmo (Finland), J.M. Prieto (Spain), R. Roe (the Netherlands), M. Smith (UK), H. Schuler (Germany), C. de Wolff (the Netherlands), and B. Zverko (Croatia).

References

Altink, W. M. M., Roe, R. A., & Greuter, M. A. M. (1991). Recruitment and selection in the Netherlands. *European Review of Applied Psychology, 41*(1), 35–46.

Antalovits, M., Roe, R. A., & Spaltro, E. (1988). *European methodologies in work and organizational psychology.* Budapest: Coordinating Council of Work Psychology.

Aubret, J., Aubret, F., & Damiani, C. (1990). *Les bilans personnels et professionnels.* Paris: EAP.

Aubret, J., & Blanchard, S. (1991, mai–juin). Les pratiques de portefeuille de compétences. *La Documentation Francaise,* 23–27.

Bakalar, E., Kobliha, V., & Slikar, J. (1980). *The alternative method for testing and assessing drivers.* Prague: USMD.

Bartram, D. (1987). The development of an automated testing system for pilot selection. *Applied Psychology: An International Review, 36,* 279–298.

Beavan, S., & Fryatt, J. (1988). *Employment selection* (UK, IMS Rep. No. 160). Sussex: Institute of Manpower Studies.

Blasco, R. (1987). Algunas consideraciones sobre la entrevista en seleccion de personal. *Revista de Psicologia del Trabajo y de las Organizaciones, 3,* 133–151.

Bruchon-Schweitzer, M., & Ferrieux, D. (1991). Une enquête sur le recrutement en France. *European Review of Applied Psychology, 41*(1), 9–17.

Bruchon-Schweitzer, M., & Lievens, S. (1991). Le recrutement en Europe [Special issue]. *Psychologie et Psychométrie, 12,* 2.

Cook, M. (1988). *Personnel selection and productivity.* Chichester, England: Wiley.

de Witte, K., Van Laere, B., & Vervaecke, P. (1992). *Assessment techniques: Toward a new perspective?* Paper presented at the workshop on Psychosocial Aspects of Employment, Sofia, Bulgaria.

Downs, S. (1985). *Testing trainability.* London: LFER–Nelson Personnel Library.

Drenth, P., Thierry, H., Willems, P. J., & de Wolff, C. J. (Eds.).(1984). *Handbook of work and organizational psychology.* Chichester, England: Wiley.

Drenth, P., & Sijtsma, K. (1990). *Testtheorie.* Houten, Belgium: Van Loghum.

Greuter, M. A. M., & Roe, R. A. (1982). Met het oog op selectie. *De gids, 61*(16), 21–27.

Guion, R. M. (1991). Personnel assessment, selection, and placement. In M. D. Dunnette & L. M. Hough (Eds.), *Handbook of industrial and organizational psychology* (2nd ed., vol. 2, pp. 327–398). Palo Alto, CA: Consulting Psychologists Press.

Herriot, P. (1984). *Down from the ivory tower: Graduates and their jobs.* Chichester, England: Wiley.

Herriot, P. (1989a). Selection as a social process. In M. Smith & I. Robertson (Eds.), *Advances in selection and assessment methods.* Chichester, England: Wiley.

Herriot, P. (1989b). Interactions with clients in personnel selection. In P. Herriot et al. (Eds.), *Assessment and selection in organizations.* Chichester, England: Wiley.

Herriot, P., Drenth, P., Dulewicz, V., Jones, V., Robertson, I., & Roe, R. (Eds.).(1989). *Assessment and selection in organizations.* Chichester, England: Wiley.

Hessel Commissie. (1977). *Een sollicitant is ook een Men.* Den Hague: Sociale Zaken.

Jansen, P. G. W., Roe, R., Vijn, P., & Algera, J. A. (1986). *Validity generalization revisited.* Delft, the Netherlands: Delft University Press.

Johnson, C. E., Wood, R., & Blinkhorn, S. F. (1988). Spuriouser and spuriouser, the use of ipsative personality tests. *Journal of Occupational Psychology, 61*(2), 153–162.

Jones, A., & Harrison, E. (1982). Prediction of performance in initial officer training using reference reports. *Journal of Occupational Psychology, 55,* 35–42.

Jones, A., Herriot, P., Long, B., & Drakeley, R. (1991). Attempting to improve the validity of a well-established assessment center. *Journal of Occupational Psychology, 64,* 1–21.

Kerr, S., & Davenport, H. (1989). Unpublished document mimeographed by British Telecom.

Lévy-Leboyer, C. (1991a). *Evaluation du personnel, quelles méthodes choisir?* Paris: Editions d'organisation.

Lévy-Leboyer, C. (Ed.). (1991b). Pratiques de recrutement en Europe [Special issue]. *European Review of Applied Psychology 1*(41).

Lévy-Leboyer, C. (1993). *Les bilans de compétences.* Paris: Editions d'organisation.

Lévy-Leboyer, C., & Sperandio, J. C. (1987). *Traité de psychologie du travail.* Paris: P.U.F.

Lyon-Caen, G. (1991). *Les libertés publiques et l'emploi.* Paris: Rapport pour le Ministère du Travail.

Mabey, B. (1989). The majority of large companies use occupational tests. *Guidance and Assessment Review, 5*(3), 1–3.

Munsterberg, H. (1914). *Psicologia de la Actividad Industrial.* Madrid: Daniel Jorro.

Poortinga, Y. H., Coetsier, P., Meuris, G., Miller, K., Samsonowitz, V., Seisedos, N., & Schlegel, J. (1982). A survey of attitudes toward tests among

psychologists in six western European countries. *International Review of Applied Psychology, 31,* 7–34.

Prieto, J. M., Blasco, R. D., & Quintanilla, I. (1991). Recrutement et sélection du personnel en Espagne. *European Review of Applied Psychology 41*(1), 47–62.

Robertson, I., & Downs, S. (1989). Learning and the prediction of performance: Development of trainability testing in the United Kingdom. *Journal of Applied Psychology, 64,* 42–50.

Robertson, I., Gratton, L., & Sharpley, D. (1987). The psychometric properties and design of managerial assessment centers: Dimensions into exercises won't go. *Journal of Occupational Psychology, 60,* 187–195.

Robertson, I., & Kandola, R. S. (1982). Work sample tests: Validity, adverse impact, and employee reactions. *Journal of Occupational Psychology, 55,* 171–183.

Robertson, I., & Makin, P. J. (1986). Management selection in Britain: A survey and critique. *Journal of Occupational Psychology, 59,* 45–57.

Roe, R. A. (1989). Designing selection procedures. In P. Herriot et al. (Eds.), *Assessment and selection in organizations.* Chichester, England: Wiley.

Saville, P., Nyfield, G., Sik, G., & Hackston, J. (1990). *Enhancing the person-job match through personality assessment.* Paper presented at the annual meeting of the American Psychological Association, San Francisco.

Schmitt, N., & Robertson, I. (1990). Personnel selection. *Annual Review of Psychology, 41,* 289–319.

Schooman, W. (1989). *An applied study on computerized adaptive testing.* Lisse, the Netherlands: Swets and Zeitlinger.

Schuler, H. (1989). Construct validity of a multimodal employment interview. In B. J. Fallon, H. P. Pfister, & J. Brebner (Eds.), *Advances in industrial and organizational psychology.* Amsterdam: Elsevier.

Schuler, H. (1991). Methodological issues in personnel selection research. *International Review of Industrial and Organizational Psychology, 6,* 159–213.

Schuler, H. (1993). Social validity of selection situations: A concept and some empirical results. In

Schuler, J. L. Farr, & M. Smith (Eds.), *Personnel selection and assessment: Individual and organizational perspectives*. Hillsdale, NJ: LEA.

Schuler, H., Frier, D., & Kauffmann, M. (1991). Use and evaluation of selection methods in German companies. *European Review of Applied Psychology*, 20–25.

Schuler, H., & Funcke, U. (1989). The interview as a multi-modal procedure. In R.W. Eder & G. F. Ferris (Eds.), *The employment interview* (pp. 183–193). London: Sage.

Schuler, H., & Fruhner, R. (1993). Effects of assessment center participation on self-esteem and on evaluation of the selection situation. In H. Schuler, J. L. Farr, & M. Smith (Eds.), *Personnel selection and assessment: Individual and organizational perspectives*. Hillsdale, NJ: LEA.

Schuler, H., & Guldin, A. (1990). Methodological issues in personnel selection. In C. Cooper & I. Robertson (Eds.), *International review of industrial and organizational psychology*. Chichester, England: Wiley.

Shackleton, N. J., & Newell, S. (1989). Selection procedures in practice. In P. Herriot et al., *Assessment and selection in organizations*. Chichester, England: Wiley

Shackleton, N. J., & Newell, S. (1991). Management selection: A comparative survey of methods used in top British and French companies. *Journal of Occupational Psychology, 64*, 23–36.

Shimmin, S. (1989). Selection in a European context. In P. Herriott et al., *Assessment and selection in organizations*. Chichester, England: Wiley.

Smith, M. (1987). Selection in high risk and stressful occupations. In P. Herriot et al., *Assessment and selection in organizations*. Chichester, England: Wiley.

Smith, M. (1991). Recruitment and selection in the U.K. with some data on Norway. *European Review of Applied Psychology, 41*(1), 27–34.

Smith, M., & Robertson, I. (1986). *The theory and practice of systematic staff selection*. London: Macmillan.

Smith, M., & Robertson, I. (1989). *Advances in selection and assessment methods*. Chichester, England: Wiley.

Tyler, B., & Miller, K. (1986). The use of tests by psychologists: Report on a survey of BPS membership. *Bulletin of the British Psychology Society, 39*, 495–410.

van der Flier, H. P. G., Jansen, W., & Zaal, J. (1990). *Selektie research in de praktijk*. Lisse, the Netherlands: Swets and Zeitlinger.

Visser, R. S. H., Vliet-Muilder, J. C., Van Evers, A., & Laak, J. L. (1982). *Documentatie van tests entestresearch*. Amsterdam: Nederlands Institute van Psychologen.

Wieby, M. M., Altink, R. A., Roe, R., & Greuter, M. A. (1991). Recruitment and selection in the Netherlands. *European Review of Applied Psychology, 41*, 35–43.

Zamek-Gliszczynska, X. (1980). *Work psychology in Europe*. Warsaw: Poland Scientific Publisher.

CHAPTER 4

Technological Change in a Multicultural Context: Implications for Training and Career Planning

Beryl Hesketh
Stephen Bochner
University of New South Wales, Sydney, Australia

This chapter argues that traditional approaches to training and career development must adapt to deal with the accelerated pace of technological change and increasing intercultural contact. We draw attention to the growing body of cognitive and applied research on developing learning skills and training for transferable skills, little of which appears in the industrial training literature. Australian examples of the problems associated with training for new technology and intercultural communication are covered, together with recent research on methods of training that foster schema acquisition and confidence in ability to learn. We demonstrate the comparative advantage of trainee-centered work-related social skills training over traditional trainer-centered approaches to culture training. Career planning is the key to motivation for training. The accelerated pace of change demands that individuals and organizations take a more active and vigilant approach to career development. We discuss the application of traditional career decision theories to changed circumstances in the workplace; the management of career transitions, plateauing, and career paths; the role of realistic job previews in integrating individual and organizational perspectives; and new approaches to assessment that foster flexibility. Finally, by way of summary, we raise several issues and questions that require further research.

Introduction

ONE OF THE major weaknesses in industrial and organizational psychology has been its failure to integrate sufficiently the different fields that have developed under its umbrella. The speciality areas of selection, training, career development, ergonomics, and organizational development each follow their own course, and it is not uncommon for problems to be defined in terms of the preferred specialty of the consultant or researcher. A complete understanding of work behavior and problems requires a less fragmented approach.

Figure 1 illustrates the way in which institutional (selection) and individual (career development) decisions interact with training, ergonomics, and job design processes to determine levels of satisfactory performance, satisfaction, mental health, and well-being. Furthermore, all this complexity is located within a broader organizational and societal context. There is no doubt that industrial and organizational psychology would benefit from a greater integration of the theory, research, and practices in each of the major domains indicated in Figure 1. One of the aims of this chapter is to work toward achieving such an integration, which is particularly important in light of technological and social change.

In this chapter our starting point is to identify the broad issues in the world of work facing society in the nineties. Our choice of topics and perspectives will be colored by the society we live in, and some of our comments could have a distinctly eucalypt flavor. Still, this may not be such a bad thing. One of the limiting characteristics of industrial and organizational psychology is its heavy dependence on Euro-American theories, practices, and values. As outsiders in that sense, we may be able to bring to bear perspectives that might not readily occur to an insider. At the same time, the issues facing Australia are similar to those facing most industrialized societies (Offermann & Gowing, 1990), so that the core

aspects underlying local research should be broadly generalizable beyond the confines of this continent. These issues fall into two broad groups: those arising from the introduction of new technology and those resulting from social change.

Introduction of New Technology

A core issue in the world of work facing industrialized societies today is technological development (Shenkar, 1988; Tornatzky, 1986). Such development can best be understood within Emery's (1969) model of organizations as consisting of three interacting systems—technological, social, and managerial. The introduction of new technology has a direct impact on the technological system, but also has implications for the associated managerial and social systems. In particular, the human resources techniques, practices, and approaches must keep in step with changes in the technological system, or the overall production systems will lack *joint optimization* between their various components, to use a concept often referred to in the sociotechnological literature (Elden, 1986; Emery, 1969; Pava, 1986; Susman & Chase, 1986). Some of the consequences of technological innovation for industrial and organizational psychology considered in this chapter include items below.

Skilling of the Work Force. Jobs that in the past required manual, repetitive, or clerical skills have changed in the direction of requiring more cognitive, intellectual, and self-starting abilities. Examples might include typists who now have to deal with the cognitively more complex task of word processing, which may also require autonomous decisions about the use of fonts and styles; bank tellers who work with computer screens and large data sets rather than with calculators and restricted computations; and at the professional level, naval architects using computer-based models to design racing yachts and their sail wardrobes.

FIGURE 1

Fields of Industrial and Organizational Psychology

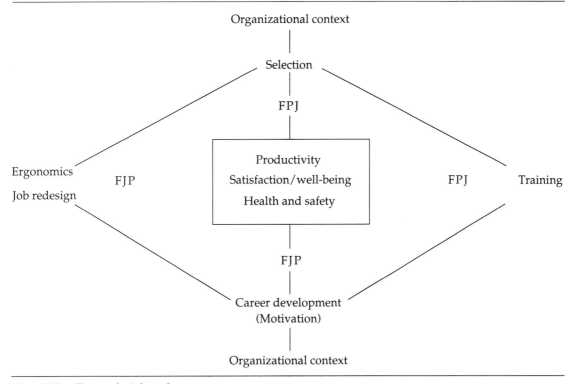

Note: FJP = Fitting the job to the person
      FPJ = Fitting the person to the job

Multiskilling of the Work Force. The tradition in this part of the world, shared by many Western industrialized societies, has been to classify workers into narrow, highly specialized single-skill trades. The guild system and the Taylorist approach to job design (Taylor, 1911) entrenched this form of skill structure, which in Australia was further supported by an arbitration system that laid down legally enforced awards based on job categories, and by a centralized trades union organization that used its industrial muscle to ensure compliance with these provisions.

Among some of the less beneficial consequences of a specialized trades structure were demarcation disputes, poor career paths, and jobs that lacked meaning (Emery, 1977). With the advent of modern technology, many new jobs have come into being, many of the existing jobs are undergoing radical change, and some jobs have disappeared altogether. In practical terms, the new jobs are increasingly complex and require a merging and broadening of skills. The old specialization of functions and duties no longer fits the current job market. In Australia, the 1988 national wages case decision of the Arbitration Commission (Stilwell, 1988) included a structural efficiency principle that aimed to broaden the range of tasks performed by each worker (multiskilling) and to establish skills related to career paths. More recently, the Australian National Training Board has been established with a brief to develop competency-based standards for all occupational levels following a procedure similar to that of the United Kingdom (National Training Board, 1991). Currently, organizations are grappling with the implementation of these principles.

There is another sense in which workers are forced into becoming multiskilled. Not only must a particular individual concurrently possess a broad set of skills in order to survive and thrive in the new climate, but it is also quite likely that during a person's lifetime, he or she may be required to adapt to changing technological circumstances and become multiskilled serially. For example, as timber fittings on yachts are being superseded by modern materials, a shipwright has had to learn how to work in fiberglass. In the future, such a shipwright may need to become an expert in even more exotic materials such as Kevlar. Not only do jobs change around employees but careers increasingly consist of a series of negotiated contracts (Herriot, 1992), requiring ongoing contract negotiation skills, decision making, and rapid learning in a new environment.

Introduction of Social Change

The changes in society that have consequences for the development and practice of industrial and organizational psychology include changes in the internal ethnic composition of the work force in some societies, an increase in between-society work-related contacts, a reduction in work-related discrimination in regard to specially defined categories of workers, an aging work force, and major changes in attitudes toward all of these issues.

Changes in the Ethnic Composition of the Work Force.   Worldwide, many societies now have work forces that are becoming increasingly multicultural in their composition

(Furnham & Bochner, 1986). In Australia, in the immediate postwar era, the blue-collar manufacturing and construction industries were heavily dependent on recent immigrants, with the building of the Snowy Mountains hydroelectric scheme passing into folklore and legend as a living symbol of cross-cultural cooperation in the workplace (McHugh 1989). Relatively few skilled migrants were attracted to Australia, and those who came were mostly from Great Britain (Salter, 1978), a culturally similar society. However, that too is changing. For instance, in contemporary Australia, a shortage of skilled personnel in the information processing industry has forced the banks, insurance companies, and other organizations to recruit such staff worldwide, so that a large part of this professionally based work force is now composed of culturally diverse, recent immigrants (Bochner, Hesketh, & Barker, 1993).

Between-society Work-related Contacts. Worldwide, bilateral and multilateral trade and aid, including the "export" of education, is increasing at an ever expanding rate. What is often left out of the statistics is that this process has created new work opportunities involving large numbers of people who carry out the functions of international marketing and supply as part of their work. During the last twenty or thirty years, a whole new set of jobs has emerged to service international commerce.

Reduction of Work-related Discrimination. A major trend in most industrialized societies is the growing participation of women in the work force. In Australia, according to the latest figures available, females constitute 40 percent of the work force (Castles, 1988). Another major development in modern society is the trend toward the reduction of both positive and negative discrimination in the workplace, usually supported by equal opportunity legislation. In Australia and New Zealand, as in most Western countries, employers are forbidden by law to discriminate against potential or actual employees on the basis of gender, race, religion, physical disability, and now also age (to the extent that in some states the mandatory retirement age of 60 for females and 65 for males is shortly to be declared void).

Aging Work Force.   Although Australia still has a relatively young population compared to other developed nations, the aged population is growing faster than in most comparable countries. The median age of the population is expected to increase from 31.4 years in 1987 to 39 years in 2021 (Department of Immigration, Local Government, and Ethnic Affairs, 1988). This increase will occur despite a continued intake of relatively young immigrants. As in most Western countries, the average age of people in the work force, and hence the age dependency ratio, is likely to increase. The challenge for industrial and organizational psychologists will be to design jobs and training programs that cater to an older work force.

Attitudes Toward Social Change.   In the best of all possible worlds, community attitudes and values would move in synchrony with the advent of social change. Alas, we do not live in a perfect world. In each of the domains discussed so far, tensions and divisions exist. Thus, for quite a while there was trade union opposition to the introduction of new technology on the grounds that this would erode traditional jobs. A classic example of this was the ban placed on the issuing of video cameras to television crews in the Australian Broadcasting Commission, on the grounds that this would destroy the jobs of the personnel working with film (Bochner, Ivanoff, & Watson, 1974). Elsewhere in the world, the introduction of new technology, particularly in the case of office automation, has been resisted by both business and labor on the grounds that it would lead to increased cost, deskilling, physical and mental stress, and electronic surveillance to monitor performance (Turnage, 1990). However, if due

regard is given to the manner in which new technology is designed and introduced, both management and the workers will be more willing to adapt to change. For instance, recently in Australia, some of the more enlightened trade unions, such as the Amalgamated Metal Workers, have been ahead of the employers in seeking to restructure their industry in line with the structural efficiency principle and are lobbying for more training to be provided within the National Training Board structure (National Training Board, 1991) so that their members can better cope with technological change.

Similar to many other countries, Australia faces a combination of moderately high unemployment levels (between 10 and 11%) and a chronic skill shortage. Although training would seem to be an obvious way of dealing with this problem, until recently the employers' preferred method was to recruit skilled labor overseas. This presents interesting challenges for within-society culture training, but the growing recognition of the importance of increasing the skill level of native-born Australians (National Training Board, 1991) places all forms of training high on the agenda.

To sum up the discussion so far, current industrial and organizational work-related problems fall into two general domains: those resulting from the changing technological component of work and those resulting from the changing social, human resources component of work. The problems include rapid technological change and its introduction and the consequent requirement of the work force to become more skilled absolutely as well as more flexible in the sense of being multiskilled in both the concurrent and serial sense. In the human resources domain, they include an increase in within- and between-nation work-related cross-cultural contacts, an aging work force, and the mandatory inclusion in the work force of groups previously excluded or discouraged from full participation, including women, ethnic minorities, some categories of disabled persons, and older persons. Each of these developments has implications for the kinds of solutions that industrial and organizational psychology has to offer.

Basis for the Choice of Industrial and Organizational Solutions

It is one of the major contentions of this chapter that the solutions currently offered have not kept pace with the developments in society that we have described.

Applied psychologists as practitioners provide a range of services. In this chapter we will take two particular procedures, training and career development, and link these to the work-related problems we have identified so far. We will argue that because the problems have changed, the existing approaches are inadequate; and we will then show what changes are necessary in the practical domains of training and career development in order to bring these procedures into line with the issues of the nineties. Although we are not alone in drawing attention to the changes currently taking place in organizations (Offermann & Gowing, 1990) and the likely future systems that will emerge to cope with these developments (e.g., Goldstein & Gillam, 1990), previous discussions have tended to be at a general organizational level, rather than looking at particular methods of training and individual career decision making.

In giving more detailed and specific attention to training and career development in this chapter, we do not wish to imply that these are the only areas of industrial and organizational psychology in need of a new approach. Traditional methods of job analysis and selection also have to adapt to the changes. For example, job analysis should identify likely future skill requirements, not only those currently required on the job; these analyses should take into account changes in ability requirements at different stages of skill acquisition (Ackerman, 1992); and individuals

should be selected for their capacity to adapt to frequent changes (Hesketh & Robertson, in press).

Training in the Twenty-first Century. Technological change on a continuing and accelerating basis requires training techniques that will prepare people for the lifelong acquisition of new skills. Most existing training approaches, even competency-based approaches (National Training Board, 1991), rely on an outmoded view that once people have acquired a set of skills, they will be able to use those qualifications for the rest of their lives. This might be called the *full bottle* approach to training and is enshrined in certificates, degrees, and diplomas, regarded as meal tickets that give people the right to pursue a particular trade or profession until retirement. The problem is that in a dynamic environment, by the time the bottle has been filled, there may be very little interest in its contents. The alternative might be called the *four-minute-mile* approach to training, drawing on the view that sporting records are made to be broken and that last month's personal best has about as much currency as yesterday's newspaper, which is only useful for wrapping up the fish and chips. More conventionally stated, a vital part of the process is to not just teach people a set of static skills but to give them a foundation for acquiring new ones on a continuing basis.

Career Development in the Twenty-first Century. Borrowing a phrase from racing parlance, career decision making has been included as the second leg of this double, because it covers the motivational side of the process. Peoples' concepts of what constitutes a career will influence their view of what is acceptable and appropriate in the domain of training, both as consumers and providers. Both individual workers and organizations contribute to what we have characterized primarily as a decision-making process, which in time will affect the extent to which individuals and organizations avail themselves of different work-related and culture training opportunities.

Conceptual Frameworks

In this chapter we will take seriously the notion that an applied science has a core discipline from which the ideas, theories, and procedures were derived. To illustrate this approach, the knotty problem of developing transferable skills will be linked to recent developments in cognitive and learning psychology; career planning will draw on decision theories; Herriot's (1989) model of the selection process as an implicit social contract and careers as a sequence of contracts will be used to account for the mutual obligations of worker and employer in pursuing achievable goals; theories of work adjustment and career transitions will be used to explain adult career development; and social skills and culture learning theories will provide the context for the discussion of multicultural issues.

Rather than dwelling on the existing literature traditionally covered under training and career development, we have instead at times chosen to deal with the emerging ideas and models that will serve as the basis for future directions in this area.

Training

Dissatisfaction With Traditional Approaches to Training

The main principles underlying industrial training appear in most major textbooks and review articles (Goldstein, 1986, 1991; Latham, 1988; Noe & Ford, 1992; Tannenbaum & Yukl, 1992; Warshouer, 1988). These include (a) assessment of training needs, through both task and person assessment; (b) setting of learning objectives; (c) design of the training program, taking into account the context, learning principles, and the characteristics of trainees; and, finally, (d) evaluation of the program. There are well-established technologies for each of these stages, yet many practitioners continue to offer training programs without following any systematic procedure. There are in fact sound reasons for questioning the conventional wisdom in the industrial training literature, but the nonadherence to training principles probably relates more to practitioners' desires to engage in "cherry picking" (Blacker, 1988) for immediate gain (namely, payment from an organization), rather than to any soundly based rejection of these principles.

Although traditional approaches do continue to offer useful guidelines, they warrant some critical analysis. For example, Alliger and Janak (1989) have expressed dissatisfaction with Kirkpatrick's (1959, 1960) levels of training criteria (reactions, learning, behavior, and results), long considered the ideal in the evaluation of training programs (Goldstein, 1986). Research reviewed by Alliger and Janak (1989) failed to support the assumptions implicit in Kirkpatrick's model, namely that the criteria are hierarchically organized, causally linked, and correlated. Fortunately, new ideas are appearing, such as those of Kraiger and Ford (1992), who suggest that the assessment of changes in knowledge structures may be useful in training evaluation.

The rapid change in skill requirements resulting from the ongoing introduction and updating of equipment in industry poses a more serious problem for traditional approaches to training. Much of the traditional training technology is based on an assumption of relative stability in skill requirements in jobs and in job availability generally. There can be no guarantee that future jobs will require a range of skills similar to those currently influencing training at an levels in society. Traditional training technologies were not designed to deal with job-related tasks that change frequently and individuals who change jobs regularly.

Although several writers acknowledge the need for new approaches (e.g., Noe & Ford, 1992), only limited reference is made to the growing literature on training for transferable skills. Fortunately, as we hope to demonstrate, recent research does point to the existence of effective methods of training for new technology and for developing transferable skills.

Another major criticism of the traditional approaches to training is that they tend to be trainer-directed rather than learner-oriented (Downs & Perry, 1984). This issue will be raised in relation to training for cross-cultural competence, which also suffers from not being sufficiently trainee-centered. Although individual differences are sometimes acknowledged, such as in the learning styles literature, instructors tend to retain the control for training. This reflects a paternalistic attitude prevalent in many organizations. Such paternalism has been challenged in the area of "manpower planning," where it is no longer accepted that an organization has the right to manipulate individuals' career paths without consulting and involving the individuals themselves. A similar challenge in the training literature is long overdue. Individuals need to take responsibility for their own learning within the context of planning their own careers, although there are dangers in failing to honor training preferences (Baldwin, Magjuka, & Loher, 1991). Training technology will have to adapt to cope with the consequent increase in "consumerism." The mystique of training must be reduced, and methods of learning must be shared with people so that they can equip themselves better against obsolescence. These are the intentions expressed in some of the work of Downs and Perry (1982, 1984).

The traditional approaches to training such as those outlined by Goldstein (1986, 1991) remain important, but they are not sufficient. Training should not only help people learn how to do a particular task, but should also develop transferable skills and skills of learning. Hence, each of the major steps involved

in training should be more future oriented in order to take into account an accelerated pace of change. The job should be analyzed for what is required immediately, as well as for how it is likely to change, perhaps using technical conference methods (Gael, 1988). Training objectives should refer to specific job content as well as to the skills and attitudes involved in the learning process. The methods of training chosen should be influenced by the growing body of research on transferable skills, and evaluation should include an assessment of how well the training course has fostered the acquisition of specific skills, generalizable skills, and developed learning skills. Training evaluation will need to establish whether people are more trainable at the end of the course than they were before it. Trainability assessments (Robertson & Downs, 1979) could be adapted to serve this purpose.

Flexibility, Transfer, and Development Generalizable Skills

In recent years, educationalists and industrial trainers have searched for methods of instruction that retain flexibility, facilitate the transfer of skills, and develop an ability to learn new skills efficiently. This interest has been reflected in a growing body of literature with a practical emphasis (e.g., Adams, 1987; Annett & Sparrow, 1986; Banks, Jackson, Stafford, & Warr, 1983; Downs, 1985; Duncan & Reiersen, 1988; Geller, 1991; Jelsma, Van Merrienboer, & Bijlstra, 1990; Kamouri, Kamouri, & Smith, 1986; Singley & Anderson, 1985; Smith, 1977; Sternberg, 1988; Zeitz & Spoehr, 1989). Two trends emerge from this and other literature. The first suggests that the content of training should be relevant to a broad range of jobs but ignores the actual learning process (ways of training that foster generalizable skills). The second trend places more emphasis on the process of learning and the training methods that develop generalizable skills (Hesketh, Andrews, & Chandler, 1989).

Training in Generic Skills. Banks et al. (1983) illustrate the first trend. They used the *Job Components Inventory* to identify skills that were common to many jobs entered by young unqualified school dropouts. Hayes, Fonda, Pope, Stuart, and Townsend (1983) similarly attempted to use the concept of occupational training families to locate skills common to particular groups of jobs. Earlier work by Smith (1977) also emphasized the importance of training in generic skills that were thought to be common to a wide range of jobs. Smith's approach was based on the underlying assumption that such skills were more fundamental, and not merely common to different jobs.

Although there are advantages in acquiring skills that are common to many of the jobs available at a particular time, this fails to prepare people for ongoing changes resulting from the introduction of new technologies. This leads to the importance of the second trend evident in the literature, which deals with the process of training. Here the focus is on the methods of training that develop learning skills and facilitate the extraction of schemas and principles in order to foster transfer. These methods aim to develop the confidence and skills necessary to engage in future learning (Annett & Sparrow, 1986; Downs & Perry, 1984; Geller, 1991; Hesketh, Andrews, & Chandler, 1989; Hill, Smith, & Mann, 1987; Polumbo, 1990; Zeitz & Spoehr, 1989).

Developing Learning Skills. A learning skill is one that is used to increase other skills or knowledge. Examples include knowing that there are different ways of learning and when to use each method, knowing how to read manuals, being able to learn from mistakes, knowing what types of questions to ask, solving problems, and being able to judge one's own performance (Downs & Perry, 1984; Myake & Norman, 1979) as well as learn from errors (Frese & Altmann, 1989). Since intelligence increases learning skills, Sternberg's (1988)

recent work on teaching "intelligence" is also relevant. Sternberg (1988) outlines several approaches than can be used to help develop some of the component skills or strategies that contribute toward behavior typically considered intelligent. The importance of learning skills is highlighted by Downs and Perry's (1982) finding that less academically able young people possessed fewer ways of learning and the methods they did use were often applied inappropriately. For example, they would use rote learning for things that required understanding and assumed that facts could be memorized by passively reading text. In response to questions about how they learned various things, less academically able young people often mentioned *who* had taught them or *where* they had learned the task in question, rather than *how* they learned. The performance of less academically able young people was improved by helping them recognize different ways of learning and the particular applications of each method (Downs & Perry, 1982).

Downs and Perry (1984) can be credited with having translated important learning-to-learn ideas into a framework that is easily understood by first-line supervisors and those responsible for the day-to-day training in industry. As part of the training program, supervisors are shown that the methods of training that foster the development of specific skills are not necessarily the same as those that also encourage learning to learn. The course is designed to allow supervisors (and hence eventually all trainees) to discover a simple learning taxonomy of methods of learning: learning by memorizing, understanding, and doing, which is easily remembered as MUD. The three categories can be related to the five types of content that Wulfeck, Ellis, Richards, Merrill, and Wood (1978) identified. Facts and rules need to be memorized; concepts and principles need to be understood; and the best way of learning procedures is by doing. In the Downs and Perry (1984) program, several exercises are designed to help the supervisors discover the ways of learning by each method. Examples include the use of mnemonics for memorizing, the use of questioning to grasp cause and effect relationships for understanding, and the use of a silent demonstration for learning by doing. Downs and Perry argue that training should help trainees to develop strategies that facilitate learning by memorizing, understanding, and doing, while also imparting relevant knowledge and skill content. Since the work of Downs and Perry (1982, 1984), several studies have explored the best methods of learning. By way of illustration, examples of recent studies on how to improve learning skills are discussed below.

The use of mnemonics is a well-known strategy for improving memorizing. Cook (1989) provides a review of the applicability of verbal mnemonics for different populations and contrasts these with visual or imagery mnemonics. Verbal mnemonics can be of a sentence type, in which the items to be learned form a sentence such as "little beer bottles crack nicely on fires" for memorizing the chemical elements lithium, beryllium, boron, carbon, nitrogen, oxygen, and fluorine. Alternatively, they can be acronyms in which the letters of a word represent the items to be learned, such as MUD for learning by memorizing, understanding, and doing, discussed above. Visual mnemonics involve forming visual images to link items or procedures that need to be learned (Mastropieri, Scruggs, & Levin, 1985; McDaniel & Pressley, 1987). The use of either verbal or visual mnemonics is more effective in improving recall than other strategies such as rehearsal, but not uniformly so. For people who have difficulty visualizing, the use of verbal mnemonics gives better results. Furthermore, verbal mnemonics are superior when the material to be learned is abstract, such as the first row of the periodic table, while visual mnemonics are better for concrete facts, such as the population size of different countries. Unfortunately, most of the research on mnemonics has used student populations,

and there is an urgent need to examine the effectiveness of mnemonics generally with adults, particularly in light of retraining needs. Mnemonic training was effective in improving memory among ordinary healthy older people (Verhaeghen, Marcoen, & Goossens, 1992).

Interestingly, Belezza and Buck (1988) have drawn attention to the role that expert knowledge plays as a mnemonic or cognitive cue. Belleza and Buck demonstrated that experts (in the areas of football and clothing) were better able to recall information in their area of expertise than were nonexperts, even when the facts to be remembered were contrary to knowledge in the particular domain. The knowledge structures that experts have allow them to engage in advance organization of material, thereby facilitating recall. Kraiger and Ford (1992) suggest that the changes that occur in knowledge structures as expertise develops (Ericcson & Smith, 1991) can be used to evaluate training.

Many work-related situations require integrated sequences of activities or procedural skills (e.g., wire wrapping in the electronics industry, starting up a complex piece of equipment), and hence we need to know ways of optimizing learning about procedures. Learning by observation, either live or on video, is one common method; following written or verbal instructions is another. Often a combination of methods is required. Baggett (1987) compared six different methods of learning a procedural task such as building a model helicopter from an assembly kit. Baggett was interested in comparing the effects of varying the order of hands-on practice and the presentation of visual, auditory, and written material. The best performance was found, both immediately and a week later, in the group that had hands-on practice (learning by doing) before seeing the film or reading about the task. Future research may well show that the best order is related both to the ability and prior knowledge of the learner and to the nature of the task.

Because of the growing interest in skill transfer and generalization, most of the recent research has been directed at exploring methods of training that facilitate an understanding of underlying principles or schemas (e.g., Cooper & Sweller, 1987; Geller, 1991; Gick, 1991; Gick & Holyoak, 1983; Jelsma et al., 1990; Lewis, 1988; Sweller, 1988). Lewis (1988) discusses the importance of the attributions that learners make about the relationships between actions and outcomes, since these affect the adequacy of their understanding and the models and principles they extract for future generalizations. Understanding principles should involve obtaining an accurate picture about the cause-and-effect relationships in the domain to be understood. Methods of training that foster an accurate understanding of cause-and-effect relationships and the extraction of schemas and principles will help develop transferable skills.

Learning Principles and Extracting Schemas

Models, schemas, and principles are terms that are often used interchangeably. A schema has one or more of the following aspects: (a) It is a prototype or abstraction of the real thing; (b) it is obtained from past experience together with examples of whatever it represents; (c) it can guide and help to organize incoming information; and (d) it provides a basis for completing a picture if information is missing (Thorndyke & Hayes-Roth, 1979). For example, one might have a schema of how word processing packages work that divides them into the two major components of editing and printing. Within editing, the schema may include functions such as inserting, deleting, finding, block-moving operations, file operations, and so on; within printing, the schema may include formatting and the use of fonts.

There is general agreement in the literature that transfer is facilitated through understanding principles and developing schemas rather than by merely knowing procedures (Annett & Sparrow, 1986; McGehee & Thayer,

1961; Murphy & Mitchell, 1986). Several reasons have been offered to account for the role of principles in transfer: Principles are more general than procedures and hence can be applied in more contexts; they play a role in the organizing of knowledge in memory and its retrieval (Thorndyke & Hayes-Roth, 1979); and in general, principles are remembered more easily than procedures, perhaps because they have been used in a range of situations. Procedures, in turn, are remembered better if people know the underlying principles (Katona, 1940; Kieras & Bovair, 1984; Wertheimer, 1959). Any method of training that fosters abstraction of schemas and principles warrants attention. The appropriate use of examples and methods of training that do not place a heavy cognitive load on the learner are important, as are many of the procedures used in discovery or exploration-based learning.

Zeitz and Spoehr (1989) varied the presentation of material in a manual for a troubleshooting program by presenting either an overview explanation first (top down) or the detailed information first (bottom up). Several performance criteria indicated that the top down organization resulted in better integration and learning of principles. Advance organizers such as the top down approach help to reduce cognitive load during learning. Schema extraction and the organization of knowledge structures require sufficient spare attentional capacity; Kanfer and Ackerman (1989) and Kanfer, Dugdale, Nelson, and Ackerman (1990) also identify the importance of spare attentional resources if self-regulatory motivational processes are to be effective.

Use of Examples.   Although examples have always been used by educators and trainers (e.g., Pirolli & Anderson, 1985), until quite recently little was known about the best way of using them to facilitate learning. Fortunately, there is considerable research now available to guide trainers and learners in the appropriate use of examples (Gams, Drobnic, & Petkovsec,

1991; see Hesketh, Andrews, & Chandler, 1989, for a review).

In the fields of artificial intelligence and cognitive science, attention has been given to how generalizations are extracted from examples. Chi, Bassok, Lewis, Reimann, and Glaser (1989) examined how better students successfully managed to extract principles from a single example in which a solution had been partially worked out. They found that these students tended to overcome the incompleteness of worked examples by engaging in covert statements and explanations while they worked. The covert statements helped them acquire the underlying principles. Lewis (1988) found that subjects learning a computerized task used several different strategies or heuristics, not all of which were optimal. Often superstitious connections were made simply because a string of actions were linked in a sequence. Another heuristic commonly used was to link together two loose ends. Causal links were assumed between an input and an outcome simply because each was a loose end; the input had no companion output, and the output no companion input. These heuristics may help learners, but they can also lead to false models or generalizations that could hinder transfer.

Research undertaken at the University of New South Wales has shown that worked mathematical examples (examples that include the solution as well as the problem) facilitate the extraction of schemas (Sweller, 1988). Sweller and others (Sweller & Cooper, 1985; Tarmizi & Sweller, 1988) found that worked examples provided a better learning environment for extracting schemas. Sweller (1988) argues that worked examples reduce the cognitive load placed on learners, who do not need to be concerned with the mechanics of additions and subtractions. Worked examples allow sufficient spare capacity to attend to the nature of the problem and hence facilitate the categorization of problem types and the development of domain-specific schemas, which are a feature of expert knowledge (see also the arguments by Kanfer et al., 1990, and Kanfer & Ackerman, 1989, with respect to attentional resources and self-regulatory processes).

Sweller, Chandler, Tierney, and Cooper (1990) examined the best ways of using worked examples in areas such as numerical control programming and logic circuits. When the text or numerical code is integrated with diagrams, transfer was better than when examples were presented with the code or text separated from the diagram. The explanation they offered for the disadvantage of separating text from the diagram relates to the consequent divided attention, which interferes with schema acquisition. These findings and those from other studies are relevant to the best ways of presenting information in technical manuals. For example, simple formatting of text can improve comprehension in average readers (Jandreau & Bever, 1992). In Australia and New Zealand, where much computer-based and other technical equipment is imported, learning from manuals and the examples provided in manuals is often the only way in which skills can be acquired (Hesketh & Chandler, 1990). It is not unusual for an employee to be left alone to learn how to operate equipment from a manual. Research into the best methods of formatting text and of presenting information and examples in these manuals is long overdue.

Perhaps even more important than the nature of the examples used is the number of examples. It is now well established that principles are learned more effectively through the use of a variety of relevant training stimuli and examples (Ellis, 1965; Gick & Holyoak, 1983). Gick and Holyoak (1983) have provided quite convincing evidence of the importance of multiple examples. Their research made use of problems presented in story form (e.g., how to remove a tumor without removing the tissue in the path of the laser ray), together with one or two hypothetical situations illustrating the solution to a different problem based on the same principle as the target problem. Factors varied including whether one or two examples were provided and whether these were presented with or without either a graphic or a verbal statement of the principle underlying the solution to the problem.

Gick and Holyoak (1983) found that the inclusion of a statement or graphic representation of the underlying principle increased the percentage of students solving the target problem, but only when two examples were used together with the principle. With one example only, neither the statement of the principle nor its graphic representation improved performance. Gick (1991) reports more recent research that explored whether additional contrasting examples can further enhance learning and transfer.

The importance of multiple examples is further highlighted by the lack of transfer obtained in two field studies undertaken by Fotheringhame (1984, 1986). Fotheringhame (1984) found that trainees who had learned how to use a micrometer one year previously relearned the use of the micrometer easily but performed no better on the vernier gauge than trainees who were exposed directly to the vernier gauge with no prior experience on a micrometer. In this study, a set of quite specific procedures transferred rather than general principles required to facilitate skill acquisition in another measurement context. The experience on a single example (training was undertaken on either verniers or micrometers, not both) without explicit instruction about principles did not result in generalizable skills.

Examples also serve a useful role in reminding learners of relevant principles and how they solved previous similar problems. Access to an original example is easier if there is a similarity between the new problem and the original example (Gentner & Landers, 1985; Gentner & Toupin, 1986; Ross, 1987). The use of multiple and varied examples during training not only fosters the extraction of principles but also increases the chances that a relevant example can be accessed at a later

stage. Interestingly, exemplar-based models of social judgment (Smith & Zarate, 1992) may provide the key to integrating research in cognition and learning with culture training, as will be discussed later.

To summarize, it seems that multiple worked examples, presented in a form that does not divide attention, are likely to be effective in acquiring principles and in exposing learners to a range of problems, easing later access to relevant examples. The advantage of multiple examples is that learners are less likely to confuse the principle with the idiosyncratic aspects of the particular example. Presenting them with the principle draws attention to the salient features common to the two examples (Hesketh, Andrews, & Chandler, 1989). Furthermore, presenting examples in a way that does not place excessive cognitive load on learners further facilitates the extraction of domain-relevant schemas and the learning of principles (Sweller, 1988). These issues are relevant to the development of expertise (Ericcson & Smith, 1991).

Exploration-based or Discovery Learning. Exploration-based or discovery learning involves several features that are likely to contribute to schema acquisition and understanding (Hesketh, Andrews, & Chandler, 1989; Kamouri et al., 1986). In contrast with traditional instruction-based methods, discovery learning (a) removes time pressure, (b) encourages questioning (to help relate new to existing knowledge), and (c) encourages learners to develop their own rules.

One of the key features of exploration-based learning is self-pacing or the removal of time constraints. Learning under time pressure has several disadvantages. Time pressure increases anxiety (Broadbent, 1985; Hesketh & Shouksmith, 1986); learning in the presence of anxiety is likely to affect individuals' self-efficacy (perceptions of their ability to perform particular tasks; Bandura, 1977, 1982). High anxiety is likely to reduce the efficiency of the attentional mechanisms that Sweller (1988) and others have shown to be important for the abstraction of schemas or other self-regulatory processes (Kanfer et al., 1990). Furthermore, time pressure removes one of the options that is available to increase attentional resources for a particular task, namely the sequencing of activities (Pashler, 1989). Chandler (1989) examined the effects of placing high school students under time constraints while solving mathematical problems and found that it increased the use of a particular approach (means-ends analysis) that Owen and Sweller (1985) found was less likely to lead to the development of mathematical schemas. Hence, the removal of time pressures during some phases of learning has advantages for all age groups.

A second feature of discovery learning is that it allows trainees to ask questions of the trainer, enabling them to relate new information to their own learning needs and to previous knowledge. Questioning also increases the probability that trainees will develop their own rules, the third component of discovery learning. Such self-generated rules can be beneficial in some circumstances. In a study that involved behavioral modeling training of supervisory communication skills, Hogan, Hakel, and Decker (1986) showed that trainee-generated rules transferred better than trainer-provided rules, probably because of the greater personal relevance of the individually generated rules.

Kamouri et al. (1986) were able to demonstrate conclusively that exploration-based methods or discovery learning procedures resulted in the extraction of relevant and accurate schemas. Instruction-based training gave rise to less complete and less accurate schemas. In contrast, exploration-based training resulted in more accurate schemas and comparatively better performance on a transfer task that was based on a similar schema to the one underlying the training task.

The advantages of using discovery or exploration-based learning can be understood in terms of the factors that facilitate the learning of principles and the development of schemas outlined above. By removing time constraints, a learner is able to extract similarities and differences, facilitating spontaneous comparison between examples and the schema. During traditional instruction, learners are usually presented with the material they need to know, and hence they have neither the time nor a requirement to compare and contrast the new with the old material. Thus, there is no encouragement for spontaneous comparison and questions.

One of the reasons discovery learning or exploration-based methods are not widely used in industrial contexts relates to concern about the cost of mistakes on expensive equipment and the possibility of physical harm to trainees or others in the work area. One way of overcoming these difficulties is to use simulations during the learning phase. In the context of diagnostic problem solving, reducing the fidelity or completeness of a simulation has in fact been found to produce an improvement in the transfer of performance from training to the real system (Boreham, 1985). Webb and Kramer (1990) found that learning an analogy-based simulation before being exposed to the actual data base was more effective than direct exposure to a specific literal simulation. Simulations that are not identical to real situations may in fact foster schema acquisition. The factors that are important when a skill is being learned are often different from those that operate when the task is performed routinely. Simulation systems allow these differences to be taken into account, thereby maximizing the learning environment (Hesketh, Andrews, & Chandler, 1989; Kamouri et al., 1986).

In short, there are several features of exploration-based or discovery learning that are advantageous in developing schemas. Although the early work on discovery learning arose from an interest in retraining older workers (Belbin, 1969), the ideas are relevant to all age groups. Obviously there are many situations in which exploration-based learning is not appropriate. Certain basic skills do require automation (e.g., keyboard skills), and repeated practice in the form of drill may be suitable; some facts simply need to be memorized, and the strategies such as the use of mnemonics outlined earlier may be appropriate; but when understanding of cause-and-effect relationships is important, and when there are advantages in developing relevant schemas, the approaches typical of discovery or exploration-based learning offer clear advantages.

Artificial Intelligence and Cognitive Science

Not surprisingly, training in the use of computer-based systems, particularly software packages, has received extensive attention in recent years (e.g., Gist, Rowen, & Schwoerer, 1988). More is known about the nature of the errors made during such learning because of the capacity of the computer to record in detail every action of a learner (Frese & Altmann, 1989). An increasing number of studies have asked subjects to verbalize while carrying out various functions, providing insight into the cognitive models learners use to drive their actions (Annett, 1988). Some of these studies, examining the ways in which examples are used, were reviewed earlier (Chi et al., 1989; Lewis, 1988).

In the area of expert systems and artificial intelligence, system developers attempt to analyze, in extreme detail, various tasks and actions in order to build simulations. Developers of expert systems are concerned first with acquiring knowledge of various types of expertise and then converting this knowledge into a computerized system so that the expertise can be generalized to other settings. In other words, developers of expert systems access knowledge and decision-making

procedures in order to facilitate the transfer of the knowledge to new applications. Here again, we see an illustration of the importance of transfer. Technologies have developed around the area of knowledge acquisition that should be relevant to psychologists. Gains (1987), writing about knowledge engineering, suggests that one of the ways in which people can acquire knowledge about knowledge is to examine closely the acquisition process (see Clement, 1992, for an example). Gains (1987) mentions different types of learning procedures that knowledge engineers could explore, including how the learning environment is managed, how examples are used, trial-and-error learning, and analogical reasoning. These are the issues that concern us in industrial training. Zeitz and Spoehr (1989) illustrate the ways in which designers of computer-based learning systems take into account the best structures to use, not only to facilitate the acquisition of the particular domain-specific knowledge, but to improve learners' thinking skills generally. Even computer-based training systems should address how best to train for immediate skills while also improving more general learning and thinking skills to facilitate future learning.

Expert systems researchers are drawing on cognitive psychology, learning theory, and cognitive science (Clement, 1992; Glaser & Bassok, 1989; Mrozek, 1992) in order to develop approaches and produce techniques and models to facilitate the transfer of knowledge. Research in the area of artificial intelligence and cognitive science offers ideas and approaches that industrial psychologists and those interested in training for future technologies can no longer afford to ignore.

Aging and Training

Some of the earliest classic studies on transfer arose in the context of retraining older workers. Entwisle (1959) examined how well adults at various ages who previously drove horse-drawn carriages learned to drive motor vehicles. Shooter, Schonfield, King, and Welford (1956) reported several studies, including one that compared the success at different ages of two different methods used by taxi drivers to learn the location of the streets of London. Tannenbaum and Grenholm (1962) reported the results of an analysis of training data in four U.S. companies that examined differences in learning among younger and older workers. In general, where the new tasks to be learned were not particularly complex and hence little attention was paid to careful selection of trainees, older workers learned less well than younger workers. However, where a task was more complex, resulting in greater care in selecting and briefing appropriate trainees, older workers performed comparably with younger ones. Tannenbaum and Grenholm (1962) also highlighted the role of education as a moderator in the relationship between age and retraining. Older workers with higher levels of general education tended to perform better than their counterparts with less education. Hence much of the poorer performance of older workers could be attributed to their relatively lower level of education compared to younger workers. There were, however, some courses (e.g., optical tooling) in which even educated older workers learned less efficiently than younger workers.

Since these early studies on the adaptability and trainability of older workers, research on the effects of aging on cognitive skills has increased vastly (Bulgaev, 1987; Hotes, 1986; Welford, 1985a, 1985b; see also the chapter by Warr in this volume). In particular, it has been found that age affects performance on speeded tasks and that new learning does take longer (Elias, Elias, & Robbins, 1987). Older people have more difficulty learning material that has no logical or semantic meaning. Welford (1985b) has shown that older people are slower at learning sensory motor tasks that involve complex movements, although they are not affected when the tasks are simple.

Welford (1988) stresses the importance of integrating the knowledge that we have about the effects of aging into the ergonomic design of work environments and retraining programs for adults.

More recent research offers additional ideas to supplement the procedures used in discovery learning (Belbin, 1969), which was designed originally for the conversion training of older workers. For example, Gist et al. (1988) compared a behavioral modeling training method (video based) with a nonmodeling computer-based tutorial method of teaching computer skills to both younger and older workers. The modeling condition consisted of observing a videotape of a middle-aged male demonstrating the use of the spreadsheet. The model sat at the computer, described each step, and then carried out the actual procedure. The results of the actions were then shown by focusing on the computer screen. The procedure involved a "tell then show," not a "show then tell" method as suggested by Baggett (1984, 1987). After each demonstration, the tape was stopped and participants practiced the procedure. The nonmodeling condition involved a typical computerized tutorial, but with exactly the same sequencing as in the video model. Trainees had to successfully perform a function before being able to move on to the next one.

In both conditions older trainees were less efficient in learning to use the spreadsheet than were the younger trainees. The video modeling method was far superior to the computerized tutorial method for both older and younger trainees. Gist et al. (1988) had predicted that the video model would reduce the age effect, but this did not occur. However, the improved performance of both younger and older trainees in the video modeling condition points to the value of using this type of approach to training all workers.

In the fight against obsolescence, managers and many other older workers are going to need to know how to use word processors, spreadsheets, and other computerized software.

Cost-effective methods of training need to be developed that will also foster confidence in future learning. Several ideas from the literature reviewed in earlier sections of this chapter can be used to achieve this.

Training for New Technology: An Australian Illustration

When new technology, particularly computer-based methods, are introduced to a work environment, they often necessitate the use of very different skills from those required before the innovation occurred. This is illustrated in the engineering field where the introduction of numerical control (NC) and computerized numerical control (CNC) machine tools has radically changed the skills required to effectively perform certain jobs in this field. In a field study, Hesketh and Chandler (1987, 1990) described the impact of these systems in several companies in Australia. The analyses were carried out on three large companies and one small company. The companies were selected because of the variety in the nature of their manufacturing work—small-run batch-type jobs to large-scale and long-run production. There was also a range in the level of sophistication of the computer-based equipment used by the three companies.

All companies made use of a mix of old and new technology, a factor that caused considerable difficulty in both training and maintenance. The old technology included lathes, mills, grinders (surface and cylindrical), borers (floor, horizontal, vertical, and jig), and drilling machines. The most frequently used new technology included a wide variety of makes and models of NC and CNC systems, although one company was involved with CAD-CAM systems.

The skills required for the old and new technologies were contrasted. The results were similar to those obtained by Hazelhurst, Bradbury, and Corlett (1969) and Zicklin (1987). Compared with the use of conventional

equipment, NC machines require a reduction in physical effort and motor skills, with an increase in demands for vigilance, monitoring, and conceptual skills. In particular, the programming of NC machines requires many more conceptual skills (Hesketh & Chandler, 1990), especially those that relate to mathematics (e.g., geometry and trigonometry; Chandler, Waldron, & Hesketh, 1988). Furthermore, since standard keyboards are increasingly used for data entry in NC and CNC systems, simple keyboard skills are also important to overcome the search-and-peck methods typically used.

In addition to charting the changes in skill requirements that follow from the introduction of NC and CNC machines, the field research provided an opportunity to examine the methods of training that were being used (Hesketh & Chandler, 1990) and to identify several blockages to learning (Hesketh & Chandler, 1987). The blockages identified included (a) a high level of anxiety when workers were first introduced to expensive equipment, (b) lack of keyboard skills, (c) inappropriate methods of training, particularly when first being exposed to equipment, and (d) insufficient mathematical background for learning NC programming.

Two major lines of research arose from the field studies. The first examined methods of training that fostered self-efficacy (Bandura, 1977, 1982) in switching on and starting up complex equipment. The second line of research examined methods of teaching mathematics to middle-ability students, those likely to enter the trade area. Since mathematics are a critical filter in learning NC programming, it seemed particularly important to examine ways of developing mathematical self-confidence.

One study examined how best to introduce trainees to equipment to foster a sense of mastery and self-efficacy. According to Bandura (1977, 1982), successful accomplishment is the most powerful method of developing self-efficacy and hence is likely to be important in fostering subsequent confidence in learning to operate other similar equipment (Hill et al., 1987). In a simple laboratory study (Hesketh & Chandler, 1988), three methods of training in the initial start-up procedures and basic operations on an EMCO NC training lathe were compared. The three methods were a traditional show *and* tell, which involved showing while telling; a videotape demonstrating the same instructions and procedures; and a method that involved show *then* tell, in which the instructor separated each demonstration from the verbal description of each procedure.

We predicted that the traditional show-and-tell method would result in the lowest task-specific self-efficacy and test performance, and that the show-then-tell method would provide the best results. These predictions were based on several theoretical considerations. First, with show and tell the trainee's gaze is likely to be directed at the eyes of the trainer rather than on the screen and panel, which contain important information. Argyle (1967) has shown that people look at a speaker while listening. The problem of the direction of the gaze can be overcome through the use of video, with the camera focusing on the important bits of the equipment while the instructor speaks. The show-then-tell method also overcomes the direction-of-gaze problem. Second, the show-and-tell and video methods may result in divided attention because of the need to process visual and verbal information simultaneously (Logan, 1979). Baggett (1984, 1987) reports studies that suggest greater retention when visual information precedes verbal information.

In each of the three conditions, 8 males and 8 females (a total of 48 subjects) received training. The training methods were compared in terms of subsequent performance and task-specific self-efficacy ratings for the steps involved in turning on, starting up, and performing basic operations on the system. For males, the show-then-tell method was better than video-based instruction, which was better than

show and tell on both the performance and self-efficacy measures. Interestingly, for females, performance and self-efficacy in the video-based instruction condition was much lower than in either of the other two training methods. We suspect that the equipment was highly novel for the female subjects and that they had difficulty translating what they saw on video to the real equipment. As predicted, the performance of the females was better in the show-then-tell method of training than in the show-and-tell (Hesketh & Chandler, 1988). The data provided support for abandoning traditional methods of show and tell in favor of the show-then-tell method when complex screens and keyboards are involved.

Incidentally, there is an additional advantage in using a show-then-tell method of training with complex procedural tasks when dealing with non-English-speaking workers. Language difficulties tend to increase the tendency to look closely at the face of the person speaking (with the hope of picking up extra cues), yet this is counterproductive when visual information must be processed to learn how to do the task.

The second line of research examined whether removing time constraints during learning improved mathematics self-efficacy. Because of the importance of mathematics to NC programming, a study was designed to examine the effect of solving mathematics problems on both performance and self-efficacy under timed or untimed conditions (Chandler, 1989). The results showed that for students of average ability (the group most likely to enter trade training), time constraints produced worse performance and lower math self-efficacy. This result was not found for high- or low-ability students; high-ability students have sufficient spare capacity to cope with time constraints and the low-ability students were unable to cope with the problems irrespective of the time constraints. Gattiker (1990) also found that middle-ability groups were most negatively affected by time pressure in a task involving microcomputer literacy skills. Further research is needed to examine the effect of ability levels and the interaction of ability and time constraints on the quality of what is learned. Much of the current research in cognitive psychology makes use of university students as subjects, individuals who would fall in the higher ability levels. For industrial applications, additional research using a wider cross-section of the population is essential.

Transfer of Training Generally

Traditionally, the phrase *transfer of training* was used to apply to the generalization of learning from the training context to the work situation (Baldwin & Ford, 1988; Baldwin & Magjuka, 1991). Factors that might affect the efficacy of transfer include trainee characteristics (ability, personality, motivation), the training design (methods used, content, and the extent to which generalizable skills were achieved), similarity between the training and work environment, and the work environment itself (the support and opportunity to use the skills learned; Baldwin & Magjuka, 1991).

In dealing with the importance of training for transferable skills, the emphasis of the literature reviewed in the earlier sections of this chapter is on methods of training that facilitate the extraction of principles and that develop learning skills. These approaches help to make future learning easier, but do not address directly the problems of generalizing from the learning environment to the work environment. Baldwin and Ford (1988) rightly point to the relevance of some approaches in clinical and counseling psychology to training in a manner that will enhance the transfer of skills back to the working environment. Examples cited include the buddy system, in which trainees are paired to reinforce each other in order to maintain their learning, and the use of booster sessions. Relapse prevention, used in clinical treatment, is exactly what trainers in industrial settings should be aiming to achieve (Marx, 1982). Cognitive and behavioral strategies are available that

can be used to guard against relapse and to increase persistence, but few of these have found their way into the industrial literature. One hopes that the increased interest in training for transferable or generalizable skills will assist all forms of training in the goal of maximizing transfer.

Dawis and Lofquist (1984) and Greenhaus (1987) suggest that one should carefully look at the nature of the reinforcers in the training environment and compare them with those functioning in the work environment. Behaviors being reinforced in the training environment may not be maintained in the work environment because of differences in the nature of reinforcement available in the two environments. The classic International Harvester study (Fleishman, 1953) bears witness to this. Problems associated with the generalizability of training are also implicit in many of the issues raised in the next section of this chapter, which is on culture training.

Culture Training

A broad overview of the topic of culture training, as well as a survey of the relevant literature, has already been provided by Triandis in chapter 2 of this volume. Rather than duplicate that material, in this section we will instead concentrate on the major issues, refer to some of the literature not covered by Triandis, and then describe one particular approach to culture orientation consistent with the general model of training being developed in this chapter. The section ends with a practical illustration from a recent Australian training application.

Between-society Culture Training

In the introduction to this chapter we distinguished within-society from between-society work-related cross-cultural contacts.

The bulk of the training literature deals with the preparation and orientation of persons intending to work or study abroad. This is not surprising because culture training is a costly business, and only institutions that have the resources and hope to gain some benefit from the process will engage in it. Historically, the research into and development of between-culture training programs came into being when large Western organizations developed global interests and started to deploy their employees to overseas branches and subsidiaries. To give some idea of the magnitude of the globalization of industry and commerce, about 100,000 American companies have overseas business dealings. Of these, 25,000 have offices abroad or are affiliated with a foreign organization, and 3,500 are major multinational companies. One-sixth of the jobs in the United States depend on foreign trade (Cascio, 1992).

Two unexpected consequences of globalization soon became apparent. First, workers who were effective in their home countries did not necessarily exhibit the same qualities overseas, so that predeparture performance could not be used as a predictor of competence in a different cultural setting (Guthrie, 1975). Second, even though an employee might appear on the company books as an individual, most workers are in fact members of a closely knit social group, the nuclear family. This tends to be ignored by most Western institutions because the financial costs of this neglect are usually not very substantial in home-based industries. But a very different picture soon emerged in the case of multinational companies. Even if employees soon adjusted to their new cultural environment and began to perform adequately, the family often continued to suffer from culture shock. Theoretically, this is to be expected because adaptation to a new environment is a function of the psychological distance between the culture of origin and the new culture (Babiker, Cox, & Miller, 1980; Furnham & Bochner, 1986). Employees tend to move around in different worlds than their

families; the difference between working in an air-conditioned office in New York and one in Bangkok is less extreme than the difference between a New Jersey supermarket or schoolroom and their Thai counterparts.

In practice, this meant that two months into a five-year contract, sometimes the executive, spouse, three children, two cars, sundry household appliances, billiard tables, and four-poster beds had to be shipped back to their port of origin. More precisely, in 1983, the direct costs to an American company for one expatriate family's early return was estimated at $70,000 (Rippert-Davila, 1985). A more recent and detailed analysis of the cost components of the failure to complete an overseas assignment include the price of the initial recruitment, relocation expenses, repatriation and resettling costs, replacement costs, and the losses resulting from poor performance. According to Cascio (1992), when an overseas assignment fails, it costs a company at least 2.5 times the employee's base salary.

The available research, summarized by Arvey, Bhagat, and Salas (1991), confirms that problems within the family circle are one of the major contributors to employee failure or poor performance abroad. Arvey et al. (1991) go so far as to suggest that the spouses and children of potential international employees should be included in the selection process to assess their ability and willingness to function in an unfamiliar physical and cultural milieu, but note that this is rarely done.

According to Harris and Moran (1987), the executive search company Korn/Ferry International has experienced repatriation rates that could reach up to 50 percent in some instances. Other studies support the conclusion that between 20 and 50 percent of personnel on foreign assignment return prematurely (Torbiorn, 1982; Tung, 1987). So, when the accountants did their sums, the sending organizations realized that they had a problem on their hands, but the solution to this day is rather elusive, as the literature on culture orientation indicates (see Triandis' conclusion in chapter 2 of this volume).

Perhaps that is why many companies simply do not bother with training. Inman (1985) surveyed 300 American multinationals that sent executives abroad. The Far East was the second most frequent destination after Western Europe. Inman reports that 23 percent of the companies gave no cultural training whatsoever to their employees prior to departure; 31 percent had no official policy on training; and in those companies in which predeparture cultural training was conducted, it averaged only 16 hours per employee. Other surveys reviewed by Harris and Moran (1987) confirm that cross-cultural training is not a high priority among American multinational companies.

Hindsight and the application of a more rigorous theoretical analysis of the problem than is customary in this area give some hints about why culture orientation did not live up to its expectations. Initially, the solution was considered to be in the domain of improving selection for overseas service. Probably the largest single group ever exposed to a systematic orientation program was the U. S. Peace Corps. In the sixties and seventies, tens of thousands of Peace Corps volunteers from the United States were dispatched to most parts of the less-developed world to engage with local counterparts in community welfare projects. The Peace Corps has a special place in the culture contact literature because, almost uniquely and virtually from its inception, the program was monitored, evaluated, partly guided, and written up by a large team of psychologists (Guthrie, 1975, 1981; Guthrie & Zektick, 1967; J. G. Harris, 1973; M. B. Smith, 1966; Textor, 1966). Of interest here is what the data have to say about the role of selection for overseas service.

The Peace Corps kept good records, which enabled Harris (1973) to calculate attrition rates for the decade 1961 to 1971. Attrition was defined as those volunteers who quit or were repatriated before their tour of duty had ended. The results showed that the worldwide attrition rate exceeded 40 percent in seven of the years listed, and in the text Harris reckons that 50 percent is probably closer to the real figure. Bear in mind that we are dealing with volunteers who were mostly young, idealistic, and part of a well-funded and organized government program. The high attrition rate stimulated a great deal of research into its determinants. Initially, the Peace Corps had devoted most of its social science resources to selection, but it became obvious that neither self-reports of personality (Mischel, 1984) nor predeparture effectiveness back home were able to predict successful performance abroad.

Of all of the psychologists working with the Peace Corps, George Guthrie (1975, 1981) was the most explicit in declaring selection to be useless, backing up his judgment with hard supporting data. For instance, in one prospective study (Guthrie & Zektick, 1967), the ratings by the final selection board of 278 volunteers headed for the Philippines were correlated with the performance of those volunteers in the field as rated by local Filipinos. The obtained correlation was .004, and peer ratings of the volunteers taken during training, as well as tests of interests and abilities, likewise lacked predictive power. In another prospective study, Guthrie (1981) collaborated with a team of psychiatrists who identified six individuals whom they considered to be at risk; all six went to the Philippines and completed their tours without serious difficulties, whereas three other volunteers who had shown no indication of any symptoms during training returned prematurely. Guthrie concluded that it was not possible to predict the performance of the volunteers in alien cultural settings.

The reason we have dwelt here on the Peace Corps experience is that it has implications for selection and training in general. One advantage of going cross-cultural in psychological research is that by so doing the phenomenon under investigation often becomes enlarged, and aspects that are normally obscured come into high relief (Bochner, Brislin, & Lonner,

1975). In speculating about why selection in the Peace Corps failed, Guthrie came to the conclusion that it was due to the qualitative discontinuity between the predictive and criterion settings, which would explain why what worked in one cultural environment did not and could not be expected to work in an entirely different one. Technically, the data indicated that most of the variance in performance in the field was due to situational influences and only a small amount of the variance was due to the enduring personality characteristics of the volunteers. In the intervening years, there has appeared a large body of literature on the buffering effects of social support against stress (Argyle, 1987; Cohen & Wills, 1985; Furnham & Bochner, 1986; Kessler, Price, & Wortman, 1985; Rodin & Salovey, 1989), providing a theoretical basis for these early empirical findings.

The practical implication for culture orientation of the principle of situational primacy is to concentrate on providing post-entry and continuing social support during the early stages of the assignment abroad, in the phase when the person is engaged in learning the culture. And because any employee joining a new company can be regarded as entering a new and unfamiliar environment, we feel that this principle is also applicable to training schemes in general, not just second-culture orientations.

It follows that during the transition period, one of the conditions contributing to the reduction of the attrition rate (or labor turnover, as it is more commonly called in within-culture settings) will be the continuing on-the-job support that the person receives. Usually this is not done systematically—new employees receive their training from those old hands willing to take on this role. Studies have shown that an excellent source of culture training is the old hand serving as a cultural mediator (Bochner, 1981). A few programs have deliberately adopted this technique (Furnham & Bochner, 1986; Guthrie, 1981; Mestenhauser,

1983), but the old hands largely remain an underutilized source of orientation.

We are not suggesting that all work-related selection is useless. Clearly, it makes sense to give preference to applicants with particular qualifications for jobs that require specific technical skills, whether this be basic literacy and numeracy for future bank tellers, logical reasoning for computer programmers, or mechanical aptitude for aircraft mechanics. Arvey, Bhagat, and Salas (1991) list five criterion domains that should feature in an expatriate selection system. They are (a) the technical skills associated with the performance of the job, including administrative and managerial competence; (b) personal qualities, such as tolerance for ambiguity, behavioral flexibility, nonjudgmentalism, cultural empathy, and low ethnocentrism; (c) appropriate motivation, such as a belief in the task, congruence with the person's career path, an interest in gaining overseas experience, and an interest in the specific host country and its culture; (d) a supportive family situation; and (e) language skills, in particular some acquaintance with the host country's language.

In a recent study of repatriated U.S. staff, Dunbar (1992) found that the possession of culturally relevant knowledge and skills and appropriate goals for undertaking the overseas assignment were significantly related to general satisfaction with the sojourn abroad. It seems, from this and other studies (e.g., Bochner, 1981), that the preconditions for success in an overseas assignment are broadly as stated. But how do you go about actually using that information in deciding who should or should not be sent abroad? Based on the validity generalization literature, there is ample evidence that selecting for cognitive abilities is both feasible and highly desirable. But what the cross-cultural literature does highlight is that selecting for personality attributes is a waste of time, in the sense that there is no hard evidence to support the validity of the process and the resources of organizations would be better spent in the provision of on-the-job training and support on a continuing basis.

Training for Cross-cultural Work-related Competence

To some extent, predeparture training suffers from the same conceptual difficulties as predeparture selection. We will now briefly review and provide a critique of the major existing approaches to training (for a fuller treatment, see Brislin, Landis, & Brandt, 1983). The limitations of the current techniques reflect the lack of a sound theory of cultural competence, a confusion not unknown in industrial and organizational psychology, where it comes under the heading of the criterion problem. We will then propose a clearly stated criterion of intercultural competence and suggest a training approach that is consistent with those criteria.

Information Giving.   The most common form of cross-cultural orientation consists of providing persons intending to work or study abroad with information about their destination. Travelers are given facts and figures about the climate, food, customs, and social relations through lectures, booklets, or films. There are several reasons why the effectiveness of such cognitively based programs is limited. The facts tend to be too general, so that their application to particular situations is not always self-evident; they tend to emphasize the exotic, such as the existence of ancestor worship, rather than providing more down-to-earth information on how much to tip in a restaurant. More generally, fact-giving programs tend to convey a mostly superficial, incoherent, and misleading view of a society, fail to deal with its more fundamental aspects, and give the false impression that a culture can be learned instantly. Because the approach is trainer-centered, the program director decides what should go into the course, so that the curriculum may

not necessarily coincide with the needs of the traveler. Finally, even if the facts are retained, they may not lead to action, or to the correct action.

Cultural Sensitization.   The aim of programs based on the principle of cultural sensitization is to make people aware of what the anthropologists have called the *doctrine of cultural relativity*—namely, that very few human values are absolute and universal. Empirically, there is no doubt that different societies have different norms of behavior. It is also the case that, due to the process of primary socialization, people will acquire the belief that their particular customs are true and correct and that anyone not following those practices is in error. Self-awareness programs aim to bring home the fact that value judgments have this cultural bias.

Two procedures that have been widely used to develop awareness of cultural differences are the Contrast-American and BAFA BAFA simulations (for a fuller description of the methods and their origins, see Gudykunst & Hammer, 1983). In the Contrast-American role-play, a series of situations is created in which Americans interact with an actor who has been trained to manifest values and assumptions that are in marked contrast to those of the trainee; this is followed by a discussion period. In the BAFA BAFA game, trainees are randomly divided into two teams representing hypothetical cultures that differ in their core values. The groups are given names (Alpha and Beta), receive written descriptions of the customs of their respective societies, and are then sent off into separate rooms where they are instructed to learn their new cultures, in an analogy of the process of primary socialization. After this phase, the groups exchange visitors, so that members of the Alpha culture interact with members of the Beta culture in visiting as well as host roles. This is followed by a discussion period. The game may last up to four hours and is said to be an effective method of achieving cultural awareness. Other methods in addition to the Contrast-American and BAFA BAFA games exist, based on a similar rationale (for a recent listing and description see Harris & Moran, 1987).

However, even if people intellectually come to accept that values are culture-bound, it may still not persuade them to adopt practices they regard as abhorrent. The problem is that when the chips are down—meaning when fundamental rather than trivial values are involved, particularly if there are also behavioral consequences—most people will revert to their primary socialization. One of the authors of this chapter, who has written learnedly on the construct of cultural relativism (e.g., Bochner, 1979), once offended his Filipino hosts by declining to join them to watch a cockfight, a popular recreational pastime in that country. More generally, greater mutual understanding does not necessarily lead to greater mutual sympathy and respect; indeed, the opposite can and does occur. Still, in practical terms, travelers who do have an understanding of the concept of cultural relativity and develop a culturally sensitive orientation to their host culture will be more effective or at least get into less trouble than the legendary ugly Americans or Australians.

Isomorphic Attributions. Effective intercultural relations—indeed, effective interpersonal relations in general—require making isomorphic attributions of each other's behavior, which in practice means "I explain their behavior in the same way as they would to themselves." As a general principle, when the distance between the subjective cultures (Triandis, 1975) of the participants increases, so does the likelihood of making nonisomorphic attributions. The proposed solution to this problem is to train people in each others' subjective cultures, using a programmed learning manual called the *culture assimilator* (Fiedler, Mitchell, & Triandis, 1971; Foa & Chemers, 1967).

Each booklet contains descriptions of unsatisfactory encounters between culturally different individuals. The reader is then given a choice of several alternate explanations of what went wrong, corresponding to different attributions. Only one of the attributions is correct from the perspective of the culture being learned, although the other attributions are plausible and consistent with the learner's own culture. The learners are told to select the answer they think is the correct one and are then instructed to turn to a subsequent page, where they are praised if they have selected the right answer or told why they were wrong if they had chosen one of the incorrect alternatives. This method is teacher-centered and cognitively based. Furthermore, a great deal depends on which particular incidents are included in the assimilator, whether the incidents are relevant to the particular learner, and more generally, whether there is in fact sufficient host culture consensus about their solution.

Experiential Learning. Cognitively based, teacher-centered information-imparting programs may be relatively easy to develop and administer, but their effect on the trainee is rather limited. This has led to the development of learning-by-doing programs, in which trainees are systematically exposed to real or simulated second-culture encounters. Once again, the Peace Corps led the way in the seventies when they built a model Southeast Asian village on the island of Hawaii, staffed by natives of the target countries. American volunteers stayed in this village for awhile and were given a supervised experience of what it is like to live in rural Asia. Most organizations do not have the resources to provide experiential learning at such a high level of realism. In practice, behaviorally based culture training programs consist of role-played encounters between trainees and actors pretending to be, or better still being members of, the target culture. Some of the more elaborate programs also contain an evaluation component, with psychologists measuring and fine-tuning the subsequent field performance of the candidates (Textor, 1966). In industrial and organizational psychology, there is a long tradition of using simulations in the training of managers (for a recent review, see Thornton & Cleveland, 1990), but not for cross-cultural competence.

Learning by doing, particularly if it is accompanied by cognitive information, ought to be more effective than mere information giving. But even here, as Triandis (1975) has pointed out, what evidence there is does not provide unequivocal support for the procedure, although some studies have shown experiential learning to be superior to other methods (McDaniel, Jr., McDaniel, & McDaniel, 1988). One limitation of most existing experiential learning techniques is that they are still teacher-centered, with the trainer deciding what is to go into the program. To put this matter into perspective, a recent review by Black and Mendenhall (1990) of 29 empirical studies evaluating the effectiveness of cross-cultural training came up with only qualified support for the claim that current training programs are able to enhance cross-cultural performance and adjustment. Certainly training is better than no training at all, but the difference is often not very dramatic. Some of the reason for the gap between promise and delivery will be referred to later in this chapter, together with suggestions on how the effectiveness of cross-cultural training might be increased.

Social Skills: Student-centered Culture Training. In the discussion so far, we have identified two major limitation of most existing culture training approaches. The literature on selection revealed that personality traits do not, and to some extent cannot, predict effectiveness in a second culture. The literature on training revealed that many current programs rely heavily on the one-way imparting of cognitive information that is teacher-centered. Since selection and training are, or should be, inextricably linked, the construction of integrated programs must overcome these two limitations in a systemic fashion.

Let us return to the issue of selection by having another look at the criterion variable, meaning what it is that we are selecting for. Most existing programs are rather vague on this point. The goals are usually stated in general terms and will sound familiar to the readers of this *Handbook*, invoking as they do the traditional twin concerns of industrial and organizational psychology: improving organizational efficiency and increasing personal satisfaction, goals which in the cross-cultural training literature are expressed in terms of increasing the on-the-job effectiveness of the travelers and reducing their culture shock. But exactly how these aims are to be achieved is not made explicit, reflecting the absence of a systematic rationale (Hannigan, 1990). That, too, should be a refrain familiar to industrial and organizational psychologists, although recent developments in job analysis procedures are beginning to provide a more focused approach to this problem.

More basically, the construct of culture adjustment contains three separate strands that are often confounded in the literature: (a) a subjective, intrapsychic component, referring to the development of feelings of well-being, with its roots in clinical psychology; (b) the development of realistic perceptions, expectations, and attitudes, with its roots in social cognition models; and (c) a behavioral, interpersonal, interactive component, with its roots in social learning theory, referring to the ability of the traveler to achieve second-culture competence and fit into the social structures of the new society. Although the three categories of variables may be correlated, they are conceptually distinct. It is also likely that progress through the three domains will be at a different rate.

When adjustment is defined as developing positive feelings and perceptions, the literature indicates that the process by which travelers arrive at that state is U-shaped (Church, 1982; Deutsch & Won, 1963; Gullahorn & Gullahorn, 1963; Lysgaard, 1955; Selltiz & Cook, 1962; Torbiorn, 1982). Typically, on arrival, travelers will experience feelings of optimism and excitement, which soon give way to a period of frustration and confusion. This in turn is followed by a gradual improvement in mood, leading to greater satisfaction with their new lives. However, adjustment defined as second-culture competence would presumably follow the conventional incremental linear progression found with most learning tasks, and not a curvilinear one. This discrepancy in the change rates and patterns of the two variables has some interesting theoretical consequences that are beyond the scope of this chapter to explore. For instance, does the descent into gloom serve to motivate or inhibit culture learning, and are there critical values of discomfort that affect this process? We are not aware of any empirical studies dealing with this issue.

To give a sharper focus to the problem, Bochner (1986a, 1986b) has suggested that, for the purpose of training, the most useful conceptualization of the overseas stay is to regard it as a process of culture learning, and that the problems and their solutions reside in the transactions between the individuals and their other-culture counterparts, rather than in the intrapsychic condition of the traveler. This model of culture shock disentangles and extricates the construct from its clinical origins, locates it in the social psychology of culture contact, and defines cultural adjustment primarily in terms of achieving competence (Dinges, 1983), with appropriate perceptions and expectancies playing a supporting role in that process.

In particular, cross-cultural competence is taken as a special case of being socially skilled (Argyle, 1982), reflecting the more basic principle that when individuals interact, they are in effect engaged in a mutually organized, skilled performance. Argyle (1989) defines social competence as an individual's ability to produce the desired effects on others in social situations. In work-related settings, these skills come into play in the actions of managers, supervisors, and sales personnel, and in selection and appraisal interviews, setting targets and arousing motivation, chairing meetings, negotiating, and presenting material to an audience. In more general terms, the model regards individuals who are socially inadequate as not having mastered the conventions of their society, either because they are unaware of the prevailing rules of social behavior or because they are unwilling to abide by them. Turning this idea around suggests the interesting possibility that people newly arrived in an unfamiliar culture will be in the same position as the indigenous socially inadequate individual.

The implication of this model for selection is that it draws attention away from the search for the desirable but elusive personality characteristics that are supposed to predict adaptation to a second culture. Rather, the research effort is directed at testing the much more plausible assumption that the enabling condition for second-culture success is a capacity and a willingness to learn new social skills. This is very similar to the notion of *learning to learn*, which was described earlier in this chapter in relation to developing generic, learning, decision, and transfer skills. Selecting for adaptation to a second culture can now be demystified and placed within a more general framework of work-related competence. To the extent that selection has a role to play, its function will be to identify prospective travelers who are trainable, with respect to both job-related and culture-related skills.

The implications of the social skills model for training are equally explicit. If culture shock is attributed to a character disorder that assumes travelers with "weak" personalities will succumb to second-culture stress, then training efforts tend to concentrate on the often futile and ethically dubious practice of trying to change people's attitudes and self-concepts. Another characteristic of this approach is to deal with a vague, heterogeneous collection of work-related contacts, rather than concentrating on deliberately selected instances. If, however, culture shock is attributed to a social skills deficit, then training efforts can be deployed to teach specific, culturally relevant behaviors known to be lacking in the person's repertoire. Furthermore, such training programs by their very nature tend to be at least in part student-centered because the content has to be tailored to the needs of the trainees. Finally, behaviorally oriented interventions lend themselves more readily to empirical outcome evaluations, a most desirable component of any applied procedure. As Guthrie (1977) has written, "if a supplementary school feeding program is accomplishing its objectives the results should show up on a set of bathroom scales rather than attitude scales" (p. 137).

Many specific work-related social skills and attitudes are highly culture-bound. These include leadership behavior, such as the use of sanctions, reasoning, appeals to higher authority, friendliness, assertiveness, and coalition formation, all of which differ cross-culturally (Schmidt & Yeh, 1992); leadership style (Rubin, DeHart, & Heintzman, 1991; P. B. Smith, Peterson, Misumi, & Bond, 1992); corporate communication patterns and networks (Erez, 1992); and determinants of job satisfaction (Kumara, Hara, & Yano, 1991; Shwalb, Shwalb, Harnisch, Maehr, & Akabane, 1992).

Strategies of conflict resolution and resource allocation (Bond, Leung, & Schwartz, 1992; Leung, Au, Fernandez-Dols, & Iwawaki, 1992; Lind & Earley, 1992) are also culturally determined, and bargaining style has been found to vary across cultures, causing tension among culturally unaware negotiators (Adler, Doktor, & Redding, 1986; Morley, 1981). Cognitive information processing also varies cross-culturally. According to Adler et al., the Japanese prefer to go from the general to the specific, whereas Westerners like to get the details out of the way before tackling the larger issues. Role plays could be readily devised to develop these particular skills. The cognitive style of field independence (Witkin, 1967) has been found to vary cross-culturally among managers and technicians (Gruenfeld

& MacEachron, 1975), being positively related to a country's economic development.

There are cross-cultural differences in how people perceive technological and other risks (Kleinhesselink & Rosa, 1991; Vaughan & Nordenstam, 1991; Watson & Kumar, 1992), a variable that has implications for the decision-making process. Hofstede (1986) has shown that teaching and learning strategies differ cross-culturally. This will lead to difficulties in any learning situation in which the teachers and students come from markedly different backgrounds, unless the gap is acknowledged and then closed with suitable remedial action. The involvement of managers with their families varies cross-culturally (Misra, Ghosh, & Kanungo, 1990), another potential source of trouble in culturally diverse workplaces. In another study, Furnham and Bochner (1982) asked 150 foreign students in Britain how much difficulty they had experienced in each of 40 different social situations. The ten most difficult categories of encounters all involved establishing and maintaining personal relationships with English people, consequently isolating the visitors from the host community. This diagnostic study provided empirical justification for constructing a training program around personal-relationship episodes. We will present another example of such program development later in this chapter.

More generally, the models, theories, approaches, procedures, and solutions generated by Western industrial and organizational psychology do not readily transfer to non-Western settings (Bochner, 1992). This has profound consequences for the effectiveness of those overseas operations that have installed a replication of their head office management systems without taking into account local cultural variations.

The Training of Trainers. Up to now we have been discussing the training process as it affects travelers. However, culture training is not a self-service activity, but is conducted and administered by specialists, although we have not been able to ascertain exactly how many practitioners there are. They must number in the thousands worldwide, and yet surprisingly little has been written about how these people are selected, trained, and regulated. One exception is an article by Paige (1986), which discusses this topic. It is beyond the scope of this chapter to go into details, except to mention the major issues, which include ethical considerations and the various criteria that distinguish competent cross-cultural trainers, including their personal attributes. The reader is referred to Paige (1986) and Paige and Martin (1983) for a comprehensive account. Incidentally, the training of trainers is an issue that has just as much relevance in monocultural work settings as it does in cross-cultural ones (Downs & Perry, 1984).

Within-society Culture Training

As we stated earlier, the bulk of the training literature refers to the problems of the traveler. However, in the nineties there will certainly be a greater demand for within-society culture training, as work forces become more culturally diverse in those societies accepting immigrants. Following is a brief description of such a project.

An Australian Example.   Due to a local shortage of skilled information systems personnel, a major bank has resorted to a deliberate policy of recruiting its computer programmers from overseas. The bank recognized that this culturally diverse work force could have unforeseen effects and approached us (Bochner & Hesketh, in press) to set up a training program to forestall any problems that might arise. The resulting study is therefore unusual in that the intervention was proactive and preventive rather than palliative and reactive, which tends to be the norm in these matters. In keeping with the diagnostic approach whose virtues were extolled earlier, the study went through several stages.

In stage 1, individual managers were interviewed to find out what work-related problems, if any, they attributed to cultural differences. In stage 2, group discussions were held with several work teams in which staff involved gave examples of culturally affected, job-related problems. In stage 3, a questionnaire was constructed based on both empirical and theoretical considerations. Many of the items reflected the topics that had emerged from our observations and interviews, but there were also items derived from Hofstede's (1980) model of cross-cultural differences in work-related values. In particular, there were questions relating to the individualism/collectivism and power distance components of the model (for a fuller account of these concepts, see Shackleton & Ali, 1990; Triandis, 1989, 1990; Triandis, Bontempo, & Villareal, 1988).

The questionnaire was administered to over 400 staff in the information systems division of the bank, taking care to sample for ethnicity, status in the hierarchy, and gender. The aims were to determine the generality of the problems uncovered by the earlier case studies, whether there were any systematic effects due to the three demographic conditions and whether these interacted with the Hofstede factors. On the basis of this information the fourth stage was devised, but for practical reasons the implementation was deferred. The planned fourth phase consisted of role plays and social skills exercises aimed at particular problems known to exist amongspecific sections of the work force. These included cultural differences in job-related help-seeking and help-giving, relationships with superiors and subordinates, between-gender interactions and attitudes, and differences in values and perceptions (e.g., the Southeast Asians thought that Australians did not work as hard as other groups; some of the workers of non-English speaking backgrounds felt that their prospects for promotion were negatively affected by their cultural status).

Summary

The nineties will see a further increase in work-related cross-cultural contacts as many societies become more culturally diverse and international trade and commerce expands. These trends will be accompanied by a corresponding increase in the demand for culture training programs. One of the uncompleted tasks in this area is to establish clear criteria for cross-cultural work-related competence, and the social skills model may provide a useful framework in that regard. Ideally, culture training programs should proceed through a diagnostic, implementation, and evaluation cycle, and they should consist of tailor-made, behaviorally oriented, experiential learning exercises that provide the trainees with specific culturally related social skills lacking in their repertoire.

The first two major sections of this chapter dealt with training. In the introduction we referred to the requirement for career planning to be closely integrated with training programs particularly when the aim is to use trainee-centered approaches. The willingness of individuals to seek out and participate in training will be determined by their subjective view of how it relates to their career structure and prospects. Career planning provides the missing link because it makes the potential benefits of training explicit; it therefore has the capacity to increase motivation for learning.

Career Planning and Decision Making

Vocational psychology is increasingly drawing on and being integrated with industrial and organizational psychology. This is evidenced in review articles in the *Journal of Vocational Behavior* (Fitzgerald & Rounds, 1989; Morrow, Mullen, & McElroy, 1990) and the growing body of research on organizational career development (Arthur, Hall, & Lawrence,

1989; Greenhaus, 1987; Stout, Slocum, & Cron, 1988; Wakabayashi, Graen, Graen, & Graen, 1988). Integration is particularly relevant in the current climate of organizational restructuring, which means that career planning is required throughout life while training becomes an integral part of career development.

Implications of Change for Career Planning

Restructuring has radically altered the job opportunity structure, with major consequences for individuals' career plans. The changing needs and expectations of individuals during the career life cycle are not being matched by the changes occurring in society (Herriot, 1992; McEnrue, 1989). For example, many people who had linear career aspirations for hierarchical promotions (Brousseau, 1990) are finding that these cannot be met because of flatter organizational structures and the increase in contract work (Offermann & Gowing, 1990).

Currently, organizations want greater flexibility, and consequently, they no longer wish to be in the business of managing the careers of their employees. In part, this is because it is no longer possible to guarantee security and promotions in return for motivation, commitment, and loyalty. Since this implicit exchange has been an informal part of many work contracts in the past, there is a sense in which employees perceive that a psychological contract has been broken (Herriot, 1992; Rousseau, 1990). Understanding the nature of the psychological contract helps to throw light on the intensity of feelings that surround job loss and restructuring (Rousseau & Anton, 1991). In the current climate, individuals need to be in a state of watchful anticipation for organizational changes that can be predicted and must develop skills for dealing with those that are unexpected. In particular, they can no longer assume that their careers will be taken care of by the organization, and in order to survive, they will need to become expert self-managing career planners.

However, as highlighted by Herriot (1992), organizations cannot leave their employees to cope with the increased requirements for flexibility and self-reliance without providing developmental support. Organizations will need to help individuals make the necessary transitions. It is in the interest of organizations to provide this developmental support because in the future their success may depend on (a) how they manage to motivate staff under new work arrangements, (b) how well they can arrange a mix of tenured and contract staff to deal flexibly with change (Barker, 1990), and (c) how well they use training approaches that develop staff with flexible and transferable skills. These are the issues that have informed the discussion that follows on how to adapt career planning approaches to deal with the changed circumstances.

Career Development Theories and Frameworks

Many of the current theories of career development (Brown & Brooks, 1990) can be adapted to deal adequately with increased change. In recent years there has been a renewed interest in person–environment fit and interaction models, as indicated by several special issues of the *Journal of Vocational Behavior* (Vol. 31, No. 3, in 1987; Vol. 40, No. 2, in 1992; and one on the theory of work adjustment, in press). Perhaps the most widely known model is that of Holland (1985), who describes environments and people in terms of six major types: Realistic, Investigative, Artistic, Social, Enterprising, and Conventional. Although Holland's theory is useful, it fails to separate motivational preference factors, such as interests, from the supply factors, such as abilities, and hence it is unable to provide a comprehensive framework for adult career development. Furthermore, it does not have a process component capable of dealing with change. The Minnesota theory of work adjustment (Dawis & Lofquist, 1984) is a more comprehensive person–environment interaction model that has many similarities to Holland's theory but is better able to deal with change processes (Dawis, in press; Hesketh & Dawis, 1991).

The theory of work adjustment (Dawis & Lofquist, 1984) provides a structure for assessing both people and jobs and for evaluating the relationship between people and their work in terms of satisfaction, satisfactory performance, and tenure. According to the theory, tenure—the length of time an individual remains in an environment—is a function of how satisfied a person is and how well he or she is performing in the environment. Satisfaction, in turn, is related to the extent to which an environment offers outlets for an individual's needs, interests, and values. Satisfactory performance is related to the extent to which the requirements and demands of the environment are matched by a person's performance capabilities and limitation. Style variables deal with the ways in which organizations and individuals are mutually responsive to the requirements and supplies of the other. The style variables address adjustment and change and describe processes that are similar to those of Arthur and Kram (1989). The model is sufficiently general to provide a framework for career development, rehabilitation, occupational health, selection, training, and ergonomics (Hesketh, in press; Hesketh & Dawis, 1991).

The theory of work adjustment is particularly useful in accounting for problems that arise from work transitions and from change in either the individual or the work setting. Transitions may be from school or university to work, from unemployment to a job, from one job or contract to another, or from work to retirement. Change may also occur without a physical move. The widespread introduction of computer-based technologies into the workplace has resulted in jobs changing while the workers adjust (Downs, 1985).

Furthermore, the skills, abilities, needs, and values of individuals may alter during their life cycle, all introducing possible mismatches. The source of the discrepancy can be identified by assessing and comparing people and environments before and after change or before and after a transition. Identifying the cause of a mismatch is often an important first step in responding to it.

There are four major assessment domains that are common to many theories of career development (Dawis & Lofquist, 1984). Information in relation to these four variables is critical to understanding transitions and to decision making about any work contracts or other career-related issue. Interestingly, they are also the four areas of information that employers should consider in selection decision making (Hesketh, 1993; Hesketh & Robertson, 1993). The four factors are:

- Individual requirements—their needs, interests, and values

- Individual supplies—their skills, abilities, and work-related experience

- Employer requirements for skills and abilities and the likely ways in which these might change in the future

- Employer supplies in terms of what they have to offer and what outlets are provided for interests, values, and needs

The information must also be utilized effectively, giving rise to additional requirements:

- Decision-making skills to integrate the four types of information in order to choose a sensible course of action

- Implementation skills relevant to marketing oneself effectively

- Transition skills to manage a transition once it occurs

These steps can be summarized in a simplified graphic form (after Watts & Herr, 1976) as indicated in Figure 2.

Adults should regularly ask themselves, What do I want? What do other employers, including my own, want? What have I to offer to my own employer and other employers? And what do employers, including my own, have to offer? These are also the questions to ask in relation to negotiating a contract. People may need formal procedures such as psychological tests and job analyses to help them obtain accurate answers to these four questions and may also need decision-making aids such as balance sheets (Janis & Mann, 1977; Mann, 1989) and computerized decision programs (Hesketh, Gleitzman, & Pryor, 1989) to integrate the information, once obtained. Finally, in light of the changes in the nature of work contracts, implementation and transition skills will be used frequently and throughout life.

A major aspect of transition involves adaptation and adjustment. The Minnesota theory of work adjustment has a systems component (Dawis, in press) in which dissatisfaction on the part of either party provides the driving force to initiate active and reactive modes of adjustment aimed at reducing any discrepancy between the individual and the work context. Typical adjustment strategies initiated by individuals or employers include training, ergonomic interventions, job redesign, and the renegotiation of work arrangements (Hesketh & Dawis, 1991; Rounds & Hesketh, in press). If individuals are to use skill acquisition and training as part of their career management and adjustment strategy, it will be important that they construe new learning as an opportunity rather than as a threat (Ashford, 1988). For example, Martocchio (1992) found that when training in microcomputers was framed as an opportunity rather than as having neutral outcomes, motivation to participate was higher.

The Minnesota theory of work adjustment is also relevant to adjustment following a

FIGURE 2

Graphic Representation of Career Planning Steps

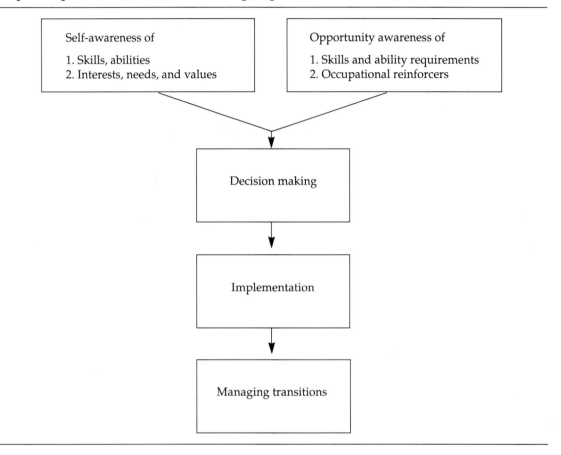

major transition, such as from school to work, from university to work, or from one job to another. Nicholson (1984) presents an alternate but similar model relevant to the mini-transitions that occur in career development. Both the theory of work adjustment and ideas arising from Nicholson's model were used together with research findings to outline practical suggestions for dealing with transitions. We will discuss these using the university-to-work transition as an example.

Career Transition Management

The shift from university to corporate life offers one example of a major career transition. Nicholson and Arnold (1989a, 1989b) identified two primary sources of disillusionment and frustration for new graduates. The first related to the inflated expectations on the part of graduates generated prior to joining the organization. The second related to misallocation and mismanagement of early tasks and roles in the organization. Inflated expectations were generated in part by selection processes and in part by the graduates' general expectations of life in a large corporation.

Similar themes emerged in a study involving 100 graduate employees in a large Australian bank (Hesketh & McLachlan, 1991). Of the 100 graduates, 30 felt that their jobs in the bank involved a compromise of their career plans, with compromise perceptions being related to lower levels of satisfaction (particularly with opportunities to use skills and abilities, outlets for enterprising interests, and the prestige level of their work). Compromise was also associated with higher intentions to leave the bank. Graduates had a number of expectations about the bank (such as it providing challenging work, regular job rotations, and good training) that were not met once they commenced work. This was a major source of dissatisfaction.

One solution to the problem of overcoming frustrated expectations is to be more applicant-centered in the provision of relevant job information during the selection process (see the discussion on realistic job previews given later). Drawing on relevant literature and findings from the Australian study, Hesketh and McLachlan (1991) outlined methods that an organization such as a bank might adopt in order to overcome some of the transition difficulties experienced by graduates. Table 1 provides a summary of these suggestions together with ways in which graduates themselves could prepare for the transition. Several of the issues raised in the table will be discussed presently as mechanisms for integrating the individual and the organizational perspective.

Integrating the Individual and Organizational Perspective

The Minnesota theory of work adjustment applies equally to individual career and organizational selection decisions. Both parties need good information to make decisions, and an awareness of the information needs of the other can only facilitate the outcome for both. Traditionally, selection has not taken into account the individual perspective, with the realistic job preview literature (e.g., McEvoy & Cascio, 1985; Wanous, 1992) offering the only exception. Individuals need to know realistically what the organization has to offer them in the short and the long term and what it requires of them. Information of this sort will help establish realistic expectations (Wanous, Poland, Premack, & Davis, 1992) by helping applicants self-assess whether there are sufficient outlets for their needs, interests, and values, and whether they have the skills and abilities needed to perform effectively.

Herriot (1989) argues that selection is a process of negotiating and establishing a contract. Recruitment and selection procedures constitute the first stage of a developing psychological contract between an individual and the organization. As such, these procedures offer the opportunity to convey expectations about the role that the applicants will play in the organization. One way of formalizing the provision of realistic information is through the use of realistic job previews (Dugoni & Ilgen, 1981; McEvoy & Cascio, 1985; Wanous, 1992;). A realistic job preview refers to the information given to applicants about important aspects of the job. Both positive and negative information must be supplied, without any distortions (Dugoni & Ilgen, 1981). Unfortunately, several recent reviews have appeared that conclude that realistic job previews have only modest effects on satisfaction and turnover (e.g., McEvoy & Cascio, 1985; Premack & Wanous, 1985; Wanous, 1992). A closer examination of these studies reveals that the previews have a greater effect when the jobs are more complex. Thus, in positions such as a supermarket checkout clerk, the realistic job previews do little to add to what applicants already know about the job. However, in more complex jobs, the preview information can be helpful to applicants. The success of the realistic job preview in more complex jobs may

TABLE 1

Managing Graduate Transitions

What the Individual Can Do	*What the Organization Can Do*
Prior to taking a job, seek out realistic information about work done by other graduates, type of stressors encountered, ways of coping, and typical speed of job rotation and progression	As part of recruitment and selection provide realistic job preview information about the nature of the work to be done (initially and later), likelihood of encountering resentment toward graduates, and ways of coping with resentment and *typical* career paths (Herriot & Wingrove, 1984; Hesketh & McLachlan, 1991)
Prepare for work by acquiring basic employability skills, such as telephone and interpersonal skills and basic business sense (Fitzgerald, 1986)	
Once on the job, seek out opportunities to use and develop skills acquired during tertiary training; volunteer for projects or become involved in professional associations (Hesketh & McLachlan, 1991)	Use the interview and recruitment generally to communicate expectations and start the process of negotiating a contract with potential recruits (Herriot, 1989)
	Make some use of graduate skills, perhaps by setting "assignments" in the first year of employment
Read about the role of mentors in career development and look for opportunities to use mentors in own career (Kram, 1985; Noe, 1988)	
Proactively seek feedback once on the job in order to help clarify role requirements (Ashford & Cummings, 1985)	Allocate a mentor to each graduate, particularly in early years (Nicholson & Arnold, 1989a, 1989b)
	Provide regular feedback to graduates, who may be used to more frequent and specific feedback in educational settings than is typically available in organizations

relate to its role in the development of anticipatory coping behavior. Dilla (1987), based on the work of Gommersall and Myers (1966), points to the potential role of previews in the provision of information about how to cope in the initial period on a job. In this respect, the approaches are not dissimilar to the use of relapse prevention strategies in training (Marx, 1986), in which difficulties that are likely to arise in the work context are anticipated and methods for dealing with these are developed.

One problem for the realistic job preview approach is that some evidence suggests that career decision makers bias the processing of information to fit the preliminary decisions that they have already made. For example, applicants may not give sufficient weight to the negative information included in a realistic job preview if they have already decided that they want the job (Blustein & Strohmer, 1987; Gati & Tikotzki, 1989). Clearly there is a need for more research about the ways in which individuals process the information provided in realistic job previews. Nevertheless, realistic job previews do offer the opportunity for organizations and individuals to cooperate in making appropriate selection and career decisions and in anticipatory preparation for transition difficulties. The role of the previews may be much broader. Realistic information of this sort could be used to help staff anticipate difficulties following organizational restructuring and mergers. They could also be used to help overcome unrealistic expectations about the content and outcome of training courses and to convey sufficient information to help overcome any perceived threat in training.

Career Plateauing

Although increased change and frequent transitions are likely to place strain on career planning, it is well documented that insufficient change can also be debilitating, especially if change was expected as part of career progression (Buunk & Janssen, 1992; Caplan, 1987; Nicholson & West, 1988). Currently, many people are having to come to terms with the reduced promotion prospects resulting from organizational restructuring and the increase in contract work. Even though some employees may not have lost their jobs in the wake of downsizing, many may feel they have plateaued.

Career plateauing is defined as the point in a career where the likelihood of additional hierarchical promotions is very low (Ference, Stoner, & Warren, 1977). Organizational career plateauing occurs because there are insufficient positions higher up the hierarchy. Individual plateauing is the result of the person not having the skills and abilities required for higher position. As indicated earlier, organizational career plateauing is on the increase. Individual plateauing is likely to occur if workers fail to keep up with the requirements for new skills in an increasingly technologically sophisticated environment. Subjective feelings of plateauing are also likely to increase, since many adults currently in midcareer came to expect a rapid sequence of promotional opportunities because of their earlier experiences of easy progress during the heady days of economic growth in the sixties and early seventies (Brousseau, 1990). Several writers have suggested that a key factor in the success of organizations in the future will be the manner in which they are able to deal with plateaued staff (Greenhaus, 1987).

Although there is a growing body of literature on career plateauing (Feldman & Weitz, 1988; Gerpott & Domsch, 1987), many of the findings are contradictory, some suggesting devastating motivational consequences for individuals (e.g., Near, 1980), others finding that plateauing may be healthy in certain circumstances (Levinson, 1986; Near, 1985). The most common research approach involves examining differences between plateaued and nonplateaued employees (e.g., Bardwick, 1986; Slocum & Cron, 1985). These studies suggest that nonplateaued people are more concerned with the exploration and establishment stages in their careers and have a future orientation. Plateaued employees are more concerned with the maintenance stage, with holding on to what they have got, than they are with seeking new challenges.

Bardwick (1986) suggested that career-plateaued individuals initially pass through a resistance stage, which is followed by a feeling of resignation or a reluctant acceptance of the plateaued state. During the resistance stage, initially motivation may be high as staff work hard and keep trying to meet promotional criteria, but after they come to realize that their efforts lead nowhere, there is a tendency to withdraw from work and become passive. Significantly, Evans and Gilbert (1984) found that supervisors and managers gave less feedback to plateaued than to nonplateaued staff.

Eventually, plateaued employees have lower aspirations for promotions, work shorter hours, and produce less work (Evans & Gilbert, 1984). They also tend to report interacting with a significantly larger number of people outside their work than nonplateaued people (Gerpott, Domsch, & Keller 1986). It would appear that one of the adaptive responses to plateauing from the individual's perspective is to devalue the role of work. Methodologically, much of the research on plateauing lacks rigor, and it is not surprising that data are inconsistent. The first difficulty relates to obtaining an index of plateauing. Measures can be objective, such as an examination of salary curves and promotions, or subjective, such as individuals stating that they have plateaued. Furthermore, one might expect individuals to differ in their responses to plateauing, depending on whether they are innovators or adaptors (Dawis & Lofquist, 1984; Kirton, 1987).

We would argue that, to date, the research into career plateauing has failed to integrate predictions with the more general career development theories such as the Minnesota theory of work adjustment (Dawis & Lofquist, 1984). In order to understand plateauing, it will be necessary to make use of person–environment fit and interaction models. The descriptive taxonomy of career plateauing offered by Feldman and Weitz (1988) can easily be understood within this framework. Plateauing results from nontransitions, yet neither people nor jobs are stable, and hence mismatches may occur simply because of the passage of time. An interesting extension of the person–environment fit ideas relates to examining the correspondence between career path preferences and the availability of career paths.

Career Paths

Within Australia there is much discussion about the need to create career paths for all levels in an organization. The structural efficiency principle in the 1988 national wages case (Stilwell, 1988) identified career paths as one of the essential components of award restructuring. The use of the term *career path* in this context refers to ongoing opportunities for skill development and potential increases in earnings. Whether industry will be able to live up to the expectations outlined in the structural efficiency principle is doubtful. However, expectations have been raised at all levels, and there is a growing demand for professionalization

of all forms of work. We have recently become acquainted with the training and recruitment of security guards, a large area of employment receiving almost no attention in the industrial and organizational psychology literature. It would appear that one of the reasons for the high turnover among guarding personnel relates to the lack of status given to the work, a feature that is associated with poor training opportunities and insufficient pay and career prospects.

Career paths for Australian academics too are changing. Entrekin and Everett (1981) examined the relationship between age and academics' attitudes toward their careers. Cosmopolitanism (an outward orientation) and an emphasis on teaching were related to age. Among the 45- to 50-year age group there was a decreased emphasis on teaching and an increased cosmopolitan orientation. Academic institutions in Australia have not been immune from changes occurring in organizations. Entrekin and Everett (1981) are in the process of repeating their study ten years later, and the results will provide an opportunity to identify any changes in career attitudes and orientations that have occurred over the past decade.

A major concern among professional engineers in Australia, as in several other countries, relates to the lack of career paths for those with a high level of technical expertise. The lack of a technical career path often requires that the engineer switch to management for adequate promotion. Hesketh, Gardner, and Lissner (1992) interviewed 150 senior and trainee engineers and found that the managerial career path was usually perceived as the most readily available, although preferences for a technical career path or for research opportunities were stronger. The managerial career path was perceived as carrying more status, money, and power than a technical career path. Senior engineers who were in the career path that matched their preference were more satisfied than those in a path that did not correspond to their preferences. Based on a review of the literature and interviews with the senior and trainee engineers, suggestions for dealing with the inherent conflict between the technical and managerial career path were outlined. These included job rotation with incentives to management for keeping up their technical skills, review of the job evaluation systems, encouragement of research opportunities with recognition for publications, and more technical and managerial training (Hesketh et al., 1992).

The problem of insufficient incentives for technical work encountered in this organization is common in other areas of Australian industry. If a country is to develop its technology base, it will need to recognize and reward technical competence. Job evaluation systems may well be the source of these difficulties. Interestingly, a recent issue of the professional newsletter for engineers in Australia (*The Professional Engineer*, 1990, Vol. 44, No. 1) outlined advice to members about how to respond to job analyses and job evaluation interviewers. The concern expressed by the engineers was that those conducting the job analyses had little basis for understanding the technical complexity of the work performed and hence were unable to provide sufficient detail to ensure that the jobs received appropriate evaluation. In support of the engineers' argument, Taber and Peters (1991) found that technical staff were the least satisfied with the job evaluation system. This concern is perhaps justified, since job evaluation systems commonly used in Australia do reflect a bias against technical competencies in favor of generalist managerial skills. This bias occurs through the choice of compensable factors and the weightings attached to the factors. These job evaluation systems have probably evolved to reflect the lack of value placed on technical skills in the Australian culture, a feature that does not appear to be a problem in several other countries such as Germany and Japan, where technical skills are valued highly. A cross-cultural study of compensable factors in job evaluation systems offers an interesting way of establishing

cultural differences in values, something that to our knowledge has not been explored.

In this latter part of the chapter, we have examined general career development frameworks that can be adapted to deal with the recurrent transitions and ongoing career change. The discussion has covered issues and research relevant to career transitions, the role of realistic job previews, career plateauing, and career paths. Throughout, an attempt has been made to integrate the individual and organizational perspective in the context of change. Before summarizing areas for future research, we would like to draw attention to a novel approach to measurement that offers a way of assessing flexibility in career assessment, performance measurement, and possibly in evaluating training.

Fuzzy Preferences and Perceptions

A novel approach to measurement has arisen out of research testing Gottfredson's (1981) theory of career compromise. In order to measure zones of preference, a computerized fuzzy graphic rating scale was developed that allows respondents to specify a preferred point on a modified semantic differential and to indicate asymmetrical latitudes of acceptance on either side of the most preferred point (Hesketh, Elmslie, & Kaldor, 1990; Hesketh, McLachlan, & Gardner, 1992; Hesketh, Pryor, Gleitzman, & Hesketh, 1988). An example follows.

Ask yourself which job you would prefer, one that:

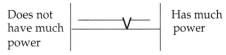

Does not have much power | Has much power

This rating mechanism can be used with several different anchors and provides a basis for assessing fuzzy preferences and job perceptions. The fuzzy rating procedure encourages individuals to recognize that preferences can be flexible and that job environments are also flexible, something that may become increasingly important to work adjustment in the future. The computerized nature of the measure means that personally relevant attributes or values can be entered into a decision structure (Hesketh et al., 1990). Traditionally, the content of factors to be considered in career decision making have been derived from research in countries with a Western orientation. The use of computerized fuzzy ratings makes it easy to include personally relevant attributes and to adapt the content of measures when assessing preferences, interests, and values among people from different cultures.

Another possible advantage of the fuzzy rating lies in its potential to capture distributional information. For example, in performance appraisal, there is some evidence that distributional ratings contain more valid information (Steiner, Rain, & Smalley, 1992). With respect to training, one might expect that changes could occur in the distribution or variability of attributes as well as in mean scores (Kraiger & Ford, 1992). It is possible that traditional training outcome measures have not been sufficiently sensitive to these types of changes.

Summary and Suggestions for Future Research

In this chapter we have sought to bring together ideas relevant to training and career planning in a context of technological and social change, an aging work force, and increased contact between cultures. Although we have chosen to focus on training and career development, we are aware that other areas of industrial and organizational psychology also need to adapt to the accelerated pace of change and that problem solving requires attention to all areas of industrial and organizational psychology. This is demonstrated graphically in Figure 1, presented at the start of the chapter.

Drawing on research in cognitive psychology, several ideas were presented about ways

of developing learning skills and training for transferable skills. In particular, we gave considerable attention to approaches that help learners extract schemas and acquire an understanding of underlying principles. We do not pretend that the literature reviewed is comprehensive; there is an ever increasing body of research in cognitive psychology and cognitive science highly relevant to industrial training. Our hope is that our drawing attention to this literature may interest industrial and organizational psychologists in consulting the research being undertaken in these related areas of psychology. We have used Australian examples to illustrate research relevant to the training problems created through the introduction of new technology (e.g., NC machines) and through a multicultural work force.

Several of the training themes identified in the first section of this chapter are taken up in the second section dealing with work-related culture training. The approach to culture training that appears most successful, namely trainee-centered, work-related social skills development, follows principles similar to those found to be successful in developing generalizable and learning skills. We made the point that selection for work in other cultures, and for work more generally, will need to focus on identifying individuals who have the interest and capacity to keep on learning—that is, we should be assessing trainability or openness to experience. It is with these motivational issues in mind that the final section of the chapter dealt with career planning and decision making.

In the final section, we outlined general models of career planning and transition that can apply to the increased pace of change. Drawing on examples of Australian research, we presented ideas for managing the transition from university to work and stressed the role of realistic job previews in integrating the individual and organizational perspective. Finally, we reviewed literature on career plateauing and identified a major problem in Australian industry relating to career paths for technical staff.

Our review of the relevant literature served to raise as many questions as it answered. By way of summary, we will outline possible areas where more research is required.

- *Developing generalizable and transferable skills.* There is a need for laboratory and field studies examining in greater depth the approaches that help or hinder schema acquisition during training, that foster transfer between training context and target situations, and that develop learning skills and adaptability. In particular, research is needed that makes use of subjects other than university or college students. The most effective methods of training vary across ability levels. Unfortunately, much cognitive psychology research makes use of college students, who represent the upper end of the ability levels. Considerable research is also available on methods of training among developmentally delayed individuals. We need to know more about methods that optimize learning among the middle-ability groups who constitute the large pool of employees in industry.

- *Trainee-centered learning.* Research in the area of work-related culture training, and training more generally, identifies the importance of trainee-centered learning. Yet, in practice, few training programs meet this requirement. Perhaps what is needed is research into the reasons related to such resistance: What is it about the training context that makes it difficult for trainers to share control of training with trainees?

- *Cross-cultural issues.* The social skills approach to culture training offers a sound behavioral basis for training in cross-cultural communication, yet systematic evaluation of programs based

on this approach are needed. Other areas, such as an analysis of differences in the compensable factors in job evaluation systems in different countries, offer an interesting indirect way of obtaining information about cultural differences in the nature of work that is valued. There may be a degree to which job evaluation systems perpetuate the status quo with respect to career paths, inhibiting flexibility in the development of required skills.

- *Processing of career-related information.* As individuals take a more active role in managing their own training and career development, and as organizations attempt to provide the required information to help them do this, we will need to understand more fully the biases in the processing of information about the self and job or occupational opportunities. Industrial and organizational psychology offers plenty of real-world settings for testing theories in the field of social cognition and decision making.

- *Career transitions and plateauing.* Carefully planned longitudinal research may help clarify some of the conflicting results arising from the work on career plateauing and the processes of compromise and adjustment. Inevitably, it will be necessary to understand career motivation within a broader context of lifestyle factors, and increasingly to include a sequence of negotiated contracts as part of the career concept.

- *Fuzzy ratings.* There are other areas in which fuzzy ratings could be applied, such as in obtaining distributional performance ratings, in the evaluation of training programs to determine whether training increases flexibility, and in knowledge engineering to elicit imprecise information from experts, to name a few. Further development is required in terms of methods of analyzing and dealing with fuzzy data collected.

The theory and practice of industrial and organizational psychology will need to adapt to the social and technological changes we are experiencing. We have attempted to offer some suggestions of how this might be achieved in at least two major areas of the field, training and career development.

References

Ackerman, P. (1992). Predicting individual differences in complex skill acquisition: Dynamics of ability determinants. *Journal of Applied Psychology, 77*, 598–614.

Adams, J. A. (1987). Historical review and appraisal of research on the learning, retention, and transfer of human motor skills. *Psychological Bulletin, 101*, 41–74.

Adler, N. J., Doktor, R., & Redding, S. G. (1986). From the Atlantic to the Pacific century: Cross-cultural management reviewed. *Journal of Management, 12*, 295–318.

Alliger, G. M., & Janak, E. A. (1989). Kirkpatrick's levels of training criteria: Thirty years later. *Personnel Psychology, 42*, 331–342.

Annett, J. (1988). Motor learning and retention. In J. Patrick & K. D. Duncan (Eds.), *Training, human decision making and control* (pp. 371–382). Amsterdam: North-Holland.

Annett, J., & Sparrow, J. (1986). Transfer of training: A review of research and practical implications. *Programmed Learning and Educational Technology, 22*, 116–124.

Argyle, M. (1967). *The psychology of interpersonal behaviour.* Harmondsworth, Middlesex, England: Penguin.

Argyle, M. (1982). Inter-cultural communication. In S. Bochner (Ed.), *Cultures in contact: Studies in cross-cultural interaction.* Oxford, England: Pergamon.

Argyle, M. (1987). *The psychology of happiness.* London: Methuen.

Argyle, M. (1989). *The social psychology of work* (2nd ed.). London: Penguin.

Arthur, M. B., Hall, D. T., & Lawrence, B. S. (Eds.). (1989). *Handbook of career theory.* Cambridge, England: Cambridge University Press.

Arthur, M. B., & Kram, K. E. (1989). Reciprocity at work: The separate, yet inseparable possibilities of individual and organizational development. In M. B. Arthur, D. T. Hall, & B. S. Lawrence (Eds.), *Handbook of career theory.* Cambridge, England: Cambridge University Press.

Arvey, R. D., Bhagat, R. S., & Salas, E. (1991). Cross-cultural and cross-national issues in personnel and human resources management: Where do we go from here? *Research in Personnel and Human Resources Management, 9*, 367–407.

Ashford, S. (1988). Individual strategies for coping with stress during organizational transitions. *Journal of Applied Behavioral Science, 24*, 19-36.

Ashford, S. J., & Cummings, L. L. (1985). Proactive feedback seeking behaviour: The instrumental use of the information environment. *Journal of Occupational Psychology, 58*, 67–79.

Babiker, I. E., Cox, J. L., & Miller, P. M. (1980). The measurement of cultural distance and its relationship to medical consultations, symptomatology and examination performance of overseas students at Edinburgh University. *Social Psychiatry, 15*, 109–116.

Baggett, P. (1984). The role of temporal overlap of visual and auditory material in forming dual media associations. *Journal of Educational Psychology, 76*, 408–417.

Baggett, P. (1987). Learning a procedure from multimedia instructions: The effects of film and practice. *Applied Cognitive Psychology, 1*, 183–195.

Baldwin, T. T., & Ford, J. K. (1988). Transfer of training: A review and directions for future research. *Personnel Psychology, 41*, 63–105.

Baldwin, T. T., & Magjuka, R. J. (1991). Organizational training and signals of importance effects of pre-training perceptions on intentions to transfer. *Human Research and Development, 2*, 25–36.

Baldwin, T. T., Magjuka, R. J., & Loher, B. T. (1991). The perils of participation: Effects of choice of training on trainee motivation and learning. *Personnel Psychology, 44*, 51–65.

Bandura, A. (1977). Self-efficacy: Toward a unifying theory of behavioral change. *Psychological Review, 84*, 191–215.

Bandura, A. (1982). Self-efficacy mechanisms in human agency. *American Psychologist, 37,* 122–147.

Banks, M. H., Jackson, P. R., Stafford, E. M., & Warr, P. B. (1983). The job component inventory and the analysis of jobs requiring limited skill. *Personnel Psychology, 36,* 57–66.

Bardwick, J. (1986). *The plateauing trap.* New York: Amacom.

Barker, R. (1990, March). Changing employee needs—A challenge for employers. *Personnel Today,* p. 6.

Belbin, R. M. (1969). *The discovery method: An international experiment in retraining.* Paris: Organization for Economic Cooperation and Development (O.E.C.D.).

Belezza, F. S., & Buck, D. K. (1988). Expert knowledge as mnemonic cues. *Applied Cognitive Psychology, 2,* 147–162.

Black, J. S., & Mendenhall, M. (1990). Cross-cultural training effectiveness: A review and a theoretical framework for future research. *Academy of Management Review, 15,* 113–136.

Blacker, F. (1988). Information technologies and organizations: Lessons from the 1980s and issues for the 1990s. *Journal of Occupational Psychology, 61,* 113–127.

Blustein, D. L., & Strohmer, D. C. (1987). Vocational hypothesis testing in career decision-making. *Journal of Vocational Behavior, 31,* 45–62.

Bochner, S. (1979). Cultural diversity: Implications for modernization and international education. In K. Kumar (Ed.), *Bonds without bondage: Explorations in transcultural interactions.* Honolulu: University Press of Hawaii.

Bochner, S. (Ed.). (1981). *The mediating person: Bridges between cultures.* Cambridge, MA: Schenkman.

Bochner, S. (1986a). Coping with unfamiliar cultures: Adjustment or culture learning? *Australian Journal of Psychology, 38,* 347–358.

Bochner, S. (1986b). Training inter-cultural skills. In C. R. Hollin & P. Trower (Eds.), *Handbook of social skills training. Vol. 1: Applications across the life span.* Oxford, England: Pergamon.

Bochner, S. (1992). The diffusion of organizational psychology across cultural boundaries: Issues and problems. In J. Misumi, B. Wilpert, & H. Motoaki (Eds.), *Organizational and work psychology.* Hove, England: Erlbaum.

Bochner, S., Brislin, R. W., & Lonner, W. J. (1975). Introduction. In R. W. Brislin, S. Bochner, & W. J. Lonner (Eds.), *Cross-cultural perspectives on learning.* New York: Sage.

Bochner, S., & Hesketh, B. (in press). Power distance, individualism/collectivism, and job related attitudes in a culturally diverse work group. *Journal of Cross-Cultural Psychology.*

Bochner, S., Ivanoff, P., & Watson, J. (1974). Organization development in the A.B.C. *Personnel Practice Bulletin, 30,* 219–233.

Bond, M. H., Leung, K., & Schwartz, S. (1992). Explaining choices in procedural and distributive justice across cultures. *International Journal of Psychology, 27,* 211–225.

Boreham, N. C. (1985). Transfer of training in the generation of diagnostic hypotheses: The effect of lowering fidelity of simulation. *British Journal of Educational Psychology, 55,* 213–223.

Brislin, R. W., Landis, D., & Brandt, M. E. (1983). Conceptualizations of intercultural behavior and training. In D. Landis & R. W. Brislin (Eds.), *Handbook of intercultural training: Vol. 1. Issues in theory and design.* New York: Pergamon.

Broadbent, D. E. (1985). The clinical impact of job design. *British Journal of Clinical Psychology, 24,* 33–44.

Brousseau, K. R. (1990). Career dynamics in the baby boom and bust era. *Journal of Organizational Change Management, 3,* 46–58.

Brown, D., & Brooks, L. (Eds.). (1990). *Career choice and development: Applying contemporary theories to practice.* San Francisco: Jossey-Bass.

Bulgaev, V. N. (1987). Age-related changes in working capacity restricting work performance in the elderly. *Human Physiology, 13,* 198–203.

Buunk, B. P., & Janssen, P. P. M. (1992). Relative deprivation, career issues, and mental health among men in midlife. *Journal of Vocational Behavior, 40,* 338–350.

Caplan, R. E. (1987). Person-environment fit theory and organizations: Commensurate dimensions, time perspectives and mechanisms. *Journal of Vocational Behavior, 31,* 248–267.

Cascio, W. F. (1992). *Managing human resources: Productivity, quality of work life, profits* (3rd ed.). New York: McGraw-Hill.

Castles, I. (1988). *Census 86—Australia in profile: A summary of major findings.* Canberra, Australia: Australian Bureau of Statistics.

Chandler, P. (1989). *The effects of time constraints on mathematical self-efficacy, performance and cognitive problem solving strategies.* Unpublished master's thesis. University of New South Wales, Sydney, Australia.

Chandler, P., Waldron, R., & Hesketh, B. (1988). Math teaching can be relevant: Mathematical problems in NC programming. *The Australian Mathematics Teacher, 44*(1), 28–32.

Chi, M. T. H., Bassok, M., Lewis, M. W., Reimann, P., & Glaser, R. (1989). Self-explanations: How students study and use examples in learning to solve problems. *Cognitive Science, 13,* 145–182.

Church, A. T. (1982). Sojourner adjustment. *Psychological Bulletin, 91,* 540–572.

Clement, R. P. (1992). Learning expert systems by being corrected. *International Journal of Man-Machine Studies, 36,* 617–637.

Cohen, S., & Wills, T. A. (1985). Stress, social support, and the buffering hypothesis. *Psychological Bulletin, 98,* 310–357.

Cook, M. M. (1989). The applicability of verbal mnemonics for different populations: A review. *Applied Cognitive Psychology, 3,* 3–32.

Cooper, G., & Sweller, J. (1987). The effects of schema acquisition and rule automation on mathematical problem solving transfer. *Journal of Educational Psychology, 79,* 347–362.

Dawis, R. V. (in press). Career choice and development theory and the theory of work adjustment. In M. Savickas & R. Lent (Eds.), *Convergence in theories of career choice and development.* Palo Alto, CA: Consulting Psychologists Press.

Dawis, R. V., & Lofquist, L. H. (1984). *A psychological theory of work adjustment.* Minneapolis: University of Minnesota Press.

Department of Immigration, Local Government, and Ethnic Affairs. (1988). *Australia's population trends and prospects.* Canberra, Australia: Australian Government Publishing Service.

Deutsch, S. E., & Won, G. Y. M. (1963). Some factors in the adjustment of foreign nationals in the United States. *Journal of Social Issues, 19*(3), 115–122.

Dilla, B. L. (1987). Descriptive versus prescriptive information in a realistic job preview. *Journal of Vocational Behavior, 30,* 33–48.

Dinges, N. (1983). Intercultural competence. In D. Landis & R. W. Brislin (Eds.), *Handbook of intercultural training: Vol. 1. Issues in theory and design.* New York: Pergamon.

Downs, S. (1985). Retraining for new skills. *Ergonomics, 28,* 1205–1211.

Downs, S., & Perry, P. (1982). How do I learn? *Journal of European Industrial Training, 6,* 27–32.

Downs, S., & Perry, P. (1984). Developing learning skills. *Journal of European Industrial Training, 8,* 21–26.

Dugoni, B. L., & Ilgen, D. R. (1981). Realistic job previews and the adjustment of new employees. *Academy of Management Journal, 24,* 579–591.

Dunbar, E. (1992). Adjustment and satisfaction of expatriate U.S. personnel. *International Journal of Intercultural Relations, 16,* 1–16.

Duncan, K. D., & Reiersen, C. S. (1988). Long-term retention of fault diagnostic skill. In J. Patrick & K. D. Duncan (Eds.), *Training, human decision making and control* (pp. 93–118). Amsterdam: North-Holland.

Elden, M. (1986). Sociotechnical systems ideas as public policy in Norway: Empowering participation through worker-managed change. *Journal of Applied Behavioral Science, 22,* 239–255.

Elias, P. K., Elias, M. I., & Robbins, M. A. (1987). Acquisition of word-processing skills by younger, middle-age and older adults. *Psychology and Aging, 2,* 340–348.

Ellis, H. C. (1965). *The transfer of learning.* New York: Macmillan.

Emery, F. E. (Ed.). (1969). *Systems thinking.* Harmondsworth, England: Penguin.

Emery, F. E. (1977). *The emergence of a new paradigm of work.* Canberra, Australia: Australian National University Press.

Entrekin, L. V., & Everett, J. E. (1981). Age and midcareer crisis: An empirical study of academics. *Journal of Vocational Behavior, 19,* 84–97.

Entwisle, D. G. (1959). Aging: The effects of previous skill on training. *Journal of Occupational Psychology, 33,* 239–243.

Erez, M. (1992). Interpersonal communication systems in organizations and their relationships to cultural values, productivity, and innovation: The case of Japanese corporations. *Applied Psychology: An International Review, 41,* 43–64.

Ericcson, K. A., & Smith, J. (Eds.). (1991). *Toward a general theory of expertise: Prospects and limits.* Cambridge, England: Cambridge University Press.

Evans, M. G., & Gilbert, E. (1984). Plateaued managers: Their need gratifications and their effort-performance expectations. *Journal of Management Studies, 21,* 99–108.

Feldman, D. C., & Weitz, B. A. (1988). Career plateaus reconsidered. *Journal of Management, 14,* 69–80.

Ference, T. P., Stoner, J. A. F., & Warren, E. K. (1977). Managing the career plateau. *Academy of Management Review, 2,* 602–612.

Fiedler, F. E., Mitchell, T., & Triandis, H. C. (1971). The culture assimilator: An approach to cross-cultural training. *Journal of Applied Psychology, 55,* 95–102.

Fitzgerald, L. F. (1986). On the essential relations between education and work. *Journal of Vocational Behavior, 28,* 254–284.

Fitzgerald, L. F., & Rounds, J. B. (1989). Vocational behavior, 1988: A critical analysis. *Journal of Vocational Behavior, 35,* 105–163.

Fleishman, E. (1953). Leadership climate, human relations training, and supervisory behavior. *Personnel Psychology, 6,* 205–222.

Foa, U. G., & Chemers, M. M. (1967). The significance of role behavior differentiation for cross-cultural interaction training. *International Journal of Psychology, 2,* 45–57.

Fotheringhame, J. (1984). Transfer of training: A field investigation of youth training. *Journal of Occupational Psychology, 57,* 239–248.

Fotheringhame, J. (1986). Transfer of training: A field study of some training methods. *Journal of Occupational Psychology, 59,* 59–71.

Frese, M., & Altmann, A. (1989). The treatment of errors in learning. In L. Bainbridge & S. A. R. Quintanilla (Eds.), *Developing skills with information technology.* Chichester, England: Wiley.

Furnham, A., & Bochner, S. (1982). Social difficulty in a foreign culture: An empirical analysis of culture shock. In S. Bochner (Ed.), *Cultures in contact: Studies in cross-cultural interaction.* Oxford, England: Pergamon.

Furnham, A., & Bochner, S. (1986). *Culture shock: Psychological reactions to unfamiliar environments.* London: Methuen.

Gael, S. (Ed.). (1988). *Handbook of job analysis for business, industry and government.* New York: Wiley.

Gains, B. R. (1987). An overview of knowledge-acquisition and transfer. *International Journal of Man-Machine Studies, 26,* 453–472.

Gams, M., Drobnic, M., & Petkovsek, M. (1991). Learning from examples: A uniform view. *International Journal of Man-Machine Studies, 34,* 49–68.

Gati, I., & Tikotzki, Y. (1989). Strategies for collection and processing of occupational information in making career decisions. *Journal of Counseling Psychology, 36,* 430–439.

Gattiker, U. E. (1990). Acquiring microcomputer literacy: Factors affecting end-user training. In U. E. Gattiker (Ed.), *Technological innovations and human resources* (Vol. 2). New York: Walter de Gruyter.

Geller, J. (1991). Propositional representation for graphical knowledge. *International Journal of Man-Machine Studies, 34,* 97–131.

Gentner, D., & Landers, R. (1985). Analogical remindings: A good match is hard to find. *PIEEE proceedings of the International Conference on Cybernetics and Society.* Tuscon, AZ: Institute of Electrical and Electronic Engineers.

Gentner, D., & Toupin, C. (1986). Systematicity and surface similarity in the development of analogy. *Cognitive Science, 10,* 277–300.

Gerpott, T., & Domsch, M. (1987). R & D professionals' reactions to the career plateau: An exploration of the mediating role of supervisory behaviors and job characteristics. *R & D Management, 17,* 103–118.

Gerpott, T. J., Domsch, M., & Keller, R. T. (1986). Career events, communication activities, and working hours investment among research and development employees. *IEEE Transactions on Engineering Management, 33,* 188–196.

Gick, M. L. (1991). Transfer in insight problems: The effects of different types of similarity. In K. J. Gilhooly, M. T. G. Keane, R. H. Logie, & G. Erdos, *Lines of thinking: Reflections on the psychology of thought.* Chichester, England: Wiley.

Gick, M. L., & Holyoak, K. J. (1983). Schema induction and analogical transfer. *Cognitive Psychology, 15,* 1–38.

Gist, M., Rowen, B., & Schwoerer, C. (1988). The influence of training method and trainee age on the acquisition of computer skills. *Personnel Psychology, 41*, 253–265.

Glaser, R., & Bassok, M. (1989). Learning theory and the study of instruction. *Annual Review of Psychology, 40*, 631–636.

Goldstein, I. L. (1986). *Training in organizations: Needs assessment, development and evaluation.* Pacific Grove, CA: Brooks/Cole.

Goldstein, I. L. (1991). Training in work organizations. In M. D. Dunnette & L. Hough (Eds.), *Handbook of industrial and organizational psychology* (2nd ed., vol. 2, pp. 507–620). Palo Alto, CA: Consulting Psychologists Press.

Goldstein, I. L., & Gillam, P. (1990). Training systems issues in the year 2000. *American Psychologist, 45*, 134–143.

Gommersall, E. R., & Myers, M. S. (1966, July–August). Breakthrough in on-the-job training. *Harvard Business Review,* pp. 62–72.

Gottfredson, L. S. (1981). Circumscription and compromise: A developmental theory of occupational aspirations [Monograph]. *Journal of Counseling Psychology, 28*, 545–579.

Greenhaus, J. H. (1987). *Career management.* Chicago: Dryden.

Gruenfeld, L. W., & MacEachron, A. E. (1975). A cross-national study of cognitive style among managers and technicians. *International Journal of Psychology, 10*, 27–55.

Gudykunst, W. B., & Hammer, M. R. (1983). Basic training design: Approaches to intercultural training. In D. Landis & R. W. Brislin (Eds.), *Handbook of intercultural training: Vol. 1. Issues in theory and design.* New York: Pergamon.

Gullahorn, J. T., & Gullahorn, J. E. (1963). An extension of the U-curve hypothesis. *Journal of Social Issues, 9*(3), 33–47.

Guthrie, G. M. (1975). A behavioral analysis of culture learning. In R. W. Brislin, S. Bochner, & W. J. Lonner (Eds.), *Cross-cultural perspectives on learning.* New York: Sage.

Guthrie, G. M. (1977). Problems of measurement in cross-cultural research. *Annals of the New York Academy of Sciences, 285*, 131–140.

Guthrie, G. M. (1981). What you need is continuity. In S. Bochner (Ed.), *The mediating person: Bridges between cultures.* Cambridge, MA: Schenkman.

Guthrie, G. M., & Zektick, I. N. (1967). Predicting performance in the Peace Corps. *Journal of Social Psychology, 71*, 11–21.

Hannigan, T. P. (1990). Traits, attitudes, and skills that are related to intercultural effectiveness and their implications for cross-cultural training: A review of the literature. *International Journal of Intercultural Relations, 14*, 89–111.

Harris, J. G., Jr. (1973). A science of the South Pacific: Analysis of the character structure of the Peace Corps volunteer. *American Psychologist, 28*, 232–247.

Harris, P. R., & Moran, R. T. (1987). *Managing cultural differences.* Houston: Gulf.

Hayes, C., Fonda, N., Pope, M., Stuart, R., & Townsend, K. (1983). *Training for skill ownership.* Sussex, England: Institute of Manpower Studies.

Hazelhurst, R. J., Bradbury, R. J., & Corlett, E. N. (1969). A comparison of the skills of machinists on numerically controlled and conventional machines. *Occupational Psychology, 43*, 169–182.

Herriot, P. (1989). Selection as a social process. In M. Smith & I. T. Robertson (Eds.), *Advances in slection and assessment* (pp. 171–187). Chichester, England: Wiley.

Herriot, P. (1992) Careers in recession? *British Journal of Guidance and Counselling, 20*, 231–238.

Herriot, P., & Wingrove, J. (1984). Graduate preselection: Some findings and their guidance implications. *British Journal of Guidance and Counselling, 12*, 166–174.

Hesketh, B. (1993). Measurement issues in industrial and organizational psychology. In C. L. Cooper & I. T. Robertson (Eds.), *International review of industrial and organizational psychology, 1993.* Chichester, England: Wiley.

Hesketh, B., Andrews, S., & Chandler, P. (1989). Training for transferable skills: The role of examples and schemas. *Education and Training Technology International, 26*(2), 156–165.

Hesketh, B., & Chandler, P. (1987). Training for new technology: Adaptability and developing learning skills. *Training and Development in Australia, 14*(3), 8–10.

Hesketh, B., & Chandler, P. (1988). *A comparison of "show then tell," video based instruction and traditional "show and tell" methods of training.*

Paper presented at the International Congress of Psychology, Sydney, Australia.

Hesketh, B., & Chandler, P. (1990). Training in the use of numerically controlled and computerised numerically controlled systems in industry. In U. E. Gattiker (Ed.), *Technological innovations and human resources* (Vol. 2). New York: Walter de Gruyter.

Hesketh, B., & Dawis, R. V. (1991). The Minnesota theory of work adjustment: A conceptual framework. In B. Hesketh & A. Adams (Eds.), *Psychological perspectives on occupational health and rehabilitation*. Marrickville, Sydney, Australia: Harcourt Brace.

Hesketh, B., Elmslie, S., & Kaldor, W. (1989). Career compromise: An alternative account to Gottfredson's (1981) theory. *Journal of Counseling Psychology, 37*, 49–56.

Hesketh, B., Gardner, D., & Lissner, D. (1992). Technical and managerial career paths: An unresolved dilemma. *International Journal of Career Management, 4*, 9–16.

Hesketh, B., Gleitzman, M., & Pryor, R. (1989). Tailoring computerised interventions to client vocational needs. *British Journal of Guidance and Counselling, 17*, 19–33.

Hesketh, B., & McLachlan, K. (1991). Career compromise and adjustment among graduates in the banking industry. *British Journal of Guidance and Counselling, 19*, 191–208.

Hesketh, B., McLachlan, K., & Gardner, D. (1992). Work adjustment theory: An empirical test using a fuzzy rating scale. *Journal of Vocational Behavior, 40*, 318–337.

Hesketh, B., Pryor, R., Gleitzman, M., & Hesketh, T. (1988). Practical applications and psychometric evaluation of a computerised fuzzy graphic rating scale. In T. Zetenyi (Ed.), *Fuzzy sets in psychology*. Amsterdam, NTLDS: Elsevier Science Publishers.

Hesketh, B., & Robertson, I. T. (1993). Personnel selection: A process model for research and practice. *International Journal of Selection and Assessment, 1*, 3–18.

Hesketh, B., & Shouksmith, G. (1986). Job and non-job activities, job satisfaction and mental health among veterinarians. *Journal of Occupational Behaviour, 1*, 325–339.

Hill, T., Smith, N. D., & Mann, M. F. (1987). Role of efficacy expectations in predicting the decision to use advanced technologies: The case of computers. *Journal of Applied Psychology, 72*, 307–313.

Hofstede, G. (1980). *Culture's consequences: International differences in work-related values.* London: Sage.

Hofstede, G. (1986). Cultural differences in teaching and learning. *International Journal of Intercultural Relations, 10*, 301–320.

Hogan, P. M., Hakel, M. D., & Decker, P. J. (1986). Effects of trainee-generated versus trainer-provided rule codes on generalization in behavior-modeling training. *Journal of Applied Psychology, 71*, 469–473.

Holland, J. L. (1985). *Making vocational choices: A theory of vocational personalities and work environments.* Englewood Cliffs, NJ: Prentice-Hall.

Hotes, R. W. (1986). Aging and productivity: An agenda for OD research. *Organizational Development Journal, 4*(4), 54–58.

Inman, M. (1985). Language and cross-cultural training in American multinational corporations. *Modern Language Journal, 69*, 247–255.

Jandreau, S., & Bever, T. (1992). Phrase-spaced formats improve comprehension in average readers. *Journal of Applied Psychology, 77*, 143–146.

Janis, I. L., & Mann, L. (1977). *Decision-making: A psychological analysis of conflict, choice and commitment.* New York: Free Press.

Jelsma, O., Van Merrienboer, J. J. G., & Bijlstra, J. P. (1990). The ADAPT model: Toward instructional control and transfer. *Instructional Science, 19*, 89–120.

Kamouri, A. L., Kamouri, J., & Smith, K. H. (1986). Training by exploration: Facilitating the transfer of procedural knowledge through analogical reasoning. *International Journal of Man-Machine Studies, 24*, 171–192.

Kanfer, R., & Ackerman, P. L. (1989). Motivation and cognitive abilities: An integrative/aptitude-treatment interaction approach to skill acquisition. *Journal of Applied Psychology, 74*, 657–690.

Kanfer, R., Dugdale, B., Nelson, L., & Ackerman, P. L. (1990). *Goal setting and complex task performance: A resource allocation perspective.* Paper presented at the 6th meeting of the

Society of Industrial and Organizational Psychology, Miami.

Katona, G. (1940). *Organizing and memorizing.* New York: Columbia University Press.

Kessler, R. C., Price, R. H., & Wortman, C. B. (1985). Social factors in psychopathology: Stress, social support, and coping processes. *Annual Review of Psychology, 36,* 531–572.

Kieras, D. E., & Bovair, S. (1984). The role of a mental model in learning to operate a device. *Cognitive Science, 8,* 255–273.

Kirkpatrick, D. L. (1959,1960). Techniques for evaluating training programs. *Journal of the American Society of Training Directors, 13,* 3–9, 21–26; *14,* 13–18, 28–32.

Kirton, M. J. (1987). *Kirton Adaption-Innovation Inventory (KAI) manual* (2nd ed.). Hatfield, Herts: Occupational Research Centre.

Kleinhesselink, R. R., & Rosa, E. A. (1991). Cognitive representation of risk perceptions: A comparison of Japan and the United States. *Journal of Cross-Cultural Psychology, 22,* 11–28.

Kraiger, K., & Ford, J. K. (1992). *Comprehensive training evaluation.* Paper presented at the 7th annual meeting of the Society for Industrial and Organizational Psychology, Montreal.

Kram, K. E. (1985). *Mentoring at work: Developing relationships in organizational life.* Glenview, IL: Scott Foresman.

Kumara, U. A., Hara, Y., & Yano, M. (1991). On understanding behavior characteristics of Japanese manufacturing workers: An analysis of job climate. *International Journal of Intercultural Relations, 15,* 129–148.

Latham, G. P. (1988). Human resource training and development. *Annual Review of Psychology, 39,* 545–582.

Leung, K., Au, Y. F., Fernandez-Dols, J. M., & Iwawaki, S. (1992). Preference for methods of conflict processing in two collectivist cultures. *International Journal of Psychology, 27,* 195–209.

Levinson, D. J. (1986). A conception of adult development. *American Psychologist, 41,* 3–13.

Lewis, C. (1988). Why and how to learn why: Analysis-based generalization of procedures. *Cognitive Science, 2,* 211–256.

Lind, E. A., & Earley, P. C. (1992). Procedural justice and culture. *International Journal of Psychology, 27,* 227–242.

Logan, G. D. (1979). On the use of concurrent memory load to measure attention and automaticity. *Journal of Experimental Psychology Human Perception and Performance, 5,* 189–207.

Lysgaard, S. (1955). Adjustment in a foreign society: Norwegian Fulbright grantees visiting the United States. *International Social Science Bulletin, 7,* 45–51.

Mann, L. (1989). Becoming a better decision maker. *Australian Psychologist, 24*(2), 141–155.

Martocchio, J. J. (1992). Microcomputer usage as an opportunity: The influence of context in employee training. *Personnel Psychology, 45,* 529–552.

Marx, R. D. (1982). Relapse prevention for managerial training: A model for maintenance of behavioural change. *Academy of Management Review, 7,* 433–441.

Marx, R. D. (1986). Development through relapse prevention strategies. *Journal of Management Development, 5,* 27–40.

Mastropieri, M. A., Scruggs, T. E., & Levin, R. J. (1985). Maximizing what exceptional students can learn: A review of research on the keyword method and related mnemonic techniques. *Remedial and Special Education, 6,* 39–45.

McDaniel, Jr., C. O., McDaniel, N. C., & McDaniel, A. K. (1988). Transferability of multicultural education from training to practice. *International Journal of Intercultural Relations, 12,* 19–33.

McDaniel, M. A., & Pressley, M. (1987). *Imagery and related mnemonic processes.* New York: Springer-Verlag.

McEnrue, M. P. (1989). Self development as a career management strategy. *Journal of Vocational Behavior, 34,* 57–68.

McEvoy, G. M., & Cascio, W. F. (1985). Strategies for reducing employee turnover: A meta analysis. *Journal of Applied Psychology, 70,* 342–353.

McGehee, W., & Thayer, P. S. (1961). *Training in business and industry.* New York: Wiley.

McHugh, S. (1989). *Snowy: The people behind the power.* Melbourne, Australia: Heinemann.

Mestenhauser, J. A. (1983). Learning from sojourners. In D. Landis & R. W. Brislin (Eds.),

Handbook of intercultural training: Vol. 2. Issues in training methodology. New York: Pergamon.

Mischel, W. (1984). Convergences and challenges in the search for consistency. *American Psychologist, 39,* 351–364.

Misra, S., Ghosh, R., & Kanungo, R. N. (1990). Measurement of family involvement: A cross-national study of managers. *Journal of Cross-Cultural Psychology, 21,* 232–248.

Morley, I. (1981). Negotiation and bargaining. In M. Argyle (Ed.), *Social skills and work.* London: Methuen.

Morrow, P. C., Mullen, E. J., & McElroy, J. C. (1990). Vocational behavior, 1989: The year in review. *Journal of Vocational Behavior, 37,* 121–195.

Mrozek, A. (1992). A new method for discovering rules from examples in expert systems. *International Journal of Man-Machine Studies, 36,* 127–144.

Murphy, E. D., & Mitchell, C. M. (1986). Cognitive attributes: Implications for display design in supervisory control systems. *International Journal of Man-Machine Studies, 25,* 411–438.

Myake, N., & Norman, D. A. (1979). To ask a question one must know enough to know what is not known. *Journal of Verbal Learning and Verbal Behavior, 18,* 357–364.

National Training Board. (1991). *National competency standards: Policy and guidelines.* Canberra, Australia: National Capital Printing.

Near, J. P. (1980). The career plateau: Causes and effects. *Business Horizons, 23,* 53–57.

Near, J. P. (1985). A discriminant analysis of plateaued versus nonplateaued managers. *Journal of Vocational Behavior, 26,* 177–188.

Nicholson, N. (1984). A theory of work role transitions. *Administrative Science Quarterly, 29,* 172–191.

Nicholson, N., & Arnold, J. (1989a). Graduate entry and adjustment to corporate life. *Personnel Review, 18,* 23–25.

Nicholson, N., & Arnold, J. (1989b). Graduate early experience in a multinational corporation. *Personnel Review, 18,* 2–14.

Nicholson, N., & West, M. (1988). *Managerial job change: Men and women in transition.* Cambridge: Cambridge University Press.

Noe, R. A. (1988). An investigation of the determinants of successful assigned mentoring relationships. *Personnel Psychology, 41,* 457–479.

Noe, R. A., & Ford, J. K. (1992). Emerging issues and new directions for training research. *Research in Personnel and Human Resource Management, 10,* 345–384.

Offermann, L. R., & Gowing, M. K. (1990). Organizations of the future: Changes and challenges. *American Psychologist, 45,* 95–108.

Owen, E., & Sweller, J. (1985). What do students learn while solving mathematics problems? *Journal of Educational Psychology, 77,* 272–284.

Paige, R. M. (1986). Trainer competencies: The missing conceptual link in orientation. *International Journal of Intercultural Relations, 10,* 135–158.

Paige, R. M., & Martin, J. N. (1983). Ethical issues and ethics in cross-cultural training. In D. Landis & R. W. Brislin (Eds.), *Handbook of intercultural training: Vol. 1. Issues in theory and design.* New York: Pergamon.

Pashler, H. (1989). Dissociations and dependencies between speed and accuracy: Evidence for a two-component theory of divided attention in simple tasks. *Cognitive Psychology, 21,* 469–514.

Pava, C. (1986). Redesigning sociotechnical systems design: Concepts and methods for the 1990s. *Journal of Applied Behavioral Science, 22,* 201–221.

Pirolli, P. L., & Anderson, J. R. (1985). The role of learning from examples in the acquisition of recursive programming skills. *Canadian Journal of Psychology, 39*(2), 240–272.

Polumbo, D. B. (1990). Programming language/problem solving research: A review of relevant issues. *Review of Educational Research, 60,* 65–89.

Premack, S., & Wanous, J. (1985). A meta-analysis of realistic job preview experiments. *Journal of Applied Psychology, 70,* 706–719.

Rippert-Davila, S. (1985). Cross-cultural training for business: A consultant's primer. *Modern Language Journal, 69,* 238–246.

Robertson, I., & Downs, S. (1979). Learning and the prediction of performance: Development of trainability testing in the United Kingdom. *Journal of Applied Psychology, 64,* 42–50.

Rodin, J., & Salovey, P. (1989). Health psychology. *Annual Review of Psychology, 40,* 533–579.

Ross, B. H. (1987). This is like that: The use of earlier problems and the separation of similarity effects. *Journal of Experimental Psychology: Learning, Memory and Cognition, 13,* 629–639.

Rounds, J. & Hesketh, B. (in press). The theory of work adjustment: Unifying principles and concepts. In M. Savickas & R. Lent (Eds.), *Convergence in theories of career choice and development.* Palo Alto, CA: Consulting Psychologists Press.

Rousseau, D. M. (1990). New hire perceptions of their own and their employer's obligations: A study of psychological contracts. *Journal of Organizational Behavior, 11,* 389–400.

Rousseau, D. M., & Anton, R. (1991). Fairness and implied contract obligations in job terminations: The role of contributions, promises and performance. *Journal of Organizational Behavior, 12,* 287–299.

Rubin, D., DeHart, J., & Heintzman, M. (1991). Effects of accented speech and culture-typical compliance-gaining style on subordinates' impressions of managers. *International Journal of Intercultural Relations, 15,* 267–283.

Salter, M. J. (1978). *Studies in the immigration of the highly skilled.* Canberra, Australia: Australian National University Press.

Schmidt, S. M., & Yeh, R. S. (1992). The structure of leader influence: A cross-national comparison. *Journal of Cross-Cultural Psychology, 23,* 251–264.

Selltiz, C., & Cook, S. W. (1962). Factors influencing attitudes of foreign students towards the host country. *Journal of Social Issues, 18*(1), 7–23.

Shackleton, V. J., & Ali, A. H. (1990). Work-related values of managers: A test of the Hofstede model. *Journal of Cross-Cultural Psychology, 21,* 109–118.

Shenkar, O. (1988). Robotics: A challenge for occupational psychology. *Journal of Occupational Psychology, 61,* 103–112.

Shooter, M. N., Schonfield, A. E. D., King, H. F., & Welford, A. T. (1956). Some field data on the training of older people. *Occupational Psychology, 30,* 204–215.

Shwalb, D. W., Shwalb, B. J., Harnisch, D. L., Maehr, M. L., & Akabane, K. (1992). Personal investment in Japan and the U.S.A.: A study of worker motivation. *International Journal of Intercultural Relations, 16,* 107–123.

Singley, M. K., & Anderson, J. R. (1985). The transfer of text editing skill. *International Journal of Man-Machine Studies, 22,* 403–423.

Slocum, J., & Cron, W. (1985). Job attitudes and performance during three career stages. *Journal of Vocational Behavior, 26,* 126–145.

Smith, M. B. (1966). Explorations in competence: A study of Peace Corps teachers in Ghana. *American Psychologist, 21,* 555–566.

Smith, A. D. (1977). *Generic skills: Key to job performance.* Ottawa, Canada: Employment and Immigration Commission.

Smith, E. R., & Zarate, M. A. (1992). Exemplar-based model of social judgment. *Psychological Review, 99,* 3–21.

Smith, P. B., Peterson, M., Misumi, J., & Bond, M. (1992). A cross-cultural test of the Japanese PM leadership theory. *Applied Psychology: An International Review, 41,* 5–19.

Steiner, D. D., Rain, J. S., & Smalley, M. M. (1992). *Rating distributions of performance: A new type of rating format.* Paper presented at the 7th annual meeting of the Society for Industrial and Organizational Psychology, Montreal.

Sternberg, R. J. (1988). Applying cognitive theory to the testing and teaching of intelligence. *Applied Cognitive Psychology, 2,* 231–255.

Stilwell, F. (1988, October). Wages: The policy debate and the 1988 national wage decision. *Economics,* pp. 36–39.

Stout, S. K., Slocum, J. W., & Cron, W. L. (1988). Dynamics of the career plateauing process. *Journal of Vocational Behavior, 32,* 74–91.

Susman, G. I., & Chase, R. B. (1986). A sociotechnical analysis of the integrated factory. *Journal of Applied Behavioral Science, 22,* 257–270.

Sweller, J. (1988). Cognitive load during problem solving: Effects on learning. *Cognitive Science, 12,* 257–285.

Sweller, J., Chandler, P., Tierney, P., & Cooper, M. (1990). Cognitive load as a factor in the structuring of technical material. *Journal of Experimental Psychology: General, 119,* 176–192.

Sweller, J., & Cooper, G. (1985). The use of worked examples as a substitute for problem solving in learning algebra. *Cognition and Instruction, 2,* 59–89.

Taber, T. D., & Peters, T. D. (1991). Assessing the completeness of a job analysis procedure. *Journal of Organizational Behavior, 12,* 581–593.

Tannenbaum, A. S., & Grenholm, G. (1962). Adaptability of older workers to technological change: Performance in retraining. *Bulletin of the International Association of Applied Psychology, 2(2),* 73–85.

Tannenbaum, S., & Yukl, G. (1992). Training and development in work organizations. *Annual Review of Psychology, 43,* pp. 399–441.

Tarmizi, R. A., & Sweller, J. (1988). Dual effects of guidance during mathematical problem solving. *Journal of Educational Psychology, 80,* 424–436.

Taylor, F. W. (1911). *The principles of scientific management.* New York: Harper.

Textor, R. B. (Ed.). (1966). *Cultural frontiers of the Peace Corps.* Cambridge, MA: MIT Press.

Thorndyke, P. W., & Hayes-Roth, B. (1979). The use of schemata in the acquisition and transfer of knowledge. *Cognitive Psychology, 11,* 82–106.

Thornton, G. C., III, & Cleveland, J. N. (1990). Developing managerial talent through simulation. *American Psychologist, 45,* 190–199.

Torbiorn, I. (1982). *Living abroad: Personal adjustment and personnel policy in the overseas setting.* Chichester, England: Wiley.

Tornatzky, L. G. (1986). Technological change and the structure of work. In M. S. Pallak & R. P. Perloff, *Psychology and work: Productivity, change and employment* (pp. 53–84). Washington, DC: American Psychological Association.

Triandis, H. C. (1975). Culture training, cognitive complexity and interpersonal attitudes. In R. W. Brislin, S. Bochner, & W. J. Lonner (Eds.), *Cross-cultural perspectives on learning.* New York: Sage.

Triandis, H. C. (1989). The self and social behavior in differing cultural contexts. *Psychological Review, 96,* 506–520.

Triandis, H. C. (1990). Cross-cultural studies of individualism and collectivism. In J. J. Berman (Ed.), *Nebraska symposium on motivation, 1989: Vol. 37. Cross-cultural perspectives.* Lincoln, NE: University of Nebraska Press.

Triandis, H. C., Bontempo, R., & Villareal, M. J. (1988). Individualism and collectivism: Cross-cultural perspectives on self-ingroup relationships. *Journal of Personality and Social Psychology, 54,* 323–338.

Tung, R. L. (1987). Expatriate assignments: Enhancing success and minimizing failure. *Academy of Management Executive, 1,* 117–125.

Turnage, J. J. (1990). The challenge of new workplace technology for psychology. *American Psychologist, 45,* 171–178.

Vaughan, E., & Nordenstam, B. (1991). The perception of environmental risks among ethnically diverse groups. *Journal of Cross-Cultural Psychology, 22,* 29–60.

Verhaeghen, P., Marcoen, A., & Goossens, L. (1992). Improving memory performance in the aged through mnemonic training: A meta-analytic study. *Psychology and Aging, 7,* 242–251.

Wakabayashi, M., Graen, G., Graen, M., & Graen, M. (1988). Japanese management progress: Mobility into middle management. *Journal of Applied Psychology, 73,* 217–227.

Wanous, J. P. (1992). *Organizational entry: Recruitment, selection, orientation and socialization.* Reading, MA: Addison-Wesley.

Wanous, J. P., Poland, T. D., Premack, S. L., & Davis, K. S. (1992). The effects of met expectations on newcomer attitudes and behaviors: A review and meta-analysis. *Journal of Applied Psychology, 77,* 288–297.

Warshouer, S. (1988). *Inside training and development: Creating effective programs.* San Diego: University Associates.

Watson, W. E., & Kumar, K. (1992). Differences in decision making regarding risk taking: A comparison of culturally diverse and culturally homogeneous task groups. *International Journal of Intercultural Relations, 16,* 53–65.

Watts, A. G., & Herr, E. L. (1976). Career(s) education in Britain and the U.S.A.: Contrasts and common problems. *British Journal of Guidance and Counselling, 4,* 129–142.

Webb, J. M., & Kramer, A. F. (1990). Structuring effective worked examples. *Cognition and Instruction, 7,* 1–39.

Welford, A. T. (1985a). Changes of performance with age: An overview. In N. Charness (Ed.), *Aging and human performance* (pp. 333–369). Chichester, England: Wiley.

Welford, A. T. (1985b). Practice effects in relation to age: A review and a theory. *Developmental Neuropsychology, 1,* 173–190.

Welford, A. T. (1988). Preventing adverse changes of work with age. *International Journal of Aging and Human Development, 27,* 283–291.

Wertheimer, M. (1959). *Productive thinking.* New York: Harper & Row.

Witkin, H. A. (1967). A cognitive-style approach to cross-cultural research. *International Journal of Psychology, 2,* 233–250.

Wulfeck, W. H., Ellis, J. A., Richards, R. E., Merrill, M. D., & Wood, N. D. (1978). *The instructional quality inventory: Introduction and overview* (NPRDC Tech. Rep. No. 79-3). San Diego.

Zeitz, C. M., & Spoehr, K. T. (1989). Knowledge organization and the acquisition of procedural expertise. *Applied Cognitive Psychology, 3,* 313–336.

Zicklin, G. (1987). Numerical control machining and the issue of deskilling: An empirical view. *Work and Occupations, 14,* 452–466.

CHAPTER 5

An Underlying Structure of Motivational Need Taxonomies: A Cross-cultural Confirmation

Simcha Ronen
Tel Aviv University, Israel

Cross-cultural studies can serve as an alternate approach to the examination and integration of work motivation theories. This chapter reports research conducted in various countries and cultures. It summarizes the available data pertaining to the taxonomies of various need categories, concentrating on those theories that have been developed primarily in the United States but which have been found to have external validity in other cultures as well. This theoretical integration is based on an analysis of work values and the underlying dimensions that persist across cultures. Applied primarily to need theories, these underlying dimensions suggest a multidimensional structure discernible through multivariate techniques. The chapter suggests that valence categories of various job characteristics form universal dimensions that can serve as a basis for understanding culturally bound organizational reward systems. In order to guide the reader through the assumptions that underlie our conclusions, I will first summarize the relevant theories in the field of motivation. I will begin with basic concepts in motivation, followed by a discussion of their application to the work environment, with an emphasis on need theories, and, finally, I will introduce the rationale for the employment of work values as a justifiable basis for establishing the dimensions of the underlying structures of these theories. These dimensions are based on empirical data reviewed here and are confirmed in other psychological areas. Finally, I will show how these dimensions can help us integrate the various taxonomies of needs in industrial and organizational motivation theories.

Introduction

MOTIVATION THEORIES HAVE been based on the assumption of the pleasure principle, or hedonism, which means that organisms behave in order to increase pleasure and avoid pain. The basic goal of behavior is to maintain a homeostatic balance; in the process, people will strive to maximize positive affect and minimize negative affect. Weiner's (1991) recent review offers a categorization of motivation theories: One group of theories asks the question, "What turns behavior on and off"? Another group of theories asks the question, "What choices do individuals make to maximize their hedonic pursuits"? Weiner points out that the latter group assumes that individuals are perfectly rational, are aware of possible alternative goal-related actions, know the likelihood of each action resulting in goal attainment, and have determined the value of each goal (p. 925). These theories, referred to as *expectancy-value* theories of motivation, were originally represented in the writing of Lewin (1935, 1951), Tolman (1955), Rotter (1954), and Atkinson (1957, 1964).

Weiner (1991) criticizes these assumptions based on claims that people fail to reach decisions that are in their best interest and often make decisions that are not based on rational or normative principles (Dawes, 1988; Tversky & Kahneman, 1974). The tendency of more recent theories, according to Weiner (1991), is "to rely more on emotionality and less on rationality, more on evaluation and less on decision making and choice, and are more focused on the external social world and less on hedonic maximization" (p. 926).

The dilemmas arising between emotionality and rationality, and between subjective evaluation and objective decision-making processes, are also prevalent issues within the area of *work* motivation theories. They have implications not only for the theoretical conceptualization of the theories but also for the operational definitions of these concepts and for the methods of investigation. Within the field of work motivation, different models have also attributed various degrees of emotionality and rational decision making to their conceptualization. Some of the assumptions underlying these theories are relevant to this chapter, particularly those related to needs and valences.

Traditional theories in the industrial and organizational domain, such as need theories and expectancy/valence models, are based on the assumption that people choose and engage in activities that will provide the greatest perceived positive overall value or utility (Kanfer, 1991). Because the assumptions underlying these theories are relevant to the thesis of this chapter, they will be briefly summarized in the next section.

The Role of Needs in Work Motivation Models

I will concentrate now on the domain of the work environment. As expected, work motivation theories have long been a central field of investigation. Katzell and Thompson (1990) have defined work motivation as a "broad construct pertaining to the conditions and processes that account for arousal, direction, magnitude and maintenance of effort in a person's job" (p. 144).

One group of work motivation theories is based directly on the concept of needs. The term *needs* became useful mainly because it did not differentiate between primary and secondary (learned) motives. Murray (1938) defined need as "a force which organizes perception, apperception, intellection, conation and action" (p. 123). Such forces energize and motivate through the creation of a state of tension that an individual attempts to relieve through appropriate actions. They are also "specific in their ability to influence the perceived attractiveness of various actions or outcomes in terms of their ability to relieve tension," according to Campbell and Pritchard (1976, p. 68).

Lewin (1951) developed the conceptual framework that related needs to the perceived attractiveness (incentive) of an activity or an outcome by referring to the latter's *valence*. This paved the way for the incorporation of cognitive deliberation into motivation models, particularly expectancy theory. Although this approach does not exclude the importance of past experience, in terms of the reinforcement properties of an incentive, *it allows needs to be part of the process of establishing a valence for an act or an outcome.*

The incorporation of valence into work motivation theory has become widespread, but with somewhat different theoretical interpretations. The predominant theories during the last decades have used cognitive models of individual motivation for investigating organizational membership and task performance (Hackman & Porter, 1968; Lawler, 1971; Locke, 1975, 1976; Porter & Lawler, 1968; Staw, 1977; Vroom, 1964).

Of the cognitive models, expectancy theory has become a main framework for the study of work motivation. A few similar models have been developed, with some slight variation in terminology among their major proponents (Lawler, 1971; Porter & Lawler, 1968; Staw, 1977; Vroom, 1964). None of them specifies any source or a priori directionality of needs or valences. In using the expectancy model for prediction, only the ultimate perception of the valence of a particular outcome is necessary (multiplied by the expectancy and instrumentality—that is, their perceived probability). Indeed, Vroom (1964), in the original conceptualization of work expectancy theory, does not even discuss drives or needs as sources affecting the degree of importance (valence) that is attached to an outcome. Lawler (1971) and Staw (1977), on the other hand, are very explicit about the theoretical and practical implications of combining instrumentality theory with a theory of needs, primarily because it allows better prediction about the conditions that affect the cognition of outcomes likely to

be valued and the factors that affect those values. These assertions are applicable notwithstanding the question of the stability of these needs (Salancik & Pfeffer, 1977).

In a similar vein, the literature has also emphasized the application of reinforcement models (Bolles, 1967; Skinner, 1971), but some have also delineated the incentive properties of reinforcement (Bindra, 1969; Black, 1969; Campbell & Pritchard, 1976). Surely, in terms of incentives, a model that combines instrumentality theory with a theory of needs can make predictions about conditions that affect the importance of different outcomes (Lawler, 1971; p. 24). Although previous experience assigns importance, through reinforcement, to certain outcomes, it seems reasonable to assume that the rewarding properties of the outcomes must be derived initially from some system of needs and values.[1]

In her thorough review and analysis of motivation theories, Kanfer (1991) categorizes need and expectancy theories under the heading of "Need-Motive-Value Approaches." These approaches stem from internal tension or arousal and view person-based factors as a major determinant of behavior. According to Kanfer, "individual differences in needs and values, as well as activation of commonly held intrinsic motives, are posited to influence the mediating cognitive processes that result in behavioral variability" (p. 83). Because this chapter deals with need theories, a review of the major models is called for.

Maslow's formulation of need theory (Maslow, 1954, 1959) postulates a few basic assumptions:

- A person may experience five distinct need categories: physiological needs, safety needs, belongingness needs, esteem needs, and self-actualization needs.

- These needs are arranged in a declining hierarchy of importance from basic needs to self-actualization needs.

- This hierarchy is manifested in a pre-potency principle, by which a lower-level need—higher in importance—must be satisfied before the next need becomes the energizer of motivational forces.

- The fifth need, self-actualization, is not satiable—it is never fully fulfilled.

- These needs can be considered universal.

Another formulation of need theory is offered by Alderfer's (1969) existence-relatedness-growth theory (ERG). Alderfer empirically identified three needs that encompass the five needs suggested by Maslow. However, in contrast to Maslow's prepotency principle based on a set hierarchy of needs, Alderfer proposed that the three needs may operate simultaneously and, furthermore, that the dynamic of attributing importance to a need is such that it may shift from a frustrated need, the fulfillment of which is perceived to be unattainable by the environment, to either a lower-level (regression) or upper-level need.

As we will see later, some of the reasons for the recent declining interest in these theories, following the period of their popularity during the 1960s and the 1970s, are associated with the failure to obtain additional empirical support.

In summary, we may conclude that the concept of needs, in addition to being fundamental to the original need motivation models, is also compatible with, and possibly useful for, motivation theories based on cognitive and behavioral models. Because in most cases the investigation of needs is approached through the study of the associated valence of different *work characteristics,* several pressing questions may be asked:

- Has the construct of needs in work settings been empirically verified? That is, is there a consistent pattern or organization in the assignment of valence to work characteristics (values) that could support the concept of underlying needs?

- Assuming that the answer to the above question is positive, what job characteristics can be grouped together as having the same need as the main source of their valence? This knowledge could prove useful in predicting, for example, the compensatory value of one job outcome from another one in the same grouping.

- Several needs may contribute valence to one particular job characteristic or outcome (e.g., pay). What are they, and what individual or cultural differences influence the valences attributed to various job characteristics by affecting the associated needs?

- In a more empirical vein, what contribution will the knowledge of an underlying structure of needs have on our ability to understand and predict behavioral and attitudinal outcomes in the work environment?

One more point should be emphasized before we proceed. Most theories of need motivation in the work environment attempt to identify and classify the content of motivation. Thus, beyond explaining the process itself, these models can be seen as taxonomies of motivational variables. A comparison of three theoretical taxonomies of work motivation is presented in Figure 1.

The purpose of this chapter is twofold: (a) to offer an integrated model of the taxonomy of needs and (b) to examine its universality.

Let's now turn to a review of some of the research pertaining to the investigation of needs and to some of the possible reasons for the unsuccessful efforts in the literature to establish such need categories as those proposed by Maslow.

FIGURE 1

Comparison of Three Theoretical Taxonomies of Work Motivation

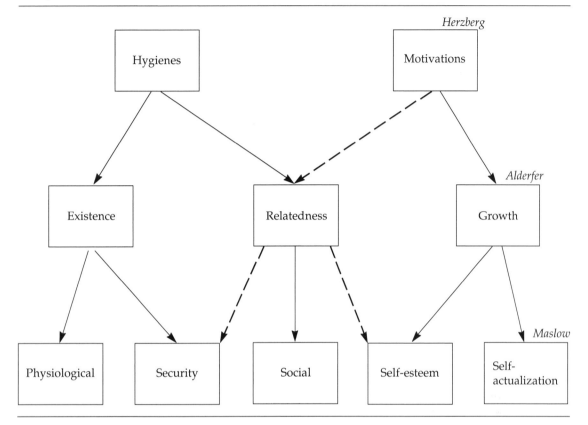

From "A Nonmetric Scaling Approach to Taxonomies of Employee Work Motivation" by S. Ronen, A. I. Kraut, J. C. Lingoes, and N. Aranya, 1979, *Multivariate Behavioural Research, 14*, p. 391. Copyright 1979 by Multivariate Behavioral Research. Reprinted by permission.

Need Theories and Empirical Verification

There have been a number of need theories that have stimulated research in the field of work motivation, of which Maslow's has been without doubt the most popular.

The fact is that a number of studies, relying primarily on factor analysis, have not been able to produce the expected grouping of items designed to represent Maslow's categories

(Herman & Hulin, 1973; Imperato, 1972; Payne, 1970; Roberts, Walter, & Miles, 1971; Water & Roach, 1973).

In view of this, Alderfer (1969, 1972) attempted to regroup Maslow's categories into three sets of needs: existence, relatedness, and growth. Alderfer has been able to develop items that have clustered in the way he predicted, even though the more widely known Maslow model has not been so fortunate. However, Rauschenberger, Schmitt, and Hunter

(1980) failed to find support for either Maslow's prepotency proposition or for Alderfer's frustration/regression proposition.

Indeed, reviews of Maslow's theory by Miner and Dachler (1973), Wahba and Bridwell (1976), and Campbell and Pritchard (1976) have concluded that the evidence for the five categories is nonexistent, that the theory has been received with uncritical acceptance, and that the intrinsic–extrinsic model seems to best incorporate the general thrust of the data.

In my view, two major shortcomings may have contributed to the failure to find empirical support for Maslow's taxonomy: One is associated with the items used, the other with the method of analysis.

Items Used in the Past

Most studies attempting to examine need taxonomies have employed job satisfaction items, following the assumption that needs and job satisfaction are related (e.g., Wofford, 1967, 1971). Guion (1958) defined job satisfaction as "the extent to which the individual's needs are satisfied and the extent to which the individual perceives that satisfaction as stemming from his total job situation" (p. 62). Wolf (1970) also defines satisfaction and dissatisfaction in terms of the level of gratification and threat of nongratification of needs. He specifically relates those needs to Maslow's conceptualization. However, operationalizing these assumptions by using job satisfaction to investigate general needs has serious drawbacks. By definition, *needs transcend immediate job occupancy. Job satisfaction does not; rather, it is modified by the perceptions of the immediate job conditions and its expectancies.*

Furthermore, the results of investigating needs through the reported level of job satisfaction may be clouded by an individual's compensatory processes (e.g., across different life domains), as well as the perceptual adaptability to the reward's availability in the particular job (e.g., Deci, 1971). It has been suggested, for example, that under some conditions of limited extrinsic rewards, individuals may cognitively reevaluate the intrinsic characteristics of their particular jobs in order to justify or explain their behavior (Ronen, 1978; Staw, 1977). Staw has further indicated that Bem's (1967) self-perception theory supports such a process. All these considerations may have contributed to the difficulty in categorizing job satisfaction items into clusters that resemble Maslow's need categories.

Shortcomings of the Analysis Used in the Past

The second shortcoming of the studies mentioned earlier that have failed to extract need taxonomies may be related to the employment of factor analysis. In particular, statistical rigidities and indeterminancies with respect to both rotation and stopping criteria put serious limitations on the technique. For example, the classification of a large number of variables into factors based on a variety of rotational criteria may obscure rather than clarify the relationship of the variables to one another within and across the factors.

Indeed, recent studies have shown that *nonmetric multivariate techniques* are likely to reveal fundamental patterns in the experimental data, and hence increase the likelihood of finding an underlying structure of needs, if such a structure exists. A few examples of such studies are reported below.

Recently, researchers (Borg, 1990, 1991; Elizur, 1984) have postulated a facet definition of work outcomes using two facets: modality of outcome (material, social, and psychological) and relation to performance (reward, resource). Smallest space analysis of sample data indicates some support for this definition, although the results are open to alternative explanations.

A different approach was taken by Billings and Cornelius (1980). They asked respondents to assess the similarity of different work outcomes and then used a method developed by Kruskall and Young (multidimensional scaling; MOS) to locate linear axes having psychological meaning. They found that the popular dichotomy of intrinsic–extrinsic rewards is not sufficient to distinguish between a variety of possible work outcomes. They suggested two further descriptive dimensions based on empirical data: "[association with an] Underlying Need" and "Extent Inherent in Work."

Like the examples just given, the studies to be presented in this chapter employ multivariate techniques. They have been published elsewhere but receive here a different treatment, as will be shown in the following sections.

Overcoming the Limitations

I have pointed out the two limitations that I assume have contributed to the failure to empirically extract Maslow's need taxonomy in the past. One was associated with the items, the other with the methodology.

A number of empirical studies have dealt with these two limitations and have indeed succeeded in extracting Maslow's need categories (Ronen, 1979; Ronen & Barkan, 1985; Ronen & Kraut, 1980; Ronen, Kraut, Lingoes, & Aranya, 1979; Shenkar & Ronen, 1987b). They used a nonmetric multivariate analysis, (such as smallest space analysis (SSA), which, as will be explained later, overcomes some of the limitations of factor analysis in achieving the clustering intended here. More importantly, these researchers employed a work values questionnaire rather than job satisfaction items, thus enabling them to tap the individual's attribution of importance to different work characteristics. It was assumed that questions investigating the importance of job characteristics or outcomes in general would reflect the valence associated with these outcomes as a result of needs, without the interference of expectations associated with particular job conditions. Indeed, Maslow's categories, as well as the other need taxonomies, were clearly extracted in these studies, which will be further elaborated and reanalyzed in the following sections. The studies reported here incorporated both need and

satisfaction dimensions, tapping importance rather than satisfaction and employing a nonmetric multidimensional analysis.

These two issues need further elaboration and theoretical underpinning. I will attempt to do so in the next two sections. The first section deals with the definitions of values and the other with the method of data analysis used in analyzing the data employed in these studies.

Relating Needs to Values

In this chapter, the analysis of the data is based on work values. It is necessary, then, to lay the theoretical groundwork underlying the assumptions employed. But first a recapitulation of the relationship between needs and valences is necessary.

Need satisfaction models of job attitudes consist of two bodies of theory: expectancy theory and need theory (Alderfer, 1977). The two can be viewed as complementary (Campbell, Dunnette, Lawler, & Weick, 1970; Hackman & Oldham, 1976; Porter & Lawler, 1968). This complementarity is possible because *expectancy* models have been considered a process theory of motivation, while *need* models have been viewed as content theories of motivation, concerned with what within the individual or the environment energizes and sustains behavior (Alderfer, 1977; Campbell & Pritchard, 1976). *The valence associated with the outcomes produced in performing an act may be viewed as the link between the two theories. Need theory provides input in the determination of the type and level of the valence associated with an act, while expectancy theory adds the perceived probability of the outcomes.*

Alderfer (1972) proposes that need satisfaction affects human desires. There is a continuous dynamic cycle of changing individual satisfactions and desires as a function of individual–organizational interaction. An individual interacting with a complex environment subjectively determines the level of relative importance of various valences associated with job outcomes or job characteristics and assigns priority to their attributes.

Notwithstanding the issue of whether the individual bases the level of importance of various job aspects on a predetermined hierarchy (prepotency) or in combination with the influence of his or her desires and satisfactions, in this chapter we will consider only items describing job characteristics and the individual's report of his or her level of importance (as an approximation of attribution of valences). It should again be emphasized that I do so because I am not interested in the process aspect, nor in the dynamic properties of prepotency and hierarchy of needs, but rather because I am interested in investigating the degree to which these values can be grouped to reflect established categories or needs.

Also, in order to avoid unnecessary disputes over the meaning of needs and their antecedents, we will not concern ourselves with the issue of whether self-reported levels of importance (or work values) are primarily innate or socially induced, affective or cognitive. Instead, we will concentrate on how they operate in the determination of outcome and their evaluation in the work situation. Moreover, because in my view these items—which we will call *work values*—transcend the immediate job situation (as influenced by the individual's perception of the immediate environment), I will assume that they can be grouped into categories that reflect a needs structure. This means that even if a certain need is temporarily satisfied, it can still be identified regardless of the variation in its intra- or interpersonal strength. Since these items are considered to reflect work values, and because with some variations we consider them to be universally applicable, some assumptions regarding values will be delineated in the next section.

Work Values

The research presented here uses data based on items presumed to reflect work values. Certain assumptions are associated with this assertion. First, it is assumed here that if one can indeed identify values associated with the work domain, they can be regarded as possessing characteristics usually associated with more basic values, those presumed to transcend various life domains (see Kluckhohn, 1951; Rokeach, 1968, 1973, 1979). Kluckhohn (1961) defines a value as "a conception, explicit or implicit, distinctive of an individual or characteristic of a group, of the desirable which influences the selection from available modes, means and ends of actions" (p. 395).

The features of these values, therefore, incorporate concepts of beliefs, pertain to desirable end states or behaviors, guide selection or evaluation of behavior and events, and may be ordered in terms of relative importance (Schwartz & Bilsky, 1987, 1990).

Second, it is assumed that these features of basic values may be associated with work motivation models through the employment of valences attributed to job characteristics and expected outcomes.

This assumption is reflected in the definition of work values proposed by Kalleberg (1977), in terms of the range of gratifications available from work and its environment, and therefore suggests the possibility of assessing value preferences by means of individual priorities regarding job rewards and characteristics.

Third, it is assumed that importance ratings—as relative weights of various job characteristics, outcomes, or orientations—reflect work goals or, alternatively, work values (e.g., Elizur, 1984; Jurgensen, 1978; Quinn & Cobb, 1980).

Fourth, these kinds of items are applicable cross-culturally (Bass & Burger, 1979; Haire, Ghiselli, & Porter, 1966; Mow, 1987; Ronen,

FIGURE 2

Needs, Values, and Motivation: Individual, Organizational, and Environmental Antecedents

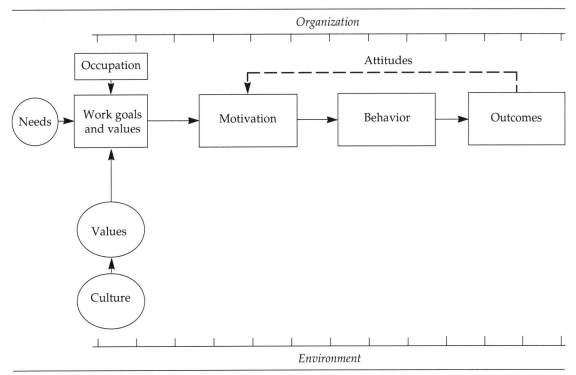

From *Comparative and Multinational Management* (p. 137) by S. Ronen, 1986, New York: Wiley. Copyright 1986 by Wiley. Reprinted by permission.

1986). The issue of comparability of items across cultures is relevant here and is also recognized (Poortinga, 1989). However, the purpose of this chapter is not to compare *levels* of importance across samples but rather to analyze the data separately for each national sample, which reduces the relevance of the cross-cultural eticemic dispute for the data somewhat (Ronen, 1986; Ronen & Shenkar,1989).

Figure 2 depicts my basic approach guiding the relevance of the cultural and organizational environment to the established work values of an individual.

The most hazardous leap in the assumptions just mentioned is probably the one associated with interpretating data based on work values to reflect the concepts employed in need theories (my second assumption). I also recognize here that the meaning of *importance* may be ambiguous in terms of the individual's perspective. He or she may relate the items to such functions as choosing a job, getting one to work harder, or staying in the organization. Still, such an approach is definitely an improvement over the studies reported earlier that employed job satisfaction items to investigate need theories.

As indicated earlier, the other innovation in my research is associated with the data analysis technique employed, which will be introduced in the next section.

The Method and Analysis of the Data

Analysis

Nonmetric analysis[2] seems especially appropriate for exploring the grouping among various motivational variables. As noted by Karni and Levin (1972), as well as by Schlesinger and Guttman (1969), nonmetric techniques may be more powerful than metric analysis for some studies because they can reveal more fundamental order relations. (*Order*, of course, refers here to classification and not to the prepotency of motivational factors.) In addition, such multidimensional scaling techniques are less sensitive to measurement difficulties such as noninterval level measurement, distributional properties due to scaling, or attenuation due to changes in reliability. Perhaps most appealing of all to the practically minded psychologist is the parsimony of the technique in regard to the number of dimensions required for an adequate geometric representation. Meaningful displays of complex data can often be graphed in only two dimensions, making the results visually accessible to the researcher.

The correlation matrices of each country's sample were analyzed using smallest space analysis (SSA-I), a nonmetric multidimensional scaling technique developed by Guttman (1959, 1968) and Lingoes (1965, 1977). This procedure provides a geometric representation of the variables (work values, in this instance) as points in Euclidean space, often representing them in only two or three dimensions, such that distances are inversely related to correlations. It

should be noted that with but minor exceptions, all of the intercorrelations were positive and consistent with Guttman's First Law of Attitude, which states that if any two items are selected from the universe of attitude items toward a given object, and if the population observed is not selected artificially, then the population regressions between these two items will be monotone, with positive or zero sign (Gratch, 1973, p. 36).

The resulting display reflects the relationship among all possible pairs of variables, provides a total picture of the multiple interactions among the variables, and facilitates abstraction of the most dominant concepts of the universe under consideration. The structure obtained is then compared to the a priori structure of the variables, which in our case were the taxonomies based on Maslow's and Alderfer's needs categories and the extrinsic–intrinsic dichotomy offered by Herzberg. The validation of the a priori structures depends on how well the SSA's empirically based structure can be partitioned into contiguous regions corresponding to the a priori structure.

As Karni and Levin (1972) point out, the SSA technique differs in several respects from factor analysis. The factor analytic approach treats the correlation coefficient as a measure of the common variance to be decomposed, whereas SSA uses the correlation coefficient as an index of similarity. Unlike factor analysis, which assumes an interval level of measurement, SSA requires only ordinal measurement, which, in general, leads to dimensional parsimony. A two- or three-dimensional space is often sufficient to adequately represent an observational structure that may require many factor analytic dimensions (Schlesinger & Guttman, 1969). In addition, factor analysis takes a reductionist point of view in trying to account for common variance through a limited number of presumed underlying variates. In SSA, the focus is on the configuration of the variables and the interpretation of the order of relations among the data.

Sample

The samples and the resulting SSA maps were taken from various published articles: The samples from Canada, France, the United Kingdom, Germany, and Japan were taken from Ronen (1979). Two samples from Germany were taken from Ronen and Kraut (1980) and Ronen et al. (1979). The Chinese sample was taken from Shenkar and Ronen (1987a). The sample from Israel was taken from Ronen and Barkan (1985).

The data for all but one sample (the Israeli sample) were collected as part of a longer questionnaire in which employees rated the importance of 14 different aspects of a job, as shown in Table 1. The 14 work values were selected to represent a wide variety of work-related expectations popular in many theoretical and empirical studies of job attitudes (Hofstede, 1980; Hofstede, Kraut, & Simonetti, 1977). Employees rated these 14 values on a five-point scale from "most important" to "very little or no importance" in terms of *rated importance* in an ideal job. Table 1 gives the values label and the actual questionnaire wording. This table also shows each item's a priori assignment to the categories in Maslow's, Alderfer's, and Herzberg's taxonomies.

For the Israeli sample, a longer questionnaire was used and another multivariate analysis technique employed (a version of the ALSCAL algorithm; Takane, Young, & De Leeun, 1976). In this case, the number of dimensions of the representation space were chosen with the aid of two criteria: (a) Young's s-stress formula and (b) economy of the interpretation.[3]

Multidimensionality of Work Values

The geometric representations—or maps—of data found by Ronen and associates (Ronen, 1979; Ronen & Barkan, 1985; Ronen & Kraut, 1980; Ronen et al., 1979; Shenkar & Ronen, 1987b), and which appeared in the original articles, are presented and reanalyzed in this chapter. The original papers had in common both the employment of a multivariate analysis technique and the goal of investigating the possibility of identifying need taxonomies, particularly Maslow's categorization. In the original published analysis, the maps were partitioned by drawing boundaries around the hypothesized regions. These boundaries are *excluded* from the presentation here, and only the maps are used. These maps include the geometric representation of the intercorrelation matrices, in the form of the work values location on a two-dimensional computer printout.

However, after the accumulation of the maps from the different country samples (over a few years) and a comparison was made among them, a consistency became apparent. This consistency is presented here with the assistance of the following:

- The geometric presentations—the maps—that appeared in the published studies were rotated for visual convenience by placing items presumed to represent lower needs at the bottom of the figure. Note that the axes in the maps carry no a priori theoretical meaning. The only meaningful interpretation concerns the relative distances among the items.

- A comparative appraisal of the geometric representation of the data reveal some startling similarities that to some degree became apparent in each of the original published analyses. The following characteristics appear in all the configurations:

  a. Work values relating to security and benefits are placed opposite those relating to challenge and autonomy.

TABLE 1

Questionnaire Wording of 14 Work Values and Assignment to Various Motivational Taxonomies

Work Goal	Questionnaire Wording	Category of Various Taxonomies		
		Maslow's	*Alderfer's*	*Herzberg's*
Physical	Have good physical working conditions (good ventilaton and lighting, adequate work space, etc.)	Physiological and security	Existence	Hygienes
Area	Live in an area desirable to you and your family			
Time	Have a job which leaves you suffient time for your personal or family life			
Security	Have the security that you will be able to work for your company as long as you want to			
Benefits	Have good fringe benefits			
Earnings	Have an opportunity for high earnings			
Co-workers	Work with people who cooperate well with one another	Social	Relatedness	
Manager	Have a good working relationship with your manager			
Recognition	Get the recognition you deserve when you do a good job	Self-esteem	Growth	Motivators
Advancement	Have the opportunity for advancement to higher level jobs			
Training	Have training opportunities (to improve your skills or to learn new skills)			
Autonomy	Have considerable freedom to adopt your own approach to the job	Self-actualization		
Skills	Fully use your skills and abilities on the job			
Challenge	Have challenging work to do—work from which you get a personal sense of accomplishment			

From "A Nonmetric Scaling Approach to Taxonomies of Employee Work Motivation" by S. Ronen, A. I. Kraut, J. C. Lingoes, and N. Aranya, 1979, *Multivariate Behavioral Research*, 14, p. 392. Copyright 1979 by *Multivariate Behavioral Research*. Reprinted by permission.

FIGURE 3

**A Smallest Space Analysis Map of U.K. Sample,
With Diagonals Inserted (*n* = 1,535)**

From "Cross-national Study of Employee Work Goals" by S. Ronen, 1979, *International Review of Applied Psychology, 28,*
p. 7. Copyright 1979 by *International Review of Applied Psychology.* Reprinted by permission.

b. Between these two clusters, values relating to promotion/advancement and social interaction, also diametrically opposed, are to be found.

■ As a result of the observation presented in the second point, *diagonal lines were drawn separately for each map.* The SSA maps and the diagonal lines are presented in Figures 3 through 10. Although there are some modifications and variations in the groupings—differences that were discussed in the original papers—the two-dimensionality of the data delineated by these diagonal lines is apparent.

A close look at the actual items reveals some structural information. For example, most of the items contained in the lower right half of the maps, separated by one of the diagonals, are those associated with the collectivity of employees rather than with the individual—items such as social benefits, tenure, and interpersonal relations. In contrast, the upper left half of the maps, the other side of the same

FIGURE 4

**A Smallest Space Analysis Map of German (I) Sample,
With Diagonals Inserted (*n* = 800)**

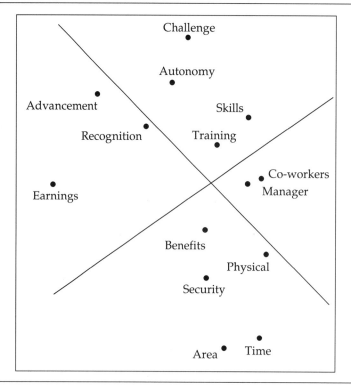

diagonal, contains items associated primarily with the individual employee, such as promotion, autonomy, and challenge.

From a different perspective, using the other diagonal as a boundary, it can be further seen that the lower left half of the maps contain items that are by and large material in nature, such as pay, tenure, and promotion. On the other hand, the items contained in the upper right half of the maps are nonmaterial by nature, such as interpersonal relations, autonomy, and challenge.

These apparent structural features suggest that the simple two-factor intrinsic–extrinsic taxonomy of job characteristics is inadequate. Rather, an interpretation based on the *quadrants* seems more compelling.

The multiple replications of the same data structure suggest a reconsideration of the original interpretations given in each of the studies and suggest the presence of an underlying structure *common* to all the empirical data. Furthermore, such an underlying structure should ideally be compatible with

FIGURE 5

A Smallest Space Analysis Map of German (II) Sample, With Diagonals Inserted (*n* = 2,720)

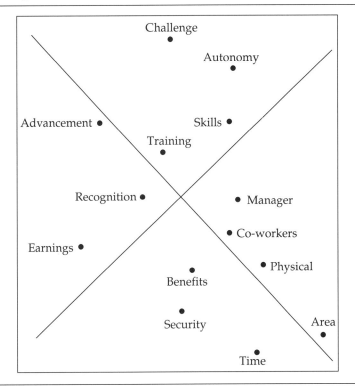

From "An Experimental Examination of Work Motivation Taxonomies" by S. Ronen and A. I. Kraut, 1980, *Human Relations, 33.* Copyright 1980 by Plenum. Reprinted by permission.

existing motivational need taxonomies, such as those of Maslow (1954), Herzberg, Mausner, and Snyderman (1959), McClelland (1961, 1975), and Alderfer (1972), and which we shall later examine.

The interpretation of the data in terms of a *two-dimensional configuration* is not surprising in view of published research in other psychological areas. We shall turn now to that literature in order to draw the potential conceptual and theoretical interpretations of such dimensions before drawing final conclusions.

The Underlying Dimensions of Work Values

There is a considerable literature on dual-dichotomous (or two-dimentional) models in human behavior, most of it in the field of interpersonal trait perception. Wiggins (1979) has summarized the literature on the structural analysis of interpersonal behavior while showing that a two-dimensional model can adequately explain the variation among individuals with respect to such behavior. Researchers

FIGURE 6

**A Smallest Space Analysis Map of French Sample,
With Diagonals Inserted (*n* = 1,966)**

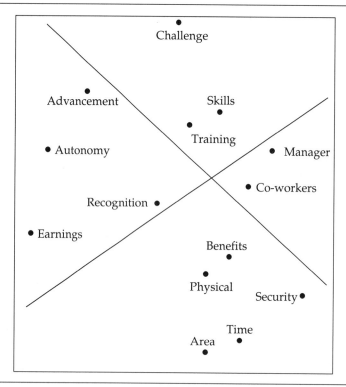

have consistently found dichotomous dimensions, such as dominance–submission and love–hate (Carson, 1969; Foa, 1961; Leary, 1957; Wiggins, 1979) or individual prominence–sociability (Borgatta, Cottrell, & Mann, 1958; Carter, 1954).

It should be noted that Wiggins (1979) advocates use of a circumplex model to describe the structure of interpersonal trait perception. This model will support many bipolar, axial representations but nonetheless always remains a two-dimensional structure.

An additional area of human behavior where dual-dichotomous models are to be found is that of values. Bengston (1975), in the course of a study on values associated with socialization, summarized a body of literature devoted to empirical analysis of the structure of values. In this context, values are considered desirable ends that serve as guides to action. They are assumed to be patterned and organized according to superordinate cognitive categories. Using factor analysis and citing several similar studies by Scott (1965), Flacks (1967), and Payne, Summers, and Stewart (1973), he found two orthogonal conceptual axes: humanism–materialism and individualism–collectivism.

FIGURE 7

**A Smallest Space Analysis Map of Japanese Sample,
With Diagonals Inserted (*n* = 1,695)**

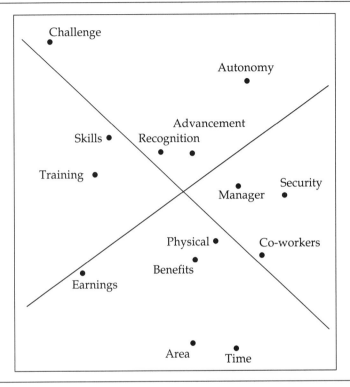

From "Cross-national study of Employee Work Goals" by S. Ronen, 1979, *International Review of Applied Psychology, 28, p. 8.*
Copyright 1979 by *International Review of Applied Psychology.* Reprinted by permission.

Bengston (1975) also constructed a typology of values as determined by the two independent bipolar dimensions. This typology consists of four ideal-type sets of values: (a) values reflecting individualism, (b) values reflecting collectivism, (c) values reflecting materialism, and (d) values reflecting humanism. In a subsequent study on the relationship between occupation and work value preferences, Samuel and Lewin-Epstein (1979) applied this dual-dichotomy model of values and revealed differences in preferences among different occupations.

The two dimensions fit well into our data representation. The extreme points on each continuum are associated with the *orientation* of the values on the resulting maps and define the composition of these values in terms of the four *quadrants*.

A note is necessary to illuminate the collectivistic aspect of work values. In his chapter on cross-cultural industrial and organizational psychology, Triandis (this volume) describes collectivistic cultures as those in which people define the self in group terms, (e.g., "I am an employee of General Motors"). Our

FIGURE 8

**A Smallest Space Analysis Map of Canadian Sample,
With Diagonals Inserted (*n* = 1,088)**

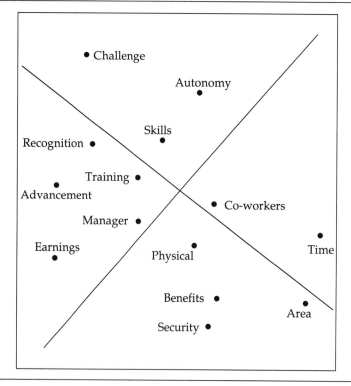

From "Cross-national Study of Employee Work Goals" by S. Ronen, 1979, *International Review of Applied Psychology, 28*, p. 6.
Copyright 1979 by *International Review of Applied Psychology*. Reprinted by permission.

interpretation of the collectivistic orientation in our model resembles this interpretation (i.e., little attention to or regard for individual differences).

Indeed, Meindle, Hunt, and Lee (1989) found collectivistic societies to be characterized by lower values on achievement, esteem, independence, and growth and higher values on benefits, security, pay, recognition, and working conditions. The assumptions associated with cultures are applicable to the dimensions of our model: Collectivists use the group as the unit of analysis of social relationships, while individualists use individuals. While various work values depict both individualistic and collectivistic components, individuals from varied cultural backgrounds are expected to assign different importance levels to these values. However, *both individualism and collectivism (group orientation) are components of every work value.*

The Resulting Quadrants and Need Taxonomies

The two dimensions, and the resulting composition of the content area of each quadrant, are

FIGURE 9

**A Smallest Space Analysis Map of Chinese Sample,
With Diagonals Inserted (*n* = 163)**

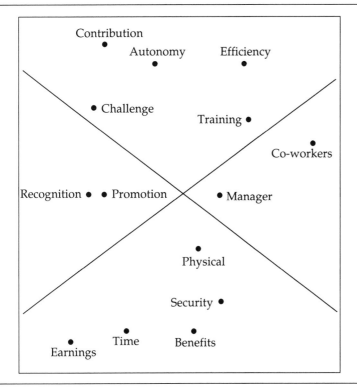

From "The Structure and Importance of Work Goals Among Managers in the People's Republic of China" by O. Shenkar and S. Ronen, 1987, *Academy of Management Journal, 30*(3), p. 569. Copyright 1987 by *Academy of Management Journal.* Reprinted by permission.

presented in Figure 11. They seem to define the clusters of values in each quadrant in terms of Maslow's needs taxonomy, as depicted in Figures 3 through 10. The lower-level needs (physiological and security) have their orientation in the combination of materialism and collectivism and appear in the bottom quadrant. These are job aspects that are financially quantifiable and are usually allotted to employees because they belong to a group (e.g., same organizational level, fulfilling similar tasks, or having similar seniority). The left-hand quadrant is associated with the ego, or esteem, need; it is inherently materialistic and based on individual differences, and contains job aspects such as recognition and promotion. The right-hand quadrant consists primarily of interpersonal relations and is therefore primarily nonmaterialistic and group or system oriented (collectivism). The top quadrant (self-actualization) is defined as consisting of individualism and nonmaterialism (or humanism), and contains such job aspects as challenge and autonomy. Figure 12 illustrates the quadrants by using the sample presented in Figure 4.

FIGURE 10

**Two-dimensional Plot of Work Outcomes Importance
Using ALSCAL Algorithm of Israeli Sample (*n* = 186)
(Young's S = stress = 0.22; Kruskal's stress = 0.21)**

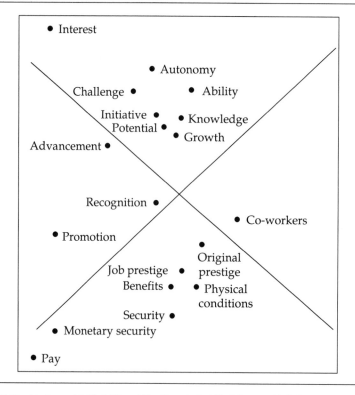

From "A Multivariate Approach to Work Values: A Two Facets Analysis" by S. Ronen and S. Barkan, 1985, Israel
Research Institute, Tel Aviv University.

The dimensions designated as facets *A* and *B*, therefore, can be considered facets in a multiple model. Figure 13 represents this relationship. *A* represents the nonmaterialism/ humanistic (a_1)–materialism (a_2) facet, while *B* represents the individualism (b_1)–collectivism (b_2) facet. By designating each *quadrant* containing a cluster of work values as a composition of either facet *a* or facet *b*, we can now proceed to try to account for the various taxonomies of need theories.

It should be noted that the SSA results of both the Chinese and Japanese samples suggest that the category of self-actualization may need some modification. In Japan, a society that may be categorized as collectivistic, the value of recognition tends to group together with advancement, autonomy, and challenge. The value of recognizing a person as a worthy contributor to the group may offer an aspect that may be conceptualized as a kind of a collectivistic–self-actualization

FIGURE 11

**The Dimensions and Their Combined
Contribution in Forming Need Categories**

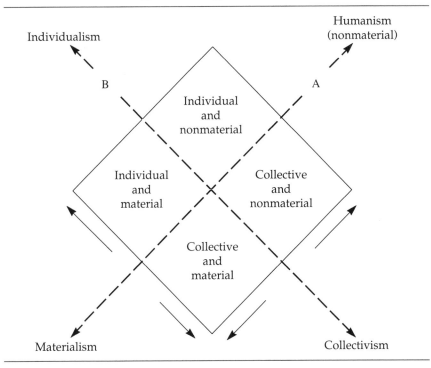

(Triandis, personal communication, March, 1993). A similar interpretation may be applied to the inclusion of the value of contribution to society in the self-actualization quadrant of the Chinese sample.

Accounting for "Order" of Needs in Various Taxonomies

Figure 14 relates the two-dimensional underlying structure of work values to the various motivational need taxonomies with a close approximation to their theoretical derivations.

It is apparent from Figure 14 that the two-dimensional structure may account, on the one hand, for the unidimensional assumptions of such theories as Maslow's, Alderfer's and Herzberg's (in which levels are designated by the dotted lines) and, on the other hand, for the difficulty in verifying these models empirically. With the full realization that we set out to investigate the taxonomic aspects of these theories, some propositions about the order relationships among the needs will also be offered in the discussion.

Discussion and Concluding Remarks

In their review of motivation theory, Campbell and Pritchard (1976) mention that "after

FIGURE 12

**Representation of Figure 4 With Maslow's Needs Inserted
into the Appropriate Quadrons Presented in Figure 11**

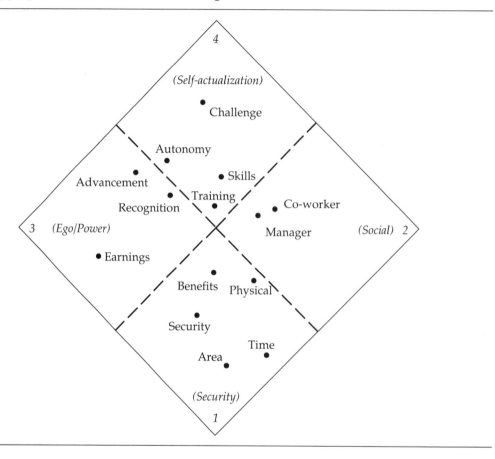

looking at the available information it was surprising to realize that there have been relatively few comprehensive programs of research that have tried to define and sample systematically the overall domain of possible job outcomes; and that most of what is available has used some variant of the factor analytic procedure" (p. 100). Later they state: "We are badly in need of both substantive and methodological innovation in this area" (p. 122).

This chapter attempts to employ and integrate innovations in both areas: first, to suggest an explanation for the underlying dimensions of the different need motivation taxonomies, and second, to demonstrate how these dimensions are consistent throughout the different need taxonomies by employing a multidimensional methodology to analyze relevant empirical data. In addition, this chapter is based on cross-cultural data that lend

FIGURE 13

**The Proposed Facet Structure That Forms
the Underlying Dimensions of Work Values**

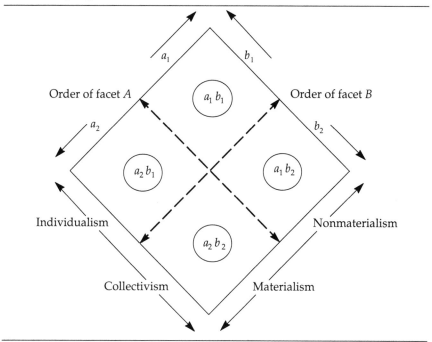

initial support for the universality of the findings and conclusions. Naturally, this is relevant only if the reader accepts the assumptions regarding work values as a legitimate approximation of employees' expressions of their needs.

The structural definition offered here suggests a way of characterizing the underlying cognitive pattern of work motivation. Several sets of empirical data revealed a fundamental structure corresponding to the definition. This definition, exhibited in Figure 13, supposes the existence of a motivational directionality with two facets to it—an individualism versus collectivism orientation and a humanistic, nonmaterial versus material orientation. The various models may be now reevaluated in terms of the two facets (Levy, 1982).

The facets may be considered different aspects of the traditional intrinsic–extrinsic dichotomy, thus possibly solving a long-standing controversy with respect to the classification of work value characteristics: Because there are two facets playing a *joint* role in determining the hierarchy of work characteristics, it becomes legitimate for ambiguous work goals such as "co-workers" (see Table 1) to be intrinsic in one sense (say, nonmaterialistic or humanistic) and extrinsic in another (say, collectivistic). Similarly, "recognition" may be viewed in terms of both facets, intrinsic in terms of individualism, and extrinsic in terms of materialism.

In addition to the intrinsic–extrinsic dichotomy, other previously mentioned taxonomies are also clearly visible in the structure of

FIGURE 14

**The Underlying Two-facet Structure and the
Corresponding Motivational Need Taxonomies**

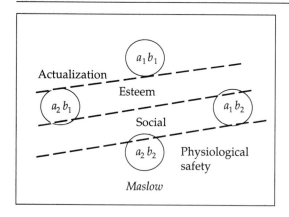

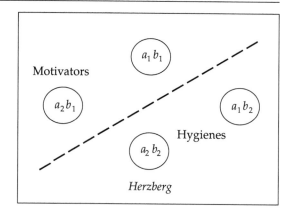

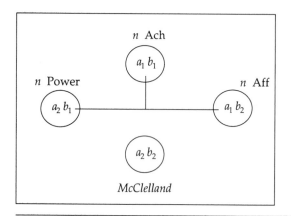

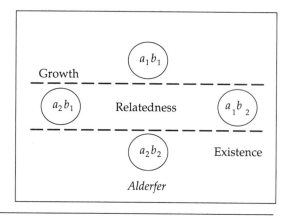

the empirical data. This is made possible by the existence of a partial order, allowing several different substructures, as opposed to the determinate structure of a complete, unidimensional order, such as Maslow's theory. Figure 14 illustrates the different ways one can interpret the data in order to reveal the compatibility of this underlying multidimensional structure with each taxonomy.

The correspondence between the various classifications is also quite clear. For example,

in terms of Maslow's and Alderfer's need classifications, there is complete agreement between the facet combination "nonmaterial-individual" and their categories of self-actualization and growth. Similarly, the combination "materialism-collectivism (group)" coincides with Maslow's two lowest categories, physiological and safety needs, and closely resembles Alderfer's existence category. The presentation of Alderfer's taxonomy in Figure 14 does not, however, fully capture his model (e.g., that certain aspects of security are associated with relatedness, as shown in Figure 2). Nevertheless, our definition of the basic needs does include the collectivistic orientation.

The regional approach to interpreting geometric representations allows the researcher to examine the adequacy of the sample of variables (or items) he or she has chosen. In the present case, examination of the results in Figures 3 through 10 shows a dearth of work values in the various samples, particularly relating to the facet combinations a_2b_1 (associated with Maslow's Ego needs and McClelland's *nPo*) and a_1b_2 (associated with Maslow's Social needs and McClelland's *nAff*). Further research, with broader item sampling, should provide an additional test of the adequacy of the proposed structure.

From the available data, I have shown that at the very least we are faced with a dual dichotomy: collectivistic (group) versus individualistic items and materialistic versus nonmaterialistic (humanistic) items. Furthermore, these dimensions are well anchored in previous research on the dimensionality of social values.

It was my intent in this chapter to offer support to need theories—in terms of their *taxonomies* of needs and their universality. In addition, I intended to show that the various theoretical taxonomies are compatible.

The significance of this discussion lies in the conclusion that two-dimensional structures account for the need taxonomies offered by various motivation theories. Still, one should not overlook the finding that Maslow's need taxonomies are indeed extracted by a multidimensional data analysis—a finding consistent throughout all the samples used. It should be also noted that these samples were taken from various countries—most of which, with the exception of China and Japan, were from Western societies—and lend partial support for the universality of these taxonomies.

Nonetheless, one should not disregard the criticism of need theory that is associated with its "inability to predict specific behavior nor the mediating processes that direct a person's motivational energy to such a specific behavior" (Kanfer, 1991, p. 17). However, in terms of the contribution of need theories to motivation models in industrial and organizational psychology, remember that need theory proposes that innate human needs energize a person's behavior and that these needs, including psychological growth needs, direct behavior toward the satisfaction of unmet needs. Furthermore, concerning intrinsic motivation, Kanfer concludes that "intrinsic motives may be universal in that they reside latently within all persons, but only influence cognitive process and behavior when activated" (p. 36). In other words, need theories can provide essential although incomplete information. And indeed, Hackman and Oldham (1976, 1980), for example, in their job characteristic theory, have hypothesized that growth needs reside within individuals, but at various levels of strength.

In a more practical vein, in reviewing studies of employee needs and expectations in various countries, it appears that what motivates people to work depends both on what the job can provide and on what people will lack if they do not work. Barrett and Bass (1976) have concluded that when the motivation to work is closely tied to basic survival, the pattern and diversity of motives that induce people to work are restricted. Thus, in developed countries, employees often express the desire for more challenging work and autonomy, but most people elsewhere in the world still work for basic survival; for them, job security is paramount (Ronen, 1986). It seems that the relevance of motivational need theories to the work environment is still applicable.

In their review of work motivation theory and practice, Katzell and Thompson (1990) note that "the motivational imperative inherent in motive/need theory is that it is important to ensure that workers have motives and values relevant to the type of organization and to the jobs in which they are placed" (p. 146).

They also note that in spite of criticism of this theory (Salancik & Pfeffer, 1978), it remains central to two basic strategies for improving work motivation: (a) selecting workers whose motives match a situation, and (b) reinforcing those motives within the workers.

The dual-dimensional structure of employee needs proposed here may assist us in matching more effectively workers' motives and work values with the organizational and cultural environment. It reaffirms the validity of various taxonomies of needs—particularly Maslow's—but also offers an explanation for the difficulty in establishing empirically a unidirectionality of a needs hierarchy (or prepotency).

Although I had previously stated that the taxonomies of the various theories are not contradictory since they are but subsets of one another, one should favor the strongest theory (i.e., Maslow's) if it is consistent with the results (which in this case, it is), since more implications flow from it (Ronen et al., 1979).

Moreover, in addition to variations resulting from individual differences, this model offers an explanation of a universal employee need structure. Variations accounted for by cultural values and national conditions can be reflected in the composition of the two dimensions. Although other relevant dimensions may be offered in terms of analyzing work values, the model offered here seems parsimonious enough to capture the variation in employee importance ratings of various job characteristics.

Notes

1   This does not negate the importance of social information processing of the immediate environment in contributing to the outcome's valence (Salancik & Pfeffer, 1978). However, there are sufficient reasons to assume that motives may influence human information processing.

2   The discussion of the analysis is based on the articles from which the data and results were taken.

3   Note that sets of data with larger numbers of variables are permitted using Young's formula to obtain higher stress values, especially when the intention is to display them in a uniform way—that is, along the same number of dimensions (in this case, two).

References

Alderfer, C. P. (1969). An empirical test of a new theory of human needs. *Organizational Behavior and Human Performance, 4,* 142–175.

Alderfer, C. P. (1972). *Existence relatedness and growth: Human needs in organizational settings.* New York: Free Press.

Alderfer, C. P. (1977). A critique of Salancik and Pfeffer's examination of need-satisfaction theories. *Administrative Science Quarterly, 22,* 658–669.

Atkinson, J. W. (1957). Motivational determinants of risk-taking behavior. *Psychological Review, 64,* 359–372.

Atkinson, J. W. (1964). *An introduction to motivation.* Princeton, NJ: Van Norstrand.

Barrett, G. V., & Bass, B. M. (1976) Cross-cultural issues in industrial and organizational psychology. In M. D. Dunnette (Ed.), *Handbook of industrial and organizational psychology* (pp. 1639–1686). Chicago: Rand McNally.

Bass, B. M., & Burger, P. C. (1979). *Assessments of managers: An international comparison.* New York: Free Press.

Bem, D. J. (1967). Self-perception: The dependent variable of human performance. *Organizational Behavior and Human Performance, 2,* 105–121.

Bengston, V. L. (1975). Generation and family effects in value socialization. *American Sociological Review, 40,* 358–371.

Billings, R. S., & Cornelius, E. T. (1980). Dimensions of work outcomes—A multidimensional scaling approach. *Personnel Psychology, 33,* 151–162.

Bindra, D. (1969). The interrelated mechanisms of reinforcement and motivation, and the nature of their influence on response. In W. J. Arnold & D. Levine (Eds.), *Nebraska symposium on motivation.* Lincoln: University of Nebraska Press.

Black, R. W. (1969). Incentive motivation and the parameters of reward in instrumental conditions. In W. J. Arnold & D. Levine (Eds.),

Nebraska symposium on motivation. Lincoln: University of Nebraska Press.

Bolles, R. C. (1967). *Theory of motivation*. New York: Harper & Row.

Borg, I. (1990). Multiple facetisations of work values. *Applied Psychology: An International Review, 39*, 401–412.

Borg, I. (1991). On the relationship between importance and satisfaction ratings of job aspects. *Applied Psychology: An international Review, 40*, 81–92.

Borgatta, E. F., Cottrell, L. S., Jr., & Mann, J. M. (1958). The spectrum of individual interaction characteristics: An interdimensional analysis. *Psychological Reports, 4*, 279–319.

Campbell, J. P., & Pritchard, R. D. (1976). Motivation theory in industrial and organizational psychology. In M. D. Dunnette (Ed.), *Handbook of industrial and organizational psychology* (pp. 63–130). Chicago: Rand McNally.

Campbell, J. P., Dunnette, M. D., Lawler, E. E., & Weick, K. E. (1970). *Managerial behavior, performance, and effectiveness*. New York: McGraw-Hill.

Carson, R. C. (1969). *Interaction concepts of personality*. Chicago: Aldine.

Carter, L. F. (1954). Evaluating the performance of individuals as members of small groups. *Personnel Psychology, 7*, 477–484.

Dawes, R. M. (1988). *Rational choice in an uncertain world*. San Diego: Harcourt Brace Jovanovich.

Deci, E. L. (1971). The effects of externally mediated rewards on intrinsic motivation. *Journal of Personality and Social Psychology, 18*, 105–115.

Elizur, D. (1984). Facets of work values: A structural analysis of work outcomes. *Journal of Applied Psychology, 69*, 379–389.

Flacks, R. (1967). The liberated generation: An exploration of the roots of student protest. *Journal of Social Issues, 23*, 52–72.

Foa, U. G. (1961). Emergences in the analysis of the structure of interpersonal behavior. *Psychological Review, 68*, 241–353.

Gratch, H. (Ed.). (1973). *25 Years of social research in Israel*. Jerusalem: Jerusalem Academic Press.

Guion, R. M. (1958). Industrial morale: The problem of terminology. *Personnel Psychology, 11*, 59–64.

Guttman, L. (1959). A structural theory for intergroup beliefs and action. *American Sociological Review, 24*, 318–328.

Guttman, L. (1968). A general nometric technique for finding the smallest coordinate space for a configuration of points. *Psychometrika, 33*, 461–469.

Hackman, J. R., & Oldham, G. R. (1976). Motivation through the design of work: Test of a theory. *Organizational Behavior and Human Performance, 16*, 250–279.

Hackman, J. R., & Oldham, G. R. (1980). *Work redesign*. Reading, MA: Addison-Wesley.

Hackman, J. R., & Porter, L. W. (1968). Expectancy theory predictions of work effectiveness. *Organizational Behavior and Human Performance, 3*, 417–426.

Haire, M., Ghiselli, E. E., & Porter, L. W. (1966). *Managerial thinking: An international study*. New York: Wiley.

Herman, J. B., & Hulin, L. (1973). Managerial satisfactions and organizational roles: An investigation of Porter's need deficiency scales. *Journal of Applied Psychology, 57*, 118–124.

Herzberg, F., Mausner, B., & Snyderman, B. (1959). *The motivation to work* (2nd ed.). New York: Wiley.

Hofstede, G. (1980). *Culture's consequences: International differences in work-related values*. Beverly Hills, CA: Sage.

Hofstede, G., Kraut, A., & Simonetti, S. H. (1977). Development of a core attitude survey questionnaire for international use. *JSAS Catalog of Selected Documents in Psychology, 7*(1439), 7–21.

Imperato, N. (1972). Relationship between Porter's need satisfaction questionnaire and the job description index. *Journal of Applied Psychology, 56*, 397–405.

Jurgensen, C. E. (1978). Job preferences (What makes a job good or bad?). *Journal of Applied Psychology, 63*, 267–276.

Kalleberg, A. L. (1977). Work values and job rewards: A theory of job satisfaction. *American Sociological Review, 42*, 124–143.

Kanfer, R. (1991). Motivation theory and industrial and organizational psychology. In M. D. Dunnette & L. M. Hough (Eds.), *Handbook of industrial and organizational psychology* (Vol. 1, pp. 75–170). Palo Alto, CA: Consulting Psychologists Press.

Karni, E. S., & Levin, J. (1972). The use of smallest space analysis in studying scale structure. *Journal of Applied Psychology, 56*, 341–346.

Katzell, R. A., & Thompson, D. E. (1990). Work motivation: Theory and practice. *American Psychologist, 45,* 144–153.

Kluckhohn, C. (1951). Values and value-orientations in the theory of action: An exploration in definition and classification. In T. Parsons & E. Shils (Eds.), *Toward a general theory of action* (pp. 388–433). Cambridge, MA: Harvard University Press.

Kluckhohn, C. (1961). The study of values. In D. N. Barrett (Ed.), *Values in transition.* Notre Dame, IN: University of Notre Dame Press.

Lawler, E. E. (1971). *Pay and organizational effectiveness: A psychological view.* New York: McGraw-Hill.

Leary, T. (1957). *Interpersonal diagnosis of personality.* New York: Ronald Press.

Levy, S. (1982). Lawful roles of facets in social theories. In I. Borg (Ed.), *Multidimensional data analysis: When and why.* Ann Arbor, MI: Mathesis Press.

Lewin, K. (1935). *A dynamic theory of personality.* New York: McGraw-Hill.

Lewin, K. (1951). *Field theory in social science.* New York: Harper & Row.

Lingoes, J. C. (1965). An IBM-7090 program for Guttman-Lingoes smallest space analysis. *Behavioral Science, 10,* 183–184.

Lingoes, J. C. (1977). Identifying regions in the space for interpretation. In J. C. Lingoes (Ed.), *Geometric representations of relational data.* Ann Arbor, MI: Mathesis Press.

Locke, E. A. (1975). Personnel attitudes and motivation. *Annual Review of Psychology, 26,* 457–480.

Locke, E. A. (1976). The nature and causes of job satisfaction. In M. D. Dunnette (Ed.), *Handbook of industrial and organizational psychology* (pp. 1297–1349). Chicago: Rand McNally.

Maslow, A. H. (1954). *Motivation and personality.* New York: Harper & Row.

Maslow, A. H. (Ed.). (1959). *New knowledge in human values.* New York: Harper & Row.

McClelland, D. C. (1961). *The achieving society.* Princeton, NJ: Van Nostrand.

McClelland, D. C. (1975). *Power: The inner experience.* New York: Irvingston/Halstead Press/Wiley.

MOW. Meaning of Work International Research Team. (1987). *The meaning of work.* London: Academic Press.

Meindle, J. R., Hunt, R. G., & Lee, W. (1989). Individualism-collectivism and work values: Data from the United States, China, Taiwan, Korea and Hong Kong. *Research in Personnel and Human Resources Management,* Suppl. 1, 59–77.

Miner, J. B., & Dachler, H. P. (1973). Personnel attitudes and motivation. In P. H. Mussen & M. R. Rosenzweig (Eds.), *Annual Review of Psychology, 24.* Palo Alto, CA: Annual Reviews.

Murray, H. A. (1938). *Exploration in personality.* New York: Oxford University Press.

Payne, R. (1970). Factor analysis of a Maslow-type need satisfaction questionnaire. *Personnel Psychology, 23,* 251–268.

Payne, S., Summers, D. A., & Stewart, T. R. (1973). Value differences across three generations. *Sociometry, 36,* 20–30.

Porter, L. W., & Lawler, E. E. (1968). *Managerial attitudes and performance.* Homewood, IL: Irwin-Dorsey.

Poortinga, Y. H. (1989). Equivalence of cross-cultural data: An overview of basic issues. *International Journal of Psychology, 24,* 737–756.

Quinn, R. P., & Cobb, W., Jr. (1980). What workers want: Factor analyses of importance ratings of job facets. In D. Katz & J. S. Adams (Eds.), *The study of organizations.* San Francisco: Jossey-Bass.

Rauschenberger, J., Schmitt, N., & Hunter, J. E. (1980). A test of the need hierarchy concept by a Markov model of change in need strength. *Administrative Science Quarterly, 25,* 654–670.

Roberts, K. H., Walter, G. A., & Miles, R. E. (1971). A factor analytic study of job satisfaction items designed to measure Maslow need categories. *Personnel Psychology, 24,* 205–220.

Rokeach, M. (1968). *Beliefs, attitudes, and values.* San Francisco: Jossey-Bass.

Rokeach, M. (1973). *The nature of human values.* New York: Free Press.

Rokeach, M. (Ed.). (1979). *Understanding human values.* New York: Free Press.

Ronen, S. (1978). Job satisfaction and the neglected variable of job seniority. *Human Relations, 31,* 297–308.

Ronen, S. (1979). Cross-national study of employee work goals. *International Review of Applied Psychology, 28,* 1–12.

Ronen, S. (1986). *Comparative and multinational management.* New York: Wiley.

Ronen, S., & Barkan, S. (1985). *A multivariate approach to work values: A two facets analysis.* [Working Paper]. Israel Research Institute, Tel Aviv University.

Ronen, S., & Kraut, A. I. (1977). Similarities among countries based on employee work values and attitudes. *Columbia Journal of World Business, 12*(2), 89–96.

Ronen, S., & Kraut, A. I. (1980). An experimental examination of work motivation taxonomies. *Human Relations, 33,* 565–616.

Ronen, S., Kraut, A. I., Lingoes, J. C., & Aranya, N. (1979). A nonmetric scaling approach to taxonomies of employee work motivation. *Multivariate Behavioral Research, 14,* 387–401.

Ronen, S., & Shenkar, O. (1989). Clustering variables: The application of non-metric multivariate analysis techniques in comparative management [Special Issue: Strategic Management Research]. *International Studies of Management and Organization, 28*(3), 72–87.

Ronen, S., & Shenkar, O. (1985). Clustering countries on attitudinal dimensions: A review and synthesis. *Academy of Management Review, 10*(3), 435–454.

Rotter, J. B. (1954). *Social learning and clinical psychology.* Englewood Cliffs, NJ: Prentice-Hall.

Salancik, G. R., & Pfeffer, J. (1977). An examination of need-satisfaction models of job attitudes. *Administrative Science Quarterly, 22,* 427–456.

Salancik, G. R., & Pfeffer, J. (1978). A social information processing approach to job attitudes and task design. *Administrative Science Quarterly, 23,* 224–253.

Samuel, Y., & Lewin-Esptein, N. (1979). The occupational situs as a predictor of work values. *American Journal of Sociology, 85,* 625–639.

Schlesinger, I. M., & Guttman, L. (1969). Smallest space analysis of intelligence and achievement tests. *Psychological Bulletin, 71,* 95–100.

Schwartz, S. H., & Bilsky, W. (1987) Toward a psychological structure of human values. *Journal of Personality and Social Psychology, 53,* 550–562.

Schwartz, S. H., & Bilsky, W. (1990). Toward a theory of the universal content and structure of values: Extensions and cross-cultural replications. *Journal of Personality and Social Psychology, 58,* 878–891.

Scott, W. A. (1965). *Values and organizations.* Chicago: Rand McNally.

Shenkar, O., & Ronen, S. (1987a). The cultural context of negotiation: The implications of Chinese interpersonal norms. *Journal of Applied Behavioral Science, 23,* 163–275.

Shenkar, O., & Ronen, S. (1987b). The structure and importance of work goals among managers in the People's Republic of China. *Academy of Management Journal, 30*(3), 564–576.

Shenkar, O., & Ronen, S. (1990). Culture, ideology, or economy: A comparative exploration of work-goals importance among managers in Chinese societies. In S. B. Prasad (Ed.), *Advances in international comparative management* (Vol. 5, pp. 117–134). Greenwich, CT: JAI Press.

Skinner, B. F. (1971). *Beyond freedom and dignity.* New York: Knopf.

Staw, B. M. (1977). Motivation in organization: Towards synthesis and redirection. In B. M. Staw & G. R. Salancik (Eds.), *New directions in organizational behavior.* Chicago: St. Clair Press.

Takane, Y., Young, F., & De Leeun, J. (1976). Nonmetric individual differences multidimensional scaling: An alternating least squares method with optimal scaling features. *Psychometrika, 42,* 7–67.

Tolman, E. C. (1955). Principles of performance. *Psychological Review, 62,* 315–326.

Tversky, A., & Kahneman, D. (1974). Judgments under uncertainty: Heuristics and biases. *Science, 185,* 1124–1131.

Vroom, V. H. (1964). *Work and motivation.* New York: Wiley.

Wahba, M. A., & Bridwell, L. (1976). Maslow reconsidered: A review of research on the need hierarchy theory. *Organizational Behavior and Human Performance, 15,* 212–240.

Water, L. K., & Roach, D. (1973). A factor analysis of need fulfillment exams designed to measure Maslow need categories. *Personnel Psychology, 26,* 185–195.

Weiner, B. (1991). Metaphors in motivation and attribution. *American Psychologist, 46,* 921–930.

Wiggins, J. S. (1979). A psychological taxonomy of trait-descriptive terms: The interpersonal domain. *Journal of Personality and Social Psychology, 37,* 395–412.

Wofford, J. C. (1967). Behavior styles and performance effectiveness. *Personnel Psychology, 20,* 461–495.

Wofford, J. C. (1971). The motivational basis of job satisfaction and job performance. *Personnel Psychology, 24,* 501–518.

Wolf, M. G. (1970). Need gratification theory. *Journal of Applied Psychology, 54,* 87–94.

CHAPTER 6

Action as the Core
of Work Psychology:
A German Approach

Michael Frese
Dieter Zapf
University of Gissen, Gissen, Germany

*To establish a general theory of work behavior, one must begin with the concept
of action. Action is goal-oriented behavior that is organized in specific ways by
goals, information integration, plans, and feedback and can be regulated consciously or via routines. We will describe general theory along these lines. This
is quite a different theory from the typical American theories in industrial and
organizational psychology. This becomes quite clear when this general theory
is applied to understanding certain phenomena:*

- *Errors. Errors are the converse of efficient action. We will present an action
  theoretic taxonomy of errors and some empirical results. The concept of error
  management allows an active approach to dealing with errors.*

- *Interrelationship between work and personality. From an action theory point
  of view, a person develops his or her personality by acting. Thus, working has
  some impact on the development of personality. From this, it follows that work
  should enhance personality. Action styles provide a way
  to understand personality from an action theory perspective.*

- *Development of competence at the workplace and training. A particularly
  important concept is the issue of the superworker in action theory. The
  superworker uses better and long-term strategies, has a better understanding
  of the work tasks, and organizes things better than other workers, but does
  not work more than they do. Training enhances worker skills in the direction
  of the superworker and, therefore, the area of training has been of traditional*

importance to German action theory. We will discuss issues in training (e.g., active approach in learning, understanding, accidental learning, the use of heuristics, learning from feedback and errors, automatization of skills, and transfer).

- *Task characteristics. We will present task characteristics from an action theory perspective, including task analysis instruments developed in Germany, and will discuss resources for action regulation, regulation requirements, and action regulation problems (stress).*

- *Work design. Finally, we will discuss the issue of work design from an action theory point of view.*

Introduction

THE BASIC ISSUE of a psychology of work has to be concerned with actions. Actions are goal-oriented behaviors. Without a conscious goal, there is hardly any possibility for a person to take action. A goal may be to develop a new motor, to achieve a certain career post, to write a letter, to finish one piece of work at the assembly line. Additional goals may be to earn money with one's work or to do one's job well.

Therefore, the basic starting point for industrial and organizational psychology has to be work action. This is what persuaded German industrial and organizational psychology to develop an action theory.

This is not the typical starting point in the United States. Here, the phenomena studied the most seem to be two types of prerequisites of action: abilities used in selection research and motivation. While they undeniably play an important role, one has to deal with the fact that people demonstrating the highest performance in a job are not always the most motivated workers, but rather those who have the best cognitive understanding of the job and the better work strategies (Hacker, 1992). In this chapter we will deal with a set of issues for which an action theory orientation proved useful. At the same time, we will see that the theory of action provides an integrative account of what happens with, to, and from the person working.

Three kinds of readers will profit from this chapter: (a) those who would like to become familiar with a rather well-developed cognitive theory of work behavior and who do not have access to the German literature in this area; (b) those who want to get to know an alternative theory to some of the dominant paradigms of American industrial and organizational psychology; and (c) those who are interested in the specific topics of this chapter: errors, work and personality (including action styles), superworkers and training, task characteristics (including job discretion, complexity, and stress at work), and work design. In general, action theory is a "grand theory" that provides quite a broad approach to understanding work actions in general. Unfortunately, this chapter may not be easy to read. Since it is necessary to first develop the theory in an abstract way, the reader will only become aware of its usefulness, and empirical underpinnings, after he or she has looked at the specific action theory topics.

Action theory is a cognitive theory. But unlike many cognitive theories, it is tied to behavior. It is an information processing theory. But unlike many information processing theories, it is tied to objective work environments and to the objective work outcome. It is a behavior-oriented theory. But unlike behavioristic theories, it is concerned with the processes that intervene between environmental input and behavior: the regulatory function of cognitions.

German psychology has by and large been more interested in grand theories than has the Anglo-American tradition. Action theory builds on the grand theory of Lewin and its newer system theory version of Miller, Galanter, and Pribram (1960). At the same time, it has been influenced by Soviet psychology, particularly Rubinstein (1962, 1968), Leontiev (1978, 1981), Vygotski (1962), and Luria (1959, 1970). Other influential figures were Oschanin (1976), Galperin (1967), and, in Polish praxeology, Tomaszewski (1964, 1978).

It should be added, however, that there are English versions of action theory that resemble the kind of theory we will discuss. For example, Carver and Scheier (1982) and Anderson (1983) have presented such theories. It should also be pointed out that the use of such theories in German work psychology is much older (the first books on this topic were Hacker, Skell, & Straub, 1968, and Volpert, 1971) and better developed.

Grand theories or frameworks are very often empirically and theoretically not as well developed as some readers may think they should be. One reason that it is fun to work with action theory is that it has been used—or promises to be used—to provide a unified framework to human factors, industrial psychology, and organizational psychology—namely, work psychology. Since all of these disciplines are facets of our knowledge of people's work, an analytical framework of work action is capable of integrating otherwise isolated issues of stress, errors, job performance, and skill development.

Action Theory: Toward a General Theory of Work Behavior

It is naive to think of general theories as ideas to be simply applied in work (Schönpflug,

in press; Semmer, 1993). The degree of specification of a theory has to be adequate for its application. It is finer in general psychology and less fine in work psychology. Moreover, external validity questions are more important in work psychology than in general experimental psychology. Finally, work psychology problems often involve many variables that are not completely tested.

An action can be described from two points of view. First, an action proceeds from a goal to a plan, to its execution and to feedback being received. This is the action process. Second, an action is regulated by cognitions; the regulation processes can be conscious (called "controlled" by Schneider & Shiffrin, 1977) or automatic. This is the structure of action. Both points of view are combined in action theory. For purposes of exposition, we will present these two aspects of action consecutively.

The Action Process

The action process consists of the following steps (Dörner, 1989; Frese & Stewart, 1984; Hacker, 1985, 1986a; Norman, 1986; Tomaszewski, 1964, 1978): (a) development of goals and decision between competing goals; (b) orientation, including prognosis of future events; (c) generation of plans; (d) decision to select a particular plan from available plans; (e) execution and monitoring of the plan; and (f) the processing of feedback.

Figure 1 presents these action steps. This model presents the action process as an orderly affair. Of course, actions are often quite chaotic; for example, goals may change in the middle of an execution. Moreover, later steps in the action process may change earlier ones; for example, a goal may be changed after one notices that the plan is not good. The figure presents a good first approximation. In the text that follows, we will discuss each of these action steps.

FIGURE 1

The Action Process

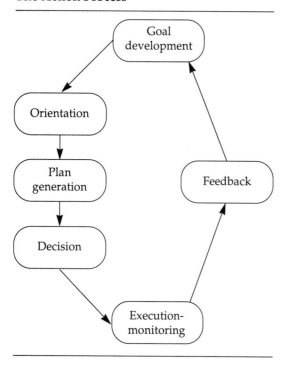

Goal Development and the Role of Tasks.
The goal is certainly the most important concept in action theory, since action is defined as goal-oriented behavior. Hacker (1986a, p. 73) defines an *action* as the smallest unit of behavior that is related to a conscious goal. The concept of goal integrates motivational and cognitive concepts. The goal is a point of comparison for the action (the cognitive aspect), and the action is "pulled" by the goal (the motivational aspect).

Actually, it is a gross oversimplification to begin a description of the action process with a goal. As Heckhausen and Kuhl (1985) have pointed out, at first there is really a wish. This wish may be translated into a want. When there are potential opportunities, the time is right, and there is some urgency and importance,

these wants may translate into an intention and then act as action-guiding goals.

While this is generally true of actions, the starting point for work actions is the task (Hacker, 1986a, p. 69). Usually a person is given a task at work and is expected to proceed with the task according to some rules. A *task* is the intersection between the individual and the organization (Volpert, 1987b). Via tasks, an individual or a subgroup takes over a part of the overall organizational goals.

It is useful to differentiate between an *external* and an *internal* task. People are developing goals either when they are creating their own tasks or when they are taking over external tasks. The external task is presented by the organization, though sometimes in a very general manner.

The result of an external task has to be anticipated as a goal, and conditions for its execution have to be taken into consideration. Making an internal task out of an external one is accomplished through the *redefinition process* (Hacker, 1982b, 1986a; Hackman, 1970). The task presented by an organization to an individual worker must be understood—it is interpreted on the basis of prior knowledge and general terms of the trade, and it is taken over in light of standards and certain implications. For example, if a supervisor asks a person to tend a machine, the worker can respond in two possible ways when the machine breaks down. The worker might simply wait until the supervisor comes by again to mention the problem, or the worker might fix the problem or actively report the problem to the supervisor. Many social conflicts can occur when different redefinitions collide, such as when a supervisor sees different implications in a particular action than a worker does.

Thus, the redefinition process depends on the degree of understanding of the external task and its clarity; the expectations, the values, the degree of acceptance, and the willingness to carry out the task; and the workers' prior experiences (Hackman, 1970).

The fact that goals are implied by tasks should not be mistaken to mean that people passively respond to environmental stimuli. Rather, according to action theory, people influence and shape their environment as well. Goals are changed according to one's accomplishments, usually in the direction of higher efficiency on the environment (White, 1959). Thus, most humans will proceed to develop new goals, even when a certain goal has been achieved.

Goals anticipate future results; therefore, goals should be considered anticipative cognitive structures (Hacker, 1986a, p. 115) that guide the action process. Goals are to a certain extent invariant—that is, they do not change very quickly (Hacker, 1985). A person still knows and pursues his or her goal even if the plan of action led astray. Only by being invariant to a certain extent can goals function as set points to interpret feedback.

While the actual behavior guiding goals is usually conscious, it does not have to be in the focus of attention all the time. Once a certain action pattern is put into effect, it is not necessary to keep the goal in consciousness unless the action pattern fails. This is particularly true for supergoals (like life goals; e.g., to be honest or successful in what one is doing). Often action patterns have the status of an implicit goal.

Actions are often directed toward multiple goals, and while acting on one goal, people scan the environment for opportunities to act on other goals. This leads to several problems. One practical problem is that the various goals may be contradictory (e.g., the goals of being honest and polite, increasing the profit rate, or trying to make people feel good at work). A theoretical problem is which goal will be operative at any particular time. The latter has been emphasized in the various theories of expectancy x valence theories (e.g., Heckhausen, 1991; Vroom, 1964). Since these theories, which also originated from Lewin, have been well developed in the Anglo-American literature (and are

discussed by Kanfer, 1990, in the first volume of this *Handbook*), they do not need to be discussed here.

Reither and Stäudel (1985) have pointed out that goal development requires effort and is therefore usually reduced to a minimum. Goals are developed while the task is being carried out. Since often little thought is put into goal development, people have a tendency to overlook contradictions between different goals. Also, goals are often developed without reference to potential negative effects that occur after the goal has been achieved (e.g., what to do with the atomic waste that is created once a nuclear power plant has been built).

In general, important—and partly interrelated—parameters of goals are the following:

- *Difficulty.* Goal difficulty has to be distinguished from goal or task *complexity.* While complexity is related to the number of units in a system and their relationships to each other, difficulty has a more restricted meaning: A given degree of complexity may still pose various degrees of difficulty. For example, to shout louder than 90 decibels is more difficult than to shout louder than 60 decibels but not necessarily more complex.

- *Specifity of the goal.* Specific goals can be described in detail; a specific goal, therefore, usually has clearer implications for action than a more global goal. An example of a manager's global goal is that people should be satisfied in their jobs; an example of a specific goal is that the profit rate should be increased by 10 percent (Dörner, 1989; Locke & Latham, 1990).

- *Hierarchization of goals and subgoals.* This implies that subgoals are formed (goal decomposition; Dörner, 1989). This is not identical to goal specificity. For example, raising the profit rate by 10 percent is highly specific, but it may be very difficult to describe the sub-goals necessary for reaching that goal.

- *Connectedness of goals and subgoals.* This implies that the different goals and subgoals are checked for potential contradictions.

- *Time range.* It is self-evident that goals can be oriented toward the future (long range) or toward the near future (short range).

- *Valence.* This is one of the better re-searched areas of psychology, referring to the positive or negative value that is attached to a goal state and its relation-ship (instrumentality) to other goal states (Heckhausen, 1991).

- *Process versus end-state goals.* Process goals are goals directly related to an action. Thus, the action itself is the goal. For example, a ballet dancer's goal is to move in a certain way. Often, process goals can be conceptualized as standards that should be maintained, such as behaving politely or conserv-ing energy while working. In contrast, producing a commercial product is an end-state goal.

- *Efficiency divergence of goals.* This con-cept (Oesterreich, 1981, 1982) suggests that one should choose subgoals with the highest number of options (diver-gence) to reach potential other goals with a high likelihood (efficiency). For example, in a career path, a person may choose a low-salary position in a prestigious university because it opens many options for later jobs. Subgoals with high efficiency divergence should be approached when it is difficult to develop a whole plan in advance. Computer simulation experiments showed that high efficiency diver-gence subgoals were actually prefer-red by the subjects, even when other

more favorable possibilities existed (Resch & Oesterreich, 1987). Moreover, subjects preferred action domains that included many points of high efficiency divergence, and they were more success-ful in reaching their goals within such action domains (Oesterreich, Resch, & Weyerich, 1988).

Orientation, Prognosis, and Signals. The ori-entation reflex is a basic response of human beings. Orienting oneself toward something novel is the lowest level of analysis of situational and object conditions. In dynamic systems, objects may change even without an intervention by the actors. Here, prognoses of future states must be calculated (e.g., the infla-tion rate when investing money).

Prognosis and orientation have been studied by Dörner and his group in problem-solving approaches using highly complex com-puter simulation programs (Dörner, 1987b, 1989; Dörner, Kreuzig, Reither, & Stäudel, 1983; Reither & Stäudel, 1985). To orient one-self within a system, one must search for and collect information, develop good analogies, and use abstract schemata. Of particular im-portance is a problem's *level of decomposition*. For example, repairing a machine re-quires a fine level of decomposition, as the various parts of the machine must be known. On the other hand, knowing everything about the particulars of the machine is of much less use to the production worker who must know how to operate the machine. (As a matter of fact, the repairperson may be less efficient us-ing the machine, although he or she knows much more about it than the production worker.)

Orientation often means to attend to signals, because signals are action-relevant stimuli that are integrated into some knowl-edge system on the work task. This means that the worker has to know different forms of a certain signal prototype and process characteristics and how they are translated into observable signals. The worker also must have an action plan associated with the signal at his or her disposal (Hacker, 1986a, p. 118).

The following are important issues of signals (see also Hacker, 1986a, p. 232):

- The number of signals that need to be reacted to

- How easy it is to differentiate a signal from background noise and other signals (contrast and number of alternative signals; e.g., see Patterson, 1990)

- Compatibility and population stereotype (e.g., a red signal meaning stop and a green signal meaning go; e.g., see Hoyos, 1974)

- The predictability of when a signal appears and what kinds of signals one can expect

- Transparency of signals in terms of understanding the meaning of the signal within a system

- Consistency of the signal—that is, whether a particular signal has the same meaning all the time

- The active search for signals and the active construction of signals versus waiting for signals to come

In every case, the signals are related to the knowledge and the mental models that the worker has about the work process. (Later, the concept of mental model from an action theory point of view will be discussed.) Signal detection and the actions taken are therefore highly dependent on this knowledge.

Plan Generation and Decision.   Some kind of plan is usually developed before the action occurs. This plan is, of course, not necessarily worked out in detail. Most often it is a simple list of subgoals. Sometimes the plan consists of an elaborate structure of a plan and backup plans in case something goes wrong. These plans can be more or less consciously represented or automatized (more on this later).

The action theory concept of *plan* is not to be confused with everyday uses of the term. The theoretical concept of plan means everything from a first idea of *how* to proceed to an elaborated blueprint (Miller et al., 1960). Also, a representation of well-automatized sensorimotor skills (like walking) is conceptualized to be a plan. Because of the different meanings of *plan* in action theory and everyday life, the term *action program* was introduced. *Action program* and *plan* are used interchangeably in this chapter.

Many aspects of the concepts of plans, strategies, and tactics will be discussed in the various application areas of action theory in this chapter. Therefore, only the important parameters of plans need to be mentioned at this point.

- *Detailedness*. As pointed out, a plan may or may not be developed in detail before action is taken. When the plan is not detailed beforehand, then it is worked out during the action itself.

- *Inclusive of potential problems—backup plans*. This is a variant of detailedness, but of a specific sort: One may develop backup plans in case something goes wrong, and even plan for events that are unlikely to happen.

- *A priori hierarchization of plans*. Plans can be broken up into subplans before the decision is made to take action. When acting, plans always have to be connected to lower-level plans; otherwise, no action would occur. Of course, the hierarchy of plans is related to the hierarchy of goals, but the two things are not the same. It is possible to have goals (or subgoals) without having a plan for how to achieve them. This will be discussed in more detail later.

- *Long range versus short range.* Similar to goals (and, of course, related to them), plans can have a long range into the future (e.g., a career plan) or a short range (what to do during the next few minutes).

- Miller et al. (1960) thought plans to be the bridges between thought and action. They are made up of TOTE (test, operate, test, exit) units. Thus, a plan is always a combination of thought and action. A TOTE unit consists of testing how far one has moved in one's action, performing an operation to get nearer to the goal, and testing again. If the goal (or subgoal) is achieved, one exits from this TOTE unit into the next one. Thus, there is no plan completely outside action and there is no action completely outside planning.

- The decision concerning which plan (or goal) to pursue has not been researched much within the tradition of action theory. There is, of course, a large body of research on decision theory that concerns itself with these questions (Baron, 1988).

Execution-Monitoring.   Insofar as planning always implies some kind of operation, it is actually superfluous to include a separate phase of execution. However, from the perspective of higher-order plans, it is important to distinguish between the execution of a plan and the waiting period. For example, the overall plan to achieve a professorship at a prestigious university is not dealt with at each point in time. But it is important for the individual to note and take advantage of certain opportunities, such as when meeting a professor from that university. Thus, timely subplans should be used (see the concept of triggering in Norman's, 1981, activation-trigger-schema theory).

Various aspects are important for plan execution.

- *Flexibility.* How quickly is a plan abandoned if it does not work out immediately? Volpert (1974) suggests that efficient action implies steering a middle course between flexibility of the plan and keeping one's goals. Thus, one should be flexible enough to adjust plans to environmental demands but stable enough not to give up goals too easily.

- *Speed.* Speed of plan execution has been researched heavily within other theories (and one of the important concepts, of course, is the speed–accuracy tradeoff; e.g., Wickelgren, 1977). Within action theory, speed has been emphasized as important in dynamic situations (Dörner, 1989).

- *Sharing and coordination of plans.* In many cases, tasks have to be accomplished cooperatively. This requires communication about goals and plans in several respects. Tasks have to be redefined in the same manner, leading to compatible and supplemental goals and plans. Furthermore, the time frame of plan execution must be coordinated (Cranach, Ochsenbein, & Tschan, 1987; Cranach, Ochsenbein, & Valach, 1986).[1]

- *Overlapping plan execution.* One can either follow only one plan at one time or follow several. Hannover (1983) has shown that there are individual differences in how people do several tasks—consecutively or overlapping in time. This is related to the issue of multiple goals—whether they are pursued consecutively or not.

The execution of the action is at the boundary of the subjective and objective world.

Therefore, action theory is not subjectivistic because actions change the objective world and the person receives feedback from the (changed) objective world. For this reason, practitioners of action theory feel comfortable with the behavioristic emphasis on the real stimulus situation; however, they are interested in the process of the interactions between the objective and subjective worlds.

Feedback Processes. Generally speaking, feedback is information about how far one has progressed toward the goal. Feedback is neither completely outside the person nor completely inside. It is partly outside because feedback puts the person in touch with the real world of objects. On the other hand, without a goal in mind, there is no chance to understand or conceptualize feedback—thus, feedback is a relational concept. Therefore, feedback can only be interpreted with reference to a goal. There is no doubt that without knowledge of results, there is no progress, such as in learning or performance improvement (Annett, 1969; Volpert, 1971). Thus, feedback is of particular importance for work performance.

There are some useful distinctions between various aspects of feedback, most of them developed in the area of sensorimotor skills (see Holding, 1965; Semmer & Pfäfflin, 1978a; Volpert, 1971):

- *Concurrent versus terminal feedback.* There is feedback concurrent to one's actions (like proprioceptive feedback) and knowledge of results after a certain action plan has been completed.

- *Extrinsic versus intrinsic feedback.* Extrinsic feedback, also called artificial or augmented feedback (Annett, 1969; Holding, 1965), is introduced for the purpose of training (e.g., a ringing bell telling us that we have reached a target). Intrinsic feedback is given during the execution of the real-world task itself. Intrinsic feedback can be proprioceptive (information from the vestibular system; kinesthetic information) or exterioceptive (i.e., tactile, visual, auditive, or olfactory information).

- *Immediate versus delayed feedback.* Research shows how difficult it is for people to use delayed feedback to guide behavior (Brehmer & Allard, 1991; Cratty, 1973; Dörner, 1989; Lee, 1950).

- *Verbal versus nonverbal feedback.* Verbal feedback is usually more effective. One reason is that it comprises more information than nonverbal feedback (Holding, 1965).

Certain parameters can be differentiated in feedback processing.

- *Amount of "realism" versus self-serving interpretations.* Dörner (1989) found in his simulation experiments that people who processed feedback in a self-serving manner showed lower performance. Receiving negative feedback may affect the self-concept. When feedback is interpreted within a framework of keeping up the self-concept instead of dealing with the problem, actions are less effective.

- *Reaction to the social content of feedback versus reaction to the performance content.* Since feedback is often communicated via people, the social content of feedback may be important. Some people react primarily to the social rather than the performance content of feedback. This may lead to defensive strategies (e.g., when a superior only notices that a subordinate criticizes him or her).

- *Feedback search rate.* In highly uncertain dynamic situations, it is important to actively search for feedback and react

FIGURE 2

The Hierarchic Structure of TOTE Units

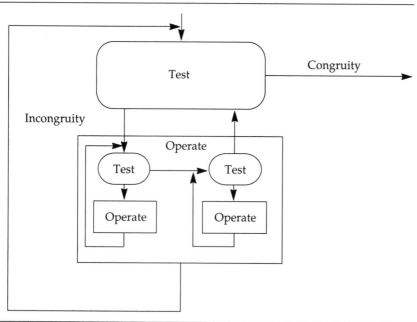

From *Plans and the Structure of Behavior* (p. 36) by G. A. Miller, E. Galanter, and K. H. Pribram, 1960, London: Holt.
Copyright 1960 by Holt. Adapted by permission.

quickly to it (Dörner, 1992). A high feedback search rate and planning activities may be opposed to each other, since a high feedback search rate may in and of itself lead to working memory overload.

The Hierarchical Structure of Action

The structure of action must be organized hierarchically. If actions were regulated by internal models in a nonhierarchical and sequential way, then models for every action would have to be stored in memory. Obviously, this behavioristic approach is not feasible. As Chomsky (1957) and Carver and Scheier (1982) have pointed out, the infinite number of potential concrete operations must be organized and generated by higher levels of regulation.

Tayloristic time and motion studies in work psychology are equivalent to behaviorist concepts in general psychology. Only the surface structure of the behavior of work is looked at. Action theory attempts to understand the "deep structure of action" as well (Hacker, 1982b, p. 91).

The hierarchy of action regulation is composed of so-called functional units (Volpert, 1982). The starting point of discussing functional units was the TOTE unit by Miller et al. (1960; see also Hacker, 1985, 1986a; Volpert, 1974, 1982); the TOTE units may be nested hierarchically (see Figure 2). Its basic technical analogy is the cybernetic feedback loop.

One can have several points of critique with the TOTE model (and action theorists in Germany have discussed these in depth). For example, the model does not clearly indicate that there are goals and feedbacks within this model (they are tucked away under the terms of *test* and *incongruity*). Moreover, the model looks too self-contained (or like a closed loop; Hacker, 1986a; Kuhl, 1983). There is, of course, an environment that may, for example, change the goals or plans. People will also sometimes construct the feedback themselves; thus, there is an active process of developing feedback. Moreover, goals can change, and therefore there is a dynamic development of action structures that is not well represented in Miller et al.'s theory. Every new goal leads to another set of actions because of new discrepancies between the world and the goals. There are also multiple goals that lead the concert of actions; for example, when working on a specific task, one may also want to do it efficiently and at the same time elegantly. In sensorimotor skills, parallel movements are organized by multiple goals as well (Broadbent, 1985; Fuhrer, 1984).

Finally, one critique is that action theory is concerned only with single actions pertaining to a single goal. Some of the conclusions in the discussion on multiple actions and the issue of heterarchy within action theory (Broadbent, 1985; Fuhrer, 1984; Gallistel, 1980; Kaminski, 1973; Turvey, 1977; Volpert, 1983) include:

- It is in principle not difficult to include multiple actions within action theory. Since planning must be anticipative to a certain extent, action anticipation goes beyond the particulars of the action itself. This means that a certain amount of parallel processing has always been assumed in action theory.

- Two actions running their course can be intertwined with each other; often this is done by some time-sharing process on the intellectual level of regulation.

- A hierarchy does not imply that the lower levels of regulation have no regulatory functions except those delegated from above. Of course, lower levels

react to feedback (even if, as in the case of proprioceptive feedback, conscious processes are not involved) and adjust the action to situational conditions without involvement of higher levels.

- Lower-level actions can lead to changes in the goals at higher levels when it turns out that one cannot pursue them adequately.

- Some errors show that lower levels can have "a life of their own." This implies that there is no "dictatorial power" of the higher over the lower level, but rather a sort of "negotiation" process (Turvey, 1977). The primary example is capture errors (Reason, 1979), in which a habitual routine takes precedent over a conscious plan, as in the case of a driver who takes a direct route home, although she had planned to divert to buy clothing. These actions that don't go as planned appear as intact sequences of action, perfectly coherent in all respects except that they were not what was intended at that time (Reason, 1988). This suggests that low-level habits can take over the action path vis-à-vis conscious higher-level plans.

For these reasons, the concept of hierarchy may be too strong. However, *heterarchy* is not really a good term, since *hetero* means "different" in Greek. We prefer the term *weak hierarchy* (Turvey, Shaw, & Mace, 1978). These points of critique should not divert attention from the fact that functional units are nested in some kind of upper- and lower-level processing.

Volpert (1982, p. 39) describes in Figure 3 how the functional units can be grouped into a hierarchic-sequential pattern. This model assumes a temporal organization: First an overall goal is set and then a series of functional units are produced and executed in a top–down manner. This means that once the lower-level units have been completed, the

FIGURE 3

The Hierarchic-Sequential Model of Action Regulation

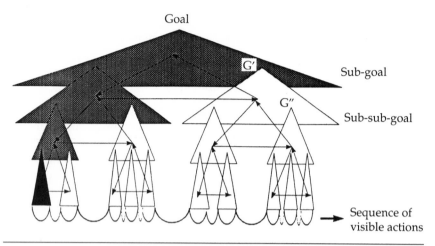

From "The Model of the Hierarchical-Sequential Organization of Action" by W. Volpert. In *Cognitive and Motivational Aspects of Action* (p. 39) by W. Hacker, W. Volpert, and M. Cranach (Eds.), 1982, Berlin: Hüthig Verlagsgemeinschaft GmbH. Copyright 1982 by Hüthig Verlagsgemeinschaft GmbH. Reprinted by permission.

goal of the upper-level unit is accomplished. Some functional units (the gray areas) are resident but not in the foreground of attention, while the black unit is the one acted upon. The white units are not yet really thought out or fully activated—they will be elaborated and activated during the course of action. The regulations are elaborated before they actually are used in the action process—the term *breadth of anticipation* is used here (Hacker, 1973). The ascending arrows signify feedback (this is the bottom–up part of this figure). If the subgoal has been attained, the unit is completed.

A concrete example of such a hierarchic process is Hacker's (1986a, p. 137) description of how a tree along the street is replaced (see Figure 4).

This hierarchy is usually described as going from higher levels (the intellectual level) that control and monitor the action process to lower levels directly linked to muscular activities (the sensorimotor level). Actually, we think there are two, albeit related, dimensions

involved. One goes from conscious thought to automatized behavior, the other from thought to muscular action.

The first dimension goes from consciousness to automaticity. Consciousness does not necessarily imply that a thought is verbalizable; it can also be a vivid thought, picturing a certain action (e.g., Shephard & Metzler, 1971). Conscious strategies are necessary when a new problem is tackled or when a more routinized strategy fails to work.

With practice in redundant environments, actions become routinized and automatic. Then they tend to have the following characteristics (Semmer & Frese, 1985): (a) They become more situationally specific, (b) they require less effort, (c) they involve overlap between different operations, (d) they require less feedback from the environment, (e) they require fewer (or no) decisions to be made, and (f) movements take on a more parsimonious form.

The second dimension implies that thoughts can translate into muscular movements. Newer

FIGURE 4

The Hierarchic Structure of Action: An Example

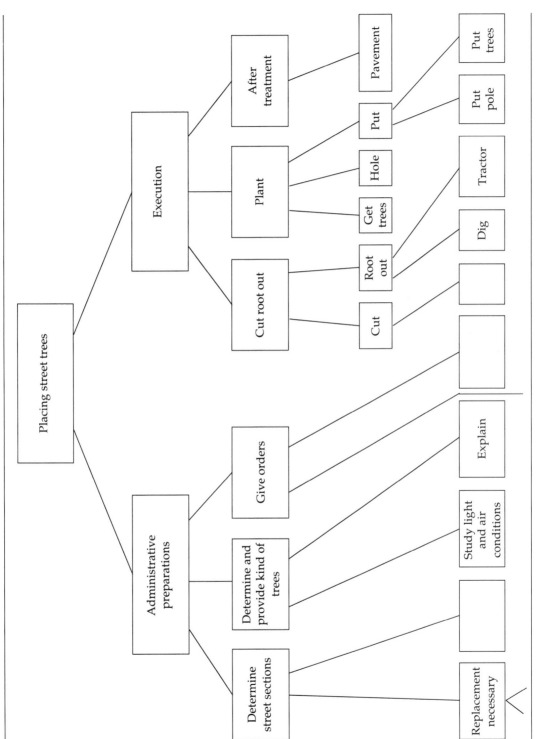

From *Arbeitspsychologie* (p. 137) by W. Hacker, 1986a, Bern, Germany: Huber. Copyright 1986 by Huber. Reprinted by permission.

research, particularly by Gallistel (1980), whose theory was strongly influenced by the German biologist von Holst, shows the mediating mechanisms between a general goal and muscular movements, and does not need to be repeated here. A separate set of research on mental training (Vandell, Davis, & Clugston, 1943), taken as evidence for action theory, showed that just mentally imaging a certain movement led to an improvement in the skills of using these movements (Ulich, 1967, 1974). This phenomenon is documented well (Heuer, 1985). Moreover, mental training leads to physiological arousal in the muscle used in the imagined movement (Wehner, Vogt, & Stadler, 1984) and in pulse and breathing rate; however, the latter is somewhat reduced in comparison to actually doing a certain task, but is stronger than just watching the task (even the latter implies an increase in pulse and breathing rate; Rohmert, Rutenfranz, & Ulich, 1971).

It is interesting to note that the upper halves of both dimensions are related to conscious thoughts. Moreover, sensorimotor skills can combine both dimensions as well: They usually are highly routinized and related to muscular movements. For these reasons and for economy of exposition, these two dimensions are usually combined into one, and different levels are differentiated. The following four levels[2] seem to be most useful (Hacker, 1973; Semmer & Frese, 1985).

The Sensorimotor Level of Regulation.   The sensorimotor level is the lowest level of regulation. Stereotyped and automatic movement sequences are organized without conscious attention. Regulation takes place with the help of proprioceptive and exterioceptive feedback. This type of regulation is largely unconscious and is done with little subjective effort (Kahneman, 1973). The concept of automatic processing (Shiffrin & Schneider, 1977) can be applied here. Information processing at this level is parallel, rapid, effortless, and without apparent limitations. Conscious regulation has

some difficulty to modify action programs at the sensorimotor level. It can stop the action, but it is much more difficult to modify an automatized action.

At this regulation level, different levels of complexity of movements may occur. For example, performing a delicate ballet figure is more complex than driving a nail into a wall. Because of parallel information processing at this level, the execution and coordination of parallel movements is possible, but training for the movement must be done to a great extent at this level. For this reason, the ballet figure has to be practiced repeatedly for one to become accustomed to it. What makes the actions at this level difficult is the number of movements to be coordinated, their timing, and their accuracy.

The Level of Flexible Action Patterns.   Action patterns can be conceptualized as schemata (see Norman, 1981, 1986; Schmidt, 1975). These are ready-made action programs that are available in memory and must be specified to situationally defined parameters. These action programs have been previously established and must be activated and integrated into an action chain for a specific situation. Moreover, the action patterns can be adjusted to the situation (Volpert, 1974). According to Hacker (1986a), these action programs are largely dependent on the perception of signals. Since in his view signals are well-trained concepts, they can trigger these well-trained action schemas.

The Intellectual Level of Action Regulation.   On the intellectual level, complex analyses of situations and actions concerning problem solutions are regulated (Hacker, 1973). New action programs are designed comprising analysis of goals and environmental conditions, problem solving, and decision making. Execution on this level is necessarily conscious. It is slow, laborious, resource-limited, and works in a serial mode, interpreting feedback step by

TABLE 1

A Model of Levels of Regulation

Levels of Action Regulation	Sensorimotor Level	Level of Flexible Action Pattern	Intellectual Level	Heuristic Level
Consciousness of regulation	Unconscious; normally no access to consciousness	Access to consciousness possible, but not necessary	Conscious representation necessary	Both conscious and automatic use of heuristics
Elements of the operative image system	Movement-oriented schemata; not necessarily conscious	Flexible action schemata	Complex, intellectually mediated image systems	Generalized heuristics, possibly automatized
Goals	No independent goals available	Subgoals	Goals	Standard and metagoals
Action programs	Blueprints of elementary movement patterns and cognitive routines	Well-known action patterns with situational specifications	Conscious complex plans, strategies	Metaplans, heuristics
Feedback/ signals	Stereotype test programs, unconscious processing of kinesthetic and proprioceptive feedback signals	Processing of known signals/ feedback	Analysis and synthesis of new information	Abstract (nonobject-oriented) checks, logical inconsistencies

After Hacker, 1985, 1986a; Semmer & Frese, 1985; Volpert, 1975, 1987b.

step (see Shiffrin & Schneider's, 1977, controlled processing).

A similar kind of trichotomization has been developed by Rasmussen (1982, 1987a, but without reference to Hacker, 1968, 1973, or German action theory). He differentiates between knowledge-, rule-, and skill-based strategies.

The Heuristic Level.   The intellectual level is object oriented; metacognitive heuristics cannot be regulated on this level. Therefore, an additional heuristic level was introduced by Semmer and Frese (1985).[3] On this level, the

heuristic functions of how to go about a certain problem or a class of problems in a certain area are regulated, logical inconsistencies are tested, and abstract heuristics are generated. The concept of metacognitions is related to regulation at this level (e.g., Brown, 1988; Gleitman, 1985).

The different levels of regulation are presented in Table 1 in a summary form. They are quite important concepts in action theory. They have only been sketched out briefly at this point, but the issues of levels of regulation will be taken up again when we discuss the applications of action theory.

The Operative Image System
as the Knowledge Base for Regulation

In addition to the levels of regulation, there is
the so-called operative image system. The operative image system can be considered as the
sum of internal long-term representations of
condition–action–result interrelations (Hacker,
1986a). It is the cognitive base for action regulation and comprises the knowledge that enables a person to act. Long-term representations comprise movement-oriented schemata
to be regulated largely unconsciously at the
sensorimotor level, flexible action schemata
regulating routinized actions at the level of
flexible action patterns, more complex schemata and strategies to be related to the intellectual level, and metaplans and heuristics referring to the heuristic level.

In other cognitive systems, procedural and
declarative knowledge have been differentiated (e.g., see Anderson, 1976). This should not
be confused with the difference between
plans and goals and the operative image system. The operative image system is itself action
oriented. Action theory does not deny that
there is knowledge that is not linked to action
at all. However, it is seen as the uninteresting
part of mental events—at least of little relevance for applied psychology.

Operative image systems do not directly
regulate actions. The correctness and sophistication of the operative image system determines the quality of the actions via goals, information processing, plans, and so on. Hacker
(1986a) describes the operative image system
of a process control operator. The operator
knows which processes take place, how they
are related to technological parameters, how
this is part of the total structure of the plant;
and the operator knows a lot of signals and
how to act if they appear and the consequences
of potential actions. The better the operator's
operative image system, the more efficient the
operator's actions will be.

There is some relation of the concept of the
operative image system with the "mental
model" (Gentner & Stevens, 1983; Norman,
1983). Mental models and operative image
systems are similar insofar as the information
they store is not a true copy of reality. Both
share properties like selection of information and incompleteness. However, the term
operative emphasizes the action-oriented character of operative image systems. They are
developed by actions and comprise action-
oriented images (e.g., how to print a text double-
spaced). The concept of mental models is more
an internal model of an external system—for
example, a computer program (e.g., how formatting functions are organized in submenus).
Action theory emphasizes the fact that operative image systems are learned and built by
acting.

Properties of the Operative Image System.
Operative image systems are prerequisites of
the regulation processes. They include knowledge on goals, plans, and feedback. During
action preparation (goal development, orientation, and plan development), operative image
systems have guiding functions. They guide
orientation and lead to parsimonious search
strategies.

They are usually selective and even dis-
torted because operative image systems do
not have to represent a complete picture of the
work situation. They need only represent those
issues that are important for the tasks done.
They can, for example, exaggerate differences
of important signals and underrate irrelevant
ones. Thus, operative image systems work with
generalized schematic features (Bartlett, 1932;
Piaget, 1969).

Not every action is represented. Thus, the
problem of storage space is solved: The operative images imply rough outlines of actions that
do not exceed storage space and can be comple-
mented during the action process. Operative
image systems are cost-optimizing systems.

FIGURE 5

Applications of Action Theory: An Overview

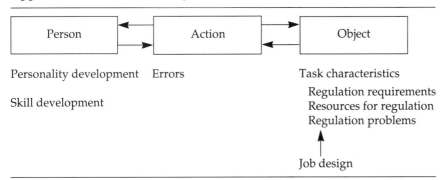

For example, they generate strategies that meet job requirements with the least amount of effort. The cost of storing information is optimized as well. Therefore, expenditures of decoding and encoding are minimized and stored in terms of rules and heuristics.

Operative image systems have to be differentiated from short-term processes of regulation (e.g., goal and plan development, monitoring, feedback processes). While operative image systems are elements of long-term memory, action programs must be kept at least partly in the working memory (Reason, 1990). The goals present information that certain parameters have to be retrieved from long-term memory to working memory.

Operative image systems comprise long-term knowledge on the input conditions of one's task, the throughput conditions, and the expected and prescribed results (Hacker, 1982a, 1985). The knowledge of the input conditions includes the intervention points, the laws of technological processes, and the conditions of the raw material. The throughput conditions imply knowledge of plans, tool use, signals, typical errors, and expected probability of success. The knowledge on expected and prescribed performance results should include

in-between outcomes, standards, set points, and prediction of consequences, including unwanted ones.

Applications: An Action Theory Understanding of Phenomena in Industrial and Organizational Psychology

Action theory is useful in understanding certain phenomena that are typical of industrial and organizational psychology: errors, personality and work, competence and training, task characteristics, and work design. Figure 5 describes action as the mediator between the person and the work object. Without action, there is no change in the work object. The objective world of work, again, influences the actions. Personal prerequisites have an impact on action, but action also has an impact on the person.

The following presentation will be organized along the lines of Figure 5. At first we shall continue to concentrate on action as the centerpiece of the theory. Up to this point, action has been assumed to work out. Errors are the converse.

On the left side of Figure 5, aspects of the person are described; the two most important issues are personality development and competence. On the right side—the object side—the task characteristics are most important and will be presented next. Work design influences the task characteristics (and thereby also influences, for example, the development of competence, mediated by actions); work design is discussed last.

Errors in Actions

Action theorists have always been interested in the efficiency of action (Semmer & Frese, 1985; Volpert, 1974). Therefore, there has been great interest in the converse: inefficiency and errors. First we will discuss a definition of errors. Second, we will present a taxonomy of errors. Third, we will summarize some validity hypotheses that both support the error classification scheme as well as the basic theory. Finally, we will discuss some practical implication of error analyses.

Definition of Errors.   There are three elements of a definition: (a) errors only appear in goal-oriented action, (b) they imply the nonattainment of goals, and (c) an error should have been potentially avoidable (Frese & Zapf, 1991b; Zapf, Brodbeck, Frese, Peters, & Prümper, 1992).

This definition is, for example, contrary to a phenomenological approach, which defines an error as an out-of-tolerance action, or a technical approach, which defines error as the violation of a rule or not meeting the normal system standard. Since one could purposely deviate from externally imposed actions or purposely violate a rule, this would not be considered erroneous from a psychological point of view (see Sellen, 1990). For example, risky behavior is often an intended deviation from a prescribed course of action (Hoyos, 1980; Hoyos & Zimolong, 1988). This definition of errors is in line with other cognitive and action-oriented approaches (see Arnold & Roe, 1987; Norman, 1984; Rasmussen, 1987b; Reason, 1987a, 1990).

Errors and inefficient behavior have a large conceptual overlap. A detour to reach a goal may be conceptualized as inefficiency but also as error, because usually one's goal is to proceed in the most straightforward manner (see Volpert, 1974). Pragmatically, behavior is inefficient even when it is successful in attaining a goal if the goal should have been more easily attained in a more direct manner (*direct* implies that each subaction leads closer to the goal and that no subaction has to be undone; Zapf, Brodbeck, & Prümper, 1989).

Since an action-oriented approach to human errors looks at errors in human action, this could easily lead to the assumption that it is always the human being that fails. However, scientifically it is quite difficult to give one clear cause of an error. Usually there is a chain of causes, and it is more or less arbitrary where one should stop seeking further causes (see Rasmussen, 1987c). Errors should therefore be considered the result of mismatched conditions within a sociotechnical system (Rasmussen, 1982, 1985).

A Taxonomy of Errors.   Errors can be differentiated according to steps in the action process and the different levels of action regulation. In addition to the levels of regulation, there are errors in the knowledge base for regulation.[4]

Figure 6 depicts a general taxonomy of errors (Frese & Zapf, 1991b, p. 21). Since there are hardly any theoretical criteria on what and how many types of errors should be differentiated, practical criteria are important: A taxonomy proves its relevance if different error types lead to different practical consequences, such as in training and system design.

The following categories exist (some examples stem from the domain of human–computer interaction for which the taxonomy was originally developed; for details, see Frese

FIGURE 6

A General Taxonomy of Errors

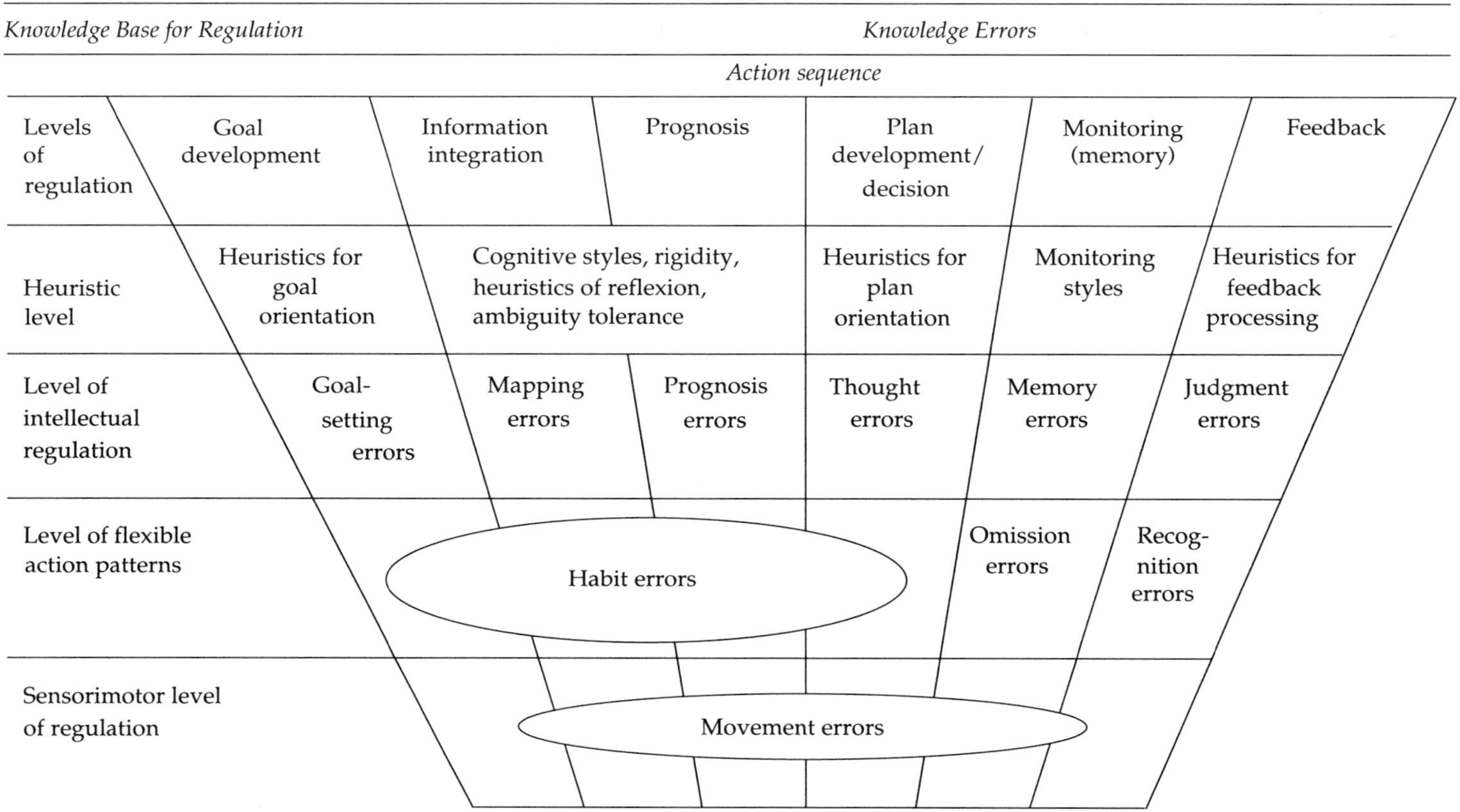

Knowledge Base for Regulation

Knowledge Errors

Action sequence

Levels of regulation	Goal development	Information integration	Prognosis	Plan development/ decision	Monitoring (memory)	Feedback
Heuristic level	Heuristics for goal orientation	Cognitive styles, rigidity, heuristics of reflexion, ambiguity tolerance		Heuristics for plan orientation	Monitoring styles	Heuristics for feedback processing
Level of intellectual regulation	Goal-setting errors	Mapping errors	Prognosis errors	Thought errors	Memory errors	Judgment errors
					Omission errors	Recognition errors
Level of flexible action patterns	Habit errors					
Sensorimotor level of regulation	Movement errors					

From "Fehlersystematik und Fehlerentstehung: Ein theoretischer Überblick" by M. Frese and D. Zapf. In *Fehler bei der Arbeit mit dem Computer. Ergebnisse von Beobachtungen und Befragungen im Bürobereich* (p. 21) by M. Frese and D. Zapf (Eds.), 1991b, Bern, Switzerland: Huber. Copyright 1991 by Huber. Reprinted by permission.

& Altmann, 1989; Frese & Zapf, 1991a; Zapf et al., 1992).

Knowledge errors occur when there is a lack of knowledge of facts about the tasks and the tools to carry out the tasks.

At the *heuristic level*, action styles, cognitive styles, and the impact of a lack of self-reflection can be discussed. *Cognitive styles* and *action styles* can be described as generalized and automatized heuristics. Cognitive styles are typically investigated with reference to errors (Messer, 1976); for example, reflexivity versus impulsivity using the matching familiar figures test (see Kagan, Rosman, Day, Albert, & Phillips, 1964) or field dependence using the embedded figures test (Witkin, Dyk, Faterson, Goodenough, & Karp, 1962). Dörner (1981, 1987b) described lack of self-reflection as an important prerequisite for errors in problem solving. Good problem solvers showed more self-reflections than bad problem solvers. Furthermore, the number of self-reflections decreased under conditions of failure.

On the *intellectual level* of action regulation, errors occur because the information processing capacity is limited (see Reason, 1990). *Errors in goal setting* occur when goals are inadequately developed. Examples for typical errors described by Dörner (1989, 1991) are the deficient decomposition of global goals into subgoals. Goals are sometimes unclear: There is only a vague criterion that helps in deciding whether the goal is achieved or not (e.g., the library should become more user-friendly).

Mapping errors occur in gathering, integrating, and elaborating information (Dörner, 1991). Here, the goals are correct, but information needed to reach the goals is ignored or processed incorrectly. In complex situations it is often necessary to search actively for information. A series of simulation studies showed the difficulties people have in predicting the behavior of dynamic systems (Dörner, 1987a; Dörner et al., 1983). For example, *prognosis errors* occur in predicting nonlinear system states (e.g., prognosis of AIDS incidents;

Badke-Schaub, 1990; Dörner, 1989). *Thought errors* occur when plans are inadequately developed or when wrong decisions are made in the assignment of plans and subplans. Typical planning errors occur when long-term and side effects are not considered, or in methodism, which is the unreflected replication of a course of action that has been successful before (Dörner, 1991; also Luchins & Luchins, 1959). *Memory errors* occur when a certain part of the plan is forgotten and not executed, although the goals and plans were initially correctly specified. *Judgment errors* appear when one cannot understand or interpret the feedback.

Errors on the *level of flexible action patterns* occur when well-known actions are performed. *Habit errors* imply that a correct action is performed in a wrong situation. Some examples from human–computer interaction are presented by Zapf et al. (1989, 1992): A person switches from the use of one word processing system to the next one. Doing this, she still uses the function keys that were correct in the former system but which are now incorrect. There is a tendency to use more routinized behaviors even if they are not adequate (Semmer & Frese, 1985; see also Reason's [1990] frequency gambling and Rasmussen's [1982] model). *Omission errors* occur when a person does not execute a well-known subplan. An example may be that a person forgets to save a file after he is interrupted by a telephone call, although he usually does this routinely at the end of a session. *Recognition errors* occur when a well-known message is not noticed or is confused with another one.

Movement errors are placed at the *sensorimotor skill level*. There is only one category here because at this level it is empirically difficult to differentiate between planning, monitoring, and feedback. For example, typing errors or stumbling could be classified at this level (for more on this, see Gentner, 1987; Grudin, 1982).

Though there are other error taxonomies (e.g., Arnold & Roe, 1987; Heckhausen &

Beckmann, 1990; Norman, 1981; Rasmussen, 1982; Reason, 1987b, 1990), they are usually not validated in field studies. A field validation study was carried out by Frese and Zapf (1991a; Zapf et al., 1992). In this study on computerized office work, a reduced version of the taxonomy described above was used (see Figure 6).

As hypothesized, errors at the intellectual level of regulation and knowledge errors required more error-handling time. This is the case because the in-tellectual level implies conscious thoughts that are processed in a slow, sequential mode. Additionally, the errors are more complicated at this level. Knowledge errors imply a need for additional time because one must either look information up (e.g., in a handbook) or explore to find the correct procedure. Errors at the intellectual level and knowledge errors can often be corrected only with some external support (such as from co-workers; Brodbeck, Zapf, Prümper, & Frese, 1990).

Errors at the lower levels are related to well-known actions; moreover, handling of a wrong action step is usually not complicated at lower levels (Zapf, Lang, & Wittmann, 1991). Therefore, errors at lower levels can usually be corrected without any external help.

Knowledge errors appear more frequently in novices. Novices do not have enough knowledge about, for example, functions or commands. They also make more thought errors because they have more difficulty applying their computer knowledge to their tasks. In contrast, expert users make more habit errors. This is expected because expert users regulate more actions at the lower levels (Prümper, Zapf, Brodbeck, & Frese, in press). Thought and memory errors appear more often in highly complex jobs (Zapf et al., 1992) because complex jobs require more regulation at the intellectual level.

Sensorimotor errors fall into a separate class. First, there is no need for support. Second, differences from habit errors are apparent in the distribution of novices and experts. These empirical results are encouraging and support a taxonomy of the type suggested here.

The Error-handling Process. Error handling can be defined as the process from error detection to recovery from an error (or quit to recover). The error-handling process comprises the following stages (see Bagnara & Rizzo, 1989; Reason, 1990; Zapf et al., 1991): error occurrence, error diagnosis (including error detection and explanation), and error recovery.

Error detection is defined as the user's realization that an error has occurred independently from knowing what the error is like and how it came about (Zapf, Maier, Rappensperger, & Irmer, in press). To know whether an error has occurred or not implies some knowledge about the user's goal. Thus, error detection is essentially related to the feedback that there is a deviation from the goal. In many cases, the people involved in the action themselves are the only ones who know about their goals. In all these cases, only they can detect the error. For example, say a user wants to adjust the page layout margins but instead presses the print key. In this case, only the user knows that an error has occurred, since the result looks reasonably correct. In such a case, error detection cannot be done by a computer. The results of both a field study and some experiments showed that error detection by computer systems has clear limitations (Zapf, Frese, et al., 1991; Zapf, Lang, E. Whittmann, 1991; Zapf et al., in press).

The Concept of Error Management. There are essentially two ways to deal with errors: error prevention and error management. The more typical strategy used by software designers, trainers, and industrial engineers is the attempt to reduce the number of errors. In contrast, an error management strategy does not reduce the number of errors per se but attempts to make error handling easier rather than trying to avoid errors under all circumstances (Frese, 1991; Frese & Altmann, 1989). To understand the concept of error management, one must differentiate between the error occurrence and the negative error consequences. For example, one negative error consequence is time loss due to an error. An error management strategy exists when a system supports quick and effective recovery procedures.

There are several reasons for using error management (Frese, 1991):

- It is often assumed that errors occur more often in complex work environments. The most important strategy to reduce complexity is to increase the division of labor. A reduction of complexity should lead to a reduction of errors as well. Our data show a relationship between complexity and errors for thought and memory errors but not for all other kinds of errors (Zapf et al., 1992).

Increasing the division of labor was, of course, the strategy suggested by Taylor and his followers (Taylor, 1913). Taylor's strategy stands in contrast to work design concepts developed by action theory (see the section on work design later in this chapter).

- One strategy for solving the problem of human errors is automatization. The less people actually do, the fewer errors there should be. In one sense, this strategy works. However, the long-term consequences might be rather negative. This has to do with the "ironies of automatization" (Bainbridge, 1983). The automated production or data flow must be supervised by human beings. This means that error-prone human beings should interrupt production if something goes wrong with a machine. However, such actions are rarely practiced anymore and skills not practiced will not run smoothly and without problems.

- Some argue that errors can be avoided by qualification. However, qualification does not reduce the number of errors

per se; as a matter of fact, in some cases experts commit even more errors than novices (fewer knowledge but more habit errors; Prümper et al., 1992).

- The data on error detection show that it is not possible to automatize error recovery because only a small percentage of errors can be detected by the system (Zapf et al., in press). Undetected errors cannot be handled by the system.

- Last, but not least, empirical studies both in psychology and engineering show that it is impossible to avoid errors completely.

The concept of error management tries to overcome the potential negative side effects of error prevention. Error management is a special case of giving control to the worker.

With these empirical findings in mind, the advantages of an action theory approach to human errors can be summarized.

- Unlike phenomenological approaches, an action theory approach to errors is based on underlying psychological mechanisms (see Rasmussen, 1987a). Based on phenomenological error descriptions, it would be difficult to develop measures to overcome error situations.

- The model integrates different approaches to human errors—for example, errors in complex problem solving (Dörner, 1987a, 1987b, 1989, 1991); the analysis of action slips (Heckhausen & Beckmann, 1990; Norman, 1981; Reason & Mycielska, 1982); taxonomies based on Rasmussen's skills, rules, and knowledge classification (Rasmussen, 1982, 1987a, 1987b; Reason, 1987b, 1990); and taxonomies oriented to the action process (e.g., Rouse & Rouse, 1983). Errors in complex problem solving are located at the higher levels of regulation; action slips at the lower levels.

- The model clarifies the differentiation between mistakes (wrong intention) and slips (correct intention but wrong execution; Norman, 1984; Reason & Mycielska, 1982). The concept of slip indicates first that there is an error in a routine action and second, that it is an execution error but not an error in the intention. However, errors of execution are not necessarily at the lower levels of action regulation; they can also occur at the intellectual level. If someone wants to do a multivariate analysis of an empirical problem and chooses, for example, the multivariate variance analysis procedure correctly (correct goal), then the decision for a wrong parameter is still the result of intellectual regulation but at the same time part of the wrong execution of the correct goal (i.e., slip). According to our model, this would be an error at the intellectual level of regulation.

- Action theory distinguishes between errors at the intellectual level of action regulation and knowledge errors, which is not done by Rasmussen (1982, 1987a) and Reason (1987b, 1990). Errors at the intellectual level are more dependent on the complexity of a task; knowledge errors are mainly dependent on users' qualifications (Zapf et al., 1992).

- Action theory is able to explain the somewhat surprising finding (Prümper et al., in press) that additional expertise does not necessarily lead to fewer errors. The person with a higher level of expertise delegates regulation to lower levels (routine levels). This implies that the chances of committing

errors at these levels increase with expertise.

- Finally, the concept of feedback-driven actions implies that errors and correct actions are two sides of one coin. Feedback drives behavior by comparing the current state with the goal. Errors are essential feedback components of human actions. Errors often tell us that our picture of reality is not congruent to reality. Therefore, errors also have a positive function (Frese, Brodbeck, Heinbokel, Mooser, Schleiffenbaum, & Thiemann, 1991). They support the construction of realistic models of the world and are necessary steps toward achieving a goal.

Work and Personality

In the Anglo-American literature, personality is usually taken as the independent variable in industrial and organizational psychology. Action theory presupposes that this may not necessarily be the case. Since work is the prototype of action and since in work action personality is changed, personality may be the dependent variable (Hacker, 1986a; Rubinstein, 1968).[5]

This is the area of occupational socialization (Frese, 1982). Needless to say, action theory quite enthusiastically embraced the concept of lifelong development (Baltes, Reese, & Lipsitt, 1980), with work being a major factor in the adolescent and adult years.

Moreover, German-speaking work psychology has turned the issue around in the sense that it is believed that work should allow further chances for the enhancement of the personality[6] ("Persönlichkeitsförderlichkeit der Arbeit"; Hacker, 1986a; Ulich, 1978b; Volpert, 1989). Quite a bit of the discussion in German-speaking work psychology surrounds the question of what constitutes prerequisites of good work design. Since work psychology is supposed to provide a methodology for work design, criterion issues on the adequacy of a work situation are important. Much of this is ontological—for example, the criterion that work should not damage a person's mental and physical health in the long run or that work should allow social interactions to take place.

One of these criteria is the chance for personality development. This criterion emphasizes particular aspects of personality—namely, a set of cognitive and procedural skills developed in work, like problem-solving, social, and general metacognitive skills (Hacker, 1986a). One should be able to use one's abilities, develop one's own goals and plans for work, and use creative ideas in work. Two important issues are the chance for the individual to be active in work and the acceptance of the job in the society (Hacker, 1986a; Ulich & Baitsch, 1987).

Personality enhancement should lead to a transfer from work to active and enjoyable leisure activities (Hoff, 1986; Hoff, Lempert, & Lappe, 1991). It should also be related to productivity because of the higher level of qualification of the workers and because of better work strategies (see the issue of superworkers discussed later).

Empirically, there are some well-established effects of work complexity on intellectual functioning and flexibility that are about as strong as the impact of education (Häfeli, Kraft, & Schallberger, 1988; Kohn & Schooler, 1978, 1983; Schleicher, 1973). Research has been done with different methodologies and different dependent variables. While Kohn and Schooler (1978) have used a measure of intellectual flexibility that has not been validated independently (Greif, 1978), Schleicher (1973) has used a traditional IQ measure (the Intelligence-Structure-Test of Amthauer, 1955) and essentially found a similar relationship. These empirical results suggest that certain skills developed in complex work situations generalize to some kind of general use of flexible intellectual functioning.

Moreover, the relations between work and leisure activities (Hoff, 1986; Karasek, 1976, 1978; Meissner, 1971; see also Ulich & Baitsch, 1987) show some spillover from work into leisure time; however, these relations are certainly complex and difficult to interpret, and causal relations have not yet been well analyzed.

One concept helpful in understanding how work can translate into personality development is action styles (Frese, 1983; Frese, Kreuscher, Prümper, Schulte-Göcking, & Papstein, in press; Frese, Stewart, & Hannover, 1987; Sonnentag, Frese, Stolte, Heinbokel, & Brodbeck, 1992). For example, if the work environment encourages the development of long-range goals, this may transfer to actions outside work. Two concrete action styles researched were goal orientation and planfulness (Frese et al., 1987). Goal orientation means that a long-range goal is developed in detail and that it is particularly persistently pursued. Similarly, planfulness implies that the plan is long-range–oriented, that the plan is not given up quickly, and that it is developed in detail before action is taken (e.g., there are backup plans available in case something goes wrong).

The functioning of these action styles is assumed to be related to the following process (Frese, 1983; Frese, Stewart, & Hanover, 1987): To have long-range goals is a metacognitive heuristic that is developed on the heuristic level (see the earlier discussion of the levels of regulation). The use of this heuristic can be automatized as well. Thus, if a person is often in a situation that requires long-range goal setting, this heuristic to set goals with a long-term orientation will be automatically used. Automaticity implies that the first thought for a person with high goal orientation in unconstrained (or weak) situations (Weiss & Adler, 1984) may be questions like, "What does this imply in the long run?" Automaticity does not imply, of course, that this person always uses a long-range goal because she may consciously decide to use a different strategy in this particular situation or the situation may suggest the use of a certain strategy in the first place.

Since automaticity develops with practice, the job can either strengthen the use of a heuristic used before entering the job (since it is now practiced repeatedly, it will become automatized) or a new heuristic can be developed at work and automatized there. Finally, a prior heuristic can be reduced in its applicability. This may mean that the generality of the action style is reduced.

A questionnaire on goal orientation and planfulness was shown to have adequate reliability and validity (Frese et al., 1987). Goal orientation has been related:

- Negatively with depression in several studies (Frese et al., 1987, Frese et al., in press)

- Positively to the Type A behavior pattern (Frese et al., 1987)

- To growth need strength (Frese et al., 1987)

- To students' grade point average (Frese et al., 1987)

- To leaders' goal orientation with performance in software development groups (Sonnentag et al., 1992)

- To good performance in insurance agents (Frese et al., in press)

- To programmers with high goal orientation who can recognize important material in programs more quickly (Albrecht, 1988)

Planfulness was less clearly related to work variables, although one study shows that there is a weak positive correlation with work complexity and with certain forms of inefficiency (Stumpf, 1991).

We would assume that the action-style goal orientation might be a moderator in goal-setting studies, although we do not have empirical support for this supposition yet.

Another action style is action versus state orientation (Kuhl, 1983, 1992). Kuhl (1982) argues that people are in different metacognitive states when they have formed an intention; they may either be occupied with goal-irrelevant cognitions about the situation and about their emotional state or they may be oriented toward planning and acting. The former is called *state orientation*, the latter *action orientation*. A scale measuring the construct was shown to mediate between the intention and the action (Kuhl, 1982). State orientation also leads to a perseverance effect in which people stick to an unattractive task that they have begun (switching is more action oriented; Kuhl, 1983, 1992). Moreover, this action style moderates the influence of noncontrol situations on helplessness, with only state-oriented people showing the helplessness effects (Kuhl, 1981). On the other hand, managers with high state orientation are probably better decision makers in complex and risky situations, while action-oriented managers are better decision implementers (Kuhl, 1992).

Another issue relating work and personality is control. Control at work implies a certain amount of autonomy with regard to the sequence, time frame, and content of the work goals; work plans; the use of feedback; and the conditions of work (Frese, 1989). Not having control implies that the goals and plans of work are outside the person working (this is related to Hackman & Oldham's, 1975, concept of autonomy). An example would be that a person is told in detail how to perform a certain procedure at work. Control at work may have an influence on control cognitions. While this has been shown to be true in cross-sectional studies, there is no longitudinal evidence for this assertion (Frese & Zapf, 1988). One would assume that this leads to less self-confidence in one's goal and plan development—a notion similar to self-efficacy (Bandura, 1986). For this reason, people with low control at work should also be more passive and less productive (Karasek & Theorell, 1990). In situations that require independent actions, such as using and applying a new software program to one's work, control at work is an effective moderator (Papstein & Frese, 1988). Thus, knowing that one is in control of one's goals and plans may have its own impact on productivity (Hacker, 1986a).

In a study on East German blue collar and white collar workers (Frese, Zempel, Kring, & Soose, in press), the relationship between control at work and developing initiative vis-à-vis work issues has been shown to be true as well. Moreover, people with less control at work rely on more authoritarian principles in education (Kohn, 1969).

For this reason (and for the effect of control in health issues; see Frese, 1989; Karasek & Theorell, 1990), control cognitions have been of interest to action theorists.

Thus, personality is seen as the dependent variable within action theory research. Obviously, action theory does not deny the importance of personality variables as predictors of work performance and adjustment. As a matter of fact, there are suggestions to adapt the work situation to personal prerequisites, including personality variables of a person. This is one issue of work design that is taken up in the last section of this chapter.

Competence and Its Development

One of the crucial variables for action theory is competence. Therefore, there has been quite a lot of research in this area and on the question of training. It is in the area of performance that action theory has the most promise. Anglo-American work psychology has usually focused on motivation when looking at performance. The most important interest of action theory has been in knowledge of the background of the production process and in the work strategies used.

Performance, Knowledge, and the Super-worker.   There is, of course, more than one way to increase performance. Hacker (1986a) distinguishes the following methods.

General Increase of Activation.   This is a pure motivational approach. It does not change the

direction of task performance but just the intensity. While this is certainly useful over short periods of time, in the long run activation has more negative effects by increasing fatigue and the number of errors, including a decrease in error detection. For this reason, Hacker (1986a) suggests use of the following strategies, which are all based on some kind of learning.

Sensibilization.   This implies that signal differences can be perceived adequately. For example, steel workers can perceive very small differences in color of the melt in a blast furnace. This gives them a signal concerning whether the iron is ready or not. Similarly, radiologists can discover the smallest abnormalities in an X-ray picture with phenomenal speed (Dahm et al., 1991). Of course, sensibilization is a result of practice and the development of a good operative image system.

Psychological Automatization.   With practice in redundant environments, skills become routinized. This has the advantage that the use of automatized skills does not require a high level of cognitive effort; additionally, the movements are smoother and more parsimonious because different movements, thoughts, and actions overlap to a greater degree (Hacker, 1986a). Moreover, cognitive operations can be performed while acting because automatized operations do not require a lot of attention.

However, there are also disadvantages: Automatization carries with it a certain degree of rigidity. This rigidity is partly due to the fact that there is no conscious attention to the action and to the feedback. It is also difficult to unlearn automatized skills. Reintellectualization of an automatized skill is not only effortful, it is also very slow. Particularly under stressful conditions, there is a tendency to revert back to prior automatized skills (Semmer & Pfäfflin, 1978b).[7]

Verbalization.   Verbalization may mean two things. First, it may mean conscious verbalizable knowledge of some facts or some work procedure. If something is explicitly verbalized, it helps to orient one's attention toward the right signals. It also facilitates flexible knowledge. Second, and more importantly, the learning process is facilitated by verbalization. Galperin (1967) has suggested that learning is facilitated by interiorization of speech. Thus, it would help to verbalize a certain work procedure. This verbalization is then interiorized, which means the verbalization is shortened until an abbreviation of a command is used to regulate behavior. Thus, more and more, external speech becomes inner speech. Elssner (1972) has shown the viability of such a procedure in training (more on this later in the section on training).[8]

Intellectual Penetration. By this, Hacker (1986a) means a deep intellectual understanding of the task and of the activities necessary to accomplish the task. Intellectual penetration is what differentiates superworkers from average workers. Superworkers have a better operative image system. For example, excellent blue collar workers are more realistic about how long it will take to carry out a task (Hacker, 1986a); excellent white collar workers are more realistic concerning the time it will take to perform a computer task, and they can anticipate better what another person would want to do with a certain procedure (Lang, 1987a). Because of their higher anticipation, superworkers perform fewer work activities and produce more, as in the case of weavers with semiautomatic looms (Herrmann, 1967). A North American study on managers yielded similar results: The best managers anticipated more problems, knew more about the implications of an event, predicted events more accurately, and avoided negative ones (Klemp & McClelland, 1986). Similarly, Jeffries, Turner, Polson, and Atwood (1981) found that expert programmers used more time to understand the problems at hand than nonexpert programmers.

In another set of studies, Rühle (1979) and Schneider (1977) have shown the differences between excellent and average blue collar workers in a textile factory. Table 2 shows Hacker's (1992) summary of their results. This table is another indication that it is not the greater motivation to work hard that distinguishes superworkers from nonsuperworkers, but rather a better operative image system and better work strategies.

While Hacker and his co-workers usually looked at blue collar work, in another set of experiments Dörner and his colleagues (Dörner et al., 1983) have used very complex computer simulations. For example, subjects had to work as a dictatorial mayor of a city. These computer simulations included 4,000 variables that were interdependent and dynamic (e.g., inflation increased even when nothing was done, the number of unemployed in the city changed when investments were low). Each experiment lasted for several days.

Successful subjects had more precise goals and asked more questions, particularly more "why" and more abstract questions. The questions were also on the right level of decomposition; in other words, they made sure to develop an adequate operative image system that was useful in understanding the problems at hand. This allowed them to set clearer and better priorities (e.g., economic priorities of inflation reduction instead of providing every citizen with a public telephone). They also developed more hypotheses and tested their hypotheses. They planned more, directed their actions more toward their goals once they were established, and did not act impulsively. They made more decisions and had more goals. They were more self-reflective and thought more actively about changing things rather than just describing them (Dörner et al., 1983; Reither & Stäudel, 1985).

They were also less neurotic, but there were no differences in IQ compared to the bad performers (Dörner et al., 1983; Dörner & Kreuzig, 1983; Dörner & Pfeifer, 1991). This result is, of course, akin to Sternberg's

TABLE 2

Empirical Results on the Superiority of Superworkers in Two Studies

Area	Criteria	Direction of Results	Significance
Intensity of work	Use of work time; speed	—	n.s.
Sensorimotor skills	Skills in two areas	—	n.s.
Operative image system	Search time for causes of errors	Shorter	Sig.
	Error prevention	More frequent	Weak sign
	Disruption of normal work for planning	More frequent and longer	Sign
	Organizing periods of machine use without tending them	More frequent and longer	Sign
	Interviews		
	Knowledge of frequency of errors	More comprehensive	Sig.
	Knowledge of signals of error causes	More comprehensive	Sig.
	Knowledge of duration of repair and other operations	More exact	Sig.
	Knowledge of efficiency of strategies	More comprehensive	Sig.

Adapted from "Expertenkönnen. Erkennen und Vermitteln" by W. Hacker. In *Arbeit und Technik* (Vol. 2; p. 15) by M. Frese and H. Oberquelle (Eds.), 1992, Stuttgart, Germany: Verlag für Angewandte Psychologie. Copyright 1992 by Verlag für Angewandte Psychologie. Reprinted by permission.

discussion of practical intelligence (e.g., Sternberg, 1986).

More Active Approach. A more general description of the work strategies of superworkers is Hacker's (1986a) differentiation of momentary versus planning strategies.[9] Momentary strategy implies that one reacts to the situation that exists at the moment. In contrast, a person using a planning strategy plans ahead and actively structures the situation, including potential feedback. Thus, planning strategy implies a more comprehensive and more penetrating intellectual representation of the work process, a longer time frame to plan ahead, a larger inventory of signals, a better knowledge and anticipation of error situations, and a more active orientation toward work.

This comparison also sheds some light on the riddle that superworkers sometimes seem to work less yet produce more. Because of their planning strategy, they are more efficient in the sense of getting a higher yield with less effort than people using a momentary strategy. Hacker and Vaic (1973) found that superworkers were not significantly different from other workers in their actual work time (time spent in production), but there were significant differences in preparatory activities (e.g., getting supplies), in having exact goals in work, and in presenting work rationalization ideas to the company.

The concept of superworkers is somewhat different from the concepts of novice versus expert. There is certainly some conceptual overlap between them. The novice versus expert concepts are quite fuzzy but are often based on the dimension of experience. In contrast, the superworker concept refers to the notion of efficient strategies of action, which may very well be different from experience.

Thus, there is ample evidence that superworkers in real-life work situations show a better understanding of work processes and potential strategies, and also use more active strategies to control the work situation rather than have it govern them. This is not only true of blue collar workers, but also of managers and subjects in a very complex simulation. Superworkers do not necessarily work harder (they usually do not, and sometimes show even less work behavior) than other workers, but work more efficiently.

Skills and Skill Acquisition. Much of the literature on training in action theory was done in the area of sensorimotor skills (e.g., Ulich, 1964, 1967, 1974; Volpert, 1971, 1976) and learning computer skills (Frese et al., 1988; Greif, 1989). However, there is also an active literature on training in social skills (Hartwich & Okonek, 1979; Kühbauer & Schmidt-Hieber, 1978; Rieger & Rummel, 1979; Semmer & Pfäfflin, 1978a), although there is less research in this area.

From action theory comes the following propositions on skill acquisition and training:

- People are active learners.

- The action is regulated by an operative image system. The better a training program improves this system, the better is the action.

- Every person begins a learning situation with a rudimentary operative image system. Accidental learning results will be incorporated into this system.

- Cognitive strategies and heuristics structure the training process and

lead to a better operative image system for the training process.

- People learn from feedback and errors.

- In the beginning of the learning process, the rules and plans are conscious. With practice, they are transferred to lower levels of regulation.

- Transfer of training to everyday work depends on task orientation and practice support at work.

- Mental training should have an effect on physical performance.

People Are Active Learners. One assumption of action theory is that people are active toward their environment (Rubinstein, 1968). As a matter of fact, learning is facilitated by action. Only through action is it possible to develop routines. In principle, one can have thoughts that are not related to actions. In such a case, these thoughts will not really regulate action (Semmer & Frese, 1985). Only thoughts that are actually connected to actions will result in better performance. It is easier to solve a problem that is action oriented than one that is not (Johnson-Laird, 1983). Even perception may be much more action oriented than classical perception theory held to be true (Gibson, 1979; Hofsten, 1985; Neisser, 1985). Again, it is easier to learn something about the environment when we are acting on it than when we are sitting still.

In the training literature, an active approach has been discussed under the rubric of exploratory learning (Bruner, 1966; Greif, 1992; Greif & Keller, 1990). There is ample evidence that this approach is superior to learning that does not allow an active approach (Carroll, Mack, Lewis, Grischkowsky, & Robertson, 1985; Frese et al., 1988; Greif & Janikowski, 1987, Greif & Keller, 1990; see however, contrasting discussion by Ausubel, Novak, & Hanesian, 1968). In one study (Hiltscher, 1992; Hiltscher & Frese, 1992), two training procedures were compared—one attempted not to allow any exploration (sequential training); the other necessitated exploration. One result was that the exploration group learned more than the sequential group. However, there was a second, more important finding: Our hypothesis was that some people in the sequential training would deviate from the instruction and would explore anyway. We found that those subjects learned more than the people who actually followed the instruction.

The Importance of an Operative Image System. Ausubel et al. (1968) were critical about exploration because it always involves a certain amount of "blind trial and error." They suggest giving trainees a clear cognitive orientation—an advanced organizer—to enhance training. This is also in line with trainees' preferences to be able to first observe the skill that they are to learn and then use more active approaches of learning (Volpert, 1969). Thus, these concepts speak for the importance of the operative image system.

A good operative image system leads to better performance. It is developed by providing good background knowledge on the work process involved and a set of principles by which the work process and the task execution is done effectively (Freier & Huybrechts, 1980; Josif & Ene, 1980; Rühle, Matern, & Skell, 1980).

The operative image system must have two characteristics. First, it should be in some way holistic; thus, it should include the important parameters of the task. In tasks that are too complex to learn in one practice session, an overall global concept of the task should be given to the trainee (Volpert, 1971). This stands in sharp contrast to the sequential orientation that Seymour (1954) suggested. The sequential orientation leads to one-sided and low-level training procedures and thus produces little intellectual insight into the task.

Second, the operative image system has to be action oriented. In an observational study on computer users, only those parts of the mental model that had direct relevance to actions were useful (Lang, 1987b).

There is a certain contradiction between the issue of exploration just discussed and the issue of providing a good operative image system. In fact, exploration implies a certain amount of trial and error, though this may be hypothesis-driven. In contrast, presenting a good operative image system in the beginning of training helps to avoid trial-and-error periods, although discovery learning is minimized. In actuality, most training programs do not pit discovery learning against giving a good mental model before the training—rather, they use both. For example, Greif and Janikowski (1987) have first presented an orientation poster that provides a hierarchy of the program commands to be learned. Next, they gave the subjects a chance to explore.

In one experiment, these two procedures were tested against each other (Frese et al., 1988). One group of computer-naive subjects received an orientation poster (Greif & Janikowski, 1987) and a good introductory handbook. The other group—the exploratory group—was asked to develop some hypotheses on how the computer program might function and tried out to work with these hypotheses (at some point, the trainer would provide a correct answer). Both groups did about equally well with an insignificant superiority of the exploratory group. In another experiment simulating a chemical process control, performance was better for a group that received a set of optimal rules than it was for a group that developed its own set (Freier & Huybrechts, 1980). One explanation for the superiority of the rule presentation may have been that feedback—which is crucial for exploratory learning—was not optimal.

Thus, there may be two different processes by which a high degree of learning takes place—the learning made by active exploration and the learning made by using good rules. Both may also lead to high performance. Note that both involve practice. However, exploratory training emphasizes learning through action to a higher degree than learning through the use of good rules (which may prove positive), but it may invariably lead to certain errors and pitfalls. They may in turn lead to incorrect conceptualizations that need to be eradicated over the long run (which may work against efficient learning). In contrast, initially giving a good operative image system reduces the amount of active learning (which may actually reduce good learning). This is true even though it will give a good mental model initially, thus minimizing wrong turns and dead-end roads (which may prove positive). Of course, a combination of the two approaches would be best from an action theory point of view.

The action theory perspective in training implies that pure drill has its limits (Frese et al., 1988; Semmer & Pfäfflin, 1978a). Drill may provide certain experiences in performing a task. However, drill reduces the chances to develop a good mental model. Drill may work with very rudimentary types of tasks, but if the task has a certain amount of complexity, important task characteristics will be missed because they are not self-evident (not even when a model is presented). Drill just produces skill acquisition on a lower level of regulation. Therefore, an intellectual understanding will be minimized. Additionally, drill does not guarantee flexible reactions when environmental changes occur because action patterns have been learned as invariants.

Rudimentary Operative Image System and Accidental Learning.   People start out with a rudimentary operative image system. This is usually some kind of metaphor or analogy. For example, a typewriting metaphor is often used by computer novices when they are learning a word processing system. This leads to characteristic errors, such as in the interpretations of blank spaces and the possibility to overwrite a blank. A blank has no particular meaning when one is working with a typewriter, while

it has its own representation in a word processing program. In contrast, using the metaphor of building block letters leads the subjects to avoid creating blanks, since a block letter "blank" is conceptualized to exist (Waern & Rabenius, 1987).

Humans beings are uniquely adjusted to changing environments by drawing inferences very quickly. This has the disadvantage that a mental model is formed even when there is actually not enough information available. In one training, we observed a computer novice perform the following process with a word processing system: When inserting a letter, he would first "make room" for it by inserting a blank space, then, he would insert the letter and delete the blank space that was now unneeded. He had been using this procedure quite consistently for a long period of time. People develop operative image systems quite quickly and without having an adequate knowledge base (Norman, 1983). This means that trainees should be cautioned against developing a fixed operative image system too early. Exploration may help to reduce a premature fixation because people are encouraged and sometimes forced to test new hypotheses. Additionally, trainees should learn to look for disconfirming experiences (this may be an advantage of error training, as will be discussed later).

Cognitive Strategies and Heuristics.   One way to sharpen the operative image system and avoid premature fixtures on one type of explanation is to give heuristics to trainees. Training with heuristics has been shown to be superior to training without heuristics. Skell (1972, p. 48) has, for example, given the following heuristics to tool and dye maker apprentices (nonliteral translation by the authors):

- Compare the drawing with the raw material. What do you have to do to achieve the changes demanded by the drawing?

- Are there any prerequisites not immediately observable in the drawing?

- Is there anything else to do after you have performed all the steps?

- Try to eliminate movements that are not necessary; you can do this by thinking about the following questions:

  Can different types of actions be performed with the material clamped the same way into the vise?

  Can the clamped item be used again?

  If you have a choice between the same clamp setting or the same tool, ask yourself which one is more time-consuming!

  If a different clamp setting is used for the material, can it be used to do different things at the same time?

Skell (1972) and others (e.g., Höpfner, 1983; Sonntag, 1989; Sonntag & Schaper, 1988; Volpert, Frommann, & Munzert, 1984) showed that heuristics such as these produce work performance superior to that which results when these suggestions are not given.

Rühle, Matern, and Skell (1980) reported two experiments on giving heuristics to switchpersons in railway stations and to multiple machine operators. The use of heuristics and their interiorization increased optimal decisions in the switchpersons and increased the work performance of the multiple machine operators. Additionally, the operators with the new training procedure experienced less monotony and satiation in their work than those trained with the traditional procedure.

Heuristics were not only used in skills for blue collar workers. Computer training (Frese et al., 1991; Greif, 1989, 1992; Irmer, Pfeffer, & Frese, 1991) and social competence training (e.g., discussion and negotiation skills) were

also advanced by using heuristics (Hartwich & Okonek, 1979; Kühbauer & Schmidt-Hieber, 1978).

The theoretical importance of heuristics is, first, that they further a clear and action-oriented operative image system, and, second, that they provide a set of easy-to-remember rules of thumb that help prevent pitfalls. Third, it is important that they do not attempt to present a complete orientation that would be too difficult for the novice to remember and that would only produce a partial information extraction leading to a lopsided mental image; heuristics leave room for exploration. Fourth, at the same time, a set of heuristics can be complete enough to present a mental image that is in some ways holistic. Fifth, heuristics can be used in the sense of progressive interiorization of commands. That is, in the beginning they have to be spoken out loud; after a while, a shortened version is used, this version is then only mumbled, and finally, only an abbreviated version of inner speech is used (Skell, 1980).

Learning From Feedback and Errors.   There is no doubt that feedback is necessary for learning to occur (Annett, 1969). This is, of course, one issue that has led to the development of action theory in the first place, with its heavy orientation toward a feedback loop. However, feedback is only useful when it is similar to real-life feedback. For example, augmented feedback (i.e., feedback used only in training) leads to worse real-life performance because one has become accustomed to the feedback in training (Volpert, 1971). Moreover, feedback is of no use if there is no external task or internal goal to compare the feedback with. Without a set point, feedback has no guiding function for action.

Feedback has a number of functions in the learning process. First, one knows from feedback whether a certain movement is still oriented toward the goal or is leading away from it. Second, negative feedback tells the trainee what he or she has not learned yet, and positive feedback reveals what is known. Third, negative feedback describes the boundaries of the operative image system as it exists now—what cannot be solved with the particular mental model one has developed so far. Fourth, feedback connects the trainee to the objectivity of the world. Fifth, feedback has a motivating function; positive feedback encourages one to persist on the path, and negative feedback encourages one to correct the path and orient oneself toward the environment to scan it for unnoticed clues.

In comparison with behavioristic and humanistic views, action theory has a higher opinion on negative feedback. An error is one type of negative feedback, and a particularly useful one. Errors have been shown to improve training in a number of studies from different groups in Germany (Frese & Altmann, 1989; Frese et al., 1991; Greif, 1992; Greif & Janikowski, 1987).

Errors have several advantages. First, errors help people understand that a certain part of the operative image system is *not correct* (possibly a boundary condition). For example, some trainees had difficulties with the use of rulers in a computer system because it was not used to underline text (as subjects thought) but to set margins (Frese & Altmann, 1989). This error led the subjects to know that they should expect exceptions to underlying metaphors. Moreover, the trainee may realize that he or she does not know something well enough, which may lead to self-reflective thoughts.

Second, errors can sometimes lead to new phases of exploration and to creative solutions. Many scientists have reported that errors led to new discoveries.

Third, errors can bring about a reintellectualization of the action. Potential premature routinization of behavior will be broken up. This gives the person a chance to think consciously of the adequacy of the operative image system. Moreover, premature routinization is a problem in training and needs to be broken up before automatization is developed too far because alternative learning is then very difficult.

Fourth, errors produce a more complete operative image system because they sharpen the knowledge on potential pitfalls, potential problems, and difficult areas in the task structure. Therefore, more caution and enhanced attention is used in these areas, and therefore quicker detection and correction.

Fifth, error making helps to develop skills in error handling. Since errors appear quite frequently in real work life (Zapf et al., 1992), skills in error handling help to use errors productively and efficiently.

Sixth, errors always have the negative effect of being frustrating. But since they occur regularly, it is useful for people to learn to deal with this frustration. Thus, using errors in training in some ways provides stress management training (Greif, 1986).

Errors have been experimentally researched by comparing one group that received ample opportunities for making errors (essentially by being given tasks that were too difficult to do) with another group that was given instruction in how to go through the difficult tasks. The instruction did not allow someone following it to make an error. The error training group consistently fared better than the group that received no training (Frese et al., 1991; Greif & Janikowski, 1987; Hiltscher, 1992; Thiemann, 1990). Most of these trainings also presented general heuristics to the subjects on how to deal with errors, such as "I have made an error. Great!" or "There is a always a way to leave the error situation" (Frese et al., 1991, p. 83). Since these were all laboratory experiments with volunteers as subjects, error training was also used in a normal school for teaching computer skills (Irmer, Pfeffer, & Frese, 1991). Again, various error training groups were superior to groups receiving standard training in a performance test given after the training.

Automatization of Action Regulation. With practice, there is a change from conscious regulation to lower levels of regulation: Action theory presupposes that with practice, skills become automatized. For example, the novice driver cannot talk while driving—all of the person's attention is oriented toward driving. In contrast, the expert driver shifts gears without thinking about it and talks while driving without problems ocurring (except when he or she gets into a difficult situation and when something does not work properly). Routinization develops rather quickly. As a matter of fact, after doing something for a few times in a redundant environment, routines develop. As discussed before, it is hard to break up routines; particularly when people are under stress, there is a tendency to stick to old routines.

This implies for training that it is necessary to prevent premature routinization. This can be done by keeping the environment non-redundant. It may be one of the advantages of an exploratory form of training that the environment is kept nonredundant. In contrast, sequential training (Seymour, 1954) deliberately introduces redundancy to increase the routinization of skills in partial tasks. While this leads to a quick routinization of these partial tasks, it is more difficult to connect different parts of the complete action because organizing the parts into a whole requires new strategies. The different parts may form some kind of gestalt. This gestaltlike character is more difficult to achieve in sequential training. If the partial tasks have been prematurely routinized in separate practices, it may be very difficult to combine the parts.

A general problem of automatic behavior is the difficulty in changing it. This implies that verbal forms of retraining are useless. The alternative actions must be practiced until one has achieved a certain routine in this new behavior. This is the case, for example, in leadership behavior. Alternative leadership behavior will not be used in the real work situation as long as one has not practiced the alternative behaviors. Thus, practice is an important part of training. It is not so much a problem of changing cognitions, but one of making the new cognitions regulatory significant; much of the work is in getting the person to really act according to the new rules (Semmer & Frese, 1985).

Transfer of Training to Everyday Work. Transfer of training should be enhanced by a clear orientation toward the task at work and a chance to practice in safe environments and with task-oriented support.

We have discussed the importance of the task for an action theoretic conceptualization. Since the reason for action is to accomplish tasks, it is little wonder that action theorists have looked at the role of task orientation in transfer. Papstein and Frese (1988) have suggested that there is a difference between training tasks and work tasks. Usually in training, the development of system knowledge stands in the foreground. For example, most trainers will explain in great detail how to use the computer as a system but not how to apply it in the specific tasks at hand. To transfer this to the work task requires a separate set of principles and new knowledge: task application knowledge. Task application knowledge implies knowledge on how the system can be used in practical work situations (e.g., knowing concrete examples). In a study involving training people on a computer program, task application knowledge was an effective mediator between performance after the training and the use of the software six months later (Papstein & Frese, 1988).

Moreover, goal orientation and planfulness (both related to long-term orientation and precise goal setting and planning) proved to be an effective moderator (Papstein & Frese, 1988). Thus, people who think about the long-term use of the training material show a higher degree of transfer.

The more decision latitude the work situation allows, the easier it is for employees to develop such safe environments for themselves. This may be one reason why work situations with a high degree of job discretion show more transfer than work situations with little autonomy in work (Papstein & Frese, 1988).

Of course, task orientation can be incorporated into the training itself, either by using normal work tasks as examples or by asking the trainees to apply the training content to their normal work tasks. This was suggested in cognitive therapy (Kanfer, 1975; Watson & Tharp, 1972) and social competence training; application contracts that specify how and when to use what one has learned can help to further this goal (Greif, 1976; Semmer & Pfäfflin, 1978a).

One way to understand theoretically the difficulties in transferring knowledge learned in training is to look at the action structure. In the beginning of the learning process, the actions are conceptualized as a global structure without specific relations with the actual performance of these actions (Volpert, 1971). Slowly, the regulatory processes are strengthened and the global structure is replaced by an operative image system that has regulatory power to control the particular acts. At this point, actions are regulated at the intellectual level. It is an important issue to connect this intellectual level with lower levels.

Since the tasks have usually been done before and are therefore well routinized, there is a necessity to unlearn old routines and to establish new ones. This may be of greater importance than all other issues in training because lack of support for this transmission from training to work and from intellectual understanding to actual routine use of new action patterns is largely responsible for the inefficiency of training as an instigator of on-the-job-behavior.[10]

The Effects of Mental Training. Evidence that purely imagining a movement leads to an improvement has strengthened the concept of cognitive regulation of action. Therefore, mental training—or, as it was also often called, mental practice—was one of the first issues taken up by action theorists (e.g., Däumling et al., 1973; Rohmert, Rutenfranz, & Ulich, 1971; Ulich, 1964, 1967; Volpert, 1969, 1971; Wunderli, 1978). In mental training, the movements must be imagined very concretely (e.g., in skiing, how one uses the legs in turning left).

Obviously, so-called behavioristic concepts like systematic desensitization are easily reinterpretable within this framework (Semmer & Frese, 1985). Similarly, in training assertiveness skills, it is useful to imagine how one talks about a sensitive issue.

Mental training probably works through two different mechanisms. One is related to the training of cognitive aspects of the movement. Movements that are more cognitively regulated, such as learning to go through a maze, will be better after cognitive training. However, mental training additionally shows a practice effect even with more motoric movements (e.g., dart throwing). The function may be to integrate thoughts and muscular actions, or more specifically to integrate motoric and kinesthetic schemata (Heuer, 1985).

Task Characteristics

Hackman (1970) differentiated four approaches in job analysis: behavior description, behavior requirement, ability requirement, and task description. From an action theory perspective, task characteristics are described with reference to regulation processes—the regulation requirement approach. This actually constitutes a fifth approach, although there are certain similarities to the behavior requirement approach.

Three aspects are distinguished: the regulation requirements of a task, the resources for regulation, and the regulation problems (see Figure 7).

FIGURE 7

Classification of Task Characteristics

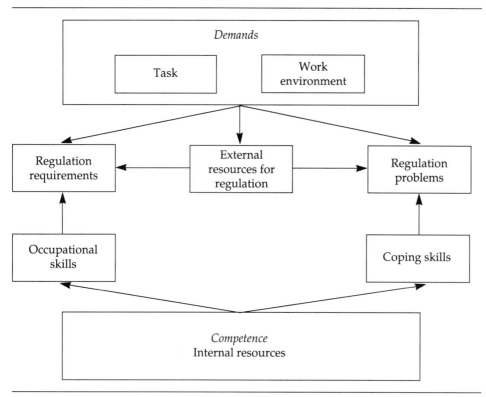

Resources for Regulation: Control at Work. A central variable for work design is control. Many different terms are used in this area: control (Frese, 1977, 1989; Oesterreich, 1981), *Handlungsspielraum* (room for action; Semmer, 1984; Ulich, 1972), degrees of freedom (Hacker, 1986a), decision latitude (Karasek, 1979), and autonomy (Hackman & Oldham, 1975, 1980). There is high conceptual overlap between these terms, and all of them can be subsumed under the term *control.*

Control means to have an impact on the conditions and on one's activities in correspondence with some goal (Frese, 1977). Decision possibilities exist with regard to the sequence

of the action steps, the time frame, and the content of goals and plans (see Figure 8). Decision points with regard to sequence include which tasks are carried out first, in which sequence plans are performed, and in which sequence feedback information is processed. *Time frame* refers to both when and for how long a certain task is performed. *Content* refers to the substance of the decisions, such as what particular task is done and what plan is performed.

A high amount of control might allow one to define the general goal of the work itself. A lower level of control might only allow one to choose between goals and plans at lower levels of action regulation.

FIGURE 8

Aspects of Control

	Decision Possibilities		
Action sequence	Sequence	Time frame	Content
- - - - -	- - - -	- - - -	- - - -
Tasks			
(Goals)			
- - - - -	- - - -	- - - -	- - - -
Plans			
- - - - -	- - - -	- - - -	- - - -
Feedback			
(Signals)			
=========	======	======	=====
Conditions			

From "A Theory of Control and Complexity: Implications for Software Design and Integration of the Computer System into the Work Place" by M. Frese. In *Psychological Issues of Human Computer Interaction in the Work Place* (p. 316) by M. Frese, E. Ulich, and W. Dzida (Eds.), 1987b, Amsterdam: North-Holland. Copyright 1987 by North-Holland. Reprinted by permission.

In the context of action theory, the goal-oriented nature of control is emphasized. Without a goal, there is no issue of control (see Frese, 1987b). This differs, for example, from Seligman's (1975) concept of control as noncontingency of events (i.e., an event appears or disappears regardless of a person's action). According to Seligman's (1975) definition, a person would have control if he or she accidentally and contrary to his or her intention produced a mistaken outcome. A goal-oriented definition would suggest that this person had no control.

Several issues have to be emphasized in this context (Frese, 1987b, 1989). First, the goal-oriented nature of control: Decisions are made with some goal in mind. As long as something is irrelevant to a goal, noncontrol is not an issue. Second, control and risks: Real

freedom exists only when decisions do not involve high risks. High-risk decisions are aversive. Third, the personal meaning of control: There is only control if the decision possibilities make sense and they are relevant to the person. There must be real alternatives of goal attainment (e.g., sorting out eggs in a hen farm for breeding does not offer real decision possibilities; Hacker, 1986a).

Subjective and objective control can be distinguished (Frese, 1978; Hacker, 1986a; Oesterreich, 1981; Ulich, 1972). Objective control consists of potential decision points with regard to a goal. Objective control is determined by the logic of work products; means and machinery and their physical, chemical, or biological structures and regularities; and organizational variables that, for example, determine the division of work or prescribe work procedures. Subjective control is the control a person perceives in a situation. Skills are particularly important as prerequisites of control. They determine whether objective decision possibilities are actually perceived and whether the perceived decision parameters can be realized. Perceived control might sometimes be higher than objective control. However, since feedback conditions are usually more obvious in work life, illusion of control should be lower in the work domain than in other settings (Frese, 1992).

Functionality, Transparency, and Predictability: Prerequisites for Control. Functionality, transparency, and predictability have become important issues in human–machine systems (Ulich, 1991). An action theoretic concept of control allows one to integrate these concepts into a theoretical framework (Frese, 1987b; Hacker, 1986a).

Functionality refers to whether a tool, such as a computer program, permits or enhances the completion of a task. Without the functionalities of tools, there is no control because goals cannot be achieved at all or must be changed (see Zapf, 1991c). However, a high degree of functionality does not necessarily imply control. For example, a typist with a powerful word processor whose task is writing standard letters has little control.

Transparency implies that one can easily develop an operative image system of the tool (see Maass, 1983). Under conditions of non-transparency, one cannot make adequate goal, planning, and feedback decisions. However, transparency is not identical to control because it is possible to develop a system that is completely transparent but does not offer any control (Frese, 1987b)—for example, a computer system that explains every step it takes in a process and provides clear prompts but does not allow the user to make any decisions.

Predictability has some overlap with transparency. Transparency refers to the present and the predictability to the future. If a system's behavior cannot be foreseen, it is not predictable. As with transparency, a system can be predictable but noncontrollable. Take the typist example: When writing standard letters, it is easy for the typist to predict what will happen next, but the person has little control over the task.

Regulation Requirements.   From an action-oriented perspective, regulation requirements are related to properties of the hierarchic-sequential organization of action. In this section we will differentiate between the complexity, variety, and completeness of actions.

Complexity.   In contrast to control as a set of decision possibilities, complexity implies *decision necessities*. Thus, high complexity leads to a high degree of regulation requirements necessary to perform a particular task. *Complexity is an interactive term.* It refers to a person's skills and the requirements of the situation. For example, if a person has done a certain task frequently, the person will have routinized the decisions necessary for performing the task; thus, the complexity of the task is rather low. In contrast, the task will have a high

degree of complexity for the novice, even if it may turn out to be a noncomplex task after practice. This is in contrast to, for example, Kieras and Polson's (1985) concept of complexity as completely independent of a person's experience.

Thus, a high level of regulation always implies more complexity than a low level of regulation. An example for low-complexity work is certainly assembly line work, which can be almost completely regulated at the lower levels of regulation after a short period of practice. Thus, the altitude of the hierarchy illustrated in Figure 3 is a good approximation of complexity.

The situational parameters of complexity can be described in analogy to Figure 8. Decision *necessities* are based on the following parameters (Dörner, 1976; Frese 1987b; Fuhrer, 1984):

- The number of different goals, plans, and signals (feedbacks) that have to be regulated and put into a time frame

- The dissimilarity of the goals, plans, and signals

- The number of relationships within and between goals, plans, and feedback

- The number of conditional relationships

It makes sense to differentiate complicatedness from complexity. A system becomes complicated when it is complex *and* when one of the following additional conditions apply (after Frese, 1987b, p. 322): little control, little functionality, little transparency, little predictability, fewer decision possibilities than necessary, and when the complexity is neither socially nor technically necessary or adequate. Complicatedness is related to the regulation problems to be discussed presently.

This view has implications for work design. Work may allow too little complexity. However, it does not help to induce complicatedness into the process because this would just increase negative stress effects. Rather, true complexity and control have to be increased at the same time.

Complexity and Control.   There are some approaches that confound complexity and control (Karasek, 1979; Karasek, Baker, Marxer, Ahlbom, & Theorell, 1981; Volpert, Oesterreich, Gablenz-Kolakovic, Krogoll, & Resch, 1983). This is understandable from an empirical perspective, since complexity and control are usually highly correlated (Semmer & Zapf, 1989). Theoretically, however, control and complexity can be differentiated. While control can be considered as the amount of *decision possibilities,* complexity represents the amount of *decision necessities.* In other words, a complex task requires complex decisions whether the person wishes this or not. In a sense, complexity is a prerequisite of control: If there is no complexity (e.g., only decisions at the sensorimotor level are required), then little control is possible (decision possibilities at the level of movements). But even if a task is very complex, there might be little room for deciding how to perform the task. Since control is seen as a positive factor within action theory (Frese, 1989; Hacker, 1986a; Semmer, 1984; Ulich, Grosskurth, & Bruggemann, 1973) while complexity can have negative influences in some cases, it is important to distinguish control from complexity. Semmer (1984) pointed out that workplaces with high complexity and low control are particularly stressful.

The major reasons complexity can be negative are that it leads to overload and responsibility. Responsibility is related to complexity and control in a curious way. First, responsibility usually implies that a certain number of decisions must be made. Second, these decisions often imply high risks or high negative consequences. This may be aversive, although it often enlarges the freedom of action on the job. Since we have defined control as decision possibilities and complexity as decision necessities, responsibility should only be aversive if

it implies too much complexity and/or too little control.

Variety.   Variety as an indicator of job content was used by Hackman and his colleagues (Hackman & Lawler, 1971; Hackman & Oldham, 1975; Jenkins, Nadler, Lawler, & Cammann, 1975). According to action theory, variety can be interpreted as the amount of different actions required by the tasks, independent of the complexity. Since having many different tasks in a given job implies variety, the amount of hierarchies needed to do the job constitutes variety. Thus, variety refers to the latitude of the pyramid of the hierarchic-sequential model. The pyramid of hierarchic-sequential action regulation would either be very narrow or very wide.

Completeness of Action.   From the perspective of action theory, the completeness of action can be added as a further concept of work content (Hacker, 1985). Completeness refers to both completeness of the action process and completeness of the hierarchy-of-action regulation. The action process is complete when all steps in the action process (goal setting, plan development, plan decision making, monitoring, and feedback processes) are carried out. Actions are, for example, incomplete when there are no possibilities to define goals (because they are defined by supervisors) or when there is no feedback to the worker (e.g., quality control).

The hierarchy is complete when all levels of regulation are used. When a person can regulate all of his or her actions on a low level of regulation (as, e.g., at the assembly line), the action is not complete.

The completeness of an action has been discussed as a sort of ontological given within action theory. Volpert (1978) argued that the nature of humans was to act and perform complete actions. He introduced the concept of "partialization of actions" to describe the phenomenon that higher levels of regulations are cut off (Volpert, 1975). In his view, modern industrialization has led to a reduction of complete actions. Certain problems arise from partialized actions, such as a reduced level of competence and a reduced ability to deal with problems from more than one perspective.

Research has shown that work regulated on the lower levels only is related to a lower degree of competence and job satisfaction and higher stress (evidence in Hacker, 1982a, 1982b, 1985, 1986a; however, there is also contradictory evidence, e.g., in Zapf, 1991b). While it is clearly possible to develop other hypotheses to explain these results, they have been taken as a starting point to demand that work design be oriented toward allowing complete actions.

Stress and the Concept of Regulation Problems.　Action and stress can be related in two ways: (a) The action process can be influenced and changed under stressful conditions, and (b) actions can produce stress.

The Action Process Under Stress Conditions.　We will discuss two aspects here how the action process is changed under stress conditions in general, and a taxonomy of stressors developed from the perspective of how it influences the regulatory processes in actions.

Planning and feedback under stress conditions. Stress conditions can influence the various elements of action regulation, such as goal setting, planning, and the levels of regulation.

For example, under stress (time pressure and noise), subjects show a higher number of operations, a lower efficiency (Schulz & Schönpflug, 1982), and more sensorimotor errors (Zapf, 1991a) than subjects working under nonstress conditions.

Under stress, people compensate for past inefficiencies. Schulz (1980) simulated clerical work by giving subjects a series of decisions to make regarding such things as checking bills, replying to customer complaints, and responding to credit applications. The subjects were able to look for additional information in computerized directories. A highly effective strategy was to memorize the directories, because otherwise the subjects had to interrupt their work frequently. The results indicated that people under stress tended to give up long-term planning and fall back on more short-term strategies; for example, they did not memorize the directories and had to request information frequently.

Simple performance studies do not always lead to the effects just described. People compensate for stressors and misregulations. For example, Dörner and Pfeifer (1991) reported that subjects working with a fire-fighting simulation under stress used less adequate strategies but compensated for this by working harder (i.e., giving more commands to the fire-fighting units).

Other experiments on mental load have shown its impact on the action dynamics (Hacker & Richter, 1980; Hockey & Hamilton, 1983; Schönpflug & Wieland, 1982). The interesting point here is that action theory might present a way to integrate these findings. For the sake of brevity, we will not be able to elaborate in this chapter.

A taxonomy of stressors.　Many reviewers of stress research have criticized the fact that there is no theoretically derived taxonomy of stressors (e.g., Kasl, 1978; one exception being role conflict and ambiguity, Katz & Kahn, 1978). For example, many studies treat nearly every work characteristic as a stressor (e.g., Frone & McFarlin, 1989; Spector, Dwyer, & Jex, 1988). Action theory suggests a taxonomy of stressors on the basis of how the stressors affect the action regulation.

From an action theory perspective, stressors can be considered to disturb the regulation of actions (Semmer, 1984). These regulation problems can be differentiated into the following groups: regulation obstacles, regulation uncertainty, and overtaxing regulations (see Figure 9).[11] The content of Figure 9 (after Leitner, Volpert, Greiner, Weber, & Hennes, 1987; and Semmer, 1984) will be discussed in the following section.

FIGURE 9

A Classification of Regulation Problems

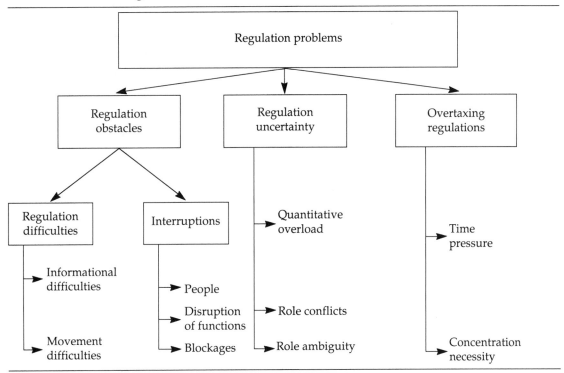

Note: The content of this figure is taken from Leitner et al. (1987) and Semmer (1984). We have changed the English terminology used by Greiner and Leitner (1989) because we think ours better conveys the theoretical meaning.

After K. Leitner, W. Volpert, B. Greiner, W. G. Weber, & K. Hennes, 1987, and N. Semmer, 1984.

Regulation obstacles. According to Leitner et al. (1987), "regulation obstacles are events or conditions that are directly related to the task at hand" and make it harder or even impossible to pursue a goal and to regulate an action. "The actor has to expand additional effort or has to use more risky actions" (p. 21; translation by the chapter authors). An example is a crane operator who has to make sure that there are no people underneath the crane before being able to swing the crane across some space. An obstacle exists if the operator is not able to oversee this space without any difficulty. Obstacles have a negative influence on an otherwise intact action. They can be conceptualized to be "daily hassles" (Kanner, Coyne, Schaefer, & Lazarus, 1981) in the workplace.

Additional effort may imply that one has to give up on a particular task or start anew, that some steps have to be repeated again, or that detours are necessary. It may also mean more physical strength is necessary in some cases.

One subcategory of regulation obstacles is regulation difficulties: It is in principle possible to do a task, but it is made more difficult than is necessary. Examples are lack of information or bad tools. Regulation difficulties do not directly pertain to the external task. If a person's task is to look for information, a lack of information is not a regulation difficulty (e.g., a telephone operator looking for a number that is difficult to find). However, other difficulties that make it hard to find the information fall under this concept (e.g., no computer being available).

Another subcategory refers to interruptions that are produced by unpredictable outside events. Interruptions can appear because of other people (colleagues, supervisors), technical problems (machine breakdown), and organizational problems (lack of supplies). Semmer (1984) has shown organizational problems to be one of the best predictors of psychosomatic complaints among the various stressors ascertained.

Regulation uncertainty. Regulation uncertainty means that one does not know how to achieve a certain goal, which kinds of plans are useful, and what feedback can be trusted (Semmer, 1984). Qualitative overload is a related category (Frankenhaeuser & Gardell, 1976).

Another issue is uncertainty caused by insufficient or delayed feedback. For example, a process control operator who never knows if his or her decisions really produce a chemical correctly until much later must live with this stressor even when he or she is optimally performing all the time.

The traditional concepts of role ambiguity and conflicts fall under this category (Kahn, 1973). From an action theory point of view, uncertainty is the underlying concept of role ambiguity and role conflict, such as when a supervisor has to push production but is supposed to keep safety first and does not know how to achieve these two goals simultaneously.

Overtaxing regulations. Overtaxing regulation does not mean that it is impossible to develop adequate goals, plans, and feedback, as in the case of uncertainty. Rather, the problem is the speed and intensity of regulation. For example, time pressure taxes the person's capabilities because of the high speed required. One response is for the person to expend a higher degree of energy. The resulting arousal is not a problem over a short time span, but becomes one over a long time span (Rissler, 1979). The problem is to find out what the normal maximum speed is. We know that people can compensate for higher demands for some time—that is, they can work with a higher speed (with a higher physiological arousal level) and thus work beyond their capacity (see Frankenhaeuser & Gardell, 1976).

Speed of processing (time pressure) produces problems because action regulation cannot be done as planned within a given time frame. A second problem is information overload of the short-term working memory during action execution (concentration). Too much information has to be kept in the working memory at the same time (Zapf, 1991b).

Actions and Their Influence on Stress. A somewhat novel issue is action theory's emphasis on the influence of action on stress. Stress theory is by and large very optimistic postulating that, once a person acts, there is little stress because one can deal and cope with stress (Gal & Lazarus, 1975). Proponents of this kind of theory include Lazarus and co-workers (Lazarus & Folkman, 1984). Although Lazarus and Folkman certainly see a potential negative impact of coping on the stress process, they do not really emphasize this point. From an action theory point of view, Schönpflug and his co-workers (Battmann, 1984; Schönpflug, 1979, 1983, 1985, 1986a, 1987; Schulz, 1979, 1980, 1982) have taken a different perspective: that actions consume energy and require effort in setting goals, planning, and processing feedback. Thus, actions can aggravate stress or even produce new stress. This can lead to a vicious cycle. While stress itself can produce certain problems in the action process, the actions taken up under stressful conditions may themselves increase the stress problems. Resulting misregulations must be compensated for by additional actions, and these compensating actions can lead to even more stress

The various aspects of the action process can be discussed from this perspective (Schönpflug, 1985). For example, planning takes extra effort, particularly if there are little resources available. Realistic and detailed feedback can be used for effective action execution. However, looking for feedback can be very laborious if it is not at hand. This may contribute to stress (Battmann, 1988).

From an action theory perspective, disengagement can be considered a strategy to cope with stress. Schönpflug (1985) suggests two different patterns: disengagement as giving up and disengagement as an instrumental act. Disengagement as giving up is an avoidance strategy that comes about when negative outcomes of actions outweigh the positive ones. For example, not being able to solve a work task may result in complete inactivity (Schulz & Schönpflug, 1982). In social systems, disengagement may also be a strategy to engage other people's help, thus transferring a task to someone else.

Applications of Action Theory in Job Analysis Instruments. In order to be able to design and change workplaces, German work psychologists were always interested in how objective work conditions affect people.

Since action theory emphasizes its relatedness to the outside world, it is not surprising that job analysis instruments based on this theory claim to measure objective rather than subjective representations of work characteristics (Oesterreich & Volpert, 1987). This is by no means common sense, since it is often argued that the perception of work characteristics should be measured because they are the best predictors of such aspects as performance and health outcomes. This is particularly true in the stress field.

However, both practical and methodological reasons for an objective conceptualization and measurement of work characteristics (Frese & Zapf, 1988; Oesterreich & Volpert, 1987; Zapf, 1989) include the following:

- Practically, one needs objective parameters to redesign work independently of a particular worker (institutional approach). This institutional approach can only be used if objective work characteristics are shown to have an impact on people's behavior, ill health, or personality development. If objective work characteristics do not have any impact on the individual but all variance is explained by individual cognitive appraisals, it would not make sense to redesign working conditions. In this case, the only sensible approach would be to change the individual.

- Methodologically, objective measures can overcome the problems of trivial correlations between subjective measures of work characteristics and psychological well-being and ill health (Frese & Zapf, 1988; Kasl, 1978).

Based on action theory, several job analysis instruments were developed: an instrument to identify regulation requirements in industrial work (VERA: Verfahren zur Ermittlung von Regulationserfordernissen in der Arbeitstätigkeit; Oesterreich & Volpert, 1991; Volpert, Oesterreich, Gablenz-Kolakovic, Krogoll, & Resch, 1983), the activity evaluation system (TBS: Tätigkeitsbewertungssystem; Hacker, Iwanowa, & Richter, 1983), an instrument to identify regulation obstacles in industrial work (RHIA: Leitner, Volpert, Greiner, Weber, & Hennes, 1987), and an instrument for stress-oriented job analysis (ISTA: Semmer, 1984; Semmer & Dunckel, 1991). These instruments have several characteristics in common. First, they are related to the objective environment. Second, they are based on the concept of the ideal typical worker (an average worker with sufficient skills to perform the necessary tasks;

TABLE 3

The VERA Model of Regulation Requirements*

Level 5	*Development of new action spheres*
	The result of the work task cannot not be predetermined in detail. The result can only be achieved by developing new ways of production. Thereby, it is open [as to] exactly what needs to be produced. Thus, new production areas are opened up or inferred (e.g., research).
Level 5	Plans for new tasks and technological processes have to be developed and coordinated.
Level 5R**	Plans for changes of existing tasks and technological processes have to be developed and coordinated, but the existing conditions should be changed as little as possible.
Level 4	*Coordination of action spheres*
	The result of the work task cannot not be predetermined in detail. Several action spheres have to be coordinated and sometimes initiated in the work process. This means tha developing subgoals in one area has implications for dealing with the subgoals in a second area. The functions of the action spheres are interrelated and influence each other. Therefore, they have to be coordinated (e.g., repair of a complex system).
Level 4	Several interrelated subgoals of the work domain have to be planned and coordinated.
Level 4R	Only one subgoal has to be planned. However, other interrelated subgoals have to be taken into consideration.
Level 3	*Subgoal planning*
	The result of the work task cannot not be predetermined in detail. Reaching the production goal cannot be done by using a preprogrammed plan. The result can only be achieved by developing a set of subgoals that are worked through step by step. Achieving the subgoals cannot be one by planning everything in detail beforehand (e.g., the work of a tool-and-dye maker).
Level 3	Only a rough series of subactivities can be planned. After achieving a subgoal, the plan to attain the next subgoal has to be thought through. Each subgoal is reached by regulation on level 2.
Level 3R	As in level 3, but the sequence of subgoals and respective sequences of subactions are preplanned by external order or in the way the production system is organized. Therefore, there is no own planning of subgoals, but the sequence of subgoals has to be recapitulated. Each subgoal is reached by regulation on level 2.
Level 2	*Action planning*
	The result of the work task cannot be produced by a movement program alone. Different movement programs have to be combined in a new way (e.g., cutting and installation according to a plan).
Level 2	The sequence of work steps has to be planned. By combining different movement programs, it is possible to plan the whole task in advance, since the task is familiar to the worker.
Level 2R	There is a given sequence of work steps by external order or by the way the production system is organized, but with some variations. Therefore, there is no own planning of the worker, but the plan of the work steps has to be recapitulated.
Level 1	*Sensorimotor regulation*
	The result of the work task is produced by a sequence of movements that have been used frequently (e.g., assembly line work).
Level 1	An initiated action program can be carried out without conscious regulation; however, small variations in work material, work results, and tool use occur.
Level 1R	Same as level 1, but there is no occasional use of a different tool and variations of material seldom occurs.

From "Task Analysis for Work Design on the Basis of Action Regulation Theory" by R. Oesterreich and W. Volpert, 1986, *Economic and Industrial Democracy, 7*, pp. 42–45. (Translation of original work by W. Volpert, R. Oesterreich, S. Gablenz-Kolakovic, T. Krogall, & M. Resch, 1983). Copyright 1986 by Sage. Reprinted by permission.

* This is not a literal translation of Volpert et al. (1983, pp. 42–45). However, we have tried to be true to the text as much as possible. However, we have at times changed the terminology used by Oesterreich and Volpert (1986) in an English-language publication. We think (and hope) that our translation better conveys the theoretical meaning.

**R = restricted level

Oesterreich & Volpert, 1987). From a practical point of view, any worker who knows how to do a certain work task can be considered as an ideal typical worker (e.g., employees who have worked at least one year after their education for the job). Third, the instruments make use of "observational interviews" in which the observer who is familiar with the underlying theory both observes the work actions and asks questions to understand his or her observations. Fourth, the instruments are not concerned with the individual qualities of the workers but with general regulation requirements; that is, they take no account of interindividual differences in mental regulations. *Objective* implies here that the measures are independent of an individual's cognitive processing (Frese & Zapf, 1988; Oesterreich & Volpert, 1987).

VERA: Instrument to Identify Regulation Requirements in Work. The instrument VERA (Verfahren zur Ermittlung von Regulationserfordernissen in der Arbeitswelt), which identifies regulation requirements in work, was developed to assess the requirement of planning and thought processes in certain jobs (Oesterreich, 1984; Oesterreich & Volpert, 1986, 1991; Volpert et al., 1983).

A VERA analysis breaks down the job into tasks. Two criteria are used to distinguish tasks: (a) If units refer to a common identifiable goal, they are grouped together as a task; (b) if two units cannot be performed independently by two people without them giving information to each other, they belong to the same task.

Each task is then analyzed to determine at which levels the task accomplishment should be regulated. The levels are based on Oesterreich's (1981) five-level model of action regulation (Table 3). This model differs to a certain degree from the levels of regulation described earlier. The lowest level corresponds to Hacker's (1986a) sensorimotor level. The level of action planning roughly represents the level of flexible action patterns. The higher

levels of regulation in the VERA instrument all refer to intellectual levels.

The so-called "restricted level" R was introduced to further differentiate the VERA model. This applies if regulations arising at this level only need to be performed in an incomplete and restricted form (examples in Oesterreich & Volpert, 1986).

VERA can be used to analyze blue collar work, but not white collar, engineering, or management work. Separate versions of VERA were developed to evaluate flexible manufacturing systems (Volpert, Kötter, Gohde, & Weber, 1989; Weber & Oesterreich, 1989) and office work. This was done within the framework of another instrument—the *Contrastive Job Analysis* (Dunckel, 1989; Dunckel & Volpert, 1990; Dunckel, Volpert, Zölch, Kreutner, Pleiss, & Hennes, 1993; Volpert, 1987a, 1992). The *Contrastive Job Analysis* asks which parts of a job should be computerized and which parts should remain with the worker. Work tasks that are regulated at the sensorimotor level are candidates for computerization.

VERA is constrained, however, to one important aspect of work. It does not measure work stressors or communication. Therefore, it should be applied together with other instruments, such as the RHIA instrument. A weak point of VERA is that it does not differentiate between work complexity and decision latitude, as was described earlier.

RHIA—Instrument to Identify Regulation Obstacles in Industrial Work. The instrument RHIA (Regulationshindernisse in der Arbeitstätigkeit; an instrument to identify regulation problems in industrial work) was developed to identify, describe, and quantify task-related mental stress in industry (Greiner & Leitner, 1989; Leitner et al., 1987). Our section on regulation problems was largely based on the background theories of the RHIA instrument (see Figure 9).

RHIA was developed to measure stressors at work through observational interviews, independent of whether the particular conditions are evaluated by the worker as disturbing. In this sense, work characteristics are considered to be stressors when they require additional efforts for people to carry out a particular task.

The instrument is based on the theory described in Figure 9; the emphasis is on regulation obstacles and overtaxing regulations. Regulation obstacles influence the action regulation directly and require immediate reaction from the workers. They are measured on a common dimension—the length of additional time required to respond to the obstacles. Capacity overtaxing appears when continuous conditions reduce the mental and physical achievement capacity of the worker over the course of the workday.

Most prominent for this instrument is the measurement of regulation obstacles. These have to be identified by the job analyst with the help of observations, interviews with the job incumbents and supervisors, or document analysis.

The value of this instrument is certainly its strong theoretical basis and its clear theoretical distinction between several types of regulation obstacles. The method leads to concrete descriptions of stress events that can be easily communicated to practitioners. The observed stressors show moderate size correlations with psychosomatic problems and irritation/ strain (Greiner & Leitner, 1989). A disadvantage is that it only tackles a part of potential stressors at work (Semmer & Dunckel, 1991).

Like the VERA instrument, RHIA was developed to analyze blue collar work. An integrated VERA/RHIA instrument for the analysis of office work is available (Leitner, Lüders, Greiner, Ducki, Niedermeier, & Volpert, in press).

TBS—Tätigkeitsbewertungssystem (Activity Evaluation System).   The TBS is an instrument for evaluating the chances for personality enhancement in a job (Hacker & Iwanowa, 1984; Hacker, Iwanowa, & Richter, 1983; Iwanowa &

Hacker, 1984). This instrument evaluates the completeness of actions in several respects. A complete action according to this instrument includes sequential completeness (including goal and plan development and preparatory phases of the action process) and hierarchical completeness (including regulation at all levels). As additional features, cooperation and communication made during work are measured. Based on this concept, five groups of scales were developed, as shown in Table 4.

There are several variants of the TBS for different jobs and a special version for mental activities such as software development (Rudolph, Schönfelder, & Hacker, 1987).

The instrument provides cutoff values for each scale, resulting in a typical job profile. Given minimum values, personality enhancement at work should be possible. Scale values that are below the cutoff points indicate job areas that need to be redesigned.

The TBS covers the full range of job content variables. The most important part of the TBS is certainly the measure of complete activities at the workplace (which are assumed to enhance personality). In this way, the TBS is a typical theory-driven form of job analysis and evaluation instrument that can be used to support the need for the redesigning of jobs. Since there is no concept of personality enhancement at the workplace in the Anglo-American literature, there is also no comparable instrument available. There are, however, certain areas of overlap with the *Job Diagnostic Survey* (Hackman & Oldham, 1974, 1975).

Action Theory and Work Design

In Germany, work psychology is seen not just as a descriptive science of work behavior but as a prescriptive science that should contribute to work design. Unlike the situation in the United States, this is regarded to be of utmost importance, and issues related to work design take up a large proportion of the professional discussion in German industrial and

TABLE 4

The Scales of the Job Evaluation System (TBS)

The TBS Scales

A. Organizational and technological conditions that determine the completeness of action.
   A.1. Completeness of the action process. The amount of so-called preparatory activities are of particular importance. Furthermore, items for error checks and organizational activities are included here.
   A.2. Variety of work tasks and cycle time
   A.3. Possibilities for psychological automatization
   A.4. Transparency of the production process
   A.5. Predictability of job requirements and time constraints
   A.6. Controllability (degrees of freedom)
   A.7. Physical (bodily) variety, including variety in posture and bodily movements

B. Cooperation and communication
   B.1. The range of necessary cooperative work
   B.2. Types of cooperative work
   B.3. Variety of cooperative work
   B.4. Communication

C. Responsibility resulting from the external task
   C.1. Content of individual responsibility
   C.2. Amount of responsibility for results
   C.3. Collective responsibility for performance

D. Required cognitive performance
   D.1. The level of action regulation required
   D.2. Information required by the job (ranging from simple signals to complex states and processes)
   D.3. Intellectual information processing required (problem-solving activities, ranging from algorithmic cognitive operations to creative problem solving)

E. Skill requirements
   E.1. Required formal education for the job
   E.2. Actual use of occupational education
   E.3. Job requires constant learning

Adapted from A. Iwanowa and W. Hacker, 1984, and W. Hacker, A. Iwanowa, and P. Richter, 1983; translated and extended by the chapter authors.

organizational psychology. Certain prerequisites must be met if design is to be taken seriously:

- There should be strong relationships to the engineering sciences, like machine construction and computer sciences.

- One should know the psychological parameters that are affected by work design.

- Design always implies certain value decisions; they must be made transparent and tied to scientific knowledge. For example, it is a value decision to answer the question, "Is it more important that work contributes to health, or is productivity more important even if it damages health?"

- Design decisions can never be completely based on empirical work because future use of a technology or a machine to be designed for the first time cannot be studied empirically (Ulich, 1991). Thus, they have to be derived from a design theory that is anchored in other empirical work.

Many of the action theory concepts discussed earlier were developed to justify design work. The central variables from an action theory perspective are the completeness of action, the increase of regulation requirements and control, the reduction of regulation problems, and the concept of personality enhancement. Ontological givens, such as being active or the necessity to develop one's own goals and plans, were hypothesized. Moreover, action theory may also provide a theory that can help determine how new machines should be designed. A discussion of the most important criteria for work design appears below.

There is no one best way, in the sense of Taylor (1913). Since regulation necessities and regulation possibilities usually go hand in hand, action theory takes a nondeterministic view (Frese, 1987b). A situation may require complex regulations, but may not prescribe a particular way of accomplishing them. Since people have different priorities, styles, and mental models, different work strategies result. This is partly in contrast to the concepts of Newell and Simon (1972) or the GOMS-model of Card, Moran, and Newell (1983; see the critique of the GOMS model by Greif & Gediga, 1987). The more complex a situation is, the greater are the chances of there being

individual strategies (see Ulich's [1990, 1991] principle of individualization of work). Empirically, different strategies may lead to a similar productivity (Ackermann & Ulich, 1987; Triebe, 1981; Ulich, 1990). For this reason, it is useful to allow a person to choose his or her own work strategy.

Volpert (1975, 1978) and Hacker (1986a) maintain that an action is an ontological given and that phylogenetic development of the person involved the possibility to use action with control over goal setting, planning, and the use of feedback and involves all levels of regulation. This contrasts with the notion of partialized action (Frese, 1978; Volpert, 1975), in which certain levels of regulation are not under the control of the individual. For example, in assembly line work, the worker only works on the lowest level of regulation but has little conscious problem-solving activities; thus, higher levels of regulation are not at his or her disposal but are concentrated in the engineers who set up the assembly line. Another example is a job that does not give feedback or a job that does not allow one to develop one's own plans and goals. Complete activity is related to better health effects and higher productivity (Hacker, 1987b).

An action should be allowed to run its course. It is aversive when it is interrupted by outside events that do not belong to the task (Frese, 1987b; Semmer, 1982). Any obstacles to doing one's work should be reduced. Very often these obstacles result from bad organization (see our earlier discussion on stress).

People should be allowed to be active in their work (Hacker, 1986a; Volpert, 1987b). Again, this is related to the ontological given that people are better when they are acting than when they are just observing. Phylogenetically, people are not cognitive or mental beings, but rather actors who use cognitions to regulate their actions. Therefore, work should allow people to be active. Any task that takes away action will lead to problems, as the difficulties of vigilance tasks amply show

(Mackworth, 1970). From this follows the concept of the active operator (cited in Hacker, 1986). In contrast to complete automatization of, for example, piloting, the active operator concept allows the person to stay in active control of the process. He or she still must act. Lomov and co-workers (cited in Hacker, 1986) show that active pilots perform better than pilots working with highly automated machines (see also Wiener, 1985).

The issue of control has come up repeatedly and is one of the central issues in work design. In contrast to Emery and Trist (1960) and Emery and Thorsrud (1976), who similarly prefer work to be designed to allow more control, action theory's arguments are not based on the grounds that control is a prerequisite of democracy at work. Nor is the basis a humanistic type of psychology. It is also not a motivational theory, as is the one by Hackman and Oldham (1980). Rather, action theory's idea is that people who have control can do better because they can choose adequate strategies to deal with the situation. For example, they can plan ahead better and are more flexible in the event that something goes wrong (see our earlier discussion of the superworker concept). Skills can only be acquired in a lifelong process when there is control at work.

This view is supported by recent studies of Wall and collaborators (Jackson & Wall, 1991; Wall, Corbett, Martin, Clegg, & Jackson, 1990; Wall, Jackson, & Davis (1992). In a job redesign study in advanced manufacturing technology, computer numerical control (CNC) operators' jobs were restricted to merely loading, monitoring, and unloading machines. In the case of a machine fault, they had to alert specialists. In a field experiment (Wall et al., 1990), the operators were trained in fault diagnosis and fault management (e.g., recalibrating mechanisms that worked out of tolerance, resetting machines, editing programs to cope with variations of raw material). Fault diagnosis and fault management then became a part of the operators' jobs, and specialists were only called upon in situations with more fundamental difficulties. The results showed a decrease of machine downtime and a corresponding increase in output. These results were not only due to a quicker response to machine breakdowns that could be caused by higher motivation and the time saved because no experts had to be called; a reanalysis by Jackson and Wall (1991) revealed that there was a long-term learning effect that produced a reduction of faults. This result appeared gradually over several weeks. The explanation is that the increase of complexity and control by job redesign provided the possibility to develop a more differentiated operative image system and better strategies to prevent machine faults.

The basis for any good work design is the good qualification of the worker. Therefore, qualifications are necessary prerequisites for good work design but are also important consequences. If work does not allow the use of qualifications, they will be lost due to disuse. Any work reorganization program must also involve a qualification program (Ulich et al., 1973).

Qualifications can only be upheld if work has a certain complexity. For this reason, action theory is much more concerned than other approaches in psychology with keeping complexity in the job and even increasing complexity. For example, cognitive psychology applied to tool use seems to have quite an opposite approach (e.g., Card, Moran, & Newell, 1983; Kieras & Polson, 1985). It may be useful to differentiate between complexity, which increases the amount of intellectual work in the job, and complicatedness, which increases mental load. "With an increase of memory load, the quantity and quality of performance deteriorates and fatigue increases. In contrast, increasing the complexity of intellectual tasks does not yield such a deterioration, at least as long as memory load remains constant" (Hacker, 1987a, p. 123; see Hacker, 1986b).

Obviously, it follows from action theory that work should provide feedback. This feedback should be natural; that is, it should result from doing the work itself and not from some system superimposed (e.g., feedback only given by the supervisor).

Work should minimize the amount of information that must be kept in memory at any one time. One way to reduce this amount is by chunking (Miller, 1956), and being able to chunk is a function of good qualifications and experience. This suggestion is not necessarily opposed to having a certain amount of complexity in the job, as Hacker's earlier quote shows.

Thus, there are certain design criteria developed from an action theory perspective. Work design concepts can be put into a different perspective within an action theory orientation, such as in job rotation and job enlargement. These concepts have been interpreted to be restricted design concepts because tasks of a very similar nature are combined (Herzberg, 1966). From an action theory perspective, regulation requirements and control are certainly the same across the tasks. However, there may be different regulation problems in the tasks combined (stressors, errors). One result may be that job rotation and enlargement decrease one-sided physical and mental loads. In contrast, job enrichment and semiautonomous work groups imply an increase of regulation requirements and control. More complex goals and plans can be developed and may allow for the use of complete actions in work. The effects on regulation problems may be the same as for job rotation and enlargement. However, insofar as increased control functions as a moderator, job enrichment may lead to fewer stress problems, given a certain amount of stressors.

Design can mean several things. Ulich (1991) has suggested differentiating the following design strategies:

- *Corrective work design.* This is the typical situation for the work psychologist—to be called in to suggest a redesign because certain problems have arisen

(e.g., a high accident rate, high staff turnover, or high absenteeism).

- *Preventive work design.* That is, design of machines and workplaces that do not yet exist. This is preferred because cooperation with the design engineer allows for workplaces to be developed from scratch from a work psychologist's perspective.

- *Prospective work design.* While preventive work design aims at the potential negative impacts of the job, prospective work design attempts to anticipate the positive impacts for personality development.

- *Differential work design.* This implies that the job is adapted to an individual's personality (Ulich, 1978a, 1983). Therefore, such a work design leads to productivity gains (Ulich, 1990). One disadvantage is, of course, that many different designs must be realized. Moreover, the design may cast a person into a certain mold that may not fit after a while. Therefore, Ulich (1983) suggests complementing this with the principle of dynamic work design.

- *Dynamic work design.* This means that the work design is adjusted to the growing aspirations of the job holder.

Since work design is influenced by new technology, it follows that action theorists have a keen interest in issues related to new technologies. The use of new technologies has been studied intensively. The above design strategies imply that one would prefer blue collar workers to become programmers and supervisors of their machines (e.g., tool-and-dye machines), rather than just the monitors of them. Thus, results like the one by Wall and Clegg (1981) fall well in line with this thinking.

Another aspect of work design involves looking at the tools used in work. For this reason, software ergonomics became an important field for German work psychology (see Frese, 1987c, and Frese, Ulich, & Dzida, 1987, for English-language overviews). The following aspects are important in tool design (see Ulich, 1986, 1991).

- Tools change the action process at work. Thus, tool design is always work design to a certain extent (Hacker, 1987a, 1987b; Ulich, 1989, 1991) because, depending on the tools, important parameters of the jobs change (e.g., help provided, which strategy is supported, complexity and control at work). For this reason, tools have to be evaluated according to how they interact with general work dimensions and what effects they have on the general work situation.

- Tools should truly support the task accomplishment. Since the task is the primary goal of the worker, tools must be well adapted to the task, their use must be learned within a reasonable time, and they should not interrupt task completion or the usual routines of task completion. Whenever a tool has its own logic—aside from the support of the task actions—it hinders task completion.

- Tools should be consistent. This means two things: (a) consistency with the specialist knowledge in the field of application and (b) internal consistency. The former implies that users can rely on their specialist nomenclature and on their prior concepts of how the work is to be done when using the tool; the latter means that all the parts of the tool should react in the same way. Examples are that error messages should always appear in the same line or that function keys should operate

consistently throughout a software program. Inconsistencies produce problems because people develop complete operative image systems and automatize their behavior very quickly.

- Tools must be transparent, meaning that users can develop a good operative image system from using the tool. This means that the original intentions of the designer are clear (Keil-Slawik & Holl, 1987; Maass, 1983).

- Controllability of a tool means that users can adapt the system to the task and to their own strategies and preferences. Moreover, it should support flexible use, since strategies change and should be allowed to change over time (e.g., with fatigue; Sperandio, 1971). One implication of this is that the tool should not adjust itself (adaptiveness), but its change should be under the user's control (Haaks, 1992). In contrast, some cognitive human factors scientists suggest that a computer system should adapt to the user automatically (Kass & Finin, 1988).

- One variant of controllability is individualization (Ackermann & Ulich, 1987; Greif & Gediga, 1987; Ulich, 1990). This means that a user can adjust a system to his or her work strategies. This may be done through macroprograms. It may also be done through systems that grow with the knowledge a person has of a system (the so-called genetically growing system; Greif, 1988).

- Finally, the tool should support error management. We already discussed error management in the section on training. From an action theory point of view, errors are ubiquitous because they can be seen as aberrations on the way toward the goal. Overcoming the error is more important than error making per se. Moreover, the cognitive apparatus of human beings is error prone, precisely because it is so well adapted to an environment in which one must react quickly.

Error management is also useful because it reduces costs. What makes errors costly, both in terms of stress effects and economic costs, are the error consequences, such as error handling time, but not the error per se (Frese, 1991). Thus, error handling time should be reduced by supporting error management strategies. Computer systems often offer features, such as the UNDO key on a computer's keyboard, that support error management. Many additional features can be developed (for an overview, see Zapf, Frese, Irmer, & Brodbeck, 1991).

Postscript

This chapter provides an introduction to action theory. First, a general concept of action theory was developed by describing action as goal-oriented behavior. The core of action is the feedback cycle. This implies that there is a goal, which constitutes the set point to which action outcomes are compared. The theory describes an action process, consisting of goals, information integration, plans, monitoring, and feedback. In addition, action regulation is hierarchically structured. There are four levels of regulation—the sensorimotor level, the flexible action patterns level, the intellectual level, and the heuristic level. The most important differentiation is between actions that are consciously regulated and those that are routinized. Long-term knowledge of these processes is stored in the operative image system.

In the second part of this chapter, the general theory was applied to understanding certain phenomena such as errors, the interrelationship between work and personality, the development of competence, tasks characteristics, and work design.

It is tempting to contrast American with German industrial and organizational psychology, but such a contrast is very often misleading. Clearly, both American and German industrial and organizational psychology are rather heterogeneous. Even when there are differences, it is really hard to say whether one has used sufficiently representative materials from each country. Moreover, the differences that one finds are often more a matter of degree of emphasis rather than a clear-cut distinction between the approaches used in the two countries. Nevertheless, we feel that there are some differences, and that action theory has something to contribute to American psychology. Here we offer a few speculative remarks.

We think that the major advantage of action theory is not its cognitive orientation, but rather the ease with which it can relate cognitive issues to applied field settings. Cognitive psychology tends to be rather elementaristic, as with mechanistic concepts. This makes it hard to use such concepts in a field of application. In contrast, action theory is much less fine-grained but allows an easy application to such issues as task analysis, task design, and training. Moreover, action theory encompasses within one theoretical orientation a far broader range of issues. This provides the advantage that one can integrate findings of middle- and small-range theories and various practically important phenomena of industrial and organizational psychology.

The other side of the coin, however, is that action theory has not been clearly defined or as well tested as some cognitive theories. At times, action theorists seem to have been content with being able to use a concept in the field rather than to verify it independently.

Still, we think that action theory has a lot to offer. For example, American industrial and organizational psychology tends to look largely for motivational concepts when explaining differences in job performance. In contrast, the concept of the superworker allows a different approach. Similarly, issues of participation in decision making are typically related to motivation. Again, in action theory, participation in decision making implies that knowledge is shared. This has practical implications: With a pure motivation concept in mind, one might suggest setting up group discussion sessions designed to make persons feel important to the overall work effort. Our concept of participators implies simply that maximal transfer of knowledge must be organized and implemented.

We do not want to say that motivation is unimportant.[11] In the concept of goals, cognitive and motivational aspects of action are closely related. Also, there is certainly a motivational side to having complete actions (e.g., as discussed by Hackman & Oldham, 1980). But motivation does not constitute the whole picture. As a matter of fact, a simple increase in motivation does not produce higher productivity, while a better understanding of a job does.

Moreover, action theory is objectivistic. A purely cognitive point of view often negates the function of cognition for human beings—namely, to be able to act properly. Experiments often show that illusions exist. This view has been quite prominent in American industrial and organizational psychology as well (Salancik & Pfeffer, 1977). An action theory concept implies that this is only true if the person cannot act (Neisser, 1985; Sabini, Frese, & Kossman, 1985) because generally the perceptual cycle (Neisser, 1976) is supplemented by feedback received from the objects acted upon. Obviously, there are limits to this objectivity. These

different views have practical implications. From an action theory point of view, one would, for example, be much more cautious in expecting a reduction of stress from a change of subjective perceptions without also changing the objective stressors and resources. This may lead to illusions that cannot be upheld against reality over the long run—an issue that becomes particularly clear when optimism is confronted with grim realities (e.g., in the case of unemployment; see Frese, 1987a).

Moreover, the job analysis instruments attempt to be objective as well. Of course, the practical reason is most important: An objective instrument allows the design of jobs to be done independently of a particular individual. Without the concept of an objective environment that affects the individual, the only sensible approach would be to change the individual. The concept of object-oriented action—that is, changing the objective world—will correspond well to the practical requirements of work analysis.

As we see it, personality is usually conceptualized as an independent variable in the United States. We do not quarrel with this point of view, but feel the full picture should also include the view that personality develops through action. This produces a different orientation, the most important result being the concept of personality enhancement in the workplace. From this perspective, it is obvious that selection may be seen differently. At times, selection procedures assume that there is a stable personality that is not affected by the job at all. Again, this has practical consequences: In a typical concurrent validation program, a correlation between person characteristics and performance is used as a good approximation of the prediction of performance from the person characteristics. From an action theory perspective, working effectively in a job produces certain person effects that may partly explain the correlations in a concurrent validation procedure. Thus, interpreting them as *predictors* of performance only may oversimplify the case.

Since action theory is an integrative theory, it allows for a higher degree of integration of areas that are rather differentiated in the United States. For example, there seems to be little integration between human factors and industrial and organizational psychology. Action theory allows such an integration to a larger extent because it specifically integrates upper and lower levels of regulation. This implies, for example, that motor movements are not seen as completely distinct from thinking.

From a historical perspective, the following three points made action theory a powerful paradigm in German industrial and organizational psychology:

- It superseded the stale controversy between cognitive theory and behaviorism.

- Work action is taken as the legitimate starting point of work psychology.

- People are seen as active rather than passive beings who change the world through work actions and thereby change themselves.

Superseding the Controversy Between Cognitive Theory and Behaviorism

The nearest thing to an action concept is, of course, behaviorism. However, behaviorism does not allow a closer look at the goals and tasks of working people and the thought processes that take place while they are working. While behaviorism was at one time a useful theory for looking at work from a time and motion study perspective, modern technology made simple time and motion studies obsolete. When supervising a machine, simple physical action was not the important contributor to the work outcome. Rather complex, thoughtful, and goal-oriented actions like setting, servicing, and controlling the machine and checking the output were most important. Those activities were not usefully described within

the tradition of time and motion studies. Thus, an action theory that was connected to cognitive processes was needed. (After it was developed, one result of the theory and its studies was that even simple work could not be well described with time and motion studies that were disconnected from cognitive processes, either; see Hacker, 1986a.)

Behaviorism developed a high methodological sophistication to study behavior, its antecedents, and its consequences. Additionally, it allowed the study of psychology with a clear objective reference point—the behavior of people. On the other hand, it was not consistent with the knowledge that such aspects as expectancies, thoughts, and mental models guide actions above and beyond antecedents and consequences. The apparatus of a behavioristic animal would simply be too unwieldy and nonorganized to survive in reality (e.g., Chomsky, 1959, suggested that a few transformation rules allow the generation of language, while learning language in the sense of behaviorism would take too long and be too complicated).

One of the most important arguments of behaviorism against early cognitive theorists was that a goal referred to something in the future that could not have an impact on the behavior that was occurring right now. Moreover, it was a metaphysical concept and therefore not worthy of study for the new natural science of psychology (Hull, 1943). The cybernetic feedback cycle (Miller et al., 1960) has allowed the understanding at a purely mechanical level that goals and feedback can have the function of regulating behavior toward a goal. The computer analogy helped to overcome this largely philosophical behavioristic argument.

Cognitive theory, on the other hand, keeps the human animal lost in thought (Guthrie, 1935). The phylogenetic function of thought was not just to understand but to be better able to act because of the good understanding of a situation (Hofsten, 1985; Neisser, 1985).

Miller et al. (1960) set out to bridge the gap between cognition and action. The major link was the concept of plan. Since a plan is hierarchically organized, action theory is a molar as well as a molecular kind of theory. It is possible to discuss the trajectory from a specific thought to a specific muscle movement (Gallistel, 1980), as well as the trajectory from a wish to action (Heckhausen & Kuhl, 1985) within the same kind of theory.

Work Action as the Starting Point of Work Psychology

Work in the sense of developed and systematic tool use is unique to human beings (Dolgin, 1985; Schurig, 1985). Thus, the starting point for an industrial psychologist should be the human being at work. The ultimate purpose of work is to produce a product (which can, for example, be a physical object, an intellectual concept, or a certain emotion). Production means acting on the world in a systematic way. Work action is therefore the theoretical and empirical starting point of industrial and organizational psychology. From this perspective, it is surprising that the earlier edition of this *Handbook* did not even mention the concept of action in its subject index (Dunnette, 1976; this is also true of its equivalent in Germany; see Mayer & Herwig, 1970).

Work means accomplishing a task via action. A task is a conglomerate of redefinitions and objective demand characteristics (Hackman, 1970). But a task cannot usually be accomplished without some reference point in the world of objects. The tasks of work may be to hunt an animal, produce a new automobile, sell a computer, design a software program, or make a customer happy. In each case, there is an object that needs to be changed (or at least it has to change hands) in an objective sense. With the development of culture, the object of action may not be directly tied to a physical object, such as in the case of working out a theory. But even such a theory will be of little use if there is not some tie to real-world objects. Thus, in the final analysis, work psychology must be rooted in the objective world. Work psychology cannot be just the study of cognition at work or just the symbolism involved in work. (This does not mean, of course, that symbols are not important— they are, and they must be incorporated into an action theory of work.)

Moreover, work uses tools in changing objects. Such tools are either physical or mental (e.g., a pair of scissors or a brainstorming session). A tool is more than just some material shaped in a certain way. It is always an objectification of a certain procedure to work—the tool as a plan of action. The same is true of social tools, like the organization of work. An organization is an objectification of how one deals socially with a certain object (Berger & Luckmann, 1966).

The Human as an Active Rather Than a Passive Being

In contrast to the perspective of behaviorism, here human beings are not seen as only responding to their environment; instead, they are seen as influencing and shaping their environment as well. Moreover, living is acting. Thus, we usually have a goal and some kind of idea of how to proceed with it (at least as long as the action is not routinized). Goals change in accordance with one's accomplishments, usually in the direction of higher effect on the environment (White, 1959). Thus, an active person will continue to be active, even when he or she has achieved a goal.

The conceptualization of humans as active does not imply, however, that the environment is unimportant. When working, physical objects are changed directly or indirectly. By changing physical objects, workers are changed as well. The example of tool use demonstrates this. When producing a tool, a procedure for doing something is developed materially. When using this tool afterward, the person is to a certain extent bound to the procedure. Thus, the person changes because of work. After the invention of the spoon, eating soup changed; at the same time, a spoon can only be used in a certain way and a spoon actually produces an affordance (in the sense of Gibson, 1979) to use it for bringing watery substances to the mouth.

Changes in objects and social organizations produce cultures and also produce changes in the people working. Thus, work action is something that shapes people collectively and individually. Thus, by working, people change the world and thereby change themselves. For this reason, work socialization has been an interesting issue for action theorists (Frese, 1982; Hacker, 1986a; Volpert, 1975).

Action theory has been a useful theory, both in terms of integrating various areas pertaining to work and in providing a structured approach to studying and researching work psychology. Certainly it is not yet a fully developed theory, but it consists of fragments that have been studied in detail and areas that have heuristic value. It is a tool to be used in gaining a better understanding of one area—work—that differentiates the human animal so clearly from other animals.

Thanks to the following people who read the manuscript and gave us recommendations: F. Brodbeck, C. Clegg, N. Semmer, S. Sonnentag, and W. Volpert.

Notes

1   Actually, there is a whole tradition of a social action theory that is not covered in this chapter (see Cranach & Harré, 1982).
2   For a different approach, see Oesterreich (1981, 1984).
3   They used the term *level of abstract thought* then.
4   There are several concepts for internal representations: the operative image system, with its emphasis on plans and actions; and mental models, with their emphases on structural parameters of the envi-

ronment. To use a term that embraces both of them, knowledge base for regulation was introduced.
5   Of course, there is no doubt that personality may also be a prerequisite for doing some kinds of work well.
6   It is interesting to note that enhancement of personality or growth in personality is the major psychological variable discussed in the German constitution—quite a contrast to the more hedonistic pursuit of happiness in the United States.
7   It is interesting to note that learning theorists have used this as a paradigm of regression—the rat reverts back to the more routinized route if under stress (Mowrer, 1950).
8   Of course, Meichenbaum (1977) has popularized this concept in the United States in the area of stress immunization training.
9   Hacker published in East Germany under socialist rule. One can assume that the concept of planning strategy was used to accommodate the leading ideology of socialist planning. This may very well be so. As it turns out, however, it might be a myth that socialist countries were planning well or were planning at all. While there was quite a lot of metaplanning on the societal level, there was very little planning of production. This lack of planning of the particulars of work and the little use of feedback (and the little attempt to look actively for realistic feedback) may have been two factors leading to the low work efficiency in the Eastern European countries.
10   In this connection it is interesting to note that in the recent *Frontiers* book of the Society for Industrial and Organizational Psychology on training, there is no mention of the problem of transfer and *transfer* is not even in the index (Goldstein, 1989).
11   We have left out an action theory approach to the area of motivation that is quite unique and potentially very interesting for applied psychology (e.g., Gollwitzer, 1990; Heckhausen, 1991). This area was left out because these motivational constructs have not been used in industry up to this point.

References

Ackermann, D., & Ulich, E. (1987). The chances of individualization in human–computer interaction and its consequences. In M. Frese, E. Ulich, & W. Dzida (Eds.), *Psychological issues of* human–computer interaction in the work place (pp. 131–145). Amsterdam: North-Holland.

Albrecht, K. (1988). *Einflüsse personenspezifischer Variablen auf die Programmierung*. München, Germany: Universität München: Unveröff. Diplomarbeit.

Amthauer, R. (1955). *Intelligenz-Struktur-Test*. Göttingen, Germany: Hogrefe.

Anderson, J. R. (1976). *Learning, memory, and thought*. Hillsdale, NJ: Erlbaum.

Anderson, J. R. (1983). *The architecture of cognition*. Cambridge, MA: Harvard University Press.

Annett, J. (1969). *Feedback and human behavior*. Baltimore: Penguin Books.

Arnold, B., & Roe, R. A. (1987). User errors in human–computer interaction. In M. Frese, E. Ulich, & W. Dzida (Eds.), *Psychological issues of human computer interaction in the work place* (pp. 203–220). Amsterdam: North-Holland.

Ausubel, D. P., Novak, J. D., & Hanesian, H. (1968). *Educational psychology: A cognitive view*. New York: Holt, Rinehart and Winston.

Badke-Schaub, P. (1990). *AIDS-Bekämpfung in Pannenburg. Wie unterscheiden sich Gruppen und Einzelpersonen bei der Bearbeitung eines komplexen Simulationsproblems?* (Working paper No. 6). Berlin: Project Group Cognitive Anthoroplogy, Max-Planck-Gesellschaft.

Bagnara, S., & Rizzo, A. (1989). A methodology for the analysis of error processes in human–computer interaction. In M. J. Smith & G. Salvendy (Eds.), *Work with computers: Organizational, management, stress and health aspects* (pp. 605–612). Amsterdam: Elsevier Science Publishers.

Bainbridge, L. (1983). Ironies of automatization. *Automatica, 19*, 775–779.

Baltes, P. B., Reese, H. W., & Lipsitt, L. P. (1980). Life-span developmental psychology. *Annual Review of Psychology, 31*, 65–110.

Bandura, A. (1986). *Social foundation of thought and action: A social cognitive theory*. Englewood Cliffs, NJ: Prentice-Hall.

Baron, J. (1988). *Thinking and deciding*. Cambridge, UK: Cambridge University Press.

Bartlett, F. C. (1932). *Remembering: A study in experimental and social psychology*. Melbourne: Cambridge University Press.

Battmann, W. (1984). Regulation und Fehlregulation im Verhalten IX: Entlastung und Belastung durch Planung. *Psychologische Rundschau, 26*, 672–691.

Battmann, W. (1988). Request of feedback as a means of self-assessment and affect optimazation. *Motivation and Emotion, 12*, 57–74.

Berger, P. L., & Luckmann, T. (1966). *The social construction of reality*. New York: Doubleday.

Brehmer, B., & Allard, R. (1991). Dynamic decision making: The effects of task complexity and feedback delay. In J. Rasmussen, B. Brehmer, & J. Leplat (Eds.), *Distributed decision making: Cognitive models for cooperative work* (pp. 319–334). New York: Wiley.

Broadbent, D. E. (1985). Multiple goals and flexible procedures in the design of work. In M. Frese & J. Sabini (Eds.), *Goal directed behavior: The concept of action in psychology* (pp. 285–295). Hillsdale, NJ: Erlbaum.

Brodbeck. F. C., Zapf, D., Prümper, J., & Frese, M. (in press). Error handling in office work with computers: A field study. *Journal of Occupational and Organizational Psychology*.

Brown, A. L. (1988). Metacognition, executive control, self-regulation, and other, even more mysterious mechanisms. In F. E. Weinert & R. H. Kluwe (Eds.), *Metacognition, motivation, and understanding*. Hillsdale, NJ: Erlbaum.

Bruner, J. S. (1966). *Toward a theory of instruction*. Cambridge, MA: Harvard University Press.

Card, S. K., Moran, T. P., & Newell, A. (1983). *The psychology of human–computer interaction*. Hillsdale, NJ: Erlbaum.

Carroll, J. M., Mack, R. L., Lewis, C. H., Grischkowsky, N. L., & Robertson, S. R. (1985). Exploring a word processor. *Human-Computer Interaction, 1*, 283–307.

Carver, C. S., & Scheier, M. F. (1982). Control theory: A useful conceptual framework for personality, social, clinical, and health psychology. *Psychological Bulletin, 92*, 111–135.

Chomsky, N. (1957). *Syntactic structures*. S. Gravenhage, the Netherlands: Mouton.

Chomsky, N. (1959). Review of Skinner's verbal behavior. *Language, 35*, 26–58.

Cranach, M. v., & Harré, R. (Eds.). (1982). *The analysis of action: Recent theoretical and empirical advances*. Cambridge, UK: Cambridge University Press.

Cranach, M. v., Ochsenbein, G., & Tschan, F. (1987). Actions of social systems: Theoretical and empirical investigations. In G. R. Semin & B. Krahé (Eds.), *Issues in contemporary German social psychology: History, theories and application* (pp. 119–155). London: Sage.

Cranach, M. v., Ochsenbein, G., & Valach, L. (1986). The group as a self-active system (outline of a theory of group action). *European Journal of Social Psychology, 16,* 193–229.

Cratty, B. J. (1973). *Movement behavior and motor learning.* Philadelphia: Lea & Febiger.

Däumling, M., Engler, H. J., Smieskol, H., Tiegel, G., Triebe, J. K., Ulich, E., & Wilke, K. (Eds.). (1973). *Beiträge zum mentalen Training.* Frankfurt: Limpert.

Dahm, M., Glaser, K., Jansen-Dittmer, H., Keizers, A., Meyer-Ebrecht, D., Münker-Haupp, K., Rudolf, H., Schilling, Ch., Selbmann, A., & Winkler, W. (1991). DIBA: Der digitale Arbeitsplatz. In D. Ackermann & E. Ulich (Eds.), *Software-Ergonomie '91. Benutzerorientierte Software-Entwicklung* (pp. 342–351). Stuttgart, Germany: Teubner.

Dörner, D. (1976). *Problemlösen als Informationsverarbeitungsprozeß.* Stuttgart, Germany: Kohlhammer.

Dörner, D. (1981). Über die Schwierigkeiten menschlichen Umgangs mit Komplexität. *Psychologische Rundschau (Sonderdruck), 31,* 163–179.

Dörner, D. (1987a). On the difficulties people have in dealing with complexity. In J. Rasmussen, K. Duncan, & J. Leplat (Eds.), *New technology and human error.* Chichester, UK: Wiley.

Dörner, D. (1987b). *Von der Logik des Mißlingens: Denken, Planen und Entscheiden in Unbestimmtheit und Komplexität.* Bonn-Bad Godesberg: Lehrstuhl Psychologie II, Universität Bamberg, Projekt "Mikroanalyse" DFG 200/5-7 No. 54.

Dörner, D. (1989). *Die Logik des Mißlingens.* Hamburg: Rowohlt.

Dörner, D. (1991). The investigation of action regulation in uncertain and complex situations. In J. Rasmussen, B. Brehmer, & J. Leplat (Eds.), *Distributed descision making: Cognitive models for cooperative work* (pp. 349–356). New York: Wiley.

Dörner, D. (1992). *Wissen, Emotionen und Handlungsregulation oder Die Vernunft der Gefühle.* Bamberg, Germany: University of Bamberg, Department of Theoretical Psychology.

Dörner, D., & Kreuzig, H. W. (1983). Problemlösefähigkeit und Intelligenz. *Psychologische Rundschau, 34,* 185–192.

Dörner, D., Kreuzig, H.W., Reither, F., & Stäudel, T. (1983). *Lohhausen—Vom Umgang mit Unbestimmtheit und Komplexität.* Bern, Switzerland: Huber.

Dörner, D., & Pfeifer, E. (1991). Strategisches Denken, Stress und Intelligenz. *Project Group Cognitive Anthropology* (Working Paper No. 11). Berlin: Max-Planck-Gesellschaft.

Dolgin, K. G. (1985). An action theory perspective of the tool-using capacities of chimpanzees and human infants. In M. Frese & J. Sabini (Eds.), *Goal directed behavior: The concept of action in psychology* (pp. 35–44). Hillsdale, NJ: Erlbaum.

Dunckel, H. (1989, March). Contrastive task analysis. In K. Landau & W. Rohmert (Eds.), *Recent trends in job analysis: Proceedings of the International Symposium on Job Analysis: University of Hohenheim* (pp. 125–134). London: Taylor & Francis.

Dunckel, H., & Volpert, W. (1990). A guide for contrastive task analysis in clerical and administrative work. In P. Richter & W. Hacker (Eds.), *Mental work and automation* (pp. 61–67). Dresden, Germany: Technical University.

Dunckel, H., Volpert, W., Zölch, M., Kreutner, U., Pleiss, C., & Hennes, K. (1993). *Kontrastive Aufgabenanalyse im Buero. Der KABA-Leitfaden.* Zuerich: Verlag der Fachvereine; Stuttgart: Teubner.

Dunnette, M. D. (Ed.). (1976). *Handbook of industrial and organizational psychology.* Chicago: Rand McNally.

Elssner, G. (1972). Erlernen motorischer Arbeitshandlungen auf der Grundlage von Sprechimpulsen—dargestellt an einer Anlernmethodik für das Aufstrecken von Kuoxamseide in einem Kunstseidenwerk. In W. Skell (Ed.), *Psychologische Analyse von Denkleistungen in der Produktion* (pp. 173–189). Berlin: Deutscher Verlag der Wissenschaften.

Emery, F. E., & Thorsrud, E. (1976). *Democracy at work.* Leiden, the Netherlands: Martinus Nijhoff.

Emery, F. E., & Trist, E. L. (1960). Socio-technical systems. In C. H. Churchman & M. Verhulst (Eds.), *Management science, models and techniques* (Vol. 2, pp. 83–97). Oxford, UK: Pergamon.

Frankenhaeuser, M., & Gardell, B. (1976). Underload and overload in working life: Outline of a multidisciplinary approach. *Journal of Human Stress, 2,* 35–46.

Freier, B., & Huybrechts, R. (1980). Untersuchung zum Training kognitiver Grundlagen von Arbeitsverfahren. In W. Hacker & H. Raum (Eds.), *Optimierung von kognitiven Arbeitsanforderungen* (pp. 229–235). Bern, Switzerland: Huber.

Frese, M. (1977). *Psychische Störungen bei Arbeitern.* Salzburg, Germany: Otto Müller Verlag.

Frese, M. (1978). Partialisierte Handlung und Kontrolle: Zwei Themen der industriellen Psychopathologie. In M. Frese, S. Greif & N. Semmer (Eds.), *Industrielle psychopathologie* (pp. 159–183). Bern, Switzerland: Huber.

Frese, M. (1982). Occupational socialisation and psychological development: An under emphasized research perspective in industrial psychology. *Journal of Occupational Psychology, 55,* 209–224.

Frese, M. (1983). Der Einfluß der Arbeit auf die Persönlichkeit. Zum Konzept des Handlungsstils in der beruflichen Sozialization. *Zeitschrift für Sozialisationsforschung und Erziehungssoziologie,* 3(1), 11–28.

Frese, M. (1987a). Alleviating depression in the unemployed: Adequate financial support, hope and early retirement. *Social Science Medicine, 25,* 213–215.

Frese, M. (1987b). A theory of control and complexity: Implications for software design and integration of the computer system into the work place. In M. Frese, E. Ulich, & W. Dzida (Eds.), *Psychological issues of human computer interaction in the work place* (pp. 313–338). Amsterdam: North-Holland.

Frese, M. (1987c). The industrial and organizational psychology of human-computer-interaction in the office. In C. L. Cooper & I. T. Robertson (Eds.), *International review of industrial and organizational psychology* (pp. 117–165). Chichester, UK: Wiley.

Frese, M. (1989). Theoretical models of control and health. In S. L. Sauter, J. J. Hurrel, & C. L. Cooper (Eds.), *Job control and worker health* (pp. 108–128). New York: Wiley.

Frese, M. (1991). Error management or error prevention: Two strategies to deal with errors in software design. In H. J. Bullinger (Ed.), *Human aspects in computing: Design and use of interactive systems and work with terminals* (pp. 776–782). Amsterdam: Elsevier Science.

Frese, M. (1992). A plea for realistic pessimism: On objective reality, coping with stress, and psychological dysfunctioning. In L. Montada, S. H. Filipp, & M. J. Lerner (Eds.), *Life crises and experiences of loss in adulthood* (pp. 81–94). Hillsdale, NJ: Erlbaum.

Frese, M., Albrecht, K., Altmann, A., Lang, J., Papstein, P., Peyerl, R., Prümper, J., Schulte-Göcking, H., Wankmüller, I., & Wendel, R. (1988). The effects of an active development of the mental model in the training process: Experimental results in a word processing system. *Behaviour and Information Technology, 7,* 295–304.

Frese, M., & Altmann, A. (1989). The treatment of errors in learning and training. In L. Bainbridge & A. Ruiz Quintanilla (Eds.), *Developing skills with information technology* (pp. 65–86). Chichester, UK: Wiley.

Frese, M., Brodbeck, F. C., Heinbokel, T., Mooser, C., Schleiffenbaum, E., & Thiemann, P. (1991). Errors in training computer skills: On the positive function of errors. *Human Computer Interaction, 6,* 77–93.

Frese, M., Brodbeck, F. C., Zapf, D., & Prümper, J. (1990). The effects of task structure and social support on users' errors and error handling. In D. Diaper, D. Gilmore, G. Cockton, & B. Shackel (Eds.), *Human–computer interaction—INTERACT '90* (pp. 35–41). Amsterdam: Elsevier Science.

Frese, M., Kreuscher, R., Prümper, J., Schulte-Göcking, & Papstein, P. (in press). *Action styles and performance: The role of planfulness and goal-orientation in five ecologically valid performance studies.* Giessen, Germany: University of Giessen, Department of Psychology.

Frese, M., & Stewart, J. (1984). Skill learning as a concept in life-span developmental psychology: An action theoretic analysis. *Human Development, 27,* 147–162.

Frese, M., Stewart, J., & Hannover, B. (1987). Goal-orientation and planfulness: Action styles as personality concepts. *Journal of Personality and Social Psychology, 52,* 1182–1194.

Frese, M., Ulich, E., & Dzida, W. (Eds.). (1987). *Psychological issues of human–computer interaction at the work place.* Amsterdam: North-Holland.

Frese, M., & Zapf, D. (1988). Methodological issues in the study of work stress: Objective vs. subjective measurement and the question of longitudinal studies. In C. L. Cooper & R. Payne

(Eds.), *Causes, coping, and consequences of stress at work* (pp. 375–411). Chichester, UK: Wiley.

Frese, M., & Zapf, D. (Eds.). (1991a). *Fehler bei der Arbeit mit dem Computer. Ergebnisse von Beobachtungen und Befragungen aus dem Bürobereich.* Schriftenreihe "Arbeitspsychologie," Band 52, (Hrsg. E. Ulich). Bern, Switzerland: Huber.

Frese, M., & Zapf, D. (1991b). Fehlersystematik und Fehlerentstehung: Ein theoretischer Überblick. In M. Frese & D. Zapf (Eds.), *Fehler bei der Arbeit mit dem Computer. Ergebnisse von Beobachtungen und Befragungen im Bürobereich* (pp. 14–31). Bern, Switzerland: Huber.

Frese, M., Zempel, J., Kring, W., & Soose, A. (1993). *Everyday entrepreneurship in Germany; Differences in personal initiative.* Unpublished manuscript, University of Giessen, Department of Psychology, Giessen, Germany.

Frone, M. R., & McFarlin, D. B. (1989). Chronic occupational stressors, self-focussed attention, and well-being: Testing a cybernetic model of stress. *Journal of Applied Psychology, 74,* 876–883.

Fuhrer, U. (1984). *Mehrfachhandeln in dynamischen Umfeldern.* Göttingen, Germany: Hogrefe.

Gal, R., & Lazarus, R. S. (1975). The role of activity in anticipating and confronting stressful situations. *Journal of Human Stress, 1* (4), 4–20.

Gallistel, C. R. (1980). *The organization of action: A new synthesis.* Hillsdale, NJ: Erlbaum.

Galperin, P. I. (1967). Die Entwicklung der Untersuchungen über die Bildung geistiger Operationen. In H. Hiebsch (Ed.), *Ergebnisse der sowjetischen Psychologie* (pp. 367–405). Berlin: Akademie Verlag.

Gentner, D. R. (1987). Timing of skilled motor performance: Tests of the proportional duration model. *Psychological Review, 94,* 255–276.

Gentner, D. R., & Stevens, A. L. (Eds.). (1983). *Mental models.* Hillsdale, NJ: Erlbaum.

Gibson, J. J. (1979). *The ecological approach to visual perception.* Boston: Houghton Mifflin.

Gleitman, H. (1985). Some trends in the study of cognition. In S. Koch & D. E. Leary (Eds.), *A century of psychology as science: Retrospections and assessments* (pp. 420–436). New York: McGraw-Hill.

Goldstein, I. L. (Ed.). (1989). *Training and the development in organizations.* San Francisco: Jossey-Bass.

Gollwitzer, P. M. (1990). Action phases and mind sets. In E. T. Higgins & R. M. Sorrentino (Eds.), *Cognition: Foundations of social behavior* (Vol. 2, pp. 53–92). New York: Guilford Press.

Greif, S. (1976). *Diskussionstraining.* Salzburg, Germany: Otto Müller.

Greif, S. (1978). Intelligenzabbau und Dequalifizierung durch Industriearbeit? In M. Frese, S. Greif, & N. Semmer (Eds.), *Industrielle psychopathologie* (pp. 232–256). Bern, Germany: Huber.

Greif, S. (1986). Neue Kommunikationstechnologien —Entlastung oder mehr Streß? Beschreibung eines Computer-Trainings zur "Streßimmunisierung." In K. K. Pullig, U. Schäkel, & J. Scholz (Eds.), *Streß im Unternehmen* (pp. 178–200). Hamburg: Windmühle.

Greif, S. (1988, December). *Genetic growing systems and self-controlled training.* Paper presented at the Swedish-German Hda/MDA-Workshop on the Humanization of Working Life, Stockholm. *Ergebnisse des Projektes MBQ.* Universität Osnabrück, 9–89.

Greif, S. (1989). Exploratorisches Lernen durch Fehler und qualifikationsorientiertes Software-Design. In S. Maaß & H. Oberquelle (Eds.), *Software-Ergonomie '89. Aufgabenorientierte Systemgestaltung und Funktionalität* (pp. 204–212). Stuttgart, Germany: Teubner.

Greif, S. (1992). Computer systems as learning environments. In J. Valsiner & H. G. Voss (Eds.), *The structure of learning processes.* Norwood, NJ: Ablex.

Greif, S., & Gediga, G. (1987). A critique of one-best-way models in human–computer interaction. In M. Frese, E. Ulich, & W. Dzida (Eds.), *Psychological issues of human–computer interaction in the work place* (pp. 357–377). Amsterdam: North-Holland.

Greif, S., & Janikowski, A. (1987). Aktives Lernen durch systematische Fehlerexploration oder programiertes Lernen durch Tutorials? *Zeitschrift für Arbeits-und Organisationspsychologie, 31,* 94–99.

Greif, S., & Keller, H. (1990). Innovation and the design of work and learning environments: The concept of exploration in human–computer interaction. In M. A. West & J. L. Farr (Eds.), *Innovation and creativity at work* (pp. 231–249). Chichester, UK: Wiley.

Greiner, B., & Leitner, K. (1989, March). Assessment of job stress: The RHIA-Instrument. In K. Landau & W. Rohmert (Eds.), *Recent developments in job analysis*. Proceedings of the International Symposium on Job Analysis, University of Hohenheim (pp. 53–66). London: Taylor & Francis.

Grudin, J. T. (1982). Error patterns in novice and unskilled transcription typing. In W. E. Cooper (Ed.), *Cognitive aspects of skilled type writing* (pp. 121–144). New York: Wiley.

Guthrie, E. R. (1935). *The psychology of learning*. New York: Harper & Row.

Haaks, D. (1992). *Anpaßbare Informationssysteme. Auf dem Weg zu aufgaben- und benutzerorientierter Systemgestaltung und Funktionalität*. Göttingen, Germany: Verlage für Angewandte Psychologie.

Hacker, W. (1968). Zur Entwicklung der Arbeitspsychologie in der wissenschaftlich-technischen Revolution. In W. Hacker, W. Skell, & W. Straub (Eds.), *Arbeitspsychologie und wissenschaftlich-technische Revolution* (pp. 11–39). Berlin: Deutscher Verlag der Wissenschaften.

Hacker, W. (1973). *Allgemeine Arbeits- und Ingenieurspsychologie*. Berlin: Deutscher Verlag der Wissenschaften.

Hacker, W. (1982a). Action control. On the task dependent structure of action-controlling mental representations. In W. Hacker, W. Volpert, & M. Cranach (Eds.), *Cognitive and motivational aspects of action* (pp. 137–149). Berlin: Deutscher Verlag der Wissenschaften.

Hacker, W. (1982b). Objective and subjective organization of work activities. In M. Cranach & R. Harré (Eds.), *The analysis of action* (pp. 81–98). Cambridge, UK: Cambridge University Press.

Hacker, W. (1985). Activity: A fruitful concept in industrial psychology. In M. Frese & J. Sabini (Eds.), *Goal directed behavior: The concept of action in psychology* (pp. 262–284). Hillsdale, NJ: Erlbaum.

Hacker, W. (1986a). *Arbeitspsychologie*. Bern, Switzerland: Huber.

Hacker, W. (1986b). What should be computerized? Cognitive demands of mental routine tasks and mental load. In F. Klix & H. Wandke (Eds.), *Man Computer Interaction Research MACINTER-I* (pp. 445–461). Amsterdam, North Holland: Elsevier Science Publishers.

Hacker, W. (1987a). Computerization versus computer aided mental work. In M. Frese, E. Ulich, & W. Dzida (Eds.), *Psychological issues of human–computer interaction in the work place* (pp. 115–130). Amsterdam: North-Holland.

Hacker, W. (1987b). Software-Ergonomie: Gestaltung rechnergestützter geistiger Arbeit? In W. Schönpflug & M. Wittstock (Eds.), *Software-Ergonomie '87* (pp. 31–54). Stuttgart, Germany: Teubner.

Hacker, W. (1992). Expertenkönnen. Erkennen und vermitteln. Goettingen, Germany: Hogrefe, Verlag Fuer Angewandte Psychologie.

Hacker, W., & Iwanowa, A. (1984). Zur psychologischen Bewertung von Arbeitsmerk-malen. *Zeitschrift für Psychologie, 192*, 103–121.

Hacker, W., Iwanowa, A., & Richter, P. (1983). *Tätigkeits-Bewertungssystem*. Berlin: Diagnostisches Zentrum.

Hacker, W., & Richter, P. (1980). Psychische Fehlbeanspruchung: Psychische Ermüdung, Monotonie, Sättigung und Streß. In W. Hacker (Ed.), *Spezielle Arbeits- und Ingenieurpsychologie, Lehrtext 2*. Berlin: Verlag der Wissenschaften.

Hacker, W., Skell, W., & Straub, W. (Eds.). (1968). *Arbeitspsychologie und wissenschaftlich-technische Revolution*. Berlin: Deutscher Verlag der Wissenschaften.

Hacker, W., & Vaic, H. (1973). Psychologische Analyse interindividueller Leistungsdifferenzen als eine Grundlage von Rationalisierungsbeiträgen. In W. Hacker, W. Quaas, H. Raum, & H. J. Schulz (Eds.), *Psychologische Arbeitsuntersuchung*. Berlin: Deutscher Verlag der Wissenschaften.

Hackman, J. R. (1970). Tasks and task performance in research on stress. In J. E. McGrath (Ed.), *Social and psychological factors in stress* (pp. 202–237). New York: Holt, Rinehart & Winston.

Hackman, J. R., & Lawler, E. E. (1971). Employee reactions to job characteristics. *Journal of Applied Psychology, 55*, 259–286.

Hackman, J. R., & Oldham, G. R. (1974). *The job diagnostic survey: An instrument for the diagnosis of jobs and the evaluation of job redesign projects*. Technical Report No. 4. New Haven, CT: Yale University, Department of Administrative Science.

Hackman, J. R., & Oldham, G. R. (1975). Development of the job diagnostic survey. *Journal of Applied Psychology, 60*, 259–270.

Hackman, J. R., & Oldham, G. R. (1980). *Work redesign*. Reading, MA: Addison Wesley.

Häfeli, K., Kraft, U., & Schallberger, U. (1988). *Berufsausbildung und Persönlichkeitsentwicklung*. Bern, Germany: Huber.

Hannover, B. (1983). *Handlungsstile. Ein handlungstheoretischer Beitrag zur psycho-logischen Persoenlichkeitsforschung*. Unpublished diploma thesis, Department of Psychology, Technical University of Berlin.

Hartwich, C., & Okonek, K. (1979). *Diskussionstraining für die gewerkschaftliche und betriebliche Interessensvertretung*. Unpublished diploma thesis. Berlin: Free University Berlin, Department of Psychology.

Heckhausen, H. (1991). *Motivation and action*. Berlin: Springer.

Heckhausen, H., & Beckmann, J. (1990). Intentional action and action slips. *Psychological Review, 97,* 36–48.

Heckhausen, H., & Kuhl, J. (1985). From wishes to action: The dead ends and short cuts on the long way to action. In M. Frese & J. Sabini (Eds.), *Goal directed behavior: The concept of action in psychology* (pp. 134–160). Hillsdale, NJ: Erlbaum.

Herrmann, G. (1967). Psychische Anforderung bei Mehrmaschinenbedienung. *Probleme und Ergebnisse der Psychologie, 20,* 21.

Herzberg, F. (1966). *Work and the nature of man*. New York: Mentor Books.

Heuer, H. (1985). Wie wirkt mentale Übung? *Psychologische Rundschau, 36,* 191–200.

Hiltscher, T. (1992). *Schulungsstrategien für das Erlernen von Computerprogrammen: Eine Anaylse der psychologischen Aspekte verschiedener Trainingskonzeptionen*. Unpublished diploma thesis. University of Giessen, Giessen, Germany.

Hiltscher, T., & Frese, M. (1992). *Process characteristics of error training: The role of exploration*. Giessen, Germany: University of Giessen, Department of Psychology.

Hockey, R., & Hamilton, P. (1983). The cognitive patterning of stress states. In R. Hockey (Ed.), *Stress and fatigue in human performance* (pp. 331–362). Chichester, UK: Wiley.

Hoff, E. H. (1986). *Arbeit, Freizeit und Persönlichkeit. Wissenschaftliche und alltägliche Vorstellungsmuster*. Bern, Germany: Huber.

Hoff, E. H., Lempert, W., & Lappe, L. (1991). *Persönlichkeitsentwicklung in der Facharbeiterbiographie*. Bern, Germany: Huber.

Hofsten, C. (1985). Perception and action. In M. Frese & J. Sabini (Eds.), *Goal directed behavior: The concept of action in psychology* (pp. 80–96). Hillsdale, NJ: Erlbaum.

Holding, D. H. (1965). *Principles of training*. Oxford, UK: Pergamon Press.

Höpfner, H. D. (1983). Untersuchungen zum Einsatz heuristischer Regeln beim Üben im berufspraktischen Unterricht. *Forschung der sozialistischen Berufsbildung, 17,* 28–33.

Hoyos, C. Graf. (1974). *Arbeitspsychologie*. Stuttgart, Germany: Kohlhammer.

Hoyos, C. Graf. (1980). *Psychologische Unfall- und Sicherheitsforschung*. Stuttgart, Germany: Kohlhammer.

Hoyos, C. Graf, & Zimolong, B. (1988). *Occupational safety and accident prevention*. Amsterdam: Elsevier.

Hull, C. L. (1943). *Principles of behavior*. New York: Appleton-Century-Crofts.

Irmer, C., Pfeffer, S., & Frese, M. (1991). Praktische Konsequenzen von Fehleranalysen für das Training: Das Fehlertraining. In M. Frese & D. Zapf (Eds.), *Fehler bei der Arbeit mit dem Computer: Ergebnisse von Beobachtungen und Befragungen im Bürobereich* (pp. 151–165). Bern, Germany: Huber.

Iwanowa, A., & Hacker, W. (1984). Das Tätigkeitsbewertungssystem. Ein Hilfsmittel beim Erfassen potentiell gesundheits- und entwicklungsfördernder objektiver Tätigkeits-merkmale. *Psychologie und Praxis, 28,* 57–66.

Jackson, P. R. & Wall, T. D. (1991). How does operator control enhance performance of advanced manufacturing technology? *Ergonomics, 34,* 1301–1311.

Jeffries, R., Turner, A. A., Polson, P. G., & Atwood, M. E. (1981). The processes involved in designing software. In J. R. Anderson (Ed.), *Cognitive skills and their acquisition* (pp. 255–283). Hillsdale, NJ: Erlbaum.

Jenkins, G. C., Nadler, E. E., Lawler, E. E., III, & Cammann, C. (1975). Standardized observations: An approach to measuring the nature of jobs. *Journal of Applied Psychology, 60,* 171–181.

Johnson-Laird, P. N. (1983). *Mental models. Towards a cognitive science of language, inference, and consciousness*. Cambridge, MA: Harvard University Press.

Josif, G., & Ene, P. (1980). Entwicklung der Diagnosetätigkeit bei Operateuren in Wärmekraftwerken. In W. Hacker & H. Raum (Eds.), *Optimierung von kognitiven Arbeitsanforderungen* (pp. 248–251). Bern, Germany: Huber.

Kagan, J., Rosman, B. L., Day, D., Albert, J., & Phillips, W. (1964). Information processing in the child. *Psychological Monographs, 78* (1, Whole No. 578).

Kahn, R. L. (1973). Conflict, ambiguity, and overload; three elements in job stress. *Occupational Mental Health, 3,* 2–9.

Kahneman, D. (1973). *Attention and effort.* Englewood Cliffs, NJ: Prentice-Hall.

Kaminski, G. (1973). Bewegungshandlungen als Bewältigung von Mehrfachaufgaben. *Sportwissenschaft, 3,* 233–250.

Kaminski, G. (1982). What beginner skiers can teach us about actions. In M. v. Cranach & R. Harré (Eds.), *The analysis of action* (pp. 99–114). Cambridge, UK: Cambridge University Press.

Kanfer, F. H. (1975). Self-managing methods. In F. H. Kanfer & A. P. Goldstein (Eds.), *Helping people change.* New York: Pergamon.

Kanfer, R. (1990). Motivation theory and industrial and organizational theory. In M. D. Dunnette & L. M. Hough (Eds.), *Handbook of industrial and organizational psychology* (Vol. 1, pp. 75–170). Palo Alto, CA: Consulting Psychologists Press.

Kanner, A. D., Coyne, J. C., Schaefer, C., & Lazarus, R. S. (1981). Comparison of two modes of stress measurement: Daily hassles and uplifts versus major life events. *Journal of Behavioral Medicine, 4,* 1–39.

Karasek, R. A. (1976). *The impact of the work environment on life outside the job: Explorations in the associations between job content and leisure behavior and mental health using national survey data from Sweden and the United States.* Unpublished doctoral dissertation, Massachusetts Institute of Technology, Cambridge, MA.

Karasek, R. A. (1978). *Job socialization. A longitudinal study of work, political and leisure activities.* Stockholm: Swedish Insitute for Social Research.

Karasek, R. A. (1979). Job demands, job decision latitude and mental strain: Implications for job redesign. *Administrative Science Quarterly, 24,* 385–408.

Karasek, R. A., Baker, D., Marxer, F., Ahlbom, A., & Theorell, T. (1981). Job decision latitude, job demands, and cardiovascular disease: A prospective study of Swedish men. *American Journal of Public Health, 71,* 694–705.

Karasek, R. A., & Theorell, T. (1990). *Health work: Stress, productivity, and the reconstruction of working life.* New York: Basic Books.

Kasl, S. V. (1978). Epidemiological contributions to the study of work stress. In C. L. Cooper & R. Payne (Eds.), *Stress at work* (pp. 3–48). Chichester, UK: Wiley.

Kass, R., & Finin, T. (1988). A general user modelling facility. In E. Solloway, D. Frye, & S. B. Sheppard (Eds.), *CHI '88 Conference proceedings: Human factors in computing systems* (pp. 145–150). Reading, PA: Addison-Wesley.

Katz, D., & Kahn, R. L. (1978). *The social psychology of organizations.* New York: Wiley.

Keil-Slawik, R., & Holl, F. (1987). Transparenz von Dialogsystemen: Rückmeldungen, Systemmeldungen, Fehlerverstehen. *Abschlußbericht der Arbeitsgruppe 1 der 7. Mensch-Maschine-Kommunikationstagung.* Unpublished manuscript, Peiting, Germany.

Kieras, D., & Polson, P. G. (1985). An approach to the formal analysis of user complexity. *International Journal of Man–Machine Studies, 22,* 365–394.

Klemp, G. O., & McClelland, D. C. (1986). What characterizes intelligent functioning among senior managers. In R. J. Sternberg & R. K. Wagner (Eds.), *Practical intelligence: Nature and origins of competence in the everyday world* (pp. 51–83). Cambridge, UK: Cambridge University Press.

Kohn, M. L. (1969). *Class and conformity. A study in values.* Homewood, IL: Dorsey Press.

Kohn, M. L., & Schooler, C. (1978). The reciprocal effects of the substantive complexity of work on intellectual flexibility: A longitudinal assessment. *American Journal of Sociology, 48,* 24–52.

Kohn, M. L., & Schooler, C. (1983). *Work and personality. An inquiry into the impact of social stratification.* Norwood, NJ: Ablex.

Kühbauer, B., & Schmidt-Hieber, E. (1978). *Beratungstraining für die gewerkschaftliche und betriebliche Interessensvertretung. Theoretische Grundlagen und Entwicklung eines Kategoriensystems zur Evaluation eines Trainings.* Berlin: Institut für Psychologie, Freie Universität Berlin, Unveröff. Diplomarbeit.

Kuhl, J. (1981). Motivational and functional help-lessness: The moderating effect of state vs. action orientation. *Journal of Personality & Social Psychology, 40*, 155–170.

Kuhl, J. (1982). Action vs. state-orientation as a moderator between motivation and action. In W. Hacker, W. Volpert, & M. Cranach (Eds.), *Cognitive and motivationational aspects of action* (pp. 37–46). Amsterdam: North-Holland.

Kuhl, J. (1983). *Motivation, Konflikt und Handlungskontrolle*. Berlin: Springer.

Kuhl, J. (1992). A theory of self-regulation: Action vs. state orientation, self-discrimination, and some applications. *Applied Psychology: An International Review, 41*, 97–129.

Lang, J. (1987a). Mentale Modelle bei Experten: Eine empirische Untersuchung zur elektronischen Ablage eines Bürosystems. In W. Schönpflug & M. Wittstock (Eds.), *Software Ergonomie '87* (pp. 98–109). Stuttgart, Germany: Teubner.

Lang, J. (1987b). *Mentale Modelle bei Experten. Eine empirische Untersuchung der elektronischen Ablage eines Bürosystems*. Unpublished diploma thesis. University of Munich, Department of Psychology, Munich.

Lazarus, R. S., & Folkman, S. (1984). *Stress, appraisal and coping*. New York: Springer.

Lee, B. S. (1950). Effects of delayed speech feedback. *Journal of the Acoustic Society of America, 22*, 824–826.

Leitner, K., Lüders, E., Greiner, B., Ducki, A., Niedermeier, R., & Volpert, W. (1993). *Analyse psychischer Anforderungen und Belastungen in der Büroarbeit. Das RHIA/VERA-Büro-Verfahren*. Göttingen, Germany: Hogrefe, Verlag für Psychologie.

Leitner, K., Volpert, W., Greiner, B., Weber, W. G., & Hennes, K. (1987). *Analyse psychischer Belastung in der Arbeit. Das RHIA-Verfahren*. Cologne, Germany: TÜV Rheinland.

Leontiev, A. N. (1978). *Activity, consciousness, and personality*. Englewood Cliffs, NJ: Prentice-Hall.

Leontiev, A. N. (1981). *Problems of the development of the mind*. Moscow: Progress.

Locke, E. A., & Latham, G. P. (1990). *A theory of goal setting and task performance*. Englewood Cliffs, NJ: Prentice-Hall.

Luchins, A. S., & Luchins, E. H. (1959). *Rigity of behavior: A variational approach to the effects of Einstellung*. Eugene, OR: University of Oregon Books.

Luria, A. R. (1959). The directive function of speech in development and dissolution. *Word 15*, 341–352, 453–464.

Luria, A. R. (1970). *Die höheren kortikalen Funktionen des Menschen und ihre Störungen bei örtlichen Hirnschädigungen*. Berlin: Deutscher Verlag der Wissenschaften.

Maass, S. (1983). Why systems transparency? In T. R. G. Green, S. J. Payne, & G. C. van der Veer (Eds.), *The psychology of computer use* (pp. 19–28). London: Academic Press.

Mackworth, J. F. (1970). *Vigilance and attention*. Harmondsworth, UK: Penguin Books.

Mayer, A., & Herwig, B. (Eds.). (1970). *Handbuch der Psychologie, Band 9: Betriebspsychologie*. Göttingen, Germany: Hogrefe.

Meichenbaum, D. (1977). *Cognitive-behavior modification: An integrative approach*. New York: Plenum Press.

Meissner, M. (1971). The long arm of the job. A study of work and leisure. *Industrial Relation, 10*, 239–260.

Messer, S. B. (1976). Reflection-impulsivity: A review. *Psychological Bulletin, 83*, 1026–1052.

Miller, G. A. (1956). The magical number seven, plus or minus two. *Psychological Review, 63*, 81–97.

Miller, G. A., Galanter, E., & Pribram, K. H. (1960). *Plans and the structure of behavior*. London: Holt.

Mowrer, O. H. (1950). *Learning theory and personality dynamics*. New York: Ronald Press.

Neisser, U. (1976). *Cognition and reality: Principles and implications of cognitive psychology*. San Francisco: Freeman.

Neisser, U. (1985). The role of invariant structures in the control of movement. In M. Frese & J. Sabini (Eds.), *Goal directed behavior: The concept of action in psychology* (pp. 97–109). Hillsdale, NJ: Erlbaum.

Newell, A., & Simon, H. A. (1972). *Human problem solving*. Englewood Cliffs, NJ: Prentice-Hall.

Norman, D. A. (1981). Categorization of action slips. *Psychological Review, 88*, 1–15.

Norman, D. A. (1983). Some observations on mental models. In D. R. Gentner & A. L. Stevens (Eds.), *Mental models* (pp. 7–14). Hillsdale, NJ: Erlbaum.

Norman, D. A. (1984). *Working papers on errors and error detection* [unpublished manuscript]. San Diego: University of California.

Norman, D. A. (1986). Cognitive engineering. In D. A. Norman & S. W. Draper (Eds.), *User centered system design* (pp. 31–61). Hillsdale, NJ: Erlbaum.

Oesterreich, R. (1981). *Handlungsregulation und Kontrolle*. München, Wien, Baltimore: Urban & Schwarzenberg.

Oesterreich, R. (1982). The term "efficiency-divergency" as a theoretical approach to problems of action-planning and motivation. In W. Hacker, W. Volpert, & M. Cranach (Eds.), *Cognitive and motivational aspects of action* (pp. 99–110). Berlin: Deutscher Verlag der Wissenschaften.

Oesterreich, R. (1984). Zur Analyse von Planungs- und Denkprozessen in der industriellen Produktion. Das Arbeitsanalyseinstrument VERA. *Diagnostica, 30*, 216–234.

Oesterreich, R., Resch, M. G., & Weyerich, A. (1988). Bevorzugung und inhaltliche Bewertung von Handlungsfeldern unterschiedlicher Natur. *Sprache und Kognition, 7*, 144–161.

Oesterreich, R., & Volpert, W. (1986). Task analysis for work design on the basis of action regulation theory. *Economic and Industrial Democracy, 7*, 503–527.

Oesterreich, R., & Volpert, W. (1987). Handlungstheoretisch orientierte Arbeits-analyse. In U. Kleinbeck & J. Rutenfranz (Eds.), *Arbeitspsychologie. Enzyklopädie der Psychologie, Themenbereich D, Serie III, Band 1* (pp. 43–73). Göttingen, Germany: Hogrefe.

Oesterreich, R., & Volpert, W. (Eds.). (1991). *VERA Version 2. Arbeitsanalyseverfahren zur Ermittlung von Planungs- und Denkanforderungen im Rahmen der RHIA-Anwendung (Handbuch und Manual)*. Berlin: Technische Universität Berlin.

Oschanin, D. A. (1976). Dynamisches operatives Abbildsystem. *Probleme und Ergebnisse der Psychologie, 59*, 37–48.

Papstein, P., & Frese, M. (1988). Transfering skills from training to the actual work situation: The role of application knowledge, action styles and job decision latitude. In E. Soloway, D. Frye, & S. B. Sheppard (Eds.), *Proceedings of the CHI '88 conference of human factors in computing systems* (pp. 55–60). Reading, PA: Addison-Wesley.

Patterson, R. D. (1990). Auditory warning sounds in the work environment. In D. E. Broadbent, A. D. Baddely, & J. T. Reason (Eds.), *Human factors in hazardous situations* (pp. 485–491). Oxford, UK: Clarendon Press.

Piaget, J. (1969). *Das Erwachen der Intelligenz bei Kinde*. Stuttgart, Germany: Klett.

Prümper, J., Zapf, D., Brodbeck, F. C., & Frese, M. (1992). Errors of novices and experts: Some surprising differences between novice and expert errors in computerized office work. *Behaviour and Information Technology, 11*, 319–328.

Rasmussen, J. (1982). Human errors: A taxonomy for describing human malfunction in industrial installations. *Journal of Occupational Accidents, 4*, 311–335.

Rasmussen, J. (1985). *Human error data: Facts or fiction*. Roskilde, Denmark: Riso National Laboratory.

Rasmussen, J. (1987a). Cognitive control and human error mechanisms. In J. Rasmussen, K. Duncan, & J. Leplat (Eds.), *New technology and human error* (pp. 53–61). London: Wiley.

Rasmussen, J. (1987b). The definition of human error and a taxonomy for technical system design. In J. Rasmussen, K. Duncan, & J. Leplat (Eds.), *New technology and human error* (pp. 23–30). Chichester, UK: Wiley.

Rasmussen, J. (1987c). Reasons, causes, and human error. In J. Rasmussen, K. Duncan, & J. Leplat (Eds.), *New technology and human error* (pp. 293–301). London: Wiley.

Reason, J. T. (1979). Actions not as planned: The price of automation. In G. Underwood & R. Stevens (Eds.), *Aspects of conciousness* (Vol. 1, pp. 76–89). London: Academic Press.

Reason, J. T. (1987a). A preliminary classification of mistakes. In J. Rasmussen, K. Duncan, & J. Leplat (Eds.), *New technology and human error* (pp. 15–22). London: Wiley.

Reason, J. T. (1987b). Generic error-modelling system (GEMS): A cognitive framework for locating common human error forms. In J. Rasmussen, K. Duncan, & J. Leplat (Eds.), *New technology and human error* (pp. 63–83). London: Wiley.

Reason, J. T. (1988). Framework models of human performance and error: A consumer guide. In L. Goldstein, H. B. Andersen, & S. E. Olson (Eds.), *Mental models, tasks, and errors* (pp. 35–49). London: Taylor & Francis.

Reason, J. T. (1990). *Human error*. New York: Cambridge University Press.

Reason, J. T., & Mycielska, K. (1982). *Absent-minded? The psychology of mental lapses and everyday errors.* New York: Prentice-Hall.

Reither, F., & Stäudel, T. (1985). Thinking and action. In M. Frese & J. Sabini (Eds.), *Goal directed behavior: The concept of action in psychology* (pp. 110–122). Hillsdale, NJ: Erlbaum.

Resch, M. G., & Oesterreich, R. (1987). Bildung von Zwischenzielen in Entscheidungsnetzen. *Zeitschrift für experimentelle und angewandte Psychologie, 34,* 301–317.

Rieger, A., & Rummel, M. (1979). *Analyse des Trainerverhaltens in der Kleingruppenarbeit.* Institut für Psychologie, FU Berlin: Unveröff. Diplomarbeit.

Rissler, A. (1979). A psychobiological approach to quality of working life: Costs of adjustment to quantitative overload. In R. G. Sell & P. Shipley (Eds.), *Satisfaction in work design: Ergonomics and other approaches* (pp. 113–119). London: Taylor & Francis.

Rohmert, W., Rutenfranz, J., & Ulich, E. (1971). *Das Anlernen sensumotorischer Fertigkeiten.* Frankfurt, Germany: Europäische Verlagsanstalt.

Rouse, W. B., & Rouse, S. H. (1983). Analysis and classification of human error. *IEEE Transactions on Systems, Man, and Cybernetics, 13,* 539–549.

Rubinstein, S. L. (1962). *Sein und Bewußtsein.* Berlin: Verlag der Wissenschaften.

Rubinstein, S. L. (1968). *Grundlagen der allgemeinen Psychologie.* Berlin: Verlag deutscher Wissenschaften.

Rudolph, E., Schönfelder, E., & Hacker, W. (1987). *Tätigkeitsbewertungssystem—Geistige Arbeit (TBS-GA).* Göttingen, Germany: Hogrefe.

Rühle, R. (1979). *Inhalte, Methoden und Effekte der Analyse und Vermittlung operativer Abbilder bei Bedientätigkeiten der Mehrstellenarbeit.* Unpublished doctoral dissertation, Technical University of Dresden, Dresden, Germany.

Rühle, R., Matern, B., & Skell, W. (1980). Training kognitiver Regulationsgrundlagen. In W. Hacker & H. Raum (Eds.), *Optimierung von kognitiven Arbeitsanforderungen* (pp. 223–241). Bern, Germany: Huber.

Sabini, J., Frese, M., & Kossman, D. (1985). Some contributions of action theory to social psychology: Social actions and social actors in the context of institutions and an objective world. In M. Frese & J. Sabini (Eds.), *Goal directed behavior: The concept of action in psychology* (pp. 249–257). Hillsdale, NJ: Erlbaum.

Salancik, G., & Pfeffer, J. (1977). An examination of need-satisfaction models of job attitudes. *Administrative Science Quarterly, 22,* 427–456.

Schleicher, R. (1973). Die Intelligenzleistung Erwachsener in Abhängigkeit vom Niveau der beruflichen Tätigkeit. *Probleme und Ergebnisse der Psychologie, 44,* 25–55.

Schmidt, R. A. (1975). A schema theory of discrete motor skill learning. *Psychological Review, 82,* 225–260.

Schneider, N. (1977). *Untersuchungen zur Effektivität von kognitiven Lehr- und Trainingsmethoden.* Unpublished doctoral dissertation, Technical University of Dresden, Dresden, Germany.

Schneider, N., & Shiffrin, R. M. (1977). Controlled and automatic human processing I: Detection, search, and attention. *Psychological Review, 84,* 1–66.

Schönpflug, W. (1979). Regulation und Fehlregulation im Verhalten I: Verhalten-sstruktur, Effizienz und Belastung —theoretische Grundlagen eines Untersuchungsprogramms. *Psychologische Beiträge, 21,* 174–202.

Schönpflug, W. (1983). Coping efficiency and situational demands. In R. Hockey (Ed.), *Stress and fatigue in human performance* (pp. 299–330). Chichester, UK: Wiley.

Schönpflug, W. (1985). Goal directed behavior as a source of stress: Psychological origins and consequences of inefficiency. In M. Frese & J. Sabini (Eds.), *Goal directed behavior: The concept of action in psychology* (pp. 172–188). Hillsdale, NJ: Erlbaum.

Schönpflug, W. (1986a). Behavior economics as an approach to stress theory. In M. Appley & R. Trumbull (Eds.), *Dynamics of stress.* New York: Plenum Press.

Schönpflug, W. (1986b). The trade off between internal and external information storage. *Journal of Memory and Language, 25,* 657–675.

Schönpflug, W. (1987). Beanspruchung und Belastung bei der Arbeit—Konzepte und Theorien. In U. Kleinbeck & J. Rutenfranz (Eds.), *Arbeitspsychologie. Enzyklopädie der Psychologie, Themenbereich D, Serie III, Band 1* (pp. 130–184). Göttingen, Germany: Hogrefe.

Schönpflug, W. (1993). Applied psychology: Newcomer with a long tradition. *Applied Psychology: An International Review, 42,* 5-30.

Schönpflug, W., & Wieland, R. (1982). *Untersuchungungen zur Äquivalenz schwankender Schallpegel. Schwankende Schallpegel, Leistungshandeln und der Wechsel von Arbeit und Erholung.* (Research Rpt. No. 82–105 01 204). Berlin: Umweltbundesamt.

Schulz, P. (1979). Regulation und Fehlregulation im Verhalten II: Streß durch Fehlregulation. *Psychologische Beiträge, 21,* 597–621.

Schulz, P. (1980). Regulation und Fehlregulation im Verhalten V.: Die wechselseitige Beeinflussung von mentaler und emotionaler Beanspruchung. *Psychologische Beiträge, 22,* 633–656.

Schulz, P. (1982). Regulation und Fehlregulation im Verhalten. VII. Entstehungsbedingungen und Erscheinungsweisen der emotionalen Belastung in Leistungssituationen. *Psychologische Beiträge, 24,* 498–522.

Schulz, P., & Schönpflug, W. (1982). Regulatory activity during states of stress. In W. Krohne & L. Laux (Eds.), *Achievement, stress and anxiety* (pp. 51–73). Washington, DC: Hemisphere.

Schurig, V. (1985). Stages in the development of tool behavior in the chimpanzee (pantroglodytes). In M. Frese & J. Sabini (Eds.), *Goal directed behavior: The concept of action in psychology* (pp. 20–33). Hillsdale, NJ: Erlbaum.

Sellen, A. J. (1990). *Four chapters on human error and human error detection.* Unpublished doctoral dissertation, Institute for Cognitive Science, University of California, San Diego.

Semmer, N. (1982). Stress at work, stress in private life, and psychological well-being. In W. Bachmann & I. Udris (Eds.), *Mental load and stress in activity* (pp. 42–55). Amsterdam: North Holland.

Semmer, N. (1984). *Streßbezogene Tätigkeitsanalyse.* Weinheim, Germany: Beltz.

Semmer, N. (1993). Differentiation between social groups: The case of basic and applied psychology. *Applied Psychology: An International Review, 42,* 40–46.

Semmer, N., & Dunckel, H. (1991). Streßbezogene Arbeitsanalyse. In S. Greif, E. Bamberg, & N. Semmer (Eds.), *Psychischer Streß am Arbeitsplatz* (pp. 57–90). Göttingen, Germany: Hogrefe.

Semmer, N., & Frese, M. (1985). Action theory in clinical psychology. In M. Frese & J. Sabini (Eds.), *Goal directed behavior: The concept of action in psychology* (pp. 296–310). Hillsdale, NJ: Erlbaum.

Semmer, N., Pfäfflin, M. (1978a). *Interaktionstraining.* Weinheim, Germany: Beltz.

Semmer, N. (1993). Differentiation between social groups: The case of basic and aplied psychology. *Applied Psychology: An International Review, 42,* 40–46.

Semmer, N., & Pfäfflin, M. (1978b). Streß und das Training sozialer Kompetenzen. In R. Bösel (Ed.), *Streß. Einführung in die psychosomatische Belastungsforschung* (pp. 188–203). Hamburg: Hoffmann & Campe.

Semmer, N., & Zapf, D. (1989). Validity of various methods of measurement in job analysis. In K. Landau & W. Rohmert (Eds.), *Recent developments in job analysis* (pp. 67–78). London: Taylor & Francis.

Seymour, W. D. (1954). *Industrial training for manual operations.* London: Pitman.

Shepard, R. N., & Metzler, J. (1971). Mental rotation of three-dimensional objects. *Science, 171,* 701–703.

Shiffrin, R. M., & Schneider, W. (1977). Controlled and automatic human information processing, II: Perceptual learning, automatic attending, and a general theory. *Psychological Review, 84,* 127–190.

Skell, W. (1972). Analyse von Denkleistungen bei der Planung und praktischen Durchführung von Produktionsarbeiten in der Berufsausbildung. In W. Skell (Ed.), *Psychologischen Analysen von Denkleistungen in der Produktion* (pp. 13–100). Berlin: Deutscher Verlag der Wissenschaften.

Skell, W. (1980). Erfahrungen mit Selbstinstruktionstraining beim Erwerb kognitiver Regulationsgrundlagen. In W. Volpert (Ed.), *Beiträge zur Psychologischen Handlungstheorie* (pp. 50–79). Bern, Germany: Huber.

Sonnentag, S., Frese, M., Stolte, W., Heinbokel, T., & Brodbeck, F. C. (1992). *Goal orientation of team leaders: Its effects on performance and group interaction in software development projects.* Giessen, Germany: Department of Psychology, University of Giessen.

Sonntag, K. (1989). *Trainingsforschung in der Arbeitspsychologie.* Bern, Germany: Huber.

Sonntag, K., & Schaper, N. (1988). Kognitives Training zur Bewältigung steuerungstechnischer Aufgabenstellungen. *Zeitschrift für Arbeits- und Organisationspsychologie, 32,* 128–138.

Spector, P. E., Dwyer, D. J., & Jex, S. M. (1988). Relation of job stressors to affective, health, and performance outcomes: A comparison of multiple data sources. *Journal of Applied Psychology, 73,* 11–19.

Sperandio, J. C. (1971). Variations of operator's strategies and regulating effects of work load. *Ergonomics, 14,* 571–577.

Sternberg, R. J. (1986). Introduction: The nature and scope of practical intelligence. In R. J. Sternberg & R. K. Wagner (Eds.), *Practical intelligence: Nature and origins of competence in the everyday world* (pp. 1–12). Cambridge, UK: Cambridge University Press.

Stumpf, J. P. (1991). *Handlungsstile und Fehler. Eine Auswertung von Beobachtungen an betriebswirtschaftlichen Softwarepaketen.* Unpublished doctoral dissertation, University of Munich, Department of Psychology.

Taylor, F. W. (1913). *Die Grundsätze wissenschaftlicher Betriebsführung.* Neuauflage 1977, hrsg. von W. Volpert. Weinheim, Germany: Beltz.

Thiemann, P. (1990). *Aus Fehlern lernen? Fehlervermeidung vs. Fehlermanagement in der Mensch-Computer-Interaktion.* Unpublished doctoral dissertation, University of Munich, Department of Psychology.

Tomaszewski, T. (1964). Die Struktur der menschlichen Tätigkeiten. *Psychologie und Praxis, 8.*

Tomaszewski, T. (1978). *Tätigkeit und Bewußtsein.* Weinheim, Germany: Beltz.

Triebe, J. K. (1981). *Aspekte beruflichen Handelns und Lernens. Feld- und Längsschnittuntersuchung zu ausgewählten Merkmalen der Struktur und Genese von Handlungsstrategien bei einer Montagetätigkeit.* Bern, Gemany: Unpublished doctoral dissertation, University of Bern, Department of Psychology.

Turvey, M. T. (1977). Preliminaries to a theory of action with reference to vision. In R. Shaw & J. Bransford (Eds.), *Perceiving, acting and knowing: Toward an ecological psychology.* Hillsdale, NJ: Erlbaum.

Turvey, M. T., Shaw, R. E., & Mace, W. (1978). Issues in the theory of action: Degrees of freedom, coordinative structures and coalition. In J. Requin (Ed.), *Attention and performance* (Vol. 7). Hillsdale, NJ: Erlbaum.

Ulich, E. (1964). Das Lernen sensumotorischer Fertigkeiten. In R. Bergius (Ed.), *Lernen und Denken. Handbuch der Psychologie* (Vol. 1–2, pp. 326–346). Göttingen, Germany: Hogrefe.

Ulich, E. (1967). Some experiments on the function of mental training in the acquisition of motor skills. *Ergonomics, 10,* 411–419.

Ulich, E. (1972). Aufgabenwechsel und Aufgabenerweiterung. *REFA-Nachrichten, 25,* 265–275.

Ulich, E. (1974). Formen des Trainings für das Erlernen und Wiedererlernen psychomotorischer Fertigkeiten. *Rehabilitation, 13,* 105–110.

Ulich, E. (1978a). Über das Prinzip der differentiellen Arbeitsgestaltung. *Industrielle Organisation, 47,* 566–568.

Ulich, E. (1978b). Über mögliche Zusammenhänge zwischen Arbeitstätigkeit und Persönlichkeitsentwicklung. *Psychosozial, 1,* 44–63.

Ulich, E. (1983). Differentielle Arbeitsgestaltung—ein Diskussionsbeitrag. *Zeitschrift für Arbeitswissenschaft, 37,* 12–15.

Ulich, E. (1986). Aspekte der Benutzerfreundlichkeit. In W. Remmele & M. Sommer (Eds.), *Arbeitsplätze morgen (Berichte des German Chapter of the ACM)* (Vol. 27, pp. 102–122). Stuttgart, Germany: Teubner.

Ulich, E. (1989). Arbeitspsychologische Konzepte der Aufgabengestaltung. In S. Maass & H. Oberquelle (Eds.), *Software-Ergonomie '89: Aufgabenorientierte Systemgestaltung* (pp. 51–65). Stuttgart, Germany: Teubner.

Ulich, E. (1990). Individualisierung und differentielle Arbeitsgestaltung. In C. Graf Hoyos & B. Zimolong (Eds.), *Enzyklopädie der Psychologie, Themenbereich D, Serie III, Band 2, Ingenieurspsychologie* (pp. 511–535). Göttingen, Germany: Hogrefe.

Ulich, E. (1991). *Arbeitspsychologie.* Stuttgart, Germany: Poeschel.

Ulich, E., & Baitsch, C. (1987). Arbeitsstrukturierung. In U. Kleinbeck & J. Rutenfranz (Eds.), *Enzyklopädie der Psychologie, Themenbereich D, Seire II, Bd. 1: Arbeitspsychologie* (pp. 493–532). Göttingen, Germany: Hogrefe.

Ulich, E., Grosskurth, P., & Bruggemann, A. (1973). *Neue Formen der Arbeitsgestaltung.* Frankfurt: Europäische Verlagsanstalt.

Vandell, R. A., Davis, R. A., & Clugston, H. A. (1943). The function of mental practice in the acquisition of motor skills. *Journal of General Psychology, 29,* 243–250.

Volpert, W. (1969). *Untersuchungen über den Einsatz des mentalen Trainings beim Erwerb einer sensumotorischen Fertigkeit.* Cologne, Germany: Deutsche Sporthochschule.

Volpert, W. (1971). *Sensumotorisches Lernen. Zur Theorie des Trainings in Industrie und Sport.* Frankfurt: Limpert.

Volpert, W. (1974). *Handlungsstrukturanalyse als Beitrag zur Qualifikationsforschung.* Cologne, Germany Pahl-Rugenstein.

Volpert, W. (1975). Die Lohnarbeitswissenschaft und die Psychologie der Arbeitstätigkeit. In P. Großkurth & W. Volpert (Eds.), *Lohnarbeitspsychologie* (pp. 11–196). Frankfurt: Fischer.

Volpert, W. (1976). *Optimierung von Trainingsprogrammen. Untersuchungen über den Einsatz des mentalen Trainings beim Erwerb einer sensumotorischen Fertigkeit.* Lollar, Germany: Achenbach.

Volpert, W. (1978). Struktur und Entwicklung menschlicher Handlung—Der Ansatz der psychologischen Handlungstheorie. In G. Rückriem, F. Tomberg, & W. Volpert (Eds.), *Historischer Materialismus und menschliche Natur* (pp. 266–277). Cologne, Germany: Pahl-Rugenstein.

Volpert, W. (1982). The model of the hierarchical-sequential organization of action. In W. Hacker, W. Volpert, & M. Cranach (Eds.), *Cognitive and motivational aspects of action* (pp. 35–51). Berlin: Hüthig Verlagsgemeinschaft GmbH.

Volpert, W. (1983). An den Grenzen der hierarchisch-sequentiellen Handlungsorganisation. *Berliner Hefte zur Arbeits- und Sozialpsychologie, 3.*

Volpert, W. (1987a). Contrastive analysis of the relationship of man and computer as a basis of system design. In K. Fuchs-Kittowski, P. Docherty, P. Kolm, & L. Matthiassen (Eds.), *System design for human development and productivity.* Amsterdam: North-Holland.

Volpert, W. (1987b). Psychische Regulation von Arbeitstätigkeiten. In U. Kleinbeck & J. Rutenfranz (Eds.), *Arbeitspsychologie. Enzyklopädie der Psychologie, Themenbereich D, Serie III, Band 1* (pp. 1–42). Göttingen, Germany: Hogrefe.

Volpert, W. (1989). Work and personality development from the viewpoint of the action regulation theory. In H. Leymann & H. Kornbluh (Eds.), *Socialization and learning at work: A new approach to the learning process in the work place and society* (pp. 215–232). Aldershot, UK: Avebury.

Volpert, W. (1992). Work design and human development. In C. Floyd, H. Züllighoven, R. Budde, & R. Keil-Slawik (Eds.), *Software development and reality construction* (pp. 336–349). Berlin: Springer-Verlag.

Volpert, W., Frommann, R., & Munzert, J. (1984). Die Wirkung allgemeiner heuristischer Regeln im Lernprozeß—eine experimentelle Studie. *Zeitschrift für Arbeitswissenschaft, 38,* 235–240.

Volpert, W., Kötter, W., Gohde, H. E., & Weber, W. G. (1989). Psychological evaluation and design of work tasks: Two examples. *Ergonomics, 32,* 881–890.

Volpert, W., Oesterreich, R., Gablenz-Kolakovic, S., Krogoll, T., & Resch, M. (1983). *Verfahren zur Ermittlung von Regulationserfordernissen in der Arbeitstätigkeit (VERA).* Cologne, Germany: TÜV-Rheinland.

Vroom, V. H. (1964). *Work and motivation.* New York: Wiley.

Vygotski, L. S. (1962). *Thought and language.* Cambridge, MA: MIT Press.

Vygotski, L. S. (1978). *Mind in society: The development of higher psychological processes.* Cambridge, MA: Harvard University Press.

Waern, Y., & Rabenius, L. (1987). On the role of models in instructing novice users of a word processing system. *Zeitschrift für Psychologie, Suppl. 9.*

Wall, T. D., & Clegg, C. W. (1981). A longitudinal field study of group work redesign. *Journal of Occupational Behaviour, 2,* 31–49.

Wall, T. D., Corbett, J. M., Martin, R., Clegg, C. W., & Jackson, P. R. (1990). Advanced manufacturing technology, work design and performance: A change study. *Journal of Applied Psychology, 75,* 691–697.

Wall, T. D., Jackson, P. R., & Davis, K. (1992). Operator work design and robotics system behavior: A serendipitous field study. *Journal of Applied Psychology, 77.*

Watson, D., & Tharp, R. (1972). *Self-directed behavior: Self-modification for personal adjustment.* Belmont, CA: Brooks/Cole.

Weber, W. G., & Oesterreich, R. (1989, March). VERA microanalysis: Applied to a flexible manufacturing system. In K. Landau & W. Rohmert (Eds.), *Recent developments in job analysis: Proceedings* of the International Symposium on Job Analysis, University of Hohenheim (pp. 91–100). London: Taylor & Francis.

Wehner, T., Vogt, S., & Stadler, M. (1984). Task-specific EMG-characteristics during mental training. *Psychological Research, 46*, 389–401.

Weiss, H. M., & Adler, S. (1984). Personality and organizational behavior. In L. L. Cummings & B. M. Staw (Eds.), *Research in organizational behavior* (Vol. 6, pp. 1–50). Greenwich, CT: J Press.

White, R. W. (1959). Motivation reconsidered: The concept of competence. *Psychological Review, 66*, 297–333.

Wickelgren, W. A. (1977). Speed–accuracy tradeoff and information processing dynamics. *Acta Psychologica, 41*, 67–85.

Wiener, E. L. (1985). Beyond the steril cockpit. *Human Factors, 27*, 75–90.

Witkin, H. A., Dyk, R. B., Faterson, H. F., Goodenough, D. R., & Karp, S. A. (1962). *Psychological differentiation*. New York: Wiley.

Wunderli, R. (1978). Psychoregulativ akzentuierte Trainingsmethoden. *Zeitschrift für Arbeitswissenschaft, 32*, 106–111.

Zapf, D. (1989). *Selbst- und Fremdbeobachtung in der psychologischen Arbeitsanalyse. Method-ische Probleme bei der Erfassung von Streß am Arbeitsplatz.* Göttingen, Germany: Hogrefe.

Zapf, D. (1991a). Handlungsfehler, Streß und organisationaler Kontext. In M. Frese & D. Zapf (Eds.), *Fehler bei der Arbeit mit dem Computer: Ergebnisse von Beobachtungen und Befragungen im Bürobereich* (pp. 106–117). Bern, Germany: Huber.

Zapf, D. (1991b). Stressbezogene Arbeitsanalyse bei der Arbeit mit unterschiedlichen Bürosoftwaresystemen. *Zeitschrift für Arbeits- und Organisationspsychologie, 35*, 2–14.

Zapf, D. (1991c). Taxonomie von Handlungsfehlern bei der Computerarbeit. In M. Frese & D. Zapf (Eds.), *Fehler bei der Arbeit mit dem Computer: Ergebnisse von Beobachtungen und Befragungen im Bürobereich* (pp. 32–46). Bern, Germany: Huber.

Zapf, D., Brodbeck, F.C., Frese, M., Peters, H., & Prümper, J. (1992). Errors in working with computers: A first validation of a taxonomy for observed errors in a field setting. *International Journal of Human-Computer Interaction, 4*, 311–339.

Zapf, D., Brodbeck, F. C., & Prümper, J. (1989). Handlungsorientierte Fehlertaxonomie in der Mensch-Computer-Interaktion. Theoretische Überlegungen und eine erste Überprüfung im Rahmen einer Expertenbefragung. *Zeitschrift für Arbeits- und Organisationspsychologie, 33*, 178–187.

Zapf, D., Frese, M., Irmer, C., & Brodbeck, F. C. (1991). Konsequenzen von Fehleranalysen für die Softwaregestaltung. In M. Frese & D. Zapf (Eds.), *Fehler bei der Arbeit mit dem Computer: Ergebnisse von Beobachtungen und Befragungen im Bürobereich* (pp. 177–191). Bern, Germany: Huber.

Zapf, D., Lang, T., & Wittmann, A. (1991). Der Fehlerbewältigungsprozeß. In M. Frese & D. Zapf (Eds.), *Fehler bei der Arbeit mit dem Computer. Ergebnisse von Beobachtungen und Befragungen im Bürobereich* (pp. 60–79). Bern, Germany: Huber.

Zapf, D., Maier, G. W., Rappensperger, G., & Irmer, C. (in press). Error detection, task characteristics and some consequences for software design. *Applied Psychology: An International Review.*

CHAPTER 7

Time and Behavior at Work

Henk Thierry
Tilburg University, The Netherlands

Theo Meijman
The University of Amsterdam

Time offers opportunities and imposes limitations on behavior at work. These opportunities and limitations can be examined at different levels, such as the individual level (e.g., income per unit of time), at the corporate level (e.g., return on investment), and at the societal level (e.g., unemployment during a specific time period). This chapter emphasizes the individual level, and especially the effect of different working time arrangements (WTA's) (e.g., hours worked, shiftwork, part-time work, flextime, overtime, the work-leisure interface) and rhythms on health, well-being, work accidents, absenteeism, turnover, and productivity.

An overview will be given of major themes relevant to research on working time arrangements and to applications in practice.

The first section of the chapter presents a general model for the analysis of WTA's. In addition, the history of WTA's is addressed and some general time aspects of labor conditions are discussed. The second section addresses the major schedules and dimensions of shiftwork. Major research data are discussed as well as interventions and experiences gained in practice. The third section deals with various flexible WTA's. The rather scarce research data are discussed and, given the relatively widespread use of some flexible arrangements, the necessity of a major research effort in the near future is stressed. The chapter concludes with several considerations of future research needs in the area of time and behavior at work.

Introduction and Theoretical Perspectives on Time

TIME PERVADES OUR life and work in a multitude of ways. Perhaps one of the most frequently used expressions in industrialized societies is "I have no time." Symbolically, this phrase may have several meanings in social interactions. The expression signals that time is a scarce commodity and thus a valuable resource. Moreover, it usually conveys that a person is loaded with work, facing deadlines that should be kept, and, thus, rather heavily pressed. It may also reflect a person's slightly higher status or merely indicate a lack of interest in one or more other people making a request on the person's time. In other words, the concept of time is used to express and structure social relationships. It denotes, for example, the accessibility of a person as well as a part of his or her way of life.

In this chapter, in which an overview will be given of major themes relevant to research on working time arrangements (WTA's) and to applications in practice, first some other perspectives on time will be discussed. Then we will present a general overview of WTA's and a model for their analysis. After a brief glimpse into the history of WTA's, this section ends with a discussion of time aspects of labor conditions. The second section of this chapter addresses the major schedules and dimensions of shiftwork. In addition to considering major research data, several interventions will be discussed, including experiences gained in practice. The third section deals with various flexible WTA's. Research data are unfortunately rather scarce in this area. The relatively widespread use of some flexible arrangements, however, necessitates a major research effort in the near future.

Perspectives on Time

Most people in society are on a daytime pattern: They sleep at night, and engage in activities such as work and leisure during the day and evening. The language that goes along with this, however, may be rather normative in nature. Usual daily working time patterns are often called "normal." Employees operating in shift schedules are said to work during unsocial hours or on an irregular basis. Those working longer hours than has been agreed by contract work overtime, while employees working fewer than the average 36 to 40 hours per week are labeled part-timers. All this assumes the existence of a real, basic, or natural working pattern. The history of WTA's, however, shows—as we will see later—that this assumption is erroneous. Working time arrangements, including current ones, are to some extent the arbitrary outcome of a host of factors. Yet the language used to describe them is far from innocent. It reflects the notion that daytime work between, say, 6:00 A.M. and 7:00 P.M. for five days a week (excluding the weekend) is the standard working pattern, and that work facilities and recreational opportunities are also frequently geared to this norm. As a result, employees who have other WTA's may actually be faced with inadequate support and opportunities. This leads to negotiations on particular forms of compensation for nonstandard WTA's. Thus, time is conceptually used to differentiate (if not discriminate) between certain categories of employees. In a wider context, this use of the concept of working time may act as a slight barrier to adjustment and change.

Other "normative" examples are probably more innocent. The terms that identify nonworking time, such as spare time and free time, indicate primarily what the time is not: It is time during which a person is not occupied with something and is free from duties. Leisure time denotes, according to its Latin stem *lic~ere,* the permission to spend time according to one's wishes and needs.

Concepts of time may highlight other perspectives. An expression like "last night, when we met these youngsters" is an example of an *endogenous* use of the concept of time. It is narrative: It tells a short local story that refers to a particular moment in time in terms of a specific social event. An *exogenous* wording dispenses with any reference to social events and would be something like "yesterday, at 8:45 P.M." This abstract, universal indication (Elchardus, 1988) also touches on the *chronological* concept of time. The use of one or the other concept depends, among other things, on prevailing societal cultural patterns. Endogenous time references characterize more stable social and societal patterns, such as those found in rural communities (Durkheim, 1912). Exogenous time expressions are more typical of highly differentiated, if not segmented, societal structures. Current exogenous time concepts stress, for example, the exchange value of time. As a kind of currency, time is a resource allowing some people to have more access, and thus more power, than others. This is one of the major reasons why working time is a recurrent subject for negotiation in labor contracts. Elchardus (1985) states, interestingly, that since modern time goes so very fast (e.g., in data networks) or cannot even be noticed anymore, endogenous concepts may return.

Time may also be conceived in terms of *individual* perspective. This refers to the temporal orientation of a person. Some individuals primarily look backward: For example, they base their self-esteem on past achievements. Others are driven by the challenge to meet particular goals in the future, while still others focus primarily on maintaining their current way of life. According to Nuttin and Lens (1985; Lens, 1986), the individual time perspective can be defined as the extent to which a person's past and future are psychologically integrated into his or her present life. This perspective includes issues such as a shorter or longer time frame, makes use of means–end connections, sets particular goals, and is heavily influenced by a person's age. As a personality

factor, it structures a person's motivation and behavior.

Another point of view conceives time in terms of *rhythms*. Rhythmic patterns affect all life on earth incisively. The diurnal light–dark alternation determines (interacting with the season of the year) major physiological processes in plant and animal life. Many human biological processes also show a circadian (around 24 hours) pattern, such as body temperature, pulse rate, hormonal secretion, and brain activity (Aschoff, 1978; Minors & Waterhouse, 1985a). These rhythmic processes in humans are not only determined by the day–night pattern but also interact with social and societal stimuli (Wever, 1979, 1985). Thus, an airline passenger crossing various time zones usually experiences jet lag (which is actually a desynchronization of biological rhythms) as a slight discomfort. After several days, his or her rhythms are resynchronized. That is not what happens to shiftworkers who are employed in night shifts. Instead, each time they sleep during the day and work at night, society conveys to them the message that they are out of phase (Thierry & Jansen, 1984), both biologically and socially. As will be discussed later, the effects of this may cause problems of health and well-being, particularly over a long period of time.

In this chapter we will focus on time from the perspective that it offers opportunities as well as places limitations on an individual's behavior at work. Thus, we will consider WTA's as they determine both the hours that employees are engaged in their jobs and, by definition, the hours during which they are "free." Shift schedules will also be discussed. Shiftwork occurs when the operating time of a company considerably exceeds the length of employees' average working time, resulting in the need for more than one group (or shift) of employees during a 24-hour period. In one particular form of shiftwork—so-called continuous shift schedules—work must be performed 24 hours a day, 7 days a week. Flexible WTA's will also be reviewed. This umbrella term covers a variety of arrangements that are implemented to cope with the different flexibility needs of companies (e.g., fluctuating consumer demands) or of employees (e.g., childcare needs). Also common to flexible WTA's is the fact that often the company's operating time exceeds the employees' average working time, such as when a working week is compressed. For example, employees work four days (for 10 hours) per week, or three days (for 12.5 hours), while the company operates 5 to 7 days a week. In some cases, there is a gray area between what is defined as a flexible WTA and what is defined as a shift schedule.

General Overview

Figure 1 may help to explain both the general discussion of WTA's and the review of specific WTA's. First, a WTA will be described in terms of its structural design. The clock shown in Figure 1 is helpful in some cases, such as when flextime is at issue. This arrangement implies that core times are set by a company—during which all employees should be at their work: for example, from 10:00 A.M. to 4:00 P.M.—while each employee may choose when to begin and end the workday according to his or her preferences. An average amount of hours should be worked per day, week, or month. Regarding other arrangements, such as shiftwork with a 10-week cycle, the clock in Figure 1 is merely symbolic. To display all such possible shifts, we would need 70 clocks. In these cases, a set of design dimensions will be introduced.

Second, arguments for adopting a particular WTA will be analyzed. In general, shiftwork may be introduced because of services needed at a societal level, such as health care, public utilities, customs and safety, and morning newspapers. Transportation facilities for cargo and passengers offered by airlines, railways, and road and water transportation companies can be subsumed under the same heading, but

relevant WTA's are often indicated as irregular schedules (Rutenfranz, Knauth, Küpper, Romann, & Ernst, 1979). At the company level, shiftwork may be needed on a seasonal basis. For example, perishable agricultural products such as sugar beets and corn must be processed very soon after they are harvested. There may also be a technical necessity for shiftwork, such as in the iron, steel, chemical, and nuclear power industries, that would make it unsafe or virtually impossible to make daily stops and starts. But the most important argument for shiftwork at the company level is economic. In particular, when capital equipment is employed, a more intensive use may lead to a higher return on investment (Bosworth & Dawkins, 1979; Maurice, 1975). As a consequence, products such as cars may be sold at a lower price. When this occurs on a larger scale, shiftwork is macroeconomically assessed in terms of its contribution to national income (Iwema & Hofman, 1974). Interestingly, many companies appear not to know how to evaluate whether their current shift WTA is at an economic optimum (de Jong & Bonhof, 1974; Walker, 1978). This suggests that factors like tradition, habit, and market trends can also affect decision making on WTA's, as in, for example, a supermarket becoming "continuous" because a nearby store recently did so.

On the level of the individual employee (or applicant), shiftwork is usually not favored, and the more a schedule departs from daytime working hours during the usual five working days per week, the more it is disfavored. However, a job requiring shiftwork may be the sole alternative available to a person. Also, the extra income such work brings often provides a compelling argument to do shiftwork. An additional consideration is that work at night may afford employees more decision latitude, since most managers and staff work during daytime hours (Thierry & Jansen, 1984). It is important to keep in mind that U.S. companies employ fixed shifts more than European companies do. With fixed shifts, each employee

FIGURE 1

Description and Benefits of Working Time Arrangements

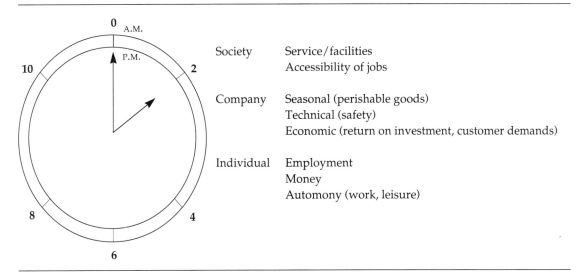

Society	Service/facilities
	Accessibility of jobs
Company	Seasonal (perishable goods)
	Technical (safety)
	Economic (return on investment, customer demands)
Individual	Employment
	Money
	Automony (work, leisure)

opts, according to his or her seniority, for a particular shift during a six-month period. In Europe, shiftworkers rotate, usually once or twice a week; schedules are highly varied, as will be discussed later. Employees may also prefer to work at night, when access to resources is easier (and often less expensive), such as when communication with a mainframe is needed for doing computing work.

The major societal arguments for the introduction of a flexible WTA—such as flextime, part-time work schedules, a compressed work week, and variable retirement age—focus on making jobs more accessible to various categories of people (Maric, 1977; Rosow, 1979). Thus, particular arrangements may suit groups of people, such as working parents (often mothers), handicapped employees, and older workers (professionals, managers, and others) who have a great deal of experience to share. Some flexible WTA's are also thought to contribute to increasing employment rates, as, for example,

when two part-time employees occupy one full-time position.

For companies, major arrangements for a flexible WTA are often rooted in customer demands for products and services (Loen & Van Schilfgaarde, 1990). Clients' needs for supermarket services vary across hours and days; these patterns are usually fairly predictable. But the demand for a new product or service may be hardly foreseeable, as, for example, may be the case with the effects of a massive advertising campaign. Another argument for a flexible WTA bears upon the delivery of goods (and information) at all times of the day or night, such as when foreign facilities (in another time zone) forward data to a company headquarter's mainframe. Likewise, stock-trading firms face markets that operate 24 hours a day throughout the world. These examples show that the introduction of flexible WTA's may in certain cases be a step toward the application of continuous shiftwork.

Another argument may reside in the collective preference of categories of employees.

Employees' preferences often relate to things that affect individual living conditions, such as childcare, commuting time, and household duties. Moreover, they may stem from the wish to have more opportunities for additional education and training, particular leisure time pursuits, more time to recover from a tiring work schedule, or a second job (Levitan & Belous, 1979; Tepas, 1985; Thierry, 1980).

A Model for the Analysis of Working Time Arrangements

Now that the design of a WTA and the main arguments for its applications have been described, research data on the effects of WTA's will be reviewed. Figure 2 outlines our main variables of interest.

The core part of the model in Figure 2 addresses the performance behavior of an employee in terms of a cognitive motivational cycle (Campbell & Pritchard, 1976; Kanfer, 1990; Lawler, 1973). We assume that the person wants to satisfy various motives through such things as setting particular goals (Locke & Latham, 1990) or meeting certain standards (Klein, 1989; Thierry, Koopman, & Van der Flier, 1992), and expects to be able to do this, to some extent, through performing job tasks (box 1). Thus, the person engages in actions relevant to his or her job tasks and puts forth effort on the job (box 2). This results (box 3), on the one hand, in some level of task performance (quality of output, accuracy of inspection) and, on the other hand, in particular states. States, based on objective and subjective reports, refer to fatigue (Meijman, 1991), sleep quality and quantity, and so on, or, more generally, to the availability of resources. Changes in both performance and state lead to certain outcomes, such as more or less recognition by others, self-esteem or salary, and a changing need for time to recover or opportunities for leisure time.

Many outcomes are usually moderated to some extent by performance appraisal yardsticks and by the roles of the concerned appraisers (box 16). Appraised outcomes cause the employee to have more or less satisfaction (Thierry, 1989; box 4), also in comparison to how relevant others' outcomes are appraised. Satisfaction is among the determinants of health (box 5), well-being (box 6), absenteeism (box 7), turnover (box 8), and productivity (box 9). Feedback ties, which are not indicated in the figure, cause this cycle to occur again or bring about changes, depending on the degree to which the person's goals have been met and the kind of attributions the person has made.

Many variables may moderate one or more components of this cycle. Task characteristics (box 10) such as identity, variability, and autonomy (Algera, 1990; Hackman & Oldham, 1980) affect incisively the opportunities the person has for furthering his or her motives, the task actions that are engaged in, performance levels, and various states. Aspects of organizational structure (box 13), such as size, hierarchical configuration, and systems of control (Mintzberg, 1983), are of comparable importance and may also have an impact on task characteristics. The impact of WTA's (box 11) will concern us throughout this chapter. WTA's also affect the time scheduling and the amount of nonworking time, as well as the nature of leisure pursuits (box 12). Both variables moderate most components of the cycle. Moreover, the importance of work and nonworking time activities may interact in various ways (Kabanoff, 1980). There may be a compensatory relationship in which one domain (e.g., club life) is characterized by high personal involvement, while the other (e.g., work) is not. The relationship might also be characterized by spillover: Attributes (e.g., *Central Life Interests;* Dubin, Champoux, & Porter, 1975) characteristic to one domain also apply to the other. Both domains may also be unrelated in some respects (Elizur, 1991).

FIGURE 2

Major Determinants and Effects of Working Time Arrangements

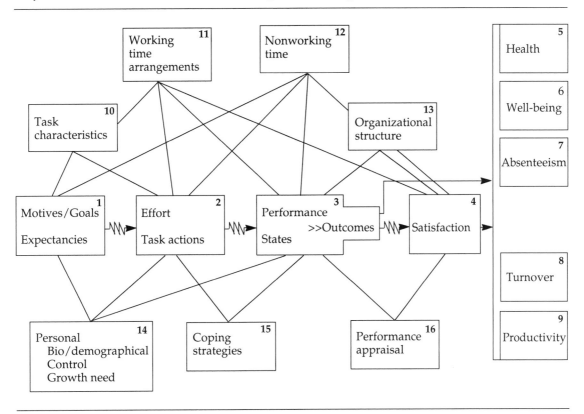

Personal characteristics (box 14) affect the motivational cycle in various ways. Age, family, and housing conditions are among the more important biographical and demographical variables conditioning consequences of WTA's. Dispositional variables, such as the need for control, may, for example, affect the impact of employee participation in designing or administering WTA's. Coping strategies (box 15) refer on the one hand to particular facilities, such as a sound-protected sleeping room and food intake tuned to work requirements and bodily rhythms at night. On the other hand, personal strategies are at stake,

such as the opportunity to take late afternoon naps (Gillberg, 1985) when working an early morning shift, the taping of favorite TV programs, and shopping at flexible times.

The model outlined in Figure 2 should help in assessing the effects of any WTA. Obviously, more variables can be included. Interestingly, however, most research on WTA's ignores the vast majority of variables outlined here. Regarding shiftwork, a fair amount of data are available; yet the evidence is inconclusive in many respects, as our review will show. In regard to flexible WTA's, research is very fragmented and addresses variables in only a few boxed areas shown, as will be explained later in this chapter.

In general, there are various theoretical perspectives to assess the nature and the effects of a WTA. One approach conceives a WTA in terms of an *additional factor*. That is, any WTA that differs from the usual (normative) daytime pattern from Monday through Friday is assessed in terms of the effects it causes in the various boxes in Figure 2, as well as in the relationships among these elements. It implies that a WTA is characterized in terms of the labor conditions it affects. This makes some sense in the case of shiftwork, as will be illustrated in the labor conditions section. In many countries, particular laws and/or collective agreements between employer federations and unions have been enacted that specify conditions within and outside of traditional working hours. Moreover, particular labor agreements may apply, such as the shift bonus and a reduced number of working hours. Also, a WTA specifies nonworking time in terms of number of hours worked and time of work. Again, this makes sense when shiftwork is applied; however, comparable evidence regarding flexible WTA's is virtually unavailable.

Assessing a WTA as a factor in addition to what is considered usual or traditional, though, creates serious problems when most variables in Figure 2 are taken into account. As other chapters in this *Handbook* demonstrate, there is no such thing as normal motivation, usual social relationships, normative task content, or normal leadership style. Consequently, it is impossible to estimate the independent effects of a WTA. Of course, researchers have tried to overcome this by studying the changes of a WTA longitudinally, or by comparing the effects of one WTA with those of another on different samples. A major problem here is that the ceteris paribus clause often does not apply (see also Shiftwork and Other Environmental Factors). First, job content, work load, and work climate are among the more important variables that often vary through successive diurnal shifts. Consider, for example, the job

of a hospital nurse on night duty: Just a few other nurses are on duty (compared to their numbers during other shifts); doctors are only available on call; very calm periods alternate with hectic moments; most routine care is provided during the day; and so on. In industry, the content of jobs across shifts may vary much less; yet organizational climate and supervision are often different at night. In regard to flexible WTA's, there are few studies in which the lack of similarity of job conditions is even considered as a potential problem. Second, it has been shown in various studies that employees who are exposed to shiftwork for an extensive period of time may leave shiftwork (Aanonsen, 1964; Frese & Okonek, 1984; Frese & Semmer, 1986; Thiis-Evensen, 1969). Since these workers experience some problem of health or well-being, they opt for another job. On an individual level, this may be interpreted as a coping strategy. It causes a selection effect, however, when shiftwork employees are compared to traditional daytime workers. Workers who remain with shiftwork are probably more healthy, have more positive attitudes, perform better, and so on. To our knowledge, the possibility of a selection effect has never been studied regarding flexible WTA's. Consequently, determining the effects of a WTA as separate from other influences creates serious problems.

A second perspective for assessing the effects of a WTA focuses on *rhythmic patterns*. As outlined earlier, many important human biological processes show a circadian rhythm. These processes are kept in phase by the internal body clock, which resides in the lower frontal hypothalamus, or *supra-chiasmaticus* (Schmidt & Thews, 1983). Additionally, social and societal rhythms affect the synchronization of these processes (Aschoff, 1978). Assume that somebody awakens during twilight, unaware of the time of day, wondering whether it is dawn or dusk. When the environment is familiar, the person will observe all kinds of noises—dogs barking, cars passing, children shouting, doors creaking, and the like—that tell him or her about what time it is. Likewise, performing work during the day, going to a theater in the evening, exercising early in the morning, and so on structure a person's life and keep him or her "in phase."

Research based on this perspective highlights the consequences of WTA's that require regular work between, say, 11:00 P.M. and 7:00 A.M. In practice, this boils down to shift and irregular schedules; flexible WTA's are left out of consideration. Thus, effects of successive night shifts on biological rhythms are analyzed, for example, in terms of the risks extensive exposure may have on a person's health and psychological well-being (Jansen, 1987b; Reinberg, Andlauer, & Vieux, 1981; Reinberg, Vieux, & Andlauer, 1980). Also, possible consequences for task actions, performance results, and leisure pursuits are monitored (Colquhoun & Rutenfranz, 1980; Folkard & Monk, 1985; Monk & Folkard, 1985). Interventions may refer to selection of employees (in practice, primarily on rather general medical yardsticks), coping strategies (e.g., sleep), and shift schedules (Kogi, Miura, & Saito, 1984; Thierry & Jansen, 1981). Schedules may be designed so that the amount of successive "risky" night shifts is minimized, which implies moderately fast rotation (Thierry & Jansen, 1984). Their design may also focus on minimal change in phasic patterns. This means that being constantly out of phase is considered preferable to returning, each time, to usual daytime patterns (Akerstedt, 1985).

This perspective will be taken up in the second part of this chapter. But it runs into problems comparable to those mentioned in the first approach. Moreover, shiftwork during more usual hours—say between 7:00 A.M. and 11:00 P.M.—is often not considered to be a particular problem.

The third perspective might apply primarily to flexible WTA's. It conceives the work organization as a whole in terms of change and adaptation. Considered as a system, the organization needs to permanently regulate its transactions with the environment, as well as the interrelations among subsystems (Katz & Kahn, 1978). Contingency theory would stress concepts like a good fit between organization and environment: Managerial choice processes should effectuate a good mix of departmental differentiation and organizational integration (Burns & Stalker, 1961; Pennings, 1990) as well as adequate (more mechanical or more organic) adaptation strategies (Morgan, 1986). Population–ecology theory emphasizes the reversed direction: Environments select organizations that will survive. Applied to flexible WTA's, two routes might be taken. The first considers the introduction of such a WTA, for example, flextime, as a reflection of ongoing processes or organizational adaptation. Thus, setting core times by the organization jointly with choosing start and stop times by employees mirrors how a new fit can be sought that accommodates the needs of both the organization and the employee. The other route takes the adoption of a WTA, for example, a *min-max* contract, in which an employee is paid for a minimum amount of hours and is on call for a specified maximum amount of time. That is, since the internal and external adaptation of the organization comes out rather poor, flexible WTA's are needed to compensate. It highlights the possibility that costs are primarily carried by employees and the gains taken by the organization. Of course, this perspective may also have a bearing on shiftwork.

Most WTA research has failed to include variables of interest to this perspective. In general, the research that is reviewed later in this chapter hardly enables one to make consistent generalizations.

The History of Working Time Arrangements

Are WTA's that diverge from the common Monday through Friday working pattern characteristic of modern times—that is, the twentieth century? Certainly not. Scherrer (1981), whose overview will be referred to frequently, begins his account of WTA's with the Roman Empire. Although most work was performed during daytime hours, the Roman army marched and occasionally battled at night, and used nocturnal guards when the army was at rest. Religious duties also required work at night, such as when Vestal Virgins guarded the sacred fire. Scherrer points out, moreover, that births and deaths frequently occurred during the night (as is also the case in present times), necessitating midwives, physicians, and others to provide professional help at night. Some transportation service also took place at night, such as delivering the imperial mail and supplying shops in cities that were difficult to reach during the day. During the Middle Ages, night work decreased, first as the Roman Empire fell. In its Western part, other than in the Byzantine area, civilization and urbanization regressed for quite some ages (Boissonnade, 1987). One of the consequences of this was that transportation decreased considerably, and, thus, so did work at night. But from the thirteenth century on—and this is a second point—corporate socioeconomic structures were developed in some western European countries. Professional rules held that crafts were to be performed in full view of everyone—thus, during daytime hours—allowing customers to verify the quality of products visually. But some groups continued to work occasionally at night during these ages, such as the military and the clergy.

According to Scherrer, important changes were initiated with the onset of the Renaissance. In the mining industry, a three-shift system was introduced in the sixteenth century, although the night shift was only needed from time to time. Sailing ships, which were used primarily for transportation purposes across continents but also for deep-sea fishing, continued their activities at night. Transportation by coach and horse increased incisively, also primarily at night. But the Industrial Revolution during the eighteenth and nineteenth centuries witnessed the greatest change. The

large supply of coal allowed the continuous operation of furnaces in factories, and mechanization routinized and multiplied many kinds of operations. The invention of gas lighting and, later, of the kerosene lamp, made "work around the clock" possible. Normal working hours varied with the season of the year. At the end of the eighteenth century, work began at about 5:45 A.M. and ended at about 8:00 P.M. from November through March in British and French companies. During the rest of the year, work extended from 5:00 A.M. to around 9:00 P.M., although about two hours were provided for breaks. Thus, workers, including women and children, were required to work an average of 12 to 13 hours per day. In the late nineteenth century, several countries enacted laws on child labor and weekly periods of rest.

Excessive working hours occurred, for example, in the transportation and in the baking industries. The Netherlands set a record in the Franeker brickworks (Ruppert, 1953). Including mealtimes, the average workday totaled 20 hours! Available data show that the average working week in some European countries and the United States did not differ very much at the end of the nineteenth century: around 60 hours (Levitan & Belous, 1979). According to Scherrer, night work occurred, for example, in metal factories, sugar refineries, paper plants, glass foundries, and mines. Technology brought about an increase in the number of jobs that allowed or required shiftwork, but it also led, jointly with social pressure, to a decrease in the proportion of employees subject to shiftwork. In some British mines, 12-hour shifts were operating. There is no evidence, however, that workweeks were to any extent compressed.

During the twentieth century, average working time decreased gradually. After World War I, the 8-hour workday was introduced on a larger scale. In the beginning of the 1960s the five-day workweek was implemented in quite a few countries. In western European countries and Japan, workweeks totaled 44 to

45 hours. In the United States, they totaled slightly less at 40 to 41 hours. These patterns changed in the 1970s. Current full-time contracts usually amount to 36 to 42 hours in the United States and western Europe and total 46 hours in Japan (Kogi, 1991). This sizable reduction of working hours in many countries is in most instances the result of tight labor negotiations, fierce social struggles, continued strikes, the onset of unions, and the like. Interestingly, major arguments of workers' representatives, unions and/or governments in favor of reduced working hours changed throughout the decades. First, protection against excessive demands made on particular categories of workers, such as women and children, as well as on workers at large, was stressed. Later on, health considerations in general were voiced (de Koning, 1980), followed by desires to claim a share in the gains brought about by the enormous increase in productivity (Levitan & Belous, 1979). In the 1960s the desire for more free time arose, jointly with a concern for improved quality of life in which work, rest, and leisure were balanced (Maric, 1977). More recently, a further reduction in working time has been pursued, often in connection with increasing the operating hours of a company, with the objective to create more jobs, thus curbing unemployment rates.

This sketchy review shows that current WTA's, particularly concerning the amount of daily and weekly working hours, are to some extent arbitrary. Historically, there is no ground to assume the existence of an original pattern of working hours throughout the day, both in number and location. Of course, human beings tend to work during the day and sleep at night. But most WTA's now in use in many companies throughout industrialized countries just happen to be what they are. There is no compelling argument, at least not historically, to prevent a further reduction or, on the contrary, an increase in average working hours. Rather, market considerations (in the European Community/United States

at large, within a given country, or across a given sector), customs, and traditions affect decision making on working hours. It is a tenet of this chapter that behavioral science arguments should affect decision making to a greater extent.

The review also shows that shiftwork has a rather long history. This is probably not the case with most flexible arrangements. Most authors agree that flextime originated in the 1960s in the German enterprise Messerschmidt-Bölkow-Blohm, which tried to meet its employees' commute and parking problems (Thierry & Jansen, 1984). Poor (1970) and Maric (1977) have different opinions about whether the compressed workweek is an American or European invention. Other flexible WTA's, highlighted later, also have a rather short history.

Labor Conditions

Another part of the framework for assessing the nature and effects of shiftwork and of flexible WTA's relates to labor conditions. In most countries, these are regulated by international conventions such as the International Labour Office in Switzerland, national laws, and collective contracts between organizations of employers and employees. In legislation, agreements on working times, breaks or rest periods, and nonworking times are based on a society in which day work is the traditional pattern. For example, in the Netherlands the standard prescriptions are as follows: work hours must be between 6:00 A.M. and 7:00 P.M. or 8.00 A.M. and 9:00 P.M.; the maximum workday is 9.5 hours; workdays are from Monday to Saturday (no work is done on Sunday); the minimal uninterrupted nonworking time in a 24-hour period is 11 hours; the minimal weekly nonworking time is 38 hours; the norm for a maximum four-week period is 190 work hours, and the maximum three-month norm is 552.5 work hours. Schedules that do not follow these prescriptions, such as systems with night work, need a special permit from the Dutch Labour Inspectorate. In practice, such permission is always granted when some specific conditions are fulfilled and when the necessity of the deviating schedule is recognized. Officially, however, day work is the rule.

Accordingly, norms and recommendations with respect to the admissibility of working conditions are based on the notion of regular day work. American Threshold Limit Values (TLV) and Dutch/German Maximum Admissible Concentrations (MAC) of toxic agents at the workplace presuppose day work—in most Western countries for 8 to 8.5 hours during a five-day week (American Conference of Governmental Industrial Hygienists [ACGIH], 1988; Mason & Johnson, 1987). Norms and recommendations concerning noise level, whole body vibrations, climate, and other physical working conditions also refer to day work. One can hardly find discussions on the validity of standards regarding WTA's that differ from the normal daily work routines in chapters on these factors in ergonomics textbooks (e.g., Kantowitz & Sorkin, 1983; Salvendy, 1987). When discussions focus on these issues, they are relegated to a special chapter on shiftwork. The same reasoning applies to recommendations about acceptable levels of work load, which originate from energetic sources (Astrand & Rodahl, 1986), biomechanical aspects (Chaffin & Andersson, 1984), and sense organs and aspects of mental load and information processing (Gopher & Donchin, 1986), though any recommendation with respect to the admissibility of specific levels of information load in real working tasks is still missing in the relevant literature.

In most industrialized countries, the length of the workday is constrained. In the Netherlands, for example, a workday cannot exceed 9.5 hours. Dutch law prescribes a rest period of 30 minutes for every 4.5 hours of work in industry, and for every 5.5 hours of work in most other branches. Overtime is also limited to a maximum of 11 hours of

work per day and 62 hours per week. These maximum limits also apply in principle to shiftwork. The Dutch Labour Inspectorate, however, adheres in its policy on night shiftwork permissions to a stricter regime. But, again, in the official regulations, day work states the norm.

The modern literature on the acceptability of the length of working times is surprisingly limited. Apart from several recent studies on the 12-hour shift (for an overview, see Costa, Cesena, Kogi, & Wedderburn, 1990), which will be discussed later, one must go back to the years immediately following the World Wars and to the turn of the century in order to find any empirical data. The most comprehensive studies by the U.S. Department of Labor after World War II recommended, in general, the 8-hour workday and the five-day/40-hour workweek. Longer work hours were associated with lower productivity and higher absenteeism and accident rates (Kossoris & Kohler, 1947). Alluisi and Morgan (1982) subscribe to this conclusion in their review, stating in addition that the effects of the total hours of work on human performance and productivity interact with many other factors, both temporal and nontemporal.

The early studies on fatigue in industry (e.g., Vernon, 1921) suggest that there is also an optimum working time of about eight to nine hours a day and a maximum of 45 hours a week for manual work in industry, but much depends, of course, on the work intensity and quantity of the work load. A more recent study by Rissler and Elgerot (1978) presented evidence on the impact of lengthening the workday and/or the workweek, in this case as a result of overtime. Elevated adrenaline levels were observed for several weeks after workers had completed six weeks of overtime work for up to 12 to 14 hours a day in clerical work. Studies on the optimal length of working hours in relation to various forms of information processing work, in which both performance and fatigue measures are used, are very scarce in the recent literature. This applies to studies on the length and scheduling of rest periods during modern working tasks. Continuing the German tradition on the study of *optimal pausing (lohnende Pausen;* Graf, 1922), Schmidt, Kleinbeck, and Knauth (1988) presented evidence that short rest periods, equally scheduled over the workday, could have beneficial effects on the subjective strain of the worker at the end of the day. A recent study by Meijman, Mulder, Van Dormolen, and Cremer (1992) found that an intensified workday—one without any intermittent pauses between successive working tasks—resulted in elevated adrenaline levels during the evening following the workday. Related to this *overactivation syndrome*, the workers also experienced sleeping problems. Such sustained activated adrenaline levels were not observed after workdays with scheduled pauses of two to five minutes between successive working tasks (in this study, making a formal examination of a trainee driver every 40 minutes).

The evidence on psychosocial aspects of work load and stress suggests that various factors from this rather diverse domain may contribute, sometimes separately but primarily in combination with each other, to problems of well-being and health. Among these are short-cycled jobs, machine pacing, heavy work demands and continuous time pressure, low levels of decision latitude, and lack of support from superiors and colleagues. The evidence is predominantly based on cross-sectional studies; longitudinal evidence is fairly scarce (House, 1987). With respect to health impairments, the literature is still fragmented (Kasl, 1986). Thus, only very general recommendations may be deduced from the literature on psychosocial risk factors in work. Norms or specific prescriptions are very hard to give. The well-known combination of job stressors, high work demands, and low decision latitude (Karasek & Theorell, 1990) is related to various outcome measures with respect to problems of well-being and health (see Figure 2). Yet it is extremely difficult to derive acceptable norms or even recommendations on both parameters from this literature.

Shiftwork, particularly night work, is included on many lists of psychosocial risk factors. The status of this factor, however, is quite different from other psychosocial risk factors. Shiftwork is not just an additional aspect of working conditions like noise or level of decision latitude; it is a specific arrangement in time of the working and living conditions, posing its own demands on the worker and thus on the acceptability of the other factors.

Shiftwork

This section begins with a description of the main characteristics or design dimensions of shiftwork schedules and a review of the prevalence of shiftwork. Next, we will discuss methods for analyzing these dimensions. Referring back to Figure 2, boxes 11 and 12 are of concern to us in these sections. We will then review evidence on the effects of shiftwork on performance, individual health and well-being, and on the social life of the shiftworker and his or her family. In this discussion, boxes 3 to 9 in Figure 2 will be addressed. Lastly, we will discuss the job stressors that categories of shiftworkers are more subject to than others, such as daytime workers. In this discussion, boxes 10 and 13 in Figure 2 will be our main concern. The discussion on these factors leads to a review of evidence concerning combined factors and effects. We end with a look at the issue of countermeasures to overcome the disadvantageous aspects of shiftwork.

Definitions, General Design Dimensions, and Prevalence

Definitions.   According to the International Labour Office (1986), shiftwork is defined as a method of work organization under which groups or "crews" of workers succeed each other at the same work stations to perform the same operations, each crew working a certain schedule or "shift" so that the undertaking can operate longer than the stipulated weekly hours for any worker.

Thus, in shiftwork the working times deviate from the regular pattern, which is working from 7:00 A.M. to 7:00 P.M. during conventional workdays with a work-free weekend. The succession of shifts, however, follows a certain schedule. The term *irregular working hours* is used to describe all those deviating or abnormal working hours that do not adhere to a fixed schedule. It makes sense to differentiate between shiftwork and irregular working hours. The former is characterized by some regularity in the changes of working and nonworking times over a longer period of weeks or months. The latter is characterized by a greater irregularity and, hence, a greater unpredictability of working and nonworking times. This last factor may have a negative impact of its own on the leisure activities and social life of the worker and his or her family (Ernst, Nachreiner, & Volger, 1986).

General Design Dimensions.   There are several forms of shiftwork. Traditionally, a distinction is made between *permanent* systems and *rotating* systems.

In permanent systems, the same crew works during a longer period—months or even years—at the same hours that deviate from the regular daytime work hours. For example, the morning shift works between 6:00 A.M. and 2:00 P.M., or the afternoon/evening shift between 2:00 P.M. and 10:00 P.M., or the night shift between 10:00 P.M. and 6:00 A.M. Permanent systems were much more common in the United States prior to the 1980s. In Europe, they were and continue to be exceptional except for some industries, such as the baking industry, the newspaper printing industry, and certain parts of the safety services.

Rotating systems are becoming more popular in the United States, while they are the rule in Europe. In these systems, a crew rotates from one shift during a certain number of days to the other, with one or more free days in between. It is suggested that adjustment to night work is better in permanent systems than in rotating systems (Akerstedt, Patkai, & Dahlgren, 1977; Patkai, Akerstedt, & Pettersson, 1977), particularly for workers who are able to schedule their lives predominantly around their WTA (Folkard, Monk, & Lobban, 1979). However, even permanent night workers are confronted with a regular shift from a nocturnal way of life to a day-oriented pattern, at least during their free days. Such changes of biological rhythms and social activity may eventually cause problems of well-being. In a study of permanent night working newspaper printers, Lortie, Foret, Teiger, and Laville (1979) observed sleeping problems and feelings of fatigue and malaise not so much during the (night) working week, but on the Monday following the free weekend when the printers had changed from their working nightlife to their leisure daylife (see also Teiger, 1984). Similar observations were reported by Alfredsson, Akerstedt, Mattsson, and Wilborg (1991). They compared a sample of permanent night working security guards with a representative sample of the Swedish day-working population. Age standardized morbidity ratios were computed, controlling for various background variables. Results showed that the occurrence of sleep disturbances and fatigue was two to three times higher in permanent night workers than in the national sample. No differences were found on gastrointestinal problems and other psychosomatic problems. It may be concluded that sleep/wake disturbances are more common in permanent night workers than they are in the day-working population as a whole. Direct comparisons of permanent night workers with rotating night shift-workers point out, however, that the former experience fewer sleep disturbance problems than do rotating shiftworkers (Akerstedt, 1988).

In a survey on nurses in permanent or rotating shifts (Jamal & Baba, 1992), rotating nurses experienced more job stress and strain, more health problems, and less commitment and job satisfaction than their colleagues in permanent shifts.

Traditionally, rotating systems may be divided into three broad categories: discontinuous, semicontinuous, and continuous systems (Knauth & Rutenfranz, 1982; Rutenfranz, Knauth, & Angersbach, 1981).

Discontinuous systems mainly involve two, and sometimes three, different crews. These crews do not work during the night or during some part of the weekend. Thus, discontinuous systems are interrupted during the night and during the weekend. Conventional day-work systems of five days a week result in an effective company operation time of 38 to 48 hours, depending on the length of the workday. Discontinuous systems result generally in an effective company operation time between 64 and 88 hours, with individual employees working between 32 and 48 hours a week. The operating hours in discontinuous systems are from Monday through Friday between 5:00 A.M. and 1:00 A.M., and on Saturday between 5:00 A.M. and 6:00 P.M. In the literature, these systems are mostly referred to as *two-shift systems* or *discontinuous systems*.

Semicontinuous systems involve three, and sometimes four, different crews. These systems involve night work, but they are always interrupted by some period without work during the weekend (mainly between 11:00 A.M. on Saturday and 9:00 P.M. on Sunday). Semicontinuous systems generally result in an effective company operation time between 96 and 144 hours a week. These systems are mostly referred to in the literature as *three-shift* or *semicontinuous* systems.

Continuous systems involve mainly four, and sometimes five or even six, different crews. Night work is included, and the system

is not interrupted by some period without work during the weekend. Continuous systems result in more than 160 hours a week of effective company operating time. These systems are referred to as *continuous shift systems*.

Apart from the differentiations mentioned above, several other characteristics must be mentioned that group shift systems into subcategories. Most important are direction of rotation and pacing or speed of rotation.

Systems are called *forward rotating* when they follow the sequence morning–afternoon/evening–night. The shifts of the same crew succeed each other in a clockwise fashion. Systems in which the same crew rotates from morning to night to afternoon/evening are called *backward rotating*. Forward rotating systems are generally recommended (Knauth & Rutenfranz, 1982), thought to be optimal for chronobiological reasons (Czeisler, Moore-Ede, & Coleman, 1982; Wegmann & Klein, 1985). However, the literature provides some indications that backward rotating systems are preferred by shiftworkers over forward rotating systems (Bonitz, Crzech-Sukalo, & Nachreiner, 1987). One of the reasons may be that in some cases the latter systems allow for more recovery time after the last night shift.

Systems may also differ with respect to speed of rotation. In fast rotating systems, the succession of the different shifts occurs rather quickly; or, stated another way, a particular shift lasts for a relatively short number of days: two or less. In slowly rotating systems, the same crew works five or more of the same shifts in succession. An example of a slowly rotating system is what in the Netherlands is called the *American continuous system*: seven morning shifts, two days off, seven afternoon shifts, two days off, seven night shifts, and three days off. Depending on the rotation speed and the number of crews, the total shift cycle (i.e., one complete succession of the different shifts) is longer or shorter. Medium rotating shift systems (a maximum of four of the same shifts in succession) are recommended (Akerstedt, 1985; Knauth & Rutenfranz, 1982). Fast rotating systems are judged as rather hectic by workers (Knauth & Kieswetter, 1987). Such systems place relatively high demands on the biological and social flexibility of the worker and his or her family. Generally, older workers and people who prefer a more stable pattern in their lives report more problems with fast rotating systems (Folkard, Monk, & Lobban, 1979; Frese & Rieger, 1981; Jansen, Thierry, & Van Hirtum, 1986). Long sequences of five or more night shifts in slowly rotating systems may lead to the accumulation of fatigue in older workers—those who are older than 40 years of age. This is due first to increased sleep loss, resulting from the decrease of daytime sleep length and quality; second, it is caused by the older workers' decreasing ability to adjust to circadian dephasing. Both factors are related to age (Akerstedt, 1980; Akerstedt & Gillberg, 1981). Younger workers, however, may report more problems associated with long sequences of morning shifts due to an increase of sleep loss resulting from less sleep during this shift period (Rutenfranz & Knauth, 1987; Ng-A-Tham & Thierry, 1993).

Table 1 presents a schedule that illustrates some of the principles we've discussed. The schedule is a three-shift continuous system, medium-speed forward rotating. In the Netherlands, schedules like this are called the *French continuous system*. There are five crews in this schedule. The effective company operation time is 168 hours a week, and the employee's working time is 33.6 hours a week. The working times in the shifts are morning (M) 7:00 A.M. to 3:00 P.M., afternoon (A) 3:00 P.M. to 11:00 P.M., night (N) 11:00 P.M. to 7:00 A.M., and days off.

The systems discussed thus far follow more or less regular schedules. There are, however, many WTA's that deviate from normal, but that do not fall into one of those schedules. In the health and/or safety services, for example, there are many professionals who are

TABLE 1

An Example of a Three-shift Medium-speed Forward-rotating Continuous System With Five Crews

	Mon.	Tue.	Wed.	Thurs.	Fri.	Sat.	Sun.
Week 1	M	M	M	—	—	A	A
Week 2	A	A	—	—	N	N	N
Week 3	—	—	—	M	M	M	M
Week 4	—	—	A	A	A	—	—
Week 5	N	N	N	N	—	—	—

on a regular day-working scheme, which is disturbed from time to time by deviations from the day-working hours during the evening or during the night, in the case of emergencies. Also, within shift schedules, there may be deviations from the regular pattern, such as in the case of multicraft systems in which extra day shifts are scheduled to allow for job rotation, training programs, or meetings. In many other systems, there are days scheduled in which employees are on call in order to cope with emergencies or to work for colleagues who are ill or on vacation.

In most systems, the length of a work shift varies around eight hours. Extended work days, up through 12 hours, and compressed workweeks are becoming more and more popular (Colligan & Tepas, 1986; Tepas, 1985, 1990). It has been argued (Nachreiner & Rutenfranz, 1975) that fast rotating 12-hour shifts, provided the work load is not too intensive (Rutenfranz & Rohmert, 1983), are preferable to eight-hour slowly rotating shift systems. Frese and Semmer (1986), however, could not find much support for this position in their study of a large group of former 8- and 12-hour shiftworkers. Ong and Kogi (1990) report on an unsuccessful experiment with the large-scale introduction of 12-hour shifts in industries in Singapore. A year after the introduction of the shifts, most industries had abandoned the system. The main reasons were widespread complaints among workers about physical health and serious disruption of social and family life. Due to the possibility of accumulation of fatigue effects (Rosa & Colligan, 1988; Rosa, Colligan, & Lewis, 1989) over successive 12-hour work periods, such extended work periods are not recommended for a longer succession (more than four working days), or for night shifts. The preference for extended work periods varies considerably among shiftworkers, depending on biographic and demographic characteristics (Colligan & Tepas, 1986). However, it seems realistic to conclude that shiftworkers prefer 8-hour shifts, as may be inferred from data presented by Tepas (1990) based on 2,115 shiftworkers in four industries in the United States. These results are presented in Figure 3.

Prevalence. The prevalence of shiftwork varies between countries and within countries between sectors, for example, between the manufacturing industry and the services sector. About 20 percent of the wage-earning population in the industrialized North Atlantic countries is engaged in work systems other than a regular daytime work schedule. In the European Community (EC), the percentage varies from 41 percent of industrial employees in Luxembourg to 18 percent in the Netherlands and 11 percent in Denmark. The overall percentage in the manufacturing industry in the EC is 21 percent. About 18 percent of the workers in the services sector in the EC does not work regular daytime schedules, with a range of 23 percent in Denmark to 10 percent in Ireland (Corlett, Queinnec, & Paoli, 1988). Similar figures are reported on the United States and Canada (Presser, 1986). About 10 to 15 percent of the wage-earning population works regularly at night, in both the United States and the EC (Corlett et al., 1988; Mellor, 1986). In

developing countries, night work is less prevalent, but it is spreading (Kogi & Thurman, 1990).

The prevalence of shiftwork also varies between industrial branches. In industrial branches such as the chemical, oil, and food processing industries, relatively high percentages of shiftworkers are employed. Mechanical engineering and construction industries have lower percentages. The services sector, the health, energy, public transportation, communication, and safety branches have higher proportions of shiftworkers, while the banking and public administration branches have lower proportions.

Even within the same branches of industry, the prevalence of shiftwork varies between occupations and jobs. During the 1970s, 41 percent of the total male work force in the former German Federal Republic was engaged in skilled clerical work, whereas only 30 percent of the male shiftworker population was (Münstermann & Preiser, 1978). In Great Britain, it was also estimated that during the 1970s, 35 percent of all manual laborers in industrial branches was engaged in some form of shiftwork and that 66 percent of them was engaged in night work, versus 7 percent of the office workers in the same branches (Clark, 1984). There is no reason to assume that these percentages have changed drastically during the 1980s.

The Analysis of
Shift Design Dimensions

The scheduling principles or design dimensions discussed thus far are rather general. Many variations are possible concerning the location of the work times in a shift, the length of the shift, the number of successive shifts and the number of crews, the direction of the rotation, and so on. Jansen (1987b) identified more than 900 different schedules, all in operation in Dutch industries and services in the mid-1980s. The proportion of discontinuous

FIGURE 3

**Worker Preference for Working Time Arrangements,
Based on Actual Shift Experience (with 8- and/or 12-hour shifts)**

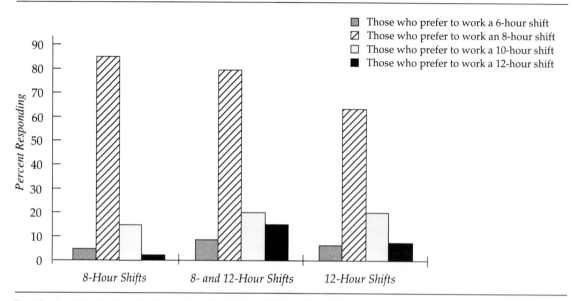

Legend:
- ▧ Those who prefer to work a 6-hour shift
- ▨ Those who prefer to work an 8-hour shift
- ☐ Those who prefer to work a 10-hour shift
- ■ Those who prefer to work a 12-hour shift

Percent Responding (y-axis: 0, 10, 20, 30, 40, 50, 60, 70, 80, 90)

x-axis categories: *8-Hour Shifts*, *8- and 12-Hour Shifts*, *12-Hour Shifts*

From "Condensed Working Hours: Questions and Issues" by D. I. Tepas, 1990. In G. Costa, G. Cesena, K. Kogi, and A. Wedderburn (Eds.), *Shiftwork: Health, Sleep and Performance* (p. 275). Frankfurt: Peter Lang. Copyright 1990 by Peter Lang. Reprinted by permission.

schedules was 51 percent, 23 percent of which was atypical. The proportion of semi-continuous schedules was 35 percent, 10 percent of which was atypical. The proportion of continuous schedules was 14 percent, 64 percent of which was atypical. *Atypical* means that a schedule adheres basically to a discontinuous, semicontinuous, or continuous arrangement but deviates from its basic principles in some particular way. This makes a universal classification system extremely difficult.

The classification of shift systems according to the criteria mentioned above is criticized by several authors (Jansen, 1987b; Nachreiner, Baer, Diekmann, & Ernst, 1984). Their main objections concern the normal character of these criteria, which do not lend themselves

sufficiently to the analysis of differential effects of various shift systems. Nachreiner's group (Bonitz et al., 1987; Bonitz, Heddon, Crzech-Sukalo, & Nachreiner, 1989; Ernst et al., 1986; Hedden, Bonitz, Grzech-Sukalo, & Nachreiner, 1989) studied shift schedules for their periodic components by using spectral analyses. The main rhythmic components are related to indicators of psychosocial impairments. Their leading hypothesis is that schedules allowing for a better synchronization with social rhythms should result in less impairment. It turned out that schedules with a main periodic component of about 96 hours approach the normal social rhythmicity in an optimal way and are therefore preferable. This classification method resulted in more homogeneous groupings of different schedules and a more coherent picture of associated impairments than does the traditional classification according to the speed and direction of the rotation. Jansen (1987a, 1987b) designed a system based on recommendations in the literature (Knauth & Rutenfranz, 1982) to assess the characteristics of a specific schedule. His typology, called the *Rota-Risk-Profile-Analysis* (RRPA), is based on 13 characteristics that are central to a more encompassing theory of differential aversive effects of schedules. These characteristics are summarized in Table 2, together with the main inconveniences associated with each.

All characteristics in Jansen's system are scaled from 0 to 10, indicating the extent of deviation from a regular day-work schedule. By means of a cluster analysis of all the 925 different schedules using the scores on the RRPA, Jansen (1987b) identified six different clusters. In Figure 4, the risk profiles of three different clusters are given. The first cluster (discontinuous system) in the figure is a two-shift system, with the five morning shifts (6:15 A.M.–2:45 P.M.) in week 1 from Monday through Friday; five afternoon/evening shifts (2:45 P.M.–11:15 P.M.) in week 2 from Monday through Friday; with the two weekend days free. The second cluster in the figure is a two-shift semicontinuous system (semicontinuous system), with five morning shifts (6:00 A.M.–3:00 P.M.) during week 1 from Monday through Friday; five night shifts (10:00 P.M.–6:00 A.M.) during week 2 from Tuesday through Saturday. The third cluster in the figure is a three-shift continuous system (continuous system); it was presented in Table 1.

From the data presented in Figure 4, one may conclude that the three schedules differ considerably with respect to their risk profiles. Due to the afternoon/evening shift each second week in schedule A, the scores on the risk characteristics OH and CH (opportunity of household/family tasks and constancy of opportunity of household and family tasks, respectively) and on OE and CE (opportunity of evening recreation and constancy of

opportunity of evening recreation, respectively) are rather low. Due to the night shifts each second week, schedule B scores on the risk characteristics ON and CN (opportunity to rest at night and constancy of opportunity to rest at night, respectively) and on OH and CH are low. In addition, there are low scores on the characteristics of weekend recreation (OW and CW). Schedule C is low on the characteristics PR (predictability) and opportunity of weekend recreation and constancy of opportunity for weekend recreation, respectively (OW and CW). Its scores on the night rest characteristics (ON and CN) are higher than in schedule B, due to the slower succession of night work weeks in this schedule compared to schedule B. Measurements on various effect variables correspond with these risk profile characteristics. For example, complaints of fatigue and sleep problems were relatively high among workers in cluster B systems, and relatively low in cluster A, with cluster C in between. Complaints of limitations on weekend recreation were relatively high among workers in clusters B and C. Both approaches, the analysis of rhythmic components and the risk profile analysis, open new ways to more analytical studies of schedule characteristics and their differential relations to effects of well-being and health than would be possible on the basis of the conventional formal criteria.

Effects on Performance, Health, and Well-being

The effects of shiftwork are intimately related to the various rhythmic timing systems of human life. There are two patterns that must be differentiated: the work–rest cycle and the sleep–wakefulness cycle (Alluisi & Morgan, 1982). Each of these cycles contains the same basic elements: sleep–rest, wakefulness–work, and wakefulness–rest. In normal daily work routine, both cycles follow a specific order over 24 hours. In shiftwork, the cycles are differentially affected, as Figure 5 illustrates.

TABLE 2

The Rota-Risk-Profile-Analysis

	Characteristic	Definition	Inconveniences
RE	Regularity	Mean number of changes in the starting times of working periods during the week	Unrest, nervous complaints, constipation
PE	Periodicity	Weekly mean of the sum of the accumulated number of successive night shifts plus half of the number of accumulated successive afternoon shifts	Sleeping problems, fatigue, stomach and intestinal complaints
LS	Load per shift	Mean shift length in hours	Fatigue, feelings of overload
LW	Load per week	Mean weekly working time in hours	Fatigue, feelings of overload
ON	Opportunity to rest at night	Mean weekly number of hours off work between 11:00 P.M. and 7:00 A.M.	Sleeping problems, insomnia, fatigue, nervous complaints
PR	Predictability	Cycle time in weeks	Planning/coordination problems
OH	Opportunity for household and family tasks	Weekly mean number of hours off work from Monday through Friday beween 7:00 A.M. and 7:00 P.M.	Frustration of partner/parental role, complaints on limitation of household tasks
CH	Constancy of opportunity for household and family tasks	Variation coefficient of weekly opportunity for household and family tasks	Lack of continuity in partner/parental role and in household tasks
OP	Opportunity for evening recreation	Mean weekly number of hours off work from Monday through Fridays between 7:00 P.M. and 11:00 P.M.	Lack of continuity in partner role, limitation of social and recreational activities
OW	Opportunity for weekend recreation	Half of the number of days off work during the weekend per week	Limitation of social and recreational activities
CW	Constancy of opportunity for weekend recreation	Variation coefficient of the number of days off during the weekend per week	Lack of continuity in social and recreational activities

From *Dagdienst en Ploegendienst in Vergelijkend Perspectief* [Day Work and Night Work Compared] by B. Jansen, 1987b, University of Amsterdam. Copyright 1987 by University of Amsterdam. Adapted by permission.

FIGURE 4

The Risk Profiles of Three Shift Systems

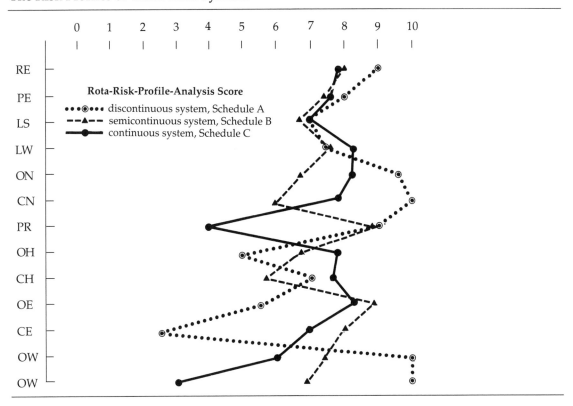

Ordinarily, an uninterrupted sleep period is followed by two uninterrupted periods of wakefulness: work and wakefulness–rest. In the morning shift, both cycles remain basically the same, though the sleep period is likely to be shortened and the wakefulness–rest period is likely to be somewhat longer. In the afternoon/ evening shift, the sleep–wakefulness cycle remains the same, but the work–rest cycle is affected in such a way that the wakefulness–rest period is interrupted by the wakefulness–work period. In the night shift, both cycles are affected.

In Figure 5, a circadian curve has also been depicted. Most physiological and psycho- logical functions that are related to the activa- tion and/or deactivation of the organism fol- low such a rhythm over the 24-hour period. Some functions reflect in their rhythms direct changes in the sleep–wakefulness cycle. This holds true for, among others, nonadrenaline secretion, heart rate, and blood pressure. Other functions, such as temperature or adrenaline and cortisol secretion, have fairly stable rhythms and are not easily modified by environmental synchronizers such as light, social timing cues, or overt activities. These functions have a strong endogenous rhythmicity and are rela- tively unaffected by behavior (Aschoff, 1978). Their speed of adjustment to a new time regime is usually about one hour per day, although this speed may differ considerably between functions. Depending on biological characteristics (Reinberg, Vieux, Ghata, Chaumont, & Laporte, 1978), age (Akerstedt, 1980), and psychological characteristics like introversion/extraversion (Blake & Corcoran, 1972; Colquhoun & Folkard, 1978) and morningness/eveningness (Moog, 1987; Ostberg, 1973), there are considerable interindividual differences in the speed of adjustment of endogenous rhythms to new time regimes or entrainment on the rhythms of a new time zone. In the reality of night shiftwork, however, a complete adjustment will never be achieved, not even after 10 or more days (Knauth et al., 1981).

Figure 5 illustrates the problems that night shiftworkers are confronted with. In contrast to transmeridian travelers in the new time zone, night shiftworkers remain in contact with the synchronizers from the normal daily routine of the physic (light/dark) and social environment. The rhythms of several functions remain entrained on the rhythmicity of the environment and, as a consequence, they are not in phase with the actual sleep–wakefulness cycle of the worker, while other functions follow this cycle. Thus, night shiftworkers have to cope with two types of desynchronization: external, in which some of the workers' rhythms are out of phase with the environment, and internal, in which the rhythms of several functions are out of phase with each other. In addition, they have to cope with the conflicts arising from the mismatch between their own work–rest cycle and the cycles of normal daily routine followed by the rest of society. These conflicts and the ways they are coped with may give rise to various problems, including those related to performance capacity and organizational outcomes, individual health and well-being, and the social functioning of the shiftworker and his or her family.

Sleep Distrubances. The most dramatic effects of shiftwork arise perhaps from the disturbances of the sleep–wakefulness cycle, which are most prominent during the night shift but which may also exist during the morning shift due to the decrease of the sleep duration. Night work and, consequently, daytime sleep, produces quantitative and qualitative changes in sleeping patterns. Compared with undisturbed night sleep, shorter REM latencies are observed during daytime sleep, together with fewer absolute minutes of REM sleep, and less total sleep duration (one to four hours shorter), whereas stage 3 and 4 sleep, which together make up slow wave sleep or deep sleep, seem to be less affected (Akerstedt, 1991; Tilley, Wilkinson, Warren, & Drud, 1982; Torsvall, Akerstedt, & Gillberg, 1981; Walsh, Tepas, & Moss, 1981). There is no conclusive evidence on the adjustment process across a series of night shifts. It has, however, been observed that sleep length does not improve a great deal (Foret & Benoit, 1978). Permanent night workers seem to sleep longer than rotating shiftworkers on night shift (Dahlgren, 1981). The decrease of sleep length during dayime sleep has been attributed to the higher noise levels at that time. A decrease is also observed under laboratory conditions, where noise levels were controlled, so noise cannot be the only factor accounting for this decrease (Akerstedt & Gillberg, 1981). Circadian factors also have a strong influence. The rise of body temperature and increased secretion of hormones (adrenaline and cortisol) during morning hours are important factors.

Based on aggregated data of 5,766 shiftworkers, Rutenfranz et al. (1981) present the following data on the prevalence of sleep disturbances. These problems are reported by:

- 15 to 20 percent of permanent day workers

- 5 percent of shiftworkers not doing night shifts

FIGURE 5

Sleep–Wakefulness and Work–Rest Cycles in Different Shift Conditions

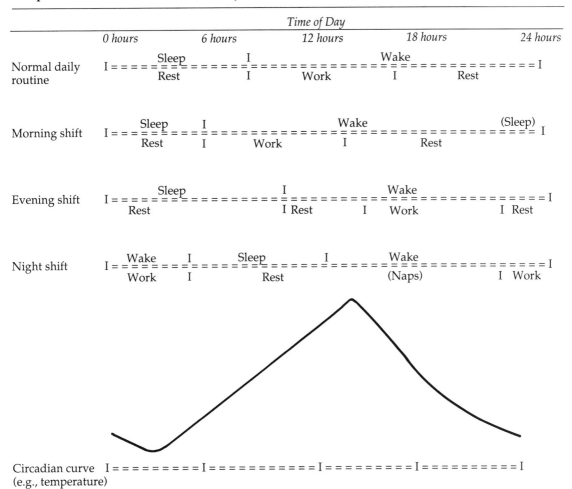

- 10 to 80 percent of shiftworkers doing night shifts in semicontinuous systems

- 60 percent of shiftworkers doing night shifts in continuous systems

- 90 percent of former shiftworkers at the time of their night shift activity; after their switch to daywork, reports

on sleep disturbances decreased to less than 20 percent

These last data suggest that sleep disturbances are among the most important reasons for leaving night shiftwork. They also suggest that these disturbances must be attributed to the affected sleep–wakefulness cycle during night shifts. There is ample evidence that sleep disturbances of night shiftworkers are related to age and years on the shift: Older workers, those past 40 to 45 years of age, have more problems that are aggravated related to the years of night shiftwork experience (Akerstedt, 1980; Akerstedt & Torsvall, 1981; Kundi, Koller, Cervinka, & Haider, 1979). Although no daytime sleep is at stake in the morning shift, sleeping problems are also observed in this condition. These stem mainly from the short duration (occasionally less than five to six hours) and the impaired sleep quality, particularly when the work begins before 6:00 A.M. (Folkard, Arendt, & Clark, 1990; Hak & Kampman, 1981; Meijman, Thunnissen, & de Vries-Griever, 1990).

Sleepiness and Fatigue.   The sleep problems have been related to feelings of fatigue, sleepiness, and lethargy, which are most widespread on the night shift, hardly appear on the afternoon/evening shift, and are in between on the morning shift (Akerstedt, 1988; Meijman, 1991). Using an EEG, Torsvall, Akerstedt, Gillander, and Knutsson (1989) recorded short sleep episodes of 25 papermill workers during night shiftwork; the sleep episodes were observed for approximately one-fourth of the subjects. These episodes were experienced as "dozing off" and were concomitant with subjective sleepiness and low rated work load. Similar observations have been reported on train personnel (Fruhstorfer, Langandke, Meinzer, Peter, & Pfaff, 1977; Torsvall & Akerstedt, 1987), military personnel (Haslam, 1982), and truck drivers (Prokop & Prokop, 1955; McDonald, 1984). The sleepiness problem seems greatest during the first night shift and during the second half of the night work period. There is no indication, however, that more than a marginal adjustment takes place over a series of night shifts (Akerstedt, 1988, 1990). The problem is also observed in permanent night workers (Folkard et al., 1979; Minors & Waterhouse, 1985b), although they seem to experience fewer

difficulties than rotating shiftworkers (Akerstedt, 1988).

Another phenomenon related to the disturbance of the sleep–wakefulness cycle is known as *night shift paralysis:* a short-lived but incapacitating immobility involving the entire voluntary musculature, although full consciousness prevails. According to Folkard and Condon (1987), who studied the phenomenon in several recent studies, it was first reported by Rudolf (1946). Folkard, Condon, and Herbert (1984) observed this paralysis in 12 percent of the night nurses surveyed in one study and in 6 percent of the air traffic controllers (Folkard & Condon, 1987) in another study. The incidence of this paralysis was found to be affected by four main factors, all of which might reasonably be assumed to influence the night worker's level of sleep deprivation and sleepiness. These factors were (a) time of night (around 5:00 A.M.), (b) the number of consecutive night shifts worked (higher incidences occurred when second or third night shifts were worked in succession), (c) the amount of recuperation time preceding the night shift, and (d) individual characteristics, particularly individual differences in sleep flexibility, and, to a lesser extent, preferences for working during the morning.

Thus, not only sleep is affected, both quantitatively and qualitatively, by the disturbance of the sleep–wakefulness cycle in the night shift; wakefulness is as well.

Performance Deterioration.   The last conclusion raises questions about the impairment of performance or capacity during the night shift. In general, productivity decreases during night work compared with daytime work levels (Agervold, 1976; Alluisi & Morgan, 1982; Carter & Corlett, 1982; Menzel, 1962; Monk & Folkard, 1985; Wyatt & Marriott, 1953). For example, Vidacek, Kaliterna, and Radosevic-Vidacek (1986) studied the productivity in assembling tasks in three shift conditions—morning, afternoon, and night—and during five successive shifts. Lowest production figures were found during the first and second night shift. Then a peak was found during the third night shift and a decline again occurred during the fourth and fifth night shift. Overall, productivity was higher during the morning and afternoon shifts compared to the night shifts. During the first three shifts of the morning and afternoon, condition production figures were steadily high and declined in both conditions during the fourth and fifth shift (but were never lower than during the night shift).

Physical working capacity is found to be less optimal during the night (Costa, Gaffuri, Perfranceschi, & Tansella, 1979; Wotjczak-Jaroszowa, & Banaskiewicz, 1974; Wotjczak-Jaroszowa, Makowsa, Rzepecki, Banaskiewicz, & Romejko, 1978), although it is hard to conclude the causes: a circadian rhythmicity of the physical working capacity itself or the rhythmicity of the physiological parameters (like heart rate), which are used in the study of physical working capacity.

With respect to mental performance capacity, the research evidence on circadian factors is rather complicated. Although there are indications that mental performance deteriorations due to a disturbed sleep–wakefulness cycle may be severe enough to establish accident risks (Mitler, Carskadon, Czeisler, Dement, Dinges, & Graeber, 1988), field studies, particularly those on time-of-day effects in the occurrence of accidents, do not provide converging evidence (de Vries-Griever & Meijman, 1987). This may be due to several confounding factors, including the following:

- Some accidents are not caused by human factors.

- Not every human error and/or lapse of attention leads necessarily to an accident.

- An error, accident, or near-accident is often registered long after its occurrence if it is registered at all; therefore, it is difficult to analyze the details of such incidents.

- Working conditions at night often differ from daytime ones, which may provide opportunities for the occurrence of accidents.

In studies that automatically register minor accidents and when no repercussions are likely or expected by the workers involved, the highest frequencies of minor accidents are found during the end of the night shift, with a secondary peak around 3:00 P.M. (Folkard et al., 1979). Such was the finding in the classical studies by Browne (1949) with teleprinter switchboard operators and by Bjerner, Holm, and Swensson (1955), who registered a nightly peak in reading errors among gas meter operators, with a smaller peak occurring in the afternoon. In a very interesting study on train drivers, Hildenbrandt, Rohmert, and Rutenfranz (1974) found that such late night/early morning and afternoon peaks in errors were related to the length of the preceding working time. Apparently, fatigue in interaction with circadian factors is an important determinant of the performance in detecting (or missing) warning signals, as is shown in Figure 6.

On the other hand, fewer errors were found at night than during the day in a field study on errors in complex monitoring and control tasks in which decisions had to be made on the basis of information stored in working memory (Monk & Embrey, 1981).

These conflicting findings on the occurrence of human errors during night and day work have led to the hypothesis that mental performance capacity is multidimensional and varies differentially during the 24 hours in a day, depending on the type of information processing operations involved and the task load (Folkard & Monk, 1985). Performance capacity in simple sensorimotor and perceptual tasks has a circadian rhythm that is more or less analogous to that of body temperature. Performance capacity in long-term memory tasks, in

FIGURE 6

Warning Signals Missed by Train Drivers in Relation to Time of Day and Hours Worked on Shift

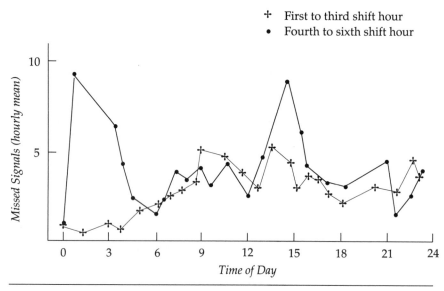

From "Variations in the Daily Rhythm of Error Frequency by Shiftworkers and the Influence of it on Tiredness" by G. Hildenbrandt, W. Rohmert, and J. Ruthenfranz, 1974, *International Journal of Chronobiology, 2*, p. 179. Copyright 1974 by Harwood Academic GmbH for Wiley. Reprinted by permission.

which information has to be stored for a longer time in order for it to be recalled later, varies accordingly. Contrary to performance in these tasks, performance in short-term memory tasks reaches its peak late at night or in the early morning and then decreases in the course of the day. Mental performance capacity rhythms are also dependent on the memory load of the task. In simple tasks with a low memory load, immediate transfer from input to output is involved—a process that seems to improve during the course of a day. On the other hand, in complex tasks with a high memory load, storage or information in the working memory is involved—a process that seems to depreciate during the course of a day.

It may be erroneous to conclude from the research findings on the differential rhythmicity of mental performance capacities that complex tasks with a high memory load during night shifts may be best assigned to the employees (de Vries-Griever & Meijman, 1987). Most of the studies on mental performance during night shifts have not focused on the human costs involved in performing complex mental tasks. Due to the compensating mechanism of mental effort, a suboptimal performance capacity does not necessarily manifest itself in decreased performance. It may become manifest, however, in parameters reflecting the human costs (Hockey, 1986; Mulder, 1986). It is only when the limits of effort are exceeded that a breakdown will occur—either in the form of an error or accident, or in the form of complaints on health and well-being and eventually, sick leave.

Attitudes Toward Shiftwork. A very large part of the research on shiftwork is devoted to individual outcomes: work-related attitudes, individual well-being and health, and social well-being of the shiftworker and his or her family.

The attitudes of shiftworkers with respect to their working conditions vary considerably, depending on the biographical and demographical characteristics of the worker and the shift system involved. Generally, just a minority (about 20%) of the workers surveyed prefers shiftwork over regular day work, particularly when night work is involved (Khaleque & Rahman, 1984; Tepas, 1990; Ulich, 1957; Wyatt & Marriott, 1953). But, as stated previously, this figure may vary. The more regular the shift system, the more it is preferred (Münstermann & Preiser, 1978). Younger workers and workers with young children more willingly accept shiftwork, among other reasons because of the monetary bonus that may increase their financial opportunities (Clark, 1984; Theiry, Hoolwerf, & Drenth, 1975). Other important factors in the acceptance of shiftwork are the labor opportunities: Work in certain professions has to be done at irregular hours or requires shiftwork (health care, safety services, fire fighting, etc.). Wedderburn (1967) pointed out that there may also be social determinants behind the acceptance of shiftwork: In some geographical regions, such as in mining districts, shiftwork has a higher status than regular day jobs.

Morning shifts are judged more positively because they provide the opportunity for a longer wakefulness period in which other activities can be performed (Sergean, 1971; Wedderburn, 1978). In addition, the morning shift is seen as the least disturbing condition of the sleep–wakefulness and work–rest cycle. On the other hand, younger workers prefer the morning shift less than older workers, and morning shifts starting before 6:00 A.M. are definitely not preferred (Hak & Kampman, 1981; Sergean, 1971). Afternoon/evening shifts are judged as the least fatiguing, at least in northern Europe, North America, and Australia. This is not the case in tropical countries, mainly because of high temperatures in the afternoon and the custom of sleeping at that time. That may explain why 42 percent of morning shiftworkers in Bangladesh report sleep complaints and 93 percent of afternoon shiftworkers report complaints (Khaleque & Rahman, 1982). Afternoon/evening shifts disturb the wakefulness–rest period and may therefore hinder social activities (Bonitz et al., 1987, 1989; Bunnage, 1979; Ernst et al., 1986). Night shifts are judged the most negatively, since they disturb both the sleep–wakefulness and the work–rest cycles. However, they have some advantage. Shiftworkers report more autonomy, generally lower work demands, fewer disruptions from maintenance personnel, and less burden from their supervisors (De la Mare & Walker, 1968; Sergean, 1971; Thierry et al., 1975). On the other hand, there are fewer opportunities for assistance and support from supervisors and/or maintenance services. Operators in process industries and nursing personnel mention these less advantageous aspects of working the night shift (Gadbois, 1980; Gadbois & Queinnec, 1984; Münstermann & Preiser, 1978).

Social Consequences. An advantage of shiftwork often mentioned relates to the idea of being off work when everyone else is working. Shiftworkers and their relatives may profit from such free hours "when everybody else is working," but they also pay a price. Because "everybody else is working," shiftworkers may have fewer opportunities for group leisure activities, either with their friends or with their families (Bunnage, 1979; Mott, Mann, McLoughlin, & Warwick, 1965; Thierry et al., 1975; Wedderburn, 1967). Thus, the quality of off-duty hours may be lower for shiftworkers than it is for day workers, particularly for afternoon and night shiftworkers (Bonitz et al., 1987, 1989; Knauth, 1987; Staines & Pleck, 1984). This may explain why relatively high percentages of shiftworker complaints relate to the issue of social life. In a large-scale study by Nachreiner and Rutenfranz (1975), workers reported they had insufficient time for involvement with the following:

- Social organizations—complaints voiced by 64 percent of shiftworkers and 11 percent of day workers

- Cultural events—complaints voiced by 61 percent of shiftworkers and 10 percent of day workers

- Friends—complaints voiced by 52 percent of shiftworkers and 10 percent of day workers

- Family—complaints voiced by 40 percent of shiftworkers and 9 percent of day workers

- Hobbies—complaints voiced by 39 percent of shiftworkers and 11 percent of day workers

Another factor to consider relates to the hours spent off duty that must be devoted to recuperation in the form of dozing off and short naps, particularly during night shift periods and after early morning shifts. Shiftworkers in night and morning shift periods compensate on their days off for the sleep missed during the working periods by sleeping more (Akerstedt, 1988; Rudat, 1977; Tepas, 1982; Tune, 1969). Moreover, the effects of the sleep disturbances associated with the night shift may be transferred to the days off that follow these shifts. Impaired sleep quality has been measured two to three days after a night shift period has been worked (Meijman, Thunnissen, & de Vries-Griever, 1990). In addition, performance deteriorations in memory search tasks were observed during the second day off after night shift periods of at least four nights (Meijman, van der Meer, & van Dormolen, 1993).

Health and Well-being. A considerable body of data has demonstrated that shiftwork, particularly when done during the night, may be detrimental to health and individual well-being. The most clear-cut effects concern sleep and wakefulness, which have been addressed previously. The digestive system may also be affected. Complaints such as gastrointestinal upset and disturbed appetite have been reported (Aanonsen, 1964; Thiis-Evensen, 1958, 1969). Rutenfranz et al. (1981) present the following overview, based on aggregated data of a large group of studies.

Complaints about and disturbances of eating habits were reported by:

- 10 to 25 percent of day workers

- 17 percent of shiftworkers not working night shifts

- 5 to 35 percent of night shiftworkers working semicontinuous systems

- 50 percent of night shiftworkers working continuous systems

- 30 to 50 percent of former shiftworkers who left shiftwork for health reasons

Ulcers are reported by:

- 3 to 7 percent of day workers
- 5 percent of shiftworkers not working night shifts

- 2.5 to 15 percent of night shiftworkers

- 10 to 30 percent of former shiftworkers who left shiftwork for health reasons

There is a considerable overlap in the figures for the various groups. However, Angersbach et al. (1980) reported confirmative evidence on the previous data, based on a well-designed retrospective cohort study. Similar results were reported by Akerstedt and Theorell (1976), Cervinka, Kundi, Koller, and Arnhoff (1984a, 1984b), and Costa, Apostoli, d'Andrea, and Gaffuri (1981). Contrary to sleeping problems, which seem at least partly to disappear after workers leave night shiftwork, complaints of gastrointestinal problems continue even after shiftwork is relinquished.

Although night shiftworkers, and former night shiftworkers, in particular, report general psychosomatic complaints and/or impaired well-being more frequently than day workers who do not have previous shift experience (Frese & Okonek, 1984; Frese & Semmer, 1986; Koller, Kundi, & Cervinka 1978), there is no firm evidence on higher incidences of psychiatric syndromes or diseases among former shiftworkers.

Early studies on cardiovascular diseases among shiftworkers were inconclusive (Harrington, 1978; Rutenfranz, Colquhoun, Knauth, & Ghata, 1977). For example, Taylor and Pocock (1972) did not find statistically significant higher mortality rates among shiftworkers, former shiftworkers, and day workers in an epidemiological study of the mortality figures in Great Britain over 12 years. There was, however, a tendency: Compared to the expectancies based on the total male population in England and Wales, these were lower actual rates for the day workers, somewhat higher actual rates for the shiftworkers, and considerably higher actual rates for the former shiftworkers, although these latter numbers were small. A cross-sectional study among oil refinery shiftworkers and former shiftworkers in Austria by Koller et al. (1978), however, indicated an increased prevalence of cardiovascular symptoms. These findings were confirmed in a five-year follow-up study of the same groups (Koller, 1983). Recently, some other evidence has been presented in several well-designed epidemiological studies. Alfredsson, Karasek, and Theorell (1982) performed a case–referent study, with aggregated work load data, and found that only exposure to monotony and shiftwork, among many other work load indicators, were significantly related to hospitalization for myocardial infarction. Akerstedt, Knutsson, Alfredsson, and Theorell (1984), Alfredsson, Spetz, and Theorell (1985), and

Akerstedt, Alfredsson, and Theorell (1986) report significantly increased standardized morbidity ratios for cardiovascular disease with increased exposure to shiftwork and work at irregular hours. Knutsson (1989) and Knutsson, Akerstedt, Johnsson, and Orth-Gomer (1986) report, among others, on a cohort study, with controls for confounders and several other risk factors such as age, smoking, ethnic group, and sex, in which the day work and the shiftwork cohorts were comparable in socioeconomic status and physical work load. Increased prevalences were also reported in this study. Moreover, Knutsson (1989) and Knutsson, Akerstedt, Johnsson, and Orth-Gomer (1986) present some evidence on higher prevalences of risk factors, such as smoking and dietary factors, among shiftworkers. Thus, evidence that night shiftwork is possibly associated with cardiovascular risk factors, or perhaps may be a potential risk factor in itself, is accumulating (see Combined Factors and Effects, this chapter).

Absenteeism.   Despite the problems in health and well-being that shiftworkers may be confronted with, the evidence on higher absentee rates among shiftworkers compared to day workers is not very consistent. There are indications that the duration of absenteeism due to sickness is somewhat higher among shiftworkers compared to day workers. The frequency, however, is not (Angersbach, Knauth, Loskant, Karvonen, Undeutsch, & Rutenfranz, 1980; Thierry et al., 1975; Walker & de la Mare, 1971; Wongphanic, Saito, Kogi, & Temmyo, 1982), or is even lower (Aanonsen, 1961; Taylor, 1967; Taylor, Pocock, & Sergean, 1972). Several factors have been offered to explain these rather counterintuitive observations. Selection mechanisms may be at stake: Only relatively healthier workers start with shiftwork, whether they are deliberately selected or not, and stay in it. Several authors have pointed to social pressure from work groups and/or solidarity with colleagues as things that may prevent shiftworkers from being absent from work for minor health reasons (Bjerner et al., 1955; Taylor, 1967). This may explain why higher percentages of shiftworkers compared to day workers report to work despite complaints of sickness. Evidence of this phenomenon has been presented by the Japanese Committee on Shiftwork (Shift Work Committee, 1978). Another factor may be the tendency of shiftworkers to underestimate slight symptoms of impaired health and well-being (Taylor, 1968). Andersen (1970) found that 70 percent of the day workers in his study with physical complaints visited their family doctor, compared to 47 percent of the shiftworkers. It seems that shiftworkers regard all kinds of slight physical symptoms as a part of the job (Agervold, 1976) and therefore have a higher threshold before visiting a physician (Akerstedt et al., 1977; Tasto, Colligan, Skjei, & Polly, 1978). The consequences of these underestimations of impairments of health and well-being among shiftworkers could be quite serious (Colligan, Frockt, & Tasto, 1979). When shiftworkers regard these symptoms as part of the job, then the figures from surveys on these problems may be systematically too low. The practical consequences could be that shiftworkers do not seek medical care in cases when it is justified. It is not clear whether this could be a factor in the development of health problems in the long run among the shiftworking population.

Shiftwork and Other Environmental Factors

In an earlier discussion we stated that shiftwork, including night work and/or working at irregular hours, is more common in production jobs and less so in administrative and office jobs. Therefore, it may be hypothesized, generally speaking, that jobs in shiftwork differ from jobs in regular day work in terms of both content and working conditions. We will now discuss the empirical evidence about such differences between the two sorts of jobs. In the next paragraph, consequences concerning some methodological aspects of comparative studies on health status and well-being between shiftworkers and day workers and the possibility of interaction effects of shiftworking and other job factors on outcomes of health and well-being will be formulated.

Subjective Data. Studies in which the opinions about job content and working conditions are compared between shift- and day workers suggest substantial differences with regard to the subjective valuation of work load and hindrance from environmental factors (Bosworth & Dawkins, 1984). Streich (1985), for example, studied nearly 4,000 shiftworkers and more than 20,000 day workers in West Germany on their judgments of various aspects of the work load. Compared with day workers, shiftworkers reported more complaints on noise (32%), environmental stressors such as heat, cold, humidity, and airstreams (21%), perceptual demands (20%), lack of decision latitude (19%), monotony (16%), and physical work load (9%). Similar findings, also in West Germany, were reported by Münstermann and Preiser (1978) and by PROSA (1981) in a survey conducted on request of the Union of Chemical Workers. More recently, these results were confirmed in a Swedish study by Akerstedt, Alfredsson, and Theorell (1986). They performed secondary analyses on aggregated data of 118 occupations stemming from a large-scale survey of more than 900,000 workers by the Swedish Central Bureau of Statistics. More than 250 different occupational characteristics were assessed, including working times and various physical and psychosocial job stressors. Akerstedt et al. (1986) computed the association by means of gamma coefficients between the exposure to irregular working hours and other work and environmental stressors. The results are summarized in Table 3.

The data suggest that working in shifts and/or working at irregular hours does covary with many other job stressors. Thus, it seems that

TABLE 3

**Correlations (Gamma Coefficients)
Between Irregular Working
Hours and Other Job Stressors**

Variable	Gamma
No influence on pace	.45
Noise	.44
Monotony	.39
Accidents	.38
No learning possibilities	.32
Heavy work	.31
Repetitive movements	.26
No visitors allowed	.26
Sweating	.25
Vibrations	.25

Note: Only values $p > .05$ presented

From "An Aggregate Study of Irregular Work Hours and Cardiovascular Disease" by T. Akerstedt, L. Alfredsson, and T. Theorell, 1986. In M. Haider, M. Koller, and R. Cervinka (Eds.), *Night and Shiftwork: Longterm Effects and Their Prevention* (p. 42). Frankfurt: Peter Lang. Copyright 1986 by Peter Lang. Reprinted by permission.

shiftworkers are engaged in the more stressful jobs and are exposed to more negative environmental factors in their working situations than day workers. The empirical evidence substantiating this statement, however, stems from the subjective valuations made by shift- or day workers of their jobs. Apart from the aforementioned conclusion, alternative explanations remain. It may be that shiftworkers complain more than day workers about environmental factors because they are more sensitive to the hindrance from these factors. Such greater sensitivity may arise from the physical and mental condition of shiftworkers, which is generally less optimal, due to the disturbance of biological rhythms and/or sleep loss and fatigue, particularly during the night, and the early morning shifts. It may also be that shiftworkers attribute the burden of their WTA's, which deviate from normal, to all aspects of their working situation, when in

reality these other aspects do not deviate from normal situations. Both explanations can be sustained. Shiftworkers do complain more about their general psychosomatic condition (Dirken, 1966; Koller et al., 1978; Kundi, Koller, Cervinka, & Haider, 1981; McCarthy, 1983; Michel-Briand, Chopard, Guiot, Paulmier, & Struder, 1981), and they do have a general feeling of "being an exception," or, as Thierry and Jansen (1981) describe it, a feeling of "apartheid." Why should such complaints and bad feelings remain restricted to their living and personal situation and not apply to assessments of their working situation?

Data From Task Analyses. Yet there are good arguments that jobs in shiftwork are more likely to be characterized by more job stressors than jobs in day work. Knauth (1983; also in Rutenfranz & Knauth, 1986) used the data of standardized job descriptions of 2,500 workplaces. These analyses were carried out by trained job analysts. The results are summarized in Table 4.

From the data presented in Table 4, at least two conclusions can be drawn. First, the differential reports by shiftworkers and day workers on the prevalence of other stressors in their work situation are confirmed by job analysts. Second, within the population of jobs in shiftwork, substantial differences can be observed in the prevailing job stressors.

Evidence to substantiate this last conclusion is presented by various studies. For example, Münstermann and Preiser (1978) compared the complaints regarding various job stressors made by 1,674 industrial day workers with those of 816 industrial shiftworkers from similar branches of industry. Their findings are summarized in Table 5. The complaints are grouped into two broad categories: physical stressors and mental stressors.

Although no intercorrelations between the stressors have been computed, we can still assume that the data in Table 5 reflect

TABLE 4

Relative Frequencies (In Percentage) of Unfavorable Environmental Conditions at 2,429 Workplaces as Analyzed by Trained Job Analysts, Dependent on the Organization of Working Times

Shift System	Noise	Unfavorable Climate	Unfavorable Lighting	Vibrations	Other Unfavorable Conditions
Day work	16	6	2	3	21
Two-shift system	32	9	7	4	22
Continuous system	31	18	12	7	27
Night shift system	35	19	13	7	32
Irregular system	29	24	14	6	47
Three-shift system	36	22	11	8	37

From *Ergonomic Contributions to Safety Aspects of Working Time Arrangements* (p. 178) by P. Knauth, 1983, Düsseldorf: VDI-Verlag. Copyright 1983 by VDI-Verlag. Printed by permission.

TABLE 5

Percentage of Complaints Made by Industrial Shiftworkers Minus the Percentage of Complaints Made by Industrial Day Workers Differentiated into Two Broad Categories

Physical Stressors	Percentage	Mental Stressors	Percentage
Noise	27	Concentration	42
Heat	15	Responsibility for people	33
Dust	14	Responsibility for machinery	28
Cold	12	Attention/alertness	15
Air stream	10	Time pressure	14

Note: Only differences >9% are reported.

From *Schichtarbeit in der Bundesrepublik Deutschland* [Shift work in the German Federal Republic] by J. Münstermann and K. Preiser, 1978, Bonn, Germany: Forschungsbericht Humanisierung des Arbeidslebens 8, Bundesministerium Arbeit und Sozialordnung. Copyright 1978 by Forschungsbericht Humanisierung. Adapted by permission.

two general kinds of jobs in shiftwork: production work, which is characterized by traditional physical stressors, and process control work, characterized by mental task demands.

Environmental Factors. Even within the same jobs in shiftwork, differences with respect to aspects of the work organization and environmental factors can be found between the various shifts. Clearly, lighting conditions may vary substantially during the day—in the early morning, late afternoon, and night. Workers in transportation branches or maintenance operators who work partly outdoors on chemical plants, for example, are confronted with this variation in working conditions during their work times. Several studies (Pokorski, Oginski, & Knauth, 1986; Queinnec, Chabaud, & de Terssac, 1986) reported the observation that work pace is generally slower and there is generally less time pressure during the night shift. Also, the social climate and communications on the workplace are reported to be more "easygoing," probably because the general atmosphere is more quiet at night and the workers are together in their own crew. There is less of a burden of being under "the eye of the boss," simply because of the absence of higher management during the night. There are also fewer disturbing events, such as activities from maintenance operators, quality control officials, and transportation activities. Similar observations are reported outside industry—for example, in hospitals (Folkard et al., 1979; Verhaegen et al., 1987). Gadbois (1980) paid attention to the fact that there is often less work to be done during the night shift in hospitals, compared with the morning shifts and/or the day shifts. Shiftworkers often mention these aspects as the positive side of working night shifts. On the other hand, it must be mentioned that the same level of work demands may require physical and/or mental effort (de Vries-Griever & Meijman, 1987; Knauth, 1988) due to a worse psychophysiological condition of the worker during the night, and, in particular, during the last hours of the shift. Gadbois and Queinnec (1984) and Queinnec et al. (1986) have observed that among other things, shiftworkers adapt their working strategies during the night shift to compensate for their generally worse psychophysiological condition during those hours.

Combined Factors and Effects

The fact that shiftworkers are exposed to other environmental stressors in their work situation raises the issue of the combination of such factors and their combined effects. The Münstermann and Preiser study (1978) summarizes the number of stressors that various categories of shiftworkers complain about. Unskilled workers mention a mean of 3.99 other stressors in their jobs apart from shiftworking itself. Skilled workers in shiftwork mention a mean of 2.61, whereas shiftworkers in administrative and office jobs have a mean score of 1.75 other stressors. Civil servants in shiftwork, such as postal workers, fire fighters, and truck drivers, mention a mean of 3.53 other stressors. Knauth (1988) also gives information on the combination of more than one other environmental stressor and shiftwork. His study concludes that combinations of two and more environmental stressors are rare in day work and in jobs with a two-shift system (relative frequencies are lower than 3%). However, the combination of noise and unfavorable climate (see Table 4) occurs in 11 percent of jobs in continuous systems and in 15 percent of jobs in three-shift semicontinuous systems. A threefold combination of noise, unfavorable climate, and unfavorable lighting is found in 3.9 percent of jobs in continuous systems and in 7.5 percent of jobs in irregular systems (occurring in less than 0.5% of both day work and two-shift system jobs). Fourfold combinations (noise, vibrations, lighting, and climate) are not observed in day work jobs and in jobs in two-shift systems. They do occur in 1.1 percent of jobs in continuous systems and in 1.8 percent of jobs in three-shift semicontinuous systems.

Thus, shiftworkers are not only exposed to the burden caused by the conflicts between their own circadian rhythms and the prevailing physical and social rhythms, compared with day workers, they are also more likely to be exposed to other stressors in their jobs. This leads to two points of consideration: The first deals with the methodological consequences in studies comparing shiftworkers with day workers on issues of health and well-being; the second deals with the nature of the possible effects of these combined factors.

Comparative studies between subjects in jobs with different WTA's have only a limited value for drawing conclusions on the direct effects of a specific WTA, without provisions in the research design for the control of other factors pertaining to the job content and the working conditions (Colligan, 1981). For example, Wongphanic et al. (1982) compared female day and shiftworkers within the same textile industry on well-being and health outcomes. About 78 percent of the shiftworkers in this study came from the weaving and/or spinning mill, while 27 percent of the day workers did; 54 percent of the day workers had clerical jobs or did sewing work, versus only 9 percent of the shiftworkers. Direct conclusions from this study on the differential effects of the two WTA's are open to question, simply because of the covarying differences in job content and working conditions between the two groups of workers. It is difficult to perform field studies in which both factors—WTA and other working conditions—can be separated. One way to do this is to use statistical procedures to assess interaction effects and to differentiate between main effects of factors stemming from a specific WTA and those pertaining to other work aspects. In the Akerstedt et al. (1986) study, mentioned above, which is based on a Swedish large-scale (n = 958,096) epidemiological survey, such procedures were followed. Standardized (age adjusted) morbidity ratios (SMR's), for males and females separately, of the hospitalization for ischemic heart disease and myocardial infarction were computed for occupations with high versus low exposure to irregular work hours and for other work environment variables that were assessed in the study. The ratios pertaining to irregular work hours were found to be higher than 1 (p < 0.05) for males and females for both cardiovascular health outcomes, even after statistical adjustments were made for a number of potential confounders such as income, smoking, marital status, and place of residence.

Several other job stressors also have significant SMR's. In order to study the status of the factor "working at irregular hours," Akerstedt and his co-workers computed the SMR's of each work-related predictor with respect to a list of diagnoses other than the two cardiovascular diseases already mentioned. Compared with all other work-related factors that yielded significant ratios, the SMR's of "working irregular hours" turned out to be the best predictors of the two cardiovascular outcomes. Moreover, "working irregular hours" did not, or in just two cases only weakly, predict other diagnoses that were predicted by the other work-related stressors. Thus, evidence is accumulating that irregular work hours are related to cardiovascular diseases. However, despite the fact that none of the other stressors mentioned in Table 3 had a separate significant relationship with the cardiovascular outcomes, it is still not possible to conclude which aspect of working at irregular hours is related to these outcomes. The combination of all job stressors, or a subset of them, might account for the correlations. As they are common to working at irregular hours, this last factor may be the overall denominator.

Shiftwork as Detrimental Factor on Its Own. There are, however, some indications that suggest that working shifts, and night work in particular, may have detrimental effects of its own on outcomes of well-being and health. The evidence stems from various sources: direct follow-up studies of shiftworkers and day workers, cross-sectional studies of age cohorts in shiftwork and day work, and studies of former shiftworkers. Verhaegen, Maassen, and Meers (1981, 1986) followed 40 male shiftworkers doing night work for 12.5 years. This group remained from an original group of 104 workers. At the beginning of the study, the mean age of the group was 24 years. The authors performed four measurements during the 12.5 year follow-up using the same instrument: a standardized questionnaire on psychosomatic complaints. It was found that the score on this scale increased (meaning there were more complaints) during the first seven years and stabilized afterward to a high level of complaints. This level was significantly higher than it was for day workers of the same age who were in similar jobs but who did not have previous exposure to shiftwork. No differences were found between the two groups on a neuroticism questionnaire, which may indicate that a "general complaining factor" or "negative affectivity factor" (Watson & Pennebaker, 1989) could not account for the observed difference in psychosomatic problems. Moreover, measures after four years and again after seven years indicated that the workers from the original group who had left shiftwork retained the level of complaints measured at the time of their departure, whereas the shiftworkers' scores had increased. Despite the methodological weaknesses of this follow-up study, such as the small size of the groups and the uncontrolled selection effects, the results suggest at least the possibility of effects of night work (as a separate detrimental factor) on general well-being. Similar conclusions may be drawn from a five-year follow-up study by Kundi, Koller, Cervinka, and Haider (1986) of 91 shiftworkers and 34 day workers from comparable work sites. Selection effects were somewhat better controlled in a study by Bohle (1990), in which 130 student nurses were followed for 15 months after they were either assigned to a day and evening shift system without night shifts or to a shift system with night shifts. No differences on psychosomatic complaints were found between the non-night and the night shiftworkers at the start of the period. After 15 months, however, it was found that the night shift group showed a higher level of complaints on well-being and subjective health—even when statistical corrections were performed for differences in neuroticism between the two groups. Moreover, it was found that the nurses who reported serious problems with work and nonwork conflicts showed a higher level of subjective health problems after 15 months of night shiftwork.

Akerstedt and Torsvall (1978) administered a questionnaire on 400 workers on different shift schedules (day schedule, two-shift schedule, three-shift schedule, and four-shift schedule) shortly before and a year after the schedules of 131 of them had been changed. Those workers who had changed from three- or four-shift schedules working with night shifts to two-shift schedules working without night shifts, showed a significant increase in well-being with respect to sleep, gastrointestinal functioning, and social functioning. Those who changed from shift to day work reported increased social well-being from improved attitudes toward their work. Their absence rates due to illness were also reduced. From this follow-up study, it might be concluded that the abolition of night work results in an improvement in mental, physical, and social well-being.

Studies of aging and shiftwork also suggest that night shiftworking may have detrimental effects of its own, independent of other work-related factors. It is well known that younger workers report fewer problems of adjustment to night shiftwork (Aanonsen, 1964; Bruusgaard, 1969; Koller, 1983), particularly with respect to sleep disturbances and deteriorated sleeping quality (Akerstedt & Torsvall, 1981; Foret, Bensimon, Benoit, & Vieux, 1981). One of the reasons may be that older workers have more difficulty sleeping during the day. Other reasons may be that older people—those over 45 years of age—are more vulnerable to desynchronization problems and, consequently, have problems with the psychobiological adjustment to changing sleep–wake cycles (Wever, 1974). Some cross-sectional age cohort studies have observed that these problems aggravate after age 40 to 45, in relation to the number of years the person has been exposed to night shiftwork (Akerstedt, 1980; Haider, Kundi, & Koller, 1981). In a large-scale study of 2,659 shiftworking and 1,303 day working police officers, similar observations were made (Ottmann, Karvonen, Schmidt, Knauth, & Rutenfranz, 1989). It turned out, however, that not every outcome was equally affected. As they relate to age and exposure, complaints of musculoskeletal disorders, appetite, and digestion and pulmonary problems were aggravated by shiftwork. Nervous complaints and stomach problems increased with age, but they were relatively independent of shiftworking and were additively related to it. Thus, these studies suggest that during the first years of shiftworking, habituation processes and selection (quitting shiftwork) conceal the accumulation of problems. With increasing age and increasing exposure, these "safety valves" may cease to function, and the results of the accumulated negative effects of night shiftworking become manifest.

A third line of reasoning that may substantiate the thesis that night shiftworking may have detrimental effects of its own stems from studies of former shiftworkers. It is known that higher levels of impairment of health and well-being are found among former shiftworkers—in particular, among those who left night shiftwork for reasons of health and well-being—than among shiftworkers and day workers who do not have shiftwork experience (Aanonsen, 1964; Frese & Okonek, 1984; Frese & Semmer, 1986; Koller et al., 1984; Rutenfranz et al., 1981). These apply to general health problems, gastrointestinal disturbances, and cardiovascular complaints. In most studies, no improvements of these complaints are reported after workers leave shiftwork for health reasons. It therefore seems that once a certain threshold that forces the worker to leave shiftwork is passed, complaints are likely to remain. Some authors, however, have reported that sleeping problems decrease during the years after workers leave shiftwork. Rutenfranz et al. (1981) state in their review of the relevant literature that approximately 90 percent of former shiftworkers reported sleep disturbances at the time of their night shift activity. After switching over to day shifts, their sleep problems decreased to less than 20 percent. Such marked changes could not be affirmed in a recent study by Frese and Semmer (1986). Nonetheless, it may be concluded from their study that night shiftwork may have a separate effect on health and well-being, independent from other job stressors that former shiftworkers have been exposed to.

Combined Effects.   Related to these issues surrounds the question of what the nature of the interaction of combined effects is. Such effects could be in principle additive, subtractive, or multiplicative. In a recent overview of the relevant literature, van Dormolen, Hertog, Van Dijk, Kompier, and Fortuin (1990) underlined the general conclusion made by Poulton (1978) on the nature of the effects of combined stressors. These combined effects can be described sufficiently by simple additive models. Most studies on possible combined effects of working irregular hours and being exposed to environmental stressors agree with this conclusion. For example, Smith and Miles (1986) found in a laboratory experiment with students that noise and night work had different and independent effects on a variety of human functions, including temperature, alertness, and performance in several mental tasks. Similar findings were reported by Seibt, Friedrichsen, Jakubowski, Kaufman, and Schuring (1986) in a field study of shiftworkers on the effects of noise and night work. In another laboratory study, Rutenfranz et al. (1986) found no coherent effects of the combination of night work and heat stress on adrenaline excretion and some, but not very strong, effects on mental performance, particularly in divided attention tasks. A separate line of research that is relevant in this context pertains to the interaction of the effects of toxic agents and the irregularity of working hours, or, more generally, the possible fluctuations in vulnerability to chemical compounds during the day. There is a growing interest in this field, both from industrial toxicology and hygiene and from pharmacology (Bolt & Rutenfranz, 1988; Brief & Scala, 1986; Koopmans, 1988; Reinberg & Smolensky, 1983). Toxicological experts recommend that the regular threshold limits for chemical compounds at the workplace should be adapted when the total number of working hours is increased from eight to more than ten and when the number of consecutive shifts is more than five. The regular threshold values are based on a five-day workweek, consisting of eight-hour days. Chronopharmacological research provides some evidence that the vulnerability to certain chemicals fluctuates over the 24 hours in a day. Koopmans (1988) studied the effects of midazolam, which is common in sleeping drugs, and caffeine in coffee, at various hours of the 24-hour period. The sleeping drug did affect day sleep, but despite the better period of sleep preceding it, the feelings of fatigue remained high during the following night. Caffeine taken at night turned out to have measurable effects that were detrimental for the day sleep following the night it was consumed. There is some relevance of these findings for night shiftworkers who use coffee in considerable amounts during the night as a remedy to fight off fatigue and sleepiness.

In summary, the fact that jobs in shiftwork are also more likely to be characterized by other unfavorable working conditions and job stressors than jobs in day work has raised some important research issues. Corlett et al. (1988) hypothesize that shiftwork may aggravate negative effects that may possibly result from being exposed to other job stressors. On the other hand, Rutenfranz and Knauth (1986) discuss the possibility that the negative effects of shiftwork are not only caused by the phase differences between circadian rhythms and working/living conditions but also by the adverse working conditions combined with shiftwork. We tried to address these questions. As yet, however, no definitive answers can be given. Evidence is accumulating from various sources that night shiftworking is at least associated with future problems of well-being and health, independent of other factors. In this sense, night shiftworking may be considered a risk factor.

Prevention and Interventions

A distinction can be made between two general models of compensating for the disadvantageous aspects of working in shifts or at irregular hours (Thierry, 1980, 1981; Thierry & Jansen, 1981): counterweight versus counter-value models.

In *counterweight* models, disadvantageous aspects are compensated for by some global measure. Generally, it is assumed that the shift bonus compensates for these aspects. The discomfort and negative characteristics related to shiftwork are in a sense translated into monetary terms. Supplying more money usually causes an increase in the package of advantages, although its meaning is dependent on both the actual income position of the employee and his or her pattern of motivation (Lawler, 1971; Thierry, 1992; Thierry & de Jong, 1991). The shiftwork bonus may weigh against a certain amount of dissatisfaction with the shiftwork situation in general. It reflects a recognized and often welcomed strategy of summarizing a complex and multidimensional problem. But in doing so, it also tends to reduce the problem to a sheer matter of money, and thus it may even conceal the real problem and tend to sustain the status quo.

In addition to this simple counterweight model, increasing importance is being given to other potential compensatory variables. On the one hand, the potential value of having a shorter average workweek has been emphasized, for instance, by the introduction of a five-shift system or of longer vacations. On the other hand, the humanization of the workplace is also being advocated. Such a more extended model may be considered a more fruitful approach to the problem than the similar counterweight model or the mere provision of a bonus. But the extended counterweight model is also still very general. It may be questioned whether a specific inducement, such as job autonomy or a decrease of the average weekly working time, reduces or even eliminates a specific inconvenient aspect of shiftwork, such as having a broken evening or working at night.

The concept of compensation as outlined in the two preceding models has been characterized as counterweighting—that is, as operating on the general level on which the overall costs and benefits relating to a job are weighed against each other. Providing more weight to the benefits may lead to less dissatisfaction. But the costs or the specific inconveniences remain unchanged. An approach to compensation that attempts to reduce or eliminate the actual inconveniences may be more effective. Such an approach focuses on specific subbalances and not on the global balance of costs and benefits. To reflect its potential capacity to reduce or even eliminate a specific negative effect, it is called the *countervalue* model, which acts by means of specific interventions with respect to specific inconveniences. In order to acquire countervalue properties, each intervention or deliberately induced change should fulfill two requirements. First, it ought to produce positive effects that belong to the same category or lie on the same denominator as the perceived and/or experienced unfavorable aspects of the shiftwork in question. Second, its effects should be rewarding in relation to the motives and situational outcomes the workers view as important.

Clearly, the construction of each intervention in the countervalue model requires extensive analysis and careful planning. Three types of countervalue interventions can be distinguished, each of which operates at a different level of analysis. These interventions have a certain hierarchical order: Type I is more encompassing than type II, while type II may be more encompassing than type III. Type I interventions pertain to the elimination or reduction of the causes or inconveniences. An example would be changing a shiftwork scheme to be less progressive by reducing the number of consecutive night shifts. Other interventions of this type might involve changes in the shift rotation system, in the length of each shift, or in the changeover times. Assuming that some type I interventions can

be introduced in an organization and that they do provide countervalue compensation, in most cases, several inconveniences that have not been tapped will remain. This is the point at which the applicability of type II interventions should be considered. Type II interventions pertain to the reduction or elimination of the consequences of inconveniences. If the causes of inconveniences cannot be removed for the time being, then at least an attempt should be made to provide compensation for their effects. For example, shiftworkers may be unable to regularly attend on-the-job training courses or organizational meetings if they are scheduled during the day. Thus, to compensate for this negative effect, it would be necessary to duplicate, or even triplicate, such events at times that are convenient for shiftworkers: during the evening or even at night.

Assuming that type I and type II interventions have been seriously considered and whenever possible implemented, there may still remain several inconveniences that could not be eliminated. It would then, and only then, be time to consider the third type of interventions. These type III interventions pertain to the compensation for the psychological meaning of inconveniences. The following would be an example. The still-existing inconveniences, regardless of their causes and effects, may be experienced by the shiftworker as a loss of status. Then an intervention that may provide countervalue compensation should result in a gain of status.

In conclusion, the model of countervalue compensation seems to offer a different and more specific approach than counterweight compensation for attempting to improve the living and working situation of shiftworkers (e.g., Jansen, 1987b; Jansen et al., 1986). Such an approach presupposes careful analysis and flexibility in organizational potential. On the other hand, it must be stressed that some form of counterweight compensations cannot be completely dispensed with. Thus, although major contributions toward the goal of optimally designed shiftwork situations may be made via the concept of countervalue compensation, additional compensation, such as a shiftwork bonus or reduction of working hours, may still be needed.

Recommendations

The knowledge on the differential inconveniences of various shift schedules may be summarized in a list of interventions that may have countervalue properties. Table 6 provides such an overview, based on the recommendations in the relevant literature (Jansen, 1987b; Knauth & Rutenfranz, 1982; Meijman, de Vries-Griever, & Kampman, 1989). The interventions are organized according to the various schedule characteristics used in the RRPA, which were mentioned earlier. They should be considered recommendations, not fixed prescriptions. It is impossible to follow them all in one schedule. Some of them are even in conflict with one another. In practice, one should strive for an optimal schedule, following the recommendations given in Table 6.

Individual workers may react quite differently to the objective burden of shiftwork, depending on individual and situational differences. It has been established that it is best for people suffering from certain diseases or chronic health impairments not to work in shifts or irregular working hours (Rutenfranz et al., 1981). Shiftwork is not recommended for the following groups for the reasons described:

- People with a history of digestive tract disorders, since shiftwork produces special physiological problems and involves having meals at unusual times, both of which may affect gastric functions

- People with a history of cardiovascular problems, since epidemiological evidence suggests that shiftwork may be related to cardiovascular disease and its traditional risk factors

- Diabetics and thyrotoxicosics, since food intake and correct therapeutic timing can be difficult to maintain under shiftwork conditions

- Epileptics, since the reduction of sleep and the irregularity of sleeping and waking associated with shiftwork may increase the incidence of epileptic seizures

Medical examinations before an employee begins doing shiftwork are necessary. They do, however, have very limited value in predicting future absences due to illness and health problems. Therefore, it is recommended that employers periodically—once every four or five years—monitor the health of shiftworkers by means of a careful and thorough medical examination.

Although some personality and physiological differences have been detected in the way people adapt to changes of diurnal rhythms, it is extremely difficult to use this information for standard selection purposes. Most of the knowledge on interindividual differences stems from cross-sectional correlational studies on a population level. Carefully planned prospective cohort studies are still lacking. As a consequence, there are no firm data on the predictive power of the relevant measures that may justify their standard use in individual selection and guidance. On the other hand, extreme "morning-types," extreme neurotics, and people who highly value rigid living patterns should be discouraged from working in shifts or at irregular hours.

With respect to age, some guidelines are generally accepted. Beginning shiftwork after the age of 35 should be discouraged for workers who do not have any former, and successful, experience in shiftwork. After the age of 45, shiftworkers are at risk, particularly with respect to sleeping problems and overfatigue

TABLE 6

Countervalue Interventions and Recommendations for Optimal Design of Work Schedules

	Arrangement		
Viewpoint	*Day Work*	*Shiftwork Without Night Work*	*Shiftwork With Night Work*
Scheduling			
Regularity	Equal amount of working hours per week		
	Scheduling of working hours on the same days of the week		
	Regular shift periods in the schedule (begin and end shifts at the same times)		
Periodicity		Schedule working hours between 8:00 A.M. and 9:00 P.M.	
			At least 3 days off after (4 max) night shift period
Rotation		Moderate speed of rotation (2–4 shifts in succession)	
		Forward rotation	Night shift not first in the cycle
		Schedule transfer time or change overtime between consecutive shifts (i.e., a short overlap of consecutive shifts)	
Work load			
Work load per shift	Length of shift between 4 and 8 hours		
	Minimize combined load		
	Pauses	Lunch pause in the middle of shift at least 30 minutes Coffee and tea breaks 15 minutes In case of heavy physical and/or mental load, regularly scheduled breaks of 5 to 10 minutes	
			Possibility to reduce working time of nightshift (6 hours)
			Facilities for naps during night shift
Work load weekly	Working hours 10 hours maximum	36 hours maximum at least 12 hours free between consecutive shifts	33.6 hours (thus at least 5 crew system)
	Possibility of at least 3 consecutive weeks' vacation and at least 10 days off scheduled by the worker		

TABLE 6

**Countervalue Interventions and Recommendations
for Optimal Design of Work Schedules (continued)**

Viewpoint	*Arrangement*		
	Day Work	*Shiftwork Without Night Work*	*Shiftwork With Night Work*
Recovery and sleep			
Night rest		Optimizing the system in order to schedule sleeping time between 1:00 P.M. and 7:00 A.M. (i.e., morning shift not starting before 7:00 A.M., evening shift not ending after 11:00 P.M.)	
Regularity of night rest		Moderate speed of rotation	
Family and social activities			
Predictability	Simple schemes of working times	Short cycle length (maximum 12 weeks)	
Opportunity for home work	Scheduling of working hours in such a way that at least 25% of the home work and family duties between 9:00 A.M. and 9:00 P.M. can be performed outside the working time		
Constancy of home duty time	Scheduling of working times in such a way that each day contains 2 hours between 9:00 A.M. and 6:00 P.M. for home work duties		
Evening leisure time		Scheduling of working time in such a way that at least 70% of evenings have no work duties	
		Moderate rotation speed in order to guarantee regular evening leisure	
Weekend leisure time		Scheduling of working time in such a way that at least 40% of the weekend days are free	
		Regularity in scheduling of full weekends off (Friday 6:00 P.M. to Monday 7:00 A.M.) during the year	

during night shift periods, due to a decreased adaptability to circadian changes and to a diminished capacity to sleep sufficiently during the day. Special schedules are recommended for these workers. Such schedules may encompass a reduced number of consecutive night shifts, a reduction of the night shift length, the scheduling of more recuperation days between shifts, and less frequent day–night schedule changes. After the age of 55 the transfer to day work should be seriously considered. Because such a transfer may result in specific problems with respect to an income loss and probable qualifications deficiencies, provisional measures that may help overcome such problems and provide a career guidance policy for the older shiftworkers—those over age 45—are strongly recommended.

As the literature reports on phenomena such as night shift paralysis (Folkard et al., 1984; Folkard & Condon, 1987), short sleeping periods and lapses of wakefulness during the night shift (Torsvall & Akerstedt, 1989), reduced alertness around 4:00 A.M. in relation to the number of preceding working hours (Andlauer, Rutenfranz, Kogi, Thierry, Vieux, & Duverneil, 1982; Hildenbrandt et al., 1974), the established association of performance reduction during the night shift with an increased risk of accidents (Harris, 1977; Mitler et al., 1988), shiftwork jobs that have high safety risks deserve special attention. Physical exercise, particularly in sedentary watchkeeping jobs, is recommended (Härmä, Ilmarinen, Knauth, Rutenfranz, & Hänninen, 1988), as may be the reduction of the length of the night shift. Although the evidence is still scarce and somewhat conflicting, the scheduling of opportunities for a short sleep, or naps, during the shift may also have beneficial effects (Dinges, Whitehouse, Orne, & Orne, 1988; Minors & Waterhouse, 1987; Sakai & Kogi, 1986).

It is often recommended that passengers and aircrew personnel on transmeridian flights engage as soon as possible in the social activities of the time zone they have arrived in, and forget about the time-regulators or *zeitgebers* of the previous zone. This will be beneficial in overcoming the diurnal change or in adjusting to the new rhythms. This will be the case when individuals are supposed to stay for an extended period in the new time zone. When they will return to the previous time zone within 24 to 48 hours, however, it is best that they adhere as much as possible to the regime of the time zone they will return to. Obviously, such behavior will put them in conflict with the rhythms of the new time zone. Shiftworkers are regularly confronted with this conflict. Being active at night and sleeping during part of the day would be much easier if they were not confronted with *zeitgebers* from the rest of the society that regulate inverse rhythms. Moreover, as recent research indicates (Czeisler, Johnson, Duffy, Brown, Ronda, & Kronauer, 1990; Daan & Lewy, 1984; Minors & Waterhouse, 1990), light is a more powerful entrainer of circadian rhythms than was once thought to be the case (Aschoff, 1978). Although the practical problems seem very great, it may be beneficial in the adaptation to diurnal changes for night work sites to be provided with bright light (over 2,500 lux) and for more attention to be given to maintaining the sleeping rooms of night shiftworkers so that they remain dark and isolated from noise.

Shiftworkers consider the disturbances to their social life and other aspects of their work far more serious than the impairments to health and well-being. In fact, they tend to underestimate slight impairments of health and well-being (Agervold, 1976; Akerstedt et al., 1977; Andersen, 1970; Colligan et al., 1979; Tasto et al., 1978), labeling them an "inevitable part of the job." In addition to the possible implications for the assessment of health problems and absenteeism due to sickness, other consequences should be mentioned. They may be relevant for the success of interventions.

Justifying interventions solely by arguments of promoting health and well-being may be somewhat suspect in the eyes of shiftworkers. It makes an intervention vulnerable to failure. The success of an intervention is strengthened by other factors. Although authors and readers of literature reviews on the timing aspects of work behavior may have the impression that these issues are primarily the concern of the worker, this impression is wrong. Workers value the "security of their working place," "the payment," "the social contacts at work," "an understanding and cooperative supervisor," and "interesting work" more than the "working times" (Ott, 1987). Interventions aimed at improving a specific shift schedule run a high risk of failure when their possible negative side effects on other aspects of the working situation are ignored or insufficiently attended to. For example, in a project on the redesign of a shift schedule in which both authors were engaged, one of the experimental departments resigned from the experiment during the project. The reason was that the employees felt that the proposed changes endangered their autonomy in exchanging their individual schedules. The employees, working at the passenger check-in desk of a large airline company, valued this autonomy for a variety of reasons. A considerable part of this flexibility enabled them to attend educational college courses outside of their work, and they valued the flexibility of being able to exchange their work schedules with others for this reason. Others valued the autonomy that enabled them to profit from "last-minute flights," or "empty seats on interesting flights." Hence, the various subgroups of employees were, for a variety of reasons, opposed to every redesign of their schedules that might endanger these kinds of individual objectives. Despite the good intentions of the researchers and their sound proposals for the improvement of the existing schedule for the purpose of promoting health and well-being,

the intervention had to be canceled due to massive employee resistance.

There is hardly any well-documented report in the literature on such failures, or on projects that in the end bring about quite different outcomes than were foreseen by the researchers. The literature on shiftwork and irregular working hours is characterized more by reports on "fact finding on scientifically relevant relations between variables," and less by reports on experimentation with alternative schedules in field settings, which may provide systematic knowledge on the do's and don'ts in the practice of design and redesign of schedules.

Flexible Working Time Arrangements

In this part, various flexible working time arrangements will be reviewed: flextime, a compressed workday and workweek, and part-time, overtime, and temporary employment. Characteristic to these arrangements is, as was mentioned in the chapter's introduction, that flexible WTA's are expected to accommodate the flexibility needs of both companies and categories of employees. Also, the operating time of a company usually exceeds employees' average working time. We will first give a brief description of the WTA. Then, major arguments for its adoption will be discussed, subsequent to which research data will be presented. Finally, some vital research needs will be identified.

Flextime

Design.   Other terms to identify these working arrangements are *flexible working hours*—a rather unfortunate term, since the very category of this kind of working arrangement is named *flexible* or *flextime*. The flexibility in this WTA refers to the options employees have regarding the times they begin and end their workday. Figure 7 shows two examples of flexible WTA's.

The outer circle of each clock in the figure indicates 0:00 to 12:00 A.M. hours; the inner circle indicates 12:00 to 0:00 P.M. hours. Both examples are based on an eight-hour workday with at least a half-hour lunch break.

In type I of Figure 7, it is left to the employees' discretion when to start working between 7:00 and 9:00 A.M. Core time, when all personnel are expected to be present at work, extends from 9:00 A.M. to 3:00 P.M., including the fixed lunch break. It is, again, optional at which time employees leave their workplace between 3:00 P.M. and 5:00 P.M. In this example, the company's operating time totals 11 hours.

A quite different arrangement is shown in type II of Figure 7. Core times extend from 8:30 A.M. to 12:00 A.M. and from 2:30 P.M. to 4:30 P.M. In addition to optional hours from 6:30 A.M. to 8:30 A.M. and from 4:30 P.M. to 6.:00 P.M., the time for taking a lunch break between noon and 2:30 P.M. is at the employees' discretion. Company operating hours now amount to 11.5 hours.

Obviously, the main technical benefit of the flextime system is that it offers employees the opportunity to choose the "location" of the working time during the day within some boundary conditions. Arrangements in which successive start times, lunch breaks, and leave times are predetermined for all categories of employees are called *staggered hours*. These are designed to cope with things such as parking spaces, elevator space, and cafeteria or lunchroom capacity at the company's facilities, but do not lend themselves to employee discretion.

Of course, many variations of both schedules are possible. Type I schedules may be found in commercial service departments, or in companies in which the production process requires considerable start-up time as well as careful, detailed coordination of the contributions of various craftspeople. In such a case,

time options may not be individualized, but may apply to units of mutually interdependent employees. Type II schedules may be relevant to organizations with sizable desk-service activities; for example, clients' needs intake occurs during the morning, and their handling takes place in the afternoon.

Flextime may also apply to part-time workers. An interesting case is provided by a large supermarket in which the number of cashiers required varies by hour and by day of the week (Perret, 1980). Every two weeks the manager specifies the number of registers that must be opened, after which small groups of cashiers indicate their work schedule preferences to an elected coordinator. Perret also mentions an experiment in a hospital in which each nurse's task was analyzed in components that were bound to fixed times and components that could be accomplished at varying times. Consequently, obligatory attendance—which we called core time earlier—could be reduced.

In some cases, employees are not allowed to work less or more hours per day than is agreed by contract (e.g., 8 hours). In others, a minimum and a maximum amount of daily working hours is specified, and in still other arrangements, these amounts—in excess of core time—are specified for a week, a month, a three-month period, or even a year. The latter examples result in a work credit–debit system, which is often recorded through a system of time clocks (Cohen & Gadon, 1978; Fleuter, 1975; Robison, 1976; Ronen, 1981; Thierry & Jansen, 1984). This implies that whenever too many or too few hours are worked, adjustments must be made. Introducing a credit–debit system provides employees with the discretion of how many hours they will work per day, in addition to the choice of time they will begin and end their workday. It thus increases the rate of flexibility, such as would be beneficial in a large firm of consultancy accountants. In this

FIGURE 7

Two Examples of Flextime

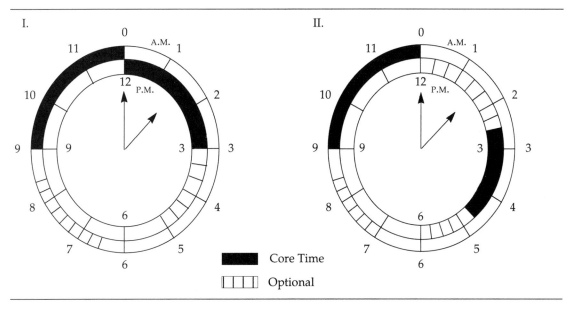

example, because firms' annual reports must be prepared for their shareholders, the accountants are expected to work more hours in the first part of the year and to balance this with fewer hours during the quieter fall. One may, however, question the extent of free choice that is available to each accountant in this example.

Main Arguments. Flextime was probably first introduced in 1967 in the German enterprise Messerschmidt-Bölkow-Blohm. However, Maric (1977) is of the opinion that a Swiss company preceded it. It is hard to estimate the spread of flextime in the EC. A rough guess would be that some 10 percent of the work force in various countries and up to about 40 percent in a few others use flextime. Presumably, the variation across sectors within each country is pretty sizable. In the late 1980s around 5 million U.S. employees were

subject to flextime (Ralston, 1989). According to the survey by Tepas (1985) among U.S. labor organizations around 1980, government organizations apply flextime to a greater extent than manufacturing firms. Both EC and U.S. figures may underestimate actual rates considerably, as Tepas rightly states. Quite a number of categories of workers, such as farmers, self-employed business professionals, and university professors, are accustomed to setting their own schedules to some extent.

Predominantly, flextime is advocated in order to provide the employee with options. Having some discretion on the location of daily working time allows the employee to care better for children, to work undisturbed (with fewer phone calls), and to commute at times other than general rush hours. It provides for more career opportunities for women, a better use of leisure time, more opportunities to learn new skills (when colleagues have to be substituted), and it is said to result in increased motivation and a better quality of working life (International Labour Office, 1978; Robison, 1976; Ronen, 1981; Sloane, 1975; Tepas, 1985). Benefits for the company relate to increased adaptability to market fluctuations (Lendfers & Nijhuis, 1989), less absenteeism, turnover, traffic accidents, tardiness, and overtime, better recruitment, and improved morale. However, more managerial coordination is needed, and increased energy costs may offset the gains of the greater number of operating hours. Moreover, Cohen and Gadon (1978) and Ronen (1981) question the benefits that are assumed to exist for employees. Many employees adjust their start and leave times just once. Let us now consider whether research data support the claims made.

Research Outcomes.   Unfortunately, there are not more than a few qualified research studies in this area. Ralston, Anthony, and Gustafson (1985) evaluated 100 studies on flextime in the period 1965 to 1985 in terms of four criteria. According to these, studies should have used direct productivity measures, a pre- and post-test design, an experimental as well as a control group, and appropriate methods of data analysis.

Consistent with Golembiewsky and Proehl's earlier review (1978), a very small minority of research met the criteria. One of the issues addressed repeatedly in the research is whether flextime affects productivity. Schein, Maurer, and Novah (1977) found two out of five clerical production units that showed increases; the other three witnessed no changes (see also Kim & Campagna, 1981). Managers objecting to the introduction of flextime for their employees appraised a four-month experiment in rather positive terms and felt that employees' productivity had increased (Schein, Maurer, & Novah, 1978). Actually, they were mistaken in this respect. Records kept by the researchers showed no change in productivity.

Ralston et al. (1985) predicted that only when employees face scarce resources—for example, computer programmers accessing the mainframe—will flextime cause an increase in productivity. Their prediction proved to be right, in particular, in the long run (12–18 months after the implementation of flextime). Various other studies show no change in productivity (e.g., Orpen, 1981).

Some research focuses on satisfaction and attitudes related to working time. Schein et al. (1978) report that managers of flextime employees reacted quite favorably. Two field experiments showed an increase in employee job satisfaction after the introduction of flextime (Orpen, 1981; Ralston, 1989). Some other studies have provided mixed results (e.g., Hicks & Klimoski, 1981; Narayanan & Nath, 1982). Ralston's data also reveal less tardiness, easier coordination of on- and off-the-job responsibilities, and more ease in commuting. No differences were observed in the use of leave time and in employer–employee relations. Absenteeism is found to decrease in some studies (Dalton & Mesch, 1990; Golembiewsky, Hillies, & Kagno, 1974; Harrick, Vanek, & Micklitsch, 1986; Krausz & Freibach, 1983; Narayanan & Nath, 1982; Pierce & Newstrom, 1983), but not in others (Kim & Campagna, 1981). A few studies even report an increase (McGuire & Liro, 1987). Turnover is usually unaffected (Dalton & Mesch, 1990). Krausz and Hermann (1991) report an interesting outcome of a study in an Israeli government unit. Employees opted more for flextime to the extent that their growth need was stronger. Apparently, flextime is appraised in terms of getting supplemental rewards, according to the authors, and not as a way to better solve existing problems. The use of flextime, as these and other authors point out, may thus contribute to experiencing more workers' autonomy.

Figure 8, which is derived from Figure 2, summarizes the main variables addressed in the studies reviewed. Variables that received the most interest are double boxed.

FIGURE 8

Research on Flextime: Scope of Variables

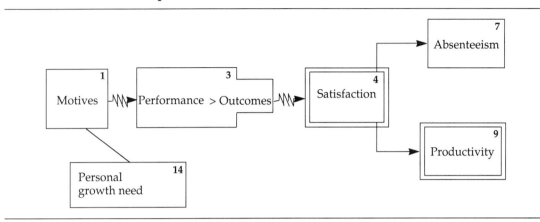

As you may recall, Figure 2 addresses main variables of interest regarding determinants and effects of all sorts of WTA's. Much more than the small amount of existing studies does, Figure 8 illustrates the narrow scope of available research on flextime. In terms of the perspectives outlined in the chapter's introduction, flextime is apparently considered to be a factor additional to a usual WTA. Consequently, rather obvious questions for research have been dealt with, such as:

- Does it affect performance or productivity?

- Is it appreciated by employees and their superiors?

- Does it have an impact on attendance?

Also, most research is exploratory in nature; that is, it is not theory-driven, but is primarily descriptive. Thus, research data are hard to interpret: What does it mean to say that performance (or satisfaction or absenteeism) is or is not affected? Moreover, most studies have been done in government settings, impeding generalization to other settings. Most surprising, important objectives such as organizational flexibility, individual discretion, and system adaptability have been left out of consideration almost completely. The list below identifies some vital issues to be addressed in future research.

- There is a strong need to map flextime consistently as an independent variable. Arrangements pertaining to choosing when to begin and end the workday have effects that are probably quite different from those created when workers are allowed to choose their number of daily working hours.

- When the time to begin work is very early (e.g., 6:30 A.M. or earlier) and the time to end it is rather late (e.g., 11:00 P.M. or later), research ought to address various circadian rhythms, fatigue levels, sleep quality, and so on. This rhythmic perspective is needed more as a debit–credit system is applied in order to regulate the number of working hours over a longer period. For periods of weeks or even months, there may be excessive amounts of working hours required. In the long term, this may deplete resources, build up fatigue, increase stress levels, and subsequently affect performance and leisure time pursuits.[1]

- Flextime may have an influence on non-working time, depending both on its time during the day and the nature of activities involved. Thus, flextime may have an additional, indirect effect on such things as satisfaction, health, and well-being.

- Finally, as the Ralston et al. study (1985) shows, it is recommended that task characteristics should be con sidered in future research. Also, organizational control systems, biological and demographical variables, and coping strategies should be systematically assessed as moderating variables. This perspective should also determine whether internal and external organizational adaptation is affected at all by applying flextime.

Compressed Workday and Workweek

Design. This arrangement is characterized by the fact first that the number of working hours per workday is more than usual, varying, say, between nine and twelve hours. Therefore, there are fewer days worked per workweek than is customary: In the case of a full-time contract it ranges from three (e.g., three 12-hour days) to four (e.g., four 9.5 hour days per week). In some cases, more days are worked, consecutively followed by a greater number of days off. For part-time employees,

the schedule may consist of a total of two weekly working days. Also, mixed forms of this kind of arrangement are possible, in which employees work, for example, for 11 hours for three days for a period of several weeks, and then alternate by working four days during other weeks.

These examples apply to compressed schedules in which work is exclusively performed during the day, and the employees' period of free time always includes the weekend. Other applications, however, place working hours during the late evening or the night, oftentimes including the weekend (Maric, 1977). Particularly in Canada and the United States, the petrochemical and chemical industries use the EOWO schedule—"every other weekend off" (Northrup, Wilson, & Rose, 1979). This usually refers to a 12-hour shift system in which free and working weekends alternate each week. In some cases, the compressed WTA only applies to the weekend, while the eight-hour shift length prevails during the other working days. In the United Kingdom, the compressed schedule is also found within the framework of the widely used two-shift system. This so-called alternating day and night shift system operates one long watch (e.g., 10 hours) during the day and another, after a break or rest period, during the night (Sloane, 1975; Walker, 1978). Since the latter cases qualify as examples of shiftwork, we will focus on the compressed daytime schedule. The concept of flexibility in this kind of arrangement refers primarily to the opportunity for the company to increase its operating time without implementing a system of shiftwork, and adjust the number of employees on the job to the fluctuating market demands. Table 7 illustrates a typical compressed WTA.

In this example the facility, which is in the retail sector, operates six days a week, 10 hours per day. Apparently, there is less business on Monday and Thursday than on the other days. Groups 1 and 2 work on four successive

---

[1] Tentative data in ongoing research show that employees of different Dutch companies consider the number of successive shifts—for example, seven consecutive afternoon shifts prior to a rest period—as the most incisive inconvenient factor (Van Limborgh, University of Amsterdam).

TABLE 7

Example of a Typical Compressed Schedule

	Mon.	Tue.	Wed.	Thurs.	Fri.	Sat.
Group 1	x	x	x	x	—	—
Group 2	—	—	x	x	x	x
Group 3	x	x	—	—	x	x
Group 4	—	x	x	—	x	x

workdays; groups 3 and 4 work two sets of two days each. Consequently, the amount of free time is distributed differently. The first two groups enjoy three successive days off, the third group has two days off in the middle of the week plus a free Sunday, while the fourth group has one day off on Thursday and a "delayed weekend" (Sunday and Monday). Obviously, a host of variations to this model is possible.

The rate of application of the compressed schedule is not very well known. In the early 1970s it was advocated in the United States as an example of managerial innovation. Tepas (1985) points out, however, that this WTA dates back to the 1940s (if not earlier), but was not then termed compressed. Maric (1977) is of the opinion that first applications were found in the early 1960s in the United Kingdom and West Germany. Based on a few surveys, it is probably safe to estimate that around 2 percent of the American work force is subject to the compressed workweek, and around 1.5 percent are in various European countries (Cohen & Gadon, 1978; Nollen, 1979; Northrup et al., 1979; Tepas, 1985; Wheeler, Gurman, & Tarnowieski, 1972). According to Colligan and Tepas (1985), the compressed workweek prevails in the government and utility sector, in the construction and health industries, and the services sector.

Main Arguments. A compressed schedule allows a company to extend its operating time and, consequently, to provide more service and to make better use of costly equipment. Also, personnel may be employed at hours that better match fluctuating market demands (as with retail customers, clients seeking help, and peripheral stations transmitting information on financial transactions at particular times of the day to the mainframe for further processing). This may go together with a decrease in the average amount of working time for employees, as experience in several European countries in recent years has shown.

Employees may profit from more consecutive free days: Opportunities arise for more leisure time, for additional education and training, and also for a better recovery from fatigue caused by work (Colligan & Tepas, 1986; Meijman, 1992). However, this WTA facilitates some to take a second job, the consequence of which may be an increase of fatigue.

We will again look at major research outcomes in order to find out whether the preceding arguments have been dealt with in most studies.

Research Outcomes. In mere quantitative terms, research is rather scarce. A first concern is the extent to which compressed schedules affect productivity. Ivancevich (1974; Ivancevich & Lyon, 1977) compared two groups of equal size in a food company. The experimental group worked four days, 10 hours per day, while the control group worked five days, eight hours per day. Repeated measurements done over a 13-month period show that employees with a 4 x 10 schedule performed better and were more satisfied than their colleagues who worked a 5 x 8 schedule. Interestingly, a follow-up study points out that these effects virtually disappeared after 25 months. A second experimental group, installed during the follow-up study, also manifested similar short-term effects. Foster, Latack, and Reindle

(1979) studied computer operators, one group of which changed to a three day, 38 hour per week schedule, while another group maintained the five day, 40 hour per week pattern. The first group manifested a higher productivity, and more satisfaction with the WTA, than the second group. However, this design prevents attributing these effects unequivocally to a particular WTA characteristic. In a county health department, Dunham, Pierce, and Castaneda (1987) studied a group of nurses, health technicians, and clerical personnel that changed from a five day, 40 hour per week schedule to a four day, 40 hour per week pattern. After operating on the new schedule for four months, the employees returned to their former routine. Measures were also taken from a control group. Data show that changing toward the compressed schedule improved one (client service) out of seven effectiveness indices, while five indices tended to point in this direction. After having returned to the five day, 40 hour per week routine, six indices showed a decline.

Various other studies also report mixed evidence (summarized in Dunham et al., 1987; Lendfers & Nijhuis, 1989; Thierry & Jansen, 1984). It is important, though, to clearly differentiate between quantity and quality of performance (Meijman, 1992). Many research data are available regarding the relationship between performance quantity and the number of hours worked, although hardly any study actually deals with compressed schedules in practice. In the case of manual labor (Ray, Martin, & Alluisi, 1961), performance decline increases sizably after 8 to 8.5 working hours. Likewise, an incisive decline in performance is observable after four days of working 8.5 hours. The more complex the task, the sooner performance quantity decreases.

Quality of performance is often more relevant to tasks than sheer quantity. Respondents usually deal in a very strategic way with this so-called *speed/accuracy trade-off* (Meijman, 1992), as many studies have demonstrated. People expecting a task to take a long time to accomplish decrease the tradeoff soon after they start working (Craig, 1988). But if it is expected that the task will soon be completed, then they maintain a higher tradeoff level. Such strategies reflect how human beings cope with increasing fatigue, contingent upon task conditions (e.g., extent of autonomy) and task goals. Evidence shows that performance quality decreases considerably when more than 7 to 8 hours are worked (Rosa & Colligan, 1988). This decrease is more apparent on the fourth and the fifth consecutive working days. Again, such data hardly stem from research in which the effects of compressed schedules in practice were analyzed. With regard to fatigue, data are slightly ambiguous. Volle, Brisson, Perusse, Tanaka, and Doyon (1979) report hardly any difference between employees in a compressed schedule and members of a control group. A few other studies (Latack & Foster, 1985) provide similar results. Pierce and Dunham (1992) found less fatigue complaints among police officers after they moved toward a schedule of four 12-hour days; however, this study had no control condition. But some research points out that employees do voice fatigue complaints (Meijman, 1992). Yet Lendfers and Nijhuis (1989) and Tepas (1990) state rightly that increased fatigue levels per se are not very indicative. The point is whether they affect performance, health, or well-being. A matter of concern, moreover, is the extent to which fatigue may build up during successive long working days.

In passing, we already mentioned data on attitudes that were rather positive regarding a compressed schedule (Pierce & Dunham, 1992). Breaugh (1983) reports 12-hour schedules being evaluated positively by employees in terms of such things as family life, sleep–wake routine, use of drugs, and commuting. Various studies show that the more employees have gained experience with a compressed system, the more positive their attitudes are for them (Breaugh, 1983; Dunham et al., 1987; Foster et al., 1979; Hodge & Tellier, 1975). This is even more so the case when Monday and Friday are the days off (making a very long weekend), although this has made it difficult for some employees to return to their work (Sloane, 1975). Also, younger single workers appreciate this WTA schedule. Yet one must keep in mind Tepas' data on American employees (Tepas, 1990; see Figure 3). He related their actual amount of daily working hours (8; alternating 8 and 12; 12) to their preferences. The vast majority preferred the eight-hour workday—more so when they actually worked for eight hours. Negative attitudes about this schedule are directed at the length of a working day, the interference with activities at night as well as with family, and the combination of a long working day with childcare responsibilities. Lendfers and Nijhuis (1989) make an interesting point in stating that positive attitudes may be interpreted in terms of escape: Employees in routine jobs are exposed to their work for fewer days and/or make better use of their free time. In other cases, compressed schedules are applied in connection with job enrichment (Ronen & Primps, 1981). Favorable attitudes might relate to the changes in job content. Also, more consecutive free days are said to increase the employee's control of time.

Evidence on employees' tardiness, absenteeism, and turnover is mixed. Traffic congestion is reduced; the availability of public transportation may be less, however, outside of peak rush hours. Some studies report an increased organizational need for coordination of interdependent work processes.

This review reveals quite a few open questions. This is, to some extent, highlighted in Figure 9, which summarizes variables addressed.

In comparison with research on flextime, there are slightly more longitudinal data available on compressed schedules, while a few studies were designed to test particular hypotheses. But the majority is of a descriptive nature, touching on rather obvious, if not superficial, issues. This apparently reflects a more general point of view: The compressed workday and workweek are considered factors additional to the usual daytime pattern of work. Another remarkable point is that available data do not allow us to assess the effectiveness of compressed schedules in terms of the main arguments that were made for their inception. It was argued that the compressed work schedule would allow more flexibility in time arrangements in order to better adapt the company to fluctuating market demands, and make a more rewarding use of employees' free time.

This suggests a series of questions that should be addressed in future research. Yet we think that a few others are even more important.

Available evidence is not yet fully adequate to provide guidelines for an optimal length of the workday and for an acceptable amount of consecutive workdays within a week, although quite a bit of data do exist. But one of the most complex issues is the differential impact on various task dimensions. First, simple tasks affect performance over time—successive hours as well as consecutive days—in quite different ways than complex tasks do. Quantity of performance is a quite different dimension compared to various quality dimensions. Second, conditions and targets of work—such as required speed, quality specifications, method of working, rate of autonomy, and extent of disturbance—are important. Third, some work is performed in potentially unhealthy environmental conditions. Thus, maximum exposure time to chemical or physical substances should be observed, including safety at work as a more general issue. Fourth, all preceding variables may affect circadian rhythms as well as various states, such as fatigue, the more so as work is done for a longer period. All this condenses in stressing, on the one hand, that task characteristics should be considered at least as important contingent variables in future research. This should clarify

FIGURE 9

Research on Compressed Schedules: Scope of Variables

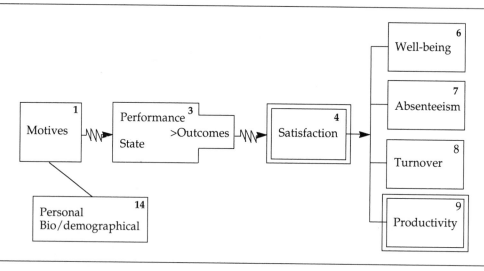

which kinds of tasks, and under which conditions, ought to be done for short periods of time, and which can be done for eight hours or more. The time of rest periods should be addressed as well. On the other hand, research ought to encompass various circadian rhythm variables.

This last subject—rhythmicity—may seem a bit foreign. How would it apply to schedules of 9 or 9.5 hours? A first point is that 10 to 12-hour schedules are also at stake. This may imply that work begins very early. It is well documented that all sorts of near accidents, and sometimes actual accidents, occur late at night and early in the morning. Also, workers usually sleep considerably less when they work early schedules. Second, consecutive workdays are involved, which also apply to 9 to 9.5-hour schedules. This may lead to a buildup of effects, each of which is perhaps minor when considered from the perspective of just one long day of work: less sleep, fatigue, slightly less

concentration, decreased mental alertness, some strain, and so on.

The idea that compressed schedules may be favored as an escape from work—or, on the contrary, as a component of enriched jobs—suggests that job satisfaction may be more fundamental than satisfaction with a WTA. Similarly, satisfaction with free and leisure time may have some independent effects.

Part-time Work

Design.   Part-time employees work on average less than 38 to 40 hours a week. But how much less? Considerably less, according to an often-quoted definition of the International Labour Organization of part-time work— "work voluntarily accepted and regularly performed in a number of working hours considerably smaller than usual." In the United States, this amounts to less than 35 hours per week (e.g., Feldman, 1990). Within the EC, some countries use the same yardstick (say, Ireland or the Netherlands), while others define a different upper limit (like 29 in Great Britain) or state a rather general rule in terms of it being fewer hours than is customary (Konle-Seidl, Ullmann, & Walwei, 1990). In most cases, this WTA is embedded in a collective labor agreement or an individual labor contract. But in others, part-time work is temporary, with usual labor conditions, such as social security and health care, not applying to it. Accordingly, some countries exclude employees who work less than about 15 hours per week from these provisions.

This is one of the few WTA's for which statistics are available. In the second part of the 1980s, around 15 percent of the EC's work force was employed part time (Commission of the European Communities, 1990; Konle-Seidl et al., 1990). Differences are great, however, ranging from 4 percent in Spain to around 24 percent in Great Britain and the Netherlands. In most countries, these numbers have been rising steadily since the early 1970s. According to Feldman (1990), around 20 percent of the American work force are part-time employees; this is twice as much as were in the mid-1950s (Kahne, 1985). Yet part-time work is unevenly distributed across categories of employees and industrial sectors. Both in the EC and in the United States, the majority of part-timers is female. Two-thirds of the American males in part-time jobs are under age 24 (many of whom are students) or over age 65 (retirees). Most part-time jobs are semiskilled or unskilled and can be found in the retail, banking, and service industries. Industrial firms employ part-time workers on a much smaller scale.

As was suggested already by the different amounts of work hours concerned, there is a great variety among part-time WTA's.

A first characteristic is the unit of time worked (de Koning, 1980):

- *Per day:* the number of working hours. The hours of work occurring during the day may be optional or fixed; the latter category can be found in cafeteria and cleaning jobs (Evans & Attew, 1986).

- *Per week:* the number of part-time workdays. Part-time contracts may include all days of the week (say, working three hours for seven days), a series of successive working days (e.g., Monday through Thursday), or a couple of half days worked throughout the week.

- *Per year:* the number of vacation days. An interesting example is given by Perret (1980). A large company in the clothes manufacturing industry is faced with seasonal peaks. When business activity is high, the amount of weekly work hours may total 45. One-quarter of each employee's credit hours are paid as overtime, while the remaining part is reserved for periods of slow activity. Then the company may close down for some days or operate just for a few hours a day.

- *Per working life:* there are not many examples of this arrangement in practice. It is advocated, though, as a system of individual "drawing rights" (Emmerij & Clobus, 1978; Maric, 1977). Every now and then an employee may opt for getting additional education and training, while working time may be reduced as the employee ages. Such a working life arrangement was practiced by Peugeot-Citroen in France: Credit points were awarded for low levels of absenteeism, working during the weekend, and working at night and in shifts. Whenever credit built up and was not spent within a particular age bracket— three of which were distinguished as < 35; 35–50; > 50—rights were doubled. However, this example is not typical for part-time work. Nonetheless, it is over time effectuated in a part-time schedule, the onset of which is primarily contingent on each employee's preference.

A second characteristic is affected by the organizational form (de Koning, 1980; Driehuis & de Vrije, 1981):

- *Split jobs:* A job is divided into two or more new part-time jobs. The main design principle is horizontal or vertical differentiation, such as production phase, skill level, and customer demand.

- *Twin jobs:* One job is performed by two part-time employees. The two are jointly responsible for all outcomes and often also for internal coordination processes.

- *Joint jobs:* Two employees work on one job, as with twin jobs, but each is only responsible for his or her part of the job.

- *Mini-shift:* Groups of part-time employees work in shifts for a short period of time. This occurs, for example, with seasonal peaks or when the amount of regular work temporarily exceeds the capacity of full-time employees.

- *Min-max:* Within terms of an agreement, a minimum number of working hours must be made within a certain time period, while excess hours are bound to a maximum within that period.

- *On call:* Whenever the employer needs it, work must be done. A pool of workers is available, usually through a hiring agency.

Main Arguments. The preceding overview of different part-time arrangements shows that part time is a bit of an umbrella term, more widely used since the early 1960s.

Accordingly, arguments to adopt this WTA are varied. Konle-Seidl et al. (1990) stress the issue of numerical flexibility: The employing organization is able, to a certain extent, to adjust its labor force to varying production requirements. These variations may be rather common and predictable, such as in the case of public transportation, the retail industry, and commercial services; or when seasonal ups and downs occur. But more often it is difficult for companies to decide whether increasing or decreasing customer demand is temporary or permanent. A second point concerning flexibility refers to the individual employee: Part-time work allows the employee to choose work hours that better meet private conditions and considerations (say, age of children or leisure pursuits; Kogi, 1991). In order to appreciate this argument, it is clearly important to be more specific. Min-max and on-call arrangements may allow employees just a marginal level of discretion. A twin job offers more discretional opportunities while an annual or even working life arrangement (regardless of its particular form) affords the employee much more autonomy.

Part-time arrangements are also advocated in order to employ people with a handicap that prevents them from working full time. More in general, the creation of more jobs in order to decrease the rate of unemployment has been one of the major arguments for part-time work in several countries. It is difficult, though, to provide unequivocal evidence that this can be accomplished. Economists state as a general rule that working a smaller number of hours tends to increase the productivity per employee per hour. Research data on quality and quantity of performance in relation to hours worked, summarized earlier, are not at variance with this statement. On a macro level, some estimates hold that the decrease in the average amount of working hours occurring in various European countries in the early 1960s resulted in some productivity improvement. More recent global evidence on part-time work in, for example, the retail and banking industries, suggests some 20 percent increase in productivity (Van Schilfgaarde, 1984). However, higher productivity may work against a sizable increase in jobs: To the extent that part-time employees are more effective performers, job increase is rather modest in the case the total amount of work to be done does not change. This is how White (1987) explains the relatively disappointing employment effects of recent working time reductions at large in several EC countries.

Moreover, part-time work may result in a disproportionate increase in costs due to benefits and social security premiums to be paid for additional workers (Driehuis & de Vrije, 1981). But capital costs may decrease as a consequence of more intensive use of expensive machinery and equipment. On the other hand, "moonlighting," usually done to supplement one's income (Feldman, 1990), makes the amount of jobs available for the unemployed smaller.

Another argument for part-time work is the emancipation of women. Over the years, the number of part-time female employees has increased sizably (de Koning, 1980; Konle-Seidl et al., 1990). Yet most part-time jobs require rather low skill levels and are not as well paying as full-time positions. Moreover, employees having to combine their work with childcare and household responsibilities may experience a relatively heavy burden. This is why the emancipatory character of part-time work is frequently criticized (Demenint-de Jong, 1989). A partly related issue is whether part-time work is always voluntarily engaged in, as the International Labour Organization suggests it should be. Konle-Seidl et al. (1990) provide results from a 1987 EC survey concerning the percentage of part-time employees who are not able to find full-time employment. These figures are generally much higher in countries with high unemployment rates. In Italy, some 45 percent of males working part-time and around 30 percent of females working part-time are not able to find full-time jobs, versus around 10 percent for both males and females in Denmark.

In this section we already mentioned some economic data as well as results from a few case studies. There are many more reports issued in various industrial sectors within several EC countries (Bosch, Eisendoorn, & Nijsen, 1988; Hegner & Kramer, 1988; Van Schilfgaarde, 1984). They often offer detailed insights, but they lack a basis in research. In the next section we will turn to what is available in behavioral science research.

Research Outcomes.   One of the subjects relatively frequently addressed is whether part- and full-time workers have different degrees of satisfaction with various aspects of their jobs. Obviously, this requires delicately matched samples and adequate data analysis techniques as well. Some studies do not allow the review of these requirements. Yet, although Miller and Terborg (1979) found part-timers to be less satisfied in various respects, and Eberhardt and Shani (1984) found them to be more satisfied, other studies show that there are hardly differences (Dijkstra, 1984; Logan, O'Reilly, & Roberts, 1973; regarding older employees, Steffy & Jones, 1990; see also Feldman, 1990). Most studies also reveal that satisfaction for full-timers encompasses more, and partly different, facets compared to part-timers (Lendfers & Nijhuis, 1989). Accordingly, part-timers do not use the frame of reference full-timers do and/or are less committed to their organization. This may lead to a lower level of expectation, which would explain why part-timers in lower status positions are often no less satisfied than their full-time colleagues.

Some studies report a slightly higher degree of perceived work load by part-time employees (Steffy & Jones, 1990) and more health complaints from employees who are 35 and older (Dijkstra, 1984) than full-timers have. Data on absenteeism and turnover are equivocal (Cohen & Gadon, 1978; Levitan & Belous, 1979).

Companies often argue that all sorts of higher line and staff jobs cannot be done on a part-time basis. Schoemaker, Van Gageldonk, Demenint, and Van Vianen (1981) and Demenint-de Jong (1989) selected jobs in a variety of Dutch companies that were assumed to be unsuitable for part-time positions. They made use of various methods to assemble data. Both studies show that each selected job lends itself in principle to be done on a part-time basis. This is not to say that part-time work is always a desirable or optimal strategy.

In one of the very few theoretical accounts on part-time work, Feldman (1990) pleads for unambiguously defining the independent variable. There are so many different part-time arrangements, while quite divergent demographic categories with different frames of reference are attracted to working part time, that these arrangements are probably theoretically distinct. In other words, they perhaps reinforce differentially. Thus, Feldman expects, for example, that employees with an annual voluntary part-time job that is their main employment will have more job satisfaction than other part-timers. Likewise, employees in temporary and seasonal arrangements will have less satisfaction with their pay, benefits, and work.

Figure 10 summarizes the variables addressed in the reviewed research on part-time WTA's.

Given the relatively widespread use of part-time arrangements, Figure 10 nonetheless shows that these have hardly been considered as relevant subjects for research. Part-time work is apparently viewed as a factor additional to the usual pattern, although the term subtractive actually fits better, and is not as an important a phenomenon in itself. We conclude this section by highlighting some issues for future research:

- We are unaware of statistics concerning part-time employment as a second or even a third job. Yet quite a few researchers, for example, in the area of shiftwork, met this problem. Individual employees may consequently face a buildup of, say, fatigue and loss of sleep, which may impair their performance, health, and well-being. Companies thus meet increased risks not only in terms of lower effectiveness and a higher illness rate but also in terms of organizational safety.

- Available evidence suggests that the concept of satisfaction may be partly different in content for part-time employees compared to those in full-time employment. By means of including more potentially determining variables—say, income, task attributes, and organization structure characteristics—this difference may be better understood. This leads to the issue of whether differential consequences of satisfaction (as outlined in Figure 2) may also occur. Moreover, it may go along with different expectations or experience regarding one's free time.

Other Flexible Work Arrangements

Some working time arrangements defined as flexible have not been considered in the previous sections. Yet they have hardly been a subject in behavioral science research. In this final section on flexible arrangements, we will consider what is known about working overtime and temporary work. Our analysis of these and previously discussed arrangements should facilitate the assessment of the wider spectrum of flexible WTA's.

Overtime.   The design of overtime is easy to define: It is working time that is longer than agreed by contract, occurring periodically or incidentally. Thus, part-time employees can work overtime. The main argument for its

FIGURE 10

Research on Part-time Schedules: Scope of Variables

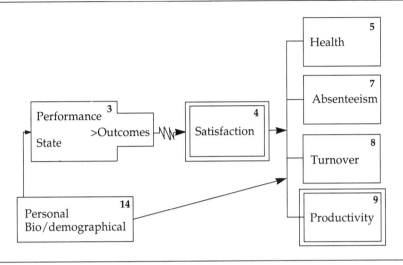

implementation is to adjust labor capacity to an increase in demand for products or services. Fluctuations in demand may have a seasonal pattern—such as retail sales during the Christmas season—but are often assumed to last for a relatively short period. Some categories of employees prefer to work overtime because of the additional earnings (Algemene Werkgevers Vereniging [General Employers' Federation], 1972; Fottler & Schaller, 1975).

Statistics regarding some industrial sectors in a few countries show, not surprisingly, that the rate of application has fluctuated over the years. But a recent survey in Dutch industry found that it is the most widely practiced method for making working time more flexible (Ministry of Social Affairs and Employment, 1991). Nonetheless, many companies and unions tend to stress the temporary nature of overtime. Contrary to flexible WTA's discussed in previous sections, it is advocated that overtime be applied as minimally as possible

(Curson, 1986). Companies facing an increase in demand may prefer to make use of temporary workers, as will be discussed later. They may also opt for a min-max arrangement. Another opportunity is to attract an additional team of employees half the size of the usual composition (or a semisized additional shift in the case of shiftwork). This arrangement was developed in a company producing candy bars, in which the effectiveness of regular television ads proved very hard to predict.

In one of the very few interesting research studies, Baird and Beccia (1980) suggest that not only increased demand may cause the introduction of overtime, but also a low productivity level within an organization due to such factors as inadequate coordination or lack of motivation. They analyzed data gathered from 42 U.S. government offices. First, a considerable negative correlation occurred between the amount of work done and the average number of overtime hours worked by each employee. Second, more overtime hours per office corresponded with the recruitment of more employees. Third, more overtime correlated with less job and pay satisfaction (see also Dijkstra, 1984). This survey obviously does not allow one to make causal inferences. But the results do at least suggest that the use of overtime may be one of the symptoms of poor internal and external organizational adaptation.

Other questions that future research ought to address relate to the buildup of fatigue and the possibility that employees lose sleep when they repeatedly work overtime. Also, the effects on performance quality and quantity must be assessed. These issues are even more important when workers in shifts are subject to overtime.

Temporary Work.   Temporary work may be described as work done voluntarily, without permanent employment, and for short periods. Actually, it is an umbrella term, encompassing quite different arrangements. First, a fixed-term employment relationship may be at stake, in which the date of termination is included in the contract. According to Konle-Seidl et al. (1990), the percentage of employees with these contracts within the EC corresponds more or less with the level of employment. Thus, in Portugal (which has a higher rate of unemployment) more than 15 percent of employees is subject to a fixed-term arrangement, while less than 5 percent has this arrangement in Luxembourg (which has a lower unemployment rate; see Commission of the European Community, 1990). Second, employees may be hired temporarily through an employment agency. This is prohibited in a few EC countries such as Greece but is a rather common practice in most others. Most sources, however, indicate recent large increases in temporary work in many countries. Third, some temporary work takes place in homes or in small shops, where migrant workers can be employed only when there is a demand for their labor. When such demand develops,

companies may contract out their regular work. Since such arrangements are illegal in many countries, there are no records of the frequency that such activities occur.

A major argument in favor of temporary work is its numerical flexibility: It allows the company to adapt its work force quickly to a decrease or increase in demand. It may also compensate for a temporary decrease in labor capacity, such as when employees are ill or on vacation. These are, to a large extent, well-known, traditional considerations. A much less traditional, and fiercely debated, consideration is a permanent reduction of the stable part of the work force. Temporary arrangements thus enable a company to invest in a smaller, well-educated group of permanent employees. Consequently, the cost of downsizing is minimized. The other side of the coin shows a segmented labor force. Since it is not in a company's interest to invest in temporary personnel, temporary jobs may be low skilled (Lendfers & Nijhuis, 1989).

Another argument relating to employment agencies in particular is that temporary work offers employees opportunities for choice. To some extent, employees change jobs until they find their preferred site (Van Haasteren & Van Overeem, 1976). A more recent Dutch survey shows that the majority of workers prefers a stable employment contract in temporary work (Allaart, Kunnen, Van Ours, & Van Stiphout, 1987). But the same issue of choice may apply to an employer: In temporary work, employees rotate until some are considered to be potential applicants.

In the case of work sites at home, the disadvantages of a high flexibility rate are primarily accruing to the workers (like being on call or unemployment). Some authors consider telework to be an example of having a work site at home. This may literally be the case, though not necessarily, but doing so would obscure a good perspective on this phenomenon. Telework implies that an employee, regardless of his or her WTA, is connected through a personal computer (located at home, at a company facility, or at a shop in which employees of other companies are also working) to a company's mainframe. Usually, telework offers the employee a number of opportunities to decide when work will be done during the day. However, since telework is not a WTA per se, we will not discuss it further here.

Behavioral science research on temporary work is almost nonexistent. A first question is whether organizational flexibility—the main argument for its use—is actually achieved. A second question centers around how different forms affect performance behavior, its outcomes, and some of the potential effects mentioned in Figure 2. Actually, any research relating to a part of that figure would be welcome.

Conclusion

Throughout this chapter we have monitored quite a number of future research needs. To a certain extent, this results from the irresistible drive that any researcher who reviews the state of the science in a particular area experiences. Researchers are usually in love with their subject and fear most strongly a divorce from it. Yet our plea for more research also stems from another concern: We expect that work organizations, both in the United States and Europe, will increasingly be faced with rapid, if not sudden, changes, particularly with regard to product and service design, consumer demand, and ecological priorities. In order to cope with such changes, a company should acquire, among other things, an advanced level of flexibility in its operations. The domain of WTA's is often among the more urgent, important subjects in this regard.

Does the available body of knowledge concerning WTA's allow psychologists and others to make justifiable inferences to applications in practice? To the extent that shiftwork is concerned, we would not be so hesitant. Of course, various issues need much more attention in

reasearch, such as the optimal length of a diurnal working period for various tasks, the frequency and length of rest periods, the long-term cost to organizations of the impaired health of employees engaged in night shifts, and so on. Yet there is some consensus, in general terms, on the potential or actual harmful effects of working in shifts and on the ways to curb such effects. This is not the case with regard to flexible WTA's. As discussed, most research on flexible WTA's has been rather superficial in nature. Descriptive and exploratory studies abound without much concern for theory development and theory testing. This state of affairs reflects the perspective that a WTA can be conceived in terms of an "additional" factor. That is, a flexible WTA is thought to merely add a "flexibility factor" to current work characteristics that are determinants of employees' performance behavior rather than affect the very character of some work characteristics and, consequently, of work behavior. We consider this perspective to be too narrow, underestimating as it does the incisive individual and organizational effects flexible WTA's may have.

In recommending a more encompassing approach for industrial and organizational psychologists to research WTA's, we briefly mention in conclusion three problem areas that summarize some of our current interests. First, through addressing problems and opportunities of shiftwork and flexible work schedules, regular daytime work may seem harmless, if not healthy. Yet we very often come across all sorts of professionals; for example, employers of very small firms who work many hours a day—say, between 12 and 16 hours—for six or seven days per week. Since we are not aware of any study in this area, we would favor research into the long-term effects of working excessive amounts of hours per day for a prolonged period of time. Second, we would welcome more research regarding the mutual relationships between the nature of a job and an employee's free time. This would require, first, the design of a free-time taxonomy, delineating quite different domains, such as time for recovery, meals and sleep, solitary and social recreation, leisure, job task preparation, escapes from the job, second jobs, and so on. Data on attributes (e.g., central life attributes) relevant to the job and to these domains should provide more insight in "compensatory" and "spillover" relationships. This should also allow better assessment of the harmful and healing effects of various free-time pursuits. Third, we came across a rather curious phenomenon as we described research on shiftwork interventions. Shiftworkers in semicontinuous schedules tend to assess health aspects and the effects of working in shifts in terms of the social characteristics of these schedules. This rather systemic translation process may reveal that individuals are rather poor judges of their health states in relation to WTA's (unless, of course, severe symtoms have occurred already). Although documented, this phenomenon is not very well understood. This suggests, first, the need for research into the determinants of this translation process, for example, levels of cognitive information processing, and second, that an intriguing line of research would focus on the long-term effects of this translation when individual scores on such things as self-efficacy, self-esteem, and internal control are considered. Would employees with a stronger self-concept perhaps be healthier than those with a weaker concept of self?

References

Aanonsen, A. (1964). *Shift work and health.* Oslo: Universitetsforlaget.

American Conference of Governmental Industrial Hygienists (ACGIH). (1988). *Documentation of threshold limit values* (5th ed.). Cincinnati: ACGIH.

Agervold, M. (1976). Shift work, a critical review. *Scandinavian Journal of Psychology, 17,* 181–188.

Akerstedt, T. (1980). Interindividual differences in adjustment to shiftwork. In W. P. Colquhoun &

J. Rutenfranz (Eds.), *Studies of shiftwork.* London: Taylor & Francis.

Akerstedt, T. (1985). Adjustment of physiological circadian rhythms and the sleep-wake cycle to shiftwork. In S. Folkard & T. H. Monk (Eds.), *Hours of work: Temporal factors in work-scheduling.* Chichester, UK: Wiley.

Akerstedt, T. (1988). Sleepiness as a consequence of shift work. *Sleep, 11,* 17–34.

Akerstedt, T. (1990). Psychological and psycho-physiological effects of shift work. *Scandinavian Journal of Work, Environment and Health, 16,* 67–73.

Akerstedt, T. (1991). Sleepiness at work: Effects of irregular work hours. In T. H. Monk (Ed.), *Sleep, sleepiness and performance.* Chichester, UK: Wiley.

Akerstedt, T., Alfredsson, L., & Theorell, T. (1986). An aggregate study of irregular work hours and cardiovascular disease. In M. Haider, M. Koller, & R. Cervinka (Eds.), *Night and shiftwork: Longterm effects and their prevention.* Frankfurt: Peter Lang.

Akerstedt, T., & Gillberg, M. (1981). Sleep disturbances and shift work. In A. Reinberg, N. Vieux, & P. Andlauer (Eds.), *Night and shift work: Biological and social aspects.* Oxford, UK: Pergamon Press.

Akerstedt, T., Knutsson, A., Alfredsson, L., & Theorell, T. (1984). Shift work and cardiovascular disease. *Scandinavian Journal of Work, Environment and Health, 10,* 409–414.

Akerstedt, T., Patkai, P., & Dahlgren, K. (1977). Field studies of shift work, II: Temporal patterns in psychophysiological activation in night workers alternating between night and day work. *Ergonomics, 20,* 261–631.

Akerstedt, T., & Theorell, T. (1976). Exposure to night work: Serumgastrin reactions, psychosomatic complaints and personality variables. *Journal of Psychosomatic Research, 20,* 479–484.

Akerstedt, T., & Torsvall, L. (1978). Experimental changes in shift schedules—Their effect on well-being. *Ergonomics, 21,* 835–847.

Akerstedt, T., & Torsvall, L. (1981). Age, sleep and adjustment to shift work. In W. P. Koella (Ed.), *Sleep.* Basel, Switzerland: Karger.

Alfredsson, L., Akerstedt, T., Mattsson, M., & Wilborg, B. (1991). Self-reported health and well-being amongst night security guards: A comparison with the working population. *Ergonomics, 34,* 525–530.

Alfredsson, L., Karasek, R., & Theorell, T. (1982). Myocardial infarction risk and psychosocial work environment: An analysis of the male Swedish working force. *Social Science and Medicine, 16*, 463–467.

Alfredsson, L., Spetz, C. L., & Theorell, T. (1985). Type of occupation and near-future hospitalization for myocardial infarction and some other diagnoses. *International Journal of Epidemiology, 14*, 378–388.

Algera, J. A. (1990). The job characteristics model of work motivation reviewed. In U. Kleinbeck, H. H. Quast, Hk. Thierry, & H. Häcker (Eds.), *Work motivation.* Hillsdale, NJ: Erlbaum.

Allaart, P. C., Kunnen, R., Van Ours, J. C., & Van Stiphout, H. A. (1987). *OSA-trendrapport 1987 (OSA trend report).* Den Haag, the Netherlands: Organisatie voor Strategisch Arbeidsmarktonderzoek.

Alluisi, E. A., & Morgan, B. B. (1982). Temporal factors in human performance and productivity. In E. A. Alluisi & E. A. Fleishman (Eds.), *Human performance and productivity, Vol. 3: Stress and performance effectiveness.* Hillsdale, NJ: Erlbaum.

Andersen, J. E. (1970). *Three shift work: A sociomedical survey.* Copenhagen, Denmark: Teknisk Forlag.

Andlauer, P. (1960). The effects of shift working on the worker's health. *OEEC Trade Union Information, 29*, 3–9.

Andlauer, P., Rutenfranz, J., Kogi, K., Thierry, Hk., Vieux, N., & Duverneuil, G. (1982). Organizational of night shifts in industries where public safety is at stake. *International Archives of Occupational and Environmental Health, 49*, 353–355.

Angersbach, D., Knauth, P., Loskant, H., Karvonen, M. J., Undeutsch, K., & Rutenfranz, J. (1980). A retrospective cohort study comparing complaints and diseases in day- and shift workers. *International Archives of Occupational and Environmental Health, 45*, 127–140.

Aschoff, J. (1978). Features of circadian rhythms relevant for the design of shift schedules. *Ergonomics, 21*, 739–754.

Astrand, P. O., & Rodahl, K. (1986). *Textbook of work physiology. Physiological basis of exercise.* New York: McGraw-Hill.

Algemene Werkgevers Vereniging (AWV). (1972). *Overwerk: Verslag van een onderzoek in vier bedrijven naar de opvattingen rond het overwerken* [Overtime: Report on an investigation of attitudes towards overtime in four firms]. Haarlem, the Netherlands: AWV.

Baird, L. S., & Beccia, P. J. (1980). The potential misuse of overtime. *Personnel Psychology, 33*, 557–565.

Bjerner, B., Holm, A., & Swensson, A. (1955). Diurnal variation in mental performance: A study of three-shift workers. *British Journal of Industrial Medicine, 12*, 103–110.

Blake, M. S. F., & Corcoran, D. W. (1972). Introversion-extraversion and circadian rhythms. In P. Colquhoun (Ed.), *Aspects of human efficiency.* London: The English University Press.

Bohle, P. (1990). The impact of night work: Individual differences in subjective health. In G. Costa, G. Cesena, K. Kogi, & A. Wedderburn (Eds.), *Shiftwork: Health, sleep and performance.* Frankfurt: Peter Lang.

Boissonnade, P. (1987). *Life and work in medieval Europe.* New York: Dorset Press.

Bolt, H. M., & Rutenfranz, J. (1988). The impact of aspects of time and duration of exposure on toxicokinetics and toxicodynamics of workplace chemicals. In W. R. F. Notten, R. F. M. Herber, W. J. Hunter, A. C. Monster, & R. Zielhuis (Eds.), Health surveillance of individual workers exposed to chemical agents. *International Archives of Occupational and Environmental Health* (Suppl.). Berlin: Springer Verlag.

Bonitz, D., Crzech-Sukalo, H., & Nachreiner, F. (1987). Differential psychosocial effects of different shift systems. In A. Oginsky, J. Pokorski, & J. Rutenfranz (Eds.), *Contemporary advances in shiftwork research.* Krakow, Poland: Krakow Medical Academy.

Bonitz, D., Hedden, I., Crzech-Sukalo, H., & Nachreiner, F. (1989). Zur klassifikation und analyse unterschiedlicher schichtsysteme und ihrer psychosoziale effekte, Teil 1: Differentielle effekte bei unterschiedlicher rotationsdauer und richtung [On the classification and analysis of different shift systems and their psycho-social effects, Part 1: Differential effects for different rota duration and direction]. *Zeitschrift für Arbeitswissenschaft, 43*, 34–41.

Bosch, L. H. M., Eisendoorn, G. Th., & Nijsen, A. F. M. (1988). *Deeltijdwerk in kleinere industriële bedrijven* [Part time work in smaller industrial firms]. Den Haag, the Netherlands: COB/SER.

Bosworth, D. L., & Dawkins. P. J. (1979). *Advantages and disadvantages of shift work—United Kingdom*. Dublin: European Foundation for the Improvement of Living and Working Conditions.

Bosworth, D. L., & Dawkins, P. J. (1984). Shiftworking and perceived working conditions: An empirical analysis. In A. Wedderburn & P. Smith (Eds.), *Psychological approaches to night and shift work*. Edinburgh: Herriot-Watt University.

Breaugh, J. A. (1983). The 12-hour work day: Differing employee reactions. *Personnel Psychology, 36*, 277–288.

Brief, R. A., & Scala, R. A. (1986). Occupational health aspects of unusual work schedules. *American Industrial Hygiene Association Journal, 47*, 199–202.

Browne, R. C. (1949). The day and night performance of teleprinter switchboard operators. *Journal of Occupational Psychology, 23*, 121–126.

Bruusgaard, A. (1969). Shift work as an occupational health problem. In A. Swensson (Ed.), *Night and shift work. Studia laboris et salutis. 4*, 9–14.

Bunnage, D. (1979). *Effects of shiftwork on social life*. Dublin: European Foundation for the Improvement of Living and Working Conditions.

Burns, T., & Stalker, G. M. (1961). *The management of innovation*. London: Tavistock.

Campbell, J. P., & Pritchard, R. D. (1976). Motivation theory in industrial and organizational psychology. In M. D. Dunnette (Ed.), *Handbook of work and organizational psychology*. Chicago: Rand McNally.

Carter, F. A., & Corlett, E. N. (1982). *Overzicht van de research van de Europese stichtingen over ploegenarbeid: 1977–1980* [Overview of research on shift work in Europe]. Dublin: European Foundation for the Improvement of Living and Working Conditions.

Cervinka, R., Kundi, M., Koller, M., & Arnhoff, J. (1984a). Ernährungsverhalten und schichtarbeit [Eating habits and shiftwork]. *Zeitschrift für Arbeitswissenschaft, 38*, 30–36.

Cervinka, R., Kundi, M., Koller, M., & Arnhoff, J. (1984b). Shift-related nutrition problems. In A. Wedderburn & P. Smith (Eds.), *Psychological

approaches to night and shift work*. Edinburgh: Herriot-Watt University.

Chaffin, D. B., & Andersson, G. B. J. (1984). *Occupational biomechanics*. New York: Wiley.

Clark, D. Y. (1984). The social consequences of rotating shift work in manufacturing industry. In A. Wedderburn & P. Smith (Eds.), *Psychological approaches to night and shift work*. Edinburgh: Herriot-Watt University.

Cohen, A. R., & Gadon, K. (1978). *Alternative work schedules: Integrating individual and organizational needs*. Reading, UK: Addison-Wesley.

Colligan, M. J. (1981). Methodological and practical issues related to shiftwork research. In L. C. Johnson, D. I. Tepas, W. P. Colquhoun, & M. J. Colligan (Eds.), *The twenty-four hour workday: Proceedings of a symposium on variations in work-sleep schedules*. Cincinnati: Niosh.

Colligan, M. J., Frockt, I. J., & Tasto, D. L. (1979). Frequency of sickness absence and worksite clinic visits among nurses as a function of shift. *Applied Ergonomics, 10*, 79–85.

Colligan, M., & Tepas, D. I. (1986). The stress of hours of work. *American Industrial Hygiene Association Journal, 47*, 686–695.

Colquhoun, W. P., & Folkard, S. (1978). Personality differences in body-temperature rhythm, and their relation to its adjustment to night work. *Ergonomics, 21*, 811–817.

Colquhoun, W. P., & Rutenfranz, J. (Eds.). (1980). *Studies of shiftwork*. London: Taylor & Francis.

Commission of the European Communities. (1990). *Employment in Europe*. Brussels: EC.

Corlett, E. N., Queinnec, Y., & Paoli, P. (1988). *Adapting shiftwork arrangements*. Dublin: European Foundation for the Improvement or Living and Working Conditions.

Costa, G., Apostoli, P., d'Andrea, F., & Gaffuri, E. (1981). Gastrointestinal and neurotic disorders in textile shift workers. In A. Reinberg, N. Vieux & P. Andlauer (Eds.), *Night and shift work: Biological and social aspects*. Oxford, UK: Pergamon Press.

Costa, G., Cesena, G., Kogi, K., & Wedderburn, A. (Eds.). (1990). *Shiftwork: Health, sleep and performance*. Frankfurt: Peter Lang.

Costa, G., Gaffuri, E., Perfranceschi, G., & Tansella, M. (1979). Reentrainment of diurnal variation of psychological and physiological performance at the end of a slowly rotated shift system in hospital workers. *International Archives of Occupational and Environmental Health, 44,* 165–175.

Craig, A. (1988). Self-control over performance in situations that demand vigilance. In J. P. Leonard (Ed.), *Vigilance, methods, models and regulations.* Frankfurt: Peter Lang.

Curson, C. (Ed.). (1986). *Flexible patterns of work.* London: Institute of Personnel Management.

Czeisler, C. A., Johnson, M. P., Duffy, J. F., Brown, E. N., Ronda, J. M., & Kronauer, R. E. (1990). Exposure to bright light and darkness to treat physiologic maladaptation to night work. *The New England Journal of Medicine, 322,* 1253–1258.

Czeisler, C. A., Moore-Ede, M. C., & Coleman, R. M. (1982). Rotating shift work schedules that disrupt are improved by applying circadian principles. *Science, 217,* 460–462.

Daan, S., & Lewy, A. J. (1984). Scheduled exposure to daylight: A potential strategy to reduce 'jet-lag' following transmeridian flight. *Psychopharmacology Bulletin, 20,* 566–568.

Dahlgren, K. (1981). Adjustment of circadian rhythms and EEG sleep functions to day and night sleep among permanent night workers and rotating shift workers. *Psychophysiology, 18,* 381–391.

Dalton, D. R., & Mesch, D. J. (1990). The impact of flexible scheduling on employee attendance and turnover. *Administrative Science Quarterly, 35,* 370–387.

de Jong, J. R., & Bonhof, W. L. (1974). *Bedriffseconomische aspecten van ploegenarbeid* [Industrial economic aspects of shiftwork]. Leiden, the Netherlands: Stenfert Kroese.

de Koning, J. (1980). *Optimalisering van de verdeling van de werkgelegenheid* [Optimalization of the distribution of employment]. Rotterdam, the Netherlands: Netherlands Economic Institute.

De la Mare, G., & Walker, J. (1968). Factors influencing the choice of shift rotation. *Journal of Occupational Psychology, 42,* 1–22.

Demenint-de Jong, M. (1989). *Arbeidsduur, organisatie en emancipatie* [Working time, organization, and emancipation]. Utrecht, the Netherlands: Lemma.

de Vries-Griever, A. H. G, & Meijman, T. F. (1987). The impact of abnormal hours of work on various modes of information processing: A process model on human costs of performance. *Ergonomics, 30,* 1287–1301.

Dijkstra, A. (1984). Leeftijdspecifieke verschillen in gezondheid en ziekteverzuim tussen deeltijdwerkers, voltijdwerkers en overwerkers [Age specific differences in health and absenteeism among part time, full time, and over time workers]. In J. J. Godschalk (Ed.), *Sociale aspekten van arbeidstijdverkorting.* Amsterdam: Swets & Zeitlinger.

Dinges, D. F., Whitehouse, W. G., Orne, E. C., & Orne, M. T. (1988). The benefits of a nap during prolonged work and wakefulness. *Work & Stress, 2,* 139–153.

Dirken, J. M. (1966). Industrial shift work: Decrease in well-being and specific effects. *Ergonomics, 9,* 115–124.

Driehuis, W., & de Vrije, P. A. (1981). *Vooronderzoek experiment bevordering deeltijdarbeid* [Preliminary study to an experiment stimulating part time work]. Part I. The Hague, the Netherlands: Dutch Ministry of Social Affairs.

Dubin, R., Champoux, J. E., & Porter, L. W. (1975). Central life interests and organizational commitment of blue-collar and clerical workers. *Administrative Science Quarterly, 23,* 411–427.

Dunham, R. B., Pierce, J. L., & Castaneda, M. B. (1987). Alternative work schedules: Two field quasi-experiments. *Personnel Psychology, 40,* 215–242.

Durkheim, E. (1912). *Les formes élémentaires de la vie religieuse* [The elementary forms of the religious life]. Paris: F. Alcan.

Eberhardt, B. J., & Shani, A. B. (1984). The effects of full time versus part time employment status on attitudes towards specific organizational characteristics and overall job satisfaction. *Academy of Management Journal, 27,* 893–900.

Elchardus, M. (1985). Het sociale substraat van de tijd [The social substrate of time]. *Tijdschrift voor Sociologie, 6,* 317–353.

Elchardus, M. (1988). The rediscovery of chronos: The new role of time in sociological theory. *International Sociology, 1,* 35–39.

Elizur, D. (1991). Work and nonwork relations: The conical structure of work and home life relationship. *Journal of Organizational Behavior, 12,* 313–322.

Emmerij, L. J., & Clobus, J. A. E. (1978). *Volledige werkgelegenheid door creatief verlof* [Full Employment through creative leave]. Deventer, the Netherlands: Kluwer.

Ernst, G., Nachreiner, F., & Volger, A. (1986). Applicability of shift work research to problems of irregular working hours. In M. Haider, M. Koller, & R. Cervinka (Eds.), *Night and shiftwork: Longterm effects and their prevention.* Frankfurt: Peter Lang.

Evans, A., & Attew, T. (1986). Emerging themes in flexible work patterns. In C. Curson (Ed.), *Flexible patterns of work.* London: Institute of Personnel Management.

Feldman, D. C., (1990). Reconceptualizing the nature and consequences of part time work. *Academy of Management Review, 15,* 103–112.

Fleuter, D. L. (1975). *The workweek revolution.* Reading, MA: Addison-Wesley.

Folkard, S., Arendt, J., & Clark, M. (1990). Sleep, mood and performance on a 'weekly' rotating (7-7-7) shift system: Some preliminary results. In G. Costa, G. Cesena, K. Kogi, & A. Wedderburn (Eds.), *Shiftwork: Health, sleep and performance.* Frankfurt: Peter Lang.

Folkard, S., Condon, R. (1987). Night shift paralysis in air traffic control officers. *Ergonomics, 30,* 1353–1364.

Folkard, S., Condon, R., & Herbert, M. (1984). Night shift paralysis. *Experientia, 40,* 510–512.

Folkard, S., Monk, T. H., (1979). Shift work and performance. *Human Factors, 21,* 483–492.

Folkard, S., & Monk, T. H. (1985). Circadian performance rhythms. In S. Folkard & T. H. Monk (Eds.), *Hours of work.* Chichester, UK: Wiley.

Folkard, S., Monk, T. H., & Lobban, M. C. (1978). Short and long-term adjustment of circadian rhythms in 'permanent' night nurses. *Ergonomics, 21,* 785–799.

Folkard, S., Monk, T. H., & Lobban, M. C. (1979). Towards a predictive test of adjustment to shift work. *Ergonomics, 22,* 79–91.

Foret, J., & Benoit, O. (1978). Etude du sommeil chez des travailleurs a horaires alternants: Adaptation et récupération dans le cas de rotation rapide de poste (3-4 jours) [Study on the sleep of rotating shift workers: Adaptation and recovery in a rapid rotating schedule (3-4 days)]. *European Journal of Applied Physiology, 38,* 71–82.

Foret, J., Bensimon, B., Benoit, O., & Vieux, N. (1981). Quality of sleep as a function of age and shift work. In A. Reinberg, N. Vieux, & P. Andlauer (Eds.), *Night and shift work: Biological and social aspects.* Oxford, UK: Pergamon Press.

Foster, L. W., Latack, J. C., & Reindle, L. J. (1979). Effects and promises of the shortened workweek. *Academy of Management Proceedings,* 226–230.

Fottler, M. D., & Schaller, F. W. (1975). Overtime acceptance among blue-collar workers. *Industrial Relations, 14,* 327–336.

Frese, M., & Okonek, K. (1984). Reasons to leave shiftwork and psychological and psychosomatic complaints of former shiftworkers. *Journal of Applied Psychology, 69,* 509–514.

Frese, M., & Rieger, A. (1981). Beschreibung und Kritik einer Skala zur Prädiktion von psychophysischem Befinden bei Schichtarbeitern [A scale on the prediction of psychophysiological well-being of shiftworkers: Description and critics]. *Zeitschrift für Arbeitswissenschaft, 35,* 13–22.

Frese, M., & Semmer, N. (1986). Shiftwork, stress and psychosomatic complaints: A comparison between workers in different shiftwork schedules, non-shiftworkers, and former shiftworkers. *Ergonomics, 29,* 99–114.

Fruhstorfer, H., Langandke, P., Meinzer, K., Peter, J. H., & Pfaff, U. (1977). Neurophysiological vigilance indicators and operational analysis of a train vigilance monitoring device: A laboratory and field study. In R. R. Mackie (Ed.), *Vigilance.* New York: Plenum.

Gadbois, C. (1980). Les exigences du travail hospitalier de nuit comme facteurs de la charge de travail [Job demands during the night shift in hospital work]. *Le Travail Humain, 43,* 17–31.

Gadbois, C., & Queinnec, Y. (1984). Travail de nuits, rhythmes circadiens et régulations des activitiés [Night work, circadian rhythms and the regulation of work activities]. *Le Travail Humain, 47,* 130–156.

Gillberg, M. (1985). Effects of naps on performance. In S. Folkard & T. H. Monk (Eds.), *Hours of work.* Chichester, UK: Wiley.

Golembiewsky, R. T., Hillies, R., & Kagno, M. S. (1974). A longitudinal study of flex-time effects: Some consequences of an OD structural intervention. *Journal of Applied Behavioral Science,* 10, 503–532.

Golembiewsky, R. T., & Proehl, C. W. (1978). A survey of the empirical literature on flexible workhours: Character and consequences of a major innovation. *Academy of Management Review, 3,* 837–853.

Gopher, D., & Donchin, E. (1986). Workload—An examination of the concept. In K. R. Boff, L. Kaufmann, & J. P. Thomas (Eds.), *Handbook of perception and human performance: Vol. 2. Cognitive processes and performance.* New York: Wiley.

Graf, O. (1922). Uber lohnenste Arbeitspausen bei geistiger Arbeit [Optimal pausing in mental tasks]. *Psychologische Arbeiten, 9,* 228–243.

Hackman, J. R., & Oldham, G. R., (1980). *Work redesign.* Reading, MA: Addison-Wesley.

Haider, M., Kundi, M., & Koller, M. (1981). Methodological issues and problems in shift work research. In L. C. Johnson, D. I. Tepas, W. P. Colquhoun, & M. J. Colligan (Eds.), *The twenty-four hour workday: Proceedings of a symposium on variations in work-sleep schedules.* Cincinnati: Niosh.

Hak, A., & Kampman, R. (1981). Working irregular hours: Complaints and state of fitness of railway personnel. In A. Reinberg, N. Vieux, & Andlauer (Eds.), *Night and shift work: Biological and social aspects.* Oxford, UK: Pergamon Press.

Härmä, M. I., Ilmarinen, J., Knauth, P., Rutenfranz, J., & Hänninen, O. (1988). Physical training intervention in female shift workers, I. The effects of intervention on fitness, fatigue, sleep and psychosomatic symptions. *Ergonomics, 31,* 39–50.

Harrick, E. J., Vanek, G. R., & Micklitsch, J. T. (1986). Alternative work schedules, productivity, leave usage, and employment attitudes: A field study. *Public Personnel Management, 15,* 159–169.

Harrington, J. M. (1978). *Shift work and health: A critical review of the literature.* London: H.M.S.O.

Harris, W. (1977). Fatigue, circadian rhythm, and truck accidents. In R. R. Mackie (Eds.), *Vigilance: Theory, operational performance and physiological correlates.* New York: Plenum.

Haslam, D. R. (1982). Sleep loss, recovery sleep and military performance. *Ergonomics, 25,* 163–178.

Hedden, I., Bonitz, D., Grzech-Sukalo, H., & Nachreiner, F. (1989). Zur Klassifikation und analyse unterschiedlicher Schichtsysteme und ihrer psychosozialen Effekte; Teil 2: Differentielle Effekte bei Gruppierung nach periodischen Merkmalen, Uberprüfung eines alternativen Klassifikationsansatzes [On the classification and analysis of different shift systems and their psycho-social effects: Part 2. Differential effects for grouping in periodic characteristics]. *Zeitschrift für Arbeitswissenschaft, 43,* 73–78.

Hegner, F., & Kramer, U. (1988). *Neue Erfahrungen mit beweglichen arbeitszeiten* [New experiences with flexible working time arrangements]. Cologne, Germany: Gesammtmetal.

Hicks, W. D., & Klimoski, R. J. (1981). The impact of flexitime on employee attitudes. *Academy of Management Journal, 24,* 333–341.

Hildenbrandt, G., Rohmert, W., & Rutenfranz, J. (1974). Variations in the daily rhythm of error frequency by shift workers and the influence of it on tiredness. *International Journal of Chronobiology, 2,* 175–180.

Hockey, G. R. J. (1986). A state control theory of adaptation to stress and individual differences in stress management. In G. R. J. Hockey, A. W. K. Gaillard, & M. Coles (Eds.), *Energetics and human information processing.* Dordrecht, the Netherlands: Mart.

Hodge, B. J., & Tellier, R. D. (1975). Employee reactions to the four-day week. *California Management Review, 18,* 25–30.

House, J. S. (1987). Chronic stress and chronic disease: Conceptual and methodological issues. *Work & Stress, 1,* 129–134.

International Labour Office. (1978). *Management of working time in industrial countries.* Geneva: International Labour Office.

International Labour Office. (1986). *Conditions of work digest.* Geneva: International Labour Office.

Ivancevich, J. M. (1974). Effects of the shorter work-week on selected satisfaction and performance measures. *Journal of Applied Psychology, 59,* 717–721.

Ivancevich, J. M., & Lyon, H. L. (1977). The shortened workweek: A field experiment. *Journal of Applied Psychology, 62,* 34–37.

Iwema, R., & Hofman, L. (1974). *Macro-economische consequenties van ploegenarbeid* [Macro-economic consequences of shift work]. Leiden, the Netherlands: Stenfert Kroese.

Jamal, M., & Baba, V. V. (1992). Shiftwork, department type and stress. *Journal of Organizational Behavior, 13,* 449–464.

Jansen, B. (1987a). Rota-Risk-Profile-Analysis. In A. Oginsky, J. Pokorski, & J. Rutenfranz (Eds.), *Contemporary advances in shiftwork research.* Krakow, Poland: Krakow Medical Academy.

Jansen, B. (1987b). *Dagdienst en ploegendienst in vergelijkend perspectief* [Day work and night work compared]. Amsterdam: Swets & Zeitlinger (Doctoral dissertation, University of Amsterdam, 1987).

Jansen, B., Thierry, Hk., & Van Hirtum, A. (1986). *Ploegenarbeidsroosters herzien* [Designing shift schedules]. Deventer, the Netherlands: Kluwer.

Kabanoff, B. (1980). Work and nonwork: A review of models, methods and findings. *Psychological Bulletin, 88,* 60–77.

Kahne, H. (1985). *Reconceiving part time work.* Totowa: Rowman & Allanheld.

Kanfer, R. (1990). Motivation theory and industrial and organizational psychology. In M. D. Dunnette & L. M. Hough (Eds.), *Handbook of industrial and organizational psychology* (2nd ed., vol. 1). Palo Alto, CA: Consulting Psychologists Press.

Kantowitz, B. H., & Sorkin, R. D. (1983). *Human factors: Understanding people-system relationships.* New York, Wiley.

Karasek, R., & Theorell, T. (1990). *Healthy work: Stress, productivity, and the reconstruction of working life.* New York: Basic Books.

Kasl, S. V. (1986). Stress and disease in the workplace: A methodological commentary on the accumulated evidence. In M. F. Cataldo & T. J. Coates (Eds.), *Health and industry, a behavioral medicine perspective.* New York: Wiley.

Katz, D., & Kahn, R. L. (1978). *The social psychology of organizations* (2nd ed.). New York: Wiley.

Khaleque, A., & Rahman, A. (1982). Sleep disturbances and health complaints of shiftworkers. *Journal of Human Ergology, 11,* 155–164.

Khaleque, A., & Rahman, A. (1984). Shiftworkers' attitudes towards shift work and perception of quality of life. *International Archives of Environmental Health, 53,* 291–297.

Kim, J. S., & Campagna, A. F. (1981). Effects of flextitime on employee attendance and performance: A field experiment. *Academy of Management Journal, 24,* 729–741.

Klein, H. J. (1989). An integrated control model of work motivation. *Academy of Management Review, 14,* 150–172.

Knauth, P. (1983). *Ergonomische beiträge zu sicherheitsaspekten der arbeitszeitorganisation* [Ergonomic contributions to safety aspects of working time arrangements]. Düsseldorf, Germany: Fortschritt-Berichte der VDI Zeitschriften Reihe 17, Nr. 18, VDI-Verlag.

Knauth, P. (1987). The value of leisure time: A field study of three-shift workers. In A. Oginsky, J. Pokorski, & J. Rutenfranz (Eds.), *Contemporary advances in shiftwork research.* Krakow, Poland: Krakow Medical Academy.

Knauth, P. (1988). Belastungen und beanspruchungen bie schichtarbeit [Workload in shiftwork]. In F. Nachreiner (Ed.), *Aktuelle probleme der belastungs- und Beanspruchungsforschung.* Frankfurt: Peter Lang.

Knauth, P., Emde, E., Rutenfranz, J., Kieswetter, E., & Smith, P. (1981). Re-entrainment of body temperature in field studies of shift work. *International Archives of Occupational and Environmental Health, 49,* 137–149.

Knauth, P., & Kieswetter, E. (1987). A change from weekly to quicker shift rotations: A field study of discontinuous three shift workers. *Ergonomics, 30,* 1311–1322.

Knauth, P., & Rutenfranz, J. (1982). Development of criteria for the design of shift work systems. *Journal of Human Ergology, 11,* 337–367.

Knutsson, A. (1989). *Shift work and coronary heart disease.* (Doctoral dissertation, Karolinska Institute, 1989). Stockholm: National Institute for Psychosocial Factors and Health.

Knutsson, A., Akerstedt, T., Johnsson, B., & Orth-Gomer, K. (1986). Increased risk of ischemic heart disease in shift workers. *Lancet, 1986(2),* 89–92.

Kogi, K. (1991). Job content and working time: The scope for joint change. *Ergonomics, 34,* 757–773.

Kogi, K., Miura, T., & Saito, H. (Eds.). (1984). *Shiftwork: Its practice and improvement.* Tokyo: Center for Academic Publications.

Kogi, K., & Thurman, J. E. (1990). Development of new international standards on night work. In G. Costa, G. Cesena, K. Kogi, & A. Wedderburn

(Eds.), *Shiftwork: Health, sleep and performance.* Frankfurt: Peter Lang.

Koller, M. (1983). Health risks related to shift work. *Internatinal Archives of Occupational and Environmental Health, 53,* 59–75.

Koller, M., Kundi, M., & Cervinka, R. (1978). Field studies of shift work at an Austrian oil refinery: I. Health and psychosocial well-being of workers who drop out of shift work. *Ergonomics, 21,* 835–847.

Koller, M., Kundi, M., Cervinka, R., & Haider, M. (1984). Health risk factors due to the sensitization process in shift work. In A. Wedderburn & P. Smith (Eds.), *Psychological approaches to night and shift work.* Edinburgh: Herriot-Watt University.

Konle-Seidl, R., Ullmann, H., & Walwei, U. (1990). The European social space: Atypical forms of employment and working hours in the European Community. *International Social Security Review, 18,* 143–179.

Koopmans, R. (1988). *Chronopharmacology and shift work.* Amsterdam: University of Amsterdam (Doctoral dissertation, Medical Faculty, University of Amsterdam, 1988).

Kossoris, M. D., & Kohler, R. F. (1947). *Hours of work and output* (U.S. Department of Labor, Bureau of Labor Statistics, Bulletin No. 917). Washington, DC: U.S. Government Printing Office.

Krausz, M., & Freibach, N. (1983). Effects of flexible working time for employed women upon satisfaction, strains, and absenteeism. *Journal of Occupational Psychology, 56,* 155–159.

Krausz, M., & Hermann, E. (1991). Who is afraid of flextime: Correlates of personal choice of a FT schedule. *Applied Psychology, An International Review, 40,* 315–326.

Kundi, A., Koller, M., Cervinka, R., & Haider, M. (1979). Consequences of shift work as a function of age and years of shift. *Chronobiologia, 6,* 123.

Kundi, M., Koller, M., Cervinka, R., & Haider, M. (1981). Job satisfaction in shift workers and its relation to family situation and health. In A. Reinberg, N. Vieux, & P. Andlauer (Eds.), *Night and shift work: Biological and social aspects.* Oxford, UK: Pergamon Press.

Kundi, M., Koller, M., Cervinka, R., & Haider, M. (1986). Health and psychosocial aspects of shiftwork results of a 5-year follow-up study. In M. Haider, M. Koller, & R. Cervinka (Eds.), *Night*

and shiftwork: Longterm effects and their prevention. Frankfurt: Peter Lang.

Latack, J. C., & Foster, L. W. (1985). Implementation of compressed work schedules: Participation and job redesign as critical factors of employee acceptance. *Personnel Psychology 38,* 75–92.

Lawler, E. E. (1971). *Pay and organizational effectiveness.* New York: McGraw-Hill.

Lawler, E. E. (1973). *Motivation in work organizations.* Monterey, CA. Brooks/Cole.

Lendfers, M. L. G. H., & Nijhuis, F. J. N. (1989). *Flexibilisering van de arbeid en gezondheids effecten* [Flexibilisation of work and health effects]. Den Haag, the Netherlands: Organisatie voor Statistisch Arbeidsmarktonderzoek.

Lens, W. (1986). Future time perspective: A cognitive-motivational concept. In D. R. Brown & J. Veroff (Eds.), *Frontiers of motivational psychology.* New York: Springer.

Levitan, S. A., & Belous, R. A. (1979). *Minder werk, meer werk* [Less work, more work]. Deventer, the Netherlands: Kluwer.

Locke, E. A., & Latham, G. P. (1990). *A theory of goal setting and task performance.* Englewood Cliffs, NJ: Prentice-Hall.

Loen, C. D., & Van Schilfgaarde, P. (1990). *Flexibiliteit binnen stabiele arbeidsrelaties* [Flexibility within stable employment relationships]. Assen, the Netherlands: Van Gorcum.

Logan, N., O'Reilly, C., & Roberts, K. H. (1973). Job satisfaction among part time employees. *Journal of Occupational Behavior, 3,* 33–41.

Lortie, M., Foret, J., Teiger, C., & Laville, A. (1979). Circadian rhythms and behavior of permanent night workers. *International Archives of Occupational and Environmental Health, 44,* 1–11.

Maric, D. (1977). *Adapting working hours to modern needs.* Geneva: International Labour Office.

Mason, R. W., & Johnson, B. L. (1987). Ergonomic factors in chemical hazard control. In G. Salvendy (Ed.), *Handbook of human factors.* New York: Wiley.

Maurice, M. (1975). *Shift work: Economic advantages and social costs.* Geneva: International Labour Office.

McCarthy, E. (1983). Job attitudes of shiftworkers. *Journal of Irish Business and Administrative Research, 5,* 86–103.

McDonald, N. (1984). *Fatigue, safety and the truck driver.* London: Taylor & Francis.

McGuire, J. B., & Liro, J. R. (1987). Absenteeism and flexible work schedules. *Public Personnel Management, 16,* 47–59.

Meijman, T. F. (1991). *Over vermoeidheid* [Fatigue]. Amsterdam: Studiecentrum Arbeid en Gezondheid.

Meijman, T. F. (1992). *Verkorten van de werkweek en verlengen van de werkdag* [Shortening the workweek and lengthening the workday]. Amsterdam: Studiecentrum Arbeid en Gezondheid.

Meijman, T. F., de Vries-Griever, A. H. G., & Kampman, R. (1989). *Rhythm and blues: Onregelmatige werk- en rusttijden als arbeids- en leefomstandigheid* [Rhythm and blues: Irregular working- and resting hours at work- and living condition]. Amsterdam: Netherlands Institute of Working Conditions (NIA).

Meijman, T. F. , & Mulder, G., Van Dormolen, M., & Cremer, R. (1992). Workload of driving examiners: A psychophysiological field study. In H. Kragt (Ed.), *Enhancing industrial performances.* London: Taylor & Francis.

Meijman, T. F., Thunnissen, M. J., & de Vries-Griever, A. H. G. (1990). The after-effects of a prolonged period of day-sleep on subjective sleep quality. *Work & Stress, 4,* 65–70.

Meijman, T. F., van der Meer, O., & van Dormolen, M. (1993). The after-effects of night work on short-term memory performance. *Ergonomics, 36,* 37–42.

Mellor, E. F. (1986). Shift work and flexitime: How prevalent are they? *Monthly Labor Review,* 14–21.

Menzel, W. (1962). *Mensliche tag-nacht rhythmik und schichtarbeit* [Human day-night rhythms and shiftwork]. Basel, Switzerland: Benno Schwabe.

Michel-Briand, C., Chopard, J. L., Guiot, A., Paulmier, M., & Struder, G. (1981). The pathological consequences of shift work in retired workers. In A Reinberg, N. Vieux, & P. Andlauer (Eds.), *Night and shift work: Biological and social aspects.* Oxford, UK: Pergamon Press.

Miller, H. E., & Terborg, J. R. (1979). Job attitudes of part time and full time employees. *Journal of Applied Psychology, 64,* 380–386.

Ministry of Social Affairs and Employment. (1991).*Veranderende arbeidstijdpatronen*

[Changing working time patterns]. Den Haag, the Netherlands: Loontechnische Dienst.

Minors, D. S., & Waterhouse, J. M. (1985a). Introduction to circadian rhythms. In S. Folkard & T. H. Monk (Eds.), *Hours of work.* Chichester, UK: Wiley.

Minors, D. S., & Waterhouse, J. M. (1985b). Circadian rhythms in deep body temperature, urinary excretion and alertness in nurses on night work. *Ergonomics, 28,* 1523–1530.

Minors, D. S., & Waterhouse, J. M. (1987). The role of naps in alleviating sleepiness during an irregular sleep-wake schedule. *Ergonomics, 30,* 1261–1274.

Minors, D. S., & Waterhouse, J. M. (1990). The influence of light on the entrainment of the circadian system: An introduction. In G. Costa, G. Cesena, K. Kogi, & A. Wedderburn (Eds.), *Shiftwork: Health, sleep and performance.* Frankfurt: Peter Lang.

Mintzberg, H. (1983). *Structure in fives: Designing effective organizations.* Englewood Cliffs, NJ: Prentice-Hall.

Mitler, M. M., Carskadon, M. A., Czeisler, C. A., Dement, W. C., Dinges, D. F., & Graeber, R. C. (1988). Catastrophes, sleep and public policy: Consensus report. *Sleep, 11,* 100–109.

Monk, T. H., & Embrey, D. E. (1981). A field study of circadian rhythms in actual and interpolated task performance. In A. Reinberg, N. Vieux, & P. Andlauer (Eds.), *Night and shift work: Biological and social aspects.* Oxford, UK: Pergamon Press.

Monk, T. H., & Folkard, S. (1985). Shift work and performance. In S. Folkard & T. H. Monk (Eds.), *Hours of work.* Chichester, UK: Wiley.

Moog, R. (1987). Optimization of shiftwork: Physiological contributions. *Ergonomics, 30,* 1249–1259.

Morgan, G. (1986). *Images of organizations.* London: Sage.

Mott, P. E., Mann, F. C., McLoughlin, Q., & Warwick, D. P. (1965). *Shift work: The social, psychological and physical consequences.* Ann Arbor, MI: The University of Michigan Press.

Mulder, G. (1986). The concept and measurements of mental effort. In G. R. J. Hockey, A. W. K. Gaillard, & M. Coles (Eds.), *Energetics and human information processing.* Dordrecht, the Netherlands: Mart. Nijhoff.

Münstermann, J., & Preiser, K. (1978). *Schichtarbeit in der Bundesrepublik Deutschland* [Shift work in the German Federal Republic]. Bonn, Germany: Forschungsbericht Humanisierung des Arbeitslebens 8, Bundesministerium Arbeit & Sozialordnung.

Nachreiner, F., Baer, K., Diekmann, A., & Ernst, G. (1984). Some new approaches in the analysis of the interference of shift work with social life. In A. Wedderburn & P. Smith (Eds.), *Psychological approaches to night and shift work*. Edinburgh: Herriot-Watt University.

Nachreiner, F., & Rutenfranz, J. (1975). Sozial-psychologische, arbeitspsychologische und arbeitsmedizinische Erhebungen in der chemischen Industrie [Social psychological, work psychological and occupational medical studies in the chemical industry]. In J. Rutenfranz, E. Werner et al. (Hrgs.), *Schichtarbeit bei kontinuierliche Produktion*. Dortmund, Germany: Bundesanstalt für Arbeits- und Unfallsforschung. Bericht no 141.

Narayanan, V. K., & Nath, R. (1982). A field test of some attitudinal and behavioral consequences of flexitime. *Journal of Applied Psychology, 67,* 214–218.

Ng-A-Tham, J. E. E., & Thierry, Hk. (1993). An experimental change of the speed of rotation of the morning and evening shift. *Ergonomics, 36,* 51–57.

Nollen, S. (1979). *New patterns of work*. Scarsdale, NY: Work in American Institute.

Northrup, H. R., Wilson, J. T., & Rose, K. M. (1979). The twelve-hour shift in the petroleum and chemical industries. *Labor Relations Review, 32,* 312–326.

Nuttin, J., & Lens, W. (1985). *Future time perspective and motivation: Theory and research method*. Leuven, Belgium: Leuven University Press.

Ong, C. N., & Kogi, K. (1990). Shiftwork in developing countries, current issues and trends. In A. J. Scott (Ed.), *Shiftwork*. Philadelphia: Hanley & Belfus.

Orpen, C. (1981). Effect of flexible working hours on employee satisfaction and performance: A field experiment. *Journal of Applied Psychology, 66,* 113–115.

Ostberg, O. (1973). Interindividual differences in circadian fatigue patterns of shift workers. *British Journal of Industrial Medicine, 30,* 341–351.

Ott, E. (1987). Arbeitswissenschaft, arbeitszeitflexibilisierung, normalarbeitszeitstandard [Science of work, flexibilization and standard working times]. *Zeitschrift für Arbeitswissenschaft, 41,* 129–133.

Ottmann, W., Karvonen, M. J., Schmidt, K. H., Knauth, P., & Rutenfranz, J. (1989). Subjective health status of day and shift working policemen. *Ergonomics, 32,* 847–854.

Patkai, P., Akerstedt, T., & Pettersson, K. (1977). Field studies of shift work, I: Temporal patterns in psychophysiological activation in permanent night workers. *Ergonomics, 20,* 611–619.

Pennings, J. M. (1990). Structurele contigentie-theorie [Structural contingency theory]. In P. J. D. Drenth, Hk. Thierry, & Ch. J. de Wolff (Eds.), *Nieuw handboek arbeids- en organisatiepsychologie*. Houten, the Netherlands: Bohn Stafleu, Van Loghum.

Perret, D. (1980). *Experiments involving productivity and "worksharing."* Paper presented at the EAPM/EFPS Congress on "Rewarding Work," Amsterdam.

Pierce, J. L., & Dunham, R. B. (1992). The 12-hour workday: A 48-hour eight-day week. *Academy of Management Journal, 35,* 1086–1098.

Pierce, J. L., & Newstrom, J. W. (1983). The design of flexible work schedules and employee responses: Relationships and process. *Journal of Occupational Psychology, 4,* 247–262.

Pokorski, J., Oginski, & Knauth, P. (1986). Work physiological field studies concerning effects of combined stress in morning, afternoon and night shifts. In M. Haider, M. Koller, & R. Cervinka (Eds.), *Night and shiftwork: Longterm effects and their prevention*. Frankfurt: Peter Lang.

Poor, R. (1970). Reporting a revolution in work and leisure: 274-day firms. In R. Poor (Ed.), *4 Days, 40 hours*. Cambridge, MA: Bursk & Poor.

Poulton, E. C. (1978). Blue collar stressors. In C. L. Cooper & R. Payne (Eds.), *Stress at work*. New York: Wiley.

Presser, H. B. (1986). Shift work among American couples: The relevance of job and family factors. In M. Haider, M. Koller, & R. Cervinka (Eds.), *Night and shiftwork: Longterm effects and their prevention*. Frankfurt: Peter Lang.

Prokop, O., & Prokop, L. (1955). Ermüding und Einschlafen am Steuer [Fatigue and sleeping during driving]. *Deutsches Zeitschrift für gesammate gerichtliche Medizin, 44,* 343.

Projektgruppe Schicht Arbeit [Projectgroup Shift Work] (PROSA).(1981). *Projekt Schichtarbeit: Gesam-tergebniss der Problemanalyse* [The shiftwork study: Overall results]. Berlin: IG Chemie-Papier-Keramik.

Queinnec, Y., Chabaud, & de Terssac, G. (1986). Shiftworker's activity considered as the interaction of 'functional capacities and tasks to be carried out.' In M. Haider, M. Koller, & R. Cervinka (Eds.), *Night and shiftwork: Longterm effects and their prevention.* Frankfurt: Peter Lang.

Ralston, D. A. (1989). The benefits of flextime: Real or imagined? *Journal of Organizational Behavior, 10,* 369–373.

Ralston, D. A., Anthony, W. P., & Gustafson, D. J. (1985). Employees may love flextime, but what does it do to the organization's productivity? *Journal of Applied Psychology, 70,* 272–279.

Ray, J. T., Martin, D. E., & Alluisi, E. A. (1961). *Human performance as a function of the work-rest cycle: A review of selected studies.* Washington, DC: National Academy of Science, National Research Council.

Reinberg, A., Andlauer, P., & Vieux, N. (1981). Circadian temperature rhythm amplitude and long term tolerance of shiftworking. In L. C. Johnson, D. J. Tepas, W. P. Colquhoun, & M. J. Colligan (Eds.), *Biological rhythms, sleep and shift work.* New York: SP Medical & Scientific Books.

Reinberg, A., & Smolensky, M. H. (1983). Biological rhythms and medicine: *Cellular, metabolic, physiopathologic and pharmacologic aspects.* New York: Springer.

Reinberg, A., Vieux, N., & Andlauer, P. (Eds.). (1980). *Night and shift work: Biological and social aspects.* Oxford, UK: Pergamon Press.

Reinberg, A., Vieux, N., Ghata, J., Chaumont, A. J., & Laporte, A. (1978). Circadian rhythm amplitude and individual ability to adjust to shift work. *Ergonomics, 21,* 763–766.

Rissler, A., & Elgerot, A. (1978). *Stress reactions related to overtime at work.* Stockholm: Department of Psychology, University of Stockholm.

Robison, D. (1976). *Alternative work patterns.* Scarsdale, NY: Work in America Institute.

Ronen, S. (1981). *Flexible working hours.* New York: McGraw-Hill.

Ronen, S., & Primps, S. B. (1981). The compressed workweek as organizational change: Behavioral

and attitudinal outcomes. *Academy of Management Review, 6,* 61–74.

Rosa, R. R., & Colligan, M. J. (1988). Long workdays versus restdays: Assessing fatigue and alertness with a portable performance battery. *Human Factors, 39,* 305–317.

Rosa, R. R., Colligan, M. J., & Lewis, P. (1989). Extended workdays: Effects of 8-hour and 12-hour rotating shift schedules on performance, subjective alertness, sleep patterns and psychosocial variables. *Work & Stress, 3,* 21–32.

Rosow, J. M. (1979). Quality-of-work-life issues for the l980's. In C. Kerr & J. M. Rosow (Eds.), *Work in America: The decade ahead.* New York: Van Nostrand Reinhold.

Rudat, R. (1977). *Freizeitmöglichkeiten von nachtschicht- und feiertagsarbeitern sowie ansätze zu deren verbesserung* [Optimalization of the opportunities for leisure of shiftworkers]. Bonn, Germany: Inst. Angewandte Sozialwissenschaft.

Rudolf, G. de M. (1946). Psychological aspects of a conscious temporary generalized paralysis. *Journal of Mental Science, 92,* 814–816.

Ruppert, M. (1953). *De Nederlandse vakbeweging* [Dutch trade unions]. Haarlem, the Netherlands: Bohn.

Rutenfranz, J., Colquhoun, W. P., Knauth, P., & Ghata, J. N. (1977). Biomedical and psychosocial aspects of shirt work: A review. *Scandinavian Journal of Work, Environment and Health, 3,* 165–182.

Rutenfranz, J., & Knauth, P. (1986). Combined effects: Introductory remarks. In M. Haider, M. Koller, & R. Cervinka (Eds.), *Night and shiftwork: Longterm effects and their prevention.* Frankfurt: Peter Lang.

Ruenfranz, J., & Knauth, P. (1987). *Schichtarbeit und Nachtarbeit* [Shiftwork and nightwork]. München, Germany: Bayerisches Staatsministerium für Arbeit und Sozialordnung (2 Auflage).

Rutenfranz, J., Knauth, P., & Angersbach, D. (1981). Shift work research issues. In L. C. Johnson, D. I. Tepas, W. P. Colquhoun, & M. J. Colligan (Eds.), *The twenty-four hour workday: Proceedings of a symposium on variations in work-sleep schedules.* Cincinnati: Niosh.

Rutenfranz, J., Knauth, P., Küpper, R., Romann, R., & Ernst, G. (1979). *Model study on physiological and psychological consequences of shift work in some branches of the service sector.* Dublin: European

Foundation for the Improvement of Living and Working Conditions.

Rutenfranz, J., Neidhart, B., Ottmann, W., Schmidt, B., Plett, R., Knauth, P., & Klimmer, F. (1986). Circadian rhythms of physiological functions during experimental shiftwork with additional heat stress. In M. Haider, M. Koller, & R. Cervinka (Eds.), *Night and shiftwork: Longterm effects and their prevention*. Frankfurt: Peter Lane.

Rutenfranz, J., & Rohmert, W. (1983). *Arbeitszeitprobleme* [Problems with working times]. In W. Rohmert & J. Rutenfranz (Eds.), *Praktische Arbeitsphysiologie*. Stuttgart, Germany: Thieme Verlag.

Sakai, K., & Kogi, K. (1986). Conditions for three-shift workers to take night-time naps effectively. In M. Haider, M. Koller, & R. Cervinka (Eds.), *Night and shiftwork: Longterm effects and their prevention*. Frankfurt: Peter Lang.

Salvendy, G. (1987). *Handbook of human factors*. New York: Wiley.

Schein, V. E., Maurer, E. H., & Novah, J. F. (1977). Impact of flexible hours on productivity. *Journal of Applied Psychology, 62*, 463–465.

Schein, V. E., Maurer, E. H., & Novah, J. F. (1978). Supervisors' reactions to flexible working hours. *Journal of Occupational Psychology, 51*, 333–337.

Scherrer, J. (1981). Man's work and circadian rhythm through the ages. In A. Reinberg, N. Vieux, & P. Andlauer (Eds.), *Night and shift work: Biological and social aspects*. Oxford, UK: Pergamon Press.

Schmidt, K-H., Kleinbeck, U., & Knauth, P. (1988). Uber die Wirkung von Leistrungsvorgaben auf das Pausenverhalten und das Beanspruchungserleben bei freier Arbeit [On the effects of goalsetting with respect to performance on pausing and work load]. *Zeitschrift für Arbeitswissenschaft, 42*, 96–101.

Schmidt, R. F., & Thews, G. (1983). *Human physiology*. New York: Springer-Verlag.

Schoemaker, N., Van Gageldonk, A., Demenint, M., & Van Vianen, A. (1981). *Deeltijdarbeid in het bedrijf* [Part time work in the company]. Alphen a/d Rijn, the Netherlands: Samsom.

Seibt, A., Friedrichsen, G., Jakubowski, A., Kaufman, O., & Schuring, U. (1986). Investigations on the effect of work-dependent noise in combination with shiftwork. In M. Haider, M. Koller, & R.

Cervinka (Eds.), *Night and shiftwork: Longterm effects and their prevention*. Frankfurt: Peter Lang.

Sergean, R. (1971). *Managing shift work*. London: Gower Press.

Shift Work Committee, Japan Association of Industrial Health. (1978). Opinion on night work and shift work. *Journal of Science of Labor, 55*(8), 1–36.

Sloane, P. J. (1975). *Changing patterns of working hours*. London: Department of Employment Manpower Paper No. 13, HMSO.

Smith, A., & Miles, C. (1986). The combined effects of nightwork and noise on human function. In M. Haider, M. Koller, & R. Cervinka (Eds.), *Night and shiftwork: Longterm effects and their prevention*. Frankfurt: Peter Lang.

Staines, G. L., & Pleck, J. H. (1984). Nonstandard work schedules and family life. *Journal of Applied Psychology, 69*, 515–523.

Steffy, B. D., & Jones, J. W. (1990). Differences between full time and part time employees in perceived role strain and work satisfaction. *Journal of Organizational Behavior, 11*, 321–329.

Streich, W. (1985). *Fünf Jahre Schichtarbeitsforschung im Aktionsprogramm Humanisierung des Arbeitslebens* [Five years of shift work research in the program 'humanisation of working conditions']. Dortmund, Germany: Gesellschaft für Arbeidsschutz- und Humanisierungsforschung.

Tasto, D. L., Colligan, M. J., Skjei, E. W., & Polly, S. J. (1978). *Health consequences of shift work*. Washington, DC: Niosh.

Taylor, P. J. (1967). Shift and day work: A comparison of sickness absence, lateness, and other absence behaviour at an oil refinery from 1962 to 1965. *British Journal of Industrial Medicine, 24*, 93–102.

Taylor, P. J. (1968). Sickness absence resistance. *Transport Social Occupational Medicine, 18*, 96–100.

Taylor, P. J., & Pocock, S. J. (1972). Mortality of shift and day workers 1956–1968. *British Journal of Industrial Medicine, 29*, 201–207.

Taylor, P. J., Pocock, S. J., & Sergean, R. (1972). Shift and day workers' absence: Relationship with some terms and conditions of service. *British Journal of Industrial Medicine, 29*, 338–340.

Teiger, C. (1984). Overmortality among permanent nightworkers: Some questions about adaptation. In A. Wedderburn & P. Smith (Eds.), *Psychological approaches to night and shift work*. Edinburgh: Herriot-Watt University.

Tepas, D. I. (1982). Shiftworker sleep strategies. *Journal of Human Ergology, 11*, 325–336.

Tepas, D. I. (1985). Flexitime, compressed workweeks and other alternative work schedules. In S. Folkard & T. H. Monk (Eds.), *Hours of work: Temporal factors in work-scheduling*. Chichester, UK: Wiley.

Tepas, D. I. (1990). Condensed working hours: Questions and issues. In G. Costa, G. Cesena, K. Kogi, & A. Wedderburn (Eds.), *Shiftwork: Health, sleep and performance*. Frankfurt: Peter Lang.

Thierry, Hk. (1980). Compensation for shiftwork: A model and some results. In W. P. Colquhoun & J. Rutenfranz (Eds.), *Studies of shiftwork*. London: Taylor & Francis.

Thierry, Hk. (1981). Compensation for shift work. In L. C. Johnson, D. I. Tepas, W. P. Colquhoun, & M. J. Colligan (Eds.), *The twenty-four hour workday: Proceedings of a symposium on variations in work-sleep schedules*. Cincinnati: Niosh.

Thierry, Hk. (1989). Motivatie en satisfactie [Motivation and satisfaction]. In P. J. D. Drenth, Hk. Thierry, & Ch. J. de Wolff (Eds.), *Nieuw handboek arbeids- en organisatiepsychologie*. Houten, the Netherlands: Bohn, Stafleu, Van Loghum.

Thierry, Hk. (1992). Pay and payment systems. In J. F. Hartley & G. M. Stephenson (Eds.), *Employment relations: The psychology of influence and control at work*. Oxford, UK: Blackwell.

Thierry, Hk., & de Jong, J. R. (1991). Arbeidsanalyse ten behoeve van beloning [Work analysis and payment]. In J. A. Algera (Ed.), *Analyse van arbeid vanuit verschillende perspectieven* [The analysis of work from various perspectives]. Amsterdam: Swets & Zeitlinger.

Thierry, Hk., Hoolwerf, G., & Drenth, P. J. D. (1985). Attitudes of permanent day and shift workers towards shiftwork: A field study. In P. Colquhoun, S. Folkard, P. Knauth, & J. Rutenfranz (Eds.), *Experimental studies of shiftwork*. Opladen, Germany: Westdeutscher Verlag.

Thierry, Hk., & Jansen, B. (1981). Potential interventions for compensating shift work inconveniences. In A. Reinberg, N. Vieux, & P. Andlauer (Eds.), *Night and shift work: Biological and social aspects*. Oxford, UK: Pergamon Press.

Thierry, Hk., & Jansen, B. (1984). Work and working time. In P. J. D. Drenth, Hk. Thierry, P. J.

Willems, & Ch. J. de Wolff (Eds.), *Handbook of work and organizational psychology*. Chichester, UK: Wiley.

Thierry, Hk., Koopman, P. L., & Van der Flier, H. (1992). *Wat houdt ons bezig: Recente ontwikkelingen rond motivatie en arbeid* [Points of concern: Recent developments in motivation and work]. Utrecht, the Netherlands: Lemma.

Thiis-Evensen, E. (1958). Shift work and health. *Industrial Medical Surgery, 27*, 493–497.

Thiis-Evensen, E. (1969). Shift work and health. *Studia Laboris et Salutis, 4*, 81–83.

Tilley, A. J., Wilkinson, R. T., Warren, P. S. G., & Drud, M. (1982). The sleep and performance of shift workers. *Human Factors, 24*, 624–641.

Torsvall, L., & Akerstedt, T. (1987). Sleepiness on the job: Continuously measured EEG changes in train drivers. *Electroenceph. Clinical Neurophysiology, 66*, 502–511.

Torsvall, L., Akerstedt, T., Gillander, K., & Knutsson, A. (1989). Sleep on the night shift: 24-hour EEG monitoring of spontaneous sleep/wake behavior. *Psychophysiology, 26*, 352–358.

Torsvall, L., Akerstedt, T., & Gillberg, M. (1981). Age, sleep and irregular work hours: A field study with electroencephalographic recordings, catecholamine excretion and self ratings. *Scandinavian Journal of Work, Environment and Health, 7*, 196–203.

Tune, G. S. (1969). Sleep and wakefulness in a group of shiftworkers. *British Journal of Industrial Medicine 26*, 54–58.

Ulich, E. (1957). Zur Frage der Belastung des arbeitenden Menschen durch Nacht und Schichtarbeit [On the workload in night and shiftwork]. *Psych. Rundschau, 8*, 42–61.

van Dormolen, M., Hertog, C. A. W. M., Van Dijk, F. J. H., Kompier, M. A. J., & Fortuin, R. (1990). The quest for interaction studies on combined exposure. *International Archives of Occupational and Environmental Health, 62*, 279–287.

van Haasteren, F. C. A., Van Overeem, M. (1976). *Arbeidà la carte* [Work at discretion]. Scheveningen, the Netherlands: Stichting Maatschappij en Onderneming.

Van Schilfgaarde, P. (Ed.). (1984). *Werk in delen* [Work in parts]. Deventer, the Netherlands: Kluwer/COB.

Verhaegen, P., Cober, R., de Smedt, M., Dirkx, J., Kerstens, J., Ryvers, D., & Van Daele, P.

(1987). The adaptation of night nurses to different work schedules. *Ergonomics, 30,* 1301–1310.

Verhaegen, P., Dirkx, I., Maassen, A., & Meers, A. (1986). Subjective health after twelve years of shift work. In M. Haider, M. Koller, & R. Cervinka (Eds.), *Night and shiftwork: Longterm effects and their prevention.* Frankfurt: Peter Lang.

Verhaegen, P., Maassen, A., & Meers, A. (1981). Health problems in shiftworkers. In L. C. Johnson, D. I. Tepas, W. P. Colquhoun, & M. J. Colligan (Eds.), *The twenty-four hour workday: Proceedings of a symposium on variations in work-sleep schedules.* Cincinnati: Niosh.

Vernon, H. M. (1921). *Industrial fatigue and efficiency.* London: Routledge.

Vidacek, S., Kaliterna, L., & Radosevic-Vidacek, B. (1986). Productivity on a weekly rotating shift system: Circadian adjustment and sleep deprivation effects? *Erogonomics, 29,* 1583–1590.

Volle, M., Brisson, G. R., Perusse, M., Tanaka, M., & Doyon, Y. (1979). Compressed workweek; psychophysiological and physiological repercussion. *Ergonomics, 22,* 1001–1010.

Walker, J. (1978). *The human aspects of shift work.* London: Institute of Personnel Management.

Walker, J., & de la Mare, G. (1971). Absence from work in relation to length and distribution of shift hours. *British Journal of Industrial Medicine, 28,* 36–44.

Walsh, J. K., Tepas, D. I., & Moss, P. D. (1981). The EEG sleep of night and rotating shiftworkers. In L. C. Johnson, D. I. Tepas, W. P. Colquhoun, & M. J. Colligan (Eds.), *The twenty-four hour workday: Proceedings of a symposium on variations in work-sleep schedules.* Cincinnati: Niosh.

Watson, D., & Pennebaker, J. W. (1989). Health complaints, stress and distress: Exploring the central role of negative affectivity. *Psychological Review, 96,* 234–254.

Wedderburn, A. A. I. (1967). Social factors in satisfaction with swiftly rotating shifts. *Journal of Occupational Psychology, 41,* 85–107.

Wedderburn, A. A. I. (1978). Some suggestions for increasing the usefulness of psychological and sociological studies of shift work. *Ergonomics, 21,* 827–833.

Wegmann, H. M., & Klein, K. E. (1985). Jetlag and aircrew scheduling. In S. Folkard & T. H. Monk (Eds.), *Hours of work: Temporal factors in work-scheduling.* Chichester, UK: Wiley.

Wever, R. A. (1974). Bedeutung der circadianen Periodik für das Alter [Circadian rhythms and age]. *Naturwissenschaftliche Rundschau, 27,* 475–479.

Wever, R. A. (1979). *The circadian system of man: Results of experiments under temporal isolation.* Berlin: Springer.

Wever, R. A. (1985). Man in temporal isolation: Basic principles of the circadian system. In S. Folkard & T. H. Monk (Eds.), *Hours of work.* Chichester, UK: Wiley.

Wheeler, K. E., Gurman, R., & Tarnowieski, D. (1972). *The four-day week.* New York: American Management Association.

White, M. (1987). *Working hours: Assessing the potential for reduction.* Geneva: International Labour Office.

Wongphanic, M., Saito, H., Kogi, K., & Temmyo, Y. (1982). Conditions of working life of women textile workers in Thailand on day and shift work systems. *Journal of Human Ergology, 11,* 165–175.

Wotjczak-Jaroszowa, J., & Banaskiewicz, A. (1974). Physical work capacity during day and night. *Ergonomics, 17,* 193–198.

Wotjczak-Jaroszowa, J., Makowsa, Z., Rzepecki, H., Banaskiewicz, A., & Romejko, A. (1978). Changes in psychomotor and mental task performance following physical work in standard conditions and in a shift working situation. *Ergonomics, 21,* 801–809.

Wyatt, S., & Marriott, R. (1953). Night work and shift changes. *British Journal of Industrial Medicine, 10,* 164–172.

CHAPTER 8

Cross-cultural Leadership Making: Bridging American and Japanese Diversity for Team Advantage

George B. Graen
University of Cincinnati

Mitsuru Wakabayashi
Nagoya University, Japan

Developing reciprocal bonds of harmony, obligation, and trust between two or more people from different cultures who work together over time is a process called cross-cultural leadership making. This process is more complicated than leadership making within a single culture, but it may provide the opportunity to observe both cultural differences and leadership making together in the case of newly established Japanese corporations' manufacturing plants in the United States. Clearly, effective cross-cultural leadership making must take place before these Japanese transplants can match the effectiveness of their homeplants. In this chapter we focus on bridging the cultural differences between Japan and the United States by describing some of the problems relevant to cross-cultural leadership making, presenting a model of unicultural leadership making, including critical research, and reviewing applications of cross-cultural leadership making and discussing their implications for research.

Introduction

CROSS-CULTURAL LEADERSHIP MAKING is the process of developing mature leader–follower relationships, both vertical and horizontal, between people from different cultures. While leadership making is a complicated process for two people from the same culture, the process becomes doubly complicated when it involves people from different cultures. However, this added complication may actually present an opportunity to observe the relationship between cultural differences and leadership making together. This research opportunity results from the direct foreign investment in manufacturing plants by Japanese corporations in North America. These plants, which use lean Japanese organization methods and mostly American employees, require cross-cultural leadership making to be successful.

Cross-cultural leadership making is necessary for the successful internationalization of the corporation (Starr, 1988). Contemporary Japanese corporations are faced with the difficult challenge of creating ways to develop cross-cultural leadership in their foreign plants (Negandhi, 1985). This is particularly true in the United States, where so-called Japanese transplants have been established at increasing rates in recent years: approximately 550 by 1987; 837 by 1988; 1,039 by 1989; and 1,443 by the end of 1990 (Taga, 1992).

A *Japanese transplant* is a manufacturing plant owned by a Japanese parent company and located in a foreign country. Such plants typically are established using the latest technology available to the parent company. The idea is to make the plant a long-term investment by providing it with every advantage the parent company can afford. This includes a developmental plan, advanced technology, skilled workers, long-term capital, starter markets, and reliable suppliers (Abo, 1988).

Leadership presents special problems for Japanese transplants in the United States because of the cultural and contextual differences between the two countries (Fucini & Fucini, 1990; Johnson, 1988). Cultural differences between the United States and Japan are well known and deeply rooted. In fact, the two cultures are polar opposites on many dimensions (Hofstede, 1980). In addition, the contextual differences between the two countries are also substantial in that the Japanese transplant uses the *Toyota system* or *lean organization system* (described later in this chapter), while most Americans have experience only with the scientific management or mass production system (Pucik & Hanada, 1990). Despite these cultural and contextual differences, leadership relationships must be developed in these transplants between the Japanese associates and the American workers (Wakabayashi & Graen, 1988).

The hope is that transplants will become the vanguards of cross-cultural leadership making by developing leaders who can translate their cross-cultural learning into concepts shared by colleagues who live in another culture. In a sense, these leaders learn two cultures to make a separate third culture (Useem, Useem, & Donghue, 1963). If two parties representing two different cultures at a transplant struggle to retain their separate cultures, then serious cultural conflict will emerge. However, if cross-cultural learning is done by both parties, we believe a third, hybrid culture can emerge that will benefit the organization by enhancing associates' commitment to the organization and promoting associates' participation in corporate issues. Managers at a typical hybrid culture transplant have found that their associates see themselves neither as Japanese at the home plants nor as other Americans working in the same industry in the United States. Rather, they see themselves as part of a unique corporate culture that has developed.

In this chapter, we will consider cross-cultural leadership making by first discussing some current cross-cultural leadership-making problems in Japanese transplants. Second, we will review the literature on leadership making within single cultures, present a model of the process, and report on some new research approaches. Third, we will describe some important differences between Western and Eastern leadership contexts. Fourth, we will report on recent applications of cross-cultural leadership making to Japanese transplants in the United States. Finally, we will discuss our conclusions and the implications for research.

Problems Relevant to Cross-cultural Leadership Making

Our studies of Japanese transplants in the United States reveal a set of problems that are clear by-products of early cross-cultural leadership-making efforts. These problems can be resolved either by accepting one culture or the other, or by creating a third culture for leadership making. Some of the problems found in Japanese transplants in the United States are the following.

Language differences complicate communications and cooperation at managerial levels. Very few domestic managers are able to interpret communications from the Japanese home office, and few expatriate managers can discuss abstract issues in English. Communication is therefore restricted to concrete issues without the benefit of any rationale or subtlety. Although fax machines run throughout the night, only Japanese managers can understand their messages. Domestic managers receive their home office communications via expatriates. Several transplants we became familiar with assigned expatriate advisers to each domestic manager to help deal with communication difficulties. The immediate array of unresolved language problems keeps managers from confronting the underlying cultural issues. We can expect that these cultural issues will continue to surface long after any language problems are resolved.

*Japanese managers and workers are shocked by what they perceive as American managers' seem-*ingly *underdeveloped sense of obligation to their company and co-workers.* Japanese managers often believe that American managers place their personal interests above those of the company and their co-workers. For example, one company engaged in launching a new product during deer hunting season asked its hourly workers to postpone taking days off until the product launch was completed. Japanese managers were gratified that hourly rank-and-file absenteeism only increased by 5 percent during hunting season. However, they were aghast that absenteeism among American managers also increased by 5 percent during this period. They complained that managers should feel a stronger obligation to the company and lead their workers by setting a good example. This perceived underdeveloped sense of obligation makes it difficult for expatriate managers to trust or rely on domestic managers to perform critical tasks.

Domestic managers appear to have difficulty subordinating their personal need for power to the good of the team. Domestic managers may experience a sense of control loss when they follow the advice of their Japanese trainers and allow their subordinates to participate in critical decision making. This is especially true when the managers have a technically superior solution to a problem that their workers resist. At a cognitive level, domestic managers need to understand that the quality of a decision has two dimensions—technical adequacy and effective implementation—and that participation by those who will implement the decision strengthens the latter. However, these managers may feel powerless when they allow this kind of participation to operate in their work units. This uneasiness contrasts greatly with the feelings of expatriate managers, who are comfortable with this process.

Domestic managers have difficulty with the absence of punishment for insubordination as an ideal. According to this Toyota principle, workers should not necessarily be punished for resisting a legitimate request by their managers. Instead, this philosophy considers the possibility that it is the manager who may be at fault for making a request that is resisted. Without insubordination as a punishable offense, a manager must develop a sense of obligation and ownership in his or her workers through leadership-making activities. Although the leadership-making process takes time and involves the investment of valuable outcomes for each party, it builds mutual obligations that render insubordination superfluous. This leadership process is described in detail by Graen (1989).

Domestic managers see a lack of office perks as a loss of status. The absence of status symbols such as private offices, reserved parking spaces, and management lunchrooms, meeting rooms, and washrooms—as well as the de-emphasis of status symbols in general—reduces the gulf between hourly workers and managers. In addition, some transplants require all plant management personnel to work on the shop floor at least one day a month and get their hands dirty. Though domestic managers understand at a conceptual level that such equal treatment helps reduce the social distance between hourly workers and managers, they feel the loss of status signaled by a lack of perks at a deeper, emotional level. Compared to their cohorts in domestic companies, they feel that their situation is inferior and that they are not treated as well (Thibault & Kelley, 1959).

Domestic managers do not commit their entire career to a single company. One of the most serious challenges transplants face surrounds the issue of management mobility in the United States. Japanese transplants very carefully recruit and select domestic managers for operations and personnel, often from presidents on down. They hope that everyone hired will retire with their company. When domestic managers leave the transplant for another company, expatriate managers feel the loss doubly. First, they must repair their extensive networks by assuming the obligations of their departed peer and prepare for a new person to grow into the numerous company networks. This kind of adjustment is especially difficult for the Japanese leadership system because it is based on stable interlocking teams of committed managers. Over time, managers grow into critical roles in numerous networks based on their capabilities and the changing needs of the company. Second, expatriate managers feel the loss at a personal level as a failure of obligation. Many Japanese managers have difficulty accepting that a domestic manager can proclaim allegiance to a company and then leave within a year or two for another company—especially if it is a direct competitor.

The average expatriate manager is usually thought more deserving of leadership-making investment than the best domestic manager. This is largely because expatriot managers have demonstrated orientation toward lifetime commitment to the company and their shared sense of obligation, teamwork, and sense of harmony. Moreover, they have a superior understanding of the home plant management system, which serves as the ideal. Domestic managers need to counter the advantages expatriates hold over them by earning respect for their capabilities and motivations. Clearly, expatriate management must engage in cross-cultural leadership making with their domestic managers if they hope to build their professional ranks with people other than visitors who will leave after a short time.

In the face of these challenges to leadership making in transplants, cross-cultural solutions are needed. We view this situation as a unique opportunity to further understand and apply the process of cross-cultural leadership making. We will next turn to a review of what we understand about leadership making from both American and Japanese studies before discussing the application of cross-cultural leadership making in transplants.

A Model for Leadership Making[*]

Leadership involves an "influential increment" over and above that which is formally prescribed in the work unit (Katz & Kahn, 1978). By exerting this extra influence, effective leaders are able to develop additional resources within their work units beyond those that are formally defined (Zalesny & Graen, 1986). Leadership influence may vary from extremely effective, where the leadership influence dominates the structural influences, to nonexistent, where no additional increment of influence is exerted (Ferris, 1985; Graen, Liden, & Hoel, 1982). Moreover, leadership can lead to an internalization of team interests—a transformation of self-interests to team interests (Burns, 1978).

In a series of longitudinal studies investigating role-making processes in ongoing organizations, Graen and colleagues (Graen, 1969; Graen & Cashman, 1975; Graen, Orris, & Johnson, 1973; Graen, Novak, & Sommerkamp, 1982; Graen & Scandura, 1987; Graen, Scandura, & Graen, 1986; Graen, Wakabayashi, Graen, & Graen, 1990; Liden & Graen, 1980), through the development of a leadership making model called the *leader-member exchange* (LMX) model, have identified ways in which effective leadership processes can be attained as a by-product of role making by organizational participants. These studies found that truly effective leadership—the type of leadership in which leaders are able to exert considerable incremental influence with their workers, and the workers with their leaders—occurs when leaders develop mature leadership relationships with their followers. Within mature leadership relationships (high LMX), leaders and members experience reciprocal influence; extracontractual behavior; mutual

trust, respect, and liking; and internalization of common goals (Crouch & Yetton, 1988; Duchon, Green, & Taber, 1986; Hosking & Morley, 1988; Zalesny & Graen, 1986). In contrast, the working relationships of leaders and members who have not developed mature leadership relationships (or low LMX) are characterized by unidirectional downward influence, contractual behavior exchange, formal role-defined relations, and loosely coupled goals (Dansereau, Graen, & Haga, 1975; Graen, 1976; Graen & Schiemann, 1978; Vecchio, 1982). Because of the transformation that occurs in mature leadership relationships when followers agree to take on additional responsibilities, leaders can rely on these followers to act as trusted associates who will aid in the design and management of the work unit. Such workers are willing to exert extra effort in their work—to outgrow their formally defined work roles—by engaging in activities that are not specifically prescribed by the organization, such as taking personal initiative, exercising personal leadership to make their work unit more effective, and taking career risks to accomplish assignments (Graen, 1989). These are the individuals with whom leaders can effectively earn incremental influence beyond what is formally defined by the employment contract—the individuals with whom effective leadership processes are achieved (Fairhurst & Chandler, 1989; Fairhurst, Rogers, & Sarr, 1987).

Clearly, leadership within an organization is not simply a leader's downward influence over a follower. Leadership also involves upward influence, from a follower to a leader (Mowday, 1978; Porter, Allen, & Angle, 1981). Studies on the effect of follower behaviors on leader reactions (Farris & Lim, 1969; Fodor, 1974; Gardner & Martinko, 1988) have clearly demonstrated that followers also influence their leaders through a process of reverse causality (Farris & Lim, 1969; Herold, 1977; Lowin & Craig, 1968). This influence may be intentional, through the use of influence tactics (Dienesch &

---

* This section was written by George Graen in collaboration with Mary Uhl-Bien.

Liden, 1986; Gardner & Martinko, 1988; Graen, Vasudevan, & Bell, 1992; Kipnis, Schmidt, & Wilkinson, 1980; Liden & Mitchell, 1989; Porter, Allen, & Angle, 1981), or unintentional, through such things as the effect of performance level on managerial style (Lowin & Craig, 1968). Regardless of intent, however, the influence does occur (House & Baetz, 1979).

Because of this upward influence, organizational leadership is not simply a leader exerting influence over a follower, it is also a follower influencing a leader—a process of reciprocal influence (Bandura, 1977; Sims & Manz, 1984). Leadership, then, does not lie simply with a leader, but involves both parties.

What exactly are the roles of the leader and follower in the leadership process? Simply stated, if leadership is both a downward influence and an upward influence, where does the leadership process occur? To address this question, an expanded model of leadership will be presented in the following section. This model incorporates the ideas developed in the role-making literature but progresses beyond the contemporary leader-member exchange ideas by addressing the methods through which leadership making can be developed. Moreover, this model has implications not only for direct-reporting relationships but also for leadership relations that may occur between any two individuals. We will then discuss the leadership-making model and its implications for the development of leadership at both the individual and team level.

The Leadership-making Model in Detail

The leadership-making model is based on the three-component model of leadership illustrated in Figure 1. As illustrated in the figure, leadership consists of three primary components: (a) the characteristics of the leader, (b) the characteristics of the follower, and (c) the maturity of the leadership relationship. This model illustrates the leadership influence

process described in the previous section. Of particular significance is the fact that the three-component model of leadership suggests that the leadership influence process occurs within the context of the leadership relationship. According to this model, leaders and followers can independently contribute to the effectiveness of teamwork, but these will only be base contributions that are motivated by a formal work contract, whereas leadership-motivated contributions to teamwork effectiveness result in incremental influence (Katz & Kahn, 1978). More specifically, leadership relationships that are more highly mature will contribute more positively to teamwork effectiveness through incremental influence than those relationships that are less mature. In addition, the maturity of the leadership relationship contributes to internalization of the team goals, structure, and process through its effect on the values adopted by team members. Through the establishment of a highly mature leadership relationship, team members undergo a transformation process in which they outgrow their jobs by expanding their interests from an individual focus to a team focus.

The development of mature leadership relationships is initiated when reciprocal investments are made between leaders and high-potential members. These high-potential members are identified by their ability to convince their leaders that they deserve to outgrow their present positions and by their leader's readiness to encourage it. Through a process of reciprocal investments, leaders and selected members are able to successfully accomplish complicated and difficult tasks despite apparent obstacles and impediments (Graen, 1989). To better understand this process, the leadership relationship may be thought of as a dyadic psychological account to which the leader and follower give investments and take withdrawals (Graen & Scandura, 1987). Because the account is a socioemotional relationship, the units of measure are psychological, not material. Each party therefore interprets both

FIGURE 1

Three-Component Model of Leadership

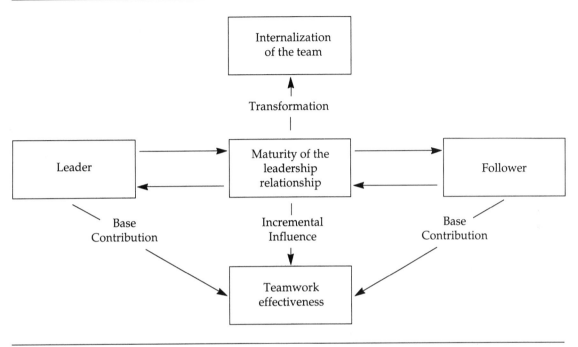

From "The Transformation of Professionals Into Self-managing and Partially Self-designing Contributors: Toward a Theory of Leadership Making" by G. B. Graen and M. Uhl-Bien, 1991, *Journal of Management Systems, 3* (3), p. 30. Copyright 1991 by Maximilian Press. Reprinted by permission.

investments and withdrawals subjectively and in terms of the account's history. Moreover, these psychological accounts have a life cycle. At first, they are between two strangers; later they are between two acquaintances. Finally, under certain circumstances, the accounts transform into mature relationships.

When a leader attempts to influence a follower (or, conversely, when a follower attempts to influence a leader), the attempts at influence are recognized and considered by the follower in terms of his or her relationship with the leader. This relationship may be in its early stages, in which case the attempts at influence will occur within a process of role making (or team making) (Graen & Scandura, 1987). In the case of a well-established relationship, the

person who is targeted for influence may consider the request in terms of past experiences with the person who is attempting to do the influencing (e.g., based on idiosyncratic credits described by Hollander, 1958, 1980). In either case, the follower will respond to the leader's attempts at influence based on impressions of the leader that have been formed by the relationship; high-quality relationships will result in greater mutual influence, and low-quality relationships will result in contractual influence.

As it is developing, the reciprocal investment process between leaders and selected followers resembles a partnership. The leader and the selected followers collaborate to capitalize on both the hidden opportunities and resources of the work unit and the unique mix of abilities and motivations of people within and around the work unit. Thus, individual workers are integrated into cohesive, coordinated, and adaptable teams at the work unit level, and they are integrated into larger collaborative competence networks at the organizational level.

Life Cycle of Leadership Maturity

As noted, the development of mature leadership relationships in the leadership-making process may be viewed as a life cycle of leadership relationship maturity. In this life cycle, the relationship-building process between leaders and followers occurs over three stages, as shown in Figure 2. In the first stage of the leadership making life cycle, leaders and followers come together as *strangers* who occupy interdependent organizational roles. In this stage, interactions between the leader and follower occur on a more formal basis where leaders and followers engage in a "cash-and-carry" and immediate exchange (see Characteristics B and C in Figure 2). Within this relationship, exchanges are purely contractual: Leaders provide followers only with what they need to perform, and followers perform only as they are required. In the second, *acquaintance* stage, leaders and followers progress in their relationship from strangers to acquaintances. In this stage, increased exchanges occur between leaders and followers, not all of which are contractual. Leaders and followers may begin to share greater information and resources on both a personal and professional level. These exchanges are still limited, however, and constitute a testing stage: An equitable return of favors is expected within a limited time period. Finally, in the third, *mature* stage, exchanges between leaders and followers are highly developed: They are mutual exchanges and may have a long time span of reciprocation (Characteristics B and C in Figure 2). Leaders and followers can rely on

one another for loyalty and support. Exchanges are not only behavioral but also emotional. In this stage, the amount of incremental influence occurring between leaders and followers is extremely high.

Progression through the life cycle varies in real time according to leadership dyads. In some dyads, the relationship may not progress much beyond the stranger stage—the leader and member have limited interactions, and those that do occur are strictly contractual. These types of dyads have been documented in the LMX research (Graen & Scandura, 1987) as low-LMX dyads (Characteristic D in Figure 2). In these situations, the leadership process is essentially nonexistent, since incremental influence is not achieved. This is analogous to the transactional leadership model as defined by Bass (1985; see F.1 in Figure 2), in that the exchange is based on subordination to the leader. In this case, the leader makes requests based on his or her hierarchical status within the organization, and the follower complies because of a formal obligation to the leader and because of the rewards the leader controls. Similarly, the motivations of the follower are based on the satisfaction of his or her own self-interests, without consideration of the good of the group (Characteristic F.2 in Figure 2). Rather than being based on an exchange of favors, this conception of transactional leadership is based more on the fundamental ideas of behavior modification (Skinner, 1953).

In other dyads, leaders and followers may advance beyond the stranger stage into the acquaintance stage. In these cases (medium-LMX dyads), leaders and members may develop a somewhat more involved relationship; however, the incremental influence (Characteristic E in Figure 2) is still limited. Leadership processes in these dyads are more effective than those in the stranger stage, but the high degree of trust and loyalty necessary for truly effective leadership still has not been fully developed. That kind of relationship is only possible for those

FIGURE 2

Life Cycle of Leadership Making

	Time		
Stage	*Stranger* ⟶	*Acquaintance* ⟶	*Mature*
Characteristic			
A. Relationship building phase	Role finding	Role making	Role implementation
B. Type of reciprocity	Cash and carry	Mixed	In kind
C. Time span of reciprocity	Immediate	Some delay	Indefinite
D. Leader–member exchange	Low	Medium	High
E. Incremental influence	None	Limited	Almost unlimited
F. Type of leadership:			
1. Transactional	Behavioral management (Bass, 1985)	⟶	Reciprocal favors (Burns, 1978)
2. Transformational	Self-interest	⟶	Team interest

From "The Transformation of Professionals Into Self-managing and Partially Self-designing Contributors: Toward a Theory of Leadership Making" by G. B. Graen and M. Uhl-Bien, 1991, *Journal of Management Systems, 3* (3), p. 33. Copyright 1991 by Maximilian Press. Reprinted by permission.

who progress to the third stage, the mature leadership stage.

The payoffs can be tremendous for those dyadic members who progress to the mature stage (high-LMX). In mature relationships, the potential for incremental influence is virtually unlimited, due to the enormous range of exchange of favors (transactions) that are possible as defined by Burns (1978). In Burns' conception of transactional leadership (in contrast to Bass' [1985] interpretation), transactions are exchanges of favors that may or may not be influenced by hierarchical position within the organization. Instead, the transactions are based on the history of the exchange relationship between the dyadic members. Thus, in this stage, the mature transactional relationship

developed between the dyadic members results in a high degree of mutual trust, respect, and obligation within the relationship (Characteristic F.1 in Figure 2), subsequently leading members to engage in activities they otherwise would not. Leaders can rely on the followers to provide them with special assistance when needed. For example, they may rely on followers to take on extra assignments without pay or provide honest, constructive criticism in situations that others may find intimidating. Likewise, followers may rely on leaders for needed support, encouragement, or advice. It is this trust, respect, and confidence in leaders that encourages followers to grow beyond a formalized work contract: to grow out of their jobs and help *redesign the unit and its context*

(Characteristic F.2 in Figure 2). In this transformation process (Burns, 1978), followers in mature relationships progress beyond their own self-interests to a focus that is more on team interests. These individuals recognize that by satisfying team interests they are also able to fulfill their own interests. Moreover, because of their special relationship with the leader, they have the resources and support which allow them to take on the additional responsibilities that accompany this transformation. The hypotheses derived from the type of leadership being considered—either transactional or transformational (Characteristics F.1 and F.2 in Figure 2)—have been supported empirically by Sridhar (1991), Deluga (1992), and Basu (1991). In all three studies, behavior management (Bass, 1985) and self-interest were more strongly associated with immature leadership relationships than they were with mature ones, while reciprocal obligations (Burns, 1978) and team interest were more strongly associated with mature leadership relationships than they were with immature ones.

Leadership Making Upstairs, Downstairs, and Across the Hall

Given that leadership is an interpersonal influence process, the leadership-making model describes a process that is applicable to the cultivation of more effective cross-cultural teamwork. As networks of interdependent dyadic leadership relationships, teams are also affected by the types of relationships developed among their members. Since teams are composed of every possible combination of dyadic leadership relationships, how each of these interdependent relationships is developed and managed will influence the outcome of teams. Thus, relationships within teams are not merely collections of leadership relationships between members and leaders: *They also include the entire set of leadership or incremental influence relationships between team members*. In

addition to teammate relationships, the concept of team in our extended model also includes leadership relationships between team members and co-workers outside of the nuclear team (Graen & Uhl-Bien, 1991b; Seers, 1989). Specifically, a person's competence network is composed of anyone who has nontrivial interdependent relationships with him or her (Graen, 1990).

Let us draw boundaries around our conception of the extended team by describing the two additional kinds of leadership-making relationships within our concept. Leadership making occurs both between prospective teammates as part of team making, and between prospective teammates and their competence networks as part of role making.

Leadership Making With Teams.   One kind of leadership making, that which occurs among prospective teammates as a group, is necessary in order to tap into members' personal reserves. Ideally, teams go through a team-making process to develop cooperative and harmonious relationships among all of their teammates based on the mutual theory in practice that career progress is best enhanced through team achievement (Graen, 1989). Therefore, no individual should be rewarded for self-enhancement at the expense of the team, but all teammates should be rewarded through team success (Uhl-Bien & Graen, 1992b).

Individuals in the end must decide for themselves the extent to which they are willing to contribute from their personal reserves. These kinds of contributions cannot be required by either organizational superiors or peers. Therefore, team-making processes ultimately need to be employed to create that which can be given and to influence what will be given. In one study of team making in a commercial bank (Graen, 1989), the team members effectively convinced themselves that they needed to tap into their collective competence networks or risk failure. Their traditional market segments were becoming unprofitable, but promising new markets were emerging. Although the teammates had not developed relationships with influential leaders in these new segments, workers in their competence networks had. Thus, by redeeming some owed favors and asking for new favors, teammates were able to "leapfrog" over their competition into emerging market segments. Following this team success, the team sponsors recorded the contributions of teammates in their personnel files.

Leadership Making With Competence Networks. A second kind of leadership making, that which occurs between prospective teammates and their competence networks as part of role making, is required in order for team *backup systems* to develop (Graen, 1989). These backup systems tap into information intelligence, influence, resource, and expertise reserves. Such backup systems can be mediated by teammates through their leadership relationships with colleagues outside of the team. Furthermore, the probability of accessing such backup systems depends on the maturity of the leadership relationships. Teammates with mature relationships are more likely to gain access to these systems than teammates with acquaintance-level relationships.

As a team progresses on its assigned mission, it often finds itself in need of these backup systems. Moreover, these systems may supply needed elements that are unavailable through sponsors. For example, a team may need confidential information about what a sister team is really doing rather than relying on what that team reports upstairs (intelligence). As another example, the team may need someone outside of itself and its sponsors to put in a good word for it to receive some favorable administrative ruling (influence). Or the team may find a critical resource or vital expertise unavailable from other sources within the allotted time (resource or expertise). In such emergencies, backup systems composed of the leadership networks that cross the boundaries of the team

may be able to save the day. The ultimate test of a mature leadership relationship is whether it helps when it is most needed.

Both kinds of leadership making are required as backups for deficiencies in what Hackman (1986) calls *enabling performance conditions*. Enabling performance conditions fall into five categories: (a) clear and engaging direction, (b) an enabling unit structure (including tasks, people, and expectations), (c) a supportive organizational context (rewards, education, and information), (d) available expertise and coaching, and (e) adequate material resources (Hackman, 1986). Theoretically, when all five of these enabling performance conditions are met, effective team performance outcomes are assured. Moreover, when one or more of these conditions are not met, team performance can suffer. When such deficiencies in enabling conditions exist, teammates must look for substitutes or allow team performance to decline (Kerr & Jermier, 1978). Such substitutes can be mediated by leadership relationships. The probability of acquiring needed substitutes depends on the maturity of the leadership relationships between the teammates and the outside resource people. Teammates who have mature relationships with outside resource people are more likely to be given innovative substitutes than teammates who have acquaintance-level relationships.

Effective teams do not put all of their faith in the five enabling conditions. They understand that enabling conditions may change as the team progresses toward its mission. Such teams realize their limitations by realistically prescribing before the fact what will be needed in the end (Graen, 1989). Therefore, they expend a fair amount of energy building pipelines for needed substitutes for enabling conditions. As the team progresses toward its mission and the inadequacies in enabling conditions become apparent, the team turns to whatever substitutes are needed. In this way, teams can meet the challenges presented by their environments.

TABLE 1

Differences Between Managership and Leadership

	Managership	*Leadership*
Where	Jobs	Projects
When	Business as usual	Innovation and change
Why	Overdetermine routine	Create integrated teamwork
How	Efficient use of rules and resources	Transformation of self-interest into team interest via incremental influence
Cost	Elaborate communication and control	Investment in relationships
Benefit	Role compliance	Continuous improvement

From "Self-management and Team Making in Cross-functional Work Teams: Discovering the Keys to Becoming an Integrated Team" by M. Uhl-Bien and G. B. Graen, 1992, *Journal of High Technology Management Research, 3* (2), p. 228. Copyright 1992 by JAI Press. Reprinted by permission.

In summary, leadership making in organizations is usually an inclusive process of building networks one relationship at a time with competent people who are *inside* as well as *outside* of one's team. By engaging in role making to build one's professional network of competent others who have a vested interest in one's career success, a person can become more professional and contribute more effectively as a team player. Put simply, the career strategy of professionals seeking to become team players includes proactive role making with competent people who can intervene when the cumulative personal and professional resources of all the professionals' other teammates prove inadequate. At such times, favors may be called in by teammates or from competence networks of team members.

Next we will turn to new research on leadership making that focuses on observable interaction patterns. These patterns are important both to validate the far-reaching impact of leadership relationships and to illustrate the flavor of leadership interactions.

Interaction Research on Leadership Making

Leadership making is a process that requires dyadic communications to negotiate and implement both a managership contract and a leadership contract. The distinction between managership and leadership contracts as shown in Table 1. As the table illustrates, managership is the use of role-prescribed behavior involving the efficient use of rules, resources, and elaborate communication and control procedures. In contrast, leadership is the use of interpersonal incremental influence and transformational appeals. Managership involves the formal side of the employment relationship between two people—that is, how two people relate to each other according to their respective job descriptions. Leadership is the informal side of the dyadic relationship—or, how two people relate to each other when they are collaborating on projects outside their respective job descriptions.

A managership contract might, for example, specify the job-focused relationships between the two parties in terms of the five questions suggested by Graen (1989):

- What do managers need from their direct reports in order to do their jobs?

- What do direct reports need from their managers in order to do their jobs?

- What are each person's responsibilities?

- What are the priorities about what actually gets done?

- How do things get done when new situations arise?

It is important that both parties agree on the answers to these five questions. A leadership contract, in contrast, might specify the answers to the same five questions but focus on the professional relationship of members over and above the job-focused aspects of the relationship.

The so-called leadership contract is typically extended by the leader through an offer. For example, a top-down offer typically involves an indication that the leader is willing to invest valuable resources in the career development of the follower in exchange for the follower's willingness to outgrow the narrow definition of his or her job through self-investment in development, more responsible supra-job assignments, and more mature leadership. Bottom-up and peer offers involve similar exchanges. This offer signals that a relationship more mature than what would be possible under managership is feasible. The power of this offer was demonstrated in a series of field experiments by Graen and his associates (Graen, Novak, & Sommerkamp, 1982; Graen, Scandura, & Graen, 1986). In these investigations, leaders were trained in the leadership-making theory and instructed in a model procedure for making an offer of a leadership contract to all of their followers. Results of these offers were gratifyingly positive for both the leaders and followers who accepted an offer. Over the six-month time period of the studies, these consenting followers showed a 50 percent improvement in hard productivity and demonstrated greater commitment to both their team and their leader. Moreover, they found that collaborating with their leader to make their unit look good added personal value to their work. Clearly, they did not want to return to the previous style of management. Such a leadership contract cannot be ordered but must be voluntarily accepted. Upon acceptance, the leadership contract can be negotiated and implemented. It is important to note, however, that not every follower who receives an offer accepts it. Hence, within most units, relationships vary in maturity from low to high. However, in sociological terms, the lows are no "outgroup" and the highs are no "ingroup." Some merely have more mature leadership relationships with their supervisors than others (Yukl & Van Fleet, 1992).

Discovering Communication Patterns

A method rooted in anthropological linguistics was employed by Fairhurst (1991) to examine leadership relationships. Anthropological linguistics examines naturally occurring discourse in terms of some cultural group membership (Gumperz, 1982; Tannen, 1984). The goal is to identify patterns of communications and the rules of their operation from naturally occurring conversations. Fairhurst (1991) derived her "culture grouping" from the leadership-making theory and research of Graen and his associates. This theory and research were used as an overarching logic that made description of the patterns meaningful. Thus, stranger relationships were characterized as low-maturity cultural groups, acquaintance relationships as middle-maturity cultural groups, and mature relationships as high-maturity cultural groups.

TABLE 2

Dyadic Communication Patterns of High, Middle, and Low Maturity of Leadership Relationships

	Maturity of Leadership Relationship		
Pattern	*High*	*Middle*	*Low*
Contracting			
Value convergence	X		
Nonroutine problem solving	X		
Reciprocal support	X		
Insider argot	X		
Cooperating			
Role negotiation	X	X	
Choice framing	X	X	
Polite disagreement	X	X	
Coaching		X	
Competing			
Performance monitoring		X	X
Face-threatening acts			X
Power games			X
Unresolved conflicts			X

From "The Leader-Member Exchange Patterns of Women Leaders in Industry: A Discourse Analysis" by G. T. Fairhurst, in press, *Communication Monographs*, Arizona State University, Tempe. Copyright 1993 by the Speech Communication Association. Reprinted by permission.

Using a case comparison method, several passes through the transcripts of 30-minute conversations must be made for this type of analysis to be effective. Although each of the three leadership maturity cultures were sought in this analysis, the coders were blind as to the quality of the particular leader and member relationship under assessment. In fact, a test of the analysis is the agreement between the maturity of the relationship suggested by the conversational patterns and the actual assessments using the member-completed LMX scale and norms provided by Graen and Scandura (1985). In the Fairhurst (1991) investigation, the hit rate was 80 percent correct.

Using this method, Fairhurst, in a breakthrough investigation, discovered the twelve communication patterns shown in Table 2. As the table illustrates, the communication patterns were found to be different levels of leadership maturity—high, middle, or low. These communication patterns were identified through discourse analysis of 30-minute audiotapes of conversations between female managers and their direct reports in manufacturing plants. As the table indicates, high-maturity relationships included all of the contracting patterns and all but one of the cooperating patterns. Middle-maturity relationships included all cooperating and only one of the competing patterns. Finally, low-maturity relationships included only the competing patterns. Pattern types are defined below.

These three distinct patterns from the Fairhurst study can be further analyzed in terms of key moves and attributions shown in Table 3. *Value convergence* extends beyond simple agreement and involves the

TABLE 3

Leader-Follower Communication Patterns, Key Moves, and Attributions

Communication Patterns	Key Moves	Attributions	
Contracting			
Value convergence	Beyond simple agreement	(L&F)	We think alike
Nonroutine problem solving	Collaborate on unstructured task	(L&F)	We participate in decision making
Reciprocal support	Stand behind agreements	(L&F)	We back each other when threatened
Insider argot	Dyadic language	(L&F)	We have need to talk in code
Cooperating			
Role negotiation	Role outgrowth	(L&F)	We shape our roles
Choice framing	Choice with preference	(F)	I decide within limits
Polite disagreement	Nonagreement	(F)	I am a "Yes but..." person
Coaching	Investment in career	(F)	I get career advice
Competing			
Performance monitoring	Checking	(F)	I get asked for reports
Face-threatening acts	Blunt evaluations	(F)	I'm free to criticize my boss
Power games	Hidden agenda	(F)	I'm free to play one-upmanship
Unresolved conflicts	Open old wounds	(F)	I'm free to complain

Note: (L&F) indicates that both leader and follower hold this view; (F) indicates that only follower holds this view.

attribution by both the leader and the follower that "We think alike." In the case of *nonroutine problem solving*, the key moves are collaborating on unstructured tasks, and the attribution by both parties is "We participate in decision making." Clearly, this interaction pattern is a construct-valid definition of participation in decision making. (The two people involved in the conversation were making a nonroutine decision.) *Reciprocal support* refers to mutual obligation, with both parties committing themselves to being available when needed. *Insider argot* involves references to previous dyadic experiences and the use of nonpublic references. These four *contracting* patterns were found for only high-maturity relationships. These patterns appear to involve the implementation of leadership contracts.

Cooperating patterns shown in Table 3 were found for both high- and middle-maturity dyads and included role negotiation, choice framing, polite disagreement, and coaching. *Role negotiation* involves suggestions and countersuggestions for outgrowing prescribed roles. It implies a certain dynamic of change which is under discussion by both parties. *Choice framing* is the process by which a leader offers a choice to a member but first places a limiting frame on it. Clearly, the follower gets the message "I decide within limits." *Polite disagreement* is really nonagreement and implies that the follower is not a "yes person." Allowing a follower to play the "devil's advocate" role would fall into this pattern. Finally, *coaching* consists of providing advice and direction regarding career-relevant matters. Coaching was the only cooperating pattern not found for the high-maturity relationships, but this may have been a function of the number of conversations studied. These

TABLE 4

**Communication Pattern
Categories and Dyadic Contracting**

Communication Pattern	Managership Contract Negotiated	Leadership Contract Negotiated	Leadership Contract Implementation
Contracting	Yes	Yes	In progress
Cooperating	In progress	In progress	Not yet
Competing	In progress	No	No

cooperating patterns seem to involve the negotiation of leadership contracts.

Competing patterns were found primarily for low-maturity relationships. In fact, only performance monitoring was also found for the middle group. Competing patterns include performance monitoring, face-threatening acts, power games, and unresolved conflicts. *Performance monitoring* refers to asking for verbal progress reports and periodic updates on progress (Komaki & Citera, 1990). *Face-threatening acts* are blunt evaluations that imply a criticism of the leader. *Power games* are attempts to establish dominance over the leader. Finally, *unresolved conflicts* are references to continuing problems by the follower. These competing patterns suggest negative relationships that may deteriorate further.

These communication patterns and those found by Waldron (1991) suggest that followers can influence the development of mature leadership relationships with their leaders by using appropriate career management styles. A study by Vasudevan (1992) demonstrated that more and less effective career management styles (CMS) were identifiable. For example, those professionals whose CMS expressed values reflected long-term gratification, proactive problem solving, optimism, and

willingness to exchange obligation for team interest were clearly strong contributors to mature leadership relationships. The strong contribution of these CMS dimensions to the maturity of leadership relationships has been found for both technical and nontechnical professionals (Graen, Vasudevan, & Bell, 1992).

Turning to the dynamics of the three communication patterns, Table 4 illustrates what may be occurring. As shown in Table 4, contracting patterns may indicate that the leader and follower dyad has negotiated a managership contract and a leadership contract and is in the process of implementing a leadership contract. In contrast, cooperating patterns may indicate that the dyad is in the process of negotiating both a managership and a leadership contract. Finally, competing patterns may indicate that the leader and member are struggling to negotiate a managership contract. A leadership contract would be an unlikely topic under the competing pattern. Clearly, these formulations are speculative, but based on our model they are quite consistent.

Returning to the leadership-making life cycle, we may add communication patterns to the characteristics that evolve over the life cycle from acquaintance to mature relationships.

TABLE 5

Leadership-making Life Cycle Stage and Communication Pattern

Acquaintance ——————————▶ *Mature*

Performance monitoring
Coaching
    Role negotiation
    Choice framing
    Polite disagreement
            Insider argot
            Value convergence
            Nonroutine problem
               solving

As shown in Table 5, the acquaintance stage may begin with performance monitoring ("How are things going?") and coaching ("Here's some good advice") and progress to role negotiating ("Can I help you?"), choice framing ("Here are your options"), and polite disagreement ("Yes, but I have a somewhat different idea"). Finally, the mature leadership relationship may be approached with insider argot ("We talk in code"), value convergence ("We think alike"), reciprocal support ("We back each other"), and nonroutine problem solving ("We collaborate on decision making").

The significance of Fairhurst's program is that she demonstrated not only that one can reliably assess the maturity of leadership relationships by simply listening to 30-minute dyadic conversations but that one can reliably identify communication patterns that refer to various phases of the leadership-making process. Clearly, Fairhurst was able to find the high-, middle-, and low-maturity patterns she was looking for. Planned future research in this program is scheduled to collect 30-minute audiotapes from leaders and followers each week beginning with their first day working together until the time that the relationships reach a plateau. In this way, additional communications from the managership and leadership contract negotiations and the leadership contract implementation can be identified and illustrated. Because so much of leadership making is reflected in communications about work activities and because the nucleus of leadership making consists of symbolic interaction, the discourse analysis of Fairhurst represents a promising opportunity for cross-cultural leadership-making research. Triandis and Albert (1987) provide a summary of some of the more traditional research and theory on cross-cultural communications within organizations.

American Versus Japanese Leadership-making Context

A major difference between American and Japanese leadership making lies in their leadership contexts. American contexts rely on the scientific management system; Japanese contexts rely on a version of the Toyota system or lean organization (Womack, Jones, & Roos, 1990).

The scientific management system can be characterized by these factors:

- Job holders as variable costs

- Minimized on-the-job education

- Reliance on individual competition and obedience to rules

- Tall hierarchies and clear job definitions

- Services for pay

- Supervisors linked by chains of command

- Emphasis on quarterly profit

In sharp contrast, the Toyota system context can be characterized by these factors:

- Job holders as enhanceable assets

- Optimized on-the-job education

- Reliance on team cooperation and group harmony

- Shallow hierarchies and ambiguous team definitions

- Services as reciprocal obligation

- Team leaders without subordination linked by overlapping teams

- Emphasis on long-term market positions

As can be seen, the American model makes a clearer separation between a managership contract and a leadership contract than does the Japanese model. The characteristics of the Toyota system come close to those we find for the American leadership contract:

- Treat employees as assets to be enhanced in value through investments

- Train and cross-train employees to enhance career opportunities

- Promote team cooperation and team interest above self-interests

- Encourage employees to outgrow their jobs as soon as possible and support team self-management

- Build the reciprocal obligations we refer to as mature leadership relationships

- Develop leadership contracts with both one's staff and one's colleagues

- Orient the team to long-term objectives

In summary, the leadership contracts of the East and West appear much more similar than their respective managership contracts. This is due in no small measure to the vast differences in their leadership contexts.

Team Type

Next we will turn our attention to a study of an American organization that had a need for both the more traditional scientific-management-compatible self-leadership (Manz & Sims, 1980) and the newer team-oriented leadership making. Clearly, the concept of self-leadership is more compatible with the American value of individualism.

A two-year study by Uhl-Bien, Graen, and Baugh (1992) of 184 technical professionals organized within 35 functional work sections (home base) and assigned to cross-functional project teams suggests different appropriate uses for self-leadership (Manz, 1986) and leadership making (Graen & Uhl-Bien, 1991b). In the study, self-leadership made positive contributions to overall performance and effective unit process in functional sections, but made negative contributions to overall performance and effective team process in cross-functional projects. In contrast, leadership making made no contribution to either overall performance or effective unit process in functional sections, but made positive contributions to both performance and process in cross-functional projects.

Further investigation of this organization revealed that the work patterns of the functional sections consisted primarily of coacting rather than interacting between and among professionals. Coacting professionals worked on their own tasks from start to finish with minimal assistance from their section colleagues. Moreover, this type of work pattern was evaluated as productive for the functional sections by higher-ups. Therefore, the larger the proportion of self-leaders in a functional section, the higher the performance rating of the section. In this kind of unit, performance was attributable to the amount of quality work completed relative to the number of professionals. Thus, the proportion of the section that worked independently (coacting) contributed positively to section performance. The developmental goal of the section leader was to encourage each professional to grow from dependence to independence as soon as possible. This is the goal of self-leadership development (Manz, 1986).

In contrast, the work patterns of the cross-functional project teams consisted primarily of interacting rather than coacting. (There notions are analogous to Thompson's, 1967, ideas). Interacting professionals worked in close collaboration with their project colleagues from the start to finish of their contribution. This work pattern is also called interdependent or integrated teamwork. This integrated teamwork was evaluated by higher-ups as productive for cross-functional project teams. Therefore, the better the professionals integrated their contributions appropriately with those of their project teammates, the higher the performance rating of the project team. Performance was a function of the quality of the team's cross-function project. Thus, the proportion of mature leadership relationships (leadership making) in a project team was a positive contributor to project performance. The developmental goal of the project leader was to develop mature leadership relationships into an integrated project team as soon as possible. This is the goal of leadership making (Graen & Uhl-Bien, 1991a).

Leadership making was inappropriate to the functional sections discussed earlier because the performance of a section was based on its cumulative individual output relative to its size and not its integrated performance. This functional section is analogous to academic departments in a research university where department performance is a function of the average output of individual faculty members. Here the prima donna is a valued role model (Tierney, 1992).

Self-leadership was inappropriate to the cross-functional project teams because the performance of a project team was based on the quality of its integrated project. Self-leadership, based as it is on individual

self-determination, renders interdependent collaboration and teamwork more difficult, and, at its worst, impossible. This cross-functional project team is typical of teams that are employed for functions such as research and development, product design for manufacturability, quality enhancement, and various special projects. Here the prima donna can be a problem, and the valued role model is that of the team player (Uhl-Bien & Graen, 1992a).

Organizations like the one just described face a peculiarly American dilemma of developing and rewarding functional self-leadership while hoping for cross-functional leadership making and teamwork. For the past 40 years, a most popular organizational design in the West has been the so-called functional organization, in which activities are grouped into homogeneous functions and assigned to single-discipline units. In such models, people are trained as functional specialists and spend their entire careers within the same function. This produces strong loyalties toward one's functional group and corresponding suspicion of other functional groups. At its worst, a functional group might develop a "fortress-mentality" and only deal with other functions by throwing their products over the wall. This fortress mentality has become a major concern of many American organizations as the team-based Toyota system (Womack, Jones, & Roos, 1990) becomes widely adopted in Japanese companies and is rapidly proving that the functional design of American organizations is obsolete. Despite many attempts by American organizations to establish cross-functional project team organizations in place of functional designs, a reliable method has not yet been found.

Applications of Cross-cultural Leadership Making

Next we will examine Japanese transplants in the United States as a natural laboratory for our investigation of cross-cultural leadership making. But before we can begin to understand what we are observing there, we need to study the home plant practices of the Japanese parent companies. This was the focus of a series of investigations beginning with the Japanese management progress study (Graen, Wakabayashi, Graen, & Graen, 1990), which addressed the following questions:

- What is the nature of leadership making over the careers of Japanese managers in leading corporations?

- What characteristics render advantage, and how, when, and with what impact?

- What opportunities are offered and how are they capitalized upon?

Most importantly, what can this tell us about the nature of leadership making in transplants?

Japanese Management Progress Study

The Japanese management progress study began in 1972 with an investigation of that year's college graduates who joined four leading Japanese corporations, tracing the "hidden" leadership-making process between them and their immediate supervisors and its effects on their careers up until the point of retirement. The "hidden" process refers to the way newcomers demonstrated leadership talent by earning investment in their careers from their supervisors. The effects of this process were evaluated in three companies over a period of 3 years (Wakabayashi, Minami, Hashimoto, Sano, Graen, & Novak, 1980) and in one company over 7 years (Wakabayashi & Graen, 1984) and over 13 years (Wakabayashi, Graen, Graen, & Graen, 1988).

The study found first that the newcomers' progress into middle management 13 years after joining the company was influenced more by what happened to them during their first three years on the job involving their

relationships with their supervisors and their assessed promotability (process variables) than by the combined effects of their university, first job, and entry performance (antecedent variables). This indicates that newcomers were clearly differentiated in terms of their relationship with their supervisors and their promotability early on—by the end of their third year. Moreover, it found that these factors accounted for a large amount (up to 50%) of the variations that occurred in speed of promotion, salary, and bonus levels in their thirteenth year. Thus, early career differentiation rather than deferred evaluation was the basic feature of managerial career progress in these Japanese organizations (Drucker, 1971; Ouchi, 1981; Ouchi & Johnson, 1979).

Second, regarding the effect of leadership relations, one might hypothesize that the newcomers' career progress was triggered by a mature relationship with their supervisors, which afforded them critical developmental opportunities. They were able to acquire needed skills, knowledge, and expertise, which in turn could help them develop an even stronger relationship with their supervisors. Thus, the quality of their relationship combined with assessed promotability during the first three years appears to have acted as a catalyst for future career development. These findings suggest that the environment for managerial career progress under the lifetime employment system in these Japanese organizations was far from benign. Rather, it entailed obstacles and opportunities involving the relationship with the supervisor (Graen & Scandura, 1987), and disenchantment with or challenge from the work (Dunnette, Arvey, & Banas, 1973). In fact, this study found that those who enjoyed mature leadership relationships with their immediate supervisors early in their careers achieved superior career progress. This "hidden investment" in one's direct reports should be distinguished from "mentoring," which involves no direct reporting relationships but may produce similar career outcomes.

Third, promotion to middle management involved very intense competition among cohort members. A promotion tree analysis suggested that the promotion process followed a pattern in which the less qualified were screened out (Rosenbaum, 1979). Those who received an early first promotion were more likely to win early second and third promotions than their slower-starting colleagues. It should be emphasized that the newcomer's speed of moving up the promotion tree was predictable to a considerable extent based on the quality of vertical exchange with leaders and promotability. These results suggest that early merit promotion rather than deferred merit promotion was another principal feature of career progress in these Japanese corporations (Yoshino, 1968).

In many leading Japanese organizations, this underlying process of early differentiation may go largely unnoticed as a result of the egalitarian personnel practices used in the lifetime employment system. These personnel practices notwithstanding, early differentiation of management talent may contribute to a growing number of ineffective middle managers at later stages under the lifetime employment system. Because managers who receive early first promotions tend to get more than their share of challenging growth opportunities, they tend to monopolize the developmental resources of the corporation. Consequently, those who do not receive early first promotions become relatively less developed middle managers. Several more progressive corporations, challenged by keen market competition and rapid technological change at home and abroad, have begun to study concepts for dealing with this problem.

The Japanese management progress study will continue to follow this panel of managers through the tournament process that divides managers into executives and early retirees. Next, several hypotheses about leadership making derived from this longitudinal investigation—which focus on the role of leadership in shaping managerial careers—were investigated in a study of a cross-section of line managers in Japan.

Japanese Hidden Investment Study

Five leading Japanese corporations were sampled for this hidden investment study. Three of them were in manufacturing and two were in service industries. Within these companies, data were collected from 1,075 college-educated male line managers: 261 management trainees, 417 lower-level managers, 146 lower-middle managers, and 251 upper-middle managers (Uhl-Bien, Tierney, Wakabayashi, & Graen, 1990; Wakabayashi, Graen, & Uhl-Bien, 1990).

Results indicated that the maturity of the leadership relationship with one's supervisor contributed greatly to the investment in a manager's career and his leadership development activities on the job. These findings clarify the effect of leadership development on a manager's career progress suggested by the preceding 13-year investigation. Specifically, the study found that the maturity of the leadership relationship was related to various investments made in a manager's career—for example, utilization of potential, appreciation of contribution, training, and attention of the superior and the personnel department. More opportunities for role development were provided to managers who had more mature leadership relationships. These opportunities make it possible for such managers to promote their discretional job-enrichment activities on their jobs based on the trust and support of their supervisors. This finding has important implications for career progress among Japanese managers. Apparently it was these discretional role development activities, rather than age and tenure, that contributed to the career progress of the Japanese managers in the study. Moreover, allowing individual efforts directed toward career enhancement on the job makes upward tournament mobility in Japanese organizations very competitive. Perhaps the view of slow and steady "lock-step" movement up the ladder by Japanese managers based on age and seniority is a cultural stereotype rather than an accurate description of career progress (Abeggler & Stalk, 1985).

The hidden investment hypothesis derived from the 13-year longitudinal investigation of management progress was supported in this study of 1,075 line managers in the five corporations. The study found that the maturity of the leadership relationship between a salaried employee and his immediate supervisor resulted in strong and significant contributions to individualized career investments and role development opportunities, which supports the generalizability of this hypothesis. Moreover, these overall findings were replicated within each of the five companies and in each of the four levels of management with them. Clearly, the path to the executive suite is enhanced by hidden investment in people's careers by their immediate superiors at each rank (Graen, 1989).

Once this hidden investment process is initiated, it places a competitive advantage on the individual's career. Individualized opportunities are offered and capitalized on, and new capabilities are acquired by a person thus favored. This early advantage is magnified over time by cumulative hidden investments by successive superiors in their more promising and faster-developing workers (Graen, 1990; Graen & Cashman, 1975). We next turn to an investigation of how this hidden investment in leadership development plays out in the lower levels of the organization in manufacturing plants in Japan and the United States.

Comparative Home Plant and Transplant Practices Study

The picture that emerges from our investigations of the Japanese leadership-making process in home plants suggests potential problems in exporting this process to America. To investigate these problems and the larger issues surrounding the exportation of Japanese leadership practices, a comparative study of leadership practices in home plants and transplants in the United States was undertaken.

The design of these comparative studies incorporated a two-phase research plan in which we investigated the home offices and selected plants of ten leading manufacturing firms in central Japan during one- to three-day visits. In phase one, we conducted patterned interviews with operations, personnel, and foreign affairs managers, collected written documentation and case material, and took plant tours. The purpose of this phase of the investigation was to explore how well these firms were globalizing their businesses. Specifically, we sought to identify the major processes associated with their globalization efforts. In phase two of the study, we visited six U.S. plants of Japanese corporations for at least one day. During these visits, we interviewed plant management, collected documentation, and toured plants.

All of the transplants we visited were new start-ups that were wholly owned by the parent firms in Japan. All were located in the midwestern United States and were engaged in manufacturing auto parts production, car assembly, machine tool manufacturing, or elevator assembly operations. The research procedure for this phase of the study required sending a lengthy interview schedule to the participating plants several weeks before the planned visits so that the participants had ample time to gather relevant information and documentation.

Forming the Transplant

In all six plants we visited, an integrated team concept guided hiring, training, and organizing employees and their jobs. Most importantly, team leaders received special training for their role in socializing and developing their team members. People were hired specifically to be members or leaders of particular work teams within the organization. Team leaders, who were mostly skilled and experienced technicians, were hired very carefully prior to the recruitment of unskilled, rank-and-file team members.

These skilled employees were normally selected and trained specifically to be future team leaders in the United States. They went to the Japanese home plants for the more rigorous team-leader training and education. After returning from Japan, they were appointed to the position of team leader and began building their own teams by training newly recruited team members, who were normally less skilled and had less tenure. Therefore, from the beginning of the new operation, team leaders were developed internally. As the team building process unfolded and team leaders were promoted, they were to be replaced by the internally developed team subleaders or experienced senior associates.

First Stage—Role Designing. During the first stage of forming a transplant, skilled, more experienced technicians were hired as vanguards of cross-cultural learning as well as transfer agents of the target systems from Japan to the United States. These selected technicians were also prime candidates for being future team leaders at the U.S. plants. In most of the plants we visited, these vanguard groups of skilled employees were recruited 6 to 12 months before the unskilled group. Most received introductory cross-cultural courses about Japanese society and culture as well as indoctrination into the company's history and its present business state. They then were sent to the Japanese home plants to engage in on-the-job training for production skills and knowledge, working alongside Japanese colleagues. The production lines used for their training at the home plants were those designed for use at the companies' U.S. plants.

Japanese coaches were selected carefully for their technical expertise and communication skills. Japanese managers in the home plants we visited emphasized that English proficiency itself was not an essential prerequisite for effective coaching. Instead, emphasis was placed on coaches having the ability to respond to the questions of American co-workers by utilizing all possible forms of communication, including nonverbal and paper-and-pencil methods. Sponsor employees, the homeplant employees selected to serve as coaches for the American trainees, also underwent a systematic training session to acquire English vocabulary and idioms necessary for technical communication associated with production and machine operations. Along with language drills, introductory cross-cultural training was provided to selected coaches involving such issues as the typical American way of doing business and how to get along with Americans.

Second Stage—Role Finding. During the second stage, a new group of selected U.S. trainees were sent to the Japanese home plants for on-the-job training assignments. They worked with Japanese colleagues who had become experienced in training American partners on the job and in providing sponsorship on personal issues during the typical two- to three-month stay in Japan. During this training period, trainees usually spent half of their day in a classroom and the other half working on a shop floor. Production lines were the same as or similar to the ones to be exported to the U.S. plants. It was common for the U.S. plants to receive slightly modified but very technically advanced production facilities. In addition to instruction on technical matters, American trainees were encouraged to observe and discuss all aspects of the work culture in the Japanese home plant. For example, in one company, work culture issues involved topics such as working as a team, cooperating with team members, maintaining a clean work environment, working under broader job classification and job rotation systems, customer-oriented services, quality control, and corporate philosophies and policies.

In addition, American trainees were introduced to such Japanese company practices as quality control circle activities, suggestion and improvement activities, and a Just in Time system (Whitehill, 1991). Specific aspects of work culture were studied using videotapes, written materials, lectures, on-the-job observations, and informal discussions with Japanese co-workers. Training officials in one of the home plants in Japan emphasized that the purpose of training American workers on work culture is to provide enhanced understanding about how things are done in the Japanese home plants and why they are done that way.

Third Stage—Role Making. During the third stage, production lines were exported and installed at the U.S. plants. Following the transfer of the *hardware system*, an attempt was made to transplant components of the so-called *humanware system* by moving a trainee-coach unit (buddy system) from Japanese home plants to the U.S. transplants. They would then serve as the core element for team development at the transplants. In two companies, in addition to this trainee–coach unit, skilled technicians, engineers, and managers were sent to the U.S. plants to help work teams start to operate the production lines at the newly established plants. Frequently, the old trainee–coach relationships were maintained in the United States, but American employees helped their Japanese colleagues understand American culture. The major goals in the third-stage transfer efforts were to establish in the U.S. plants the basic skills and knowledge for operating the new production lines in a different industrial and sociocultural environment. Also important at this stage of the process was a transfer of team leadership from the Japanese to the U.S. employees. The trained U.S. employees began to play team leader roles in the transplants, working with

coaches, technicians, managers, and engineers from Japan.

Along with the transfer of people and machines from Japan to the United States, the process of recruiting unskilled team members began at this stage in all six transplants. Selection processes for these rank-and-file employees, who were called *associates,* followed a well-established pattern involving two or three screening stages with paper-and-pencil tests, interviews, reference checks, and physical examinations. These procedures were rationalized with a very low selection ratio. In all of the transplants, this selection stage was the beginning of an organizational socialization of employees to the companies' unique corporate society and work culture. This period also served as a time to provide information that would modify unrealistic expectations held by overzealous newcomers desiring to work for a Japanese organization. Some of these newcomers referred to certain practices in the transplants as "un-Japanese," believing that they contradicted their initial expectations. For example, some newcomers complained that their Japanese managers did not take their suggestions as seriously as they should have. Instead they were told that it is appropriate for a person to offer suggestions only after he or she has mastered a particular task.

Managers at each plant were able to identify the most desirable type of workers for recruitment. Desirable employees were characterized as having a willingness to develop themselves, to grow with the company, to be good team players, and as being able to adapt to flexible work conditions.

Fourth Stage—Role Implementing. During the fourth stage, employees who had been trained in both the Japanese home plant and the U.S. plant were appointed formally as team leaders. These team leaders then began to build their own work teams by organizing newly hired team members. New team members were assigned to a rather rigorous training program at a company training center, but they were expected to develop further job mastery while doing their jobs under a team leader's supervision. In most of the plants we visited, one of the important responsibilities of team leaders was deciding what kind of on-the-job training and eventual job assignment each team member should receive. At this stage, Japanese coaches and technicians also helped group members acquire the necessary skills and knowledge that would enable them to grow quickly out of their initially assigned tasks and become effective associates who could perform multiple team responsibilities within the group. (Rapid growth out of initial job assignments is a key to the success of the team-making process.)

To facilitate smooth on-the-job training and job rotation, all the plants had a very simplified job classification system. Typically all hourly workers, or associates, were grouped into two broad job categories such as production and maintenance. However, jobs were usually structured into a hierarchically ranked system based on conventional American job titles for the purposes of promotion and wage determination. New group members were expected to start at the lowest-ranking level, acquire skills and knowledge through on-the-job training and job rotation, and be promoted to higher ranks over time in their work group. In addition to this skill development process, group members were exposed to different aspects of the unique work culture in the plants concerning such issues as corporate philosophies and policies, ideas on quality work, customer orientation, teamwork, and employee relations. In summary, team leaders were required during this stage to function as reliable sponsors for new employees during their socialization into established team members. Staff employees from Japan—coaches, technicians, engineers, and managers—also helped team leaders develop their teams.

Final Stage—Team Making. By the time employees from the home plants returned to Japan, work teams in the U.S. plants had become self-reliant work groups led by experienced team leaders. It was critical at this stage that managers and engineers provided continuing support to the team concept. They were expected to provide resources for running production systems based on autonomous work groups organized around the team leaders. A team leader (called "honcho" in Japanese) in Japanese home plants typically receives broad discretionary authority from management in the areas of production, maintenance, and human resource utilization and development. Thus, team leaders are responsible for producing high-quality products that meet deadlines and budgets and for maintaining a cohesive work team. Therefore, it is critical to establish team control over production processes at the shop-floor level under the strong leadership of the group leader at the final stage of team development (Uhl-Bien & Graen, 1992a).

The transfer of technology across vastly different cultures cannot be accomplished without a supportive human organization. Relevant organizational structures must be developed to support new skills and knowledge, a new pattern of behaviors, a new work culture, and new workers. Organizational development that provides a supportive environment for practicing the team concept in the U.S. plants becomes an important element in facilitating cross-cultural transfers of production systems from Japan to the United States.

Throughout the team-building process, on-the-job training and job rotation were practiced to help develop team leaders. Workers were encouraged to become effective team members, and eventually to be promoted to team leaders. In fact, three of the six companies reported that effective team leaders had been developed internally as a result of implementing an integrated team concept on the shop floor over the course of a decade.

In all of the transplants, shallow hierarchies were used to facilitate the mobility of the work force and more flexible utilization of human resources within the plants. For example, the status hierarchy in one company consisted of only two status categories in the plant: manager and associate. Associates were further differentiated into ranks based on the content of the jobs they held. The key to this system was the different paths through ranks and positions that were used to develop associates within the organization. For example, in two companies, new bottom-ranking technical employees are expected to move up the hierarchy step by step through job rotation and on-the-job training to a team leader position within seven to eight years. Since all jobs are classified into a single associate category, no formal barriers exist to prevent associates from moving to different areas in the plant. This was the case at all plants we visited. Promotion decisions and recommendations for job rotation and training were made based on semiannual performance evaluations. This made promotions to the position of team subleader and then to team leader fairly competitive (based on merit) rather than being based on an automatic progression based on seniority.

Team Leader

A team leader position is a salaried position, although it is not formally categorized as a management position. This team leader position is described by the formal job description, which reveals that a qualified team leader (a) is expected to have extensive and detailed knowledge of production processes, (b) can execute judgment and problem solving on interfunctional issues, (c) is able to implement long-range plans, (d) can communicate cross-functionally as well as across organizational hierarchies, and (e) is able to direct and train team members.

It is clear that these functions of a team leader overlap with those of manager and engineer. This indicates that a team leader must be highly qualified in both technical and team leadership skills. To meet these qualifications, potential team leaders must first become qualified associates, then acquire the necessary skills to be qualified subleaders, and finally make the transformation into team leaders.

Moreover, to successfully discharge his or her responsibilities, it is critical for a team leader to have authority delegated from managers and engineers. Successfully performing the job of team leader requires having the authority to write operating rules, introduce changes in production processes, handle emergency situations, and train subleaders and associates. All are vital resources that enable a team leader to function effectively on the shop floor.

In addition to the formal job responsibilities just described, team leaders in all the transplants we visited were expected to help team members solve personal problems, including those that could potentially lead to disciplinary action. In one company, team leaders were given training to enhance their counseling skills so that they could better deal with these issues, and staff specialists at the company's personnel department were available to support team leaders' attempts to solve the complicated personal problems of their team members. It was emphasized that management and staff as a rule did not bypass a team leader's authority on the shop-floor level. In general, team leaders were given resources such as information, decision-making authority, and material and budgetary support so that they could function as resource people rather than managers.

Plant Leadership

Plant organization is designed to shift managerial resources to the shop-floor level where team leaders control the day-to-day operations, including production, maintenance, quality control, and human relations. Team leaders are provided with resources so that they can perform the team-leader functions. Using these resources, the following occurs. First, team leaders provide team members with training opportunities, and members learn at different rates to perform the more complex jobs in the team. As a result, hierarchical distinctions based on skill differences develop among team members. Second, all members gradually learn to solve routine problems by themselves and nonroutine problems with the help of team leaders. Also, leaders invite some team members to participate in cross-functional problem solving to broaden their perspective. Third, team members are trained so that they can make suggestions to continuously improve the processes and efficiency of production. Fourth, team members are encouraged by the team leader to cooperate and collaborate within their team to devise solutions to problems that confront the team. Fifth, team members become members of self-managing teams capable of solving most day-to-day problems, working together with team leaders to "troubleshoot" large problems in the case of emergencies. Finally, managers and engineers realize that helping teams develop themselves so that they can solve routine as well as nonroutine problems is key to achieving corporate goals for product quality, production efficiency, and operational flexibility. The team management process described here is called *shop floor control* in Japanese home plants.

Leadership making in the transplants we investigated was directed at the long-term goal of implementing a teamwork system that is functionally equivalent to the home plant's. Although all the transplants began their operations using Western-style supervisor positions and concepts, all have or plan to develop team leaders and coordinators and gradually abolish both supervisory positions and concepts. In all the transplants we visited, expatriate managers are firmly committed to implementing a functional equivalent of the lean organization system. They clearly know what they want and are searching for ways to make the system work. Some of the transplants were much further along in this developmental path than others. For example, some of the more mature plants had already abolished supervisory positions and concepts. Unfortunately, these techniques have worked much better on the shop floor than in the office. The challenge remains to discover a cross-cultural leadership-making process that will be effective for professionals in the transplants.

Conclusions and Implications for Research

During the leadership-making process in Japanese transplants in the United States, American and Japanese colleagues face different fears. The Americans may fear that adopting the Toyota system could subvert traditional American values of individualism. On the other side, the Japanese may fear that adopting the scientific management system could undermine traditional Japanese values of teamwork. Neither of these polar fears is productive in this situation. Instead, functional solutions to this dilemma can be found when both parties are willing to learn each other's culture and work together to create a third culture for leadership making.

At the professional level in the transplants, leadership making between Americans and Japanese may require a much more interdependent buddy system than that described earlier for rank-and-file-level associates. Each party must at the very least feel compelled to understand the set of culturally based conceptual tools of his or her partner (Swidler, 1986). To accomplish this interdependence, dyadic teams of an American and a Japanese may be assigned to important projects that require interacting as opposed to coacting interdependence. Moreover, appropriate training in comparative problem-solving techniques and cross-cultural leadership making might be given to such teams to enhance the development of their third culture.

After such a dyadic team has explored its cultural options (role finding), it is ready to begin the delicate task of testing its most promising options (role making). Clearly, it will make mistakes, but a system should be in place to minimize any negative consequences resulting from them. Finally, those promising options that work for a dyadic team can form the foundation for a mature leadership relationship (role implementing). Perhaps in this way a new generation of bicultural professionals will emerge that can take the best from each culture and produce a far better third culture through cross-cultural leadership making.

Research is needed that is designed to sort out those cultural variables that make a difference at the macro level (Weber, 1958) or the micro level (Hofstede, 1980) to cross-cultural leadership making from those that do not. A step in this direction would be to view culture not as a system of predispositions but as a set of conceptual tools to be used to solve different kinds of problems (Swidler, 1986). These conceptual tools could be learned by someone from a different culture during a process of cross-cultural leadership making. One could observe how people from Japan and America learn each other's techniques and how they integrate these techniques into their leadership making. We agree that this approach, which we have used, in retrospect appears to explain a great deal about our own leadership making over the past 20 years. Initially we worked to understand and become comfortable with each other's cultural techniques. Next we tried to integrate our two different sets of techniques into a new, third set of conceptual tools. Finally, we are striving still to refine our problem-solving procedures despite numerous examples of old cultural habits.

Based on 20 years of our own personal cross-cultural leadership-making experience, our 20-plus years of research on Japanese and

American leadership making, and our 5 years of research on cross-cultural leadership making in Japanese transplants in the United States, we believe that the process is researchable and that the transplants represent a unique research opportunity. Clearly, the transplants have significant needs for critical cross-cultural bridges from one culture's concepts to the other's in order to help associates work together, and the process for building such bridges is cross-cultural leadership making. Everything we have learned about this process and the transplants leads us to expect that this process must and will unfold in the transplants within the next few years. We recommend that researchers be available to observe and document this process as it unfolds.

Furthermore, we recommend that this research not simply be an adaptation of some U.S. study of foreign-owned companies, using some foreign research assistants. Instead, the research should be a cross-cultural partnership on both sides of the measuring instruments, because to begin the process by using only U.S. researchers would likely build in a certain amount of cultural contamination (Lynn, 1991). By using cross-cultural research partnerships, each researcher's ethnocentricities can be removed through cross-cultural leadership making. Through this procedure, research designs would focus on cohort panels by taking samples of cross-cultural leadership-making behaviors, evaluations, and outcomes over time. Given the parent companies' commitments to the long-term success of their transplants, longitudinal panel designs for research that incorporates periodic assessments using audiotapes, patterned interviews, questionnaires, and archival records appear feasible. Finally, the tenet of the Toyota system that new problems should be actively sought because they present the opportunity for highly valued achievement of solutions and new learning reinforces the transplants' interest in finding a functionally equivalent solution to this set of problems.

This we believe is a win-win situation for both researchers and transplants.

The authors would like to thank Joan Graen, Mike Graen, and Marty Graen for their research assistance, and Hal Angle, Gail Fairhurst, Amit Raturi, Pam Tierney, Harry Triandis, and Mary Uhl-Bien for reading an earlier version of this chapter.

References

Abeggler, J. C., & Stalk, G. Jr. (1985). *Kaisha: The Japanese corporation.* Tokyo: Charles E. Tuttle.

Abo, T. (1988). *Local production by Japanese automobile and electric manufacturers in the United States: Application and adaptability of Japanese-style management practices.* Tokyo: Toyokezai Publishing.

Bandura, A. (1977). *Social learning theory.* Englewood Cliffs, NJ: Prentice-Hall.

Bass, B. M. (1985). *Leadership and performance beyond expectations.* New York: Free Press.

Basu, R. (1991). *An empirical examination of leader-member exchange and transformational leadership as predictors of innovation behavior.* Unpublished doctoral dissertation, Purdue University, West Lafayette, IN.

Burns, J. M. (1978). *Leadership.* New York: Harper & Row.

Crouch, A., & Yetton, P. (1988). Manager-subordinate dyads: Relationships among task and social contact, manager friendliness, and subordinate performance in management groups. *Organizational Behavior and Human Decision Processes, 41,* 65–82.

Dansereau, F., Graen, G., & Haga, W. (1975). A vertical dyad linkage approach to leadership in formal organizations. *Organizational Behavior and Human Performance, 13,* 46–78.

Deluga, R. J. (1992). The relationship of leader-member exchanges with laissez-faire, transactional, and transformational leadership in naval environments. In K. E. Clark, M. B. Clark, & D. P. Campbell (Eds.), *The impact of leadership.* West Orange, NJ: Leadership Library of America.

Dienesch, R. M., & Liden, R. C. (1986). Leader-member exchange model of leadership: A critique and further development. *Academy of Management Review, 11,* 618–634.

Drucker, P. E. (1971). What can we learn from Japanese management? *Harvard Business Review, 49,* 110–122.

Duchon, D., Green, S., & Taber, T. (1986). Vertical dyad linkage: A longitudinal assessment of antecedents, measures, and consequences. *Journal of Applied Psychology, 71,* 56–60.

Dunnette, M. D., Arvey, R. D., & Banas, P. A. (1973, May–June). Why do they leave? *Personnel,* 25–76.

Fairhurst, G. T. (1991). *Leadership making and dyadic communications patterns among women leaders in industry: An anthropological linguistics approach.* Paper presented at the Society of Organizational Behavior, Albany, NY.

Fairhurst, G. T., & Chandler, T. A. (1989). Social structure in leader-member exchange interaction. *Communication Monograph, 56,* 215–239.

Fairhurst, G. T., Rogers, L. E., & Sarr, R. A. (1987). Manager-subordinate control patterns and judgments about the relationship. In M. McLaughlin (Ed.), *Communications Yearbook, 10,* 395–415.

Farris, G. F., & Lim, F. G., Jr. (1969). Effects of performance on leadership, cohesiveness, influence, satisfaction, and subsequent performance. *Journal of Applied Psychology, 53,* 490–497.

Ferris, G. R. (1985). Role of leadership in the employee withdrawal process: A constructive replication. *Journal of Applied Psychology, 70,* 777–781.

Fodor, E. M. (1974). Disparagement by a subordinate as an influence on the use of power. *Journal of Applied Psychology, 59,* 652–655.

Fucini, J. J., & Fucini, S. (1990). *Working for the Japanese: Inside Mazda's American auto plant.* New York: Free Press.

Gardner, W. L., & Martinko, M. J. (1988). Impression management: An observational study linking audience characteristics with verbal self-presentation. *Academy of Management Journal, 31,* 42–65.

Graen, G. B. (1969). Instrumentality theory of work motivation: Some experimental results and suggested modifications. *Journal of Applied Psychology, 53,* Whole No. 2, Part 2.

Graen, G. B. (1976). Role making processes within complex organizations. In M. D. Dunnette (Ed.), *Handbook of industrial and organizational psychology* (pp. 1201–1245). Chicago: Rand McNally.

Graen, G. B. (1989). *Unwritten rules for your career: 15 secrets for fast-track success.* New York: Wiley.

Graen, G. B. (1990). Designing productive leadership systems to improve both work motivation and organizational effectiveness. In E. Fleishman (Ed.), *International work motivation* (pp. 200–233). Hillsdale, NJ: Erlbaum.

Graen, G. B., & Cashman, J. (1975). A role-making model of leadership in formal organizations: A developmental approach. In J. G. Hunt & L. L. Larson (Eds.), *Leadership frontiers* (pp. 143–166). Kent, OH: Kent State University Press.

Graen, G. B., Liden, R., & Hoel, W. (1982). Role of leadership in the employee withdrawal process. *Journal of Applied Psychology, 67,* 868–872.

Graen, G. B., Novak, M., & Sommerkamp, P. (1982). The effects of leader-member exchange and job design on productivity and satisfaction: Testing a dual attachment model. *Organizational Behavior and Human Performance, 30,* 109–131.

Graen, G. B., Orris, D., & Johnson, T. (1973). Role assimilation processes in a complex organization. *Journal of Vocational Behavior, 3,* 395–420.

Graen, G. B., & Scandura, T. (1987). Toward a psychology of dyadic organizing. In B. Staw & L. L. Cumming (Eds.), *Research in organizational behavior* (Vol. 9, pp. 175–208). Greenwich, CT: JAI Press.

Graen, G. B., Scandura, T., & Graen, M. (1986). A field experimental test of the moderating effects of growth need strength on productivity. *Journal of Applied Psychology, 71,* 484–491.

Graen, G. B., & Schiemann, W. (1978). Leader-member agreement: A vertical dyad linkage approach. *Journal of Applied Psychology, 63,* 206–212.

Graen, G. B., & Uhl-Bien, M. (1991b). The transformation of professionals into self-managing and partially self-designing contributions: Toward a theory of leadership-making. *Journal of Management Systems, 3*(3), 33–48.

Graen, G. B., Vasudevan, D., & Bell, L. M. (1992). *Career management style: Effective role-making on the job.* Unpublished report. Center for the Enhancement of International Competitiveness. University of Cincinnati, OH.

Graen, G. B., & Uhl-Bien, M. (1991a). Job redesign: Managing for high performance. *Productivity Press Proceedings,* pp. 157–164.

Graen, G. B., Wakabayashi, M., Graen, M. R., & Graen, M. G. (1990). International generalizability of American hypothesis about Japanese management progress: A strong inference in-vestigation. *The Leadership Quarterly, 1*(1), 1–11.

Gumperz, J. J. (1982). *Discourse strategies.* Cambridge, UK: Cambridge University Press.

Hackman, J. R. (1986). The psychology of self-management in organizations. In M. S. Pollack & R. O. Perloff (Eds.), *Psychology and work: Productivity, change and employment* (pp. 85–136). Washington, DC: American Psychological Association.

Herold, D. M. (1977). Two-way influence processes in leader-follower dyads. *Academy of Management Journal, 20,* 224–237.

Hofstede, G. (1980). *Culture's consequences: National differences in thinking and organizing.* Newbury Park, CA: Sage.

Hollander, E. P. (1958). Conformity, status, and idiosyncrasy credit. *Psychological Review, 65,* 117–127.

Hollander, E. P. (1980). Leadership and social exchange processes. In K. J. Gergen, M. S. Greenberg, & R. H. Willis (Eds.), *Social exchange: Advances in theory and research.* New York: Plenum.

Hosking, D. M., & Morley, I. (1988). The skills of leadership. In J. G. Hunt, B. R. Baliga, H. P. Dachler, & C. A. Schriesheim (Eds.), *Emerging leadership vistas* (pp. 80–106). Boston: Lexington.

House, R., & Baetz, M. (1979). Leadership: Some empirical generalizations and new research directions. In B. Staw (Ed.), *Social exchange: Advances in theory and research.* New York: Plenum.

Johnson, C. (1988). Japanese-style management in America. *California Management Review,* 34–45.

Katz, D., & Kahn, R. L. (1978). *The social psychology of organizations* (2nd ed.). New York: Wiley.

Kerr, S., & Jermier, J. (1978). Substitutes for leadership: Their meaning and measurement.

Organizational Behavior and Human Performance, 22, 375–403.

Kipnis, D., Schmidt, S. M., & Wilkinson, I. (1980). Intraorganizational influence tactics: Exploration in getting one's way. *Journal of Applied Psychology, 65,* 440–452.

Komaki, J. L., & Citera, M. (1990). Beyond effective supervision: Identifying key interactions between superior and subordinate. *Leadership Quarterly, 1*(2), 91–105.

Liden, R., & Graen, G. B. (1980). Generalizability of the vertical dyad linkage model of leadership. *Academy of Management Journal, 23,* 451–465.

Liden, R. C., & Mitchell, T. R. (1989). Ingratiation in the development of leader-member exchanges. In R. A. Giacalone & P. Rosenfeld (Eds.), *Impression management in organization.* Hillsdale, NJ: Erlbaum.

Lowin, A., & Craig, J. R. (1968). The influence of level of performance on managerial style: An experimental object-lesson in the ambiguity of correlation data. *Organizational Behavior and Human Performance, 3,* 440–458.

Lynn, L. H. (1991). Technology and organizations: A cross-national analysis. In P. S. Goodman & L. S. Spoull (Eds.), *Technology and organizations* (pp. 174–199). San Francisco: Jossey-Bass.

Manz, C. (1986). Self-leadership: Toward an expanded theory of self-influence processes in organizations. *Academy of Management Review, 11,* 585–600.

Manz, C., & Sims, H. (1980). Self-management as a substitute for leadership: A social learning theory perspective. *Academy of Management Review, 5,* 361–367.

Mowday, R. T. (1978). The exercise of upward influence in organizations. *Administrative Science Quarterly, 23,* 137–156.

Negandhi, R. (1985, Summer). The management practices of Japanese subsidiaries overseas. *California Management Review,* No. 4, 125–133.

Ouchi, W. G. (1981). *Theory Z: How American business can meet the Japanese challenge.* Reading, MA: Addison-Wesley.

Ouchi, W. G., & Johnson, J. B. (1979). Types of organizational control and their relationship to emotional well-being. *Administrative Science Quarterly, 23,* 293–317.

Porter, L. W., Allen, R. W., & Angle, H. L. (1981). The politics of upward influence in organizations.

In L. L. Cummings & B. Staw (Eds.), *Research in organizational behavior,* Vol. 3 (pp. 109–149). Greenwich, CT: JAI Press.

Pucik, V., & Hanada, M. (1990). *Corporate culture and human resource utilization of senior managers in Japanese corporations in the United States.* Tokyo: Egon Zehnder International. (in Japanese)

Rosenbaum, J. E. (1979). Tournament mobility: Career patterns in a corporation. *Administrative Science Quarterly, 24,* 220–241.

Seers, A. (1989). Team-member exchange quality: A new construct for role-making research. *Organizational Behavior and Human Decision Processes, 43,* 118–135.

Sims, H., & Manz, C. (1984). Observing leader verbal behavior: Toward reciprocal determinism in leadership theory. *Journal of Applied Psychology, 69,* 222–232.

Skinner, B. F. (1953). *Science and human behavior.* New York: Macmillan.

Sridhar, B. (1991). *A path analytic examination of the impact of transactional and transformational behavior on follower empowerment: A vertical dyad linkage perspective.* Paper presented at the annual meeting of the Association of Management, Atlantic City.

Starr, M. (1988). *Global competitiveness: Getting the U.S. back on track.* New York: Norton.

Swidler, A. (1986). Culture in action. *American Sociological Review, 51,* 273–286.

Taga, T. (1992). *Marketing strategy of Japanese firms operating in the United States.* Paper presented at the annual meeting of the Association of Japanese Business Studies, Denver.

Tannen, D. (1984). *Conversational style: Analyzing talk among friends.* Norwood, NJ: Ablex.

Thibault, J. W., & Kelley, H. H. (1959). *The social psychology of groups.* New York: Wiley.

Thompson, J. (1967). *Organizations in action.* New York: McGraw-Hill.

Tierney, P. (1992). *The contribution of leadership, supportive environment, and individual traits of creative performance in an industrial setting.* Unpublished doctoral dissertation, University of Cincinnati, OH.

Triandis, H. C., & Albert, R. (1987). Cross-cultural perceptives on organizational communication. In F. M. Jablin, L. Putman, K. H. Roberts, & L. M. Porter (Eds.), *Handbook of organizational communication* (pp. 264–295). Beverly Hills, CA: Sage.

Uhl-Bien, M., & Graen, G. B. (1992a). Leadership-making in cross-functional project teams. *The Journal of High Technology Management Research, 3*(2), 225–241.

Uhl-Bien, M., & Graen, G. B. (1992b). Leadership-making in self-managing professional work teams: An empirical investigation. In K. E. Clark, M. B. Clark, & D. P. Campbell (Eds.), *Impact of self-leadership*. West Orange, NJ: Leadership Library of America.

Uhl-Bien, M., Graen, G. B., & Baugh, G. (1992). *Impact of self-leadership and leadership making in professional coacting and interacting work.* Unpublished paper, University of Cincinnati, Cincinnati.

Uhl-Bien, M., Tierney, P., Wakabayashi, M., & Graen, G. (1990). Paternalism as an indicant of "right type" of manager in the Japanese organization. *Group and Organization, 15,* 415–431.

Useem, J., Useem, R., & Donghue, J. (1963). Men in the middle of the third culture. *Human Organization, 22*(3), 169–179.

Vasudevan, D. (1992). *Identifying the determinants of career intentions among undergraduate engineering students.* Unpublished doctoral dissertation, University of Cincinnati, OH.

Vecchio, R. (1982). A further test of leadership effects due to between-group and within-group variation. *Journal of Applied Psychology, 67,* 200–208.

Wakabayashi, M., & Graen, G. B. (1984). The Japanese career progress study: A 7-year follow-up. *Journal of Applied Psychology, 69,* 603–614.

Wakabayashi, M., & Graen, G. B. (1988). Human resource development of Japanese managers: Leadership and career investment. In K. Rowland & G. Ferris (Eds.), *International human resources management.* Greenwich, CT: JAI Press.

Wakabayashi, M., Graen, G. B., Graen, M. R., & Graen, M. G. (1988). Japanese management progress: Mobility into middle management. *Journal of Applied Psychology, 73,* 217–227.

Wakabayashi, M., Graen, G. B., & Uhl-Bien, M. (1990). Generalizability of the hidden investment hypothesis among line managers in five leading Japanese corporations. *Human Relations, 43,* 1099–1116.

Wakabayashi, M., Minami, T., Hashimoto, M., Sano, K., Graen, G., & Novak, M. (1980). Managerial career development: Japanese style. *International Journal of Intercultural Relations, 4,* 391–420.

Waldron, V. R. (1991). Achieving communications goals upward. *Communications Monographs, 58,* 289–306.

Weber, M. (1958). *The protestant ethic and the spirit of capitalism.* New York: Scribner's. (Originally published 1904–1905)

Whitehill, A. M. (1991). *Japanese Management.* London: Routledge.

Womack, J. P., Jones, D. T., & Roos, D. (1990). *The machine that changed the world.* New York: Macmillan.

Yoshino, M. (1968). *Japan's managerial system.* Cambridge, MA: MIT Press.

Yukl, G., & Van Fleet, D. (1992). Theory and research on leadership in organizations. In M. D. Dunnette & L. M. Hough (Eds.), *Handbook of Industrial and Organizational Psychology* (2nd ed., vol. 3, pp. 147–197). Palo Alto, CA: Consulting Psychologists Press.

Zalesny, M. D., & Graen, G. (1986). Exchange theory in leadership research. In A. Kieser, G. Reber & R. Wunderer (Eds.), *Encyclopedia of leadership* (pp. 714–727). C. E. Poeschel Verberg. Stuttgart, Germany.

CHAPTER 9

Aging and Work Behavior

José A. Forteza
José M. Prieto
Complutense University, Madrid

Demographic trends indicate that the population in industrial countries is aging. It is likely that an increasing percentage of the work force will consist of older workers. Therefore, industrial and organizational psychologists must become more concerned with this segment of the work force. An examination of life cycles and labor cycles indicates what changes in psychological functioning occur during the life cycle and what implications these have for the labor cycle. Special difficulties (e.g., stereotypes of employers) encountered by older workers are examined. The performance of older workers is reviewed. The relationship between aging and training, job satisfaction, and other variables is examined. The human side of retirement in several countries is considered, and suggestions are made for improvements in the adjustment of older workers to both the work setting and retirement. The chapter ends with a discussion of public policy toward retirees.

Aging in the Labor Market

DEMOGRAPHIC STUDIES POINT to a clear tendency toward an aging of the world population. Even though there is a concurrent improvement in life and working conditions, hygiene, and available sanitary services, it creates problems and conflicts that affect even the most advanced industrial societies.

Figure 1 shows the available data on and estimations of the percentages of populations aged 65 or older in the European Community (EC). Just after the end of World War II, people aged 65 or older represented approximately 10 percent of the population of each country. In the 1990s, that age group represents approximately 15 percent, increasing to 20 percent by the year 2040.

FIGURE 1

Percentage of Populations in the EC Aged 65 or Older

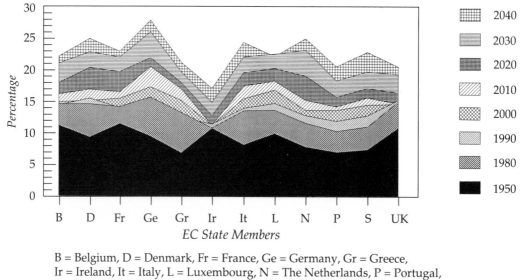

B = Belgium, D = Denmark, Fr = France, Ge = Germany, Gr = Greece,
Ir = Ireland, It = Italy, L = Luxembourg, N = The Netherlands, P = Portugal,
S = Spain, UK = United Kingdom

From *Employment Outlook 1989* by the Organization for Economic Cooperation and Development (OECD), 1989, Paris: Author. Copyright 1989 by OECD. Adapted by permission.

Another way of looking at the phenomenon of aging in the labor market is to examine the percentages of *active population* members (15 to 64 years old) versus *retired people* (65 years or older). Figure 2 compares these percentages in the EC in 1985, in the year 2000, and in the year 2025. The number of retired people increases, and the number of people of working age decreases, though slightly,[1] which may increase the economic dependence of retired people on those who work. Figure 3 shows that this tendency is similar in all the member countries except Ireland.[2]

If the data from the surveys of the active population are analyzed, certain differences with respect to age become evident between countries. Figure 4 compares the percentages of males and females in the work force by age in the United States and Spain in the year 1988. Parallel tendencies occur among men but not among women. This may be attributed to the different socialization patterns among adult married women in the respective countries.

As can be seen in Figure 5, in Spain the highest rate of participation in the work force is maintained by married men, followed by single men and then single women. Married women are more likely to either leave the labor market or never become a part of it (Casanueva, 1990; García, 1990). Men who marry young enter the Spanish labor market between the ages of 16 and 19.

There is evidence of a rapid decline in the presence of men and women between the ages

FIGURE 2

Percentage of Retired People Versus Active Population in the EC in 1985, 2000, and 2025

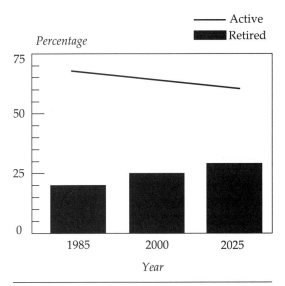

Source: EUROSTAT, 1988

of 55 and 64 in the Spanish labor market. The result is early retirement or long-lasting unemployment. In Spain the age of retirement is not fixed. Industrial reconversions as well as personnel policies are behind this noteworthy decline. Nevertheless, in both Spain and the United States, early retirement occurs more frequently among people who have lower levels of formal education, as is evidenced in Figure 6. Companies retain their most qualified employees, or the most qualified resist giving up their jobs, perhaps because they reach higher positions in the organizations. In addition, both the aged and the qualified remain active in the growing productive sectors.

Life Cycles and Labor Cycles

This chapter does not cover the aging of organizations (Boerlijst, 1989) in detail. However, the relationship of the average age of workers to organizational life cycles is considered (Ekvall, 1986; Schrank & Waring, 1981). For example, the role of older workers in a large Spanish firm in which 77 percent of employees had a seniority of at least nine years was clearly different from their role in another company in which most of the workers had little seniority (Rodriguez, 1989). The age distribution within the organization and rules about seniority create different attitudes and values in the work setting and planning (Bouza, Asenjo, Vargas, & Borges, 1990; Johnston, 1976).

Chronological Phases in Human Life

The life span of an individual is a vast concurrence of causes and conditions. During different chronological age periods, people go through phases of changing life conditions.[3] Forteza (1985) calls these phases *successive lives.*[4] The consequence is that the developmental sequence of an individual becomes an unstable process in the face of further change.

Life transitions come and go. For example, people pass from being single to being married, and from marriage to separation, divorce, or the death of a spouse. They convert to different religions, militancies, or ideologies. Migratory workers go to the city or to other countries to obtain a desired job. All of these transitions cause a change in people's lives and necessarily affect their social relationships, skills, feelings of adequacy or inadequacy, and attitudes. Chronological age in itself is usually an inadequate predictor of people's accomplishments and behavior. Interindividual differences predominate.

In aging, three differentiated processes come together, all of which develop separately even though they are not independent (as in Bromley, 1990; Riley, 1979). They are *biological aging, psychological aging,* and *social aging.* The respective ages at which these processes occur do not usually correspond exactly, year for year, in people. In fact, there are often significant differences in these phases.

FIGURE 3

Ratio of Retired People to the Active Population in the EC

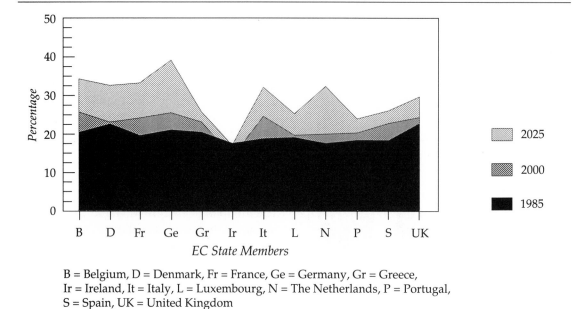

B = Belgium, D = Denmark, Fr = France, Ge = Germany, Gr = Greece,
Ir = Ireland, It = Italy, L = Luxembourg, N = The Netherlands, P = Portugal,
S = Spain, UK = United Kingdom

Source: EUROSTAT, 1988

FIGURE 4

Work Force in Spain and the United States in 1988 Classified by Age and Sex

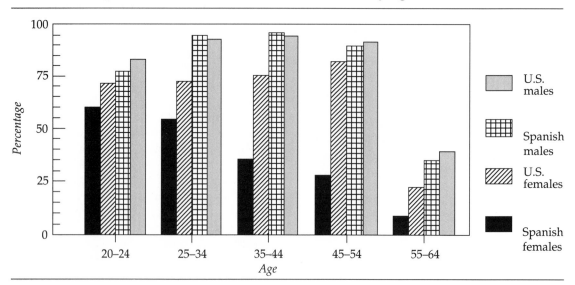

From *Employment Outlook 1989* by the Organization for Economic Cooperation and Development (OECD), 1989, Paris: Author. Copyright 1989 by OECD.
Adapted by permission.

FIGURE 5

Work Force in Spain in 1987 Classified by Sex, Age, and Marital Status

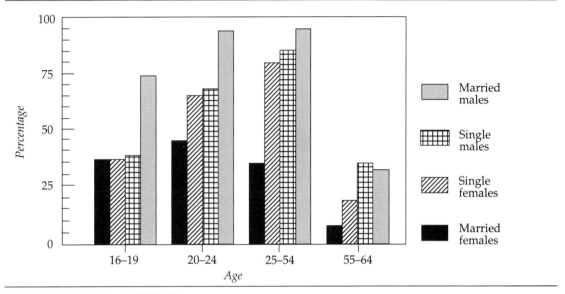

Source: Instituto Nacional de Empleo (INEM), 1987

FIGURE 6

**Percentage of U.S. and Spanish Males and Females
in the Work Force Aged 55 to 64 Classified by Level of Education**

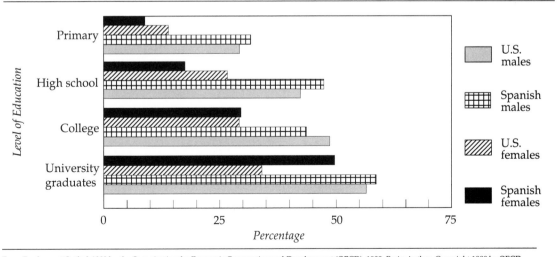

From *Employment Outlook 1989* by the Organization for Economic Cooperation and Development (OECD), 1989, Paris: Author. Copyright 1989 by OECD. Adapted by permission.

From a subjective point of view, "one is not old." Rather, "one is older than." The relational and comparative aspects stand out. At the same time, cultural and economic surroundings attach various specific meanings to any given event. In certain settings, an 18-year-old woman is at the optimum age at which to proceed with the socialization process. In other settings, the socialization process may have already been completed. In history texts, there is an account of Emperor Charles V giving up the throne and retiring to the Monastery of Yuste as "an aged and decrepit man." He was 55.

In spite of these considerations, many authors have developed models concerning the course of human life (Kalish, 1983; Lehr, 1980; Pikunas, 1976). Each proposes a series of periods, each of which is characterized by its own specific set of tasks and activities, motives and expectations, and problems and concerns (Levinson, 1978).

The biological paradigm identifies three phases: growth, stabilization, and deterioration. The first lasts from birth to 25 years, the second up to age 65, and the third covers the remaining years.

In the psychological paradigm, a characterization of the different chronological phases was sought. One of the most ambitious projects was begun at the University of Vienna in the 1930s by Karl and Charlotte Bühler and later continued in California under the direction of Charlotte. This project was intended to analyze in each stage of the life-span cycle (Bühler, 1933):

- The most representative facts and peculiarities

- The internal experiences of the subjects— their desires, expectations, and attitudes

- The most substantial achievements and accomplishments

Five stages were identified, beginning with childhood, in which dependency predominates. This is followed by a stage of self-determination, which lasts from age 17 to 28. In this second stage, activities of an exploratory nature are carried out and skills accumulated. The stabilization stage spans the ages of 28 to 50. In this period, people make their most important contributions and take on greater responsibilities. The transition stage covers the period between the ages of 50 and 65, in which achievements are evaluated and the sense of finality of human life is strong. In the last stage, activities decrease and restrictions increase, there is an acceptance that life has gone by, and the reality of death is reckoned with. In numerous cultures, the idea of a posthumous message has been institutionalized in the form of memoirs, wills, or death poems (Hoffman, 1986).

Life-span Developmental Psychology

Life-span developmental psychology serves as a frame of reference for analyzing the changes that come about in individuals with age (Baltes, 1987; Baltes, Reese, & Lipsitt, 1980; Birren, Cunningham, & Yamamoto, 1983). In a simplified form, some of the fundamental suppositions of this line of research are as follows:

- Aging begins with birth (or even conception) and ends with death. There is a close connection between all the life-span stages.

- Aging is a continuous process in which biological, psychological, and social influences are interrelated and become more interdependent with age.

- The behavior norms of any person or cohort of persons are affected by the social and environmental changes that occur during the course of human existence. Nevertheless, it is believed that cohort and other time-related cultural influences on the factor structure of psychological variables are relatively small (Cunningham & Birren, 1976).

- The fundamental concepts are *change* and *aging patterns*.

This point of view emphasizes concomitant causality and interaction: Individual behavior is the result of the resources of the person and the peculiarities of the situation and surroundings in which he or she moves. Instead of being concerned with the differences between groups by age, the object of study refers to the modifications being generated in the psychological processes throughout one's life.[5]

Methodological Issues

When researching the links between age and work, it is not a practicable procedure to manipulate the independent variables. As a result, industrial and organizational psychologists resort to comparative, quasi-experimental methods. The main difference between experimental and the quasi-experimental methods is that in quasi-experimental methods neither the independent nor the predictive variables are under the control of the researcher; they have been previously modified. Additionally, it is not very likely that the differences that have been found among groups—differences that concern the dependent variable or criterion—can be attributed to a causal relationship whose origin can be found exclusively in the independent variables.

Two general research models stand out from among the comparative methods and are used when analyzing the changes in a specific variable that come about with age. These are the *cross-sectional* and *longitudinal* models. *Mixed* models have also been developed, which have been determined in accordance with the purpose of the studies and by the available means or resources. The following is assumed for both models:

- The individual behavior of adults is relatively stable throughout the life span (Johnson, Nagoshi, & Ahern, 1983; Krauss, 1980).

- The measurements or the observations made throughout the life span are identical or equivalent in their meaning (Labouvie, 1980).

The cross-sectional model is the one that has been used in most of the research regarding aging and work. lt basically consists of the comparison of the data obtained with representative samples of workers who belong to different subpopulations. The observations or measurements are collected during one time period; a comparison of the scores is made at a later period. These scores are obtained from groups of workers who have been differentiated by age using statistical tests. The results are usually used in personnel decisions that affect workers of different ages.

The internal validity of these models is affected by the following factors:

- Differences in the rates of human maturation and identifying themes inherent to a specific age or generation

- Biases in the selection of samples, since some cohorts are better represented than others

- The selection of the specific psychological tests (differential validity and reliability)

- Different subjective reactions and interpretations of the scores, depending on the age of the testees

Three variants are used in the cross-sectional model: cross-cultural methods, cross-national methods, and cross-organizational methods.

The longitudinal model is of a diachronic sort and in essence consists of repeating the observations and measurements with the same sample of adults throughout the time they remain in the company. This is especially appropriate for checking hypotheses in which the independent variable exerts a cumulative effect over time on the dependent variable.

The internal validity of longitudinal models is affected by the following:

- Attrition, since employment vacancies are not arbitrary or casual

- The degree of familiarity with the tests and instruments that are used

- The specific demands of these workers at different points in their lives

Career development programs can be cataloged as typical longitudinal models. The personnel department files usually accumulate much information about each individual employee; thus, this type of research is practicable within a company. When these studies are carried out, they result in internal reports of a confidential sort and are rarely published.

In addition, mixed models described by Schaie (1973) include time-lag, cohort-sequential, time-sequential and cross-sequential designs.

The choice of statistical procedures appropriate for each type of data poses a problem (Horn & McArdle, 1980): Analysis of variance and covariance are still widely used, but they are in fact special cases of the general linear model. Multivariate approaches lend themselves to this type of analysis better, but in many cases the assumptions on which they are based are not met by the samples studied. Time-series analyses and log-linear models are more appropriate. Future research ought to examine nonlinear developments, known as *mathematics of chaos*, that might be applied to this kind of data.

There are few industrial and organizational psychologists who have adequate training in life-span research methodology. That is unfortunate because they usually have data at their disposal from the files of human resources departments that ought to be analyzed from the perspective of life-span research. The results mentioned under the following heading were carried out by researchers using this framework.

Changes in Psychophysiological Processes During the Life Cycle

The available literature indicates which physiological and psychological functions are most relevant in the work setting during the life span (Birren & Schaie, 1977; Charness, 1985a; Craik & Threhub, 1982; Maddox, 1987; Perlmutter & Hall, 1985; Ward, 1984).

Sensory Functions.   Changes with age of the most important sensory functions, sight and hearing, are an established fact. Nevertheless, there are important individual differences with respect to the timing, speed, and seriousness of the losses.

With respect to sight, four characteristics are taken into account: acuity, accommodation, adaptation, and chromatic discrimination.

Between the ages of 40 and 50, there is a gradual decrease in the capacity for seeing objects at a distance. The size of the pupil is reduced and the crystalline lenses become more opaque. Older people often need more intense lighting in order to work without difficulty. However, excess light can create discomfort.

Around 45 years of age, people begin to have difficulties focusing on close objects. The decrease in the elasticity of the crystalline lens of the eye begins during childhood and stops by the age of 60. This phenomenon is known as "tired vision" or farsightedness (presbyopia).

The losses of acuity and accommodation together usually create problems for reading and for signal detection.

Older people also experience difficulties in adapting to the dark. The pupil dilates more slowly, and recovery after a glare also decreases considerably. There is also a narrowing of the field of vision, which results in greater difficulty distinguishing bright objects.

With respect to chromatic discrimination, older people can distinguish colors well, but with age there is yellowing of the crystalline lens, reducing sensitivity to hues with shorter wavelengths. Older people can easily distinguish yellows, oranges, and reds, but confuse blues, gray-blues, and violet.

The loss of hearing with age is gradual. The deterioration affects high-pitched sounds first and low-pitched sounds later. The incidence of deafness increases linearly after age 50. Temporal auditory discrimination—that is, the ability to distinguish two concurrent sounds—also gets notably worse. This results in difficulties in understanding conversations. Instead of shouting at elderly workers, one must speak more slowly.

Elderly workers are more sensitive to sound interferences. Background noises easily distract them. Defective localization of the source of sounds is also frequent.

There is a certain amount of confusion with regard to the effects that can be attributed to age and those that can be attributed to surroundings. Minimal deficits have been found in elderly people who live in geographical areas that are not very noisy. People who normally work in very noisy workshops generally manage well in that atmosphere—that is, accommodate to the noise; nevertheless, with age the appearance of "professional deafness" increases.

There also appear to be some links between deafness and certain personality traits that increase with age, such as distrust, hypersensitivity, and paranoid tendencies.

The data concerning the remaining senses point in the same direction but are less conclusive. Because of their relevance in the work environment, certain deficits in the sense of touch and in the vestibular functions—which generate problems of balance and continuous discomfort—stand out. Vestibular problems often require a job change or modification in order to avoid falls and work accidents.

Sensation and Perception. In work surroundings, the delimitation between sensation and perception is not clear. Sensation precedes perception and is essential to produce perception. The cortical elements, linked to the mechanisms of control of the nervous system, play a major role. Perception is a psychological process more complex than sensation. It includes the interpretation and evaluation of the stimuli as well as the central processing of the information.

Research carried out in laboratories with technology such as tachistoscopes, the projection of films, and sound devices indicates that aging reduces the speed and amplitude of perception (Fozard, Wolf, Bell, McFarland, & Poldosky, 1977; Minton & Schneider, 1980, chap. 11; Willerman, 1979, chap. 13).

The following is regarded as true of elderly people:

- They take longer to identify and interpret information presented in an incomplete and disorganized way.

- They encounter difficulties when identifying concealed and disguised elements in a context of complex structures.

- They detect with difficulty those stimuli relevant to carrying out a task when those stimuli are presented in a complex context.

- They have a tendency not to modify the perceptions that have been consolidated, even when the available information suggests the advantages of doing so.

- They usually perceive discrete stimuli that are presented serially as fused sounds forming a whole.

- They need more time to process information and to carry out appropriate motor tasks.

A typical characteristic of the aging process is a behavioral slowdown when activation of the central nervous system is needed.

In tasks that require alertness, the elderly make more mistakes and suffer more distractions. It appears that this is a result of the interaction between anxiety, speed, and the diversity in the stimuli inherent in the task they are doing.

Psychomotor Performance.   Another facet that has been analyzed has to do with psychomotor performance (Welford, 1977). Psychomotor skills require body movements, especially of the limbs. Movements are carried out by means of the action of the striated muscles in response to afferent stimulation.

The critical loss in these abilities is less pronounced than those discussed earlier and may be compensated by practice. Nevertheless, healthy elderly people take longer to react to a range of diversified stimuli, use more time when carrying out specific movements, are less strong, and in general usually perform worse at tasks that require coordination, vigor, and speed. All of this must be considered in relation to the tasks that the elderly must carry out, the equipment required, the required postures and movements, as well as the range and presentation format of the stimuli to which the elderly must react.

With age, there is a decrease in psychomotor performance. The problem is knowing to what extent this decrease seriously affects performance in different common activities and tasks. For example, muscular strength reaches its peak at age 20. From that age on, the decrease is gradual and moderate. By age 70 muscular strength is between 15 to 35 percent lower than at age 20. A similar decrease can be noted in maximum and continuous hand pressure when squeezing a dynamometer. In most jobs, however, it is not necessary to employ maximum muscular strength or to maintain it for a prolonged time period.

Reaction time studies show significant differences with age (Jensen, 1982). These differences are small for simple tasks but large for complex ones, especially when the stimuli are varied and appear at irregular intervals.

The interchange of information between laboratory and field studies within factory workshops has determined at which phases of the aging process difficulties are likely to occur.

Initially the deterioration was attributed to certain losses in peripheral processes: an inadequate perception of the stimuli or certain difficulties in the execution of movements. Welford (1977) demonstrated that the deterioration affects decisions regarding movements and how they are to be monitored. This happens especially when complex, nonrepetitive tasks are concerned.

In situations in which there is enough time to examine the signs and to control movements, elderly people are usually slower but more precise. When the work rate is determined by the production system, elderly people are usually less precise than younger people. For well-learned tasks it is possible to compensate for certain deficiencies (Downs & Roberts, 1977).

Analysis of accidents has emphasized the differences that are concomitants of age and patterns of psychomotor performance (Dillingham, 1981). Older employees have lower rates of accidents but suffer more severe injuries.

Intelligence.   The myth of intellectual deterioration with age is still widespread. According to this myth, intelligence increases, at a rapidly decreasing rate, from childhood until the end of the teens. This is followed by a leveling-off phase that lasts approximately 10 years. Afterward, there is a slow and gradual decline, which becomes faster after age 70.

The first studies that emphasized significant differences in intellectual performance all through the life span were based on data from cross-sectional studies. Researchers examined groups of subjects of different ages only once. They reached the conclusion that systematic differences were found in general intelligence or in specific abilities that could be attributed— without further explanation—to chronological age.

Many of these studies did not use rigorous controls and ignored measurement errors that may have affected ability scores. The consistency of findings from different countries and periods resulted in the *deficiency* model of intelligence. According to this model, a maximum level of intellectual performance is reached at a given moment during childhood. From that time on, there is an irreversible, slowly accelerating linear decrease. However, several outside factors may contribute to this decrease. Among elderly people the probability of cardiovascular and cerebral illness is higher than among younger people. Furthermore, older individuals were educated differently from the way the young are educated today.

The deficiency model is now being questioned (Horn, 1982; Horn & Donaldson, 1976). The assumption that decline begins just after reaching the age of 20, as well as the idea of inexorable and universal deterioration, is under scrutiny.

There is a great deal of data that supports the need for an in-depth revision of this model:

- The results obtained from longitudinal studies, with the same cohort of subjects, show that the scores are maintained and that the point of inflection is not clear.

- The elderly who are in good health do not deteriorate after age 60 (J. Birren, 1974).

- The scores obtained by the elderly today and 30 years ago are remarkably similar.

- The content of many intelligence tests is irrelevant when applied to the elderly.

- Certain personality traits such as anxiety, caution, depression, and rigidity interfere with performance on these tests.

Nevertheless, the cross-sectional and longitudinal studies suggest the following:

- There is a greater variability in the scores among people of a greater

age. Some elderly people surpass the average score of younger people.

- The decline on tests of mental speed is greater than on tests of mental power.

- There is a differentiation among abilities; some deteriorate faster than others. There is little similarity across individuals in the time at which the decline begins, its speed, and the degree. The verbal factors are maintained, and even improve, until after age 50. Perceptual and spatial factors begin decreasing sooner and show a more pronounced deterioration.

We can conclude that until a very advanced age there is no confirmation of a consistent decline either in all abilities or in all individuals (Botwinick, 1984; Schaie, 1980; Schaie & Willis, 1986).

For most people after the age of 70, we can observe a decrease in abilities that require rapid responses and measures that are sensitive to the deterioration of the nervous system. Furthermore, losses occur in most abilities among those who suffer serious cardiovascular illness or who live in impoverished sociocultural surroundings, no matter what their age.

In most abilities the variance attributable to aging is relatively slight in comparison to the variance between distant and distinct cohorts. Psychological test scores and survival are positively associated.

To summarize, in populations of healthy subjects who have a high level of education and who are exposed to acceptable stimulation within their surroundings, the ontogenic changes in the intellectual variables are minimal. Many elderly workers show an average level of intellectual performance similar to that of younger people. As a result, researchers have questioned the idea of intellectual deterioration and have moved to the study of which factors, in addition to the age of the subjects, may be responsible for behavioral changes. In addition, research examines what improvements in the surroundings can minimize behavioral changes. This view is supported also by data, gathered over three decades, in the only longitudinal study of senescent twins reported to date (Jarvik & Bank, 1983).

Learning and Memory.   Studies of learning and memory constitute another significant chapter of psychogerontology (Kliegl, Smith, & Baltes, 1986; Poon, 1985). They have followed the current shifts of paradigms in psychological research (Hartley, Harker, & Walsh, 1980).

Differences among groups of distinct ages in the phases of acquisition, retention, and retrieval have been studied. Many studies used verbal materials and analyzed diverse forms of presentation of stimuli and intervals of retention under various conditions. Elderly people take almost twice as long to learn a series of associated pairs but once learned they remember them as well as young people do.

Cognitive psychology and the study of patterns of information processing have permitted a better understanding of the difficulties encountered and the strategies followed by elderly workers. In fact, memory losses—although they are normative and substantial—can be minimized (Arenberg, 1980).

In short-term memory, the differences that can be attributed to age are minimal as long as a series of conditions is met:

- Subjects perceived the stimuli correctly.

- Subjects do not have to reorganize the materials.

- Subjects are not distracted or disturbed during learning.

However, if the materials exceed the capacity of short-term memory, elderly workers experience some deficiencies.

In order to overcome these deficiencies, different strategies for classifying information have been explored. For example, including familiar contents or contents with a specific meaning

among the materials that have to be retained can be helpful. These strategies are relevant when designing training and retraining programs.

Research has examined the effects of personality factors such as rigidity, carefulness, consistency, depression, anxiety, lower ego strength, thoughtfulness, friendliness, dependency, inhibition, introversion, locus of external control, and lower need achievement on the behavior of the elderly (Prieto, 1977). Nevertheless, longitudinal studies of personality change show persuasive evidence of stability of adult personality, reflected in levels of disposition, age-invariant personality structure, and time consistency of individual differences (Costa, McCrae, & Arenberg, 1983).

With maturation, changes are brought about at specific ages. It is unclear that these ontogenic changes are the only ones that influence individual differences in human performance.

Career Development and Aging

Vocational choice is like choosing among paths in a forest. The paths chosen inevitably leave other paths behind. The following factors influence the choice of professional careers:

- Socioeconomic determinants such as social class, profession of the parents, circle of friends and relatives, place of residence, institutional facilities, cultural attitudes regarding the value of studying and working, and the political and economical situation of the country

- Certain personal traits, such as aptitudes, emotional and personality behavioral patterns, social skills, and interests

- Degree of competence acquired by means of regular education and accumulated experience

The transition from school to the world of work constitutes one of the crucial moments in the life of an individual and does not always come about without tension (Burton, Forrest, & Stewart, 1989; Hall, 1986; Peiro & Moret, 1987; Schein, 1978). The preparatory period has reached its end, and the range of occupations to which an individual can devote him or herself in the future becomes clearly outlined.

On all levels there is usually a difference in phase between academic training and the demands of the productive system of which the individual becomes a part. Additionally, a high percentage of youths who are looking for a job must still be considered *unclassifiable;* that is, they cannot easily commit themselves to the exercise of a specific work activity. New technological developments can complicate the horizon for those who do not possess the means to keep up to date.

Quite often university graduates enter jobs that do not have a direct relationship to their training and professional aims. This results in underemployment.

The admission of an individual to the work environment is the result of a double process of visibility (of the company and the candidate) and of decision making between individuals and organizations. The socialization process begins with admittance to the organization. More specifically, the new hire has to:

- Adapt to an unknown work environment and to many physical and social aspects that are different from the previous environment

- Take on new responsibilities that are generally specific to each company, production unit, or assigned job

- Assimilate or adapt to the management style that exists in the organization and that the worker perceives in interactions with a supervisor

- Sympathize with the rules, customs, traditions, values, relational networks,

power groups, myths, and rituals that define the culture of the organization

This early socialization is a normal phenomenon in 20-year-old new hires. This same process with new hires who are more than 30 years of age and who have no previous work experience (because of chronic unemployment or other personal reasons) is considered an intricate process. Companies are usually hesitant about hiring candidates who are older than is typical for a given job—for instance, university graduates who might be underemployed or women who interrupted their careers to raise children. Often the cost of employing such people is greater than the cost of employing younger people. After getting job experience, their rate of turnover is higher than it is among younger people. In some of the local communities in Spain, many of those who receive social welfare are precisely those who—because of their age and skills—have fewer and fewer job possibilities.

The admission phase is followed by a long period in which personal goals determine the channels through which status is reached. Successful employees assimilate the goals, values, rules, styles, and performance that allow them to be promoted, change jobs, and attain proximity to those who hold positions of power within the organization (Blanco, 1977). In this way they achieve a balance between their own career needs and the organization's requirements.

As workers approach the age of 50, they begin to review past achievements (Dupuis, Brunet, St. Germain, Hamel, & Lavoie-Ste. Marie, 1986). They do not consider themselves "old," yet they realize they are no longer young. There is still time to do things, but they have to decide, and—above all—they have to hurry.

In this period there is also an awareness of one's own mortality, and a significant number consider looking elsewhere to pursue other personal and professional directions. There is evidence of a turning inward and a refusal to identify what the future holds. Past ideals and illusions are readjusted in light of changes produced in the professional sphere and family circle. It is usually a period of profound emotional tension, most of it intimate and nontransferable. In some companies employee assistance programs provide adequate psychological counseling to those elderly workers experiencing these crises, which may include a transitory deterioration of work performance (Beaudoin, 1986).[6]

In this phase, successful older workers know that they have reached the top or are about to reach it. They are holding a consolidated position; they have acquired ease, mastery, and control of the situation. They know well the tasks they have to carry out and the essential functioning of the organization they are working for. They place their own distinctive stamp on the activities they carry out or initiate.

At the same time they become aware of their limitations and may find themselves unable to adjust to new demands that are a direct result of technological changes within the organization. These senior employees realize that they are losing initiative and inventiveness, so they usually take refuge in that which is familiar to them—the methods that allowed them to be successful—without properly determining if those methods are still the most efficient. Younger collaborators are perceived as a threat, especially those with a high level of education. All of this generates an excessive preoccupation with security. Senior employees take pains to make and keep themselves indispensable.

Oncoming retirement generates in many workers a state of restlessness, uneasiness, distress, and nervousness, which interferes with their expected performance. The people who are most satisfied with their work or most identified with the organization are those who are most weakened. In some firms, courses are offered to prepare workers for retirement.[7] These courses center on two objectives: (a) to generate ideas and suggestions for better

performance in old age and (b) to encourage future personal projects with open attitudes of achievement and acceptance.

On the subject of retirement, psychological points of view contradict political, legal, and trade union traditions. It is necessary to seek and stimulate formulas for voluntary, flexible, and gradual retirement that allow part-time work, as opposed to mandatory retirement at a fixed age, which means total and sudden abandonment of employment (Forteza, 1990). Recent labor legislation in the European Community allows for this option (Prieto & Martin, 1990), although in practice its effective utilization is minimal.[8] It doesn't make any sense to continue with the idea that employment is the time for work and retirement is the time for idleness. Human activity and work continue independently of employment conditions.

Working and Family Life

Throughout the life span, workers perform different roles, simultaneously and regularly. In each one of these roles, such influences as norms of behavior, expectations, motives, responsibilities, and social relations come into play. In recent years the links between work environment and family environment have been taken into consideration (Burke & Greenglass, 1987; Voydanoff, 1987). This is an old subject, whose importance was already mentioned in the Hawthorne studies.

Many young workers still live in their parents' homes when they take on their first job. A work contract consolidates the possibilities of effective independence with respect to the family circle and places the individual in a new context of direct dependence under the protection of immediate supervisors.

During adult life, people take on both work and personal commitments. Organizations reinforce those who manage to give more to the work environment and less to the personal environment. As a result, promotion policies favor those employees who show a dependence on work as a means of maintaining self-esteem and self-worth. These policies are not necessarily discriminating against women; they simply reflect management emphasis on the goals of the organization (Schwartz, 1989). Organizations make assumptions that must guide the personal lives of employees. On most occasions, personal matters must be resolved outside of work hours or employees must arrange for other people to take care of their personal matters. Single-career couples and women with a total dedication to career adopt this assumption as a standard condition. The majority of dual-career couples and women who try to balance career and family view it as an unfavorable condition.

Career factors such as planning, promotion, and relocation challenge spouses' or partners' expectations, both at work and at home.[9] The massive entrance of women into public and private organizations has modified male and female roles. The degree of centrality of work and home has a direct influence on individual goals and family plans.

Three hypotheses have been proposed to explore the influence of life experiences in one area on behavior in the other.

- *Segmentary model*—People adapt their attitudes and behavior to the immediate demands of each situation.

- *Compensatory model*—People look for satisfaction, achievement, and prestige in an area that compensates for what they are missing in another area.

- *Generalization model*—Attitudes that take form in one sphere tend to be extended to another, affecting the orientation adopted toward oneself, one's partner, and the workplace.

Empirical data—still divergent—basically sustain the generalization model.

An overview of the few studies that have explored the relationship between family life and work life generally have been limited to the following topics (Voydanoff, 1987):

- Studies that directly relate the effects of the work environment on the quality of family life

- Studies that analyze the direct consequences of family life conditions on the work situation

- Studies that analyze the circular relationships of variables from both areas

Among the studies that examine the effects of the work environment on quality of family life, the following issues are noteworthy:

- The influence of income on family life, quality of life, satisfaction, and inter-family relations—one of these studies (Aldous, Oxmond, & Hicks, 1979) concludes that marital happiness is higher in families whose primary wage partner achieves only moderate professional success

- The influence on family life of such job structural conditions as length and distribution of work time, job site, change in work responsibility, and geographical mobility

- The influence on family life of such psychological dimensions as degree of work involvement, self-esteem, and satisfaction with the position

Among the studies that analyze the direct consequences of the conditions of family life on the work situation, the following observations are noteworthy:

- Family conditions have an influence on work. Important variables include educational background, family atmosphere, family requirements and responsibilities, family structure, and members' contributions to total family income. These variables are related to such factors as types of employment, hours worked, multiple employment, levels of performance, rates of absenteeism and rotation, and degree of fatigue and stress.

- Certain sporadic and specific incidents that occur within the family, such as accidents, conjugal disputes, illnesses, concern for children, and deaths, seem to have a real—but transitory—effect on work behavior.

Work life, as reflected in job satisfaction, styles of decision making, job conflicts and stability, and how individuals and couples use time and view their lives, influence family life (McCook, Folzer, Charlesworth, & Scholl, 1991; Mortimer, Lorence, & Kumka, 1986).

The Aging of the Active Adult Population

In this section, age constitutes a criterion for the classification of workers. The aggregate of the workers of a company makes up the roster of personnel. In this way, a genuine distribution of a segmented and specific population in a given moment within the history of each organization can be obtained. Periods of economic growth or decline imply different ratios of employment among cohorts in the same firm.

In many professional groups, the distribution by age differs substantially from that which exists within the general population. As an example, 82.1 percent of Spanish psychologists are under 40 years of age and only 1.7 percent are over 55. However, 23.7 percent of industrial and organizational psychologists are over 40 years of age. And 25.5 percent of Spanish psychologists obtained their predoctoral degrees in psychology before 1980. However, 44.7 percent of industrial and organizational psychologists obtained their degrees before 1980. Both distributions differ significantly from that which can be found within the general population and within the population of Spanish university graduates (Diaz-Sanchez, 1991).

The statistics currently available at the Ministry of Labor show important differences between the active or working population and the population census. Similar differences are also found when comparing the distribution of the population according to professions with the population pyramid. The population pyramid reflects the distribution of ages in a country, as reflected in the population census. The statistics of the Ministry of Labor show important differences between the age distribution of the working population and this pyramid. Similar differences have been identified when the age distribution of specific professions is compared with this pyramid (Smith, 1975). These differences exemplify an old dispute that exists between personnel psychologists with a sound background in demography and those psychometricians who emphasize the general population standardization norms. Currently, there are significant differences among the age-related variance in the general population and in the active population. The consequence is that, quite often, the *age effects* correction in standardization norms cannot be applied to the active population or to the distribution according to professions.

In examining the distribution of workers by age, some additional trends appear:

Men are overrepresented with respect to women in certain labor pools. Furthermore, the percentage of women decreases as age increases. This effect is accentuated when previous experience is a prerequisite for employment. Both ends of the age curve are overrepresented among the chronically unemployed—the young, because they lack experience, and the old, because their experience is no longer relevant to the new technology. This results in governments establishing formulas for tax incentives or reductions in social security costs that encourage the hiring of the younger (less than 25) and older (more than 45) segments of the population (Comision Asesora para el Desarrollo de los Recursos Humanos, 1987; Organization for Economic

Cooperation and Development [OECD], 1989).

Internal promotion is usually connected to seniority, but in a biased way. Companies identify desirable age ranges for specific jobs. Thus, access to these jobs is closed to those within the company who are above or below that age range but is open to outsiders who have higher levels of educational attainment and are not in that age range.

Age constitutes one of the determinants that shapes the existence of informal groups within companies. To a great extent, being a member of a specific cohort creates cohesion.

There are industrial sectors in which certain age groups predominate. For example, young people are more prevalent in computer science, television, and advanced electronics. Mature people predominate in the steel, metallurgy, banking, and insurance industries.

The age of mandatory retirement is another point of stratification of the working population. Those who were active become inactive. In phases of industrial reconversion or company mergers, premature retirement is encouraged, which results in younger retirees. For 1991, in Spain, 22.9 percent of the forecasted expenses of the state were used to guarantee the buying power of pensioners. In the United States, this was the item that forced a standoff between President Bush and the Congress when the 1991 national budget agreement was reached.

Attitudes Toward Aged Workers

The beliefs and attitudes—often prejudices—that govern modern society with respect to the elderly are widespread. In some cases, even 40-year-old workers are considered old. For instance, in the United States the Age Discrimination in Employment Act defines older workers as those over the age of 40. In the Spanish legislation, people 45 and older are considered older workers. These criteria

are widely shared by company owners, management, and employees. Even some human resource specialists currently view as old any individual age 40 and above who is still an active adult. Employers discriminate in areas such as hiring, promotion, training opportunities, and termination. It is estimated that three out of every four older workers believe that they have been the object of discrimination at some time. However, as the average age of a sample increases, the attitudes toward older people become less negative (Bird & Fisher, 1986).

Older workers are perceived as less efficient, less creative, less promotable, more resistant to change, slower, disinterested in training or retraining, incapable of adapting to change, and more rigid and prone to illnesses and accidents (Charness, 1985b; Doering, Rhodes, & Schuster, 1983; Rhodes, 1983; Rosen & Jerdee, 1978; Schwab & Heneman, 1978).

These perceptions are in conflict with research findings. The size of the age effect is relatively small. Nevertheless, in modifying attitudes, it is not enough to simply point out the facts. The involvement of those workers whose attitudes must be changed is necessary. In this sense, the pioneering study by Marrow and French (1945) about the change of stereotypes is a paradigmatic model that should be considered systematically.

The Generation Gap in the Workplace

The generation gap in the workplace has been studied very little. Confidential reports that circulate within companies show problems of communication between employees of different ages. This gap is manifested in several different facets of work life.

Language. In Spain, for example, over 90 percent of older workers in industrial centers come from rural backgrounds (Martinez, 1970; Tezanos, 1989). Their speech, acquired during childhood, is full of nature-oriented nuances that are irrelevant in urban contexts. In contrast, the younger generation commands a reduced vocabulary, with ambiguous words and terms. In addition, the new technology has introduced specific English words that do not fit into the customary syntax of the Spanish language. All of this generates difficulties in the composition and reading of letters, in telephone communication, and in referring to objects, as well as in the specification of instructions that are to be followed.

Authority Issues.   In Spain there has been a transition from an authoritarian and paternalistic regime to a democratic and egalitarian one. People who grew up with the slogan "The boss is always right" find themselves in serious conflict with young employees who maintain "The boss *may* be right." Supervisors who instigate a discussion want to hear opinions. The younger employees expect that the final decision will be made based on the opinion of the majority.

Concepts of Leadership.   Catholic and monarchical traditions have prevailed for centuries in Spain. Hence, leaders were expected to be "infallible," their source of power ineff-able, their commitment unquestionable, their behavior faultless (Prieto, 1989). They were appointed and acted in the name of God. They were *caudillos*, sovereign kings, bishops, cardinals, and abbots. Older workers have been educated in this tradition. Younger workers reject this view in their daily life, and they do not want these beliefs in their workplace.

Guidelines for Sexual Conduct.   In Spain the entry of women into the workplace has been slow but constant. At the same time, after the age of 25, many married women leave the workplace (see Figure 5). The average number of male workers is usually greater than the average number of female workers. Gender-based expectations that are considered

normal for one cohort lead to misunderstandings or misperceptions of others' intentions and behaviors (Abbey, 1982; Saal, 1990). Men tend to attribute more sexuality to single or young women's normal behavior than do other women. Sexual harassment might result from this disparity. In addition, differences in age complicate the attraction-rejection exchanges. In one company, one author of this chapter noted that those who most regularly worked overtime were married men and single women. This profile predicted more than 50 percent of the "sexual incidents" reported to the personnel department.

Views of Labor Ethics.   Older workers in Spain consider their jobs a scarce resource. As a consequence of the civil war, older workers grew up in an economy of scarcity (Spain was excluded from the Marshall plan). They use the ethics of a job well done as a source of reward and stability on the job. Younger employees grew up in a more affluent economy and are more concerned with the ethics of leisure—a job is carried out properly only if it is rewarding. Older employees had to pass a probationary period in order to become permanent workers. Younger employees face different indentures of apprenticeship or training contracts before having access to a tenured job. All of this turns into a dialogue of the deaf concerning the meaning of work and the rights and obligations of employees.

Labor Union Ideologies.   During the 1960s and early 1970s, by the end of Franco's regime, free trade unions became a social demand of the Spanish work force (Mella, 1989). Their attainment implied a series of Marxist ideological developments. Older workers who are members of a union are loyal to a specific ideological position. In contrast, younger employees become members of a union because they are dissatisfied with the company or because they want to assure themselves of a specific role as leaders among their fellow workers (Bouza et al., 1990). Thus, labor conflicts and strikes are interpreted differently by the two age groups.

Promotion Systems. In Spain, promotions based on seniority or favoritism were seen as natural. Merit was a secondary element. The new cohorts are against seniority or favoritism and favor equal opportunity and valid and reliable methods in performance evaluation and assessment of merit. However, recent judicial decisions have favored seniority.

Role of Work Motivation and Satisfaction. The economic environment (e.g., periods of inflation or recession) changes the valence of many of the elements that appear in models of work motivation and job satisfaction (Lévy-Leboyer, 1984). Incentives that motivate and satisfy older workers are irrelevant to younger workers. Differences in age and seniority result in different answers to the question, What is it that is worthwhile in this firm? While the preceding discussion draws on examples from Spain, the barriers between generations may be the rule, not the exception, in most countries. These barriers reflect different ways of understanding the reality of working among people who have to communicate and work together.

Performance Among Aged Workers

The changes mentioned earlier concerning the effect of aging on psychological and physiological processes undoubtedly result in deficiencies in the execution of some specific tasks by older workers. Similarly, we have pointed out the negative influences that technological and organizational changes can have on older workers. This may lead to underestimation of the importance of the greatest resource of older workers: experience. In specific cases, experience is seen as a drawback. By contrast,

in other cases, experience is at a premium. Historically, for instance, expert systems were developed because experienced and competent employees were few and far between or were about to retire.

We have mentioned prejudices and negative stereotypes toward older workers. Even though they may be false, these prejudices and negative stereotypes determine behavior patterns toward older workers and standards of judgment when evaluating their actual performance. Such stereotypes have often undermined the self-esteem of older workers. Changes in interests and motivation throughout life must also be considered. In this context, it may be helpful to note the following findings:

- Even though some workers experience a certain decrease in their skills with the passing of time, their capacity is still sufficient to meet the demands of normal activity (Salthouse, 1979).

- In jobs that have been carried out for many years, and in which drastic modifications have not been introduced, experience can compensate for the losses attributed to age (Charness, 1985a).

- With age, speed is lost (Birren, Robinson, & Livingston, 1986; Salthouse, 1979). But in those jobs where extreme speed is not an essential factor, older workers can perform similarly to younger workers (Welford, 1977).

- When workers can control their own time, they are not affected by the decrease in their skills. On the other hand, they may be affected in jobs that require a specific performance rate (Salthouse, 1979).

- Moderate physical effort is not a cause of premature aging (Lehr, 1980). For this reason, it is unadvisable to shift elderly workers to more comfortable positions. In these jobs, instead of physical effort, often perceptual abilities are required or the workers are forced to stay in the same position for prolonged time periods, which may be uncomfortable to them or even harmful.

- When comparisons are made with respect to performance quotas among people of different ages, the seniority factor moderates the link between age and performance (Salthouse, 1988).

- Groups of older workers may be affected by biases of a different type. The most common one is selection: The best are promoted, and the ones who do not adapt to the jobs are terminated (Arnold & Feldman, 1982).

The relationship between age and performance is the focus of many studies (Davies & Sparrow, 1985; Doering et al., 1983; Meier & Kerr, 1976; Riley, Hess, & Bond,1983; Sterns & Alexander, 1987). The results, obtained with many samples of factory employees, are inconsistent. In some cases a positive relationship has been found, in others a negative relationship, and, in still others, no relationship. In some studies the very young and very old do better than those in the middle of the age distribution.

However, most of these studies suffer from a series of limitations, such as bivariate designs of a cross-sectional type, poor control of variables, samples of convenience, or poor representativeness and reliability of the criteria. The conclusions of a meta-analytic study (Waldman & Avolio, 1986), based on the most rigorous studies, indicate that subjective performance reports are less favorable to older workers than the objective measurements. These studies suggest that performance improves with age, stabilizes around midlife, and then goes on increasing or decreasing in accordance with certain moderating variables. It is necessary to point out that the decrease in

manual work is only 8 to 10 percent among workers at age 65 compared to those at age 40. In normal clerical jobs, the differences with age are not significant. Many older workers perform better than younger workers. Additionally, they have a more constant production rate, with fewer oscillations and greater precision.

Among employees in the commercial sector, sales rates tend to increase with age and experience (Maher, 1959). The most productive and stable groups are usually in the 51- to 55-year-old age bracket. Additionally, the most successful employees have been promoted to supervisory positions.

In addition to actual job performance, other related work behaviors have been investigated. With respect to absenteeism, older workers miss fewer work hours, although their absences may be longer due to illness (Bartley, 1977). Punctuality is greater and rotation among firms hardly exists (Porter & Steers, 1973). The accident rate is similar, although the causes are usually different in older people. Their recovery and rehabilitation are slower. The older employees are more dependable and responsible, which implies greater care taken with equipment and machinery, less waste of materials, and greater energy savings. In isolated jobs—frequently due to automation—older workers are more reliable and consistent. In terms of creativity, reflected in suggestions and proposed innovations, nearly 80 percent of the suggestions that are accepted come from people over 40 years of age. With respect to mental health, the data appear to be contradictory. Trends indicate that among workers in their forties, few require psychiatric treatment.

At the same time, there are other lines of research that have taken up the links between age and performance in the scientific and artistic areas (Cole, 1979; Dennis, 1966; Diamond, 1986). By analyzing the publishing history of authors from diverse sectors, an effort has been made to find answers to the following questions:

- At what age in the life of an author are the most noteworthy contributions made?

- How is an author's work distributed throughout his or her lifetime?

The classical research of Lehman (1953, 1960) showed evidence that the most outstanding contributions, in nearly all disciplines, are produced between the ages of 30 and 39. The slope is positive until the age of 30 and negative after the age of 40.

The research of Dennis (1966), however, indicated that there is constant productivity in the following categories:

- Humanities scholars between the ages of 30 and 70

- Science scholars between the ages of 30 and 60 (they generate 68% of their previous productivity at the age of 70)

- Art scholars between the ages of 30 and 50 (at 60 years of age such scholars generate only 54% of their previous productivity and 23% at age 70)

Lehman identifies 16 aspects of the personal and professional lives of the researchers that may be mediating in the decrease in production. At the same time, production in itself facilitates:

- A positive transfer in the development and accumulation of compatible previous knowledge

- A negative transfer with respect to incompatible contemporary developments or the difficulty of rejecting what has already been learned

It is also apparent that in the humanities and sciences, new developments prevail through teamwork, whereas in the arts new developments result from individual effort.

Aging and Training

From the point of view of company management, there is a certain hesitancy to invest in the training of older workers (Robinson, Livingston, & Birren, 1984; Slater & Kingsley, 1976). Nevertheless, technological innovation creates needs for training and retraining of tenured employees. Often reference is made to the lack of skills among adult and older incumbents, when in reality it is often a question of a lower level of formal education or work motivation. Frequently, reference is made to the short time that the older workers will stay in their companies, without mentioning the fact that they are the people with the greatest stability in their jobs, since their rates of external rotation are low (Downs & Roberts, 1977).

On the other hand, such factors as corporate dynamics, technological changes, and the disappearance of certain positions and redesign and reconversion of others require the introduction of learning programs. Older workers ask for retraining when performance is not up to standard and when they want updated knowledge or skills; management is often hesitant to accommodate. According to one study, "by lowering the chances of failure, older trainees' feelings of self-confidence can be enhanced" (Wexley & Latham, 1991, p. 284).

Several studies (Cross, 1981; Mullan & Gorman, 1972; Tucker, 1985) show that, under the same conditions, older workers benefit more than younger workers from programs designed to equip them with new job skills. They progress more in their work performance as a consequence of the training activities. The fact that they are chosen for retraining and participants in special programs serves as an incentive that increases their competence and level of self-esteem, along with upgrading their skills. The effect of these programs lasts longer in older workers than in younger workers.

From the pioneering research of Belbin and Belbin (1972) and Welford (1977), it is clear that conventional training methods do not work well with adult learners (Fernández-Ballesteros, Izal, Diaz, Gonzalez, & Souto, 1988;

Schmidt, Murphy, & Sanders, 1981; Willis, 1985). Thus, when designing a course for older workers, the following must be taken into consideration:

- Their slowness of comprehension may lead them to miss relevant details or key points in a lecture.

- The amount of information presented at one time should not surpass the extent of their retention level.

- The modification of concepts or erroneous ideas takes more time to process in older workers than in younger ones.

The instructor must be aware of these added difficulties in order to allow for them. Teaching must necessarily be slow, deliberate, repetitive, and distributed in units of time with material that makes sense by itself and that can easily be connected with other material. Additionally, the teaching style must be more personal and direct because older adults often develop self-directed methods of organizing information and experience (Gonzalez, 1983; Knowles, 1984; Kolb, 1984).

Valid methods such as active learning, discovery training, and experimental learning are especially pertinent for older workers. These approaches involve tasks of graded difficulty and reduced description and memorization, with organized consecutive activities that are error-free. The consequence is that aged trainees discover for themselves how things work and, often, why things work.

When using audiovisual resources, sensorial and perceptual losses must be taken into account. When the course is long, exercises that encourage active participation and practical execution must be programmed. Programmed learning—aided or not through the use of computers—may be especially relevant for aged workers who require a high level of instruction because they have a strong motivation to learn; and self-regulation of time, which is an aspect of this type of learning, can be especially beneficial for them (Sieman, 1976).

Keeping in mind the previously mentioned conditions, training programs can be open to older workers. The short-lived character of new technologies has led to a noteworthy expansion of training programs. Older workers are just as suitable for training programs as are younger workers. According to one study, some of the shortcomings "may be related to learning and individual differences variables, rather than to chronological age" (Sterns & Doverspike, 1989, p. 313).

Aging and Work Satisfaction

When using global measurements of work satisfaction with age, it is usual to find an inverted U relationship. The upper extreme is usually accentuated by the tension that is a result of the nearness of retirement (Adams, 1971).

It then becomes necessary to break down and analyze separately the different elements that make up this general satisfaction. It would appear that the indicators vary in a different way, depending on the age of the subjects (Loitegui, 1990). Generational effects as well as the professional level moderate the age-satisfaction relationships. For example, relations with the supervisor and recognition are important for the satisfaction of young people, while in veteran workers those indicators lose significance. In older workers, the type of work and income have relatively greater effect on satisfaction, whereas autonomy, collaboration, and the job itself lose relevance.

In this way, Weaber's (1980) review of the evolution of satisfaction during the 1970s found the relationship to be linear instead of a U-shaped curve. The youngest people were more dissatisfied, while the older workers showed greater satisfaction. One possible explanation may be that the youngest people held positions that were less pleasant or more overloaded, or that the workers who were dissatisfied had already left the company. Higher aspirations and expectations of the young people have also been mentioned

(Pond & Geyer, 1987) as factors in this linear relationship.

Some personality aspects, such as introversion and extroversion, intervene in the levels of activity and satisfaction of older workers.

The Human Side of Retirement

The age of retirement is a relatively clear concept, but comparisons by country reveal certain nuances. As is shown in Table 1, there is a noteworthy variability among the EC countries. The retirement age range is between the ages of 55 and 67 for women and between 60 and 67 for men. The mode for men is 65 years of age, whereas for women there are two modes, at ages 60 and 65.

In the United States, the Age Discrimination in Employment Act was amended to remove the maximum age restriction and to partially abolish mandatory retirement. In Japan large companies enforce compulsory retirement between the ages of 55 and 60. In EC members during the last decade, there has been an effective decrease in the legal age for retirement, but an increase is expected in the future.

These variations reflect different political and legislative traditions and indicate that retirement age is not a concept that can be unequivocally determined. There is evidence of variability among nations and variability among cohorts within a country concerning minimum working age and retirement plans.

The effect of the aging process on the national systems of social security will be pronounced in all EC members except Ireland (see Figures 1 and 3). The number of beneficiaries of retirement benefits will increase, whereas the number of workers who are paying into the security systems will decrease.

The Existing Context

Retirement refers to explicitly leaving the workplace. Any consideration related to retirement and its consequences necessarily alludes to the meaning that work has for those who

TABLE 1

Normal Retirement Age and Minimum Working Age in the EC for December 1991

	Retirement Age		Minimum Working Age
	Males	*Females*	
Belgium	65	60	15
Denmark	67	67	15
France	60	60	16
Germany	65	65	15
Greece	65	60	15
Ireland	65	65	16
Italy	60	55	15
Luxembourg	65	65	15
The Netherlands	65	65	15
Portugal	65	62	14
Spain	65	65	16
United Kingdom	65	60	16

continue working (MOW International Research Team, 1987) or for those who have stopped (Forteza, 1990).

In fact, healthy adults spend a large part of their time and energy working. These activities structure their lives by determining, for instance, the distribution of time, schedules, and places they frequent. A large part of personal interactions and even the value of personal standing (prestige, status, influence) are directly or circumstantially related to employment. In addition, the greater share of such qualities as aptitudes, skills, knowledge, competence, creativity, and attitudes are put into play at work.

As a result, when the responsibilities of work are abruptly interrupted, there is necessarily a crisis or at least a violent break that requires a period of readaptation (Bynum, Cooper, & Acuff, 1978; Forteza, 1990; Karp, 1989; Mutran & Reitzes, 1981).

All throughout their lives, adults experience numerous processes of adaptation: to school, to the first job, to marriage, to the death of loved ones. When retirement comes, older workers attempt to adapt to the new condition by reconstructing and recreating the advantages and disadvantages in order to live in an unknown psychosocial territory often perceived as hostile.

The institution of retirement is a relatively recent phenomenon. As we study its evolution and the mores and values that characterize it in an advanced society, we note a series of undeniable advances. At the same time, we must point to a series of problems that do not have short-term solutions (Parker, 1982):

- In comparison with previous generations, there are now more people who reach an advanced age with acceptable health conditions (at least three out of four retirees in Spain) and physical surroundings.

- The standard of living of retired people is better now than it was a few generations ago.

- The average retirement age is decreasing; thus retired people are more "youthful," not only physically but in their lifestyles, plans, and projects for the future.

Along with these signs of hope, there are also specific problems for an affluent society:

- As the age pyramid becomes taller, because people live longer, there will be pressures to delay the retirement age of those who are effective, in good health, and want to work. This effect is already observed in socially oriented free market economies, where the readjustment of pensions is supported by a narrowed active population, and is important in technical and managerial jobs, where expert knowledge and experience is necessary to keep up with technological changes or the survival of the organization. The age of retirement, mentioned in Table 1, has been postponed in Spain exclusively for university professors, judges, and

individuals in senior posts. The continuity of highly trained personnel has a marginal influence in unemployment rates and contributes to an increased productiveness.

- There is a latent conflict between the interests of retirees and those of the active population. In those countries where the social security and retirement systems are based on the capitalization of payments made by beneficiaries during their work life, this type of conflict occurs to a lesser degree. However, in those countries where pensions are paid from the contributions of those who are currently working, this conflict becomes more intense. The better systems in the future will use both capitalization of payments of those who work and contributions of those currently working. In Spain there now coexist contributory pensions, funded pension plans, graduated pension schemes, insured pension plans, profit sharing and stock bonus plans, and so forth.

- It is becoming more and more difficult to satisfy the wishes of older people who prefer to continue working. Many people in good physical and mental health are forced to retire against their will.

- For some people, mandatory and abrupt retirement is accompanied by negative effects, such as problems of personal adjustment, integration, or loss of a sense of identity.

- When the values and symbols typical of youth (e.g., speed, competitiveness) receive more emphasis in a society, old age loses value, and workers nearing retirement age are relegated to marginal functions. Thus, a stereotype that dismisses the elderly as rigid, fragile, and unfit may prevail.

- The relationships between retired and nonretired people at times become tense, or at least distant. Working is the rule; being retired is different or distinct. This is accentuated by the actual physical separation that occurs with retirement.

- Retirement is usually seen as a period of passivity, exaggerating the degree of inactivity in older people (Harris, 1975). The date of retirement is turned into a date of premature death.

The retirement context described above differs considerably among countries and cultures. Nevertheless, it is typical of advanced industrial societies. Other traditions, often considered more primitive, grant a higher status to older people. Notwithstanding, it is a period of adult life that is eminently fragile.

Attitudes Toward Retirement

The quality of life of retired people becomes better or worse in accordance with the political and economic changes within a country. It has improved in countries such as Spain, which have gone from an economy of scarcity to an economy of abundance. Furthermore, welfare economies make gerontological services available by law to all retired people through "benevolent funds," while liberal economies offer such services on the market.[10]

Retirement is sustained by scarcity in underdeveloped countries. The changes are noteworthy in those Third World countries in which traditional values of respect toward the elderly have been rejected. In advanced societies, retirees usually receive a pension by their employer or by the government. This is often not the case in underdeveloped countries (Touraine, 1989).

The attitudes and cultural changes that have been observed in advanced industrial societies will be discussed in this section,

and evidence will be provided that the geopolitical frame of reference is biased. This bias has become apparent throughout the lectures that the first author has given to graduate students of psychology from Spain and other European Community countries, the Middle East, and Latin America. The first question has almost always been the same: "How is a retired worker viewed in your country?" The answers to this question group retirees into three categories:

- People who have the right to a subsidy in accordance with payments during work life and who have access to specific services in the community, but who are no longer relevant within the community

- "Wise" people who have acquired fame within the community, who have a right to specific social benefits, and who in some cases receive some economic subsidies

- People who rarely receive subsidies and who are socially discriminated against (unless supported by charity organizations) and who become directly dependent on the generosity of the nearest relatives

In conversations in situ with qualified people from eastern European countries, a fourth category has been detected:

- People who have worked all their lives for a centralized system that has collapsed—the new system gives a low priority to their needs. They receive devalued subsidies and can contribute very little to the new society

Developed countries with a relatively stable economic system show acceptance and consideration of retired workers. They have pension funds that are relatively current and guarantee some minimal levels of quality of life. In the European Community, the national budgets usually fund such pensions. In the United States and Canada, these allocations occur through privately developed pension schemes.

Attitudes of disappointment or confidence from the retiree are therefore the result of planning at the individual or state level. A reduction in income is nevertheless the rule. The critical point is the subjective perception of the availability of sufficient resources (Palmore, 1968). The degree of uncertainty is high, since it depends on such factors as the retiree's state of health, longevity, the economic situation of the country, the results of national and local elections, the personal relationships with sons and daughters, and unexpected expenses.

In addition to the loss of buying power, people who are about to retire are on the alert to other limitations. Forteza and Burgaleta (1991) used a Likert scale with a group of 150 pre-retired people to obtain the following results:

- There is agreement among two out of three workers who are about to retire that retirement is annoying and un-pleasant because they perceived it to be the point after which all possibilities have been used up and after which there are no more possibilities of success or personal development, the moment of breaking off from the interesting world of work, and the point of transition toward a boring life.

- Attitudes differ on whether life can still be enjoyed after retirement and on whether retirement implies a feeling of uselessness.

Analyses of the effect that different facets of work can have on retirement attitudes have not provided convincing, convergent, or generalizable results. Complex relationships, which are difficult to discern by means of a quantitative approach, have been detected.

Taking one by one the variables that are internal and external to the subject, linear relationships have not been found. There is no agreement between different studies. For example, crossing work satisfaction with attitudes toward retirement resulted in a quite balanced distribution among the four possible combinations:

- Satisfied older workers with a negative attitude toward retirement emphasize that they are forced to give up work.

- Satisfied older workers with a positive attitude toward retirement usually emphasize that after a successful professional life, they are going to be able to enjoy aspects of life unexplored until now.

- Dissatisfied workers with a negative attitude toward retirement feel frustrated for not having been able to do what they would have wanted to do. A feeling of incomplete fulfillment predominates.

- Dissatisfied workers with a positive attitude toward retirement emphasize feelings of relief for giving up an unpleasant job and being able to embark only on matters that are gratifying to them.[11]

The only relationship that appears stable is the attitude maintained with respect to the date of retirement. Younger people emphasize the positive aspects, while older people place more emphasis on the negative aspects. Younger people believe that the date should be earlier and older people feel that it should be postponed. With increasing age, the attitude is less and less positive; people feel defenseless.

The Meaning of Retirement

Work is central to adult life in the twentieth century in developed countries, especially in urban and industrial areas. Furthermore, the work ethic has dominated the leisure ethic. The interruption of work life generates a vacuum. It is necessary to establish another center. Retirement results in feelings of uselessness.[12]

For many adults, that means (a) a reduction in the quality of life, (b) an increase in shameful privations, (c) relinquishment of specific tasks that once gave structure to life, (d) changes in life-style and in friendships, which are then necessary to reestablish, (e) the loss of a functional role in society, with all of its consequences, (f) a limitation of opportunities for interpersonal communication and of selective access to the information that is considered pertinent, (g) isolation, and (h) lack of predetermined timetables (Fernández-Ballesteros, Diaz, Izal, & Hernandez, 1988).

On the other hand, the end of several awkward, annoying, workaday aspects of employment becomes salient. It may imply recovering interpersonal relationships and intimacy. Time is available and can be programmed at will.

The meaning of retirement is subjective regarding both facts and circumstances. A recovery of that which is idiographical, compared to that which is nomothetic, enables aged people to anticipate the consequences and particular problems of their adjustment to retirement.

The leisure ethic expanded to more social classes after the 1968 revolution in several European Community countries. The increased unemployment rates during the 1970s or 1980s (depending on the country) has affected the way today's adults perceive free time. The battles waged by unions to increase the number of vacation days and to reduce the number of work hours per week contributed to these changes. This may lead to different approaches to free time.[13]

One aspect of retirement that has not been studied from a psychological point of view is relocation and changes in residence once people retire. Numerous retired people from different European countries reside in Spain. Most of these retirees come from countries with a Protestant tradition; consequently, the work ethic predominates. The retired people from Catholic countries, on the other hand, tend to remain where they are or return to their birthplaces. Many retirees who move from the North to the South of Europe often begin new cycles of economic part-time activities. Legally they are retirees in one country but not in the other. Those who stay recover old hobbies or start new activities, for instance, becoming involved in missionary organizations.

Facilitating an Appropriate Adjustment

To assure a healthy adjustment that allows the retired worker to reorganize his or her life and take advantage of the available resources, the retired worker must be able to count on the following:

- An adequate state of health and physical functioning (Fernández-Ballesteros, 1985)

- A level of economic solvency that allows him or her to pay for at least the bare necessities

- Some type of affective bonds with relatives, neighbors, and friends

The integration of these three conditions affects the degree of autonomy and independence of the retired worker. Retirees determine their frame of reference when it comes time to manage on their own and not to have to depend on others in matters that affect the organization of their own lives. From then on, they can make decisions with respect to place of residence, type of housing, appropriate companions, and medical services and physicians they are going to use.

If one or more of these necessary conditions is missing, the adaptation can be seriously compromised. However, other conditions can affect adaptation to retirement as well. These include:

- The vital professional experiences that have been accumulated, where significant differences between men and women can still be found

- The characteristics of the profession, as well as the education and income level the individual has reached

- The degree of personal involvement in the job and the achievements one must relinquish

- The personality or cognitive style of the individual, such as rigidity versus flexibility, tolerance toward ambiguity, locus of control, and self-esteem

- The characteristics of the retired person's family circle, including the attitude of the spouse or significant other and the part that person plays in shaping the adaptation process

- Attributes of the place of residence, including sociological, climatic, cultural, recreational, and religious factors—with retirement the space within which people live is reduced, yet the distances that have to be covered become subjectively greater; what is close at hand determines the new environment of the retiree

- Home conditions, including the individual's personal belongings and objects—many retired people rediscover their homes and work to improve and beautify them, taking advantage of tools and equipment they had previously paid little attention to

After retirement all these elements take on significant meaning and importance, and help to determine the direction the retiree takes toward his or her retirement.

Preparing Aged Workers for Retirement

One gets old in accordance with the way one has lived. In general, previous lifestyle is the best predictor of the later behavior of the retired worker. Retirees can take advantage of accumulated knowledge, hobbies that have been pursued, and programs that are offered in the community or country that are organized for the general population or specifically for senior citizens. However, many workers of retirement age need some institutional support to benefit from the advantages retirement offers (Odenwald, 1986). Most do not think about what they can do until they find themselves with the retirement notification in their hands.

In order to facilitate a smooth transition, two factors are important for adaptation:

- *Having skills, interests, and hobbies that are different from the ones that were at play during the period of employment.* There are many retired people who continue doing practically the same things they were doing when they were active. Furthermore, they appear hesitant to switch to new activities. Some activities require learning or practice and can be acquired only with time. Other activities presuppose that specific habits are already acquired—for example, the habit of reading, of traveling, of keeping things neat and clean. Those who during their work life have reached a balance between their work and free time already have greater resources for retirement.

- *Having a specific preparation that includes knowledge of the concrete circumstances of the new environment and of the possible strategies that will facilitate adaptation.* Public and private initiatives to provide such preparation increased rapidly in recent years, including conferences, individual support programs, and brief courses (Autores Varios Endesa, 1991; Eckerdt, 1989). Topics of such courses include biology and the psychology of aging, diet and physical exercise, pension plans and retirement funds, local and national programs for senior citizens, specific benefits for senior citizens, and learning techniques that allow senior citizens to develop new hobbies and entertainment.

Priority must be given to helping retirees acquire a realistic image of their future situation. They should be encouraged to:

- Realize what their opportunities and limitations are

- Become aware of dangerous fantasies and mental images with respect to their future selves

- Dissipate unfounded fears

- Acquire new communication skills

- Learn to manage new technologies shaping the environment in which they are about to enter

Realistic plans and attitudes that are open to achievement, usefulness, and personal satisfaction are needed. At the same time, it is necessary to make senior citizens aware of the illnesses that one day they may have to face.

Table 2 presents the major topics of a week-long workshop given by a Spanish firm for its older workers. The program, held off-site, addressed a variety of issues in different-sized groups.

Short lectures followed by discussion were given by retired workers relating their own experiences. The workshop included visits to interesting places, contests, and collective games.

Participation was voluntary, and the age of the participants ranged between 59 and 65. In a later phase, complementary sessions were organized to which spouses or partners were invited. Their presence lent support to the process. The workshop objective was to help pre-retired employees find new ways of dealing with the stress of retirement planning, relocation, and everyday work life.[14]

Hobbies and Leisure Time

There are many classifications of leisure activities (Kelley, 1983). Some of them are suitable for retired people. Table 3 lists possible activities carried out during free time.

Using these lists as a starting point, retirees can explore preferences. Several studies have examined preferences in relation to age and personality (Havighurst, 1976; Klemeier, 1961). However, certain confusion exists between the effects of age and the effects of the cohort.

In studies whose objective was to determine the actual distribution of free time among retired people, some of the most consistent and generalized results included the following:

- Retirees spend a lot of time watching television or playing board games; passive and relaxed hobbies prevail.

- They spend very little time studying and reading.

- There is a lot of physical exercise, such as strolling and taking excursions.

- They usually go to shows, expositions, or cultural activities for which they receive discounts.

The meaning and personal contribution of these activities varies in accordance with the social conditions, the retirees' roles, and the immediate living context.

In Spain there are often cases in which retirees perform tasks to help children or close relatives. For example, they help in family businesses, take care of grandchildren, and run routine errands. This subsidiary function is accentuated in the case of dual-career couples whose parents—retired—reside in the same place.

In a more structured way, Gordon, Gaitz, and Scott (1976) proposed five categories, ordered on a passive versus active-expressive dimension. Each of these include several related activities as follows:

- *Resting activities,* such as naps or calm rest periods in one's favorite place

- *Fun activities,* such as watching television, reading, going to the movies or football games, or playing sedentary games with friends

TABLE 2

**Preretirement Program Agenda
Offered by a Spanish Firm**

1. *Introduction*

   Objectives of the program
   Why should one prepare for retirement?
   The worker and retirement

2. *Physical Health*

   Prevention of common illnesses:
      rheumatism, arthritis, prostate,
      and circulation problems
   Diet
   Hygiene and physical exercise
   Accidents in the home

3. *Psychological Aspects*

   Retirement as an adaptation to a new way
      of life
   Developmental growth
   Changes in the psychological processes
   Attitudes, stereotypes, and prejudices
   Relaxation and self-control techniques

4. *Family and Social Relations*

   Communication with one's mate
   Sexuality
   Family life
   Use of social services: clubs, homes, residences

5. *Economic Aspects*

   Economic and legal affairs specific to
      retirement
   Sources of income
   Social security: pensions
   How to reduce expenses without diminishing
      the quality of life
   Income tax
   Discounts and economic benefits

6. *Use of Free Time*

   How to enjoy free time
   Physical activities and sports
   Social and cultural activities

TABLE 3

Leisure Activities

Studying and publishing
Do-it-yourself activities within the home
Housework
Religious practice
Participation in civic and political affairs
Participation in professional or union affairs
Affiliation to recreational or informal organizations
Informal interpersonal relationships
Physical exercise
Attending cultural and artistic functions
Trips
Games or sports
Developing inventions or new technologies
Personal hobbies

- *Developmental activities,* such as excursions, fishing, physical exercise, or belonging to clubs and societies

- *Creative activities,* such as home improvements, arts and crafts, or attending debates and training forums

- *Activities of a sensual kind,* such as attending dances, participation in competitions, sexual activities, consumption of stimulants, or religious experiences of a mystical sort

This classification has served as a basis for an extensive study carried out in Houston, Texas, on leisure and mental health by Gordon et al. (1976). The available results confirm the tendencies that have been mentioned.

Alternatives to Existing Policies

The underlying philosophy of much legislation concerning retired people takes for granted that retirement is a phase of human life in which people are no longer busy. On the other hand, the psychological perspective offers a very different point of view:

- Employees who work, keep themselves in good condition, and wish to remain active in their employment should not be forced to stop working only because of age. This view favors voluntary and flexible retirement. As opposed to the sudden discontinuance of work, it suggests the slow and gradual discontinuance of work.

- There are activities that are ecological, cultural, artistic, educational, and strategic in which people with experience can take part on a voluntary basis and without interfering in the employment conditions of younger employees.

- There are other forms of justifiable and satisfying activities in which retired people can be involved and fulfill themselves. For instance, they may participate in any number of voluntary activities, such as teaching crafts and traditions, counseling and advising, investigating and classifying historical documents, or reconstructing historical passages of local history.

- The institutionalization of preretirement programs can be beneficial. However, these programs must keep the retired person integrated in the society.

The ideal balance between work and leisure activities during retirement is uncertain. Adequate preparation for retirement, though, will result in suggestions and the development of ideas and projects for that time. Retired people have at their disposal a wide range of activities, including those that are active versus passive, individual versus collective, physical versus intellectual, and home-based versus community-based.

They should be reminded of the range of possibilities and should not be excluded because of stereotypes or legislation. The community can offer them access to the resources already available to most citizens.

Retirees usually want to be active. It is typically the society that deactivates them. Society advances as it understands that the "retirement problem" is a pseudoproblem.

Retirees can also be viewed as consumers buying new products. There is a new area in marketing research: the analysis of consumer behavior among retirees. One consequence has been that private firms have created luxury real estate offers for retired people that include:

- Independent housing, with services for leisure and recreational activities

- Modern health care for those who require special medical and psychological services

- Location in geographical areas that have a pleasant, stable climate, far from crowded cities

- Separation of products and services in accordance with the degree of activity that future tenants will maintain

All of this reflects changes in viewpoint and in commercial strategies that are mainly addressed to those retired people who have a comfortable standard of living.[15] In Spain, banks, building contractors, and multinational real estate firms are directing large investments to projects aimed exclusively at senior citizens. Investors are creating new communities that ensure quality of life after retirement. There are hotels built and designed to provide the services that people over 65 years of age require. In many cases, they are joint ventures among strong economic groups in different countries of the European Community. Low pensions in one city may be sufficient income in another country or in a properly designed area in which general costs are shared.

Retirement plans appear to be pervasive as a force in the future evolution of the quality of working life. The importance of positive self-images among aged employees and retirees is so great that it is important to have a healthy regard for meeting their needs. This chapter provides a framework for longer range planning and strategic thinking for industrial and organizational psychologists concerned with aging and the working behavior of older employees.

We are indebted to Professor Harry Triandis and Kathleen Hummel, who read the English draft of this chapter and provided constructive suggestions and corrections.

We have avoided a review of the Spanish industrial and organizational psychology literature. However, we refer the reader to Peiro (1986) and to Prieto, Blasco, and Quintanilla (1991). There are two journals in which researchers and practitioners have regularly published their papers and main contributions: Revista de Psicologia General y Aplicada *(since 1954) and* Revista de Psicologia del Trabajo y de las Organizaciones *(since 1985). In 1993 a monographic issue of* Applied Psychology: An International Review *reviewed in English the topic of applied psychology in Spain.*

Notes

1   There are several groups, such as college students, conscripts, and convicts, who are not included in the statistics of the labor force.
2   The birth rate in Ireland is very high and it compensates for the migration loss. The number of migratory workers is also very high. Their native language is English and it favors their "job-hunting" strategies.
3   *"Caminante, no hay camino; se hace camino al andar"* ("Way-faring man, there is no path, the path is made

by walking"). This is a verse by the Spanish poet Antonio Machado.
4   This is a very old idea that can be traced back to Plato (the *anamnesis*) and Pythagoras (the myth of the *metempsychosis*). At that time, both concepts were understood in the context of the recollection of past lives. But authoritative sources interpret the idea behind them as the recollection of successive lives in the real existence of an individual. Probably both ideas originated in India and came to Europe during the empire of Darius or Alexander (Kolm, 1982, chaps. 17 & 18).
5   Etymologically, the terms *individual* and *atom* mean just the same: "indivisible," "inseparable." In fact, *individuus* is a Latin translation of "ατομος" in ancient Greek. Conceptual frameworks like "life-span of the individual" and "life-span of the atom" are based on a similar set of ideas and abstract principles about the notion of causality.
6   During the last five years, the midcareer burnout phenomenon has been approached in several symposia and seminars held in the context of the International Congresses of Applied Psychology.
7   Preretirement programs started in the 1960s in the United States but have received increased attention during the 1980s in EC countries. Some of these programs are sponsored by firms and some by community-based groups, such as the American Association for Retired Persons (Nadler & Nadler, 1989, p. 68).
8   In fact, absolute age is only relevant in terms of the legislation governing retirement and social security. Table 1 shows that there is no absolute age of retirement or minimum working age among EC State Members. In Spain, for instance, the Colegio Libre de Profesores Emeritos and the Asociacion de Empresarios Seniors (professors and businessmen) do not accept the 65-year retirement cap.
9   Now leading firms sponsor regular seminars to help dual-career couples balance work and family concerns.
10   The economic crisis and the political transition in eastern European countries now have negative consequences on the living conditions of retired people. The elderly are living on a state pension (e.g., 250 rubles per month—1 U.S. dollar equals 32 rubles). Inflation rates are very high.
11   Perhaps the key resides in the term *satisfaction*. Etymologically, this can be broken into two Latin components: *satis* and *facere*. Whoever is about to retire has a mental image of what he or she has done

or plans on doing (*facere*). Individual differences revolve around the image that each person considers is enough (*satis*) and sufficient. Fuzzy logic prevails.

12 François Mauriac, the well-known French novelist, coined the following description: *"Cette horreur de la viellese que c'est de non plus servir"* [This horror of old age, that one is no longer serving others].

13 The situation in Japan is just the reverse. Their workweeks are longer than in Western economies, and the average number of vacation days is six per year.

14 People continue working even after they retire. They maintain the status of *homo faber.*

15 Pensions insufficient in a developed country are adequate in nearly all undeveloped countries, where the pensions are considered a "high income."

References

Abbey, A. (1982). Sex differences in attributions for friendly behavior: Do males misperceive females' friendliness? *Journal of Personality and Social Psychology, 42,* 830–838.

Adams, D. (1971). Correlates of life satisfaction among the elderly. *Gerontologist, 11*(4), 64–68.

Aldous, J., Oxmond, M., & Hicks, M. (1979). Men's work and men's families. In W. Burr (Ed.), *Contemporary theories about the family.* New York: Free Press.

Arenberg, D. (1980). Memory and learning do decline late in life. In S. M. Grabowski & W. D. Mason (Eds.), *Education for the aging.* Syracuse, NY: Syracuse Press.

Arnold, H. J., & Feldman, D. C. (1982). A multivariate analysis of the determinants of job turnover. *Journal of Applied Psychology, 67,* 350–360.

Autores Varios Endesa. (1991). *El jubilando ante su futuro: Plan de preparacion a la jubilacion.* Madrid: Narcea.

Baltes, P. B. (1987). Theoretical propositions of life-span developmental psychology: On the dynamics between growth and decline. *Developmental Psychology, 23*(5), 611–626.

Baltes, P. B., Reese, H. W., & Lipsitt, L. P. (1980). Life-span developmental psychology. *Annual Review of Psychology, 31,* 65–110.

Bartley, D. L. (1977). Compulsory retirement: A reevaluation. *Personnel, 4,* 62–66.

Beaudoin, O. (1986). *Le counseling en milieu de travail: Programmes d'aide aux employés.* Montreal: Agence D'Arc.

Belbin, E., & Belbin, M. (1972). *Problems in adult retraining.* London: Heineman.

Bird, C. P., & Fisher, T. D. (1986). Thirty years later: Attitudes toward the employment of older workers. *Journal of Applied Psychology, 71,* 515–517.

Birren, J. E. (1974). *Human aging* (Department of Health, Education, and Welfare Publication No. AMD-DHEW). Rockville, MD: National Institute of Mental Health.

Birren, J. E., Cunningham, W. R., & Yamamoto, K. (1983). Psychology of adult development and aging. *Annual Review of Psychology, 34,* 543–575.

Birren, J., Robinson, P., & Livingston, J. (1986). *Age, health and employment.* Englewood Cliffs, NJ: Prentice-Hall.

Birren, J., & Schaie, K. W. (1977). *Handbook of the psychology of aging.* New York: Van Nostrand Reinhold.

Blanco, J. M. (1977). *Factores de personalidad en jefes administrativos medidos a traves del 16 PF.* Unpublished master's thesis, Complutense University, Madrid.

Boerlijst, J. G. (1989). *Does the aging of the working population really pose a threat?* Paper presented at the Fourth European Congress on the Psychology of Work and Organizations, Cambridge, UK.

Botwinick, J. (1984). *Aging and behavior* (3rd ed.). New York: Springer.

Bouza, F., Asenjo, A., Vargas, M. T., & Borges, F. (1990). *Perfil, actitudes y demandas del delegado y afiliado a la Union General de Trabajadores.* Madrid: Fundación Largo Caballero.

Bray, D. W., & Howard, A. (1983). The AT&T longitudinal studies of managers. In K. W. Schaie (Ed.), *Longitudinal studies of adult psychological development* (pp. 266–312). New York: Guilford.

Bromley, D. B. (1990). *Behavioral gerontology.* Chichester, UK: Wiley.

Bühler, C. (1933). *Der menschische Lebenslauf als psychologisches problem.* Leipzig, Germany: Hirzel.

Burke, R. J., & Greenglass, E. R. (1987). Work and family. In C. L. Cooper & I. T. Robertson (Eds.),

International review of industrial and organizational psychology 1987 (pp. 273–320). Chichester, UK: Wiley.

Burton, P., Forrest, R., & Stewart, M. (1989). *Growing up and leaving home.* Dublin: The European Foundation for the Improvement of Living and Working Conditions.

Bynum, J., Cooper, B. L., & Acuff, G. (1978). Retirement reorientation: Senior adult education. *Journal of Gerontology, 33,* 253–261.

Casanueva, G. (1990). El proceso de selección y la discriminación laboral de la mujer. *Revista de Psicología del Trabajo y de las Organizaciones, 6*(15), 32–48.

Charness, N. (Ed.). (1985a). *Aging and human performance.* New York: Wiley.

Charness, N. (1985b). Aging and problem-solving performance. In N. Charness (Ed.), *Aging and human performance* (pp. 225–259). New York: Wiley.

Cole, S. (1979). Age and scientific performance. *American Journal of Sociology, 84,* 958–977.

Comision Asesora para el Desarrollo de los Recursos Humanos. (1987). *Encuesta para el diagnóstico del desarrollo de los recursos humanos en España.* Madrid: Ministerio de Trabajo y Seguridad Social.

Costa, P. T., Jr., McCrae, R. R., & Arenberg, D. (1983). Recent longitudinal research on personality and aging. In K. W. Schaie (Ed.), *Longitudinal studies of adult psychological development* (pp. 222–265). New York: Guilford.

Craik, F., & Threhub, S. (1982). *Aging and cognitive processes.* New York: Plenum.

Cross, K. P. (1981). *Adults as learners: Increasing participation and facilitating learning.* San Francisco: Jossey-Bass.

Cunningham, W. R., & Birren, J. E. (1976). Age changes in human abilities: A 28-year longitudinal study. *Developmental Psychology, 12,* 81–82.

Davies, R., & Sparrow, P. (1985). Age and work behavior. In N. Charness (Ed.), *Aging and human performance.* New York: Wiley.

Dennis, W. (1966). Creativity productivity between the ages of twenty and eighty years. *Journal of Gerontology, 21,* 1–18.

Diamond, A. (1986). The life-cycle research productivity of mathematicians and scientists. *Journal of Gerontology, 41*(4), 520–525.

Diaz-Sanchez, R. (1991). *La identidad profesional de psicologo en el Estado español.* Unpublished doctoral dissertation, University of Valencia, Valencia, Spain.

Dillingham, A. (1981). Age and workplace injuries. *Aging and Work,* 1–10.

Doering, M., Rhodes, S., & Schuster, M. (1983). *The aging worker,* London: Sage.

Downs, S., & Roberts, A. (1977). The training of underground train guards: A case study with a field experiment. *Journal of Occupational Psychology, 50,* 111–120.

Dupuis, P., Brunet, L., St. Germain, P., Hamel, M. J., & Lavoie-Ste. Marie, P. (1986). *Le mitan de la vie et la vie professionnelle.* Montreal: Agence d'Arc.

ERUOSTAT. (1988). *Rapid Reports 3,* Luxembourg.

Eckerdt, D. J. (1989). Retirement preparation. *Annual Review of Gerontology and Geriatrics, 9,* 321–356.

Ekvall, G. (1986). El clima organizacional: Una puesta a punto de la teoría e investigaciones. *Revista de Psicología del Trabajo y de las Organizaciones, 2,* 95–113.

Fernández-Ballesteros R. (1985). Hacia una vejez competente: Un desafio en la ciencia y en la sociedad. In M. Carretero, J. Palacios, & A. Marchesi (Eds.), *Psicología evolutiva, 3.* Madrid: Alianza.

Fernández-Ballesteros, R., Diaz, P., Izal, M., & Hernández, J. M. (1988). Conflictive situation in the elderly. *Psychological Reports, 63,* 171–176.

Fernández-Ballesteros, R., Izal, R., Diaz, P., González, J. L., & Souto, E. (1988). Training of conversational skills with institutionalized elderly: A preliminary study. *Perceptual and Motor Skills, 66,* 923–926.

Forteza, J. A. (1985). Procesos de envejecimiento y problemática laboral. In Forum Universidad-Empresa, *Presente y futuro de la psicologia del trabajo en la empresa* (pp. 25–42). Madrid: Fundacion Universidad-Empresa.

Forteza, J. A. (1990). La preparación para el retiro. *Anales de Psicología, 6*(2), 101–113.

Forteza, J. A., & Burgaleta, R. (1991). *Programa de preparacion a la jubilacion.* Unpublished report, Complutense University, Retirement Educational Program, Madrid.

Fozard, J. L., Wolf, E., Bell, B., McFarland, R. A., & Poldosky, S. (1977). Visual perception and communication. In J. Birren & K. W. Schaie (Eds.), *Handbook of the psychology of aging.* New York: Van Nostrand Reinhold.

García, Y. (1990). La dualidad del rol de la mujer trabajadora. *Revista de Psicología del Trabajo y de las Organizaciones, 6*(15), 13–20.

Gonzalez, R. M. (1983). *Influencia de la naturaleza de los estudios universitarios en los estilos de aprendizaje de los sujetos.* Published doctoral dissertation, Complutense University, Madrid.

Gordon, C., Gaitz, C., & Scott, J. (1976). Leisure and lives. Personal expressivity across the life-span. In R. Birstock & E. Shanas (Eds.), *Handbook of aging and the social sciences.* New York: Van Nostrand Reinhold.

Hall, R. (1986). *Dimensions of work.* Beverly Hills, CA: Sage.

Harris, L. (1975). *The myth and reality of aging in America.* Washington, DC: The National Council on Aging.

Hartley, J. T., Harker, J. O., & Walsh, D. A. (1980). Contemporary issues and new directions in adult development of learning and memory. In L. W. Poon (Ed.), *Aging in the 80s* (pp. 239–252). Washington, DC: American Psychological Association.

Havighurst, R. J. (1976). Leisure and aging. In A. Hoffman (Ed.), *The daily needs and interests of older people* (pp. 165–174). Springfield, IL: Thomas.

Hoffman, Y. (1986). *Japanese death poems: Written by Zen monks and haiku poets on the verge of death.* Tokyo: Charles E. Tuttle.

Horn, J. L. (1982). The theory of fluid and crystallized intelligence in relation to concepts of cognitive psychology and aging in adulthood. In F. I. M. Craik & S. E. Trehub (Eds.), *Aging and cognitive processes* (pp. 847–870). New York: Plenum.

Horn, J. L., & Donaldson, G. (1976). On the myth of intellectual decline in adulthood. *American Psychologist, 31,* 701–719.

Horn, J. L., & McArdle, J. J. (1980). Perspectives on mathematical/statistical model building (MASMOB) in research on aging. In L. W. Poon (Ed.), *Aging in the 80s* (pp. 503–541). Washington, DC: American Psychological Association.

Instituto Nacional de Empleo (INEM). (1987). Mercado de Trabajo en Espaua, [Labor Market in Spain] Madrid: Ministry of Labor.

Jarvik, L. F., & Bank, L. (1983). Aging twins: Longitudinal psychometric data. In K. W. Schaie (Ed.), *Longitudinal studies of adults' psychological development* (pp. 40–63). New York: Guilford.

Jensen, A. R. (1982). Reaction time and psychometric g. In H. J. Eysenck (Ed.), *A model for intelligence* (pp. 93–132). Berlin: Springer-Verlag.

Johnson, R. C., Nagoshi, C. T., & Ahern, F. M. (1983). Correlations of measures of personality and of intelligence within and across generations. *Personality and Individual Differences, 4*(3) 331–338.

Johnston, H. R. (1976). A new conceptualization of source of organizational climate. *Administrative Science Quarterly, 21,* 95–103.

Kalish, R. (1983). *La vejez, perspectivas sobre el desarrollo humano.* Madrid: Piramide.

Karp, D. (1989). The social construction of retirement among professionals 50–60 years old. *The Gerontologist, 29*(6), 750–760.

Kelley, J. R. (1983). *Leisure identities and interactions.* London: Allen & Unwin.

Klemeier, R. (1961). *Aging and leisure: A research perspective into the meaningful use of time.* New York: Oxford.

Kliegl, R., Smith, J., & Baltes, P. B. (1986). Testing the limits, expertise and memory in adulthood and old age. In F. Klix & H. Hagendorf (Eds.), *Human memory and cognitive capabilities: Mechanisms and performances* (pp. 395–407). Amsterdam: North-Holland.

Knowles, M. (1984). *The adult learner: A neglected species* (3rd ed.). Houston, TX: Gulf.

Kolb, D. A. (1984). *Experiential learning: Experience as the source of learning and development.* Englewood Cliffs, NJ: Prentice-Hall.

Kolm, S. C. (1982). *Le bonheur-liberté.* Paris: Press Universitaires de France.

Krauss, I. K. (1980). Between and within group comparisons in aging research. In W. Poon (Ed.), *Aging in the 80s* (pp. 542–551). Washington, DC: American Psychological Association.

Labouvie, E. W. (1980). Identity versus equivalence of psychological measures and constructs. In L. W. Poon (Ed.), *Aging in the 80s* (pp. 493–502). Washington, DC: American Psychological Association.

Lehman, H. C. (1953). *Age and achievement.* Princeton, NJ: Princeton University Press.

Lehman, H. C. (1960). The age decrement in outstanding scientific creativity. *American Psychologist, 15,* 128–134 .

Lehr, U. (1980). *Psicología de la Senectud* (Spanish translation). Barcelona, Spain: Herder.

Levinson, D. J. (1978). *The seasons of man's life.* New York: Knopf.

Levy-Leboyer, C. (1984). *La crise des motivations.* Paris: Press Universitaires de France.

Loitegui, J. R. (1990). *Determinantes de la satisfaccion laboral en empleados de la administracion foral de Navarra.* Unpublished doctoral dissertation, Complutense University (Determinants of work satisfaction among employees in the local administration of Navarra), Madrid.

Maddox, G. L. (1987). *The encyclopedia of aging.* New York: Springer.

Maher, H. (1959). Age and performance of two work groups. *Journal of Gerontology, 10,* 448–451.

Marrow, A. J., & French, J. (1945). Changing a stereotype in industry. *Journal of Social Issues, 1*(3), 32–37.

Martinez, L. A. (1970). *La emigración española a examen.* Madrid: Edicusa.

McCook, L. I., Folzer, S. M., Charlesworth, D., & Scholl, J. N. (1991). Dueling careers. *Training and Development Journal, 45* (8), 41–44.

Meier, E. L., & Kerr, E. (1976). Capabilities of middle-aged and older workers: A survey of the literature. *Industrial Gerontology, 3*(3), 147–156.

Mella, M. (1989). Los grupos de presión en la transición política. In J. F. Tezano, R. Cotarelo, & A. Blas (Eds.), *La transición Democrática Española* (pp. 149–181). Madrid: Sistema.

Minton, H. L., & Schneider, F. W. (1980). *Differential psychology.* Pacific Grove, CA: Brooks/Cole.

Mortimer, J. T., Lorence, J., & Kumka, D. S. (1986). *Work, family and personality.* Norwood, NJ: Ablex.

MOW International Research Team. (1987). *The meaning of working.* London: Academic Press.

Mullan, C., & Gorman, L. (1972). Facilitating adaptation to change: A case study in retraining middle-aged and older workers at Aer Lingus. *Industrial Gerontology, 15,* 20–39.

Mutran, E., & Reitzes, D. (1981). Retirement, identity and well-being realignment of role relationships. *Journal of Gerontology, 6,* 733–740.

Nadler, L., & Nadler, Z. (1989). *Developing human resources.* San Francisco: Jossey-Bass.

Odenwald, S. (1986). Pre-retirement planning gathers steam. *Training and Development Journal, 40,* 62–63.

Organization for Economic Cooperation and Development. (1989). *Employment outlook 1989.* Paris: OECD.

Palmore, E. (1968). The effects of aging on activities and attitudes. *Gerontologist, 8,* 259–263.

Parker, S. (1982). *Work and retirement.* London: Allen & Unwin.

Peiro, J. M. (1986). An historical view on I/O psychology in Spain. In G. Debus & H. W. Schroiff (Eds.), *The psychology of work and organisations: Current trends and issues.* Amsterdam: North-Holland.

Peiro, J. M., & Moret, D. (1987). *Socializacion laboral y desempleo juvenil: La transición de la escuela al trabajo.* Valencia, Spain: Nau Libres.

Perlmutter, M., & Hall, E. (1985). *Adult development and aging.* New York: Wiley.

Pikunas, J. (1976). *Human development* (3rd ed.). New York: McGraw-Hill.

Pond, S. B., & Geyer, P. D. (1987). Employee age as a moderator of the relations between perceived work alternatives and job satisfaction. *Journal of Applied Psychology, 72,* 552–557.

Poon, L. (1985). Differences in human memory with aging. In J. Birren & W. Schaie (Eds.), *Handbook of the psychology of aging* (2nd ed.). New York: Van Nostrand Reinhold.

Porter, L., & Steers, R. M. (1973). Organizational work and personal factors in employee turnover and absenteeism. *Psychological Bulletin, 80,* 151–176.

Prieto, J. M. (1977). *Estudio comparativo de las Formas A & B del 16 PF en su adaptacion española.* Unpublished masters thesis, Complutense University, Madrid.

Prieto, J. M. (1989). Liderazgo como enredo en la empresa española. *Boletín de Estudios Económicos, 44*(136), 35–59.

Prieto, J. M., Blasco, R. D., & Quintanilla, I. (1991). Recrutement et sélection du personnel en Espagne. *European Review of Applied Psychology, 41*(1), 47–62.

Prieto, J. M., & Martin, J. (1990). New forms of work organisation. *The Irish Journal of Psychology, 11*(2), 202–217.

Rabinowitz, S., & Hall, D. T. (1977). Organizational research on job involvement. *Psychological Bulletin, 84,* 265–288.

Rhodes, S. R. (1983). Age-related differences in work attitudes and behaviors: A review and conceptual analysis. *Psychological Bulletin, 93,* 328–367.

Riley, M. W. (1979). *Aging from birth to death.* Boulder, CO: Westview.

Riley, M. W., Hess, B., & Bond, K. (1983). *Aging in society: Selected reviews of recent research*. Hillsdale, NJ: Erlbaum.

Robinson, P. K., Livingston, J., & Birren, J. E. (Eds.). (1984). *Aging and technology*. New York: Plenum.

Rodriguez, J. L. (1989). *Viejo valores y nuevas burocracias: El caso de una empresa semipública*. Madrid: Ministerio de Trabajo y Seguridad Social.

Rosen, B., & Jerdee, T. H. (1978). The influence of age stereotypes on managerial decisions. *Journal of Applied Psychology, 63*, 573–578.

Saal, F. E. (1990). Sexual harassment in organizations. In K. R. Murphy & F. E. Saal (Eds.), *Psychology in organizations: Integrating science and practice* (pp. 217–239). Hillsdale, NJ: Erlbaum.

Salthouse, T. (1979). Adult age and speed accuracy trade-off. *Ergonomics, 22*(7), 811–821.

Salthouse, T. (1988). Aging and skilled performance. In A. Colley & R. J. Beech (Eds.), *The acquisition and performance of competitive skills*. Chichester, UK: Wiley.

Schaie, K. W. (1973). Methodological problems in descriptive developmental research on adulthood and aging. In J. R. Nesselroade & H. W. Reese (Eds.), *Life-span developmental psychology: Methodological issues* (pp. 253–298). New York: Academic Press.

Schaie, K. W. (1980). Age changes in intelligence. In R. Sprott (Ed.), *Age, learning ability and intelligence*. New York: Van Nostrand Reinhold.

Schaie, K. W., & Willis, S. L. (1986). Can decline in adult intellectual functioning be reversed? *Developmental Psychology, 22*, 223–232.

Schein, E. (1978). *Career dynamics: Matching individual and organizational needs*. Reading, MA: Addison-Wesley.

Schmidt, F. A., Murphy, M. D., & Sanders, R. (1981). Training older adults' free-recall rehearsal strategies. *Journal of Gerontology, 36*, 329–337.

Schrank, H. T., & Waring, J. M. (1981). Aging and work organizations. In B. B. Hess & K. Bond (Eds.), *Leading edges: Recent research on psychosocial aging* (pp. 91–118). Washington, DC: Department of Health and Human Services.

Schwab, D. P., & Heneman, H. G. (1978). Age stereotyping in performance appraisal. *Journal of Applied Psychology, 63*, 573–578.

Schwartz, F. N. (1989). Management women and the new facts of life. *Harvard Business Review*, January–February, 65–76.

Sieman, J. R. (1976). Programmed materials as a training tool for older persons. *Industrial Gerontology, 3*, 183–190.

Slater, R., & Kingsley, S. (1976). Predicting age-prejudiced employers: A British pilot study. *Industrial Gerontology, 3*, 121–128.

Smith, J. M. (1975). Occupations classified by their age structure. *Industrial Gerontology, 2*, 209–215.

Sterns, H. L., & Alexander, R. (1987). Industrial gerontology: The aging individual and work. *Annual Review of Gerontology and Geriatrics, 7*, 243–264 .

Sterns, H. L., & Doverspike, D. (1989). Aging and the training and learning process. In I. L. Goldstein (Ed.), *Training and development in organizations* (pp. 299–332). San Francisco: Jossey-Bass.

Tezanos, J. F. (1989). Modernizacion y cambio social en España. In J. F. Tezanos, R. Cotarelo, & A. Blas (Eds.), *La transición democrática española* (pp. 63–115). Madrid: Sistema.

Touraine, A. (1989). *America Latina: Politíca y sociedad*. Madrid: Espasa Calpe.

Tucker, F. (1985). A study of the training needs of older workers. *Public Personnel Management Journal*, 85–95.

Voydanoff, P. (1987). *Work and family life*. Beverly Hills, CA: Sage.

Waldman, D. A., & Avolio, B. J. (1986). A meta-analysis of age differences in job performance. *Journal of Applied Psychology, 71*, 33–38.

Ward, R. (1984). *The aging experience*. New York: Harper & Row.

Weaber, C. (1980). Job satisfaction in the United States in the 70s. *Journal of Applied Psychology, 65*(3), 364–367.

Welford, A. T. (1977). Motor performance. In J. E. Birren & W. K. Schaie (Eds.), *Handbook of the psychology of aging*. New York: Van Nostrand Reinhold.

Wexley, K. N., & Latham, G. P. (1991). *Developing and training human resources in organizations*. New York: Harper Collins.

Willerman, L. (1979). *The psychology of individual and group differences*. San Francisco: Freeman.

Willis, S. L. (1985). Towards an educational psychology of the adult learner. In J. E. Birren & K. W. Schaie (Eds.), *Handbook of the psychology of aging* (pp. 818–847). New York: Van Nostrand Reinhold.

CHAPTER 10

Age and Employment

Peter Warr
University of Sheffield, Sheffield, England

*This chapter examines two principal issues: the impact of aging on work behavior
and attitudes, and the influences of work characteristics on aging itself. These
issues are introduced through a consideration of age-related social roles, age
stereotypes, national labor force projections, and the key features of cross-sectional
and longitudinal investigations. Age differences in job performance are reviewed,
and some determinants of positive or negative age/performance relationships are
examined. A four-category framework is presented in terms of possible declines
in basic capacities that occur in conjunction with potential gains through the
accumulation of relevant experience. Research into different aspects of cognitive
performance is also reviewed within that framework, covering psychometric
test scores, expertise, attention, response speed, learning and memory, and
physical health. Age differences in job-related well-being, job satisfaction, work
values, and personality are examined to identify possible explanations for the
observed findings. Investigations into the chapter's second issue, the influence of
work characteristics on aging, are shown to be rather limited, but the importance
of the issue suggests that it will be addressed more vigorously in the future.
Finally, guidelines for organizational policies and procedures that will help
procure the effective employment of older workers are outlined.*

ABOUT HALF A century ago, there was concern in the United States, the United Kingdom, and other countries that older people comprised an increasing proportion of the population and that this demographic shift would give rise to significant economic and social problems. Some of the anticipated difficulties concerned people at work, and research into occupational aspects of aging was expanded. Key research themes were identified that remain important today (Cowdry, 1942; Fox, 1951; McFarland, 1943; Welford, 1976; see also Miles, 1933).

By 1960, revised population estimates suggested that the postwar baby boom would redress any serious imbalance in the demographic structure, and research into industrial and organizational psychology became less concerned with age-related issues. Currently, however, baby boomers are progressing into middle age, many young people have delayed parenthood, and families in industrialized countries have become smaller. For many countries, the issues surrounding an aging population that were prominent 50 years ago have surfaced once again.

In the meantime, the pattern of jobs has changed so that older employees are now liable to experience task demands that are quite different from those they experienced earlier in their careers. All developed countries have seen a major shift away from agriculture and manufacturing industry to the services sector, which in many cases now accounts for more than two-thirds of all jobs. Hard manual labor is less common in developed countries than it once was, and the work activities of younger as well as older employees are more likely to require cognitive and interpersonal skills, rather than physical strength.

Changes have also been brought about by the widespread introduction of computer-based equipment. Many jobs now depend on information technology, and employees need knowledge and skills that were unheard of a decade or two ago. Greater international interdependence and commercial rivalry have also increased the pace of change in many employment sectors (Triandis, 1993). For these reasons, people in the middle of their working lives are now particularly likely to be faced with a need to modify their work behavior and to learn new job tasks. These changes in conjunction with an aging labor force raise questions that are of both scientific and practical importance.

This chapter will examine these issues. The central themes can be approached from two different directions. One addresses the question, how does aging affect work behavior and attitudes? Research into that question examines the pattern of age differences in occupationally relevant variables and seeks to explain the differences observed: What factors associated with development through the adult years are likely to influence work behavior and attitudes? The second general approach, which is much less common, examines the reverse process of how work affects aging: Are there particular aspects of jobs that accelerate or slow down key aspects of physiological or psychological aging? How are different dimensions of aging influenced by particular work experiences and job characteristics?

Many early studies in this area examined age only as a variable of subsidiary interest, or without a theoretical framework of influences that might affect the course of aging. Some of the field is thus rather atheoretical. In part, this has occurred because of the low levels of research interest in this area in previous decades, and changes may now be expected. In part, however, some concern for issues of age and employment will always have a practical focus. Organizations need to know what procedures of personnel selection, training, and job design are likely to be most effective in current economic and technological circumstances. Age-related issues of that pragmatic kind will also be considered in this chapter. The terms *older* and *younger* will be used without a single definition. Several conventions occur in the literature, with the lower age of "older" workers most commonly understood to be 40 or 45 years. In this chapter, the "older" age group of interest extends up to about 65 years, although information about more elderly people will sometimes also be examined.

Age and Social Roles

First, let us consider several macroscopic issues. Anthropologists and sociologists have emphasized that age is a key factor contributing to the organization of any society and the control of its members. All societies divide time and the human life span into socially meaningful units. For example, age strata are commonly established in relation to infancy, childhood, adolescence, stages of adulthood, and old age. Each age group carries its own rewards, rights, and duties, and transitions between age categories are sometimes marked by social events and public recognition.

Every society has a system of social expectations for appropriate behavior in each age grade, internalized as age norms by members of that grade as well as by others. Personal identities and meanings are created partly in light of a person's age within his or her cultural setting (e.g., Heise, 1987). Middle-aged workers tend to view a particular level of personal achievement as appropriate or inappropriate by comparing it with the achievements of other members of their age group. For example, in the organization studied by Lawrence (1988), "40 is the age at which people begin to move to level two, and 55 is the make-or-break age for promotion to the highest levels" (p. 332). Employees develop attitudes about themselves and their own competence, which are influenced by social norms about their age group as well as through direct knowledge about themselves (Lawrence, 1984).

It is, of course, incorrect to consider time or age on their own as causal variables. Changes are a result of physiological, psychological, and social influences that occur over time. These influences may be viewed as either *normative* (occurring to most members of an age group) or nonnormative (experienced more idiosyncratically, being relatively independent of chronological age; e.g., Baltes, Reese, & Lipsitt, 1980; Schroots & Birren, 1988). Nonnormative life events include periods of ill health, movement to another part of the country, job transitions, and specific educational experiences.

Normative influences can be described as either *history-graded* or *age-graded.* History-graded influences include events in the world that affect all members of a particular society, irrespective of their age. For example, a severe economic depression, a war, or a major technological innovation may be specific to a particular time in history and affect everyone living at that time. These history-graded events may influence the development of the people who live through them but have no impact on people who live at earlier or later times.

Normative age-graded influences, on the other hand, are expected to influence everyone at approximately the same point in their lives. These influences derive from physiological or psychological changes that occur as people grow older, or from membership in age-related social categories, as people become socialized into age-graded roles with their associated norms, obligations, and prerogatives. In considering possible factors that give rise to observed differences between age groups, it is thus important to recognize the potential impact of three types of processes: nonnormative life events, normative history-graded influences, and normative age-graded influences of physiological, psychological, and social origin. In practice, of course, any investigator is likely to have only limited information about this wide range of possible factors, so attention is often directed at one restricted set of potential causal variables.

Different age strata in society typically receive different rewards, for example, in terms of wealth, prestige, and power. Cultures differ in their treatment of different age groups, and socially generated reward patterns vary from time to time. Microcosms of the greater society may be seen in organizations, with their own systems of age grades and differential rewards. An employee's age might be treated as a rough index of his or her relevant knowledge and capability, and age stratification is often sustained by requirements of training and experience before individuals can be promoted (e.g., Schrank & Waring, 1983). In forming an impression of someone, inferences based on age and assumed age-graded performance may sometimes be more influential than judgments about directly relevant characteristics.

Stereotypes

These different perceptions of people in different age groups have been referred to as *age stereotypes*. Several authors have documented the common tendency to view older workers as slower, less interested in new training, less flexible, and more likely to become weary than their younger colleagues; conversely, older people are often considered to be more reliable, loyal, careful, and conscientious than their younger colleagues (e.g., Doering, Rhodes, & Schuster, 1983; Heron & Chown, 1961; Stagner, 1985). Attitudes toward older workers or toward older people in general tend to be more negative than are attitudes toward younger people (e.g., Bird & Fisher, 1986; Kirchner & Dunnette, 1954), although the magnitude of that difference is reduced when attitudes toward specific individuals rather than attitudes toward groups as a whole are considered (Kite & Johnson, 1988).

The important point to remember about stereotypes is not that they are completely false. Rather, although they may sometimes be appropriate in general terms, people who use them frequently fail to recognize the existence of considerable variability around a stated average. As we will discuss later, a number of differences between younger and older employees have been identified, but so have wide variations between people who are the same age. Forming impressions on the basis of chronological age alone, excluding other kinds of information, is inaccurate, just as other forms of unidimensional perception are often inaccurate.

However, there is ample evidence that negative age stereotypes can have a marked impact on employment decisions. Surveys of employers (e.g., Fox, 1951; Rosen & Jerdee, 1977) and reports by workers themselves (e.g., Kasschau, 1976; McCauley, 1977) make it clear that age discrimination is not uncommon. Such discrimination occurs when individuals are refused employment, dismissed from jobs, paid less, or denied promotions, training, or other benefits because of their age. Such actions are prohibited by law in some countries, but it is often difficult to determine whether age or other factors are the primary causes of a decision in any one case. For example, older employees in general have less formal education, less recent training, and less physical strength than younger employees, and it would be difficult to demonstrate that age itself was the key factor behind a decision against an older person who is characterized in all of these ways.

Despite negative age stereotypes and the existence of age discrimination, older people who remain in full-time employment in general receive larger incomes than their younger colleagues. Earnings of full-time workers increase on average to a level that plateaus at about age 40, remaining at that high level before tending to decline somewhat after about age 50 (Jablonski, Rosenblum, & Kunze, 1988; Makeham, 1980; National Commission for Employment Policy, 1985; Rones, 1988). The higher wages of older employees are particularly linked to years of work experience itself rather than to chronological age alone (Mincer, 1979). The association between income and work experience is particularly apparent among women. Female employees who spend intermittent periods outside the labor market are subsequently likely to have lower incomes than continuously employed women their same age (Stewart & Greenhalgh, 1984). Older people's higher levels of pay often result from their longer tenure in a single company and their accumulation of skills that are of particular value to the employer.

Age-related Transitions

Formal or informal procedures exist in many industries for older employees to be transferred to alternative work if they begin to experience difficulties with strenuous or machine-paced jobs (e.g., R. M. Belbin, 1953; Davies & Sparrow, 1985; Teiger, 1989). In a study of British coal miners, Powell (1973) observed that after the age of about 45, men were likely to move to less physically strenuous work or to leave the industry altogether. Heron and Chown (1961) noted a similar tendency in the manufacturing industry, although in a minority of jobs. Transfers were at that time most likely to occur after workers were about 50 years old. Murrell's (1962) analysis revealed that older workers were particularly likely to leave jobs that made heavy demands of a perceptual kind, and Richardson's (1953) results indicated that a change to lighter work often led to a reduction in skill use.

If they lose a job after long service with one company, older workers tend to experience larger decreases in wages in their new positions than do reemployed younger people. These reductions can be attributed in part to the nontransferability of company-specific skills and knowledge associated with considerable job seniority in the previous

organization (Shapiro & Sandell, 1987). After losing their jobs, older people tend to have greater difficulty than their younger counterparts in finding new positions, and they more often have to move into work that is at a lower skill and/or income level (e.g., Daniel, 1974; Makeham, 1980). This is partly because their previous experience is of limited value to a new employer (being narrowly focused on one firm's requirements) and partly because of employers' widespread reluctance to hire older individuals when younger applicants are available.

In terms of the negative psychological impact of unemployment, it appears that, among principal family wage earners, people in their 30s and 40s can be especially affected (e.g., Warr & Jackson, 1985; Warr, Jackson, & Banks, 1988). For that medium-age group, financial and family stress and issues of personal self-worth can be especially pressing during unemployment. However, older unemployed workers tend to report less financial stress (although it may still be considerable), and they may come to view themselves as having retired from the labor market, thus being in a role that is personally and socially more acceptable.

General age-related patterns are modified in particular cases by other personal or social attributes. For example, older workers who belong to minority ethnic groups or who suffer from physical disabilities are likely to be particularly disadvantaged (e.g., Haber, 1970). These individuals face multiple difficulties finding work after a period of unemployment, and both their age and other factors operate against them.

Official statistics indicate that unemployment rates are generally relatively low for older members of the labor force. This arises partly from their retention by employers because of accumulated job seniority and company-specific skills. Table 1 presents some recent unemployment rates for the United States and the United Kingdom. The elevated

TABLE 1

**Unemployment Rates (Percentages) at Different Ages
in the United States and the United Kingdom in July 1989**

| | *Age Group* | | | | | | | |
	18–19	20–24	25–39	40–49	25–54	50–59	55+	60+
U.S.A.	12	9	—	—	4	—	3	—
U.K.	9	9	7	4	—	7	—	2

Sources: *Monthly Labor Review* and *Employment Gazette* (1989, November)

figure (7%) for British workers in their 50s derives partly from a large number of long-term unemployed people who have been unable to obtain employment after large-scale layoffs, particularly in economically depressed areas of the country. The low rates of unemployment in the oldest category (3% and 2% in the two countries) are particularly notable. However, these official figures underestimate true levels of joblessness, since many older people, unable to obtain work, prefer to define themselves as retired or permanently sick.

In the United Kingdom, the conventional retirement age (at which a government pension becomes payable) is 60 for women and 65 for men (though equalization between the sexes has been promised, at a currently unspecified standard age). In the United States, the Age Discrimination in Employment Act prohibits employers from requiring workers to retire before they reach the age of 70, although partial retirement benefits are available at 62. (The age for receiving full retirement benefits will gradually be raised to 67 over the next four decades.) In practice, retirement before the age of 65 has become common in both countries (e.g., National Commission for Employment Policy, 1985; Sheppard & Rix, 1977), as older people find it difficult to retain or obtain

employment and employers encourage withdrawal from the labor force through earlier payment of pensions. Up to a third of older people work while receiving a pension, perhaps on a part-time basis or for intermittent periods. Pay rates are typically lower for jobs undertaken after retirement (e.g., Rones, 1988).

Participation Rates

The labor force participation rate is the proportion of the adult population who considers themselves to be in the labor market (whether they are unemployed or employed at the time). Labor force participation rates for 1986 in the United States and United Kingdom are shown in Table 2. Male rates are consistently higher than female rates, and for both men and women there is sharply reduced participation for the two oldest groups.

Factors influencing the decision to retire have frequently been investigated (e.g., Atchley, 1979; Davies, Matthews, & Wong, 1991; Parnes, 1988; Robinson, Coberly, & Paul, 1985; Talaga & Beehr, 1989). Two main groups of influences are personal (e.g., financial resources, health, attitudes, and social pressures) and institutional (e.g., employer policies, national regulations, economic conditions, and job availability). Withdrawal from the labor market stems

TABLE 2

Civilian Labor Force Participation Rates (Percentage of Each Age Group) in the United States and the United Kingdom in 1986

	Age Group							
	16–19	*20–24*	*25–34*	*35–44*	*45–54*	*55–64*	*65+*	*Total*
U.S.A. men	56	86	95	95	91	67	16	76
U.S.A. women	53	72	72	73	66	42	7	55
U.K. men	74	86	94	95	92	67	9	86
U.K. women	71	70	64	72	71	36	3	67

Sources: Fullerton (1987) and *Employment Gazette* (1988)

from a combination of these factors, but societal attitudes and local employment opportunities are likely to be particularly important. Since job seekers around age 60 tend to be comparatively unattractive to employers, they are less likely to gain the jobs they would like in times of high unemployment. Their persistence in hunting for those jobs depends on social norms and the attractiveness of financial benefits available outside the labor market through their previous employers or through official welfare programs.

The labor force participation rates of older people are generally higher in nonindustrialized countries than they are in developed countries, partly because of the lack of welfare benefits in the former. Participation rates in five developing countries are shown in Table 3, which indicate that many people (particularly men) are active in the labor market past 65. Data from five industrialized countries are also shown; Japan is notable for its unusually high rates of participation at all the ages.

Labor Force Projections

Research into psychological, physiological, or social aspects of age is of potential interest at any time, but it takes on particular importance in periods of marked demographic change. Many developed countries are currently experiencing a steady increase in the average age of their populations. Some examples, calculated from the comprehensive data provided by Zachariah and Vu (1988), are given in Table 4.

Population projections for the years 1990, 2000, and 2010 are shown for principal age groups between 15 and 69 years of age, with percentage distributions provided for each year. In the final column are the projected numbers for each group in the year 2010 as a percentage of that age group's 1990 figure. Projections of this kind are based on specific assumptions about trends in fertility rates, mortality levels, and migration into and out of each country. Such assumptions can, of course, become invalid, especially when distant future periods are considered (the source document extends up to the year 2150), but the overall patterns in Table 4 are firmly based on actual population figures and are likely to be substantially correct.

Consider first the data for the United States. The total population between 15 and 69 years of age is projected to increase by 14 percent up to the year 2010. However, there

TABLE 3

Civilian Labor Force Participation Rates
(Percentage of Each Age Group) in Ten Countries

	Men			Women		
	55–59	*60–64*	*65+*	*55–59*	*60–64*	*65+*
Developing countries						
China (1982)	83	64	30	33	17	5
Indonesia (1980)	85	77	53	41	33	19
Mexico (1980)	91	86	69	26	24	19
Peru (1981)	95	88	63	24	23	12
Thailand (1980)	84	68	39	59	43	19
Industrialized countries						
France (1989)	70	23	4	45	18	2
Italy (1989)	68	35	8	20	10	2
Japan (1989)	92	71	36	52	39	16
The Netherlands (1989)	65	24	3	24	9	1
West Germany (1989)	79	34	5	41	11	2

From "Aging and Work" by D. R. Davies, G. Matthews, and C. S. Wong, 1991. In C. L. Cooper and I. T. Robertson (Eds.), *International Review of Industrial and Organizational Psychology* (Vol. 6). Chichester, England: Wiley. Copyright 1991 by Wiley. Reprinted by permission.

will be a decline in the number of people aged between 20 and 39, and most of the increase is concentrated in the above-40 group. This trend is apparent in the right-hand column of the table, but it is also visible in the figures shown to the left of that column. The largest age group in 1990 is between 30 and 39, and this remains the biggest cohort in subsequent years, becoming the 40 to 49 age group in 2000, and the 50 to 59 age group in 2010.

The pattern for the United Kingdom and Australia is similar, with the largest age group in these countries being between 20 and 29 in 1990, which later becomes the 40 to 49 age group by 2010. There will be a decline in the

number of younger people, under 40 years in the United Kingdom and under 30 in Australia. The number of 50- to 59-year-olds will increase substantially in both countries; note that the smaller increment for this group in the United Kingdom (22%) partly reflects the fact that the total population between 15 and 69 is projected to increase by only 1 percent during this period.

Table 4 also contains projections for unified Germany. This is the only country in these examples that will experience an overall decline in population between 15 and 69 over this period. This decline is particularly large for those under the age of 40. (Some commentators have speculated about whether high levels of

TABLE 4

**Population Projections (In Thousands,
Aged Between 15 and 69) for Five Countries**

Age Group	Population in			Percentage in			2010 Population as Percentage of 1990
	1990	*2000*	*2010*	*1990*	*2000*	*2010*	
United States							
15–19	16,287	18,625	17,099	9	10	9	105
20–29	39,539	34,071	36,929	23	18	18	93
30–39	42,756	40,088	34,182	24	21	17	80
40–49	33,294	42,660	39,818	19	23	20	120
50–59	22,324	32,330	41,414	13	17	21	186
60–69	20,819	20,263	29,581	12	11	15	142
Total 15–69	175,019	188,037	199,023	100	100	100	114
United Kingdom							
15–19	3,886	3,570	3,542	10	9	9	91
20–29	8,939	7,171	7,083	22	18	17	79
30–39	7,812	8,842	7,113	19	22	18	91
40–49	7,497	7,696	8,736	19	19	22	116
50–59	6,104	7,227	7,449	15	18	18	122
60–69	5,922	5,491	6,553	15	14	16	111
Total 15–69	40,160	39,997	40,476	100	100	100	101
Australia							
15–19	1,387	1,263	1,260	12	10	9	91
20–29	2,782	2,668	2,525	23	20	18	91
30–39	2,664	2,854	2,680	22	22	19	101
40–49	2,174	2,680	2,839	18	21	21	131
50–59	1,551	2,118	2,604	13	16	19	168
60–69	1,377	1,407	1,936	12	11	14	141
Total 15–69	11,935	12,990	13,844	100	100	100	116

TABLE 4

**Population Projections (in Thousands,
Aged Between 15 and 69) for Five Countries (continued)**

Age Group	Population in			Percentage in			2010 Population as Percentage of 1990
	1990	2000	2010	1990	2000	2010	
Germany							
15–19	4,361	4,041	3,773	8	7	7	87
20–29	12,712	8,357	7,975	22	15	15	63
30–39	11,544	12,684	8,322	20	23	16	72
40–49	10,174	11,399	12,505	18	20	24	123
50–59	10,575	9,779	10,998	18	18	21	104
60–69	8,137	9,494	8,800	14	17	17	108
Total 15–69	57,503	55,718	52,373	100	100	100	91
Japan							
15–19	10,023	7,630	7,459	11	8	8	74
20–29	17,133	18,525	14,824	19	20	16	86
30–39	16,817	17,068	18,462	18	18	20	110
40–49	19,824	16,668	16,938	22	18	19	85
50–59	15,927	19,273	16,225	17	21	18	102
60–69	11,707	14,561	17,751	13	16	19	152
Total 15–69	91,431	93,725	91,659	100	100	100	100

migration into Germany might moderate this decline somewhat.) The number of young employees is also projected to decrease in Japan, but that country will have an abundance of 20- to 29-year-olds in the year 2000, who will be aged between 30 and 39 in 2010.

Some countries have developed detailed breakdowns of their national population projections. For example, Wetrogan (1988) has presented figures for different regions of the United States and examined likely trends for major ethnic groups. The population in the southern and western United States is expected to grow most rapidly, and the black population is projected to increase more than twice as quickly as the white population.

The figures in Table 4 summarize the number of people between the ages of 15 and 69 in each country in the three years shown. However, not all of these people will be active in the labor market, and before we can make projections about labor force numbers we must also consider labor market participation rates. Examples of previous rates are given in Tables 2 and 3, and projections about employment rates require that assumptions about future labor market participation be made for each of the countries.

This is fairly easy for, say, young middle-aged men, for whom activity rates above 90 percent can be safely assumed. But, as indicated earlier, the participation of older men in the labor force is particularly dependent on economic circumstances, welfare benefits, and social norms. These are not always predictable a decade or two in advance. Women's labor market participation has increased in many countries in recent years. For example, 44 percent of American women were in the labor market in 1972, but this figure had increased to 55 percent by 1986. At that time, more than 70 percent of women between the ages of 25 and 54 were economically active (e.g., Fullerton, 1987; Shank, 1988). In slightly different terms, women made up 41 percent of the American labor force in 1976, 45 percent in 1988, and are projected to make up 47 percent in the year 2000 (Fullerton, 1989).

Some labor force projections for the United States up to the year 2000 are based on the assumption that the employment participation rate for males over age 54 will decline somewhat but that more women of all ages up to 65 will be in the labor market (Fullerton, 1987). These assumptions yield a pattern of labor force changes up to the year 2000 that are very similar to the population projections shown in Table 4. Silvestri and Lukasiewicz (1989) have provided parallel projections that focus on probable skill requirements, emphasizing the need for a work force that is more highly educated than is currently the case.

In the United Kingdom, labor force projections to the year 2001 by the Department of Employment (1992) have assumed that unemployment levels will remain unchanged and that economic activity by women under age 55 will increase slightly. These assumptions generate a predicted increase in the labor force (for men between the ages of 16 and 64 and for women between the ages of 16 and 59) of 3 percent between 1991 and 2001, with a decline of 16 percent among 16- to 24-year-olds and an increase of 16 percent for those between the ages of 35 and 54. Spence's (1990) projections are very similar.

In overview, the figures summarized in this section suggest that there will be a future shortage of younger employees in many developed countries, while the numbers of older workers will increase, and the proportion of women in the labor force is likely to continue growing. Older people will occupy a greater percentage of jobs in many countries. However, there will be variations between different industrial sectors. For instance, organizations needing to recruit large numbers of well-educated young people will have particular difficulty, whereas the declining number of companies dependent on unskilled older employees will continue to have sufficient applicants.

Research Designs: Cross-sectional and Longitudinal

Hundreds of studies have involved cross-sectional comparisons between the behavior or attitudes of younger and older adults. Such a research design is essential for gathering currently valid information about the members of a society or a particular organization. In many cases, the research objective is merely descriptive and comparative across ages, and a cross-sectional design is adequate. However, the use of cross-sectional information to suggest explanations of observed differences in terms of processes of intraindividual aging is more problematic.

Cross-sectional Research

Suppose that a cross-sectional difference were found between groups of 20-year-olds and 60-year-olds, with the former obtaining significantly higher scores. Can we then infer that this disparity is evidence for some process of aging between 20 and 60? Three assumptions need to be made before such a developmental explanation can be accepted.

First, an explanation based on age depends on the assumption that the sample of 60-year-olds would have performed 40 years ago like the sample of 20-year-olds does now. This is, of course, not open to investigation. Second, we must assume that the difference (assumed to develop after the age of 20) derives from influences that are age-graded rather than history-graded. As explained earlier, normative age-graded influences are those physiological, psychological, and social processes influencing all members of an age group, at whatever point in history the group is studied. History-graded influences vary from time to time, influencing all members of an age group at one point in history, not because of their age but because of environmental developments.

It is often difficult to exclude some form of history-graded influence from cross-sectional data. For example, the younger group will have been educated in ways that are qualitatively and quantitatively different from the 60-year-olds. The existence of potentially important history-graded influences means that, in interpreting cross-sectional differences, we cannot separate out possible aging effects from possible differences between cohorts (groups of people who are born at the same time). Cohort effects arise because separate cohorts are subject to different, history-graded environmental influences.

A third concern about the interpretation of cross-sectional research is that, regardless of any cohort effect, the younger and older samples may be differentially representative of their respective populations. For example, researchers often have difficulty recruiting older people for investigation. In research in the community, the older participants may be members of elderly persons' associations or live in sheltered residential accommodations. Younger samples are often made up of university students, themselves an atypical group. In comparing older employees with younger employees who have the same job, the older group may be self-selected to a greater degree. Older people who cannot cope adequately with the job will in all likelihood have already left; conversely, those with special skills may have been promoted out of the group.

These limitations are well known to researchers who investigate cross-sectional differences between age groups. In many cases, attempts are made to ensure that the groups are matched in terms of education, socioeconomic status, physical health, verbal ability, task motivation, or other possibly relevant factors. However, in attempting to understand and explain processes of intraindividual aging, it is clear that research designs that are longitudinal have particular strengths that are lacking in cross-sectional studies.

Longitudinal Research

Only a few longitudinal investigations have extended across the substantial periods required in adult aging research. Several of these will be described later. They have clear advantages in recording changes in the same individuals over time, in identifying interrelationships between changes in different variables, and in obtaining time-ordered information that can support causal interpretations of development.

However, longitudinal studies also have problems (e.g., Baltes, 1968; Dixon, Kramer, & Baltes, 1985; Schaie, 1983a, 1983b). First is the fact that their initial sample is likely to be reduced over time through attrition that is not random. It is usually found that over the course of a longitudinal study, the less capable, less motivated, and/or less healthy members of a cohort end their participation. After those individuals have been omitted from the longitudinal data analyses, the findings are biased toward smaller decrements across the years than would otherwise be the case (e.g., Willis & Baltes, 1980).

Longitudinal studies are also open to testing effects. These fall into two categories: practice and reactivity. In the first, respondents completing the same test of, say, intellectual ability on several occasions may improve their scores as a result of practice. Reactivity effects might occur if participants recall their earlier responses and choose to respond in the same way or differently on a second or third occasion.

Time of measurement effects can also be important in longitudinal research: Environmental influences on a dependent variable may occur at one point of measurement but not at another (e.g., Palmore, 1978). Occasion-specific measurement effects are expected to influence all age levels at that time, rather than having an impact only on a certain age group, as in the case of cohort effects. However, in a longitudinal study, their occurrence may affect the scores of the cohort under investigation at one time but not at another, creating the appearance of an age change which in reality was caused by temporary variations in the environment.

It is usually difficult to determine whether such a time-of-measurement effect has occurred, or to determine the direction of its influence. The effects seem likely to be more troublesome in studies of attitudes and values than they are apt to be in research on intellectual abilities. Studies of abilities measure the maximum performance that people can attain, something that is less likely than an attitude to be affected by occasion-specific environmental features.

Potential problems arising from time-of-measurement effects would be reduced by a sequential cohort design, which examines a series of longitudinal trajectories, each covering the same segment of participants' lives (e.g., between the ages of 20 and 60), but starting at different points in time, say, in 1930, 1940, and 1950 (e.g., Schaie, 1983a, 1983b). Time-of-measurement effects are unlikely to occur systematically at the same life stage for each cohort, and the repeatability of patterns across time could be investigated. Such sequential projects are complex and expensive, and, not surprisingly, uncommon; examples of such investigations will be cited later.

A final point about the conduct of research in this area concerns the analysis and presentation of findings. It is common for the results observed in a particular group to be summarized in terms of the mean score and its standard deviation. This allows straightforward tests of significance of the difference between mean values, for example, between an older and a younger group.

Such a procedure has often given rise to research reports that describe a significant difference between age groups. However, these reports or others in this area often also draw attention to large individual differences that occur at each age, so that despite the mean difference, there is considerable overlap between the two distributions of scores. If results were also presented in terms of the number of people falling within certain ranges or, in the case of longitudinal studies, in terms of the proportions increasing or decreasing on the variable in question, a different interpretation might often be drawn.

Job Performance

In investigating associations between age and job behavior, reliance has through practical necessity been placed almost entirely on cross-sectional research designs. As pointed out earlier, these are valuable for providing descriptive information about a current situation, but they are unable to document intra-individual changes that occur over time. This section will first examine cross-sectional information about work performance, then consider labor turnover, absenteeism, and workplace accidents.

In terms of job performance, Waldman and Avolio (1986) and McEvoy and Cascio (1989) have presented meta-analyses of studies published in the past four decades. The average association between age and job performance was in both cases almost zero; for example, in the second (larger) analysis, the mean correlation was 0.06. Hunter and Hunter's (1984) separate investigation yielded a comparable value of –0.01. Subsequently reported studies of specific samples have found correlations between age and rated job performance of 0.07 (Avolio, Waldman, & McDaniel, 1990), –0.08 (Cleveland & Shore, 1992), –0.19 (Ferris & King, 1992), 0.17 (Jacobs, Hofmann, & Kriska, 1990), and –0.04 (Lawrence, 1988). There are wide variations between individual studies, with age/performance correlations in the McEvoy and Cascio analysis ranging from –0.44 to 0.66.

In interpreting these findings, a number of issues need to be considered. First is the usual problem concerning the potential unreliability and invalidity of the criteria. Job performance has been scored either by measured output or, more commonly, through ratings made by a person's supervisor. In both cases, variance in scores is likely to be limited by the fact that clearly unacceptable performance would already have led to the voluntary or involuntary departure of low-performing employees. Objective performance data are available in only a few situations, restricted to that minority of jobs in which each person's achievements are documented, attributable to his or her own activities, and sufficiently comparable across groups of people to permit this kind of analysis. In practice, studies of recorded output have been restricted to employees on piecework payment systems. Performance ratings are open to several biases and inaccuracies, and it is possible that raters' age stereotypes sometimes

influence results in a way that is disadvantageous to older people (e.g., Stagner, 1985).

A second problem concerns the numbers of and characteristics of older employees in a study. Many investigators have focused on the relatively small number of people over 50 in samples that cover all age groups within a single job (e.g., Clay, 1956; King, 1956; McEvoy & Cascio, 1989; Sparrow & Davies, 1988; but see Bowers, 1952, and Breen & Spaeth, 1960, for post-60 samples). This imbalance arises from the fact, as noted earlier, that in many occupations people are likely to move into alternative work in their later years. It seems likely that the people moving on to new positions will often be less able to cope than those who remain in the same job, and that the movement of less competent employees out of positions might encourage a more positive observed association between age and performance than would occur in the population as a whole.

On the other hand, some jobs act in part as steps on a career ladder, out of which better-performing employees are promoted after spending some years in the position. Cross-sectional comparisons in such cases will be biased toward the observation of a negative age gradient. The older employees remaining in that position will be employees deemed to have limited promotion potential, whereas their younger colleagues will represent two groups—particularly effective employees who are likely to be promoted later and employees who have less promotion potential.

A third feature might sometimes lead to the overestimation of intraindividual changes. Cohort differences can result in younger people being better educated and better able to deal with recent technological advances. Currently, this is evident in many countries where there is greater computer literacy among 20-year-olds than among 50-year-olds. In some jobs, such a disparity in educational levels between cohorts gives rise to performance discrepancies that favor the younger group. Yet these differences might be less marked if the younger group were followed longitudinally, or if it were included in subsequent cross-sectional comparisons after technological change has slowed down.

Fourth, in some circumstances, it is important to consider maximum possible performance as well as typical levels. Data in terms of average output or ratings might represent the pattern of typical performance, but people can often raise their performance substantially above its normal level in cases of emergencies or special needs. Such elevated performance can be maintained for considerable periods through increased personal effort. In cases where an age difference is observed in average level of work performance, we do not know whether age is also related to maximum possible performance—and that is sometimes the more important piece of information.

Relevant Experience

A fifth issue concerns the causal factors that might underlie any observed age difference in job behavior. Different influences are likely to be important in different kinds of work. For example, in jobs requiring fast psychomotor responses to externally paced information, physiological and cognitive deterioration in later years may give rise to a decline in performance. Examples of such changes as they relate to age will be cited later.

In other cases, where job performance is positively associated with increased age, continued learning through experience on the job (or in similar contexts) may be the key underlying feature. Previous relevant experience has been shown to be significantly correlated with rated job performance by Avolio et al. (1990; $r = 0.18$), Hunter and Hunter (1984; $r = 0.18$), and McDaniel, Schmidt, and Hunter (1988; $r = 0.21$); positive associations of experience with work-sample and job-knowledge tests have also been described by Schmidt, Hunter, Outerbridge, and Goff (1988). Since the variables of age and job-relevant experience are positively

intercorrelated (often above 0.60), between-age comparisons also in part reflect differences in experience.

After statistically controlling for years of relevant experience, positive associations between age and performance tend to be reduced. For example, Schwab and Heneman (1977b) observed a correlation of 0.29 between age and output in a sample of American assembly workers. After partialing out years of experience with the firm, that value dropped to 0.04. In research with two samples of American manual workers under age 25 to over age 65, Giniger, Dispenzieri, and Eisenberg (1983) found that correlations of age with hourly piecework rate of 0.33 and 0.26 were reduced to 0.02 and –0.03 after statistical correction was made for experience.

The role of experience was also investigated by Murrell, Powesland, and Forsaith (1962). In a study of engineering drilling work in Britain, older workers (between the ages of 44 and 60) were in general found to be slower. However, this effect was confined to inexperienced operators; among experienced drillers, age was unrelated to speed of operation. Salthouse's (1984) study of typists with an average job experience of more than 10 years revealed that older workers could type as rapidly as younger ones, despite reduced speed in reaction-time tests. In a similar manner, small positive age gradients in the performance of American office workers were found to disappear when analyses were restricted to those with nine months or more experience on the job; younger workers were as effective as older ones if they were appropriately experienced (Kutscher & Walker, 1960). Walker (1964) reported the same finding for federal mail sorters.

Bowers (1952) presented overall performance appraisals separately for male employees with different amounts of experience; the sample contained "an appreciable number over 65" (p. 299). The positive association with age observed for people who had recently joined the company was absent for those who had been employed with the company for more than two years. In a study of American fire fighters, Jacobs et al. (1990) found that years of experience in a job were positively associated with rated performance for those in the position for less than five years, but not for longer-serving employees. Schmidt, Hunter, and Outerbridge (1986) observed the same pattern among U.S. military personnel. The positive value of job experience is thus likely to be nonlinear.

This nonlinearity may arise from two sources. First are the diminishing returns from continued practice on a task, as one's level of competence approaches its maximum. Second is the fact that extended exposure to the same conditions can give rise to boredom and reduced enthusiasm. Employees who become locked into a job with no prospect of advancement may be less proactive and energetic than those with fewer years in that job. Extremely long periods of experience in a particular position can thus be disadvantageous, despite the benefits that result from experience in general.

Observed benefits of relevant experience are consistent with more general research into practical intelligence and expertise, where aging is increasingly found to be accompanied by a deepening of knowledge and skills in specialized areas (Rybash, Hoyer, & Roodin, 1986; Warr & Conner, 1992). In cases where age is *negatively* associated with performance, it seems likely that experience will also often be beneficial (reducing the size of the negative correlation), and this possibility will be discussed later (e.g., Tables 5 and 6).

Nonlinearity

A sixth issue in interpreting job performance findings is that in drawing inferences from correlational data about age and performance, we need to consider the possible nonlinearity of relationships with age. The use of only linear coefficients of correlation rules out the possibility in many studies of finding curvilinear associations between age and job performance. For example, increasing but negatively accelerating curves or an inverted-U pattern might sometimes be expected in addition to linear relationships of the kind described earlier (e.g., Doering, Rhodes, & Schuster, 1983; Rhodes, 1983).

Several earlier investigators reported results in terms of subgroup averages, rather than simply in terms of correlation coefficients, sometimes identifying an inverted-U relationship between age and output (Clay, 1956; Kutscher & Walker, 1960; Mark, 1956, 1957; Walker, 1964). A more recent study of equipment maintenance engineers in the United Kingdom also found that quality of work was associated with age in this inverted-U manner (Sparrow & Davies, 1988). Scientists' productivity reveals a similar pattern, with the greatest number of publications and citations received for those between the ages of 40 and 44 (Cole, 1979; Horner, Rushton, & Vernon, 1986). Simonton (1988) has developed a model to account for such an inverted-U pattern in a wide range of creative activities through age 80.

Within the inverted-U patterns that are found, the deterioration observed at older ages is usually small. In Clay's study, performance of employees over age 50 was on average more than 95 percent of the level it was for the 40 to 50 age group. In the data published by Kutscher and Walker, performance after age 55 was on average about 1 percent lower than it was for 45- to 54-year-olds; considerable variation existed within each age group. Mark's findings showed a decrement of between 5 percent and 10 percent for those over age 55, and in the study by Sparrow and Davies, age was found to account for less than 1 percent of variance after experience, training, and other variables were considered. Furthermore, in some cases curvilinear relationships are observed without a decrement at the oldest ages, in terms of increases in performance up to a

TABLE 5

**Four Categories of Job Activity and Expected Relationships
of Performance With Age During the Years of Labor Market Participation**

Task Category	Basic Capacities Are More Exceeded With Increasing Age	Performance Is Enhanced by Experience	Expected Relationship With Age	Illustrative Job Content
A	No	Yes	Positive	Knowledge-based judgments with no time pressure
B	No	No	Zero	Relatively undemanding activities
C	Yes	Yes	Zero	Skilled manual work
D	Yes	No	Negative	Continuous, paced data processing

plateau from middle age to retirement (e.g., Avolio et al., 1990).

We may draw the following general conclusions. There is no single relationship between age and job performance; negative, positive, and inverted-U patterns are all observed. On average, the relationship is around zero, and in most cases, the negative or positive influence of chronological age is small or nonexistent. However, much research has examined only the two variables of age and performance, rather than also including other factors that might account for any association that is observed.

A Four-Category Framework

A number of ambiguities remain in the available data, and more complex research designs and theorizing are needed. In particular, it would be helpful to develop models that can explain why different relationships with age occur in different kinds of jobs. An outline possibility of these relationships is summarized in Table 5. Activities are placed into groups according to the importance of age-related capacity-limitation or potential enhancements that result from experience.

Let us think in terms of four main types of activities, recognizing that the variations are in fact continuous rather than discrete in this simplified manner. The four categories can be defined in terms of two features—that they are concerned with either basic capacities or relevant experience.

In the first case, do task requirements exceed basic capacities known to decline with age? Those "raw capacities" (Salthouse, 1985b, p. 86) ultimately derive from physiological processes, which tend to deteriorate over the years (e.g., Birren, Woods, & Williams, 1980; Laville, 1989). Examples include speed of information processing or effectiveness of sensory mechanisms. Declines in capacity are likely to be more influential after age 60 or 70. Our concern here is with the years of paid employment. We should also consider whether the acquisition of knowledge and skills is likely to improve performance as workers age. Some activities benefit from accumulated experience, and others do not; in the former case, more experienced (and thus on average older) employees are likely to be more effective.

In many cases, job performance will be a function of both accumulated experience and declining raw capacities, and an observed relationship with age will reflect the relative strength of the two types of age-related influences. There are, of course, empirical problems associated with specifying in advance the relative importance of each type of influence for any one task. And a single job may be made up of tasks in more than one category, so that age may have different associations with different aspects of performance in the same job.

Type A activities in Table 5 are those that remain within basic capacities despite advancing age and in which performance benefits from experience. (As discussed earlier, the gains from experience may be nonlinear, stabilizing after a number of years.) For example, positive associations between age and job performance are likely in situations that are relatively stable, in which knowledge and skills can continue to be developed by older workers. In a study of an American company's sales staff, Maher (1955) observed that older employees (over age 50) were rated as more effective in almost every respect. A particularly strong positive association (0.67) was found between age and rated product knowledge. However, "since the company carries over 1,000 items in its catalog, a man may require many years to know the technical characteristics of the majority of them" (Maher, 1955, p. 451); years of job experience are clearly useful in such settings. The acquisition of social knowledge and interpersonal skills through accumulated experience was particularly emphasized by Perlmutter, Kaplan, and Nyquist (1990). In

their study of food-service employees between the ages of 20 and 69, age was correlated 0.36 with performance effectiveness.

Other situations in which older employees are likely to be viewed as more effective include those demanding personal characteristics that are more often found in older people. For example, Walker (1964) observed in a study of mail sorters a steady increase in consistency, with less variation in output from week to week, across groups from under 25 years to 60 and over; the oldest group was 60 percent more consistent than the youngest group. British shoe-leather cutters were found by De la Mare and Shepherd (1958) to work more slowly at older ages, but older employees produced work of a higher quality, at least up to age 60. In a sample where ages extended into the late 60s, Bowers (1952) reported more positive appraisals of conscientiousness and attendance for older workers. The significant positive association between age and rated performance of paraprofessional family advisers might also be accounted for in terms of enhanced reliability, as well as increased job knowledge, at older ages (Holley, Feild, & Holley, 1978).

On the other hand, a negative linear or nonlinear relationship with age is expected in tasks where basic capacities are exceeded to a greater extent for older people and where experience cannot help. That possibility corresponds to category D in Table 5 and includes continuous rapid information processing or some kind of strenuous physical activity that becomes more difficult with advancing years. Laboratory research will be reviewed later in this chapter, but there are few investigations in organizations of age differences in the performance of jobs that require continuous rapid processing of complex material. In part, this imbalance is due to employee self-selection into other work as they age, as mentioned earlier.

The studies of age and performance by Kutscher and Walker (1960), Mark (1956, 1957), and Walker (1964) described earlier all belonged to a series of studies that used the same procedures and analyses. Comparison between results indicates that, although older office workers and mail sorters were almost as productive as their younger colleagues, factory workers were more likely to demonstrate a decrement in productivity after age 55. This differential pattern may reflect the greater physical demands in the factory settings that were studied.

Other circumstances in which a negative age gradient can be anticipated include jobs whose content changes rapidly, so that previous knowledge and skills can easily become obsolete. For example, Dalton and Thompson (1971) reported a marked (cross-sectional) decline in the performance of professional engineers after the age of about 40, as their technical knowledge became increasingly outdated. This process was viewed in part as a negative spiral: An older engineer who lacks current knowledge receives poorer appraisals and less challenging assignments, so that he or she comes to feel discouraged and is less willing to make efforts at retraining; such discouragement in turn leads to more negative appraisals and further discouragement. Such a process has been analyzed in more formal theoretical terms by Fossum, Arvey, Paradise, and Robbins (1986).

Many job activities fall within category B in Table 5. Work is routine and nonproblematic, requiring either limited skill or skill that is firmly established so that behavior is fairly automatic. In such circumstances, age differences in task performance are not expected.

Type C activities are also very common in jobs. Older people may have increasing difficulties because of some decline in information processing or physical capacities, but they are able to compensate for that decline in some way. Older employees may have additional knowledge or helpful habits, they may take more written notes, or they may modify their behaviors so they can capitalize on personal

strengths or avoid situations known to present difficulties. For instance, Birren (1969) has described how middle-aged managers may have learned to conserve their time and energy by operating through day-to-day tactics that reduce cognitive and affective load. Other forms of compensation will be discussed in a later section of this chapter.

The four-part framework summarized in Table 5 draws attention to the fact that type D activities (those for which we might expect a negative age gradient) comprise only a minority of job behaviors. Some job tasks are clearly of this kind, but many jobs are made up primarily of the other three types of activity— for example, knowledge-based judgments with no time pressure, relatively undemanding activities, and skilled manual work. Furthermore, in considering the relationships between age and *overall* job performance, evaluative combinations have to be made across a number of component activities. Only in cases where performance is impaired by age in the majority of job components (or in those which are especially salient) will an overall evaluation be lower for older workers; such a situation may be relatively uncommon.

This four-category framework will be further developed later in this chapter, when laboratory studies of information processing are examined. The applicability of laboratory findings to age differences in job situations will also be considered then.

Other Aspects of Work Behavior

A separate issue is concerned not with effectiveness, but with the characteristics of work behavior itself. Between groups of older and younger workers who are all competent in the same job, are there differences in the way work is carried out? Griew and Tucker (1958) examined this question among employees of a British engineering factory and observed considerable similarity between the work practices of manual workers in the 24-to-30 and 48-to-61 age groups. For example, there was no age difference in the amount of lifting or speed of working (which was under an individual's control). However, older employees were less likely to work in a stooping position, and their machines were running (rather than being set up) for higher proportions of the work cycle. This approach to age differences in job performance appears not to have been followed up. Investigations of different kinds of jobs, for example, in information or service work, would now be of interest in order to learn about the effects of experience or to learn about how older people compensate for their physical limitations.

The relationship between shiftworking and age has also received attention. In many industries, there is a marked tendency for workers over the age of about 40 to move out of shiftwork (e.g., Monk & Folkard, 1985; Teiger, 1989), so that cross-sectional comparisons between age levels are particularly confounded by differential self-selection. Problems of unsatisfactory sleep are reported by shiftworkers of all ages, and they tend to be greater among older employees (e.g., Foret, Bensimon, Benoit, & Vieux, 1981). In an experimental environment isolated from time cues, middle-aged men have been found to adjust less rapidly to a shift in their imposed time schedules than men between the ages of 18 and 25 (Moline et al., 1992).

In research conducted in Sweden, Akerstedt and Torsvall (1980) observed that older shiftworkers (over age 45) had greater difficulty with night shifts than their younger colleagues, although they coped better with morning shifts. This difference was linked to the preference of older workers to take sleep periods at earlier times than younger individuals, so that the early-night sleep required by morning shifts was more acceptable to older workers. Such a preference for earlier sleep at older ages is consistent with findings from the more general study of nonshiftworkers reported by Tune (1969).

Aspects of managerial decision making have been investigated in some studies. For example, Taylor (1975) studied Canadian managers between the ages of 23 and 57 in an individual decision-making exercise. After controlling for years of management experience, he reported that older managers were slower in reaching conclusions (having obtained greater amounts of information), but were better able to diagnose accurately the value of information and were more flexible in altering decisions in the face of adverse consequences of choices they made. A similar study by Pinder and Pinto (1974) found that American managers between the ages of 40 and 55 were less autocratic than those between the ages of 20 and 29, and that they were more effective in information gathering and in interpersonal relationships. In an investigation of managers' written responses to hypothetical choice situations, older managers were found by Vroom and Pahl (1971) to favor less risky options.

Streufert, Pogash, Piasecki, and Post (1991) studied American managers (aged 28 to 35 and 45 to 55) in a computer-based group decision-making environment. Fifteen indices of decision-making style were computed, on twelve of which there were no differences between the groups. However, significant differences were found concerning the number of decisions taken, the amount of search activity, and the diversity of actions taken to achieve goals: Younger teams had higher scores in each case. (A third group, between the ages of 65 and 75, was somewhat less effective. Since this group contained volunteers who were retired, results may not reflect the behavior of currently employed managers of that age.)

Staff Turnover

Other sets of investigations have examined staff turnover, absenteeism, and labor accidents. In the case of staff turnover, research findings indicate that older employees are significantly less likely than younger ones to leave their employer in order to move to alternative work (e.g., Doering et al., 1983; Rhodes, 1983). Turnover is influenced both by factors in a present job and by the availability of alternatives. Older people tend to receive higher pay (partly as a result of longer service as discussed earlier) and to be more satisfied with their positions and more committed to their organization (as discussed below). It is also the case that older people are less likely to be attractive to other employers, so that fewer employment alternatives are available to them elsewhere.

In order to identify directly the influence of employee age, rather than age in conjunction with job tenure, it would be useful to trace the behavior of people from the time they joined a company. Downs (1967) examined staff turnover in this way, identifying the probability of a person leaving in several consecutive periods after employment began. She studied two British organizations that provided training for new recruits in the first few weeks of employment, and observed that older people (those over age 35) were more likely to quit during the training period, but thereafter had a higher probability of staying in their job. She noted that older employees may face special problems during training and that instruction should be designed with the special needs of older employees in mind. Issues of age and learning will be examined later.

Employee age may also influence turnover rates through the composition of a work group or organization. McCain, O'Reilly, and Pfeffer (1983) have drawn attention to the ways the cohort membership of an organization can influence its attractiveness to employees. There may sometimes be substantial discontinuities in an age distribution, for example, when an organization employs an older cohort, a younger cohort, and no people of medium ages. These discontinuities, and associated within-cohort cohesiveness, can make communication more difficult and may increase conflict and power struggles so that employees tend to leave the organization more often than they would in other cases. Examining data from a U.S. university, McCain and colleagues obtained some evidence for this possibility.

Absenteeism

In terms of absenteeism, it is important to distinguish between voluntary or casual absences—those that occur because an employee chooses not to attend work—and involuntary absences—those that occur when sickness or some other factor prohibits attendance. However, it is rarely possible to assess directly the voluntariness of particular incidents of absence, and measurement approximations are usually required. It is common to assess voluntary absence in a given period in terms of the *frequency* of a person's nonattendance (thus giving equal weight to short and long periods of absence); involuntary absence is often assessed by looking at a person's total *duration* of nonattendance during a given period, thus emphasizing long periods of illness.

Two recent meta-analyses in this area, which overlap only partly in their source studies, agree that voluntary absenteeism is inversely associated with the age of male employees, although there appears to be no association in the case of female employees (Hackett, 1990; Martocchio, 1989). Involuntary absenteeism is widely thought to be positively associated with age, since older people are expected to experience more extended periods of illness. However, the results of the meta-analyses rather surprisingly point to a small negative correlation with age (between -0.05 and -0.10).

Makeham (1980) described findings from a British national earnings survey, which obtained information about absenteeism for specified reasons during the preceding month. These data contained information on the percentages of workers in each age group who were absent for specified reasons; they are not directly comparable to the frequency and duration scores examined in the meta-analyses. In comparisons between full-time male manual workers under age 25 and those between age 50 and 64, absence defined as voluntary in the sense just described was almost three times as common among the younger group, and absence that resulted from medically certificated sickness occurred almost twice as frequently among older workers. Among women, voluntary absenteeism was also more common for younger workers (by a factor of about two), but there was no difference between age groups in the frequency of certificated absence. Overall absenteeism (for all reasons) was more frequent among younger workers of both sexes.

It is important not to view absenteeism, either voluntary or involuntary, as determined purely by an individual worker. Individual characteristics, such as age-related social roles and physical health, may influence attendance at work, but an organization's norms and sanctions are also particularly important considerations. The *absence culture* of a company has a considerable impact on the nature and amount of absenteeism that is informally considered appropriate (Nicholson & Johns, 1985). Unmeasured variations between these cultures in different studies can affect findings about patterns of age and absence.

Workplace Accidents

In relation to workplace accidents, some studies have examined frequency (rate of accidents as a proportion of the number of employees at risk or the amount of time worked), and others have analyzed severity in terms of duration of injury. The most common finding is that accidents occur less frequently among older employees, but those that do occur in older groups on average lead to longer subsequent absences (e.g., Doering et al., 1983; Rhodes, 1983). Root (1981) drew attention to the fact that employees of different ages are susceptible to different kinds of accidents. Examining data covering employees between the ages of 16 to 65 and over, he found that

fractures, hernias, and multiple injuries were more frequent in older groups, whereas burns, cuts, and lacerations were more common among younger workers.

It is clearly important in these analyses to account for differential exposure to danger in different jobs. Dillingham (1981) examined separately the frequency of compensated injury at different ages in three occupational groups in New York state: white collar, service, and blue collar jobs. For men, a negative association was found between age and accident frequency in each group, although the probability of injury in blue collar employment was about eight times what it was for white collar work. The pattern for women was more variable, with a clear negative relationship present only among blue collar workers. In general, the very young subgroups (those under 25 years) were particularly prone to injury.

O. S. Mitchell (1988) introduced statistical controls in relation to different occupational groups in a study of injury data from nine U.S. states. Combined results for men and women indicated that, after controlling for occupation and industry, the frequency of compensated temporary injury was unrelated to age. A similar result was obtained for permanent injury, up to age 65, when the rate increased considerably.

These studies examined injuries that are severe enough to warrant compensation claims. Most accidents are less serious than that; indeed, the large majority are minor and are never recorded. Van Zelst (1954) studied dispensary visits linked to accidents in one American company. He found that older employees (whose mean age was 41) made fewer such visits, but that the length of a person's tenure in the company (and thus in most cases, in the job) was a crucial factor. For both older and younger groups, accidents were particularly frequent during the first five months of employment. In two British construction companies, Stubbs and Nicholson (1979) also observed a negative association between age and frequency of accidents for employees between the ages of 17 and 63 and over, drawing particular attention to the need for inexperienced workers to be trained in materials handling to help reduce accidents. A similar relationship between age and experience was reported in American coal-mining companies by Butani (1988).

Most of the published studies of age and accidents concern manual work of the kind that is currently less common than was once the case. Basic findings have been established for jobs requiring physical labor in potentially hazardous situations, but there is now a need to examine in more detail the importance of age and experience in accidents that may be more prevalent in information processing work and in the provision of services. Many performance errors, some of which lead to accidents, may be traced back to cognitive difficulties that will be described later in the chapter.

Physical Health and Illness

To what degree are differences in employees' physical condition implicated in the findings outlined so far? It is clear that people experience more illness and disability as they grow older. For example, surveys of American workers indicate that severe functional limitations in performing key sensory and physical activities are reported by 55- to 64-year-olds about four times as frequently as they are by 25- to 34-year-olds (Berkowitz, 1988; Haber, 1970). Other surveys have asked respondents whether their physical condition limited the amount and kind of work they are able to do. In the 55 to 64 and 25 to 34 age groups, about 24 percent and 5 percent, respectively, of Americans report such a limitation (Berkowitz, 1988).

It is clear that decreased physical effectiveness that occurs as workers age can have some negative impact on performance in certain job tasks. For example, reduced visual acuity or aerobic power may cause problems in some cases (e.g., Robinson, 1986). However, much ill health is temporary and would not be

expected to affect the behaviors examined in this section apart from involuntary absence. Chronic impairment is often under personal control to an acceptable degree. Furthermore, everyone is restricted in the kind of work he or she can successfully perform, in terms of knowledge, experience, ability, or physical attributes, and the increased physical limitations of some older people do not imply that they will be ineffective in every job. In the course of their careers, individuals tend to move into jobs they can cope with, and those who are seriously disabled may leave the labor market altogether.

Note, incidentally, that cross-sectional data about differences in physical condition at different ages can be subject to cohort effects. In many countries there have been health improvements in recent decades, so that younger people are now on average in better physical condition than their counterparts were 30 years ago. Physical deterioration through time may be smaller than that indicated in cross-sectional comparisons.

Longitudinal research into physical performance among workers is rare. One exception is the follow-up after three and a half years of a sample of middle-aged Finnish employees by Nygard, Luopajarvi, and Ilmarinen (1988). The study recorded significant deterioration in handgrip strength, trunk flexion strength, and trunk extension strength among both men and women. Longer-term studies would clearly be useful.

Reviews of investigations into age and job performance often reach conclusions similar to Robinson (1986, p. 70), that "in general, variability in performance measures within age groups far outweighs differences among age groups." This large variability within an age group again draws attention to the inappropriateness of making personnel decisions on the basis of chronological age alone. It has also been the source of arguments for using the term *functional age*. This refers to the fact that individuals' functioning can be above or below the level expected for their chronological age (e.g., Birren & Cunningham, 1985; McFarland, 1973; Stafford & Birren, 1986).

For that reason, there could be merit in seeking to measure people's functional capacities in relevant areas and using that information instead of chronological age to make personnel decisions. Some attempts have been made to create a single overarching indicator of functional age, using psychomotor, sensory, and biomedical information; in other cases, attempts have been made to profile functional scores that range over key tasks of interest in a particular setting. As pointed out by Salthouse (1986), these procedures are of limited practical use in occupational situations, since the functions needed in different forms of employment have rarely been ascertained with any accuracy and would in any case differ widely from job to job. In addition, the use of the term *age*, in relation to *functional age*, appears to be inappropriate, since the focus is on functional *capacities* rather than age itself. It seems fair to conclude that a more accurate measurement of specific abilities and competencies should be sought and that the term *functional age* is not really helpful in employment settings.

Financial Issues

Finally in this section, what is known about the financial costs of employing people of different ages? Such information is rarely available, although material published by Billings (1983) is informative. He analyzed costs that might vary by age within a single American company, noting that overall costs approximately doubled between the lowest age group (those under 25) and employees between the ages of 55 and 64. The greatest cost element was for health insurance claims, which were greatest for employees between 45 and 54 years; most of these expenditures were incurred on claims by dependents of employees. This form of company expenditure is not typically found outside of the United

States, where national provisions or personal insurance schemes are more typical.

Other costs are associated with staff turnover, sick leave, and personal absence. In total, Billings calculated that younger American employees were more expensive in these respects. Actual expenditure will vary from country to country and within individual organizations, but in the absence of major health insurance claims it seems likely that the overall cost of employing older and younger workers will in general be very similar. As pointed out earlier, performance differences associated with age are on average also absent.

Well-being, Work Values, and Personality

This section will examine research into people's feelings about their environments and themselves, with particular emphasis on job-related well-being and attitudes. Most investigations in this area have focused on the relationship between age and job satisfaction.

Job Satisfaction

As with other constructs, satisfaction can be viewed at different levels of generality. Overall job satisfaction reflects a person's feelings about his or her job as a whole, whereas facet satisfactions concern specific features of that job. Research into age and satisfaction has most often dealt with the more general construct.

Overall job satisfaction is typically found to be significantly higher among older workers (e.g., Doering et al., 1983; Glenn, Taylor, & Weaver, 1977; Rhodes, 1983), although the positive correlation is not high, usually falling between 0.10 and 0.20. The pattern of association is often observed to be linear, although the review of early research by Herzberg, Mausner, Peterson, and Capwell (1957) pointed to a U-shaped relationship. They concluded that overall job satisfaction was likely to be especially high for young adults, when the novelty of working encourages positive feelings about a job. However, between the ages of 20 and 30, increasing boredom and perceptions of diminishing opportunities may lead to some reduction in job satisfaction. Their review suggested that over time a person comes to terms with his or her job (perhaps after having moved out of relatively unrewarding positions), and some increase in satisfaction is observed.

A cross-sectional increase in job satisfaction after age 30 is widely observed, but many investigators have failed to find evidence of increased job satisfaction in very young employees. This discrepancy is difficult to explain, but it may be due to the limited sampling of young workers in certain studies. Furthermore, there may be no decline in satisfaction among young workers who receive training and advancement early in their careers; variations in these factors may influence results from any one study.

More focused satisfaction, with a specific job facet, is related to age in various ways, depending on the facet under investigation. It is generally found that satisfaction with the work itself is greater in older groups of workers. This relationship remains significant after controlling for job or organizational tenure (Kacmar & Ferris, 1989; Rhodes, 1983; Schwab & Heneman, 1977a). The same findings occur for measures of intrinsic satisfaction, perhaps because intrinsic satisfaction and satisfaction with the work itself are both highly correlated with overall job satisfaction (e.g., Cook, Hepworth, Wall, & Warr, 1981, p. 54). Satisfaction with pay is sometimes found to be positively associated with age (e.g., Kacmar & Ferris, 1989; Rhodes, 1983), but an age gradient is usually absent in relation to extrinsic satisfaction, and in relation to satisfaction with promotion, co-workers, and supervisors. This does not exclude the possibility that significant relationships are sometimes present, and

findings about facet satisfaction are likely to depend on the nature of the sample, the organization, and the measures investigated.

Extended longitudinal studies of job satisfaction are rare. Cook et al. (1981, pp. 23 and 52) have summarized test-retest correlations across periods between 12 and 16 months, reporting a median value around 0.60. A coefficient of 0.37 across five years for overall job satisfaction in the same job, and 0.17 in different jobs, was reported by Staw and Ross (1985). Longer-term investigations would be valuable, as would research into the level of scores across time as well as their stability.

There are some suggestions in sequential U.S. national surveys of a small cohort effect in terms of overall job satisfaction, with people born earlier in the century having more positive attitudes regardless of their age (Glenn & Weaver, 1985). However, "the evidence was far from conclusive" (p. 85), and an explanation of the cross-sectional association in terms of cohort differences cannot easily account for the fact that only certain forms of facet satisfaction exhibit positive age gradients. A cohort explanation is also contradicted by the finding that commitment to having a paid job of any kind (another form of positive attitude) is *less* strong among workers in older age groups (Hanlon, 1986; Warr, 1982, 1992).

As in other parts of this chapter, we might expect factors associated with age—such as tenure in an organization or in a job, current income, or job level—to account for some variance in the relationship between age and job satisfaction. The characteristics of a job and their desirability or undesirability are likely to be particularly important in that relationship. Wright and Hamilton (1978) focused on American workers' preferences for different job features at different stages in their lives and found that employees were more concerned early in their careers with promotion opportunities and income, and later in their working lives with security and pleasant social relations. Wright and Hamilton analyzed national survey data to suggest that older workers are more likely to have moved into jobs whose characteristics they value, and that the differences in personally desirable job content can partly explain the positive association between overall job satisfaction and age.

An examination of data from the same survey by Kalleberg and Loscocco (1983) also showed that a substantial portion of the age–satisfaction relationship could be traced to work values and job rewards, but that chronological age remained a significant predictor, independent of the other variables. Investigating more restricted sets of potentially explanatory variables, Lee and Wilbur (1985) also reported an independent age effect, but White and Spector (1987) found that age was linked to overall job satisfaction only through other factors in their study. In an Australian investigation, O'Brien and Dowling (1981) found that age remained an independent predictor of job satisfaction for women but not for men.

Job-related Anxiety

A second important dimension of job-related well-being concerns feelings of anxiety or strain associated with the job. Although these have often been examined as they relate to specific job stressors, there is only limited information about age differences. Maslach and Jackson (1981) found that older members of their American human service sample reported lower levels of burnout in terms of emotional exhaustion and depersonalization. Warr (1992) observed a U-shaped relationship between age and job anxiety/contentment among British employees between the ages of 18 and 64, with those between 25 and 34 reporting the lowest well-being. In determining possible explanations for this relationship, additional personal and job variables were included in multiple regression analyses. A significant correlation between age and job-related anxiety contentment was retained after controlling for differences in job tenure, job level, decision latitude, work demands, working conditions, income, employment commitment, education, and other potentially relevant variables.

It appears that, after controlling for the fact that older people had moved into better jobs, there is still a positive age gradient in occupational well-being. It may be possible to account for more variance in that relationship by including additional occupational variables—for instance, environmental clarity or opportunity for interpersonal contact (Warr, 1987)—but part of the age gradient in job-related affect is likely to be attributable to nonjob differences between older and younger people.

For example, there is a small but significant cross-sectional increase in general measures of life satisfaction occurring with age (Campbell, Converse, & Rodgers, 1976; Diener, 1984); reported psychiatric symptoms have been found with less frequency among older factory workers (Siassi, Crocetti, & Spiro, 1975); and there is generally less nonjob anxiety (Warr, 1990) and depression (Ryff, 1989) among older members of the work force. Within a life course, the period spent raising young children is often relatively stressful (e.g., House & Robbins, 1983); older individuals perceive themselves as less stressed than younger people (Aldwin, 1991); and older workers experience fewer negative life events and daily hassles than their younger counterparts (Folkman, Lazarus, Pimley, & Novacek, 1987). There is also evidence that middle-aged people tend to employ more effective procedures to cope with stress than do younger people, having learned by experience that instrumental reactions are more appropriate than escapist responses (Aldwin, 1991).

The fact that older employees report higher job satisfaction and other forms of occupational well-being than younger people is thus likely to be partly attributable to broader differences of these kinds. The causes of the positive age gradient are not entirely occupational.

In general, workers over the age of 30 tend to view themselves as feeling younger than their chronological age (Barnes-Farrell & Piotrowski, 1989). However, those who report feeling older than their years are likely to experience more job strain and sleep difficulties and to report lower work performance than other people (Barnes-Farrell & Piotrowski, 1991). This form of perceived personal age deserves further examination as a possible predictor of well-being and work performance.

Work Values

Turning to work values that have been investigated, it is usually found that involvement in one's current job is greater among older employees, with a median correlation with age of about 0.25. However, an independent effect does not always remain after controlling for job and organizational factors (Doering et al., 1983; Hanlon, 1986; Morrow & McElroy, 1987; Rhodes, 1983). Additional research to identify the underlying causes would be useful.

Similar conclusions are appropriate in relation to the broader notion of organizational commitment (e.g., Mowday, Porter, & Steers, 1982), which has been defined in a number of ways, encompassing a person's acceptance of his or her organization's goals, willingness to work hard toward those goals, and feelings of being bound to a current employing organization because of personal investments already made. Measures of organizational commitment are usually associated positively with employee age; the average correlation was 0.20 in the meta-analysis reported by Mathieu and Zajac (1990).

Key elements of the so-called Protestant work ethic have been measured through a number of scales. These cover, for instance, the importance of work as an end in itself, the moral value of disciplined activity, and the possible harmful effects of excessive leisure (Furnham, 1990a). Scores on these scales tend to be positively associated with age, and these relationships remain after partialing out income, job level, tenure, and education (Cherrington, Condie, & England, 1979; Furnham, 1990b). Beyond any possible cohort effects, we are again left with the question, what aspects of growing older, beyond those that have been included in previous analyses, are responsible for changed values of these kinds? A broad examination of personal, family, social, and occupational developments over the life course is needed to answer that question.

One form of work value that is negatively correlated with age is nonfinancial employment commitment. Several investigators have asked the question, "If you were to get as much money to live as comfortably as you like for the rest of your life, would you continue to work or would you stop working?" National surveys in both the United States and the United Kingdom have found that overall between 65 percent and 70 percent of people of working age in the two countries indicate that they would continue working (Lacy, Bokemeier, & Shepard, 1983; Vecchio, 1980; Warr, 1982). Men are more likely to respond positively than women, as are full-time rather than part-time workers, but older respondents are less likely to want to continue working in the absence of financial need. For instance, in Warr's British study, 74 percent of full-time male employees between the ages of 16 and 44 expressed a desire to continue working, but only 58 percent of those between 45 and 64 did. Hanlon (1986) reported from American data that this age difference was retained despite statistical controls for income, education, seniority, job prestige, sex, and job satisfaction.

These findings suggest that, although older members of the labor force are more committed to the jobs they currently hold, they would be more willing than younger workers to give them up if paid work were no longer financially essential. Older employees also tend to hold stronger views about the moral value of work. It seems possible that this established work ethic often carries over into a style of retirement in which active, goal-oriented behavior is valued both by individuals themselves and by friends, relatives, and professional counselors. Such a "busy ethic" in retirement has been illustrated and interpreted by Ekerdt (1986).

Personality

What about personality differences that occur over the course of the working years? Here, three main topics have been addressed. First is the degree of consistency of personality characteristics, as indicated, for example, by test-retest correlations across a period of time. Second, research has examined the similarity of personality structure at different ages, indicated, for example, by factor analyses. A third set of findings concerns the stability or change in mean personality scores: Do people on average obtain different scores at different ages?

The test-retest consistency of personality scores is often high (coefficients around 0.50) over several decades (Conley, 1984; Costa, McRae, & Arenberg, 1983; Howard & Bray, 1988; Kogan, 1990; Ormel, 1983). Structural changes are also uncommon (e.g., Costa et al., 1983; McRae, Costa, & Arenberg, 1980). However, there is more uncertainty about the possible existence of age differences in mean scores.

Personality may be viewed at varying levels of abstractness. For example, the broad component of extraversion subsumes more limited attributes such as sociability, liveliness, impulsiveness, and sensation-seeking tendencies. Many theorists accept that both extraversion and neuroticism (anxiety, depression, guilt, etc.) are two main personality components of the broader kind.

It appears that scores on both of these components decline cross-sectionally with age across the years of employment (Costa et al., 1983; Costa & McRae, 1988; Eysenck, 1987; McRae & Costa, 1990), but that the decrement is quite small. Furthermore, psychometrically assessed depression tends to increase cross-sectionally with age after retirement (Mirowsky & Ross, 1992; Newmann, 1989). There is less agreement about the nature of other broad personality constructs, but evidence suggests that both psychoticism (Eysenck, 1987) and openness to experience (Costa & McRae, 1988) are lower in samples of older workers.

However, the pattern of relationships with age becomes mixed when more restricted aspects of personality are considered, with no change, an increase, and a decrease all reported (Colligan & Offord, 1992; Costa & McRae, 1988; Howard & Bray, 1988; Lachman, 1989; Müller, 1991; Ryff, 1989; Stevens & Truss, 1985). Furthermore, longitudinal investigations may fail to confirm the patterns observed in cross-sectional research (Costa et al., 1983), sometimes because cohorts born at different times exhibit somewhat different personalities. For example, Schaie and Willis (1991) showed in a sequential cohort study that later generations have more flexible personalities than earlier ones, so that "the inferences previously drawn from cross-sectional data regarding the life course of flexibility-rigidity are unduly pessimistic" (p. P283).

Of course, a standard pattern of change for all specific attributes of personality is extremely unlikely. Different personality characteristics will be open to modification in different ways, and we need different models of potential normative and nonnormative influences from personal, family, and occupational processes as they relate to particular attributes. Marked differences exist in the way people experience these processes, and research needs to record events in people's lives as well as measure the personality feature of interest. It may be helpful to examine specific phases and transitions during people's life course, identifying more precisely than has been done in previous research

TABLE 6

**Four Categories of Laboratory Tasks and Expected Relationships
of Performance With Age During the Years of Labor Market Participation**

Task Category	Basic Capacities Are Exceeded With Increasing Age	Performance Is Enhanced by Experience	Expected Relationship With Age	Illustrative Laboratory Tasks
A	No	Yes	Positive	Verbal comprehension; crystallized intelligence
B	No	No	Zero	Immediate ("primary") memory
C	Yes	Yes	Zero	Complex reasoning in areas of personal expertise
D	Yes	No	Negative	Reaction time; working memory; fluid intelligence

the linkages between particular life events and aspects of personality (e.g., Davis & Tagiuri, 1988; Levinson, 1986). The complexity of theoretical issues in this area and the practical difficulty of gathering adequate information are clearly very great.

Cognitive Performance

There have been hundreds of investigations of age differences in cognitive performance. Many of these have involved laboratory tasks, and attention has most often been focused on declining performance that occurs with age. Welford (1958, pp. 2–3) observed that "almost all the research on ageing which has been done so far has the depressing characteristic that the changes are downward with the years," and Cunningham and Owens

(1983, p. 21) pointed out that in the 1950s "the substantive view of aging was that it involved inevitable decline." For people within the working population, that view has by now been substantially modified.

It is clear that in some respects cognitive performance improves with age, and that in other respects varying degrees of decline occur. For many activities, there is no age variation across the working years. These possibilities may be illustrated with the same framework that was applied to job performance earlier in this chapter.

Four types of activity are shown in Table 6. In keeping with the focus of this chapter, this discussion covers primarily the age range up to about the mid-60s. The later pattern for many activities is likely to change, with more shifts into categories C and D, since physiological deterioration then becomes more rapid.

As with job performance above, the two extreme possibilities are identified as type A and type D. Type A activities are those that do not exceed basic capacities with increasing age and in which performance is enhanced by experience. With these activities, we may predict a positive relationship to exist between performance and chronological age.

The opposite is true for type D activities, in which basic capacities are increasingly exceeded as people grow older and experience cannot help performance. The capacities in question are physiologically based (usually through the nervous system) and are liable to deteriorate with age. Most psychological research into this category has investigated aspects of information processing, concerned with inductive reasoning, speed of psychomotor reaction, learning, and other cognitive processes. However, type D activities might also involve strenuous manual work of an essentially noncognitive kind.

Other tasks neither exceed basic capacities nor are improved through experience; these are identified as type B. Finally, in Table 6 are type C activities—those subject to a decrement because of increasingly limited capacities and an increment through the benefits of experience. Generally, the two factors may in these cases cancel each other out. In overall terms, the two influences will operate in opposition to each other, with an observed pattern of age development or cross-sectional difference arising from the relative impact of each. The boundaries between categories are thus less distinct than Table 6 suggests.

Type A Activities:
The Benefits of Experience

Crystallized Intelligence. Research from several standpoints has shown that certain types of cognitive functioning can improve with age during the working years. For example, scores on some tests of intellectual ability are regularly found to be higher among older people

(e.g., Berg & Sternberg, 1985; Denney, 1984; Dixon et al., 1985; Labouvie-Vief, 1985). Such tests measure what has been referred to as *crystallized* intelligence (e.g., Cattell, 1963; Horn, 1970), covering cognitive processes and primary abilities that are embedded in learned cultural meanings. They reflect what may be viewed as the crystallized residue of prior experience. Crystallized intelligence (as opposed to fluid intelligence, to be discussed later) is investigated through tests of verbal comprehension, analogies, and vocabulary; it improves through practice and new learning.

As an illustration, consider Stankov's (1988) study of Australians between the ages of 20 and 70: Crystallized intelligence was correlated 0.27 with age, whereas for fluid intelligence that value was −0.31. Longitudinal studies of American samples have revealed significant increases in crystallized intelligence through time: in verbal tests, such as reading comprehension, synonyms, and analogies, between the ages of 19 and 50 (Cunningham & Owens, 1983); in verbal ability between the ages of about 22 to 42 (with a test-retest correlation of 0.89; Howard & Bray, 1988); in vocabulary between the ages of 21 and 46 (Schaie, 1983a); and in comprehension between the ages of 18 and 54 (with no significant change at later ages up to 61; Sands, Terry, & Meredith, 1989).

Practical Knowledge. Several recent theoretical approaches to the nature and measurement of intelligence have emphasized the central role of accumulated practical knowledge and cultural understanding. For instance, Sternberg's (1985) "triarchic theory" of intelligence contains a "contextual" component, which focuses on intelligent behavior in practical situations. The theory emphasizes the acquisition through experience of knowledge required for intelligent behavior, and considers several ways in which people might intelligently modify their environment or select particular settings to enter. In terms of age, Sternberg argues that, despite a core of common features, key components of everyday intelligent behavior are different for, say, 30-, 50-, and 70-year-olds (see also Berg & Sternberg, 1985). He considers intellectual abilities requiring established knowledge and use of experience to be important aspects of intelligence in middle-aged and older adults than among young people.

A similar view has been taken by Baltes and his colleagues (e.g., Baltes, 1991; Baltes et al., 1984; Dixon et al., 1985). These authors attempted to create a theory of intelligence more comprehensive than the frameworks underlying traditional psychometric approaches (e.g., Warr & Conner, 1992). A *dual-process* model is proposed, covering what are referred to as the *mechanics* and *pragmatics* of intelligence. The mechanics of intelligence derive from basic information processing activities (which will be considered shortly), and the pragmatics are seen in terms of functional adaptation to the environment. They are taken to subsume systems of knowledge that are quite general, as seen in crystallized intelligence, and also specialized knowledge and skills for application in particular settings. The development of intelligence is said to differ between life stages. In the first third of life, cognitive development is proposed to involve basic information processing (the mechanics), whereas in adulthood pragmatic intelligence builds on basic abilities that have already been formed.

Other researchers have examined the appropriateness of using different types of tests at different ages. Demming and Pressey (1957) set out to identify principal features of adult activity and framed new tests of practical knowledge considered "indigenous to adult life"; older individuals obtained higher scores than younger people. This approach was extended by Gardner and Monge (1977), who constructed 28 tests that were intended to be appropriate for adults of different ages. Emphasis was placed on vocabulary

and knowledge in various areas, including finance, transportation, and death and dying. Scores were higher in middle-aged and older groups, with (cross-sectional) deterioration occurring by the 60s.

Also focusing on changes in knowledge that occur with age, Cornelius and Caspi (1987) developed an instrument to assess practical problem solving. Family, work, and other situations relevant to daily life were described, and American respondents between the ages of 20 and 78 were required to select the most appropriate of four alternative actions. (Pretesting had provided a reliable scoring key to define the most effective solutions.) This measure of everyday problem-solving performance indicated a linear (cross-sectional) improvement with age. A vocabulary test of crystallized intelligence was also administered, and a positive age gradient was again observed.

Denney (1989) has reviewed her own and other studies of realistic problem-solving tasks, pointing out that middle-aged people have repeatedly been found to be most effective in these activities. However, results depend on the nature of the problem being examined; high scores tend to be associated with extensive experience in the area under examination.

Expertise.   Indeed, it seems that a key feature of aging is the development of expertise in specific areas. The cognitive performance of older people can exceed that of their younger counterparts, since the older adults have acquired expertise through extended practice and exposure to new situations. For instance, Rabbitt (1991) reports findings about the competence of experts and novices in the completion of crossword puzzles. The experts' performance was unrelated to their age (between 55 and 75), whereas the (less competent) performance of novices declined over that range.

Comparisons between the performance of novices and experts have distinguished between *declarative* and *procedural* knowledge (e.g., Anderson, 1982). Expertise is accompanied by greater knowledge of both kinds. In declarative knowledge, a person acquires information about individual facts and their relationships in different situations. During learning, this declarative knowledge is gradually converted into a set of behavioral procedures through which it is applied in dealing with the environment. These procedures become collapsed into increasingly long strings of action, which the person can execute as a whole, and which he or she can readily assess for appropriateness and generalizability.

Expertise thus includes greater automatization of behavior, as people move from controlled, effortful cognition to execute fast strings of action, which are not under direct control once initiated but which permit the simultaneous processing of new information. Other aspects of expertise have been reviewed by Charness (1985, 1989), Glaser (1988), Salthouse (1987), and Warr and Conner (1992). For instance, experts perceive and recall large meaningful patterns in their domain, made possible by their superior and more organized knowledge base. However, research has emphasized that expertise is very much domain specific; an expert in one area may be quite ineffective in other areas.

Several of these themes come together in models of *selective expertise* (Salthouse, 1985b) or *selective optimization with compensation* (Baltes, 1991; Baltes et al., 1984; Baltes & Baltes, 1990a; Dixon et al., 1985). These models are based on the fact that, as people age, they are able to increase their effectiveness in areas of specialization. Continued interest and practice in a limited number of areas permit the growth of knowledge-based competence, and individuals are sometimes able to learn how to make the necessary compensations when faced with limitations that arise from deteriorating basic capacities. (Examples of this type C process will be considered later.) In Baltes' (1991) terms,

"knowledge and pragmatics are often more important than cognitive mechanics" (p. 845).

However, outside their areas of specialization, older people may find it more difficult to acquire new skills. This may be due to greater capacity limitations that occur with age, and/or through the reduced confidence older adults can experience in some kinds of new situations. Older people may also experience greater cognitive interference between well-learned behaviors in their areas of expertise and the new skills and knowledge that have to be learned in other settings.

A similar perspective is taken by the *encapsulation model* of Rybash et al. (1986). This argues that "the growth and encapsulation of domain-specific knowledge is the most salient feature of adult cognition" (p. 147). Encapsulation is thought to be accompanied by greater expertise of the kinds outlined previously in this chapter, but increasing cognitive limitations that occur with age are expected to inhibit development in less familiar areas. In a similar manner, Ceci (1990) has emphasized the importance of "elaborated knowledge domains" (specific to each individual) in the production of intelligent behavior. The work performance of older employees will often remain within those areas of maintained expertise, being embedded in familiar contexts, although the individuals might have more difficulty with new and complex activities.

Type D Activities: Reductions in Basic Capacities

The cognitive activities considered in the previous section (type A) were those in which basic capacities were not exceeded and relevant experience could enhance job performance. The type D activities shown in Table 6 are of the opposite kind: Basic capacities are liable to be exceeded and experience is of no benefit to performance. A negative association between age and performance is expected, since the capacities required for these activities tend to decline with age.

Numerous studies illustrate this negative association. Some of these deal with sensory processes of visual and auditory functioning, while others focus on motor activity and muscular strength (e.g., Fozard, 1990; Kline & Schieber, 1985; Schieber, 1992; Schneider & Rowe, 1990; Stones & Kozma, 1985; Verillo & Verillo, 1985; Welford, 1985), but most of the research that is relevant to this chapter concerns cognitive processes. Almost all of this research has been carried out in the laboratory. As illustrated by three additional categories in Tables 5 and 6, type D activities make up only a proportion of job activities. Indeed, it can be argued that tasks in category D become on average less important as employees become older and move into jobs that permit them increasingly to draw on accumulated knowledge in specialized areas.

Psychometric Tests. Type D research may be roughly divided into investigations with psychometric tests and studies of particular components of information processing, such as attention, reaction time, and learning. The psychometric tests of relevance to this section are those introduced earlier as tapping fluid intelligence, concerned with effectiveness in situations where new material has to be processed, often under time constraints. Abilities represented by the factor of fluid intelligence include seeing relationships among patterns, drawing inferences from relationships, and understanding implications. Tests to measure these abilities are usually made up of abstract, nonverbal problems and are sometimes said to measure nonverbal intelligence.

It has long been established that older people within the working population (and of course beyond this age group) perform less well on these tests than do their younger counterparts (e.g., Dixon et al., 1985; Heron & Chown, 1967; Horn, 1970; Labouvie-Vief, 1985; Rybash et al., 1986; Salthouse, 1985b, 1991b). Despite some

variability between findings, it appears likely that the magnitude of decline in fluid intelligence is similar within groups of high- and low-ability individuals (Christensen & Henderson, 1991).

Most investigations have been cross-sectional and, as noted earlier, may be subject to differential cohort effects. Since educational differences between cohorts are likely to favor younger people, it is possible that these cross-sectional comparisons overstate the longitudinal effects of aging (e.g., Willis, 1989a). The few available longitudinal studies of fluid intelligence reveal smaller decrements than suggested by the cross-sectional comparisons, although the observed decline is usually statistically significant when data are included from people in their 70s and older. Even within the working population, Cunningham and Owens (1983) reported a significant average intraindividual decline in abstract numerical reasoning (around 6%) between the ages of 19 and 61.

Schaie's (e.g., 1983a, 1989) cohort-sequential study of Seattle residents is particularly useful. Partly overlapping samples were drawn in 1956, 1963, 1970, and 1977, so that it was possible to analyze data both cross-sectionally and longitudinally (see also Schaie & Hertzog, 1983; Willis, 1985; Willis & Baltes, 1980). Respondents completed tests of five primary mental abilities, originally developed by Thurstone, of which two—inductive reasoning and spatial orientation—are particularly relevant here. Inductive reasoning involves the identification of abstract logical principles or rules, to be inferred from presented sequences of letters; spatial orientation requires the mental rotation of abstract figures to match a stimulus item.

Consistent with other investigations, there was a significant decline from the 30s in terms of cross-sectional comparisons. However, this difference was less marked in the longitudinal analyses, with significant intraindividual declines over the preceding 21 years occurring only at the ages of 74 and 67 for inductive reasoning and spatial orientation, respectively. As explained earlier, longitudinal investigations can underestimate the progress of decline through selective sample attrition, and it appears appropriate to conclude that the most likely developmental pattern exists somewhere between the two sets of results. Small average declines in inductive reasoning and spatial orientation are thus likely to occur by the age of 60, although there are wide interindividual differences, and sharper deterioration occurs thereafter (Schaie, 1989).

Components of Information Processing. Another set of studies has examined performance on abstract problem-solving tasks, such as those involved in concept formation, logical reasoning, the solution of anagrams, and twenty-questions games. Cross-sectional deterioration is commonly found in such studies, although it is rarely large until after middle age (e.g., Charness, 1985; Denney & Palmer, 1981). Some longitudinal decline has been observed over a six-year period, but not before age 70 (Arenberg, 1988).

Research into specific components of information processing (within the general framework of cognitive psychology) has examined age differences in several different tasks. As illustrations of type D activities in Table 6, let us consider attention, reaction times, learning, and memory. These processes overlap each other, although individual researchers tend to focus on them separately.

Attention.   The concept of attention has been characterized in different ways (e.g., Plude & Doussart-Roosevelt, 1990; Plude & Hoyer, 1985; Wickens, 1984), but heavy demands on attention are seen during both visual search and dual-task performance. In each of these activities, individuals have to direct their limited attention toward particular targets in the

presence of other stimuli that can themselves capture some of that attention. In the first case, a typical visual search task is one in which people have to locate as quickly as possible a particular letter among a set of nontarget letters. Older individuals are known to be less effective at this kind of selective attention task than are younger people (e.g., Rabbitt, 1965; Stankov, 1988).

The second type of task requires that attention be divided between activities involving different stimulus modalities (e.g., visual or auditory), different stimulus locations, or different response modes (e.g., manual or vocal). In the course of responding to one set of information, a person must also deal with a second set of stimulus demands. Age is negatively correlated with performance on this type of dual-task activity, with success on one task increasingly being traded off against poorer performance on the other (e.g., Plude & Hoyer, 1985). This negative age gradient may not exist for people under age 60 (Ponds, Brouwer, & van Wolffelaar, 1988) or in relatively easy dual-task activities (McDowd & Craik, 1988).

In general, it appears that older people may be more distractible, being less able to suppress task-irrelevant information during the selection of task-relevant material (e.g., Connelly, Hasher, & Zacks, 1991; Hasher & Zacks, 1988; McDowd & Birren, 1990). That would present greater problems at older ages, as cognitive resources are devoted to the processing of irrelevant stimuli at the expense of speed or accuracy in dealing with task-relevant information (McDowd & Filion, 1992). However, the magnitude of that decrement during the years of paid employment has not been clearly established.

Reaction Time. Reaction time in a wide range of tasks is known to become longer as people grow older. Salthouse (1985a) illustrated this by presenting more than 50 correlations between age and speed of performance on laboratory tasks (e.g., single and choice reaction time, card sorting, and digit-symbol substitution). The median correlation was –0.45, with a range from –0.15 to –0.64. Most values were derived from samples that included people who were past working age, but even within the 15 groups aged below 65, the median correlation with age was –0.43. This consistent finding has been discussed by Birren et al. (1980); Hale, Myerson, Smith, and Poon (1988); Myerson, Hale, Wagstaff, Poon, and Smith (1990); Rybash et al. (1986); Salthouse (1985b); Welford (1958); and others.

Reduced speed of information processing with age can possibly account for a wide range of apparently diverse findings (e.g., Salthouse, 1985b). Older people's slower handling of information may give rise to poorer performance on tasks that require rapid cognitive processing. This is obvious in the case of reaction time and similar activities, but it can also be expected in situations where active mental rehearsal, comparison between alternatives, and temporary storage in memory are needed. Cognitive capacities are limited, and there is a need to pass information through the system as rapidly as possible before it is lost or overtaken by other material. Particularly complex tasks, requiring a larger number of processing steps, are especially likely to be susceptible to cognitive slowing (e.g., Myerson et al., 1990).

Scores on tests of fluid intelligence have been shown to reflect the speed with which people process information (e.g., Vernon, Nador, & Kantor, 1985), and the attention tasks just illustrated are themselves heavily speeded. Memorizing complex new information is also likely to benefit from more rapid execution of the necessary cognitive components (e.g., Fozard, 1980; Salthouse, 1985b). It is therefore plausible to argue that certain age-related physiological changes are accompanied by reduced speed of information processing, which is itself causally involved in some impairment of key cognitive capacities. This point is taken up again later in this chapter, in relation to working memory.

Time is necessary for the utilization of any postulated cognitive resource. Therefore, some overlap necessarily exists between general explanations of age and information processing in terms of reduced speed and those envisaging age-dependent depletion of particular resources, such as cognitive energy or specific types of communication channels (e.g., Salthouse, 1988). Alternative general models that relate to age changes in assumed signal-to-noise ratio, for example (Layton, 1975; Welford, 1976, 1985), are also plausible. However, it is not clear how one should choose between these general theoretical alternatives, or how we can determine whether one single processing resource or several resources can better account for the large body of research findings in this area (e.g., Morris, Gick, & Craik, 1988; Rabbitt & Maylor, 1991; Salthouse, 1985b).

Learning and Memory. What about age differences in learning and memory? As elsewhere in this chapter, we need to distinguish between tasks that exceed an individual's capacities and those less difficult activities that are within an individual's capacities. In the latter situations (which in daily life may be more common than those that exceed individual capacity), older people can perform as well as younger ones, insofar as their relevant capacities have not declined beyond the requirements of the task. Such activities are shown in task categories A and B in Table 6. In this section, our concern is with type D tasks, those in which basic capacities are exceeded more at older ages and experience does not enhance performance.

Thorndike, Bregman, Tilton, and Woodyard (1928) recognized the need to distinguish between learning in which previous knowledge and training could be helpful and situations involving what they termed "sheer modifiability little influenced by the fund of ideas and habits which the individual starts with" (pp. 96–97). In order to exclude the benefits of experience (as in our type D activities), aspects of sheer modifiability were examined through a range of unfamiliar tasks. Cross-sectional declines were found in association with people between the ages of about 20 and 45 (the upper age limit in these studies), and this negative relationship has since been frequently replicated and extended into older age groups.

For example, Herzog and Rodgers (1989) obtained data from people between the ages of 20 and 80 on two memory tasks, assessing either recall or recognition. Correlations with age were –0.29 and –0.39, respectively. (Incidentally, scores on self-report questionnaires of memory ability were not significantly correlated with actual performance; see also Arbuckle, Gold, & Andres, 1986; Rabbitt & Abson, 1990.) Salthouse (1985b, ch. 11) has collated findings from several dozen studies (e.g., of digit span, free recall of lists, spatial memory, and paired associate learning); these have consistently indicated a negative relationship with age. Using nine different cognitive and sensorimotor tasks with French railway operatives, Paccaud (1990) obtained lower scores from older people (about age 50) in nearly all activities. American air traffic control trainees were found by Trites and Cobb (1964) to have progressively greater difficulty in acquiring job skills between the ages of 21 and 51. Research and theories in this field have been reviewed by Fozard (1980), Poon (1985), Rybash et al. (1986), Salthouse (1989), Welford (1958), and others. Related studies of occupational training will be examined in the penultimate section of this chapter.

Particular interest has recently focused on the notion of *working memory* (Baddeley, 1986; Baddeley & Hitch, 1974; Salthouse, 1990c). Much information processing requires that operations be carried out on one set of material, while information is retained in temporary storage (one's working memory) before being brought into active operations later in the activity. For example, in a laboratory investigation of working memory, people might be presented with a list of words to keep in mind, then asked to carry out a task of logical reasoning before recalling the initial list of words. Other working memory investigations have required individuals to repeat a list of digits in reverse order, a task that requires a person to retain the list in memory store while determining the correct reversal.

Mental activities of this kind (involving simultaneous storage and processing of information) are very common in daily life—in problem solving, mental arithmetic, and many forms of reasoning—and the demands frequently exceed available cognitive capacity. It has been established that older people perform less well than younger people in situations in which working memory is heavily loaded (e.g., Campbell & Charness, 1990; Fozard, 1980; Gick, Craik, & Morris, 1988; Hasher & Zacks, 1988; Hultsch & Dixon, 1990; Morris et al., 1988; Rybash et al., 1986; West & Crook, 1990). This differential effectiveness may underlie age-related decrements in many types of information processing activities, including those in tests of fluid intelligence.

Salthouse (1991) studied performance on several reasoning tasks as a function of age in people between age 20 and 84. Separate measures were also taken of each person's working memory effectiveness and speed of responding to presented stimuli. It was found that the observed age decrement in reasoning performance was largely explained (in hierarchical regression analyses) by individuals' working memory effectiveness and that the latter was itself significantly predicted by response speed (see also Salthouse & Babcock, 1991; Salthouse & Skovronek, 1992). Salthouse (1991a) concluded that "only a small proportion of the age-related variance in measures of cognitive functioning is not mediated by reductions in either working memory or perceptual comparison speed" (p. 182). Other research into age variations in the recall of words and of text has led to a similar conclusion: "Individual differences in abilities, particularly those involving verbal speed and working memory, contribute substantially to age differences on complex memory tasks" (Hultsch, Hertzog, & Dixon, 1990, p. 365).

The importance of working memory for many forms of information processing is clear, as is the fact that working memory becomes less effective with age. However, much of the published research has examined older people who were past conventional retirement age, and negative age gradients are not always observed within the labor force. Both West and Crook (1990) and Foos (1989, experiment 1) found no difference in working memory up to the age of 60. However, West and Crook pointed out that the magnitude of age decrement depended on the complexity of a task. When more heavy demands were made on working memory, age differences became more apparent. This "complexity effect" is discussed later in this chapter; for now it seems appropriate to conclude that age decrements in working memory occur within the labor force, but that such decreases are most evident in especially complex activities.

In general, age decrements in the type D cognitive activities illustrated here appear particularly likely when people have to rely entirely on their own internal representation of a problem and its elements. In such circumstances, information must be processed entirely within the head. In other cases, where at least some of the stimuli are present in writing or in another external form, older people are less likely to exhibit a decrement (e.g., Craik, 1990; McDowd & Craik, 1988). The role of this kind of environmental support in information processing will be considered again later.

One process that has been suggested to be particularly problematic for older learners is interference or negative transfer from one set of material to another. For example, Kay (1951) studied a serial learning task in which people between the ages of 20 and 70 had to learn by trial and error which key to press in response to the illumination of one light from a set of ten. As in other investigations, older people were less competent learners, and Kay observed that they were particularly likely to repeat the errors they had made on previous trials. Their difficulties were in part due to their inability to unlearn the incorrect associations they had made initially, which were interfering with their future progress.

Belbin and Downs (1965) examined learning by British postal workers (ages 18 to 49) of geographical information and concluded that those in middle age suffered particularly from interference from previous activity. In an American study, Hultsch (1974) also reported greater negative transfer of new work activity among older groups of workers. Questions about the effects of interference in learning have been unfashionable in recent years, and the available data (with their limited analyses or small samples) are inconclusive in their findings about whether major age differences associated with interference actually exist: Perhaps interference is equally a problem at all ages (see also Welford, 1958, ch. 9). This topic deserves new attention in future studies.

In keeping with researchers' interest in sheer modifiability, described earlier, most of the studies of learning and memory summarized here have examined unfamiliar, abstract laboratory tasks. However, the age decrement observed in these tasks is also present in more familiar activities, providing that substantial demands are placed on people's cognitive resources. For instance, Kausler (1985) reported an experiment in which younger and older Americans (mean ages 21 and 68 years) were required to recall each of 12 brief conversations they had participated in. A significant main effect of age was observed. Several other familiar tasks exhibiting an age-related decrement have been noted by Salthouse (1987).

One set of studies has investigated the learning and recall of extended prose passages. The growing literature in this area has been reviewed by Hartley (1989), Meyer and Rice

(1989), and Zelinski and Gilewski (1988). There is widespread agreement that an age decrement exists in the acquisition and recall of prose. However, studies have almost always been concerned with elderly people rather than older members of the labor force, and there are many discrepancies of detail in the investigations that have been done thus far. A theme of interest to this chapter concerns the possible importance of variations in learners' verbal ability, usually indexed in terms of a vocabulary score.

Taub (1979), Stine and Wingfield (1987), and others have reported that age differences in the learning and recall of prose are smaller for individuals with substantial verbal ability than for people who are less verbally skilled. This would be expected in the terms of our current discussion, if raised verbal ability reduced the demands on cognitive capacity in this task, perhaps as a result of increased facility through accumulated experience. The meta-analysis by Zelinski and Gilewski (1988) of 36 studies in this area confirmed the general conclusion: Observed cross-sectional age decrements were reliably greater in studies comparing low-verbal participants than in those comparing high-verbal ones (see also Hartley, 1989).

The studies of learning and memory illustrated in this section have in common the explicit assessment of information storage and retrieval, usually in circumstances in which processing capacity is exceeded. Results presented here make it clear that age decrements in such tasks are typically observed, although their magnitude is not always great within the working population.

However, learning may also be demonstrated in other ways, when information is memorized as part of another activity. Such "implicit" activities are in several ways different from the explicit forms of learning considered so far (Hultsch & Dixon, 1990; Reber, 1989; Schacter, 1987), and it may be that implicit information processing is relatively less impaired in older people. A finding that older people are less able than younger people to recall material that has been explicitly presented for learning does not necessarily indicate that they have acquired no information. People are not always able to verbalize what they have learned.

Implicit learning is very common in work and other tasks, but being outside consciousness, it is difficult to investigate in everyday situations. Instead, it has been studied in the laboratory in terms of *repetition priming,* being indexed by a subsequent reduction in response time to previously presented stimuli. For example, individuals might first be asked to name as quickly as possible the objects presented to them in pictures. Subsequent (explicit) recall tests are likely to show that older people have a poorer storage and retrieval of the identity of the objects. However, older people may respond just as quickly as younger people to subsequent presentations of the original pictures for naming, while being slower at identifying newly presented pictures. There is some sense in which they have remembered the earlier stimuli, even though they cannot explicitly recall them.

Several studies have suggested that age decrements in this form of implicit memory (where people cannot verbalize what they have learned) are either small or nonexistent (Hashtroudi, Chrosniak, & Schwartz, 1991; Howard & Howard, 1989; D. B. Mitchell, 1989). Given that everyday activities provide many opportunities for implicit learning, as well as require intentional time-limited activities of the kind investigated in the laboratory, it may be that age declines in learning in daily life are overall less marked than indicated by experimental research using direct measures of learning alone.

This topic is complicated by the fact that research results are influenced by a range of factors not yet fully understood. In some circumstances, an age decrement in implicit learning has been found (Howard, Fry, & Brune, 1991; Hultsch, Masson, & Small, 1991), but the conditions associated with different findings are not yet clear (cf. Hashtroudi et al., 1991). One possibility is that older people's implicit learning is slower than younger people's (as is their explicit learning), so that more extended practice is required.

Most laboratory research into learning has focused on discrete facts that must be memorized under time constraints. However, a great deal of adult learning serves to increase a network of understanding, rather than increase the number of separate items in a memory store. In these cases, factual knowledge is already present, and new learning involves the interpretation and assimilation of material within that framework, perhaps extended across time and as a result of social interaction and idiosyncratic questioning.

Limited evidence from studies of *guided discovery learning*, which will be discussed later, suggests that age decrements may not be substantial when workers set out to understand complex processes by means of interactive questioning to fill gaps in their own understanding. Such a possibility is consistent with the widespread importance of type A activities. Older people retain or expand their crystallized or practical intelligence, and this can be applied without age decrement to enhance understanding of new processes within current domains of knowledge. However, as with other activities described here, older people are disadvantaged if the form of learning has to be carried out with severe time constraints.

Physical Health.   Finally in this section, let us consider the relevance of physical health or ill health to age differences in information processing. Type C and D activities in Table 6 are defined as those in which basic capacities are exceeded. Such capacities have physiological underpinnings (unidentified in most cases) and tend to decline with age. It is possible that certain forms of physical ill health will be associated with greater decline in these basic capacities and, through them, with poorer information processing. Particular attention has focused on cardiovascular illnesses, which may affect cortical blood flow or the death of brain cells, but research has also looked more widely at the possible impact of physical ill health of other kinds.

Some studies have compared healthy individuals with patients who have coronary heart disease, for whom medical data are already available. In a number of samples, nonpatients exhibited faster reaction times, but in other cases they did not (Baltes et al., 1984; Birren et al., 1980; Salthouse, 1985a). The influence of physical ill health on speed of responding may be more pronounced in elderly groups than it is among people who are still in the labor market (Milligan, Powell, Harley, & Furchtgott, 1984), or observed differences may depend on the severity of the ill health in question.

Hertzog, Schaie, and Gribbin (1978) examined longitudinal associations between cardiovascular disease and deterioration in intellectual functioning across a wide age range. Significant associations were found with several, but not all, cognitive tests, but some analyses were limited by small sample sizes resulting from the tendency of less healthy people to withdraw from the study (see also Schaie, 1983a, 1989). In a general review of physical fitness, aging, and psychomotor speed, Spirduso (1980) drew attention to probable psychomotor benefits flowing from physical activity and concluded that a positive relationship is likely to exist despite the unavailability of directly confirmative evidence.

Recent research with healthy volunteers has more strongly indicated that defined neurological factors can account for much of the age-related decline in cognitive processes. For example, Houx, Vreeling, and Jolles (1991) distinguished between people who had been exposed to processes which might damage optimal brain functioning and people not affected by such factors. Factors defined as neurologically damaging included recurrent migraine, epilepsy, head injury, frequent exposure to general anesthesia, and heavy consumption of alcohol. Age-related decrements for those between the ages of 20 and 80 on several cognitive tasks were substantially greater for the former group; age differences were very small for the neurologically healthy individuals.

Interindividual differences in aerobic fitness, assessed in terms of lung functioning, have been examined among male British white collar workers by Bunce, Warr, and Cochrane (1993). The frequency of mental blocks in a choice reaction time task was found to increase between the ages of 17 and 63, and that increase was significantly greater for unfit individuals than it was for men who were relatively more fit. Future research is likely to identify more precisely the physiological bases of different kinds of age-dependent cognitive processes.

Type C Activities:
Capacity Reduction and Gains
Through Experience

So far, this review of cognitive performance has examined the two extreme categories in Table 6. In the case of type A activities, basic capacities are not exceeded and performance is enhanced by experience; a positive association between performance and age is therefore expected. The opposite is true for type D activities, in which basic capacities, declining with age, are increasingly exceeded and experience cannot help a person compensate for them.

Most real-life activities fall within the remaining two categories in Table 6. In type C situations, basic capacities are exceeded more at older ages, so that, as with type D activities, decrements with age are possible; however, in this case a person is able to use the products of previous experience to cope with his or her deficiencies. There is a continuous interplay

between growth and decline. This joint impact of the two processes has been recognized in the literature for some decades (e.g., Baltes & Baltes, 1990b; Salthouse, 1985b, 1990b) and is frequently visible in work and other situations.

Benefits of Experience. Relevant experience may benefit people in at least five different ways. First is the general development of expertise, in the sense of enriched job knowledge and skills, as discussed earlier with respect to type A activities. Such expertise (associated with years of relevant experience, but not necessarily linearly) permits more appropriate responses to new situations, generates more rapid and accurate decisions, and also frees cognitive capacity to cope with particularly demanding stimuli (e.g., Charness & Bosman, 1990; Glaser, 1988).

Second, in terms of category C activities, older individuals may be able to compensate for certain limitations through specific learned behaviors or other gains. For example, an older person may take written notes to compensate for possible memory limitations; experience may have given rise to more effective time management, compensating for reduced energy at older ages; older people may simply work harder for brief periods in order to keep up with their younger colleagues; and such aids as eye glasses and hearing aids can help reduce the problems brought about by sensory deterioration.

Older people's successful compensation in cognitive activities has been documented in relation to chess playing and transcription typing. In chess playing, Charness (e.g., 1989) points out that successs depends heavily on an individual's ability to think ahead, which in turn makes continuing demands on working memory. He has shown that, among equivalently skilled players, older people have a poorer memory for chess positions than younger people. On the other hand, older players were found to be equally good at choosing the best moves from specified chess positions. They searched less widely (although they looked ahead to the same extent as younger players), and as a result of this more economical (and more rapid) procedure they were as effective as younger players, despite some memory deficits associated with age.

Salthouse (1984) examined the performance on several tasks of experienced typists aged between 19 and 72. Consistent with findings summarized earlier in relation to type D activities, older typists were found to respond more slowly in a serial choice reaction time task and in digit-symbol substitution. However, there was no age difference in actual typing speed. By manipulating the length of preview available (the number of characters visible ahead of the current position), Salthouse showed that older typists in this experienced group looked farther ahead than their younger counterparts. On average, typists in their 60s had an extra 300 milliseconds of preparation time in comparison with typists in their 20s.

These findings "suggest that one mechanism used to compensate for declining perceptual-motor speed with increased age is more extensive anticipation of impending keystrokes" (Salthouse, 1984, p. 356). From results of a later study, Salthouse and Saults (1987) emphasized that this form of compensation by older typists is contingent upon them being extensively experienced in the task. Research into the reading and transcription of text by Marquié and Paumes (1988) has also pointed to the greater use of anticipation by older people (mean age, 53 years).

A third possible consequence of relevant experience is behavioral accommodation, in which individuals alter their activities to avoid situations that might reveal defects (e.g. Salthouse, 1990a). For example, older employees may have progressed into positions from which they can delegate activities in which they are relatively ineffective. In extreme cases, accommodation can be seen in the selective migration of older workers out of jobs that they have come to find difficult.

Fourth, experience may suggest ways through which a particular goal can be achieved by new methods. For instance, a specific task may be treated as less important to goal attainment, as other, more manageable, procedures are employed. Alternatively, the duration or sequencing of tasks may be modified to remain within an older person's cognitive or physical capacity.

Finally, processes of cognitive compilation may occur with increased experience, as higher-order or more automatic skills are assembled to become relatively independent of difficult lower-order procedures, as described in the earlier discussion of procedural knowledge; age-related declines in lower-order procedures may occur in parallel with the maintenance of effective higher-order skills. For example, only about one third of the speeding up that Charness and Campbell (1988) observed in a two-digit mental squaring task was due to faster execution of elementary arithmetic operations; most of the increase in speed resulted from people learning how to chain together the subgoals quickly and efficiently.

The precise outcomes from the opposed influence of declining capacities and increasing experience in type C activities will depend on the relative strength of each in the particular behavior under study. Research into this category is rather sparse. Nevertheless, in many employment situations, age patterns are often likely to fall into the type C category, where performance is stabilized by relevant experience, rather than the type D category, where experience cannot compensate for impaired capacities.

Remedial Training. Both type C and D activities, in which basic capacities are exceeded more at older ages, have been shown to be open to improvement through brief training interventions. For instance, Schaie and Willis (1986) provided five hours of training to improve the inductive reasoning or spatial orientation of elderly people (mean age 73 years); relevant rules were taught and opportunities for practice were provided (see also Willis & Schaie, 1986). Significant improvements were found in immediate post-tests in both cases. Baltes, Dittmann-Kohli, and Kliegl (1986) reported that beneficial training effects were retained six months after a training intervention. The investigation by Anderson, Hartley, Bye, Harber, and White (1986) suggested that older people (average age 71) showed benefits that were proportionately as large as younger trainees (age 41). This approximate equivalence of gains in cognitive test scores at different ages was also suggested by Willis' (1987) review of the field. However, findings to date point to rather limited generalizability of training benefits (e.g., Baltes et al., 1986). Training focused on specific aspects of information processing appears to improve only the aspects emphasized.

Research into the training of fluid intelligence and similar processing activities (mainly for people retired from the labor force) has been reviewed by Berg and Sternberg (1985), Dixon et al. (1985), Poon (1985), Salthouse (1985b, 1987), Willis (1985, 1987, 1989b), Willis and Schaie (1986), and others. Denney's (1984, 1989) model of cognitive development distinguishes between unexercised potential and optimally exercised potential. *Unexercised potential* refers to a person's performance in the absence of practice or training, and *optimally exercised potential* is predicted after maximum training. The gap between the two levels can be bridged through learning and training. Denney points out that different abilities will be subject to different learning opportunities as well as to different degrees of decline, so that many different patterns of development are possible. Her model accounts for both increases and decreases in cognitive performance with increasing age.

Charness (1989) has illustrated the potential impact of training in type C activities by estimating the amount of practice necessary to bring an average older person to the same performance level as that of an average younger adult. Examining published findings for digit-symbol substitution (one of the laboratory tasks that is particularly age-sensitive), he concludes that age effects on this task can be eliminated by allowing three minutes of practice for every year of age difference. Thus, an average 60-year-old can equal the performance of the average 20-year-old on this task after three hours of practice.

Type B Activities: No Changes With Age

Finally, what about type B activities, those for which capacities are not exceeded, and experience yields no benefit? In these very common activities, variations occurring across the different age groups are not expected.

This uniform performance at different ages is regularly found in quite easy tasks. For instance, primary memory is apparently unaffected by age: Older people are as able as their younger counterparts to retain in memory small amounts of information (within their span of primary memory) that are being used in uncomplicated cognitive activities (e.g., Poon, 1985). Furthermore, while increased age is associated with slower learning of new material, it is unrelated to the speed of forgetting material after it has been acquired (Rabitt & Maylor, 1991). Age differences are also absent in what Miles (1933) described as *spontaneous imagination,* generating ideas based on ambiguous stimuli.

In certain more difficult cognitive tasks, increases in experience are assumed to cancel out a potential age decline (type C), or some age-related deterioration might be anticipated (type D). Task characteristics giving rise to this deterioration with increasing age have sometimes been discussed in terms of the *complexity effect.*

Figure 1 presents the results of Kay's (1954) laboratory study of problem solving. Research

FIGURE 1

The Relationship Between Age, Total Errors, and Degree of Difficulty

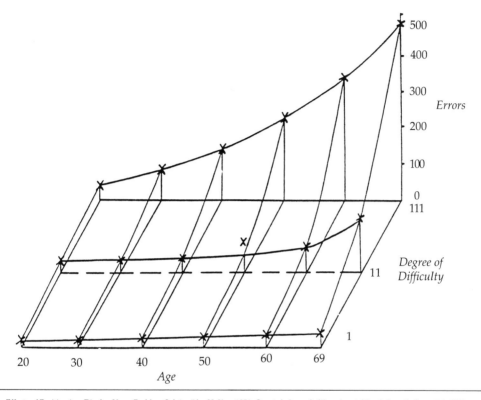

participants were required to learn the relationships between the position of lights (in a series of 12) and particular response buttons, using the transformation code on a separate strip of card. The card was presented in three different locations, giving rise to different degrees of difficulty in each case. As the figure illustrates, at the lowest level of difficulty, people of all ages could perform the task equally well. At the intermediate difficulty level, a small age effect became apparent; and at the third level, older people were particularly ineffective.

The easiest form of the task in this framework might be thought to be of the type B category, with responses being within people's basic capacities at all ages. The complexity effect is illustrated through increasing information processing loads in conditions two and three, with greater age decrements in performance occurring in proportion to the difficulty of the task.

In a similar manner, Morris, Craik, and Gick (1990) reported age differences in working memory performance, with an age-related decrement that became greater with increasing task difficulty. This pattern has been observed in many other situations (e.g., Charness, 1985; Gick et al., 1988; McDowd & Craik, 1988; Madden, 1990; Myerson et al., 1990; Salthouse, 1985b; Welford, 1958). The complexity effect is methodologically important, in that apparently contradictory findings in different investigations may in practice be due to variations in the difficulty of the task being studied. For our purposes, it serves to make the point that type C activities can easily become type D activities (where capacities are exceeded) as a result of a task's increasing complexity.

More generally, it appears that age decrements occur primarily when cognitive tasks of any kind require information processing that is especially complex. The nature of *complexity* is at present ill-defined. Tasks that are more complex might involve a greater number of processing stages, or increased complexity may derive from the required cognitive manipulation of increased amounts of information. Another perspective takes into consideration the extent to which required cognitive processes are either internally generated or are supported by the environment, as in recognition or relearning tasks. In the absence of external support, greater demands are placed on a person through the need, for instance, to retrieve information without external cues or to operate entirely "within the head." Such an absence of environmental support may generate another form of complexity, associated with the finding that it is internally generated processing activities that are particularly subject to negative age effects (e.g., Craik, 1990). In practice, these three characteristics of tasks (number of stages, amount of material, and absence of environmental

support) tend to be intercorrelated so that the specific reasons for this general "complexity effect" remain difficult to define.

Cognitive Performance: An Overview

Laboratory research into cognitive performance at different ages has made it clear that age gradients differ considerably between different tasks. In many cases, there are improvements with increasing age (type A activities in the current framework), and in a large number of activities (type B and type C), no age decrements are expected within the working population. These three categories of activity are likely to encompass the majority of tasks undertaken in almost any job; additional examples have been considered in the section on job performance.

Nevertheless, some type D activities (where a decrement in maximum performance is exhibited with increasing age) are present in all jobs, and laboratory research has examined this category of behavior in particular. From the extensive research summarized in this section, can we make a general statement about the average magnitude of decline that occurs during the working years in the activities known to be affected by age? Such activities are especially likely to make high demands on working memory and to introduce heavy time pressure.

Specifying an average age gradient in these tasks is difficult for a number of reasons. First, the magnitude of decrement is a function of the complexity of the task being studied, and complexity has varied unsystematically between studies. For exceedingly complex cognitive tasks under time pressure, there is more likely to be a marked difference between age groups than there is for simple tasks, especially within the age range of employed people. Second, cross-sectional investigations point to a greater decrement than do longitudinal studies. We need to determine which information is more acceptable in a particular setting. Third, the metric employed to specify age differences varies between tasks and studies, and it is not possible to integrate different results to produce an overall statement about average changes that occur with age.

It is also difficult to reach a conclusion about the importance of the decrements that have been found in laboratory investigations. In part, this concerns the difference between statistical and practical significance. In many studies, the variation between scores from different age groups, although statistically significant, is extremely small, and it may have no practical consequences. Conversely, the combination in practical situations of a number of small differences could sometimes be extremely important.

Extending this point, what can be said about the implications of laboratory findings of decrements in type D activities for work behavior? There has so far been very little research in job settings regarding age differences that occur in specific cognitive processes of the kind described here. Few attempts have been made to map onto work performance those activities that reveal a negative age gradient in the laboratory, although it is clear that they are central to some kinds of jobs. There is now a need for cognitive job analyses and investigations of age gradients in key cognitive activities among people working in those jobs (Warr & Conner, 1992).

Even in cases where age decrements are observed in cognitive processes considered to be important in a job, successful job performance still derives from more than basic information processing activities. Effective work behavior also involves appropriate social interactions, requisite motivation, and sustained energy input, as well as integrated processes of long-term planning and self-management. Prolonged competence over a period of work may be more important in a job than rapid information processing on a brief task. As pointed out by Heron and Chown (1967, p. 138), "within wide limits [cognitive test scores] probably bear little relation to a man's ability to perform many real-life tasks, just as measures of 'health' tell little about a man's capacity to do his job unless his condition is markedly abnormal." It would thus be incorrect to infer from a negative age gradient in a specific cognitive activity that older employees are overall less effective in their jobs.

Nevertheless, the decrements (as well as the increments) reviewed here are certain to have some implications for job performance. There is currently a need to develop a greater interchange between laboratory and organizational investigators and to identify and interpret age-related variations in cognitive processing in jobs whose key cognitive components have been defined. For example, there would be great value in studies that seek to account in multiple regression analyses for an age-related decline in job performance through interindividual variations in particular cognitive, as well as motivational and interpersonal, processes.

The Influence of Jobs on Aging

Studies reviewed in earlier sections have focused primarily on the ways in which age-related processes can affect behavior and attitudes at work: What age differences exist at work, and how can they be explained? Most attention has focused on influences identified at the beginning of the chapter as normative age-graded, although opportunities for individuals to derive benefits from their idiosyncratic experience have also been stressed. Causal processes in the reverse direction are also important: How do jobs affect the processes of aging? The emphasis here is on nonnormative influences, seeking to account for observed interindividual variation arising from the different conditions of employment.

In that way, Teiger (1989) has distinguished between "natural" aging in work and aging "induced" by work, emphasizing that some jobs can make employees physiologically or psychologically older than would otherwise be the case. Conversely, workers in certain positions might be supported and developed by their jobs, so that the aging process is in some ways slowed down.

This perspective is becoming more widely important in gerontological research. Aging, as evidenced by changes in physiological and psychological functioning, is not determined solely by a standard set of factors that give rise to an unalterable rate of change; changes occurring during the life course are influenced by social and physical environments and by psychological processes underpinning a person's interactions with those environments (e.g., Abeles & Riley, 1987; Labouvie-Vief, 1985). Some environments are more conducive to successful aging than are others (Baltes & Baltes, 1990b).

Environmental differences are likely to contribute to the increased variability in cognitive performance between people that is regularly observed with increasing age. In cases where a negative age gradient exists in terms of average values, the older subsample necessarily contains more low scorers, but it is not unusual for some older people to be as effective as the best performing young person (e.g., Rabbitt, 1991). This increased interindividual variability is likely to have developed slowly over a number of years.

In examining possible influences on the pace of aging, we are in part concerned with the consequences of long-term exposure to certain forms of environmental demands and opportunities. The centrality of paid employment in most people's lives means that certain features of jobs can have substantial impacts on mental health and development (e.g., Warr, 1987). However, jobs are located in the broader network of a socioeconomic structure, and it is difficult to extract solely occupational influences

from those arising from a person's place in that structure. For example, unskilled workers in comparison with professional workers tend to live in greater poverty, have more exposure to stressors, and have less healthy lifestyles and eating habits. They are subject not only to particular job conditions but also to this wider set of sociocultural processes.

Evidence about the long-term influence of jobs on aging thus tends to be indirect; no longitudinal study with appropriate controls and comparison groups has been undertaken. However, significant positive associations between extended job experience and individual expertise have been demonstrated in several studies. It is also clear that short-term training interventions can improve intellectual functioning, and we may envisage that some job holders are exposed to intellectual stimulation throughout their careers, whereas others work in roles that require more limited cognitive activity.

Environmental Complexity. This difference has sometimes been discussed in terms of the environmental complexity provided by different jobs. Complex environments expose a person to more varied stimuli, require more decisions and the consideration of more features in making those decisions, and contain greater ambiguity than do simple environments (e.g., Schooler, 1987). By presenting more challenges and requiring more complicated information processing and activity, complex environments embody the types of experience and training that have been shown earlier to assist cognitive functioning across the life span.

Cross-sectional and longitudinal research has pointed to the causal importance of this aspect of jobs. Kohn and Schooler (1983) have summarized an extensive program in which several forms of intellectual flexibility were found to be influenced by the complexity of a person's current job and one the person held ten years previously. Avolio and Waldman (1987) examined the correlations between age and cognitive functioning in workers (aged 19 to 62) defined as being exposed to different degrees of intellectual stimulation in their work. Within a single American company, skilled and unskilled employees were compared on a range of tests, including verbal, numerical, and mechanical reasoning. Negative correlations with age (holding constant level of education) were significantly greater for the unskilled group (exposed to less complex work environments) than for the skilled workers; for example, values were –0.28 versus –0.05, respectively, for numerical reasoning.

In secondary analyses of data collected for 111 different test validation studies, Avolio and Waldman (1990) defined the complexity of nonmanagerial jobs on the basis of inferences derived from job titles rather than through examination of the content of each job itself. Correlations between job holders' age (between 18 and 74) and scores on general cognitive ability did not differ according to this very indirect measure of environmental complexity. However, negative correlations between age and cognitive ability did vary between different categories of occupation. Clerical workers exhibited the lowest associations (median $r = -0.06$), whereas the value for service employees (e.g., salespeople, drivers) was –0.19. These data, collected from many separate investigations, are potentially subject to unreliability of several kinds, and (as the authors point out) longitudinal processes of self-selection cannot be excluded from this kind of study; furthermore, results are so far difficult to interpret. However, the approach of viewing differential aging as a function of particular job characteristics is a promising one, and additional investigations would be worthwhile. Potential impacts on personality as well as cognitive variables should be examined.

A related, simple example was provided by LaRiviere and Simonson (1965). They recorded the maximum speed with which people between 40 and 69 could copy a sheet of one-digit numbers. For manual laborers and managers, speed of writing was significantly negatively associated with age, but for clerical workers (who practice this task regularly in their jobs), no cross-sectional decrement was shown to exist with increasing age. A similar finding has been reported by Smith and Greene (1962).

Differential aging as a result of long-term exposure to particular job conditions may be seen more dramatically in terms of potential impacts on physical health. One set of investigations has focused particularly on the health consequences of shiftworking. For example, in an Austrian study, Koller (1983) compared shiftworkers between the ages of 25 and 50 against day workers who had similar lengths of work experience. The health of both groups was found to decline cross-sectionally with age, but the deterioration was greater for the shiftworkers. Older shiftworkers were particularly prone to circulatory and digestive ailments (see also Rutenfranz, Haider, & Koller, 1985; Teiger, 1989). Knutsson, Akerstedt, Jonsson, and Orth-Gomer (1986) examined ischemic heart disease in Swedish shiftworkers and day workers. Although no differences were found in groups with less than 10 years of shiftwork experience, significantly higher rates of heart disease were observed among longer-term shiftworkers than comparable day workers.

In addition to the practical importance of learning more about the influence of jobs on differential rates of aging, this area is of particular theoretical interest. Research into issues of the kind illustrated here will require more careful attention to the definition of key features of successful aging. It will also be necessary to specify more precisely possible pathways of influence across time, from particular long-term environmental features (including those in jobs) to aspects of physiological and psychological functioning.

Currently, knowledge and theory in this area are limited.

Organizational Policies and Procedures

How should organizations respond to changing technological conditions and demographic shifts in the labor force? As pointed out earlier, jobs increasingly require cognitive rather than physical skills, and there will be a growing need for a work force that is more educated and trained than was previously the case. There may be sufficient numbers of job applicants, but competition for the best workers will often be severe.

For example, companies accustomed to tapping into a regular pool of young applicants may have difficulty attracting adequately capable new recruits from that age group. Effective women employees may be available but not interested in the company's traditional work hours. Many women returning to paid employment after a period spent away from the labor force while caring for children may also lack necessary skills; personnel selection schemes will frequently need to be strengthened to identify the minority of applicants who can most benefit from training to qualify for particular positions. Similarly, older male applicants may have work experience that does not translate directly to new positions, and their suitability for retraining may need behavioral and/or psychometric investigation.

The general need is therefore to confront both the changing demographic structure and recent changes in the nature of work. Organizations require human resources policies that address the needs of older workers. Such organizational policies embrace a wide range of traditional concerns, including health and safety, communications, and working conditions. In this chapter, we should concentrate on issues that specifically concern different age groups.

An essential first step is for companies to think through their personnel requirements and investigate likely developments in the local labor market. This should be linked with actions that will be summarized shortly, to yield an overall strategy for the employment of older people and other demographic groups. For example, should primary emphasis be placed on retraining current employees to meet changing job needs, or should companies seek to attract new employees who have particular attributes they are interested in? Can appropriately trained staff be recruited from elsewhere, or will it be necessary to create new training procedures? If the emphasis is to be placed on enhancing the skills of current staff in a highly competitive labor market, what changes will be necessary in career development and other procedures? How should the increasing number of part-time employees be addressed in terms of changed organizational systems and working hours? Should the company compete more vigorously for the best workers among new entrants to the labor market, or should it focus primarily on older people? The costs and benefits of these and other approaches need to be assessed.

The development and content of age-related organizational policies in this area have been discussed by Dennis (1988), Humple and Lyons (1983), Meier (1988), Robinson (1983), Rosen and Jerdee (1985), Sonnenfeld (1978), and others. The need to be better informed about age discrimination legislation is typically emphasized, as is the value of examining the organization's current age structure (sometimes referred to as carrying out an "age audit"). Explicit statements about the company's attitude toward older staff should be introduced, together with the necessary training of key managers in the policy's rationale and accompanying procedures. Key facts about the normal aging process need to be disseminated and discussed with employees. Programs of preretirement planning are increasingly recommended to assist employees and to maximize the probability of attracting and retaining high-quality workers.

Human Resources Management

Issues considered in this chapter are likely to give particular impetus to the creation of more sophisticated procedures at the heart of human resource management. Decisions about personnel selection, retention, and promotion need to be soundly based and publicly defensible, especially with respect to older people. Many applicants for newly developed jobs will have no directly relevant experience that can assist in personnel selection decision making. It will therefore be essential to develop and validate effective procedures for carrying out individual testing and appraisal, based on careful job analyses and the identification of employee attributes required for specific activities (see the earlier discussion on functional age). Selection and placement decisions can then more effectively match individuals to tasks, irrespective of their age. Within this area, companies will sometimes need to examine evidence about the validity of particular forms of selection instruments at different ages; it seems likely from the pattern of cognitive age differences reviewed earlier that validity coefficients for some psychometric measures may differ significantly between age groups.

It would be useful to specify the types of cognitive activities required in key jobs that might be filled by older workers. Cognitive job analyses can identify task demands likely to be problematic for some older people so that appropriate selection, training, or job redesign initiatives can be taken. More generally, jobs should be examined to identify their degree of suitability for older employees, beginning with the recognition that older people are more widely capable than some stereotypes about them might suggest.

Many companies should particularly investigate their performance appraisal and career development practices. In addition to permitting greater effectiveness in personnel decision making as a whole, such a review might help retain older staff who have demonstrated an ability to meet company objectives, and might support discussions of possible retirement with those who have proven to be less productive. Effective older employees might continue in their present jobs, or find that lateral transfers or temporary positions can be valuable in enhancing motivation and learning. Productive and satisfying career development for employees in their 40s and older can be encouraged by regular performance reviews (say, every five years) that explicitly consider the possibility of such lateral moves. Improved assessments of actual competence in job settings will increasingly be needed, both to practice sound human resource management and to address instances of alleged age, racial, gender, and other discrimination.

Within an overview of personnel procedures, consideration should be given to the possibility of redesigning some aspects of work identified to be potentially troublesome for older employees. Standard ergonomic investigations of lighting, posture, displays, and controls are likely to be particularly helpful for older employees. In addition, cognitive analyses, in terms of typical and maximum loads on working memory, information processing speed, and so on, can lead to task or equipment modifications that reduce the probability of age-related differences in performance (e.g., Fozard, 1981).

Training

Particular attention should be given to training older staff. This is likely to become more pressing, both in order to prepare current employees to meet the demands of new working procedures, and to enable recent recruits to reach the required standards in work they are unfamiliar with. As emphasized previously, cognitive skills are increasingly needed at work, while physical competence is less significant than previously (e.g., Downs, 1985; Rosen & Jerdee, 1985).

Older workers tend to see themselves as unsuited to substantial new learning and lack confidence in training situations (e.g., Plett & Lester, 1991; Sterns, 1986). Belbin and Belbin (1972) have examined in detail the anxieties of older trainees and suggested ways in which the confidence of these workers might be raised. In general, however, older workers do not learn as quickly as their younger colleagues (e.g., R. M. Belbin, 1965; Sterns & Doverspike, 1989). Paced instruction, where speed of information transmission is beyond a trainee's control, is particularly problematic for older workers, as would be expected from the research into cognitive performance we have already reviewed. Most learning situations exceed people's capacity to process and store all the material provided (type C and D activities in Tables 5 and 6). However, it is clear from the success of training itself and from studies of the enhancement of fluid intelligence in elderly people (see the review of type C activities) that, given appropriate opportunities, older as well as younger employees can acquire additional job skills and perform effectively in new kinds of work. Furthermore, there is no evidence that older workers forget their new knowledge and skills at a faster rate than younger workers, in circumstances where continuing practice can maintain the standard of performance (Charness & Bosman, 1990; Rabbitt & Maylor, 1991).

A topical concern is with information technology training. In addition to the need for advanced courses of a technical or professional kind, basic use of computer and word processing equipment has become central to many jobs. Recent research has compared the performance of younger and older people in the acquisition of skills of this kind.

For example, Elias, Elias, Robbins, and Gage (1987) compared three groups of learners (aged 18 to 28, 37 to 48, and 55 to 67, respectively) in the acquisition of word processing skills.

Training was self-paced, with an instructor available to give advice throughout the training. No differences were observed in training time, assistance sought, or examination performance between the two younger groups. However, the older trainees were significantly worse in all these respects, by a factor of approximately one-third. Similar findings have been reported by Gist, Rosen, and Schwoerer (1988); see also Czaja (1988) and Sterns and Doverspike (1989).

Note that, in addition to possible age-related deterioration, a cohort effect is particularly likely to be found in relation to information technology. Recently educated young people will already have become more skilled and confident with computers than older employees, who are often experienced only with earlier forms of equipment.

What processes are likely to contribute to greater difficulty in learning as one becomes older? Reduced information processing capacities and a general cognitive slowing have already been described, as have older trainees' anxiety and lower self-confidence as learners (see also Charness, Schumann, & Boritz, 1992). The special value of external information aids for older learners is suggested by the laboratory research mentioned earlier; information processing that is to be done entirely in the head can be particularly difficult for older employees.

Older learners are sometimes at an initial disadvantage in that they lack underlying knowledge that trainers normally take for granted. For example, some older employees may not have a basic knowledge of the terminology and operation of a computer-linked keyboard. Competence in that respect is widespread among young cohorts, arising from their previous experiences, but older people's initial lack of basic knowledge (if not corrected) may prevent them from progressing rapidly in training. It is thus essential for employers to ensure that opportunities for advanced familiarization are provided when necessary. Older trainees are able to acquire the necessary basic knowledge quite readily, and such an initial gain also helps reduce their anxiety. Training is provided relatively infrequently for older employees, and the initial anxiety they experience in an unfamiliar setting needs to be addressed.

Problems of unlearning initial errors have been stressed by E. Belbin (1964), R. M. Belbin (1965), and Belbin and Belbin (1972). Consistent with laboratory research by Kay (1951), these authors argued that older people were better able to learn if their activities were constrained so that errors were minimized early in the process. A careful start was therefore advisable, allowing trainees to experience early success, rather than making mistakes that would be difficult to eradicate later. This procedure has the advantage of sustaining confidence as well as minimizing potential negative interference.

Cumulative (or progressive) part learning is an associated control over material to be learned. E. Belbin (1964) and Belbin and Belbin (1972) have suggested that older learners gain particular benefit if material is broken down into successive segments. They recommend that presentation and practice should be first given in terms of the initial segment, then that initial segment and the next segment, then the first three segments, and so on. In some cases, this will be best achieved through the creation of special learning tasks, embodying controlled simulations of parts of the overall activity. Abstract concepts should be presented through the use of concrete and familiar examples, and training should develop out of individuals' prior knowledge and experience.

It is possible that older learners have more difficulty than younger ones transferring their new skills to tasks that appear to be novel, even though the underlying features may be similar (Myers & Conner, 1992). If so, it is particularly important to provide training in a variety of interconnected tasks so that the potential for widespread transfer is similar at all ages.

Older trainees may gain special benefit from guided activity (or discovery) learning.

This approach creates situations in which individuals are encouraged to learn by finding out principles and relationships for themselves; the emphasis is on active learning rather than through verbal or physical instruction. Material to be learned must be structured and introduced by instructors in ways that recognize the issues addressed in previous paragraphs, and trainees should be guided in their understanding of processes and interrelationships rather than being required only to memorize facts. Discovery learning can be encouraged by asking trainees to generate and answer questions about the subject matter, rather than merely presenting them with information to be learned. Their answers to personally relevant questions will permit them to build on individual experience, and a successful process of discovery can give rise to a shift from the experience of extrinsic rewards to more intrinsic achievements (e.g., Knowles, 1984).

Discovery learning has been shown to be helpful in the training of older workers by E. Belbin (1964), R. M. Belbin (1965, 1969), Belbin and Downs (1964), Mullan and Gorman (1972), and Sterns and Doverspike (1989), and the detailed suggestions made by these authors deserve further consideration. However, although significant beneficial results of guided discovery learning have been observed among older groups, the investigations published to date leave it unclear whether the benefit is differentially greater for older trainees than it is for younger people. It may be the case that discovery learning is equally helpful for trainees of all ages.

Older employees are often out of the practice of learning itself, and they may need help relearning how to learn. Their potential learning ability can be much greater than the actual ability they exhibit when they first begin training. Perry and Downs (1985) have considered a number of procedures to develop the learning skills of people (for instance, through the use of self-questioning, time management, and hypothesis testing), and these procedures are particularly helpful for older people.

However, one form of learning to learn was found by Czaja and Drury (1981) not to reduce the difference in learning performance between older and younger trainees. In a simulated industrial inspection task, half of the learners received pertraining in organizing incoming material for better learning. Although this pretraining improved learning performance in expected ways, the performance of older trainees remained at a significantly lower level than it did for younger trainees. Age-group differences were as great as they were when no learning-to-learn pretraining was provided.

Older employees have also been found to need more time in psychotherapy than younger employees. In a study of professional and managerial workers experiencing job-related depression and/or anxiety, Barkham, Firth-Cozens, and Shapiro (1989) found that the older clients responded more slowly and made less progress during therapy. Cognitive and motivational factors underlying this difference may be similar to those introduced earlier.

Looking more widely at companies' policies and programs for older employees, it is important not to forget broad-range training for managers and the work force as a whole. Special efforts may be necessary to change attitudes toward older members of the company, to ensure widespread understanding of personnel selection and training policies, and to create a consistent corporate culture that encourages high levels of performance for workers of all ages.

For example, many managers believe that the payback period for recouping the expenditure that their companies make on training is too short for older employees, in that their potential time with the company is shorter than it is for younger people (Thompson, 1991). In practice, however, the lower labor turnover of older employees often means that training investments are especially cost-effective in their case.

There is sometimes tacit collusion between older and younger staff memnbers of a company, encouraging the belief that training should be reserved for younger workers. Older workers' motivation for learning and self-development can be enhanced through lateral transfers or fixed-term projects that expose them to new challenges and activities. The factors limiting their learning primarily concern expectations and corporate norms rather than major deficits in information processing abilities.

Incentives for training and procedures to encourage older workers to undertake new learning should also be reviewed.

Nontraditional Working Arrangements

Company policymakers in this area should also consider alternative working arrangements. In order to attract valuable employees in times of scarcity, it may be necessary to introduce more varying types of employment contracts. Part-time work is widely popular among women workers and may become increasingly attractive for older workers of both sexes, both prior to and after formal retirement. Allowing employees to take career breaks to care for young children or other relatives can sometimes help employers retain valued staff members.

Other nontraditional options include "rehearsal retirement" (allowing older employees to take an unpaid leave of absence without the accrual of benefits; e.g., Humple & Lyons, 1983), or phased retirement, which permits employees to gradually reduce their work hours (e.g., Meier, 1988). In some circumstances, retired people might be hired on a part-time basis, or for specific projects, or for particular periods of time. For example, a number of companies have created their own internal employment agencies to recruit, hire, and (if necessary) train retirees to fill temporary employment needs. The quality of work from such employees is reported to be extremely high (Libassi, 1988).

The policy mix will, of course, vary between companies and particular local labor markets. In some cases, procedures adopted to meet specific objectives will have the general benefit of signaling to potential recruits that the company is a caring employer with whom they might want to be associated. To ensure that the policy is effectively developed and comprehensively applied, a senior manager or director should be made responsible for all the company's activities in this area.

Concluding Remarks

In looking back on the large amount of research that has been examined in this chapter, two general themes may be noted. The first concerns the location of psychologists' investigations into aging; these have most commonly been undertaken outside organizational settings. The extensive laboratory and psychometric research has undoubtedly advanced our understanding, but perhaps at the expense of giving us a realistic picture. Studies have often focused on abstract information processing in brief, prestructured tasks, and have underemphasized the importance of specialized knowledge, expertise, social relationships, and personal decisions about which working environments should be entered or avoided. The full range of age-related topics in organizational behavior has not been adequately explored.

Two factors suggest that now may be the time to redress this imbalance. First, a sound foundation of research findings is available, as reviewed here. Second, practical impetus for this work comes from the demographic changes described earlier. The concerns of 50 years ago, as described in the chapter's opening paragraph, have returned, and are likely, as then, to promote fresh investigations into this area.

A second theme concerns the growing concern for empirical research that can support causal explanations of observed age differences.

Although many early studies were restricted to bivariate associations between age and a specific variable of interest, researchers have increasingly also investigated other factors, which might be causally responsible for age-related differences in that variable. For instance, job experience, activities that promote particular kinds of expertise, cardiovascular functioning, or aspects of personality have all been considered as possible causal factors in explaining variations in age gradients.

Research into the influence of age is thus becoming more a question of research into the long-term influence of environmental factors, sustained personal behaviors, and physiological changes. These features, extended in time, may covary with age, but not always to a high degree. People of the same age behave and feel very differently, and these variations need to be accounted for in terms of different environmental influences, frequently repeated behaviors, and certain physiological changes. Age gradients may be more (or less) steep for individuals who have specific characteristics or who spend long periods in certain kinds of environments. By investigating a range of potential causal factors, within a specific explanatory model about a given age-related variable, research is more likely to contribute to theoretical progress than has sometimes been the case in the past.

Two perspectives were introduced at the outset in this chapter. In relation to the first question—how does aging affect work behavior and attitudes?—some rephrasing is now required. Beyond the collection of descriptive data about age differences at work, attention is increasingly being focused on possible causal factors underlying the age differences that are found. Researchers' interest increasingly focuses on the question, how are work behavior and attitudes influenced in the long term by particular environmental features, sustained patterns of behavior, and age-related physiological changes? Employee age can be a rough indicator of some of these variables, but the variables also require investigation as potential causal factors in their own right.

The second question—how does work affect aging?—has been examined less often by psychologists. We need to learn about the same sets of potential causal factors as we have explored with the issue of how age affects work behavior and attitudes but with respect to work settings. How do long-term work demands, sustained work behaviors, and the physiological impact of working influence the pace of psychological aging, outside of as well as in employment? Research to answer both questions must, of course, investigate chronological age, but other long-term features should receive greater theoretical and empirical attention than have been the case to date.

References

Abeles, R. P., & Riley, M. W. (1987). Longevity, social structure, and cognitive aging. In C. Schooler & K. W. Schaie (Eds.), *Cognitive functioning and social structure over the life course* (pp. 161–175). Norwood, NJ: Ablex.

Akerstedt, T., & Torsvall, L. (1980). Age, sleep and adjustment to shiftwork. In O. Benoit (Ed.), *Sleep 1980*. Basel, Switzerland: Karger.

Aldwin, C. M. (1991). Does age affect the stress and coping process? Implications of age differences in perceived control. *Journal of Gerontology, 4*, P174–P180.

Anderson, J. R. (1982). Acquisition of cognitive skill. *Psychological Review, 89*, 369–406.

Anderson, J. W., Hartley, A. A., Bye, R., Harber, K. D., & White, O. L. (1986). Cognitive training using self-discovery methods. *Educational Gerontology, 12*, 159–171.

Arbuckle, T. Y., Gold, D., & Andres, D. (1986). Cognitive functioning of older people in relation to social and personality variables. *Psychology and Aging, 1*, 55–62.

Arenberg, D. (1988). Analysis and synthesis in problem solving and aging. In M. L. Howe & C. J. Brainerd (Eds.), *Cognitive development*

in adulthood (pp. 161–183). New York: Springer.

Atchley, R. C. (1979). Issues in retirement research. *The Gerontologist, 19*, 44–54.

Avolio, B. J., & Waldman, D. A. (1987). Personnel aptitude test scores as a function of age, education and job type. *Experimental Aging Research, 13*, 109–113.

Avolio, B. J., & Waldman, D. A. (1990). An examination of age and cognitive test performance across job complexity and occupational types. *Journal of Applied Psychology, 75*, 43–50.

Avolio, B. J., Waldman, D. A., & McDaniel, M. A. (1990). Age and work performance in nonmanagerial jobs: The effects of experience and occupational type. *Academy of Management Journal, 33*, 407–422.

Baddeley, A. D. (1986). *Working memory*. Oxford, UK: Oxford University Press.

Baddeley, A. D., & Hitch, G. J. (1974). Working memory. In G. H. Bower (Ed.), *The psychology of learning and motivation* (Vol. 8, pp. 47–89). New York: Academic Press.

Baltes, P. B. (1968). Longitudinal and cross-sectional sequences in the study of age and generation effects. *Human Development, 11*, 145–171.

Baltes, P. B. (1991). The many faces of human aging: Toward a psychological culture of old age. *Psychological Medicine, 21*, 837–854.

Baltes, P. B., & Baltes, M. M. (1990a). Psychological perspectives on successful aging: The model of selective optimization with compensation. In P. B. Baltes & M. M. Baltes (Eds.), *Successful aging* (pp. 1–34). Cambridge, UK: Cambridge University Press.

Baltes, P. B., & Baltes, M. M. (Eds.). (1990b). *Successful aging*. Cambridge, UK: Cambridge University Press.

Baltes, P. B., Dittmann-Kohli, F., & Dixon, R. A. (1984). New perspectives on the development of intelligence in adulthood: Toward a dual-process conception and a model of selective optimization with compensation. In P. B. Baltes & O. H. Brim (Eds.), *Life-span development and behavior* (Vol. 6, pp. 33–76). Orlando, FL: Academic Press.

Baltes, P. B., Dittmann-Kohli, F., & Kliegl, R. (1986). Reserve capacity of the elderly in aging-sensitive tests of fluid intelligence: Replication and extension. *Psychology and Aging, 1,* 172–177.

Baltes, P. B., Reese, H. W., & Lipsitt, L. P. (1980). Lifespan developmental psychology. *Annual Review of Psychology, 31,* 65–110.

Barkham, M., Firth-Cozens, J., & Shapiro, D. A. (1989). Change in prescriptive versus exploratory therapy: Older clients' responses to therapy. *Counselling Psychology Quarterly, 2,* 395–403.

Barnes-Farrell, J. L., & Piotrowski, M. J. (1989). Workers' perceptions of discrepancies between chronological age and personal age: You're only as old as you feel. *Psychology and Aging, 4,* 376–377.

Barnes-Farrell, J. L., & Piotrowski, M. J. (1991). Discrepancies between chronological age and personal age as a reflection of unrelieved worker stress. *Work and Stress, 5,* 177–187.

Belbin, E. (1964). *Training the adult worker.* London: Her Majesty's Stationery Office.

Belbin, E., & Belbin, R. M. (1972). *Problems in adult retraining.* London: Heinemann.

Belbin, E., & Downs, S. M. (1964). Activity learning and the older worker. *Ergonomics, 4,* 429–437.

Belbin, E., & Downs, S. M. (1965). Interference effects from new learning: Their relevance to the design of adult training programs. *Journal of Gerontology, 20,* 154–159.

Belbin, R. M. (1953). Difficulties of older people in industry. *Occupational Psychology, 27,* 177–190.

Belbin, R. M. (1965). *Training methods for older workers.* Paris: Organisation for Economic Cooperation and Development.

Belbin, R. M. (1969). *The discovery method in training.* London: Her Majesty's Stationery Office.

Berg, C. A., & Sternberg, R. J. (1985). A triarchic theory of intellectual development during adulthood. *Developmental Review, 5,* 334–370.

Berkowitz, M. (1988). Functioning ability and job performance as workers age. In M. E. Borus, H. S. Parnes, S. H. Sandell, & B. Seidman (Eds.), *The older worker* (pp. 87–114). Madison, WI: Industrial Relations Research Association.

Billings, A. E. (1983). Age-related employment costs at the Travelers Companies in 1981. *Aging and Work, 6,* 7–14.

Bird, C. P., & Fisher, T. D. (1986). Thirty years later: Attitudes toward the employment of older workers. *Journal of Applied Psychology, 71,* 515–517.

Birren, J. E. (1969). Age and decision strategies. *Interdisciplinary Topics in Gerontology, 4,* 23–36.

Birren, J. E., & Cunningham, W. R. (1985). Research on the psychology of aging: Principles, concepts and theory. In J. E. Birren & K. W. Schaie (Eds.), *Handbook of the psychology of aging* (2nd ed., pp. 3–34). New York: Van Nostrand Reinhold.

Birren, J. E., Woods, A. M., & Williams, M. V. (1980). Behavioral slowing with age: Causes, organization, and consequences. In L. W. Poon (Ed.), *Aging in the 1980s* (pp. 293–308). Washington, DC: American Psychological Association.

Bowers, W. H. (1952). An appraisal of worker characteristics as related to age. *Journal of Applied Psychology, 36,* 296–300.

Breen, L. Z., & Spaeth, J. L. (1960). Age and productivity among workers in four Chicago companies. *Journal of Gerontology, 15,* 68–70.

Bunce, D. J., Warr, P. B., & Cochrane, T. (1993). Blocks in choice responding as a function of age and physical fitness. *Psychology and Aging, 8.*

Butani, S. J. (1988). Relative risk analysis of injuries in coal mining by age and experience at present company. *Journal of Occupational Accidents, 10,* 209–216.

Campbell, A., Converse, P. E., & Rodgers, W. L. (1976). *The quality of American life.* New York: Russell Sage Foundation.

Campbell, J. I. D., & Charness, N. (1990). Age-related declines in working-memory skills: Evidence from a complex calculation task. *Developmental Psychology, 26,* 879–888.

Cattell, R. B. (1963). Theory of fluid and crystallized intelligence: A critical experiment. *Journal of Educational Psychology, 54,* 1–22.

Ceci, S. J. (1990). *On intelligence:...more or less.* Englewood Cliffs, NJ: Prentice-Hall.

Charness, N. (1985). Aging and problem-solving performance. In N. Charness (Ed.), *Aging and human performance* (pp. 225–259). Chichester, UK: Wiley.

Charness, N. (1989). Age and expertise: Responding to Talland's challenge. In L. W. Poon, D. C. Rubin, & B. A. Wilson (Eds.), *Everyday cognition in adulthood and late life* (pp. 437–456).

Cambridge, UK: Cambridge University Press.

Charness, N., & Bosman, E. A. (1990). Expertise and aging: Life in the lab. In T. M. Hess (Ed.), *Aging and cognition: Knowledge organization and utilization* (pp. 343–385). Amsterdam: Elsevier.

Charness, N., & Campbell, J. I. D. (1988). Acquiring skill at mental calculation in adulthood: A task decomposition. *Journal of Experimental Psychology: General, 117*, 115–129.

Charness, N., Schumann, C. E., & Boritz, G. M. (1992). Training older adults in word processing: Effects of age, training technique, and computer anxiety. *International Journal of Technology and Aging, 5*, 79–106.

Cherrington, D. J., Condie, S. J., & England, J. L. (1979). Age and work values. *Academy of Management Journal, 22*, 617–623.

Christensen, H., & Henderson, A. S. (1991). Is age kinder to the initially more able? A study of eminent scientists and academics. *Psychological Medicine, 21*, 935–946.

Clay, H. M. (1956). A study of performance in relation to age at two printing works. *Journal of Gerontology, 11*, 417–424.

Cleveland, J. N., & Shore, L. M. (1992). Self- and supervisory perspectives on age and work attitudes and performance. *Journal of Applied Psychology, 77*, 469–484.

Cole, S. (1979). Age and scientific performance. *American Journal of Sociology, 84*, 958–977.

Colligan, R. C., & Offord, K. P. (1992). Age, stage, and the MMPI: Changes in response patterns over an 85-year age span. *Journal of Clinical Psychology, 48*, 476–493.

Conley, J. J. (1984). Longitudinal consistency of adult personality: Self-reported psychological characteristics across 45 years. *Journal of Personality and Social Psychology, 47*, 1325–1333.

Connelly, S. L., Hasher, L., & Zacks, R. T. (1991). Age and reading: The impact of distraction. *Psychology and Aging, 6*, 533–541.

Cook, J. D., Hepworth, S. J., Wall, T. D., & Warr, P. B. (1981). *The experience of work.* London: Academic Press.

Cornelius, S. W., & Caspi, A. (1987). Everyday problem solving in adulthood and old age. *Psychology and Aging, 2*, 144–153.

Costa, P. T., & McCrae, R. R. (1988). Personality in adulthood: A six-year longitudinal study of self-reports and spouse ratings on the NEO personality inventory. *Journal of Personality and Social Psychology, 54*, 853–863.

Costa, P. T., McCrae, R. R., & Arenberg, D. (1983). Recent longitudinal research on personality and aging. In K. W. Schaie (Ed.), *Longitudinal studies of adult psychological development* (pp. 222–265). New York: Guilford Press.

Cowdry, E. V. (Ed.). (1942). *Problems of aging* (2nd ed.). Baltimore: Williams and Wilkins.

Craik, F. I. M. (1990). Changes in memory with normal aging: A functional view. *Advances in Neurology, 51*, 201–205.

Cunningham, W. R., & Owens, W. A. (1983). The Iowa State study of the adult development of intellectual abilities. In K. W. Schaie (Ed.), *Longitudinal studies of adult psychological development* (pp. 20–39). New York: Guilford Press.

Czaja, S. J. (1988). Microcomputers and the elderly. In M. Helander (Ed.), *Handbook of human computer interaction* (pp. 581–598). North Holland, the Netherlands: Elsevier.

Czaja, S. J., & Drury, C. G. (1981). Aging and pretraining in industrial inspection. *Human Factors, 23*, 485–494.

Dalton, G. W., & Thompson, P. H. (1971). Accelerating obsolescence of older engineers. *Harvard Business Review, 49*(5), 57–67.

Daniel, W. W. (1974). *National survey of the unemployed.* London: Political and Economic Planning.

Davies, D. R., Matthews, G., & Wong, C. S. K. (1991). Aging and work. In C. L. Cooper & I. T. Robertson (Eds.), *International review of industrial and organizational psychology* (Vol. 6, pp. 151–210). Chichester, UK: Wiley.

Davies, D. R., & Sparrow, P. R. (1985). Age and work behaviour. In N. Charness (Ed.), *Aging and human performance* (pp. 293–332). Chichester, UK: Wiley.

Davis, J. A., & Tagiuri, R. (1988). Using life stage theory to manage work relationships. In H. Dennis (Ed.), *Fourteen steps in managing an aging work force* (pp. 123–140). Lexington, MA: Heath.

De la Mare, G. C., & Shepherd, R. D. (1958). Aging: Changes in speed and quality of work among leather cutters. *Occupational Psychology, 32*, 204–209.

Demming, J. A., & Pressey, S. L. (1957). Tests "indigenous" to the adult and older years. *Journal of Counseling Psychology, 4,* 144–148.

Denney, N. W. (1984). A model of cognitive development across the life span. *Developmental Review, 4,* 171–191.

Denney, N. W. (1989). Everyday problem solving: Methodological issues, research findings, and a model. In L. W. Poon, D. C. Rubin, & B. A. Wilson (Eds.), *Everyday cognition in adulthood and late life* (pp. 330–351). Cambridge, UK: Cambridge University Press.

Denney, N. W., & Palmer, A. M. (1981). Adult age differences on traditional and practical problem solving measures. *Journal of Gerontology, 36,* 323–328.

Dennis, H. (Ed.). (1988). *Fourteen steps in managing an aging work force.* Lexington, MA: Heath.

Department of Employment. (1992). Projected trends in the labour force 1992–2001. *Employment Gazette, 100,* 173–184.

Diener, E. (1984). Subjective well-being. *Psychological Bulletin, 95,* 1105–1117.

Dillingham, A. E. (1981). Age and workplace injuries. *Aging and Work, 4,* 1–10.

Dixon, R. A., Kramer, D. A., & Baltes, P. B. (1985). Intelligence: A life-span developmental perspective. In B. B. Wolman (Ed.), *Handbook of intelligence* (pp. 301–350). New York: Wiley.

Doering, M., Rhodes, S. R., & Schuster, M. (1983). *The aging worker: Research and recommendations.* Beverly Hills, CA: Sage.

Downs, S. (1967). Labour turnover in two public service organisations. *Occupational Psychology, 41,* 137–142.

Downs, S. (1985). Retraining for new skills. *Ergonomics, 28,* 1205–1211.

Ekerdt, D. J. (1986). The busy ethic: Moral continuity between work and retirement. *The Gerontologist, 26,* 239–244.

Elias, P. K., Elias, M. F., Robbins, M. A., & Gage, P. (1987). Acquisition of word-processing skills by younger, middle-age, and older adults. *Psychology and Aging, 2,* 340–348.

Eysenck, H. J. (1987). Personality and aging: An exploratory analysis. *Journal of Social Behavior and Personality, 3,* 11–21.

Ferris, G. R., & King, T. R. (1992). The politics of age discrimination in organizations. *Journal of Business Ethics, 11,* 341–350.

Folkman, S., Lazarus, R. S., Pimley, S., & Novacek, J. (1987). Age differences in stress and coping processes. *Psychology and Aging, 2,* 171–184.

Foos, P. W. (1989). Adult age differences in working memory. *Psychology and Aging, 4,* 269–275.

Foret, J., Bensimon, G., Benoit, O., & Vieux, N. (1981). Quality of sleep as a function of age and shift work. In A. Reinberg, N. Vieux, & P. Andlauer (Eds.), *Night and shift work: Biological and social aspects* (pp. 149–154). Oxford, UK: Pergamon Press.

Fossum, J. A., Arvey, R. D., Paradise, C. A., & Robbins, N. E. (1986). Modeling the skills obsolescence process: A psychological/economic integration. *Academy of Management Review, 11,* 362–374.

Fox, H. (1951). Utilization of older manpower. *Harvard Business Review, 29*(6), 40–54.

Fozard, J. L. (1980). The time for remembering. In L. W. Poon (Ed.), *Aging in the 1980s* (pp. 273–287). Washington, DC: American Psychological Association.

Fozard, J. L. (1981). Person-environment relationships in adulthood: Implications for human factors engineering. *Human Factors, 23,* 7–27.

Fozard, J. L. (1990). Vision and hearing in aging. In J. E. Birren & K. W. Schaie (Eds.), *Handbook of the psychology of aging* (3rd ed., pp. 150–170). San Diego: Academic Press.

Fullerton, H. N. (1987). Labor force projections: 1986 to 2000. *Monthly Labor Review, 110*(9), 19–29.

Fullerton, H. N. (1989). New labor force projections, spanning 1988 to 2000. *Monthly Labor Review, 112*(11), 3–12.

Furnham, A. (1990a). A content, correlational, and factor analytic study of seven questionnaire measures of the protestant work ethic. *Human Relations, 43,* 383–399.

Furnham, A. (1990b). *The protestant work ethic.* London: Routledge.

Gardner, E. F., & Monge, R. H. (1977). Adult age differences in cognitive abilities and educational background. *Experimental Aging Research, 3,* 337–383.

Gick, M. L., Craik, F. I. M., & Morris, R. G. (1988). Task complexity and age differences in working memory. *Memory and Cognition, 16,* 353–361.

Giniger, S., Dispenzieri, A., & Eisenberg, J. (1983). Age, experience, and performance on speed and skill jobs in an applied setting. *Journal of Applied Psychology, 68*, 469–475.

Gist, M., Rosen, B., & Schwoerer, C. (1988). The influence of training method and trainee age on the acquisition of computer skills. *Personnel Psychology, 41*, 255–265.

Glaser, R. (1988). Thoughts on expertise. In C. Schooler & W. Schaie (Eds.), *Cognitive functioning and social structure over the life course* (pp. 81–94). Norwood, NJ: Ablex.

Glenn, N. D., Taylor, P. A., & Weaver, C. N. (1977). Age and job satisfaction among males and females: A multivariate, multisurvey study. *Journal of Applied Psychology, 62*, 189–193.

Glenn, N. D., & Weaver, C. N. (1985). Age, cohort, and reported job satisfaction in the United States. In Z. S. Blau (Ed.), *Current perspectives on aging and the life cycle* (Vol. 1, pp. 89–109). Greenwich, CT: JAI Press.

Griew, S., & Tucker, W. A. (1958). The identification of job activities associated with age differences in the engineering industry. *Journal of Applied Psychology, 42*, 278–282.

Haber, L. D. (1970). Age and capacity devaluation. *Journal of Health and Social Behavior, 11*, 167–182.

Hackett, R. D. (1990). Age, tenure, and employee absenteeism. *Human Relations, 43*, 601–619.

Hale, S., Myerson, J., Smith, G. A., & Poon, L. W. (1988). Age, variability, and speed: Between-subjects diversity. *Psychology and Aging, 4*, 407–410.

Hanlon, M. D. (1986). Age and commitment to work. *Research on Aging, 8*, 289–315.

Hartley, J. T. (1989). Memory for prose: Perspectives on the reader. In L. W. Poon, D. C. Rubin, & B. A. Wilson (Eds.), *Everyday cognition in adulthood and late life* (pp. 135–156). Cambridge, UK: Cambridge University Press.

Hasher, L., & Zacks, R. T. (1988). Working memory, comprehension, and aging: A review and a new view. In G. H. Bower (Ed.), *The psychology of learning and motivation* (Vol. 22, pp. 192–225). San Diego: Academic Press.

Hashtroudi, S., Chrosniak, L. D., & Schwartz, B. L. (1991). Effects of aging on priming and skill learning. *Psychology and Aging, 6*, 605–615.

Heise, D. R. (1987). Sociocultural determination of mental aging. In C. Schooler & K. W. Schaie (Eds.), *Cognitive functioning and social structure over the life course* (pp. 247–261). Norwood, NJ: Ablex.

Heron, A., & Chown, S. M. (1961). *Ageing and the semi-skilled: A survey in manufacturing industry on Merseyside*. London: Her Majesty's Stationery Office.

Heron, A., & Chown, S. M. (1967). *Age and function*. London: Churchill.

Hertzog, C., Schaie, K. W., & Gribbin, K. (1978). Cardiovascular disease and changes in intellectual functioning from middle to old age. *Journal of Gerontology, 33*, 872–883.

Herzberg, F., Mausner, B., Peterson, R. O., & Capwell, D. F. (1957). *Job attitudes: Review of research and opinion*. Pittsburgh: Psychological Service of Pittsburgh.

Herzog, A. R., & Rodgers, W. L. (1989). Age differences in memory performance and memory ratings as measured in a sample survey. *Psychology and Aging, 4*, 173–182.

Holley, W. H., Feild, H. S., & Holley, B. B. (1978). Age and reactions to jobs: An empirical study of paraprofessional workers. *Aging and Work, 1*, 33–39.

Horn, J. L. (1970). Organization of data on life-span development of human abilities. In L. R. Goulet & P. B. Baltes (Eds.), *Life-span developmental psychology: Research and theory* (pp. 424–466). New York: Academic Press.

Horner, K. L., Rushton, J. P., & Vernon, P. A. (1986). Relation between aging and research productivity of academic psychologists. *Psychology and Aging, 1*, 319–324.

House, J. S., & Robbins, C. (1983). Age, psychosocial stress, and health. In M. W. Riley, B. B. Hess, & K. Bond (Eds.), *Aging in society* (pp. 175–197). Hillsdale, NJ: Erlbaum.

Houx, P. J., Vreeling, F. W., & Jolles, J. (1991). Age-associated cognitive decline is related to biological life events. In K. Iqbal, D. R. C. McLachlan, B. Winblad, & H. M. Wisniewski (Eds.), *Alzheimer's disease: Basic mechanisms, diagnosis and therapeutic strategies* (pp. 353–358). Chichester, UK: Wiley.

Howard, A., & Bray, D. W. (1988). *Managerial lives in transition*. New York: Guilford Press.

Howard, D. V., Fry, A. F., & Brune, C. M. (1991). Aging and memory for new associations: Direct versus indirect measures. *Journal of*

Experimental Psychology: Learning, Memory and Cognition, 17, 779–792.

Howard, D. V., & Howard, J. H. (1989). Age differences in learning serial patterns: Direct versus indirect measures. *Psychology and Aging, 4*, 357–364.

Hultsch, D. F. (1974). Learning to learn in adulthood. *Journal of Gerontology, 29*, 302–308.

Hultsch, D. F., & Dixon, R. A. (1990). Learning and memory in aging. In J. E. Birren & K. W. Schaie (Eds.), *Handbook of the psychology of aging* (3rd ed., pp. 258–274). San Diego: Academic Press.

Hultsch, D. F., Hertzog, C., & Dixon, R. A. (1990). Ability correlates of memory performance in adulthood and aging. *Psychology and Aging, 5*, 356–368.

Hultsch, D. F., Masson, E. J., & Small, B. J. (1991). Adult age differences in direct and indirect tests of memory. *Journal of Gerontology, 46*, P22–P30.

Humple, C. S., & Lyons, M. (1983). *Management and the older workforce.* Washington, DC: American Management Association.

Hunter, J. E., & Hunter, R. F. (1984). Validity and utility of alternative predictors of job performance. *Psychological Bulletin, 96*, 72–98.

Jablonski, M., Rosenblum, L., & Kunze, K. (1988). Productivity, age, and labor composition changes in the U.S. *Monthly Labor Review, 110*(9), 34–38.

Jacobs, R., Hofmann, D. A., & Kriska, S. D. (1990). Performance and seniority. *Human Performance, 3*, 107–121.

Kacmar, K. M., & Ferris, G. R. (1989). Theoretical and methodological considerations in the age–job satisfaction relationship. *Journal of Applied Psychology, 74*, 201–207.

Kalleberg, A. L., & Loscocco, K. A. (1983). Aging, values, and rewards: Explaining age differences in job satisfaction. *American Sociological Review, 48*, 78–90.

Kasschau, P. L. (1976). Perceived age discrimination in a sample of aerospace employees. *The Gerontologist, 16*, 166–173.

Kausler, D. H. (1985). Episodic memory: Memorizing performance. In N. Charness (Ed.), *Aging and human performance* (pp. 101–141). Chichester, UK: Wiley.

Kay, H. (1951). Learning of a serial task by different age groups. *Quarterly Journal of Experimental Psychology, 3*, 166–183.

Kay, H. (1954). The effects of position in a display upon problem solving. *Quarterly Journal of Experimental Psychology, 6*, 155–169.

King, H. F. (1956). An attempt to use production data in the study of age and performance. *Journal of Gerontology, 11*, 410–416.

Kirchner, W. K., & Dunnette, M. D. (1954). Attitudes toward older workers. *Occupational Psychology, 7*, 257–265.

Kite, M. E., & Johnson, B. T. (1988). Attitudes toward older and younger adults: A meta-analysis. *Psychology and Aging, 3*, 233–244.

Kline, D. E., & Schieber, F. (1985). Vision and aging. In J. E. Birren & K. W. Schaie (Eds.), *Handbook of the psychology of aging* (2nd ed., pp. 296–331). New York: Van Nostrand Reinhold.

Knowles, M. (1984). *The adult learner: A neglected species* (3rd ed.). Houston, TX: Gulf Publishing.

Knutsson, A., Akerstedt, T., Jonsson, B. G., & Orth-Gomer, K. (1986). Increased risk of ischemic heart disease in shift workers. *The Lancet*, July 12, 89–91.

Kogan, N. (1990). Personality and aging. In J. E. Birren & K. W. Schaie (Eds.), *Handbook of the psychology of aging* (3rd ed., pp. 330–346). San Diego: Academic Press.

Kohn, M. L., & Schooler, C. (1983). *Work and personality: An inquiry into the impact of social stratification.* Norwood, NJ: Ablex.

Koller, M. (1983). Health risks related to shift work. *International Archives of Occupational Environmental Health, 53*, 59–75.

Kutscher, R. E., & Walker, J. F. (1960). Comparative job performance of office workers by age. *Monthly Labor Review, 83*(1), 39–43.

Labouvie-Vief, G. (1985). Intelligence and cognition. In J. E. Birren & K. W. Schaie (Eds.), *Handbook of the psychology of aging* (2nd ed., pp. 500–530). New York: Van Nostrand Reinhold.

Lachman, M. E. (1989). Personality and aging at the crossroads: Beyond stability versus change. In K. W. Schaie & C. Schooler (Eds.), *Social structure and aging: Psychological processes* (pp. 167–189). Hillsdale, NJ: Erlbaum.

Lacy, W. B., Bokemeier, J. L., & Shepard, J. M. (1983). Job attribute preferences and work commitment of men and women in the United States. *Personnel Psychology, 36,* 315–329.

LaRiviere, J. E., & Simonson, E. (1965). The effect of age and occupation on speed of writing. *Journal of Gerontology, 20,* 415–416.

Laville, A. (1989). Vieillissement et travail. *Le Travail Humain, 52,* 3–20.

Lawrence, B. S. (1984). Age grading: The implicit organizational timetable. *Journal of Occupational Behaviour, 5,* 23–35.

Lawrence, B. S. (1988). New wrinkles in the theory of age: Demography, norms, and performance ratings. *Academy of Management Journal, 31,* 309–337.

Layton, B. (1975). Perceptual noise and aging. *Psychological Bulletin, 82,* 875–883.

Lee, R., & Wilbur, E. R. (1985). Age, education, job tenure, salary, job characteristics, and job satisfaction: A multivariate analysis. *Human Relations, 38,* 781–791.

Levinson, D. J. (1986). A conception of adult development. *American Psychologist, 41,* 3–13.

Libassi, F. P. (1988). Integrating the elder into the labor force: Consequences and experience for insurance. *The Geneva Papers on Risk and Insurance, 13,* 350–360.

Madden, D. J. (1990). Adult age differences in attentional selectivity and capacity. *European Journal of Cognitive Psychology, 2,* 229–252.

Maher, H. (1955). Age and performance of two work groups. *Journal of Gerontology, 10,* 448–451.

Makeham, P. (1980). *Economic aspects of the employment of older workers.* London: Department of Employment.

Mark, J. A. (1956). Measurement of job performance and age. *Monthly Labor Review, 79,* 1410–1414.

Mark, J. A. (1957). Comparative job performance by age. *Monthly Labor Review, 80,* 1467–1471.

Marquié, J. C., & Paumes, D. (1988). Age related changes in visual information intake in a transcription task. *European Bulletin of Cognitive Psychology, 8,* 107–124.

Martocchio, J. J. (1989). Age-related differences in employee absenteeism: A meta-analysis. *Psychology and Aging, 4,* 409–414.

Maslach, C., & Jackson, S. E. (1981). The measurement of experienced burnout. *Journal of Occupational Behaviour, 2,* 99–113.

Mathieu, J. E., & Zajac, D. M. (1990). A review and meta-analysis of the antecedents, correlates, and consequences of organizational commitment. *Psychological Bulletin, 108,* 171–194.

McCain, B. E., O'Reilly, C., & Pfeffer, J. (1983). The effects of departmental demography on turnover: The case of a university. *Academy of Management Journal, 26,* 626–641.

McCauley, W. J. (1977). Perceived age discrimination in hiring: Demographic and economic correlates. *Industrial Gerontology, 4,* 21–28.

McCrae, R. R., & Costa, P. T. (1990). *Personality in adulthood.* New York: Guilford Press.

McCrae, R. R., Costa, P. T., & Arenberg, D. (1980). Constancy of adult personality structure in males: Longitudinal, cross-sectional and times-of-measurement analyses. *Journal of Gerontology, 35,* 877–883.

McDaniel, M. A., Schmidt, F. L., & Hunter, J. E. (1988). Job experience correlates of job performance. *Journal of Applied Psychology, 73,* 327–330.

McDowd, J. M., & Birren, J. E. (1990). Aging and attentional processes. In J. E. Birren & K. W. Schaie (Eds.), *Handbook of the psychology of aging* (3rd ed., pp. 222–233). San Diego: Academic Press.

McDowd, J. M., & Craik, F. I. M. (1988). Effects of aging and task difficulty on divided attention performance. *Journal of Experimental Psychology, 14,* 267–280.

McDowd, J. M., & Filion, D. L. (1992). Aging, selective attention, and inhibitory processes: A psychophysiological approach. *Psychology and Aging, 7,* 65–71.

McEvoy, G. M., & Cascio, W. F. (1989). Cumulative evidence of the relationship between employee age and job performance. *Journal of Applied Psychology, 74,* 11–17.

McFarland, R. A. (1943). The older worker in industry. *Harvard Business Review, 21,* 505–520.

McFarland, R. A. (1973). The need for functional age measurements in industrial gerontology. *Industrial Gerontology, 19,* 1–19.

Meier, E. L. (1988). Managing an older work force. In M. E. Borus, H. S. Parnes, S. H. Sandell, & B. Seidman (Eds.), *The older worker* (pp. 167–189). Madison, WI: Industrial Relations Research Association.

Meyer, B. J. F., & Rice, G. E. (1989). Prose processing in adulthood: The text, the reader, and the task. In L. W. Poon, D. C. Rubin, & B. A. Wilson (Eds.),

Everyday cognition in adulthood and late life (pp. 157–194). Cambridge, UK: Cambridge University Press.

Miles, W. R. (1933). Age and human ability. *Psychological Review, 40*, 99–123.

Milligan, W. L., Powell, D. A., Harley, C., & Furchtgott, E. (1984). A comparison of physical health and psychosocial variables as predictors of reaction time and serial learning performance in elderly men. *Journal of Gerontology, 39*, 704–710.

Mincer, J. (1979). Progress in human capital analyses of the distribution of earnings. In A. Atkinson (Ed.), *The personal distribution of income* (pp. 136–192). London: Allen and Unwin.

Mirowsky, J., & Ross, C. E. (1992). Age and depression. *Journal of Health and Social Behavior, 33*, 187–205.

Mitchell, D. B. (1989). How many memory systems? Evidence from aging. *Journal of Experimental Psychology, 15*, 31–49.

Mitchell, O. S. (1988). The relation of age to workplace injuries. *Monthly Labor Review, 111*(7), 8–13.

Moline, M. L., Pollak, C. P., Monk, T. H., Lester, L. S., Wagner, D. R., Zendell, S. M., Graeber, R. C., Salter, C. A., & Hirsch, E. (1992). Age-related differences in recovery from simulated jet lag. *Sleep, 15*, 28–40.

Monk, T. H., & Folkard, S. (1985). Individual differences in shiftwork adjustment. In S. Folkard & T. H. Monk (Eds.), *Hours of work* (pp. 227–237). Chichester, UK: Wiley.

Morris, R. G., Craik, F. I. M., & Gick, M. L. (1990). Age differences in working memory tasks: The role of secondary memory and the central executive system. *Quarterly Journal of Experimental Psychology, 42A*, 67–86.

Morris, R. G., Gick, M. L., & Craik, F. I. M. (1988). Processing resources and age differences in working memory. *Memory and Cognition, 16*, 362–366.

Morrow, P. C., & McElroy, J. C. (1987). Work commitment and job satisfaction over three career stages. *Journal of Vocational Behavior, 30*, 330–346.

Mowday, R. T., Porter, L. W., & Steers, R. M. (1982). *Employee-organization linkages*. New York: Academic Press.

Mullan, C., & Gorman, L. (1972). Facilitating adaptation to change: A case study in retraining middle-aged and older workers at Aer Lingus. *Industrial Gerontology, 15*, 20–39.

Müller, M. M. (1991). The stability of anger across age and sex in German cohorts born between 1930 and 1972. *Personality and Individual Differences, 12*, 417–425.

Murrell, K. F. H. (1962). Industrial aspects of aging. *Ergonomics, 5*, 148–153.

Murrell, K. F. H., Powesland, P. F., & Forsaith, B. (1962). A study of pillar-drilling in relation to age. *Occupational Psychology, 36*, 45–52.

Myers, C., & Conner, M. (1992). Age differences in skill acquisition and transfer in an implicit learning paradigm. *Applied Cognitive Psychology, 6*, 429–442.

Myerson, J., Hale, S., Wagstaff, D., Poon, L. W., & Smith, G. A. (1990). The information-loss model: A mathematical model of age-related cognitive slowing. *Psychological Review, 97*, 475–487.

National Commission for Employment Policy. (1985). *Older workers: Prospects, problems and policies*. Washington, DC: NCEP.

Newmann, J. P. (1989). Aging and depression. *Psychology and Aging, 4*, 150–165.

Nicholson, N., & Johns, G. (1985). The absence culture and the psychological contract—who's in control of absence? *Academy of Management Review, 10*, 397–407.

Nygard, C. H., Luopajarvi, T., & Ilmarinen, J. (1988). Musculoskeletal capacity of middle-aged women and men in physical, mental and mixed occupations. *European Journal of Applied Physiology, 57*, 181–188.

O'Brien, G. E., & Dowling, P. (1981). Age and job satisfaction. *Australian Psychologist, 16*, 49–61.

Ormel, J. (1983). Neuroticism and well-being inventories: Measuring traits or states? *Psychological Medicine, 13*, 165–176.

Pacaud, S. (1990). Performance in relation to age and educational level: A monumental research. *Experimental Aging Research, 3*, 123–136.

Palmore, E. (1978). When can age, period, and cohort effects be separated? *Social Forces, 57*, 282–295.

Parnes, H. S. (1988). The retirement decision. In M. E. Borus, H. S. Parnes, S. H. Sandell, & B. Seidman (Eds.), *The older worker* (pp. 115–150). Madison, WI: Industrial Relations Research Association.

Perlmutter, M., Kaplan, M., & Nyquist, L. (1990). Development of adaptive competence in adulthood. *Human Development, 33,* 185–197.

Perry, P., & Downs, S. (1985). Skills, strategies and ways of learning: Can we help people learn how to learn? *Programmed Learning and Educational Technology, 22,* 177–181.

Pinder, C. C., & Pinto, P. R. (1974). Demographic correlates of managerial style. *Personnel Psychology, 27,* 257–270.

Plett, P. C., & Lester, B. T. (1991). *Training for older people: A handbook.* Geneva: International Labour Office.

Plude, D. J., & Doussard-Roosevelt, J. A. (1990). Aging and attention: Selectivity, capacity, and arousal. In E. A. Lovelace (Ed.), *Aging and cognition: Mental processes, self awareness and interventions* (pp. 98–133). Amsterdam: Elsevier.

Plude, D. J., & Hoyer, W. J. (1985). Attention and performance: Identifying and localizing age deficits. In N. Charness (Ed.), *Aging and human performance* (pp. 47–99). Chichester, UK: Wiley.

Ponds, R. W. H. M., Brouwer, W. H., & van Wolffelaar, P. C. (1988). Age differences in divided attention in a simulated driving task. *Journal of Gerontology, 43,* P151–P156.

Poon, L. W. (1985). Differences in human memory with aging: Nature, causes, and clinical implications. In J. E. Birren & K. W. Schaie (Eds.), *Handbook of the psychology of aging* (2nd ed., pp. 427–462). New York: Van Nostrand Reinhold.

Powell, M. (1973). Age and occupational change among coal-miners. *Occupational Psychology, 47,* 37–49.

Rabbitt, P. M. A. (1965). An age-decrement in the ability to ignore irrelevant information. *Journal of Gerontology, 20,* 233–238.

Rabbitt, P. M. A. (1991). Management of the working population. *Ergonomics, 34,* 775–790.

Rabbitt, P. M. A., & Abson, V. (1990). "Lost and found": Some logical and methodological limitations of self-report questionnaires as tools to study cognitive ageing. *British Journal of Psychology, 81,* 1–16.

Rabbitt, P. M. A., & Maylor, E. A. (1991). Investigating models of human performance. *British Journal of Psychology, 82,* 259–290.

Reber, A. S. (1989). Implicit learning and tacit knowledge. *Journal of Experimental Psychology, 118,* 219–235.

Rhodes, S. R. (1983). Age-related differences in work attitudes and behavior: A review and conceptual analysis. *Psychological Review, 2,* 328–367.

Richardson, I. M. (1953). Age and work: A study of 489 men in heavy industry. *British Journal of Medicine, 10,* 269–284.

Robinson, P. K. (1983). *Organizational strategies for older workers.* New York: Pergamon.

Robinson, P. K. (1986). Age, health, and job performance. In J. E. Birren, P. K. Robinson, & J. E. Livingston (Eds.), *Age, health and employment* (pp. 63–77). Englewood Cliffs, NJ: Prentice-Hall.

Robinson, P. K., Coberly, S., & Paul, G. E. (1985). Work and retirement. In R. H. Binstock & E. Shanas (Eds.), *Handbook of aging and the social sciences* (pp. 503–527). New York: Van Nostrand Reinhold.

Rones, P. L. (1988). Employment, earnings, and unemployment characteristics of older workers. In M. E. Borus, H. S. Parnes, S. H. Sandell, & B. Seidman (Eds.), *The older worker* (pp. 21–54). Madison, WI: Industrial Relations Research Association.

Root, N. (1981). Injuries at work are fewer among older employees. *Monthly Labor Review, 104*(3), 30–34.

Rosen, B., & Jerdee, T. H. (1977). Too old or not too old? *Harvard Business Review, 7*(6), 97–108.

Rosen, B., & Jerdee, T. H. (1985). *Older employees: New roles for valued resources.* Homewood, IL: Irwin.

Rutenfranz, J., Haider, M., & Koller, M. (1985). Occupational health measures for nightworkers and shiftworkers. In S. Folkard & T. H. Monk (Eds.), *Hours of work* (pp. 199–210). Chichester, UK: Wiley.

Rybash, J. M., Hoyer, W. J., & Roodin, P. A. (1986). *Adult cognition and aging.* New York: Pergamon Press.

Ryff, C. D. (1989). In the eye of the beholder: Views of psychological well-being among middle-aged and older adults. *Psychology and Aging, 4,* 195–210.

Salthouse, T. A. (1984). Effects of age and skill in typing. *Journal of Experimental Psychology: General, 113,* 345–371.

Salthouse, T. A. (1985a). Speed of behavior and its implications for cognition. In J. E. Birren & K. W. Schaie (Eds.), *Handbook of the psychology of aging* (2nd ed., pp. 400–426). New York: Van Nostrand Reinhold.

Salthouse, T. A. (1985b). *A theory of cognitive aging*. Amsterdam: North Holland.

Salthouse, T. A. (1986). Functional age. In J. E. Birren, P. K. Robinson, & J. E. Livingston (Eds.), *Age, health, and employment* (pp. 78–92). Englewood Cliffs, NJ: Prentice-Hall.

Salthouse, T. A. (1987). The role of experience in cognitive aging. *Annual Review of Gerontology and Geriatrics, 7,* 135–158.

Salthouse, T. A. (1988). The role of processing resources in cognitive aging. In M. L. Howe & C. J. Brainerd (Eds.), *Cognitive development in adulthood* (pp. 185–239). New York: Springer.

Salthouse, T. A. (1989). Aging and skilled performance. In A. M. Colley & J. R. Beech (Eds.), *Acquisition and performance of cognitive skills* (pp. 247–264). Chichester, UK: Wiley.

Salthouse, T. A. (1990a). Cognitive competence and expertise in aging. In J. E. Birren & K. W. Schaie (Eds.), *Handbook of the psychology of aging* (3rd ed., pp. 310–319). San Diego: Academic Press.

Salthouse, T. A. (1990b). Influence of experience on age differences in cognitive functioning. *Human Factors, 32,* 551–569.

Salthouse, T. A. (1990c). Working memory as a processing resource in cognitive aging. *Developmental Review, 10,* 101–124.

Salthouse, T. A. (1991a). Mediation of adult age differences in cognition by reductions in working memory and speed of processing. *Psychological Science, 2,* 179–183

Salthouse, T. A. (1991b). *Theoretical perspectives on cognitive aging*. Hillsdale, NJ: Erlbaum.

Salthouse, T. A., & Babcock, R. L. (1991). Decomposing adult age differences in working memory. *Developmental Psychology, 5,* 763–776.

Salthouse, T. A., & Saults, J. S. (1987). Multiple spans in transcription typing. *Journal of Applied Psychology, 72,* 187–196.

Salthouse, T. A., & Skovronek, E. (1992). Within-context assessment of age differences in working memory. *Journal of Gerontology, 47,* P110–P120.

Sands, L. P., Terry, H., & Meredith, W. (1989). Change and stability in adult intellectual functioning assessed by Wechsler item responses. *Psychology and Aging, 4,* 79–87.

Schacter, D. L. (1987). Implicit memory: History and current status. *Journal of Experimental Psychology: Learning, Memory, and Cognition, 13,* 501–518.

Schaie, K. W. (1983a). The Seattle longitudinal study: A 21-year exploration of psychometric intelligence in adulthood. In K. W. Schaie (Ed.), *Longitudinal studies of adult psychological development* (pp. 64–135). New York: Guilford Press.

Schaie, K. W. (1983b). What can we learn from the longitudinal study of adult psychological development? In K. W. Schaie (Ed.), *Longitudinal studies of adult psychological development* (pp. 1–19). New York: Guilford Press.

Schaie, K. W. (1989). The hazards of cognitive aging. *The Gerontologist, 29,* 484–493.

Schaie, K. W., & Hertzog, C. (1983). Fourteen-year cohort-sequential analyses of adult intellectual development. *Developmental Psychology, 19,* 531–543.

Schaie, K. W., & Willis, S. L. (1986). Can decline in adult intellectual functioning be reversed? *Developmental Psychology, 22,* 223–232.

Schaie, K. W., & Willis, S. L. (1991). Adult personality and psychomotor performance: Cross-sectional and longitudinal analyses. *Journal of Gerontology: Psychological Sciences,* P275–P284.

Schieber, F. (1992). Aging and the senses. In J. E. Birren, R. B. Sloane, & G. D. Cohen (Eds.), *Handbook of mental health and aging* (2nd ed., pp. 251–306). San Diego: Academic Press.

Schmidt, F. L., Hunter, J. E., & Outerbridge, A. N. (1986). Impact of job experience and ability on job knowledge, work sample performance, and supervisory ratings of job performance. *Journal of Applied Psychology, 71,* 432–439.

Schmidt, F. L., Hunter, J. E., Outerbridge, A. N., & Goff, S. (1988). Joint relation of experience and ability with job performance: Test of three hypotheses. *Journal of Applied Psychology, 73,* 46–57.

Schneider, E. L., & Rowe, J. W. (Eds.). (1990). *Handbook of the biology of aging*. San Diego: Academic Press.

Schooler, C. (1987). Psychological effects of complex environments during the life span: A review and theory. In C. Schooler & K. W. Schaie (Eds.), *Cognitive functioning and social structure over the life course* (pp. 24–49). Norwood, NJ: Ablex.

Schrank, H. T., & Waring, J. M. (1983). Aging and work organizations. In M. W. Riley, B. B. Hess,

& K. Bond (Eds.), *Aging in society* (pp. 53–69). Hillsdale, NJ: Erlbaum.

Schroots, J. J. F., & Birren, J. E. (1988). The nature of time: Implications for research on aging. *Comprehensive Gerontology, 2,* 1–29.

Schwab, D. P., & Heneman, H. G. (1977a). Age and satisfaction with dimensions of work. *Journal of Vocational Behavior, 10,* 212–220.

Schwab, D. P., & Heneman, H. G. (1977b). Effects of age and experience on productivity. *Industrial Gerontology, 4,* 113–117.

Shank, S. E. (1988). Women and the labor market: The link grows stronger. *Monthly Labor Review, 111*(3), 3–8.

Shapiro, D., & Sandell, S. H. (1987). The reduced pay of older job losers. In S. H. Sandell (Ed.), *The problem isn't age* (pp. 37–51). New York: Praeger.

Sheppard, H. L., & Rix, S. E. (1977). *The graying of working America.* New York: Free Press.

Siassi, I., Crocetti, G., & Spiro, H. R. (1975). Emotional health, life and job satisfaction in aging workers. *Industrial Gerontology, 2,* 289–296.

Silvestri, G. T., & Lukasiewicz, J. M. (1989). Projections of occupational employment, 1988–2000. *Monthly Labor Review, 112*(11), 42–65.

Simonton, D. K. (1988). Age and outstanding achievement: What do we know after a century of research? *Psychological Bulletin, 104,* 251–267.

Smith, K. U., & Greene, D. (1962). Scientific motion study and aging processes in performance. *Ergonomics, 5,* 155–164.

Sonnenfeld, J. (1978). Dealing with the aging work force. *Harvard Business Review, 56*(6), 81–92.

Sparrow, P. R., & Davies, D. R. (1988). Effects of age, tenure, training, and job complexity on technical performance. *Psychology and Aging, 3,* 307–314.

Spence, A. (1990). Labour force outlook to 2001. *Employment Gazette, 98,* 186–198.

Spirduso, W. W. (1980). Physical fitness, aging, and psychomotor speed: A review. *Journal of Gerontology, 35,* 850–865.

Stafford, J. L., & Birren, J. E. (1986). Changes in the organization of behavior with age. In J. E. Birren, P. K. Robinson, & J. E. Livingston (Eds.), *Age, health, and employment* (pp. 1–26). Englewood Cliffs, NJ: Prentice-Hall.

Stagner, R. (1985). Aging in industry. In J. E. Birren & K. W. Schaie (Eds.), *Handbook of the psychology of*

aging (2nd ed., pp. 789–817). New York: Van Nostrand Reinhold.

Stankov, L. (1988). Aging, attention, and intelligence. *Psychology and Aging, 3,* 59–74.

Staw, B. M., & Ross, J. (1985). Stability in the midst of change: A dispositional approach to job attitudes. *Journal of Applied Psychology, 70,* 469–480.

Sternberg, R. J. (1985). *Beyond IQ: A triarchic theory of human intelligence.* Cambridge, UK: Cambridge University Press.

Sterns, H. L. (1986). Training and retraining adult and older adult workers. In J. E. Birren, P. K. Robinson, & J. E. Livingston (Eds.), *Age, health and employment* (pp. 93–113). Englewood Cliffs, NJ: Prentice-Hall.

Sterns, H. L., & Doverspike, D. (1989). Aging and the training and learning process. In I. L. Goldstein (Ed.), *Training and development in organizations* (pp. 299–332). San Francisco: Jossey-Bass.

Stevens, D. P., & Truss, C. V. (1985). Stability and change in adult personality over 12 and 20 years. *Developmental Psychology, 21,* 568–584.

Stewart, M. B., & Greenhalgh, C. A. (1984). Work history patterns and the occupational attainment of women. *The Economic Journal, 94,* 493–519.

Stine, E. A. L., & Wingfield, A. (1987). Levels upon levels: Predicting age differences in text recall. *Experimental Aging Research, 13,* 179–183.

Stones, M. J., & Kozma, A. (1985). Physical performance. In N. Charness (Ed.), *Aging and human performance* (pp. 261–291). Chichester, UK: Wiley.

Streufert, S., Pogash, R., Piasecki, M., & Post, G. M. (1991). Age and management team performance. *Psychology and Aging, 5,* 551–559.

Stubbs, D. A., & Nicholson, A. S. (1979). Manual handling and back injuries in the construction industry: An investigation. *Journal of Occupational Accidents, 2,* 179–190.

Talaga, J., & Beehr, T. A. (1989). Retirement: A psychological perspective. In C. L. Cooper & I. Robertson (Eds.), *International review of industrial and organizational psychology* (Vol. 4, pp. 185–211). Chichester, UK: Wiley.

Taub, H. A. (1979). Comprehension and memory of prose materials by young and old adults. *Experimental Aging Research, 5,* 3–13.

Taylor, R. N. (1975). Age and experience as determinants of managerial information processing and decision making performance. *Academy of Management Journal, 18*, 74–81.

Teiger, C. (1989). Le vieillissement differentiel dans et par le travail. *Le Travail Humain, 52*, 21–56.

Thompson, M. (1991). *Last in the queue? Corporate employment policies and the older worker.* Brighton, UK: Institute of Manpower Studies.

Thorndike, E. L., Bregman, E. O., Tilton, J. W., & Woodyard, E. (1928). *Adult learning.* New York: Macmillan.

Triandis, H. C. (1993). Cross-cultural industrial and organizational psychology. In M. D. Dunnette, L. M. Hough, & H. C. Triandis (Eds.), *Handbook of Industrial and Organizational Psychology* (2nd ed., vol. 4). Palo Alto, CA: Consulting Psychologists Press.

Trites, D. K., & Cobb, B. B. (1964). Problems in air traffic management III. Implications of training-entry age for training and job performance of air traffic control specialists. *Aerospace Medicine, 35*, 336–340.

Tune, G. S. (1969). The influence of age and temperament on the adult human sleep-wakefulness pattern. *British Journal of Psychology, 60*, 431–441.

Van Zelst, R. H. (1954). The effect of age and experience upon accident rate. *Journal of Applied Psychology, 38*, 313–317.

Vecchio, R. P. (1980). The function and meaning of work and the job: Morse and Weiss (1955) revisited. *Academy of Management Journal, 23*, 361–367.

Vernon, P. A., Nador, S., & Kantor, L. (1985). Reaction times and speed-of-processing: Their relationship to timed and untimed measures of intelligence. *Intelligence, 9*, 357–374.

Verrillo, R. T., & Verrillo, V. (1985). Sensory and perceptual performance. In N. Charness (Ed.), *Aging and human performance* (pp. 1–46). Chichester, UK: Wiley.

Vroom, V. H., & Pahl, B. (1971). Relationship between age and risk taking among managers. *Journal of Applied Psychology, 55*, 399–405.

Waldman, D. A., & Avolio, B. J. (1986). A meta-analysis of age differences in job performance. *Journal of Applied Psychology, 71*, 33–38.

Walker, J. F. (1964). The job performance of federal mail sorters by age. *Monthly Labor Review, 87*(3), 296–301.

Warr, P. B. (1982). A national study of non-financial employment commitment. *Journal of Occupational Psychology, 55*, 297–312.

Warr, P. B. (1987). *Work, unemployment, and mental health.* Oxford, UK: Oxford University Press.

Warr, P. B. (1990). The measurement of well-being and other aspects of mental health. *Journal of Occupational Psychology, 63*, 193–210.

Warr, P. B. (1992). Age and occupational well-being. *Psychology and Aging, 7*, 37–45.

Warr, P. B., & Conner, M. T. (1992). Job competence and cognition. In B. M. Staw & L. L. Cummings (Eds.), *Research in organizational behavior* (Vol. 14, pp. 91–127). Greenwich, CT: JAI Press.

Warr, P. B., & Jackson, P. R. (1985). Factors influencing the psychological impact of prolonged unemployment and of re-employment. *Psychological Medicine, 15*, 795–807.

Warr, P. B., Jackson, P. R., & Banks, M. H. (1988). Unemployment and mental health: Some British studies. *Journal of Social Issues, 44*, 47–68.

Welford, A. T. (1958). *Ageing and human skill.* Oxford, UK: The Nuffield Foundation.

Welford, A. T. (1976). Thirty years of psychological research on age and work. *Journal of Occupational Psychology, 49*, 129–138.

Welford, A. T. (1985). Changes of performance with age: An overview. In N. Charness (Ed.), *Aging and human performance* (pp. 333–369). Chichester, UK: Wiley.

West, R. L., & Crook, T. H. (1990). Age differences in everyday memory: Laboratory analogues of telephone number recall. *Psychology and Aging, 5*, 520–529.

Wetrogan, S. I. (1988). *Population estimates and projections* (Series P-25, No. 1017). Washington, DC: Bureau of the Census.

White, A. T., & Spector, P. E. (1987). An investigation of age-related factors in the age-job-satisfaction relationship. *Psychology and Aging, 2*, 261–265.

Wickens, C. D. (1984). *Engineering psychology and human performance.* Columbus, OH: Merrill.

Willis, S. L. (1985). Towards an educational psychology of the older adult learner: Intellectual and cognitive bases. In J. E. Birren & K. W. Schaie (Eds.), *Handbook of the psychology of aging*

(2nd ed., pp. 818–847). New York: Van Nostrand Reinhold.

Willis, S. L. (1987). Cognitive training and everyday competence. *Annual Review of Gerontology and Geriatrics, 7*, 159–188.

Willis, S. L. (1989a). Cohort differences in cognitive aging: A sample case. In K. W. Schaie & C. Schooler (Eds.), *Social structure and aging* (pp. 95–112). Hillsdale, NJ: Erlbaum.

Willis, S. L. (1989b). Improvement with cognitive training: Which old dogs learn what tricks? In L. W. Poon, D. C. Rubin, & B. A. Wilson (Eds.), *Everyday cognition in adulthood and late life* (pp. 545–569). Cambridge, UK: Cambridge University Press.

Willis, S. L., & Baltes, P. B. (1980). Intelligence in adulthood and aging: Contemporary issues. In L. W. Poon (Ed.), *Aging in the 1980s* (pp. 260–272).

Washington, DC: American Psychological Association.

Willis, S. L., & Schaie, K. W. (1986). Training the elderly on the ability factors of spatial orientation and inductive reasoning. *Psychology and Aging, 1*, 239–247.

Wright, J. D., & Hamilton, R. F. (1978). Work satisfaction and age: Some evidence for the "job change" hypotheses. *Social Forces, 56*, 1140–1158.

Zachariah, K. C., & Vu, M. T. (1988). *World population projections.* Baltimore: Johns Hopkins University Press.

Zelinski, E. M., & Gilewski, M. J. (1988). Memory for prose and aging: A meta-analysis. In M. L. Howe & C. J. Brainerd (Eds.), *Cognitive development in adulthood* (pp. 133–158). New York: Springer.

Industrial and Organizational Psychology in Collectivist Cultures

The chapters in this section are written by authors from or living in Asia. This is demographically the most important part of the world. Thirty-five percent of humans live in just two countries: China and India. The population of China is approaching 1.2 billion. At the turn of the century the population of the *world* was 1.5 billion! The population of India is approaching .9 billion and is expected to surpass (!) China sometime around the year 2020. The world now has a population of 5.5 billion and it is not expected, according to a U.N. population study, to reach a stable asymptote until the population reaches 14 billion, sometime in the middle of the next century. The asymptote will be reached because of a low quality of life and a high infant mortality rate, rather than because of the triumphs of population planners.

A recent report called "Warning to Humanity," signed by the Academies of Science of all the major industrial countries and 1,000 scientists from 70 countries, warns that the earth's ability to provide for growing numbers of people is finite and we are fast approaching many of the earth's limits.

Vast regions of Africa and Asia are becoming unproductive and uninhabitable due to desertification, flooding, hurricanes, and other environmental disruptions. In 1950, 40 percent of the surface of Ethiopia was forested; today only 1 percent is in this condition. The rate of these disruptions has doubled between 1960 and 1980 because the ecosystems have been made more vulnerable by human pressures on the land, forests, and soils. Serious water shortages are occurring in 80 countries, containing 40 percent of the world's population. Rivers carrying large amounts of eroded soil and industrial, municipal, agricultural, and livestock waste, some of it toxic, are destroying the oceans near some of the coastlines that produce most of the world's fish. At present rates of destruction, critical forests will disappear in just a few years; since 1945, 11 percent of the earth's vegetated surface has been degraded. Per capita food production is declining in many parts of the world.

Changes in the troposphere due to pollution, and ozone depletion in the stratosphere, are increasing the ultraviolet radiation at the earth's surface and have prompted some scientists to suggest that we should stay out of the sun and protect our skin with sunscreens, while others have argued that sunscreens release destructive free radicals and should be used sparingly. When you ask the experts which side to believe, they tell you that we just do not have enough research on the subject, so we really do not know.

The worse offenders in environmental pollution are the developed countries. We now know that industrialization without concern for the environment leads to disaster. The developed countries produce most of the acid precipitation, the urban pollution, the reduction in the visibility of the atmosphere that airline pilots have reported during the last 20 years, the haze over the north pole that used to be one of the pristine regions of the globe, the hazardous wastes, the agricultural chemicals that have been found to be responsible for many cancers, and so on. The largest monument of the ancient world, in cubic meters, was the Temple of the Sun in Mexico; the largest garbage dump of the modern world is five times the size of that monument!

If we were to "clean up" the environment in developed countries, we would have to devote a substantial fraction of our GNP to that task. Some experts estimate that the cost of cleaning the environment in eastern Germany alone would approach one trillion dollars—one quarter of the U.S. national debt! Of course, such investments are politically impossible. We already see shortages of funds all over the globe. The former Soviet Union and countries formally in its sphere of influence are good examples. These changes will unquestionably affect industrial and organizational psychology. The trends of migration from poor to rich countries will accelerate unless conditions in the poor countries improve dramatically, while the work populations of some countries, such as Germany, will decline, making room for migrants who will be available as *Gastarbeiter* to do the undesirable jobs. Diversity will be the name of the game.

At the same time, outsourcing and the establishment of large trading blocks, like the EC and the Mexico–U.S.–Canada bloc will make many production activities international.

One way to reduce the flood of refugees from the developing world is to help that part of the globe create conditions that are sufficiently attractive to keep its population from migrating. The East Asian countries are doing this successfully. In some of the chapters that follow, we will examine why they are so successful. But they are apparently using some of the resource-intensive development models of the European and North American countries. As we have seen, if these models were implemented in the overpopulated regions of the world, the resources of five or six planets would be required. Obviously, this will not work in the long run.

We need new models of the "good life" that are not so dependent on consumption and do not overutilize the environmental resources. We cannot hope to continue to become richer and richer, and more wasteful of resources, while the hungry multitudes watch our lifestyle on their television screens.

Furthermore, one of the realities of overdevelopment is the emergence of pockets of the poor in every country. Idle, sitting in front of their TVs, they look at the overemployed (who have much more to do than they can possibly do) with envy, knowing that their own incomes are but a fraction of the incomes of these people. The distribution of the population between the overemployed, the employed, and the underemployed (on public welfare, on unemployment insurance, retired, environmental refugees) will keep shifting in favor of the latter, unless we redesign our economic, educational, and employment systems. Some of the effects of overpopulation on organizational behavior can be seen in Sinha's chapter in this section.

We need to spend much more of our GNP on education, training, and job redesign than we have considered so far. We have to determine whether or not we can develop models of the good life that do things differently. We probably have much to learn from the developing countries *who as yet are not overusing the resources of the planet.* For example, the Japanese use energy at a fraction of the per capita rate of the United States. This section of the *Handbook* is based on data from that part of the world. It examines both successful and unsuccessful organizations in that part of the world and thus provides one more perspective on the future of industrial and organizational psychology in the next century.

Erez, in chapter 11, provides a bridge between the West and the East by examining the role of individualism and collectivism in industrial life. She argues that cross-cultural industrial and organizational psychology needs to bring culture into its important models and reports two surveys that indicate that culture is one of the important determinants of the choice of the problems we study.

Her model places the differences between the independent and the interdependent self in the center and contrasts the self-derived needs, the emphasis on self-enhancement, efficacy, and consistency of the individualists with the emphasis on group-derived needs, the emphasis on ingroup harmony, and virtuous action among collectivists. She then examines the implications of these differences for work behavior. Culture is shown to be an antecedent of the kind of self found in a society as well as a consequent of work behavior. Managerial motivational techniques work well or not well depending on culture, and depending on the kind of self that is most commonly found among the employees. She reviews data from Israeli urban and U.S. individualists and Israeli kibbutz collectivists and shows that goal setting and participation strategies can be successful or not successful, depending on culture.

Erez also discusses her studies carried out in Japan, thus introducing chapter 12 by Kashima and Callan, which examines the Japanese work group. Kashima and Callan use the family metaphor of Japanese organization as a contrast with the machine metaphor of Western organization.

They show that the family metaphor has a long history in Japanese culture and is most important in understanding the operation of Japanese organizations. For example, the Japanese assign work to the group, and the group functions according to interpersonal bonds and power relationships to assign work to individuals according to each worker's competence, knowledge, and job experience. In Japanese organizations, there is clear differentiation of ranks, but there is a great deal of interaction among the ranks that facilitates group performance and group decision making. The quality of the working relationship between superiors and subordinates is an important component of performance evaluation in Japanese organizations. The ideology of harmony is emphasized during work socialization and is an important factor in creating a family atmosphere.

Of special importance in this chapter is the use of Japanese language terms with their translations that provide to an outsider a better sense of the Japanese way of functioning. For example, the presentation of the Japanese addressing system, with several status levels for *I* and several levels for *you* and corresponding grammatical forms, can be very useful for those who want to understand that culture.

They argue that features of the Japanese work group are likely to improve productivity but not job satisfaction or even commitment. They finally examine whether the Japanese methods can be transferred to other cultures and use the collectivism-individualism contrast as one of the ways to develop their analysis of this problem.

In chapter 13, Redding, Norman, and Schlander argue that the organization has different meanings in every culture, and as a result, the attachment of the individual to the organization varies across cultures. Each individual's predisposition to cooperate is absorbed from the culture. In addition, culture influences forms of labor laws, wage legislation, skills development, and so on. For example, in a culture where security is a very important value, laws make it more difficult to lay off workers. The organization itself must be viewed as an artifact of the culture.

Redding et al. examine East Asian organizations as case studies of organizations in successful economies. What is it about China, Japan, South Korea, Taiwan and Hong Kong, and Singapore that has resulted in such success in international competition? Are the Confucian cultural heritage and the economic philosophies of laissez-faire export orientation behind this success?

These authors end with an examination of the importance of culture for organizational, motivation, and leadership theory. For example, while *consideration* may be a universal variable, the way it is manifested is strongly influenced by culture, so that in individualistic cultures a considerate leader respects a subordinate's autonomy, and in a collectivist culture a considerate leader interacts more with a subordinate. Or to take another example, *pressure for production* is an aspect of *performance emphasis by the supervisor* to a greater extent in the West than the East, while *planning* and *goal facilitation* are more important elements of *performance* in the East than in the West.

Wang, in chapter 14, examines the role of culture in economic reform and industrial and organizational psychology in China. He starts with a review of ancient Chinese traditions that are still influential in China. He outlines the close collaboration of Chinese psychologists and practitioners, such as managers and government officials, in applying theories of industrial and organizational psychology to economic reform.

Several interesting experiments are reviewed. For example, in one field experiment carried out in an assembly line, a 2 x 2 x 2 design (individual vs. group rewards, success vs. failure, male vs. female) was used. These independent variables were linked to the determinations made by the workers of whether success or failure could be attributed to effort, ability, cooperation from others, the task, or chance. It was shown that the individual versus group responsibility facet resulted in differences in the attributes used. Under the group reward system, workers attributed their success to group cooperation, whereas under the individual reward system, they used personal factors or the difficulty of the task to explain their performance.

From industrial and organizational psychology in the most populous country in the world, we move to the second most populous country, India, in chapter 15 by Sinha. In India, about two-thirds of the industrial enterprises are in the public sector, and the government exerts pressure on them to solve social and macroeconomic problems as well as to produce goods. Technology, efficiency, and profitability are compromised in order to provide employment and to stimulate economic growth. The culture is collectivist, emphasizing hierarchy and personalized relationships. Centralization is high, especially in the large enterprises.

Sinha contrasts *synergetic* to *soft* organizational cultures in Indian enterprises. The former use the cultural ethos appropriately and manage organizations that are effective. The latter are characterized by helpful patrons and loyal subordinates and ignore criteria of profitability and effectiveness.

One can identify the effects of overpopulation and the corresponding pressures to meet human needs in statements such as, "The leading private sector iron and steel company has 7,000 employees (out of 33,000) who are really not needed and is committed to hire 4,000 more, though these additional employees are also not needed. Most organizations are under constant pressure to employ more people." Is this the wave of the future in the overpopulated parts of the planet?

An interesting contrast can be seen between India, where most of the Western management techniques have been tried, and China, which is proud to have invented its own managerial systems. The cultural fit between the Western techniques and Indian realities has often been poor, and the techniques have been abandoned in favor of Indian ones. Of special interest is Sinha's own theory of leadership effectiveness, which apparently is quite useful in India. It uses the ideas of *nurturance* (N) and *task orientation* (T) to define the nurturant–task nuturance–task-oriented leadership style (NT). If we use Ohio State terminology, we would say that this leader is high in both consideration and initiating structure. Sinha describes this leader vividly: He or she dispenses N contingently on the subordinate's task performance and provides close supervision and feedback. Sinha also reviews a number of complicating factors, such as when participative management is optimal for NT leaders.

Thus, Sinha identifies industrial and organizational psychology variables that are universal but are modified in the Indian context. This may well be the wave of the future in most of the developing world, as Western trained industrial and organizational psychologists try to fit their Western theories and methods into the indigenous contexts.

—The Editors

CHAPTER 11

Toward a Model of Cross-cultural Industrial and Organizational Psychology

Miriam Erez
Technion-Israel Institute of Technology, Haifa

The conceptual framework developed in this chapter was stimulated by the limitations of theories of industrial and organizational psychology to explain empoyees' behavior across cultures. Culture is identified as an important contextual factor that moderates the effects of managerial practices and motivational techniques on employees' behavior. The chapter is organized around six research questions that address the absence of the cultural factor in traditional research and the need for developing a new model. The answers to these questions led to the development of a new cross-cultural model that consists of four major factors: (a) cultural values and norms that serve as criteria for evaluating management practices; (b) types of managerial practices and motivational techniques in the work setting; (c) the self as the function of self-regulating processing, and as the interpreter and evaluator of management practices; and (d) employees' work behavior. The model proposes that management practices and motivational techniques are evaluated by the self according to a set of criteria represented in the self and shaped by cultural values and norms, and with respect to their potential contribution to the notion of self-worth and well-being. Positive evaluations have a positive effect on employees' behavior, whereas no effects or negative effects are expected when management practices do not fit in with the cultural values and norms. The model serves to interpret the effects of various managerial and motivational techniques across cultures and to explain the differential priority given to research topics in different cultures. The chapter discusses the contribution of cross-cultural research to understanding employees' behavior within a particular culture.

Introduction

THE LACK OF a cross-cultural perspective on organizational behavior has limited our understanding of the reasons why motivational approaches and managerial practices are not smoothly transferred across cultures, and the reasons why prediction of the potential effectiveness of managerial techniques across cultures is limited. These questions concerning the effect of culture cannot be answered by current models of industrial and organizational psychology because they overlook cross-cultural factors. The purpose of this chapter is to formulate key research questions concerning the cross-cultural aspect in understanding industrial and organizational psychology. These questions serve as guidelines for the development of a conceptual model of cross-cultural psychology.

The following six research questions that are proposed provide the organizational structure for this chapter.

- Is there a need for developing models of cross-cultural industrial and organizational psychology?

- Why does traditional research in industrial and organizational psychology tend to ignore cultural influences on employee behavior in organizations?

- Is it possible to develop a theoretical model of cross-cultural industrial and organizational psychology that integrates cultural factors into models of employee work behavior?

- How effective are similar managerial and motivational techniques across cultures?

- Does culture influence the choice of research topics?

- What can be learned from cross-cultural research in industrial and organizational

psychology that may benefit research within a particular culture?

The answers to these questions are based on four sources: (a) an in-depth review of the literature in industrial and organizational psychology and in related topics in cross-cultural psychology; (b) a development of a new model of cross-cultural industrial and organizational psychology that integrates cultural factors, managerial approaches, and employee behavior; (c) the use of the new model of cross-cultural industrial and organizational psychology for reexamining and understanding existing research findings across cultures; and (d) data collection concerning the focus of research topics in different cultures. In the data collection, more than two thousand articles published during the eighties in the leading journals of industrial and organizational psychology and cross-cultural psychology were reviewed to examine the differences and similarities in research topics in industrial and organizational psychology across cultures. The review process was conducted with the use of two major data sources: *Psychlit* and *Psychological Abstracts*. *Psychlit* is a computerized data source, and it was used to review the following English-language journals published between 1982 and 1990: *Applied Psychology: An International Review, British Journal of Psychology, British Journal of Social Psychology, International Journal of Psychology, Journal of Applied Psychology, Journal of Applied Social Psychology, Journal of Business and Psychology, Journal of Cross-cultural Psychology, Journal of Occupational Psychology, Journal of Organizational Behavior, Journal of Vocational Behavior, Leadership and Organizational Behavior, and Organizational Behavior and Human Decision Processes.* The *Psychological Abstracts* was used to review studies in industrial and organizational psychology that were published in five countries that are influential in Europe and Asia: Scandinavia, West Germany, Japan, India, and Israel.

Need for Developing Cross-cultural Models

The field of industrial and organizational psychology pertains to the application of psychology to the way individuals, groups, and organizations behave when creating products or rendering services as a means of maintaining and enhancing their own survival. In line with the discipline of psychology, the vast majority of research has centered on the individual level of analysis, overlooking cultural and contextual effects.

Cross-cultural psychology can be defined as a field that studies "similarities and differences in individual psychological and social functioning in various cultures and ethnic groups" (Kagitcibasi & Berry, 1989, p. 494). Until very recently, these two fields of psychology were developed with only a limited amount of influence on each other. Cross-cultural research has mainly focused on the relationship between individual and societal psychological variables in the cultural, social, economic, ecological, and biological spheres. The field of industrial and organizational psychology has occupied only a small niche within the wide scope of cross-cultural research, and vice versa—research in industrial and organizational psychology has not taken a cross-cultural perspective on employee behavior in organizations.

Research in cross-cultural psychology still lacks a strong conceptual framework (Kagitcibasi & Berry, 1989). On the other hand, highly developed conceptual models with strong empirical support have been developed in industrial and organizational psychology. Included in these models are the goal-setting theory of motivation (Locke & Latham, 1990), expectancy models (Vroom, 1964), job design (Hackman & Oldham, 1980), theory of behavior in organizations (Naylor, Pritchard, & Ilgen, 1980), integrative resource model of learning and task performance (Kanfer & Ackerman,

1989), decision-making models (Beach & Mitchell, 1990; Staw, 1987; Vroom & Yetton, 1973), and models of employee–organization interaction (Schneider, 1987).

In the presence of highly developed theories in industrial and organizational psychology, it is legitimate to ask whether these theories are necessary and sufficient for understanding employee behavior in organizations across cultures, or whether there is a need to develop a new conceptual framework of cross-cultural industrial and organizational psychology. A comprehensive theory of human behavior should take into consideration the interrelationship between individual difference characteristics and contextual factors. This chapter focuses on culture as a major contextual factor, and its role in explaining and predicting employee behavior.

Models of industrial and organizational psychology centered mainly on individual difference characteristics may capture all the variance in behavior when contextual factors are held constant. However, when the context varies across jobs, organizations, and cultures, its effect on behavior cannot be ignored. A good illustration of the interplay between individual differences and differences in work assignments in explaining behavioral outcomes is brought up in the following case. Teacher evaluation scores during a period of six years were highly correlated when the course subject was held constant. Yet, lower correlations were obtained among evaluation scores for the same teachers across courses and for the same courses across teachers. Thus, consistency in teachers' performance as accounted for by personal characteristics is high only when the course subject is held constant (Hanges, Schneider, & Niles, 1990). An extrapolation from the effect of a relatively minor contextual change in course subject to major changes in the work context from local to global markets suggests that contextual factors cannot be held constant and that cultural diversity, in particular, should be examined in relation to organizational behavior.

Significant changes in the world market make clear the cultural changes in work context and the resulting need to study the cultural factor and its effect on organizational behavior. These changes are presented below.

- *Cultural diversity of the labor force.* Demographical changes all over the world intensify the cultural diversity of the labor force. These trends in the United States suggest that by the year 2000 about one-third of the labor force will be black and Hispanic, and managers of the future will have to cope with cultural diversity (see Triandis, in this volume). The unification of Europe as well as the political changes in the former Soviet republics have resulted in waves of immigrants across cultural borders. Israel, in particular, is in the process of absorbing about 400,000 new Russian immigrants within a three-year period, which is a 10 percent population growth (*Monthly Bulletin of Statistics,* 1992). The Russian immigration is going to have a significant impact on the labor market, and the recognition of the cultural factor may help in the process of acculturation of the new immigrants into the labor force.

- *Scope of the work environment.* The work environment has changed from local to global and international in scope. In the United States, for example, more than 100,000 American companies do business overseas, including 3,500 multinational companies. It is estimated that one-third of the profit of U.S. companies is derived from international business, along with one-sixth of the nation's jobs (Cascio, 1989). The competitive global market sets new rules for survival. Companies and their employees must become

more competitive to survive, and they must learn to compete against foreign competitors not only in their home courts but also in their rivals' courts. The level of ambiguity and risk taking increases, and there is a growing need to learn about the characteristics of the global market in order to adjust.

The eagerness to know more about foreign competitors has led to the development of numerous university-affiliated educational programs and research centers on international management, and the growing concern of Americans for the economic competition with Japan has been documented in a significant number of publications. Yet the current body of knowledge and processes in the field of organizational behavior is still limited by geographical, cultural, temporal, and conceptual parochialism (Adler & Jelinek, 1986; Boyacigiller & Adler, 1991).

- *Mergers and acquisitions.* A substantial number of companies have gone through processes of mergers, acquisitions, and downsizing. In the United States alone, between 1987 and 1989 there were 11,428 mergers, with a total value of $645,386 million (*M & A Demographics of the Decade,* 1990). Of these, 1,412 were foreign acquisitions of U.S. companies, and only 621 were U.S. acquisitions overseas. Two of the more famous cases, which may have a symbolic meaning, are the acquisition of the Rockefeller Center in New York and the acquisition of Columbia Pictures by Japanese companies.

Mergers and acquisitions result in organizational downsizing and massive layoffs. A 1989 survey of the American Management Association showed that 39 percent of the 1,084 companies surveyed reduced their work forces during 1990 (Offermann & Gowing, 1990). From 1985 to 1988, approximately 15 million workers were affected by mergers and acquisitions, and nearly three-quarters of the senior executives in an acquired company left within three years. These processes have a strong impact on those who were forced to leave, as well as on the survivors (Offermann & Gowing, 1990). For the survivors, restructuring meant a high level of uncertainty and dissatisfaction, stress, and increasing distrust. Very often a confrontation between different organizational cultures results when two or more companies are merged. Those who were forced to leave experienced economic problems, a high level of stress, and loss of personal worth that often resulted in physiological symptoms. This cost was paid not only by the individual but by society at large.

- *Organizational restructuring.* Following the process of globalization, organizations no longer have distinct physical entities (Miles & Snow, 1984). Headquarters of organizations can be located in one country, manufacturing in another location, sales and distribution in a third country, and service close to the customer in a nonlocal market. As a result, organizations change their structures to become flatter, with fewer layers of management and more diversification. Each distinct part of the business is responsible for the day-to-day operations, whereas the corporate office is responsible for the overall financial control of the division and the overall strategic development (Hill, Hitt, & Hoskisson, 1988). Globalization requires more joint ventures and results in a network of contracted relationships and strategic alliances that often cross cultural borders (Galbraith & Kazanjian, 1988).

- *Customer orientation.* Customer satisfaction is considered a key factor in a competitive market. Experts of total quality management recognize customer satisfaction as the ultimate criterion of quality (Feigenbaum, 1983). To cope with customer needs, organizations to date emphasize the formation of self-contained, close-to-the-customer work groups that learn customer preferences and feed the information to other divisions. As a result, there is a growing emphasis on teamwork and team building, which brings into focus sociocultural group characteristics that were overlooked as long as the unit of analysis was the individual employee (Sundstrom, De Meuse, & Futrell, 1990). This shift toward teamwork in Western cultures is of special interest to industrial and organizational psychologists, since Western cultures are known for their individualistic as opposed to group-oriented values. Empirical research on the group level in industrial and organizational psychology still lags behind the needs of organizations in today's changing world.

- *Emergence of high technology and telecommunication systems.* The revolution in telecommunication systems introduced into the market electronic mail, fax machines, cellular phones, and teleconferences. New technology has facilitated communication across geographical borders and significantly reduced the time needed to process information. New developments of simultaneous computer-based translation of written documents from one language to another will overcome language barriers. Parallel to this, the technological revolution in office and manufacturing automation continues to develop. All these changes will accelerate cross-cultural communication and exposure to different systems of values, norms, and behavior. Management and employees of the future will have to deal with cultural diversity more than ever in the past.

- *Financial forces.* The market is mainly driven by financial considerations of shareholders. The world centers of stock exchange in New York, Tokyo, and Europe are not bounded anymore by geographical borders. Shareholders from all over the world can buy stocks in any one of the stock markets and influence the market values of companies in a particular country. Thus, companies should learn to cope with the cultural diversity of their shareholders.

- *The political arena.* Significant changes are taking place in the political arena, and as I write this chapter, the political map around the world is changing. On the one hand, we witness the process of unification, in particular, the unification of Europe and of East and West Germany, the end of the Cold War, and the political agreement between South and North Korea. The process of unification allows for an influx of immigration from one country to another that crosses not only political but also cultural borders.

On the other hand, we witness the process of deunification in Eastern Europe due to the emergence of national-ethnic forces, such as the declaration of independence of the Baltic Republics and the three major republics of the former USSR—Russia, Ukraine, and Belarus. The declarations of independence stress the hidden cultural diversity that supports the political processes. In both cases, the awareness of the cultural factor increases.

All these changes support the notion that the variance among situations has become as important for understanding work behavior as the variance among individuals.

Traditional Research and Cultural Influences

The previous section reviewed the major changes toward a global work environment that call attention to the cultural factor. Yet this factor has not been incorporated into existing models of industrial and organizational psychology. Present models focus mainly on the individual level of analysis and attempt to explain employee behavior by looking at individual difference characteristics, individual goals, expectancies, self-efficacy, and need satisfaction.

For example, individual job enrichment was found to have positive effects on employee intrinsic motivation (Hackman & Oldham, 1980); the setting of specific and difficult individual goals was positively related to employee performance (Locke & Latham, 1990); incentive plans were developed to reinforce employee performance (Lawler, 1986); and models of human resource management have taken an individualistic approach by concentrating on job analysis, staffing, performance appraisal, compensation, and career management, disregarding activities at the group and societal level such as communication, team building, and cultural values (Cascio, 1989). All of these models were developed and implemented in the United States. Some of the models were tested in other cultures as well (e.g., goal setting), but in most cases the potential moderating effect of culture has been overlooked.

This section attempts to explain why culture has been overlooked by industrial and organizational psychologists. The reasons summarized below were previously suggested by Cappeli and Sherer (1991) for explaining the missing role of context in organizational behavior.

The Use of "Fixed" Research Paradigms

Paradigms serve as road maps for guiding research; therefore, they seriously limit the number and kind of variables under study (Roberts, Hulin, & Rousseau, 1978). Research paradigms comprise the cognitive schema necessary for sampling, selecting, and interpreting empirical evidence. Information cannot be processed unless it can be recognized and interpreted. It is therefore reasonable to argue that existing research paradigms cause biases in information search and block opportunities for collecting and interpreting data that contradict existing paradigms. The system tends to preserve itself and attenuate opportunities for change.

Research paradigms of industrial and organizational psychology were developed in line with the individualistic stream in psychology, which focuses on the individual level of analysis and studies individual characteristics as major explanatory causes of human behavior. This approach overlooks situational effects, including cultural factors, as will be further discussed.

The Individual as the Unit of Analysis

The focus on the individual as the unit of analysis, especially in American industrial and organizational psychology, which dominates the research literature, has distracted attention from broader units of analysis. From a historical perspective, the focus on the individual is anchored in the dominant stream of liberal individualism in psychology, which views individuals as self-contained, autonomous sovereigns in charge of their own lives. This approach calls for a detachment of individuals from the ties that formerly bound them to their community and that define who or what they are or could be. This detachment sets people free to determine their own self-definitions. Communal associations are established by people who existed independently of those associations and who can withdraw their consent to belong as freely as they give it (Sampson, 1989). Under this theory of a person, a "well-ordered society is...one in which people are free to pursue their various aims" (Sandel, 1982, p. 116), and the task of government is to assure the conditions needed to allow individuals to choose their own aims and purposes in life, not to set these aims for the individual. The liberal-individualistic approach has nourished the values of personal freedom, responsibility, and achievement and has served as the basis for all political and human rights. The spirit of individualism is reflected in the amendments to the Constitution of the United States, which state that all American citizens have equal protection under the law (Article XIV, Section 1) and are granted the "freedom of religion, speech, of the press, and the right of petition" (Article 1 of the amendments to the Constitution of the United States).

However, in its extreme form, an individualistic approach views individuals as self-contained and detached from their social milieu, and it ignores the importance of interpersonal relationships in shaping self-identity. The self is, in fact, anchored in the social system, and it is shaped by the shared understanding among members of a particular culture of what it is to be human (Cahoone, 1988; Cushman, 1990; Sandel, 1982). This shared understanding is transmitted from one generation to another through the process of socialization. Extreme individualism limits the development of the self by reducing the role played by interpersonal relationships in shaping self-identity.

The individualistic paradigm confines the level of analysis mainly to the individual level, disregarding sociocultural effects. The neglect of contextual factors often leads to a false attribution of contextual effects to individuals (Ross, 1977).

The focus of American psychology on the individual level of analysis coincides with the dominant individualistic culture of the

United States, unlike collectivistic cultures, which pay more attention to contextual and cultural factors (Boyacigiller & Adler, 1991; see also chapter 2 by Triandis in this volume). Furthermore, citizens of large countries such as the United States are less likely to speak foreign languages or to know about other countries than citizens of small countries (Hofstede, 1991). Consequently, the latter develop more awareness of cultural differences.

In the new era of globalization, the individualistic approach does not provide the conceptual framework and methodology for understanding cross-cultural differences in the formation of cognitive schemas, self-identity, and individual behavior. A new theory is therefore needed for understanding individual behavior in the global era (Sampson, 1989).

The Cognitive Paradigm

The rise of the cognitive paradigm in industrial and organizational psychology is considered the most important reason for the shift from external environmental factors to internal factors of cognitive information processing, including perceptions, interpretations, and evaluations (Cappelli & Sherer, 1991). The cognitive paradigm focuses on individual perceptions and on the internal representations of the external environment, which is partially shaped by individual difference characteristics (Ilgen & Klein, 1989). Individual perceptions do not provide accurate information on the objective characteristics of the perceived environment. Rather, perceptions are the product, or interaction, of environmental and personal characteristics. The same situational characteristics may lead to different perceptions of individuals who differ in their personality, in their experience, and in their social values and norms. Thus, perceptions do not fully correspond to the objective environment.

It can be argued that cognitive processes mediate the relationship between contextual effects and individual behavior and that both contextual and mediating effects have to be studied in order to understand and predict behavior. Yet the mediating role of cognitive processes has not been recognized, and some researchers contend that although endogenous theories that deal with cognitive mediating processes help explain what is going on in motivation, it is the exogenous theories that provide the "action lever" that can be employed to change work motivation (Katzell & Thompson, 1990). Therefore, these researchers emphasize the need to improve the technology of work motivation—including methods of incentive plans, goal setting, and job design—rather than to develop the cognitive mediating models.

Knowledge of the mediating processes per se does not convey specific information on the nature of the situational characteristics. Hence, any attempt to control or change situational effects requires the identification of the situational factors and their causal relationships with the mediating processes and their consequent behavior. Unfortunately, the gradual rise of the cognitive paradigm in industrial and organizational psychology distracts attention from the situational factors and is accompanied by a gradual erosion in the role of context in ongoing research of organizational behavior. This happens because according to the cognitive paradigm, "if individuals construct their own images of the environment which vary across individuals, then why bother with the objective environment?"(Cappelli & Sherer, 1991, p. 82). Culture is a characteristic of the social context, and as such it is not part of the existing cognitive paradigm.

Bridging the Micro-level of Individual Behavior and the Macro-level of Contextual Factors

Cappelli and Sherer (1991) argue that "there is no way to relate macro theories with their focus on the environment, to micro behavior or visa versa" (p. 87). Their solution to the problem is to focus on the organizational level of analysis as a midpoint on the macro–micro continuum. They argue that the organizational context can more easily be related to employee behavior than the macro-level of societal factors. Among the organizational variables that were found to affect individual behavior are demographic (Pfeffer, 1983), structural (Pugh, 1976), and technological characteristics (Hulin & Rosnowski, 1985). Yet the mere relationship between various organizational variables and employee behavior does not contribute to our understanding of causality. The causal link may be explained by mediating cognitive processes (Hulin & Roznowski, 1985).

Developing a Theoretical Model

New models are developed in response to identified weaknesses in past models of individual behavior. Models and theories are being tested under changing conditions, and their boundary conditions are identified along the dynamic process of theory development. The process of globalization in the eighties has changed the work context and has opened up opportunities for transferring managerial techniques across cultures. Attempts to implement Japanese management techniques in U.S. companies were driven by the crisis in the American auto industry, which lost part of the market in competition with the Japanese. Following the common wisdom that if you can't beat them, join them, Japanese management techniques were transferred to the United States, with only limited success. In particular, attempts to implement quality circles in the United States were far less successful than their counterparts in Japan (Lawler, 1986). These failures have brought into focus the potential moderating effect of culture on work behavior. Similarly, in the field of consumer behavior, the recognition of cultural diversity has led companies to develop different advertisements for their products in different cultures (Schiller, 1989). Thus, culture is becoming a significant moderator of the

effectiveness of various managerial and marketing techniques.

The recognition of culture as a moderator has stimulated research that centers on the identification of cultural dimensions and on the similarities and differences in values across cultures. Among the typologies are ones developed by Elizur (1984), England (1983), Hofstede (1980), Ronen & Shenkar (1985), Schwartz and Bilsky (1990), and Triandis, Bontempo, Vilareal, Masaaki, and Lucca (1988).

The typologies vary in the cultural dimensions they measure and in the methodology they use for assessing cultural differences. Hofstede (1980) developed the most popular typology to date, consisting of four major dimensions of work values: collectivism/individualism, high/low power distance, high/low tolerance of ambiguity, and masculinity/femininity. He used the typology to differentiate among 40 IBM subsidiaries across 40 countries.

Cultural typologies contribute to our knowledge and understanding of cross-cultural differences, but they do not help us understand how culture moderates the effect of managerial practices on employee behavior. The question still remains how the three factors—culture, managerial techniques, and individual work behavior—are interrelated. To answer this question, a new model should be developed, since existing models do not offer a conceptual framework for understanding the causal relationship between culture, managerial and motivational techniques, and employee behavior. The development of a new model involves two major steps. The first step is to critically examine previous models by using analytic criteria, empirical criteria, and criteria of peer evaluation. These criteria are used in the second step, searching for a new model, which is described below.

Searching for a New Model

The development of a new theory is not an end in itself. Rather, a better theory is a means to an end. Therefore, a theoretical model should generate a series of steps in a problem diagnosis/solution generation process (Campbell, 1990). The improvement of conceptual models could be reached by using three criteria: (a) It can be derived analytically; (b) it can come about as a result of evaluations of experts in the field of study; and (c) it is evaluated empirically (Campbell, 1990). All three criteria are considered in the process of formulating a new model of cross-cultural industrial and organizational psychology.

Analytic Evaluation. In line with the analytic approach, I choose to critically reexamine two conventions in industrial and organizational psychology: (a) that cognitive models of information processing inhibit the inclusion of cultural factors in models of organizational behavior (Cappelli & Sherer, 1991), and (b) that there is at present no way to relate the individual-based explanations of individual behavior in microresearch to the environment or context-based explanations of organizations in macroresearch.

An analytic examination of the nature of cognitive models may lead to a counter argument concerning the two conventions: namely, that cognitive models may help incorporate cultural factors into behavioral models and link micro- and macroresearch levels. Cognitive models of human information processing provide the theoretical foundation for understanding persons as processors of information and as allocators of cognitive resources. Within the social domain, models of cognitive information processing are known as models of social cognition. Such models enable us to understand how information from the social environment, as well as from internal cues, is sampled, processed, interpreted, and stored in cognitive schemas. Information that fits the cognitive schema is more likely to be accepted than conflicting information (Wyer & Srull, 1989).

A cognitive framework can be used for defining culture. In cognitive terms, culture is viewed as a set of shared meaning, transmitted by a set of mental programs that affect individual responses in a given context (Hofstede, 1980; Shweder & LeVine, 1984). As such, culture shapes the cognitive schemas that ascribe meaning and values to motivational variables and guide our choices, commitments, and standards of behavior. Culture serves as a criterion for evaluating the meaning of various managerial techniques and the valences of their behavioral outcomes.

An in-depth analysis of the cognitive process of information reveals that individuals not only process information but also have an awareness and knowledge about these internal processes. This knowledge serves as a source of influence on a person's behavior (R. Kanfer, 1990). An awareness of one's own cognitive processes resides in the self. Individuals are capable of self-regulating their behavior toward goal attainment by taking these steps: (a) *self-monitoring*, which pertains to the attention people pay to their own behavior; (b) *self-evaluation*, which takes place through personal judgment of the discrepancies between a person's behavior and the goals and standards for behavior; and (c) *self-reaction*, achieved by creating incentives for one's own actions and by responding evaluatively to one's behavior (Bandura, 1986).

Using a cognitive framework of self-regulatory processes, the self can be viewed as an interpreter of managerial practices and motivational techniques in light of cultural values and norms and in relation to the fulfillment of self-generated needs. Thus, the self bridges the gap between the macro-level of culture and managerial practices and the micro-level of individual behavior. Following this analysis process, the following is proposed: *Cognitive models of self-regulation facilitate rather than inhibit the integration of cultural variables into models of organizational behavior, and they mediate the relationship between the macro-level of cultural factors and the micro-level of employee behavior.*

Expert Evaluation. This is the second criterion for evaluating the quality of theoretical models. Researchers in the field of cross-cultural psychology admit that their theoretical models of cross-cultural psychology are poorly developed. Although the field of industrial and organizational psychology has a longer tradition of theory development than that of cross-cultural psychology, "the state of theory in industrial and organizational psychology is not what it should be and improvement is needed," Campbell (1990, p. 40). In particular, theories have been criticized for lacking validity generalization across cultures (Boyacigiller & Adler, 1991).

Empirical Validation. The generalizability of present theories of industrial and organizational psychology has been empirically validated mainly in the United States. Yet the theories failed to explain the variance in research findings across cultures (Adler, 1986; Amir & Sharon, 1988). What happens to a theory when it is not supported by empirical findings? The answer to this question is guided by two different approaches. One approach represents the school of logical empiricism, which asserts that some theories are right and others are wrong and that the empirical confrontation is a test of whether a given theory is valid. The second approach represents the position of contextualism, which maintains that empirical confrontation is a continuing process of discovery of the contexts under which hypotheses are true and those under which hypotheses are false (McGuire, 1983). According to this approach, "the role of the empirical side of science is not to test which of the opposite formulations is valid but rather to explore and discover the range of circumstances in which each of the opposite formulations holds" (McGuire, 1980, p. 79). For example, failures to generalize the

validity of a motivational technique across cultures would lead to the search of the boundary conditions in which the motivational technique is found to be effective. A theory is refuted only when it does not predict in any context.

The contextual paradigm can serve for studying the level of generalization of behavioral rules across cultures. Two sets of behavioral rules were identified in the past: the *emic* rules, which are culture-specific, and the *etic* rules, which are universal and generalizable across cultures (Berry, 1979). A more recent classification distinguishes between three levels of generalizations across cultures: Relativism conveys the emic approach by proposing that "explanations of psychological variation across the world's people are to be sought in terms of cultural variations with little recourse to other factors" (Berry, Poortinga, Segall, & Dasen, 1992, p. 256). Theoretically, relativists do not show much interest in the existence of similarities across cultures. Methodologically, they focus on research within a particular culture and develop psychological assessments and procedures within the local cultural terms, thus avoiding cross-cultural comparisons and generalizations.

In contrast, absolutism implements the etic rules by viewing all psychological phenomena to be basically the same across cultures. For example, the essential character of equity, leadership, and commitment is considered to be the same everywhere, and the possibility is ignored that the researchers' knowledge is rooted in their own cultural conceptions of these phenomena. Methodologically, cross-cultural differences are frequently studied based on the use of the same instruments in many cultures.

The third level of generalization across cultures is universalism, which proposes that "basic psychological processes are likely to be common features of human life everywhere, but their manifestations are likely to be influenced by culture" (Berry et al., 1992, p. 258). The degree of variance in the manifestation of psychological processes is a function of the variability in cultural characteristics. Of the three approaches, universalism is most congruent with the contextual paradigm, and it is considered to be the most fruitful orientation for cross-cultural psychology (Berry et al., 1992).

A model of interpersonal relations driven by the universalistic approach has been developed by Fiske (1991). He distinguishes between four relational models of behavior: *communal sharing*, which is characterized by the fact that people attend to group membership and have a sense of common identity; *authority ranking*, which is a relationship of inequality and a transitive asymmetrical relationship; *equality matching*, which is an egalitarian relationship among peers who are distinct but coequal individuals; and *market pricing*, which is a relationship determined by a market system of exchange. In the market pricing relationships, individuals interact with others when they decide that it is rational to do so, and they denominate value in a single universal measure, typically price, by which they can compare any two persons or associated commodities quantitatively. The four relational models are considered by Fiske to be universal. However, they are implemented differently across cultures according to certain implementation rules, such as the domain to which each model is applied (e.g., family, work) and the persons who are eligible to relate in each way (e.g., spouses, parents–children, superiors–subordinates). In the domain of marriage, for example, the implementation rule in some American families is that of communal sharing, but in other cultures the rule of authority ranking, market sharing, or equality matching may dominate the relationship. Furthermore, the meaning of communal sharing may differ across cultures. In some cultures it reflects unity and identity, whereas in other cultures it involves the sharing of tangible resources. Fiske's (1991) model is by and large conceptual, and it has not yet been tested systematically.

The universalistic approach has guided another line of research designed to test empirically the universality of the structure and content of human values (Schwartz & Bilsky, 1990). Values are defined as beliefs that pertain to desirable end states or behaviors that transcend specific situations, guide selection or evaluation of behavior and events, and are ordered by relative importance. The typology of values proposed by Schwartz and Bilsky (1990) is based on three universal human requirements: biological needs, requisites of coordinated social interaction, and survival and welfare needs of groups. An empirical study across thirty countries (Schwartz, 1992) supports the universal existence of seven motivational domains and the basic structure of compatible and conflicting domains. Schwartz (in press) proposes that, against the background of what is common, it is now possible to compare cultures and groups and to detect genuine variation in value priorities and in the relationship between values and behavior.

The distinction between values and needs can be clarified by using the universalistic paradigm. Needs constitute the starting point of motivation, and they do not differentiate people from each other because all people have the same fundamental needs (e.g., existence, relational, self-esteem; Locke, 1991). In contrast to needs, values are conscious rather than being innate; they are acquired, and unlike needs, a value system "makes each person a unique individual...and guides his actual choices and actions" (Locke, 1991, p. 297). On a macro-level of aggregation, values can be viewed as unique characteristics of members of a particular culture, since culture is formed around shared meaning and values. Hence, according to the universalistic approach, cultural differences in values may affect the interpretation and meaning conveyed by motivational techniques across cultures. It can be argued that research in industrial and organizational psychology is dominated by absolutism, disregarding cultural differences.

In line with the universalistic approach, Erez and Earley (1993) developed a new model of cultural self-representation that integrates the following factors for explaining employee behavior across cultures: cultural factors; managerial and motivational practices; the self, which evaluates managerial techniques according to cultural norms and criteria and in relation to their contribution to the fulfillment of self-derived needs; and employee work behavior as guided by the self in response to the practice of certain managerial and motivational techniques. The model is based on the premise that the basic psychological processes of self-regulation are likely to be common features of human life everywhere. But the meaning ascribed to various managerial and motivational techniques in the process of evaluation varies across cultures in line with cultural differences in the values and criteria used for evaluation. The model is further evaluated in the following section.

A Model of Cultural Self-representation

The model of cultural self-representation is probably the first model of cross-cultural industrial and organizational psychology, and it incorporates the four major components necessary for understanding employee behavior across cultures that were referred to above. The model, illustrated in Figure 1, was first developed by Erez and Earley (1993), and each one of its components, including their causal links, are further examined.

Culture

Culture is often defined in cognitive terms. For example, culture is viewed as consisting of patterned ways of thinking (Kluckhohn, 1954), as a set of shared meaning systems (Shweder & LeVine, 1984), and as a set of mental programs that control individuals' responses in a given context (Hofstede, 1980). The cognitive terms facilitate the integration of culture into the model of cultural self-representation.

Culture, or the set of mental programs and shared meaning, is developed within a certain

ecological environment (Berry, 1979). Adaptation to the environment requires different levels of sophistication and of cognitive complexity. As a result, cognitive schemas across cultures vary in both their level of complexity and their content parameters (Witkin & Berry, 1975). Members of different cultures develop different ways of viewing and perceiving the world. Their level of cognitive complexity was found to be positively related to indexes of economic growth (Gruenfeld & MacEachron, 1975).

Shared meaning conveys the sharing of core values, norms, and modes of action by members of a particular culture. These values are shared and transmitted from one generation to another through social learning processes of modeling and observation, as well as through the effects of individual actions (Bandura, 1986). Any definable group with a shared history can have a culture, and within one nation or one organization there can therefore be many subcultures (Schein, 1990; Schneider, 1975; Triandis, 1972). Once a group has learned to hold common assumptions about adaptation to the environment, its members respond in similar patterns of perception, thought, emotion, and behavior to external stimuli.

In homogeneous societies, the norms and values shared by various ingroups are relatively homogeneous, and they form tight cultures, as in Japan. A loose culture is formed in heterogeneous societies consisting of groups of partly similar and partly dissimilar norms and values, as in the United States (Triandis, 1989).

Four core values differentiate among cultures (Hofstede, 1980, 1991): collectivism/individualism, high/low power distance, masculinity/femininity, and uncertainty avoidance.

Collectivism/individualism, a major cultural characteristic, captures the patterns of relationship between the individual and the group (Hofstede, 1991; Triandis et al., 1988). The major themes of individualism are being distinct and separate from the group, having an emphasis on personal goals, and showing

FIGURE 1

Cultural Self-representation Theory

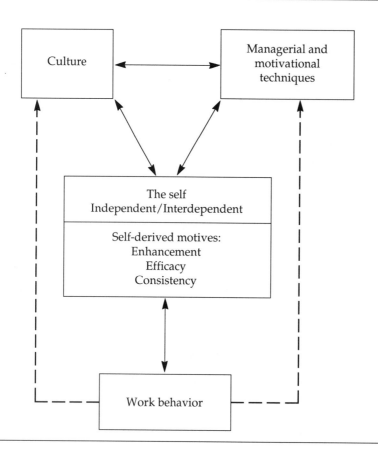

less concern and emotional attachment to the ingroups. In contrast, collectivism conveys self-definitions as part of the group, subordination of personal goals to group goals, concern for the integrity of the group, and intense emotional attachment to the ingroup (Triandis et al., 1988). Collectivism/individualism has a direct implication for the workplace. Workers in individualistic cultures are expected to act according to their personal needs and self-interests. In collectivistic cultures, in which the work group is the ingroup, employees are expected to act according to the interest of their group, which may not always coincide with their individual interests. Human resource management practices differ between individualistic and collectivistic cultures: Hiring and promotional decisions in individualistic cultures depend on the personal characteristics and on the performance level of the individual employee, whereas in collectivistic cultures they depend on the relationship of the individual to the group and on his or her contribution to group performance (Hofstede, 1991).

High/low power distance reflects the degree of inequality in society. Power distance in the workplace can be observed between superiors and subordinates. In cultures with high levels of power distance, organizations are likely to be hierarchical; subordinates are expected to be told what to do, and they are afraid to express their ideas openly in front of their superiors. In such cultures, there are visible signs of status differences, the salary gap between superiors and subordinates is high, and superiors are entitled to privileges. In contrast, status differences and high salary gaps are not tolerated in cultures of small power distance.

Masculinity/femininity provides another source of distinction among cultures. *Masculinity* pertains to societies in which social gender roles are clearly distinct, men are supposed to be assertive and tough and to focus on material success, and women are expected to be modest, tender, and concerned with quality of life. Organizations in masculine societies provide unequal opportunities for men and women to advance in the managerial echelon and stress work centrality over family life, independence over interdependence, decision over intuition, assertiveness over consideration, results over process, equity over equality, and an adversary over a mutual style of conflict resolution and negotiation. *Femininity* pertains to societies in which social gender roles overlap.

Uncertainty avoidance reflects the level by which members of a culture feel threatened by uncertain or unknown situations. In uncertainty avoidance societies, there are many formal rules controlling the rights and duties of employers and employees and many rules and regulations controlling the work process.

Cultural values have an immediate impact on organizational structures and processes and on employee behavior. Managerial practices and motivational techniques that are considered to be legitimate and acceptable in one culture may not be acceptable in another culture. Therefore, culture should be taken into consideration when evaluating the effectiveness of various managerial and motivational techniques.

A developmental perspective on cultural evolution of societies points at a shift from traditional-collectivistic cultures to modern-individualistic cultures, with a focus on exchange rather than communal relations and on the independent rather than the interdependent self. The shift toward individualism has been found to be associated with high levels of gross national product (GNP; Hofstede 1991; McClelland, 1961; Triandis, 1989). Furthermore, Hofstede (1991) suggests that the GNP per capita is positively and linearly related to individualism. Countries dominated by individualistic values have higher levels of GNP per capita than countries dominated by collectivistic values, as shown in Figure 2. Yet a careful examination of the graph suggests that many of the countries that scored above the regression line on collectivism had higher scores on GNP per capita compared to the prediction made by the regression line. Among those countries are Singapore, Hong Kong, Japan, and Scandinavia.

Furthermore, the advantage of individualistic over collectivistic countries may depend on the criteria being used. For example, comparative measures of stress and health problems indicate that Western individualistic countries suffer from these problems more than collectivistic cultures and that there is a trade-off relationship between affluence and stress in Western countries (Henry & Stephens, 1977). Keeping GNP per capita constant, the advantage of collective groups in reducing health problems and prolonging life expectancy is evident in the kibbutzim in Israel. Research data collected between 1975 and 1980 by Leviatan (Leviatan, 1983; Leviatan & Cohen, 1985) demonstrated that the life expectancy of elderly people in the kibbutzim in Israel was significantly higher than that of elderly people in urban areas. In the kibbutz, life expectancy

FIGURE 2

1970 Individualism Index Scores Versus 1987 GNP Per Capita for 49 Countries

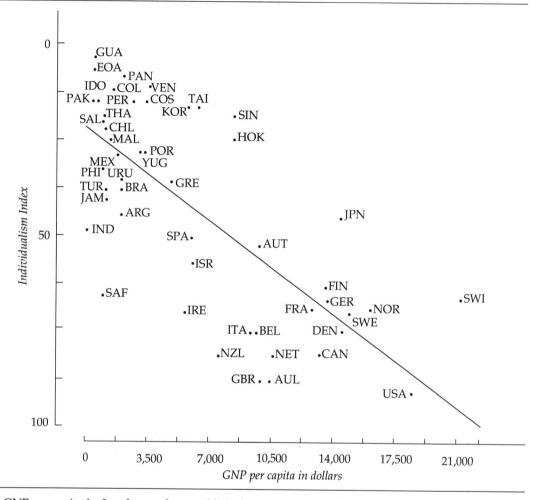

Note: GNP per capita for Iran has not been published since 1977. For multicountry regions, GNP per capita data are not a meaningful criterion.

From *Culture and Organizations: Software of the Mind* (p. 75) by G. Hofstede, 1991, London: McGraw-Hill. Copyright 1991 by McGraw-Hill. Reprinted by permission.

for men was 74.4 years, and for women it was 78.9, compared to the total population figures in Israel of 71.9 and 75.4, respectively. Leviatan (1983) attributed this increased life longevity to the social support system for the elderly people in the kibbutzim.

The emergence of Japan and other Confucian-culture countries as economic powers in the 1980s, with more rapid economic growth patterns than Europe and North America, suggests that collectivism can be compatible with rapid development. What is not clear, however, is whether rapid growth occurs *only* when countries are "catching up" with the more developed countries.

Management Practices and Motivational Techniques

Employee behavior in organizations is partly directed by management practices, including human resource management and motivational techniques. A typical model of human resource management in the United States is tailored to fit in with an individualistic approach (Cascio, 1989). For example, selection of individual employees is based on individual difference characteristics, performance appraisals are centered on the individual and his or her personal achievement, individual compensation plans are commonly implemented in American companies, and job enrichment is designed for the individual employee.

Unlike American models of HRM, Japanese models of HRM center on the group level and on the philosophy of mutuality between management and employees, as realized in many of the large corporations by the principle of lifetime employment, by an emphasis on interpersonal communication, and by group participation. Employees are evaluated on their contribution to their group and their organizational unit (Erez, 1992). Therefore, it is reasonable to argue that managerial practices that are consistent with Japanese culture may not be effective in American companies, and vice versa.

Cultural values and norms serve as criteria for evaluating and interpreting the meaning of various managerial practices and motivational techniques for the individual employee. Information concerning management practices and motivational techniques is processed by the individual self and evaluated in terms of its potential contribution to a person's sense of well-being and self-worth. Management practices perceived to make a positive contribution are more likely than others to be accepted and to have a positive effect on employee behavior.

Similar methods of managerial practices and motivational techniques are likely to be evaluated differently by the self in individualistic and collectivistic cultures, depending on their contribution to the notion of well-being and self-worth in each culture. The role played by the self as an evaluator and an interpreter for understanding the relationship between culture, managerial techniques, and employee behavior will be discussed in the next section.

The Self

"The self consists of all statements made by a person, overtly or covertly, that include the words 'I,' 'me,' 'mine,' and 'myself'" (Triandis, 1989, p. 506). According to this definition, a person's attitudes, intentions, roles, and values represent the self.

People everywhere are likely to develop an understanding of themselves as physically distinct and separable from others (Hallowell, 1955). Beyond a physical self, individuals have a private self that conveys the awareness of internal thoughts and feelings that are private to the extent that they cannot be directly known by others (Markus & Kitayama, 1991). Yet these thoughts and feelings are shaped to a great extent by the shared understanding within a particular culture of what it is to be human (Cahoone, 1988; Cushman, 1990). The enduring attachments and commitments to the social environment help define who the persons are (Sandel, 1982). The self is a composite view of oneself that is formed through direct experience and evaluations adopted from significant others. In cognitive terms, the self is viewed as a person's mental representation of his or her own personality. It is formed through both experience and thought and encoded in memory alongside mental representations of other objects, reflected and imagined, in the physical and social world (Kihlstrom et al., 1988). The self is both the knower and what is known (Markus & Wurf, 1987), or the mind and the basic values, knowledge, and skills stored in the mind. The self can be described on both structural and dynamic dimensions.

The Structural Dimensions of the Self. On the structural level, the self is viewed as a collection of schemas, prototypes, goals, or images that are arranged in a space (Sherman, Judd, & Bernadette, 1989). Each schema is a generalization about the self. It contains descriptive information about traits, roles, and behavior, as well as procedural knowledge of rules and procedures for making inferences and evaluations for its own functioning and development (Kihlstrom & Cantor, 1984).

The various attributes of the self seem to be organized along two dimensions: from general to specific, and from central to peripheral. The general attributes of the self are further divided into more specific self attributes (Cantor & Khilstrom, 1987; Shavelson & Marsh, 1986; Sherman et al., 1989). The central traits are more substantial for the self-concept than the peripheral traits (Cantor & Kihlstrom, 1987). Individuals are known to be more committed to their central roles because these roles are more consequential to their behavior (Gecas, 1982).

Not all the information stored in the self is accessible at any particular moment. The aspects of personality brought to our attention at any particular time are determined by contextual factors, which stimulate the cognitive processing of information relevant to the context (Khilstrom et al., 1988). The part of the self active at any moment is defined as the "working self," or "the self-concept of the moment," and it directly encounters the environment (Markus & Kunda, 1986; Markus & Wurf, 1987). Compared to the deeper levels of the self-concept, it is more accessible, active, malleable, and tied to the prevailing circumstances. The configuration of the immediate social environment determines the facet of the self that is to be most accessible.

The Dynamic Processes of the Self. The self has been conceived of in terms of dynamic self-regulatory processes. These processes consist of (a) the setting of goals that represent proximal and enduring self-definitions; (b) planning and strategy selection to facilitate goal attainment; (c) self-monitoring, which takes place as people attend to various aspects of their behavior, including intensity, direction, and quality; (d) judgmental processes, which evaluate the behavior in line with certain standards, and (e) self-reaction, including self-reinforcement (Bandura, 1986; F. H. Kanfer, 1980; Markus & Wurf, 1987).

Self-regulatory processes operate in the service of developing and maintaining a positive representation of the self, namely, in developing a sense of self-worth and well-being. Thus, the self-concept is to a large extent an agent of its own creation (Gecas, 1982). The positive representation of the self is maintained by satisfying three basic motives (Gecas, 1982; Markus & Wurf, 1987): (a) self-enhancement, as reflected in seeking and maintaining a positive cognitive and affective state about the self; (b) self-efficacy, which is the desire to perceive oneself as competent and efficacious; and (c) self-consistency, which is the desire to sense and experience coherence and continuity. All three motives—self-enhancement, self-efficacy, and self-consistency—are part of the self-regulatory processes, and their fulfillment is evaluated by the self on the basis of their contribution to a positive representation of the self and to a sense of self-worth and well-being.

The process of self-evaluation requires the use of a set of criteria and guidelines. Three reference sources of criteria are recognized (Breckler & Greenwald, 1986). The first is the public evaluation that a person gains from others. The second is the self-evaluation, as determined by personal, internal standards. The third is based on the contribution that one makes to the collective, or the reference group to which the individual relates him or herself. These three criteria that are represented in the self pertain to three facets of the self. The public self represents cognition concerning others' view of the self. It is sensitive to the evaluations of significant others and seeks to gain their approval (Breckler & Greenwald, 1986; Triandis, 1989). The private self represents cognition that involve traits, states, or behaviors of the person, and it seeks to satisfy internal standards of achievement. The private self represents a person's view of what makes him or her unique and unlike other people. The collective self is guided by the criteria of achieving the goals of and fulfilling one's role in a reference group. The collective self corresponds to the notion of social identity, which, according to Tajfel (1978), is "the part of the individual's self-concept which derives from his or her knowledge of his/her membership in a social group, together with the values and the emotional significance attached to this membership" (p. 63).

The criteria for evaluation used by the self vary across cultures along with differences in cultural values, and they end up shaping different meanings of self-worth. Criteria used by the private self are supported by individualistic values, whereas those representing the collective self are dominant in collectivistic cultures. The public self is considered to be an extension of the private or the collective self, depending on the culture (Triandis, 1989). In individualistic cultures it is assumed that the generalized others will reinforce autonomy and independence, whereas in collectivistic cultures they will reinforce the subordination of the private goals to the collective goals.

The development of the three reference points of the self is anchored in the cognitive discrimination between self and others. The sequence of development is from the public to the collective self (Breckler & Greenwald, 1986). The first developmental stage of the public self reflects conformity to external rules, with conscious preoccupations centering on appearance and social acceptability (Piaget, 1965). The private self is developed as the individual internalizes the valuative standards of others. It is seen as the conscientious stage of ego development, with an emphasis on long-term self-evaluated goals, self-set standards for achievement, differentiated self-criticism, and a sense of responsibility (Loevinger, 1976). The collective self represents a further developmental step in which the goals of the reference groups have become internalized and the individual is

capable of effective collaboration with others (Piaget, 1965). The three facets of the self have a direct correspondence to Kelman's (1961) analysis of social influence in terms of compliance, internalization, and identification.

Although the structural and dynamic dimensions of the self are considered to be universal, the relative differentiation between self and others varies across cultures. People who live in the same cultural environment share similar values and cognitive schemas, and they use similar criteria for evaluating the contribution of certain types of behavior to the development of a sense of self-worth (Triandis, 1989). Western cultures are known for their individualistic values. In these cultures the self is less connected and more differentiated from the social context. The normative imperative is to become independent from others, self-reliant, and to discover and express one's unique attributes. Western cultures reinforce the formation of the independent self, "whose behavior is organized and made meaningful primarily by reference to one's own internal repertoire of thoughts, feelings, and actions" (Markus & Kitayama, 1991, p. 226).

In contrast, the predominant values in cultures of the Far East are collectivism and group orientation, with an emphasis on harmony, conformity, obedience, and reliability. These cultures tend to be homogeneous, share a common fate, and emphasize interdependence and a sense of collectivity, mainly when they are exposed to external threat and competition with outgroups (Triandis, 1989). People in collectivist cultures stress similarities with other group members that strengthen their group identity. Collectivistic cultures emphasize the connectedness of human beings to each other, and they cultivate the interdependent construing of the self (Markus & Kitayama, 1991). The interdependent self, according to Markus and Kitayama (1991, p. 227), entails "seeing oneself as part of an encompassing social relationship recognizing that one's behavior is determined, contingent on, and, to a large extent organized by what the actor perceives to be thoughts, feelings, and actions of others in the relationship." The focus of the interdependent self is on the relationship of the person to others.

Empirical findings demonstrate that people from East Asia tend to describe themselves in terms reflecting their collective-interdependent self more frequently than do Europeans or North Americans (Bond & Cheung, 1983; Trafimow, Triandis, & Goto, 1991). Furthermore, students from a Western cultural background perceive their selves to be less similar to others compared to students from an Eastern cultural background. However, students from an Eastern background perceive others to be less similar to themselves than do students from Western cultures. This finding suggests that for individuals from a Western background, self-knowledge is more distinctive and elaborate than knowledge about others; whereas for individuals from an Eastern background, knowledge about others is more distinctive and elaborate than knowledge about the self (Kitayama, Markus, Tummala, Kurokawa, & Kato, 1990). Chinese, who are driven by the interdependent self, have higher social needs than needs for autonomy and for personal achievement (Bond, 1986).

The typology of the three self-derived motives—enhancement, efficacy, and consistency—and the typology of the private and collective self, or independent and interdependent self, were developed as two separate systems. The question of how these two systems relate to each other has not yet been addressed. It is reasonable to argue that the fulfillment of the three self-derived motives should have a different meaning in reference to the independent or the interdependent self.

For this purpose the two systems should be integrated, as presented in Figure 1: The three self-derived motives are nested within the two facets of the self—the independent and interdependent self. The different criteria for evaluation driven by the independent and the interdependent facets of the self determine what kind of actions and situations will be perceived as satisfying the self-derived motives. According to this model, self-enhancement driven by the independent facet of the self motivates individuals toward personal achievement. Situations and managerial practices that provide opportunities for individual success are positively evaluated by the independent self. On the other hand, enhancement driven by the interdependent facet of the self motivates individuals to contribute to the success of the group (Erez, 1992), to avoid social loafing (Earley, 1989), and to meet expectations of significant others (Bond, 1986; Markus & Kitayama, 1991).

Perceptions of self-efficacy become salient in face of the independent self, whereas perceptions of collective efficacy, which pertain to people's sense that they can solve their problems and improve their lives through concerted effort (Bandura, 1986), become salient in face of the interdependent self. Finally, self-consistency is evaluated by the independent facet of the self in line with previous individual behavior. Consistency with the interdependent self pertains to the enduring relationship between a person and his or her reference group.

The self, including the self-derived motives, constitutes the link between the contextual factors of culture and managerial practices, which operate on the macro- and mesolevels respectively, and the microlevel of employee behavior. Management practices are evaluated by the self in line with the cultural values as they are represented in the self, and with respect to the fulfillment of the self-derived motives, which are driven by the independent and interdependent facets of the self.

Generalized Work Behavior

The broad concept of work behavior encompasses work-related behavioral processes that take place on the individual, group, and organizational levels. These processes can be measured according to both objective and subjective criteria. Among the objective criteria are performance quantity and quality, withdrawal behavior of absenteeism and turnover, and extra-role behavior, namely, behavior that is over and above expectations. Subjective criteria involve perception and attribution, attitude formation, motivation, and commitment.

Work behavior, as described above, is strongly affected by managerial practices and motivational techniques. Managerial practices are evaluated according to their contribution to employee self-worth and well-being. Cultural values and norms serve as criteria for evaluating the potential contribution of management practices to employee self-worth. A positive evaluation results in a positive effect on work behavior. Thus, the self, which carries a representation of cultural values, mediates the relationship between managerial practices and work behavior.

No study has ever tested the integrated model of cultural self-representation. However, portions of the model are supported by previous research. For example, previous research has examined the relationship between culture and self (Markus & Kitayama, 1991; Triandis, 1989); the relationship between culture, self, and motivated behavior (Markus & Kitayama, 1991); the moderating effect of culture on the relationship between motivational techniques and employee behavior (Earley, 1986; Earley, 1989; Erez, 1986; Erez & Earley, 1987); and the relationship between managerial techniques and the self. Research in this last domain proposes that charismatic leaders operate by implicating the self-concept of their followers and recruiting their self-expressive motivation (Shamir, House, & Arthur, in press). Although research on charismatic leadership did not explicitly examine cultural dimensions, it is implied that charismatic leaders have the ability to empower their followers by identifying the factors that strengthen their followers' sense of enhancement, efficacy, and consistency within their particular culture. Charismatic leaders facilitate followers' intrinsic motivation by emphasizing the symbolic and expressive aspects of the effort they are expected to exert for attaining the goal. Thus, charismatic leaders should be sensitive to cultural values and norms in order to ascribe meaning to the behavioral outcomes they expect to get from their followers.

The model of cultural self-representation helps us understand in retrospect the meaning of previous research. For example, differences in leadership styles between the United States and Japan can be understood in light of the model of cultural self-representation. In Japan, the most effective leader is one who incorporates both performance and maintenance orientations, regardless of the task or the situation examined (Misumi, 1989), whereas in the United States, leadership effectiveness is contingent upon situational characteristics. Task-oriented leaders are most effective in situations that are either most favorable or least favorable for the leader, whereas the employee-oriented leader is most effective in situations that are moderately favorable (Fiedler & Chemers, 1974). One possible explanation is that in an interdependent culture, the personal attachment to the leader most strongly motivates people to do their work, regardless of the situation (Markus & Kitayama, 1991).

The following section reviews and analyzes the effectiveness of similar managerial and motivational techniques across cultures in light of the present model of cultural self-representation.

Managerial and Motivational Techniques

Research in cross-cultural industrial and organizational psychology enriches our knowledge of the reasons that certain motivational techniques are developed and become effective in some cultures but not in others. Cross-cultural studies on work values, work motivation, and human resource management clearly demonstrate that there are significant differences among cultures in collectivistic versus individualistic values and in values of power distance, which is the psychological distance between different levels in the organizational hierarchy (Hofstede, 1980; Triandis, 1989; Triandis et al., 1988). Such differences correspond to the differential effectiveness of various motivational techniques and management practices. Managerial techniques that fit in with individualistic values—individual job enrichment, individual goal setting, and individual incentives—emerge and become effective in individualistic cultures. In contrast, the management practices that correspond to collectivistic, group-oriented values—quality circles, autonomous work groups, group goals, and participation in goal setting and decision making—emerge in more collectivistic cultures such as Scandinavia, Japan, China, and Israel (Earley, 1989; Erez, 1986; Erez & Earley, 1987; Matsui, Kakuyama, & Onglatco, 1987). In the following section, the moderating effect of culture on the effectiveness of four motivational techniques—participation in goal setting, job design, quality control circles, and reward allocation—will be examined.

Participation in Goal Setting

Participation in goal setting and decision making is not value free. In fact, according to Locke and Schweiger (1979), "no issue in the field of organizational behavior and industrial relations is more loaded with ideological and moral connotations than that of worker participation in decision-making" (p. 266). From a political perspective, it increases workers' control over the production and conveys the belief that participatory democracy is a social value in itself. Ideological differences between the United States and Europe led the proparticipation voice in the United States to advocate voluntary adoption of participative practices, whereas, in Europe, compulsory participation is advocated by government legislation. In general, European countries, in comparison to those in the United States, are known to be more collectivistic and to have lower levels of power distance (Hofstede, 1980). It is therefore reasonable to propose that the cultural background can either support or not support participatory management. In fact, European researchers suggest that the strongest predictors of attitudes toward participation and of actual involvement are values, institutionalized norms, and experience with a participative approach (England, 1983; Heller, Drenth, Koopman, & Ruz, 1988; Heller & Wilpert, 1981). In the next section, I will review a number of studies on participation in goal setting and decision making that exemplify the moderating effect of culture on the relationship between participation and employee behavior.

One of the early studies of participation in the work setting was conducted by Coch and French (1948) in the United States. They found that group participation resulted in a higher level of goal commitment and performance than in two other conditions of no participation and participation by a representative. In contrast, a replication of the study in Norway was not successful and group participation was not more effective than participation by a representative. A cross-cultural perspective helped resolve the inconsistencies between the two studies. The authors identified institutionalized differences between the United States and Norway with respect to participation. Norwegian workers were unionized. Therefore, union representatives were perceived to be the legitimate management liaisons. On the other hand, voluntary participation was more acceptable in the United States than institutionalized participation. Direct group participation coincided with the American philosophy of participation but not with the Norwegian philosophy where the legitimate power of union representatives was threatened by direct group participation.

In a more recent study, Earley (1986) discovered that cultural differences explained the differential effectiveness of a goal-setting method that was implemented in the United States and England. A goal-setting technique initiated by shop stewards was more effective than one initiated by supervisors in England. No such differences were found in a U.S. sample. Earley (1986) concluded that English workers, as contrasted with American workers, placed greater trust in their stewards than in their supervisors and therefore responded more favorably to a goal program sponsored by a steward than by a manager. Using the model of cultural self-representation in Figure 1, it can be argued that the managerial practice that was more congruent with the cultural norms satisfied the self-derived motives. It contributed to self-enhancement by making the workers feel good about the collaboration with the stewards, whom they trusted. It increased the level of self-efficacy because employees in England trusted their stewards and therefore were more confident that they could accomplish the goals set by their shop stewards. It also helped maintain self-consistency by being consistent with previous norms of behavior.

Erez and Earley (1987) conducted a cross-cultural study in the United States and in Israel to test for the moderating effect of culture on the relationship between participation in goal setting and performance. The United States is known for its individualistic values and moderate levels of power distance in organizations. In contrast, Israel is known for its collectivistic values and for a low level of power distance (Hofstede, 1980). In Israel, employee

participation programs are institutionalized in the labor relations system. They take the form of work councils in the private and public sectors and of employee representatives in management in the Histadrut sector, which is the general federation of unions and the employer of about 23 percent of the industry (Rosenstein, Ofek, & Harel, 1988). The highest level of participation is implemented in the kibbutz sector, which symbolizes the values of collectivism, group orientation, and egalitarianism. Ultimate decision-making power in the governance of the kibbutz resides with the general assembly of all the kibbutz members (Leviatan & Rosner, 1980).

Participants in this study (Erez & Earley, 1987) were 180 university students, of whom 120 were Israeli (60 of whom were kibbutz members) and 60 were Americans. They were all asked to perform a task under one of three goal-setting conditions: group participation, participation through a representative, and no participation. The results, as portrayed in Figure 3, demonstrate that performance of the Israeli students was significantly lower when goals were assigned to them than when goals were participatively set. In addition, Israeli students who were assigned goals performed significantly lower than their American counterparts. There were no significant differences between the Israeli and the American students when goals were participatively set. This finding clearly demonstrates the moderating effect of culture. The more collectivistic and lower-power-distance Israeli students reacted adversely to the nonparticipative assigned goals as compared to the more individualistic and higher-power-distance American students. A nonparticipation approach was inconsistent with the cultural norms in Israel and hence was negatively interpreted by the self. The results led to the conclusion that the differences between the two countries are not so much in terms of the beneficial effect of participation as they are in terms of the adverse

FIGURE 3

**Presentation of Adjusted Performance Means
Across Goal-setting Strategies and Countries**

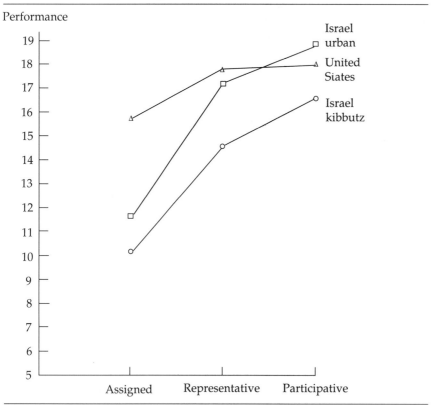

reaction of individuals to their assigned
goals.

Cultural differences may occur between
subcultures within one country and may lead
to a differential effect of participation. Erez
(1986) examined the effectiveness of three levels of participation in three industrial sectors
within Israel, which represent three different
points on a continuum of participative values:
(a) the private sector—guided by utilitarian
goals with no explicit policy of employee
participation; (b) the Histadrut, which is the

federation of most unions in Israel; and (c) the
kibbutz sector—known for its strong collectivistic values, with emphasis on group rather
than individual welfare and on egalitarian
rather than utilitarian approaches to profit sharing (Leviatan & Rosner, 1980). The three sectors
convey different work environments and
provide different opportunities for participation. Results of this study, as portrayed in
Figure 4, demonstrate that group participation was most effective in the kibbutz sector,
participation by a representative was most ef-

FIGURE 4

**The Relationship Between
Goal-setting Strategies, Sector, and Performance**

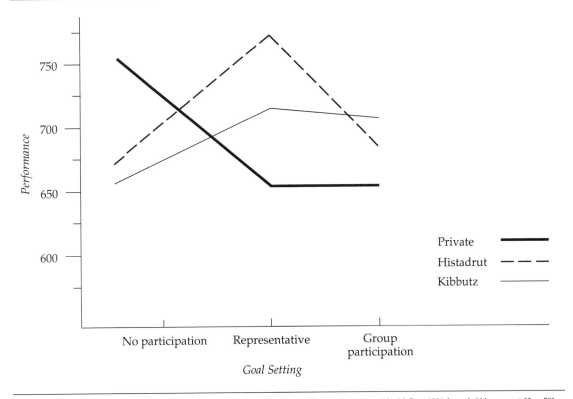

From "The Congruence of Goal Setting Strategies With Socio-cultural Values, and its Effect on Performance" by M. Erez, 1986, *Journal of Management, 12*, p. 591. Copyright 1986 by *Journal of Management*. Reprinted by permission.

fective in the Histadrut sector, and no participation was most effective in the private sector. The interaction effect was statistically significant ($p < .05$). Once again, culture was found to moderate the effect of participation on performance.

The effectiveness of group goals versus individual goals varies across cultures. It was found that in Japan the combination of group and individual goals was more effective than individual goals alone (Matsui, Kakuyama, & Onglatco, 1987). However, in individualistic cultures, group goals very often result in social loafing and free riding because group members in individualistic cultures do not share responsibility to the same extent as group members in collectivistic cultures (Earley, 1989). Perhaps one way to make group performance effective in individualistic cultures is to have the group members become personally accountable for their performance (Weldon & Gargano, 1988).

Participative management can be formed as a subculture in some of the departments within a given organization (Schneider, 1975). For example, French, Kay, and Meyer (1966) examined the effect of participation in the setting of goals as part of a performance appraisal system in the General Electric Company. They found that participation in goal setting was more effective in a department with a participative climate. Assigned goals were more effective in a department with a nonparticipative climate, in particular when employees felt threatened by the appraisal process.

A study conducted in Israel on the implementation of quality circles demonstrated that the technique was successfully implemented in industrial plants in which other mechanisms of employee participation were already in existence, such as labor management councils (Erez, Rosenstein, & Barr, 1990). Again, past experience with participatory management facilitates the adoption of new participative techniques.

In another line of research, Latham, Erez, and Locke (1988) designed a joint series of experiments to identify the conditions that moderate the effect of participation on performance. In a brainstorming session that preceded the study, the researchers discovered that they conceptualized the episode of participation in different ways. For Erez, participation was conceived of as a group discussion process, whereas for Latham, participation took the form of a dyadic relationship between one superior and one subordinate. This example demonstrates how researchers from different cultures have different interpretations of the participation episode.

It is concluded that participative management is effective mainly when it is supported by the cultural values of group orientation, collectivism, and a low level of power distance. In addition, prior experience with participation and appropriate training facilitates the implementation of participative methods.

Job Design

Differences in collectivistic versus individualistic values may explain why different models of job design were developed in the United States as compared to Norway, Sweden, or Japan. Hackman and Oldham's (1980) model of job enrichment, which was developed in the United States, focuses on the design of jobs for the individual employee. The underlying theme of the job enrichment approach is that work can be structured so that it is performed effectively, and at the same time job holders find the work personally rewarding and satisfying. The critical psychological states that mediate the relationship between job dimensions and work motivation are attributes of the independent self. They consist of experienced meaningfulness of the work, experienced responsibility, and knowledge of results. However, the job enrichment model does not include psychological dimensions that pertain to the interdependent facet of the self, such as the formation of group identity and social support.

Although Hackman and Oldham (1980) examine the manifestation of the principles of job enrichment on the group level, they recommend that "unless the case of self-managing work groups is compelling, it may be more prudent in traditional organizations to opt for the less radical alternative of enriching the jobs of individual employees" (p. 225).

The difficulties associated with the group level stem from the lack of knowledge and experience on the part of American managers in managing teams and in dealing with the interpersonal aspect of teamwork. This problem may be less prevalent in collectivistic and group-oriented societies such as Japan and Israel.

Parallel to the development of the individual job enrichment approach in the United States, a similar approach, known as the *sociotechnical system,* or *autonomous work groups,* was developed on the team level in

North European countries such as England, Sweden, and Norway (Thorsrud, 1984; Trist, 1981). The sociotechnical approach attempts to optimize the integration of the social and technical aspects of the work system. Furthermore, the sociotechnical approach takes into consideration the interplay between the organization and its environment and, in particular, the cultural values that specify the norms, rules, and regulations of behavior in organizations. Sociotechnical interventions almost always involve the design of jobs on the group level. They implement the core principles of individual job enrichment on the group level—team autonomy, team responsibility, feedback on performance, and task meaningfulness as enhanced by skill variety and by task identity and significance. One of the disadvantages of the sociotechnical system as viewed by American experts, according to Hackman and Oldham (1980), is that it "does not adequately deal with differences among organization members in how they respond to work that is designed for the sociotechnical perspective" (p. 65). This critique conveys the individualistic value of American culture, which is more concerned with individual difference characteristics than with groups.

The development of the individual job enrichment approach in the United States and of autonomous groups in Northern European countries suggests that the motivation potential of the job has taken two different forms on the basis of cultural differences. In the United States, which is an individualistic culture, the motivation potential of the job is directed to satisfy the independent facet of the self, whereas in Northern European countries, which are more collectivistic compared to the United States, the motivation potential of the job is directed to satisfy the interdependent facet of the self. It is interesting to note that in the kibbutz sector in Israel there is a special unit known as the Unit of Sociotechnical Design that develops and implements sociotechnical

projects in the kibbutz industry. This approach was adopted by the kibbutz sector because it fits with the kibbutzim's cultural values.

The most famous sociotechnical project has been implemented in the Volvo auto company in Sweden. A sociotechnical system substitutes for the traditional assembly line in the Kalmar plant. The work is organized in teams. Each team is responsible for a particular, identified portion of the car, such as electrical systems or interior doors. Team members have the opportunity to develop task identity by assuming responsibility for an identifying portion of the work. In addition, all group members develop multiple skills that allow them to rotate positions and substitute for each other. The multiple skill approach enhances task meaningfulness. A sense of responsibility is developed by self-inspection of product quality. The immediate feedback on quality performance available through inspection provides knowledge of results and enhanced work motivation and performance. In another Volvo plant, located outside Gotenburg, a similar approach has been implemented on the departmental level by delegating as much autonomy as possible to the four main departments (pressing, body work, painting, and assembly). Each department forms working groups to solve unique problems of the department. On the managerial level, industrial democracy has taken the form of work councils, consultation groups, and project groups. These groups have their own budgets to spend for the improvement of working conditions. The main function of management is to create an organizational climate in which people are committed to work and are encouraged to develop ideas for improvement and try them out (Gyllenhammar, 1977). The implementation of the sociotechnical system helps reduce the turnover rate and improves the level of product quality compared to the traditional assembly line. The sociotechnical system has recently been implemented in a new plant in Uddevalla (Kapstein & Hoerr,

1989). This plant is divided into six assembly plants, each of which has eight teams. The teams largely manage themselves, handling scheduling, quality control, hiring, and other duties.

Although morale seems high at Uddevalla, absenteeism is only 8 percent, and the quality level is high, the productivity level, measured in number of hours per car assembly, is lower than that in mass production systems (Prokesh, 1991). The question still remains whether the savings resulting from the high level of quality and the low cost of absenteeism, including the training of new employees, could balance the lower level of productivity in terms of time cycle of car assembly in the new Volvo plants.

Quality Control Circles

The congruence between participation and culture is clearly exemplified by the participative management techniques in Japan. The Japanese set of values is characterized by collectivism, group orientation, and respect for seniority (Hofstede, 1980; Odaka, 1986; Triandis et al., 1988). Group orientation conveys the priority given to the continuity and prosperity of the social system. Collectivism is reflected in self-definition as part of groups, subordination of personal goals to group goals, concern for the integrity of the ingroup, and intense emotional attachment to the group (Triandis et al., 1988). In this culture, the interdependent facet of the self dominates the cognitive processes of sampling, evaluating, and interpreting information from the work environment (Triandis, 1989). The core values of the Japanese culture were implemented into the corporate level and have shaped Japanese management practices. Concern for continuity of the organization and for the integrity of the group has led to the development of a system of lifetime employment. The terms *management familism* (Kume, 1985) and *corporate collectivism* (Triandis, 1989) were used to describe Japanese

management, implying that both management and employees have a high level of lifelong mutual commitment. Japanese managers attribute their success to the lifetime employment system, which enables them to develop mutual commitment between employees and employers, as well as teamwork and group cohesiveness (Erez, 1992). Employee participation displays the value of corporate collectivism. It takes the form of small group activities, including quality circles on the shop floor level and management improvement activities at higher organizational levels. Quality control circles are based on the implicit recognition that workers understand their work better than almost anyone else and they can significantly contribute to its improvement (*Canon*, 1987; *Q.C. Circle Koryo*, 1980; *How to operate Q.C. Circle Activities*, 1985).

Quality control (QC) circles are small groups in the same workshop that voluntarily and continuously undertake quality control activities, which include the control and improvement of the workplace (Onglatco, 1988, p. 15). In Japan, quality control circles have two main objectives: to enhance the company-wide quality level and to contribute to the self-growth of employees.

The QC circles activity in Japan has significantly increased over the years, from about 6,000 circles in 1975 to almost 230,000 circles in 1985 (Onglatco, 1988). QC circles in Japan significantly contribute to the improvement of product quality, enhance the level of efficiency and cost reduction, and facilitate innovation. For example, a software company reported a 70 percent reduction of error rate since the implementation of the system, and a bank reports a significant relationship between a circle activation index and an efficiency index (Onglatco, 1988). QC circles were found to have a significant positive effect on employee attitudes in Japan, in particular on social understanding, enhanced sense of participation, and fulfillment of higher-order needs.

In an attempt to compete against the Japanese, many American companies have implemented QC circles. However, these have not been highly successful (Cole, 1979; Lawler, 1986). One of the reasons for the lack of success in the United States is attributed to cultural differences. QC circles are a form of bottom-up communication, and in the long run they raise expectations for high levels of participation. Yet American management is driven by a different philosophy from Japanese management. Participation does not necessarily fit in with the individualistic approach in the United States, which lacks a group focus and lifetime commitment to the organization. Successful implementation of QC circles requires the involvement of staff support, and of middle- and top-level management. The circles fail to implement their ideas without such a support. Therefore, successful implementation of QC circles seems to require an infrastructure of supportive and participative management.

The Japanese example demonstrates that when motivational techniques are congruent with cultural values, they satisfy the self-derived needs and result in a high performance level. In Japan, the interdependent facet of the self is more dominant than the independent self. Therefore, enhancement, efficacy, and consistency are experienced when an individual makes a contribution to the group and gets recognition for his or her contribution. As a result, motivational techniques that facilitate the contribution of the individual to group success are found to be effective. Reciprocally, effective group performance reinforces perceptions of collective efficacy, which further affect group and organizational performance.

The development of individual job enrichment in the United States, autonomous work groups in Northern Europe, and quality control circles in Japan is not a coincidence. Rather, it supports the idea that different cultures enhance the development of different forms of motivational techniques. Cultural criteria are used for evaluating the motivational techniques.

Motivational techniques that contribute to the fulfillment of the self-derived needs are presumably congruent with the cultural values. In the United States, individual job enrichment satisfies the private self, which is cultivated by the value of individualism. In Northern Europe, the sociotechnical system provides opportunities for the enhancement of the interdependent self, which is nourished by the collectivistic values. And in Japan, QC circle activities fit in with the collectivistic and group-oriented values and provide opportunities for the fulfillment of the interdependent self.

Reward Allocation

Rewards can be allocated on the basis of at least three principles: the principle of *equity*— to each according to contribution; the principle of *equality*—to each equally; and the principle of *need*—to each according to need. Theories of motivation and managerial practices developed in the United States are mainly guided by the equity rule, namely, that the rewards are differentially distributed and that they are contingent upon performance. This rule is embedded in the expectancy model of motivation, in the equity model, and in models of merit-based compensation plans. Methods of individual performance appraisal have been developed extensively and implemented in the United States because performance appraisal serves as a major criterion for compensation. The scientific management school advocates the philosophy of performance-based compensation and the installment of individual wage incentive plans (Taylor, 1967). The superiority of the equity rule over the rule of equality or the rule of need has continually been advocated by American managers and has never been questioned. When the same allocation rule is so widely used within a particular culture, it seems obvious and is not questioned. However, the same allocation rule may not be taken for granted when implemented in a different culture. Thus, decisions on allocation rules become a meaningful research topic when taking a cross-cultural perspective.

Allocation preferences are influenced by three types of factors: beliefs about the personal utilities of specific distributions, situational demands, and cultural influences (Leventhal, Karuza, & Fry, 1980). Motivational research has mainly been concerned with personal beliefs, and to a lesser extent with specific situational factors. Interest in the cultural influences has stemmed from research in cross-cultural psychology. This research has mainly been published in cross-cultural journals and has not been incorporated into the mainstream of research on work motivation. The meaning and effectiveness of reward allocation systems by using the model of cultural self-representation is examined below.

The model of cultural self-representation proposes that pay level and pay structure are evaluated with respect to their contribution to the fulfillment of self-derived motives—enhancement, efficacy, and consistency—and that cultural norms and values serve as criteria for evaluation. Thus, the significance of pay to a person is determined by the extent to which it conveys information about the domains relevant to his or her self-concept (Thierry, 1992b).

Cultural values of individualism and collectivism modify the principle of reward allocation dominant in a particular culture. The rule of equality fits better with group-oriented, collectivistic values, and it satisfies the interdependent self, whereas the rule of equity fits in with individualistic values and satisfies the independent facet of the self.

Empirical support for the differential implementation of allocation rules comes from observations that individuals with high interpersonal orientation tend to use equality norms to a greater extent than individuals who scored low on interpersonal orientation. The opposite was found for the rule of equity (Swap & Rubin, 1983). A comparative study between China and the United States demonstrated that Chinese,

who are guided by collectivistic values, used the equality rule in allocating rewards to ingroup members more than did Americans, who were guided by individualistic values (Bond, Leung, & Wan, 1982; Leung & Bond, 1984).

Additional research has demonstrated that there are boundary conditions for the implementation of the rule of equality in collectivistic cultures and the rule of equity in individualistic cultures: Collectivists make clear distinctions between ingroup and outgroup members. Therefore, in collectivistic cultures, the rule of equality may not hold for outgroup members. In individualistic cultures, a distinction can be made between public and private reward allocation. Public allocation brings into salience the interpersonal dimension that may attenuate the use of the equity rule and enhances the use of the rule of equality. In fact, a study conducted by Leung and Bond (1984) demonstrated that in both the Chinese and the American samples participants allocated to themselves more resources in the private condition when the social pressure was removed. Furthermore, high performers in both cultures allocated to themselves more rewards than low performers. Chinese males use the rule of equality more than Americans both for ingroup and outgroup members. However, for outgroup allocation, they use the rule of equality when the allocation is public and the rule of equity when allocation is made privately. Thus, in addition to the main effects of culture and situation (level of publicness, and ingroup/outgroup), cultural characteristics interacted with the level of publicness to affect allocation decisions.

The specific characteristics of the situation may bring into salience the collective or the private self. The collective self brings into attention the rule of equality, whereas the private self supports the rule of equity. For example, Leung and Park (1986) compared two environments within the United States and Korea—a work setting, which was guided by performance goals, and a neighborhood, which was guided by the goal of enhancing friendship. They hypothesized that the rule of equity will be implemented in the work setting and the rule of equality will dominate the neighborhood. Their findings supported the situational effect. In both countries, the rule of equity was more highly regarded in the work setting, and allocators who used the equity rule in the work setting were more highly evaluated on social competence than others. In contrast, in the neighborhood situation, the equality rule was more highly preferred than the equity rule. Yet Koreans, compared to Americans, evaluated allocators using the equality rule higher than those using the equity rule. Again, both cultural and contextual attributes influenced the rule of reward allocation.

The strategy of paying individuals by results, which fits in with the individualistic culture, differs considerably between countries (Thierry, 1992a). A survey conducted within the European communities showed that payment by results was most highly implemented in the U.K. and in the Irish Republic (40 to 45% of all employed workers), and lowest in the Netherlands (19%; Thierry, 1992a). These two countries differ in their level of individualism, which is higher in the U.K. than in the Netherlands (Hofstede, 1980).

Of special interest is a case of implementing the management-by-objective (MBO) program in the Israel National Water Company (Gluskinos, 1988). The MBO program consists of setting performance goals, providing individual performance appraisals, and offering individual monetary incentives. The results, at the end of one year, demonstrate that the setting of goals has led to a significant cost reduction, mainly in energy costs. However, mixed attitudes were expressed toward the individual appraisal system and monetary rewards. The appraisal procedure was perceived as quite threatening. In fact, the local union used incidents concerning possible improper appraisal to demand a halt to the written appraisal procedure. The opposition against the written appraisal procedure existed despite the fact that the mean evaluations were above average and only a few employees received really negative evaluations. The bonus system, although it increased the net income of employees, was opposed by 40 percent of them. The objection was related to envy among those not rewarded and the lack of opportunities of showing excellence in certain jobs. Most comments on how to improve the bonus system suggested rewarding teams rather than individuals.

The negative responses to the differential system of performance appraisal and rewards become meaningful only when they are interpreted in light of the dominant cultural values in the company: The company is in the public sector, its employees are all unionized, and they have lifetime employment. Salary and compensation are distributed according to the rule of equality, and promotion is determined mostly by seniority. The organizational culture in the company represents the general dominant cultural values in Israel of collectivism and low power distance. The differential reward and performance appraisal systems were designed for an individualistic culture, and they were not congruent with the cultural values of the company. This incongruence resulted in negative responses to parts of the MBO system. Such negative responses could have been avoided by taking into consideration the organizational culture and adjusting the MBO system accordingly.

Tornblom, Jonsson, and Foa (1985) compared the use of the three allocation rules—equity, equality, and needs—in the United States and Sweden. The Swedish value system (Tomasson, 1970) is oriented more toward equality than the American system. The Swedish education system discourages competition in favor of cooperation. Teamwork and solidarity are encouraged rather than individual achievement. The equality rule fits in with the Swedish system of values, whereas the equity rule fits in with the American system. Tornblom et al. (1985) hypothesized that the order of preference of allocation rules for the Swedes is equality, followed by need and by equity, and that the three rules are more highly differentiated by the Swedes than by the Americans. The results clearly support the predicted preference order. The equality rule is significantly stronger among Swedes than among Americans. The equity rule is stronger in the United States than in Sweden, and the need rule is negatively viewed by Americans, whereas the Swedes are indifferent to this rule. The degree of differentiation among rules is higher for Swedes than for Americans.

The high value given in Sweden to interpersonal orientation is emphasized in the criteria for advancement. A positive correlation was found between cooperativeness and rate of advancement in Scandinavia and Japan but not in ten other countries, including the United States, the Netherlands, Belgium, and Germany (Rosenstein, 1985).

The three allocation rules were examined with respect to a positive and negative allocation—bonus and cut in pay, respectively—both in the United States and India (Berman & Singh, 1985). Results demonstrated that for Indians the order of preference of the three rules was need, equality, and equity across situations. The Americans distributed on the basis of equity in the positive resource condition, but on the basis of need in the negative resource condition. Several explanations could be offered for the results. First, allocation on the basis of need predominates in collectivistic cultures, due to the high level of personal interdependence and a greater sensitivity to other people's needs (Murphy-Berman, Berman, Singh, Pachauri, & Kumar, 1984). Second, the rule of need is more likely to be implemented when many people live below the poverty line, as in the case of India. A third explanation is that Indians are less sensitive to merit since status in their society is determined by affiliation and not so much by achievement (Berman & Singh, 1985).

These studies clearly demonstrate that cultural factors are related to preferences for rules of reward allocation. The application of an inappropriate distribution rule may cause feelings of injustice and may demotivate employees. Therefore, knowledge about cross-cultural differences with regard to preferences of allocation rules is vital for implementing motivational techniques.

To summarize, the emergence of different motivational techniques in different cultures is not a coincidence. Rather, it reflects the congruence between the cultural values and the motivation potential of managerial techniques. Managerial and motivational techniques are interpreted by the self in light of the cultural values and in relation to their potential contribution for the fulfillment of self-derived motives. The criteria and standards of evaluation in cultures that cultivate the interdependent self are different than the ones used in cultures that emphasize the independent self. In the former case, enhancement is experienced by contribution to group success, whereas in the latter case it is experienced by personal achievements. Therefore, different motivational techniques are expected to be effective in different cultures.

Influence of Culture on Research Topics

Science is considered to be universalistic and value free (Merton, 1957). Yet in applied psychology, the relevance of various research topics may vary across cultures and work contexts. Some research questions may become more salient than others, depending on the culture of the researchers involved. Researchers may be blind to the fact that their interests are driven not only by pure scientific curiosity but also by the relevance of certain research questions to their immediate sociocultural context. The purpose of this section is to examine the thesis that research topics vary across cultures and that they are affected by cultural characteristics.

To examine these hypotheses I conducted two reviews. The first review includes 714 articles published during the eighties in four countries—Scandinavia (including Sweden, Norway, and Finland), West Germany, Japan, and India—based on listings in the *Psychological Abstracts*. These countries were selected for the following reasons. Scandinavia is a mature, stable European industrial region. West Germany is the growing economic power in Europe and is the only Western country with a positive balance of payments. Japan represents the growing economic power in the Far East. India represents the largest country in mid-Asia. The countries selected represent a high level of cultural diversity.

Articles for the first review were taken from the listings under the heading of "Applied Psychology" from those sections relevant to organizational psychology. The 714 articles comprise all the relevant articles listed in the *Psychological Abstracts* from 1980 to 1989. Articles were classified by country according to the institutional affiliation of the authors. For example, an article by an author affiliated with a Japanese university was classified as Japanese. An article by an author with a Japanese name but who was affiliated with an American university was not included.

The second review included all of the articles published in English-language journals of applied and organizational psychology on topics of organizational psychology. Altogether, 1,700 articles were reviewed in the following 13 journals:

- *Applied Psychology: An International Review* (1982–1989)
- *British Journal of Psychology* (1982–1989)
- *British Journal of Social Psychology* (1982–1989)
- *International Journal of Psychology* (1986–1989)
- *Journal of Applied Psychology* (1982–1989)
- *Journal of Applied Social Psychology* (1982–1989)
- *Journal of Business and Psychology* (1986–1989)
- *Journal of Cross-Cultural Psychology* (1982–1989)
- *Journal of Occupational Psychology* (1982–1989)
- *Journal of Organizational Behavior* (1988–1989)
- *Journal of Vocational Behavior* (1982–1989)
- *Leadership and Organizational Behavior* (1982–1989)
- *Organizational Behavior and Human Decision Processes* (1982–1989)

Articles in this review were classified by country according to the institutional affiliation of the author. The countries examined were the United States, Canada, Great Britain, and Israel. The first three countries were selected because their predominant language is English. Israel was selected because Israeli industrial and organizational psychologists publish mainly in journals written in English.

A list of topics was prepared and each article was coded by two judges—myself and one doctoral student—according to the topics covered. The topics are the ones that best represent the articles under review. An article was coded as covering a particular topic if that topic was identified by the two judges as the main focus of the article.

The research topics used for classification are presented in alphabetical order in Table 1. In addition, articles were classified into five categories according to the group sampled as follows: nonmanagers, managers, entrepreneurs, military personnel, and students.

First Review

The first review consisted of articles published in four countries: Scandinavia, West Germany, Japan, and India, listed in the *Psychological Abstracts* between 1980 and 1989. The classification of countries by source of sample and research topics is summarized in Table 1.

One of the most interesting findings is that more than half of the articles (*n* = 379) were written by authors affiliated with Indian institutions. Scandinavia came next with 171 articles, followed by 95 articles from West Germany and 69 from Japan.

Another interesting aspect of the articles, from all four countries, is that the majority of them are field studies in actual organizations, compared to the smaller number of lab experiments with students.

Scandinavia. Research in the Scandinavian countries focused on workers rather than managers. Only 5 percent of the articles reviewed were about managers, while 82 percent dealt with workers and 10 percent with the military. The topic most highly studied in Scandinavia concerned the physical and mental health of workers. About 53 percent of the articles centered on this topic. Some of those articles focused on physical well-being and on the relationship between stress and mental health. Accident prevention, fatigue, and work in difficult environments such as offshore rigs were addressed. Affiliations of authors of articles were consistent with their emphasis on health issues (e.g., The National Board of Occupational Safety, National Institute of Psychological Factors and Health, Institute of Occupational Health).

Fifteen percent of the articles addressed shiftwork, an issue that has relevance for blue collar workers and that has serious health implications. Other topics were related to the work environment and economic conditions. Nine percent of the articles dealt with the effects of unemployment, particularly its effect on health. Seven percent of the articles concerned new technology, specifically computer technology. Some of these articles examined the physical aspect of working with computers. Training was a concern in 6 percent of the articles, and work satisfaction and motivation were addressed in 4 percent and 2 percent of the articles, respectively. Career-related issues, values, cross-cultural research, unions, and age each represented 2 percent of the articles.

West Germany. The West German research was similar to the Scandinavian research in its focus on workers over managers. Sixty percent of the articles examined workers' behavior, while only 16 percent were concerned with managers. Another 10 percent of the studies came from the military, and only 8 percent were conducted on students. Fourteen percent of the articles centered on worker health and stress, with an additional 10 percent on effects of the physical environment and 3 percent on shiftwork. Thus, altogether, 27 percent of the studies focused on employee physical and mental well-being. Motivation (13%) and training (11%) were two additional topics of high concern in Germany, followed by career-related issues (8%), aging (7%), cross-cultural research (7%), gender differences (6%), selection (6%), and unemployment, turnover, and absenteeism (6%).

Japan. Of the Japanese articles, 23 percent were done under the auspices of the military, specifically the air force. The other articles were almost equally divided between workers (27%) and managers (25%). Students participated in only 4 percent of the studies.

Leadership as well as health and stress problems were the most prevalent topics in Japan, with 25 percent of the articles written on each of the two topics. The majority of the leadership articles used the performance-maintenance construct of leadership developed by Misumi (1989). One could argue that the emphasis on leadership in Japan might be accounted for by

TABLE 1

Distribution in Percentages of Samples and Research Topics in Six Countries

	Countries					
	Scandinavia (*n* = 171)	Germany (*n* = 95)	Japan (*n* = 69)	India (*n* = 379)	United States (*n* = 1,255)	Israel (*n* = 80)
Sample						
Nonmanagers	82	60	27	46	35	34
Managers	5	16	25	46	9	8
Entrepreneurs				5		
Military personnel	10	10	23			3
Students		8	4	4	32	32
Research Topics						
Age	2	7				
Career issues	2	8	11	1	11	13
Communication		2	2			
Cross-cultural research		7		4		10
Decision making		1			2	
Environment—physical		10	2		1	
Environment—psychological					2	2
Family issues					2	
Gender differences	10	6		5	8	6
Health/stress	53	14	25	11	5	4
Leadership		2	25	9	9	5
Legal issues				5	1	
Motivation	2	13	11	18	7	10
Organizational climate		1		7	1	
Performance appraisal		1	2		11	10
Pay system			2		3	6
Satisfaction	4	2	3	20	6	10
Segmentation				13		
Selection		6			14	5
Shiftwork	15	3				
Technology	7		2		2	
Training	6	11		3	2	
Unemployment, turnover, absenteeism	9	6	7	2	5	5
Unions	2			3	2	1
Values				2	4	11

the high energy level and influence of one distinguished researcher in this area. However, a counterargument may suggest that the choice of leadership as a research topic by Misumi (1989), and the fact that this topic attracted the interest of other researchers in Japan who chose to collaborate with him, is not a coincidence. Yet it is surprising that given the Western interest in Japanese management techniques, particularly quality control circles, there was only one article on this topic.

Worker health and well-being in Japan were of concern in 25 percent of the articles, with 14 percent of the articles addressing such topics in nonmilitary organizations and 11 percent of them in military settings. Worker health and safety tended to focus on such physical phenomenon as eye strain and fatigue.

Motivational and career issues each were examined in 11 percent of the studies. Turnover and dropout mainly in the military sector was a concern of 6 percent of the studies. Additional research was about equally distributed between communication (2%), performance appraisal (2%), pay system (2%), satisfaction (3%), and technology (2%).

India. Articles published in India had a broad scope. Research on managers and nonmanagers was equally emphasized, with 46 percent of the studies in each category.

The most prevalent topic, appearing in 20 percent of the articles, was job satisfaction, followed by work motivation with 18 percent. A unique research topic in India was concerned with segmentation and stratification. Thirteen percent of the articles involved comparisons of the private and public sectors, of different levels of the corporate hierarchy, and of different professions. A typical article examined differences in job satisfaction between various organizational layers. Another area of differentiation was that of gender differences, which was the subject of 5 percent of the studies. The

studies examined problems of women executives and dual-career couples and seemed to reflect the growing number of women in the labor force.

Studies on health and stress problems in India were also salient (11%), particularly in relation to job satisfaction. Hence, the focus of Indian research on stress differs from that in Europe because the latter is concerned with stress in relation to physical health.

Seven percent of the articles in India examined organizational climate characteristics, and 4 percent centered on cross-cultural differences. It is interesting to note that career issues were of low concern, possibly because of the stratified society and the limited freedom of career choice.

Second Review

The second review consisted of English journals of applied and organizational psychology. This review covered 1,699 articles on topics of organizational psychology published in 13 journals, mostly between 1982 and 1989. It focused on articles written by authors affiliated with institutes in the following countries: the United States, Canada, Great Britain, and Israel. Table 1 summarizes the classification of articles written by American and Israeli authors. Although Canada and Great Britain were also included in the review, they are not reported in the table because they have a similar distribution to that in the United States, as will be described presently.

United States. The vast majority of the articles published in the journals that we considered came from the United States (1,255 out of 1,699 articles). About 35 percent of the articles published in these journals collected data on nonmanagers, 9 percent on managers, and 32 percent on students. This review differs from the previous one by the larger number of studies conducted on students and in lab experiments.

The most prevalent U.S. topic was selection (14%), followed by performance appraisal (11%) and career-related issues (11%). These three topics concerned issues of personnel psychology. The fourth dominant topic was that of leadership (9%), followed by gender differences (8%), motivational issues (7%), work satisfaction (6%), turnover (5%), health and stress problems (5%), and work values (4%). Pay systems were less frequently studied (3%), as were environmental issues (physical, 1%; psychological, 2%). It is of interest to note that health and stress problems were examined in only 5 percent of the articles compared to their high rate in the first review. Cross-cultural issues were among the least researched topics in the United States.

Canada and Great Britain. A similar distribution to the U.S. one was found in two other Anglo-Saxon countries, Great Britain and Canada. There were 136 articles published in the journals by authors affiliated with British institutes. On the top of this list were articles on selection (21%), followed by articles on turnover (9.5%), leadership (8.8%), stress, and gender differences (8% each).

In Canada, out of 72 articles, an equal number were published on selection, leadership, and stress (12% each), followed by articles on career development (8%), gender differences, and work values (7% each).

It is noted that in the journals considered for the second review there was no article published by affiliates of Scandinavian or German institutes, whereas eleven articles were published by affiliates of Japanese institutes and six by affiliates of Indian institutes. The Japanese published two articles on career development and work motivation and one article each on the topics of work satisfaction, groups, gender differences, physical environment, leadership, pay system, and performance appraisal. The authors from India published three articles on leadership, two articles on work satisfaction, and one on gender differences.

Israel. Eighty articles in this review were published by Israeli authors. It is of interest to note that the distribution of samples in Israel is very similar to that in the United States: 34 percent of the studies were on workers, 8 percent on managers, 3 percent on military samples, and 32 percent on students. The most prevalent topic in Israel was that of career-related issues (13%), followed by studies on work values (11%). Of equal salience were cross-cultural research, work satisfaction, motivation, and performance appraisal (10% each). The rest of the articles were almost equally distributed between gender differences (6%), pay systems (6%), and leadership, selection, and turnover (5% each).

A Comparative Analysis of the Relationship Between Cultural Dimensions and Research Topics in Industrial and Organizational Psychology

Hofstede's (1980) four-value system serves as the conceptual framework for analyzing the differences in research topics among the countries under review. Table 2 classifies the six countries according to the four cultural values.

Collectivism/Individualism.

> Individualism pertains to societies in which the ties between individuals are loose. Collectivism as its opposite pertains to societies in which people from birth onwards are integrated into strong, cohesive ingroups, which throughout people's lifetime continue to protect them in exchange for unquestioning loyalty. (Hofstede, 1991, p. 51)

According to Hofstede, Japan and India are the most collectivistic countries in the present review, followed by Israel, Scandinavia, and West Germany. The United States was found to be the most individualistic country compared

TABLE 2

Classification of Six Countries to Hofstede's Cultural Dimensions

		Collectivism	*Power Distance*	*Uncertainty Avoidance*	*Masculinity*
High	1	Japan	India	Japan	Japan
	2	India	Japan	Israel	West Germany
	3	Israel	United States	West Germany	United States
	4	Scandinavia	Scandinavia	United States	India
	5	West Germany	West Germany	India	Israel
Low	6	United States	Israel	Scandinavia	Scandinavia

to all the 40 countries that participated in Hofstede's study.

As reported in Table 1, the most highly researched topics in the United States were selection, performance appraisal, and career-related issues. It is important to note that the review does not include the journal *Personnel Psychology,* which specializes in these research areas. Thus, it is proposed that U.S. researchers focused on the area of individual difference characteristics. This focus coincides with the individualistic values of American culture (Hofstede, 1980; Triandis et al., 1988). The least researched topics concern cross-cultural issues and topics related to concern for employee psychological and mental health. The individualistic values of the society may explain the small level of attention paid by U.S. researchers to the macro-level of cross-cultural research. A similar distribution of research topics appeared in two other Anglo-Saxon countries, Great Britain and Canada, which are similarly rated as highly individualistic.

Concern for the physical and mental health of employees is mainly advocated by the unions and by legislation. It is plausible that a combination of collectivistic values and a low level of power distance strengthen the power of

employees as a collective, and thus more resources are allocated for dealing with problems related to the physical and mental health of employees, as found in Scandinavia and West Germany, but not in the United States. Indeed, research in industrial and organizational psychology in these countries centers on employee physical and mental well-being.

India and Japan both are characterized by a high level of collectivism (Hofstede, 1980). Indeed, concern for employee physical and mental well-being was prevalent in both countries, but in different forms. In Japan, one of the two most frequently studied topics concerned health and stress problems, whereas in India more attention was given to employee mental well-being and in particular to work satisfaction.

In Israel the two most frequently researched topics were career development and work values. The former pertains to an individualistic orientation, whereas the latter is related to social collectivistic issues. It seems that a similar percentage of topics driven by individualistic and collectivistic values in Israel is not a coincidence. Rather, Israeli society is known to be both collectivistic and individualistic. The culture is classified as collectivistic by Hofstede's (1980) classification. On the other hand, the level of individual aspiration and achievement orientation is considered to be high. For example, work centrality in Israel was found to be higher than in the United States, and mostly because "working is basically interesting and satisfying," according to MOW International Research Team (1987) in their comparative study *The Meaning of Working.*

Ronen and Shenkar (1985) used a small space analysis to classify various cultures into clusters based on attitudinal dimensions. They identified eight clusters (Nordic, Germanic, Anglo, Latin European, Latin American, Far Eastern, Arab, Near Eastern) and four independent clusters (Israel, India, Japan, and Brazil). Although Israel was identified as an independent cluster, it was relatively close to the Anglo cluster, which includes the United States, Canada, and the United Kingdom, countries known for their individualistic values, a low to middle score on power distance, and a low to middle score on uncertainty avoidance. One possible explanation suggested by the authors is that Israel was influenced by the Anglo culture while it was under the British rule before its independence.

Power Distance. Power distance is defined as "the extent to which the less powerful members of institutions and organizations within a country expect and accept that power is distributed unequally" (Hofstede, 1991, p. 28). Japan and India are known for their high level of power distance compared to the other counties under review—the United States, Scandinavia, West Germany, and Israel. Power distance may explain why there is a great interest in the study of leadership in India and Japan. Leadership was the most frequently studied topic in Japan, together with employee well-being (25% of the articles each). Furthermore, the proportion of studies conducted on managers was similar to that of nonmanagers (27% nonmanagers and 25% managers). In

addition, a significant number of studies were conducted in a military context (23%), and part of them focused on officers. Thus, the total number of studies conducted on managers is at least as high as that conducted on nonmanagers.

In India, the percentage of studies conducted on managers was equal to that conducted on nonmanagers (46% each), and it was the highest compared to other countries in our present review. In India, power distance is operated not only through the managerial hierarchy but also through the social system of segmentation and stratification (13%). The dominance of the caste system in India may explain why a significant number of studies focused on differentiation and segmentation in the work setting. Differentiation was studied in the context of industrial sectors—public versus private, differences between managerial levels, differences among professionals, as well as gender differences. The heavy focus on segmentation is unique to India, and it seems to be related to its cultural characteristics.

Uncertainty Avoidance. Uncertainty avoidance is defined as "the extent to which the members of a culture feel threatened by uncertain or unknown situations " (Hofstede, 1991, p. 113). Extreme uncertainty creates high anxiety. Uncertainty is alleviated by technology, law, and religion, and by written and unwritten codes of behavior. Hofstede (1991) suggests that uncertainty avoidance is related to the search for absolute truth. Cultures with high levels of uncertainty avoidance tend to believe that there is only one truth. Israel is known for a relatively high level of uncertainty avoidance, compared to Scandinavia, India, the United States, and West Germany. This cultural characteristic may explain the significant number of studies on work values conducted in Israel. Furthermore, a high level of uncertainty is one of the causes of experienced stress. Although there were only three studies on stress published by Israelis in the journals written in

English that were reviewed, stress has been a significant research topic in Israel. There is a great body of research on stress related to military activity and war. Very often, international conferences on stress are held in Israel. In addition, Haifa University has a research center dedicated to the study of stress.

Israeli researchers were highly involved in cross-cultural research (11% of the studies), and in particular in the study of values from a cross-cultural perspective. This characteristic may be related to the dimension of uncertainty avoidance. It reflects the need to look for the meaning of life and of absolute truth, as portrayed by the interest in values, and the need to reduce ambiguity by knowing more about other cultures. The fact that Israel is relatively isolated geographically, because it is surrounded by Arab countries with which there is a peace agreement only with Egypt, may accelerate the need to relate to other countries and to know more about them.

Masculinity/Femininity.

> Masculinity pertains to societies in which social gender roles are clearly distinct (i.e., men are...assertive...and focused on material success whereas women are...tender, and concerned with the quality of life); femininity pertains to societies in which social gender roles overlap (i.e., both...are concerned with the quality of life). (Hofstede, 1991, pp. 82–83)

According to this value, Japan is identified by Hofstede as the most masculine country, followed in our sample by West Germany, the United States, India, Israel, and Scandinavia. In line with Hofstede's definition, it was found that the most feminine country (Scandinavia) was the one most concerned with employee well-being, including physical and mental health. Israel and India, also characterized by a relatively low level of masculinity, were concerned with topics related to employee mental

health, motivation, and satisfaction. Work satisfaction was the most frequently studied topic in India (20%), followed by work motivation. Thus, the cultural value of masculinity/femininity has an impact on the study of employee well-being and related issues.

To summarize, it is proposed that cultural values draw researchers' attention to some topics more than to others. Cultural values may influence decisions on allocating research grants for different topics. Priorities in resource allocation influence the scope of research conducted in certain areas. For example, in Sweden and Norway, most of the research on the physical and mental well-being of employees is conducted under the auspices of research institutes in these areas, such as the National Institute of Occupational Health in Sweden.

Our reviews demonstrate that a cultural perspective ascribes meaning to the research topics selected by researchers in different cultures. Individual researchers may not be aware of the driving forces behind their research interests. Researchers are reluctant to admit that their selected topics are affected by cultural factors. Yet researchers in Israel, for example, might be surprised to hear that work values are one of the most salient research areas in the country. In fact, I could list at least one researcher in each one of the universities in Israel who studies values from a cross-cultural perspective or in the context of subcultures within Israel: for example, Shalom Schwartz, the Hebrew University (Schwartz, 1992); Dov Eden, Amira Galin, Simcha Ronen, Oded Shenkar, and Teodor Weinshall, Tel-Aviv University (Dubin & Galin, 1991; Eden & Leviatan, 1980; Ronen, 1986; Ronen & Shenkar, 1985; Weinshall, 1977); Yehuda Amir and Dov Elizur, Bar-Ilan University (Amir & Sharon, 1988; Elizur, 1984); Itzhak Harpaz, Uri Leviatan, Baruch Nevo, Ofra Nevo, Michal Palgi, Menachem Rosner, and Moshe Zeidner, Haifa University (Bartolke, Eschweiler, Flechsenberger, Palgi, & Rosner, 1985; Eden & Leviatan, 1980; Harpaz, 1990;

Nevo & Nevo, 1983; Zeidner & Nevo, 1987); and Miriam Erez, Chanoch Jacobsen, Bilha Mannheim, and Yeshayahu Rim, Technion-Israel Institute of Technology, Haifa (Erez, Borochov, & Mannheim, 1989; Jacobsen, 1983; Rim, 1970). Thus, perhaps our focus of attention, preferences, and choices are more highly guided by cultural values than we tend to believe.

Cross-cultural Research and the Individual Culture

Research in cross-cultural industrial and organizational psychology opens up not only cross-cultural perspectives but also new avenues for understanding organizational behavior within a particular culture. When I visited Japan in 1988 and 1989 to study Japanese management, I was accompanied to all the interviews with top managers by Professor Tamao Matsui from Surugadai University. I wondered why he was willing to dedicate so much of his time to listen to what he had already known as a Japanese professor of industrial and organizational psychology until he said to me, "I am blind to the system since I am part of it. Please, open my eyes and let me know what you see in Japanese management." His statement is true for each one of us. Being part of a closed system limits the opportunity to explore and understand the unique characteristics and boundary conditions of one's own culture.

The model of cultural self-representation presented in this chapter proposes the link between culture, managerial and motivational practices, self-concept, and the consequent behavior. Organizational goals and managerial practices are interpreted and evaluated in terms of their contribution to one's well-being. Cultural norms and values serve as criteria for evaluation. The evaluation process affects employee goals, which are the immediate regulators of behavior (Locke & Latham, 1990). For example, the cultural value of social equality

affects perceptions of fairness in reward allocation. Social equality is more highly evaluated in cultures with a low level of power distance. A salary gap between two levels in the organizational hierarchy may be acceptable in a culture with a high level of power distance, but unacceptable in a culture of low power distance. The kibbutz in Israel serves as a model of culture with probably the lowest level of power distance in the world and with a high level of collectivism. This value determines to a great extent the equality of reward allocation in the kibbutz. Indeed, the allocation of rewards in the kibbutz is egalitarian and unrelated to individual performance. The kibbutz movement is now going through a transition of cultural values, which is the result of the need to survive economically and to compete in the marketplace. This transition weakens the collectivistic values and strengthens the achievement-oriented, individualistic values ("The Kibbutz in the Transition of the Century," 1991). This change in the value system may lead to the development of a different system of reward allocation in the future. A differential system of reward allocation will not be acceptable in the kibbutz unless there is a change in the value system.

The identification of one's own cultural characteristics could serve several purposes: (a) evaluating the potential effectiveness of various managerial techniques, (b) adopting decisions concerning new managerial and motivational techniques, and (c) making decisions concerning organizational development and initiated changes in organizational culture.

There is a growing body of organizational consultants and practitioners who serve as agents of various managerial techniques, and they advise management how to implement certain techniques in their organizations based on success stories in other places. Our review leads to the argument that a technical approach to management is doomed to fail. A successful implementation of managerial techniques depends on their congruence with the cultural values of the particular organization and its social environment.

The model of cultural self-representation presented here attempts to explain how and why situational variables influence validities. Previous research in industrial and organizational psychology has tended to ignore situational effects and to focus mainly on individual difference characteristics. This philosophy has led to the development of meta-analytic techniques that enabled researchers to test for validity generalizations across situations while ignoring possible situational effects (Schmidt & Hunter, 1977). The latter were often explained as artifacts. However, it is now time to treat situational effects not as a noise but rather as a signal.

An excellent paper written recently by James, Demaree, Mulaik, and Ladd (1992) suggests that some artifacts are not really artifacts, because their occurrence may be traced back to the situational causes that produce variation in the true validities over situations. Therefore, the researchers developed a statistical model that integrates situational variables into the validity generalization estimation process. They proposed that situational variables should be identified by taking a proactive approach "in which a theory is constructed pertaining to situational moderation of validities, in which theory is then used to design empirical investigations that include assessment of situational variables" (James et al., 1992, p. 10). The model of cultural self-representation in this chapter is perhaps the first model in industrial and organizational psychology to provide a theoretical basis for testing situational effects on validity generalization.

The value and potential contribution of this model could be examined in line with the different roles that theories should play (Campbell, 1990), listed below.

Theories tell us that certain facts among the accumulated knowledge are important, and others are not. Our model tells us that culture is an important determinant of the effectiveness of managerial techniques. Cultural values provide the criteria for determining whether certain motivational techniques will be perceived as enhancing or inhibiting self-worth and well-being. Positive evaluations result in a desired behavior, whereas negative evaluations result in undesired behavior. Thus, the model identifies culture as an important moderator of the relationship between management practices and employee behavior.

Theories can give old data new interpretations and new meaning. Our model helps us understand the boundary conditions of culture and why certain managerial techniques were found to be effective in certain cultures but not in others. Prior to this model, situational effects were ignored because there was no conceptual framework to capture their effects. The model gives old data new interpretations and new meanings by discovering the moderating effect of culture on the relationship between management practices and employee behavior. Some of the core topics of organizational behavior, such as motivation, leadership, groups, and communication, have been reexamined in this chapter from the perspective of the new conceptual model.

Theories identify important new issues and prescribe the most critical research questions that need to be answered to maximize understanding of the issue. Our model is driven by both theoretical and practical considerations. On the practical level, it has two major concerns: the lack of validity generalization of various motivational techniques across cultures, and the failure to successfully transfer managerial techniques from one culture to another. On the theoretical level, it aims at bridging the gap between the macro-level of culture and the micro-level of employee behavior and at identifying the causal relationships between the four major components of the model: culture, managerial techniques, the self as an interpreter of the meaning of management practices for a person's notion of self-worth and well-being, and employee behavior.

Theories provide a means by which new research data can be interpreted and coded for future use. The impact of our model on the field will be tested by the extent to which it will be used for designing new research and for interpreting new data. Two ongoing studies conducted in Israel will have the benefit of using this model. One focuses on the adaptation of Russian scientists and engineers to Israeli culture. The second examines the implementation of new motivational techniques in the kibbutz sector, which is undergoing modifications through a process of ideological changes. I hope the model will stimulate a new wave of research in cross-cultural organizational behavior.

Theories provide a means for identifying and defining applied problems and for prescribing and evaluating solutions to applied problems. Our model provides criteria and guidelines for evaluating the potential effectiveness of transferring motivational techniques and managerial practices across cultures. It proposes that cultural values serve as criteria for evaluating the meaning of managerial and motivational techniques; the self-regulatory processes serve for evaluating the contribution of managerial and motivational techniques to a person's sense of self-worth and well-being. As such, the self mediates between contextual effects—cultural values on the macro-level and managerial and motivational techniques on the organizational level—and the micro-level of employee behavior. A given motivational technique is likely to result in a different evaluation, depending on whether it is appraised with respect to the independent or the interdependent facet of the self. Thus, cultural values as they are represented in the independent and interdependent facets of the self moderate the relationship between motivational techniques and employee behavior.

Theories provide a means for responding to new problems that have no previously identified solution strategy. Our model provides such a means: It incorporates culture as a factor that influences the evaluation of various motivational techniques by the employees. It defines the mediating role played by cognitive processing of information concerning cultural values and motivational techniques with respect to the self-concept. It introduces the self as the link between the macro-level of context and the micro-level of employee behavior. It defines the relationship between cultural values, motivational techniques, the self, and work behavior. These relationships determine the potential effectiveness of transferring motivational techniques across cultures.

The successful implementation of managerial techniques depends on their congruence with cultural values. Cultural values serve as criteria for evaluating the contribution of various managerial practices to employee well-being. Employees will be motivated to allocate all their resources to the attainment of work goals when management practices are perceived to contribute to the enhancement of the notion of self-worth and well-being.

I would like to thank Lynda Sagrestano and Christina Ahmadjian from the University of California at Berkeley for their great help in data collection and analysis of the frequency distribution of research topics in six different countries.

The comments, suggestions, and support of Harry Triandis were invaluable for the writing of this chapter. Special thanks to Ed Locke, who played the role of devil's advocate and helped me balance some of the ideas concerning the positive and negative outcomes of extreme individualism versus extreme collectivism. Finally, I would like to thank my friend Nilli Diengott for the in-depth editorial comments she made, which significantly improved the writing of this chapter.

References

Adler, N. J. (1986). *International dimensions of organizational behavior.* Boston: Kent.

Adler, N. J., & Jelinek, M. (1986). Is "organizational culture" culture bound? *Human Resource Management, 25,* 7–90.

Amir, Y., & Sharon, I. (1988). Are social psychological laws cross-culturally valid? *Journal of Cross-Cultural Psychology, 18,* 383–470.

Bandura, A. (1986). *Social foundations of thoughts and action: A social cognitive theory.* Englewood Cliffs, NJ: Prentice-Hall.

Bartolke, K., Eschweiler, W., Flechsenberger, D., Palgi, M., & Rosner, M. (1985). *Participation and control.* Spasdorf, Germany: Verlag René F. Wilfer.

Beach, L. R., & Mitchell, T. R. (1990). Image theory: A behavioral theory of decision making in organizations. In B. M. Staw & L. L. Cummings (Eds.), *Research in organizational behavior* (Vol. 12, pp. 1–41). Greenwich, CT: JAI Press.

Berman, J. J., & Singh, P. (1985). Cross-cultural similarities and differences in perceptions of fairness. *Journal of Cross-Cultural Psychology, 16,* 55–67.

Berry, J. W. (1979). A cultural ecology of social behavior. In L. Berkowitz (Ed.), *Advances in experimental social psychology* (Vol. 12). New York: Academic Press.

Berry, J. W., Poortinga, Y. H., Segall, M. H., & Dasen, P. R. (1992). *Cross-cultural psychology: Research and applications.* Cambridge, UK: Cambridge University Press.

Bond, M. H. (1986). *The psychology of the Chinese people.* New York: Oxford University Press.

Bond, M. H., & Cheung, T. S. (1983). College students' spontaneous self-concept. *Journal of Cross-Cultural Psychology, 14,* 153–171.

Bond, M. H., Leung, K., & Wan, K. C. (1982). How does cultural collectivism operate? The impact of task and maintenance contributions on reward distribution. *Journal of Cross-Cultural Psychology, 13,* 186–200.

Boyacigiller, N., & Adler, N. J. (1991). The parochial dinosaur: Organizational science in a global context. *Academy of Management Review, 16,* 262–290.

Breckler, S. J., & Greenwald, A. G. (1986). Motivational facets of the self. In R. M. Sorrentino & E. T. Higgins (Eds.), *Handbook of motivation and cognition: Foundations of social behavior* (pp. 145–164). New York: Guilford.

Cahoone, L. E. (1988). *The dilemma of modernity: Philosophy, culture and anti-culture.* Albany, NY: State University of New York Press.

Campbell, J. P. (1990). The role of theory in industrial and organizational psychology. In M. D. Dunnette & L. M. Hough (Eds), *Handbook of industrial and organizational psychology* (2nd ed., vol. 1, pp. 39–73). Palo Alto, CA: Consulting Psychologists Press.

Canon Corporate Communication Center. (1987). *Canon handbook.* Tokyo: Author.

Cantor, N., & Kihlstrom, J. F. (1987). *Personality and social intelligence.* Englewood Cliffs, NJ: Prentice-Hall.

Cappelli, P., & Sherer, P. D. (1991). The missing role of context in OB: The need for a meso-level approach. In B. M. Staw and L. L. Cummings (Eds), *Research in organizational behavior* (Vol. 13, pp. 55–110). Greenwich, CT: JAI Press.

Cascio, W. F. (1989). *Managing human resources: Productivity, quality of work life, profits.* New York: McGraw-Hill.

Coch, L., & French, J. R. P. (1948). Overcoming resistance to change. *Human Relations, 1,* 512–532.

Cole, R. E. (1979). *Work, mobility and participation.* Berkeley, CA: University of California Press.

Cushman, P. (1990). Why the self is empty: Toward a historically situated psychology. *American Psychologist, 45,* 599–611.

Dubin, R., & Galin, A. (1991). Attachments to work: Russians in Israel. *Work and Occupation, 18,* 172–193.

Earley, P. C. (1986). Supervisors and shop stewards as sources of contextual information in goal-setting: A comparison of the U.S. with England. *Journal of Applied Psychology, 71,* 111–118.

Earley, P. C. (1989). Social loafing and collectivism: A comparison of the United States and the People's Republic of China. *Administrative Science Quarterly, 34,* 565–581.

Eden, D., & Leviatan, U. (1980). Farm and factory in the kibbutz: A study in agrico-industrial psychology (pp. 34–42). In U. Leviatan & M. Rosner (Eds.), *Work and organization in kibbutz industry.* Norwood, PA: Norwood Editions.

Elizur, D. (1984). Facets of work values: A structural analysis of work outcomes. *Journal of Applied Psychology, 69*, 379–389.

England, G. W. (1983). Japanese and American management: Theory Z and beyond. *Journal of International Business Studies, 14*, 131–141.

Erez, M. (1986). The congruence of goal setting strategies with socio-cultural values, and its effect on performance. *Journal of Management, 12*, 588–592.

Erez, M. (1992). Interpersonal communication patterns in Japanese corporations: Their relationships to cultural values and to productivity and innovation. *Applied Psychology: An International Review, 41*, 43–64.

Erez, M., Borochov, O., & Mannheim, B. (1989). Work values of youth: Effects of sex or sex role typing? *Journal of Vocational Behavior, 4, 3* 50–666.

Erez, M., & Earley, P. C. (1987). Comparative analysis of goal-setting strategies across cultures. *Journal of Applied Psychology, 72*, 658–665.

Erez, M., & Earley, P. C. (1993). *Culture, self-identity, and work.* New York: Oxford University Press.

Erez, M., Rosenstein, E., & Barr, S. (1990). *Antecedents and supporting conditions for the success of quality circles* (Research Rep. No. 193–720). Haifa, Israel: Technion Institute of Research & Development.

Feigenbaum, A. (1983). *Total quality control* (3rd ed.). New York: McGraw-Hill.

Fiedler, F. E., & Chemers, M. M. (1974). *Leadership and effective management.* Glenview, IL: Scott Foresman.

Fiske, A. P. (1991). *Structure of social life: Four elementary forms of human relations (communal sharing, authority ranking, equality matching, market pricing).* New York: Maxwell MacMillan International.

French, J. R. P., Israel, J., & As, D. (1960). An experiment in a Norwegian factory: Interpersonal dimension in decision-making. *Human Relations, 19*, 3–19.

French, J. R. P., Kay, E., & Meyer, H. H. (1966). Participation and the appraisal system. *Human Relations, 19*, 3–20.

Galbraith, J. R., & Kazanjian, R. K. (1988). Strategy, technology, and emerging organizations. In J. Hage (Ed.), *Futures of organizations* (pp. 29–41). Lexington, MA: Lexington Books.

Gecas, V. (1982) The self concept. *Annual Review of Psychology, 8*, 1–33.

Gluskinos, U. M. (1988). Cultural and political considerations in the introduction of Western technologies: The Mekorot Project. *Journal of Management Development, 6*(3), 34–46.

Gruenfeld, L. W., & MacEachron, A. E. (1975). A cross-national study of cognitive style among managers and technicians. *International Journal of Psychology, 10*, 27–55.

Gyllenhammar, P. G. (1977, July–August). How Volvo adapts work to people. *Harvard Business Review*, 102–113.

Hackman, J. R., & Oldham, G. R. (1980). *Work redesign.* Reading, MA: Addison-Wesley.

Hallowell, A. I. (1955). *Culture and experience.* Philadelphia: University of Pennsylvania Press.

Hanges, P. J., Schneider, B., & Niles, K. (1990). Stability of performance: An interactionist perspective. *Journal of Applied Psychology, 75*, 658–667.

Harpaz, I. (1990). *The meaning of work in Israel: Its nature and consequences.* New York: Praeger.

Heller, F. A., Drenth, P., Koopman, P., & Ruz, V. (1988). *Decisions in organizations: A three country comparative survey.* Newbury Park, CA: Sage.

Heller, F. A., & Wilpert, B. (1981). *Competence and power in managerial decision making: A study of senior levels of organization in eight countries.* Chichester, UK: Wiley.

Henry, J. P., & Stephens, P. M. (1977). *Stress, health, and social environment.* New York: Springer.

Hill, C. W. L., Hitt, M. A., & Hoskisson, R. E. (1988). Declining U.S. competitiveness: Reflection on a crisis. *Academy of Management Executive, 2*, 51–60.

Hofstede, G. (1980). *Culture's consequences: International differences in work related values.* Beverly Hills, CA: Academic Press.

Hofstede, G. (1991). *Culture and organizations: Software of the mind.* London: McGraw-Hill.

How to operate Q. C. Circles Activities. (1985). Tokyo: Q. C. Circle Headquarters, JUSE.

Hulin, C. L., & Rosnowski, M. (1985). Organizational technologies: Effects on organizations' characteristics and individuals' responses. In B. M. Staw & L. L. Cummings (Eds.), *Research in organizational behavior* (Vol. 7, pp. 39–85). Greenwich, CT: JAI Press.

Ilgen, D. R., & Klein, H. J. (1988). Organizational behavior. *Annual Review of Psychology, 40,* 327–351.

Jacobsen, C. (1983). What it means to be considerate: Differences in normative expectations and their implications. *Israel Social Science Research, 1,* 24–33.

James, L. R., Demaree, R. G., Mulaik, S. A., & Ladd, R. T. (1992). Validity generalization in the context of situational models. *Journal of Applied Psychology, 77,* 3–14.

Kagitcibasi, C., & Berry, J. W. (1989). Cross-cultural psychology: Current research and trends. In *Annual Review of Psychology, 40,* 493–531.

Kanfer, F. H. (1980). Self-management methods. In F. H. Kanfer & A. P. Goldstein (Eds.), *Helping people change* (2nd ed., pp. 334–389). New York: Pergamon Press.

Kanfer, R. (1990). Motivation theory and industrial and organizational psychology. In M. D. Dunnette & L. Hough (Eds.), *Handbook of industrial and organizational psychology* (2nd ed., vol. 1, pp. 75–170). Palo Alto, CA: Consulting Psychologists Press.

Kanfer, R., & Ackerman, P. L. (1989). Motivation and cognitive abilities: An integrative/aptitude-treatment interaction approach to skill acquisition [Monograph]. *Journal of Applied Psychology, 74,* 657–690.

Kapstein, J., & Hoerr, J. (1989, August). Volvo's radical new plant: "The death of the assembly line"? *Business Week,* pp. 92–93.

Katzell, R. A., & Thompson, D. E. (1990). Work motivation: Theory and practice. *American Psychologist, 45,* 144–153.

Kay, E., Meyer, H. H., & French, J. R. P., Jr. (1965). Effects of threat in a performance appraisal interview. *Journal of Applied Psychology, 49,* 311–317.

Kelman, H. C. (1961). Processes of opinion change. *Public Opinion Quarterly, 25,* 57–78.

The kibbutz in the transition of the century. (1991). [Report]. Tel Aviv: YAD TABENKIN.

Kihlstrom, J. F., & Cantor, N. (1984). Mental representations of the self. In L. Berkowitz (Ed.), *Advances in experimental social psychology* (Vol. 17). New York: Academic Press.

Kihlstrom, J. F., Cantor, N., Albright, J. S., Chew, B. R., Klein, S. B., & Niedenthal, P. M. (1988). Information processing and the study of the self. *Advances in experimental social psychology* (Vol. 21, pp. 145–178). San Diego: Academic Press.

Kitayama, S., Markus, H., Tummala, P., Kurokawa, M., & Kato, K. (1990). *Culture and self cognition.* Unpublished manuscript.

Kluckhohn, C. (1954). *Culture and behavior.* New York: Free Press.

Kume, T. (1985). Managerial attitudes toward decision-making: North America and Japan. In W. P. Gudykunst, L. P. Stewart, & S. Ting-Toomey (Eds.), *Communication, culture and organizational processes* (pp. 231–257). Beverly Hills, CA: Sage.

Latham, G. P., Erez, M., & Locke, E. A. (1988). Resolving scientific disputes by the joint design of crucial experiments by the antagonists: Application to the Erez-Latham dispute regarding participation in goal setting [Monograph]. *Journal of Applied Psychology 73,* 753–772.

Lawler, E. E., III (1986). *High involvement management.* New York: Jossey-Bass.

Leung, K., & Bond, M. (1984). The impact of cultural collectivism on reward allocation. *Journal of Personality and Social Psychology, 47,* 793–804.

Leung, K., & Park, H. J. (1986). Effects of interactional goal on choice of allocation rule: A cross-national study. *Organizational Behavior and Human Decision Processes, 37,* 11–120.

Leventhal, G. S., Karuza, J., & Fry, W. R. (1980). Beyond fairness: A theory of allocation preferences. In G. Mikula (Ed.), *Justice and social interaction: Experimental and theoretical contributions from psychological research* (pp. 167–218). New York: Springer-Verlag.

Leviatan, U. (1983). Work and aging in the kibbutz: Some relevancies for the larger society. *Aging and Work, 6,* 215–226.

Leviatan, U., & Cohen, J. (1985). Gender differences in life expectancy among kibbutz members. *Social Science Medicine, 21,* 545–551.

Leviatan, U., & Rosner, M. (1980). *Work and organization in kibbutz industry.* Norwood, PA: Norwood Editions.

Locke, E. A. (1991). The motivation sequence, the motivation hub, and the motivation core. *Organizational Behavior and Human Decision Processes, 50,* 288–299.

Locke, E. A., & Latham, P. G. (1990). *A theory of goal setting and task performance.* Englewood Cliffs, NJ: Prentice-Hall.

Locke, E. A., & Schweiger, D. M. (1979). Participation in decision-making: One more look. In B. M. Staw (Ed.), *Research in organizational behavior* (Vol. 1, pp. 265–339). Greenwich, CT: JAI Press.

Loevinger, J. (1976). *Ego development.* San Francisco: Jossey-Bass.

M&A demographics of the decade: The top 100 deals of the decade. (1990). *Mergers & Acquisitions, 25,* 107–112.

Markus, H. R., & Kitayama, S. (1991). Culture and the self: Implications for cognition, emotion, and motivation. *Psychological Review, 98,* 224–253.

Markus, H., & Kunda, Z. (1986). Stability and malleability of the self concept. *Journal of Personality and Social Psychology, 51,* 858–866.

Markus, H., & Wurf, E. (1987). The dynamic self-concept: A social psychological perspective. *Annual Review of Psychology, 38,* 299–337.

Matsui, T., Kakuyama, T., & Onglatco, M. L. (1987). Effects of goals and feedback on performance in groups. *Journal of Applied Psychology, 72,* 407–415.

McClelland, P. C. (1961). *The achieving society.* Princeton, NJ: Van Nostrand.

McGuire, J. W. (1980). The development of theory in social psychology. In R. Gilmow & S. Duck, *The development of social psychology* (pp. 53–80). London: Academic Press.

Merton, R. K. (1957). *Social theory and social structure.* Glencoe, IL: Free Press.

Miles, R. E., & Snow, C. C. (1984). Fit, failure, and the Hall of Fame. *California Management Review, 26,* 10–28.

Misumi, J. (1989). Research on leadership and group decision in Japanese organizations. *Applied Psychology: An International Review, 38,* 321–336.

Monthly Bulletin of Statistics. (1992, January, p. 10, Table E-3). Jerusalem: Central Bureau of Statistics.

MOW International research team. (1986). *The meaning of working.* London: Academic Press.

Murphy-Berman, V., Berman, J., Singh, P., Pachauri, A., & Kumar, P. (1984). Factors affecting allocation to needy and meritorious recipients: A cross-cultural comparison. *Journal of Personality and Social Psychology, 46,* 1267–1272.

Naylor, J. C., Pritchard, R. D., & Ilgen, D. R. (1980). *A theory of behavior in organizations.* New York: Academic Press.

Nevo, O., & Nevo, B. (1983). What do you do when asked to answer humorously? *Journal of Personality and Social Psychology, 44,* 188–194.

Odaka, K. (1986). *Japanese management: A forward looking analysis.* Tokyo: Japan Productivity Organization.

Offermann, L. R., & Gowing, M. K. (1990). Organizations of the future: Changes and challenges. *American Psychologist, 45,* 95–108.

Onglatco, M. L. U. (1988). *Japanese quality control circles: Features, effects & problems.* Tokyo: Asian Productivity Center.

Pfeffer, J. (1983). Organizational demography. In L. L. Cummings & B. M. Staw (Eds.), *Research in organizational behavior* (Vol 5, pp. 357–399). Greenwich, CT: JAI Press.

Piaget, J. (1965). *The moral judgement of the child.* New York: Free Press.

Prokesh, S. (1991, July). Kinder, gentler plant a failure. *Chicago Tribune.*

Pugh, D. (1976). The "Aston approach" to the study of organizations. In G. Hofstede & S. Kassem (Eds.), *European contributions to organization theory* (pp. 62–77). Assen, the Netherlands: Van Garcum.

Q. C. Circle Koryo: General Principles of the Q. C. Circle. (1980). Tokyo: Q. C. Circle Headquarters, JUSE.

Rim, Y. (1970). Values and attitudes. *Personality, 1,* 243–250.

Roberts, K. H., Hulin, C. L., & Rousseau, D. (1978). *Developing an interdisciplinary science of organization.* San-Francisco: Jossey-Bass.

Rokeach, M. (1973). *The nature of human values.* New York: Free Press.

Ronen, S. (1986). *Comparative and multinational management.* New York: Wiley.

Ronen, S., & Shenkar, O. (1985) Clustering countries on attitudinal dimensions: A review and synthesis. *Academy of Management Review, 10,* 435–454.

Rosenstein, E. (1985). Cooperativeness and advancement of managers: An international perspective. *Human Relations, 38,* 1–21.

Rosenstein, E., Ofek, A., & Harel, G. (1988). Organizational democracy and management in Israel. *International Studies of Management and Organizations, 17,* 52–68.

Ross, L. (1977). The intuitive psychologist and his shortcomings: Distortions in the attribution process. In L. Berkowitz (Ed.), *Advances in experimental and social psychology* (Vol. 10, pp. 174–221). New York: Academic Press.

Sampson, E. E. (1989). The challenge of social change for psychology: Globalization and psychology's theory of the person. *American Psychologist, 44*, 914–921.

Sandel, M. J. (1982). *Liberalism and the limits of justice.* Cambridge, UK: Cambridge University Press.

Schein, E. (1990). Organizational culture. *American Psychologist, 45*, 109–119.

Schiller, Z. (1989, August). Stalking the new consumer. *Business Week*, pp. 54–62.

Schmidt, F. L., & Hunter, J. E. (1977). Development of a general solution to the problem of validity generalization. *Journal of Applied Psychology, 62*, 529–540.

Schneider, B. (1975). Organizational climate: An essay. *Personnel Psychology, 28*, 447–479.

Schneider, B. (1987). The people make the place. *Personnel Psychology, 40*, 437–453.

Schwartz, S. H. (1992). Universals in the content and structure of values: Theoretical advances and empirical tests in twenty countries. In M. P. Zanna (Ed.), *Advances in experimental social psychology* (Vol. 25, pp. 1–65). San Diego: Academic Press.

Schwartz, S. H., & Bilsky. (1990). Toward a theory of the universal content and structure of values: Extensions and cross-cultural replications. *Journal of Personality and Social Psychology, 58*, 878–891.

Shamir, B., House, R. J., & Arthur, M. B. (in press). *The transformational effects of charismatic leadership: A motivational theory.* Organizational Science.

Shavelson, R. J., & Marsh, H. W. (1986). On the structure of self-concept. In R. Schwarzer (Ed.), *Anxiety and cognitions* (pp. 305–330). Hillsdale, NJ: Erlbaum.

Sherman, S. J., Judd, C. M., & Bernadette, P. (1989). Social cognition. *Annual Review of Psychology, 40*, 281–326.

Shweder, R., & LeVine, R. (1984). *Culture theory.* New York: Cambridge University Press.

Staw, B. M. (1987). Escalation situation. In B. M. Staw & L. L. Cummings (Eds.), *Research in*

organizational behavior (Vol. 9, pp. 39–78). Greenwich, CT: JAI Press.

Sundstrom, E., De Meuse, K. P., & Futrell, D. (1990). Workteams: Applications and effectiveness. *American Psychologist, 45*, 120–133.

Swap, W. C., & Rubin, J. Z. (1983). Measurement of interpersonal orientation. *Journal of Personality and Social Psychology, 44*, 208–219.

Tajfel, H. (1978). *Differentiation between social groups: Studies in the social psychology of intergroup relations.* London: Academic Press.

Taylor, F. W. (1967) *Principles of scientific management.* New York: Norton. (Original work published 1911)

Thierry, H. (1992a). Payment and payment systems. In J. F. Harthley & G. M. Stephenson (Eds.), *Employment relations.* Oxford, UK: Blackwell.

Thierry, H. (1992b). Payment: Which meanings are rewarding? *American Behavioral Scientist, 35*, 694–707.

Thorsrud, E. (1984). The Scandinavian model: Strategies of organizational democratization in Norway. In B. Wilpert & A. Sorge (Eds.), *International perspectives on organizational democracy* (pp. 337–370). Chichester, UK: Wiley.

Tomasson, R. F. (1970). *Sweden: Prototype of modern society.* New York: Random House.

Tornblom, K.Y., Jonsson, D., & Foa, U. G. (1985). Nationality resource class and preferences among three allocation rules: Sweden vs. USA. *International Journal of Intercultural Relations, 9*, 51–77.

Trafimow, D., Triandis, H. C., & Goto, S. G. (1991). Some tests of the distinction between the private self and the collective self. *Journal of Personality and Social Psychology, 60*, 649–655.

Triandis, H. C. (1972). *The analysis of subjective culture.* New York: Wiley.

Triandis, H. C. (1989). The self and social behavior in differing cultural contexts. *Psychological Review, 96*, 506–520.

Triandis, H. C., Bontempo, R., Vilareal, M. J., Masaaki, A., & Lucca, N. (1988). Individualism and collectivism: Cross-cultural perspectives on self-ingroup relationships. *Journal of Personality and Social Psychology, 54*, 328–338.

Trist, E. (1981). *The evolution of socio-technical system.* Toronto: Ontario Quality of Working Life Center.

Vroom, V. H. (1964). *Work and motivation.* New York: Wiley.

Vroom, V. H., & Yetton, P. W. (1973). *Leadership and decision-making.* Pittsburgh: University of Pittsburgh Press.

Weinshall, T. D. (1977). *Culture and management: Selected readings.* Middlesex, UK: Penguin.

Weldon, E., & Gargano, G. M. (1988). Cognitive loafing: The effects of accountability and shared responsibility on cognitive effort. *Personality and Social Psychology Bulletin, 14,* 159–171.

Witkin, H. A., & Berry, J. W. (1975). Psychological differentiation in cross-cultural perspective. *Journal of Cross-Cultural Psychology, 6,* 4–87.

Wyer, R. S., & Srull, T. K. (1989). *Memory and cognition in its social context.* Hillsdale, NJ: Erlbaum.

Zeidner, M., & Nevo, B. (1987). The cross-cultural generalizability of moral reasoning research: Some Israeli data. *International Journal of Psychology, 22,* 315–330.

CHAPTER 12

The Japanese
Work Group

Yoshihisa Kashima
La Trobe University, Australia

Victor J. Callan
The University of Queensland, Australia

In this chapter, we examine the role of Japanese culture in shaping the operation of organizations in Japan, focusing on the system of the Japanese work group. We adopt the conception of culture that is consistent with the information processing approach and use the concept of organizational metaphors to explain the mechanism by which Japanese culture continues to influence a wide range of practices and behaviors in Japanese organizations. In particular, the family (ie), the metaphor used for Japanese organizations is contrasted with the machine metaphor used for Western organizations. We trace the emergence of the family metaphor during Japan's industrialization and demonstrate its continuing influence in many Japanese organizations today by showing similarities between the structural features of the traditional ie *household and modern Japanese organizations.*

We then analyze the Japanese work group system from a social psychological point of view. We first examine features of culture and socialization practices in Japan that prepare people for life in organizations. Against this background, the dynamics of the Japanese work group are described at the individual, interpersonal, and group levels of analysis. We conclude that features of the Japanese work group are likely to improve productivity in the sociocultural context of Japan, but may not necessarily lead to high levels of organizational satisfaction and commitment even in Japan. We offer some speculation about the cross-cultural transferability of the Japanese work group system on the basis of Hofstede's etic dimensions of individualism and collectivism, and power distance, amended by further consideration of which specific features of a culture the system may be transferred to.

Introduction

ASSESSMENTS OF THE effectiveness of Japanese organizational practices have reached quite divergent conclusions during the last 50 years. In the recent past, Japanese management was labeled by many Western and Japanese observers as inefficient and even backward. Yet in more recent times, as Japanese corporations have begun to dominate world industrial markets, Japanese management practices have been hailed by researchers and industrialists as a panacea for organizational ineffectiveness in the West. Some have even identified Japanese management practices as the universal point of convergence for welfare corporatism (see Dunphy, 1987; P. B. Smith & Misumi, 1989, for recent reviews).

In light of such claims, it is a significant challenge for organizational researchers to provide an understanding and balanced assessment of Japanese management and organizational behavior. Toward this goal, our focus is on one element of Japanese organizational behavior—the operation of the Japanese work group. While we do not deny the importance of many other factors contributing toward the success of Japanese industry (e.g., central economic planning, lifetime employment, seniority-based wage system), it is the small, face-to-face work group that is the key to understanding the nature of Japanese organizations. The work group is the building block of the Japanese organization.

Our aim is to provide a theoretically coherent explanation of the general pattern of small group behaviors in the Japanese organization. In the discussion that follows, we first use the conceptual framework provided by organizational metaphors to explain the similarities and differences in organizational structure and behavior in Japan and North America. Second, we examine the history behind Japanese industry, and the emergence and evolution of a metaphor that likens the organization in Japan to the family. Cross-cultural comparisons of studies of Japanese, North American, and Western European organizations reveal that the family metaphor of organizations continues to influence the structure and behavior in Japanese organizations. In the final sections of this chapter, we provide a sociopsychological analysis of Japanese work groups, and speculate about the extent to which Japanese work group practices are transferable to other cultural contexts.

Culture, Symbols, and Metaphors

We define culture as a set of symbols that represents meanings shared by a population. This set of shared symbols makes the population distinct from other groups of people (for more discussion of the concept of culture, see Triandis, this volume). Our definition of culture adopts an information processing approach to understanding psychological functioning. In this framework, a symbol is defined as something that refers to or stands for something else: Cultural symbols represent the cultural meanings that people process in their lives. Within the symbolic system, however, there are multiple subsystems. Each subsystem describes a domain of shared meanings that are associated with work, family, play, and the like. Although these domains may be somewhat autonomous, such subsystems are often loosely integrated into analogical relationships. Consider the example, "Time is money." This metaphor maps a subsystem of symbols about time onto another subsystem of symbols about money. For instance, in English we might say, "You're wasting my time"; "This gadget will save you hours"; "I don't have the time to give you"; "How do you spend your time these days?"; "This flat tire cost me an hour"; and "I've invested a lot of time in her" (Lakoff & Johnson, 1980, pp. 7–8). We can waste, spend, and invest time, just as we can waste, spend, and invest money.

Metaphor maps the structure of one domain of knowledge to another domain, enabling people to draw upon the familiar in order to deal with the unfamiliar (Gentner, 1983). However, this structural mapping is necessarily partial. Metaphors structure thoughts by highlighting some aspects of an unfamiliar domain, while allowing other aspects to fade into the background. Metaphors may even create structural similarities between two concept domains. In the example "Time is money," for instance, there may be no inherent similarity between the domains of time and money. Moreover, metaphors that Lakoff and Johnson call *ontological metaphors* can dictate what we count as reality. The metaphor "Time is money" invites us to think about and deal with time *as if* we were thinking about and dealing with money.

The selectivity afforded by metaphors, while somewhat constraining to our thoughts and actions, can also lead to efficient learning and creative problem solving. As various theorists have pointed out (e.g., Collins & Gentner, 1987; Sackmann, 1989), metaphors can holistically convey rich information about a phenomenon without resorting to a high level of abstraction. People can simply draw upon their own experiences in the familiar domain in order to make sense of an unfamiliar domain. In addition, good metaphors can facilitate creative problem solving by shifting perspective. This generative function of metaphors is well illustrated by Schön (1979; also see Gick & Holyoak, 1980, 1983; Reason, 1990; Stein, 1991). He recounts how a team of product development researchers attempted to improve the performance of a new paintbrush made from synthetic bristles. After many failures, a researcher observed that a paintbrush is a kind of pump: Paint is sucked into and forced out of the spaces between the brush's bristles just as water is sucked into and forced out of a pump's cylinder. This metaphorical insight led to a successful research and development effort and further inventions. Thus, in organizational and other contexts, metaphors not only help conceptualize the unfamiliar but also help generate new solutions to problems (Morgan, 1986; Sackmann, 1989).

Organizational Metaphors in Japan and the United States

Industrialization made it necessary to organize human and technological resources in the most effective way possible to transform materials into goods and services. Both industrialists and workers had to solve what was then the novel problem of managing a large-scale modern organization, involving such tasks as the use of capital, the need to control costs, and the coordination of a large unskilled work force. The answer to the founders of organizations and to classical theorists (e.g., Taylor, 1911) was that organizations are machines. The machine metaphor provided at that time, and still today, a mental model that allowed managers and workers to understand and plan how to deal with many new problems. Weber (1958) also discerned this mechanistic trend and provided a critical analysis of bureaucratic rationalization of human social institutions. The machine metaphor dominated Western managerial practice in the 1930s. Even today, the metaphor is still influential and is intuitively appealing to managers in Western contexts (Merkle, 1980; Morgan, 1986; Ott, 1989).

The organization theory that is often labeled the machine or mechanical theory (see Burns & Stalker, 1961; Worthy, 1950) has at least seven interrelated characteristics (Katz & Kahn, 1978): the specialization of tasks, the standardization of role performance, a unity of command and centralized decision making, uniform practices, no duplication of functions, rewards for merit, and the depersonalization of office. That is, organizations ideally are assumed to have a set of elementary operations that are mutually exclusive and jointly complete. The people in such organizations are seen as "adjuncts to machines" (J. G. March & Simon, 1958).

In contrast, the founders of Japanese industry chose a very different metaphor to manage material and human resources—"organizations are families." The use of the family or household (*ie*) metaphor characterizes a unique approach adopted by Japanese managers to achieve economic and other goals (Abegglen, 1958; Bennett & Ishino, 1963; Karsh, 1984). The family, rather than the machine, provided the domain from which Japanese people launched their design of organizations and their strategies to motivate workers to meet the demands for large-scale production in modern industry. A family-nationalistic framework (*kazoku-kokkakan*) successfully integrated the value of cooperation and the need to be subordinate to authority. Applied to organizational life, company familism (*keiei-kazoku-shugi*), or a belief in the one-enterprise family (*kigyo-ikka*), served to integrate workers and worker groups in the Japanese factory (Karsh, 1984; Okochi, Karsh, & Levine, 1974).

In the Japanese context, the concept of *ie*, or household, signifies a concept somewhat different from the Western notion of family (see also Hayashi, 1988; Kondo, 1990). According to Nakane (1970a, 1970b), the *ie* household is a social unit that "once established assumes its continuity regardless of changes to its members, and exists at a core of the social system as an indivisible social unit" (p. 102). Nakane emphasizes that *ie* is a social institution that consists of members who live together and share their work (*kagyo*). Most importantly, the household is an independent unit that controls its own assets (*kasan*).

The *ie* keeps its work and assets through a family structure in which one son usually inherits control from the father. The successor is often the eldest son, either from a natural birth or adoption. Other children are not entitled to household assets and usually remain under the control of the head of the family. In the Japanese family system, households may form a larger grouping called the *dozoku* when a

branch household is established by giving it a portion of the family assets. The first household is known as the *honke,* and the branch is known as the *bunke.* If there are numerous branch households in this emerging alliance, the *honke* remains the leading household. In addition, the establishment of a bunke does not need to be through kinship, and at times a competent employee of the household can be rewarded with *norenwake.* This allows the employee to form a *bunke* in the same area of the mercantile industry. This is a significant aspect of the *ie* household: Those who receive *norenwake* do not need to have kinship ties with the family. Similarly, non-kin employees are often treated as members of a household, thus making it possible to expand a family structure beyond its immediate relatives.

The *ie* household has at least five obvious features. First, it is a social unit that has its own traditions, a sense of continuity, and sometimes considerable economic assets that are handed down from generation to generation. Second, the household is the focus of the working lives of its members, and it organizes how they relate to each other and share work. Third, it has a paternalistic structure in which the eldest son inherits the wealth and control of the household. Fourth, the household has mechanisms, like the establishment of *bunke,* that enable it to expand. And fifth, those allowed to establish such branch households do not necessarily have to be kin, and the establishment of *bunke* can be a reward given to a competent, loyal worker. In short, *ie* exists as the socially constructed locus of assets and shared work.

Significantly, many of the features of the *ie* household have become structural features of modern industrial organizations in Japan. For instance, the organization is built on a core of economic assets that have been generated by the cooperative efforts of its workers. Employees who are not related to each other by obvious kinship ties work closely together in small groups. In addition, these small autonomous work groups are linked together in ways that are quite similar to the *honke-bunke* relationship. In short, nineteenth-century Japanese industrialists quite clearly fell back on the familiar—the structure and characteristics of the *ie* household—to find a metaphor that enabled them to deal with the then novel challenge of establishing modern industrial companies in their country. Most importantly, the *ie* metaphor worked, and so it has continued to be the guiding metaphor for running organizations in Japan.

Functions of the Organizational Metaphor

The organizational metaphor allows managers and employees to understand unfamiliar tasks and situations in terms of what is familiar to them. As Tsoukas (1991) suggests, metaphors provide an economical method for vividly communicating experiential information that cannot be imparted through more literal language. For example, the use of the machine or family metaphor can assist management and employees in understanding the strategic objectives, management philosophy, and structure of an organization. Organizational metaphors assist new employees in learning about the organization's culture, particularly when they grapple with its unstated assumptions and tacit agreements.

The organizational metaphor also has a generative function. Managers and their employees can solve problems by drawing upon the more familiar domain of knowledge. In time, the base domain to which organizations are likened is often taken for granted and becomes a feature of the taken-for-granted assumptions that determine the cognition, affect, and action of organizations' members. These assumptions allow new employees to understand the ambiguous and sometimes contradictory activities and decisions pursued by organizations (Martin & Meyerson, 1988; Schein, 1990).

To clarify further what is meant by organizational metaphors and their functions, it is instructive to compare this perspective to other approaches that have since been used by theorists to understand organizational structure. Theories X versus Y (McGregor, 1960) and A versus Z (Ouchi, 1981), for example, convey important assumptions about people and organizations. Such assumptions, however, are not as clear cut and reflective as the word *theories* tends to imply. Theoretical and practical knowledge are two different kinds of knowledge (Sandelands, 1990). We believe that the rules people follow in organizations are not derived from theories, but are rather reflections of tacit practical knowledge of how people should think and act (Bourdieu, 1990; Giddens, 1979). Organizational metaphors invite people to draw upon their theoretical as well as practical knowledge in a familiar domain (e.g., the machine or family) and apply this knowledge to the domain of organizational life.

The concept of organizational culture has captured this fuzziness in its focus on the implicit assumptions that operate in many modern organizations (see Schein, 1985, 1990). Employees' behavior is not only restrained or directed by formal rules and the actions of management but also by a pattern of practical assumptions about how things ought to be done in the organization. What is also significant is that the concepts of organizational metaphor and organizational culture are similar in their acceptance of the role of the sociocultural context in influencing the operation of the organization. However, while organizational cultures are specific to organizations and their members, organizational metaphors map a domain of knowledge that is readily available to all members of a society into the domain of organizational behavior, irrespective of their organizational membership. The organizational metaphor is in part generative of organizational culture and constitutes part of the culture.

The notion of organizational metaphor also provides an insight into how culture shapes and structures organizational practices. Rather than cultural (Abegglen, 1958) or ecological determinism (Ouchi, 1981), Japanese management has actively orchestrated the choice of metaphor. The founders of Japanese organizations quite aptly drew upon their own culture to generate the *ie*, or family, metaphor. They utilized their knowledge and familiarity with the *ie* household, which most Japanese shared at the time. However, once chosen and its utility proven, organizational metaphors act not only as a device of management but also as a structure through which both management and employees view their organizations. The following section examines the historical and social factors that shaped the emergence and evolution of the family metaphor of organizations.

The History of Japanese Industrial Organizations

This brief review examines the influence of Japanese culture and its traditions, as well as various socioeconomic conditions, on the adoption of the *ie* metaphor of organization. It covers five periods in Japanese cultural history: the Tokugawa feudal period (1615–1868), the Meiji restoration and early forms of industrialization (1868–1890), the labor movement and factory legislation (1890–1920), World War II (1920–1945), and the postwar period (1945–1980s). This review is based on several excellent discussions of the history of Japanese industrialization, including Clark (1979), Dore (1969), Hirschmeier and Yui (1975), Marshall (1967), Taira (1970), and Yoshino (1968).

The history of modern industrial organizations in Japan began after the Tokugawa shogunate relinquished its 300-year-old policy of social and cultural isolation. The Meiji restoration occurred when the last shogun returned power to the emperor in 1868. The history of merchant houses during the Tokugawa era, however, provides the context from which modern organizations emerged. Toward the end of the Tokugawa period, there was a rise

in domestic trade between different regions in Japan. As a result, the merchant class, despite its low rank, amassed considerable capital. Merchant houses were essentially *ie* households. They were economic and legal units that were the locus of economic assets and cooperative work activities. To put it simply, merchant houses were corporations. It should be noted, however, that they were different from family-owned businesses. As Clark (1979) describes them, families in Japanese merchant houses did not so much own the business, as did the European business family. Rather, the house itself was the business: The enterprise and the family were united in the same corporation.

Only a few merchant houses (e.g., Mitsui) survived the turmoil of the Meiji restoration and the social, political, and economic changes that occurred during the transition from the Tokugawa period to the Meiji period. To this extent, modern Japanese organizations are not a direct outgrowth of the traditional merchant houses. Nevertheless, they could have been taken as models of large-scale organizations by Japanese industrialists who were familiar with this earlier system.

With the Meiji restoration of imperial power, the new government had to modernize the nation. It did this by abolishing the feudal class system, building a modern military, and industrializing the nation. During this period of economic difficulty, the new government took the lead in establishing heavy industry such as mines, shipyards, and engineering workshops. These industries were expanded from inheritance from the Tokugawa government, as were light industries such as cotton spinning, silk filature, and cement and glass manufacturing. Modern communication, mail and telegraph services, as well as railroads were built to provide an infrastructure for further industrialization. These government-initiated industries were eventually sold to various private entrepreneurs at much lower prices than their establishment cost.

Industrialists who had government connections, such as Yataro Iwasaki (founder of Mitsubishi), Rizaemon Minomura (a steward of Mitsui), and Eiichi Shibusawa, benefited immensely from these sales. Such private entrepreneurs were to become the major force behind the industrialization of Meiji Japan.

The major exporters in early Meiji Japan (up to around 1900) were the light industries, especially the textile industry. The majority of the textile industries were run by small industrialists from the family workshops. Most employees were young women from rural villages who were contracted out by their household heads or village elders until they returned to the village to marry. Although small in size, this industry was an important precursor to the heavy industry that developed soon after this period. The workers accepted the paternalistic attitude toward them in these workshops. These young women had previously been subjected to the power of their household heads. They now worked in a small factory (with probably 30 to 40 other women), and although room and board were provided, conditions were very poor. Indeed, when the hideous conditions of the workshops became known to villagers, this source of cheap labor disappeared.

The labor shortage was acutely felt in the metalworking and engineering industries, which came to prominence from around 1900. Skilled laborers, whom these heavy industries required, moved from firm to firm for higher wages, resulting in frequent disruptions to production. This prompted industrialists to adopt a paternalistic employment scheme in which employees were offered a career path with better jobs and higher pay after an appropriate length of service. Welfare schemes and profit-related bonuses were also offered as further inducements for workers to stay with an employer.

Around the 1920s, companies began to adopt the *ie* household metaphor of organization. There were both intrinsic and extrinsic

reasons for this development. An intrinsic factor was the appropriateness of the *ie* household as a model for modern organization. The *ie* household was a small-scale corporation much concerned about its continued ability to gather assets and produce work. Furthermore, the *ie* household offered an expandable model. It could expand by using people without kinship ties. It could also expand by forming a subsidiary *ie* (*bunke*). Thus, the *ie* household had the mechanisms for including non-relatives among its members. With slight modification, the *ie* household provided a model for modern industrial organizations, meeting a need to coordinate many people who were unrelated by kinship or marriage.

The extrinsic reasons for the adoption of the family metaphor were both social and cultural. In the early twentieth century, labor movements emerged in Japan. Industrialists were concerned about labor laws, and in order to fend off pressure from the government and the labor movement, industrialists of the Meiji era espoused familism by asserting that their relationships with workers were not exploitative. Thus, as they argued, labor protection was not needed because the industry looked after its workers just as a family would. In addition, a cultural factor behind the rise of familism was its congruence with Japanese cultural values of the time. Meiji Japan adhered to an ideology of ultranationalism, in which Japanese society was likened to a family with the emperor as its head. If all Japanese people were a family, any subsets within it (e.g., economic organizations) should also take the form of a family. As was argued earlier, the family metaphor allowed workers and industrialists to draw upon familiar domains of knowledge (the *ie* household) to model activities in the unfamiliar domain of modern economic life. The metaphor served to link knowledge domains about the family and organizations. The metaphor assisted employee–management communication, while management and workers could take action to achieve a shared vision, even when there were no clear rules or guidelines.

It is important to note that the *ie* metaphor emerged as a model for justifying paternalistic employment practices that were forced upon Japanese industry by a labor shortage. It was also a convenient doctrine to argue against the need for union movements or government legislation. It certainly helped mask problems such as poor industrial relations and the enormous inequality that existed in the treatment of managers and employees. Familism, however, was not simply an excuse or a justification for paternalistic management styles; it provided industrialists and employees with a shared framework in which to operate and to think about the structure and functions of modern Japanese organizations.

After the Second World War, the Japanese economy plummeted into severe recession. This eventually culminated in Japan's military expansion in search of raw materials, human resources, and new markets. When Japan was finally defeated and occupied by the allies after the war, drastic political changes occurred, including the rewriting of the constitution and the reinstatement of democracy. Japanese economic organizations also envisaged a new start. *Zaibatsu*, a conglomerate under the same family such as Mitsui and Iwasaki, was dismantled by the allies to create a free market. New companies (e.g., Sony, Sanyo) also emerged to revitalize Japan's economy. However, the dismantled *Zaibatsu* was eventually allowed to reform as loosely connected groups, which have continued to be major forces in the Japanese economy. In addition, a "dualism" in the Japanese economy continued with the divergence of small and large companies. Large corporations engaged in capital-intensive modern industry, paying high wages to employees. Small companies continued as a complementary feature of this dualism, mainly in the labor-intensive industry, typically paying lower wages.

In 1955, *Nihon Seisansei Honbu* (the Japanese Overseas Exchange) was established, partly sponsored and initiated by the United States government, to improve the productivity of Japanese industries. In the subsequent decade, many high-level managers were sent to the United States on study tours. It was a historical accident that many of these visitors encountered the views of the human relations school of organizational theorists, such as McGregor and Likert. There were remarkable similarities between Likert's model of organizations and the structure of indigenous organizations in Japan. Likert's (1961) linking pin theory of organizations argues that organizations consist of "families" that are tied together through shared members who act as linking pins. Each family consists of a supervisor and members who report to him or her. In turn, the supervisor belongs to another group, which is located at a higher level in the organization, and this arrangement provides peers who report to a supervisor. The supervisor then acts as a "linking pin" for the two groups in adjacent levels of the hierarchy. This model of the company as a hierarchical organization of family-like groups is extremely similar to the Japanese *ie* metaphor, with its hierarchical structuring of groups.

The post–Second World War period reinforced the Japanese *ie* metaphor. In keeping with the dualism of the Japanese economy, the *ie* metaphor took on two forms in this period. On the one hand, larger corporations began to adopt the well-known managerial practices of *shushin-koyo* (lifetime employment), *nenko-chingin* (seniority-based wage system), and *kigyobetsu-kumiai* (company-based labor union) from the 1950s to the 1970s. These practices are generally consistent with the *ie* metaphor; however, they are universalistic policies that imply a bureaucratization of the organization (e.g., Fruin, 1978, 1980). On the other hand, smaller companies did not have these practices, but persisted with the more traditional form of *ie* type organization (Kondo, 1990).

During the post-war period, social and economic conditions in Japan were compatible with the use of collectivistic work groups. The goals of Japanese firms to improve productivity and expand marketshare were generally consistent with their employees' personal goals of achieving higher standards of living. If employees worked hard for the company, the company rewarded them with promotions and higher wages. As Japan's economy expanded, companies were able to deliver these higher standards of living to motivate their employees.

Still, the persistence of the *ie* metaphor of organization in Japan is more remarkable when considered against the background of the social and economic changes that have taken place in this century. Studies by Whitehill and Takezawa (1968) and Takezawa and Whitehill (1981) reveal that the difference between Japanese and U.S. workers' attitudes actually widened from the 1960s to the 1970s. Such findings challenge the argument that Japanese organizational behaviors are converging to North American behaviors (see also Maguire & Kroliczak, 1983). Changes in Japanese management practices have actually involved an assimilation of Western practices into Japanese culture rather than their wholesale adoption (see also Smith & Misumi, 1989).

The dynamics of such cultural assimilation is well illustrated by Dore's (1983) discussion of relational contracting in Japan. A section of textile industry, which was dominated by large companies in the 1950s, is now predominantly occupied by small family enterprises that are associated with large textile firms through the *honke-bunke*, family-like relationship. Typically, an economy evolves by integrating a collection of small enterprises into large corporations; however, the direction of evolution was reversed in this case, taking the form of fragmentation of large corporations into small enterprises. Dore argues that a Western-style modern business was modified to suit the Japanese cultural pattern, in which

family-like relationships underlie many economic activities.

Lay theories about Japanese society and culture (*Nihonjinron*) also contribute to this dynamic. They typically depict Japan as a group-oriented, collectivist society that suppresses individuality while emphasizing harmony. This group model of Japan and its people is a stereotype held by many Japanese people (Mouer & Sugimoto, 1986), which is likely to reproduce social behaviors that are consistent with this self-held stereotype. Although the *ie* metaphor is not entirely consistent with this self-held stereotype (see a later section for detailed discussions), the *Nihonjinron* often acts as a constant reminder of the *ie* metaphor.

In the future, how likely is it that the *ie* metaphor of organization will be retained in its current form? As argued earlier, and noted by others (Dunphy, 1987), the Japanese management system in general and the use of the Japanese work group in particular are deliberate decisions, influenced by the *ie* metaphor. Over periods of Japanese cultural history, Japanese industrialists and their organizations have endorsed the *ie* metaphor and have gone to great lengths to maintain it (Mouer & Sugimoto, 1986; Rohlen, 1974a). They will continue to support the *ie* metaphor as long as they believe it is useful, but when it loses its utility, it is very likely that Japanese organizations will abandon it. As Smith and Misumi (1989) also argue, the likely future is a contingent one. Where the *ie* metaphor is useful, it will remain; where it is not, it will have to go.

Cross-cultural Comparisons of Work Group Attitudes and Behaviors

The *ie* metaphor operates today as the prototype for Japanese organizations. The metaphor is socially and culturally embedded and survives today as it continues to be useful. One way of demonstrating the persistence of the family metaphor is through an analysis of the match between the structures of the *ie* household and Japanese work groups. In this section, we will analyze the Japanese small work group, using role theory (e.g., Biddle, 1986; Biddle & Thomas, 1966; Katz & Kahn, 1978) as a conceptual framework for examining cross-cultural differences due to the machine and family metaphors used for organizations. Role theory is sufficiently general, enabling us to avoid the imposition of pseudoetic or imposed etic assumptions in which the investigator's own cultural assumptions are incorrectly applied to the target culture (see Berry, 1980; Malpass, 1977).

According to role theory, organizational members complete different parts of a process. Patterns of action become distributed across the organization as job roles. These roles are either assigned by the organization or negotiated by its employees. *Functional roles* are about the achievement of organizational objectives. For example, a worker might have the functional role of doing searches through the company computer system to retrieve relevant information about the company's monthly outputs. *Structural roles*, on the other hand, are more concerned about maintaining and regulating relationships between members of the organization. An example is how supervisors and workers tend to assume specific roles in their relationships with each other. The distinction between functional and structural roles in an organization is analogous to Bales' (1958) task and social roles in problem-solving groups. In organizations, structural roles can be either between employees of different status (i.e., vertical role differentiation) or between people of the same status (i.e., horizontal role differentiation). Typically, manager-worker relationships are vertical, while worker-worker relationships are horizontal (e.g., Nakane, 1970b). In the following section, we will argue that the family and machine metaphors imply different patterns of functional and structural roles, while even the most current research findings suggest the

persistence of cross-cultural differences that are consistent with this conception.

Functional Roles in Organizations

A fundamental question in modern organizations is the choice managers make about the most appropriate work unit to which functional roles can be assigned. According to the Japanese *ie* metaphor, the family-like work group should be the functional unit for organizations. U.S. organizations tend to assign functional roles to individuals, but in Japan the work group is responsible for achieving the major organizational objectives of the organization (Clark, 1979; Lincoln, Hanada, & McBride, 1986; Ouchi, 1981). The etic concepts of individualism and collectivism (Hofstede, 1980; Triandis, 1990) nicely capture these different cultural answers to the question of what is the best way to allocate the tasks to workers. In collectivist cultures, groups are likely to be treated as work units, while in individualist cultures, individuals are social units.

The importance of the work group emerges in various social models of Japanese group processes (Befu, 1982) and in theories of social groups (Ouchi, 1981). Nakane (1978), in describing face-to-face small groups in Japanese organizations, went so far as to describe work groups as "sociological units." In addition, this sociological unit "as an indivisible unit to the Japanese is not a living organism as it is to Westerners, but a group...made up of people who always (or almost always) see each other and share their work and life" (p. 21; translated by first author). Others have similarly characterized Japanese work groups as individual (*shutai*) systems, which autonomously process information, evaluate opinions, and select and execute appropriate action. In short, just as the Japanese *ie* household is a functional unit, so is the Japanese work group.

The Japanese practice of total quality control provides a concrete example of organizations' use of small work groups as semi-autonomous functional units. A quality circle is typically a small group of workers who meet to discuss and solve problems related to quality and the cost of productivity (Ohmae, 1982; Schonberger, 1982). Group leaders emphasize participative decision making in the choice of problems and the range of alternative actions that are considered. Leaders, in particular, trust the ideas of their work groups because they believe that their employees are familiar with the task. Working out a problem of quality is aided by a cooperative team spirit and the physical proximity that workers have with each other almost every day. In addition, the foundations of Japanese quality control include an adherence to the work group, the expectation of permanent employment in the company, and a strong commitment to the organization's objectives. Interestingly, in the U.S. adaptation of quality circles, membership is often voluntary (Ferris & Wagner, 1985), while in Japanese companies it is usually institutionalized. Also, U.S. companies do not have the levels of shared co-worker interdependence that are characteristic of quality control in Japan, and workers are less willing to make personal sacrifices.

Physical features of the Japanese organization are also consistent with the use of groups as functional units. The cooperative work team involves supervisors and employees working in close proximity. In many factories they are able to see and talk to each other, and communicate verbally and nonverbally about their work experiences. The U-shaped production line, for example, is believed to create a long-term bonding between workers. If a job is not finished by the end of a shift, managers and the work group expect to work back. While surveys reveal that business executives in South Korea and Taiwan prefer a worker who adheres to work hours, managers in Japan expect workers to stay on the job until the task is completed (Hayashi, 1988). Also, compared to U.S. managers, the Japanese manager has a quite different view of the role of groups. This is apparent in their preference for group-based performance appraisal and, compared to U.S. managers, their stronger belief in the role of groups in facilitating performance (Kelly & Worthley, 1981).

If a group is chosen to be the functional unit, it follows that individuals are unlikely to have clear job descriptions. In Japan, the exact nature of jobs for each individual may be quite ambiguous. On the other hand, the machine metaphor of U.S. organizations implies that functional roles should be clearly specified. Indeed, studies of Japanese organizations show that this tends to be the case (see Dore, 1973; Nakane, 1970a, 1970b; Yoshino, 1968). For instance, in a survey of 54 Japanese business organizations in California, Lincoln, Olson, and Hanada (1978) found that reduced job specifications were one of the few differences between these organizations and U.S.-owned companies. This suggests that Japanese companies became similar to U.S. companies in general; however, the ambiguous job specification remained a significant feature of these Japanese organizations. Similarly, Marsh and Mannari (1976) found a relative lack of division of labor in Japanese factories. Japanese employees preferred ambiguous functional roles. Of 594 employees, only 21 percent showed a clear preference for specialized jobs. This is consistent with the findings of Lincoln, Hanada, and Olson (1981). Japanese and Japanese-American employees were more satisfied with their jobs when their companies assigned them to less specialized jobs. In contrast, U.S. employees in the same firms did not demonstrate this relationship between job specialization and job satisfaction.

In summary, one of the characteristic differences between Japanese and U.S. organizations is the Japanese practice of assigning specialized functions and responsibilities to the work group rather than to individual workers. According to Nakane (1978), Japanese work groups are integrated into their organizations through institutional rules and assumptions about how things ought to be done; however, formal rules do not bind individual members within work groups to specific functional roles. Rather, the activities of the small work group are governed largely by interpersonal bonds and power relationships between group members. On the basis of the worker's competence, knowledge, and job experience, individual functional roles are often negotiated rather than assigned (Iwata, 1982; Nakane, 1978; Tawara, 1981). Furthermore, differences between Japanese and U.S. workers in work attitudes and the use of work groups can be described in terms of the etic dimension of collectivism and individualism. At the same time, this etic cultural dimension may be further understood using each culture's own emic metaphor of organization.

Structural Roles in Work Groups

Organizations not only regulate the production of goods and services but also the nature of interpersonal relationships between their employees (see Trist & Bamforth, 1951). In modern complex social organizations, the assignment and negotiation of structural roles is influenced by beliefs about power, control, and status. Within Japanese organizations and their work groups, clear structural roles regulate the relationships between supervisors and subordinates (e.g., *oyabun-kobun*; Bennett & Ishino, 1963; Cole, 1971; Nakane, 1970a, 1970b). The nature of these vertical relationships is even predictive of promotional opportunities in Japanese organizations (M. Wakabayashi, G. Graen, M. R. Graen, & M. G. Graen, 1988).

Characteristically, Japanese organizations have more vertical differentiation than U.S. companies (Cooney, 1989; Lincoln & Kalleberg, 1985). The consequences of vertical differentiation, however, are somewhat unclear. One study (Lincoln et al., 1981) reported that greater differentiation is associated with higher job

satisfaction among Japanese and Japanese-American workers employed in Japanese subsidiaries in the United States, while the job satisfaction of U.S. workers in the same companies was not linked to levels of vertical stratification within the companies. On the other hand, other studies have failed to establish any link between vertical differentiation and increased job satisfaction in Japanese and U.S. companies (e.g., Lincoln & Kalleberg, 1985).

One important feature of vertical roles is their level of clarity within the organization. In Hofstede's (1980) HERMES survey of work values, Japan was medium in power distance compared to other cultures. In other words, Japanese workers felt more power distance between people of different status than did workers in New Zealand, Israel, and Austria. As Hofstede's study revealed, greater power distance between people is associated with more centralization of authority, more vertical differentiation in the form of taller organizational pyramids, and greater differences in pay between workers. Nonetheless, each worker has a place in the company and as a result tends to feel protected by this power structure.

In Japan, the vertical structure is associated with a range of emotional and interpersonal responses by workers and management. There is a special form of personal involvement between supervisors and workers. While Nakane (1970a, 1970b) describes Japanese vertical relationships as being colored by mutual involvement, Doi (1967) argues that the Japanese attempt to suffuse institutionalized interpersonal relationships through their need for involvement with others. Bennett and Ishino (1963) have labeled this suffusion as "paternalism." The paternalistic posture of Japanese managers is widely expected by workers. In one survey (Whitehill, 1964), more than 70 percent of Japanese workers expected to receive personal advice from their superiors, while only 27 percent of U.S. workers expected their superiors to be involved in their lives. Cole (1979) suggests that it is this paternalistic involvement in the lives of their workers that sets Japanese organizations apart from companies in other countries. He compares Japan to Germany, for instance, where there is little involvement between people connected to each other in vertical relationships.

Fruin (1978) provides an interesting case study of changes in paternalism in a Japanese company in a period spanning from before to after the Second World War. Prewar paternalism in the company was associated with friendships and personal relationships between the company, kin, and other family. The form of postwar paternalism, on the other hand, was considerably more impersonal and institutionalized. Others like Cole (1979) and Yoshino (1968) have also commented on the changing nature of Japanese paternalism, and their observations are consistent with wider changes occurring in Japanese society. Yet despite changes in the nature of paternalism, it is still a marked feature of Japanese organizations. Employees of both Japanese- and U.S.-owned companies in Japan, compared to employees in U.S. companies, believe that their supervisors are more likely to pitch in, get their hands dirty, listen to personal problems, and encourage them to seek their advice (Pascale & Maguire, 1980).

Frequent exchanges of information and shared involvement in decision making also characterize Japanese vertical structural roles. Empirical studies show that Japanese managers' preference for two-way communication is greater than it is for managers of other countries, including the United States and India (Bass & Burger, 1979). Also, compared to U.S. workers, Japanese workers have more face-to-face communication with their superiors and more frequently initiate upward communication (Pascale, 1978b). In addition, Japanese managers appear to be better at communicating to their employees than managers in other cultures (Bass & Burger, 1979).

In contrast to traditional North American and Western European organizations, two-way communication between members of different ranks and consultative decision making are prevailing features of the Japanese organization. *Ringi* serves as one formal channel for the two-way communication and influence (e.g., Clark, 1979; Yoshino, 1968). In the *ringi* system, a proposal for a new policy is circulated through the firm for comment by those who might be affected by the policy if it is implemented. Typically, a junior member of the organization initiates the proposal, which then goes up the organization's ranks for approval. According to Smith and Misumi (1989), this system, which began as early as the Meiji period, is increasingly being modified to adapt to the demands for efficiency required in modern industrial organizations. For instance, an organization may use *ringi* only for important decisions and give discretionary control to managers at certain seniority levels. For less important decisions, proposals may be circulated only among lower- and middle-level managers, and they may never reach the organization's top level.

Furthermore, the *ringi* system is often preceded by more informal communication and processes of negotiation called *nemawashi*. In this process, members of the organization may informally talk with those who will be affected by their proposals to "test the water." When the proposals are likely to be approved, written *ringi* proposals are circulated. This *nemawashi* process acts to facilitate two-way communication between members of different ranks in the organization with even greater efficiency than *ringi*. It also prevents conflicts within the organization. The general rule is that such nonconfrontation strategies must be exhausted by workers before other forms of communication are tried (Lebra, 1976, 1984; Wetzel, 1988). Smith and Misumi (1989) further suggest that the *ringi* system is currently used more as a method of reporting and recording decisions than as a method of decision making due to the increased popularity of the more informal *nemawashi* method (see also Takahashi & Takayanagi, 1985).

While *ringi* and *nemawashi* may be the major methods of communication and decision making among managers, the suggestion system may be more frequently used as a formal channel for upward communication from the shop-floor level. Workers are officially asked to give their ideas about ways of improving worker productivity and quality. In major Japanese companies, one employee may conceive and implement an average of 40 to 100 new suggestions every year for solving problems. Basadur (1992) reports that one Japanese research and development company with 9,000 employees received 660,000 employee suggestions in one year. Some 6,000 suggestions were for new products or product improvements; the rest involved suggestions for new methods of production. Such ideas are evaluated and may be rewarded by the organization with bonuses, medals, or prizes.

Various structural and spatial arrangements also facilitate informal communication between managers and workers (see Schonberger, 1982). Many Japanese organizations adopt an open plan layout in which very few managers have separate offices. Except for very senior executives, company cafeterias are not segregated and work areas are often large open rooms. Indeed, the company cafeteria often serves as the venue for worker presentations about new problems and solutions. According to Rohlen (1974b), the layout of Japanese factories allows employees to know where to go for help and to understand where they and their ideas fit in the organization. Senior employees can be seen discussing issues with staff members of all levels, while also instructing new staff members.

As Erez (1989) points out, Japanese organizations make the assumption that in two-way communication, those who are working on a particular task know the task better than anyone else. Employees at all levels are expected to be experts at what they do. They are expected to be thinking, creative workers who engage in problem solving on and off the job.

The tasks of the small group leader are not only to ensure that daily production targets are achieved, but also that there is sufficient opportunity for the communication of suggestions about solving problems, even if overtime is necessary for this to be achieved. These opportunities for two-way communication may help the members of Japanese organizations reduce levels of uncertainty and maintain levels of motivation. As Hofstede (1980) notes, Japanese workers are high on uncertainty avoidance, which also suggests a strong aversion to a lack of information. Two-way communication should facilitate the flow of information within the organization, thereby reducing levels of uncertainty among workers. Also, many Japanese organizations believe that opportunities for work teams to engage in problem solving and to communicate solutions to problems is central to keeping workers motivated (Basadur, 1992).

The Value of Harmony

The concept of harmony provides an ideological underpinning for the role relationships in the Japanese work group. The adoption of the *ie* metaphor by Japanese industrialists can be seen as a direct antecedent of the ideological emphasis on harmony. *Wa* is variously described as the quality of relationships, teamwork, and team spirit (see Rohlen, 1974a, 1974b). It is the ideology sponsored by the company to enhance social identity (Tajfel, 1982) and a sense of belonging to the company among employees. An emphasis on *wa* also promotes work group cohesiveness. Whether or not employees internalize this ideology of harmony, it seems to reduce explicit expressions of conflict between members of work groups.

Japanese companies make deliberate efforts to socialize workers into the values of cooperation and harmony. Rohlen (1974b) described the efforts of a Japanese bank to train its employees in its company philosophy of "harmony and strength." Their use of company ceremonies and songs and morning exercises is not unusual. Many Japanese companies sponsor recreational activities such as athletic and cultural festivals, dances, and sports tournaments. Significantly, more than 85 percent of employees participate in such activities (Marsh & Mannari, 1976). Cross-cultural comparisons (e.g., Lincoln & Kalleberg, 1985) reveal that more than U.S. companies, Japanese organizations have formal ceremonies, company-sponsored activities, in-house training programs, formal orientation programs for new employees, morning exercise sessions, and "pep talks," or gatherings at which management discusses ways of achieving company objectives. There is also a trend for U.S. companies to incorporate such activities as features of their organizational cultures (Peters & Waterman, 1982).

Summary

Various characteristics of Japanese workers and their managers are quite different from those in other countries. Most significantly, the Japanese work group has ambiguous institutionalized functional roles and relatively clear vertical structural roles. There are strong expectations about personal involvement in these vertical relationships. There is a deliberate emphasis on *wa,* or harmony, in that individual workers have been socialized to try to maintain harmony in their relations with others. Together these characteristics of the Japanese small group reveal that the *ie* metaphor still operates in modern Japanese organizations: The structure of Japanese work groups resembles the characteristics of the *ie* household. There is a rigid formal structure within which there are more flexible informal arrangements for the performance of functional behaviors. In this sense, the Japanese work group is not a totalitarian system that regiments its members through the use of coercion or power. Structural roles may be rigid, but the system affords flexibility for

individuals toward achieving the goals of the work group and their organization.

This flexibility and freedom emerges in the findings of several studies that compare Japanese managers to managers in other countries. Compared to Dutch managers, Japanese managers are more openly critical of each other in their group discussions (Hesseling & Konnen, 1969). In addition, Haire, Ghiselli, and Porter (1966) found that Japanese managers favored participative approaches more than managers from other countries. They were similar to U.S. managers in their support for the need for people to show leadership and initiative. Thus, despite vertical structural roles being rigid in Japanese organizations, there is still considerable flexibility about the nature of functional roles.

In contrast to Japan, the work group in North America assigns clearly defined functional roles to its individual members. Vertical structural roles are quite ambiguous. In particular, the demarcation of functional roles for the individual worker implies that a machine metaphor still operates in these organizations. While there are relatively flexible and egalitarian personal relationships between co-workers and between supervisors and workers, there are rigid functional roles. The North American system may be egalitarian, but it applies the rigidity implied by the machine metaphor to the operation of its functional parts.

There is the temptation to explain these cultural differences in attitudes, behaviors, and roles in terms of the group model of Japanese society: The Japanese are in general group oriented and happily work toward group goals. Yet as Befu (1982) and Mouer and Sugimoto (1986) painstakingly point out, the group model oversimplifies the many issues that have created these cultural differences. One major problem is that the group model tends to suggest that there is little conflict in the group. On the contrary, the Japanese organizational behaviors are fraught with conflict, dissent, and discontent. Kondo (1990) provides a vivid example of workers' discontent and fierce criticisms of their company in her recent ethnography. These are voiced in conversations with their co-workers. This is clearly not an isolated case.

All the same, the fact that such criticisms are voiced in the work group suggests the importance of the small work group in Japanese organizations. In such settings, Japanese workers feel free to express their criticisms to those members within their family-like work group who share the workday with them. It is this small face-to-face work group in which their primary sense of obligation lies: The people with whom employees form personal relationships command their loyalty. The particularistic work group constitutes the most significant in-group for the workers, though they may not feel a strong commitment to the companies they belong to.

Even with this caveat, the *ie* metaphor of organization is not meant to suggest that the small work group is a humanistic, utopian entity. Just as some families anywhere can be maladaptive (e.g., domestic violence, child abuse, and exploitation of the powerless), some Japanese work groups can exploit and abuse their members. The family metaphor defies the mechanical versus humanistic opposition that many organizational theorists (e.g., McGregor, 1960) have used to characterize Western organizations. The Japanese work group is often treated by its members *as if* it were a family, with all the shades of meanings, both pleasant and unpleasant, that the concept of family can signify.

It is difficult to determine the impact of the characteristics of Japanese work groups identified here without a detailed analysis of Japanese culture, socialization practices, and the dynamics of work groups. In the next section, we will briefly examine the sociocultural context in which Japanese work groups operate. A focus on sociocultural issues provides information about the prototypical experience of many Japanese workers as they enter their

work groups. Our discussion also examines the dynamics of work groups to investigate the conditions that are necessary for the successful operation of Japanese work groups. Finally, we will return to the consequences of being a member of a Japanese work group and what can reasonably be expected from the work group in terms of job satisfaction, organizational commitment, and quality and quantity of production.

A Social Psychological Analysis of the Japanese Work Group

Symbolic Culture and Socialization in Japan

The Japanese culture and various socialization practices prepare people for their working lives in Japanese organizations. In this section, features of Japanese culture and socialization practices are briefly considered. First, it is known that the Japanese addressing system is an indicator of status differences in interpersonal relationships. Most importantly, the addressing system fosters a social sensitivity to structural relationships, especially the vertical relationships that exist in Japanese organizations. Second, concepts related to *amae*, or a desire for close interpersonal relationships, have considerable influence on the lives of Japanese workers. Other notions like *on* and *gimu* indicate a sense of indebtedness and obligation. We will discuss how together these features of Japanese culture motivate, as well as influence, the response of workers to the organizational system. Third, we will take a brief look at the typical school experiences of the Japanese prior to their entry into the work force. From their schooling and school relationships, Japanese students are given many opportunities to become skilled in handling group situations and vertical relationships. Finally, organizations themselves also provide extensive training not only in technical skills but also in such social skills. In particular, we will review some procedures used to promote the acceptance of company philosophies and to establish a sense of social identity based on organizational membership (for further general discussions of Japanese society, see Lebra, 1976; Plath, 1980; Smith, 1983).

The Japanese System of Address

How we address others is an important aspect of our everyday interactions with family, friends, and co-workers. An addressing system can reflect the operation of implicit rules of interpersonal conduct, and provides a vital insight into how interpersonal relationships are regulated in a society. In English, the personal pronoun *I* features strongly in our interpersonal communication. The existence of a single word for the first person in the European languages (e.g., I, Ich, Je) has provided a building block for the sense of individuality that dominates Western thought and behavior (Benveniste, 1971).

The Japanese addressing system is also a good indicator of the nature of interpersonal relationships, although it does not fully determine relations between people. In particular, the addressing system trains people for vertical structural relationships. In Japan, one needs to be sensitive to differences in vertical status in order to use various forms of address. In relationships between a supervisor and a subordinate, the addressing system constantly reminds the interactants of the differences in their status. In addition, to use the Japanese addressing system appropriately, the speaker has to be sensitive to the context and the social situation. This greater awareness of status, context, and social sensitivity are the major differences between Japanese and Western styles of interpersonal communication and personal relationships (Howard & Teramoto, 1981).

In the Japanese addressing system, there is a greater range of words used to denote the first and second person than are used in English (Mouer & Sugimoto, 1986). Instead of the single pronoun *I*, a number of words can be used to signify the speaker (e.g., *watakushi*, *boku*, and *ore*). Similarly, a wide range of words may be used for the second person (e.g., *anata*, *kimi*, and *omae*), depending on various situational cues. This range of words means that Japanese speakers need to be sensitive to the social situation in order to choose the correct phrase. Moreover, Japanese grammar allows the speaker to drop such words, thereby deemphasizing the self–other distinction in social interactions. This may serve to increase the sense of ingroup belongingness between the interactants, as Moeran (1988) has suggested.

The form of address used is a function of the formality of the situation and the degree of perceived interpersonal distance between interactants (Suzuki, 1973). As they manage their interpersonal relationships, speakers must consider the differences in their status. For instance, a supervisor would call a subordinate either *kimi* or by the subordinate's surname. The subordinate would call a supervisor by his or her position, with or without a surname (e.g., Tanaka *ka-cho*, Section Leader Tanaka). Also, the form of address between people may change across different social contexts. For example, in a more informal situation, a supervisor could call a subordinate *omae*.

There are numerous rules that must be followed in the correct use of the addressing system. Some rules function to make an interactant define the interpersonal relationship in terms of the lower status person. While such rules do not guarantee that a Japanese supervisor would seriously consider the opinions of a subordinate, such rules are yet another reminder of the existence of status-marked obligations in Japanese culture. In families, an example of the use of this rule would be when seniors call themselves the same name as more junior members of the family do (Suzuki, 1973). If a son calls his father *otosan*, for example, the father then refers to himself as *otosan.* If a niece calls her aunt *obasan,* the aunt will call herself *obasan.* In addition, this same rule applies in nonfamilial relationships. Teachers often call themselves *sensei* (teacher) when they talk to their students. Similarly, an elderly male may refer to himself as *ojiisan* (grandfather) when he talks to a child who is not related to him. Perhaps the situation sensitivity of the Japanese addressing system is most clearly illustrated by the following example. A father and son will address each other as grandfather and father in the presence of the son's child (the most junior member in the family hierarchy); however, the same individuals would call each other father and son when the child is not present. It is the perspective of the most junior person involved in the interaction that determines the choice of address.

The Japanese Concept of Interpersonal Relationships. Japanese culture provides a view of interpersonal relations that differs from what is found in Western cultures. According to Markus and Kitayama (1991), interpersonal relationships are so important in Japan that they constitute the central aspect of the Japanese self-concept. From childhood, the Japanese are taught to be able to maintain harmony with others (see Wetzel, 1988), and in the workplace, concerns about interpersonal relationships influence the behavior of work group members. Cultural concepts of *amae, on,* and *gimu* describe the significant aspects of interpersonal relationships that help the Japanese work group become a highly cohesive functional unit.

Amae and Amaeru. Amae psychology, or simply *amae* (Doi, 1971), is central to an analysis of the interpersonal behavior of the Japanese worker. *Amaeru* is the verb, meaning both to express *amae* and to satisfy it. In its broadest sense, *amae* is a person's desire to be loved or to have social acceptance. These needs emerge from the bond between mother and child, and, according to Doi, the desires initially fulfilled in these relationships continue to emerge as

needs that can be met through interpersonal relationships later in life.

Amae is a highly elaborate cultural concept that underlies a number of Japanese concepts about interpersonal relationships. In his discussion of the concept, Doi (1967) has included the following glossary of terms: *kodawari,* which is a level of hypersensitivity that results when a person's needs for *amae* are unfulfilled; *amai* (literally meaning sweet) describes a person who is too soft or benevolent in relating to others and lets them *amaeru; tori-iru* (literally to take in) describes how a person skillfully maneuvers others into allowing him or her to *amaeru; higamu* is the behavior of someone who feels unfairly treated compared to others who are more favored with *amae; tereru* is the intimate behavior that shows one wants *amae;* and *hinekureru* is the use of devious strategies to fulfill denied *amae.* The list goes on. Doi's discussion provides an understanding of the psychology of the Japanese people, their need for gaining the goodwill and acceptance of others, and, ultimately, their reluctance to do anything that will undo their relationships with others.

Amae is often described in the vertical relationships that exist in Japanese organizations (see Doi, 1971). While the supervisor–subordinate relationship is based on work-related goals and social roles (a *giri* relationship), the Japanese worker often seeks to fulfill *amae* (to seek *ninjo*), even in these social rather than personal relationships. Thus, supervisors and subordinates can establish a mutually fulfilling *amae* relationship, although overt expressions of *amae* in the workplace are very likely to be perceived as inappropriate. Whether the Japanese have a greater need to be loved or be dependent on others than do people in other cultures, they are more likely to perceive their interpersonal relationships in terms of *amae.* Doi sees *amae* as the thread that runs through all activities of Japanese society, and because of the significance the Japanese attach to their working lives, the perceived importance of *amae* and of fulfilling *amae* in organizational settings cannot be underestimated.

On. The concept of *on* is a form of indebtedness that needs to be repaid. If a person of higher status does a favor for a lower status person, for instance, this act produces *on.* This *on* needs to be repaid in some way. Two stories, known by almost every Japanese adult, illustrate the concept of *on.* In the folktale "A Crane's Repayment of *On* (Tsuru no on Gaeshi)," a captured crane is released by a hunter who thus receives *on.* The crane later returns the hunter's favor by making a beautiful fabric out of her feathers. In the second story, we have the case of a dog named Hachi. This story was popular in Japanese children's readers before the Second World War. Hachi's master raised him, and so Hachi received *on.* Hachi would repay this *on* by waiting each day at the local railway station for his master. Even after his master had died at work, Hachi still waited for his master at the station until his own death. In fact, a bronze statue of Hachi can still be found outside a railway station in Tokyo. Such stories remind the Japanese that everyone needs to repay *on,* even animals.

On is related to *amae* in at least two ways. *Amae* is a desire to be loved or wanted by others. Thus, *amae* is a desire to receive *on* from other people by being wanted or loved or through being able to depend on them. Furthermore, if a supervisor fulfills a subordinate's *amae,* the subordinate receives *on.* The supervisor does the subordinate a favor by meeting his or her needs for *amae,* which in turn produces *on* for the subordinate. In combination, *amae* motivates people to want to receive *on.* The fulfilment of the need for *amae* produces *on* in the person whose *amae* was satisfied.

Prior to the Second World War, the need to fulfill *on* was a core cultural value (Benedict, 1946). Today, the repayment of *on* is not a core value to many Japanese workers. Doi (1973) attributes the decline in the importance of meeting *on* to the link between *on* and the philosophies of the totalitarian regime that ruled Japan prior to the Second World War. When this regime was removed, *on* came to be viewed also as an outmoded concept, especially among the younger Japanese. Nonetheless, the concept continues to have considerable symbolic importance among older generations of Japanese, who as children observed the repayment of

on or who were raised on pre-war stories like those about Hachi.

Gimu. The concept of *gimu* refers to a sense of feeling of being obligated to repay a favor. This feeling motivates many workers to work very hard, as a means of repaying their obligations. As Ben Dasan (1980) notes, the act of doing a favor in principle produces not only an obligation to repay the favor but also a right to demand its repayment. Japanese symbolic culture, however, places considerable emphasis on *ho-on no gimu* (an obligation to repay *on*), but gives less attention to *se-on no kenri* (the right that *on* is repaid). The latter in fact is not a common Japanese phrase, but is one of Ben Dasan's neologisms. It is expected that a person will repay *on* spontaneously out of his or her sense of obligation (*gimu*) to do so.

Whitehill and Takezawa (1968) have given a number of cases of the Japanese workers' belief in *gimu.* On the basis of this 1959 study, they concluded that gimu was an extremely important concept toward understanding the shared obligations and motivations of Japanese production workers. At the same time, even some 30 years ago, they observed a diminishing attachment among workers to *gimu.* More specifically, Tawara (1981) found that managers and workers under the age of 35 showed a weaker sense of *gimu* toward their jobs than older workers. Cole (1971) made a similar observation of blue collar workers. Compared to older workers raised in the cultural climate prior to the Second World War, younger workers were not caught as tightly in the web of social obligations as older workers.

In summary, *amae* or *gimu* and similar principles have a significant influence on the nature of interpersonal relationships on the factory floor and among members of the work group. The Japanese are socialized to seek acceptance and to feel wanted (*amae*). This sense of dependence on others and the need to be accepted by them in turn involves obligation (*gimu*) to return the favors of others (*on*). The involvement of supervisors in going out of their way to help workers in their work and personal lives creates a sense of obligation (Bennett & Ishino, 1963; Pascale & Maguire, 1980). Workers repay this sense of obligation by working hard for their supervisors and co-workers. Such concepts are features of the Japanese concept of interpersonal relationships. There is evidence, however, that young Japanese workers do not attach the same importance to these values as do older members of organizations.

Socialization Practices in Japanese Schools. The Japanese educational system is a major agent of socialization. In particular, schools provide a major influence on interpersonal behaviors in groups and in vertical relationships. Prior to formal schooling, the mother–child relationship in Japan tends to emphasize the sense of interdependence (Caudill & Weinstein, 1969). In their preschool years, Japanese children are encouraged to explore their relationships with members of their peer group (Tobin, Wu, & Davidson, 1989). Such experiences prior to entering more formal education provide children with opportunities to live and interact with their superiors and peers in a range of socially cooperative settings.

In primary schools, students are divided into classes called *kurasu*. Typically, a *kurasu* has smaller subgroups of students who tend to study together and who develop close friendships with each other. Like the work groups in Japanese factories, members of these small, highly cohesive groups see each other every day as they work on their shared activities. The Japanese primary schools are also known for their success in developing a sense of team spirit or community spirit (*shudan–ishiki*) among children (see Kiefer, 1974). This community spirit emerges in many ways, including the greater likelihood that Japanese schoolchildren will share resources equally between their classmates (Mann, Radford, & Kanagawa, 1985).

In junior high schools, the precursor of the vertical relationship in Japanese companies is the *senpai-kohai* relationship (see Rohlen, 1983). *Senpai* is a senior member of the school or a senior student in a team or club, and the *kohai* is the junior student. While the *senpai–kohai* relationship has many similarities with the supervisor–subordinate relationship in the Japanese factory or company, it does not involve any obvious system of economic rewards between the students. The relationship, however, does prepare those who end their schooling at this younger age for the vertical relationships that they will encounter as blue collar workers.

Many junior high school graduates leave the junior school system to attend senior high schools and universities in Japan. Again, the *senpai-kohai* relationship is present at these levels of education. In this case, the relationship may involve some economic rewards in that a *senpai* may help a *kohai* find a job in the *senpai's* own organization. This recruitment by the older student, however, is not always harmonious. Relationships between *senpais* and *kohais* are not always friendly or cooperative and, in fact, they can be unfriendly, oppressive, and conflict laden. In addition, many Japanese young people avoid ever establishing a *senpai-kohai* relationship. Nevertheless, compared to Western cultures, these school-based relationships result in many young people being familiar with many practices that will be adopted by their future organizations in one form or another. At the very least, a new recruit in a Japanese organization should know that structural roles exist and have some idea about how these roles operate (Copley, 1986).

Company Training. Before they enter the work force, new recruits to Japanese industry are likely to have already been involved in group activities and team work at their primary and junior high schools. If they continued on to higher education, the *senpai–kohai* relationship has also given them a model of vertical structural relationships typical in Japanese industry. Similar *senpai–kohai* relationships may exist in the workplace. In addition, most Japanese companies also train their new employees (Nonaka & Johansson, 1985; Rehder, 1983). The significance of company training is probably increasing as many organizations believe the core cultural values are being challenged by changes in the wider society. Organizational training is often used to reinforce cultural values that are consistent with the company's philosophy (Lachman, 1983).

Rohlen (1974a) provides a description of one training program used in a Japanese company. He depicted the training as being based on a philosophy "similar to the U.S. Marine Corps, but with greater emphasis on conformity and group loyalty" (p. 333). New employees spent a month in a training camp away from home. Khaki uniforms and several sports uniforms were supplied. Money was exchanged for military-like scrip for use at the training camp canteen. The day began at 5:30 A.M. and ended at 9:00 P.M., when, in military fashion, all the lights were turned out. During a typical day in the training camp, trainees performed athletic activities, attended lectures, and studied. Rohlen reported that while lectures concentrated on the operations of the company, more significant were various messages and statements about the attitudes and behaviors that were expected of company employees. Adopting a "fighting spirit" was a persistent theme, which Rohlen interpreted to mean that employees should be determined, perseverant, and loyal to the group. Company executives had made the deliberate decision to install the training program into the organization's culture to counter the Western attitudes and values that appeared to threaten the cohesion of the company and the total system of values, incentives, and rewards by which it operated.

Although Rohlen's case study might be an extreme example of the form of training implemented by Japanese managers, many directors of large organizations have decided to use company training programs to reinforce the traditional values of Japanese culture. Compared to U.S. companies, Japanese organizations in the past have been more likely to have formal orientation programs for their new recruits (Lincoln & Kalleberg, 1985). Also, even in more recent times, the focus on discipline described by Rohlen is still evident in many programs. For instance, Sataka (1987) described a program in which managers completed many group exercises and activities, as well as *misogi*, to "install the challenging spirit" in trainees (p. 90; translated by the first author). As an example of *misogi*, trainees might enter a river semi-naked on a winter night and stay in the water for about a minute. Whatever the effectiveness of activities like *misogi*, such company training is supported by organizational leaders who believe that it maintains and builds upon the sense of cooperation between its employees (see Kondo, 1990, for another example).

The Dynamics of the Japanese Work Group

The Japanese symbolic culture and socialization practices endow organizational entrants with a set of skills and expectations that assist the effective operation of the Japanese work group. In this section, we will examine the way Japanese employees with these cultural and socialization experiences interact with the features of the Japanese work group. The dynamics of the Japanese work group can be analyzed at the individual, interpersonal, and group level: that is, by the motivation of individual workers; by the interpersonal relationships between supervisors and workers, which can be understood in terms of *amae*, *gimu*, and *on*; and by the influence of the characteristics of the Japanese work group on group processes.

Individual Level of Analysis. Japanese workers are likely to have a view of interpersonal
behaviors that is influenced by their prior
membership in other groups, earlier dealings
with vertical relationships such as the *senpai–
kohai* association at school, and the cultural
expectation for people to be sensitive to social
situations. With these experiences, they are
also likely to have developed a set of social
skills that has prepared them for their work
lives. Many entrants to Japanese organizations
are likely to have skills that help them negotiate
their roles within their work group and handle
clear vertical differentiation of roles, and that
will alert them to the need to be sensitive to the
immediate situation.

These individual attributes are reflected in
the work-related attitudes of employees and
managers. Japanese workers have higher needs
for affiliation and achievement than do workers in other cultures (De Vos 1968; MOW International Work Team, 1986). Most importantly,
these needs for affiliation and achievement are
met through the success of the work group
rather than the individual. Even compared to
workers in other collectivist cultures, such as
South Korea and Taiwan, it is through teamwork that tasks are approached (Hayashi, 1988).
In other studies, Hofstede (1980) found that
work values associated with an individual
worker's independence from his or her organization were emphasized less in Japan than in
the United States. He interpreted this result to
indicate that Japanese workers are less individualistic than their counterparts in the United
States. Again, the fact that Japanese workers
put less emphasis on being independent of
their organizations can be linked to the *ie* household metaphor of Japanese organizations.

Other research has established that Japanese employees view their work as being
central to their lives. When work centrality
scores (i.e., the degree of general importance
that work has in the life of an individual) are
calculated and divided into high, medium, and
low categories, there are 12 times the number of
Japanese workers in the high category than in

the low category (England & Misumi, 1986).
Some 37 percent of Japanese workers, but
only 17 percent of U.S. workers, believe that
work is the most important part of their life.
Work is significantly more important for
every occupational group of Japanese workers
that it is for the same group of workers in the
United States.

England (1989) also reported that 32 percent of Japanese workers perceived their work
to be central to their lives and expressed that
they want to work hard. In contrast, 17 percent
of the U.S. and 15 percent of West German
workers shared this view. As many as 93 percent of the Japanese workers reported that they
would continue to work even if there were no
financial need to do so—the highest of the
seven countries studied by Harpaz (1989; i.e.,
Belgium, Great Britain, Germany, Israel, Japan,
the Netherlands, and the United States). In
addition, England and Harpaz (1990) found
that while the Japanese, like the Germans, attach a strong sense of duty and personal gain to
work, they experience relatively low levels of
positive affect in performing them. Compared
to other nations, Japanese respondents had
the highest proportion of employees who
viewed their work as something that they are
accountable for, and the largest proportion
who believed that work is something they have
to do.

However, as England and his colleagues
have repeatedly cautioned (e.g., England, 1983;
England & Koike, 1970), Japanese work attitudes are not uniform. Considerable individual,
regional, and industry-related differences exist
in work-related attitudes. Age, levels of education, and the type of industry influence the
work-related attitudes of Japanese employees.
For example, younger executives in Japanese
organizations are more likely than their older
colleagues to take time off for vacations and
relaxation (Dollinger, 1988), while the younger
Japanese are becoming more particular and
diversified in their tastes and lifestyles (Sera,
1992). Cross-cultural comparisons show only
small differences in the importance of work

between Japan and the United States for students who are about to begin employment and for new workers under 20 years of age (England & Misumi, 1986). These cross-sectional data, however, show that the importance of work increases dramatically for Japanese workers in their twenties, and this large difference is maintained throughout the life span and into the final years of their working lives.

In addition, Cole's (1971) analysis of blue collar workers shows differences between urban and rural workers. He found that the more sophisticated urban workers were more critical of their company, more independent, and more reluctant to let their company and work dominate their lives. The Tokyo diecast workers, for instance, were unwilling to fall into the stereotypical role of being submissive and completely loyal to the company. As has been observed in collectivist cultures (Triandis, 1990), there are people who place individual goals ahead of ingroup ones (i.e., idiocentrics), while others more greatly value the goals of the ingroup (i.e., allocentrics). Cole's rural workers showed this uncritical acceptance of ingroup goals and believed in the central role of the company in their personal lives. As some studies reveal (Whitehill & Takezawa, 1968), about two-thirds of Japanese workers consider the company to be equal to or more important than their personal lives. In contrast, only about a one-fourth of U.S. workers hold a similar devotion to their companies. Japanese workers expect the company to promote a paternalistic attitude toward them, and this attitude includes the offer of lifetime employment, low-cost housing, recreation facilities, and salary increments based on seniority (Dore, 1973; Farmer & Richman, 1965).

Another factor that influences work attitudes is the type of industry and region a Japanese worker is employed in. While collective team effort is still the preferred style, employees in general trading firms (*sogo shosha*) are more likely to prefer individual responsibility for a job than workers in heavy and light industry or in large retailing firms (Hayashi, 1988). This greater preference for individual work is also present in regional management style differences. For instance, the Osaka merchant style of management is perceived to be more independent and individualistic than the management style found in large organizations in Tokyo.

Interpersonal Level of Analysis. Another level of analysis of the Japanese work group involves the interpersonal relationships between group members. Japanese beliefs about interpersonal relationships are conveyed in the concepts of *amae, on,* and *gimu.* The *amae-on-gimu* system of needs and obligations provides insights into understanding worker motivation. As discussed earlier, the Japanese are socialized to conceptualize interpersonal relationships in terms of affiliation and acceptance (*amae*). Acceptance by others in turn entails an obligation (*gimu*) to repay any indebtedness (*on*). These relationships can be seen as being mediated by processes of internalization and identification rather than mere compliance to external pressures (see Kelman, 1958).

As regulators of co-worker and supervisor–subordinate relations, *amae, on,* and *gimu* shape the motivation of Japanese workers in several ways. One consequence is that Japanese workers will seek to *amaeru* their superiors in their small work groups. The vertical separation of roles provides workers with an appropriate cultural context for subordinates to *amaeru.* In response, the superiors may fulfill their *amae* by establishing a rapport with members of the work group. In addition, the so-called paternalism of Japanese work groups possibly satisfies the desire of supervisors and workers to *amaeru* (Bennett & Ishino, 1963). At the very least, the mutual involvement is likely to be perceived as a fulfillment of *amae.* In turn, subordinates may feel *on* when their *amae* is perceived to be satisfied by their supervisor. As discussed before, both supervisors and workers expect the supervisor to be interested in the family and personal lives of employees, perhaps even going out of their way to help them (Bennett & Ishino, 1963; Pascale & Maguire, 1980). Workers can feel *gimu* or a sense of obligation to their supervisors, and they can spontaneously repay *on* by working hard within their work group.

In short, the *amae-on-gimu* system provides a culturally based interpretation of the motivation of Japanese workers (e.g., D'Andrade & Strauss, 1992). *Amae* is transformed into the motivation to work hard for members of the work group. *On* and *gimu* are the cultural underpinnings that facilitate this process. As was noted earlier, however, many young Japanese workers may not take these values too seriously. This interpretation of Japanese worker motivation may be more applicable to older workers, and to those who work in more traditional sectors of Japanese industry (see Maguire & Kroliczak, 1983; Schooler & Naoi, 1988).

Group Level of Analysis.   A third perspective that assists in understanding the dynamics of the Japanese work group is to focus on the group process and performance. According to a number of social psychological models (e.g., Seashore, 1954; Turner, 1987), levels of group cohesiveness, as well as group norms, are major determinants of group performance. The more cohesive a group, the stronger the normative influences are upon its members. While cohesiveness and norms may provide ambient stimuli (Hackman, 1976), more proximal antecedents of group performance can include the nature of the task and the skills and abilities that group members bring to the task (McGrath, 1984; Steiner, 1972). This section examines the impact that characteristics of the Japanese work group have on the level of group cohesiveness. Then, the role of group norms and social influence processes within the Japanese work group are discussed. Finally, the potential effects of the practice of functional role assignments in Japanese work groups,

particularly in terms of task demands and requisite skills, are investigated.

Group Cohesiveness. Many characteristics of the Japanese work group contribute to a high level of group cohesiveness. The assignment of functional roles to groups rather than to individuals increases the level of group cohesiveness by setting a common set of goals for all members of a work group. The application of group-based performance evaluation and feedback in the workplace also enhances this sense of common fate among work group members.

Supporting the work group as a functional unit is a clear formal differentiation of vertical roles, together with expectations about mutual involvement and a sense of obligation to other workers. The Japanese manager–subordinate relationship gives the manager the formal power to control worker behavior. As Marsh and Mannari (1976) report, this vertical structure allows cohesiveness to be maintained in work groups. At the same time, the Japanese vertical relationship also involves expectations of personal involvement by the manager, relatively high levels of two-way communication, and consultative decision making between managers and workers.

The emphasis on harmony discussed earlier also promotes high levels of cohesiveness in Japanese work groups. Company-sponsored activities and ceremonies involve employees and their work groups. Such ceremonies have considerable symbolic importance in that they reinforce the sense of harmony and cooperation and, in turn, levels of group cohesiveness and organizational commitment among workers. Both in Japan and the United States there is more organizational commitment in companies that often sponsor recreational, sporting, and ceremonial activities for their workers (Lincoln & Kalleberg, 1985). The greater use of these organizational activities in Japanese companies might explain consistent survey findings that show Japanese workers to be more trusting of their companies than their counterparts in the United States.

Group Norms. An outcome of high levels of group cohesiveness is that such groups are more able to enforce norms that allow them to achieve their expected levels of productivity. In Japanese companies, there are strong norms about high levels of quality and productivity. Japanese managers emphasize productivity more than profit (England & Koike, 1970; Haire et al., 1966), while comparisons between the United States and Japan reveal that Japanese companies and their workers are more committed to high quality in their production than U.S. companies and their workers (Garvin, 1986).

Kelman (1958) suggests that social influence can take three forms: internalization, identification, and compliance. Applied to Japanese organizations, it can be argued that workers could internalize the company's philosophy about quality and productivity, and that these beliefs in turn might encourage strong expectations about the work group's performance. Workers may identify with and imitate the work-related beliefs of others in their small work groups, or they might rigidly comply with beliefs about the need to produce quality goods in order to avoid being stigmatized by their co-workers for violating work-related norms.

It is likely that all three processes influence the performance of members of the Japanese work group. Studies of the importance of work show that Japanese workers have internalized a belief in work centrality (England & Misumi, 1986). This belief is consistent with work group norms to be highly productive and to produce goods of the highest quality. A belief in work centrality motivates members of the work group to work hard, while their efforts provide models of appropriate levels of performance to other team members. Even if some members of the group do not internalize norms about

quality and production because of other factors such as a sense of attraction and obligation among group members, they are likely at least to match the job performance of other workers.

Compliance to a work group norm of productivity and quality is promoted by the sensitivity of the Japanese to situationally appropriate behaviors. The work environment is often planned so that Japanese workers can monitor each others' performance in the group (Schonberger, 1982). Co-workers are pressured to comply by the very nature of their cooperative working relationships with other members of the team, while they also know and accept that their supervisor has the formal power to discipline lazy or disobedient employees.

Role Assignment. One of the consequences of assigning functional roles to the work group is that individual workers do not have clearly assigned functional roles. Assignment of more specific functional roles is left to the members of each work group. This poses an additional task demand on work group members. Someone in the group, whether a supervisor or a subordinate, must be able to devise a specific plan to carry out the task given to the group. Undoubtedly, in many cases there would be previously established routines and blueprints that would help the group. Nevertheless, there are always opportunities to devise a better strategy for completing the group task. The effective operation of the Japanese work group requires that the goal of the group be clearly specified and that group members be skilled enough to identify the tasks necessary to achieve the group goal. In addition, group members must have the social skills that enable them to negotiate and establish specific functional roles. In addition, their members must be motivated to carry out these negotiated roles and coordinate tasks among group members.

Various practices in Japanese organizations help to satisfy many of these requirements.

It is a typical practice to specify group roles. Also, Japanese organizations usually provide incentives for workers to acquire multiple skills (Schonberger, 1982), and the practice of lateral job rotation means that members of the work group have considerable experience across many functional areas (Hatvany & Pucik, 1981). As others have noted (Ouchi, 1981; Schonberger, 1982), this generalist worker is a central component of the successful operation of the Japanese work group. The generalist Japanese worker is also motivated to work hard and negotiate and coordinate tasks because of the intrinsic importance of hard work. Work is central to the lives of employees due to deeply held interpersonal obligations among workers and to strongly held group norms about high levels of performance. As Maruyama (1992) asserts, workers in a Japanese work group have different strengths and weaknesses that complement each other through the dynamic interaction that occurs when people perform tasks as a group.

Effects of the Japanese Work Group.   What can reasonably be expected from Japanese work groups based on this analysis? We can give a fairly clear answer regarding worker motivation and productivity. The Japanese work group system should function well given that Japanese culture enhances worker motivation and productivity. Remember that the *amae-on-gimu* system can transform workers' need for social affiliation into work motivation. The sense of group cohesiveness afforded by the very nature of Japanese work groups further reinforces worker motivation. Clearly, Japanese workers have a strong belief in the intrinsic value of work. This strong motivation to work is held by multiskilled workers who not only share group norms of quality and productivity but who can also identify and devise tasks that allow their group to achieve its specific goals.

What is not clear are the effects that the Japanese work group has on job satisfaction and organizational commitment. As for job satisfaction, the wider potential job scope afforded by the ambiguous functional role assignment (Brief & Adlag, 1975; Hackman & Lawler, 1971) and the close personal ties between supervisors and workers (Stogdill, 1974; Yukl, 1989) may enhance job satisfaction. However, the very same factors may act to reduce job satisfaction. Note that functional roles for individuals are ambiguous. They may expand or contract, depending on various factors, including the distribution of power and various abilities within the group (Iwata, 1982; Nakane, 1978; Tawara, 1981). Close personal ties and the sharing of interpersonal concerns may burden the group rather than provide a source of satisfaction (Tawara, 1981). In fact, many cross-cultural studies have shown that Japanese workers are less satisfied than workers in U.S. and Western European organizations (e.g., Azumi & McMillan, 1976; Cole, 1979; Lincoln & Kalleberg, 1985, 1990; Naoi & Schooler, 1985; Odaka, 1975; Pascale & Maguire, 1980). Smith and Misumi (1989) suggest three explanations for this finding: Japanese workers may be more dissatisfied because they have to work longer hours for lower pay; Japanese workers may have higher expectations about doing their jobs than their organizations can satisfy (i.e., Cole, 1979); and Japanese workers may have a response set toward being modest in expressing their feelings about work. Possibly all three are valid explanations for these lower levels of job satisfaction.

Turning to organizational commitment, the Japanese work group system does not guarantee a high level of commitment to the organization per se. The system is most likely to create in workers a sense of interpersonal relatedness with and personal obligation to their co-workers (e.g., Nakane, 1970a, 1970b). A highly cohesive work group and the network of friends provide many Japanese workers with the core focus of their lives. Nevertheless, their organizations as abstract entities may or may not be the locus of their sense of loyalty. Both Lincoln and Kalleberg (1985) and Luthans, McCaul, and Dodd (1985) report a lower level of organizational commitment among Japanese workers than U.S. workers. Although these findings may be interpreted in terms of a response set toward avoiding extreme statements (Triandis, this volume), evidence that work centrality is higher for Japanese workers than for U.S. workers, while the reverse is true for organizational commitment, implies that these measures tap quite different aspects of the psychology of the Japanese worker.

Japanese Culture, Socialization, and the Work Group

We have shown that the work group is a product of Japanese culture and the Japanese style of management. At the core of this organizational practice is the *ie* metaphor of organizational structure. Although others (e.g., Cole, 1971) have also recognized parallels between the Japanese family and the system of group decision making in Japanese organizations, our analysis has focused on sociopsychological effects of adopting the *ie* metaphor. We have argued that the *ie* metaphor is not merely a figure of speech, but an important influence on organizational behavior and decision making. The *ie* metaphor in the past and present allows top-level and middle-level managers in Japan to use their understanding of the social and economic relationships in the *ie* household to set up culturally appropriate organizational practices in the workplace. The *ie* metaphor allows the Japanese worker to understand organizational structure and practices. Workers can use the metaphor, as can management, to generate solutions to unique problems. The *ie* metaphor also establishes shared assumptions between management and workers about belongingness, cooperation, harmony, duty, and suitable forms of social control that can be applied by management. The *ie* metaphor has allowed Japanese management to make their organizations consistent with Japanese culture. As England (England, 1983; England & Lee, 1973; England, Negandhi, & Wilpert, 1981) has consistently pointed out, this is a major lesson from the Japanese postwar experience that others can benefit from. Managers must know their organizational objectives and culture, and choose practices that are appropriate for both.

Today, the operation of the *ie* metaphor is observed in the similarity of modern work groups to the prototypical *ie* household. Both groups have semiautonomous economic activities, shared work, clearly defined structural roles with paternalistic involvement, and emphasis on harmony (*wa*). However, more so than the Japanese household, the Japanese work group is dependent on the successful socialization of its members prior to their joining the group. Japanese childrearing practices emphasize protection, conformity, and dutiful obedience (Ronen, 1986). The Japanese educational system sustains the work group through socializing young people about the appropriateness of teamwork, the utility of a collectivist orientation to task achievement, and the significance of vertical structural relationships. At school and elsewhere, training in the correct use of the Japanese address system heightens sensitivity to status differences, the importance of the social context, and the need for good interpersonal skills. All these processes play important roles in socializing Japanese workers to work effectively with others in Japanese organizations.

Our examination of the dynamics of the Japanese work group suggests that in Japan its characteristics are likely to produce high levels of worker motivation and group cohesiveness. The assignment of functional roles to groups, clear vertical roles with expectations of personal involvement, and the ideology of harmony are likely to produce high levels of group cohesion. In addition, the *amae-on-gimu* system of interpersonal relationships can transform the personal involvement expected within the vertical relationship into work motivation. Also, the ambiguous assignment of functional roles to individuals provides the opportunity for these well-motivated and multiskilled workers to make innovative contributions toward achieving the group goal.

As Triandis (this volume) points out in his review of cross-cultural organizational research, a clear message is that what works in one culture does not necessarily work in another. Our brief analysis has attempted to identify the various features of Japanese society and its culture and to present a coherent explanation of how these features contribute to the effectiveness of the Japanese work group. The use of a group as a work unit is especially effective in Japan's social and cultural context, providing an example of what Cole (1971) has noted as organizational practices that are consistent with a sociocultural context. Does this mean, though, that Japanese organizational practices, especially the activities of small work groups, are at all cross-culturally transferable? We will now explore this question.

The Question of Transferability

The impact of the Japanese style of management is increasingly being felt in many countries because of the obvious success and growth of the Japanese economy in the last decade. In particular, the Japanese system of the primary work group is often hailed as a key to the success of Japanese organizations. Although it is debatable whether managerial practices alone can explain the success of Japanese organizations (McMillan, 1985), our analysis suggests that within the Japanese sociocultural context, the system of Japanese work groups plays a significant role in achieving high levels of quality and productivity. Others have suggested that the Japanese organizational practice is no different from the policies pursued by the more progressive U.S. corporations (e.g., Pascale & Althos, 1981), implying the cross-cultural applicability of these policies.

It is important, therefore, to evaluate critically whether the system of the Japanese work group is transferable or indeed worth transferring to different cultures. Our analysis implies that the system may be effective in Japan, but that even there it may not necessarily bring about high levels of job satisfaction or organizational commitment. Furthermore, the transferability of various attributes of the Japanese work group may depend on various cultural factors. As other writers have noted (Westney, 1987; Young, 1992), an exact model or practice can never be replicated completely in another culture, nor should it be. In this final section, we will speculate about the transferability of these specific attributes of the Japanese work group that have been identified: assignment of functional roles, differentiation of structural roles, and the ideology of harmony. Hofstede's (1980) etic dimensions of individualism and collectivism, and power distance provide the framework upon which we base these speculations.

Assignment of Functional Roles to Groups

In Japanese organizations, groups are the functional unit, and individuals are assigned ambiguous functional roles. At least four conditions are necessary for these work groups to operate effectively:

- The goals of the group must be clearly specified.

- Group members must have the knowledge and skills in a wide range of tasks that allow them to identify the steps required to achieve these goals.

- Individuals in the group must have various social skills that allow them to negotiate and establish specific roles.

- Group members must be motivated enough to carry out their negotiated roles and coordinate tasks.

If these conditions are met, the assignment of functional roles, which is so characteristic of the Japanese work group, would likely be transferable to other contexts.

A first rule of thumb in testing the work group's transferability is the application of Hofstede's dimension of individualism and collectivism. In general, the use of the group rather than the individual as the functional unit is likely to be more acceptable in collectivist cultures than it is in individualist ones. In collectivist cultures such as Venezuela, Colombia, Pakistan, Peru, Taiwan, Thailand, and Singapore, workers' lives are strongly tied to their organizations. Organizations have a strong influence on workers' personal well-being; in turn, the organization is expected to look after workers like a family (Hofstede, 1980). In contrast, in highly individualist cultures such as the United States, Canada, Australia, Great Britain, the Netherlands, and New Zealand, workers are probably less prepared for highly cohesive work groups. A worker's relationship with the organization is primarily contractual: Organizations have less influence on workers' lives and well-being, while employees do not expect their companies to impinge on their personal lives. Consequently, highly cohesive work groups may be perceived as unnecessary and an excessive commitment to work in such cultures.

Nevertheless, there are varieties of individualism and collectivism (Kashima, 1987; Triandis, 1990). A more detailed examination of each country's sociocultural context is necessary in order to calculate the potential costs and benefits of transferring the use of groups as functional units into a culture. Because there are many kinds of collectivist societies, some of them may not be able to use some of these work groups. Similarly, because there are many kinds of individualistic societies, some of them may be able to use such work groups, through they may adopt methods that are not used by the Japanese. First, can management set clear goals for work groups? Certainly for Western

managers, strategic planning and goal setting are typical managerial activities. However, it is possible that in some contexts, even though managers are well trained in these skills, a country's political–economic situation does not allow these activities to be fully implemented.

Second, do workers have the knowledge and skills that enable them to identify and establish the steps necessary to achieve the goal of the group? This is very much the requirement of an organization having generalist workers. Workers need to be talented and suitably trained so that they are able to learn multiple task-related skills. They need to be encouraged to do so, and the organization and trade unions associated with the organization must be able to see the payoff from such multiskilling. In a country such as the United States, the machine metaphor of organization may not encourage the generalist worker. The mobile job market, which allows workers to move among organizations, also discourages organizations to invest in their workers (Ouchi, 1981). Also, as has been witnessed in many Western countries, many industrial unions are still reluctant to support multiskilling for their members. On the other hand, there is substantial evidence that organizational policies that mandate training about aspects of teamwork improve the implementation of programs aimed at improving quality, customer satisfaction, and productivity (see Davy, White, Merritt, & Gritzmacher, 1992).

Third, are workers interpersonally skilled enough to negotiate functional roles that may improve their performance? These social and communication skills must be not only generally well developed but also appropriate to achieving specific group goals. The Japanese collectivist style of communication differs from more individualist patterns in both its content and process (Kim & Gudykunst, 1988; Okabe, 1983). Nonetheless, different styles of communication may still enable workers to achieve the same level of efficiency in the work group. The challenge for workers and managers is to establish their own effective strategies for achieving good communication and better interpersonal relationships.

Fourth, are workers motivated to carry out the negotiated functional roles and coordinate tasks among their co-workers? Although cross-cultural studies of worker motivation show similarities in the structure of work-related value systems, there are culturally specific antecedents of intrinsic and extrinsic work motivations. The assignment of functional roles to groups alone may not lead to a high level of intrinsic work motivation. In addition, workers must be motivated enough to coordinate their behaviors to achieve the goals of the group. How can management enhance the motivation to coordinate? Is it sufficient to increase a worker's intrinsic motivation? In answering these questions, it is the management's task to find strategies that are appropriate in their sociocultural context.

In sum, the success of assigning functional roles to work groups depends on the extent that each society satisfies the four conditions specified above. Undoubtedly, other conditions could also be identified. Although Hofstede's individualism–collectivism dimension may provide a first approximation of whether the work group can be successfully transferred to a culture, a more detailed analysis is really necessary. For instance, it appears quite possible for people in relatively individualist cultures (e.g., the Netherlands, Germany) to be skilled at team activities and sports that require the spontaneous negotiation of functional roles. The work group also entails the coordination of task-directed behaviors among teammates, for which people in collectivist cultures (e.g., South America) are also well suited. Clearly, management in each culture needs to devise a set of strategies for its specific sociocultural context.

Clear Structural Roles

If people are used to it, a clear differentiation of vertical structural roles may enhance group cohesiveness (Shaw, 1976). The extent to which people can successfully manage clear vertical structural roles seems to be captured in Hofstede's other etic dimension of power distance. According to Hofstede (1980), cultures high on power distance accept a greater differentiation of power and centralization of authority, especially in the case of autocratic leadership. Thus, clear vertical structural roles may improve group cohesiveness in cultures with greater power distance (e.g., the Philippines, Mexico, Venezuela, and India), but it may even impair the development of group cohesiveness in cultures with small power distance (e.g., Austria, Israel, Denmark, and New Zealand).

Cultures that are in the mid-range on power distance are an interesting group to consider. They include countries such as Pakistan, Italy, South Africa, Argentina, Canada, and the United States. For these countries, a prognosis about transferability based on the etic dimension of power distance may be somewhat misleading. The collection of more emic information is needed. For instance, consider Hofstede's evidence that North American countries and Japan have similar levels of power distance. Yet Japanese organizations are marked by their clear vertical differentiation, while Canada and the United States are known as models of egalitarianism. One explanation for this apparent contradiction may be the Japanese use of two-way communication between supervisors and subordinates, and consultative decision making. This may be the effect of the *ie* metaphor. On the other hand, in the traditional model of North American management, the machine metaphor often leads to the use of explicit formal control systems, top-down communication, and autocratic decision making. Japan and North American countries have similar levels of power distance for different reasons. Such differences may in fact hinder a fruitful transfer of structural role differentiation.

In this respect, it is interesting to speculate on a possible interaction effect between power distance and uncertainty avoidance. The

Japanese preference for two-way informal communication within the vertical relationship may be captured by Hofstede's other etic dimension of uncertainty avoidance. As discussed before, it is conceivable that to avoid uncertainty, Japanese managers and workers may use frequent but informal communication. Therefore, in cultures relatively high on both power distance and uncertainty avoidance (e.g., Greece, Portugal, Peru, France, and Mexico), the clear differentiation of structural roles may be usefully implemented.

The Ideology of Harmony

The ideology of harmony is central to the corporate philosophy of many Japanese organizations. Japanese companies promote the concept of harmony by sponsoring activities ranging from exercise sessions and the singing of corporate songs to cultural festivals and recreational events. These particular company-sponsored activities, however, may or may not be transferable to other cultures in the exact same form. The cultural meaning attached to such events may also not be similar across nations. An appropriate mix of marketing and promotion strategies probably needs to be devised for each culture to promote the ideology of harmony. Nevertheless, in both Japan and the United States, there is evidence that workers in companies that sponsor such activities are more committed to their organizations. Among the challenges to an organization promoting harmony are decisions about what activities to sponsor.

The multicultural character of a company's employees must also be considered. In societies where populations come from relatively homogeneous cultural backgrounds (e.g., Japan, Korea), the creation of an ideology of harmony in particular may be relatively simple. In such societies, one strategy may work well for all segments of a company's work force. However, in multicultural societies such as the United States, Australia, Canada, and China, different strategies may need to be devised for different subgroups in the organization.

Conclusion

The cultural context of Japan has encouraged rather unique relationships between government and industry, and between larger companies. These relationships in turn have assisted the finance, establishment, and control of domestic and international markets. In addition, these cultural factors have encouraged the development of different solutions in Japan about the effective use of labor. One example is the use of the work group, which is a factor attributed for continued high levels of productivity and quality control in Japanese industry. The work group, which resembles the characteristics of the *ie* household with its rigid formal structure, encompasses more flexible arrangements that facilitate the performance of functional behaviors. This freedom and flexibility exists despite quite rigid vertical structural roles in Japanese organizations. The use of the work group is compatible with Japanese culture and its socialization practices.

The work group, however, is not a panacea for organizational ineffectiveness, even in Japan. The work group does not achieve all that Japanese management had hoped it would. For instance, the use of the work group may increase productivity, but it does not necessarily result in high levels of job satisfaction or organizational commitment. Therefore, the Japanese small work group should be seen as only one of many options that may be considered for cross-cultural transfers of organizational practices. Transfer of the Japanese work group is possible if there is a detailed analysis of the nature of the work group and the culture within which the work group is to be implemented. The organizational practice that is being transferred must be appropriate for the society's sociocultural context.

The *ie* metaphor has allowed Japanese management to make their organizational practices consistent with their culture. Likewise, people in each culture need to identify an appropriate metaphor for their modern industrial organizations. Instead of fighting against culture through the wholesale acceptance of organizational practices or inappropriate metaphors that have evolved in different cultures, people should make their own culture work better for them. This is probably the most important message from the findings of cross-cultural research for members of organizations in societies trying to establish a viable industrial base. An uncritical adoption of any organizational practice, whether from the North American, European, or Japanese system, is likely to fail. Members of organizations need to think creatively and make better use of their knowledge about their own culture in making decisions about organizational reforms.

References

Abegglen, J. C. (1958). *The Japanese factory: Aspects of its social organization.* Glencoe, IL: Free Press.

Azumi, K., & McMillan, C. J. (1976). Worker sentiment in the Japanese factory: Its organizational determinants. In L. Austin (Ed.), *Japan: The paradox of progress* (pp. 215–230). New Haven, CT: Yale University Press.

Bales, R. F. (1958). Task roles and social roles in problem-solving groups. In E. E. Maccoby, T. M. Newcomb, & E. L. Hartley (Eds.), *Readings in social psychology* (3rd ed., pp. 437–447). London: Methuen.

Banas, P. (1988). Employee involvement: A sustained labor/management initiative at Ford Motor Company. In J. P. Campbell & R. J. Campbell (Eds.), *Productivity in organizations* (pp. 388–416). San Francisco: Jossey-Bass.

Basadur, M. (1992). Managing creativity: A Japanese model. *Academy of Management Executive, 6,* 29–42.

Bass, B. M., & Burger, P. C. (1979). *Assessment of managers: An international comparison.* New York: Free Press.

Befu, H. (1982). A critique of the group model of Japanese society. *Social Analysis, 5/6,* 29–43.

Ben Dasan, I. (1980). *Nihon Kyoto* [Believers of Japanese religion] (S. Yamamoto, Ed. and Trans.). Tokyo: Kodansha.

Benedict, R. (1946). *The chrysanthemum and the sword: Patterns of Japanese culture.* Boston: Houghton Mifflin.

Bennett, J. W., & Ishino, I. (1963). *Paternalism in the Japanese economy: Anthropological studies of oyabroun-kobun patterns.* Minneapolis: University of Minnesota Press.

Benveniste, E. (1971). *Problems in general linguistics.* Miami, FL: University of Miami Press.

Berry, J. W. (1980). Introduction to methodology. In H. C. Triandis & J. W. Berry (Eds.), *Handbook of cross-cultural psychology* (pp. 1–28). Boston: Allyn and Bacon.

Biddle, B. J. (1986). Recent developments in role theory. *Annual Review of Sociology, 12,* 67–92.

Biddle, B. J., & Thomas, E. J. (1966). *Role theory: Concepts and research.* New York: Wiley.

Bourdieu, P. (1990). The logic of practice (R. Nice, Trans.). Cambridge, UK: Polity Press. (Original work published 1980)

Brief, A. P., & Aldag, R. J. (1975). Employee reactions to job characteristics: A constructive replication. *Journal of Applied Psychology, 60,* 182–186.

Burns, T., & Stalker, G. M. (1961). *The management of innovation.* London: Tavistock.

Caudill, W., & Weinstein, H. (1969). Maternal care and infant behavior in Japan and America. *Psychiatry, 32,* 12–43.

Clark, R. (1979). *The Japanese company.* New Haven, CT: Yale University Press.

Coates, N. (1988). Determinants of Japan's business success: Some Japanese executives' views. *Academy of Management Executive, 2,* 69–72.

Cole, R. E. (1971). *Japanese blue collar: The changing tradition.* Berkeley, CA: University of California Press.

Cole, R. E. (1979). *Work, mobility and participation.* Berkeley, CA: University of California Press.

Cole, R. E., & Byosiere, P. (1986). Managerial objectives for introducing quality circles: A U.S.–Japan comparison. *Quality Progress, 19,* 25–30.

Collins, A., & Gentner, D. (1987). How people construct mental models. In D. Holland & N. Quinn (Eds.), *Cultural models in language and thought.* Cambridge, England: Cambridge University Press.

Cooney, B. D. (1989). Japan and America: Culture counts. *Training and Development Journal, 43,* 55–61.

Copley, P. (1986). Schooling a more productive workforce: What can we learn from the Japanese. *High School Journal, 69,* 195–201.

D'Andrade, R., & Strauss, C. (1992). *Human motives and cultural models.* Cambridge, England: Cambridge University Press.

Davy, J. A., White, R. E., Merritt, N. J., & Gritzmacher, K. (1992). A derivation of the underlying constructs of just-in-time management systems. *Academy of Management Journal, 35,* 653–670.

De Vos, G. A. (1968). Achievement and innovation in culture and personality. In E. Norbeck, D. Price-Williams, & W. M. McCord (Eds.), *The study of personality: An interdisciplinary approach* (pp. 348–370). New York: Holt, Rinehart and Winston.

Doi, L. T. (1967). Giri-ninjo: An interpretation. In R. P. Dore (Ed.), *Aspects of social change in modern Japan.* Princeton, NJ: Princeton University Press.

Doi, L. T. (1971). *Amae no kozo* [Structure of amae]. Tokyo: Kobunsha.

Doi, L. T. (1973). *The anatomy of dependence.* Tokyo: Kodansha International.

Dollinger, M. J. (1988). Confucian ethics and Japanese management practices. *Journal of Business Ethics, 7,* 575–584.

Dore, R. P. (1969). The modernizer as a special case: Japanese factory legislation 1882–1911. *Comparative Studies in Society and History, 2,* 433–450.

Dore, R. P. (1973). *British factory–Japanese factory.* London: Allen and Unwin.

Dore, R. P. (1983). Goodwill and the spirit of market capitalism. *British Journal of Sociology, 34,* 459–482.

Dunphy, D. (1987). Convergence/divergence: A temporal review of the Japanese enterprise and its management. *Academy of Management Review, 6,* 469–480.

Ebrahimpour, M. (1988). An empirical study of American and Japanese approaches to quality management in the United States. *International Journal of Quality and Reliability Management, 5,* 5–24.

England, G. W. (1983). Japanese and American management: Theory Z and beyond. *Journal of International Business Studies, 14,* 131–141.

England, G. W. (1989). *A proposal to prepare a research monograph about stability and change in the meaning of working for the labor force of the United States.* Unpublished manuscript, University of Oklahoma, Norman.

England, G. W., & Harpaz, I. (1990). How working is defined: National contexts and demographic and organizational role influences. *Journal of Organizational Behavior, 11,* 253–266.

England, G. W., & Koike, R. (1970). Personal value systems of Japanese managers. *Journal of Cross-Cultural Psychology, 1,* 21–40.

England, G. W., & Lee, R. (1973). Organizational size as an influence on perceived organizational goals: A comparative study among American, Japanese and Korean managers. *Organizational Behavior and Human Performance, 9,* 48–58.

England, G. W., & Misumi, T. (1986). Work centrality in Japan and the United States. *Journal of Cross-Cultural Psychology, 17,* 399–416.

England, G. W., Negandhi, A. R., & Wilpert, B. (Eds.). (1981). *The functioning of complex organizations.* Cambridge, MA: Oelgeschlager, Guin & Hain.

Erez, M. (1989). *Interpersonal communication patterns in Japanese corporations: Their relationships to cultural values and to productivity and innovation.* Unpublished manuscript, Israel Institute of Technology, Haifa.

Farmer, R. N., & Richman, B. M. (1965). *Comparative management and economic progress.* Homewood, IL: Irwin.

Ferris, G. R., & Wagner, J. A. (1985). Quality circles in the United States: A conceptual reevaluation. *The Journal of Applied Behavioral Science, 21,* 155–167.

Fruin, W. M. (1978). The Japanese company controversy. *Journal of Japanese Studies, 4,* 267–300.

Fruin, W. M. (1980). The family as a firm and the firm as a family in Japan: The case of Kikkoman Shoyu Company Limited. *Journal of Family History, 5,* 432–449.

Garvin, D. A. (1986). Quality problems, policies and attitudes in the United States and Japan: An exploratory study. *Academy of Management Journal, 29,* 653–673.

Gentner, D. (1983). Structure-mapping: A theoretical framework for analogy. *Cognitive Science, 7,* 155–170.

Gick, M. L., & Holyoak, K. J. (1980). Analogical problem solving. *Cognitive Psychology, 12,* 306–355.

Gick, M. L., & Holyoak, K. J. (1983). Schema induction and analogical transfer. *Cognitive Psychology, 15,* 1–38.

Giddens, A. (1979). *Central problems in social theory: Action, structure and contradiction in social analysis.* London: Macmillan.

Hackman, J. R. (1976). Group influence on individuals. In M. D. Dunnette (Ed.), *Handbook of industrial and organizational psychology* (pp.1455–1525). Chicago: Rand McNally.

Hackman, J. R., & Lawler, E. E. (1971). Employee reactions to job characteristics. *Journal of Applied Psychology, 55,* 259–286.

Haire, M., Ghiselli, E. E., & Porter, L. W. (1966). *Managerial thinking: An international study.* New York: Wiley.

Hamaguchi, E. (1977). *Nihonrashisa no Saihakken* [A rediscovery of Japaneseness]. Tokyo: Nihon Keizai Shinbunsha.

Harpaz, I. (1989). Non-financial employment commitment: A cross-national commitment. *Journal of Occupational Psychology, 62,* 147–150.

Hatvany, N., & Pucik, V. (1981). An integrated management system: Lessons from the Japanese experience. *Academy of Management Review, 6,* 469–480.

Hayashi, S. (1988). *Culture and management.* Tokyo: University of Tokyo Press.

Hesseling, P., & Konnen, E. (1969). Culture and subculture in a decision-making exercise. *Human Relations, 22,* 31–51.

Hirschmeier, J., & Yui, T. (1975). *The development of Japanese business, 1600–1973.* London: Allen & Unwin.

Hofstede, G. (1980). *Culture's consequences.* Beverly Hills, CA: Sage.

Hofstede, G. (1983). The cultural relativity of organizational practices and theories. *Journal of International Business Studies, 14,* 75–89.

Holyoak, K. J. (1984). Mental models in problem solving. In J. R. Anderson & S. M. Kosslyn (Eds.), *Tutorials in learning and memory* (pp. 193–218). San Francisco: Freeman.

Howard, N., & Teramoto, Y. (1981). The really important difference between Japanese and Western management. *Management International Review, 21,* 19–30.

Iwata, R. (1982). Nihonteki keiei-soshiko no dainamizumu [The Dynamics of Japanese management systems]. In E. Hamaguchi & S. Kumon (Eds.), *Nihonteki shudanshugi* [Japanese collectivism]. Tokyo: Yuhikaku.

Karsh, B. (1984). Human resources management in Japanese large-scale industry. *Journal of Industrial Relations, 26,* 226–245.

Kashima, Y. (1987). Conceptions of person: Implications in individualism/collectivism research. In C. Kagitcibasi (Ed.), *Growth and progress in cross-cultural psychology* (pp. 104–112). Lisse, the Netherlands: Swets & Zeitlinger.

Katz, D., & Kahn, R. (1978). *The social psychology of organizations.* New York: Wiley.

Kelly, L., & Worthley, R. (1981). The role of culture in comparative management: A cross-cultural perspective. *Academy of Management Journal, 24,* 164–173.

Kelman, H. C. (1958). Compliance, identification and internalization: Three processes of attitude change. *Journal of Conflict Resolution, 2,* 51–60.

Kiefer, C. W. (1974). The psychological interdependence of family, school and bureaucracy in Japan. In T. S. Lebra & W. P. Lebra (Eds.), *Japanese culture and behavior* (pp. 342–356). Honolulu: University of Hawaii Press.

Kim, Y. Y., & Gudykunst, W. B. (1988). *Theories of intercultural communication.* Beverly Hills, CA: Sage.

Koike, H., Gudykunst, W. B., & Stewart, L. P. (1988). Communication openness, satisfaction and length of employment in Japanese organizations. *Communication Research Reports, 5,* 97–102.

Kondo, D. K. (1990). *Crafting selves: Power, gender, and discourses of identity in a Japanese workplace.* Chicago: University of Chicago Press.

Lachman, R. (1983). Modernity change of core and periphery values of factory workers. *Human Relations, 36,* 563–580.

Lakoff, G., & Johnson, M. (1980). *Metaphors we live by.* Chicago: University of Chicago Press.

Lawler, E. E., & Mohrman, S. A. (1985). Quality circles after the fad. *Harvard Business Review, 63,* 65–71.

Lawler, E. E., & Mohrman, S. A. (1987). Quality circles: After the honeymoon. *Dynamics, 15,* 42–54.

Lebra, T. S. (1976). *Japanese patterns of behavior.* Honolulu: University of Hawaii Press.

Lebra, T. S. (1984). *Japanese women: Constraints and fulfillment.* Honolulu: University of Hawaii Press.

Likert, R. (1961). *New patterns of management.* New York: McGraw-Hill.

Lincoln, J. R., Hanada, M., & McBride, K. (1986). Organizational structures in Japanese and U.S. manufacturing. *Administrative Science Quarterly, 31,* 338–364.

Lincoln, J. R., Hanada, M., & Olson, J. (1981). Cultural orientations and individual reactions to organizations: A study of employees of Japanese-owned firms. *Administrative Science Quarterly, 26,* 93–115.

Lincoln, J. R., & Kalleberg, A. L. (1985). Work organization and workforce commitment: A study of plants and employees in the U.S. and Japan. *American Sociological Review, 50,* 738–760.

Lincoln, J. R., & Kalleberg, A. L. (1990). *Culture, control, and commitment: A study of work organization and work attitudes in the United States and Japan.* Cambridge, England: Cambridge University Press.

Lincoln, J. R., Olson, J., & Hanada, M. (1978). Cultural effects on organizational structures: The case of Japanese firms in the United States. *American Sociological Review, 43,* 829–849.

Luthans, F., McCaul, H. S., & Dodd, N. G. (1985). Organizational commitment: A comparison of American, Japanese and Korean employees. *Academy of Management Journal, 28,* 2134–2219.

Maguire, M. A., & Kroliczak, A. (1983). Attitudes of Japanese and American workers: Convergence or diversity? *The Sociological Quarterly, 24,* 107-122.

Malpass, R. S. (1977). Theory and method in cross-cultural psychology. *American Psychologist, 32,* 1069–1079.

Mann, L., Radford, M., & Kanagawa, C. (1985). Cross-cultural differences in children's use of decision rules: A comparison between Japan and Australia. *Journal of Personality and Social Psychology, 49,* 1557–1564.

March, J. G., & Simon, H. A. (1958). *Organizations.* New York: Wiley.

Markus, H., & Kitayama, S. (1991). Culture and self: Implications for cognition, emotion and motivation. *Psychological Review 98,* 224–253.

Marsh, R. M., & Mannari, H. (1976). *Modernization and the Japanese factory.* Princeton, NJ: Princeton University Press.

Marshall, B. K. (1967). *Capitalism and nationalism in prewar Japan: The ideology of the business elite 1868–1941.* Stanford, CA: Stanford University Press.

Martin, J., & Meyerson, D. (1988). Organizational cultures and the denial, channeling and acknowledgement of ambiguity. In L. R. Pondy, R. J. Boland, & H. Thomas (Eds.), *Managing ambiguity and change.* New York: Wiley.

Maruyama, M. (1992). Changing dimensions in international business. *Academy of Management Executive, 6,* 88–96.

McGrath, J. E. (1984). *Groups: Interaction and performance.* Englewood Cliffs, NJ: Prentice-Hall.

McGregor, D. (1960). *The human side of enterprise.* New York: McGraw-Hill.

McMillan, C. J. (1985). *The Japanese industrial system.* Berlin: de Gruyter.

Merkle, J. A. (1980). *Management and ideology: The legacy of the international scientific management movement.* Berkeley, CA: University of California Press.

Misumi, J. (1984). Decision-making in Japanese groups and organizations. In B. Wilpert & A. Sorge (Eds.), *International perspectives on organizational democracy* (pp. 525–539). New York: Wiley.

Moeran, B. (1988). Japanese language and society: An anthropological approach. *Journal of Pragmatics, 12,* 427–443.

Morgan, G. (1986). *Images of organization.* Beverly Hills, CA: Sage.

Mouer, R., & Sugimoto, Y. (1986). *Images of Japanese society.* London: KPI.

MOW International Research Team (1986). *The meaning of working: An international perspective.* New York: Academic Press.

Nakane, C. (1970a). *Kazokuno kozo* [The structure of family]. Tokyo: Tokyo University Press.

Nakane, C. (1970b). *Japanese society.* Berkeley, CA: University of California Press.

Nakane, C. (1978). *Tate shakai no rikigaku* [Dynamics of vertical society]. Tokyo: Kodansya.

Naoi, A., & Schooler, C. (1985). Occupational conditions and psychological functioning in Japan. *American Journal of Sociology, 90,* 729–752.

Nonaka, I., & Johansson, J. K. (1985). Japanese management: What about the "hard" skills? *Academy of Management Review, 10*, 181–191.

Odaka, K. (1975). *Toward industrial democracy: Management and workers in modern Japan.* Cambridge, MA: Harvard University Press.

Ohmae, K. (1982). Quality control circles: They work and don't work. *The Wall Street Journal*, p. 16.

Okabe, R. (1983). Cultural assumptions of East and West: Japan and the United States. In W. B. Gudykunst (Ed.), *Intercultural communications theory: Current perspectives* (pp. 21–44). Beverly Hills, CA: Sage.

Okochi, K., Karsh, B., & Levine, S. B. (1974). *Workers and employers in Japan.* Princeton, NJ: Princeton University Press.

Ott, J. S. (1989). *The organizational culture perspective.* Pacific Grove, CA: Brooks/Cole.

Ouchi, W. G. (1981). *Theory Z: How American business can meet the Japanese challenge.* Reading, MA: Addison-Wesley.

Pascale, R. T. (1978a). Personnel practices and employee attitudes: A study of Japanese- and American-managed firms in the U.S. *Human Relations, 31*, 597–615.

Pascale, R. T. (1978b). Communication and decision-making across cultures—Japanese and American comparisons. *Administrative Science Quarterly, 23*, 91–110.

Pascale, R. T., & Althos, A. (1981). *The art of Japanese management.* New York: Simon & Schuster.

Pascale, R. T., & Maguire, M. A. (1980). Comparisons of selected work factors in Japan and the United States. *Human Relations, 33*, 433–455.

Peters, T. J., & Waterman, R. H. (1982). *In search of excellence: Lessons from America's best-run companies.* New York: Harper & Row.

Plath, D. (1980). *Long engagements: Maturity in modern Japan.* Stanford, CA: Stanford University Press.

Pondy, L. R. (1983). The role of metaphors and myths in organization and in the facilitation of change. In L. R. Pondy, P. J. Frost, G. Morgan, & T. C. Dandridge (Eds.), *Organizational symbolism* (pp. 157–166). Greenwich, CT: JAI Press.

Reason, J. (1990). *Human error.* New York: Cambridge University Press.

Rehder, R. R. (1983). Education and training: Have the Japanese beaten us again? *Personnel Journal, 62*, 42–47.

Rohlen, T. P. (1974a). Sponsorship of cultural continuity in Japan: A company training program. In T. S. Lebra & W. P. Lebra (Eds.), *Japanese culture and behavior: Selected readings* (pp. 332–356). Honolulu: University of Hawaii Press.

Rohlen, T. P. (1974b). *For harmony and strength: Japanese white-collar organizations in anthropological perspective.* Berkeley, CA: University of California Press.

Rohlen, T. P. (1983). *Japanese high schools.* Berkeley, CA: University of California Press.

Ronen, S. (1986). *Comparative and multinational management.* New York: Wiley.

Sackmann, S. (1989). The role of metaphors in organization transformation. *Human relations, 42*, 463–485.

Sandelands, L. E. (1990). *Journal for the Theory of Social Behaviour, 20*, 235–262.

Sataka, M. (1987). Ikiteiru messhi-boukou [Selfless service in Japan today]. *Chuokoron, 102*, 88–95.

Schein, E. H. (1968). Organizational socialization and the profession of management. *Industrial Management Review, 9*, 1–16.

Schein, E. H. (1985). *Organizational culture and leadership.* San Francisco: Jossey-Bass.

Schein, E. H. (1990). Organizational culture. *American Psychologist, 45*, 109–119.

Schön, P. A. (1979). Generative metaphor: A perspective on problem-setting in social policy. In A. Ortony (Ed.), *Metaphor and thought* (pp. 254–283). Cambridge, England: Cambridge University Press.

Schonberger, R. J. (1982). The transfer of Japanese manufacturing management approaches to U.S. industry. *Academy of Management Review, 7*, 479–487.

Schooler, C., & Naoi, A. (1988). The psychological effects of traditional and economically peripheral job settings in Japan. *American Journal of Sociology, 94*, 335–355.

Seashore, S. E. (1954). *Group cohesiveness in the industrial work group.* Ann Arbor, MI: Institute for Social Research.

Sera, K. (1992). Corporate globalization: A new trend. *Academy of Management Executive, 6*, 89–96.

Shaw, M. E. (1976). *Group dynamics: The psychology of small group behavior.* New York: McGraw-Hill.

Smith, P. B., & Misumi, J. (1989). Japanese management—A sun rising in the west? In C. L. Cooper

& I. Robertson (Eds.), *International review of organizational psychology 1989* (pp. 143–183). London: Wiley.

Smith, P. B., & Peterson, M. F. (1988). *Leadership, organizations and culture: An event management model*. London: Sage.

Smith, R. (1983). *Japanese society: Tradition, self and the social order*. Cambridge, England: Cambridge University Press.

Stein, H. F. (1991). Metaphors of organizational trauma and organizational development: A case example. *Organization Development Journal, 9*, 22–30.

Steiner, I. (1972). *Group process and productivity*. New York: Academic Press.

Stewart, L. P., Gudykunst, W. B., & Ting-Toomey, S. (1986). The effects of decision-making style on openness and satisfaction within Japanese organizations. *Communication Monographs, 53*, 236–251.

Stogdill, R. (1974). *Handbook of leadership*. New York: Free Press.

Stone, E. F. (1978). *Research methods in organizational behavior*. Glenview, IL: Scott, Foresman.

Sullivan, J. J., Suzuki, T., & Kondo, Y. (1987). Managerial perceptions of performance. *Journal of Cross-Cultural Psychology, 17*, 379–398.

Sundstrom, E., De Meuse, K. P., & Futrell, D. (1990). Work teams: Applications and effectiveness. *American Psychologist, 45*, 120–133.

Suzuki, T. (1973). *Kotoba to bunka* [World and culture]. Tokyo: Iwanami Shoten.

Taira, K. (1970). *Economic development and the labour market in Japan*. New York: Columbia University Press.

Tajfel, H. (Ed.). (1982). *Social identity and intergroup relations*. Cambridge, MA: Cambridge University Press.

Takahashi, N., & Takayanagi, S. (1985). Decision procedure models and empirical research: The Japanese experience. *Human Relations, 38*, 767–780.

Takezawa, S. I., & Whitehill, A. M. (1981). *Workway: Japan and America*. Tokyo: Japan Institute of Labour.

Tawara, J. (1981). Nihonteki taijin-kankei to motivation [Japanese interpersonal relationship and motivation]. In K. Nishida, M. Wakabayashi, & K. Okada (Eds.), *Soshiki no koudoukagaku* [Behavioral science of organization]. Tokyo: Yuhikaku.

Taylor, F. W. (1911). *The principles of scientific management*. New York: Norton.

Tobin, J., Wu, D., & Davidson, D. (1989). *Preschool in three cultures: Japan, China, and the United States*. New Haven, CT: Yale University Press.

Triandis, H. C. (1990). Cross-cultural studies of individualism and collectivism. In J. J. Berman (Ed.), *Nebraska symposium on motivation, 1989* (Vol. 37, pp. 41–133). Lincoln: University of Nebraska Press.

Trist, E. L., & Bamforth, K. W. (1951). Some social and psychological consequences of the long wall method of coal setting. *Human Relations, 4*, 3–38.

Tsoukas, H. (1991). The missing link: A transformational view of metaphors in organizational science. *Academy of Management Review, 16*, 566–585.

Turner, J. (1987). *Rediscovering the social group: A self-categorization theory*. Oxford, England: Basil Blackwell.

Wakabayashi, M., Graen, G., Graen, M. R., & Graen, M. (1988). Japanese management progress: Mobility into middle management. *Journal of Applied Psychology, 73*, 217–227.

Webber, R. H. (1969). Convergence or divergence. *Columbia Journal of World Business, 4*, 75–83.

Weber, M. (1947). *The theory of social and economic organization*. New York: Free Press.

Weber, M. (1958). Bureaucracy. In H. Gerth & C. W. Mills (Eds.), *Max Weber: Essays in sociology* (pp. 196-244). Oxford, England: Oxford University Press.

Westney, D. E. (1987). *Imitation and innovation*. Cambridge, England: Cambridge University Press.

Wetzel, P. J. (1988). Are 'powerless' communication strategies the Japanese norm? *Language and Society, 17*, 555–564.

Whenmouth, E. (1988). Is Japan's corporate style changing? Some practices and attitudes that were unthinkable in Japan two decades ago are becoming commonplace. *Industry Week, 237*, 33–35.

Whitehill, A. M. (1964). Cultural values and employee attitudes: United States and Japan. *Journal of Applied Psychology, 48*, 68–72.

Whitehill, A. M., & Takezawa, S. (1961). *Cultural values in management-worker relations*. Chapel Hill: University of North Carolina Press.

Whitehill, A. M., & Takezawa, S. (1968). *The other worker*. Honolulu: East-West Centre.

Worthy, J. C. (1950). Organizational structure and employee morale. *American Sociological Review, 15,* 169–179.

Yazinuma, M., & Kennedy, R. (1986, May). Life is so simple when you know your place. *Intersect,* pp. 35–39.

Yoshino, M. Y. (1968). *Japan's managerial system: Tradition and innovation.* Cambridge, MA: Massachusetts Institute of Technology.

Young, S. M. (1992). A framework for successful adoption and performance of Japanese manufacturing practices in the United States. *Academy of Management Executive, 17,* 677–700.

Yukl, G. H. (1989). *Leadership in organizations* (2nd ed.). Englewood Cliffs, NJ: Prentice-Hall.

Yum, Y. O. (1988). The impact of Confucianism on interpersonal relationships and communication patterns in East Asia. *Communication Monographs, 55,* 374–388.

CHAPTER 13

The Nature
of Individual Attachment
to the Organization:
A Review of East Asian
Variations

S. G. Redding
A. Norman
A. Schlander
University of Hong Kong

This chapter explores the nature of psychological attachment between individuals and organizations in the context of East Asian cultures. Psychological attachment is conceptualized as including the linkage or bonding process between individuals and organizations. Moreover, the process includes issues such as legitimizing hierarchical influence, dependency and trust, reciprocity norms, issues of obligation, and questions of identity. The chapter explores and examines East Asian organizations as case studies of organizations in successful economies. What aspects of organization and culture in China, Japan, South Korea, Taiwan, Hong Kong, and Singapore have been the basis for such success in international competition? The chapter concludes with an examination of the importance of culture in directing the development of theory and research activities in areas such as organizational, motivational, and leadership conceptualizations.

Introduction

THE THEME OF this review is psychological attachment to the organization, and the principal reason for such a focus is that this is a field in which substantial cross-cultural variation appears. Such variation lies mainly in the *way* bonding takes place, rather than in its intensity. It is also assumed that a better comprehension of the surrounding issues may lead to some reappraisal of our understanding of the nature of organizations and of the management process. And, at the end of a long causal chain (or more accurately, a web of reciprocating and interconnected determinants), it may lead to the question of variations in national economic success. The geographic area that is the focus of this inquiry is East Asia, in acknowledgment of the worldwide competitiveness of organizations in that region.

We use the word *attachment* to signify the state of the relationship, at a psychological level of analysis, between an individual and an organization. It is intended to subsume the notion of commitment within it, the latter being seen as more specific and limited in its application. Commitment remains the core notion here, but we wish to explore around its edges.

It is a contention of this chapter that the way a person of any particular culture sees his or her relationship with an organization is inevitably colored by the cultural tendency to perceive the nature of organization itself differently. If the organization is not a universal concept, paradoxical though that may seem, then attachment becomes highly contingent. To define the organization in some universal sense as a legally bounded entity is to avoid the issue of what the organization means to those whose acts of cooperation bring it to life.

In simple terms, organizations, at least in the free societies considered here, are put together from a mass of individual gestures of willingness to cooperate (Barnard, 1938). The circumstances under which those gestures are made contain a mixture of personal, environmental, and organizational components. It is

assumed that many of the personal predispositions to cooperate are influenced by values absorbed from the wider culture and carried in the minds of individuals. It is also assumed that many of the environmental components, such as labor laws, wage legislation, and skill development, are reflections of values that also can be traced back to a specific culture. The organization itself, being so embedded in a culture (Granovetter, 1985) by virtue of its human components and its surrounding circumstances, becomes in many senses an artifact of that culture. Thus, the individual carries certain predispositions, connects to an organization in a certain context, and experiences an organization with a particular character. All three of these particularities are informed by, although never totally explained by, culture.

In arguing that forms of attachment may vary significantly, we are also then arguing that so do the contexts and the objects of attachment. For the purposes of this review, however, it is unrealistic to attempt to incorporate any kind of full analysis of variations in context and in organizational type. Instead, these features will be dealt with in outline only and brought into account as part of a not fully explicated model of economic culture (Berger, 1986). In any case, the gaps in knowledge are still too great for such a model to be sensibly attempted.

The specific focus here is the nature of the link between the individual and an organization typical of a culture, which is seen from a primarily psychological perspective. It raises questions about the nature of the bonding process, the legitimizing of influence in a hierarchy, dependency, trust, reciprocity, focuses of obligation, the workings of collectivism, and the question of identity. In raising such issues, it also touches upon the contingent nature of managing and organizing, and allows the introduction of a more ethnographic perspective than that commonly found in the main body of organizational literature (for a discussion of this issue, see Redding, 1993). As Triandis has already pointed out (see chapter 2 of this volume), more than 90 percent of studies in industrial and organizational psychology use data from North America and Europe.

The choice of East Asia as a geographical sphere for this analysis carries an unstated implication and leads to the need for certain clarifying points. The implication is that East Asia contains organizations that are successful and thus of significant interest. For 30 years, East Asia has been one of the most vibrant areas of the world economically, and its organizations demonstrably compete successfully in world markets. The clarification needed is that such success is limited to certain cultures, that those cultures are very different in detail from each other, and that the environment in each culture is also different. Having said that, it must also be acknowledged that the common denominators of an originally Confucian cultural heritage and economic philosophies of laissez-faire export orientation provide some apparent unity.

East Asia is normally taken to include China, Japan, South Korea, Taiwan, and Hong Kong, with the optional addition of Singapore because of its apparent similarity to Hong Kong. Both China and North Korea present enormous difficulties for comparative organizational psychology because of the lack of research and the barriers to empirical understanding caused by the overriding state ideologies in the two countries. They are both special cases and are seen here as outside the scope of this chapter.

The real focuses of this chapter are the Japanese and the overseas Chinese. A lack of data makes it impossible to cover the South Korean case in any depth, but some propositions will be made about the Korean case from the extant literature. These are very clear cases of cultures that have worked out a way of creating especially efficient and effective organizations that differ from the Western model, and also differ from each other. This requires some redrawing of traditional geographical boundaries if the overseas Chinese are to be included. Japan and Korea both have a clear integrity within political borders. The overseas Chinese do not. They occupy a diaspora around the South China Sea.

They are dominant in Hong Kong, Singapore, and Taiwan, but they are also highly significant in the economic life of the Philippines, Indonesia, Malaysia, and Thailand (Limlingan, 1986; Redding, 1990; Yoshihara, 1988). It is thus proposed that the overseas Chinese be included as an economic culture and treated as a reasonably coherent type. We will not, however, put tight limits on its geographical distribution. There is strong evidence to suggest that these three types are notably more effective in solving the dilemmas of organizational effectiveness than other indigenous types in Asia. It is this chapter's intention to illustrate the contribution of an industrial psychology perspective to the understanding of that phenomenon.

In doing so, we shall proceed by the following stages of analysis:

- The nature of employee commitment to the organization as understood in the Western context

- Comparative studies using the Western model and including East Asian data

- East Asian contexts of organizational attachment

- Attachment in Japan

- Attachment in the Chinese family business

- The Korean case

- Implications for theory and research

Employee Commitment as Understood in the Western Context

Since the 1960s, the construct of organizational commitment has received considerable attention from management scholars and practitioners. While a complete review of this literature is inappropriate, we will focus on two main areas: first, the principal approaches used in organizational commitment; and second, its causes and outcomes. This will then lead to a brief review of comparative regional studies recently conducted on organizational commitment in East Asia, followed by a discussion of the main cultures themselves.

Approaches to Studying Organizational Commitment

Two broad approaches for studying organizational commitment may be identified within a widely varied literature. One approach labels commitment as an attitude from which behaviors follow. The second approach focuses on behaviors and the attitudes that result from such actions (Mowday, Porter, & Steers, 1982). These approaches are referred to as *attitudinal* and *behavioral*, respectively.

Attitudinal commitment is most commonly measured by a model developed by Porter, Steers, Mowday, and Boulian (1974). They define organizational commitment "in terms of the strength of an individual's identification with and involvement in a particular organization" (p. 604). The organizational commitment scale, which they designed to measure attitudinal commitment, contains three factors: "(a) a strong belief in and acceptance of the organization's goals and values; (b) a willingness to exert considerable effort on behalf of the organization; and (c) a definite desire to maintain organizational membership" (p. 604).

The notion of behavioral commitment is linked to the theories of Howard Becker. According to Becker (1960), "commitments come into being when a person, by making a side bet, links extraneous interests with a consistent line of activity" (p. 32). This theory suggests, for example, that an employee can become committed to an organization due to the benefit scheme.

Staw (1982) and Salancik (1982) also view commitment from the behavioral perspective. For Salancik (1992), "commitment is the binding of the individual to behavioural acts" (p. 4). Staw (1982) continues this line of reasoning: "Commitment is the glue that holds individuals in a line of behaviour, encompassing those psychological forces that bind individuals to an action as well as those situational forces that make change difficult" (pp. 101–102).

Measuring behavioral commitment has proven difficult. Unlike attitudinal commitment, behavioral commitment remains a field for contention as far as measurement is concerned. Two scales, created by Hrebiniak and Alutto (1972) and Meyer and Allen (1984), have often been used for this purpose.

To summarize, attitudinal commitment reflects a potentially intense moral involvement, attachment, and identification with the organization. Behavioral commitment represents the costs that tie an employee to an organization (Aven, 1988). The relationship between attitudinal and behavioral commitment is a matter of debate. Mowday, Porter, and Steers (1982) contend that the relationship between attitudinal commitment and committing behaviors is a reciprocal one. On the other hand, Meyer and Allen (1984) view these constructs as separate.

Although the relationship between attitudinal and behavioral commitment is important and deserves additional attention, we suggest for the moment that they be treated as two sides of the same coin. Measuring both sides of commitment is necessary, given that attitudes and behaviors may contradict each other. It is possible for employees to behave in a committed way—by working long hours, for example—yet not report a moral attachment to the firm. While this approach complicates the research methodology, it should result in a more thorough understanding of this complex construct.

Antecedents and Outcomes of Organizational Commitment

A large number of studies have sought to identify the antecedents and outcomes of organizational commitment, and they have resulted in long lists of variables. It is not our intention to review all of these variables, but it may be useful to illustrate the types of variables commonly proposed as either determinants or consequences.

Steers (1977) categorized antecedents into three categories: personal characteristics, job characteristics, and work experiences. He found the following variables significantly associated with organizational commitment: need for achievement, group attitudes toward the organization, education (inversely), organizational dependability, personal importance, and task identity. Other factors include age and tenure (Sheldon, 1971), gender (Hrebiniak & Alutto, 1972), group norms, job challenge, met expectations, and self-image reinforcement (Buchanan, 1974).

Compared with this varied list of antecedents, the outcomes of organizational commitment are fairly clear (Reichers, 1985). Several outcomes of commitment have been consistently correlated with it. Turnover has been found to be inversely related to organizational commitment (Angle & Perry, 1981; Porter et al., 1974; Steers, 1977). In addition, Angle and Perry (1981) also found a correlation between tardiness and commitment. Finally, employee desire and intent to remain with an organization were significant outcomes in the study conducted by Steers (1977).

This brief review points to some main themes in our current knowledge of organizational commitment, based as it is on Western employees in Western organizations. From this we know that commitment is a reaction between employee and organization, but it is also self-evident that this reaction does not occur in a vacuum. It is influenced by personal, organizational, and cultural factors and, because of this, studies of commitment need to take into account the relationship between an organization and an individual within a particular societal context.

Comparative Studies of Organizational Commitment in East Asia

Most of the Asian cross-cultural work published on organizational commitment has focused on Japan, with some studies conducted in Singapore, Taiwan, and Korea. These studies have tended to concentrate on two main areas. First, researchers have tried to determine if the variables associated with organizational commitment are universal or culture-specific. Second, studies have compared the overall commitment levels of employees from different cultures. We shall now examine the results from comparative studies that include East Asian and Western participants.

Several studies have examined the construct validity of organizational commitment. In a study of organizational commitment and turnover, Marsh and Mannari (1977) concluded that the variables associated with commitment were universal and not culture-specific for Japanese and U.S. workers. Luthans, McCaul, and Dodd (1985) compared the relationship between organizational commitment and two variables—age and tenure—for a diverse sample of U.S., Japanese, and Korean workers. It was determined that age and tenure were positively related to commitment for all three groups of employees. This supports Marsh and Mannari's (1977) proposal that organizational commitment is based on universal values. In a study conducted in Singapore, Putti, Aryee, and Lang (1989) found that the same values that were related to organizational commitment in the West also held true for Asia.

Lincoln, Hanada, and Olsen (1981) produced results that contradict those just mentioned. They found, for instance, that Japanese and Japanese American workers placed greater value on organizational paternalism than their U.S. counterparts. Yet there were no differences among employees in their level of personal ties to colleagues. Near's (1989) study of Japanese and U.S. workers found that social interaction, fairness, and job content influence commitment regardless of culture. Yet other variables remained culture-specific. These included freedom on the job for Americans and age for Japanese.

While more research is needed to determine how many and which variables associated with commitment are universally valid, results suggest that at least some determinants of commitment will hold true across societal boundaries. The nature of the cultural influence is thus limited.

There is, however, a significant cultural issue affecting the methodology of studies using questionnaires and Likert scales, and acknowledgment must be made at the outset of this review that a particular Japanese response bias may well affect many reported findings and be inadequately acknowledged. This bias stems from Japanese reticence about the assertion of personal claims, including statements about satisfaction (Smith & Misumi, 1989). This muting of claims and modest presentation of self may well be causing some distortion of conclusions in comparative studies, even in the case of large samples, and argues for some healthy skepticism over the reliance on positivist methodology. The relative shortage of ethnographic studies remains a weakness in the field, and the issue of variations in meaning remains problematic (Redding, 1993).

Possibly in consequence of this, studies that have compared overall levels of satisfaction and commitment cross-culturally have produced contradictory results. For example, Cole (1979) found that the Japanese have a higher level of organizational commitment than their U.S. counterparts, while Lincoln, Hanada, and Olsen's (1981) study of employees of Japanese origin concluded that they have a lower level of work satisfaction than U.S. workers. Luthans, McCaul, and Dodd (1985) found the level of organizational commitment to be highest among U.S. employees, with the Japanese and Korean employees exhibiting significantly lower levels of commitment.

In studies that shared data sets, Lincoln and Kalleberg (1985) and Near (1989) compared the organizational commitment levels for approximately 7,000 Japanese and American production workers. Lincoln and Kalleberg found some evidence that Japanese managers and workers had a greater level of commitment than their U.S. counterparts. Yet they admit that "it took some shifting of our data to find it" (p. 758). Near's study (1989) of Japanese and U.S. workers found Japanese participants expressed a lower level of commitment than the U.S. workers. Near concluded that the "Western conception of commitment may simply not apply to other cultures" (p. 294).

Given the popular stereotype of the East Asian work ethic, results that indicate that Asians have a lower level of organizational commitment than their Western counterparts are surprising. Well-documented behaviors, such as remaining with the company and having a willingness to work long hours, suggest to Westerners that the Japanese are highly committed to their organizations. Why, then, do they frequently report a lower level of commitment?

The most obvious response is, quite simply, that East Asians are not as committed to their employers as were workers in the West. While this is possible, there are other explanations that would render the data just mentioned incomplete, if not misleading.

Frequently, cross-cultural studies compare employees working for different organizations operating in unique cultural and economic environments. It is difficult to determine the impact of culture on commitment when you are measuring cross-cultural employee reactions to different organizations. Ideally, we should compare the commitment levels of employees from different cultural backgrounds who are working for the same organization. If this is not possible, then organizational characteristics, such as personnel policies, need to be included in the analysis.

We are also assuming that the two essential components—commitment and organization—are the same across cultures. This may not be the case. Organizations take on many different configurations and provide a variety of environments within which employees work. Given this level of complexity, it is appropriate to ask, What is the organization in organizational commitment? It may well be that Western and Asian employees perceive the organization differently. The Western conception of organization, on which the commitment models are based, may not translate to an Asian culture. What is currently reported may actually be employee reactions to different phenomena. Employee expectations must inevitably mediate their perceptions of commitment, and such expectations will reflect surrounding normal practice in defining the quality of the connection with the company and its overall meaning.

The same case can be made for the notion of commitment itself. Behaviors and attitudes Westerners consider indicative of employee commitment may not be valid from the Asian perspective. Westerners tend to equate staying with an organization and working toward its goals with commitment. Asians may or may not define commitment in the same terms.

We are not suggesting that the cross-cultural study of organizational commitment is impossible. As mentioned earlier, commitment is the outcome of a relationship between employee and organization. When examining this relationship across different cultures, it is appropriate to recall the wide variation in human values and the different roles organizations assume. Acknowledging these differences greatly complicates research, but gives us the opportunity to understand a greater variety of organizational worlds.

Below the surface of much of what follows is a fundamental ideal-type contrast described by Etzioni (1975) as a distinction between calculative and moral relationships. Hofstede (1980, 1984, 1992) argues from a very large empirical base for a connection between these forces and his proposed key cultural components, collectivism and individualism. In individualist cultures, the employer–employee relationship is a business relationship based on the calculation of mutual advantages. It can be terminated without moral transgression. Labor is a factor of production in a rational schema. In more collectivist cultures, the relationship contains moral overtones, as with the traditional mutual obligations in an extended family. Protection and loyalty become reciprocal, and change of employment is socially disapproved of. This does not rule out finding some calculative elements in a collectivist society or finding some moral elements in an individualist society, but it does argue for a strong tendency for overlaps of the collective moral and the individualist/calculative components.

Much of what we shall argue in this chapter is in line with this position, and what is described may therefore not be the sole preserve of East Asian organizational forms. It is, however, still the case that the reasons behind the more moralistic systems of East Asia are distinctly Asian reasons and that the understanding of them operates at a different level of analysis than that of these relevant but very broad categorizations.

The East Asian Contexts of Organizational Attachment

We will illustrate in greater detail later how the nature of the psychological contract between the individual and the organization is mediated by culture in distinct ways in East Asia. These transactions are, however, located in a matrix of sociological, political, and economic forces, some account of which needs to be taken if the organizational psychology is to be understood.

The particular features of the environment that can be argued to have a bearing on the emerging of specific organizational responses in East Asia have been identified by Whitley (1990) as (a) authority relations, (b) mechanisms for generating and maintaining trust and obligation relations between nonkin, and (c) the structure and policies of state agencies and financial institutions.

Authority Relations

Authority relations that become typical of a culture reflect that culture's social history and the traditional structures devised for exercising power. A marked contrast exists between the Chinese and Japanese formulae, and the Chinese heritage is maintained by the overseas Chinese.

In the case of Japan, an elaborate structure for integrating vertical loyalties typified the feudalism inherited and subsequently reinforced by Tokugawa (Moore, 1966, pp. 254–275). In this system, a landowning aristocracy served to focus the loyalties and dependence of the peasantry. A tradition grew up of exchanging protection downward for loyalty upward.

Such connections were legitimized by a code of ethics, and the structure remained rooted in landholding and was thus stable through time. Notions of obedience, subordination, and dependence may be traced to this structure, but its most significant feature for psychological understanding is the reciprocity it contains. The Samurai ethic contains a legitimizing moral force based on an ultimately Confucian notion reintroduced by Tokugawa in devising the ideological system. According to this ethic, power is only deserved if it is exercised responsibly on behalf of those dominated. Such a notion inevitably tends to reinforce and stabilize the sense of verticality seen as one of the key distinguishing features of Japanese society (Nakane, 1972).

A related feature of this distinctly Japanese social structure is that loyalty was encouraged to a collective entity that was itself locked firmly and securely into a taller vertical structure of such entities. The traditional household, or *ie*, operating in effect as an economic survival unit and thus emphasizing the pooling of work, was the most fundamental unit of identity. In turn, this was part of a larger property holding under a particular landlord, which was in turn linked to the feudal aristocratic superstructure. At each level, the same reciprocal exchange was enacted and served to maintain the system's stability. Thus, a tradition of identity with, and dependence on, large vertical structures developed. One of the outcomes for the Japanese, due to the emphasis on the collectivity, was a depersonalizing of authority relations. In other words, the power system was based less on direct personal subordination and more on collective and positional authority. Recognition of mutual dependence, common commitment to collective goals, and the intent that superiors act on the basis of competence and subservience to joint interests (Pye, 1985, pp. 163–181) all assisted in moving Japan away from the extremes of personalism exhibited in the case of the Chinese. Today, personalism is not entirely abandoned, however, and Rohlen (1974, pp. 122–134) has illuminated how personal commitments to immediate superiors and patrons

are greater in Japan than in most Western societies. But Rohlen also points out that the personalism of Japan is more a matter of shared loyalties, collective objectives, and reciprocal trust than in other East Asian cultures.

A supplementary historical factor is that for nearly three centuries prior to the Meiji restoration, the movement of people was severely restricted in Japan. People stayed in one area always. Penalties were severe for being found outside that area, and retribution could also apply to hosts. In such a context, a fierce sense of ingroup and outgroup was fostered, and its effects are arguably still traceable.

A great contrast to Japanese society can now be pointed to in the traditional structure of Chinese society, from which some of the lessons also apply to Korea. China's state structure was based on bureaucratic patrimonialism using the mandarinate, in contrast to the military-aristocratic feudalism of Japan (Jacobs, 1958). In the Chinese case, the mandarinate exercised power on behalf of the emperor, and the power structure was highly centralized. The typical mandarin was a member of an aesthetically refined and cultivated elite living in a world that was not only different from that of the mass of the population but also deliberately distanced from ordinary people. Isolated and aloof, he oversaw a region of the country without having close connections with it. He was moved at regular intervals to a new posting and never served in the area of his own upbringing. The creation of a discontinuity in the vertical structure between the mandarin and the people, designed initially to prevent corruption, served also to prevent the growth of other ties of mutual obligation and dependence. In consequence, any emotional exchange atrophied and the notion of vertical loyalty to these intermediate units of the state was weakened to the point of irrelevance.

Maintenance of power by the mandarinate was achieved by the granting to it of a monopoly on the interpretation of the state ideology, Confucianism. The system certified its own members using a legitimizing notion of ideal virtue. It did not need to legitimize its domination through reciprocal services, such as good government in the people's interests (principles which are, incidentally, precisely replicated in the Communist party structure in China today), and thus ties of vertical obligation to the base layer of society were not sponsored. Apart from the maintenance of order and infrastructure, welfare initiatives were limited. The main agenda was stability and control from the center.

Thus, Chinese society took on a quite different shape from Japanese society. For the majority of Chinese people, living in a system in which vertical loyalty had nowhere to go and in which protection was only available via the microstructures of society, the family, these became the ultimate—and for most people the sole focuses of identity. Given also that subsistence living was the norm and that resources were consequently scarce, families were competing with each other as well.

A number of significant outcomes flow from this long and continuing tradition, and they are visible as predispositions and behavior patterns typical of the culture and maintained for their value by the overseas Chinese. In the first place, because loyalties cannot be systematically integrated into large vertical structures, they cluster instead around the standard alternative unit of support, the family, together with its surrounding circles of decreasingly potent identity, the lineage group and then the regional clan. Where Chinese are an ethnic minority, Chineseness itself can form a last circle of identity. Overwhelmingly, the most significant focus is the family.

The authority system in the resulting social units, whether they be social or economic in nature, is patrimonial (Hamilton, 1984). It is, in other words, connected to an individual, almost always a father figure, and sustained on the basis of, and in proportion to, his personal moral superiority (Silin, 1976). Allegiance remains primarily personal in both China and Korea (Jacobs, 1985; Pye, 1985). A further feature of patrimonialism is the implication that the key figure owns key resources. Legitimate

use of power is through the exercise of paternalism, a theme that contains many strands of meaning, including benevolence, discipline, piety, and responsibility (Hallgren, 1986; Pye, 1985). The dominant organizational metaphor is the family.

There is a significant cross-cultural variation in East Asia over the understanding of authority within the family context (Pye, 1985, pp. 73–79), and reflections of such socialization are visible in organizational behavior and structure. In the Chinese family, authority is undifferentiated and monolithic. It belongs entirely to the father, as does the responsibility for family welfare. The mother is obliged to reinforce that authority and cannot act as an alternative focus of different values or conduct. Equally, the owner of the Chinese family business traditionally adopts what Silin (1976, pp. 127–128) has described as a "didactic" leadership style in which, as if in a teaching mode, from a superior position, he allows subordinates a glimpse of the thoughts and beliefs that enable him to be successful. He maintains a degree of aloofness from close contact with subordinates and does not traditionally share authority, something which is in any case defined as a moral quality of an individual. In this context, participative management would be taken as a sign of weakness (Silin, 1976, p. 71).

As in so many respects, the Korean case appears in a position between the Chinese and Japanese ones. Similar perceptions of the father role as omnipotent and aloof occur here, but family authority is more differentiated than in the Chinese case, and maternal and paternal roles can be played off against each other (Pye, 1985, p. 75).

The Japanese father role, in contrast, is less suggestive of omnipotence. The father can admit uncertainty, share responsibilities with others, and share power with the family mother in a way that leaves the Japanese image of authority as being largely maternal in nature (Pye, 1985, p. 74). In the organization, the use of supportive and nurturing forms of authority acknowledges the need to take account of emotional dependence and consensus seeking.

Trust and Obligation Relations

A crucial distinguishing feature that separates the environment of organization in the West from the East Asian organizational environment is the institutional support of trust (Barber, 1983; Needham, 1956, p. 290). In a society where obligations are formalized, for instance, in a contract of employment or in the sale and purchase of goods, and where that contract is backed up by an efficient legal system, the cementing of trust and thus of cooperation can be said to be handled institutionally. In the East Asian case, this is not typical, and other forms of trust bonding are used to support cooperation. These are based on reciprocity norms and vary significantly in their structure from culture to culture.

In the Japanese case, much had already occurred before the Meiji restoration to develop loyalty to large collective structures, and this had also fostered the growth of a class of professional retainers and managers who were not related to owners. Thus, the development of a body of nonowners as executives began early in Japan's industrialization (Hirschmeier & Yui, 1981, pp. 165–168). Together with a less developed sense of identity with the family compared to that of the Chinese, a long tradition of loyalty to larger collectivities laid the groundwork for a greater willingness to trust employers. This was reciprocal with the high dependence needs of the products of Japanese upbringing (Doi, 1973; Lebra, 1976), and the ground was laid for the prototypical Japanese employee–firm relationship.

Traditional Chinese society, in contrast, was structured in such a way as to negate the emergence of trust in institutions, leaving it to be transacted over a network of personally defined reciprocal bonds. Known as *guanxi* in China, this is still the basis of most economic exchanges (Boisot & Child, 1990) and has been developed in other areas by the overseas Chinese into an elaborate web of reliable connections (Dannhaeuser, 1981). For an individual, the building and maintenance of a personal

web is essential to effective functioning in the society, and in most cases it makes the resort to more formal bonding redundant. Such a response to the question of cooperation is in part made necessary by the absence of alternatives in the traditional societal design and is in part driven by the insecurities engendered in a society where families are competing for scarce resources. This latter threat is exacerbated by ethical systems that evade the notion of public good and leave the definition of moral duty contingent on relationships (Redding, 1990, pp. 41–78).

In such a context, the most natural unit for affiliation is the family, and this consequently becomes the main component around which economic cooperation is constructed (Redding, 1990). Family businesses, with paternalistic organizational climates, are understood as trustworthy, although the strength of attachment for an individual is highly contingent on the dyadic bond between an individual member and the roles of paterfamilias/owner/chief executive, all three of which are commonly collapsed into one. It is not surprising in these circumstances that the typical organization in the case of the overseas Chinese is small. The average manufacturing company in Hong Kong, for instance, employs 19 people.

Such Chinese variations in strength of identity with the collectivity are commonly depicted as concentric circles, first outlined by Fei (1939). In simple terms, in an organizational context the central circle is family itself and the next circle is the protofamily or trusted retainers, who are often in key positions and treated as if they were honorary family members. The outside circle consists of the remaining employees. For them a tension exists between the pragmatic drive to sustain their own families and thus achieve maximum income in a given labor market, and the firm's efforts to create a paternalistic atmosphere conducive to their continued existence.

The primacy of family affiliations affects all attachments and is to be seen in the light of another force in Chinese society. The ethical system of Confucianism rests upon the family structure. Without the family as a means of expressing the moral compunctions of the society, the moral base disintegrates—a threat to be resisted at all odds because of the mental wilderness it leads to. The integrity of the family has always been seen as a function of a family's wealth or property, originally expressed as landholding. Without the association of wealth and family as a driving force, behavior becomes largely purposeless, or at least not legitimate by the prevailing value system. As Moore (1966, p. 212) cryptically puts it: "No property: no family, no religion." An outcome of this is that individual motivation in the work context is heavily imbued with the urge to accumulate family wealth. Hong Kong society, for example, is seen as minimally integrated and characterized by "utilitarianistic familism" (Lau, 1982).

It is thus possible to crudely categorize Chinese organizational members into two sets: the owners, who are pursuing the financial welfare of their own families via the success of the firm, a pursuit accepted as entirely legitimate; and the employees, who are also contributing to their own family welfare. In this latter set are the potential entrepreneurs intent on building their own family businesses when the time is ripe (Tam, 1990). The majority of workers express the intent more simply by adding their wages to the family pool (Salaff, 1981, p. 265). Extra complexity is thus added to the understanding of individual motivation.

In the case of Korea, at least at this introductory level, it is possible to argue a greater similarity to Chinese social tradition than to Japanese. In a review of the literature, Kim (1988, p. 202) proposed the following themes to describe Korean social organization: authoritarianism and strong emphasis on hierarchy, sensitivity to status and prestige, family-based collectivism, particularistic social networking, personalism with an emotional content, factionalism centering on the immediate collectivity, nepotism and favoritism, and weak sense of identity with larger organizations—such connections being primarily contractual and utilitarian.

The social history of Korea, and particularly the influence of the neo-Confucianism used as the state ideology throughout the Yi dynasty from the fourteenth to the early twentieth centuries, led to an apparently harsh authoritarian regime of attempted control over the common people. This was exacerbated by the succeeding fifty years of Japanese colonialism, and the effects of authoritarian tradition are still visible in modern Korean organizational life (Jacobs, 1985).

State Policies and Institutions

In the context of understanding organizational psychology, the reason for taking account of the role of the state is to understand its influence on the kinds of organizations found in the three economic cultures of interest here, and in consequence to see better the way such distinct organizations bond employees to them. In East Asia, the state has played a strong interventionist role in two of the cultures, and the dominant organizational types in Japan and Korea cannot be comprehended without some reference to the work of the "developmental state" (Johnson, 1982, pp. 17–23) in policy implementation as well as development policy setting. There are, of course, many other ways in which government actions could be argued to influence the psychology of organizational attachment at the individual level, not the least of which is labor legislation, but such concerns are outside the scope of this chapter and will only be brought briefly into account later as particular features of attachment come to be analyzed. For the moment, the agenda is simply to acknowledge political factors and their consequences in the emergence of (a) large Japanese conglomerates, (b) Korean *chaebol*, and (c) small-scale Chinese family business.

Although the Japanese economy is not precisely represented by the large conglomerate form of organization and there is a huge base of small companies in what is essentially a dual economy, the large coordinated enterprise remains the standard-bearer and the institution in which what the West understands as Japanese management is most typically practiced. Known varyingly as *zaibatsu* (prewar conglomerates), *sogo-shosha* (general trading companies), *keiretsu* (a closely tied complex of industrial and financial corporations), or *kaisha* (stand-alone corporations), these often monolithic organizations owe much to government policies of development.

The detailed mechanisms of government influence have no place in this account, but their results do, and may be summarized as follows:

- The growth of large corporations allows for the development of internal labor markets within the firm and corporations that are highly differentiated internally.

- The national labor market becomes differentiated by ranks as larger companies offer more attractive employment packages and status.

- Government policies of low general welfare provision exacerbate the dependence of employees on firms and thus influence the context of attachment, although increasing welfare provision in recent years is lessening the effect of this.

These three features of the Japanese context are also true of Korea, where a similar pattern of the fostering of large conglomerates by government has produced the *chaebol*.

For the overseas Chinese, the context is very different. In Hong Kong, there is a low level of government involvement in business strategy. In Taiwan, where the Chinese family business also dominates, government intervention has been quite strong in the large corporate sector and in institutional fields such as banking, education, and industrial relations. It nevertheless leaves largely untouched the strategic decision making of the great majority of companies, almost all of which are small family businesses. In other countries where the Chinese family business is a significant but not dominant player in the economy, growth is only achieved after the coopting of government support, and the most typical organizational response remains the small-scale familistic organization. Cultural

influences in such organizations are the three main features of the overseas Chinese value set—paternalism, personalism, and insecurity—each of which has strong influence on the design of cooperative systems (Redding, 1990).

Attachment to the Organization in Differing Asian Contexts

We shall turn now to an analysis of the literature on the varying nature of cooperation with organizations by individuals in different Asian cultures. We shall examine information on the Japanese and the overseas Chinese, and tentatively on the Koreans.

As a means of ordering the commentary, we propose to consider the following features:

- Goal congruence
- The work ethic
- Affiliation within groups
- Mutual obligation bonding
- Role compliance

These features are connected, as suggested in Figure 1, with the three dimensions noted earlier that are now commonly taken in the Western literature as indicative of attitudinal commitment: namely, accepting organizational goals, working hard for the organization, and wishing to remain a member. They do, however, range more widely and are deliberately constructed to pick up elements likely to be salient in the more collectivist cultures of Asia and/or in cultures with more strongly perceived informal structures of authority, such as patrimonialism.

Attachment in Japan

Description and analysis of the complex relationship between organization and individual in Japan has been attempted by analysts from the full spectrum of academic persuasions. Consequently, the characteristics of the Japanese worker and Japanese organizations have been the subject of an immense volume of

FIGURE 1

Aspects of Individual Attachment to the Organization and Their Culturally Varying Antecedents

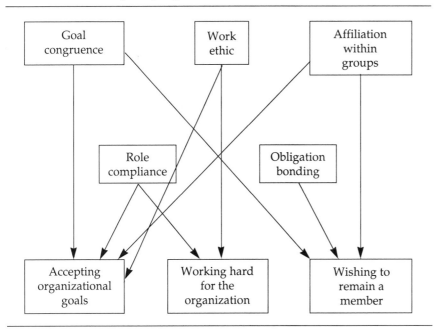

publications in academic journals and popular literature. This literature has been criticized for a tendency to concentrate on the "softer" aspects of Japanese management (Nonaka & Johansson, 1985), and some corrective is increasingly visible in the analysis of specific techniques (e.g., Abegglen & Stalk, 1985; McMillan, 1985; Murakami & Nishiwaki, 1991). Dunphy and Stening (1984) published an annotated bibliography covering approximately 500 English-language books and articles on Japanese management and organizational behavior written between 1970 and 1983. Since that time, hundreds more have been published. The following review will draw upon a relatively small proportion of that literature. It is concerned primarily with the exploration of the popular view of the Japanese worker and Japanese organizations, the accuracy of that view, and the cultural and social antecedents of individual attachment to the organization in Japan.

The differences between Japanese workers and organizations and those in the West have often been cited as the reason for the high rate of growth in productivity in Japan in the post-World War II period. Both Japanese human resource management approaches and Japanese workers have been acclaimed as superior to those in the West, and a multitude of factors have been put forward to account for this superiority. Many authors focused on those aspects of Japanese management that could be successfully adopted in the West (Ouchi, 1981a, 1981b; Ouchi & Jaeger, 1978; Vogel, 1979). Although some writers recently have claimed that Japanese success has been exaggerated (e.g., Hodgetts & Luthans, 1989), these have been in the minority.

The predominant image of the Japanese worker is that he or she is hardworking, has high loyalty to company and superiors, is strongly committed to the achievement of company goals, and possesses a self-image that reflects his or her sense of belonging to a particular company or organization. Evidence of these characteristics are the lower rate of interfirm mobility in the Japanese work force (Cole, 1979; Marsh & Mannari, 1977); the fact that the Japanese spend more hours at work, volunteer for overtime, and consistently underutilize their annual leave provisions (Cole, 1979; Smith, 1984); the ready absorption of new technology by Japanese employees (Cole, 1979; Whitehill & Takezawa, 1978); and the fact that many Japanese spend a large amount of their free time socializing with co-workers (Atsumi, 1979; Haitani, 1976). Images that have been propagated in the West of employees singing company songs, reciting company mottos, and engaging in mass exercise sessions have supported these conceptions.

The structure and policies of Japanese organizations are also different in many respects from those of Western organizations. The distinctive features of Japanese organizations have been discussed by a number of writers and include recruitment from school, lifetime employment, emphasis on internal training, importance of age and seniority rather than ability as the basis for promotion, and provision of a range of welfare services for employees and their families, including company housing, dining halls, cultural and study facilities, and recreational facilities (Dore, 1973; Haitani, 1976; Karsh, 1984; Lincoln, 1989; Lincoln & Kalleberg, 1985; Pascale & Maguire, 1980). These characteristics are reported to increase employee commitment to the organization (Cole, 1979; Lincoln & Kalleberg, 1985).

The Japanese employment system has been characterized consistently by certain features:

- High goal congruence between workers and management

- A highly developed work ethic

- A strong affiliation between employees and the organization

- A highly structured set of expectations regarding the mutual obligations of workers and management

The questions this chapter addresses are to what extent these features reflect the unique characteristics of the Japanese work force and to what extent they are the product of organizational structures set in place by management and employer groups.

Lincoln and Kalleberg (1985) discussed two theoretical perspectives, cultural and organizational, which they argued encompass most explanations for the commitment, identification, and loyalty Japanese employees exhibit toward their firms. Cultural theorists argue that "the source of modern Japanese workers' dependence on and identification with the company lies with a set of values which run deep in Japanese culture and tradition," while organizational theorists argue that "the organizational structures and employment systems of Japanese firms are so designed as to elicit commitment from the work force" (Lincoln & Kalleberg, 1985, p. 739). Organizational theorists include proponents of Dore's (1973) late development thesis and also the more radical theorists, who see the development of particular structures and processes as a means of creating dependence and submission in the work force. The supposed difference between the two theoretical positions is that one sees Japanese employee behavior as a natural outcome of the cultural heritage, whereas the other sees it as a consequence of policies, actions, and conscious manipulation by employer groups. In reality, it may simply be that such embedded management systems will inevitably reflect culturally determined predispositions, and these two perspectives are not alternatives.

These perspectives nevertheless provide useful analytical pathways, and evidence for and against these two theoretical perspectives will be evaluated through a discussion of the four key characteristics of the Japanese employment system listed above.

Goal Congruence

High goal congruence between the organization and its employees is one of the factors that distinguishes Japanese organizations from those in the West. This may be due to the fact that the corporate goals of Japanese organizations are quite different from those of most Western organizations. In Western corporate culture, maximizing the "bottom line" is seen by many as the superordinate goal and has been said to permeate "all aspects of corporate rhetoric and behaviour" (Sethi, Namiki, & Swanson, 1984, p. 125).

Clark (1979) wrote that Japanese shareholders are not primarily interested in profits and dividends and that market share was the major measure of a company's success. In fact, because of Japanese tax laws, shareholders benefit more if their company grows than if it pays dividends (Abegglen & Stalk, 1985). According to Haitani (1976), the primary goal of Japanese corporate management is to maintain a high and rising volume of sales, thus ensuring an acceptable level of profits, increased market share, increased prosperity for employees in terms of salaries, bonuses, and welfare provisions, and continued employment for production workers. In addition to paternalistic concern for company employees, Haitani also claimed that many corporate managers pronounce that their firm's activities serve the larger public purpose of economic good. Clark (1979) argued that for many employees, loyalty and service to the company were really a form of loyalty and service to the nation and an expression of nationalistic sentiments in the post-World War II era.

The concept of an overriding social responsibility is also promoted by the Japanese government. Picken (1987, p. 138) quoted the Japan Committee for Economic Development as follows:

> It is vital that modern corporate managers strive to supply products of the highest quality at the lowest possible prices through the most effective utilisation of product resources consistent with the welfare of the whole economy and the society at large. It is indeed the social responsibility of modern executives to serve as an effective instrument to develop a managerial system capable of accomplishing this mission. (p. 138)

Haitani argued that the consistency of corporate and social goals serves several important functions—enhancing prestige of the firm, encouraging a high degree of worker identification with the company, and enabling management to pressure workers to make sacrifices in the name of greater social welfare.

Logan (1984) wrote that "developing loyalty and a sense of purpose within their companies is considered by many Japanese executives to be one of their most important functions" (p. 150). He defined a sense of purpose as a common understanding of a common objective. He claimed that five principles were embodied in the purpose of most Japanese companies:

- *Universality*—the company's purpose can be embraced by all employees.

- *Transcendence*—it transcends immediate business objectives and self-centered pursuits of either manager or employee.

- *Permanence*—it does not change quickly.

- *Worthiness*—it is worthy of the employee's dedication, hard work, loyalty, and self-sacrifice.

- *Responsibility*—responsibility rests with all employees.

Research by Miyajima (1986), in which Japanese managers rated their organization as task oriented (defined as devoted to the achievement of a superordinate goal), lends further support to the emphasis on organizational goals in Japanese corporate culture. In contrast, these same managers described British organizations as power oriented, competitive, territorial, and seeking to expand control at the expense of others.

The importance of corporate goals in Japanese organizations may reflect the psychological functioning of the Japanese. Mendenhall and Oddou (1986) suggested that the cognitive framework of the Japanese may be different than that of Westerners. They claimed that in terms of information processing, Japanese prefer to begin with the whole rather than an analysis of the parts (see also Maruyama, 1974; Nakamura, 1964). Japanese managers thus spend much of their time keeping workers in tune with the "big picture" and working toward the achievement of organizational goals. They also claimed that in negotiations Japanese are more goal oriented, tending to focus on the holistic idea rather than on specific elements, much to the frustration of Western businesspeople.

It is possible that among the Japanese there may be a cultural bias toward superordinate goal-directed behavior. If so, the typical goal definitions promulgated can be expected to contribute significantly to the apparent high goal congruence between Japanese workers and organizations.

Work Ethic

Rapid increases in worker productivity in Japan in the post-World War II period have often been attributed to the Japanese work ethic. Tung (1984) claimed that this has its roots in the tradition of rice cultivation and Zen philosophy. The primary goal of Zen is for a follower to realize his or her potential as a human being. The effort one applies to a task rather than the result of one's efforts is central to the practice of Zen. The concept of *seishin-shugi* is based on a philosophy of individual development that requires self-sacrifice, gratification deferment, and sheer mental effort. This concept is often incorporated into new employee training programs and management development training programs in Japan (Mendenhall & Oddou, 1986). The Japanese government has also advocated a particular view of work that downplays the material rewards associated with work as incentive to individual effort and, instead, stresses an ethic in which work is an end in itself (Cole,

1979). Supporting evidence of high Japanese levels of achievement need, as well as affiliation need, is provided in the results from the Meaning of Work International Research Team (1986).

Cole offered three factors as evidence of the Japanese work ethic:

- A high level of personal savings, indicating a marked frugality that involves working hard and maintaining conservative consumption patterns

- A historic lag in wage increases relative to productivity increases, indicating a work ethic that emphasizes diligence and commitment to employer goals while demanding only moderate compensation in return

- Ready absorption of new technology, indicating the willingness of employees to innovate, accept management direction, and demand little monetary compensation in return

Cole (1979) argued, however, that productivity is not determined by how hard workers work but by "the interaction of technology and labor, guided by management, and influenced by the social structure and work organization prevailing in the given country...making it difficult to disentangle the contribution of the Japanese work ethic" (p. 225).

Affiliation and Group Membership

The self-image of the Japanese worker is very much a reflection of his or her sense of belonging to a particular work context, and the meeting of needs via the success of the work group rather than the individual is described in the report of the Meaning of Work International Research Team (1986). A small number of concepts go a long way toward providing an understanding of Japanese workers' strong sense of affiliation with the context of work and need for group membership.

Contextualism is the term used to describe the tendency for Japanese to define themselves by their contexts. Their personal identity is interwoven with the context or situation in which they find themselves (Mendenhall & Oddou, 1986). This is consistent with the reported high identification of Japanese employees with their company. A Japanese worker typically identifies more with the company than with a specific job or occupational classification and thus will say "I am Honda" rather than "I am a production line worker." In fact, it may take considerable questioning to find out what kind of work a person actually does (Alston, 1989; Lebra, 1976).

The principle of flux is the term Mendenhall and Oddou used to describe the relationship between the context and its members. According to this principle, the relationship is not fixed, the members' obligations to the context are unlimited, and their responsibilities are ambiguous. The members are bound to the context, but in return the context takes the ultimate responsibility for its members' lives. The strong bond between the context and its members contributes significantly to many workplace practices and characteristics, such as high loyalty, low turnover of core staff, implicit control systems, and company unions as opposed to trade unions (Mendenhall & Oddou, 1986).

A number of key Japanese concepts relating to affiliation and group membership—*ie, wa,* and *amae-on-gimu*—are discussed in detail by Kashima and Callan elsewhere in this volume but will be noted here briefly.

Ie, seen by Nakane (1972) as the primary unit of social organization in Japan, was traditionally a work group centered on a domestic family setting and is now represented in the work groups of larger organizations (Mendenhall & Oddou, 1986, p. 29). *Wa* refers to the harmony that maintains the cohesion and cooperation inside such a group, and between groups in a larger context (Haitain, 1976), and that fosters the submerging of individual goals in favor of group goals (Alston, 1989). *Amae-on-gimu* refers to the refined senses of obligation and dependence that underlie both cooperative behavior

and loyalty in the vertical relationships of an organization (Doi, 1973).

Most Japanese organizations contain structures and implement policies that seem to reinforce the strong sense of affiliation with the organization. Induction programs for new employees are one example. Rohlen (1974) discussed the way in which employees were carefully selected and then socialized into the company culture in an effort to increase commitment and promote particular cultural values.

Some widespread practices actually make it difficult for the employee to leave the organization, and job rotation within the firm is commonplace (Karsh, 1984). It has been estimated that approximately 50 percent of companies use job rotation and employee reassignments as a means of employment restructuring (Mroczkowski & Hanaoka, 1989). Thus, Japanese workers do not tend to develop skills in a particular occupational category but become familiar with many aspects of their companies' operations. Levine and Kawada (1980) examined the use of internal labor systems in Japanese enterprises and concluded that these had substantial benefits for companies in terms of developing a highly versatile and committed core of employees. From the employee point of view, this process has the disadvantage that a lack of specialist skills make an employee less attractive to potential employers.

Combined with the seniority wage system, whereby remuneration is determined by age and length of service rather than job or occupational performance, these factors tend to discourage work force mobility. Marsh and Mannari (1972) argued that it is employer incentives rather than Japanese culture that results in low employee mobility. Cole (1979) examined the incidence of intra- and interfirm mobility in Yokohama and Detroit. Although the pattern and determinants of job changes were quite similar, the volume of changes among Yokohama respondents was only about half that of the Detroit respondents, suggesting that a cultural predisposition to remain with an organization is operating.

In recent years, intercompany labor supply leasing and transfer schemes have been widely used. Information is exchanged on labor supply surpluses and shortages, and temporary or permanent employee transfers between the participating companies are arranged. In 1987, approximately 17,000 Japanese companies participated in such schemes, which effectively extend the lifetime employment principles while maintaining flexibility and economic rationality (Mroczkowski & Hanaoka, 1989).

The Japanese focus on work groups, quality circles, and consultative decision making has been extensively documented in the literature and is the object of a separate chapter (see Kashima & Callan in this volume). According to Cole (1979), work relations in Japanese organizations are structured in such a way that the focus is not on individual responsibilities and tasks but rather on integrating the individual into the group to accomplish tasks assigned to the group. Keys and Miller (1984) wrote that "Japanese management shuns individual accountability and credit in preference for collective or group responsibility resulting in a heavy emphasis on the values of teamwork and cooperation, collective decision making and participative management" (p. 351).

Lincoln and Kalleberg (1985) described the structures and policies of Japanese organizations as "corporatist," summarizing these features:

- Structures facilitating participation in decision making that diffuse responsibility and commit workers to decisions

- Structures facilitating integration, such as subunits, sections, teams, corporate symbols, and rituals

- Structures fostering individual mobility and careers, such as internal labor markets

- Structures fostering legitimacy and legal order within the firm, such as formal rules and procedures

They found that many of these features were associated with more committed and satisfied employees, not just in Japan but also in the United States. It may be concluded, then, that Japan's traditional groupism and the structures of Japanese organizations both act to strengthen the affiliation between worker and organization, whereas in other cultures the organizational structures tend to be relied on more extensively as the source of effectiveness.

Mutual Obligation Bonding

Japanese organizations are characterized by a strong sense of the obligations and mutual responsibilities of workers and management. To a large extent, the Japanese organization reflects the different psychological needs of the Japanese, and its characteristics have developed to foster the reinforcement of those needs.

In Japan, the large organization provides a range of services, such as housing, recreational facilities, educational assistance, and food allowances, many of which are provided by the state in other societies. The lifetime employment system also implies that once an employee is taken on by an organization, there is a long-term commitment from both parties. The obligations of the organization and the dependence of the employee are explained to some extent by psychological constructs that are peculiar to Japanese society, and particularly those surrounding obligation (*ie, wa, amae-on-gimu*), noted briefly earlier and discussed separately by Kashima and Callan in this volume.

Bantug-Hovarth (1985) described the large-scale Japanese organization as a "paternalistic bureaucracy." She argued that Japanese personnel policies such as job rotation encourage the formation of numerous, yet weaker, relationships within the organization rather than the strong, focused ties typical of traditional paternalism:

> As the worker is exposed to a variety of settings...he encounters a relatively uniform set of demands, rewards, and systems of control, and he learns to understand policies. From there it is only

one more step towards relating with and forming ties of loyalty to the organization. (p. 8)

Abegglen and Stalk (1985) argued that the Japanese system effectively ties individual interests to those of the organization. They argued at the same time, however, that although many aspects of their employment system were unique to Japan, they were not culture-specific and could be introduced into any organization.

There is increasing evidence that the prevalence of these paternalistic employment conditions in Japan has been exaggerated or at least oversimplified by the Western literature. Karsh (1984) described four distinct classifications of blue collar workers: regular workers employed after graduating from school, regular workers employed according to company needs (such employees have usually worked for another company), temporary workers, and outside workers. Karsh reported the results of a 1975 survey, which indicated that the proportion of regular employees varied from 11 to 63 percent in those companies surveyed. In the 1960s, it was estimated to be approximately 20 percent (Cole, 1971). Lifetime employment provisions usually only apply to those recruited directly after completing school, and benefits such as progressive wage increases, retirement allowances, and welfare facilities are available only to regular employees.

Empirical Investigation of Employee Attachment (Role Compliance)

An organizational form at odds with the prevailing attitudes and values of a society is unlikely to be successful, and the attitudes and values of the Japanese work force appear to be highly conducive to high productivity and low interfirm mobility. One would assume from these factors that the Japanese work force would also display high identification with and loyalty to the organization.

Among the first to investigate this directly were Whitehill and Takezawa (1968, 1978). From 1960 through 1962 and in 1976 these authors conducted surveys of Japanese and U.S. workers regarding aspects of relations at the workplace. In both instances, the Japanese were more loyal to and identified more strongly with their company. Respondents were asked if they would leave their company in the face of a prolonged business downturn if they could get a job with a more prosperous company. Only 3 percent of Japanese in 1962 and 5 percent in 1976 answered that they would leave their company. In the U.S. sample, the corresponding figures were 23 and 36 percent in 1962 and 1976, respectively. Among the Japanese sample, a far higher proportion claimed that the company was at least as important to them as their private life—64 percent in 1976, up from 54 percent in 1962. In the United States, the corresponding figures were 27 percent in 1962, down to 20 percent in 1976. Whitehill and Takezawa (1978) argued that the results of these and other questions in the survey indicate that Japanese workers have internalized organizational needs and that Japan is more successful in achieving "a closer identity of interests and a merger of human values and priorities between workers and managers" (Whitehill & Takezawa, 1978, p. 39).

In stark contrast to these findings, Kamata's (1973) ethnographic study of life on the production line emphasized indifference as opposed to commitment as a major theme among employees. This study created considerable interest when translated into English but generated little response among Japanese scholars. It did, however, serve to point out the experience of the disadvantaged temporary employee.

Marsh and Mannari (1976) argued that the paternalism–lifetime commitment model exaggerates the uniformity and traditionalism of Japanese organizational behavior. They investigated the validity of two forms of the model: the strong form, in which employees are highly cohesive, favor company paternalism, participate in recreational activities, identify with company goals and problems, do not change firms, and support lifetime commitment norms and values; and the weak form, in which there is high variance between employees but high correlation between the components of the paternalism–lifetime commitment model. Their data did not support either form of the model. They concluded that employees who displayed lifetime commitment behavior may do so for reasons completely extraneous to lifetime commitment attitudes and values such as job satisfaction, economic security, lack of opportunity, and personal ties—in other words, for essentially the same reasons as Western employees will stay with a firm.

Cole (1979) found that Japanese workers were slightly but significantly less committed to the organization than U.S. workers. Despite this, he argued that a strong bond existed between the Japanese employee and the company. He described this relationship as a community of fate in which failure to achieve organizational goals is damaging to the individual employee and organizational success enhances individual interests.

In a study by Luthans, McCaul, and Dodd (1985), the authors compared organizational commitment among U.S., Japanese, and Korean employees using the attitudinal commitment scale developed by Porter, Steers, Mowday, and Boulian (1974). Their results showed no difference in the level of organizational commitment between Korean and Japanese samples, but both showed significantly less organizational commitment than the U.S. employees. The authors concluded that organizational commitment is not based on culture specific norms and values and that it is not responsible for the low turnover in Japanese organizations.

Using an abridged version of the Mowday, Porter, and Steers attitudinal scale, Lincoln and Kalleberg (1985) and Lincoln (1989) found no direct evidence of higher organizational commitment among Japanese workers compared to U.S. workers. However, after controlling for the effect of low job satisfaction in Japan, they found organizational commitment in Japan to be significantly higher than in the United States. Decentralized and participatory management,

quality circle participation, and paternalistic welfare services were found to contribute to commitment in both countries. Employee tenure did not show positive links to commitment and morale.

Near (1989) used the same data set as Lincoln and Kalleberg (1985) but excluded managers from her sample. Again, the Japanese expressed lower levels of organizational commitment than the U.S. workers. In both countries, social interaction, fair treatment, and acceptable job content were related to high levels of commitment. The results did not support the argument that organization structure (e.g., centralization), context (e.g., dependence), or personnel practices (e.g., lifetime employment) have significant effects on lifetime commitment. Near concluded that personal responsibility for the employment decision may be lower in Japan and that the Western conception of commitment may not apply to other cultures.

It has long been known that Japanese workers tend to be less satisfied with their jobs than their Western counterparts (Azumi & McMillan, 1976; Cole, 1979; Naoi & Schooler, 1980; Odaka, 1975). Cole suggested that this may be because Japanese workers expect more from their jobs. Tung (1984) quoted a 1982 government survey in which the greatest sources of dissatisfaction among Japanese workers were low wages, long working hours, and short vacations. When workers were asked their reasons for staying in their current job, 33 percent said there was no difference between their company and other companies, 34 percent said that they had no alternative, and only 36 percent thought their job was worthwhile.

Thus, although the Japanese have a cultural tradition that would seem to encourage a strong bonding to the organization, and although Japanese organizations seemingly have characteristics that have been designed and are able to sponsor behavior suggesting commitment, Japanese workers express no more, if not less, underlying organizational commitment than their Western counterparts. The answer to this paradoxical situation (subject as it always is to the possibility of response bias mentioned earlier) may well lie in the history of Japanese organizational development.

A Possible Solution to the Paradox

A number of authors have argued that the practice of permanent employment did not grow out of traditional social relations but developed instead as a solution to labor unrest and the need to systematize labor market arrangements after World War I (Cole, 1971; Fruin, 1980; Nakane, 1972) and again after World War II (Cole, 1979). These paternalistic practices have been retained as an institutional pattern in postwar years. Cole (1971) claimed that a legitimizing management ideology was developed concurrently, utilizing "remoulded traditional symbols to relate the employee to the firm" (p. 52). According to his argument, Japanese leaders have used aspects of traditional attitudes and values to legitimize new economic practices. Similarly, Dore (1979) argued that while some characteristics of the Japanese employment system can be explained by the carryover of traditional patterns, the majority represent conscious institutional innovation adaptations of traditional employment and social patterns, or importations from foreign firms, or wholly indigenous inventions. Dunphy (1987) drew a similar conclusion: "Japanese managerial and political elites...used traditional values to legitimize (selected management practices), powerful socialization processes to inculcate associated behaviours, and material and moral incentives to reinforce those behaviours" (p. 454).

According to Cole (1979), "loyalty and commitment to an organization stem from the organization being the focus of normative solutions to central life problems" (p. 243). He argued that the unusual dependence of the Japanese on the organization stems from the fact that Japan has traditionally been a labor surplus economy and therefore workers had little opportunity to seek alternative employers and possessed little bargaining power. Dependence on the organization was also exacerbated by the lack

of public expenditure in social capital, a management–government alliance that inhibited worker efforts to collectively organize, and a heritage of ideology and past practices that could be mobilized to justify the dependency relationships that emerged. Cole argued that dependency alone does not result in the internalization of economic goals and may result in employee resentment and a sense of coercion. This may explain in part the low job satisfaction typically reported by Japanese workers. A reminder is also appropriate here of the general problem of questionnaire response bias noted earlier.

Cole (1971, 1979), Marsh and Mannari (1972), and Mroczowski and Hanaoka (1989) have noted changes in the Japanese economic environment that may be undermining the dependency of the worker on the organization. These include a labor shortage, a shift in emphasis away from seniority to job or skill classification as the basis for remuneration and promotion, an increase in midcareer recruitment, the legitimization of interfirm mobility via newspaper advertisements, and decreasing union membership. As Japan continues to move from a manufacturing economy toward a service economy, these trends are likely to continue, and company and work group loyalties will be replaced by greater individualism. The decreasing importance of manufacturing will be reflected in the decreasing importance of the company to the employee (Clark, 1979; Mroczowski & Hanaoka, 1989). Marsh and Mannari (1976, 1977) argued that the lack of correlation in their research between previous mobility and lifetime commitment norms and values indicated that these were becoming contingent and conditional (e.g., under certain conditions the employee will remain loyal to the company; if these conditions change, he or she will leave). As early as 1971, Cole (1971) noted that there was a shift away from cultural values that emphasized corporate loyalty to more instrumental values to be turned off and on in accordance with perceived self-interest. Cole concluded then that paternalistic employment practices had succeeded in temporarily offering sufficient psychological and economic incentives, as well as regulatory sanctions, to keep employees tied to one firm, but that changing environmental conditions would erode their efficacy.

Rohlen (1974) argued that Western theories of economic organization often assume voluntary participation by the organization's members. He claimed that his observations in Japan highlight "the fact that individual volition and the companion idea of the central labour market are only to be understood in the context of specific socio-cultural situations" (p. 91).

Adopting a similar but more extreme position, Mouer and Sugimoto (1986) argue that the group model of Japanese society is simply a very successfully propagated ideology that represents an example of how the Japanese elite controls and manipulates the rest of society. The authors do not dispute that the Japanese exhibit behavior that seems to indicate a high level of organizational commitment and loyalty but contend that there is insufficient comparative data on the underlying motivation that causes people to behave in that way. The authors discuss the manipulative and coercive controls in the workplace and society at large. While these also exist in Western society, the authors argue for the greater pervasiveness of their effects in Japanese society.

One way of summarizing and explaining the information so far accumulated is to say that Japanese organizations and their surrounding societal institutions have conspired to maximize behavioral commitment among Japanese workers; this is evident in long working hours, overt dedication to corporate ideals, conformity to corporate rules, and social bonding in the corporate context. They have not, however, succeeded in obtaining similarly high levels of underlying attitudinal commitment.

As Kashima and Callan point out in their chapter in this volume of the *Handbook*, there is a difference between the Japanese employee's commitment to work as a highly significant component of life, and the quite separate matter of commitment to a particular organization. The centrality of work itself is strongly supported by evidence from England and Misumi (1986).

An outcome of this is that, as the long-standing situation of a relative labor surplus gives way to a relative labor shortage and leaves the Japanese worker less constrained, we may observe more pursuit of self-advantages and more typically Western-type behavior. Both behavioral and attitudinal perspectives will be needed to monitor these changes, and the behavioral approach must remain suspect as an indicator of the deeper sources of commitment in the mind.

In their analysis of Japanese management, Sethi, Namiki, and Swanson (1984) put forward a strong argument for the need to study any particular management system within its social, cultural, political, and economic framework. Multidisciplinary approaches in studies of economic development and modernization are increasingly showing signs of bridge building between disciplines (Berger & Hsiao, 1988; Dernberger, 1990; Redding, 1982; Tu, 1989; Whitley, 1987, 1990). The cultural heritage of attitudes, values, and traditions and the institutional forces in the contemporary environment (including political, economic, familial, religious, and educational factors) shape the characteristics of both organization and individual and clearly influence the nature of their relationship.

Summary

The evidence presented suggests that the structure of the relationship between individual and organization in Japan takes on a distinct form. Below are features that distinguish it:

- A set of cultural values that predisposes individuals to a state of dependency

- A parallel set of predispositions for individuals to accept hierarchy and large vertical structures for attachment

- A traditionally strong affiliation with social groups related to work

- A work ethic expressed via frugality and discipline

- Traditional ethics emphasizing vertical exchanges of obligation

- A managerial ideology that offers institutional responses to the predispositions listed earlier and as a result achieves stable employee–firm relations

- A surrounding context in which neither labor mobility nor social welfare are highly developed, which thus encourages long-standing attachment

- A differentiated work force with wide variation in its reward and employment conditions

- An apparent leveling (as compared to the Western case) of the core components of satisfaction and employee commitment, as the interplay of what is offered and what is expected settle down at a conceivably (and very roughly) universal point of accommodation or balance between the individual and the organization; the Japanese are no more satisfied or committed than Westerners, but however much of these components exist is built on a different structure of forces

Attachment in the Chinese Family Business

In coming to terms with the question of organizational attachment among the overseas Chinese, it is necessary to rely more on literature that surrounds the topic rather than literature that demonstrates it empirically. It must also be admitted that less literature of this kind is available than literature on Japanese organizations.

There are a number of books about the overseas Chinese that have a historical, an anthropological, or a sociological focus. The most significant general books are by Purcell (1965), Wang (1981), Baker (1979), Godley (1981), and Pan (1990).

Studies based more specifically on subgroups of overseas Chinese in a particular country include: for Hong Kong, Osgood (1975), Lau (1982), and Wong (1988); for Taiwan, Cohen (1976); for Indonesia, Coppell (1983), Mackie (1976), and Willmott (1960); for the Philippines, Amyot (1973) and Wickberg (1965); for Malaysia, Jesudason (1989), Strauch (1981), and Hallgren (1986); and for Thailand, Skinner (1957, 1958). Valuable collections with regional coverage have also been edited by Willmott (1972), Lim and Gosling (1983), and Cushman and Wang (1988).

Studies with a more specifically economic bias include Aijmer (1979), Wu and Wu (1980), and Yoshihara (1988). Those dealing principally with business organization are Limlingan (1986), Omohundro (1981), Redding (1990), and Silin (1976).

Because so many overseas Chinese behavior patterns and values are traceable to traditional Chinese culture, the large body of literature on China itself needs also to be acknowledged as a source of ideas.

Goal Congruence

Goal congruence in the context of organization may be said to occur when the intended outcomes of work performed by organization members at different levels are similar, and when the legitimizing of authority by owners/managers is not a field of contention. It is our belief that both these conditions are met in the majority of Chinese family businesses. This is the case because (a) certain primary goals are extensively shared in the society and (b) the organization's design is a replica in many respects of the family structure seen in the society as the most natural and legitimate form of group.

A study that explored what the Chinese attribute wealth to (Furnham & Bond, 1986) provides insight into the apparent lack of tension between managers and employees. Compared to respondents in studies in Australia, Britain, and Canada, students in Hong Kong believed very strongly that wealth was the result of their own skill, effort, creativity, and timing. Thus, there is little sense that wealth is the preserve of certain sociopolitical/economic subgroups to which they are denied access. Instead, everyone is perceived to have equal chances at achieving wealth, and, consequently, those who succeed are respected rather than resented.

In this context there is little need for a managerial ideology that legitimizes the retention of power over others in terms of the managerial competence of its holders. Organizational decision power in the hands of successful owners is already legitimate and, consequencely, is stable. This in turn rests on the congruence of core values surrounding wealth, success, and social position.

A connected feature of relevance in accepting family business as natural and legitimate is the Confucian core value of filial piety and the way in which it buttresses paternalism (Redding, 1990).

In a comment on the apparent acceptance of paternalism as legitimate, Kao and Ng (1988, p. 266) observed that there were interesting inconsistencies in the image of the firm held by technicians in a large study conducted by Ng. On the one hand, such workers cherished the high trust ideal of paternalism and work community, but on the other hand, they castigated management for a tendency to exploit. Kao and Ng note the emergence of a passive fatalism in coping with the temptations of a capitalist laissez-faire context. Such passivity has also been reported among female industrial workers in Taiwan (Huang, 1977).

One is thus led to the conclusion that goal congruence in the Chinese case may be in part a function of the fatalistic acceptance of the status quo, and not entirely a matter of shared intentions. Even so, the role of Confucian culture in sponsoring the acceptance remains noteworthy.

The Work Ethic

If there is a strong work ethic generally in a population, then people entering the specific work context of an organization carry with them a tendency to behave diligently in the organization's interests as well as in their own. Dedication to the accumulation of wealth and the connected need for hard work have been commonly observed among the overseas Chinese (Lau, 1982; Ryan, 1961; Salaff, 1981) and is attributed to the general insecurity perceived by a migrant group living under uncertain political circumstances (Redding, 1990).

The general salience of what Kahn (1979) has termed the Confucian "seriousness about tasks" in the successful economic cultures of Pacific Asia has been pointed to in recent studies, which have isolated an Oriental value as an alternative to uncertainty avoidance in the Hofstede model, and as one in which the notion of persistence is dominant.

In an attempt to discern the pattern of Chinese values for comparison with Hofstede's Western values, Bond (1988) and Bond and Hofstede (1990) found three values that overlapped closely with three of Hofstede's, but one that did not. Bond labeled the nonoverlapping value "Confucian work dynamism." Its factor loadings are:

- Ordering relationships (.64)
- Thrift (.63)
- Persistence (.76)
- Having a sense of shame (.61)
- Reciprocation (−.58)
- Personal steadiness (−.76)
- Protecting your "face" (−.72)
- Respect for tradition (−.62)

The intriguing thing about this factor is its correlation of $r = .70$ with levels of economic growth from 1965 to 1984, accounting for 49 percent of the variance across 22 diverse societies. The complexities of causation in economic development make it exceptionally difficult to trace direct links between values and economic outcomes (Redding, 1982), but Bond contends that by separating the entrepreneurial factor in a manner proposed by Redding (1988), it is possible to detect connections between such values and the encouragement of the entrepreneurial role. People occupying such roles then act as catalysts in a wider context and are prone to exercise initiative in finding new wealth-creating opportunities and to have the organizing ability required for more complex business coordination, the latter skill being less universally available among them than the former (Hwang, 1990; Redding, 1990; Tam, 1990).

In a study that focused on the mutual perceptions of Japanese and Southeast Asian managers, Everett, Krishnan, and Stening (1984) provide some reflection on the Chinese work ethic. With a sample of 664 Japanese and 624 managers from the Association of Southeast Asian Nations (ASEAN) and Hong Kong, factor analysis was used to derive the main components of managerial perceptions of other managers in the region. Given 18 variables, the Singaporeans rated themselves most highly as ambitious, industrious, honest, and cautious, and the Hong Kong managers rated themselves most highly as industrious, assertive, cautious, and ambitious. The salience of industriousness and ambition is clearly high and contrasts with the perceived primary characteristics of non-Chinese ASEAN managers that emphasize more social sensitivity and factors such as politeness, patience, and cooperativeness. The predominantly Chinese groups in Singapore and Hong Kong rated themselves low on the congeniality factor and were seen similarly by others.

Closer analysis of work-related values by Hsu (1987) reveals a further important contingency, namely, the changes that may well be associated with development and modernization. His study of patterns of work goal importance among managers in Singapore and Taiwan revealed that the rankings of importance were different. In Singapore, the order was (a) job content and relationship, (b) job significance, and (c) organizational rewards. In Taiwan, the order was (a) organizational rewards, (b) job content and relationships, and (c) job significance. The different ranking in Singapore has also been noted by Redding and Richardson (1986) in a study comparing Singapore with Hong Kong, and the explanation is most likely that Singapore has distanced itself from its East Asian counterparts by moving earlier toward higher-order need satisfaction. This may be in part a result of growing wealth and clear progress in modernization, with all its ramifications. It may also be to some extent related to the Westernization of the industrial economy there, a result of which is that 55 percent of the industrial work force is employed in foreign-owned firms.

Affiliation and Group Membership

In understanding the organizational implications of collectivism, it is important to know if any particular collectivity has more salience than others. In other words, what is the primary group?

For the Chinese, the overwhelming evidence is that the primary group is the family and that it far supersedes any other as a locus of affiliation (Baker, 1979; Freedman, 1970; Lang, 1968; Lau, 1982). The importance of work group affiliation must be understood in this larger context, and any comparison with other cultures must take it into account. An organizational response to this is the construction of organizations as surrogate families (Redding, 1990, pp. 127–142), and we shall later consider paternalism as a further natural outcome. First, however, the workings of collectivism need closer scrutiny.

Studies of Chinese values have been reviewed by Yang (1986, p. 120), who considered the literature on Chinese personality and concluded that a greater emphasis on self-control and greater satisfaction in social life were what distinguished the Chinese from their counterparts in the West. There is also evidence in the data that social and moral values precede personal and competence values, thus suggesting the drives toward conformity commonly noted in Chinese behavior.

Yang (1986, p. 150) characterized the special features of traditional Chinese socialization as training in dependency, conformity, modesty, self-suppression and self-contentment, punishment preference, shaming strategy, parent centeredness, and multiple parenting (all family adults acting as parental surrogates). He concludes that these are main determinants of the Chinese personality, with its strong collectivism and its social, practical, and eclectic orientations.

It is also necessary to point out that the processes of modernization are evidently causing some transformation in this regard, and that the traditional social orientation is giving way gradually to more individual orientation (Yang, 1986, pp. 160–161).

In examining what they see as the "cultural concern for harmony-within-hierarchy," Bond and Hwang (1986, p. 216) began their discussion by naming the following as the essential elements in Confucianism:

- Man exists through, and is defined by, his relationships to others.

- These relationships are structured hierarchically.

- Social order is ensured through each party honoring the requirements in the role relationship.

The workings of a collectivist society, constructed as a dense fabric of interpenetrating networks, is then subjected to a review in which Hwang's theory of resource distribution is used to explain the processes of mutual exploitation (Bond & Hwang, 1986, p. 223). Key concepts in this are *guanxi* (relationship), *renqing* (favor), *mianzi* (face), and *bao* (reciprocation). Social resources traded between an allocator and a petitioner are allocated with regard to all four influences and result in three main categories of relationship. First, where ties are *expressive*, as within families, rules for resource distribution are based on need, more precisely, on the legitimate needs of others. Second, *instrumental* ties exist when two people interact temporarily and anonymously to achieve their own goals. Here the exchange rule is equity. Third, there are *mixed* ties in which people share some relationship—usually based on shared ascriptive characteristics such as common birthplace, school, or organization—and then use the connection in the power games surrounding the exchange of such things as money, goods, information, status, service, and affection. The affective component *(ganqing)*, or more simply "trust," can be enhanced by greater social exchange in Chinese society in the interests of this network construction and maintenance.

In a sense, the currency of much of this interaction is face, treated as a universal by Goffman (1955) and seen as the social value a person claims for him or herself. Its relevance in the organizational context has been described by Redding and Ng (1982), who found it commonly referred to in Cantonese descriptions of behavior in the fields of personnel management, marketing and sales, and the minutiae of management control and leadership behavior. Studies of its salience for the Chinese were summarized by Bond and Hwang (1986, pp. 244–246) in terms of a theory of Chinese power games—namely, that in a static society where major social resources are controlled by few allocators and distributed in line with their personal preferences, the petitioner's perceived power and status can influence an allocator's decision to help. This inevitably leads to a wide range of face behavior, but all such dyadic interactions are in turn embedded in a wider context in which everyone has an interest in the maintenance of the structural harmony, and this includes the preservation of the face of others, especially those of superiors. In a collectivist culture, one's face is more interconnected with that of others, and high-power-distance sensitivities enhance the discipline required to maintain a stable hierarchical order.

Avoidance of public conflict was found to be strong in a study by Bond, Hewstone, Wan, and Chiu (1984), and Leung and Wu (1990) have described the handling of dispute resolution in collectivist societies as being more likely to depend on mediation and arbitration than on adversarial adjudication. The related protection of group integrity and the consequent high resistance to group insult is described for the Chinese by Bond and Venus (1991) as also the tendency to deal with outsiders with less consideration for friendship (Bond & Leung, 1987).

Bond and Hwang (1986, p. 235) also report a study in which an attempt was made to discover the primary dimensions used in Chinese culture for attributing personality characteristics to others. Citing Norman (1963) and Goldberg (1980), they contend that English and American subjects use up to five dimensions: extroversion–introversion; good-naturedness–ill-temper; conscientiousness–unreliability; emotional stability–neuroticism; and cultured-ness–boorishness. Yang and Bond (1983) factor-analyzed Chinese descriptors in use and found that these yielded from three to six dimensions, depending on the target. Regardless of target, however, there was always a large first factor, labeled "social morality," which reflected the person's tendency to maintain social harmony by sacrificing self-interest (Yang & Bond, 1990). It is self-evident that the integrative capacities of people are of crucial importance in collectivist cultures.

In an empirical study of the influence of collectivism on social behavior, Wheeler, Reis, and Bond (1989) found that Chinese interact less frequently in dyads but more frequently in groups, and Chinese in groups say that they disclose more to each other than is reported by Americans. In an important clarification of the workings of collectivism, they noted that collectivists delineate sharply between ingroup and outgroups. This explains the paradox, also discussed by Triandis, Bontempo, Villareal, Asai, and Lucca (1988), that individualists may well be more sociable in individualistic societies because they have greater freedom of association and need a higher level of casual social skills to move in and out of these group allegiances.

Individual motivation appears also to be affected by the social embeddedness of people. The empirical literature on the motivational dispositions of overseas Chinese people has been usefully reviewed and summarized by Yang (1986). He concludes that compared to Western results, the pattern in terms of the *Edwards' Personal Preference Schedule* is relatively strong on Abasement, Achievement (social-oriented), Change, Endurance, Intraception,

Nurturance, and Order; moderate on Autonomy, Deference, Dominance, and Succorance, and low on Achievement (individual-oriented), Affiliation, Aggression, Exhibition, Heterosexuality, and Power.

The need to separate the important Achievement need into two components arose because of discrepancies in results from earlier studies that used only one category. Yang (1986) argues that it is valuable to distinguish between (a) social-oriented achievement motivation, which is "a kind of functionally unautonomized (hence still extrinsic and instrumental) desire in which the course of the achievement-related behaviour, the standards of excellence, and the evaluation of the performance are defined or determined by the significant others, the family, the group, or the society as a whole" (p. 114); and (b) individual-oriented achievement motivation, which is "a kind of functionally autonomized desire, in which the course of achievement-related behavior, the standards of excellence, and the evaluation of the performance or outcome are defined or determined by the actor himself or herself."

The impact of the dominant force of collectivism, already noted earlier by Triandis (this volume) and vividly evident in Hofstede's (1980) data, is clear from this pattern of motivational dispositions (see also Yu & Yang, 1992).

In the context of organization, it is then necessary to see the overseas Chinese as intensely social individuals whose behavior is mediated to an unusual degree by the social fabric. It is necessary also to acknowledge the salience of family as the primary unit of identity and the source of many motivations, especially those concerning the accumulation of wealth.

Mutual Obligation Bonding

It was noted, when considering the Japanese, that obligation bonding is both an important feature of the culture and an important component in the design of both large- and small-scale organizations. For the overseas Chinese it is also important but is acted out differently. The principal difference is that obligations are more specific and more interpersonal, and that bonding to the institution is less common. It is more a matter of bonding to the paterfamilias or his surrogate, and the process is conducted either in interpersonal terms or not at all. Loyalty to an organization per se appears to be rare.

In general discussions of societal trust processes among the overseas Chinese (Barton, 1983; Redding, 1990; Ryan, 1961; Silin, 1976; Wong, 1988), emphasis is commonly laid on two distinguishing features: first, the high importance attached to individual trustworthiness, especially in connection with its value for facilitating economic transactions; second, the highly selective nature of the bonds in a context of general mistrust. In other words, for the average Chinese, the social world is made up of those limited few who they can trust to a very high degree, and the remainder who are not trusted at all. Wong (1988) further points out, in a study of bonding, that the bonding in the economic sphere is not so much a matter of kin versus nonkin as it is a matter of the degrees of personalism in the connections.

In a study of the workings of what Hamilton (1989) has termed *"guanxi* capitalism" in Taiwan, Kao examined the workings of personal trust in 40 large companies. He concluded that personal trust is a first principle in selection decisions, especially when hiring executives. He also observed that the promotion of a relative cannot take place until the individual's networks of trust have been built inside the organization (Kao, 1990). He also cited a parallel study by Peng (1989) of 97 large companies in Taiwan that reaches the same conclusion, and summarized the position by saying, "The crucial point is that formal contractual rules are not the basic rules of the structure of everyday life-world" (Kao, 1990). A similar study in Singapore by Tong (1990) reaches the same conclusion. Kao furthermore defends the system as instrumentally rational in its capacity to reduce risk and implies that it is not a primitive

structure that is somehow prior to bureaucracy but rather a viable alternative.

The role of social networks among the overseas Chinese in the Philippines has been discussed by Omohundro (1981), who brings into the account the *compadre* (godfather) system commonly used in the Philippines to add ritual kin to the circle of blood relatives. In discussing intraorganizational relations, he notes that the most successful Chinese have the highest proportions of kinsmen and fictive kinsmen in their business lives as co-workers.

The contrast of the Chinese form of bonding with the form found in Japan has been discussed by Alston (1989), who compares the group-centered *wa* of the Japanese with the highly personalistic *guanxi* of the Chinese. Pointing out the equalizing of exchange that takes place in a typical *guanxi* tie and citing the definition by Pye (1982, p. 88) that it is best seen as friendship with overtones of unlimited exchange of favors, Alston notes that relations that are no longer profitable or equal can easily be dismantled. The result is "the economies in Taiwan and Hong Kong experience a large rate of both job mobility and entrepreneurship. Employees move whenever they see an advantage in doing so" (p. 28).

It is inevitable that, in the context of life in organizations, the *guanxi* ties of most relevance tend to be vertical and intrude into the field of leadership behavior and the workings of the authority structure. This may be seen to exhibit three characteristics, all of them aspects of paternalism—namely, clear understanding of authority relations, expectations from below about protection from above, and centralization of power and decision making.

Studies of Chinese attitudes, illuminating features more peripheral and more specific than values, have been discussed by Yang (1986) under the themes of authoritarianism and locus of control of reinforcement. Citing five substantial studies, he concluded that connections were evident between strong authoritarian attitudes among Chinese and filial piety and traditionalism. His conclusion is that Chinese are quite conspicuous in their deferential attitudes toward whomever or whatever they consider an authority (p. 127). Moreover, citing other studies on social principledness (understanding the abstract notion of sociopolitical responsibility at the societal level), he noted "a strong authoritarian orientation to defer without question to conventional authority and to accept unconditionally conventional norms and values" (p. 129).

Studies of locus of control cited by Yang (1986) indicate that Chinese beliefs in the influence of powerful others are stronger than those of Americans, although scores on internal control and the influence of chance are roughly equal.

Citing four studies in Taiwan, Bond and Hwang (1986, p. 253) concluded that Chinese leadership behavior was in part a function of organizational size and that at the typically small scale of most Chinese enterprises in Taiwan, an authoritarian style tempered by humanitarian sensitivities was the norm. They also warned, however, in line with a study by Hwang (1983), that "the more Chinese the style of management in an organization, the more deficient the perceived organizational climate" (Bond & Hwang, 1986, p. 253).

Ng has reported, from a study of 342 technicians in Hong Kong companies, that 73 percent perceived their supervisors to be "good in their job" and that 74 percent thought them to be "fair-minded" in their exercise of authority (Kao & Ng, 1988, p. 266). Such technical workers "tended to depict the employer as the head of a household," seeing this person as responsible for their welfare as opposed to seeing themselves collectively as their own protectors, an element with strong negative influence on the organization of trade union activity.

In a cross-cultural study of decision-making style comparing American, Japanese, and Chinese, Mann et al. (1990) concluded that although coping patterns of an apparently universal nature were visible, certain cultural influences were nevertheless also discernible. The strongest finding was of a difference in the level of self-confidence in decision making, held by the authors to reflect a greater emphasis on decision making as

an individual activity in the West and therefore thought to reflect its greater importance as a source of personal esteem. A second finding was that Japanese and Taiwanese (although not Hong Kong) subjects expressed higher levels of defensive avoidance (rationalization, buck passing, procrastination) than did Americans. The presumption was that group orientation would provide greater scope for individuals to leave difficult decisions to a respected authority without provoking criticism.

Bottger and Yetton (1987), in a study to determine whether participation is used for similar reasons and with similar results by both Singaporean/Hong Kong Chinese managers and Australian managers, discovered that the two groups responded in similar ways in terms of overall levels of participation. There was, however, significant variation in the conditions under which their decision making was effective. For the Chinese sample, effectiveness was more sensitive to the loss or gain of leader information than the loss or gain of leader power. For the Australians, the reverse was true, and they appeared more sensitive to changes in power than to changes in information.

These findings, which illuminate Australian and Chinese differences, are connected by Bottger and Yetton to data provided in Hofstede's (1980) survey. Power distance data indicate that Chinese managers have more fear of disagreeing with their superiors and lower preferences for consultation. Individualism data suggest that Chinese have a lower need for a sense of personal job accomplishment, lower need for personal recognition, and a higher need for working with cooperative people. In consequence, when faced with an absence of leader power, Chinese from a high-power-distance culture are still unlikely to challenge the leader. It is only when the leader does not know what to do that performance is affected.

Authoritarian leadership behavior is inevitably reflected in the structures of the organization, and this is revealed in an extension of the Aston studies of organizational structure (Redding, 1990; Redding & Pugh, 1986). Put simply, the findings indicate that Chinese organizations, which as one would anticipate, operate with relatively low structure because of their small scale, in fact use elaborate and detailed systems to control the work flow in the organization and monitor individual behavior. British and Japanese comparisons show distinctly higher levels of overall formalization than is found in Hong Kong, but do not focus especially on microcontrol of the individual. Similarly, in a study of norms of organizational design and management in Canada, Hong Kong, and China, Vertinsky, Lee, Tse, and Wehrung (1988) found that Hong Kong executives favored formalization of authority and evaluation structures more than their Canadian counterparts.

The selective use of discretion by the chief executive is visible in the decision centralization data from the Aston study (Redding, 1990), which indicate that decisions relating to people are retained by the chief executive more often than decisions in other fields, a pattern different from that in the United Kingdom and Japan. This echoes descriptions by Deyo (1978, 1983) of the overseas Chinese managerial process, in which the chief executive, by holding on to decisions about people, succeeds in sustaining his authority over the intermediate managers and supervisors, leaving them in turn in a position of dependence and limited power. The organizational limits to growth engendered by such paternalism are obvious. Perhaps less obvious is the capacity of the economic system as a whole to transcend such limitations by the use of interorganizational networking to achieve scale.

Hamilton (1984) has made an important contribution to the understanding of societal variations in processes of domination by introducing a distinction between the Western institutionalization of jurisdictions and the Chinese institutionalization of roles. An outcome is that in displaying obedience, a Chinese is not so much submitting him or herself to someone else's will as being faithful to the duties of his or her own position. Role compliance is a main

foundation of social structure and the guarantee of its stability.

The key role relationship in Chinese society is that of father–son (Hsu, 1967; Tu, 1989), a topic reviewed by Ho (1987), who concluded that

> the overall picture that emerges from a review of the social science literature is that father–child relations tend to be marked by affectional distance, perhaps even tension and antagonism, in contrast to warm and close mother–child (especially mother–son) relations. (p. 235)

In these circumstances, the maintenance of the social order comes to depend on role compliance, especially the fulfillment by the sons of the obligations of filial piety, rather than on affective bonding at the individual level.

A study by Richards (1954; reported by Yang, (1986, p. 141), which used Rorschach records on Hawaiian Chinese, revealed high levels of preoccupation with role playing as well as subjugation of basic feelings to demonstrations of polite manners. Security was evidently sought in making the correct impression, and spontaneity was hindered.

Further studies of Chinese behavior and temperament have "unanimously shown that Chinese people in general are inclined to be more restrained, cautious, patient, and self-contained and less impulsive, excitable, spontaneous, and natural than Americans" (Yang, 1986, p. 143).

Empirical Investigation of Employee Commitment

Three studies of organizational commitment using overseas Chinese samples may be considered here, with data from Singapore, Thailand, and Taiwan. Deyo studied operative work values among Chinese clerical and blue collar workers in large industrial firms in Bangkok and Singapore in an attempt to determine if ascribed values of work commitment, thrift, ambition, and economic acumen were traceable in a modern work force. He found that

Chinese white collar male workers ranked supervision and co-worker relations higher than their Thai counterparts. Among blue collar workers, this time compared with Malay equivalents, and, taking data for perceived degrees of importance, the Chinese "indicated far less personal involvement with the firm, co-workers, union, or the work itself than did their Malay counterparts" (Deyo, 1983, p. 223). There is thus evidence of psychological distancing from the firm itself, and, at least for white collar workers, the salience of co-worker relations.

In a study of employee commitment with a sample of 913 industrial workers in Taiwan, Mobley and Hwang (1982) found that patterns of response were similar to those for Western and Japanese samples and that the influences of personal, structural, role, and affective variables were also replicated. They did, however, warn that two different patterns of connection were evident for two different definitions of commitment. Although commitment defined either way was correlated with expected utility of present job, current job satisfaction, organization size, and respondent age, attitudinal commitment also yielded correlations with growth need strength and centrality of work, whereas behavioral commitment (seen as potential withdrawal) yielded correlations with expected utility of alternatives and delayed gratification. There is perhaps some circularity here as, for instance, expected utility of alternatives is predictably connected with a potential for withdrawal; but more importantly, there is clearly a need for greater definitional clarity if research is to accumulate effectively. The authors of the study conclude with this same plea.

In a study of the effects of organizational change on organizational commitment in a Taiwanese textile company with six factories, Yin (1989) reports the use of a commitment scale derived from the Mowday, Porter, and Steers model. An experiment was conducted to test the effects of two alternative means of restructuring the organization's computer-based information technology, namely by top–down implementation or by implementation after consultation. Using an experimental design with 720 pretest subjects and 720 post-test subjects (i.e., 120 subjects per factory), the aim of the research was to test the effects of restructuring on commitment. It yielded a number of findings of more specifically cross-cultural interest in addition to the main finding that computerization and restructuring do affect commitment.

The most intriguing finding was that commitment increased under the top–down implementation condition and decreased when delegation and consultation were used. Participation is clearly not a universal or automatic virtue. There were also indications that commitment is negatively correlated with structuring of activities via formalization, standardization, and specialization, and these lend support to the notion that comfort is derived from the unstructured, informally managed, more personalistic organizations that are so commonly found in the overseas Chinese culture.

Summary

No clear evidence exists to suggest that overseas Chinese as workers become more or less closely bonded to their organizations than do members of other cultures. There are, however, two specifically cultural factors that impose themselves on any consideration of the question. First, organizational control in these typically small or concentrated organizations overlaps with ownership, and ownership normally implies intense attachment and commitment for key individuals.

Second, for the general run of employees, their primary loyalties and identities are directed back into their own families. This engenders a pragmatic and calculative view of the bond with the organization, the managerial response to which is to offer a surrogate family. Legitimizing values in the Confucian ethic then supports the paternalist ethos that centralizes authority, and supports also the search for social harmony that sets the tone for much organizational behavior.

The Korean Case

Compared with Japan, relatively little has been published about employee attachment to South Korean organizations. Yet the efficiency of these organizations is suggested by four decades of successful national economic growth. While it is not our intention to focus on the South Korean economy, it is essential to understand the environment within which these organizations have prospered.

The economic miracle came in response to the five years of turmoil that accompanied liberation, independence, and war (Kim, 1988). During this time, agriculture remained the country's only large industry. Given the lack of infrastructure, industrial output during the 1960s came largely from turnkey operations (Kwak, 1989).

In an attempt to increase the country's exports, the government implemented several policies that had a profound effect on business. Laws were created to protect infant industries, and the government provided direct support to companies. Limited foreign exchange allowed for few imports, and the growing efficiency of domestic production was protected (Kwak, 1989). Over time, the economy grew in response to these economic policies, and the *chaebols* were formed (Jones & Sakong, 1980; Yoo & Lee, 1987). These family owned and controlled conglomerates continue to play a major role in the South Korean economic expansion.

Only one study has directly measured organizational commitment for Korean employees. Luthans, McCaul, and Dodd (1985) compared the overall level of attitudinal commitment for American, Japanese, and Korean employees. Using the *Organizational Commitment Questionnaire* (Porter, 1974), they concluded that the level of commitment was lower for the Korean and Japanese employees than for their U.S. counterparts. Luthans, McCaul, and Dodd also found commitment to be positively related to age and tenure. Given that age and tenure have been positively related to commitment in other countries, their data suggest that organizational

commitment levels are based, at least partly, on universal and not culture-specific values. These results raise questions about the meaning of commitment in Korea, and also pose puzzles about the sources of Korean productivity that is so visible at the macro level.

While more research is needed, it appears from this study that the attitudinal approach to commitment is unable to explain the sources of the Korean dedication to work apparent from other criteria. With so little research into Korean organizational commitment, it is necessary to turn to studies that explore managerial values, descriptive accounts of current organizational characteristics, and Korean culture for clues into employee attachment to the firm.

In a 1975 study, England compared the value systems for American, Japanese, Korean, Indian, and Australian managers. While he did not directly measure commitment levels, his focus on values is pertinent, given the assumption that values influence, among other things, a manager's participation in interpersonal relationships, acceptance of organizational goals, and perceptions of organizational success and achievement. We argue that these values have the potential to influence the way individuals perceive, attach to, and commit to an organization.

England (1975) identified several values that are characteristic of Korean managers. He found that Korean managers internalize organizational goals to a lesser extent than Japanese and American managers. In addition, we found that Koreans exhibit a high level of competence and achievement orientation, but this drive is focused more toward individual achievement than organizational achievement. The individualism, as opposed to group-centeredness, of Koreans is also suggested in a study by Graham, Campbell, and Meissner (1988, p. 14), which reported that in a series of negotiation experiments, Koreans were three times more likely than Japanese to say no and were more likely to interrupt and issue commands.

Descriptions of Korean organizational characteristics also provide insights into the employee–employer relationship. Traditionally, control of a business is held by the head of a family. Business relationships are paternalistic and founded upon family ties. People are commonly hired on the basis of personalistic ties. Roughly one-third of all executive officers in Korea's largest business groups are relatives of fellow employees or employers (Alston, 1989, p. 29). Promotions and salary are based on seniority and loyalty to the firm. Organizations are based on a natural hierarchy, with family relationships dictating upward mobility (Yoo & Lee, 1987). Supervisors and managers are to be obeyed and respected as if they were the family head.

Korean culture helps to explain the central role of this family system. The Korean family environment is influenced by classical Chinese and Confucian values (Osgood, 1951). It is also, as with the Chinese, an outcome of insecurity, here exacerbated by colonial experience, invasion, and war, since South Koreans turned to the family unit as a means of survival. This reliance on the family has remained a cornerstone of Korean society (Crane, 1978; Kim & Utterbuck, 1989).

The family system in Korea is based strictly on blood relationships (Yoo & Lee, 1987). All other loyalties (including those to organizations, personal friends, and national causes) are considered secondary to the needs of the family (Jacobs, 1985). Within the family unit itself, a strict hierarchy of unequal relationships exists following the usual Confucian model. While Western relationships are often founded on equity, Korean relationships remain hierarchical and highly emotional (Kim, 1989). It is upon this family model that organizations and business relationships are based. More than is the case in other capitalist economies, descriptions of organizational behavior refer to discipline, vertical order, and the metaphor of a military structure (Liebenberg, 1982; Woronoff, 1983). At the same time, the forces of modernization and economic prosperity have provided more young people with the education necessary to become professional managers and specialists. In turn, this education has altered their expec-

tations of the organization. These changes are influencing current management techniques; for instance, admittance to the *chaebols* is determined almost entirely by public examination.

With a larger and more educated work force, organizations in Korea are now trying to balance traditional policies based on paternalism and Confucian principles with modern policies founded on individual merit and contribution to the firm. Young people are turning away from paternalism in favor of a more impersonal system that allows them to express their own views. Some organizations are now basing promotions on ability rather than the employee's relationship with top management. Professionally qualified individuals are now rising to top management levels and providing support to the controlling family members. These changes are facing resistance from older employees, who prefer promotions and pay raises based on seniority and loyalty to the firm. Top executives are now searching for the right balance between old and new, paternalism and meritocracy (Woronoff, 1983).

The limited sources we have available suggest that in Korea, commitment is primarily a function of Confucian role compliance and its interaction with paternalist structures. The success of Korean organizations provides circumstancial evidence that employees behave in a committed way, but the nature of that psychological interaction is still very little understood.

Implications for Theory and Research

We began this chapter with the proposition that the nature of the attachment between an individual and an organization is affected by the individual's interpretation of what an organization means for him or her, and that such variations in meaning would require variations in explanatory theory.

The attachment of a person to an organization is a process of cooperation conducted with more or less intensity or commitment, depending on that individual's own guidelines for cooperation, and we take the notion of cooperation as central to our critique of universalist theorizing in the description of organization. In creating the managerial systems and in working out a particular way of exercising power in the interests of coordination, managers respond to their society's ground rules for effective cooperation and thus embed their organizations in the local cultural matrix.

Alston (1989) has succinctly captured the flavor of what we are exploring in the following précis of East Asian organizational variations:

> In Japan, business relations operate within the context of *wa,* which stresses group harmony and social cohesion.
> In China, business behaviour revolves around *guanxi* or personal relations.
> For Korea, activities involve concern for *inhwa,* or harmony based on respect of hierarchical relationships, including obedience to authority. (p. 26)

How, then, will the process of psychological bonding be different, and, in turn, how differently will organizations be perceived and defined by their members? How may our understanding be improved?

As a means of considering these issues, certain fields of theory will be considered, in the light of the information we have reviewed, to see if there are predictable needs for adjustment. These fields are organization theory, motivation theory, and leadership theory.

Organization Theory

By *organization theory* we refer here to studies that take organization structure as their *explanandum.* Two broad categories of theorizing may be identified: In the first place are the positivist explanations of structure that see it as contingent on a set of identifiable variables, such as environmental uncertainty or technology, and that describe organizations as varying along a set of dimensions such as structuring of

activities and centralization (Donaldson, 1985; Pugh & Hickson, 1976); in the second place are the theories that attempt a universal typology, the most elaborate and widely accepted of which is that of Mintzberg (1979, 1989). In this case, the theory of types revolves around the notion of coordination and the various processes and structures required to achieve it, and the organization is presented as a configuration of more or less balanced characteristics with five pure manifestations and any number of hybrids in between, in conceptual space.

Both theoretical approaches attempt to encompass all kinds of organization and, given the elasticity possible in defining concepts, will always be capable of squeezing in cases that might arguably be outside the reach of the main logics of the framework. Our concern here is not, therefore, to demonstrate that certain kinds of organization are clearly outside such frameworks, but more simply to pose the question, do the underlying logics of current Western organization theory cover the nature of East Asian organizing well enough to do justice to the problem of understanding its real nature?

In posing such a question and dealing with it in a restricted space, it is proposed simply to contend that the following key characteristics of East Asian organizations are inadequately dealt with—the variables used in the core theory do not address such influences:

- The hierarchical ordering of high-power-distance cultures that provides an invisible, informal, given vertical structure and influences the nature of hierarchical structuring required

- The influence of reciprocity norms on the achievement of cooperation between leaders and subordinates, and thus the structural implications of Oriental paternalism

- The influence of varying definitions of the *collectivity* to which a person belongs in collectivist cultures, and (especially in cases where this is a work group) the way in which coordination and cooperation are influenced

- The influence of interorganizational networking and the informal but powerful coupling of organizations on the definition of organizational boundaries; the understanding of variations in the clarity/diffuseness of what the organization actually is

Motivation Theory

Motivation theory similarly presents itself as universalist by using variables apparently capable of encompassing all determinants. Again, the issue is not whether such theory has something missing, but whether its design is not biased. One might question, for instance, the ability of standard theory to explain adequately the following forces:

- The maintenance of face and similar manifestations of interpersonal sensitivity that influence behavior

- At a deeper level, the power of social embeddedness in mediating the connections between an individual's stimulus and response pattern

- The significance of different need structures for appropriate organizational responses when the body of managerial tradition visible in the literature derives from the fostering of self-actualization

Leadership Theory

The leadership theory referred to here is the research-based, positivist, fairly micro-level study of leadership typified by the Ohio State Leadership studies and work such as that by Fiedler (1967) and other analysts of style using variables from mainly Western-based research.

Although using apparently all-encompassing categories, the assumptions about the

universality of its logic is worthy of challenge. In the East Asian context, the leader–subordinate bond is heavily influenced by cultural factors such as:

- Dependence needs, especially in Japan, which tend to widen the scope of leader–subordinate interaction and also provide it with an imported subliminal structure

- Strongly developed patterns of role compliance, buttressed by societally defined notions of authority, which prestructure many vertical relationships

- Ethics of paternalism, which, in the Confucian schema, stress responsibility for subordinate welfare as a source of legitimacy for power holders and have consequent implications for the behavior of leaders and the responses of subordinates

Conclusion

The issues just outlined become our recommended research agendas, and rather than elaborate further, we shall conclude by the reporting of a piece of research that addresses one of them precisely. Its findings are highly supportive, suggestive, and encouraging, and it may serve as an exemplar.

In studying the generality of leadership style measures across cultures, Smith, Misumi, Tayeb, Peterson, and Bond (1989) analyzed shop-floor work teams and their supervisors in Britain, the United States, Hong Kong, and Japan, with a total of 1,177 respondents. Using Misumi's notion of a distinction between a general structure in leadership and variations in its specific expression (Misumi & Peterson, 1985), they took the view that although general findings might be true and consistent with general theory, their meaning could only be understood in light of the interpretive framework of a particular setting. For example, consideration in an individualist culture might mean respecting subordinates' autonomy; in a collectivist culture, it might mean more interaction with them.

Their findings confirmed that although trans-cultural dimensions of leader style can be identified, their meaning in different cultures varies. The clearest differentiation of performance and maintenance behaviors (e.g., initiating structure and consideration) occurs in the United States. In other cultures, task behaviors can also connote consideration and considerate behaviors used to facilitate task issues.

Within the Western data, behaviors that pressure subordinates are a much more significant component of performance than they are in Eastern data. Conversely, planning and goal facilitation are much stronger in the Eastern conception of performance, and performance and maintenance are less distinct from each other.

Such research indicates that making use of general theory requires substantial local interpretation and understanding. The research work needed to provide this enrichment is only just beginning.

This research owes much to the assistance of Helga Overdyck, which is gratefully acknowledged. It has also benefited greatly from the support of the Institute for the Study of Economic Culture, Boston University, under the directorship of Peter Berger, and our gratitude is also acknowledged. This chapter has also benefited from the helpful comments of Lyman Porter, Geert Hofstede, Michael Bond, Harry Triandis, and Richard Whitley.

References

Abegglen, J., & Stalk, G. W. (1985). *Kaisha.* New York: Basic Books.

Aijmer, G. (1979). Economic man in Shatin: Vegetable gardens in a Hong Kong valley. *Scandinavian Institute of Asian Studies Monograph Series,* No. 43. London: Curzon Press.

Alston, J. P. (1989, March–April). *Wa, Guanxi,* and *Inhwa:* Managerial principles in Japan, China, and Korea. *Business Horizons,* 26–31.

Amyot, J. (1973). *The Manila Chinese: Familism in the Philippine environment.* Manila: Ateneo de Manila University Press.

Angle, H. L., & Perry, J. L. (1981). An empirical assessment of organizational commitment and organizational effectiveness. *Administrative Science Quarterly, 26,* 1–14.

Atsumi, R. (1979). *Tsukiai*—Obligatory personal relationships of Japanese white-collar employees. *Human Organization, 38*(1), 63–70.

Aven, F. F. (1988). *A methodological examination of the attitudinal and behavioural components of organizational commitment.* Unpublished doctoral dissertation, University of Colorado, Boulder.

Azumi, K., & McMillan, C. J. (1975). Culture and organization structure: A comparison of Japanese and British organizations. *International Studies of Management and Organization, 5*(1), 35–47.

Baker, H. R. D. (1979). *Chinese family and kinship.* London: Macmillan.

Bantug-Hovarth, V. (1985). Paternalism and productivity. *Euro-Asia Business Review, 4*(3), 5–8.

Barber, B. (1983). *The logic and limits of trust.* New Brunswick, NJ: Rutgers University Press.

Barnard, C. (1938). *The functions of the executive.* Cambridge, MA: Harvard University Press.

Barton, C. A. (1983). Trust and credit: Some observations regarding business strategies of overseas Chinese traders in Vietnam. In L. Y. C. Lim & L. A. P. Gosling (Eds.), *The Chinese in Southeast Asia: Vol. 1. Ethnicity and economic activity* (pp. 46–64). Singapore: Maruzen Asia.

Becker, H. S. (1960). Notes on the concept of commitment. *American Journal of Sociology, 66,* 32–40.

Berger, P. L. (1986). *The capitalist revolution.* New York: Basic Books.

Berger, P. L., & Hsiao, M. H. H. (1988). *In search of an East Asian development model.* New Brunswick, NJ: Transaction Books.

Boisot, M., & Child, J. (1990). Efficiency, ideology and tradition in the choice of transactions governance structures: The case of China as a modernizing society. In S. R. Clegg & S. G. Redding (Eds.), *Capitalism in contrasting cultures* (pp. 281–313). New York: de Gruyter.

Bond, M. H. (1988). Invitation to a wedding: Chinese values and global economic growth. In D. Sinha & H. S. R. Kao (Eds.), *Social values and development: Asian perspectives.* New Delhi: Sage.

Bond, M. H., & Venus, C. K. (1991). Resistance to group or personal insults in an ingroup or outgroup context. *International Journal of Psychology, 26*(1), 83–94.

Bond, M. H., & Hofstede, G. (1990). The cash value of Confucian values. In S. R. Clegg & S. G. Redding (Eds.), *Capitalism in contrasting cultures.* New York: de Gruyter.

Bond, M. H., & Hwang, K. K. (1986). The social psychology of Chinese people. In M. H. Bond (Ed.), *The psychology of the Chinese people.* Hong Kong: Oxford University Press.

Bond, M. H., & Leung, K. (1987). *The dynamics of cultural collectivism: Dividing a reward with a stranger in Hong Kong and the United States.* Working paper, Department of Psychology, Chinese University of Hong Kong.

Bond, M. H., Hewstone, M., Wan, K. C., & Chiu, C. K. (1984). *Group-serving attributions across intergroup contexts: Cultural differences in the explanation of sex-typed behaviours.* Working paper, Department of Psychology, Chinese University of Hong Kong.

Bottger, P. C., & Yetton, P. W. (1987). Managerial decision-making: Comparison of participative decision methods in Australian and Singaporean/Hong Kong Chinese samples. *Australian Journal of Management,* 12(2).

Buchanan, B. (1974). Building organizational commitment: The socialization of managers in work organizations. *Administrative Science Quarterly,* 12, 533–546.

Clark, R. (1979). *The Japanese company.* New Haven, CT: Yale University Press.

Cohen, M. L. (1976). *House united, house divided: The Chinese family in Taiwan.* New York: Columbia University Press.

Cole, R. E. (1971). The theory of institutionalization: Permanent employment and tradition in Japan. *Economic Development and Cultural Change,* 20(1), 47–70.

Cole, R. E. (1979). *Work, mobility and participation.* Berkeley, CA: University of California Press.

Coppel, C. A. (1983). *Indonesian Chinese in crisis.* Kuala Lumpur, Malaysia: Oxford University Press.

Crane, P. S. (1978). *Korean patterns.* Seoul, Korea: Kwangjin.

Cushman, J., & Wang, G. (Eds.). (1988). *Changing identities of the Southeast Asian Chinese since World War II.* Hong Kong: Hong Kong University Press.

Dannhaeuser, N. (1981). Evolution and devolution of downward channel integration in the Philippines. *Economic Development and Cultural Change,* 29(3), 577–595.

De Bettignies, H. C. (1973). Japanese organizational behaviour: A psycho-cultural approach. In D. Graves (Ed.), *Management research: A cross-cultural perspective.* Amsterdam: Elsevier.

Dernberger, R. (1990). *Introduction, workshop no. 1 on comparative analyses of the development process in East and Southeast Asia: An integrated interdisciplinary approach.* East-West Center, Honolulu.

Deyo, F. C. (1978). Local foremen in multinational enterprise: A comparative case study of supervisory role—tensions in Western and Chinese factories of Singapore. *Journal of Management Studies,* 15, 308–317.

Deyo, F. C. (1983). Chinese management practices and work commitment in comparative perspective. In L. A. P. Gosling & L. Y. C. Lim (Eds.), *The Chinese in Southeast Asia: Vol. 2. Identity, culture and politics.* Singapore: Maruzen Asia.

Doi, T. (1973). *The anatomy of dependence.* Tokyo: Kodansha International.

Donaldson, L. (1985). *In defence of organization theory.* Cambridge, MA: Cambridge University Press.

Dore, R. P. (1973). *British factory, Japanese factory: The origins of national diversity in industrial relations.* Berkeley, CA: University of California Press.

Dore, R. P. (1979). More about late development. *Journal of Japanese Studies,* 5, 137–151.

Dunphy, D. C. (1987). Convergence/divergence: A temporal view of the Japanese enterprise and its management. *Academy of Management Review,* 12(3), 445–459.

Dunphy, D. C., & Stening, B. W. (1984). *Japanese organization behaviour and management: An annotated bibliography.* Hong Kong: Asian Research Service.

England, G. W. (1975). *The manager and his values.* Cambridge, MA: Ballinger.

England, G. W., & Misumi, T. (1986). Work centrality in Japan and the United States. *Journal of Cross-Cultural Psychology,* 17, 399–416.

Etzioni, A. (1975). *A comparative analysis of complex organizations.* New York: Free Press.

Everett, J. E., Krishnan, A. R., & Stening, B. W. (1984). *Southeastern Asian managers.* Singapore: Eastern Universities Press.

Fei, X. T. (1939). *Rural China.* Shanghai: Guancha She.

Fiedler, F. E. (1967). *A theory of leadership effectiveness.* New York: McGraw-Hill.

Freedman, M. (1970). Introduction. In M. Freedman (Ed.), *Family and kinship in Chinese society.* Stanford, CA: Stanford University Press.

Fruin, W. M. (1980). The family as a firm and the firm as a family in Japan: The case of the Kikkoman Shoyin Co. Ltd. *Journal of Family History, 5,* 432–449.

Furnham, A., & Bond, M. H. (1986). *Hong Kong Chinese explanations for wealth.* Working paper, Department of Psychology, Chinese University of Hong Kong.

Godley, M. 1981). *Mandarin capitalists from the Nanyang.* Cambridge, MA: Cambridge University Press.

Goffman, E. (1955). On face-work: An analysis of ritual elements in social interaction. *Psychiatry, 18,* 213–231.

Goldberg, L. R. (1980, May). *Some ruminations about the structure of individual differences: Developing a common lexicon for the major characteristics of human personality.* Paper presented at the annual meeting of the Western Psychological Association, Honolulu.

Graham, J., Campbell, N., & Meissner, H. G. (1988). *Culture, negotiations, and international co-operative ventures* (International Business Education and Research Program working paper No. 8). Los Angeles: University of Southern California, Graduate School of Business Administration.

Granovetter, M. (1985). Economic action and social structure: The problem of embeddedness. *American Journal of Sociology, 91*(3), 481–501.

Haitani, K. (1976). *The Japanese economic system.* Lexington, KY: Heath.

Hallgren, C. (1986). *Morally united and politically divided: The Chinese community of Penang* (Stockholm Studies in Social Anthropology 16). Stockholm: University of Stockholm.

Hamilton, G. G. (1984). Patriarchalism in imperial China and Western Europe: A revision of Weber's sociology of domination. *Theory and Society, 13,* 393–425.

Hamilton, G. G. (1989). *Patterns of Asian capitalism: The cases of Taiwan and South Korea* (Program in East Asian Culture and Development Research Working Paper Series No. 28). Davis, CA: University of California, Institute of Governmental Affairs.

Hirschmeier, J., & Yui, T. (1981). *The development of Japanese business, 1600–1980* (2nd ed.). Boston: Allen & Unwin.

Ho, D. Y. F. (1987). Fatherhood in Chinese culture. In M. E. Lamb (Ed.), *The father's role: Cross-cultural perspectives.* Hillsdale, NJ: Erlbaum.

Hodgetts, R. M., & Luthans, F. (1989). Japanese human resource management practices: Separating fact from fiction. *Personnel, 66*(4), 42–45.

Hofstede, G. (1980). *Culture's consequences.* London: Sage.

Hofstede, G. (1984). Cultural dimensions in management and planning. *Asia Pacific Journal of Management, 1*(2), 81–99.

Hofstede, G. (1992). *Cultures and organizations.* London: McGraw-Hill.

Hrebiniak, L. G., & Alutto, J. A. (1972). Personal and role-related factors in the development of organizational commitment. *Administrative Science Quarterly, 17,* 555–572.

Hsu, F. L. K. (1967). *Under the ancestor's shadow: Kinship, personality and social mobility in village China.* New York: Doubleday.

Hsu, P. S. C. (1987). Patterns of work goal importance: A comparison of Singapore and Taiwanese managers. *Asia-Pacific Journal of Management, 4*(3), 152–166.

Huang, F. S. (1977). *Female workers and industrialization in Taiwan.* Taipei: Mutong.

Hwang, K. K. (1983). Business organizational patterns and employees' working morale in Taiwan. *Bulletin of the Institute of Ethnology, Academia Sinica, 56,* 85–133.

Hwang, K. K. (1990). The modernization of Chinese family business [Special issue]. *International Journal of Psychology, 5,* 6.

Jacobs, N. (1958). *The origin of modern capitalism and Eastern Asia.* Hong Kong: Hong Kong University Press.

Jacobs, N. (1985). *The Korean road to modernization and development.* Urbana: University of Illinois Press.

Jesudason, J. V. (1989). *Ethnicity and the economy: The state, Chinese business and multinationals in Malaysia.* Singapore: Oxford University Press.

Johnson, C. (1982). *Miti and the Japanese miracle.* Stanford, CA: Stanford University Press.

Jones, L. P., & Sakong, Il. (1980). *Government, business and entrepreneurship in economic development: The Korean case.* Cambridge, MA: Harvard University Press.

Kahn, H. (1979). *World economic development: 1979 and beyond.* London: Croom Helm.

Kamata, S. (1973). *Jidosha Zetsubo Kojo (Deadened at the auto plant: The diary of a seasonal employee).* Tokyo: Gendaisha Shuppansha.

Kao, C. S. (1990). The role of personal trust in large businesses in Taiwan. In G. G. Hamilton (Ed.), *Business groups and economic development in East Asia*. Hong Kong: Center of Asian Studies.

Kao, H. S. R., & Ng, S. H. (1988). Minimal self and Chinese work behaviour: Psychology of the grass roots. In D. Sinha & H. S. R. Kao (Eds.), *Social values and development: Asian perspectives*. New Delhi: Sage.

Karsh, B. (1984, June). Human resources management in Japanese large-scale industry. *Journal of Industrial Relations Management*, pp. 226–245.

Keys, J. B., & Miller, T. R. (1984). The Japanese management theory jungle. *Academy of Management Review, 9*(2), 342–353.

Kim, D. K. (1989). The impact of traditional Korean values on Korean patterns of management. In D. K. Kim & L. Kim (Eds.), *Management behind industrialization: Readings in Korean business*. Seoul, Korea: Korea University Press.

Kim, K. D. (1988). The distinctive features of South Korea's development. In P. L. Berger & M. H. H. Hsiao (Eds.), *In search of an East Asian development model*. New Brunswick, NJ: Transaction Books.

Kim, L., & Utterback, J. M. (1989). The evolution of organizational structure and technology in a developing country. In D. K. Kim & L. Kim (Eds.), *Management behind industrialization: Readings in Korean business*. Seoul, Korea: Korea University Press.

Kwak, S. I. (1989). Corporate strategy in Korean corporations. In D. K. Kim & L. Kim (Eds.), *Management behind industrialization: Readings in Korean business*. Seoul, Korea: Korea University Press.

Lang, O. (1946). *Chinese family and society*. New Haven, CT: Yale University Press.

Lau, S. K. (1982). *Society and politics in Hong Kong*. Hong Kong: Chinese University Press.

Lebra, T. S. (1976). *Japanese patterns of behaviour*. Honolulu: University of Hawaii Press.

Leung, K., & Wu, P. G. (1990). Dispute processing: A cross-cultural analysis. In R. Brislin (Ed.), *Applied cross-cultural psychology*. Newbury Park, CA: Sage.

Levine, S. B., & Kawada, S. B. (1980). *Human resources in Japanese industrial development*. Princeton, NJ: Princeton University Press.

Liebenberg, R. D. (1982). *Japan incorporated and "the Korean troops," A comparative analysis of Korean business organizations*. Unpublished master's thesis, University of Hawaii, Honolulu.

Lim, L. Y. C., & Gosling, L. A. P. (1983). *The Chinese in Southeast Asia: Vol. 1. Ethnicity and economic activity*. Singapore: Maruzen Asia

Limlingan, V. S. (1986). *The overseas Chinese in ASEAN: Business strategies and management practices*. Manila: Vita Development Corporation.

Lincoln, J. R. (1989). Employee work attitudes and management practice in the U.S. and Japan: Evidence from a large comparative survey. *California Management Review, 32*(1), 89–106.

Lincoln, J. R., Hanada, M., & Olsen, J. (1981). Cultural orientations and individual reactions to organizations: A study of employees of Japanese-owned firms. *Administrative Science Quarterly, 26*, 93–115.

Lincoln, J. R., & Kalleberg, A. L. (1985). Work organization and workforce commitment: A study of plants and employees in the U.S. and Japan. *American Sociological Review, 50*, 738–760.

Logan, G. M. (1984). Loyalty and a sense of purpose. *California Management Review, 27*(1), 149–156.

Luthans, F., McCaul, H. S., & Dodd, N. G. (1985). Organizational commitment: A comparison of American, Japanese, and Korean employees. *Academy of Management Journal, 28*(1), 213–219.

Mackie, J. A. C. (Ed.). (1976). *The Chinese in Indonesia*. Sydney: Nelson.

Mann, L., et al. (1990). *Cross-cultural and gender differences in self-reported decision-making style and confidence*. Working paper, Department of Psychology, Flinders University, Flinders, Australia.

Marsh, R. M., & Mannari, H. (1972). A new look at lifetime commitment in Japanese industry. *Economic Development and Cultural Change, 20*(4), 611–630.

Marsh, R. M., & Mannari, H. (1976). *Modernization and the Japanese factory*. Princeton, NJ: Princeton University Press.

Marsh, R. M., & Mannari, H. (1977). Organizational commitment and turnover: A prediction study. *Administrative Science Quarterly, 22*, 57–75.

Maruyama, M. (1974). Paradigmatology and its application to cross-disciplinary, cross-professional, and cross-cultural communication. *Dialectica, 28*(3–4), 135–196.

McMillan, C. J. (1985). *The Japanese industrial system*. Berlin: de Gruyter.

Meaning of Work International Research Team. (1986). *The meaning of work: An international perspective*. New York: Academic Press.

Mendenhall, M. E., & Oddou, G. (1986). The cognitive, psychological and social contexts of Japanese management. *Asia Pacific Journal of Management, 4*(1), 24–37.

Meyer, J. P., & Allen, N. J. (1984). Testing the side-bet theory of organizational commitment: Some methodological considerations. *Journal of Applied Psychology, 69*, 372–378.

Mintzberg, H. (1979). *The structuring of organization.* Englewood Cliffs, NJ: Prentice-Hall.

Mintzberg, H. (1985). *Mintzberg on management.* New York: Free Press.

Misumi, J., & Peterson, M. F. (1985). The Performance-Maintenance (PM) theory of leadership: Review of a Japanese research program. *Administrative Science Quarterly, 30*, 198–223.

Miyajima, R. (1986). Organization ideology of Japanese managers. *Management International Review, 26*(1), 73–76.

Mobley, W. H., & Hwang, K. K. (1966). Personal, role, structural, alternative and affective correlates of organizational commitment (Tech. Rep. No. 2-1987). College Station: Texas A and M University, Department of Management.

Moore, B. (1966). *Social origins of dictatorship and democracy.* London: Penguin.

Mouer, R., & Sugimoto, Y. (1986). *Images of Japanese society: A study in the social construction of reality.* London: KPI.

Mowday, R. T., Porter L. W., & Steers, R. M. (1982). *Employee-organization linkages: The psychology of commitment, absenteeism and turnover.* New York: Academic Press.

Mroczkowski, T., & Hanaoka, M. (1989, Winter). Continuity and change in Japanese management. *California Management Review*, pp. 39–53.

Murakami, T., Nishiwaki, T. et al. (1991). *Strategy for creation.* Cambridge, MA: Woodhead.

Nakamura, H. (1964). *Ways of thinking of Eastern peoples.* Honolulu: University of Hawaii Press.

Nakane, C. (1972). *Japanese society.* Los Angeles: University of California Press.

Naoi, A., & Schooler, C. (1980). Occupational conditions and psychological functioning in Japan. *American Journal of Sociology, 90*(4), 729–752.

Near, J. P. (1989). Organizational commitment among Japanese and U.S. workers. *Organization Studies, 10*(3), 281–300.

Needham, J. (1956). *Science and civilization in China* (Vol. 2). Cambridge, MA: Cambridge University Press.

Nonaka, I., & Johansson, J. K. (1985). Japanese management: What about the "hard" skills? *Academy of Management Review, 10*, 181–191.

Norman, W. T. (1963). Toward an adequate taxonomy of personality attributes: Replicated factor structure in peer nomination personality ratings. *Journal of Abnormal and Social Psychology, 66*, 574–583.

Odaka, K. (1975). *Toward industrial democracy: Management and workers in modern Japan.* Cambridge, MA: Harvard University Press.

Omohundro, J. T. (1981). *Chinese merchant families in Iloilo.* Athens, OH: University Press.

Osgood, C. (1951). *The Koreans and their culture.* Tokyo: Tuttle.

Osgood, C. (1975). *The Chinese: A study of a Hong Kong community.* Tucson, AZ: University of Arizona Press.

Ouchi, W. G. (1981a). Organizational paradigms: A commentary on Japanese management and Theory Z organizations. *Organizational Dynamics, 9*(4), 36–43.

Ouchi, W. G. (1981b). *Theory Z: How American business can meet the Japanese challenge.* Reading, MA: Addison-Wesley.

Ouchi, W. G., & Jaeger, A. M. (1978). Type Z organization: Stability in the midst of mobility. *Academy of Management Review, 3*, 305–314.

Pan, L. (1990). *Sons of the yellow emperor.* London: Mandarin.

Pascale, R. T., & Maguire, M. A. (1980). Comparison of selected work factors in Japan and the U.S. *Human Relations, 33*, 433–455.

Peng, H. J. (1989). *The* guanxi *of entrepreneurs in Taiwan and its transformation—a sociological perspective.* Unpublished doctoral dissertation, Graduate Institute of Sociology, Tunghai University, Taiwan.

Picken, S. D. B. (1987). Values and value-related strategies in Japanese corporate culture. *Journal of Business Ethics, 6*, 137–143.

Porter, L. W., Steers, R. M., Mowday, R. T., & Boulian, P. V. (1974). Organizational commitment, job satisfaction, and turnover among psychiatric technicians. *Journal of Applied Psychology, 59*, 603–609.

Pugh, D. S., & Hickson, D. J. (1976). *Organizational structure in its context: The Aston Programme I.* Farnborough, UK: Saxon House.

Purcell, V. (1965). *The Chinese in Southeast Asia.* Oxford, UK: Oxford University Press.

Putti, J. M., Aryee, S., & Liang, T. K. (1989). Work values and organizational commitment: A study in the Asian context. *Human Relations, 42,* 275–288.

Pye, L. (1982). *Chinese commercial negotiating style.* Cambridge, MA: Oelgeschlager, Gunn, and Hain.

Pye, L. (1985). *Asian power and politics.* Cambridge, MA: Harvard University Press.

Redding, S. G. (1982). Thoughts on causation and research models in comparative management for Asia. *Proceedings of the Academy of International Business Asia-Pacific Dimensions of International Business Conference* (pp. 1–38). Honolulu: University of Hawaii.

Redding, S. G. (1988). The role of the entrepreneur in the new Asian capitalism. In P. L. Berger & M. H. H. Hsiao (Eds.), *In search of an East Asian development model.* New Brunswick, NJ: Transaction Books.

Redding, S. G. (1990). *The spirit of Chinese capitalism.* New York: de Gruyter.

Redding, S. G. (1993). The comparative management theory zoo: Getting the elephants and ostriches and even dinosaurs from the jungle into the iron cages. In B. Toyne & D. Nigh (Eds.), *The state of international business inquiry.* Westport, CT: Greenwood.

Redding, S. G., & Ng, M. (1982). The role of "face" in the organizational perceptions of Chinese managers. *Organization Studies, 3*(3), 201–219.

Redding, S. G., & Pugh, D. S. (1986). The formal and the informal: Japanese and Chinese organization structures. In S. R. Clegg, D. C. Dunphy, & S. G. Redding (Eds.), *The enterprise and management in East Asia.* Hong Kong: Center of Asian Studies.

Redding, S. G., & Richardson, S. (1986). Participative management and its varying relevance in Hong Kong and Singapore. *Asia Pacific Journal of Management, 3*(2).

Reichers, A. E. (1985). A review and reconceptualization of organizational commitment. *Academy of Management Review, 10,* 465–476.

Richards, T. W. (1954). The Chinese in Hawaii: A Rosschach report. In F. L. K. Hsu (Ed.), *Aspects of culture and personality.* New York: Abelard-Schuman.

Rohlen, T. P. (1974). *For harmony and strength: Japanese white-collar organization in anthropologi-* cal perspective. Berkeley, CA: University of California Press.

Ryan, E. J. (1961). *The value system of a Chinese community in Java.* Unpublished doctoral dissertation, Harvard University, Cambridge, MA.

Salaff, J. (1981). *Working daughters of Hong Kong.* Cambridge, MA: Cambridge University Press.

Salancik, G. R. (1982). Commitment and the control of organizational behaviour and belief. In B. M. Staw & G. R. Salancik (Eds.), *New directions in organizational behaviour.* Melborne, FL: Krieger.

Sethi, S. P., Namiki, N., & Swanson, C. L. (1984). *The false promise of the Japanese miracle.* Boston: Pitman.

Sheldon, M. E. (1971). Investments and involvements as mechanisms producing commitment to the organization. *Administrative Science Quarterly, 16,* 143–150.

Silin, R. F. (1976). *Leadership and values.* Cambridge, MA: Harvard University Press.

Skinner, G. W. (1957). *Chinese society in Thailand.* Ithaca, NY: Cornell University Press.

Skinner, G. W. (1958). *Leadership and power in the Chinese community of Thailand.* Ithaca, NY: Cornell University Press.

Smith, P. B. (1984). The effectiveness of Japanese styles of management: A review and critique. *Journal of Occupational Psychology, 57,* 121–136.

Smith, P. B., & Misumi, J. (1989). Japanese management: A sun rising in the West? In C. L. Cooper & I. Robertson (Eds.), *International review of industrial and organizational psychology.* New York: Wiley.

Smith, P. B., Misumi, J., Tayeb, M., Peterson, M., & Bond, M. (1989). On the generality of leadership style measures across cultures. *Journal of Occupational Psychology, 62,* 97–109.

Staw, B. M. (1982). Counterforces to change. In P. S. Goodman (Ed.), *Change in organizations: New perspectives on theory, research and practice.* San Francisco: Jossey-Bass.

Steers, R. M. (1977). Antecedents and outcomes of organizational commitment. *Administrative Science Quarterly, 22,* 46-56.

Strauch, J. (1981). *Chinese village politics in the Malaysian state.* Cambridge, MA: Harvard University Press.

Tam, S. (1990). Centrifugal versus centripetal growth processes: Contrasting ideal types for conceptualizing the developmental patterns of Chinese and Japanese firms. In S. R. Clegg & S. G. Redding

(Eds.), *Capitalism in contrasting cultures.* New York: de Gruyter.

Tong, C. K. (1990). Centripetal authority, differentiated networks: The social organization of Chinese firms in Singapore. In G. G. Hamilton (Ed.), *Business groups and economic development in East Asia.* Hong Kong: Center of Asian Studies.

Triandis, H. C., Bontempo, R., Villareal, M. J., Asai, M., & Lucca, N. (1988). Individualism and collectivism: Cross-cultural perspectives on self-ingroup relationships. *Journal of Personality and Social Psychology, 54,* 323–333.

Tu, W. M. (1989). *A Confucian perspective on the rise of industrial East Asia.* Working paper, American Academy of Arts and Sciences, Cambridge, MA.

Tung, R. L. (1984). *The key to Japan's economic strength: Human power.* Lexington, KY: Lexington Books.

Vertinsky, I., Lee, K. H., Tse, D. K., & Wehrung, D. A. (1988). *Cultural and environmental determinants of norms of corporate organizational design and management.* Working paper, Faculty of Commerce and Business Administration, University of British Columbia, Vancouver.

Vogel, E. F. (1979). *Japan as number one.* Cambridge, MA: Harvard University Press.

Wang, G. (1981). *Community and nation: Essays on Southeast Asia and the Chinese.* Singapore: Heinemann.

Wheeler, L., Reis, H. T., & Bond, M. H. (1989). Collectivism-individualism in everyday social life: The middle kingdom and the melting pot. *Journal of Personality and Social Psychology, 57*(1), 79–86.

Whitehill, A. M., & Takezawa, S. (1968). *The other worker: A comparative study of industrial relations in the United States and Japan.* Honolulu: University Press of Hawaii.

Whitehill, A. M., & Takazawa, S. (1978, Fall). Workplace harmony: Another Japanese miracle. *Columbia Journal of World Business,* pp. 25–39.

Whitley, R. D. (1987). Taking firms seriously as economic actors: Towards a sociology of firm behaviour. *Organization Studies, 8,* 125–147.

Whitley, R. D. (1990). Eastern Asian enterprise structures and the comparative analysis of forms of business organization. *Organization Studies, 11*(1), 47–74.

Wickberg, E. (1965). *The Chinese in Philippine life.* New Haven, CT: Yale University Press.

Willmott, D. E. (1960). *The Chinese in Semarang.* Ithaca, NY: Cornell University Press

Willmott, W. E. (1972). *Economic organization in Chinese society.* Stanford, CA: Stanford University Press.

Wong, S. L. (1988). *Emigrant entrepreneurs: Shanghai industrialists in Hong Kong.* Hong Kong: Oxford University Press.

Woronoff, J. (1983). *Korea's economy: Man-made miracle.* Seoul: Si-sa-yong-o-sa.

Wu, Y. L., & Wu, C. H. (1980). *Economic development in Southeast Asia: The Chinese dimension.* Stanford, CA: Hoover Institution Press.

Yang, K. S. (1986). Chinese personality and its change. In M. H. Bond (Ed.), *The psychology of the Chinese people* (pp. 106–170). Hong Kong: Oxford University Press.

Yang, K. S., & Bond, M. H. (1983, March). *The Chinese orientation towards the description of personality.* Paper presented at the Conference on Modernization and Chinese Culture, Chinese University of Hong Kong, Hong Kong.

Yang, K. S., & Bond, M. H. (1990). Exploring implicit personality theories with indigenous or imported constructs: The Chinese case. *Journal of Personality and Social Psychology, 58,* 1087–1095.

Yin, S. (1989). *The effects of organizational change strategies on organizational commitment.* Paper presented at the Conference on Social Values and Effective Organizations, National Central University, Taiwan.

Yoo, S., & Lee, S. M. (1987). Management style and practice of Korean chaebols. *California Management Review, 29,* 95–110.

Yoshihara, K. (1988). *The rise of ersatz capitalism in South-East Asia.* Singapore: Oxford University Press.

Yu, A. B., & Yang, K. S. (1987). Social-oriented and individual-oriented achievement motivation: A conceptual and empirical analysis. *Bulletin of the Institute of Ethnology.* Taiwan: Academia Sinica, 64, 51–98. (In Chinese)

Yu, A. B., & Yang, K. S. (1990, July). *The nature of achievement motivation in collectivist societies.* Paper presented at the Conference on Individualism and Collectivism, Institute of Korean Studies, Seoul, Korea.

CHAPTER 14

Culture, Economic Reform, and the Role of Industrial and Organizational Psychology in China

Zhong-Ming Wang
Hangzhou University, People's Republic of China

This chapter discusses the role and development of industrial and organizational psychology in China, based on Chinese cultural tradition and recent management reform practices. We will define culture as shared beliefs, social values, and organizational norms. *Several Chinese cultural traditions in management will be described: group approach, harmony, equality, and social commitment. Ancient Chinese thinking and practices were at one time apparent in the workplace in such areas as reward design, personnel management, testing and performance evaluation, rationalization of production procedures, and systems management. Recent active training, research, and applications of industrial and organizational psychology have been linked closely with China's recent economic reforms, which have significantly modified Chinese culture. Six main areas of industrial and organizational psychology in China will be reviewed with the general theme that social and economic reforms have had a greater influence on management practices and organizational performance than culture itself. These six areas include: (a) work motivation (structure and process) and reward systems design,*

(b) group process and team effectiveness, (c) personnel systems reform and leadership assessment, (d) managerial decision making (decision process and power sharing) and worker participation, (e) management responsibility contract systems and joint-venture management, and (f) technological innovations and organizational development (strategies and action research). A Chinese approach to industrial and organizational psychology is characterized by its cultural-social orientation, links with economic reform, and joint efforts between academics and practitioners. The implications of the recent development of industrial and organizational psychology in China to international management and cross-cultural psychology include using a cross-cultural–socioeconomic perspective, emphasizing a team approach, integrating material and social aspects of work, and adopting three main strategies of organization development—expertise, systems networking, and participation. Some new directions in industrial and organizational psychology in China that will be highlighted include theory development, problem-oriented systematic research, and holistic approaches as they relate to Chinese culture and recent management reforms.

Introduction

CHINA HAS A very long history and a strong cultural tradition. The development of Chinese society has been greatly influenced throughout its history by its culture. There are discussions and studies of work and organizational issues in ancient Chinese literature (Z. M. Wang, 1990a). Many ideas, such as work ethics and morals, intrinsic rewards, systems management, performance evaluation, personnel selection practices, production procedures rationalization, and systematic quality control have been applied in Chinese work situations for centuries (e.g., D. N. Yang, 1984). Modern Chinese management practice and psychological thinking are deeply rooted in a cultural tradition that emphasizes group interests, work ethics, and social commitment. Another important factor affecting China's modern development is its social system. After the People's Republic of China was founded in 1949—particularly since China launched its national economic reform program and adopted an open-to-the-world policy in 1978—both productivity and social welfare have developed rapidly. The recent decade of economic reform has greatly

modified culture and changed organizational behavior in China. It has also provided great opportunities for the development and application of industrial and organizational psychology. Keeping Chinese cultural and social characteristics in mind, industrial and organizational psychologists have developed a unique Chinese approach linking theoretical research with applications in various aspects of social life. They are now playing more active and important roles in national reforms in areas such as reward systems, labor systems, management responsibility contract systems, personnel assessment and selection, teamwork, managerial decision making, technological innovations, joint-venture management, and organization development. Several international collaborative projects and cross-cultural studies have been conducted in Chinese enterprises. The theories and practices of industrial and organizational psychology that have developed in China certainly have important implications for management practices and the development of industrial and organizational psychology in an international context. To a large extent, culture and the reforms of socioeconomic systems determine the directions of industrial and organizational psychology within a specific country. Socioeconomic systems reform can greatly modify and improve a country's culture. It can have an even stronger impact on management and organizational behavior. The new emphasis on work efficiency, individual and team responsibility, work competition, democratic management, and, more recently, a market economy are changing work values and life in China. China's recent experience with industrial and organizational psychology may provide a model for the development of cross-cultural industrial and organizational psychology.

Ancient Chinese Thinking and Practice in Work and Management

Cultural Tradition in Management

Definition of Culture. Culture has been defined in many different ways. Psychologists, sociologists, and anthropologists have ascribed meaning to culture from their different perspectives (e.g., Hofstede, 1980; Kroeber & Kluckhohn, 1952; Smircich, 1985). Kroeber and Parsons (1958) distinguished *culture* from *social system* by defining culture as the transmitted and created content of values, ideas, and other symbolic meaningful systems, while using the term *social system* to describe the relational system of interaction among individuals and collectives. Hofstede (1980) approached culture from a cognitive perspective and regarded culture as "collective programming of the mind." Schneider (1985) regarded culture as a deeper construct that included elements such as norms and value systems. In his discussion of cross-cultural industrial and organizational psychology, Triandis (1993) defines culture as "the human-made part of the environment" that has both objective (tools, roads, and appliances) and subjective (beliefs, attitudes, norms, roles, and values) elements. The

concepts of culture and cultural tradition have recently become a topic of discussion in China (e.g., G. P. Li, 1990; Mu, 1990). A broader concept of culture includes ideology, philosophy, regulations, art and literature, folk habits, and even science and technology. However, in industrial and organizational psychology, we are inclined to define culture as shared beliefs, social norms, organizational roles, and values (e.g., Z. M. Wang, 1989a).

Confucianism, Taoism, and Buddhism. Chinese culture was at one time heavily influenced by Confucianism, Taoism, and Buddhism, which existed together for more than 2,000 years. Confucius (551–479 B.C.) was the ancient Chinese philosopher who most affected the thinking and administrative behavior of work and management. He emphasized that the rulers and the ruled should be educated, and that the ruler should first educate himself and govern with the aid of virtues (Laaksonen, 1988). He also advocated that good and capable people should be elevated and appointed to official posts and that benevolence should be regarded as the highest ideal of morality, serving as the basis of administrative power. Confucius believed that harmony could be best achieved by everyone recognizing his or her place in the world. Taoism went further and denied the hierarchical administrative system but focused less on social responsibility, whereas Buddhism focused primarily on equality, kindness, and commitment.

Several Cultural Traditions and Their Recent Changes. Since the founding of the People's Republic of China, the new social system has become a more important factor in social life, and the socialist ideology has modified Chinese culture, although the old cultural tradition is still very influential and popular. Among other things, equality, sharing, helping, organizational commitment, and a sense of workers being the masters of a company were advocated in organizations. Since 1978, China has launched economic reforms and adopted an open-to-the-world policy. The facilitation and improvement of social productivity and people's standard of living has been a major objective of the country. This has greatly changed Chinese traditional culture and social values. Two significant cultural changes have occurred: (a) a shift from egalitarianism to an emphasis on individual and team responsibility and competition and (b) a shift from social contribution alone to both social contribution and individual interests. Nationwide decentralization and participation in managerial decision making have enhanced the new organizational culture. Competition in personnel selection and management responsibility contract systems have changed a tradition that once avoided competition. The new organizational system and practice has had a significant impact on cultural traditions.

Several cultural traditions in China have had an important influence on management practice and the development of industrial and organizational psychology. First, the group approach has dominated Chinese social life. This approach, which has been reinforced since 1949, includes group decision making, teamwork, group rewards, group responsibility, and the national "Excellent Group Evaluation Campaign." During recent economic reforms, the group approach has been more strongly encouraged as one of the Chinese characteristics of managerial practice, with a new emphasis on team responsibility. Later, we will discuss recent research in this area as it relates to the Chinese economic reform program. Second, harmony relationships among team members have been greatly emphasized. Good relationships across and/or within organizational levels are considered crucial to successful management. Informal communications and indirect criticism are often seen as more acceptable and effective than direct forms of communication. Third, being equal and average, avoiding competition or conflict, and

establishing a work ethic were among the popularly accepted values, which was enhanced by an emphasis on social and economic equality during the period beginning in the late 1950s and extending through the 1960s. Workers being hardworking was greatly valued. Although recently more responsibility and competition among companies has been encouraged, many people, inculcated in egalitarianism, cannot easily adapt to the new situations that emphasize inter- and intra-organizational competition. Fourth, linking individual interests with the group and organizational interests has been greatly encouraged. The closer this linkage is, the greater the organizational commitment and effectiveness. These important cultural traditions have affected the organizational behavior in Chinese enterprises and other organizations during the last decade of economic reform.

Ancient Thinking and Practice

The study and discussion of work-related psychological issues have had a long history in China. Many ideas of work psychology have been applied for centuries in Chinese work situations, such as intrinsic motivation, systems management, performance evaluation, personnel selection based on ability and performance, rationalization of production procedures, and quality control (D. N. Yang, 1984). The Chinese cultural tradition has affected the development of work ethics and management practices throughout the country's history.

Motivation and Affectional Management. Confucius once regarded intrinsic motivation as the key aspect of learning and emphasized using affection as a major intervention to motivate people. Love and kindness were considered the basis for better moral development (Luo, 1987). According to Guan Zi, a famous Chinese ancient philosopher (around 300 B.C.) who had a strong impact on earlier management thinking in China, human drive can be categorized into two groups: (a) physiological drive, a more material and individual aspect of motivation, and (b) social drive, a more spiritual and social aspect of motivation. It was also believed that both reward and punishment were the means of maintaining certain social values and had important psychological effects on social behavior (Gao, 1985). These ideas have had a long history of influence on Chinese management practices.

Personnel Management. As early as the twelfth and eleventh centuries B.C., *The Rites of the Chou Dynasty*, China's classic work of ancient literature, clearly defined the first Chinese bureaucratic system with systematic responsibilities for six categories of official ranks. The ancient Chinese military literature, *The Art of War* by Sun Tzu, stressed the principle of "knowing your counterpart and knowing yourself and you can fight a hundred battles without disaster," advocating the importance of understanding the characteristics of subordinates, tasks, and organizational situations in management. In ancient Chinese literature (dating from about 313–238 B.C.), personnel traits and human resources were divided into three categories: (a) basic predispositions, including economic predisposition, cooperative predisposition, and specialty, which determined people's behavioral orientation; (b) capability predispositions, including study/understanding (cognitive) ability, operative/managerial (administrative) ability, and evaluation/hiring (of personnel) ability; and (c) moral predispositions, with the group value as its core element (Li, 1990). In a later section of this chapter, we will discuss some interesting links between these concepts of human resources and the practice of modern personnel assessment and selection in China.

In the personnel selection and management of ancient China, exams were given in six areas: music, archery, horsemanship, writing, arithmetic, and public affairs. Around 587 A.D.,

China initiated the world's first comprehensive national system of personnel examination and selection for civil service. Known as the *imperial examination system* (Z. M. Wang, 1991), this personnel system was used for more than 1,300 years and emphasized multilevel, public, and competitive selection with examinations on both basic knowledge and problem-solving ability (C. G. Li, Song, & J. Li, 1989). This multilevel screening system included county, provincial, and state levels of examinations. The final examination was conducted by the emperors themselves and usually consisted of essays, oral exams, and performance tests. An interesting feature of this personnel selection system was its emphasis on public competition. The selection procedure and examination rules were widely publicized. Anybody could apply for and take the examination. Final selection was based primarily on performance. A typical examination consisted of three parts: general composition (written expression ability), judgment (problem analysis), and commentary (discussion and proposals). During the Ming and Qing dynasties (1368–1911), the system became more complicated and was based on four aspects of assessment: ability, morality, performance, and seniority. Many of these ideas and practices continue to have an influence on modern personnel management in China.

Testing and Performance Evaluation. In ancient China, testing and performance evaluation was a major practice in education and management. Confucius first classified people into three categories on the basis of their intelligence levels: *great wisdom, average intelligence,* and *little intelligence,* indicating his early ideas about individual differences. Mencius (327–289 B.C.), another Chinese thinker, advocated the importance of quantitative measurement of the human mind by saying that scaling and measurement were especially true for the mind (H. C. Zhang, 1988). As early as 230 B.C.,

Han Fei (280–233 B.C.) noted that measurement of performance against organizational rules and working standards provided administrative safeguards. Around 400 B.C., some Chinese scholars proposed that work load and actual performance be prerequisites for job evaluation and reward allocation. In addition, a variety of measurement methods was developed in ancient China (C. D. Lin, 1983). During the period from 220 to 265 A.D., the interview was used for personnel evaluation. Zhu Geliang (181–234), another great thinker, designed what was perhaps the earliest version of situational interviews for measuring personal traits.

During the Tang dynasty (618–907), a type of short-answer test became popular. The promotion or demotion of Tang officials was largely based on some kind of performance evaluation, which enhanced organizational effectiveness during that period. Later during the Song dynasty (960–1279), performance evaluation was also developed and used in management.

Rationalization of Production Procedures and Systems Management.   In ancient China, mass movement was the major way of organizing large-scale projects, such as the building of the Great Wall, which used more than 300,000 laborers (306–214 B.C.) and the opening of the Great Canal, which used nearly 1 million people (585–608 A.D.). Mo D. (about 468–376 B.C.) proposed the idea of labor division, and Dong B. X. (around 1279–1368) tried to reduce unnecessary time delays in order to shorten operation processes and increase work efficiency (Z. M. Wang, 1990a). In addition, systems thought was adopted in a number of construction projects. A well-known example of Chinese ancient systems management was the implementation of the Dujiang Dam project during 306–251 B.C. (Y. L. Wang & Huang, 1984). These ancient traditions have strongly influenced the formation of Chinese culture and the development of modern management and industrial and organizational psychology in China.

The Development of Industrial and Organizational Psychology in China

A Brief History

Early Development.   Industrial and organizational psychology was originally a major part of industrial psychology in China. As a scientific subject, it began in the 1920s and emphasized work and personnel psychology. A few textbooks on industrial psychology were translated into Chinese and used in universities during the 1920s through the 1940s, such as Taylor's *Principles of Management*, translated by Mo (1916). An important landmark in the development of industrial psychology in China was the publication of the first Chinese text, *Essentials of Industrial Psychology*, by Li Chen (1935), a veteran industrial psychologist and the founder of China's industrial psychology program. In his book, Chen attempted to systematically link scientific psychological principles to the Chinese industrial practice. In his field study of a textile factory in 1937, Chen selected workers to join technical training and then improved working conditions, which greatly increased productivity in just six months. However, during this period, the management systems in most of China were mainly either bureaucrat-capitalist enterprise management or national-capitalist enterprise management, the former being controlled by government bureaucrats and the latter being managed by private capitalists. In many companies, the managerial power was highly centralized and management made all decisions on selection, staffing, wage rank, work quota, and performance evaluation. Technical training was popular at that time, but work efficiency was very low. A few trade unions functioned primarily to monitor and prevent antimanagement behaviors (Z. H. Xu & Liu, 1984). Some factories used psychological tests in personnel selection. A number of studies were carried out to improve the work environment in the mechanical and textile industries

(Executive Committee of the Chinese Psychological Society, 1982). There was also a national association of personnel psychology, although few research projects were organized. The Japanese invasion during the 1930s and 1940s brought about a decline in China's educational system. Therefore, industrial psychology in China as a whole developed very slowly during this period.

The New Period—1949–1965. After the founding of the People's Republic, the active socialist construction provided a momentum and new ground for the development of industrial psychology. Dialectical materialism became a guiding principle. However, during the 1950s and 1960s, industrial psychology in China focused more on technical and production-related topics than on organizational issues. Much of the research of work psychology in China in the 1950s was heavily influenced by the Soviet psychology. The transformation of the new socialist system and its related macroeconomic changes had a greater impact on both management practice and industrial psychology research than on culture. Among the popular topics were rationalization of production procedures, technical skill training, work creativity, and accident prevention (Li Chen & Zhu, 1959; J. H. Wang & D. R. Chen, 1985). In the early 1960s, the link between psychological research and practice was emphasized. A number of industrial psychology studies were carried out in real-life settings in areas such as technological innovations, railway signal design, power station control room displays, pilot selection, technical training, and work competition in factories (Peng, 1980; Z. M. Wang, 1990a). During this period, very little organizational research was conducted.

The Period of Disaster and Interruption—1966–1976. Unfortunately, the study and practice of psychology in China, including industrial psychology, suffered severely during the Cultural Revolution (1966–1976). Many psychologists were criticized and suffered painful consequences. Psychological teaching and research were interrupted for about ten years.

Recent Developments. Since 1978, China has launched an economic reform program and adopted an open-to-the-world policy, which offers a great opportunity for training, research, and application of industrial and organizational psychology. Industrial and organizational psychology has begun a new era of development in China. Industrial and organizational psychology is now commonly referred to as *managerial psychology* and *personnel psychology*. The Industrial Psychology Committee, which includes industrial and organizational psychology and engineering psychology, of the Chinese Psychological Society was organized in 1978. In addition, many people in universities, institutions, and enterprises have become interested in behavioral science and its applications to China. In 1983, a national symposium on behavioral sciences was held in Beijing, jointly sponsored by the Chinese Management Modernization Association, the Industrial Psychology Committee of the Chinese Psychological Society, the Preparatory Committee of Chinese Behavioral Sciences, the Chinese Mechanical Engineering Association, and other organizations (L. C. Xu, 1986). The symposium focused on three issues: (a) how to evaluate theories and methods of behavioral sciences from abroad, (b) how to apply behavioral sciences to improve enterprise management, and (c) how to develop a Chinese system of behavioral science. In 1985, the Chinese Society of Behavioral Sciences was established. Many of its members were managers and supervisors from enterprises and companies. In 1989, the Chinese Ergonomics Society was organized, in which cognitive ergonomics, management engineering, and environmental ergonomics were major divisions. In addition to the Institute of Psychology at the Chinese Academia Sinica, an Institute of Industrial Psychology and a National Key Laboratory of Industrial

Psychology have been established at Hangzhou University. There is also an Institute of Behavioral Sciences at the Dalian College of Management Training. Since 1978, many training programs have been conducted, and research projects of industrial and organizational psychology have been actively carried out in close association with the national economic reform program. Industrial and organizational psychology has played an increasingly important role in China's modernization efforts.

Recent Training and Publications

Industrial and Organizational Psychology Training. Recent industrial and organizational psychology training programs have been carried out in close relation to economic reforms as part of organizational change and development efforts. There are three levels of training—undergraduate and graduate programs, special management training programs, and on-the-job short training courses. The first level represents the industrial and organizational psychology programs for BA, MA, and Ph.D. degrees. According to the current Chinese educational system, a full-time student has to spend four years to obtain a BA, an additional three years for an MA, and another three years for a Ph.D. Students are encouraged to familiarize themselves with the management practices of organizations and carry out research projects on practical issues in real-life organizational and industrial settings to complete their theses or dissertations. In 1988, the industrial psychology program at Hangzhou University was awarded the National Key Program of Industrial Psychology and has received more attention from the government as well as industries in China. In addition to this comprehensive program, there are several MA and/or Ph.D. programs in other institutions and universities, such as the Institute of Psychology at Academia Sinica in Beijing, the College of Labour and Personnel Management at People's University in Beijing,

the Psychology Department of East-China Normal University in Shanghai, and the Management Schools of Shanghai Jiaotong University, Mid-China University of Technology in Wuhan, and Zhejiang University. Students who have graduated from these programs make up the major force of industrial and organizational psychologists teaching and applying knowledge of industrial and organizational psychology throughout China.

The second level of industrial and organizational psychology training is the special training program. Since 1978, in order to meet the new needs of economic reform tasks (especially the new enterprise-level decision-making powers envisaged), China has developed many management training programs that focus on industrial and organizational psychology. Many industries required their managers and supervisors to enroll in these programs and successfully complete them before carrying on their management responsibilities. Thousands of directors and managers from large- and medium-sized enterprises have been trained at national management training programs. The Chinese State Economic Commission has also held a number of management educational programs and MBA programs in collaboration with organizations from the United States, the United Kingdom, Germany, the European Community, Canada, and Japan. By 1989, more than 5,000 senior management personnel, 280 MBA students, and about 300 management teachers had undergone this training (Z. M. Wang, 1990b). In addition, a number of universities and research institutes have offered training programs in industrial and organizational psychology for managers, party secretaries, and supervisors from various industries. For instance, since 1981 the Psychology Department at Hangzhou University has conducted more than 20 such short management training courses. The courses generally last one-and-a-half months to two months and are geared toward industries such as mechanical engineering, electronics, textiles, petroleum, and telecommunications. A typical curriculum of the training course includes lectures on general psychology, managerial psychology, youth psychology, social psychology, and engineering psychology. The trainees are usually required to carry out field investigations in local enterprises using theories and principles of industrial and organizational psychology to analyze management cases and solve practical problems. Similar training courses have been used in Beijing, Shanghai, Tianjing, Dalian, and many other cities in China. These training courses have not only popularized the scientific knowledge and methods of industrial and organizational psychology in Chinese industrial organizations but have also established close collaborative relationships between Chinese psychologists and voluntary practitioners (managers and government officials) in applying theories of industrial and organizational psychology in economic reform activities. In fact, many recent research projects were conducted jointly by industrial and organizational psychologists and managers in various kinds of industries and organizations.

The third level of training is the on-the-job short training program. Such a training program is usually organized in relation to a field research or a consulting project of industrial and organizational psychology focusing on a particular management topic or issue. For example, in a field study on leadership assessment, L. C. Xu, L. Chen, D. Wang, and Xue (1985) carried out some training sessions that enhanced managers' self-consciousness and in turn improved their performance. In an action research project of organization development (OD) on technological innovations in 16 enterprises, Z. M. Wang (1987) used training as part of the OD intervention in computer systems development. The training focused on how principles of industrial and organizational psychology could help change attitudes and facilitate organizational change. Since 1980, many industries in China have invited industrial and

organizational psychologists to conduct short training courses in enterprises to enhance the quality of management teams and improve the organizational climate for economic reform.

Recent Publications. The recent development of industrial and organizational psychology in China has been reflected in its active publications. L. Chen (1983) applied psychological principles to China's industrial modernization and discussed this in his book, *Prospectus of Industrial Psychology*. X. S. Yang (1983) introduced principles of behavioral science in his book, *Behavioral Sciences*. S. Z. Lu and colleagues (1985) published a Chinese textbook, *Managerial Psychology*, which has been widely adopted in universities and management training programs in China. Many other textbooks have been written, among them *Managerial Psychology* (L. C. Xu & Chen, 1988), *Work and Personnel Psychology* (Z. M. Wang, 1988a), *Psychology of Industrial Management* (L. Chen, 1988a), and *Managerial Psychology* (Yu, 1985). In addition, several important books published outside China have been translated into Chinese, such as Herbert Simon's *Administrative Behavior: A Study of Decision Making Processes in Administrative Organization* (1976; translated by S. Yang et al., 1988) and *The New Science of Management Decision* (1977; translated by Z. L. Li & Tang, 1982), Kast and Rosenzweig's *Organization and Management* (1979; translated by Z. L. Li et al., 1985), and McCormick and Ilgen's *Industrial and Organizational Psychology* (1985; translated by S. Z. Lu, Z. M. Wang, and Zheng, 1990).

Most of the recent research reports have been published in two major Chinese quarterlies in industrial and organizational psychology that have been published since 1986: *Chinese Journal of Applied Psychology*, edited by the National Specialty Committees of Industrial Psychology and of Cognitive Ergonomics, attached to Hangzhou University, and *Behavior Science*, edited by the Shan-Xi Provincial Society of Behavioral Sciences in Xi-An. These publications have not only facilitated the recent development of industrial and organizational psychology in China but have also widely popularized scientific principles of psychology in national management training and greatly promoted economic reforms.

Economic Reform and Industrial and Organizational Psychology in China

Chinese Management Structure and Work Situations

China's Management Structure Pattern.

In China, there are three major kinds of enterprise ownerships: (a) *state-owned enterprise,* where the properties belong to the state and production is mainly under the state planning system; (b) *collective-owned enterprise,* where the properties belong to the collective of workers and production is relatively independent; and (c) *joint-venture enterprises,* which are jointly owned and managed by Chinese and foreign partners. The current pattern of management structure in China can be traced back to the *three-man leadership system* in the revolutionary period in the 1930s when the management team consisted of the factory director, the Communist party secretary, and the trade union leader in the enterprise. Later in the 1940s, this system was replaced by the *factory committee meeting,* in which factory director, Communist party secretary, trade union leader, technician, and worker representatives joined. After the founding of the People's Republic, the role of Chinese trade unions was changed from a concentration on management participation to an emphasis on worker welfare issues. A Soviet type of *one-man management system,* in which the director or general manager had full management power, was the major management system in China in the late 1950s and early 1960s. However, this

management pattern was inconsistent with the Chinese tradition of a group approach as well as the leadership of the Chinese Communist party in industries. It was then changed into a management system of *factory director under party committee leadership,* in which party organization, management team, and trade union were together responsible for the task management, but the party played a more important role. The one exception was during the Cultural Revolution, when the party organization became the target of criticism and was paralyzed.

New Reforms in Management Systems.

Since China started its national economic reform program in 1978, the management structure of Chinese enterprises has changed significantly. First, managerial power has been greatly decentralized, and most industrial enterprises have adopted management responsibility systems in which managers sign management contracts with the governmental bureau about profit and welfare objectives and have full power in running the enterprises. The recent development of management systems reform has undergone four stages. During the *experimental decentralization stage* (1979–1983), some 6,600 state-owned enterprises initiated pilot experiments in management to decentralize responsibility to the enterprises themselves. During the *introduction of enterprise responsibility systems stage* (1983–1985), enterprise responsibility systems with contracts of production and profit objectives were widely introduced in large- and medium-sized companies, and the Chinese State Council decided to strengthen the vitality of enterprises and expand the decision-making power of the enterprises in 10 areas, including production, sales, pricing of nonquota products, disposal of assets, organization, personnel selection and staffing, and monetary incentive. A major guideline of the reform, "China's Economic Structure Reform," was adopted in October 1984. During the *management contract systems reform stage*

(1986–1991), about 90 percent of large- and medium-sized enterprises implemented management responsibility contract systems, with output value, profits, and taxes rising significantly as a result. The national practice of "optimization through regrouping" was conducted to reorganize work groups voluntarily, which greatly enhanced team efficiency. The *management mechanism transformation stage* (beginning in early 1992), is characterized by national reforms to eliminate the "three irons"—guaranteed salary, life-positions, and "Iron Rice Bowl"—of the old management system. This is generally a transformation from the Iron Rice Bowl type of state employment system (i.e., guaranteed employment and guaranteed pay regardless of performance) to a labor contract system and from the rank wage system to a system with distribution schemes based on performance and ability rather than seniority, and a social security plan that provides pensions, health care, and life insurance. By mid-1992, nearly 40,000 enterprises involving 17.67 million employees, nearly 17 percent of China's total urban work force, have introduced changes in their employment, wage, and social security systems to strengthen enterprises and liberate social productivity. If this reform stage is completed, it will mean the end of secured jobs, guaranteed wages, and cradle-to-grave government welfare (*China Daily*, 1992a). In this reform stage, many industrial and organizational psychologists have actively worked together with managers in job analysis, performance appraisal, selection, placement, training, design, and implementation of new income distribution schemes, personnel systems, and general management systems

Second, the Chinese trade union has participated more actively in democratic management through the workers' congress organizations. There has been a clear shift of the focus of trade union activities from workers' daily interests (e.g., housing, bonuses, and other welfare arrangements) to higher level participation, including management selection,

production planning, investment evaluation, and local governmental administration. Some industrial and organizational psychologists have made general surveys and field studies on the power-influence–sharing by management and trade unions and have given useful suggestions to both the trade unions and management (Z. M. Wang & Heller, 1990). Eighty-four percent of state enterprises have set up workers' congresses, which evaluated the performance of 1.8 million managers and supervisors in 1991. Among those evaluated, 11,000 were dismissed after evaluators found them incompetent (*China Daily*, 1992b). Through the work of 610,000 grassroots trade unions, most of the country's 104 million union members have been able to participate in such policy-making issues as employment and labor reforms, new wage systems, unemployment insurance systems, and housing reform.

Third, the legal system of Chinese enterprise management has been formalized and improved by the passage of legislation such as the Enterprise Law (1988), the Joint Venture Law (1979, 1990), and the Labor Union Law (1992). Such legislation indicates that the management reforms are no longer just experiments, but formal changes that are part of the country's legal system. The Enterprise Law has defined more clearly the three organizational systems in Chinese management: the Communist party organization, the director-management responsibility system, and the trade union/workers' congress. According to the Enterprise Law for state-owned enterprises, the role of the party organization is to guarantee and supervise the implementation of the guiding principles and policies of the Communist party; the director of the management responsibility system shall be the legal representative of the enterprise and assume overall responsibility in production, operation, and management; and the trade union and workers' congress shall represent and safeguard the interests of the staff and workers and organize participation in democratic management and supervision (*China Daily Business Weekly*, 1988; Z. M. Wang, 1991). These new changes in management systems have had a significant impact on the organizational culture and behavior and have become important research areas for industrial and organizational psychologists in China. In fact, the rapid development of Chinese industrial and organizational psychology has been closely related to and greatly facilitated by the country's management reform activities.

Some Major Industrial Management Practices. A major national industrial practice that has greatly influenced management in China was the implementation of the principles of *two-way participation, one reform,* and *three-in-one combination,* which was based on the management experience from the Qinhua Tools Factory, the Jianhua Machinery Factory, and the Cangcun No. 1 Automobile Company during the late 1950s (J. Z. Xu, 1984). *Two-way participation* meant that workers participated in top-level management and that cadres (managers and supervisors) participated in daily work at the shop-floor level. *One reform* changed unreasonable management regulations and improved the management system of "director responsibility under party committee leadership." The *three-in-one combination* principle meant that technicians, workers, and cadres worked together in technical innovations and enterprise management. This national practice was successful in promoting enterprise management and participation. It later became a major part of the "Constitution of the Anshan Iron and Steel Company" (1960), a management principle stressing the importance of mass mobilization, participation, and leadership in technical innovations and management.

Another common practice found in Chinese organizations has been its community style. Since the founding of the People's Republic, most industrial enterprises and other organizations have largely provided workers with housing and health care. Many organizations are also responsible for providing employees' children with daycare and school education and organizing activities for retired employees. Employees are generally closely connected or attached to their work units, even after retirement. Therefore, many concepts of industrial and organizational psychology, such as work, team, collective, organization, and participation, have broader meanings and implications in China than they may have elsewhere.

Work Motivation and Reward Systems Design

After China began its economic reform program and shifted the country's focus toward socialist modernization in 1978, one of the important and urgent tasks in management was to restore the bonus system that was abolished and replaced by political ideology in 1966, and to develop more effective incentive or reward systems for motivating employees. Reward systems such as bonuses were then regarded as a supplementary benefit in addition to the basic wage that should be contingent on actual performance. Worker motivation and reward systems design became the first active area in industrial and organizational psychology in China in the early and mid-1980s. Many industrial and organizational psychologists were involved in field studies on work motivation and reward systems design in various enterprises and other organizations.

Structures of Basic Needs. Although both physiological and social drives were noticed and the intrinsic aspect of motivation was emphasized in ancient Chinese literature, there was no systematic research and management practice regarding employees' basic need structure. It was important, therefore, to determine the current basic need structure of Chinese employees so that more effective reward systems could be developed. Several research projects in Chinese enterprises in the early 1980s found that social needs were most important to employees. In a large-scale survey in the industries, a need hierarchy based on about 2,700 needs was categorized (L. C. Xu, 1987). Further surveys among 434 workers in two factories in northern China found that social needs, such as contributions to their own organizations and the country's modernization, were ranked highest, although wages and bonuses were among the important needs identified (L. C. Xu & L. Chen, 1988). Nevis (1983), who was among the first foreign organizational psychologists to teach in China after the Cultural Revolution, once called social needs "self-actualization in the service of society." In another field study carried out in southern China, Z. M. Wang (1988a, p. 227) found that age differences and organizational position affected what kinds of rewards employees preferred. Some intrinsic needs, such as the need for technical training and having nice jobs, were preferred mostly by young employees, while bonuses and having nice jobs were more important to middle-aged employees. Among older employees, social rewards, such as an excellent work title, appeared to be more important. People at different organizational levels and at different ages also expressed different needs. In general, receiving technical training was most important to technicians and management personnel, whereas bonuses and having nice jobs were the most important needs among ordinary workers. These results were closely related to the fact that most young employees lost their educations as a result of the ten-year Cultural Revolution and that the work program, including its reward system, needed to be redesigned. Using Maslow's hierarchy of needs framework, X. Y. Li (1988) conducted a field survey among 701 employees from eight companies in Shanghai about needs and motivation. Li found that material incentives were more important among workers, while social needs were more important to supervisors and managers. Among the factors influencing need preferences, education and family background were greatly important. Similar results were obtained in another study on work motivation emphasizing the combination of social and material incentives in human resource management in China (Yu, 1988a).

The results of field research on need structures and work motivation have had three practical implications for reward systems design in management reform in Chinese enterprises. First, different reward programs should be designed to meet the needs of employees who are of different ages and who have different jobs and organizational positions. Second, to many employees, intrinsic rewards, such as technical training and the job itself, are more important than extrinsic rewards such as bonuses. Third, a more flexible and comprehensive multiple reward structure combining social rewards with material incentives should be used in order to motivate the Chinese work force (Z. M. Wang, 1988a). A field experiment was then implemented using a flexible multireward system in some departments of a steel file company. Workers who completed their production targets could choose an incentive among five alternatives: a bonus, technical training, an earlier work schedule (flexible working time), group vacations, and having an excellent worker title. Compared with the control group, the experimental group under the multireward system had significantly higher motivation and doubled its productivity (L. Chen, 1989).

Individual Versus Group Reward Systems.
As mentioned previously, China has a long tradition of group approach in management but has suffered from egalitarianism and the Iron Rice Bowl approach during the period beginning in the 1950s and extending through the 1970s, which led to low work efficiency. In the early 1980s, in response to the Iron Rice Bowl problem in pay distribution, an individualistic approach of the piece-rate bonus system

emphasizing individual performance became popular in some Chinese industries (Z. M. Wang, 1990b). This practice discouraged collective responsibility and weakened team effectiveness. Thus, some studies of industrial and organizational psychology were carried out to compare work efficiencies between individual and group reward systems and to provide scientific evidence for improving the structure of reward systems in Chinese enterprises. Z. M. Wang (1986a) conducted a series of field experiments to determine the effect of workers' attributions on their performance under individual versus team reward systems in Chinese enterprises. The questionnaire survey was combined with a field experiment in a 2 x 2 x 2 factorial design (individual vs. group reward systems, success vs. failure, and male vs. female) using steel chain assembly tasks (similar to assembly-line tasks) and attribution measurement of five factors (effort, ability, cooperation, task, and chance). The results found that the way workers attributed their success and failure had a significant impact on their subsequent behaviors and performance, which was greatly affected by the organizational context, especially the structural characteristics of reward systems. Under the group reward system, workers tended to attribute their performance to the team cooperation and collective efforts, which may maintain or enhance their motivation and expectancy for future performance. Under the individual reward system, workers more frequently attributed their performance to personal factors or task difficulty, which may reduce their motivation. One implication of this study was that a team-oriented reward system with a clear responsibility (goal) structure would more effectively facilitate morale, cooperation, and productivity in Chinese enterprises.

Motivational Process. Weiner (1979) regarded attribution as a motivational process in which attributions with different dimensions (e.g., locus of control vs. stability) would have certain effects on people's subsequent behavior. Z. M. Wang (1986a, 1988b) studied the motivational process of workers' attributions and found that the effects of attributions on subsequent behavior and performance actually depended heavily on the kinds of work responsibility systems being used. For instance, under the team responsibility system, the work team as a whole made a contract for the production objective, and the reward was primarily based on team performance. In this case, both ability and team cooperation attributions had strong effects on workers' subsequent affect, expectation, and behavioral intention. However, under the individual responsibility system, an individual worker was fully responsible for his or her task, and rewards were based on individual output. In this case, attributions such as individual ability and effort would improve subsequent work behavior. Therefore, it is essential to take the organizational features into consideration in the attribution-motivational process. In a quasi experiment, Z. M. Wang (1988b) implemented a five-week team attributional training program in which each work team met in a workshop once a week after the workday to discuss its performance and make relevant attributions. A psychologist took part in the group discussion as an external facilitator and encouraged workers to make objective attributions about their successes and failures. Results indicated that the team attributional training reduced workers' attributional biases, enhanced work motivation, and resulted in better mutual understanding, cooperation, and performance. This indicates the importance of psychological training and team development activities in economic reforms.

In the process of establishing more stimulating and effective reward systems, attention has been paid to the goal-setting process. X. D. Xu (1986) conducted a field survey in a television factory in Hangzhou and found that formal management regulations on production quotas and rewards significantly influenced workers' goal-setting behavior and in turn their work motivation. Most employees set their goals close to the formal production quota following the organizational norm. Therefore, the formal production quota should be designed so that it could be regularly adjusted to retain its motivating nature.

Group Process and Team Effectiveness

Historically, Chinese society emphasized collectivism, social interaction, and team approaches in work situations. Particularly since 1949, team building has been popular in enterprise management. Even after the Cultural Revolution, when individual goals and responsibility were encouraged, belonging to groups was still considered a priority in the needs structure of Chinese employees (e.g., Nevis, 1983). However, in the recent national management reforms, this cultural tradition has been given new meaning, with an emphasis on group responsibility and team effectiveness (Z. M. Wang, 1986a, 1988b). A team approach has become a major strategy in the Chinese economic reform program. This approach has integrated group responsibility and authority with team interests, and enhanced work motivation and efficiency.

Excellent Team Movement and Labor Competition. Titles such as excellent team and excellent enterprise have been used in China as a form of social reward for work groups or enterprise organizations with good morale and performance. Each year, there are public campaigns at national, provincial, city, or enterprise levels to evaluate and award those who receive excellent team or enterprise titles. It is also an important approach to improve and facilitate team and organization developments. However, during the 1950s and early 1960s, this excellent team movement focused mostly on team technical innovations and cooperation. Examples of the excellent work groups include the Ma Hengchang Group, which had excellent group technical management, the Liu Changfu Group, recognized for its good

group accounting management, and the Zhao Mengtao Group, which had sound group cooperation—all of which were named by their group leaders. Since China launched its recent economic reforms in 1978, emphasis has shifted toward excellent team management and productivity and enterprise responsibility contract systems. Among the excellent team/enterprise titles, Chinese Enterprise Management Association established in 1982 an annual National Award for Excellent Enterprise Management. Some recent psychological research indicated that a high degree of group involvement and a good match between task requirements and group goals with clear member responsibility are the keys to team excellence and team goal-directed behavior (Z. M. Wang, 1991). Many excellent work teams were developed through autonomous management of the Quality Circle (QC) in national quality control activities. A national QC evaluation campaign for the Excellent Quality Circle Award is held every year. The excellent team/enterprise movement has greatly enhanced group and organizational commitment, cohesiveness, and performance in Chinese industries and other organizations.

A related team approach in Chinese management has been the labor competition, which consists of emulation campaigns and is mainly organized by trade unions in coordination with management and party organizations. The key principle of labor competition is a striving for better morale, discipline, quality, efficiency, productivity, and social contributions through competitions among individual employees, between groups, departments, and enterprises. The main forms of emulation campaigns include Advanced Worker, an award for good performance, Model Worker, an award for outstanding performance in production and technological development, and All-Excellent Industrial Project, an award for a good quality project with high productivity (Henley & Mee-Kau, 1987). This labor competition, or emulation campaign approach, has been effective in stimulating work motivation, team co-operation, and a sense of mastery in Chinese organizations.

Team Development and Optimization Through Regrouping. Although the team approach was widely adopted during the 1950s and 1960s in Chinese enterprises, work groups were exclusively organized and appointed by management. This produced problems such as overstaffing and low responsibility. Besides, most work groups suffered from the Iron Rice Bowl problem and therefore had low efficiency, especially during the Cultural Revolution, when political ideology replaced management in some organizations. During the recent decade of economic reforms, team efficiency has become a key to organizational effectiveness. Some experimental team development programs were then carried out to improve group autonomy and efficiency. Among them, a field experiment was conducted to determine the effect of volunteer grouping of work teams on group cohesiveness and productivity, using sociometric methods with 136 workers in a number of factories (L. Chen, 1987). A unique characteristic of this experiment was that the individual choice of group membership was made under the close supervision of managers, who were able to make adjustments to the experimental groupings according to an employee's ability, skills, and attitude. Comparisons were made between 14 experimental groups, which were voluntarily grouped, and 14 control groups, which were assigned by management as usual. The field experiment showed that the experimental groups as a whole had significantly higher daily output and more positive attitudes toward work and the company than did the control groups. The study provided positive psychological evidence and practical experience for implementing the recent reform action of "optimization through regrouping," a national movement to improve team efficiency by reorganizing work groups on a voluntary basis.

With the development of Chinese economic reforms, it became more and more evident that the traditional way of having management assign members to groups was not effective in enhancing team cooperation and performance. Therefore, as a major step in the economic reform program, thousands of work groups have been practicing the optimization through regrouping method since 1987 (Z. M. Wang, 1990b). This reform practice has been implemented in coordination with the introduction of the labor contract system, which is seen as a solution to the Iron Rice Bowl problem. The new system emphasizes team objectives and responsibility and allows enterprises and workers to choose each other, which has been an important development toward decentralization and high efficiency in management in China. Yu (1988b) studied the effects of such labor contract systems in three work groups in a company in Shanghai. Yu found that compared to the conventional system, the new voluntarily based team system improved interpersonal relationships and social climate within work groups, enhanced formal leadership and participation in team management, and led to better performance.

One of the characteristics of Chinese group management is that the formal group system has been more structured and influential on group behavior, whereas the informal group has been relatively weak, often coordinating well with the formal group. An attitude survey conducted at a television factory revealed that group norms for performance were primarily based on the formal production quota system rather than the informal ones (X. D. Xu, 1986).

Social Loafing in Work Groups. With an increasing interest in the group approach in management, some psychological and economic research has called into question the benefits of work groups, suggesting that it may promote reduced performance under certain circumstances—that is, that it may encourage a "social loafing" effect (e.g., Earley,

1989; Latane, Williams, & Harkins, 1979). It was believed that the social loafing effect might be closely related to cultural background factors such as individualism or collectivism. Earley (1989) tested the hypothesis that culture had a moderating influence on social loafing among 48 managerial trainees, half of whom were from the United States and half of whom were from China. The social loafing effect was observed in American managers who held individualistic beliefs but not for Chinese managers who held collectivistic beliefs. This finding is consistent with some earlier research done in China (Z. M. Wang 1986a). However, while cultural tradition alone has some influence on social loafing, management practice, such as the system through which work responsibility is impacted, may have a stronger effect on employees' psychological state and job performance. For instance, a field experiment demonstrated that employees working under a group responsibility system (group goal structure) performed better than those working under an individual responsibility system (individual goal structure) in Chinese enterprises, even though the workers were from the same culture (Z. M. Wang, 1988b). This suggests that in order to prevent or eliminate the social loafing effect, work teams must be redesigned so that they have a clear group responsibility structure.

Personnel Systems Reform and Leadership Assessment

Both the research and application of industrial and organizational psychology in China focused on work motivation and team effectiveness in the early 1980s, when the major task of the economic reform program was to reorganize and adjust the work force for the new approach to management and production. However, during the mid-1980s, the focus of economic reforms shifted to the improvement of personnel systems, especially the selection of more competent and qualified managers and supervisors. Many industrial and organizational psychologists became involved in this process and played an active role in personnel systems reform and leadership assessment.

Personnel Systems Reform. Personnel management in China has two major branches—the *labor management system* and the *cadre management system*. The *labor management system* deals primarily with the management of ordinary workers and staff members, who typically have had high school training and/or night college education, including prejob vocational training, selection, recruitment, placement, on-the-job training work quota, performance evaluation, rewards, and punishment. The *cadre management system* involves management of two categories of personnel—general administrative personnel, such as technicians, engineers, and administrative staff, and leaders, such as general managers, middle managers, party officials, supervisors, and trade union leaders. The cadre management system is responsible for the selection, transfer, promotion, assessment, training, rewarding, and punishment of cadres. Since 1978, Chinese personnel systems have undergone a series of reforms. The labor management system has emphasized the principles of public recruitment, voluntary application, comprehensive evaluation, and selection by merit, while the cadre management system has implemented the principles of selecting cadres who are more politically competent, younger, more knowledgeable, and who have specialized knowledge. These reform activities have significantly improved the quality of the work force and cadre teams, and strengthened personnel management in general.

Performance-Maintenance Leadership Assessment. Since 1984, during the process of personnel systems reform, leadership assessment has been an active area of industrial and organizational psychology in China. The objectives of leadership assessment research were to change the traditional way of evaluating enterprise leaders by personal impressions or political affiliations alone and to build up a comprehensive and scientific assessment system for cadre selection and promotion. One research project was a large-scale assessment of leadership behavior involving 16,260 respondents from 53 factories in various industries in China (L. C. Xu, 1987). In this project, a Japanese two-dimensional instrument for leadership assessment (Misumi, 1985) was adapted for use with the Chinese context of leadership assessment, measuring task performance and relationship maintenance (known as the *Performance-Maintenance Scale* or PM). Eight situational criteria were used in the PM study: work motivation, satisfaction with income, work environment, mental hygiene, teamwork, efficiency of meetings, communication, and performance. However, Chinese research data soon revealed that despite some cultural similarities between China and Japan, a third dimension of leadership assessment—moral character—was needed in addition to the original two dimensions of performance and maintenance (W. Q. Lin, L. Chen, & D. Wang, 1987). The moral character factor is an important cultural characteristic of Chinese society and includes personal characteristics such as honesty, integrity, positive attitudes, belief in team cooperation, and organizational commitment. The belief in Chinese society is that any leadership perspective that does not emphasize the moral character of leaders is incomplete (Peterson, 1988). Therefore, the PM scale was modified into a three-dimensional scale of character, performance, and maintenance—CPM, which was used in a number of Chinese governmental organizations and industrial enterprises to determine leadership styles and to make psychological diagnoses for the purpose of improving leadership behavior. The CPM proved to be a reliable and valid assessment of leadership behavior.

Other Studies on Psychological Assessment. Other Chinese studies have illustrated the psychological assessment of management and leadership behavior in companies. An early example of personnel assessment was conducted in the mechanical industry in Shanghai in 1982. A three-component assessment system was designed, which included political predisposition (such as political background, responsibility, leading role, open-mindedness, and commitment), intellectual ability (such as decision making, creativity, problem solving, verbal ability, social and interpersonal skills, and coordinating), and performance (productivity and social efficiency). More than 2,000 employees participated in the self-assessment study, which provided personnel data for selection, placement, and training (P. Q. Zhang, 1986). Later, H. J. Lu (1986) used an assessment center method that involved 52 managers. An in-basket management simulation test was designed, which included four work samples for the candidates: (a) a document review (15 common documents for middle managers), (b) a group discussion (a management meeting to determine personnel placement), (c) a supervisor-subordinate conversation (a role-playing situation), and (d) a work planning speech (a plan for new production). These simulation methods were shown to be more effective for selection than traditional paper-and-pencil tests because the simulations could be evaluated by verbal ability, written expression, interpersonal effectiveness, ability to delegate, organizational skills, analytic ability, management creativity, and effective policy implementation.

A different kind of leadership assessment was conducted as a job analysis study in 60 Chinese factories (Wu, 1986). Seven functional categories of management were found in Chinese enterprises: general administration, ideological work, production management, technical work, marketing, welfare, and personnel management. A 30-item questionnaire was then developed for use in assessing four components of leadership: political pre-disposition, knowledge structure, ability level, and work performance. Role-set methods were also developed to reflect the Chinese tradition of widespread participation in management. According to the role-set methods, several levels of measurement were adopted to accomplish assessment in many industries and governmental departments (e.g., P. Q. Zhang, 1986). Each role set involves the candidate and his or her supervisor, subordinates, and peers. These methods were used to evaluate the ability and performance of candidates being considered for management and leadership positions. These methods yielded more accurate and more comprehensive information for making personnel decisions.

Methodological concerns have been expressed about the use of quantitative measurements to assess personnel in China. One issue concerns the quality of assessment instruments. Although some instruments have been developed on the basis of information gained from job analysis, very few have been subjected to well-designed validation studies that used actual management performance measures. In fact, some psychometric or statistical methods can be misused in some assessment studies. A second issue involves the control or elimination of strong social desirability factors in leadership assessment. Since many items in leadership assessment instruments were direct expressions of socially desirable concepts, special attention needs to be given to the possibility that biases exist in the question design and ratings. A third issue concerns the training of psychometric knowledge and rating skills. Personnel evaluation and management in China from the 1950s through the 1970s were mostly qualitative, based on political criteria, and conducted by personnel departments. For the new leadership and personnel assessment method, there has been a great need for personnel training in psychological theory and assessment techniques. The focus has been on training at various levels of the

organization to eliminate rating errors and judgment biases. L. Chen (1983) called for special attention to be placed on the methodological issues surrounding Western tests and developing Chinese psychological instruments, emphasizing the importance of intensive training in psychological testing in industrial psychological research and applications. L. Chen (1987) reported the results of a recent study on the rating biases of commonly used leadership assessment scales in Chinese enterprises. Several biases were found to severely affect the ratings—leniency or severity of ratings, regression toward the mean and restriction of range, and ubiquitous halo effects. Five main deficiencies were found in the current personnel assessment activities of Chinese organizations:

- Ambiguity of the meanings of assessment items (e.g., some items were too general and global)

- Lack of training in rating skills, especially in dealing with negative statements

- Lack of familiarity and information about the ratees

- Rater attitudes or favoritism toward certain ratees

- Rater irresponsibility

This study and other relevant work proved useful in the improvement of the personnel assessment work in personnel systems reform in China.

Managerial Decision Making and Participation

To a large extent, the essence of Chinese management reform has been the improvement of managerial decision making in various organizations, especially the decentralization of decision-making power and the enhancement of decision-making quality. By 1986, developing more scientific and democratic procedures for managerial decision making became a major task of enterprise reform and organizational change in China. High involvement and participation were regarded as key to both morale and decision-making effectiveness (Z. M. Wang, 1991). Managerial decision making and participation then became a very active area in both management reform and industrial and organizational psychology in China. Research has focused on two aspects of managerial decision making—cognitive process and information utilization in decision making, and power sharing and participation in organizational decision making.

The Managerial Decision-making Process and Decision Support.   The process of managerial decision making has been one of the foci of recent studies on decision making in China. An information processing perspective was adopted in examining decision task structures, decision-making procedures, information utilization, and judgment strategies in managerial decision making. It is suggested that the characteristics of the decision-making process and information utilization are more crucial than the decision information itself (e.g., personnel assessment data). In a field study on personnel decision-making procedures in nine enterprises, Z. M. Wang and Y. B. Wang (1989) found that Chinese enterprises had a standard pattern of personnel selection, evaluation, recruitment and placement, and similar centralized procedures in which relatively strict sequences of decisions were carried out through different authority levels. However, many enterprises, especially collective-owned ones, had some local autonomy within the range of personnel management policies in decisions that concerned personnel selection and placement. In addition, the study found that the educational level of the candidate was a major criterion for selection, while psychological characteristics such as intellectual ability, personality, interests, and attitudes were deemphasized in personnel decisions. To improve personnel decisions in

Chinese enterprises, the study called for designing better decision procedures, developing decision information systems, using multiple predictors, and adopting utility analysis.

Another major task of managerial decision making, which is related to economic reform, has been the selection of directors. A contract system was developed that includes a national bidding process of public selection and competitive recruitment. This management reform has been in effect since 1987. Z. M. Wang and Fan (1990) conducted a large-scale field survey of 27 Chinese enterprises (15 state-owned and 12 collective-owned enterprises) to determine what psychological characteristics are crucial and what strategies are effective in facilitating and improving decision making when candidates are considered for the *director responsibility contract systems.* They interviewed managers, worker representatives from those companies, and supervisors from the industrial bureaus (a level above the plant) who participated in the decisions behind the director responsibility contract systems. Applications, proposals, and records of the recruitment meetings were carefully examined in order to undestand the general procedure and task structure of decision making. The procedure of public selection and competitive recruitment in Chinese enterprises were found to have several important features:

- Decision tasks were heavily based on economic and personal information but overlooked information on management tasks and human resources in enterprises.

- Information gathering relied on quantitative assessments but failed to combine quantitative findings with qualitative information and combine official performance records with evaluations by peers and/or subordinates.

- Decision tasks had fewer alternatives and more proposals with a short-term orientation and needed to coordinate objectives of the state, the collective, and individuals.

- There was a lack of participation by worker representatives at various stages of decision making.

The study provides systematic evidence and decision support strategies for improving the selection and recruitment procedure of the director responsibility contract systems in Chinese organizations.

A series of field experiments was carried out in 16 Chinese enterprises, looking at cognitive strategies and decision support information in decision making on computer systems development (Z. M. Wang, 1990c). The studies were based on the *human-computer interface hierarchy model* in which three facets or dimensions (i.e., computer expertise, system networking or connectivity, and participation) formulated a hierarchical structure of human-computer-organization interaction (Z. M. Wang, 1989b). In one experiment using verbal protocols and information search techniques, managers were asked to make decisions about the introduction and implementation of management information systems (MIS) in their enterprises. Results showed that the use of decision strategies was systematically affected by the type of decision information structures being considered. It was affected by whether decision information was arranged along a dimensional structure, where three interface facets and their related variables were grouped separately or whether decision information was organized on the basis of a causal structure, where three interface facets were centered together and were followed by intervening and dependent variables. The causal structure of decision information (facet-centered structure) proved to be more effective in simplifying information processing in complex decision making than the dimensional structure (facet-separated structure). The study demonstrated that an effective utilization of decision information depends not only on its reliability and accuracy but also on the structure of the information display being considered. The findings further suggest that a kind of facet-based information structure be adopted in the design of decision aids and decision support for enterprise management in China.

Power Sharing and Participation. Democratic management and decentralization of decision-making power have been part of recent economic reforms in China. According to the Chinese Enterprise Law (*China Daily Business Weekly*, 1988), the staff and workers' congress shall be the basic form for the practice of democratic management in enterprises and the major organ for staff and workers to exercise their democratic management powers in decision making on long-term planning, income distribution (wage and bonus), labor protection, welfare, management appraisal, and director election. Recent research has shown that worker participation has been an important factor in enhancing morale and decision effectiveness in Chinese enterprises (e.g, L. Chen, 1987). Efforts were then made to find an effective way to promote participation and skill utilization in managerial decision making. Z. M. Wang (1989a) conducted a field study of 285 Chinese managers and examined decision-making styles between top managers and their immediate subordinates (level 1 and level 2 managers, respectively). Results showed that participative decision making had positive effects on decision effectiveness and that skill utilization was closely related to job satisfaction. Using measures adapted from Heller's *Influence-Power Continuum* (IPC), Heller and Wilpert (1981) found that the centralization of managerial decision making among Chinese managers was similar to that found in the British sample. It was also evident that participative leadership styles were more closely related to decision tasks concerning the department and the employees, while decisions relating to the subordinates were more centralized. Another interesting finding was that Chinese managers thought that joint decision making could speed up decisions, since all parties shared responsibility. This relates to the Chinese leadership system and tradition of collective decision making. It also corresponds to results from some recent experiments that showed that Chinese students tended to make decisions based on opinions of the majority of participants and that group decision making often resulted in a compromise with no various alternatives rather than more risk taking or conservative decisions being made (Teng, 1989). The study of Chinese senior managers supported the idea that participation and high-influence power sharing would increase both skill utilization and managerial transparency (clear management goal perception and frequent two-way communication), which could in turn reduce organizational uncertainty in decision making and achieve better performance and satisfaction.

Laaksonen (1988) conducted field studies on the shift-of-influence power structure in six Chinese enterprises. The comparison of the results obtained in 1980 and 1984 showed that party committee influence within the enterprise and the government body had lessened, especially in terms of important strategic decisions, indicating the development of decentralization in management as a result of the economic reforms. It was also shown that managers were recently more responsible for human resources and personnel decisions, which was a key to the efficiency and profitability of the enterprise. One of the most interesting findings of Laaksonen's study is that when he compared the Chinese influence-and-power structures with those in Japan and Europe, he found that the Japanese power pattern more closely resembled the European one, although Japanese cultural values are probably much more similar to those in China than to those in Europe. This supports the view that change and development resulting from socioeconomic systems has had a greater impact on the power structure and management of enterprises than does culture.

A culture-socioeconomic perspective would be more meaningful and effective in studies and the development of cross-cultural industrial and organizational psychology than the culture perspective alone.

Management Responsibility Contract Systems

A major step in the Chinese economic reform program is the national transition from the unified leadership system of the enterprise party committee to the new director responsibility contract system, which shifts enterprise leadership to directors (Child, 1987). As a result, factory directors assume overall responsibility and power in running their enterprises, and employees have more influence on the management of their organizations (Z. M. Wang, 1990b). The main functions and powers of the factory directors are that they choose enterprise plans and administrative structures, propose the appointment or removal of leading administrative cadres at the level of vice director of the factory, appoint or dismiss the middle management cadres of the enterprise, propose plans for wage adjustment, bonus distribution and welfare programs, formulate important rules and regulations to be examined by the staff and workers' congress, and reward or punish staff members and workers according to existing laws (*China Daily Business Weekly*, 1988).

The Characteristics of Management Responsibility Contract Systems.   The key principles of management responsibility contract systems in Chinese enterprises separate ownership (e.g., state-owned or collective-owned) from management, decentralize managerial power, reduce administrative intervention, link pay directly to performance, and create a progressive organizational environment. Several factors are crucial for management responsibility contract systems to be successfully implemented.

Qualified directors for the management responsibility system should be selected by a special search committee through competitive and public recruitment procedures. Supervisors from the industrial bureau (one level above the enterprise), representatives of previous top and middle managers, representatives of the staff and workers' congress (and trade unions), and external consultants are all members of this committee (Z. M. Wang, 1990b).

Relationships among the Communist party committee, the management team, and the trade union organization should be properly coordinated. Under the director responsibility contract system, directors assume full responsibility and power in the production, operation, and management of their enterprises. Since the Communist party committee oversees the implementation of party and state policies, it is important for the director to work closely with the party committee and consult with the trade union in order to establish an effective leadership system while the trade unions organize for democratic management supervision of the enterprise.

Relationships between the factory directors and employees (staff and workers) should be carefully adjusted and enhanced. A major mechanism in this process is the staff and workers' congress, which should be formalized and strengthened in order to motivate employees, cultivate in them a sense of being masters of the company, and supervise the management.

An all-member risk sharing arrangement should be encouraged in which both management and employees contribute certain funds to cover the possible expense of failing to fulfill the objectives of the management responsibility systems. The arrangement links enterprise outcome with the interests of all members, which could facilitate a positive organizational culture with all members sharing responsibility for the enterprise.

Four types of management responsibility contract systems have proved effective in Chinese enterprise reform (Z. M. Wang, 1990b):

- The director period-objective responsibility system, under which the director signs a three- or five-year management contract with various management objectives for personnel competence, enterprise development, work efficiency, employee welfare, reward and punishment, and total profits

- The director "rolling-objective" responsibility system, in which the management objectives are "rolled" or increased each year according to new profits

- The enterprise share-holding responsibility system, in which shareholders are responsible for and elect the management teams and share its risks

- The leasing responsibility system, in which the leasing person assumes managerial power

Currently, the majority of Chinese enterprises have implemented the director period-objective responsibility system and are decentralizing management power. They have achieved good management efficiency and economic results.

Joint-venture Management. The Sino-foreign joint venture is a fruitful product of recent economic reforms and the open-to-the-world policy in China. By 1990, some 25,000 Sino-foreign joint-venture enterprises have been established (*China Daily*, 1990). Among them, more than 80 percent are in manufacturing industries. In addition to these joint ventures, there are about 1,500 foreign-run ventures and 8,500 cooperative ventures with independent foreign investment and joint management. Of the joint ventures that have been put into operation, 85 percent are doing well. Human resource management in joint ventures has been regulated under the "Law of the People's Republic of China on Joint

Ventures Using Chinese and Foreign Investment," which was introduced in July 1979 and amended in April 1990. The law includes regulations concerning the employment, recruitment, dismissal, and resignation of the staff and workers of joint ventures as well as their salary, welfare benefits, labor insurance, labor protection, and labor discipline. Human resource management in joint ventures is quite different from that found in ordinary Chinese enterprises and has therefore been the focus of attention in recent industrial and organizational studies (e.g., Tan, 1989; Z. M. Wang & Sheng, 1990). In a recent field study on managerial decision-making patterns and performance assessment models involving 21 Sino-foreign joint ventures in China, Z. M. Wang and Sheng (1990) found that Chinese and foreign partners often had different motives for establishing joint ventures. The similarity of these motives was an important factor affecting the management objectives and decision making of the joint ventures. Another important factor was the compatibility of value premises in relation to factual premises in decision making (Simon, 1976). The study showed that a key predictor of joint venture effectiveness was the locus of decision making, either in terms of the locus between partners or across different organizational levels. While the locus of decision making was affected by organizational and leadership factors, the compatibility among decision premises was influenced by the cultural and social values of Chinese and foreign managers. A model of the effectiveness of Sino-foreign joint ventures has been formulated and is being researched. It includes an assessment system with predictors (investment motives, decision premises, and locus of decision making) and criteria (organizational performance, human resource utility, and productivity). In a recent field study on this topic among 25 joint ventures, Z. M. Wang (1992) found that cultural traditions strongly influenced work behaviors in joint ventures. The value of emphasizing

interpersonal relationships and group responsibility was quite prevalent among Chinese employees. The managerial decision-making styles were largely influenced by the management traditions of the managers' respective countries. For example, in a Sino-Japanese joint-venture company, a hierarchical management organization with small steps and frequent promotions was introduced to the middle-management departments, whereas in a Sino-German joint-venture company, a German style of management training was conducted to develop a task-oriented decision-making style (instead of relation-oriented), with thorough planning and clear working responsibility. Based on these results, a survey-feedback organizational development project has been conducted to improve the organizational effectiveness in joint ventures.

Technological Innovations and Organizational Development

Technical innovation was an important activity in mass participation in Chinese enterprises, especially in the late 1950s and late 1970s. With the development of the Chinese economic reform program during the 1980s, more and more new technology, such as computer systems and automatic production lines, has been introduced into various industries and other organizations. Technological innovation is now a major goal in enterprise management. Since technological innovation is carried out at the organizational level, it has become part of recent organizational development. However, in the process of introducing and implementing technology, more attention was paid to the technical aspects rather than to the social and organizational aspects, which sometimes led to inefficiency and ineffectiveness. There is now a great need to conduct industrial and organizational research, provide useful principles of human-computer-organizational interaction and effective strategies, and enhance managerial expertise to ensure effective implementation of technological innovations (e.g., L. Chen, l986; Simon, 1987; Z. M. Wang, 1987).

Strategies in Technological Innovation. As a tradition in Chinese management, the planned mass participation in technical innovation was seen as a means of mobilizing creativity and motivation. The popular practice was to organize joint innovation teams in which cadres, technicians, and workers collaborated with each other and worked together. Both workers and technicians were encouraged to participate in team activities and to make their suggestions or proposals to improve production techniques and work procedures. As a result, the management had a much closer relationship with workers and technicians who could then combine technical knowledge with practical production experience (Tao, 1984).

There were also special reward systems for good innovation proposals and for actual productivity (e.g., based on annual actual improvement in output). In 1954, 1963, and 1982, respectively, the Chinese State Council promulgated regulations concerning awards, including both material and social rewards, for production rationalization proposals and technological improvements, which significantly facilitated mass participation in technological innovations.

Recent technological innovations in Chinese enterprises have focused more on introducing and implementing high technology or larger scale technological changes than was previously the case. Therefore, innovations have had a much larger impact on the structure and management of Chinese enterprises and have required more adaptation of organizational change and more effective psychological strategies than was the case earlier. The sociotechnical model becomes a useful way of achieving this (Heller, 1989). The model is based on two considerations—that organizational performance and effectiveness requires the joint operation of social and technical subsystems, and that both the social and technical systems must relate to the environment (Cummings & Srivasta, 1977). Here, the environment includes cultural, social, economic, and physical elements. The sociotechnical model is actually consistent with the current approach in Chinese modernization, which emphasizes both social construction (e.g., moral and sociopsychological development) and material construction (e.g., technological advancement and productivity).

On the basis of his series of field studies on computer systems development in Chinese enterprises (1986b, 1987), Z. M. Wang (1989b) built up a LISREL interface hierarchy model, which views computer expertise, system connectivity (or networking), and participation as the three facets of an interface hierarchy among people, technology, and organizations. Three psychological strategies were then proposed to facilitate technological innovations and organizational development.

- *Expertise strategy* focuses on strengthening the training of workers in the knowledge, competence, and skills necessary for the relatively high level of human-machine (computer) interaction. It is also called the *user support strategy* and includes psychological and technical support.

- *Systems strategy* emphasizes improving communication of information concerning technological and organizational development and system channels or networks for information sharing. It also includes the adaptation of new technology to the organizational structure.

- *Participation strategy* facilitates high involvement of various groups of personnel in the planning, design, and implementation of new technology and promotes positive organizational climate for new technological changes.

In a recent in-depth field survey among eight Chinese enterprises in the metallurgical, electronics, and plastics industries, Z. M. Wang and He (1989) examined the psychological characteristics of decision-making procedures used in introducing new technology. Wang and He found that in most enterprises, decisions on new technology were based solely on technical and economic analysis and ignored social and managerial information, and that few workers and supervisors participated in decision making concerning the new technology. Their survey demonstrated that frequently adopting a technology-only strategy resulted in higher decision uncertainty, organizational risk, and judgment bias when new technology was being introduced. Organizational risk was defined as high probability of incompetent and less-motivated personnel, poor interdepartmental coordination, and low organizational commitment and climate. The survey suggested that a personnel-organizational strategy be adopted jointly with the technology strategy to improve expertise, systems information networking, and organizational climate so that efficiency in technological innovations could be increased.

Action Research and Organizational Development. As the Chinese economic reform program developed into a stage of management systems change, action research has become a useful and effective approach in Chinese management reform as one of the major methods for organizational development (OD; L. Chen, 1984; Z. M. Wang, 1988a). When L. C. Xu and his colleagues (1985) carried out studies of PM leadership assessment in more than 30 enterprises, they actually used PM assessment, adapted from the Japanese scale, as a psychological instrument for survey feedback to facilitate organizational development. The results of the leadership assessment were fed back to managers, who then discussed the plans to try and improve the situation. The OD intervention increased output and productivity by about 20 percent one year after the survey feedback was given, indicating that it was feasible to adapt an OD program based on one nation's culture and socioeconomic system and apply it to another nation's context.

Given China's cultural tradition of group work and its recent reform practices that emphasize decentralization in enterprise management, industrial and organizational psychologists were interested in developing more effective OD interventions suitable for China's organizational context. In a field study in a machinery factory, workers were asked to evaluate three different OD interventions in work situations described in job descriptions: new bonus systems, job enlargement, and group participation (G. Wang, 1988). Group participation was evaluated as the most favorable and effective intervention in management reform and organizational development, whereas job enlargement was considered attractive but less practical. An interesting finding was that during the early 1980s, bonuses as a form of incentive had only a limited impact on organizational change in Chinese factories. Apparently, group participation was regarded as a kind of "social intervention," which proved to have a significant interaction with the bonus system, a "material intervention." Workers preferred a stable though small bonus under group participation but inclined toward a system of varied and unlimited bonuses when a system of group participation was not in place. Although this was just a questionnaire evaluation of different OD interventions, it did provide some evidence that an intervention that combined group participation with a bonus system could result in better organizational development in Chinese industries.

In the process of organizational reform and development, attention was also paid to the intrinsic nature of different jobs in China. Zhong (1989) tested the *Job Characteristics Model* (Hackman & Oldham, 1980) and distributed questionnaires among 215 assembly-line and nonassembly-line workers in industrial settings. Nonassembly-line employees experienced significantly higher levels of the key job characteristics, such as autonomy, identity, variety, and feedback, than did assembly-line employees. However, no difference was found between the two groups of employees in terms of their perception of job significance, which is seen as a general job characteristic in China. Moreover, there were no significant differences between the two groups of employees in terms of job meaningfulness, responsibility, and knowledge of results, but there were significant differences in how the workers responded to work motivation and satisfaction. Given that both assembly- and nonassembly-line employees experienced high job meaningfulness, responsibility, and knowledge of results, it would appear that those key psychological states were more affected by the general practice of management decentralization and incentive systems than they were by the job characteristics themselves. Further analysis showed that the relationships among job characteristics, psychological states, work satisfaction, and performance were highly dependent on the growth need strength (GNS) rating of workers. For workers with a high GNS, job characteristics were significantly correlated with work satisfaction, whereas no correlation was found among workers with low GNS ratings. The study's results have implications for job redesign implementation whenever organizational development is undertaken in Chinese enterprises.

In order to improve the nation's technological innovation (e.g., developing management information systems) as an important means of organizational development, we were able to carry out, in collaboration with the management, an action research project in 16 Chinese enterprises (Z. M. Wang, 1990d).

The project was based on field surveys and the human-computer interface model (Z. M. Wang, 1987, 1989b). Special attention was paid to assessment, diagnosis, and interventions as they relate to relationships among computer systems, users, and organizational functions so that problems could be identified and relevant actions could be determined and implemented. An *Assessment Scale of System Development* (ASSD) was developed to assess the following factors: computer skills, system link, participation, work motivation and expectation, leadership climate, human resource utilization, organizational structure, task characteristics, communication, work load, performance, and satisfaction. After some in-depth interviews at various levels of the organization, the ASSD was distributed for diagnosis among subjects in 16 enterprises, including managers overseeing management information systems development, users in relevant management departments, systems analysts and computer programmers, operators, and other employees. Both *interenterprise analysis* and *intraenterprise analysis* were made to determine the problems brought about by the implementation of management information systems, especially in terms of the three key facets of human-computer interface. Based on the assessment results, a method of *Group Feedback Consultation* (GFC) was used with working meetings, in which managers, computer programmers, users, and operators were given feedback charts of assessment results and were consulted for action plans to make improvements. The GFC was developed from the Chinese tradition of group approach and from the practice of group consultation in labor competition and technical innovation in the early 1960s, when the focus of Chinese enterprises was on technical issues and team cooperation. The major development is that the GFC is now well-structured and has more systematic assessment, data analysis, and longitudinal monitoring, while the group consultation components remain the same. The

GFC is similar to *Group Feedback Analysis* (GFA), which includes quantifiable information collection, material analysis, and group feedback (Heller, 1970). A special modification of the GFC in the present action research was that in addition to the assessment results of a particular enterprise, the average results of the whole sample were presented in the group feedback and planning sessions. This provided a comparable frame of reference and facilitated open-systems thinking, as well as comprehensive action plans and a holistic perspective. Members of the entire group then consulted with each other and with an industrial and organizational psychologist regarding key issues and useful strategies in the planning and implementation of OD actions. A follow-up interview evaluation conducted two months after the action implementation showed that the action research had resulted in the optimization of interface facets (expertise, systems networking, and participation), and in a higher level of involvement in systems development, a more positive organizational climate, and better performance (Z. M. Wang, 1990d).

While discussing the value of action research in the Chinese context, L. Chen (1984) emphasized the theoretical orientation in conducting action research as well as the open systems perspective in organizational development. In his presentation at the Eighth OD World Congress held in Hangzhou, China, Chen (1989) summarized four key principles of industrial and organizational psychology used in China's recent organization development: (a) decentralization of power and group participation, (b) the director responsibility contract system as a variation of management by objective (MBO), (c) a combination of short-term developments and long-term interests of the organization, and (d) education for better group cooperation, higher responsibility, and stronger organizational commitment in the work force. These have been the guidelines for many Chinese enterprises and other organizations.

Conclusions

The Chinese Approach to Industrial and Organizational Psychology

Recent rapid development and wide applications of industrial and organizational psychology in China have been largely based on its cultural tradition as well as its economic reform practices. To a large extent, this has in turn facilitated the development of Chinese modernization. A kind of Chinese approach to industrial and organizational psychology has emerged from recent research and practice (Z. M. Wang, 1991). Among the important characteristics of this Chinese approach are its cultural and social orientation, link with the economic reform practice, and collaborative efforts by academics and practitioners.

Cultural and Social Orientation.   Recent research and practice in industrial and organizational psychology has paid particular attention to China's cultural and social context. The three most important and influential factors have been considered. The first factor is the group orientation in organizational interventions, such as group reward systems, excellent team movement, group attributional training, group responsibility and power sharing, and group feedback consultation. The second factor is the conception and practice of combining material and social orientations, such as material rewards versus social incentives in motivating people, performance versus moral character in personnel assessment and selection, and material development versus social change in technological innovations and organization development. The third factor is the recent reform in education, which emphasizes mutual understanding, organizational commitment, social contribution, and moral dvelopment. Joint efforts are being made among party organizations, management, tradeunions, women's federations, and youth leagues in the pursuit of social and organizational development in Chinese enterprises and other organizations. These factors have been taken into consideration in the design, implementation, theoretical development, and application of recent studies in industrial and organizational psychology, which characterizes the Chinese approach in this field.

Links With Economic Reform Practices. The development of industrial and organizational psychology in China has been closely linked to the country's economic reform practices. Specifically, the focus of researchers and their applications has continuously shifted into new areas as the country has moved to new stages of economic reform. From the late 1970s through the early 1990s, the economic reform of Chinese enterprises has been moving toward management decentralization, with an emphasis on responsibility and efficiency. It has in turn gone through changes in reward and incentive systems, personnel and labor systems, management responsibility contract systems, Sino-foreign joint ventures, and high technology. In the meantime, industrial and organizational psychologists have carried out research concerning work motivation, incentive systems design, team development and optimization, personnel selection, leadership assessment, managerial decision making, participation, joint-venture management strategies, action research, and technological innovations. The close link between these factors and China's economic reform practices has not only formulated an effective approach for the development of industrial and organizational psychology as an important discipline but has also facilitated the development of the economic reforms themselves.

Collaborative Efforts With Practitioners. The recent development of industrial and organizational psychology in China should also be attributed to the close collaboration between academics and practitioners. Most recent research was conducted in collaboration with enterprises, companies, and governmental departments using workers, managers, and government officials as subjects in real organizational settings. Therefore, the results of recent studies have had more direct implications for the practice of management and for work situations. There are three major reasons why such close collaboration was possible in China. First, since 1978, the entire country has shifted its focus to modernization, which has in turn created a positive social environment for the development of new principles of industrial and organizational psychology. Second, the development of national management training and vocational education in managerial psychology in the early 1980s has popularized psychological knowledge and increased the consciousness of psychological issues among managers and workers. They are interested in applying psychological principles and methods to improve their new tasks. Third, the rapid development of various teaching and training programs of industrial and organizational psychology in universities has produced a contingent of industrial and organizational psychologists in China. They are eager to establish extensive contacts with industrial organizations and develop industrial and organizational psychology through the practice.

Cross-cultural–Socioeconomic Perspective and International Management. The recent development of industrial and organizational psychology in China cannot be separated from the advancement of industrial and organizational psychology and international management in the rest of the world. It has also been closely related to the recent economic reform program in China. A cross-cultural–socioeconomic perspective is especially useful in creating a dynamic frame of reference and formulating a new approach in the study of industrial and organizational psychology. By comparing the findings of different countries and different cultures, one can expand theories, increase the range of variables, and obtain more insights into contextual factors (Triandis & Brislin, 1984). We can also acquire a more comprehensive and accurate view of work behavior and organizational characteristics in China, which have useful implications for international management.

A Cross-cultural–Socioeconomic Perspective. China's open-to-the-world policy has had a positive impact on the recent development of industrial and organizational psychology in the country. In the early 1980s, the introduction and translation of foreign textbooks and literature in this area played an important role in formulating teaching and training programs and research projects in industrial and organizational psychology. Later, a number of Sino-foreign joint training centers played active roles in management training and education. Many research projects on industrial and organizational psychology have taken a cross-cultural perspective and have contributed to a better understanding of Chinese organizational behavior. Since 1987, we have been involved in a number of international joint research projects on managerial decision making and industrial relations and have obtained interesting results. Among the research topics, we studied participation and managerial skill utilization in enterprises (Z. M. Wang, 1989a), leadership as the management of role conflict among British, American, and Chinese managers (Smith, Peterson, & Z. M. Wang, 1992), and patterns of organizational decision making comparing 11 Chinese enterprises with 10 British companies (Z. M. Wang & Heller, 1992). The results from these studies indicate that a new approach is needed to integrate cultural factors with socioeconomic influence in cross-cultural studies (Barrett & Bass, 1983) and that a cross-cultural–socioeconomic perspective is more accurate and useful than the cross-cultural view alone in explaining the differences and similarities in organizational behaviors among different countries.

Implications for International Management. Several implications for international management have been revealed from the recent research and practice in industrial and organizational psychology in China. First, the cross-cultural–socioeconomic perspective is more useful and productive in cross-cultural industrial and organizational psychology and international management than single perspectives. Recent development of industrial and organizational psychology in China has shown that economic and social reforms have had a much greater impact on organizational behavior and human resource management practices than the cultural tradition itself. While culture still has important effects on management, it should be regarded as one of many determinants of organizational behavior in international management. Second, the Chinese team approach is of special value to international management. The core of this approach has two components: group responsibility and group consultation. Group responsibility is a task-oriented component based on a group goal structure and the task itself, whereas group consultation is a social-oriented component relevant to participation and human resource utilization and development. Using a team development method, such as group attributional training (i.e., performance attribution and group discussions) under a group responsibility system, the responsibility and group consultation components could be combined to achieve better performance (Z. M. Wang, 1986a, 1988b). This team approach has broader implications than the traditional concept of collectivism in recent cross-cultural studies (e.g., Kagitcibasi & Berry, 1989) and may greatly enhance efficiency in international management. Third, the idea and practice of integrating and adapting material and social aspects of work can have important implications for international management.

In particular, the coordination of motives and value premises between partners and across organizational levels should be a main preparation for international corporations and joint ventures. The integration of material development with encouragement of organizational commitment and workers having a sense of being the masters of their enterprises should be a major strategy in human resource management in international management. Fourth, the expertise, systems, and participation strategies developed in Chinese action research could prove valuable in achieving effective international management. These strategies should be adopted with an action research approach and adapted to the organizational situation. They are actually a kind of OD behavioral procedure, a planning process for management reform and technological innovations (Z. M. Wang, 1990d).

New Directions of Industrial and Organizational Psychology in China. Chinese economic reforms are developing into a new stage of management systems change. The implementation of the Chinese Enterprise Law, the Sino-foreign Joint Venture Law, and the Trade Union Law have promoted and consolidated the new approach in managerial practice. Industrial and organizational psychology in China is moving toward a higher level of research and applications. Although some theories and models of industrial and organizational psychology have been formulated in research and practice since 1978, the general theoretical development of industrial and organizational psychology in China has been relatively weak. As a new direction in this area, more attention is being paid to summarizing the findings from recent Chinese studies and developing a theoretical system of industrial and organizational psychology. Meanwhile, psychologists are carrying out more systematic research in wider areas of industrial and organizational psychology and are becoming problem oriented in applying

psychological principles to new tasks of economic reform. There are more interdisciplinary efforts in research and application. A holistic approach is needed to integrate principles from various branches of applied psychology with the cultural tradition and management reform practices.

Developing Theories of Industrial and Organizational Psychology. After more than a decade of research and practice, there is a great need to summarize research findings and practical experience and establish a system of industrial and organizational psychology in China. A number of relevant theoretical models have been developed in recent research in this area. Several of these models are presented here as a basis for further development.

Based on a series of field studies and experiments, Z. M. Wang (1986a, 1988b) proposed using a *motivational model of attribution and responsibility system*. This model regards work motivation as a dynamic and developmental process in which the responsibility system (goal structure) has crucial effects on the cognitive attributions, subsequent motivation, and, in turn, performance level. Under different work responsibility systems, employees have different levels of locus of control and form different patterns of attributions. Therefore, attributions are largely dependent on the kinds of responsibility system being used (team vs. individual).

In the research on leadership assessment, a *CPM leadership behavior model* (character, performance, and maintenance) was formulated (W. Q. Lin, L. Chen, & D. Wang, 1987; L. C. Xu, 1987). The model adds the dimension of moral character to the conventional divisions of performance and maintenance of leadership behavior. This is based on the Chinese tradition and practice of emphasizing moral and personal character in personnel evaluation. Therefore, the CPM model more closely adapts to the cultural context and management practice and provides a useful frame of reference for leadership studies in China.

The computer systems development has been an important part of technological innovations in various enterprises and organizations. Z. M. Wang (1989b) focused on the issue of organizational interface in systems development and formulated a LISREL *human-computer interface hierarchy model*, which included three facets: computer expertise, systems networking (connectivity), and organizational climate (participation). The interaction among these three facets determines the degree of interface uncertainty and facilitates the development of a human-computer interface hierarchy. Strengthening these key facets could therefore reduce or absorb uncertainty and increase the level of human-computer-organization interaction. The interface hierarchy model has practical implications for the task of systems development and management reform in enterprises.

Motivating people is the key to managment. Yu (1988a) proposed a *motivational model of material and social incentives,* based on a number of field surveys about employees' need structures in Chinese enterprises. The model's main theme assumes that in order to achieve maximum motivational effects, both material and social motives should be simultaneously facilitated. Material or social incentive alone fail to produce positive motivational effects. In Yu's model, material incentives include bonuses, housing, and other material benefits, while social incentives consist of positive respect, care, affection, and socially desired titles. The model proves useful in current management practice.

Based on the three-year comparative research on organizational decision making in 11 Chinese and 10 British companies, Z. M. Wang and Heller (1992) found that decision-making power was dynamic and contingent based on several organizational factors, such as the types of decisions being made, the management systems adopted, the industrial sectors represented by the enterprise, and type of ownership. They then built a *model of organizational decision power shift* and regarded the power shift as a joint function of decision task uncertainty, defined by the types of decision tasks; meso-organizational factors, such as management structure and systems (Heller & Wilpert, 1981); and macro-organizational factors, such as industry sector and ownerships. The interactions among factors such as social systems, industrial sectors, management structures, decision tasks, and leadership styles determined the decision power patterns in organizations.

Problem-oriented Systematic Research. With the development of industrial and organizational psychology in China, more research projects have been organized with more systematic methodology and improved design and measurement and are oriented toward practical problems in management reform. There are several active new areas in industrial and organizational psychology in China. The first one is the performance appraisal of both director responsibility systems and joint-venture management so that management and work efficiencies can be improved and evidence for implementing planned reform actions in Chinese enterprises can be provided.

The second area is organizational decision making, particularly the decision-making patterns found in joint ventures. Efforts are also devoted to the knowledge elicitation and acquisition among senior managers in organizational decision making. Since Sino-foreign joint ventures have different management systems and decision-making powers from ordinary Chinese enterprises, it is interesting to see how Chinese cultural, social, and organizational factors influence decision-making patterns and management behaviors, which may in turn provide a new approach for future economic reform in other Chinese enterprises.

The third area is team effectiveness. Although China has a strong tradition of group approach in management practice, there has been little systematic research on team behavior and effectiveness. One of the interesting topics in this area is team decision making. Of interest is how cultural, social, organizational, task, and personal factors interact with each other in team decision making and how decision information is processed in the team context. We are also interested in how the two components of team approach, group responsibility and group consultation, interact with each other in determining team effectiveness.

The fourth area is occupational stress, especially management stress, which is still a new area in industrial and organizational psychology in China. Some field surveys to assess occupational stress among shiftwork and nonshiftwork employees as well as management stress among supervisors and managers under different responsibility systems are in progress. In addition to these areas, there is continuing research in other areas such as Chinese motivational patterns, personnel assessment, and technological innovations.

A new trend in recent work being done in industrial and organizational psychology in China is that more attention is being paid to the methodological aspects of the research (e.g., L. Chen, 1987; Z. M. Wang, 1990e). Apart from the three-step approach of interview-questionnaire-field experiment frequently used in a number of recent studies in China, longitudinal designs are being used in research on organizational decision making as well as management training. The in-depth case analysis method is used as a necessary supplement to questionnaire surveys about industrial relations and the introduction of new technology. A parallel analysis method is used to combine interview record with questionnaire data in our Sino-British joint research project on industrial relations. Measurements with acceptable reliability and validity have been developed, and multivariate statistical analysis has been widely used in recent studies in China. One of the key issues in cross-cultural methodology is having research instruments and concepts translated into different languages (Triandis & Brislin, 1984). In the last decade of international research projects on industrial and organizational psychology in China, the back translation method was found to have some problems in matching the translations of nation- or region-specific concepts and expressions. For instance, in the translations between Chinese and English, the words "worker" or "manager" would have different translations by psychologists from mainland China, Hong Kong, and Taiwan, respectively. Therefore, a parallel translation method has been developed in our studies, in which two researchers make the first set of translations and a third researcher independently checks the two versions of translation. Then, a joint meeting between Chinese and foreign collaborators is held to check, discuss, and finalize the translation item by item. The parallel translation method has proven practical and effective in several research projects in China. All of these suggest that industrial and organizational psychology in China is developing into a higher level of scientific discipline.

The Holistic Approach: Culture, Management Practice, and Psychology. A more significant new direction in industrial and organizational psychology in China is its holistic approach in research and applications. It has two implications for industrial and organizational psychology in general. First, there has been a great need for interdisciplinary joint research in areas such as human-computer-organization interaction, job redesign, technological innovations, decision support systems, occupational stress, and training studies (Z. M. Wang, 1991). L. Chen (1988b) adopted the concepts of macroergonomics as a broader framework for the holistic approach and called for systems thinking in research and applications to integrate individual and organizational functions, short-term interests and long-term potentials, and material incentives and moral development. Second, a holistic approach should be used to integrate culture, management practice, and psychological principles in the study of industrial and organizational psychology. There are close relationships among those three components in the holistic approach: Culture has a long-term impact on management philosophy and psychological concepts; management reform practice modifies culture and facilitates theoretical development in psychology; and industrial and organizational psychology provides principles guiding management reforms and improving culture. On the basis of cultural context and the platform of economic reform, industrial and organizational psychology has played and continues to play a more and more active role in the cause of Chinese modernization.

I wish to express my appreciation to the Council for International Exchange of Scholars in the United States for the support of a Fulbright scholarship (1990) at Old Dominion University, Norfolk, Virginia, where an earlier draft of this chapter was prepared. I especially wish to thank Professor Li Chen, my mentor at Hangzhou University, for his most valuable supervision on my research. My sincere thanks go to the editors of this Volume of the Handbook of Industrial and Organizational Psychology, *Harry Triandis, Marvin Dunnette, and Leaetta Hough, for their encouragement and valuable comments on earlier drafts of this chapter.*

References

Barrett, G. V., & Bass, B. M. (1976). Cross-cultural issues in industrial and organizational psychology. In M. D. Dunnette (Ed.), *Handbook of industrial and organizational psychology* (pp. 1639–1686). Chicago: Rand McNally.

Chen, Li. (1935). *Essentials of industrial psychology.* Shanghai: Chinese Commercial Press. (in Chinese)

Chen, Li. (1983). *Prospectus of industrial psychology.* Hangzhou, China: Zhejiang People's Press. (in Chinese)

Chen, Li. (1984). Action research. *Psychology Abroad, 3,* 2–5. (in Chinese)

Chen, Li. (1986). New directions in managerial psychology. *Chinese Journal of Applied Psychology, 1*(1), 3–9. (in Chinese)

Chen, Li. (1987, September). *Recent research on organizational psychology in China.* Paper presented at the sixth annual conference of the Chinese Psychology Society, Hangzhou, China.

Chen, Li. (Ed.). (1988a). *Psychology of industrial management.* Shanghai: Shanghai People's Press. (in Chinese)

Chen, Li. (1988b). Macro-ergonomics in industrial modernization. *Chinese Journal of Applied Psychology, 3*(1), 1–4. (in Chinese)

Chen, Li. (1989). Organization development in China: Chinese version. *Chinese Journal of Applied Psychology, 4*(1), 1–5. (in Chinese)

Chen, Li, & Zhu, Z. R. (1959). Some psychological issues on training of textile workers. *Acta Psychologica Sinica, 1,* 42–49. (in Chinese)

Child, J. (1987). *Enterprise reform in China—progress and problems.* In M. Warner (Ed.), *Management reform in China* (pp. 24–52). London: Frances Pinte.

Cummings, T. G., & Srivasta, S. (1977). *Management at work: A sociotechnical systems approach.* Kent, OH: Kent State University Press.

Earley, P. C. (1989). Social loafing and collectivism: A comparison of the United States and the People's Republic of China. *Administrative Sciences Quarterly, 34,* 565–581.

Executive Committee of the Chinese Psychological Society. (1982). Retrospect and prospect of sixty years of psychology in China. *Acta Psychological Sinica, 14*(2), 127–138. (in Chinese)

Gao, J. F. (Ed.). (1985). *The history of Chinese psychology.* Beijing: Educational Press. (in Chinese)

Hackman, J. R., & Oldham, G. R. (1980). *Work redesign.* Reading, MA: Addison-Wesley.

Heller, F. A. (1970). Group feed-back analysis as a change agent. *Human Relations, 23*(4), 319–333.

Heller, F. A. (1989). On humanising technology. *Applied Psychology: An International Review, 38*(1), 15–28.

Heller, F. A., & Wilpert, B. (1981). *Competence and power in managerial decision-making*. Chichester, UK: Wiley.

Henley, J. S., & Mee-Kau, N. (1987). The development of work incentives in Chinese industrial enterprises—material versus non-material incentives. In M. Warner (Ed.), *Management reform in China* (pp. 127–148). London: Frances Pinte.

Hofstede, G. (1980). *Culture's consequences: International differences in work-related values*. Beverly Hills, CA: Sage.

Kagitcibasi, C., & Berry, J. W. (1989). Cross-cultural psychology: Current research and trends. *Annual Review of Psychology, 40*, 493–531.

Kast, F. E., & Rosenzweig, J. E. (1979). *Organization and management* (Z. L. Li, Y. J. Liu, & E. T. Su, trans.). Beijing: Chinese Social Science Press. (Chinese work published 1985)

Kroeber, A. L., & Kluckhohn, C. (1952). *Culture: A critical review of concepts and definitions*. Cambridge, MA: Peabody Museum.

Kroeber, A. L., & Parsons, T. (1958). The concept of culture and social systems. *American Sociological Review, 23*, 583–594.

Laaksonen, O. (1988). *Management in China: During and after Mao*. Berlin: Walter de Gruyter.

Latane, B., Williams, K. D., & Harkins, S. (1979). Many hands make light the work: The causes and consequences of social loafing. *Journal of Personality and Social Psychology, 37*, 822–832.

The law of the People's Republic of China on industrial enterprises owned by the whole people. (1988, May 15). *China Daily Business Weekly*.

Laws set to aid joint-ventures. (1990, September 12). *China Daily*.

Li, C. G., Song, X. H., & Li , J. (1989). *An introduction to Chinese ancient civil service systems*. Beijing: Labour and Personnel Press. (in Chinese)

Li, G. P. (1990). On personnel management in Chinese traditional culture. *Management World, 2*, 174–181. (in Chinese)

Li, X. Y. (1988). A preliminary study on employees' needs and motivation in enterprises. *Behavior Science, 4*, 5–12. (in Chinese)

Lin, C. D. (1983). Methodology of Chinese ancient psychological testing. In S. Pall & J. F. Gao (Eds.), *Studies on Chinese ancient psychological thinking* (pp. 304–312). NanChang, China: Jianxi People's Press. (in Chinese)

Lin, W. Q., Chen, L. (Long), & Wang, D. (1987). The construction of the CPM scale for leadership behavior assessment. *Acta Psychologica Sinica, 19*(2), 199–207.

Lu, H. J. (1986). An application of situational simulation assessment in selecting of managerial personnel. *Information on Psychological Sciences, 2*, 43–48. (in Chinese)

Lu, S. Z., Wu, L. L., Zheng, Q. Q., & Wang, Z. M. (1985). *Managerial psychology*. Hangzhou, China: Zhejiang Educational Press. (in Chinese)

Luo, L. J. (1987). A preliminary analysis on Confucius' thinking of affectional management. *Behavior Science, 4*, 28–30.

McCormick, E. J., & Ilgen, D. R. (1985). *Industrial and organizational psychology* (S. Z. Lu, Z. M. Wang, & Q. Q. Zheng, trans.). Beijing: Science and Technology Press. (Chinese work published 1990)

Misumi, J. (1985). *The behavioral science of leadership*. Ann Arbor, MI: University of Michigan Press.

Mu, Z. J. (1990). On characteristics of Chinese traditional culture. *Frontier of Social Science, 1*, 113–119. (in Chinese)

Nevis, E. C. (1983, Spring). Cultural assumptions and productivity: The United States and China. *Sloan Management Review, 24*(3), 17–29.

Peng, R. X. (1980). Thirty years of Chinese work psychology. *Acta Psychologica Sinica, 12*(1), 16–21. (in Chinese)

Peterson, M. (1988). PM theory in Japan and China: What's in it for the United States? *Organizational Dynamics*, 22–38.

Schneider, B. (1985). Organizational behavior. *Annual Review of Psychology, 36*, 573–611.

Simon, H. A. (1976). *Administrative behavior: A study of decision making processes in administrative organization* (S. Yang, C. L. Han, & L. Xu, trans.). Beijing: Beijing Economics College Press. (Chinese work published 1988)

Simon, H. A. (1977). *The new science of management decision* (Z. L. Li & J. C. Tang, trans.). Beijing: Chinese Social Science Press. (Chinese work published 1982)

Simon, D. F. (1987). *Managing technology in China—is the development and application of computers the answer?* In M. Warner (Ed.), *Management reform in China* (pp. 198–216). London: Frances Pinte.

Smircich, L. (1985). Is the concept of culture a paradigm for understanding organizations and ourselves? In P. J. Frost, L. F. Moore, M. R. Louis, C. C. Lundburg, & J. Martin (Eds.), *Organizational culture* (pp. 55–72). London: Sage.

Smith, P. B., Peterson, M. F., & Wang, Z. M. (1990, August). *Leadership as the management of role conflict.* Paper presented at the 22nd International Congress of Applied Psychology, Kyoto, Japan.

Tan, C. H. (1989). Human resource management reforms in the People's Republic of China. In K. M. Rowland & G. R. Ferris (Eds.), *Research in personnel and human resources management* (Suppl. 1, pp. 45–58). London: JAI Press.

Tao, D. Q. (1984). Technological innovation cell. In *Chinese encyclopedia of enterprise management* (p. 277). Beijing: Enterprise Management Press.

Taylor, F. W. (1911). *Principles of management* (X. Y. Mo, trans.). Shanghai: Chinese Publishing House. (*Scientific management* published 1916)

Teng, G. R. (1989). Decision-making in small groups: The influence of member status differences and task type on group consensus. *Acta Psychologica Sinica, 21*(1), 76–85. (in Chinese)

Trade unions play bigger role in reforms. (1992b, April 24). *China Daily.*

Triandis, H. C. (1993). Cross-cultural industrial and organizational psychology. In M. D. Dunnette, L. M. Hough, & H. C. Triandis (Eds.), *Handbook of industrial and organizational psychology* (2nd ed., vol. 4). Palo Alto, CA: Consulting Psychologists Press.

Triandis, H. C., & Brislin, R. W. (1984). Cross-cultural psychology. *American Psychologist, 39*(9), 1006–1016.

Wang, G. (1988). Three interventions and their effects on organizational change in companies. *Chinese Journal of Applied Psychology, 3*(2), 38–44. (in Chinese)

Wang, J. H., & Chen, D. R. (1985). Modern history of Chinese psychology. In *Chinese encyclopedia—Psychology: History of psychology* (pp. 6–12). Beijing: Chinese Encyclopedia Press. (in Chinese)

Wang, Y. L., & Huang, L. C. (1984). Systems thought in ancient China. In *Chinese encyclopedia of enterprise management* (pp. 27–28). Beijing: Enterprise Management Press. (in Chinese)

Wang, Z. M. (1986a). Worker's attribution and its effects on performance under different work responsibility systems. *Chinese Journal of Applied Psychology, 1*(2), 6–10. (in Chinese)

Wang, Z. M. (1986b). The interface features and psychological strategies in computer systems development. *Chinese Journal of Applied Psychology, 1*(3), 7–11. (in Chinese)

Wang, Z. M. (1987). The approach and psychological characteristics in computer applications in Chinese enterprises. *Chinese Journal of Applied Psychology, 2*, 18–21. (in Chinese)

Wang, Z. M. (1988a). *Work and personnel psychology.* Hangzhou, China: Zhejiang Educational Press. (in Chinese)

Wang, Z. M. (1988b). The effects of responsibility system change and group attributional training on performance: A quasi-experiment in a Chinese factory. *Chinese Journal of Applied Psychology, 3*(3), 7–14. (in Chinese)

Wang, Z. M. (1989a). Participation and skill utilization in organizational decision making in Chinese enterprises. In B. J. Fallon, H. P. Pfister, & J. Brebner (Eds.), *Advances in industrial organizational psychology* (pp. 19–26). Amsterdam: Elsevier Science Publishers B.V.

Wang, Z. M. (1989b). The human-computer interface hierarchy model and strategies in system development. *Ergonomics* (Special issue: *Cognitive Ergonomics*), *32*(11), 1391–1400.

Wang, Z. M. (1990a). Recent developments in ergonomics in China. *Ergonomics* (Special issue: *Ergonomics in China*), *33*(7), 853–866.

Wang, Z. M. (1990b). Human resource management in China: Recent trends. In R. Pieper (Ed.), *Human resource management: An international comparison* (pp. 195–210). Berlin: Walter de Gruyter.

Wang, Z. M. (1990c). Information structures and cognitive strategies in decision making on systems development. *Ergonomics* (Special issue: *Ergonomics in China*), *33*(7), 907–916.

Wang, Z. M. (1990d). Action research and O.D. strategies in Chinese enterprises. *Organization Development Journal,* Spring, 66–70.

Wang, Z. M. (1990e). *Research methods in psychology.* Beijing: People's Educational Press. (in Chinese)

Wang, Z. M. (1991). Recent developments in industrial and organizational psychology in People's Republic of China. In C. Cooper & R. T. Robertson (Eds.), *International review of industrial and organizational psychology* (pp. 1–15). London: Wiley.

Wang, Z. M. (1992) Managerial psychological strategies for Sino-foreign joint-ventures. *Journal of Managerial Psychology, 7*(3), 10–16.

Wang, Z. M., & Fan, B. N. (1990). The task structure and information processing requirements of decision making on director responsibility systems in enterprises. *Chinese Journal of Applied Psychology, 5*(1), 13–18. (in Chinese)

Wang, Z. M., & He, G. B. (1989). Procedural characteristics and evaluation models of decision making in introducing new technology in Chinese enterprises. *Chinese Journal of Applied Psychology, 4*(4), 18–22. (in Chinese)

Wang, Z. M., & Heller, F. A. (in press). Patterns of power distribution in managerial decision making in Chinese and British industrial organizations. *The International Journal of Human Resource Management.*

Wang, Z. M., & Sheng, J. P. (1990). Characteristics of managerial decision making in Sino-foreign joint ventures and their performance assessment. *Chinese Journal of Applied Psychology, 5*(l), 29–37. (in Chinese)

Wang, Z. M., & Wang, Y. B. (1989). Some characteristics and strategies of personnel decisions in Chinese enterprises. *Chinese Journal of Applied Psychology, 4*(3), 8–14. (in Chinese)

Warner, M. (Ed.). (1987). *Management reform in China.* London: Frances Pinte.

Weiner, B. (1979). A theory of motivation for some classroom experiences. *Journal of Educational Psychology, 71*, 3–25.

Workers support new labour reforms. (1992a, May). *China Daily.*

Wu, L. L. (1986). A job analysis of management cadres in enterprises. *Chinese Journal of Applied Psychology, 1*(3), 12–16. (in Chinese)

Xu, J. Z. (1984). Two participation, one reform and three-in-one combination. In *Chinese encyclopedia of enterprise management* (p. 90). Beijing: Enterprise Management Press. (in Chinese)

Xu, L. C. (1986). Development in organizational behavior study in China. *Acta Psychologica Sinica, 18*(4), 343–348. (in Chinese)

Xu, L. C. (1987). Recent development in organizational psychology in China. In B. M. Bass & P. J. Drenth (Eds.), *Advances in organizational psychology: An international review* (pp. 242–251). London: Sage.

Xu, L. C., Chen, L. (Long), Wang, D., & Xue, A. Y. (1985). The role of psychology in enterprise management. *Acta Psychologica Sinica, 17*(4), 339–345. (in Chinese)

Xu, L. C., & Chen, L. (Long) (1988). *Managerial psychology.* People's Daily Press. (in Chinese)

Xu, X. D. (1986). Effects of production quota increase on workers' performance. *Information on Psychological Sciences, 2*, 36–42. (in Chinese)

Xu, Z. H., & Liu, Y. F. (1984). Bureaucrat-capitalist enterprise management. In *Chinese encyclopedia of enterprise management* (pp. 48–49). Beijing: Enterprise Management Press. (in Chinese)

Yang, D. N. (1984). Management thought in ancient China. In *Chinese encyclopedia of enterprise management* (pp. 24–25). Beijing: Enterprise Management Press. (in Chinese)

Yang, X. S. (1983). *Behavioral sciences.* Shanghai: Enterprise Management Press. (in Chinese)

Yu, W. Z. (1985). *Managerial psychology.* Lanzhou, China: Gansu People's Press. (in Chinese)

Yu, W. Z. (1988a). Synchronous motivating theory as a major motivational model at socialist primary stage. *Behavior Science, 5*, 3–8. (in Chinese)

Yu, W. Z. (1988b). The motivational function of group structure under labour contract systems. *Behavior Science, 3*, 8–10. (in Chinese)

Zhang, H. C. (1988). Psychological measurement in China. *International Journal of Psychology, 23*, 101–117.

Zhang, P. Q. (1986). *Personnel assessment in industrial and governmental organizations.* Beijing: Beijing Science & Technology Press. (in Chinese)

Zhong, J. A. (1989). Perceptions of job characteristics and satisfaction. *Chinese Journal of Applied Psychology, 4*(2), 14–21. (in Chinese)

CHAPTER 15

Cultural Embeddedness and the Developmental Role of Industrial Organizations in India

Jai B. P. Sinha
A.N.S. Institute of Social Studies, Patna, India

Industrial organizations in India have adopted Western technology, structures, and systems of management. However, they remain embedded in Indian culture and are required to serve as instruments of economic development by concerning themselves with the welfare of their employees. Government exerts various types of pressure on these organizations, particularly those in the public sector, which account for about two-thirds of all industrial activities and employment in the organized sector.

As a result, structures and systems remain manifestly Western, but ways and means appear to bypass them in actual functioning. Technology, efficiency, and profitability are compromised because the societal need for providing employment, stimulating economic growth, and so on, are strongly emphasized.

The collectivism of the culture reflects a preference for hierarchy and personalized relationships. Hence, centralization is high and increases with size. Top management plays a crucial role in regulating sociopolitical influences, as well as in running the organization. If the top leaders in an organization are effective at integrating task requirements with the cultural ethos, they can establish and maintain appropriate systems of selection, appraisal, training, leadership, power and authority, reward and punishment, decision making, communication, conflict resolution, and so on. They can then create a synergetic work culture.

> *On the other hand, if an organization's management is pliant and succumbs to sociopolitical pressures, systems and procedures are ignored in favor of the personal allegiance of loyal subordinates or helpful patrons. Social modes of relationship are superimposed on the workplace and the organization falls into the hands of self-serving individuals and groups. The result is a soft work culture.*
>
> *Organizational development schemes must aim at utilizing cultural values for establishing effective systems of management.*

The Context

Industrial organizations in India have been imported from the West and contain most Western work forms. However, they are embedded in Indian culture and have been given a developmental role. As a result, they tend to assume certain features that distinguish them from their Western counterparts. This chapter will examine the ways in which industrial organizations in India have evolved and retained Western work forms and relationships, and also identify how they function differently than Western organizations because of their cultural embeddedness and developmental role.

At the time of India's independence in 1947, the country had a very weak industrial base with very few industrial activities. There were neither demands nor opportunities to conduct research. Although the first department of psychology was established in 1919, there were only 25 studies in industrial psychology through 1947 (D. Sinha, 1972). Of them, eight were surveys and general essays, six were related to work and task analysis aided by ergograph and reaction-time instruments, and five pertained to performance and job satisfaction. Only one of the studies on performance was empirical. There were three studies on estimating reliability and validity of certain foreign tests of intelligence and personality.

Expansion and Developmental Needs

The subsequent decades witnessed a phenomenal growth in industrial activities, and a corresponding increase in the number of studies in industrial psychology. From 1951 to 1985, industrial activities expanded by a factor of six (A. N. Agrawal, Verma, & Gupta, 1988, p. 114). The growth was realized through a series of *Five Year Plans*, which required industrial organizations to play a strategic role in nation building. Western technology and work forms were liberally imported and were often transplanted in undeveloped areas with virtually nonexistent infrastructure. The purpose was not necessarily to make a profit but to activate growth processes that were expected to transform the neighboring areas (De, 1979; D'Souza, 1984; Dutta, 1990; Pareek, 1968; Zahir, 1984). Thus, the origin, as well as the evolutionary process of work organizations, were different in India than in the West.

In the West, the organizational forms, particularly those aspects that are related to the management of people, are heavily "influenced by social, economic, moral, ideological, and political processes" (Nord, 1986, p. 439). The basic assumption is that organizations that survive do so because of their efficiency. Drawing on Adam Smith (1937/1976), it is further believed that "welfare is maximized if each unit pursues its self-interest efficiently" (Nord, 1986, p. 440). The only social responsibilities, apart from quality control and customer service, were pollution control, equal opportunity in employment, and employee quality of life (Heather & Surger, 1980; Kilmann & Herdner, 1976).

On the contrary, industrial organizations in India, particularly those in the public sector, while constituting about two-thirds of all industrial activities (V. K. Agrawal, 1989), were conceived as parts of a master plan of the national efforts toward development—each serving its role in coordination and in cooperation with others. "The developmental role implies that technological, strategic, and structural choices need to be made by the organization keeping in view not only the interests of the organization, but also the developmental needs of the nation" (Khandwalla, 1988, p. 102). Developmental needs might consist of providing employment, improving conditions for employees, creating surplus capacity for future use, promoting exports, and manufacturing essential commodities at higher costs. None of these is likely to improve the profit rate of an organization (FORE, 1984). The concept of organizational effectiveness naturally undergoes a qualitative modification (Khandwalla, 1988) in light of the context in which Indian organizations function.

The Controlled Environment

The government, being the custodian of developmental efforts, has to allocate resources, maintain coordination, and create a controlled environment so that resources are utilized in a planned way. There is evidence that a scarce supply of resources distorts one's need for achievement, which then becomes a disposition to monopolize and hoard surplus resources for future use (J. B. P. Sinha, 1968; J. B. P. Sinha & J. Pandey, 1970). Hence, interorganizational competition must be restricted (Dayal, 1967).

At the earlier stage, a large number of government officers were deputed to key positions in public sector industrial organizations (Nigam, 1967, p. 67). They bureaucratized management and transmitted the colonial ethos of distancing themselves from their subordinates, thereby creating a state of high power distance (Hofstede, 1980) and greater centralization in decision making, which was further supported by the cultural preference for hierarchical

relationships (J. B. P. Sinha, 1990b). Even though professional managers have subsequently assumed control to a large extent, the government still tends to centralize power and maintain control over private undertakings by putting legal constraints on their expansion and diversification (Encarnation, 1982; Khurana, 1981; Mascarenhas, 1978), over public sector enterprises by issuing directives to and appointing their chief executives (Khandwalla, 1982; Murthi, 1982; Patil, 1982), and over both by exerting influence on financial institutions (Bidani & P. K. Mitra, 1982).

The Social Identity

By the same token, the government feels, in varying degrees, an obligation to bail out the organizations that incur losses. This in turn creates a propensity to bear losses, which is then used to cover up inefficiency and poor work discipline in the name of growth and social justice. The employees misconstrue these objectives; that is, they see the organization as providing welfare for employees who do not have to work hard to earn their benefits. Primacy is given to employee needs and management's decision reflects the pressures it receives. Pervasive poverty and a high unemployment rate create a sense of insecurity and the perception of scarcity, even among those who are employed and are not so poor. There is a constant pressure for there to be additional benefits and for organizations to employ the family members and relatives of employees. Fragmented and militant trade unions often support such demands and put organizations on the defensive (J. B. P. Sinha, 1990a).

Collectivism in Indian culture (Hofstede, 1980; Triandis et al., 1986) facilitates the process. People identify with their primordial groups and tend to maintain relationships even at the expense of work performance. Quality work is performed if there is a positive relationship with members (Dayal, 1976a; J. B. P. Sinha, 1985). Otherwise, work is considered to be a favor that is likely to exhaust the person and therefore avoided if at all possible (McClelland, 1975, pp. 159–160).

As a result, organizations by and large maintain a social rather than work identity (Parikh, 1979). They do not seem to respond to Udy's (1970) recommendation that in order to be effective, work organizations must shift from socially to technologically determined work forms. If culture is defined as the human-made part of the environment (Herskovits, 1955) that includes social, economic, and political considerations, we find that Indian culture affects a major part of industrial and organizational activities, including those that are generally presumed to be the legitimate domains of technology. Triandis' (see chapter 2 in this volume) contention that culture enters where technology does not constrain does not hold to be true. The relative domains of the influence of culture and technology are illustrated in Figure 1.

Figure 1 shows that structures and systems are shaped by technological requirements, although some modifications are made to accommodate local needs and conditions. For example, the size of a standard work force is invariably indicated by the technological package imported by an organization. However, the organization must negotiate with the union and its employees the number of workers that will be employed. Or, in certain cases, the choice of a high tech machine is determined more by its image value than by the functional requirements of the organization. In certain other cases, the fully automatic plants are rendered manual either because of clumsy handling, neglect of their maintenance, or the intention to create more jobs (J. B. P. Sinha, 1990a). However, most organizations, both large and small, subscribe to functional differentiation, specialization, formalization, and standardization. Virmani and Guptan (1991) studied 44 organizations and found that most of the systems and practices of Western management exist in Indian organizations but are seldom allowed to function the way they do in the West. Virmani and Guptan

FIGURE 1

Visual Display of Relative Influences of Culture and Technology

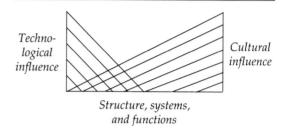

Structure, systems, and functions

From "Differences Between Psychological Domains in the Range of Cross-cultural Variation" by Y. H. Poortinga, P. M. F. Kop, and F. J. R. Van de Vijver, 1990. In J. A. Sergent and R. J. Takens (Eds.), *European Perspective in Psychology* (Vol. 3). Chichester, England: Wiley. Copyright 1990 by Wiley. Adapted by permission.

(1991) examined systems related to the flow of such things as information, financial procedures, technological upgrading, marketing, planning, recruiting, training, transfer, promotion, appraisal, delegation, grievance handling, and employee participation. In most cases, deviations and exceptions are made because of prevailing familism, patronage, a personalized approach, and a host of other cultural considerations.

Organizational Differences in Management Practices

Not all organizations are equally susceptible to cultural influences. Public enterprises, being the dominant sector and more strategic to national development, are subjected to stronger influences than large private sector, family-owned enterprises, or multinational corporations.

A number of studies have compared public and private sector organizations. Reviews by Khandwalla (1988), R. Padaki (1988), and J. B. P. Sinha (1981a) show that public enterprises are higher on such things as politicization, bureaucratization, procedural rigidity, and relationship orientation and are lower on production emphasis, profitability, and work orientation. They are comparable on safety, security, and material benefits. In certain cases, managers of public enterprises were found to be technically more competent. The sharpest contrast to the public enterprises is provided by small family managed units where the head of the unit (who is most likely to be the head of the family) and his orientations are the most critical factors of the management. The individual may have either a commercial-financial or technocratic-professional approach, each having profound consequences for running and expanding the enterprise.

There is also evidence that multinationals are more progressive and more prone to utilize formal managerial systems and practices than other businesses (Negandhi & B. S. Prasad, 1971; Parikh, 1979). Khandwalla (1983a) has identified a number of management styles, such as entrepreneurial, professional, traditional, transitional, tender, and commercial, which, he argues, are differentially adopted by different types of organizations. However, some researchers (e.g., Parikh, 1979; Virmani & Guptan, 1991) contend that organizational differences are rather minor and superficial. Putting aside the manifest differences, Indian organizations maintain a social rather than work identity.

The Evolving Research Trends

Awareness of the social identity of Indian organizations was at best latent in the initial years of research in industrial and organizational psychology. All that was striking was that increasing industrial activities created greater demands and opportunities to conduct research in a variety of settings. Hence, the number of research projects increased rapidly. Compared to 25 studies in the first 28 years (1919–1947) of industrial and organizational psychology research, 508 studies were reported (D. Sinha, 1972) in the next 21 years. J. B. P. Sinha (1981a) identified 350 during the next six years (1971–1976), and

Ganesh (1981) found twice as many during the next four years (1976–1979). R. Padaki (1988) and Khandwalla (1988) confirmed the accelerating rate of growth in industrial and organizational studies. About one-third of the studies pertained to motivation, job satisfaction, and leadership. Process variables (e.g., organizational climate, change) were much more prominent than either organizational structure (Khandwalla, 1988, p. 109) or work performance and productivity (J. B. P. Sinha, 1981a). The collectivistic concern with relationships probably sensitized social scientists only to certain aspects of working relationships.

The studies, however, have failed to generate indigenous theories, paradigms, or concepts. By all accounts (K. G. Agrawal, 1975; Chaturvedi, 1977; Ganesh, 1981; Khandwalla, 1988; R. Padaki, 1988; D. Sinha, 1972; J. B. P. Sinha, 1981a), the vast majority of them were imitative and replicative of Western theories and findings. To some extent, this was inevitable. The short history of industrial experience, the wholesale import of Western organizational forms, and the readily available and fully developed industrial and organizational literature in the West hardly allowed Indian researchers to evolve their own perspective. They were on the one hand exposed to problems arising out of the rapidly expanding industrial activities; on the other hand, the Western emphasis on specialization did not allow them to process the raw problems into manageable pieces of microscopic investigations. The temptation was to look for techniques, measures, and concepts in the Western literature and then apply them rather mechanically (J. B. P. Sinha, 1973a). Such imitative research has a "demand characteristic" to be replicated, thereby perpetuating a false etic until its inadequacy gets too conspicuous. This was exactly what happened. While the replicated findings created a false sense of universal industrial and organizational psychology, the nonconfirmed ones were left unexplained. It was these unexplained findings that led to a search for an indigenous perspective. The majority of industrial and organizational psychology research in India is still imitative and replicative but there is a growing tend to search for an alternative paradigm where even a despecialized approach (Moghaddam, 1989; D. Sinha, 1986) to larger chunks of organizational behavior may be pursued in order to appreciate the developmental role of Indian organizations (Gupta, 1991). The following sections highlight some of these efforts.

Recruitment, Appraisal, and Training

Cultural influences on the Western methods of recruitment, appraisal, and training are quite strong in Indian organizations.

Recruitment of Workers

As industrial activities expanded, there was increasing demand for human resources. It was easier to recruit workers than managers. The government policy required that at least one member of the families displaced by a new factory be given a job in the factory. Many local people—even those unskilled—were absorbed during the construction phase and later retained after the factories were commissioned. In some of the undertakings, the percentage of local workers reached as high as 93 (J. B. P. Sinha, 1990a, p. 69). Because many such local workers were unskilled, the undertaking still required skilled workers and supervisors who had to be brought initially from outside the area. Thus, most of the public undertakings and many in the private sector were burdened with overstaffing. The government rules also required that workers be recruited through the local Employment Exchange Office, and preferences were to be given to the "sons of the soil" (poor farmers), peoples from the weaker sections (underprivileged castes), the physically disabled, former military personnel, and so on.

Some organizations have developed the principle of giving jobs to the dependents of those who had put in a certain number of years of service, who had died, or who were seriously injured while on the job. According to a report by the Indian government's Ministry of Education (Ministry of Human Resource Development, 1985), 58 percent of the 15 million workers employed in public sector organizations that require technical knowledge or skills did not possess any formal education and/or training.

The leading private sector iron and steel company is estimated to have about 7,000 more employees than is necessary in a work force of about 33,600. Moreover, there are about 4,000 aspirants that the company is committed to hire, even though it does not have jobs available for them. About 1,400 are permanent workers who do not have specific jobs. They are a floating work force that receives work assignments whenever a large number of regular workers are absent. The unskilled workers constitute about 55 percent of the work force. About 70 percent of them are either native or domiciled of the state. At the supervisory and skilled levels, local employees constitute about 45 and 40 percent of the work force, respectively.

Most organizations are under constant pressure to employ more people. This is partly due to the government policy to generate employment, partly to political and trade union pressures, and partly as a result of requests made by their own employees to accommodate their kith and kin. B. P. Singh (1989, p. 123) reported that three major iron and steel plants in the public sector had about 22,000 surplus employees, which constituted about 33 percent of the work force. The plants employed about three times as many employees as is required in industrially advanced countries (p. 125). Once employed, a worker cannot ordinarily be fired—not even for nonperformance. Firing a worker implies depriving the person's family of its livelihood, which is not permissible in a welfare-oriented organization. Firing can occur only under special circumstances (e.g., for theft, criminal acts, etc.) and after less harsh disciplinary procedures have been exhausted. Hence, the pragmatic strategy is to leave the troublesome workers alone and concentrate on getting work from the few conscientious workers or to hire casual workers (on the basis of daily payment); the latter, of course, results in more overstaffing.

Recruitment of Managers

Recruitment of managers involves different issues. In the 1950s, there were hardly any management schools, but expanding industrial activities required a large number of managers. This need was met either by re-employing retired bureaucrats or former military personnel, or by placing active bureaucrats on deputation in the departments of administration, personnel, and finance. Managers in technical areas were drawn from the existing private sector or family-owned enterprises. There were not many applicants to draw upon. Hence, they were appointed after a brief interview, and received instant promotions. In order to meet the increasing demands, in 1954 the government started a number of technology institutes and asked four major universities, one in each region of the country, to start management courses. A number of management institutes, patterned after either the Sloan School of Management at MIT, the Harvard Business School, or other well-known American institutions, were then established. By 1972, there were at least 100 institutions offering management programs, besides 300 large industrial enterprises (including 50 banking organizations) that had their own management training departments. Taken as a whole, they produced fewer than 5,000 engineering and management graduates, although the industries needed more than 10,000 such individuals each year. As a result, a number of other institutions of uneven quality (D. P. Sinha, 1989) have been offering management education.

Selection of management trainees is now fairly similar to selection practices used in the United States. Large private sector organizations select the most promising candidates, including two-thirds of the graduates of the high-quality institutions. While tests are more economical than interviews, the latter are preferred because they tap more aspects of an applicant's potential. Agencies and institutions are contracted to administer and screen applicants. Hence, application forms and test are tools that are used primarily to eliminate the majority of applicants; remaining candidates are then further screened through interviews. Employers prefer to have a first-hand impression of the people they are recruiting. Culture probably sensitizes employers to be more receptive of overall impressions of applicants in person-to-person contact rather than through socially neutral tests that evaluate the elements of interest, intelligence, or aptitude that are required by specific jobs.

An absence of detailed job analyses and descriptions in many of the industrial organizations further limits the usefulness of test batteries. However, interviews are not only susceptible to subjective biases, but are also vulnerable to pressures from extraneous sources (H. Goswamy, 1985, p. 43). Favoritism based on family connections has been documented (J. B. P. Sinha & D. Sinha, 1990).

Testing through an independent agency minimizes the chance that such favoritism will occur. Work on test construction in India started in the 1920s, about the time psychologists in the United States and the United Kingdom started developing tests. By 1966, Long and Mehta (1966) identified 326 tests, of which 100 were intelligence tests, 96 achievement, 60 aptitude, 45 personality, 15 interest, and 10 were classified as miscellaneous. Since then, institutes have been established to develop batteries of selection tests (e.g., the National Institute of Bank Management, the Institute of Banking Personnel Selection, Ahmadabad

Textile Industry's Research Association, and the Indian Institute of Psychometry). The test batteries generally measure writing ability, English comprehension, perceptual acuity, mechanical aptitude, and abstract and numerical reasoning (S. Chatterji, 1985, p. 4). Critics (Mitra, 1968; B. N. Mukherjee, 1980; Rath, 1972; Shanmugam, 1972; D. Sinha, 1983) have argued that test construction in India has failed to meet expectations. They argue that tests are neither rooted in Indian realities nor based on appropriate theories. They are often developed mechanically as adaptations of foreign tests and are improperly validated. The culture probably does not promote the Western practice of analyzing individuals in terms of identifiable strands of ability, interests, and aptitudes. This may be one of the reasons that personality assessment has been more popular than ability measurement. Pareek and Rao (1974) recorded 218 instruments of personality assessment, 73 of which are adapted versions of well-known personality tests in the West: the MMPI, the *Guilford Zimmerman Temperament Survey*, Adorno's *F-scale*, Maslow's *Security-Insecurity Inventory*, and Rotter's *I-E Locus of Control Scale*. These scales, however, are used for research but not necessarily for selection.

Inductions for management and worker positions are made at their lowest levels. Thereafter, positions are generally filled by promotion. Lateral entries are rare and are strongly resented by insiders. Even for those positions where inductions from the outside may be considered desirable, cultural preference is to press for the promotion of insiders, if they are even minimally eligible. Some organizations reserve 50 percent of new positions for insiders and recruit the remaining 50 percent by a method of open competition. For the top positions, however, some inductions from outside the organization, although resented, are still made. Family-owned enterprises recruit new chief executives, and sick units (corporations losing money) bring new outsiders for turnaround management (Khandwalla, 1981c). The Bureau of Public Enterprises selects top candidates for public undertakings. However, promotion is the rule and lateral inductions are the exception. The compulsion is to build from the inside, to provide promotional opportunities to one's own people, and to minimize the potential conflicts that a newcomer might cause (S. K. Mukherjee, 1985, p. 35).

There are no tests for promotion. Seniority is by and large the basis for promotion, and interviews are conducted only to legitimize the process. In many organizations, merit is professed to be equally important. However, it is defined in such a manner that its salience is diluted, and seniority remains the only criterion, unless a competing candidate is undeniably superior. The objective ways of estimating merit are suspect and ignored at the time of promotion. Virmani and Guptan (1991) found that "in the Indian conditions, the Western emphasis on merit alone appears to go contrary to the sociocultural expectation of respect for seniority. Consequently, a loosely defined suitability is put forth that combines in itself the virtues of merit and with due deference to seniority" (p. 198).

Appraisal

A vicious circle seems to exist in regard to appraisal. Because merit is not the sole concern for either selection or promotion, neither testing nor appraisal receive appropriate use. Just as all organizations have a recruitment policy but in practice base recruitment on expediency (Virmani & Guptan, 1991, p. 204), similarly, most organizations have an appraisal system that is rarely used for either the promotion or placement of managers. If used at all, it serves as a "control device" to inculcate personal "loyalty" (Virmani & Guptan, 1991, p. 197).

The first survey of management literature in India (Dayal, 1973), which covered up until 1969, did not contain even a single reference to appraisal, nor did the survey of industrial psychology from the same period locate any studies of the appraisal systems (D. Sinha, 1972). With the notable exception of S. Chatterji and his colleagues (S. Chatterji, 1976; S. Chatterji & M. Mukherjee, 1963, 1966), A. Chatterji (1975), R. S. Das (1965), and Dayal (1976b), the area remained unexplored. Rao (1981) observed that "practically no research (of significance) has been reported on job rotation, appraisal, counseling, and strategies of human resource development" (p. 550). The exceptions were the multinationals and foreign subsidiaries (Ahmed, 1982). Shetty (1970) compared a number of firms in India and the United States and found that the U.S. firms paid greater attention to selection, training, and performance evaluation than the Indian firms, which emphasized welfare programs more than the U.S. firms.

J. B. P. Sinha (1985) argued that Indian culture does not encourage evaluating other people in objective and impersonal terms. Indians prefer relationship over performance and loyalty over efficiency. Dayal (1976b) observed that "relationship and organizational performance are not separated, loyalty having more positive meaning both for the superior and the subordinate" (p. 10). Kakar (1978) wrote that what an Indian is "sensitive to (and concerned with) are not the goals of work and productivity that are external to the relationship, but the relationship itself" (p. 125). If this is true, it is likely that evaluations would be based on the nature of the relationship between the appraiser and the appraisees. Those who are close and loyal to the appraiser would be evaluated positively, while others would be evaluated negatively. Appraisal forms are vague and abstract rather than specific and clear so that an appraiser can express liking or disliking based on the person rather than the evaluation of performance. Under such circumstances, an appraisal system is likely to lose its salience.

Training

Training seems to suffer because of the deficiencies in selection and appraisal systems. Although most organizations have a budget for training, they do not necessarily have a planned approach to training (Virmani &

Guptan, 1991, pp. 196–197). Except for the multinationals, Indian organizations, even the better organized ones, suffer from "adhocism" in their training programs. There are no systems for identifying training needs. The concern is to send a requisite number of mangers to a training course rather than have the appropriate people attend (N. K. Singh et al., 1983). Those whom employers can spare are sent to training more readily and for longer periods. Senior managers pick and choose their subordinates for attractive training programs or those that are directly linked to promotions (Dayal, 1971; S. N. Pandey, 1989, p. 70; Virmani & Gupta, 1991, p. 197).

Khandwalla (1988) reviewed the training approaches used in India and identified a number of modes. Some of the dominant ones were team building through sensitivity training (Chattopadhyaya & D. P. Sinha, 1970; Pareek & Lynton, 1965; D. P. Sinha, 1973, 1986), management by objectives (Maheshwari, 1977, 1980), sociotechnical analyses (De, 1984; D'Souza, 1984; J. P. Singh, 1981, 1983), structured interventions (Chattopadhyaya & Pareek, 1982; Lynton & Pareek, 1967), institution building (Dayal, 1977; Ganesh, 1980), and forceful management actions (Khandwalla, 1981a, 1981c). In fact, almost all the available techniques have been tried. They have some common features, most of which have been borrowed from the West. They all have their share of successes and failures. There is a growing realization that human resource development requires diversified strategies and multiple methods for training individuals who are embedded in their groups, organizations, and culture. Training individuals who are isolated from their organizations is likely to be ineffective (Baumgartel, Bennis, & De, 1968; Baumgartel & Jeanpierre, 1972).

Some (Sharma, 1972; Sharma & Warrier, 1977; J. B. P. Sinha, 1978) have commented on elitism in Indian management education. Some affluent families, most of which have urban backgrounds, can afford the tuition of Christian convents and expensive English

schools. These individuals are more often selected by the management institutes, and they
are the ones who are better in impression management during the selection interviews and
who are recruited by large public and high-
paying private undertakings. This perpetuates
elitism in management.

Training reinforces elitism further. There is
very little money available for worker training
(Virmani & Gupta, 1991). The higher the training fees, the higher are the levels of managers
who are assigned for the training, and, consequently, the greater the prestige, status, and
glamour of a training course (J. B. P. Sinha,
1978, p. M62). The smaller organizations and
the lower paid managers are naturally eliminated in this process. The high-priced courses
require luxurious settings where "the context
consumes all attention and enthusiasm, and
little room is left for concentrating on the content" (p. M62). Training materials often consist
of well-known games and exercises of alien
origin. They are interesting to indulge in but
poor in their relevance to Indian conditions.
Hence, training experiences are feathers in the
managers' cap, but not necessarily their tools
for management. As a result, many argue that
what one discusses in training sessions is not
what works in Indian organizations (D. P.
Sinha, 1989, p. 22).

A new perspective on management training is being advanced by referring to the
religiophilosophical literature on the Indian
view of an effective person (Chakraborty, 1987;
N. K. Singh, 1990). The view is contrary to what
is believed to be true in Western literature. The
training approach in the West, which has by
and large been adopted in India, is to help
managers acquire skills, knowledge, and motivation to develop systems and organize resources (material as well as human) in order to
realize goals set by the organization as well as
to develop themselves by being integrated into
the organization. The emphasis, in essence, is
on managing and organizing others. In contrast, the emphasis in the Indian approach to
training, according to Chakraborty, is on the
"purity" of the individual's mind (p. 37) because the "individual is the central focus"
(p. 233) and work is a duty meant for self-
purification (p. 124).

> The Indian thinkers have always
> stressed that such efforts [at work]
> cannot and should not be contingent
> upon whether others reciprocate the
> same attitude or not. If the cause, the
> intention, the motivation is right and
> pure, the effect, the result must be
> wholesome. (p. 125)

Having specified this orientation, Chakraborty
(p. 228) proposes that the aim of training is to
develop managers who, instead of being analytical and technical, should function as synthetic and spiritual systems. Chakraborty advocates yoga and meditation as the techniques
for experiential learning. Despite the evidence
provided by Chakraborty, the approach is still
open to further examination. Its effectiveness
in stress management is more conclusive than
in other areas of a manager's functioning.

Person-based Variables

Needs and Values

Despite pervasive poverty in the country, Indian workers in the organized sector are relatively well off. According to one estimate (Economic Intelligence Service, 1990), they earn
2.22 times more than an average Indian and
4.37 times more than workers in the unorga-
nized sector. Yet their preoccupation with
poverty persists. What an observer of the
Indian scene writes about Indians seems to
be true for workers: "How do the more fortunate manage to live amid such unending
scenes of wretchedness? They live in fear of
poverty themselves, regarding it to be a personal threat" (V. Mehta, 1967, p. 565). Two

interrelated consequences of such a preoccupation have been reported in the literature.

First, workers and, to a great extent, managers, suffer from a poverty syndrome (J. B. P. Sinha, 1977)—that is, they perceive material resources to be limited and hence experience a strong need to acquire, hoard, and monopolize them. P. Mehta (1978) reported that because of the high cost of living, unemployment, and lack of economic development, workers attach greater importance to wages than to the content of their jobs. Sharma (1983a) surveyed 2,337 employees of 23 public sector organizations and 1,417 employees of 27 private sector organizations and reported that safety, security, and monetary benefits constituted the most salient needs of the employees. Similarly, A. K. Srivastava (1977) reported that perceived physical and material factors were of prime importance in the life of workers.

The second consequence of this preoccupation with poverty is the strong need for power: One must have power to acquire resources. Elsewhere, the culture of poverty (Lewis, 1966) is believed to lead to a deficit perspective that is likely to perpetuate powerlessness and dependency (Howard & Scott, 1981, p. 147), but this is not true in the case of Indian industrial workers. The workers resort to two courses: They join or form more militant trade unions, and they attempt to get jobs for an increasing number of family members and relatives. Sengupta (1990) described the new generation of organized workers and their expectations.

Managers' needs and values present a much less clear picture. Contrasting sets of needs and values have been reported in the literature. It is also debated whether the social values are directly transmitted to a work setting or are filtered through employees' organizational experiences. Indian managers are by and large drawn from the middle classes. They are college educated, socialized in English medium schools, urbanized, and sons of white collar workers, and they cherish elitist values (Chatterjee, 1984; Dhingra & Pathak, 1972; Jain,

1971; Saiyadain & Monappa, 1977; Subramaniam, 1971). J. B. P. Sinha (1973b) reported that, irrespective of their positions or sectors, managers care more for material benefits, salary, and physical facilities than they do for social, ego, or self-actualization needs. Money, as a powerful incentive, has been mentioned by a number of investigators (T. K. Das, 1971; Kalro & Misra, 1973; Kulkarni, 1973; Roy, 1973a, 1973b). Job security seems to have a close tie with money (Kulkarni, 1973; Paliwal & Paliwal, 1974; P. Singh & Bhandarker, 1990; Singhal & Upadhyay, 1972). Agrawal and Sharma (1977), as well as Virmani and Guptan (1991), reported job security as the most salient concern of managers. Status needs similar to Hofstede's (1980) power distance were highlighted in studies by H. C. Ganguli (1974) and J. B. P. Sinha and M. Sinha (1974). Maheshwari (1983) confirmed that middle- and senior-level managers of private and public sector organizations, as well as government bureaucracies, attach the upmost importance to money. But they also give high ranks to the degree of challenge in a job and freedom of action. Power and good relationships with colleagues and subordinates were rated lower. Chattopadhyaya (1975), Pareek (1968), and J. B. P. Sinha (1970) independently reported excessive dependency and low risk propensity among Indian managers. Pareek (1968) identified the presence of a need for extension, that is, care and consideration for others, which was quite close to what J. B. P. Sinha and J. Pandey (1970) conceptualized as need for cooperation and coordination and P. Mehta (1978) operationalized as need for social achievement. Dayal (1977), J. B. P. Sinha and M. Sinha (1974), and P. Singh and Bhandarker (1990) reported Indians' preference for personalized relationships over contractual relationships, even in job matters. S. K. Singh (1989) substantiated the finding that family members are often consulted in job-related matters. Roland (1988) identified preferences for hierarchical relationships and for affective reciprocity as the typical features of the Indian psyche. Hofstede (1980) identified power distance and collectivism as typical Indian work values.

Integrating the above mentioned and other studies, J. B. P. Sinha (1990b) listed five broad social values that have a direct bearing on work behavior: (a) embeddedness, (b) harmony and tolerance, (c) duty in contrast to hedonism, (d) preference for personalized relationships, and (e) preference for hierarchy. Embeddedness of managers to their caste- and family-based ingroups is reported to be quite conspicuous. The concept is similar to N. K. Singh and Paul's (1985) "affective syndrome," Roland's (1988) "affective reciprocity," and Bond's (*Chinese Culture Connection*, 1987) "integration." Preference for harmony and tolerance are also reflected in weak task emphasis (N. K. Singh & Paul, 1985) and is similar to Hofstede's (1980) dimension of femininity, which is reported to be prevalent in Indian managers (Jaeger & Kanungo, 1990). The five values constitute a generic value, collectivism, and present a contrast from the value profiles reported in the individualist cultures of the West.

However, another set of studies provides a different profile of needs and values that underline a similarity between Indian and Western managers (J. B. P. Sinha, 1990a, p. 191). P. Singh (1979) reported that Indian managers value freedom, autonomy, challenge, and creativity more than economic gains, security, job stability, and exercise of power. Venkataraman and Valecha (1981) noted a strong work ethic in managers. Saiyadain (1980) found that management students attach greater importance to challenge, freedom in decision making, maintenance of good relationships, and the completion of work on time. J. B. P. Sinha (1990a) found that Indian managers attach greater importance to achievement, advancement, ability utilization, personal development, and peace of mind. Least importance was attached to the following: (a) social interactions, (b) comforts, (c) good social relationships, (d) low risk taking, and (e) variety. A factor analysis of 21 values (Super, 1982) yielded four factors: (a) *self-actualization* (consisting of the values of ability utilization, achievement, advancement, aesthetics, creativity, personal development, and peace of mind), (b) *status enhancement* (including the values of altruism, authority, little physical activity, and prestige), (c) *unconventional values* (including autonomy, creativity, lifestyle, low risk taking, and variety), and (d) *socioeconomic support* (including sound economics, social interactions, good working conditions, comforts, and high dependency). Self-actualization was the most important and socioeconomic support the least important of the four value clusters.

The inconsistency in findings raises a number of issues. P. Singh and G. S. Das (1977) reported a significant gap between the reported values (e.g., freedom, autonomy, etc.) of a sample of managers and their actual behaviors. In their actual behaviors, they were quite autocratic and bureaucratic. There are two possible explanations for this. Parikh (1979) argued that managers internalize two sets of values. The first set (as described earlier) is acquired from their family and community and the second is drawn from modern education, professional training, and the imperatives of modern technology. Indians are believed to be context sensitive in their functioning (Ramanujam, 1989) and associative in their thinking (Kedia & Bhagat, 1988). Hence, the salience of the two sets of values may depend on the situation in question. Secondly, it is also possible that the second set consists of espoused values, while the first may be the operative one. J. B. P. Sinha (1990b) argues that the espoused values are derived from one's concern regarding what he or she "ought" or "should" do and are derived from the Western literature on idealized values.

Work Values

The question concerning whether Indians value work has a long history and has still not been fully answered. Weber (1958) suggested that

Hindu religion is not conducive to work the way the Protestant ethic is; A. K. Singh (1967) strongly refuted Weber. Lambert (1963) studied five factories in the Western part of India and reached the conclusion that the prevailing social systems of the plants and the practices of the employees were contrary to the requirements of the industries and the work practices found in the West. Myers (1958) and Myrdal (1968) supported the contention, but Dayal (1970), Sharma (1970), and Sheth (1968) argued that Indian employees are able to adjust to industrial roles and that the traditional culture is not a serious handicap to either efficiency or achievement. Singer (1975) found Protestant-type values among industrialists of a southern Indian city. Muthuchidambaram (1972) observed that Indian workers are rational, realistic, and positive in their work behavior. In contrast, J. B. P. Sinha and M. Sinha (1974) lamented that Indians tend to prefer *aram* (rest and relaxation not preceded by hard work). J. B. P. Sinha (1985) further observed that it is not unusual to find many people in villages and cities seeming to be sitting about doing nothing. Granted that the unemployment rate is high and the casual workers may not have a full day's work, it is nevertheless striking to find that employed workers often arrive at work late and leave early unless they are forced to be punctual. During working hours, friends and relatives drop in unannounced—at times without specific purposes—and yet are entertained. People relish chatting and taking time out for tea and coffee while productivity suffers. It is customary to leave the office or plant and visit ailing friends or relatives or to meet social personal obligations. There are numerous holidays and festival days. Any occasion of joy or sorrow invariably seems to result in a holiday.

Even when actually working, the slow and clumsy manner in which some employees perform their work demonstrates indifferent attitudes and a lack of consideration for others; the emphasis on procedure rather than outcome is striking. McClelland (1975, pp. 159–160) felt that Indians perform work as

a favor to others. Work is believed to exhaust a person by draining energy from a person that should be conserved. Hence, a person is expected to work for someone who returns the favor in some form. This is one possible explanation for the prevailing corruption in Indian organizations (Khandwalla, 1988).

A completely different picture emerges when researchers focus on those who are self-employed or work for organizations that have work conducive norms and systems (J. B. P. Sinha, 1990a). Soares, Valecha, and Venkataraman (1981) noted that some Indian managers rated a good work ethic higher than interpersonal relations with colleagues, superiors, and subordinates. Besides organizational differences, the variations within an organization are generally quite wide and suggest that work values need to be examined with reference to an individual's and an organization's characteristics. Rub (1988) compared work values in a public, a private, and a cooperative sector organization. He found that the managers did not differ in their early or school socialization, which, therefore, cannot be a cause of differences in their work values. It was the organizational socialization that resulted in divergent attitudes toward work. Socialization promoting favorable working conditions, strong work norms, effective systems of reward and punishment, and assertive leadership helped the managers inculcate positive work values.

Following Super's (1982) model of importance of work, J. B. P. Sinha (1990a) differentiated cognitive, affective, and activity components of work values. The cognitive components were measured as parts of role clarity. The affect components included (a) job affect and (b) job satisfaction. The activity components consisted of (a) the time a manager spends on his or her job and (b) the extent to which he or she works hard. Although the measures were significantly intercorrelated, the relationships suggested the presence of individual differences, as well as complexity in the concept of work values.

Of the various measures, job affect and job satisfaction seemed to be the most central aspects of work values (J. B. P. Sinha, 1990a). Job affect was conceptually quite close to job involvement (Kanungo, 1981; Lodahl & Kejner, 1965; Rabinowitz & Hall, 1977), except for the cognitive elements that were removed. Thanks to the *Lodahl and Kejner Scale,* job involvement has been studied extensively in India. R. Padaki's (1988) review shows its relationship with demographic, personality, and situational variables. With few exceptions, "the job involved person had a higher designation, was older, had put in more years in service and perhaps had technical education" (R. Padaki, 1988, p. 29). One such exception was the study by G. S. Das (1983), who related length of service and a manager's position in the organization to job involvement. On both variables, the relationship assumed a U-shape, that is, the middle-level managers with 10 to 15 years of service were least involved in their job. G. S. Das also reported higher job involvement in departments of production, technical, and research and development and lower levels in personnel and public administration.

Among personality variables, locus of control, extroversion-introversion, and neuroticism have been the favorite tools of Indian organizational psychologists. They generally found that internals were more job involved and that the relationships of job involvement with extroversion and neuroticism were variable (R. Padaki, 1988). The findings may either be interpreted as artifacts of imitative research with borrowed tools or reflections of culturally invariant psychological processes, namely, that (a) longer association and success on the job generally induce greater involvement in the job and (b) internals have a stronger disposition to internalize work requirements.

The second interpretation implies that the internals hold themselves responsible for what happens on the job and have to get involved to see that the job gets done. By the same token, one might argue that the externals will depend on some external justification for getting (or not getting) involved in the job. This is the basis of the argument made by Kanungo and Misra (1988) and Misra and Kalro (1981) that job involvement is a function of the satisfaction of salient needs that may be either intrinsic or extrinsic. Khandelwal (1983) indeed reported that the fulfillment of the needs of security and pay, as well as self-actualization, led to high job involvement. Kanungo and Hartwick (1987) found that pay and promotions, as well as personal challenge, interesting work, and responsibility, resulted in high motivational effectiveness on the job.

Job Satisfaction

Most of the reviewers of studies on organizational behavior (Ganesh, 1981; Khandwalla, 1988; R. Padaki, 1988; Rao, 1981; D. Sinha, 1972; J. B. P. Sinha, 1981a) have commented that despite their large number, studies of job satisfaction have failed to develop indigenous theories. There may be many reasons. Indians' interest in job satisfaction may be intuitive and culture bound (D. Sinha, 1972, p. 188), but it has never been so articulated as to raise the question, Why? Instead, the interest drifted into an easy path of measuring job satisfaction either by a single item (i.e., How satisfied are you with your job?) or by several items (How satisfied are you with pay, service condition, etc.?). The information thus collected can be correlated with a wide range of demographic, personality, or organizational variables without much ingenuity. There were many studies, but the findings were inconsistent.

Herzberg's two-factor theory (Herzberg, Mausner, & Snyderman, 1958) hardly helped the situation. Pestonjee (Akhtar & Pestonjee, 1969; Pestonjee & Akhtar, 1969) set the ball rolling. Sarveswara Rao (1972, 1973), among others, in the early 1970s (J. B. P. Sinha, 1981a) and Dolke and R. Padaki in the late 1970s and the early 1980s (R. Padaki, 1988) systematically examined the validity of the theory. A great many others contributed. The conclusions, however, were equivocal. Some confirmed, others faulted the theory as an artifact of the method, and still others found it to be partially valid. The dichotomy of the hygiene and the motivators was, by and large, discernible, but the failure of multimethod tests rejected the theory.

Nobody, however, asked the question of whether an absence of the clear dichotomy had anything to do with Indians' weaker orientation of psychological differentiation, that is, field dependence (D. Sinha, 1980) or a collectivistic orientation (J. B. P. Sinha & J. Verma, 1987; Triandis et al., 1986). Indian employees are embedded in their work settings and work groups and may derive a sense of satisfaction as well as dissatisfaction from the same set of contextual factors. Sarveswara Rao (Ganesh, 1990, p. 97) did report that while satisfaction and dissatisfaction constitute a unidimensional variable, the so-called hygiene and motivators are bidirectional, each affecting both satisfaction as well as dissatisfaction. However, he did not identify a basic deficiency of the theory in not delineating the constructs of the intrinsic-extrinsic dichotomy in terms of the expectancy theory (Kanungo & Hartwick, 1987).

There are numerous studies on demographic, personality, and organizational correlates of job satisfaction, but they are disjointed and not grounded in theory (R. Padaki, 1988; D. Sinha, 1972). There was some evidence that age, education, income, and status were correlated with job satisfaction. However, there were exceptions. Similarly, internals and extroverts were more satisfied with their job. Then, there were counterarguments that extroverts would be more satisfied with hygiene and that introverts would be more so with motivator factors.

Similarly, K. G. Agrawal and Sharma (1977) among others (R. Padaki, 1988, Pareek, 1974, etc.) evaluated the theories of Maslow, McClelland, Herzberg, Litwin, Stringer, and McGregor and found them wanting.

However, their own efforts to develop alternative models did not go far, probably because they did not search for the roots of job satisfaction in Indian culture. They were more enamored by the prospect of developing a universalistic theory based on process analysis of how organizational and personality dispositions interact with situational factors and cause job satisfaction or dissatisfaction than they were with developing an appropriate theory to account for the data.

Leadership

Early studies on leadership were conducted under the strong influence of the Michigan University studies of leadership. Bose (1955) reported that employee-centered supervision was related to higher morale and employees' pride in their work group, which in turn resulted in productivity. H. C. Ganguli (1957, 1961) and his associates (H. C. Ganguli, S. Goswami, & Ghosh, 1957) supported Bose's findings that employee-centered supervision was related to workers' job satisfaction, morale, and higher productivity. Similarly, A. Chatterjee (1961) reported a positive relationship between democratic leadership and productivity.

The trend continued in the 1970s. Pestonjee (1973) and his associates (A. P. Singh & Pestonjee, 1974), for example, reported greater worker satisfaction under democratic leadership. Sarveswara Rao (1973) found greater trust in employees who worked under a consideration type of supervisor than those who worked under an initiating structure type. P. Singh, Warrier, and G. S. Das (1979) reported that the democratization of leadership process leads to greater job satisfaction and higher productivity. They further observed that participative leadership was conducive to the acceptance of group decisions. Prakasam, Despande, Kshirsagar (1979) used Halpin's *Leadership Behavior Description Questionnaire* and found that people-oriented leadership created a favorable climate that was conducive to higher productivity. Jaggi (1978) employed Likert's four styles and found that the leaders practiced a benevolent authoritative style in formal decision making and a consultative style in the rest of their decisions. C. N. Ganguli (1977) surveyed a large number of managers from a variety of organizations and concluded that the leaders tended to shift from a benevolent autocratic to a consultative style, particularly in organizations with participative work climates.

The evidence kept accumulating in favor of democratic, participative, and consideration type leaders. However, some fissures and gaps also began to appear. Meade (1967), for example, argued that Indian subordinates, because of their authoritarian culture, would function more effectively under an authoritarian leader. He found that groups under a democratic leader had higher rates of absenteeism and required more time to perform tasks than those working under an authoritarian leader. The latter style led to better work quality and a stronger preference for the leader. H. C. Ganguli (1964), who earlier had reported evidence in favor of employee-centered supervision, found that the majority of managers, as well as a substantial percentage of workers, preferred autocratic leaders. The reasons were different. For the managers it represented more power; for the workers it represented freedom from responsibilities. Thus, Ganguli concluded that "the autocratic leader per se is neither inefficient nor disliked by most, only when it is combined with poor intellectual and administrative abilities or is frankly tyrannical that people react to it negatively" (p. ix). Pestonjee and A. P. Singh (1973) also noted a high positive correlation between the authoritarianism of a leader and the morale among subordinates. Saiyadain (1974a, 1974b) found that employees who were socially competent felt satisfied with their autocratic supervisors and probably had the skill to manage their supervisors. J. B. P. Sinha (1974)

recorded a reversal in a planfully introduced participative style of leadership in a hospital where the surrounding culture was not quite conducive to the participative way of functioning. There was also evidence (J. B. P. Sinha, 1973b) that the participative leaders in certain cases were perceived as abdicating their responsibilities and were therefore considered weak. Ray (1970) suggested incorporating familial values in leadership. Kakar (1971) found that subordinates preferred nurturant superiors who were parental in nature, but he still felt that it was helping superiors of fraternal ideology (i.e., democratic leaders) who led to better work performance and satisfaction of subordinates.

J. B. P. Sinha (1980, 1990c) attempted to systematize the seemingly inconsistent findings into a model of leadership effectiveness in which the leader uses a combination of styles. He drew from Kakar's (1971) concept of *nurturance* and blended it with *task* orientation in order to operationalize a nurturant-task-oriented (NT) leadership style. The NT leader is warm and considerate, cares for his or her subordinates, is concerned about their well-being and growth, and guides, encourages, and directs them. The NT leader also structures his or her subordinates' roles, sets high goals, and works hard, thus acting as a role model. These leaders make their nurturance contingent on their subordinates' task performance, openly appreciate those who work hard and sincerely, and provide close supervision and feedback.

The NT style was found to work for those subordinates who prefer personalized and dependency relationships, readily accept the superiority of their leader, and work hard and sincerely if their relationship with their leader is positive. J. B. P. Sinha and Chowdhary (1981) found that managers in a leadership role are likely to employ either an authoritarian or an NT style for the subordinates who scored high on dependency and personalized relationship, status orientation, and weak work values. The authoritarian style, however, was neither effective nor satisfying. In contrast, the NT style was effective, with the exception of those subordinates who were low on the characteristics just mentioned. For the latter, the participative style was found to be effective. Thus, the model visualized a combination of NT and participative styles, which may be employed for different types of subordinates. Furthermore, Sinha (1980, 1990c) and his associates provided evidence to show that the leader-subordinate relationship changes over time. As subordinates work hard, gain experience, and acquire skills and self-confidence, their needs for dependency and personalized relationships and status orientations decrease. In order to remain effective, the leader shifts toward a more participative style. The subordinates still feel deference for the leader who remains affectionate and caring, but the relationship is now characterized by greater participation and consultation. Evidence shows that NT leaders who fail to change experience reversals toward authoritarian style, which prove to be disruptive for the relationships as well as the group task. By the same logic, in order to be effective, a leader employs a combination of styles for subordinates who manifest varying degrees of preference for dependency and personalized relationships and status and work orientations. If this is true, J. B. P. Sinha (1980) argued that the leadership styles are unassociated with the leader's personality disposition. N. Verma (1986) correlated leadership styles with leaders' ratings of self on an adjective checklist. The coefficients of correlation were by and large insignificant. Madhok (1990) did not find any relationship between leaders' needs for achievement, affiliation, nurturance, or domination with NT styles ($p > .05$). Similarly, the NT style was unrelated to Maslow's hierarchy of needs.

P. Smith, Tayeb, Sinha, and Bennett (1990) correlated the nurturant style with the degree managers approached 9,9 style and compared them with the perceived relationship of the effectiveness of their work groups. The nurturance style correlated with the 9,9 scores and both predicted group effectiveness. However, according to the authors, the nurturance style did not have the theoretical assumptions of Blake and Mouton. P. B. Smith (personal communication, 1986) also reported a higher correlation between nurturance and consideration than between nurturance and initiating structure in the United Kingdom, Japan, and India. J. B. P. Sinha (1980) has reported modest to high positive correlations between NT and participative styles. In sum, both NT and participative styles share high concern for people and task. Factor analysis of the items of participative and NT styles often load together, particularly when the leaders rate their own styles (Ansari, 1990; Hassan, 1989). Self-ratings of NT style seem to be susceptible to social desirability effects: Leaders invariably rate themselves high on NT and participative styles—more so on the NT style. Subordinates' ratings of their immediate superiors yield a more neat factor structure, with NT appearing as a distinct configuration (Ansari, 1990; Hassan, 1989). NT's difference with participative style lies in the nature of its embeddedness in the culture. Nurturance signifies care and consideration of a superior who provides patronage to those subordinates who show deference to their leader. It is more a relationship of "vertical solidarity" than of fraternal equality.

Khandwalla (1981b, 1983a) combined participative style with professional orientation in order to identify a vigorous and innovative style of managers, which he labels as *pioneering-innovative* (PI) style. The PI style is characterized by a commitment to pioneering novel and sophisticated technologies, products, and services, high risk taking, and high emphasis on creativity and adaptability. He argues that it is a modern outgrowth of the entrepreneurial tradition of the country that may enable managers to cope with a high-tech, turbulent environment. He argues that the "PI mode seemed to land the organization into a more complex, turbulent, but favorable operating environment" (Khandwalla, 1988, p. 141). Obviously, the model is more appropriate for the top leadership and places greater emphasis on task and technology and on scanning and managing the boundaries of the organization. It seems to be less concerned about the culture-specific needs of subordinates.

Recently, P. Singh and Bhandarker (1990) showed the effectiveness of transformational or charismatic leadership for corporate success at the top of an organization. Although the concept originated in the West, its relevance for the third world has been well established (House & Woycke, 1988). They trace the spirit of transformational leadership to the *karta* (i.e., head of the family) ethos in Indian culture:

> The cumulative life experiences lead the person to look for a father figure (symbolically speaking) in the work place for empowering, protection, grooming, and development. In return, the individual develops respect for his superior and demonstrates willingness to accept his authority....Indians have high need for empowering, developing, guidance, and protection. (p. 134)

Obviously, the description is quite close to what J. B. P. Sinha (1980) conceptualized as the nurturance-dependency framework for developing a model of effective leadership. The point of departure is the level of an organization for which the leadership issues are being examined. Sinha focuses on the middle levels, while P. Singh and Bhandarker have an organization's top position in mind. Naturally, they include some of the components of the PI model, too. They write:

> The style of the transformational leaders in our study has been seen to be predominantly that of demonstrating an empowering attitude, risk taking capacity, clarity of mission, goal and purpose, capability to build the team, and not losing balance in face of calamity. (p. 346)

Characteristics such as being a good boundary manager, showing care and concern for individual work as well as personal problems, being open and receptive to new ideas, and planning and evoking a sense of confidence were also considered to be crucial. In sum, leadership research in India provides, in varying degrees, a blend of concerns for task and technology as well as for cultural needs and values.

Power

Studies of power have yet to catch up with leadership research. The surveys of research in industrial psychology (D. Sinha, 1972) and management (Dayal, 1973) do not make references to power. Sporadic references to such things as political efficacy, alienation among youth, or powerlessness in the poor (P. Mehta, 1981) began to appear in the early 1970s. McClelland (1975) was the first to provide a framework for the cultural analysis of power. He pooled information from religious texts, children's stories, and his own observations to postulate that Indians have a strong need for power that expresses itself, unlike in the West, primarily through "giving." Giving, according to McClelland, is the core theme of Indian culture that is reflected in all sorts of exchanges, including the repeated exchange between the spiritual and material worlds. Giving obliges the recipient everywhere in the world and creates problems of debt management (Blau, 1964). The act of giving itself is meritorious in India, and self-sacrifice is the most meritorious form of giving. The more one gives, the more one develops power without overtly asserting him or herself over the recipient. Thus, concludes McClelland, "renunciation, yielding, and self-sacrifice often serve only to make a strong urge to power" (p. 143). McClelland further contended that power through giving has the potential to create conflict. In order to give, one must accumulate resources; and in order to do so, one must compete for resources. But then "giving," not "competing," is the core value. The built-in contradiction leads to many dubious ways of accumulating resources. Giving must be noticed in order to have an impact, which may be later utilized without the giver asking the receiver to reciprocate. Hence, unnoticed givings can cause great tension. Giving shows a superior's "moral humility which all too often is a means of getting power over others," writes McClelland (p. 144).

McClelland's otherwise excellent analysis suffers due to his attempt to integrate what is prescribed in Indian religious texts and children's stories as ideals, and what Indians are observed doing. The two co-exist in the Indian psyche, thereby baffling many foreign observers. Furthermore, a closer examination of the concept of giving and its related concepts is essential. J. B. P. Sinha (1978) mentions two such concepts: *yajna* (sacrificial worship) and *tapa* (literally meaning burning oneself). Ideally, giving (*dan*) is meant for worthy recipients without the expectation for reciprocation. Hence, it renders the donor pious. *Yajna* is performed in deference to gods and goddesses with the support of many persons. It is a collectivistic effort to gain sociospiritual merit. *Tapa* is quite personal and involves such things as yoga, meditation, renunciation of worldly comforts, and self-sacrifices and results in a kind of glow (*teja*), which is closest to the concept of power. All three are "giving away" something important. However, *dan* and *yajna* require primarily material resources, whereas *tapa* requires control over oneself through yoga, which may connect a person to the cosmic power. As a person rises on the scale of merit, the person becomes charismatic and people flock around the person to seek his or her guidance and inspiration for their own inner upliftment. That is how transformational leaders empower their subordinates. Thus, in contrast to the Western approach to power where (a) X makes Y do what Y would not do otherwise or (b) X overcomes the

resistance put forth by Y, the Indian idealized conceptualization of the power relationship does not visualize X asserting him or herself. It is Y who approaches and seeks out X's blessings. There is no resistance or conflict. X and Y are believed to be the parts of the same collective. Therefore, "giving" is a natural exchange between them.

Socioeconomic compulsions and organizational realities transform the power processes to the extent that one can see the continuities as well as the distortions. Indian managers are still found to be striving for the realization of their spiritual self (S. K. Chakraborty, 1987; J. B. P. Sinha, 1989a), but not as a power leverage. One's power lies to a great extent in one's capabilitiy to control oneself and to handle difficult problems and problem subordinates (J. B. P. Sinha, 1982b). A strong need for power seems to have roots in the country's pervasive poverty, which creates a poverty syndrome (J. B. P. Sinha, 1977), whereby even not-so-poor individuals, such as managers, perceive resources to be highly limited and, therefore, must acquire and, if possible, monopolize them. Crowding and low spatial mobility (McClelland, 1975) cause interdependence and continuing interactions. As a result, people keep comparing themselves. In sum, the perception of limited resources and a disposition to compare oneself with others creates a strong need for power, which combined with a steeply hierarchical social structure, results in centralized power (Khandwalla, 1988). Unlike organizations in the West, power tends to be more centralized in top positions as the size of an organization increases. Irrespective of the type of organization, "people are more comfortable with the tendency to centralize power and control" (Virmani & Guptan, 1991, p. 137). Large power distance is one of the typical cultural features of organizations in India (Hofstede, 1980).

In a collectivist culture (Hofstede, 1980; Triandis, 1989; Triandis et al., 1986), people are likely to categorize their superiors and subordinates in terms of ingroup versus outgroup members on the basis of family, caste, religion, language, and so on. The norms of behavior with ingroup members are vastly different from those for outgroup members. So is the power relationship. The superiors in Indian organizations are expected to be nurturant to ingroup subordinates (J. B. P. Sinha, 1980) and must provide them with guidance and patronage (Virmani & Guptan, 1991); the subordinates in turn must prove their loyalty and show deference to their superiors. In the case of outgroup members, the superior may turn out to be exploitative, and the subordinates, depending on their power, may surrender, withdraw from the relationship, or revolt against the superior (J. B. P. Sinha, 1982a, 1982b).

There are cases where the power pattern in work organizations is characterized by workers pressuring their managers to yield to all sorts of demands and harassing those who try to resist (Singh-Sengupta, 1990b; J. B. P. Sinha, 1986; 1990a). J. B. P. Sinha also provides evidence of managers trying to consolidate their power bases by distributing favors among their loyal subordinates. Ganesh (1982) reports instances of groupings and conflicts based on caste, class, family affiliations, and political and linguistic interests (p. 5). Singh-Sengupta (1990a) reported that managers, as well as nonmanagers, employ coercive power more than any other method to influence each other in a number of banking organizations.

In between the two extremes described above, there is a twilight zone where the boundaries between ingroups and outgroups are fuzzy and the loyalty of subordinates as well as the patronage of superiors are somewhat suspect. Yet, the two must work together. Such situations require pseudonurturance and pseudodependency as covers for intense games of power (J. B. P. Sinha, 1982a, 1982b). Ingratiation (Pandey, 1981) and manipulation (Tripathi, 1981) are rampant in such situations.

J. Pandey (1978, 1980a, 1980b, 1981, 1986, 1988) and his associates (J. Pandey & Bohra, 1986; J. Pandey & Kakar, 1982; J. Pandey & Rastogi, 1979; J. Pandey & Singh, 1986) have systematically examined the pervasive nature of ingratiation in Indian organizations. It is considered to be instrumental in appropriating undue resources. Therefore, managers ingratiate more when resources are perceived to be limited, and the managers have to compete to acquire and monopolize them. Junior workers ingratiate more than senior ones. Supervisors are ingratiated more than either friends or strangers. The target person shows a liking for the ingratiator and favors the person more than others. The typical forms of ingratiation are (a) self-degradation, (b) instrumental dependency, (c) name dropping, and (d) changing one's position with the situation. The cultural connections of the forms of ingratiation are obvious. The ingratiator exaggerates the power distance, demonstrates dependency on the target, and thereby evokes the latter's nurturance, draws a sense of strength by showing a connection with others who are powerful, and contextualizes his or her behavior depending on the situation.

Tripathi (1981) and his associates (Y. Sinha, Tripathi, & J. Pandey, 1982; Tripathi & Y. Sinha, 1981; Tripathi & Thapa, 1981) argue that ingratiation is a behavioral style that reflects a manipulative disposition (i.e., Machiavellianism). It is employed particularly in situations of asymmetrical power. That is, a less powerful actor ingratiates a more powerful target in order to manipulate the latter to give the former some undue favors.

In a study involving a fairly large sample of managers from a number of organizations, Ansari (1990) reported that ingratiation was the second most popular strategy used to influence one's superiors. Providing personalized help and showing dependency were the second and fifth most popular strategies for influencing subordinates, respectively. The most popular strategy in both cases was expertise and reason. Kapoor (1986) agreed with Ansari that an appeal to rationality is a universal power strategy.

Ansari (1990) goes further to show that the use of various power strategies is dependent on (a) the power bases, (b) the leadership style of the superior, and (c) the organizational climate that may facilitate one or the other kind of influence process. For example, rational tactics were found to be associated with reward, referent, and expert bases of power, while coercive power was found associated with nonrational and negative tactics. Furthermore, under a nurturant-task-oriented supervisor, managers used assertiveness to influence their subordinates, and there was less of a tendency to use negative sanctions with subordinates and blocking or defiance toward superiors. Participative managers frequently used ingratiation to influence their supervisor when the organizational climate was unfavorable; task-oriented managers used expertise, reason, and personalized help in favorable climates; bureaucratic managers frequently used ingratiation in both favorable and unfavorable climates; and autocratic managers frequently used ingratiation in favorable climates and personal help, blocking, and defiance in unfavorable climates (pp. 151–152). In an experimental study, Ansari and Kapoor (1987) found that subordinates used tactics such as blocking, upward appeal, and ingratiation to influence their authoritarian leaders. On the other hand, they rationally persuaded both participative and nurturant-task-oriented leaders. Ansari further reported that when subordinates were concerned with realizing organizational rather than personal goals, they tended to use rational persuasion, upward appeal, and blocking. To achieve personal benefits, they used ingratiation. Singh-Sengupta (1990a) replicated the study by Ansari and Kapoor (1987) and confirmed that and persuasion to realize organizational goals. They evoked dependency and ingratiation to influence their authoritarian superiors and a rational approach to do so with participative leaders. She referred to J. B. P. Sinha's (1980) conceptualization of the leader-subordinate relationship to develop a hypothesis, which

was later confirmed, that the subordinates are likely to use dependency and a personalized relationship to influence their nurturant-task leaders.

In sum, research on both leadership and power disclosed certain features that are culture specific and others that are universal. Indian culture fosters dependency, personalized relationships, the centralization of power, and power distance, thereby creating a preference for nurturant-task leadership. The task experiences and skills create a universal need to participate or at least be consulted (De, 1974; Maheshwari, 1978; D. P. Sinha, 1989), although deference for the leader remains important. The advent of high technology seems to promote a pioneering innovative style in certain enterprises. The fast-changing development-oriented environment requires transformational leadership, which again has culturally specific as well as universal components. Similarly, the pattern of relationships among the bases of power, power strategies, leadership, and organizational climate contains both universal and culture-specific components. The desire for inner transformation, peace of mind, and spiritual upliftment seems to be cultural, although its implications for stress management are also being realized outside of Indian culture. Ingratiation is universal, but its pervasiveness and locus of application are unique. Centralization of power is somewhat culture specific and has a wide range of effects on a variety of organizational behaviors.

Decision Making and Communication

Studies on decision making and communication began to appear in the management literature during the 1960s (Sharma, 1973). However, they were descriptive essays expressing concerns over the "old ways" of making decisions in modern organizations, where decentralization, delegation, and open communication were believed to be essential. The empirical studies that followed in the 1970s led to the realization that the phenomena were more than the inertia of the old ways. Decision making and communication were parts of the cultural frame, which is characterized by hierarchy and collectivism (J. B. P. Sinha, 1990b).

Formalized channels of communication and modes of decision making and delegation are parts of the package of Western work forms and modern technology that most Indian work organizations have adopted (S. N. Pandey, 1989; Virmani & Guptan, 1991). Having done so, they tended to accommodate cultural preferences by adopting means of bypassing the formalized systems. They see that decision making is centralized and delegation is restricted to trustworthy subordinates (Ganesh, 1990; Khandwalla, 1988; S. N. Pandey, 1989; Virmani & Guptan, 1991). Communication flows so as to favor one's ingroup and discriminate against outgroup members (S. K. Singh, 1989).

Besides cultural preferences, developmental roles also facilitate centralization of decision making. Managers from a variety of organizations in one study (Virmani & Guptan, 1991) reported that centralized decision making helps realize planned targets. Five-year plans are prepared at the national level and distributed to various organizations who must then find their share of responsibilities. The top leader in the organization in turn can take strategic decisions accordingly. Mishra (1982) found that perceived centralization of decision making at the top was significantly correlated with a composite measure of the top leader's efficiency. The top leader can mobilize subordinates and make them work hard. J. B. P. Sinha (1990a) reported that when combined with other factors, centralization can play a critical role in creating a synergetic work culture. But the opposite can also be true. Centralized decision making can alienate the other managers and thereby affect the organization adversely.

S. N. Pandey (1989) reported that despite an elaborate structural arrangement for effective communication in the premier private sector steel company, decision making was centralized and procedures were bureaucratic, time consuming, and cumbersome. There was inadequate information sharing, insufficient communication at the middle levels, poor horizontal communication, and, consequently, instances of rumor mongering. Earlier, R. Agrawal (1974) had found that large status differentials among managers restrict communication, delay and distort the information as it makes its way down an organization's hierarchy, and thereby render it inadequate and difficult to use. Singhal (1973) showed that information tends to travel downward and seldom sideways or upward in an organization. The communication flow seemed to assume an L-shape. That is, high-level managers directed their communications to their subordinates, who then relayed it to their peers. L. Prasad (1978) reported that higher level managers received more communication and preferred to receive only favorable information. Subordinates felt their obligation to provide information, but only if it was information that their supervisor preferred to hear. The supervisor did not like to hear any criticism of management policies or decisions. The supervisor often dominated subordinates in meetings and conferences, thereby restricting the flow of communication.

In sum, the nature of communication depended on the superior's response to the communication. Orpen (1978) reported that higher level managers initiated more communication but that the quality of downward communication declined toward the lower levels of organizations in terms of adequacy, timeliness, and clarity. Chaudhury (1978) investigated downward communication in a large public sector organization. He supported Orpen's point that higher level managers communicated with their subordinates more than lower level managers. He further observed that while the higher level managers' communications were task oriented, the communications of lower level managers were nurturant. Virmani and Guptan (1991) examined upward and downward communications in a variety of organizations. They reported that subordinates tended to be formal while communicating with their superiors, who were free to be much more informal. Furthermore, top managers felt free to communicate down directly to any level of an organization, thereby tending to erode the authority of the middle level managers.

A striking feature of Indian organizations, according to Virmani and Guptan (1991), is that the top leaders have to be available to anyone who wants to see them at any time. In fact, anyone can approach any other person in an organization, despite the highly formalized channels of communication. In some organizations, the top leader allows individuals to bypass the grievance handling systems and procedures and approach the leader for redress. This reminds one of the centuries' old tradition of the king making himself available to any subject who prayed to him for redressal or mercy. The approach is claimed to have a highly reassuring effect on employees. Yet communications are adjusted to the status, moods, and reactions of superiors, the nature of interpersonal relationships, and the social and professional relationships in the organization.

In the preceding section it was pointed out that middle and lower level managers seem to suffer from a power deficit. This is also reflected in their decision making and communication. Ayyar (1976) stated that the originality, creativity, and personal contributions of middle and lower level managers are not duly appreciated. Hence, their participation in management is often ineffective. J. B. P. Sinha and Singh-Sengupta (in press) showed that managers of a binding organization did not perceive having any say in the recruitment and transfer of their nonmanagers. All they could do was assign work and grant leave. Maheshwari (1978) examined the decision styles of middle and lower

level managers. The styles were neither authoritarian nor fully participative; rather, they were consultative. That is, the managers were highly dependent on their superiors and did not have a high need for participation, preferring instead to be consulted. Earlier, De (1974) found that managers want to be kept in touch and consulted as they do in their joint families. They respond to a personalized approach. A similar trend was reported in the literature on workers' participation (J. B. P. Sinha, 1981b), as well as in other work settings (Maheshwari, 1978; D. P. Sinha, 1989). Despite many attempts through government directives, workers' participation schemes have failed to be adopted. Even in the best organizations, they have enjoyed a limited success at best (J. B. P. Sinha, 1989b).

S. K. Singh (1989) explored managers' preferences for consulting with either members of work groups or social groups concerning work and family problems. He reported that family members are consulted more often than work group members, even in the case of job-related problems. The preference for consulting family members demonstrates cultural influence. Roland (1988) has made a clinical analysis of the typical Indian ways of communicating that have direct implications for organizational behavior. He finds that the modes of communication are highly complex and multilayered. There is emphasis on being subtle rather than explicit. Others are expected to sense what is being communicated and to respond appropriately. There is de-emphasis on asking for any help or favor, lest the refusal might hurt the relationship. Relationship is important, and mutual face-saving is necessary to maintain it. Therefore, anger and disagreements are often expressed by a person who suddenly stops talking, leaves the room, or simply walks around with an unhappy expression (p. 257). There are frequent references to the language of silence and how profound meanings can be conveyed without the use of words. While such subtleties may work within an ingroup, they are likely to cause problems in task-related communications.

Conflict Resolution

Conflict and its resolution are closely related to decision making and communication and are therefore partly culture bound and partly culture free. L. Prasad (1976) identified three possible types of conflicts in organizations, namely, vertical, horizontal, and intergroup and suggested control, coordination and competition, and bargaining, respectively, to resolve them. U. Kumar and B. N. Srivastava (1979) found that facing problems was the most desirable and that forcing was the least desirable way of resolving conflicts among managers. B. Srivastava (1974) provided details of a process analysis of how senior and middle level managers were helped to establish collaborative and cooperative relationships, thereby resolving their conflicts. Sayeed (1990) and Sayeed and Mathur (1980) listed a number of ways of resolving conflicts: avoiding arguments, following rules, accommodation, consultation, toning down differences, forcing, compromising, and confrontation.

These mechanisms for resolving conflicts may be available to managers anywhere in the world. What the culture does is sensitize managers to use them differentially and to provide a more parochial context and content for this mechanism. Collectivism in the culture expresses itself in a preference for structuring relationships hierarchically and taking ingroups and outgroups into account. The former leads to larger power distance and the latter to "affective reciprocity" within the ingroup and mistrust and hostility toward outgroups (J. B. P. Sinha, 1990b). Within one's ingroup, people of near equal power deny, suppress, tone down, or present conflict as generosity. People in asymmetrical power relationships also tend to show generosity within their ingroup. The more powerful person in a relationship is likely to give in more to the less powerful one, who is expected to yield without much coaxing. If forcing has to be resorted to, one form that it might take is the *use of fasting unto death*—that is, a suicide threat

(McClelland, 1975). Disagreement is prevented from blowing up by a withdrawal: to suddenly stop talking, to leave the room, or to convey an unhappy expression (Roland, 1988). Mutual face-saving is important. So the people in conflict may ask for a third party to mediate (Thingaajan, 1972).

Conflicts with an outgroup member are likely to be resolved differently. If the people in conflict have near equal power, they may compromise in order to avoid retaliation (J. B. P. Sinha, 1982a), but they are more likely to drift toward retaliation and cutthroat competition (J. B. P. Sinha & S. R. Sinha, 1975). In the case of unequal power relationships, the more powerful individual forces the less powerful one to surrender. The latter in some cases may withdraw or retaliate (J. B. P. Sinha, 1982a). When the ingroup–outgroup relationship is equivocal and the power relationship is asymmetrical, the less powerful individual tends to use ingratiation with good effects (J. Pandey, 1981). This is particularly true in the case of conflicts between senior and junior managers in family-managed organizations. The seniors and the juniors often differ in their values, the seniors valuing close supervision, conservatism, and so on, while the juniors value autonomy, professionalism, and so on. Integration is an affective method for the juniors in such cases.

Manager–worker conflicts have been one of the continuing concerns of industrial relations in India. Earlier studies (Chadha, 1966; P. Chakraborty, 1969; Devasagayam, 1949; Kannappan, 1958; Nallasivam, 1963), as well as the more recent ones (Chaubey, 1986; Sharma, 1979; R. B. P. Singh & J. B. P. Sinha, 1992), examined them. Taken as a whole, they reveal a whole range of behavioral strategies for resolution: forcing, yielding, accommodating, third-party mediations, and so on. R. B. P. Singh and J. B. P. Sinha have made an interesting observation about how manager–worker conflicts are often resolved. Imagine that a worker abuses a manager, who then lodges a complaint to top management. The worker comes to the manager's house or office the next day and brings a co-worker or union leader who apologizes on behalf of the worker. The worker, the third party explains, was drunk or afflicted with family problems and was not in a normal frame of mind. The manager is persuaded to pardon the worker, and then withdraws the charges against the worker, who then runs some personal errands for the manager in order to restore, symbolically, the manager's authority. Similarly, suppose that a manager abuses a worker, who then complains to the union, which then takes up the matter. A higher level manager brings the manager, the worker, and the union leader together. The manager dwells at length on how much he or she cares for the workers, how much he or she has helped them in the past, how it was never the manager's intention to hurt the worker, and that the manager's action to reprimand the worker was for the sake of the worker or the organization. The worker might even say that he or she was sorry and was misunderstood. The worker returns to work happy. In sum, third-party mediation, good intentions, mutual face-saving, as well as accommodation, mark the way conflicts are often resolved.

Organizational Climate and Work Culture

Indians are known to have *context sensitive* ways of thinking and functioning (Ramanujam, 1989; Roland, 1988). Hence, Indian managers, compared to their counterparts in the West, are more likely to look into organizational climate for the genesis, as well as the justification, of their behavior.

Organizational Climate

Organizational climate is the shared perception of an organization. It is "a snapshot of institutionalized values and practices" (Khandwalla, 1988, p. 173) and is jointly determined by the

structure of an organization and the psychological properties of its employees. Because it is perceptual and global in nature, investigators have been looking at it from different angles. Reviews of the literature (Khandwalla, 1988; R. Padaki, 1988; J. B. P. Sinha, 1981a) suggest two trends: First, almost all aspects of the organization (e.g., objectives, structures, processes, outcomes, etc.) have been studied by one or more scholars; second, organizational behavior is presumed to be an aggregate of individuals' behavior. Therefore, organizational properties such as climate are perceived to be prototypical of the characteristics of individuals. A few illustrative examples of both trends are as follows: J. B. P. Sinha (1973b) studied managers' perceptions of the importance attached by various organizations to objectives such as (a) profit, (b) welfare, (c) developmental needs, and (d) good relationships. He also studied whether the organizations were perceived as providing opportunities for promotion, good working conditions, efficient functioning, responsibility, getting due reward and punishment, and so on. R. Padaki (1982, 1983a, 1983b), explored job clarity, responsibility, reward, warmth, support, risk taking, and work norms. A factor analysis of the various components yielded a dominant general factor, which was labeled *progressive paternalism*. It was a blend of Western as well as Indian values. Virmani and Guptan (1991) reported that the organizational climate is characterized by the centralization of power in top positions and the resultant powerlessness in the middle levels to initiate innovation. Only top management can take the initiative on major issues. Criticism of supervisors is very unlikely.

N. K. Singh and Paul (1985) identified some of the characteristics of managers in the majority of Indian organizations. They seem to suffer from a lack of trust in each other, lack of credibility, too much emotionality and not enough rationality, concern for immediate gains, fear of being considered inferior and the resultant desire to be superior, ambiguities regarding their job requirements, and the habit of mobilizing their efforts only when a problem turns into a crisis. Khandwalla (1983a) delineated a three-dimensional framework for mapping organizational climate: (a) *modernity* (consisting of entrepreneurship, professionalism, and participation), (b) *tenderness* (i.e., adapting soft options by rewarding seniority and personal loyalty, emphasizing welfare versus being tough and pragmatic), and (c) *mutuality* (by seeking enlightened self-interest, cooperation with rivals versus a mercenary orientation to destroy the competition). Many Indian organizations are characterized by low modernity, high tenderness, and high mutuality. These characteristics reflect a culture-specific profile.

Some aspects of organizational climate, as described above, seem to be continuities of individuals' needs, preferences, and beliefs, as was described earlier. There are studies establishing the continuity between individual and climatic variables quite explicitly. Sharma (1983a, 1983b) ascertained the potentials of 27 organizations to meet the needs of individuals for such things as safety, security, monetary benefits, advancement, and grievance handling. P. Singh and G. S. Das (1978) asked managers to rate the extent to which their organizations were benevolent-autocratic, consultative, and democratic. Habibullah and J. B. P. Sinha (1980) measured six dimensions of motivational climate: expert power, concern for extension, achievement, affiliation, dependency, and control. Affiliation, dependency, and control were positively correlated and formed a *feudal* climate profile, while achievement, expert, and extension concerns constituted a *dedicated professional climate* profile. J. B. P. Sinha (1980) attempted to correlate authoritarian, nurturant-task, and participative styles of leadership to the climate dimensions of authoritarianism, nurturant-task orientation, participativeness, and so on. The authoritarian and nurturant-task styles were indeed correlated with the authoritarian and task-oriented climates, respectively, of the organizations. This shows the bidirectional but content-specific influence between leadership style and organizational climate, although there are investigators (e.g., M. Sinha, 1983) who argue that the influence of climate on leadership is stronger than the influence of leadership on climate. This line of argument is extended by A. K. Sinha (1991), who postulated that the effectiveness of a leadership style is moderated by the attributes of the organization, society, and culture.

Because organizational climate consists of shared images of the organization, it is expected that interdepartmental differences would be smaller than interorganizational differences (Ansari, 1980), although the intraorganizational variance may not be insignificant (J. B. P. Sinha, 1980). Sutaria (1979a) and Sutaria and V. Padaki (1976) showed that traditional textile organizations were more bureaucratic than high-tech electronic, chemical, and precision engineering organizations; Negandhi and B. S. Prasad (1971) found that multinationals were more progressive than private companies; and Jaggi (1978) confirmed that multinationals were more participative than domestic organizations.

The most frequent of the various interorganizational comparisons is the one made between private and public sector organizations. As stated earlier, the public sector has rapidly climbed to a position of dominance. There are high national stakes involved in them, yet their performance is not quite satisfactory. The reviews (Ganesh, 1981; Khandwalla, 1988; R. Padaki, 1988; J. B. P. Sinha, 1981a) document a large number of studies tracing the reason for their limited success to organizational climate. Most of the studies revealed that managers perceive the public sector organizations as having less favorable climate than those in the private sector. This was the case despite the fact that public sector managers were generally younger and equally qualified, and public sector organizations had generally more modern technology than their counterparts in the large private sector organizations. The public sector is characterized by too many objectives (Kidwai, 1987). There is high bureaucratization with too many rigid rules and regulations (Virmani & Guptan, 1991), and there is too much political interference (J. B. P. Sinha, 1973b, 1980). The climate values connections rather than merit (J. B .P. Sinha, 1990a). There is lack of managerial firmness but more of procedural rigidity (P. Singh, 1979). Relationship takes priority over task accomplishment (Dwivedi, 1980 & 1983; Sharma, 1983c). The effort-outcome linkages are quite weak (K. Kumar, 1982). There is too little scope for satisfaction of salient needs, for advancement, or for the utilization of skill and knowledge (Sharma, 1983a; R. P. Verma & R. P. Sinha, 1983). One could go on listing the negative images that the Indian public sector evokes.

Work Culture

Because organizational climate reflects both aggregated individual-level needs, values, and behavior as well as organizational objectives, structures, and processes, it has the potential to serve as an integrative framework for the various facets of an organization. In such an integrative role, organizational climate enlarges itself into the concept of work culture. Work culture signifies work-related activities and the meaning, affect, and values attached to such activities in terms of norms and managerial systems within an organizational setting (J. B. P. Sinha, 1990a, p. 16). Thus, there is often an overlap between work and organizational culture, although the two are conceptually distinct. Theoretically, each organization has a culture, the focus of which may be work or something else (e.g., welfare, good relationships.) Similarly, a large organization may have different work cultures in its different departments or divisions. Generally, however, the two overlap. Work culture has been examined in terms of (a) objectively defined organizational goals and objectives, technology, work forms, and systems within

the organizations, and (b) perceptually shared norms, values, work behavior, and the importance attached to work-related activities (J. B. P. Sinha, 1990a).

J. B. P. Sinha has identified two profiles of work culture in a number of organizations: *soft* and *synergetic*. In a *soft work culture,* work is displaced from its central place by non-work activities and interests. Employees do not work hard, do not feel positive about their work, do not derive satisfaction from their work, and do not experience role clarity. They are not punctual and tend to meet social-personal obligations at the expense of their work. The opposite is true in a *synergetic work culture.*

These two opposing ways of looking at work are directly related to organizational climate. The managers in a synergetic work culture believe that the organization rewards hard work, recognizes merit, and places appropriate importance on work. Work norms are established and strictly conformed to, and support systems are established and plants and equipment are maintained promptly and adequately. Three factors were found to be responsible for the soft or synergetic work culture. Soft work culture was associated with (a) low self-reliance (or dependency on government) and high propensity to bear losses, (b) a soft culture history, tradition, and philosophy of management, and (c) models used by top executives that translated the other two into soft management systems and practices. The top executives in synergetic work cultures develop effective means of boundary scanning, regulating the inflow of influences and resources, establishing systems, and mobilizing human resources. On the contrary, the top leaders in soft work cultures tend toward easy options, yield to extraneous pressures and internal demands, look for their own power bases, and play partisan politics inside the organization. The public sector organizations generally drift toward a soft work culture (J. B. P. Sinha, 1990a), but they do not have to do so. It depends on the interplay of various external or internal factors that render the work culture either soft or synergetic.

The Coming Years

The trends identified so far are likely to gather strength in the coming years. The bulk of research will continue to be imitative and replicative. Foreign instruments and scales will outnumber domestic ones. Surveys and self-reported data of uneven quality will keep dominating organizational research in India. Yet a number of front-runners are likely to carry on their search for indigenous concepts, theories, and methods. They are the ones who would respond to the radical changes being introduced in the industrial sector of India.

A number of measures were taken in the early 1980s to liberalize the control environment and to increase the use of high technology and the computerization of industries. Limited success of the public sector and political changes in Eastern Europe have further pushed the change process toward greater use of the private sector. The Industrial Policy (1991) of the government reflected a quantum leap toward liberalization. The protective umbrella once placed over the economy is being withdrawn to a large extent. Foreign equity is allowed to exceed 51 percent. Multinational companies are expected to use the latest technology. Licensing is being abolished in most sectors. The private sector is being allowed entry into the areas once forbidden to it. Not that the public sector is going to be significantly privatized, but both sectors will have to become open to market forces and will run the risk of liquidation if they lose their competitive edge. High technology and computerization require information-based management and will necessitate changes in work relationships and managerial practices.

Hence, there will be pressure for Indian organizations to use the systems and procedures that have been effective in organizations functioning in market economies. Such systems and procedures are primarily Western. As noted earlier, they have been formally established in Indian organizations but were bypassed in order to use cultural connections and to meet employees' needs and national priorities. Now those systems will claim to become dominant. However, it would be naive to believe that the cultural factors will readily give in to such changes.

Therefore, the issues that started taking shape in the 1980s will develop a sharper focus in the next decades. Behavioral scientists will be called upon to reexamine what Udy (1970) recommended—that is, that in order to be effective, industrial organizations must shift from being socially determined to being technologically determined. Crucial to this shift is the contractual work relationship, suppression of familial values, and an emphasis on industrial technology (pp. 95–96). Can we really realize this transformation? What if the culture, thus relegated, enters through the back door and surreptitiously undermines the systems and distorts managerial practices?

An alternative may be to try the Japanese model, where competitiveness and quality remain the central concern and cultural factors are utilized to realize them. The Indian style of integrating culture and technology is an attractive proposition to many Indian industrial and organizational psychologists, particularly because there is evidence (J. B. P. Sinha, 1990a) that some organizations have been able to use cultural factors to create a synergetic work culture, although there is also evidence that others have succumbed to cultural compulsions and have developed with a soft work culture. Some of the reasons for the differential impacts are known, but more systematic research needs to be conducted to arrive at strategies that can produce synergetic work cultures and prevent soft work cultures.

Culture probably plays a different role in organizations that vary in matters such as local versus international operations, foreign participation in equity, and technological complexities. Organizational diversity in using culture-specific systems and practices may provide fertile ground for systematic research.

Before the behavioral scientists undertake studies on the interface between culture and technology, they will need to examine the linkages between cultural, organizational, and individual-level variables. The studies reported so far have yet to prove that these three levels of analysis are isomorphic. In fact, there are instances when they are not. For example, cultural, organizational, and individual values show discrepancies that may be due to the filtering effects of organizational structures and systems, as well as individuals' characteristics. Further studies are required to identify the mechanisms (e.g., organizational socialization) that may be held responsible for the nature and extent of the inflow of macro-level forces into industrial organizations.

An important issue that is currently being glossed over in the euphoria of liberalization and high tech, is related to social justice. Soon it will emerge again and demand the attention of behavioral scientists. In a pluralistic society with large disparities among its regions and groups of people, the country probably needs a variety of organizations, some of which have promotional and welfare goals. Studies will need to identify the types of protective economic umbrellas that will need to be provided to these regions and groups.

In sum, there are exciting years ahead. The new changes are providing opportunities that were not available in previous decades. However, in order to meet these challenges, behavioral scientists will need to be much more innovative in their approaches and methods than they were in the 1980s. There are some indications that they are diversifying their methods and research designs by resorting to observations, secondary source data, archival materials, group interviews, and so on. The coming years will witness greater ingenuity and more vigorous research for identifying indigenous models for understanding industrial organizations in India.

Thanks are acknowledged to Sunita Singh-Sengupta and Sobha Mishra for their assistance in collecting references and to Jitendra Pandey for typing the chapter.

References

Agrawal, A. N., Verma, H. O., & Gupta, R. C. (1988). *India: Economic information year book* 1988–1989 (rev. 3rd ed.). New Delhi: National.

Agrawal, K. G. (1975). *Union participation and work motivation: A study among local union leaders?* New Delhi: National Labour Institute.

Agrawal, K. G., & Sharma, B. R. (1977). Gratification meta-motivation and Maslow. *Vikalpa, 2,* 265–272.

Agrawal, R. (1974). Organization structure and communication in a manufacturing sector in India. *Indian Journal of Industrial Relations, 9,* 385–386.

Agrawal, V. K. (1989). State enterprises in India: Achievements and challenges. In B. L. Mathur (Ed.), *Problems and challenges of public enterprises* (pp. 57–66). Jaipur, India: RBSA Publishers.

Ahmed, N. (1982). The making of a managerial job evaluation plan. *Vikalpa, 7,* 99–112.

Akhtar, S. S., & Pestonjee, D. M. (1969). *A study of intrinsic and extrinsic motivational factors.* Bangalore, India: St. Joseph's College, Business Administration Course.

Ansari, M. A. (1980). Organizational climate: Homogeneity within and heterogeneity between organizations. *Journal of Social and Economic Studies, 8,* 89–96.

Ansari, M. A. (1990). *Managing people at work: Leadership styles and influence strategies.* New Delhi: Sage.

Ansari, M. A., & Kapoor, A. (1987). Organizational context and upward influence tactics. *Organizational Behaviour & Human Decision Processes, 40,* 39–49.

Ayyar, S. R. (1976). Participation in management by junior and middle level managers. *Indian Manager, 7,* 196–212.

Baumgartel, H., Bennis, W., & De, N. (1968). (Eds.). *Readings in group development.* Bombay: Asia Publishing House.

Baumgartel, H., & Jeanpierre, F. (1972). Applying new knowledge in the backhome setting: A study of Indian manager's adoptive efforts. *Journal of Applied Behavioural Science, 8,* 674–694.

Bhandare, S. (1990, November). New steel policy: Liberalization sans dynamism (p. 10). *Times of India,* Patna.

Bidani, S., & Mitra, P. K. (1982). *Industrial sickness: Identification and rehabilitation.* New Delhi: Vision Books.

Blau, P. M. (1964). *Exchange and power in social life.* New York: Wiley.

Bose, S. K. (1955). Employee morale and supervision. *Indian Journal of Psychology, 27,* 117–125.

Chadha, P. P. (1966). Causes of indiscipline in industry. *Indian Management, 5,* 27–29.

Chakraborty, P. (1969). *Strikes and morale in industry in India and her principal states.* Calcutta: Chakraborty.

Chakraborty, S. K. (1987). *Managerial effectiveness and quality of work life: Indian insight.* New Delhi: Tata McGraw-Hill.

Chatterjee, A. (1961). *Satisfaction and productivity: A study of morale and team work with respect to productivity.* Unpublished doctoral dissertation, Indian Institute of Science, Banaglore, India.

Chatterjee, N. N. (1984). *Industrial relations in India's developing economy.* Bombay: Allied.

Chatterji, A. (1975). An approach to the job appraisal of managerial personnel for development: Implications of current research. *Paranassus Journal of Humanities and Social Sciences, 2*(1), 6–12.

Chatterji, S. (1976). *Collected studies on appraisal* (Rep. No. D 1–4). Calcutta: Indian Statistical Institute.

Chatterji, S. (1985, January). *Report on Indian Institute of Psychometry.* Paper presented at the International Seminar on Selection and Appraisal Systems, New Delhi.

Chatterji, S., & Mukherjee, M. (1963). A study of co-workers ratings. *Productivity, 4,* 717–720.

Chatterji, S., & Mukherjee, M. (1966). A review of merit rating method. *Indian Psychological Review, 3,* 21–32.

Chattopadhyaya, G. P. (1975). Dependency in Indian culture: From mud huts to company board rooms. *Economic and Political Weekly, 10*(1), M30–M38.

Chattopadhyaya, G. P., & Sinha, D. P. (1970). Social, organizational, and interpersonal relevance of sensitivity training. *Industrial Relations, 22,* 213–229.

Chattopadhyaya, S., & Pareek, U. (1982). *Managing organizational change.* New Delhi: Oxford and IBH.

Chaturvedi, A. (1977). Organizational behaviour in India: A review. In D. P. Sinha (Ed.), *Readings in organizational behaviour* (pp. 1–16). Hyderabad, India: ASCI.

Chaubey, R. N. (1986). *As the heart sees....* Bokaro, India: Bokaro Steel Plant.

Chaudhury, A. S. (1978). Downward communication in industrial hierarchy in public sector organizations. *Integrated Management, 13,* 11–17.

Chinese Culture Connection. (1987). Chinese values and the search for culture free dimensions of culture. *Journal of Cross-Cultural Psychology, 18,* 143–164.

Das, G. S. (1983). Some correlates of managerial job involvement: Implications for work reorganization. *Decision, 10,* 51–60.

Das, R. S. (1965). Methods of evaluating performance in industrial and educational settings: A review of research in the Indian Statistical Institute. In S. D. Kapoor (Ed.), *Psychological research in India* (pp. 115–130). Varanasi, India: Varanasi Press.

Das, T. K. (1971). Reorganization in State Bank of India. *Lok Udyog, 5*(1), 781–790.

Dayal, I. (1967). Constraint of legislation on organizational effectiveness. *Indian Journal of Industrial Relations, 2,* 315–333.

Dayal, I. (1970). *Bihar famine studies.* Ahmadabad, India: Indian Institute of Management.

Dayal, I. (1971). Organizational development: An interim balance sheet. *Economic and Political Weekly, 6,* 95–98.

Dayal, I. (1973). (Ed.). *A survey of research in management.* New Delhi: Vikas.

Dayal, I. (1976a). *Designing a work organization.* New Delhi: All India Management Association.

Dayal, I. (1976b). *Cultural factors in designing performance appraisal system.* New Delhi: RC Industrial Relations and Human Resources.

Dayal, I. (1977). *Change in work organizations: Some experiences of renewal in social systems.* New Delhi: Concept.

De, N. R. (1974). Conditions for work culture. *Indian Journal of Industrial Relations, 9,* 587–598.

De, N. R. (1979). Participative redesign of a work system. In B. C. Matheu, K. Diesh, & C. Chandrashekaran (Eds.), *Management in government* (pp. 169–189). New Delhi: Ministry of Information and Broadcasting, Publications Division.

De, N. R. (1984). *Alternative designs of human organizations.* New Delhi: Sage.

Devasgayam, A. (1949). The employer-employee partnership. *Indian Journal of Social Work, 9,* 287–295.

Dhingra, O. P., & Pathak, V. K. (1972). Professional background of the Indian personnel managers. *PACT,* 11–17.

D'Souza, K. C. (1984). Organizations as agents of social change. *Vikalpa, 9,* 233–247.

Dutta, R. C. (1990). *State enterprises in a developing country: The Indian experience, 1950–1990.* New Delhi: Abinav.

Dwivedi, R. S. (1980). Some correlates of employee performance. *Indian Journal of Industrial Relations, 15,* 563–576.

Dwivedi, R. S. (1983). A comparative study of managerial styles, leadership and trust among Indian managers. *Lok Udyog, 27,* 7–17.

Economic Intelligence Service (1990). *Basic statistics relating to Indian economy* (Vol. 1). Bombay: Centre for Monitoring Indian Economy.

Encarnation, D. J. (1982). The political economy of Indian joint ventures abroad. *International Organization, 36,* 15–27.

Foundation for Organizational Research (FORE) (1984). *A study of the indicators and process of effective management.* New Delhi: Foundation for Organizational Research.

Ganesh, S. R. (1980). Performance of management education institution: An Indian sampler. *Higher Education, 9,* 230–253.

Ganesh, S. R. (1981). *Research in organizational behaviour in India: A critique.* (Working Paper No. 372). Ahmadabad, India: Indian Institute of Management.

Ganesh, S. R. (1982). *Quality of life in Indian organizations: An irrelevant view* (Working Paper No. 407). Ahmadabad, India: Indian Institute of Management.

Ganesh, S. R. (1990). Organization behaviour. In B. L. Maheshwari (Ed.), *Research in management: 1970–1979* (pp. 83–168). New Delhi: Indian Council of Social Science Research.

Ganguli, C. N. (1977). Management styles of different organizations in India. *Management in Government, 9,* 217–234.

Ganguli, H. N. (1957). *A study supervision in a government engineering factory.* Kharagpur, India: Indian Institute of Technology.

Ganguli, H. C. (1961). *Industrial productivity and motivation.* Bombay: Asia Publishing House.

Ganguli, H. C. (1964). *Structure and process of organization.* Bombay: Asia Publishing House.

Ganguli, H. C. (1974). Role of status and money as motivators among middle management personnel. *Indian Journal of Industrial Relations, 10*(1), 189–196.

Ganguli, H. C., Goswami, S., & Ghosh, R. (1957). A railway study of differential perception of first line supervisory practices. *Indian Journal of Psychology, 32,* 39–100.

Goswamy, H. (1985, January). Views expressed at the International Seminar on Selection and Appraisal Systems, New Delhi.

Gupta, R. K. (1991). Employees and organization in India: Need to move beyond American and Japanese models. *Economic and Political Weekly, 26,* M68-M76.

Habibullah, A. H. M., & Sinha, J. B. P. (1980). Motivational climate and leadership styles. *Vikalpa, 5,* 85–93.

Hassan, A. (1989). *Dynamic of leadership effectiveness in Indian work organizations.* New Delhi: Commonwealth Publishers.

Heather, H., & Surger, B. D. (1980). The good organization. *Business Quarterly, 45,* 63–67.

Herskovits, M. J. (1955). *Cultural anthropology.* New York: Knopf.

Herzberg, F., Mausner, B., & Synderman, B. B. (1958). *The motivation to work.* New York: Wiley.

Hofstede, G. (1980). *Culture's consequences.* Beverly Hills, CA: Sage.

House, R. J., & Woycke, J. C. (1988). A comparative study of charismatic and non-charismatic leaders of the third world. In P. N. Khandwalla

(Ed.), *Social development* (pp. 145–146). New Delhi: Sage.

Howard, A., & Scott, R. A. (1981). The study of minority groups in complex societies. In R. H. Munroe, R. L. Munroe, & B. B. Whiting (Eds.), *Handbook of cross-cultural human development* (pp. 113–152). New York: Garland STPM.

Jaeger, A. M., & Kanungo, R. N. (1990). Summary and conclusions: In search of indigenous management. In A. M. Jaeger & R. N. Kanungo (Eds.), *Management in developing countries* (pp. 287–295). London: Routledge.

Jaggi, B. L. (1978). Management leadership styles in Indian organizations. *Indian Manager, 9,* 139–156.

Jain, S. C. (1971). *Indian manager.* Bombay: Somaiya Publication.

Kakar, S. (1971). Authority patterns of subordinates behaviour in Indian organizations. *Administrative Science Quarterly, 16,* 298–307.

Kakar, S. (1978). *The inner world: A psycho-analytic study of childhood and society in India.* New Delhi: Oxford University Press.

Kalro, A., & Misra, S. (1973). Salience of job instrumentality factors in pre and post-decision organizational choice. *Indian Journal of Industrial Relations, 8,* 407–413.

Kannappan, S. (1958). Management and discipline in a welfare state. *Economic Weekly, 10,* 1587–1588.

Kanungo, R. N. (1981). Work alienation and involvement: Problems and prospects. *International Review of Applied Psychology, 30,* 1–15.

Kanungo, R. N., & Hartwick, J. (1987). An alternative to the intrinsic-extrinsic dichotomy of work rewards. *Journal of Management, 4,* 751–766.

Kanungo, R. N., & Misra, S. (1988). The bases of involvement in work and family contexts. *International Journal of Psychology, 23,* 267–282.

Kapoor, A. (1986). *Some of the determinants of intraorganizational influence strategies.* Unpublished doctoral dissertation, Indian Institute of Technology, Kanpur, India.

Kedia, B. L., & Bhagat, R. S. (1988). Cultural constraints on transfer of technology across nations: Implications for research in international and comparative management. *Academy of Management Review, 13,* 559–571.

Khandelwal, P. (1983). Job involvement, perceived satisfaction, and importance of employees'

needs. *National Labour Institute Bulletin, 9,* 20–23.

Khandwalla, P. N. (1981a). Strategy for turning around complex sick organizations. *Vikalpa, 6,* 143–166.

Khandwalla, P. N. (1981b). *Performance determinants of public enterprise* (Working Paper No. 436). Ahmedabad, India: Indian Institute of Management.

Khandwalla, P. N. (1981c). Properties of competing organizations. In P. C. Nystrom & W. H. Starbuck (Eds.), *Handbook of organizational design* (Vol. 1, pp. 409–432). London: Oxford University Press.

Khandwalla, P. N. (1982). Some lessons for the management of public enterprises. *Vikalpa, 7,* 311–25.

Khandwalla, P. N. (1983a). PI management. *Vikalpa, 8,* 220–238.

Khandwalla, P. N. (1983b). The architecture of Indian top management. *Indian Management, 22,* 11–17.

Khandwalla, P. N. (1988). Organizational effectiveness. In J. Pandey (Ed.), *Psychology in India: The state of the art* (Vol. 2, pp. 97–215). New Delhi: Sage.

Khurana, R. (1981). *Growth of large business: Impact of monopolies legislation.* New Delhi: Wiley Eastern.

Kidwai, W. R. (1987). *The threatening storm over public sector in India.* New Delhi: Standing Committee of Public Enterprise (SCOPE).

Kilmann, R. H., & Herdner, P. (1976). Towards a systematic methodology for evaluating the impact of intervention on organizational effectiveness. *Academy of Management Review, 3,* 87–98.

King, A. S. (1990). Evolution of leadership theory. *Vikalpa, 15,* 43–56.

Kulkarni, A. V. (1973). Motivational factors among middle class employees. *Indian Journal of Applied Psychology, 10,* 66–69.

Kumar, K. (1982). *Organization and ownership: A comparative sectoral study of general management functions.* New Delhi: Macmillan.

Kumar, U., & Srivastava, B. N. (1979). Desirable and actual modes of conflict resolution of Indian managers and their organizational climate. In H. Eckensberger Lutry et al. (Eds.), *Cross-cultural contributions to psychology* (pp. 408–414). Lisse, the Netherlands: Swets & Zeitlinger.

Lambert, D. (1963). *Workers, factories and social change in India.* Princeton, NJ: Princeton University Press.

Lewis, O. (1966). The culture of poverty. *Scientific American, 215,* 19–25.

Lodahl, T. M., & Kejner, M. (1965). The definition and measurement of job involvement. *Journal of Applied Psychology, 49,* 24–33.

Long, L., & Mehta, P. (Ed.). (1966). *The first mental measurement handbook of India.* New Delhi: National Council for Educational Research and Training.

Lynton, R. P., & Pareek, U. (1967). *Training for development.* Homewood, IL: Irwin.

Madhok, A. (1990). *Motivational patterns and leadership styles of managers and subordinate interpersonal perception.* Unpublished doctoral dissertation, Punjab University, Chandigarh, India.

Maheshwari, B. L. (1977). Internal change agent experiences in MBO implementation. *ASCI Journal of Management, 6,* 147–187.

Maheshwari, B. L. (1978). *Decision styles and organizational effectiveness.* Hyderabad, India: ASCI.

Maheshwari, B. L. (1980). *Management by objectives: Concepts, method, and experiences.* New Delhi: Tata McGraw-Hill.

Maheshwari, B. L. (1983). Indian executives expectations from organization [Special issue]. *Management and Systems Review,* 13–27.

Mascarenhas, D. A. J. (1978). Technological progress of multinational versus domestic firms in India. *Management and Labour Studies, 4,* 20–37.

McClelland, D. C. (1975). *Power: The inner experience.* New York: Free Press.

Meade, R. D. (1967). An experimental study of leadership in India. *Journal of Social Psychology, 72,* 35–43.

Mehta, P. (1978, March). *Work motivation in Indian public sector: Some conceptualization.* Paper presented at the National Labour Institute's seminar on "Alienation, Efficacy, Motivation and Employee Participation," New Delhi.

Mehta, P. (1981). Political process and behaviour. In V. Pareek (Ed.), *A survey of research in psychology 1971–1976* (Part 2, pp. 577–615). Bombay: Popular Prakashan.

Mehta, P. (1991). *People's development, motivation, and work organization.* New Delhi: Participation and Development Center.

Mehta, V. (1967). *Portraits of India.* New York: Penguin Books.

Ministry of Human Resource Development (1985). *Challenge of education.* New Delhi: Government of India.

Mishra, R. (1982). Source determination of organizational effectiveness. *Productivity, 23,* 275–285.

Misra, S., & Kalro, A. (1981). Job involvement of intrinsically and extrinsically motivated Indian managers: To each according to his need. *Human Relations, 34,* 419–426.

Mitra, S. K. (1968). Review of tests and measurement. In S. B. Adaval (Ed.), *The third Indian yearbook on education* (pp. 124–135). New Delhi: National Council of Educational Research and Training.

Moghaddam, F. M. (1989). Specialization and despecialization in psychology: Divergent process in the three worlds. *International Journal of Psychology, 24,* 103–116.

Mukherjee, B. N. (1980). Psychological theory and research methods. In U. Pareek (Ed.), *A survey of research in psychology* (Part 1, pp. 1–135). Bombay: Popular Prakashan.

Mukherjee, S. K. (1985). Views expressed at the International Seminar on Selection and Appraisal Systems, New Delhi.

Murthi, K. K. S. (1982). Top management selection for public enterprises: Is private sector model appropriate? *Vikalpa, 7,* 9–18.

Muthuchidambaram, S. (1972). Commitment and motivation of blue collar workers in India. *Indian Journal of Industrial Relations, 7,* 569–587.

Myers, C. A. (1958). *Industrial relations in India.* Bombay: Asia Publishing House.

Myrdal, G. (1968). *Asian drama.* New York: Twentieth Century.

Nallasivam, O. (1963). Grievance procedure. *Proceedings of the Fifth Annual Conference of Human Relations* (pp. 50–51), Coimbatore.

Negandhi, A. R., & Prasad, B. S. (1971). *Comparative management.* New York: Appleton-Century-Crofts.

Nigam, R. K. (1967). Pattern of directorship in public undertakings. *Lok Udyog, 4,* 61–69.

Nord, W. R. (1986). Continuity and change in industrial/organizational psychology: Learning from previous mistakes. In F. J. Landy (Ed.), *Readings in industrial and organizational psychology* (pp. 438–447). Chicago: Dorsey Press.

Orpen, C. (1978). Interpersonal communication processes as determinants of employee perceptions of organizational goals. *Management and Labour Studies, 4*, 50–88.

Padaki, R. (1982). *A study of organizational climate and work behaviour.* Unpublished doctoral dissertation, Gujarat University, Ahmadabad, India.

Padaki, R. (1983a). *Organizational climate: What it is and what it does* (Research Rep. No. HR/142). Ahmadabad: ATIRA, Human Resources Division.

Padaki, R. (1983b). Organizational climate in nationalized textile mills. *Management Digest, 1,* 11–16.

Padaki, R. (1988). Job attitudes. In J. Pandey (Ed.), *Psychology in India: The state of the art* (Vol. 3, pp. 19–94). New Delhi: Sage.

Paliwal, M. B., & Paliwal, K. M. (1974). A study of need importance in relation to personal characteristics of industrial employees. *Psychological Studies, 19,* 118–121.

Pandey, J. (1978). Ingratiation: A review of literature and relevance of its study in organizational setting. *Indian Journal of Industrial Relations, 13,* 381–398.

Pandey, J. (1980a). Authoritarianism. *Seminar, 255,* 12–15.

Pandey, J. (1980b). Ingratiation as expected and manipulative behaviour in Indian society. *Social Change, 10,* 15–17.

Pandey, J. (1981). Ingratiation as a social behaviour. In J. Pandey (Ed.), *Perspectives on experimental social psychology* (pp. 157–185). New Delhi: Concept.

Pandey, J. (1986). Cross-cultural perspectives on ingratiation. In B. Maher & W. Maher (Eds.), *Progress in experimental personality research* (Vol. 14, pp. 205–229). New York: Academic Press.

Pandey, J. (1988). Social influence process. In J. Pandey (Ed.), *Psychology in India: The state of the art* (Vol. 2, pp. 55–94). New Delhi: Sage.

Pandey, J., & Bohra, K. A. (1986). Attraction and evaluation as a function of ingratiating style of a person. *Social Behaviour and Personality, 14*(1), 23–28.

Pandey, J., & Kakar, S. (1982). Supervisor's affect: Attraction and positive evaluation as a function of other enhancement. *Psychological Reports, 50,* 479–486.

Pandey, J., & Rastogi, R. (1979). Machiavellianism and ingratiation. *Journal of Social Psychology, 108,* 221–225.

Pandey, J., & Singh, A. K. (1986). Attribution and evaluation of manipulative social behaviour. *Journal of Social Psychology, 12,* 735–744.

Pandey, S. N. (1989). *Human side of Tata Steel.* New Delhi: Tata McGraw-Hill.

Pareek, U. (1968). A motivational paradigm for development. *Journal of Social Issues, 24,* 112–115.

Pareek, U. (1974). A conceptual model of work motivation. *Indian Journal of Industrial Relations, 10,* 16–31.

Pareek, U., & Lynton, R. P. (1965). Sensitivity training for personnel and organizational development. *Indian Management, 4,* 40–45.

Pareek, U., & Rao, T. V. (1974). *Handbook of psychological and social instruments.* Baroda, India: Samasthi.

Parikh, I. J. (1979). *Role orientation and role performance of Indian managers* (Working Paper No. 300). Ahmadabad, India: Indian Institute of Management.

Patil, S. M. (1981). *Experiences of a public sector top executive: Handicaps, disappointments and fulfillments of a public sector chief.* New Delhi: Centre for Corporate and Business Policy Research.

Pestonjee, D. M. (1973). *Organizational structure and job attitudes.* Calcutta: Minerva Associates.

Pestonjee, D. M., & Akhtar, S. S. (1969). Occupational values, preferences, and income aspirations of engineering and teacher training students. *Indian Psychological Review, 5,* 131–135.

Pestonjee, D. M., & Singh, A. P. (1973). Morale in relation to authoritarianism in supervisor. *Indian Journal of Social Work, 33,* 361–366.

Poortinga, Y. H., Kop, P. M. F., & Van de Vijver, F. J. R. (1990). Differences between psychological domains in the range of cross-cultural variation. In P. R. D. Drenth, J. A. Sergent, & R. J. Takens (Eds.), *European perspective in psychology* (Vol. 3). Chichester, England: Wiley.

Poortinga, Y. H., & Van de Vijver, F. J. R. (1987). Explaining cross-cultural differences: Bias analysis and beyond. *Journal of Cross-cultural Psychology, 18,* 259–282.

Prakasam, R., Despande, M. V., & Kshirsagar, S. S. (1979). Organizational climate in four banks: Report of a survey. *Prajnan,* 275–294.

Prasad, L. (1976). Management of conflict in organizations. *Integrated Management, 118,* 36–38.

Prasad, L. (1978). Barriers in upward communication. *Lok Udyog, 11,* 41–46.

Rabinowitz, S., & Hall, T. G. (1977). Organizational research on job involvement. *Psychological Bulletin, 84,* 275–288.

Ramanujam, A. K. (1989). Is there an Indian way of thinking? An informal essay. *Contributions to Indian Sociology, 25,* 41–58.

Rao, T. V. (1981). Psychology of work: Individual in organization. In U. Pareek (Ed.), *A survey of research in psychology, 1971–1976* (Part 2, pp. 476–570). Bombay: Popular Prakashan.

Rath, R. (1972). Social psychology: A trend report. In S. K. Mitra (Ed.), *A survey of research in psychology* (pp. 362–413). Bombay: Popular Prakashan.

Ray, A. (1970). The Indian managers in the eighties. *Economic and Political Weekly, 5,* M105–M106.

Roland, A. (1988). *In search of self in India and Japan: Toward a cross-cultural psychology.* Princeton, NJ: Princeton University Press.

Roy, S. K. (1973a). Income regulation and managerial motivation to work: An exploratory analysis. *Indian Journal of Industrial Relations, 9,* 146–160.

Roy, S. K. (1973b). Incentive motivation and organizational effectiveness. In G. K. Suri (Ed.), *Wage incentives: Theory and practices.* New Delhi: Shri Ram Centre for Industrial Relations and Human Resources.

Rub, M. M. (1988). *Antecedents of hard working behavior.* Unpublished doctoral dissertation, Patna University, India.

Saiyadain, M. S. (1974a). Personality predisposition and satisfaction with supervisory style. *Indian Journal of Industrial Relations, 10,* 153–161.

Saiyadain, M. S. (1974b). *Subordinates' personality and supervisory style.* New Delhi: ICSSR Report.

Saiyadain, M. S. (1980). Job enrichment: Prospects and problems. *Productivity, 21,* 165–172.

Saiyadain, M. S., & Monappa, A. (1977). *Profile of Indian managers.* New Delhi: Vidya Vahini.

Sarveswara Rao, G. V. (1972). Theoretical and empirical considerations of the two factor theory of job satisfaction. *Indian Journal of Industrial Relations, 7* (3), 311–330.

Sarveswara Rao, G. V. (1973). Interpersonal trust and its correlates as perceived by superiors and subordinates. *Indian Journal of Industrial Relations, 10,* 359–369.

Sayeed, O. B. (1990). Conflict management style: Relationship with leadership styles and moderating effect of esteem for co-workers. *Indian Journal of Industrial Relations, 26,* 28–52.

Sayeed, O. B., & Mathur, H. B. (1980). Leadership behaviour and conflict management strategies. *Vikalpa, 5,* 275–282.

Sengupta, A. K. (1990). New generation of organized workforce in India: Implications for management and trade unions. *Indian Journal of Industrial Relations, 26,* 1–14.

Shanmugam, T. E. (1972). Personality: A trend report. In S. K. Mitra (Ed.), *A survey of research in psychology* (pp. 266–337). Bombay: Popular Prakashan.

Sharma, B. R. (1970). Indian industrial worker. *International Journal of Comparative Sociology, 1–2.*

Sharma, B. R. (1972). What makes a manager: Merit, motivation, or money? *Economic and Political Weekly, 7,* M81–M88.

Sharma, B. R. (1973). The Indian industrial worker: His origin, experience and destiny. *Economic and Political Weekly, 8,* M38–M43.

Sharma, B. R. (1979). *Organizational correlates of indiscipline in Bokaro: Bokaro Steel Plant.* Bokaro Steel Plant, Research Cell, Personnel Department, Bokaro, India.

Sharma, B. R. (1983a). *Man-management in India: Comparison of public and private sectors* (XLRI Reprint Series No. A-5533).

Sharma, B. R. (1983b, spring). Organizational climate and employer-employee relations in India. *Abhigyan,* 45–59.

Sharma, B. R. (1983c). Man management in India: Comparison of public and private sectors. *Lok Udyog, 17,* 7–16.

Sharma, B. R., & Warrier, S. K. (1977). Selection of future managers: Relevance of admission procedure. *Management and Labour Studies, 3,* 39–51.

Sheth, N. R. (1968). *The social framework of an Indian factory.* Bombay: Oxford University Press.

Shetty, Y. K. (1970). Personnel management practices: A comparative study. *Indian Journal of Social Work, 3,* 101–115.

Shrivastava, A. K. (1977). Indian blue-collar workers: Their commitment. *Indian Journal of Industrial Relations, 13,* 223–234.

Singer, M. (1975). Industrial leadership, the Hindu ethic and the spirit of socialism. *Indian Social and Psychological Studies, 1,* 19–44.

Singh, A. K. (1967). Hindu culture and economic development in India. *Conspectus, 1*, 9–32.

Singh, A. P., & Pestonjee, D. M. (1974). Supervisory behaviour and job satisfaction. *Indian Journal of Industrial Relations, 9*, 407–416.

Singh, B. P. (1989). Problems of manpower planning in public enterprises. In B. L. Mathur (Ed.), *Problems and challenges of public enterprises in India.* Jaipur, India: RBSA Publisher.

Singh, J. P. (1983, autumn). QWL experiments in India: Trials and triumphs. *Abhigyan,* 23–27.

Singh, N. K. (1990). *The dialogues with yati: Insights on man and organization.* New Delhi: Foundation for Organizational Research and Education.

Singh, N. K., Kaul, R., & Ahluwalia, P. (1983). *A diagnostic study of training and development needs in a public sector organization.* New Delhi: Foundation for Organizational Research & Education.

Singh, N. K., & Paul, O. (1985). *Corporate soul: Dynamics of effective management.* New Delhi: Vikas.

Singh, P. (1979). *Occupational values and styles of Indian managers.* New Delhi: Wiley Eastern.

Singh, P., & Bhandarker, A. (1990). *Corporate success and transformational leadership.* New Delhi: Wiley Eastern.

Singh, P., & Das, G. S. (1977). Managerial style of Indian managers. *ASCI Journal of Management, 7*, 1–11.

Singh, P., & Das, G. S. (1978). Organizational culture and its impact on commitment to work. *Indian Journal of Industrial Relations, 13*, 511–524.

Singh, P., Warrier, S. K., & Das, G. S. (1979). Leadership process and its impact on productivity, satisfaction, and work commitment. *Decision, 6*, 25–269.

Singh, R. B. P., & Sinha, J. B. P. (1992). The darker side of worker-manager relationship in a coal area in India. In R. Th. J. DeRidder & R. C. Tripathi (Eds.), *Norm violations and intergroup relations* (pp. 90–115). London: Oxford University Press.

Singh, S. K. (1989). *Managerial decisions: Influence of ingroup.* New Delhi: Commonwealth Publishers.

Singh-Sengupta, S. (1990a). Influence strategies used on superiors. *Management and Labour Studies, 15*, 141–145.

Singh-Sengupta, S. (1990b). *Emerging patterns of power distribution.* New Delhi: Commonwealth Publishers.

Singhal, S. (1973). Psychology of men at work, communication, and job perception. *Indian Journal of Industrial Relations, 8*, 415–424.

Singhal, S., & Upadhyay, H. S. (1972). Psychology of men at work: Employees perception of job incentives. *Indian Journal of Industrial Relations, 8*, 17–30.

Sinha, A. K. (1991). The leadership enigma: What and what not to expect. *The Social Engineer, 1*, 13–14.

Sinha, D. (1972). Industrial psychology. In S. K. Mihra (Ed.), *A survey of research in psychology* (pp. 175–237). Bombay: Popular Prakashan.

Sinha, D. (1980). Sex differences in psychological differentiation among different cultural groups. *International Journal of Behavioural Development, 3*, 455–466.

Sinha, D. (1983). Human assessment in Indian context. In S. H. Iwine & J. W. Berry (Eds.), *Human assessment and cultural factors* (pp. 17–34). New York: Plenum.

Sinha, D. (1986). *Psychology in a third world country: The Indian experience.* New Delhi: Sage.

Sinha, D. P. (1973, March). Organizational development: Approach and issues. *ASCI Journal of Management,* 38–51.

Sinha, D. P. (1986). *T-Group, team building, and organizational development.* New Delhi: Indian Society for Applied Behavioural Science.

Sinha, D. P. (1989). *Indian management: Context, concerns, and trends.* Hyderabad, India: Administrative Staff College.

Sinha, J. B. P. (1968). The n-Ach/n-cooperation under limited/unlimited resource conditions. *Journal of Experimental Social Psychology, 4*, 233–246.

Sinha, J. B. P. (1970). *Development through behaviour modification.* Bombay: Allied Publishers.

Sinha, J. B. P. (1973a). Methodology of problem oriented research in India. *Journal of Social and Economic Studies, 1*, 93–110.

Sinha, J. B. P. (1973b). *Some problems of public sector organizations.* Delhi, India: National.

Sinha, J. B. P. (1974). A case of reversal in participative management. *Indian Journal of Industrial Relations, 10*, 179–187.

Sinha, J. B. P. (1977). The poverty syndrome, power motive, and democratization of the work place. *Integrated Management, 12*, 5–8.

Sinha, J. B. P. (1978). Power in superior subordinate relationship. *Journal of Social and Economic Studies, 6,* 205–218.

Sinha, J. B. P. (1980). *The nurturant task leader.* New Delhi: Concept.

Sinha, J. B. P. (1981a). Organizational dynamics. In U. Pareek (Ed.), *A survey of research in psychology, 1971–1976* (Part 2, pp. 415–475). Bombay: Popular Prakashan.

Sinha, J. B. P. (1981b). *Participation in work organizations.* Patna, India: A.N.S. Institute of Social Studies.

Sinha, J. B. P. (1982a) Power structure, perceptual frame and behavioural strategies in a dyadic relationship. In R. Rath, H. S. Asthana, D. Sinha, & J. B. P. Sinha (Eds.), *Diversity and unity in cross-cultural psychology* (pp. 308–316). Lisse, the Netherlands: Swets & Zeitlinger.

Sinha, J. B. P. (1982b). Power in Indian organizations. *Indian Journal of Industrial Relations, 17,* 339–352.

Sinha, J. B. P. (1985, January). *Cultural bias in appraisal system.* Paper presented at the International Seminar on Selection and Appraisal Systems, New Delhi.

Sinha, J. B. P. (1986). Emerging power patterns in Indian work organizations. *Management and Labour Studies, 11,* 86–96.

Sinha, J. B. P. (1989a). *Spiritualism in Indian managers.* Paper presented at the seventh Congress of World Association for Dynamic Psychiatry, West Berlin.

Sinha, J. B. P. (1989b). *Towards a participative system in Tata Steel.* Jamshedpur, India: Tata Steel Company.

Sinha, J. B. P. (1990a). *Work culture in the Indian context.* New Delhi: Sage.

Sinha, J. B. P. (1990b). The salient Indian values and their socio-economic roots. *Indian Journal of Social Science, 3,* 477–488.

Sinha, J. B. P. (1990c). A model of effective leadership style in India. In A. M. Jaeger & R. N. Kanungo (Eds.), *Management in developing countries* (pp. 252–263). London: Routledge.

Sinha, J. B. P., & Chowdhary, G. P. (1981). Perception of subordinates as a moderator of leadership effectiveness. *Journal of Social Psychology, 113,* 115–121.

Sinha, J. B. P., & Pandey, J. (1970). Strategies of high n-Ach persons. *Psychologia, 13,* 210–216.

Sinha, J. B. P., & Singh-Sengupta, S. (in press). Relationship between managers' power and the perception of their non-managers behaviour. *Indian Journal of Industrial Relations.*

Sinha, J. B. P., & Sinha, D. (1990). Role of social values in Indian organizations. *International Journal of Psychology, 25,* 705–714.

Sinha, J. B. P., & Sinha, M. (1974). Middle class values in organizational perspective. *Journal of Social and Economic Studies, 1,* 95–114.

Sinha, J. B. P., & Sinha, S. R. (1975). In response to the pressure to reduce disparity. *Indian Journal of Psychology, 50,* 108–121.

Sinha, J. B. P., & Verma, J. (1987). Structure of collectivism. In C. Kagitcibasi (Ed.), *Growth and progress in cross-cultural psychology* (pp. 123–129). Lisse, the Netherlands: Swets & Zeitlinger.

Sinha, M. (1977). Validity of the progressive matrices tests. *Journal of Psychological Researches, 21,* 221–226.

Sinha, M. (1983). *Effect of organizational climate on productivity, satisfaction, and job involvement.* Unpublished doctoral dissertation, Patna University, Patna, India.

Sinha, Y., Tripathi, R. C., & Pandey, J. (1982). Sociocultural variation in Machiavellianism. In R. Rath, H. S. Asthana, D. Sinha, & J. B. P. Sinha (Eds.), *Diversity and unity in cross-cultural psychology* (pp. 302–307). Lisse, the Netherlands: Swets & Zeitlinger.

Smith, A. (1976). *An inquiry into the nature and causes of wealth of nations.* New York: Random House. (Original work published 1937)

Smith, P. B., Tayeb, M. M., Sinha, J. B. P., & Bennett, B. (1990). Leadership style and leader behavior across cultures: The case of the 9, 9 manager. In A. Wedd, G. S. Khem, & F. Luthans (Eds.), *International human resource management review* (pp. 141–152). New York: McGraw-Hill.

Soares, R., Valecha, G., & Venkataraman (1981). Values of Indian managers: The basis of progress. *Indian Management, 20*(10), 32–38.

Srivastava, A. K. (1977). Indian blue collar workers: Their commitment. *Indian Journal of Industrial Relations, 13,* 223–234.

Srivastava, B. (1974). Management of organization's conflict: The role of process intervention. *Decision, 1,* 56–80.

Subramaniam, V. (1971). *The managerial class of India.* New Delhi: All India Management Association.

Super, D. E. (1982). The relative importance of work: Models and measures for meaningful data. *The Counseling Psychologists, 10,* pp. 95–103.

Sutaria, R. (1979). Two factor theory: A comparative study in three types of organizations. *Vikalpa, 4,* 115–123.

Sutaria, R., & Padaki, V. (1976). *Personality, organization and motivation on the job* (Research Note No. HR/85). Ahmadabad, India: ATIRA.

Thingaajan, K. H. (1972). Conflict resolution—Indian style. *Indian Management, 11,* 5–11.

Triandis, H. C. (1989). Cross-cultural studies of individualism and collectivism. In *Nebraska Smposium on Motivation* (pp. 41–133). Lincoln: Nebraska University Press.

Triandis, H. C., Bontempo, R., Betancourt, H., Bond, M., Leung, Bernes, A., Georgas, J., Hui, C. H., Marin, G., Setiadi, B., Sinha, J. B. P., Verma, J., Spandgenberg, J., Touzard, H., & de Montmollin, G. (1986). The measurement of etic aspects of individualism and collectivism across cultures. *Australian Journal of Psychology, 38,* 257–267.

Tripathi, R. C. (1981). Machiavellianism and social manipulation. In J. Pandey (Ed.), *Perspectives on experimental social psychology.* New Delhi: Concept.

Tripathi, R. C., & Sinha, Y. (1981). Social influence and development of Machiavellianism. *Psychological Studies, 26,* 58–61.

Tripathi, R. C., & Thapa, K. (1981). *Ingratiation tactics of the Machiavellianism.* Allahabad, India: Allahabad University,

Udy, S. H. (1970). *Work in traditional and modern society.* Englewood Cliffs, NJ: Prentice Hall.

Vardan, M. S. S. (1974). *Organizational development in HMT.* Banaglore, India: Center for Manpower Development and Research.

Venkataraman, S., & Valecha, G. K. (1981). Comparative motivation pattern of public and private sector managers in India. *Managerial Psychology, 2,* 31–45.

Verma, N. (1986). *Leadership styles in interpersonal perspective.* Delhi, India: P. R. Publishing.

Verma, R. P., & Sinha, R. P. (1983). A study of job satisfaction among employees of private and public sector. *Indian Journal of Labour Economics, 25,* 112–120.

Virmani, B. R., & Guptan, S. U. (1991). *Indian management.* New Delhi: Vision.

Weber, M. (1958). *The religion of India: The sociology of Hinduism and Buddhism.* (H. H. Gerth & D. Martindale, Trans. & Eds.) New York: Glencoe, C. T. Press.

Zahir, M. A. (1984). A proposed model for the study of organizational effectiveness in a developing country like India. *Lok Udyog, 18,* 7–12.

Cultural Variation and Diversity in the United States

We now return to the United States to examine cultural variations within that country and the way U.S. organizations might deal with diversity. Triandis, Kurowski, and Gelfand point out that diversity has both advantages and disadvantages, depending on the criterion that is used to evaluate its effects.

A number of political perspectives that set diversity in context can be identified. For example, is the melting pot the ideal, or should each ethnic group preserve some of its traditional culture? Should we ignore culture and emphasize that all humans are basically the same (which is partially correct), or should we pay attention to the cultural differences that distinguish each group and teach each human to respect and appreciate the views of others?

In examining diversity, we must pay attention to the "culture of relationships." Each culture of relationships has a different history. For example, African- and European-Americans have a different relationship than Laotian- and European-Americans because the former were brought to this continent forcefully and a long time ago, and the latter arrived recently and voluntarily. When an injustice is identified by an African-American, its significance is amplified; the same injustice identified by a Laotian-American is often tolerated as the price to be paid for a higher standard of living. The chapter tries to briefly capture the essence of the relationships among different groups, though because the number of the permutations involving such groups is enormous, it only touches on some of the more important relationships.

To understand each relationship, one must consider the concept of *cultural distance*. The greater the cultural distance between two people, the more probable it is that they will perceive each other as dissimilar, and when they have to interact because the job demands such interactions, the relationship can be punishing. A number of negative consequences follow. A theoretical model is used to describe the complexities of the relationships among the relevant constructs, which, however, also suggests that there are numerous ways in which we can improve interpersonal relationships. For example, cross-cultural training can be helpful.

The empirical research concerning the attributes of ethnic minority groups, women, gay men and lesbians, and the disabled in work settings indicates that each of these groups works in different social environments, that is, each experiences different schedules of reinforcement. Such differences correspond to the cultural distance mentioned earlier. By tracing the relationships between the socioeconomic environment, the culture, and the social behaviors, we can learn how to deal more effectively with diversity, so as to make it work for the organization, instead of creating difficulties for the organization.

—The Editors

CHAPTER 16

Workplace Diversity

Harry C. Triandis
Lois L. Kurowski
Michele J. Gelfand
University of Illinois

Demographic and economic changes occurring within the United States and worldwide are increasing the diversity of interpersonal and intergroup relationships in organizations. These changes are outlined and placed in historical context wherein we examine organizations' traditional response to diversity. While diversity issues have been viewed negatively in the past, the empirical research reviewed illustrates that diversity has both advantages and disadvantages that need to be balanced. In order to understand how diversity influences social behavior in industrial and organizational settings, a theoretical framework presents the major variables influencing interactions between people of different cultures. Factors that increase intergroup difficulties are examined. With this theoretical framework in mind, we next examine the empirical research on the experiences of ethnic minorities, women, gay men and lesbians, and the disabled in the workplace. Interventions that stem from the framework are discussed and areas for future research are suggested.

Introduction

ALMOST FROM THE founding of the United States, ethnic and gender diversity have characterized the American work force (Gutman, 1977). Dealing with diversity is not a novel issue for U.S. managers. What is novel about modern diversity issues is that managers will encounter diversity much more frequently and at higher levels both inside and outside their organizations, in the executive suite and on the shop floor, among their customers and their competitors. Old methods of dealing with diversity will no longer work: Workers, customers, and competitors will neither assimilate nor simply suppress their cultural distinctiveness (Nelton, 1992).

This new diverse world is already upon us. Many U.S. corporations now earn more abroad than in the United States (Adler, 1990) and face foreign competition in all their major markets. Changes in the composition of the work force are being driven by labor and market trends, legislation, and demographic realities.

For instance, the Immigration Act of 1990 makes it easier for U.S. corporations to hire skilled foreign workers, such as engineers, to compensate for shortages in labor markets. Because of their experiences in selling in the global marketplace, multinational corporations increasingly have truly multinational management, with some top managers who come from the companies' homelands and some who come from other countries.

The composition of the work force also will change in the United States at the entry level. White men, who traditionally have constituted the majority of new entrants into the labor force, will be a minority among the new entrants of the year 2000 (e.g., Goldstein & Gilliam, 1990; Johnston & Packer, 1987; Offermann & Gowing, 1990). Some estimates suggest that in the year 2000, the overwhelming majority of new entrants will be women (47%) and members of minority groups (38%). The Americans with Disabilities Act may usher in an increase in the percentages of disabled workers.

The demographic changes in the work force will, of course, be mirrored among U.S. consumers. By the year 2050, it is projected that black, Hispanic, and Asian Americans will constitute up to 47 percent of the U.S. population (Day, 1992). In the 1990 census, these groups already constituted 25 percent of the population. To market products and serve these more diverse customers effectively, most organizations will have to employ correspondingly diverse groups of marketing and sales personnel

(Jackson, 1991a). New managerial skills will be required (Jamieson & O'Mara, 1991).

Furthermore, the economy is shifting from a manufacturing base to a service base (Jackson & Alvarez, 1992); 78 percent of American jobs are in the service area. Delivering service "products" requires employees with well-developed interpersonal skills; cultural similarity between the service provider and the customer may improve the effectiveness of service delivery and the perceived quality of service. Studies have shown that race and gender affect interactions between employees and customers in service businesses (Juni, Brannon, & Roth, 1988; McCormick & Kinloch, 1986; Stead & Zinkhan, 1986).

Jackson and Associates (1992) document many forms of diversity in U.S. corporate cultures. These include diversity created by mergers, acquisitions, and strategic business alliances (e.g., Apple and IBM) caused by an increasingly competitive business environment. Nahavandi and Malekzadeh (1988) have proposed a model for the study of corporate acculturation in such new entities.

Diversity in educational qualifications and work socialization also will become more relevant in hiring. It is projected that the level of skill required for employment in the United States will rise; 65 to 75 percent of new jobs will require knowledge and proficiencies usually associated with a college education.

These changes have resulted in considerable interest in the issues raised by diversity. Of course, in some respects, this is a virgin field, lacking theoretical frameworks and intensive empirical background. Nevertheless, some books have appeared. Most notable is Jackson and Associates' (1992) compilation, which attempts to provide a framework and supplies several case studies of diversity programs in American corporations. Kavanagh and Kennedy (1992) advocate greater sensitivity to diversity issues and present a number of brief case studies that can be used in training.

About This Chapter

The focus of this chapter is on understanding how diversity influences social behavior in industrial and organizational environments. To achieve this, we will present a theoretical framework that explains how humans relate to other humans who are similar to and different from themselves. One of the important factors in understanding diversity is how culture affects social behavior. To explain this aspect, we will focus on the meaning of culture, the types of cultural patterns that distinguish groups, and the kinds of obstacles to good interpersonal and intergroup relationships that can be traced to cultural differences.

These theoretical ideas will then be used to examine the literature about attributes of ethnic groups, male–female relationships, differences in sexual/affectional orientations, and disabled individuals that affect work behavior. Finally, we will examine training interventions that are possible to improve interpersonal relations.

The primary emphasis of this chapter is on cultural factors that affect psychological processes. Thus, the chapter is especially relevant for situations in which people from different cultures (both internationally and within the United States) work together. Economic, sociological, and political issues are mentioned only in passing; no attempt is made to examine the way organizational cultures influence these factors. The depth and breadth of the literature compelled us to be selective. For example, Knouse (1991) edited a special issue on racial, ethnic, and gender issues in the military, which we do not review because the topic is more specific than the topics we have chosen to discuss.

One source for those who wish to examine wider societal issues is the book compiled by Katz and Taylor (1988) concerned with the elimination of racism. In the book, issues of assimilation and pluralism were discussed by Pettigrew. Triandis advocated additive multiculturalism, which requires members of the majority culture to learn to appreciate attributes of minority cultures; he argued that racism cannot be eliminated if some racial groups do not have jobs, so that only through a program of public works that guarantees a job for all able-bodied citizens can racism be eliminated. Sears examined symbolic racism, which blends subtle racial derogation with support for individualism ("All people of whatever color have equal opportunity, and it is up to the individual to work hard enough to succeed," p. 67). Bobo assessed the extent to which racial attitudes depend on group-interested ideology as well as irrational hostilities. Jones examined the individual, institutional, and cultural bases of racism. Ramirez explored racism toward Hispanics. Nakanishi and Trimble did the same for Japanese and Native Americans, respectively. And Reid discussed racism and sexism. The last section of the book debated the elimination of racism through school desegregation (Gerard, Cook, Armor, Hawley, & Smylie), the use of the jigsaw technique (Aronson & Gonzalez), increases in contact and cooperation (Brewer & Miller), and affirmative action (Galzer, Glasser).

Definitions

A Note on Terminology

Because of the breadth of the topic we cover here, we sometimes must use somewhat awkward terminology. In referring to studies on managers, for instance, we refer to "nontraditional" employees/workers, meaning women, ethnic minorities, and others. In another case, we refer to "old-fashioned" and "modern" racism. These phrases are meant to be descriptive; they are not value judgments. Similarly, we use various terms in referring to specific ethnic minorities, recognizing that many different terms are in use and that some people have strong preferences for certain terms.

Diversity

Our definition of diversity reflects any attribute that humans are likely to use to tell themselves, "That person is different from me." Diversity often causes misunderstandings. For example, the different socialization of men and women sometimes causes confusion about appropriate sexual behavior in the workplace. We will analyze a number of phenomena that result from diversity and reduce the effectiveness and satisfaction of interpersonal relationships.

Historical Perspective. As far as we know, all humans are ethnocentric. That is, they use their own culture as the standard for judging other cultures (Brewer & Campbell, 1976; Campbell & LeVine, 1968). Other cultures are evaluated most positively if they are similar to one's own culture. Thus, we humans tend to devalue those who are very different from us. Such devaluation has implications for interpersonal attraction, social distance, stereotyping, and other processes.

In the American workplace, ethnocentrism has been expressed in movements to "Americanize" foreign-born workers (Gordon, 1964), asking them to trade their foreign values for American ones. Very early in America's industrial history, workers' cultures (values) were cited as causes of undesirable workplace outcomes (Gutman, 1977). The move toward homogenization has been called the "difference as deficit" perspective (Fine, Johnson, & Ryan, 1990).

The work of Frederick W. Taylor, the father of so-called scientific management, and his followers might be viewed as the ultimate expression of "difference as deficit." Taylor believed that there always was only one best way in which work could be performed and that managers should be the persons to annunciate that one best way. Thus, Taylor emphasized the standardization of tasks.

The importance of workplace culture was again recognized in the 1980s by the scholars of corporate culture (e.g., Peters & Waterman, 1982; Schein, 1990). Indeed, German sociologist Claus Offe has theorized that "modern work conditions require a much greater cultural similarity between all levels of the work force than was ever the case in more traditional industries" (Wickham, 1976, p. 3). The need for such homogeneity arises from the changing nature of both organizational structures and technology, so that management controls workers through norms rather than through economic force (Offe, 1976, pp. 23–39).

With the intellectual legacy of scientific management and the modern emphasis on corporate culture, it is not difficult to understand why American managers would view diversity issues negatively rather than positively. Loden and Rosener (1991, pp. 28–29) list six assumptions "embedded in contemporary organization cultures":

- Otherness is a deficiency.
- Diversity poses a threat to the organization's effective functioning.
- Expressed discomfort with the dominant group's values is oversensitivity.
- Members of all diverse groups want to become and should be more like the dominant group.
- Equal treatment means the same treatment.
- Managing diversity requires changing the people, not the organization culture.

However, recent thinking has challenged these points. Otherness is not necessarily a deficiency; it depends on the task. For example, when "groupthink" (Janis, 1982) causes bad decisions, diversity is helpful. Organizations can function effectively even if they are diverse; one simply needs to structure them differently. Discomfort with the dominant group's values is as natural as the discomfort of the dominant group with the values of minorities. Members of diverse groups do not want to become like the dominant group. In fact, the majority want to retain significant elements of their original cultures (Lambert & Taylor, 1990). Equal treatment means showing equal respect; however, if a different approach enables a group to become more effective within the organization, it is all right to provide different treatment. Managing diversity means changing the culture—that is, the standard operating procedures. It requires analysis, data, experimentation, and the discovery of the procedures that work best for each group. It is more complex than conventional management but can result in more effective organizations.

We do not attempt to deal here with pathological reactions to diversity based on extreme ethnocentrism, such as those documented in Adorno, Frenkel-Brunswik, Levinson, and Sanford (1950). We are examining reactions of ordinary managers to the concept of diversity.

Advantages and Disadvantages. Research has shown that diversity yields both advantages and disadvantages (Jackson, 1991b) for the effective functioning of small groups. On the side of advantages, there is evidence that heterogeneous groups are more creative and more likely to reach high-quality decisions than homogeneous groups (McGrath, 1984; McLeod & Lobel, 1992; Triandis, Hall, & Ewen, 1965; Willems & Clark, 1971). On the side of disadvantages, there is evidence that diversity is related to lower levels of interpersonal attraction, more stress, and more turnover.

Overall, people of different cultures bring a variety of perspectives and outlooks to a task; such diversity may add to the pool of resources available to a group (Adler, 1990). For example, Triandis et al. (1965) examined the effects of heterogeneity of attitudes and abilities on the creativity of two-person groups. They found that dyads that were heterogeneous in attitudes and homogeneous in abilities were more creative than dyads that were heterogeneous in both attitudes and abilities or homogeneous in both attitudes and abilities. Similarly, Hoffman and Maier (1961) examined the effects of heterogeneity in values and opinions on the creativity of groups of management trainees and found that heterogeneous groups were more inventive than homogeneous groups.

Bantel and Jackson (1989) assessed the diversity of top management teams at 199 banks and correlated this measure with the degree of innovation in each of the banks. In this study, diversity was defined by examining differences in age, tenure, education level, and functional background. Innovation was operationalized as the number of new products, programs, or services that the firm had adopted and/or developed. After controlling for bank size, location, and other variables, they found that team composition still predicted innovation. The greater the diversity of the team, the greater was the level of innovation.

Another advantage is that diversity reduces the probability of *groupthink* (Janis, 1982), a phenomenon that occurs when homogeneous and cohesive groups dedicated to unanimity do not explore the full range of available solutions. Groupthink can lead to drastic errors in decision making (Janis, 1982). Diverse groups, on the other hand, have built-in protection against groupthink (Adler, 1990). While they may require more time to reach a decision (Fisher, 1980), they are more likely to explore the full range of possible solutions to the problem.

Extensive, time-consuming consideration of the issues is characteristic of groups whose members are involved with the task (Beisecker, 1969; Hoffman, Harburg, & Maier, 1962) and expend more effort and concentration on the task. Vigorous debate can result in more consensus in the end (Torrance, 1957). This is exemplified in the Japanese *ringi* system of decision making. Those who are affected by a decision are invited to debate, disagree, and modify the proposed solutions; they typically tend to reach consensus slowly. However, once consensus has been reached, implementation of the decision is very rapid.

In sum, diversity does seem to be advantageous. It can increase the potential productivity of the group (Jackson, 1991b; McGrath, 1984) and the quality of the ideas generated by the group (McLeod & Lobel, 1992). On the other hand, diversity has the effect of "greatly increasing the complexity of the process that must occur in order for the group to realize its full potential" (Adler, 1990, p. 128). Specifically, diversity often has a negative impact on communication and interpersonal attraction (Adler, 1990; Steiner, 1972; Storey, 1991; Triandis 1959; Triandis, 1960a; Zamarripa & Krueger, 1983). These potential disadvantages are examined next.

In any communicative encounter there is a sender who encodes ideas and behaviors into a symbolic representation or message, which may be in a verbal or nonverbal form. After the message has been sent through a channel, it reaches a receiver, who then must decode or attribute meaning to the symbolic behaviors and eventually respond through another encoded message (Adler, 1990). Consequently, communication is heavily influenced by social perception processes, or the process by which one selects, evaluates, and organizes stimuli to provide meaning and understanding (Singer, 1987).

The most successful communication will be one in which the participants of the interaction perceive and evaluate the message in terms of the intended idea or behavior. Barnlund (1988, p. 9) suggests that achieving this accurate understanding is a function of the similarity of the perceptual orientations, belief systems, and communication styles. Triandis (1959, 1960a, 1960b) found that people who use the same "categories of thought," or construe the situation in the same way,

communicate effectively and like each other more than people who construe the situation differently (see also Singer, 1987). Cognitive similarity leads to more intimacy (Gudykunst & Nishida, 1986), while dissimilarity leads to less self-disclosure (Storey, 1991).

Language differences can impair communication and increase the chances for errors in message transmission and decoding (Samovar & Porter, 1988). Some words simply do not have counterparts in the other languages (Pedersen, 1983). Rogers and Bhowmik (1971) found that heterogeneous groups suffered from delayed transmission of messages, message distortion, and restriction of communication channels. Zamarripa and Krueger (1983) found that in homogeneous groups communications tend to be followed by answers in the same domain, while in heterogeneous groups there is a "chaining of nonproductive behaviors" (p. 205). Landis, McGrew, Day, Savage, and Saral (1976) noted that the meanings given to the same words are often different in the white and black communities. Even sophisticated bilinguals in Canada sometimes fail to interpret correctly a monolingual's message (D'Anglejan & Tucker, 1973).

Language refers not only to verbal statements but also to paralinguistic factors, such as gestures, touching, body orientation, and eye contact, which also shape perceptions (Whorf, 1952). Cultures are known to differ on paralinguistics (Argyle, 1988).

In short, communication difficulties can result in reduced attraction and cohesion (Adler, 1990; Jackson, 1991b; O'Reilly, Caldwell, & Barnett, 1989; Shaw, 1981, p. 213; Triandis et al., 1965). Conversely, similarity in beliefs, attitudes, and values contributes to cohesiveness (Yukl, 1985). Heterogeneous groups are generally less cohesive (Adler, 1990; Lott & Lott, 1965; Shaw, 1981; Terborg, Castore, & DeNinno, 1976) and thus spend much time creating solidarity (Adler, 1990). Low levels of interpersonal attraction may affect creativity (Triandis et al., 1965; Zeleny, 1955).

The degree of creativity can also influence organizational outcomes. Jackson et al. (1991) examined 93 top management teams in bank holding companies over a four-year period and found that dissimilarity predicts high turnover. They measured similarity by examining personnel records and noting similarities in age, military service, college attended, education, and in whether an MBA degree was obtained. At the individual level of analysis, turnover was predicted by a person's dissimilarity to other group members. At the group level of analysis, team heterogeneity was a strong predictor of team turnover rates.

Specific dissimilarities, taken separately, predicted turnover: They were dissimilarities in education, in having an MBA, and in which actual college was attended. The size of specific relationships was small (e.g., which college attended and turnover correlated .2, significant at .05). However, all dissimilarity factors combined resulted in a multiple correlation that predicted 22 percent of the variance of turnover. An interesting result of this study was that distinct links between demographic similarity, cohesiveness, and low turnover were found.

O'Reilly et al.(1989) obtained similar results using age and tenure as indicators of demographic similarity. Through a survey of groups in a large convenience store chain, they demonstrated that both individual- and group-level demographic similarities affect turnover. This study made clear that demographic similarity, cohesion, and low turnover are interrelated.

Another consequence of demographic dissimilarity is stress. Triandis et al. (1965) found that heterogeneity was associated with mistrust and stress. Similarly, Fiedler, Meuwese, and Oonk (1961), working in Holland, found that heterogeneity in religion was associated with more stress.

In sum, diversity brings both advantages and disadvantages. Multicultural groups can be either highly effective or ineffective, depending on the type of task and the way diversity is managed (Adler, 1990). For example, Hayles (1991) reviewed publications that argued that "well managed diverse groups quantitatively and qualitatively outperform homogeneous groups of the same size" (p. 1). Of course, we need to find out what "well managed" means. Later in this chapter, the research under review will suggest some answers.

Similarly, Cox and Blake (1991) argue that companies that learn how to manage diversity acquire a competitive advantage over companies that do not know how to deal with diversity. They believe that the higher turnover rates and lower levels of job satisfaction among female employees relative to male employees and of minority employees relative to majority employees reflect the inability of corporations to deal with nontraditional employees. They review findings that can be interpreted as indicating that companies that learn how to manage diversity can lower their costs, attract better employees, have a competitive advantage in the multinational marketplace, be more creative, make better decisions, and adjust more appropriately to environmental changes, all of which improve their competitiveness.

Thus, those who manage diversity well are likely to gain competitive advantages, take optimal advantage of available human resources, and reduce the personal costs of intergroup conflict. The long record of national, religious, racial, communal, and tribal strife in the history of the world leaves little doubt that poorly managed diversity can be disastrous. Clearly, more research is needed to determine how to increase the effectiveness of diverse organizations.

Culture

Before we look at the theory of diversity more closely, we must define culture. *Culture* has been defined very broadly as the "human-made part of the environment" (Herskovits, 1955). This definition is very inclusive, and for this reason, individual researchers have found it more useful to limit themselves to specific aspects of culture. Nevertheless, for some purposes, this definition is quite satisfactory, as are other abstract definitions, such as "culture is a set of schedules of reinforcement" (Skinner, 1981) or "culture is a mental program that controls behavior" (Hofstede, 1980).

Characteristics. There are certain aspects that almost all researchers see as characteristics of culture. First, culture emerges in adaptive interactions with the environment. Second, culture consists of shared elements. Third, culture is transmitted across time periods and generations. Let us consider each of these aspects of culture in turn.

Adaptive Elements. Culture is to society what memory is to individuals. It is the depository of what has worked and not worked in the past. As people interact, they develop new tools, skills, and definitions of concepts, and they achieve consensus on organizing information, symbols, evaluations, patterns of behavior, intellectual, moral, and aesthetic standards, expectations, and ideas about correct behavior that are more or less effective (functional). The more effective ones (those that lead to satisfying solutions of everyday problems of existence) become shared and are transmitted to others, most importantly to the next generation. These elements often reflect unstated assumptions and result in standard operating procedures for solving the problems of everyday life. Thus, these elements become aspects of culture.

Another way to distinguish the elements of culture is to pay attention to objective aspects of culture (e.g., roads, bridges, paintings) and subjective aspects (e.g., categorization, associations, norms, roles, laws, religious beliefs, and values).

Because circumstances change, cultures are in a constant state of flux. However, cultural change tends to be slow (one or two generations are required before one can see a major transformation). What was functional in one historic period (such as having very large families when infant mortality was high) can become dysfunctional in another. Thus, many elements of culture are dysfunctional in the context of a specific time and place.

Shared Elements. Because interaction normally requires a shared language and the opportunity to interact (people who interact usually live next to each other and in the same time period), one can conveniently use (a) shared language, (b) time, and (c) place as hypotheses to identify those who are likely to belong to the same culture. However, interaction can take place among individuals who do not share a language (via interpreters), or time (one can read a book written centuries earlier), or place (via satellite). When this is the case, some elements of culture diffuse from one culture to another. In fact, diffusion and traveler acculturation are two important ways in which cultures influence each other.

Common fate and other factors that facilitate positive interaction among individuals can result in the formation of specific subcultures. Thus, nations, occupational groups, social classes, genders, races, religions, tribes, corporations, clubs, and social movements may become the bases of specific cultures.

Transmission to Others. Cultural elements are transmitted to a variety of others, such as the next generation, co-workers, colleagues, family members, and a wide range of groups. For example, new workers are socialized into a corporation. In Japan, corporate socialization is a major activity (see the Kashima and Callan chapter in this volume). Modern communication results in cultural diffusion via films and television. Tourism, commerce, war, and other factors also play a role in cultural transmission.

Emic and Etic Aspects of Culture. Universal aspects of culture are called *etic*. For example, values are an important aspect of culture, and their structures seem to be universal (Schwartz, in press)—that is, etic. On the other hand, cultures also have unique values (e.g., *amae* in Japan, *philotimo* in Greece); these are *emic*. Etic aspects of culture come about because of similarities in humans' biologies and physical environments. Emic aspects come about because of differences in the ecologies and histories of the culture.

Some students of culture assume that every culture is unique. In some sense, every object in the world is unique at some level. However, uniqueness at a trivial level is of little interest in science and is ignored.

One of the distinctions between cross-cultural psychology and anthropology is the level at which each discipline studies culture. Many of the elements of culture, such as ideas, patterns of behavior, and standards of evaluation, are specific to each culture and thus of limited interest to most psychologists wishing to find general laws of human experience and behavior. However, these elements are precisely the ones some anthropologists study. When we study cultures for their own sake, we may well focus on emic elements. Of generally greater interest to psychologists are communalities in cultural patterns. When we compare cultures, we have to work with the etic cultural elements, identifying communalities.

Emics to Etics or Etics to Emics? Social scientists observing the cultural elements of several cultures often discover similarities in the patterns. Thus they can develop constructs that are etic. Similarities identified among such different cultures as the United States, Greece, India, Japan, and China suggested the etic construct of *collectivism* (Triandis, 1990), which we describe in a later section.

Other etic constructs are the degree to which the self is embedded in the culture (Markus & Kitayama, 1991), whether norms are imposed tightly or loosely (Pelto, 1968), the emphasis on getting things done (doing) versus experiencing (being) versus changing the self (being-in-becoming; Diaz-Guerrero, 1973), the decision to exercise dominion over nature or to live in harmony/subordination to nature (Kluckhohn & Strodtbeck, 1961), and an orientation to time that emphasizes the present, future, or past, or one that considers time important or unimportant. Some patterns of child rearing also can be seen as etic (Whiting & Whiting, 1975).

Where is Culture? In the Head of the People or the Head of the Scientist? Definitions of culture sometimes reflect what is out there and sometimes what is in the head of the investigator. This contrast, between the realists and the nominalists (Rohner, 1981), is one of the controversies in modern anthropology; many of the most eminent scholars disagree. Can one obtain a satisfactory definition of culture by using only one or the other perspective? An empirical investigation by Triandis, Hui, et al. (1984) suggested that the answer is no; we need both perspectives. Geertz (1973) has provided a convincing argument that culture is a "web of significance in which actors are suspended" and must be interpreted by people who know how its many aspects hang together.

Conclusion. Because the problem of an adequate definition is difficult to solve (e.g., see Shweder & LeVine, 1984), it is best to approach it this way: There are many definitions of the concept and they are all valid. However, depending on what a particular investigator wishes to study, it may be optimal to adopt a narrower definition. For example, if the investigator is a behaviorist, Skinner's definition may be quite satisfactory; if the investigator is a cognitive psychologist, a definition that emphasizes information processing may be optimal.

In summary, for the purposes of this chapter, culture is defined as follows:

> *Culture is a set of human-made objective and subjective elements that in the past have increased the probability of survival and resulted in satisfaction for the participants in an ecological niche, and thus became shared among those who could communicate with each other because they had a common language and lived in the same time and place.*

Culture can be studied by examining its emic aspects or its etic aspects, or both. Traces of culture can be found "in the heads" of the population. For adequate interpretation, however, it is necessary also to consider historical and ecological factors that explain why the particular elements of culture have become important.

The Analysis of Diversity: A Theoretical Framework

Social psychologists have examined intergroup relations for a long time (e.g., Stephan, 1985). There are numerous studies and theoretical frameworks, but the relationships appear to be operating the way a balloon operates: If you push in one place, you get a change in many other places. To understand how the variables operate together as a *system*, we need a theoretical framework that places the main variables in relation to each other. This section will describe such a framework.

Tests of this framework are not yet available, but there is a vast literature that is consistent with it. Furthermore, the framework suggests numerous intervention strategies. If such interventions prove successful, the framework will be supported.

First we will define and suggest methods for the measurement of the key concepts of the framework. Second, we will present the framework.

Definitions and Measurements

Task Structure. Tasks differ in structure. They vary from *low structure* tasks, in which one and only one solution, method of doing it, or approach is optimal, to *high structure* tasks, which can be done with many methods and are subject to many satisfactory solutions and many approaches. Scientific management assumes that tasks can be converted to simple structure, while the current Japanese method of management favors high-structure tasks, in which the employee is the manager.

Cultural Distance. Cultures are very similar or different (distant) to the extent that they include many similar or different elements. Such elements can be objective or subjective. Objective elements include the linguistic distance of two cultures or the religion, political, or economic system in use.

For example, linguists have identified language families in which all family members share some similarities but are also different. The French, Italian, English, and Hindi languages, among others, belong to the Indo-European family. It is very easy to learn French if one already knows Italian, but more difficult to learn English, and even more difficult to learn Hindi. However, it is much more difficult for speakers of those languages to learn nonfamily languages such as Chinese, a tonal language, or one of the African languages that depend on click sounds. It is possible to measure objectively the distance between languages by noting their location in the clusters formed by language families.

Social structures are also objective. The kind of family structure, such as patrilineal, matrilineal, monogamous, polygamous, and the like, provides objective data that anthropologists use to identify cultural regions (Burton, Moore, Whiting, & Romey, 1992). Thus, Africa south of the Sahara is a different region from "the old world," which is different from South Asia, East Asia, Polynesia, North American Native, and South American Native.

These seven regions are more distant from each other than are the cultures within any one of these regions.

Other objective distances can be derived from *religion* (e.g., the different varieties of Christianity or Buddhism are closer to each other than Christianity to Buddhism), *political systems* (e.g., those political systems in which there is extensive participation of the population in policy formation are more similar to each other than they are to political systems in which only a few people or one person makes all the policies), and *economics* (those with similar incomes are more similar to each other than to those with different incomes).

Cultural distance can also be measured subjectively, by studying the attitudes, beliefs, norms, roles, values, and other elements of subjective culture (Triandis, 1972) that characterize a group of people who speak the same language and live in the same time period and geographic region. For example, one can administer a questionnaire sampling such elements and correlate the responses of every person with the responses of every other person. A cluster analysis generated from these data would provide the subjective distances among these people. If we do this analysis on the data of people from two cultures, we can test the subjective distance of the two groups by examining whether the between-group variance of the responses to the questionnaire is larger than the within-group variance. The greater the F ratio of these two variances, the greater is the distance between the two groups. One can repeat this for each of the elements of subjective culture and use an average F ratio as an estimate of the subjective distance between the two cultures.

Finally, some method must be used to combine the objective and subjective estimates of this distance. One can use as the criterion the judgments that people make (Ward & Kennedy, 1992), such as those provided by Babiker, Cox, and Miller (1980), who asked people to rate on five-point scales the extent of the differences between their own background and the background of the people in another group. Through multiple-regression analysis, one can study the combination of objective and subjective estimates of distance that predicts this criterion and develop an index of combined subjective and objective cultural distance.

There are empirical findings suggesting that distance is an important variable. For example, there is a considerable literature concerning the adjustment of foreign students to the United States that indicates that those from Europe have less difficulty adjusting to the United States than those from Africa. Suicide rates among immigrants seem to reflect cultural distance (Furnham & Bochner, 1986). Dunbar (1992) found that U.S. personnel in managerial positions abroad had less trouble adjusting to Europe than to non-Western or third-world settings.

Perceived Similarity. A considerable body of research indicates that those who see others as similar are attracted to them (for a review, see Triandis, 1977a). Perceived similarity can be obtained on simple rating scales or can be manipulated (e.g., Byrne, 1971). It is obvious that cultural distance is related to the probability that others will be perceived as similar.

A critical question is whether perceived similarity will lead to the judgment that one is dealing with "one of us" (*ingroup*) or "one of them" (*outgroup*). This distinction between ingroups and outgroups is one of the fundamental distinctions that humans make. Ingroups are "people like us": family members, coreligionists, members of our ethnic group, co-workers. This distinction is especially important in collectivist cultures (Triandis, 1990), where behavior toward ingroups differs much more from behavior toward outgroups than is the case in individualistic cultures.

People vary in their experience with others who are different from themselves. In a homogeneous, isolated tribe, people have seen few others that are different. Consequently, their level of adaptation (Helson, 1964) for similar versus different requires that the other person be very similar to be considered similar. In a cosmopolitan environment, people who differ in language, clothing, and even religion may be seen as "one of us."

Similarity has real and important effects in work settings. There is evidence of biases that can be traced to similarity. For example, Lin, Dobbins, and Farh (1992) examined the effects of interviewer and interviewee race and age similarity on interview outcomes and found substantial race effects. They suggested that the same-race effects could be avoided by using mixed-race interview panels.

Opportunities for Interaction. When people come into contact, each party may experience the contact differently. For instance, it is useful to distinguish between threatening and non-threatening contact (Stephan & Stephan, 1992). Threatening contact (e.g., in restaurants, cafés, nightclubs, bars, streets, parks, open markets) has been found to increase anxiety about the intercultural contact (Stephan & Stephan, 1992), while nonthreatening contact (in cultural events, sporting events, movies, parties, schools, hospitals) has been found to decrease anxiety.

When contact is rewarding, the number of positive interactions will be greater than the number of negative interactions. Working with marital couples, Gottman and Levenson (cited in Brody, 1992) found that those couples who discussed problem areas in ways that led to improved relationships had a positive-to-negative interaction ratio five times as large as the couples who entered a spiral of negative interactions. A ratio that high may not be necessary in the case of less ego-involving interactions, such as those that occur in ordinary job settings. Nevertheless, it seems safe to say that relationships will move into more intimate, satisfying phases only when positive interactions occur more frequently than negative interactions.

Contact. Societies differ in the extent to which they prohibit or encourage contact. For example, the Nazi policy in Germany prohibited contact with Jews, and Germans who contacted Jews in nonauthorized settings were often punished. On the other hand, Canada has a policy of multiculturalism, in which authorities encourage contact and clearly state that they hope the contact will be rewarding, while at the same time encouraging each group to maintain its own culture. This variable can be measured by examining the official policies, legal documents, and other products of the culture and by rating the extent to which authorities approve of the contact.

Acculturation. Berry (1980) has described four ways for two cultures to relate to each other. One can try to maintain one's own culture or not maintain it, and one can try to have contact or to avoid contact with the other culture. *Integration* is defined as the type of acculturation in which each group maintains its own culture and also maintains contact with the other culture. *Assimilation* occurs when a group does not maintain its own culture but maintains contact with the other culture. *Separation* occurs when the group maintains its own culture but does not maintain contact with the other culture. Finally, *marginalization* occurs when the group neither maintains its own culture nor attempts contact with the other culture. Berry has argued that integration is far better than the other processes from the point of view of mental health (see Berry, Poortinga, Segall, & Dasen, 1992, for a review). If there is contact with the other culture (i.e., in the case of integration or assimilation), a culture can move toward adopting some of the other culture's subjective culture. Such movement is called *accommodation*. However, in some cases such movement is quite extreme, so that there is *overshooting*. For example, some people in the United States with "ethnic-sounding" names have Anglicized their names or adopted completely new nonethnic names; this is over-shooting. When a group either attempts contact and is punished for such attempts, or is rejected due to discrimination, or remains satisfied with no contact, or obtains ad-vantages from emphasis on its own culture, there is *ethnic affirmation.* In ethnic affirmation, the group becomes even more extreme in manifesting its original culture than groups who have not attempted to relate to the other culture. For example, some African-Americans have rejected their familial names as "slave names" and have taken on African names. It is possible to identify these patterns of acculturation by examining the subjective cultures of people from each cultural group and seeing whether over time one group is moving toward or away from the other group (Triandis, Kashima, Shimada, & Villareal, 1986).

Cultural Identity. Individuals usually are not aware of the fact that their culture influences their behavior. It is only when they come in contact with other cultures that they realize that they have a culture. Even then, they are more likely to focus on the culture of the other group than to examine their own. However, as the other group becomes more salient, they develop a clearer view of who they are and what contrasts them from the other group. The *defining attributes* of their culture can be quite different: race, language, dialect, lifestyle, dress, neighborhood, region of the country, religion, nationality, economic status, tribe, ancestral heritage, pattern of family relationships, specific behaviors or practices (such as circumcision), and so on.

Ethnic groups differ on which of these attributes they pay attention to (e.g., the Japanese pay very little attention to religion but more attention to social class and race; Americans pay more attention to race than to nationality; see Triandis, 1967, for a review). When making a specific judgment, such as whether the other person is "good," "powerful," or "active" or whether to accept the other person in a specific social relationship, these attributes are given different weights (Triandis, 1967).

When a person pays much attention to the attributes that define an ethnic group and views these attributes as important in defining who he or she is, that person is high in cultural or ethnic identity. In short, cultural identity is the person's sense of what "constitutes membership in an ethnic group to which he or she belongs" (Ferdman, 1990, p. 183).

Stereotypes. Stereotypes are the assumed characteristics of a group of people. They can be measured through a checklist (e.g., "Check 10 out of the following 100 traits as most typical of Germans"), an estimate of the percentage of a group having the attribute (e.g., "What pecentage of Germans are warm?"), a judgment of the extent the group has an attribute (e.g., "Do Germans tend to be warm: not at all, somewhat, frequently, always?"), or through multidimensional scaling of traits and group terms (e.g., "How similar are the words *German* and *warm?*"). These methods often converge when they are used in the same study (Stephan et al., in press).

Sociotypes. While stereotypes are generally invalid, some elements of stereotypes are valid in the sense that they agree with relevant social-science research findings. Valid stereotypes are called *sociotypes.* The more contact a person has with another group, the more likely it is that the stereotype will change into a sociotype (Triandis, 1972; Triandis & Vassiliou, 1967). One way to find sociotypes is to identify the common elements between the auto- and the heterostereotypes of a group and see if the heterostereotype a group has about the target group contains many such elements. More elaborate procedures include using the heterostereotypes of many groups concerning a particular target group and extracting those elements on which the heterostereotypes converge and also agree with the target group's autostereotype.

Isomorphic Attributions. When a behavior is perceived, it is usually attributed to some cause. If P perceives O doing Y, P is likely to see X as the cause of Y. If O also sees X, or a cause similar to X, as the cause of O's behavior, then P and O are making isomorphic attributions (Triandis, 1975). That is, they give the same meaning to the behavior. To avoid misunderstandings in intercultural relations, it is desirable for those who interact to make isomorphic attributions. Measures of the extent to which people make isomorphic attributions can be obtained by presenting scenarios of social interaction to members of two groups and providing four or five attributions under each scenario. Pretest data from the target group can indicate which attribution is most probable (in a sense, correct) in that culture. If a person selects that correct attribution to explain the behavior of members of the other culture, that person is making isomorphic attributions. If several heterogeneous scenarios are used, the percent correct identification of the correct attributions is a measure of the extent to which the person is making isomorphic attributions.

Sense of Control. People in some situations feel that they have no control over the course of actions in that situation, and that is an extremely uncomfortable feeling. In fact, older people who do not feel that they are in control of their lives are more likely to die than older people who feel more in control (Langer, 1983). One way to measure this variable is to ask people to examine scenarios and to indicate what they would do in each of the scenarios and then to determine what the probability would be that such an action would obtain a desired outcome. Those who see low probabilities of successful outcomes would have a low sense of control. Bandura's (1989) concept of self-efficacy is also related to this construct.

Culture Shock. When people move from one culture to another, they experience a loss of control, and this results in both physical (e.g.,

asthma, headaches) and psychological symptoms (e.g., depression; Oberg, 1960). This condition, called *culture shock,* is explained by the lack of control over the rewards and punishments that one can obtain from the environment. Measures of well-being (e.g., Diener, Emmons, Larsen, & Griffin, 1985) may be used to estimate this variable.

Network Overlap. The more people one knows in common with another person, the more the two individuals are in the same social network, so that there is network overlap. One can use sociometric measurements to obtain an estimate of such overlap. Obviously, if two people are asked to name their friends and they name the same persons, their networks have a great deal of overlap.

Superordinate Goals. Superordinate goals are goals that each person or group cannot reach without the help of the other person or group (Sherif & Sherif, 1969); they are found in most cooperative situations. Measures can be obtained by asking people to indicate how important specific goals are and the extent to which they are committed to reaching these goals. As a second step, they can respond by giving their judgment of how important these goals are for other persons and how committed the other persons are to reaching these goals. A high correlation between one's own goals and perceived other person's goals implies the perception of superordinate goals.

The Framework

Figure 1 presents a theoretical model for the study of diversity. Most of the terms have been defined, but a few have not been defined because they are self-evident.

Let us begin with perceived similarity. The framework states that the greater the history of conflict (e.g., both length and intensity of conflict, wars, memories of one group killing members of the other group), the lower the perceived similarity.

Also, the greater the cultural distance, the lower the perceived similarity. This is simply a generalization of the Byrne (1971) research. Implicit in the concept of cultural distance is the concept of having a different cultural identity.

The greater the knowledge of the other culture, as for example when there has been effective cross-cultural training (Landis & Brislin, 1983), the higher is the perceived similarity. Intergroup relations improve with knowledge of the other culture (Stephan & Stephan, 1984). One of the methods of culture training is the culture assimilator (Albert, 1983; Fiedler, Mitchell, & Triandis, 1971); it has been shown to increase isomorphic attributions, which would increase the chances of seeing the other person as similar.

The greater the actor's language competence in the other person's language, the greater the perceived similarity. Obviously, those who speak our language appear to us to be more similar than those who do not speak our language.

The greater the network overlap with the other person, the greater the perceived similarity. The more things two people have in common, including friends and acquaintances, the more they will see each other as similar.

The more equal status contact between the two, the more they will see each other as similar, and hence the greater the perceived similarity.

The more superordinate goals there are, the more the perceived similarity. Of course, any element (age, gender) that people have in common will increase their perceived similarity, but goals are especially important.

Now let us consider what happens when two people who perceive themselves as similar have much opportunity for contact. Similarity leads to feeling good (Byrne, 1971) and interpersonal attraction. In short, the greater the perceived similarity *and* the opportunity for contact, the more rewards are experienced, which result in more interaction as well as in positive intergroup attitudes.

The rewards will be especially satisfying when authorities approve of the contact. Such approval tends to amplify the rewards.

We know that organisms emit more behaviors that have been rewarded than behaviors that have not been rewarded. In fact, behavior is shaped by its consequences (Skinner, 1981). Thus, rewards lead to more interactions.

High rates of interaction result in knowing more about the other person, and that makes intimacy possible. They also may result in higher levels of perceived similarity, if the participants are basically similar (which the model has made probable because real and perceived similarity are related; see Newcomb, 1956).

More interaction results in more network overlap. The more network overlap, the lower the probability that there will be ethnic affirmation. People who feel included in a friendship network are more likely to exhibit accommodation than ethnic affirmation.

The more interaction, the more likely it is that stereotypes will change into sociotypes (Triandis & Vassiliou, 1967).

The presence of sociotypes implies accurate perception of the other group, increasing the probability of isomorphic attributions.

Making isomorphic attributions means that one can predict much better what the other person will do, and that increases the sense of control.

Sense of control results in accommodation or even in overshooting, and there is little culture shock.

We can reverse the signs of all the variables to see how they operate. Perceived dissimilarity is greatest when there are status differences, a history of conflict, great cultural distance, little knowledge of the other culture, no knowledge of the other language, no network overlap, and no superordinate goals. An opportunity to interact will result in a punishing experience, which will lead to avoidance or aggression. Such hostile interactions will result in no network overlap and high

FIGURE 1

A Theoretical Model for the Study of Diversity

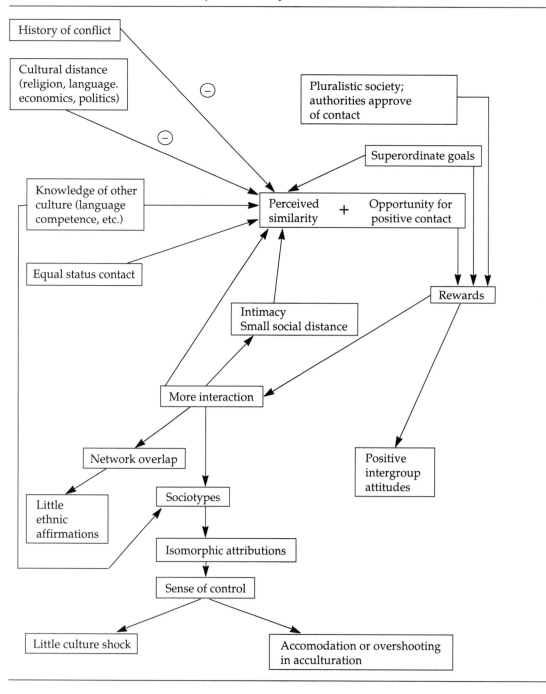

probabilities of ethnic affirmation (the feeling that my group is the best), invalid stereotypes, and nonisomorphic attributions. Under these circumstances, the best way to establish control is to kill the other! If the other is dead, one has total control of the situation.

The final point is that the framework is more applicable to persons who are open to new experiences and are nonethnocentric (Stephan & Stephan, 1992) than to people who are ethnocentric. Ethnocentrics may not be able to make isomorphic attributions and thus obtain control over the situation; thus, they may not show accommodation or overshooting, but may well always show ethnic affirmation. The framework also is more likely to work well when there is a high task structure rather than a low task structure.

In the case of low task structure, it is possible to get results through coercion. For example, the slave owners of the 17th and 18th centuries enriched themselves by exploiting their slaves. They did not have to perceive their slaves as similar to themselves or have rewarding interactions with them. In fact, in situations of large power distance between two sets of people, the powerful want to maximize their *dissimilarity* from the powerless. Because the task structure was very low on the slave owners' plantations, this framework would not be applicable.

In other words, data are more likely to support the framework as the task structure becomes higher. This implies that to adequately test the framework, we must make sure that we work with ordinary people and that the task is high in structure. The behavior of extreme (pathological) ethnocentrics probably can be modified only through clinical interventions.

Perspectives on Dealing With Diversity

This volume of the *Handbook* summarizes international perspectives on industrial and organizational psychology, and thus this chapter is especially concerned with cultural differences. However, there are two ways to approach such differences: the color-blind perspective (Ferdman, 1989) and, related to it, the categorization and labeling approaches (Ferdman, 1992). These approaches attempt to ignore cultural differences and advocate decategorization, the view that "any activity that reduces the salience of group boundaries will have an ameliorating effect on intergroup relations" (Worchel, 1986, p. 299). In short, "Do not pay attention to differences."

The second perspective accepts the presence of cultural differences and proposes to improve relationships by teaching people from each culture to appreciate the perspectives of people from other cultures.

In our judgment, the first perspective is both impractical and likely to be unsuccessful; the second has merit, and some evidence shows that it can succeed. Nevertheless, both perspectives have merit (Ferdman, 1992), and an optimal approach may emphasize both what people universally have in common and what makes them different.

Emphasizing what people have in common, Boyer (1991) identified eight kinds of communalities among humans. All humans have (a) a life cycle (birth, death), (b) language, (c) aesthetics (there is evidence of cross-cultural similarities in aesthetic judgments; see Berlyne, 1980), (d) a sense of time, (e) a tendency to adjust to institutions, (f) a shared relationship with nature, (g) a need to work or to produce something, and (h) a tendency to search for a purpose or the meaning of life. There is no doubt that similarities exist (Lonner, 1980) and that emphasis on similarities leads to interpersonal attraction (Byrne, 1971).

Emphasizing cultural differences, Triandis (1972) points to the fact that depending on the kind of environment in which we live, we are bound to consider different things as important. For example, the ancient Egyptians had the equivalent of several commandments, one of which was "I will not divert water running in a canal" (shown in the Museum of Natural History in Chicago). Clearly, in an environment where diverting water from a canal can lead to the death of a family, this is an important commandment. However, this commandment would make little sense in a society that has an abundance of water or has no canals. People can learn to appreciate the importance of this commandment for the Egyptians and respect it in that environment, and thus behave "appropriately" in that environment while behaving differently in theirs.

Triandis (1975) suggested that the ideal problem-solving group is a diverse group with members who have been trained to understand the others' point of view. Thus, when the problem's solution calls for the perspective of one cultural group more than the perspective of the other culture group, the problem-solving group would use the optimal perspective. However, diversity has a price: Communication becomes more difficult and interpersonal attraction is likely to be lower, requiring that training be used to increase attraction. To increase interpersonal attraction in that situation, it is important to view the behavior of members of other cultures as functional within a particular ecology—that is, to be able to say to oneself, "If I faced that set of circumstances, I would also behave that way." Note that such a statement creates a kind of similarity. It is, however, a different kind of similarity, in which the psychological *processes* are similar but the *situations* (i.e., ecologies and cultures) are different. In short, by emphasizing similarities we can create attraction, and we can do this two ways: by showing that there are universals and by indicating that the existing cultural differences "make sense."

One can make the case that psychologists have erred in the direction of emphasizing similarities and ignoring differences (Pepitone & Triandis, 1987), while anthropologists have erred in the direction of emphasizing differences over similarities. It is likely that the more useful perspective is to see simultaneously the enormous similarities and differences. In an analysis of 16 types of

psychological theories, Triandis (1988b) argued that four types of psychological theories are almost certainly universal, six are probably universal, and the remaining six are Western products that are not applicable to many non-Western cultures. If those numbers are taken seriously, one would argue that perhaps half of psychology is universally relevant and the other half is not. The task of cross-cultural psychology is to sort out the two halves.

Types of Cultural Patterns

To understand more clearly how culture affects social behavior we will review a literature that examines typologies of cultural patterns (Fiske, 1991; Markus & Kitayama, 1991; Triandis, 1989, 1990).

Four Basic Relational Orientations

Fiske (1991) has presented a theory (and evidence supporting it) that states that there are four "interpersonal orientations" or "structures of social behavior" that are found universally but are expressed in culture-specific forms in each culture. The four orientations are communal sharing, authority ranking, equality matching, and market pricing.

In *communal sharing*, the self is relational and includes group identities. Characteristics of communal sharing include a sense of belonging to a group; thinking more in "we" than in "I" terms; having a shared identity; fearing isolation, abandonment, and loneliness; distributing resources according to need; marrying for love so that the two spouses experience a total "oneness"; giving gifts frequently; behaving socially in intimate, nurturing, altruistic, caring, unselfish, generous, sharing ways; and giving what one can and taking only what one needs. Relationships are perceived as eternal. Children learn through direct observation of adults.

In communal sharing, the ingroup is the center of concern and protection; one is willing to fight the outgroup, which can result in racism and even genocide. Work is a collective responsibility and decisions are made by consensus. The land is emphasized.

Authority ranking is a relational system based on asymmetric power. Bosses have much legitimate and uncontested power, while subordinates obey without questioning. Subordinates show respect, deference, loyalty, and obedience. The impertinent are punished. The top boss gives gifts. There is a sense of noblesse oblige. Wars extend the authority of the boss.

In authority ranking, one marries for status, and the self reflects very strongly status-linked elements. Land belongs to high-status people (e.g., royal lands) and precedence is important in the etiquette of daily life.

Equality matching is based on reciprocity and equality. Justice and fairness are important concerns. Resources are distributed equally, work is shared equally, and land is divided equally. One marries an equal. Gifts of equal value are exchanged. In daily etiquette, people take turns, for instance, in going through a door.

Politically, the principle of "one person, one vote" is important. The self is separate and distinct from, but not dissimilar to, other selves. It is believed that misfortune should be distributed equally. Revenge is common.

In *market pricing*, people are willing to do almost anything for money. They analyze their interpersonal relationships in terms of profit and loss. They marry for money and give gifts in terms of their contribution to a relationship. Achievement is important, but people are free to "do their own thing."

The important point of the Fiske system is that each culture has a unique way of expressing the four orientations in each domain of social life or behavior setting (e.g., family,

workplace, school, religious setting, city hall). For example, in the United States, market pricing is used widely, but the social relation of marriage is based ideally on communal sharing and equality matching. In each culture, each institution or social situation is characterized by a unique pattern of elements drawn from the four orientations.

Collectivism and Individualism

A combination of these four orientations that is most common around the world is for some elements of communal sharing and authority matching to form *collectivism* and some elements of equality matching and market pricing to form *individualism*.

Collectivism reflects the way the self is defined (as part or representative of a group), and the importance of the ingroup (family, work group, country) in determining behavior. Individualism reflects an autonomous self and the importance of personality, attitudes, and other internal factors in determining behavior. In individualistic cultures, individual goals (e.g., pleasure) have primacy over group goals. Differences in self-definitions and goal structures are the two most important of some 60 attributes that have been identified as contrasting collectivists and individualists (Triandis, 1993).

Individualism is higher among affluent, socially mobile, and educated persons who have occupations that do not require much teamwork. Collectivism is higher in traditional cultures, especially those whose base is agricultural. Irrigation agriculture requires a good deal of cooperation in the construction of canals, storage facilities, and food-distribution systems. Such cultures socialize their children to obey and do their duty (i.e., be good workers and members of the ingroup). Homogeneous cultures often have clear norms; groups can impose those norms on their members. Heterogeneous cultures have many groups; if a person does not get along with one group, he or she can join another. Thus, in complex, heterogeneous cultures there is more individualism.

If the reader concludes from these comments that in some sense individualism is superior to collectivism, we wish to point out that many social pathologies, such as high rates of crime, divorce, and stress due to competition (and resulting reduction in the effectiveness of the immune system, with consequent high rates of heart attacks and cancer; see Triandis, Bontempo, Villareal, Asai, & Lucca, 1988) may be linked to individualism. On the other hand, high rates of communal conflict, superpatriotism, nationalism, and other forms of social pathology are linked to collectivism. Both social patterns are undesirable. We are only studying them, not evaluating them.

Corresponding to the cultural patterns are patterns of individual differences. Parallel to collectivism is allocentrism, and to individualism is idiocentrism (Triandis, Leung, Villareal, & Clack, 1985). There are idiocentrics in collectivist cultures who normally find their in-groups too demanding and leave them, and allocentrics in individualistic cultures who receive more social support and are less lonely than idiocentrics in such cultures (Triandis et al., 1985).

For example, the Navajo of the American Southwest have a collectivist culture. However, to succeed in the non-Navajo world in a profession such as mining engineering, a Navajo must leave the Navajo community for further education, an act that only an idiocentric Navajo finds tolerable. Navajos who succeed in becoming mining engineers are likely to be quite idiocentric, demonstrated by the fact that some Navajo mining engineers prefer not to be located in New Mexico, near their extended families (R. Stotlar, personal communication, January 25, 1991). This is a case of overshooting in the individualistic direction. Conversely, minorities who for years tried to "pass" and not be noticed as "different" (were idiocentric) sometimes show ethnic

affirmation—emphasizing their ethnic backgrounds—now that company policies have become accepting of diversity (R. Schallenberger, personal communication, January 25, 1991), thus becoming more allocentric.

All humans have both collectivist and individualist elements in their cognitive systems and sample these elements to construct their social behavior according to the situation, who they are interacting with, and the perceived consequences of the behavior. Thus, the relationships between the cultural patterns and behavior are probabilistic.

Individualism is associated with achievement and competition; collectivism with loyalty and cooperation. Cox, Lobel, and McLeod (1991) assembled groups of Asian, Hispanic, and African-Americans and assumed that they would be more collectivist and therefore more cooperative when compared with Anglo-Americans. A "prisoner's dilemma" task was used to test the hypothesis, which was supported. The authors suggest that the greater cooperativeness of minorities is an asset when organizational success depends on cooperation. However, Espinoza and Garza (1985) found, in a study of mixed groups of Anglo-American and Hispanic students, that "members of both were equally cooperative when their own group was in the numerical majority" (p. 380), but when their own group was in the numerical minority, Hispanics were significantly more competitive and Anglos were slightly less competitive. Thus, more research is needed to discover mixed-group situations that maximize cooperation.

Position of Some Ethnic Groups on Cultural Patterns. Communal sharing was the traditional pattern in Africa as well as in many of the Latino communities from which Hispanics came to the United States. Although the brutal experience of slavery somewhat distanced African-Americans from their African heritage, black communities have developed institutions such as churches and fictive kin networks for mutual support (Johnson & Barer, 1990). Nonetheless, having been exposed to American individualism for 400 years may have resulted in a sharp shift toward individualism among many African-Americans.

However, individualism is also a function of affluence, social mobility, and urban life (Triandis & Bontempo, 1988; Triandis, McClusker, & Hui, 1990). Urban African-Americans who are neither affluent nor socially mobile are subjected to contradictory forces. Hence, we expect very high variance among African-Americans on the collectivism–individualism continuum. Specifically, those who do not find emotional support in their family or community or those who are affluent should be especially individualistic. Those from emotionally supportive families who have moderate incomes should be collectivists. Thus, the relationship between social class and individualism may be curvilinear among African-Americans, with a maximum of collectivism in the lower middle class; however, this is a theoretical idea that needs testing.

Although Asian Americans and Hispanics have also been subjected to racism and discrimination, their historical and cultural circumstances differed significantly from those of African-Americans. In most cases, they were able to maintain greater contact with their original cultures than was the case for African-Americans. Thus, we expect Asian Americans and Hispanics to be more collectivist than non-Hispanic whites or blacks. In fact, the evidence (Marin & Triandis, 1985) is that many Hispanics are more collectivist than non-Hispanics, and Asian Americans are more collectivist than European Americans (Triandis et al., 1986.

The importance of collectivism in understanding minorities' work experiences is clear from results obtained in the University of Chicago Urban Poverty and Family Structure Study conducted by the National Opinion Research Center. African-Americans and Hispanics who lived in low-poverty and high-poverty areas were studied. Researcher Martha

Van Haitsma (see Reardon, 1991) reported that some of the difference between the unemployment rates of poor Mexicans and poor African-Americans may be traceable to the greater help that Mexicans receive from their families and to the fact they are more likely to live among employed people. Mexicans are likely to introduce their relatives and friends to employers, who are likely to hire them on the basis of their relative's good employment record. They also are more likely to have access to automobiles, making it easier to get to work, and to have another adult in the household to help with child care.

By contrast, due to residential segregation, many of the poorest blacks live in areas where few are employed, and thus miss this link into the employment market. They also have fewer social ties, called *social capital*, which along with their lack of economic and financial capital (Wacquant & Wilson, 1989) makes it difficult for them to overcome barriers they face in a racially biased labor market (Kirschenman & Neckerman, 1991).

Definition of Who I Am: Determining Identities. A crucial element in minority–majority contact concerns which identity the minority member adopts. Is the minority member primarily an American or an African or an African-American? Does the Hispanic see herself or himself as Mexican (or Cuban, Puerto Rican, etc.) or as an American of Mexican descent?

Brewer (1991) has proposed an "optimal distinctiveness" theory, which analyzes this problem by assuming that every person has a need for some assimilation to a group and also some differentiation from groups. The model is one of social identity, which is a variant of Solomon's (1980) opposing-processes model. She argues that each person will find a point that is most individually satisfying that lies somewhere between being totally unique and totally deindividuated. Solomon assumes this optimal level of distinctiveness or inclusiveness is a function of the relative strength of the opposing drives for assimilation and differentiation and is determined by cultural norms, individual socialization, and recent experiences.

Collectivists have greater tendencies toward assimilation into their group; individualists have greater tendencies toward differentiation from their group. This is reflected in the tendency of collectivists to describe themselves by naming more groups to which they belong than do individualists; individualists describe themselves by naming more personal traits than do collectivists (Triandis, McCusker, & Hui, 1990).

Intergroup Difficulties

Intergroup Versus Interpersonal

Collectivists are more likely to use *intergroup* and individualists to use *interpersonal* relationships. When a person relates to another person by paying attention primarily to the other's group memberships, the relationship is intergroup. When a person attends only to the other's personal attributes, the relationship is interpersonal (Tajfel, 1974).

Intergroup relationships are most probable when there is a history of conflict between groups, and individuals are physically distinct, anonymous, have incompatible goals, and are strongly attached to their own groups. Interpersonal relationships are more probable when there is no history of conflict between groups, and individuals are physically similar, know each other's names, are cooperating, and can move from one group to the other. Intergroup relations occur because people have a strong tendency to categorize others; the mere frequency of the use of the words *us* and *them* can influence intergroup bias (Perdue, Dovidio, Gurtman, & Tyler, 1990). Recategorization of a person from outgroup to ingroup can reduce bias (Gaertner, Mann, Murrell, & Dovidio, 1989).

In intergroup relations, people tend to use any attributes that happen to be available (are most salient) to make these categorizations, even if the attributes are trivial or explicitly random (Tajfel & Turner, 1979, 1986). Trust, predictability of behavior, cooperation, and common goals result in interpersonal relationships.

Factors That Increase Intergroup Difficulties

Cultural distance and any kind of difference in experience (male/female, sexual orientation, physical disability) have the potential to create low group cohesion. Differences in subjective culture add to this problem.

Such differences often result in differential evaluations of events in the social environment and in misunderstandings. For example, we judge what is worth perceiving according to our values. If we value status, we are more likely to notice status-linked clues when perceiving another person than if we do not value it. Differences in values cause us to select different information from the environment and thus to judge the same events quite differently.

We also evaluate our environment according to levels of adaptation (Helson, 1964) that reflect past experiences, particularly the most recent events to which we were subjected.

Distortions in our perceptions of the environment can be traced to differences in the framing of events (e.g., defining a situation as a profit or a loss; Tversky & Kahneman, 1981), in social comparisons (Festinger, 1954), in temporal comparisons (Albert, 1977), and in culture-shaped expectations and attributions (e.g., Hewstone, 1989, pp. 231–235). The false-consensus effect (Ross, Greene, & House, 1977; Marks & Miller, 1987), the fundamental attribution error (emphasizing internal causes more than external causes of the behavior of others; see Nisbett & Ross, 1980; Ross, 1977; Ross et al., 1977; Ross & Nisbett, 1991), and the ultimate fundamental attribution error (perceiving internal causes for undesirable behavior of outgroups and desirable behavior of ingroups, and perceiving external causes for desirable behaviors of outgroups and undesirable behaviors of ingroups; Pettigrew, 1986) further lead to judgments that are distortions of reality.

Clearly, the more a person's cultural identity is distinct from the cultural identity of others in the work environment, the more difficult it will be for people to perceive each other as similar. One plausible intervention in such cases is to attempt to change or reduce the importance of the defining attributes of the cultural identity and emphasize those attributes in which the person is similar to the other members of the work group.

Prejudice consists of negative feelings, beliefs, and behavioral dispositions toward outgroup members. Recent work suggests that prejudice is a normal aspect of ingroup–outgroup relationships (Dovidio, Gaertner, Anastasio, & Sanitioso, 1992). These authors distinguish traditional and modern aspects of the phenomenon.

Traditional aspects emphasize the psychodynamic side, as in the work on the authoritarian personality. Modern aspects emphasize cognitive processes, such as overevaluation of ingroup traits, ingroup favorability in resource distributions, increased attraction of ingroup members, having more accurate information about ingroup members, remembering less positive information about outgroups, greater cognitive accessibility of outgroup negative stereotypes, and feelings of superiority toward outgroups.

One modern bias is aversive racism. It consists of showing no discrimination against outgroups when the norms specifying fairness are clear and unambiguous, but showing bias when norms are weak, ambiguous, or conflicting, or when it is possible to justify or rationalize a negative response on the basis of some factor other than the outgroup characteristics. Dovidio et al. (1992) review numerous

empirical studies that support this conceptualization. Symbolic racism (a blend of anti-black affect and traditional American values such as the Protestant ethic and individualism) is shown to be a stronger predictor of negative attitudes toward affirmative action than old-fashioned racism, stereotyping, or self-interest. Dovidio et al. draw implications for contemporary approaches to combat bias by emphasizing the importance of breaking down the boundaries between ingroups and outgroups and spelling out the bases for affirmative action. These bases include the following points:

- Narrow definitions of equity perpetuate and exacerbate the advantaged status of people who already possess disproportionate resources.
- Equal opportunity is insufficient to reverse the effects of years of personal and institutional discrimination.
- Discrimination is more clearly seen at the societal than at the individual level.
- The focus on microjustice (the idea that one racial group should not be placed at a disadvantage just so one member of a minority group can be accepted) unnecessarily and erroneously personalizes the issue.

When a member of an ingroup behaves in a desirable way, ingroup members usually attribute it to internal factors (e.g., to superior intelligence or skill); when a member of an outgroup behaves in the *same* way, these same members usually attribute it to external factors (e.g., to good luck or coercion). Conversely, when ingroup members behave in undesirable ways, ingroup members use external attributions; when outgroup members behave in undesirable ways, ingroup members use internal attributions (Hewstone, 1989; Pettigrew, 1986).

Maass, Salvi, Arcuri, and Semin (1989) showed that people encode and communicate desirable behaviors by ingroup members and undesirable behaviors by outgroup members at a more abstract level (e.g., in terms of traits) than undesirable behaviors by ingroup members and desirable behaviors by outgroup members. The higher level of abstraction has the effect of making the stereotype more general, stable, and persistently in favor of the ingroup.

An important aspect of subjective culture consists of the attributions that individuals make spontaneously. Attributions give meaning to perceived behavior. When two groups have different subjective cultures, they are likely to make nonisomorphic attributions (Triandis, 1975) to explain the same behavior.

For example, suppose an employee, while talking to a supervisor, looks at the floor. In many minority cultures, low-status persons do not look into the eye of high-status persons. The attribution they would make to explain this behavior is that they show respect. However, in Anglo-American culture, looking into the eye is customary and expected. The attribution a mainstream American is likely to make to explain looking at the floor while talking is that the subordinate is uninterested, or distracted, or apathetic. Thus, the very same behavior has a different meaning in these two cultures.

This implies that one way to improve the relationships between minorities and the majority is to teach members of each group to extend their attributions so that they make not only their own normal attributions but also the other group's normal (modal) attributions. More formally, if Group G makes attributions A, B, C, and D and Group H makes attributions X, Y, and Z, we need to teach both groups to make attributions A, B, C, D, X, Y, and Z. This training has the additional beneficial effect of reducing the probability of each attribution. Rigid, stereotypic thinking is of the form "if K, then A," in which the attribution has a subjective probability of 1.0. Sophisticated social perception is of the form "if K, then an equal probability of A, B, C, D, X, Y, or Z," in which

each attribution has a probability of .143. The lower probability would stimulate a search for more information, leading the person to consider additional sources of evidence before making a final interpretation of the event and a decision about how to react.

Even when the two cultural groups understand a behavior approximately the same way, there may be subtle differences in meaning that can result in misunderstandings. There is much evidence that words and gestures that appear to be translation equivalent (the same in translation; Argyle, 1988) are often used in different ways (Gudykunst & Ting-Toomey, 1988).

In the area of gestures, for example, a nod can mean "I agree" or "I follow what you are saying." Clearly, serious misunderstandings can develop when the speaker thinks that the other has agreed, when in fact the other has only signaled understanding the speaker's viewpoint. To take another example, there is some evidence that blacks and women interpret advice from a supervisor as an order more frequently than white men (Asante & Davis, 1989).

The Relationship of Collectivism and Prejudice

The relationship of collectivism and individualism, on the one hand, and prejudice and discrimination, on the other hand, is complex. Collectivism is associated with simpler, two-category thinking and with having a stronger boundary between ingroup and outgroups. Specifically, it is characterized by supportive, self-sacrificing behaviors toward ingroup members, and cool, even hostile, behaviors toward outgroup members. However, outgroups are not necessarily seen as inferior; in fact, they can be seen as superior. Intermarriage with outgroup members can be seen as desirable. When this happens, a person is reclassified from outgroup to ingroup and is accepted.

Reclassification can also occur when outgroup members use communal sharing acts or act in support of ingroup goals. In short, while there is a strong boundary between ingroup and outgroup, and thus prejudice and discrimination against outgroups, reclassification is relatively easy and discrimination is not automatic.

Individualists are greatly concerned with "winning the competition," especially with attaining high status and distinctiveness. Prejudice and discrimination are mechanisms for maintaining status. The result is considerable discrimination. However, the boundary for individualists between ingroup and outgroups is weak. An outgroup member is seen as not very different from an ingroup member, provided there is cognitive and behavioral similarity—that is, provided the minority member acts like the ingroup.

This explains why Rokeach found repeatedly (e.g., Rokeach & Mezei, 1966) that European Americans feel smaller social distance from African-Americans with whom they agree (shared beliefs) than from European Americans with whom they disagree. However, while these findings hold well for relatively superficial behaviors (e.g., having a cup of coffee together), they do not hold well for intimate behaviors (Triandis, 1971). In the case of intimate behaviors, European Americans find considerable social distance from African-Americans, no matter what their beliefs. In fact, Westie and Westie (1957) identified a pyramid of social distance between African and European Americans: The largest distance occurs at the bottom of the social structure, where economic competition is most likely. The smallest social distance is found at the top of the social structure. Of course, at the top, the numbers of minority members are smaller.

Social distance is largely a function of norms. If the legal and normative environment specifies contact, people will act as if they are friendly. Norms are especially important when people are anxious about their status (Bettelheim & Janowitz, 1950) and generally insecure (Triandis & Triandis, 1960). When economic conditions favor one group over another, social distance develops to keep the groups from merging, so that the dominant group can maintain its advantage. Norms support the separation and thus the economic advantage. High individualism, with its competitive elements, is especially likely to favor such norms.

Levels of Prejudice

It is well known that cultures differ in their levels of prejudice. In general, the greater the density of a minority group in a particular environment, the greater the economic competition with that group; and the more visible the minority groups, the greater the level of prejudice toward that group. Pettigrew (1959), for instance, found that the smaller the proportion of African-Americans in the population of a school district, the more likely that district was to desegregate. One can interpret this finding as reflecting the lower likelihood that a small proportion of African-Americans will disturb the existing social structure, as well as the lower probability of economic competition and a more friendly relationship among the races. It is as yet unclear which of these factors was most important in that study.

Expressed and Controlled Prejudice

Both prejudiced and relatively unprejudiced majority-group members know the stereotypes of the larger society about members of minority groups. For instance, both prejudiced and unprejudiced whites (determined by their responses to an attitude scale) know the stereotypes of whites about African-Americans. The difference between the prejudiced and unprejudiced is that the unprejudiced have learned to control and suppress these stereotypes in their thinking about black–white relations (Devine, 1989). However, when a person must react very quickly, without the time needed to suppress the stereotype cognitively—for instance, responding to a tachistoscopically presented stimulus—the reaction is likely to reflect prejudice (Devine, 1989). In other words, all of us are prejudiced, but some of us are better at controlling our prejudices than others.

To close the gap of prejudice, one needs different strategies for cultures with collectivist and individualist emphases: The collectivists have to be exposed to communal sharing acts so they will reclassify a person from outgroup to ingroup; the individualists have to be exposed to situations in which the norms favor small social distance and to similarities in thought and action so they will see the other as a "good" person. A reduction in the perceived competitiveness of the social environment may also help reduce social distance among individualists.

Other Cultural Differences

In addition to cultural differences on individualism and collectivism, there are a myriad of cultural differences that one could describe. They include:

- *Power distance.* Power distance (Hofstede, 1980) reflects whether members of a culture see those at the top and bottom of the social structure as extremely different. It tends to be correlated with collectivism, though there are cultures that are individualistic and high in power distance (Billings, 1989).

- *Cultural tightness.* Tight cultures are those that impose norms strongly and provide sanctions for relatively minor deviations from norms. Japan is an example. Tight cultures tend to be homogeneous and relatively isolated, have often had a history of cooperation resulting in greater probabilities of survival, and often are so densely populated that people

are strongly socialized to do what is considered appropriate. Loose cultures tend to be multicultural—that is, people are aware of conflicting norms, so that in most situations it is unclear what the proper behavior is.

- *Cultural complexity.* Complex cultures have many groups, roles, lifestyles, and other elements. Complexity is a consequence of high levels of division of labor and functional specialization, social stratification, and people having many choices concerning group memberships. It is often found in affluent urban environments and is linked to individualism. Modernity is also associated with cultural complexity, but education is one of its best predictors (Inkeles & Smith, 1974). Collectivism is strongest where cultural complexity is low and tightness is simultaneously high; individualism is strongest where cultural complexity is high and tightness is low. Thus, the United States is very individualistic, but Japan is not very collectivist, because it is high in both tightness and cultural complexity.

Within the United States, minority groups differ according to their circumstances. Poor blacks have few choices; hence their environment is relatively low in complexity. However, they are also low in tightness; hence they would be intermediate in collectivism–individualism. Hispanics are in an environment that is also relatively low in complexity, but their culture is high in family tightness; hence, they tend to be collectivists (Marin & Triandis, 1985).

Several other cultural differences, such as the embedded self (Markus & Kitayama, 1991) and the willingness to change the self rather than the environment, have been identified in the literature. Both are more likely to be found in collectivist cultures where the individual is trained to adjust personal needs to fit group goals. Thus, workers in Japanese-owned industries are expected to sacrifice self-interest to benefit the corporation.

In addition, most cultures that have adopted the religions of the Old Testament and their derivatives, such as Islam, are especially concerned with the "truth" (e.g., Do you believe in my God?), while most South and East Asian cultures are most interested in "virtue" (correct action). The truth–virtue contrast may be another dimension of cultural difference (Hofstede, 1991). For example, a truth-oriented work group may insist in knowing precisely the financial conditions of the corporation, even though it recognizes that such information is the prerogative of management. A virtue-oriented work group may not ask for this information.

Other important differences include the emphasis on doing (action) versus being (experiencing) versus being-in-becoming (growth, change), differences in time orientations (past, present, future), conceptions of human nature as good or bad, and ideas about the relationship of humans to nature in the form of dominance, adaptation, or subjugation (Kluckhohn & Strodtbeck, 1961). For example, the latter contrast often results in different perceptions of how much control workers have over the outcomes of the corporation. The dominance view leads them to seek much control; the adaptation and subjugation view leads them to accept management control of outcomes.

The Culture of Relationships

When approaching the subject of workplace diversity, it is important to consider each specific relationship, such as those of men with women, old with young, Hispanics with non-Hispanics, blacks with whites, management with unions, tenured with untenured employees, educated with uneducated, upper class with lower class, one religion with another religion, and one nationality

with another nationality, and to look for the *culture of the relationship* that has developed over the centuries, especially in recent years. We need to understand this relationship to understand why members of cultures interact the way they do, or why they categorize experience the way they do. For example, why do white men, who control corporate boards of directors, use prototypes of the ideal chief executive officer that look much more like the prototypes of white men than other prototypes?

In the United States, relationships that occur in culturally diverse situations often take place within a context of unstated assumptions about white male Anglo-Saxon Protestant superiority. In 1914, an influential play in New York, *The Melting Pot*, presented the notion that America was evolving into a superior society because of a fusion of all the races (Zangwill, 1914) but also suggested that the Anglo attributes of American society are the dominant attributes of the new culture. Many minorities have resented and continue to resent (Lambert & Taylor, 1990) these assumptions, which engender antiestablishment sentiments among minorities and women.

A useful way to think about the contrast between the melting pot and the situation where each ethnic group proclaims its superiority over all other ethnic groups is to think of two types of multiculturalism (Triandis, 1976a). *Negative multiculturalism* is the condition in which an ethnic group must lose some of its essential, self-defining attributes to relate to other groups. Negative multiculturalism is close to the melting-pot view and is exemplified by the immigrant who must "lose" his mother tongue and speak only English.

Positive multiculturalism is the condition in which an individual acquires new skills and perspectives that improve one's chances of relating effectively to other ethnic groups. Positive multiculturalism is *additive,* in the sense that one maintains the essential self-defining attributes and adds skills that facilitate relationships with other groups. For example, one becomes a balanced bilingual in English and the original language.

Multicultural skills, reflecting additive multiculturalism, are characteristics of an effective modern global industrial society. One would find such skills in employees of large international organizations, such as the United Nations, or others who travel widely, whether they are English, Japanese, or Zimbabweans.

In developing multicultural skills, one can identify different domains of life. Most difficult to change (Herskovits, 1955) in order to become a member of another culture are the patterns of family life; next are one's religious and philosophical beliefs; then aesthetic, work, and political behaviors, in that order; most easy to change are consumer behavior patterns. One can change the latter, to make them part of the melting pot, much more comfortably than one can change the former. If ethnic groups are required to change their work, political, and consumer behaviors, they will not feel deprived of their most self-defining attributes, although they may not feel completely comfortable. On the other hand, having to change family, religious, or aesthetic behaviors would constitute a severe blow to their identities. By increasing skills through cross-cultural training, we can derive a solution to the conflict between the melting pot and ethnocentrism.

Some members of minority groups view the characteristics of industrial culture (e.g., emphasis on time) as aspects of the dominant culture because they are not aware of the extent the same industrial characteristics exist in other industrial countries with significantly different cultures (e.g., Japan). In that case, training of minority workers may have to be provided by their own leaders and focus on the industrial/modern versus traditional relationship, not on the majority–minority relationship in that particular culture. Training

will be discussed in the last section of this chapter.

Empirical Research on the Experiences of Ethnic Minorities, Women, and Other Groups in the Workplace

As diversity has increased in the workplace within the last 20 years, so has research on the expectations, experiences, and attitudes of ethnic minorities, women, the disabled, and gay men and lesbians in the workplace. However, research is not evenly distributed; research agendas have been influenced by current events, trends in management research, and other forces. For instance, a large body of research exists on sexual harassment and on other issues surrounding women's entry into management. Considering that the majority of the U.S. population is female, this is not inappropriate. Thus we devote considerable space to women's issues.

We will first look at research on behavioral phenomena in informal interaction that affect all nontraditional groups in organizational settings. We will then look at more specific nontraditional groups. At this point, the reader should be cautioned against overgeneralization. Within ethnic minority groups and other distinct groups (e.g., women, the disabled) one finds great within-group variation; group members and reaction to them are influenced not only by their group membership, but also by socioeconomic status and other attributes (Triandis, 1976b).

Psychological research about ethnic minorities in the workplace centers on some general areas: communication, job satisfaction, expectations and preferences in workplace behavior, leadership, and mainstream misperceptions of minorities' behavior. These are, of course, the concerns appropriate to the traditional industrial and organizational psychology perspective. Nkomo (1992) calls this approach the *ethnicity paradigm.*

However, research in the broader literature also has explored the organizational contexts in which diversity is framed (Cox & Nkomo, 1990; Nkomo, 1992). Nkomo (1992) points out that organizations are not race-neutral; other scholars have noted that neither are they, for instance, gender-neutral or neutral in regard to ethnicity, sexual/affectional orientation, or ability/disability. *Normal behavior* in most U.S. organizations is defined as the behavior of employees who are white, male, able-bodied heterosexuals from mainstream ethnic groups. Therefore, future research will benefit if researchers approach topics using not only the ethnicity paradigm but also alternative paradigms (Nkomo, 1992).

Informal Interactions

As noted in our model, positive interactions in rewarding contexts lead to perceptions of similarity. An interesting research direction in the last 15 years has been work on informal workplace interactions, such as mentoring and networking, as career development tools for women and minorities and, implicitly, as tools for managing diversity through socialization.

Some characteristic human behaviors in organizations impede the development of such informal interactions. Ibarra (1992) calls one such behavior *homophily* (from Rogers & Bhowmik, 1971), which is defined as a "preference for interaction with others who are similar on given attributes such as sex, race and education" (p. 423). Kanter (1977a) calls corporate preferences for promoting persons with certain socioeconomic characteristics *homosocial reproduction,* and for promoting persons of the same sex *homosexual reproduction* (p. 63; this term does not refer to sexual/affectional preference).

The effects of homophily and of homosocial and homosexual reproduction have been found in empirical research of both mentoring and networking.

Mentoring. Kanter (1977a) was among the first to point out the importance of *sponsorship* or mentoring in the advancement of female managers in corporations. Although mentoring now is viewed somewhat benignly as a useful tool for corporate socialization, it can also be viewed as "an elitist patron system that excludes the socially different" (Carden, 1990, p. 276; see Carden for a review of the evolution of mentoring as a career development concept).

Mentoring has two functions: the psychosocial function and the career function (Kram, 1985). Psychosocial functions include "role modeling, acceptance and confirmation, counseling and friendship," which affect individuals by building their self-esteem (Kram, 1985, p. 23). Career functions include giving information on technical aspects of performing work, providing challenging assignments, facilitating and influencing promotions, and providing protection (e.g., against discrimination; Ragins & Sundstrom, 1989).

Mentors provide invaluable inside information and guidance. Promotion often depends on understanding office politics (Ragins, 1989). In terms of individual outcomes, mentoring has been shown to result in more promotions and higher compensation (Dreher & Ash, 1990; Roche, 1979), greater job satisfaction, and greater career development for protégés (Reich, 1985). Having a mentor can be a major advantage (Collins, 1983; McIlhone, 1984).

Indeed, shortages of mentors and role models (Bhatnagar, 1988; Burke, 1984; Fernandez, 1981; Nieva & Gutek, 1981) are among the more subtle barriers to women and other nontraditional employees. Research on whether an actual shortage of mentors exists is contradictory. Some researchers have found that women and minorities may encounter difficulty finding mentors (K. Ward, n.d., cited in Gibbons, 1992), while others have found little difference in levels of mentoring either between men and women (Ragins & Cotton, 1991) or between whites and African-Americans (Thomas, 1990). Thomas (1990), who defines mentoring more narrowly, did not find a shortage of mentors in a study of 88 African-American and 107 white managers. He found that 82 percent of the blacks had had "developmental relationships" in their career and 57 percent had had mentors. However, Ragins and Cotton (1991) found that a shortage of potential mentors was one barrier women perceived to gaining mentors.

While there may not be a shortage of mentors in general, there definitely is a shortage of high-level, same-sex, same-race mentors for women, ethnic minorities, and others. Thomas (1990) found that whites had almost no developmental relationships with people of other races, while black managers formed 63 percent of such relationships with whites. Several studies (reviewed in Noe, 1988, and Ragins, 1989) have shown that women are more likely to have cross-sex mentorships than are men. Ragins and Cotton (1991) found in their study that there were 77 cross-sex mentorships and 40 same-sex mentorships among women, but 19 cross-sex and 114 same-sex mentorships among men.

The advantage of same-sex, same-race mentorships is that the mentor can better perform the psychosocial mentoring function by serving as a role model of a successful nontraditional employee. Burke, McKeen, and McKenna (1990) found psychosocial mentoring was more prevalent in mentorships involving women as either mentors or protégés, especially when both mentor and protégé were female. Ragins and McFarlin (1990) also found greater psychosocial mentoring in all-female mentoring dyads.

The larger amount of psychosocial mentoring may be related to opportunities for informal interaction with mentors. Ragins and McFarlin (1990) found that protégés in cross-sex mentorships were less likely to report engaging in after-work social interactions with their mentors than those in same-sex mentorships.

Thomas (1990) found that African-American protégés in same-race mentorships received more psychosocial support than did African-American protégés in cross-race mentorships. This may be due to the complexities of "black racial identity and white racial consciousness" (Thomas, 1990). Atkinson, Neville, and Casas (1991) found that ethnic similarity was related to evaluation ratings of mentorships by novice professional psychologists.

Some of the barriers to mentoring exist among potential mentors, and some among potential protégés (Ragins & Cotton, 1991). For instance, the few female top managers are so overworked that they generally cannot be mentors to others like them. Female managers also may feel ambivalent about mentoring other women because of the cross-pressures they experience from male managers (Bhatnagar, 1988; Yoder, 1985; Yoder, Adams, Grove, & Priest, 1985).

On the other hand, men may feel uncomfortable mentoring women because of fear of sexual tension or rumors of sexual involvement (Ragins, 1989). Men also may not sponsor women because they may perceive women as less committed to a career than men and feel sponsoring women is not a good use of male managers' time (Nieva & Gutek, 1981b). Fear that a woman may fail and that her failure will reflect badly on them may also be a factor.

Ragins and Cotton (1991) found that women who were potential protégés perceived more barriers to gaining a mentor than did male potential protégés. Women were more likely to believe that a potential mentor would mistake an approach as a sexual advance, that others would disapprove of the relationship, and that they would be rejected by potential mentors. Both men and women, however, were equally fearful about initiating a relationship with a mentor.

The perceptions of barriers found by Ragins and Cotton (1991) may explain the results obtained by Noe (1988) in a study of assigned (formal) mentorships. Noe (1988) found that protégés in cross-sex mentorships "utilized the relationships more effectively" than protégés in same-sex mentorships and that female protégées in cross-sex mentorships used the relationship the most effectively of all protégés. Because the mentorships had been formally arranged by the company, the fear of approaching mentors and the fear of misinterpretation of intent by mentors and others were eliminated.

Homosocial reproduction of traits other than race or gender—such as age, socioeconomic origins, and managerial/professional status—also appears to play a role in the formation of voluntary mentorships. Whitely, Dougherty, and Dreher (1992) found that "younger, more work-involved respondents from higher socioeconomic origins received more career-oriented mentoring" (p. 141). Whitely, Dougherty, and Dreher (1991) also found that such mentoring is related to rate of promotion and total compensation and has a greater effect on protégés from higher socioeconomic origins than on those from lower socioeconomic origins.

Networking. Inability or failure to participate in networks often hinders one's advancement in an organization (Bhatnagar, 1988). While mentoring is usually conceptualized as a vertical dyadic relationship, *networking* has been defined as maintaining many interpersonal relationships, many of them horizontal rather than vertical, to assist in one's own career development (De Necochea, 1988).

Nontraditional employees may encounter barriers to networking with white male managers, which may be caused by homophily, the scarcity of women and minorities in top management, or other organizational factors. The data presented by Rosen, Templeton, and Kichline (1981) suggest that women are placed in jobs that preclude them from making contacts with important members of management and prevent them from participating in networks. For instance, 60 percent of the women felt they had been excluded from the "informal organization." Similarly, Koontz (1979) found many women felt lonely and isolated.

Ambivalence (see the section that follows) also may play a role. Many men do not like women participating in male networks (Kanter, 1977b). Women are often excluded from informal gatherings that take place in bars and locker rooms and at sporting events (Nieva & Gutek, 1981). The "old boys' club" is still very much in evidence, although women may choose not to participate in organizational networks (Epstein, 1970) so as not to "constrain" the situation.

Indeed, women and minorities may be forced to use different networks for career purposes and for psychosocial purposes. Ibarra (1992) found that men in an advertising agency maintained same-sex friendships across multiple networks, had stronger ties, and used the same networks for career and psychosocial purposes. Women used a female network for psychosocial purposes and a male network for instrumental access to power. De Necochea (1988) found that Hispanic women in a corporation had significantly larger social networks than Hispanic men; furthermore, network utilization for career purposes was related to self-efficacy. Peterson (1988) found that lesbians had denser social networks than gay men and that "the proportion of network members who are homosexual is inversely related to loneliness." The growing field of social network analysis may provide us with more insights about the interactions of socioeconomic status, ethnicity, gender, and other differences with social networks in organizations.

Ambivalence. Another barrier to positive interaction between nontraditional employees and traditional employees in organizations is ambivalence. When confronted with difference, human beings frequently feel ambivalent. In the workplace, this ambivalence may be caused by the categorizations that people use and their irrelevance to the requirements for task performance.

All those persons whose presence raises diversity issues in the workplace have hypersalient traits, traits often used for fundamental categorization. For instance, as Gutek (1985) notes, it is nearly impossible to remember the last time one met a person whose gender one does not now remember. Similarly, obviously ethnic traits (skin color) and obvious physical and mental impairments are too salient to be overlooked for categorical purposes. Sexual/affectional preference also is a fundamental category, although ambivalence about gay men and lesbians may spring from cognitive dissonance. Because there is no obvious physical marker of sexual/affectional preference such as skin color, a person can interact with gay men or lesbians for a long time without knowing their sexual/affectional preference. Cognitive dissonance arises if one assumes that homosexuals are very different but discovers through interaction that they are not.

Indeed, Katz, Hass, and Bailey (1988) believe that ambivalence amplification operates when majority group members encounter the disabled or other "socially marginal groups." Amplification causes the ambivalent person to react in more extreme ways to those who are different.

Ambivalence amplification has been shown in research. When a minority member is better than average, there is a tendency to see that member as extremely "good," and when a member is worse than the average there is a tendency to see that member as very "bad" (Katz, Wackenhut, & Glass, 1986; Linville & Jones, 1980).

Research indicates that mainstream members of organizations feel considerable ambivalence toward women, and ambivalence amplification operates in male–female relationships in organizations. For example, in one study that used films of work samples matched for performance level, undergraduates rated the performance of high-performing women significantly higher than the performance of high-performing men (Bigoness, 1976).

Ambivalence can stem from perceptual distortions that occur when group composition within the workplace is skewed (Kanter, 1977b). Women in traditionally male-dominated occupations are often perceived as "tokens." Not only women but also African-Americans, Hispanics, and others who are not perceived as mainstream will encounter the problem of tokenism (Kanter, 1977b).

Tokens are often perceived according to preexisting stereotypes rather than according to their actions (Kanter, 1977b). Research suggests that tokens are evaluated negatively (Martin & Shanahan, 1983) even when they are perceived to be influential (Ridgeway, 1982). A number of perceptual distortions, such as visibility, polarization, and assimilation, have been associated with token status (Kanter, 1981). People have a tendency to stereotype those in the minority as having unusual attributes (Hamilton, 1982), and many such attributes are seen as undesirable. Being a token makes the person more noticeable, the target of more scrutiny (Bhatnagar, 1988), more likely to be the subject of office gossip (Kanter, 1977b), and more likely to be evaluated extremely (Taylor, Fiske, Etcoff, & Ruderman, 1978).

As a result, the token feels that any mistakes will be noticed and any actions will be attributed to the difference (e.g., sex, race; Kanter, 1977a, 1977b), and often feels extreme stress and performance pressures (Yoder et al., 1985). However, some research suggests that neither black nor white men suffer these negative consequences in some situations when they are tokens (Crocker & McGraw, 1984; Sackett, DuBois, & Noe, 1991).

We will now turn to more traditional industrial and organizational psychology research on ethnic minorities, women, and the disabled. Due to space restrictions, we have not been able to include literature on all differences, such as socioeconomic status or religious differences. A caveat is appropriate: As noted earlier, all differences occur within specific organizational contexts. Therefore, individual cultural differences cannot be separated from the context in which they are considered different.

Asian Americans

Asian Americans are the fastest-growing and most affluent minority in the country (O'Hare, 1990). However, because of the many nationalities covered by the "Asian and Pacific Islander" category, even the previous sentence is an overgeneralization. While the success of many Asian Americans has engendered the "model minority" stereotype, some Asian groups suffer disproportionately from poverty (Gould, 1988).

Among the stereotypes of Asian Americans in business is the belief that they are not assertive communicators, particularly in meetings. While some Asian American subjects have reported lower self-assertion (L. Johnson & Remus, 1985; Zane, Sue, Hu, & Kwon, 1991), such behavior may be highly situational. Zane et al. (1991) found that Asian Americans reported less self-assertion only in situations involving strangers. Sue, Zane, and Sue (1985) suggest that Asian Americans have not been promoted into top management because mainstream managers do not recognize that Asians express leadership characteristics such as aggressiveness in different ways than do non-Asians. Martini, Behnke, and King (1992) found evidence of misperception of some Asian behavior in their study of public speaking anxiety: American audiences perceived that Asian speakers were much more anxious than American speakers, although there was no significant difference between the speakers' self-reported anxiety.

Some Asian Americans prefer learning from lectures and written material to experiential learning (Ryan & Hendricks, 1989). This puts them at a disadvantage in work situations in which experiential learning is the primary training mode. For instance, Asian American social workers may be misperceived as insubordinate by non-Asian supervisors because Asians prefer carrying out written instructions to having discussions with supervisors (Ryan & Hendricks, 1989); such discussions are considered essential parts of social work training.

African-Americans

African-Americans have been the most numerous minority group in the United States, yet research on them has been relatively limited. For example, Cox and Nkomo (1990) found only 201 studies relevant to organizational behavior and race in a 25-year (1964–1989) period. We will attempt to highlight the more significant findings.

African-Americans continue to face racial discrimination in hiring (Kirschenman & Neckerman, 1991), although it is more subtle than in the past. Braddock and McPartland (1987) examine four kinds of "exclusionary barriers" found in corporations at different stages of selection and promotion. Pettigrew and Martin (1987) also look at subtle biases that place African-Americans in triple jeopardy, facing negative stereotypes, solo status, and tokenism. Thus, cultural differences between African-Americans and others must be framed in the context of the organizational racism in which they are experienced.

African-Americans and Hispanics in the United States have been shown to define satisfactory communication differently than do European Americans. Blacks are similar to whites in finding more individualistic communication satisfactory, although they prefer deeper topical involvement than whites do (Hecht & Ribeau, 1984). Blacks also perceive less aggressiveness in verbal aggression situations (Phelps, Meara, Davis, & Patton, 1991). Whites not only are more likely to perceive more aggressiveness in such situations, but they also are likely to be uncomfortable with any black assertiveness (Hrop & Rakos, 1985).

Black-white communication also reflects conflict around other dimensions. Blacks value expression in movement, sound, and the visual modalities. Whites value moderation in expression (though from a worldwide viewpoint, American whites are average on this dimension). Euro-Americans are more concerned with what they own as a determinant of identity (e.g., I am a homeowner), while blacks often emphasize what they express in personal style and movement and how they appear to others (Triandis, 1976b).

There are great differences between upper- and middle-class African-Americans and very poor African-Americans. The nonpredictability of the link between behavior and consequences for unemployed blacks (e.g., If I apply for a job will I get one? I am uncertain) results in "eco-system distrust" (Triandis, 1976b). This is a syndrome of feelings, beliefs, and behavior that includes "not trusting people, not trusting themselves, not trusting the way the establishment institutions function, and not trusting the dependability of relationships between events occurring in their environment" (Triandis, 1976b, p. 172). This syndrome is perfectly understandable as a functional reaction to an uncertain environment. How can a person plan if he or she has to hustle to make a living? How can one trust an environment that is not predictable or where one does not know if today is the last day of one's life? The previous statement is not mere hyperbole. Homicide is the leading cause of death for black men between the ages of 15 and 24.

African-American psychologist Richard Majors (Majors & Billson, 1992) argues that black men have internalized white male values of self-reliance and economic success but, due to structural barriers, cannot successfully provide for and protect their families. As a result, they assume what he calls a "cool pose" of toughness, willingness to use violence, and sexual promiscuity as a defense mechanism. However, this "cool pose" also results in more violence, abuse of women and children, accidents, fighting, and antiestablishment feelings.

Antiestablishment feelings include rejection of people who do well under the status quo. According to Triandis (1976b, p. 154), "Here blacks reject the establishment more clearly than do whites. The establishment is here seen as the police, the foremen, and others who do well under the status quo." Very poor unemployed black men see African-American professionals as "self-serving, intelligent egoists" (Triandis, 1976b, p. 173).

All of these statements, however, must be viewed within the context of two major points made in Triandis (1976b): "1. There are more similarities than differences in the responses of blacks and whites. 2. There is tremendous heterogeneity in the responses of both blacks and whites. Specifically, there are several black points of view. For example, some blacks are much more like the white middle class than they are like other blacks. The hard-core unemployed blacks are the only black sample that is consistently most different from the white middle class" (p. 174).

Hispanics

Research on Hispanic–non-Hispanic contact (e.g., Marin & Triandis, 1985) suggests that Hispanics are more collectivist than non-Hispanics. This collectivism may be reflected in Mexican-Americans' emphasis on "relational validation" in communication (Hecht & Ribeau, 1984; Hecht, Ribeau, & Sedano, 1990).

Another aspect of this collectivism is greater expectation of harmony in ingroup relationships. If the work group is to be seen as an ingroup, it has to be harmonious. Many

Hispanics use the so-called *simpatia* cultural script (Triandis et al., 1984b). That is, they value people who are *simpatico* much more than do non-Hispanics. This translates into expecting the other person to show more loyalty, dignity, friendliness, politeness, affection, respect, and behavior in socially desirable ways than is the case for non-Hispanics. They also expect the other person not to criticize them, not to demean them, and not fight with them. This *simpatia* script may be reflected in the finding from one study that a key predictor of job satisfaction for Hispanics was agreement with the statement, "My supervisor gets employees to work together as a team" (McNeely, 1987).

Of course, Hispanics have different backgrounds and different levels of acculturation to the dominant American culture, so that their culture is a mixture of the Hispanic and the dominant culture's elements, as exemplified in the study by Ferdman and Cortes (1992), published in Knouse, Rosenfeld, and Culbertson's (1992) compilation *Hispanics in the Workplace*. Marin and Marin (1991) outline important distinctions to make and issues to be addressed in research on Hispanics in organizations.

Women

Women are still dramatically underrepresented in management and tend to be clustered in the lower ranks of organizations (Dipboye, 1987). Even women who have "all the right stuff" lag behind men with equivalent qualifications with respect to salary progression and frequency of job transfers (Stroh, Brett, & Reilly, 1992). Firms reporting to the Equal Employment Opportunity Commission (EEOC) in 1990 reported that 46.1 percent of their employees were women (EEOC, 1991), but Ragins and Sundstrom (1989) estimate that women may comprise only 15 percent of entry-level managers, 5 percent of middle managers, and 1 percent of top management.

In the past, the barriers to the advancement of women were clear; now they are subtle. It could be that women have lower aspirations (Fernandez, 1981; Ragins & Sundstrom, 1989); however, studies suggest that the phenomenon is more complex and involves the effects of homophily, homosocial and homosexual reproduction, tokenism, and ambivalence, as noted earlier. It probably is correct to say that "even egalitarian males may have mixed feelings about bringing more women into management" (Dipboye, 1987, p. 143).

Another barrier that women face is the effect of sex role stereotypes on perceptions of them—for instance, in evaluations of performance—and of sex role spillover. Studies indicate that standards used to evaluate male and female managers may be based on sex role stereotypes. Sex role stereotypes are culturally based beliefs prescribing appropriate and inappropriate behavior. Stereotypes for males generally include task-oriented traits such as aggression, logic, ambition, confidence, and decisiveness.

Stereotypes for females typically include socioemotional traits such as nurturance, sensitivity, passivity, emotionality, patience, and understanding (Dipboye, 1987). Because the traits associated with leadership have been generally male sex-typed, men fit the image of a successful manager more than women (Schein, 1973). Yet research does indicate that at least managerial men and women do not differ significantly on most trait dimensions (Moore & Rickel, 1980). Moore and Rickel (1980) found that women in nontraditional occupations, such as business, and in higher levels of organizations reported having characteristics like those typically ascribed to the male sex type: objective, firm, assertive, decisive, logical, and consistent.

Nevertheless, the woman who assumes a leadership position faces a serious dilemma. She must display the traits that are defined as those of successful managers, yet she runs the risk of violating sex role stereotypes (Dipboye,

1987). In speaking of this dilemma, Bhatnagar (1988) notes, "If they want to retain the approval of people, women must be warm and expressive; if they want to succeed professionally, they must be assertive, competitive and firm" (Bhatnagar, 1988, p. 349). Thus, the professional woman can experience a double bind: She aspires to be "professional," but that is incompatible with being "feminine" (Wood & Conrad, 1983).

A sizable amount of research has concentrated on the consequences of sex role incongruence on performance and affective ratings of leaders (Bartol & Butterfield, 1976; Hagan & Kahn, 1975; Nieva & Gutek, 1980; Petty & Lee, 1975; Petty & Miles, 1976; see Ragins & Sundstrom, 1989, for a review). For instance, in a study of managers in mixed-sex training groups, Jago and Vroom (1982) found that subjects reported they would have problems working with women who used the autocratic style. On the other hand, men who used the autocratic style were rated positively.

Furthermore, in a meta-analysis of the evaluation of male and female leaders, Eagly, Makhijani, and Klonsky (1992) found that women were evaluated less favorably than men in certain circumstances; for instance, when women behaved in a stereotypically male style (i.e., autocratic or directive), they were evaluated negatively in comparison to male leaders. Moreover, these evaluations were more negative when women occupied traditionally male positions. These findings are consistent with previous research that suggested that women in traditionally male jobs do tend to receive lower performance ratings than men (Landy & Farr, 1980).

Some new areas of research on gender differences in organizations have blossomed in recent years. The area of leadership styles is one in which a great deal of debate is currently taking place. Rosener (1991) believes that women are more likely to use "transformational leadership" (influencing basic attitudes

of subordinates to build commitment to organizational objectives), a position supported by some researchers and contested by others ("Debate," 1992). Important research on gender differences in communication styles has been carried out by Tannen (1990).

However, although a great deal of research exists on certain gender issues, such as sexual harassment, more research is needed. Chusmir, Moore, and Adams (1990) examined 22 major scholarly and trade journals published from 1983 to 1988 and found "a downward trend in gender-issue publication at a time when working women are becoming an ever-increasing percentage of the work force." Paludi (1990) suggests new directions needed in research on women; one of them is research into issues confronted by dual status women, who are both female and members of other nontraditional groups. Reid and Comas-Diaz (1990) expand on possible research directions for work on dual status groups.

Sexual Harassment

Sexual harassment in the workplace is related to the problem of sex role stereotypes. It was rarely discussed until the mid-1970s, when feminists began to write about it as a women's issue. Paul (1985), in her study of the experiences of U.S. military nurses in the Vietnam conflict, received this response to a question about sexual harassment (p. 574): "One nurse reported that she was sexually harassed 'every day—but we were programmed to believe that was our lot in life.'"

In fact, the first published survey on the sexual harassment of working women was not published in a scholarly journal but in a women's magazine, *Redbook* (Safran, 1976). In her book *Sexual Shakedown*, Farley (1978) summarized contemporary knowledge about the phenomenon; MacKinnon (1979) advanced an influential argument on the legal applicability of Title VII of the Civil Rights Act of 1964 to sexual harassment. Dziech and Weiner

(1990) exposed sexual harassment in higher education.

Definition. The United States Equal Employment Opportunity Commission (EEOC) in 1980 defined sexual harassment as:

> Unwelcome sexual advances, requests for sexual favors and other verbal or physical conduct of a sexual nature when submission to such conduct is made either explicitly or implicitly a term or condition of an individual's employment; submission to or rejection of such conduct by an individual is used as the basis for employment decisions affecting the individual; or such conduct has the purpose or effect of unreasonably interfering with an individual's work performance or creating an intimidating, hostile, or offensive working environment. (p. 25024)

In this definition are the two kinds of sexual harassment actionable under federal law: quid pro quo sexual harassment and hostile environment harassment. Quid pro quo harassment occurs when sexual compliance is made mandatory for promotion, favors, or retaining one's job.

Much of the research on sexual harassment has focused on how men and women define it and whether men's definitions differ significantly from women's. Among the several studies that have found significant differences between men's and women's definitions are Gutek (1985), in which women consistently were more likely to label a behavior as sexual harassment; McKinney (1990), in which male and female faculty members at a university differed in their definition of sexual harassment by students; Padgitt and Padgitt (1986), in which women defined more behaviors as sexual harassment and were more consistent in their definitions; Popovich, Nokovich, Martelli, and Zolotny (1986); and Powell (1986).

Some researchers have found little difference between men's and women's definitions. McKinney (1990) found no difference between male and female faculty members in the definition of sexual harassment by colleagues. In the 1988 Merit Systems Protection Board study, male and female federal employees agreed that four types of behavior were sexual harassment, but disagreed on whether uninvited sexually suggestive looks or gestures and uninvited sexual teasing, jokes, remarks, or questions were sexual harassment. Generally, as an act becomes more overt and coercive, women and men are more likely to agree that it is sexual harassment. Male and female federal employees' definitions of sexual harassment had become more similar since the first Merit Systems Protection Board study in 1981 (Clode, 1988).

Costs of Sexual Harassment. In its 1988 study, the Merit Systems Protection Board estimated the cost of sexual harassment of federal employees over a two-year period to be $267.3 million. Included in this estimate were the costs of turnover, sick leave, and loss of individual and group productivity.

Incidence. The reported incidence of sexual harassment varies because of the use of slightly different definitions and different sampling techniques. Some reported rates of victimization are 76 percent among female nurses (Grieco, 1987); 21 to 53 percent among women and 9 to 37 percent among men (Gutek, 1985); and 42 percent among female federal employees (1981 and 1988), 15 percent among male federal employees (1981), and 14 percent among male federal employees (Clode, 1988).

Explanatory Models. Tangri, Burt, and Johnson (1982) described three models commonly used to explain sexual harassment: the natural/biological model, the organizational model, and the sociocultural model. The *natural/biological model*, according to the study, "asserts that sexual harassment is simply natural sexual attraction between two people"; the *organizational model* "argues that sexual harassment is simply the result of certain opportunity structures created by organizational climate, hierarchy, and specific authority relations"; and the *sociocultural model* "argues that sexual harassment reflects the larger society's differential distribution of power and status between the sexes" (p. 34).

Gutek, Cohen, and Konrad (1990) propose a model that includes frequency of contact, sex role spillover, and sexualization of the workplace. Sex role spillover (Nieva & Gutek, 1981) happens when "gender roles that are usually irrelevant or inappropriate to work" carry over into the workplace (Gutek, 1985, pp. 15–17). The sex roles that spill over into the workplace are "sex object" for women and "sexual aggressor" for men, Gutek believes (1985). Because of expectations connected with the "sexual aggressor" role, men tend to sexualize their work environments through sexual behavior such as making jokes related to sexuality, using "dirty" words, posting erotic photographs, commenting on women's physical appearance, using sexual looks and gestures, and sexual touching.

Sex role expectations for women become incorporated into traditionally female occupations, and sex role expectations for men are incorporated into traditionally male occupations. Women in traditionally male jobs are treated as role deviates. For women in traditionally female jobs, "sex-role and work-role are practically identical" (Gutek & Morasch, 1982, p. 56).

However, unequal sex ratios (caused by gender segregation of occupations) also contribute to sex role spillover. Women in traditionally male jobs and women in traditionally female jobs who interact frequently with men report more male sexual behavior than do women in traditionally female jobs who interact primarily with other women. Women in integrated jobs (in which the proportion of men and women is even) report less sexual behavior in their work groups than women in gender-segregated jobs (Gutek, 1985).

Gutek, Cohen, and Conrad (1990) found that there was more sexual harassment in environments where workers had more contact with the opposite sex; because "women are more likely to work with many men than men are to work with many women," women are more likely to be sexually harassed (pp. 570–571). For instance, a female secretary may interact primarily with her male bosses; her bosses, however, probably spend most of their time in meetings with other male executives or clients.

Victims' Responses and the Effects of Harassment. Doing nothing and ignoring harassment is the most favored response of victims (Clode, 1988; Gruber & Bjorn, 1982; Gutek, 1985). Among federal employees, 52 percent of female victims ignored the incident or did nothing, 43 percent avoided the harasser, 44 percent told the harasser to stop, 20 percent made a joke of the behavior, 14 percent threatened to tell other people about the harassment, 15 percent reported the behavior to a supervisor, 2 percent changed jobs, and 4 percent complied (Clode, 1988, p. 24).

Only 5 percent of victims filed formal complaints, a rate that may be partially attributed to the length of time required to resolve a sexual harassment complaint in the federal government: 482 days (Clode, 1988, p. 30).

The effects of harassment on victims include psychiatric injury (irritability, anxiety, anger, shame, depression, insomnia; Bursten, 1985), reduced work performance and attitudes, symptoms of stress-related mental and physical disorders (nausea, headaches, fatigue; Crull, 1982), and economic losses (Farley, 1978). Economic losses arise from job loss.

Third Parties' Perceptions. Embarrassment is believed to be one reason for the low rate of filing of formal sexual harassment complaints. Because many sexual harassment incidents have no witnesses other than the harasser and the victim, how others view the two actors is crucial to how a complaint might be resolved.

Physical attractiveness is one factor influencing third-party judgments of sexual harassment. Quinn and Lees (1984) believe that personnel departments are less likely to take seriously sexual harassment complaints from unattractive female employees than from attractive women. Pryor and Day (1988) found that remarks on physical appearance directed to unattractive women were rated as less harassing than similar remarks to women of average or high attractiveness. Castellow, Wuensch, and Moore (1990) found that female sexual harassment victims are more likely to win lawsuits against their harassers when the victims are attractive and the harassers are unattractive.

Conclusion. It seems likely that the subject of sexual harassment will continue to be an area of active research. The European Community has also recognized the problem (Rubinstein, 1988). As women participate more fully in the work forces of other countries, the question of sexual harassment specifically and the place of sexuality in the workplace generally will have to be addressed. Lobel (1993) has questioned the appropriateness of proscribing all forms of sexual relationship at work and has called for new forms of work relationships that allow sexuality at work. This is likely to become a focus of vigorous debate in the coming years.

Sexual/Affectional Orientation (Gay Men and Lesbians)

Sexual/affectional orientation has become a diversity issue as homosexuality has become more accepted in the United States; however, it is an issue precisely because that acceptance is incomplete and uncertain. While some individuals and organizations have become more tolerant of homosexual persons, homosexual sex practices are illegal in many states and municipalities. Connecticut, the District of Columbia, Hawaii, Massachusetts, New Jersey, Wisconsin, and more than 100 cities and counties currently have laws against discrimination in employment (Simon & Daly, 1992).

The amount of discrimination expressed against employing homosexuals has declined (Levine, 1979). Interestingly, a 1974 poll (Levitt & Klassen, 1974) found high support for barring homosexuals from high-status occupations (judges, teachers, ministers) but little support for barring them from low-status and stereotypically gay occupations (hairdresser, artist, musician, florist).

Such stereotypes about the occupations in which homosexuals work are inaccurate. For example, a survey of 4,000 homosexual men and women in Chicago found that "more homosexuals work in science and engineering than in social services; 40 percent more are employed in finance and insurance than in entertainment and the arts; and ten times as many work in computers as in fashion" (Stewart, 1991, p. 43).

Kinsey estimated that 10 percent of men and 2 to 3 percent of women in the United States are exclusively homosexual (Kinsey, Pomeroy, & Martin, 1948; Kinsey, Pomeroy, Martin, & Gebhart, 1953). A French survey, however, reported in the press in August 1992, agreed with a British survey that these numbers are too high. Nevertheless, there are substantial numbers of homosexual employees.

The supposed invisibility of homosexuals derives from the lack of clear identifiability; one cannot tell by looking at a person what his or her sexual/affectional orientation is. However, when applying for jobs, male homosexuals are not as invisible as many heterosexuals believe. Most employment application forms have questions about arrest records, service in the armed forces, and hospitalization that companies use to screen for male homosexuals (Levine, 1979). Because of the criminalization of homosexual acts, well-educated middle-class white homosexual men may be more likely to have arrest records than their heterosexual peers. The U.S. Armed Forces through 1992 discharged all homosexual personnel with general or unfavorable discharges; many companies will not hire anyone with such discharges. Some gays have, at some point in their lives, been subjected to treatment in psychiatric hospitals for their supposed deviance. For gays with such histories, applying for a job presents them with a double bind. If they answer the questions honestly, they will undoubtedly be rejected. However, if they answer dishonestly and are hired, they will be subject to dismissal for having lied on their applications.

Once on the job, gay workers must engage in high self-monitoring to discern if their sexual/affectional orientation will hinder them in their job (Hall, 1986; Kronenberger, 1991; Levine, 1979; Stewart, 1991). Indeed, due to such legal and professional ambiguities, the issue of whether and how to "come out of the closet" (reveal one's sexual/affectional orientation) may be a major issue in the lives of gay employees.

In a study of more than 100 gay male corporate employees, Woods (cited in Stewart, 1991) classified common responses to the "coming out" issue into these categories: *counterfeiting* a heterosexual identity (e.g., even get married to cover up), *integrating* by being openly gay, *avoiding* the issue (the most common response), and *entrepreneurial flight*, in which gays start their own businesses to escape homophobic environments.

That such environments exist is indisputable (Kronenberger, 1991; Stewart, 1991). A survey in 1987 by the *Wall Street Journal* found that 66 percent of the chief executive offices of major companies said they would "be reluctant to put a homosexual on management committees" (cited in Stewart, 1991). In testing a scale

about beliefs about employing homosexuals, O'Brien and Vest (1988) found one major factor emerging—disruption of the organization—characterized by 13 beliefs about the effects of employing homosexuals, such as undermining company morale, hurting the company image, resulting in loss of some customers, and causing some employees to quit.

Some companies may believe that there are no costs associated with overt or subtle discrimination against homosexuals. However, it is difficult to assess costs when many homosexuals counterfeit themselves as heterosexual. This so-called passing makes careful study of homosexuals within corporations extremely difficult (Weinberg, 1970). It is likely that passing has indirect consequences on the employees who have to maintain a front. These consequences may be reflected in low rates of self-esteem and high rates of substance abuse or suicide. A major problem is the loss of talent by some companies. Companies that have policies of acceptance of homosexuals (e.g., AT&T) may gain a competitive advantage in hiring; some companies take advantage of having homosexuals in their top management to increase their homosexual clientele (Stewart, 1991).

In a cross-cultural study, Ross (1989) found that the "mental health consequences of antihomosexual environments are most negative where homosexuality is more severely stigmatized" (p. 299). In an earlier study, Ross (1978) found that levels of adjustment in heterosexually married homosexual men were determined by the highly negative, stigmatic societal reaction they *anticipated* to their homosexuality rather than actual societal reaction. Ross (1990) believes that the effect of major life events is amplified by stigmatization, so that negative life events affect stigmatized persons such as homosexuals more deeply. In some major corporations, gay and lesbian support networks are officially sanctioned (Kronenberger, 1991); these groups work to mitigate the effects of stigmatization.

Openly gay men do have higher rates of alcohol and drug abuse than heterosexual men. McKirnan and Peterson (1988) speculate that homosexual men may be vulnerable to substance abuse because of the stress of stigmatization and the "bar culture" of urban gay life. Homosexuals who abuse alcohol or drugs might become less productive employees; however, in companies with antihomosexual environments, they may be afraid to take advantage of employee assistance programs. Because of the special vulnerability of some homosexuals to substance abuse, conventional treatment programs may not be as effective as programs that take the patient's sexual/affectional orientation into account (Woolsey, 1991a).

The spread of acquired immune deficiency syndrome (AIDS) gave homophobic employers yet another reason to discriminate against homosexuals (Aikin, 1988), although employees with AIDS are now protected by the Americans with Disabilities Act (Hunsicker, 1990). AIDS cases have not proved to be extraordinary burdens on employers' health insurance plans, but fear of AIDS has made some employees reluctant to work with those who are HIV-positive (Woolsey, 1991b). A leading high-technology corporation has a full-time AIDS Program Office, which sponsors educational seminars on AIDS for employees. In these seminars, leaders "encourage people to acknowledge their fears and even in some cases their disdain" (Woolsey, 1991b).

Companies who are trying to create an atmosphere in which sexual/affectional orientation is no longer an issue have extended certain benefits, such as health insurance, to the partners of gay and lesbian employees (Bulkeley, 1991). Some companies include tolerance of homosexuality in their diversity training (Stewart, 1991).

Disabled Workers

The number of disabled persons in the United States has been estimated at 43 million; about 17 percent of adults of working age were disabled in 1978. The highest unemployment rate in America is found among disabled adults (Hahn, 1983). Only one third of disabled persons ages 16 through 64 are employed; of those who are unemployed, 66 percent (8.2 million) would like to have a job (ICD, 1986). Because of this high unemployment rate, many disabled people who would like to work may lack requisite work socialization (McCarthy, 1988).

The Americans with Disabilities Act (ADA) defines disability as "(a) a physical or mental impairment that substantially limits one or more of the major life activities of such individuals; (b) a record of such an impairment; or (c) being regarded as having such an impairment" (Kohl & Greenlaw, 1992).

The passage of the ADA has rekindled interest in the integration of disabled persons into the work force. This may be a difficult task for many reasons. Disabled persons traditionally have been stigmatized, living isolated lives (Hahn, 1983; Murphy, Scheer, Murphy, & Mack, 1988; Oliver, 1990). Because of the connection between affluence and access to health care, disability is not randomly distributed in the population (Oliver, 1990). In the United States, women are more likely to be severely disabled than men, and 60 percent of low-income disabled persons are women (Mudrick, 1983). Blacks and Hispanics have higher rates of severe disability (13%) than whites (8%). There is a correlation between higher levels of disability and lower levels of education (Social Security Administration, 1980). Thus, there is "extensive overlap between the disabled and the economically disadvantaged" (Levitan & Taggart, 1977, p. 3).

Although data on disabled persons employed in the private sector are difficult to find, looking at rehabilitation literature affords a glimpse of the employment experience of the disabled. Logic suggests that large corporations might have more resources to accommodate disabled workers (Rabby, 1983). However, one study found that small companies actually are more willing to hire severely disabled workers (Craft, Benecki, & Shkop, 1980). This occurs, apparently, because small companies either have no formal job descriptions or very vague ones, making it easier to adjust positions to fit disabled workers' competencies. The "supported employment" approach attempts to integrate severely disabled workers into mainstream jobs through extensive training, counseling, and continuance of payments from government programs (Koenig & Schalock, 1991).

In the workplace, disabled persons may evoke a wide range of attitudes and behaviors in their able-bodied peers (Katz, Hass, & Bailey, 1988). Negative attitudes about the disabled have their roots both in social custom and in primal emotions such as death anxiety, anxiety about being in an unstructured/ambiguous/unpredictable situation, and fear of contamination (Livneh, 1988).

In Europe and the United States, there are very definite expectations of how disabled people should behave. Oliver (1990) calls the prevailing stereotype the "personal tragedy theory of disability," the idea being that any disability is tragedy over which disabled persons should mourn throughout their lives. Dembo, Levitan, and Wright maintain that "members of the majority group often want those who are physically different to suffer as a sign that the physical assets they lack are valuable and important" (cited in Katz, Hass, & Bailey, 1988, p. 53).

For instance, in an experiment, Katz, Hass, and Bailey (1988) found that students volunteered to help an unpleasant disabled woman more frequently than they volunteered to help a pleasant disabled woman and either pleasant or unpleasant able-bodied women. The pleasant disabled woman "apparently violated [subjects'] beliefs about how people in wheelchairs are supposed to behave. That is, instead of seeming to feel inadequate, she was out-going, competent, and achievement-oriented" (p. 53).

Such attitudes may combine with the disabled person's own lack of work socialization to create a situation that is, in itself, disabling. As the baby boom generation ages, integrating disabled workers will become even more critical. Most people cannot change their ethnic origin or their gender, but all people age. The aging process is one of progressive disability; in fact, the disabled refer to the nondisabled as "temporarily able-bodied (TABs)" (Hahn, 1983, p. 44).

Other Kinds of Diversity

We discussed the major groups that create diversity in work settings. Of course, the coverage is not complete. Thernstrom (1980) published an encyclopedia that discusses 125 ethnic groups that have significant numbers in the United States; additionally, we could mention groups resulting from socioeconomic status, from age distinctions, and others.

Dealing With Workplace Differences

Interventions designed to deal with diversity were suggested by the framework presented in Figure 1. A more general strategy for interventions can attempt to change the following:

- The structure of society, through tax incentives, government policies, and educational programs that reach large segments of the society

- The structure of organizations, through the development of standard operating procedures, affirmative action, and educational programs that reach all segments of the organization (see Pettigrew & Martin, 1987, for a discussion of "micro-remedies" and "macro-remedies")

- Interpersonal relationships, through better understanding of the point of view of members of the other culture, gender, sexual orientation, and so on

■ Internal processes, such as attitudes

Psychologists have focused mostly on the latter two levels. While there is much theoretical writing at the first two levels, empirically there are only case studies (e.g., Jackson & Associates, 1992). Space limitations preclude reviewing such writing here.

Both mainstream and minority workers bring preconceived ideas and natural human tendencies to the workplace. Minorities, women, the disabled, and gay men and lesbian women are especially alert to real or apparent denigration. Minorities are more sensitive about ethnic jokes and demeaning language than are members of the mainstream (Triandis, Kurowski, Tecktiel, & Chan, 1933); such jokes and language can be a major cause of friction in the workplace (Smeltser & Leap, 1988). Minorities, women, and others also may be less inclined to give mainstream co-workers the benefit of the doubt because white men are the majority and control most of the channels of power in business. Minorities and women see establishment law- and rule-making processes as disadvantageous to them, adding to their antiestablishment feelings. Blacks are particularly likely to feel exploited, but white women also feel more exploited than white men (Buchholz, 1978).

Many African-Americans assume that most whites are prejudiced. Consider this quote summarizing an empirical study:

> A white foreman who knows that his black workers will assume he is prejudiced whenever he gives them the slightest opportunity to think so…simply cannot assume that his behavior will be given the benefit of the doubt. (Triandis, 1976b, p. 175)

The assumption that most whites are prejudiced is reflected also in the finding that African-Americans see less discrimination in organizations that have formal rules for hiring and firing than in organizations where supervisors make personnel decisions informally (Vinson & Holloway, 1977). Blacks assume that if a supervisor has discretion, they will be subjected to discrimination.

The framework presented in Figure 1 suggests numerous interventions for dealing with diversity. One can increase similarity by making sure that those who interact are similar on as many attributes as possible—in age, sex, dress, behavior, and subjective culture. In a job setting, this would suggest clustering those who are similar and increasing the perceived similarity of those who are dissimilar by administering several treatments, such as the following:

■ Downplaying any history of conflict by pointing out the inaccuracies of historical accounts; in the classroom that would mean lightly stressing past conflict and heavily stressing previous cooperation

■ Reducing cultural distance by identifying similarities in existing subjective cultures

■ Reducing the importance of cultural distance by identifying advantages (e.g., increased creativity) of groups consisting of dissimilar individuals

■ Learning about the other culture through culture assimilators (R. Albert, 1983; Fiedler, Mitchell, & Triandis, 1971); this approach has been found to improve relationships

■ Learning the other's language

■ Finding common friends

■ Stressing what people have in common and teaching each side to understand the point of view of the other side

■ Making sure that contact is equal status by eliminating symbols of status or by making people appear equal (e.g., by using uniforms, as the Japanese do)

- Identifying and stressing the presence of superordinate goals; this can be accomplished through cooperative learning, such as that provided by Aronson (e.g., Aronson & Gonzales, 1988) or D. W. Johnson and Johnson (1983), or through profit-sharing (bonuses that can only be obtained if both groups work together)

- Adjusting the opportunities for interaction so that if there is dissimilarity there is little interaction, and the greater the similarity the greater the opportunities for interaction; this strategy suggests the use of homogeneous job settings, linked to each other through cooperative tasks

- Making sure that the interaction situation is rewarding

- Making sure that authorities stress the desirability of successful contact; this can be accomplished by having authorities organize joint enjoyable activities, such as parties, celebrations, picnics, and sports events

Intercultural Training

Intercultural training is an intervention that has been developed extensively; a three-volume handbook (Landis & Brislin, 1983) is available to detail the methods of training. We will present here only a summary of the main types of intercultural training.

One can get some idea of what is likely to happen in another culture by reading descriptions of that culture. Some of these books are useful. For example, Rowland (1985) provides an adequate description of Japanese business etiquette. However, to become really effective in another culture, an employee needs

to understand much more about the factors that underlie behavior. Company-provided cross-cultural training is essential for achieving such a goal. The purpose of such training is to (a) reduce culture shock, (b) establish good interpersonal relationships among persons from different cultural backgrounds, and (c) improve task effectiveness.

Self/Cultural Insight. Self/cultural insight is a form of training that focuses on the self-view of the trainee. It exposes the trainee to opportunities to interact with people whose culture is very different and to discuss how the trainee's culture is different from other cultures. Discussions can focus on how aspects of the ecology force particular views of the self and on the consequences of such views for interethnic behaviors. One technique is to arrange for the trainee to interact with a trained actor whose culturally based behavior is the opposite of the culture of the trainee. For example, if the trainee comes from an individualist culture, the actor performs behaviors that are typical of people in collectivist cultures. The interaction is videotaped and the training session includes an analysis of the video to explain the cultural difference in concrete terms. The main advantage of this method is that it sensitizes trainees to their own culture; such self-knowledge is applicable to interaction with members of any culture. The disadvantages are that it does not focus on the specifics of behavior in other cultures, and it is relatively expensive, in both equipment and trainer time.

Attribution Training. Attribution training can be provided by culture assimilators (Fiedler, Mitchell, & Triandis, 1971). A complete discussion of this method can be found in Albert (1983). Briefly, a set of scenarios is developed in two ways: (a) by interviewing individuals who know both cultures well and telling them to think of an episode that changed their mind about their own or the other culture, or resulted in a serious misunderstanding or interpersonal difficulty; and (b) by researching empirical studies that have identified a particular cultural difference.

After a set of 200 or so scenarios has been constructed, focus groups, consisting of about 10 people from each culture, are asked to read each scenario and provide attributions that explain why the actors in the particular scenario acted this way. An examination of these attributions identifies those that are given more frequently by members of one culture than by members of the other culture.

Next, one assembles a questionnaire that consists of the scenarios and four attributions per scenario. If one intends to develop materials for the training of members of culture A to interact effectively with members of culture B, one includes one attribution from A and three attributions from B.

Samples of about 50 subjects from each of the two cultures are given this questionnaire and asked to select one attribution per scenario. Analysis of the frequencies with which the different attributions have been selected (e.g., using chi-squares) indicates if there is a cultural difference in the way attributions are used for each scenario. For example, if 60 percent of members of culture B selected the attribution that was hypothesized to be an attribution commonly used in culture B, but only 20 percent of the members of culture A selected this attribution, there is a clear case of a cultural difference.

This scenario and the four attributions can then be used in training. If a cultural difference is not obtained in that step, the scenario is discarded. Thus, one may end with a training instrument consisting of perhaps 75 validated scenarios and the corresponding attributions.

Training can be done by presenting the scenario, the attributions, and, corresponding to each attribution, some feedback that explains why the attribution is correct (from the point of view of culture B) or incorrect.

A programmed learning format, in which the trainee turns pages to obtain the feedback found on particular pages, is used in either a book or a computer presentation. When the attribution is wrong, the feedback is brief, such as, "No, try another answer." When the selected attribution is correct, the feedback is rather complete, as much as a full page. This feedback explains cultural differences and why the correct attribution is most likely to be used in that culture.

Validation of the training using control groups has found that those who work through the assimilator do learn, and the learning makes them more comfortable and effective when they interact with members of the other culture. The disadvantage is the expensive preparation of the episodes. However, once the validated episodes are available, they can train large numbers of people.

The advantage of this form of training is that it is valid, effective, and teaches about a specific culture.

One can also provide general culture training in a culture assimilator format. Such training is applicable to any culture. Brislin, Cushner, Cherrie, and Yong (1986) have developed 100 episodes that deal with culture training in general. Validation of the general assimilator has provided encouraging results.

Another disadvantage of culture assimilator training is that unmotivated people are not likely to work through it. Some people find reading written material boring. They prefer oral learning and direct experiences with members of other cultures.

The importance of motivation cannot be overestimated. In one study, a group of high school students who were going to Central America to vaccinate villagers were given the assimilators to take home and work through. Those who had never been to Latin America showed no improvement, but those who had been to Latin America the previous summer benefited a great deal. This difference was explained by noting that taking the assimilator home does not guarantee that the trainee will actually work through the assimilator, particularly when packing and saying good-bye to friends may interfere with such activities. However, those who had been to Latin America before had many questions about their previous experience and were eager to understand the other culture. Thus, they not only worked through the assimilator but also gained cognitive categories on which to hook the new information in their existing cognitive framework.

For those who prefer oral presentation of the information, a useful way to use the assimilator is to role-play the scenarios and discuss the attributions.

Experiential Training. This training essentially takes the form of contact with members of the other culture, under conditions in which the contact can be beneficial to the relationship. Mere contact usually does not result in good relationships and is sometimes counterproductive. However, when contact occurs under specific conditions, as outlined in a review by Stephan (1985, p. 643), it can be beneficial.

For contact to be beneficial, a number of factors must be present. First, it is helpful to have an equal number of members of each group so that there are no minorities in the training situation. Second, contact must provide opportunities to interact with the other group under conditions that maximize positive outcomes. Such conditions include equal status and cooperative, intimate, voluntary contact, with superordinate goals, among individuals who are similar in beliefs and equal in competence, and sponsorship by authorities that support good intergroup relations. Third, the positive outcomes must occur in a variety of contexts and with a variety of ingroup and outgroup members. Otherwise, the trainees may consider the members of the other ethnic group, with whom they have interacted so

effectively, as special cases and not representative of most of the other members of that ethnic group.

The advantage of this method of training is that it has very high face validity; the disadvantage is that it is very expensive. The amount of training time, as well as trainer time, has to be substantial in order to obtain some positive results.

Behavior Modification. One can identify behaviors that offend each side and use behavior modification techniques to reduce their frequency, as well as identify behaviors that are welcomed by each side and use such techniques to increase their frequency.

This is the most clinical of the methods. It is very time-consuming for both trainee and trainer because it requires one-on-one training over time to extinguish undesirable behaviors and to increase the frequency of desirable behaviors. Furthermore, one does not develop a cognitive framework that explains why people in the other culture value and devalue particular behaviors. In attribution training, one does develop such a framework, so that one can generalize to behaviors that one has not yet learned. On the other hand, attribution training does not guarantee a change in behavior. One might know that a behavior is undesirable and still do it because one is responding under the control of habits. Thus, the combination of the two types of training is often desirable.

Exposure to the Strengths of Each Group. This method focuses on each group learning to appreciate the strengths of other groups. This requires focusing on dimensions that each group values and showing that the other group has desirable attributes on such dimensions.

The disadvantage here is that it may be difficult to identify such dimensions and even more difficult to generate experiences that make the dimensions salient. On the other hand, when this method is used in conjunction with other methods, it may be helpful.

Effectiveness of Cross-cultural Training

There is evidence that cross-cultural training is effective (Black & Mendenhall, 1990), yet it is not widely used by U.S. corporations. It is estimated that only 15 percent of expatriate managers receive some predeparture training, and even that is of short duration (less than one month). The result is that somewhere between 30 and 50 percent of the expatriates leave their assignment early at a cost to themselves (in lower self-esteem), their families, and their corporations that is estimated to be as high as $500,000 per case. It is estimated that U.S. corporations lose $2 billion each year because of expatriate failure.

By contrast, Japanese and Korean companies use cross-cultural training extensively. Some firms pay their employees $50,000 plus expenses to spend full time for one year to learn English and learn about American culture. Failure rates are insignificant.

Optimizing Intercultural Training—Research Gaps

A mixture of these five types of training is likely to be optimal, but research has yet to identify the optimal mixtures for different ethnic group relationships and different situations (Triandis, 1977b). We do not know, for example, how much of each of these forms of training to provide, to whom, when, where, by whom, and at what cost to provide them, and what monetary benefits might result from such training.

Nor do we know how to order the different forms of training. It may be the case that the first type to be used should be self/cultural insight training in order to provide the motivation for attribution training. Once one has learned something about the other culture, behavior modification training may be the best next step, followed by experiential training that includes some material exposing each group to the strengths of the other group.

There is also some doubt about how much language training one should receive. In general, knowing the language increases the extent one feels comfortable in other cultures and reduces culture shock. However, extensive training may take years and may not be justified in a short overseas assignment. Undoubtedly, the complexity of who is to be trained (i.e., selection of candidates), by what method, in what sequence, in what amount, when (e.g., after the person has arrived abroad), and where (in a lab or on the job) will require extensive future research.

Conclusion

Clearly, this chapter reflects what has already been done in this area, and what has been done reflects what is in the literature. There is more known about sexual harassment than is known about the psychosocial adjustments of minorities or about what efforts women and others must make to maintain their positions in mainstream or majority organizations. The trends noted here of decreasing publication of research on African-Americans and on gender issues are quite discouraging. Already there is some evidence that women (Rosen, Miguel, & Peirce, 1989) and minority managers are opting out of majority/mainstream organizations. Such losses seriously affect organizations' abilities to respond to changing work conditions and reflect an intolerance of differences that diminishes us as a diverse society. As industrial and organizational psychologists themselves become more diverse, there will be increased attention to some of these research gaps.

We thank Taylor Cox, Bernardo Ferdman, and Sharon Lobel for valuable comments made on an earlier draft.

References

Adler, N. J. (1990). *International dimensions of organizational behavior* (2nd ed.). Boston, MA: Kent.

Adorno, T., Frenkel-Brunswik, E., Levinson, D. J., & Sanford, R. N. (1950). *The authoritarian personality.* New York: Harper & Row.

Aikin, O. (1988, May). A positive response to AIDS in the workplace. *Personnel Management*, 52–55.

Albert, R. (1983). The intercultural sensitizer or culture assimilator: A cognitive approach. In D. Landis & R. W. Brislin (Eds.), *Handbook of intercultural training* (Vol. 2, pp. 186–217). New York: Pergamon Press.

Albert, S. (1977). A temporal comparison theory. *Psychological Review, 84*, 485–503.

Allen, J. P., & Turner, E. (1990). Where diversity reigns. *American Demographics, 12*(8), 34–38.

Amir, Y. (1969). Contact hypothesis in intergroup relations. *Psychological Bulletin, 71*, 319–342.

Argyle, M. (1988). *Bodily communication.* London: Methuen.

Aronson, E., & Gonzalez, A. (1988). Segregation, jigsaw and the Mexican-American experience. In P. A. Katz & D. T. Taylor (Eds.), *Eliminating racism* (pp. 301–314). New York: Plenum.

Asante, M. K., & Davis, A. (1989). Encounters in the interracial workplace. In M. K. Asante & W. B. Gudykunst (Eds.), *Handbook of international and intercultural communication* (pp. 374–391). Newbury Park, CA: Sage.

Atkinson, D. R., Neville, H., & Casas, A. (1991). The mentorship of ethnic minorities in professional psychology. *Professional Psychology Research and Practice, 22*(4), 336–348.

Babiker, I. E., Cox, J. L., & Miller, P. McG. (1980). The measurement of cultural distance and its relationship to medical consultations, symptomatology, and examination performance of overseas students at Edinburgh University. *Social Psychiatry, 15*, 109–116.

Bandura, A. (1989). Perceived self-efficacy in the exercise of personal agency. *The Psychologist:*

Bulletin of the British Psychological Society, 10, 411–424.

Bantel, K. A., & Jackson, S. E. (1989). Top management and innovations in banking: Does the composition of the top team make a difference? *Strategic Management Journal, 10*, 107–124.

Barnlund, D. C. (1988). Communication in a global village. In L. A. Samovar & R. E. Porter (Eds.), *Intercultural communication: A reader.* Belmont, CA: Wadsworth.

Bartol, K. M., & Butterfield, D. A. (1976). Sex effects in evaluating leaders. *Journal of Applied Psychology, 61*(4), 446–454.

Beisecker, T. (1969). *Communication and conflict in interpersonal negotiations.* Paper presented to the Speech Communication Association, New York.

Berlyne, D. (1980). Psychological aesthetics. In H. C. Triandis & W. J. Lonner (Eds.), *Handbook of cross-cultural psychology* (pp. 323–362). Boston: Allyn & Bacon.

Berry, J. W. (1980). Acculturation as varieties of adaptation. In A. Padilla (Ed.), *Acculturation: Theory, models, and some new findings* (pp. 9–25). Boulder, CO: Westview.

Berry, J. W., Kim, U., Power, S., Young, M., & Bujaki, M. (1989). Acculturation attitudes in plural societies. *Applied Psychology, 38*, 185–206.

Berry, J. W., Poortinga, Y., Segall, M., & Dasen, P. (1992). *Cross-cultural psychology.* New York: Cambridge Press.

Bettelheim, B., & Janowitz, J. (1950). *Dynamics of prejudice.* New York: Harper.

Bhatnagar, D. (1988). Professional women in organizations: Paradigms for research and action. *Sex Roles, 18*(5/6), 343–353.

Bigoness, W. J. (1976). Effect of applicant's sex, race and performance on employers' performance ratings: Some additional findings. *Journal of Applied Psychology, 61*, 80–84.

Billings, D. K. (1989). Individualism and group orientation. In D. M. Keats, D. Munroe, & L. Mann (Eds.), *Heterogeneity in cross-cultural psychology* (pp. 92–103). Lisse, The Netherlands: Swets & Zeitlinger.

Black, J. S., & Mendenhall, M. (1990). Cross-cultural training effectiveness: A review and a theoretical framework for future research. *Academy of Management Review, 15,* 113–136.

Boyer, E. L. (1991, October 31). *Campus life: In search of community.* Lecture given at the University of Illinois, Urbana.

Braddock, J. H. II, & McPartland, J. M. (1987). How minorities continue to be excluded from equal employment opportunities: Research on labor market and institutional barriers. *Journal of Social Issues, 43*(1), 5–39.

Brewer, M. B. (1991). The social self: On being the same and different at the same time. *Personality and Social Psychology Bulletin, 17,* 475–482.

Brewer, M., & Campbell, D. T. (1976). *Ethnocentrism and intergroup attitudes.* New York: Wiley.

Brislin, R. W., Cushner, K., Cherrie, C., & Yong, M. (1986). *Intercultural interactions: A practical guide.* Beverly Hills, CA: Sage.

Brody, J. E. (1992, August 11). To predict divorce, ask 125 questions. *New York Times,* p. C–1.

Buchholz, R. A. (1978). An empirical study of contemporary beliefs about work in American society. *Journal of Applied Psychology, 63,* 219–227.

Bulkeley, W. M. (1991, October 25). Lotus creates controversy by extending benefits to partners of gay employees. *Wall Street Journal,* pp. B–1, B–10.

Burke, R. J. (1984). Mentors in organizations. *Groups and Organizational Studies, 9*(3), 353–372.

Burke, R. J., McKeen, C. A., & McKennan, C. S. (1990). Sex differences and cross-sex effects on mentoring: Some preliminary data. *Psychological Reports, 67,* 1011–1023.

Bursten, B. (1985). Psychiatric injury in the women's workplace. *Bulletin of the American Academy of Psychiatry and the Law, 13*(4), 399–406.

Burton, M. L., Moore, C. C., Whiting, J. W. M., & Romney, A. K. (1992, February). *World cultural regions.* Paper presented to the Santa Fe, NM, meetings of the Society for Cross-Cultural Research.

Byrne, D. (1971). *The attraction paradigm.* New York: Academic Press.

Campbell, D. T., & Levine, R. A. (1968). Ethnocentrism and intergroup relations. In R. Abelson, E. Aronson, W. J. McGuire, T. M. Newcomb, M. T. Rosenberg, & P. H. Tannenbaum (Eds.), *Theories of cognitive consistency: A sourcebook.* Chicago: Rand McNally.

Carden, A. D. (1990). Mentoring and adult career development: The evolution of a theory. *Counseling Psychologist, 18*(2), 275–299.

Castellow, W. A., Wuensch, K. L., & Moore, C. H. (1990). Effects of physical attractiveness of the plaintiff and defendant in sexual harassment judgments. *Journal of Social Behavior and Personality, 15*(6), 547–562.

Chusmir, L. H., Moore, D. P., & Adams, J. S. (1990). Research on working women: A report card of 22 journals. *Sex Roles, 22*(3/4), 167–175.

Clode, Diane. (1988). *Sexual harassment in the federal government: An update.* Washington, DC: Office of Merit Systems Review and Study.

Collins, N. W. (1983). *Professional women and their mentors.* Englewood Cliffs, NJ: Prentice-Hall.

Cox, T. H., Jr., & Blake, S. (1991). Managing cultural diversity: Implications for organizational competitiveness. *The Executive, 5,* 45–56.

Cox, T. H., Lobel, S. A., & McLeod, P. L. (1991). Effects of ethnic group cultural differences on cooperative and competitive behavior on a group task. *Academy of Management Journal, 34,* 827–847.

Cox, T. H., Jr., & Nkomo, S. M. (1990). Invisible men and women: A status report on race as a variable in organization behavior research. *Journal of Organizational Behavior, 11,* 419–431.

Cox, T. H., Jr., & Nkomo, S. M. (1991). A race and gender-group analysis of the early experience of MBAs. *Work and Occupations, 18,* 431–446.

Craft, J. A., Benecki, T. J., & Shkop, Y. M. (1980). Who hires the seriously handicapped? *Industrial Relations, 19,* 94–99.

Crocker, J., & McGraw, K. M. (1984). What's good for the goose is not good for the gander. *American Behavioral Scientist, 27*(3), 357–369.

Crull, P. (1982). Stress effects of sexual harassment on the job: Implications for counseling. *American Journal of Orthopsychiatry, 52*(3), 539–544.

D'Angeljan, A., & Tucker, G. (1973). Communicating across cultures: An empirical investigation. *Journal of Cross-Cultural Psychology, 3,* 121–136.

Day, J. C. (1992). Population projections of the United States, by age, sex, race, and Hispanic origin: 1992–2050. (Current population Report P25–1092). Washington, DC: Bureau of the Census.

Debate: Ways men and women lead. (1992, January–February). *Harvard Business Review,* pp. 150–160.

De Necochea, G. (1988). An analysis of the impact of self-efficacy, acculturation and gender on the formation of career-related social networks by Hispanic managers. (Doctoral dissertation, University of California at Santa Barbara). *Dissertation Abstracts International, 50,* 02A, 482.

Devine, P. G. (1989). Stereotypes and prejudice: Their automatic and controlled components. *Journal of Personality and Social Psychology, 56,* 5–18.

Diaz-Guerrero, R. (1973). Interpreting coping styles across nations. *International Journal of Psychology, 8,* 193–203.

Diener, E., Emmons, R. A., Larsen, R. J., & Griffin, S. (1985). The satisfaction with life scale: A measure of life satisfaction. *Journal of Personality Assessment, 49,* 71–76.

Dipboye, R. L. (1987). Problems and progress of women in management. In K. S. Koziara, M. Moscow, & L. Tanner (Eds.), *Working women: Past, present, and future.* Washington, DC: Bureau of National Affairs.

Dovidio, J. F., Gaertner, S. L., Anastasio, P. A., & Sanitioso, R. (1992). Cognitive and motivational bases of bias: Implications of aversive racism for attitudes toward Hispanics. In S. B. Knouse, P. Rosenfeld, & A. L. Culbertson (Eds.), *Hispanics in the workplace* (pp. 75–108). Newbury Park, CA: Sage.

Dreher, G. F., & Ash, R. A. (1990). A comparative study of mentoring among men and women in managerial, professional, and technical positions. *Journal of Applied Psychology, 75*(5), 539–546.

Dunbar, E. (1992). Adjustment and satisfaction of expatriate U.S. personnel. *International Journal of Intercultural Relations, 16,* 1–16.

Dziech, B.W., & Weiner, L. (1990). *The lecherous professor* (2nd ed.). Urbana: University of Illinois Press.

Eagly, A. H. (1987). *Sex differences in social behavior: A social role interpretation.* Hillsdale, NJ: Erlbaum.

Eagly, A. H., Makhijani, M. G., & Klonsky, B. G. (1992). Gender and the evaluation of leaders: A meta-analysis. *Psychological Bulletin, 111*(1), 3–22.

Epstein, C. F. (1970). *Woman's place: Options and limits in professional careers.* Berkeley: University of California Press.

Equal Employment Opportunity Commission. (1980). Discrimination because of sex under Title VII of the Civil Rights Act of 1964, as amended; adoption of interim interpretive guidelines. *Federal Register, 45,* 25024–25025.

Equal Employment Opportunity Commission. (1991). *Job patterns for minorities and women in private industry 1990.* Washington, DC: U.S. Government Printing Office.

Espinoza, J. A., & Garza, R. T. (1985). Social group salience and interethnic cooperation. *Journal of Experimental Social Psychology, 21,* 380–392.

Farley, L. (1978). *Sexual shakedown.* New York: McGraw-Hill.

Ferdman, B. M. (1989). Affirmative action and the challenge of the color-blind perspective. In F. A. Blanchard & F. Crosby (Eds.), *Affirmative action in perspective* (pp. 169–176). New York: Springer Verlag.

Ferdman, B. M. (1990). Literacy and cultural identity. *Harvard Educational Review, 60,* 181–204.

Ferdman, B. M. (1992). The dynamics of ethnic diversity in organizations: Toward integrative models. In K. Kelley (Ed.), *Issues, theory, and research in industrial/organizational psychology* (pp. 339–384). Amsterdam: North Holland.

Ferdman, B. M., & Cortes, A. C. (1992). Culture and identity among Hispanic managers in an Anglo business. In S. Knouse, P. Rosenfeld, & A. Culbertson (Eds.), *Hispanics in the workplace* (pp. 246–277). Newbury Park, CA: Sage.

Fernandez, J. P. (1981). *Racism and sexism in corporate life.* Lexington, MA: Lexington Books.

Festinger, L. (1954). A theory of social comparison processes. *Human Relations, 7,* 117–140.

Fiedler, F. E., Meuwese, W., & Oonk, S. (1961). An exploratory study of group creativity in laboratory tasks. *Acta Psychologica, 18,* 100–119.

Fiedler, F. E., Mitchell, T., & Triandis, H. C. (1971). The culture assimilator: An approach to cross-cultural training. *Journal of Applied Psychology, 55,* 95–102.

Fine, M. G., Johnson, F. L., & Ryan, M. S. (1990). Cultural diversity in the workplace. *Public Personnel Management, 19*(3), 305–319.

Fisher, B. A. (1980). *Small group decision making. Communication and the group process* (2nd ed.). New York: McGraw-Hill.

Fiske, A. P. (1991). *Structures of social life.* New York: Free Press.

Furnham, A., & Bochner, S. (1986). *Culture shock: Psychological reactions to unfamiliar environments.* London: Methuen.

Gaertner, S. L., Mann, J., Murrell, A., & Dovidio, J. F. (1989). Reducing intergroup bias: The benefits of recategorization. *Journal of Personality and Social Psychology, 57,* 239–249.

Geertz, C. (1973). *The interpretation of cultures.* New York: Basic Books.

Gibbons, A. (1992). Key issue: Mentoring. *Science, 255,* p. 1368.

Goldstein, I., & Associates. (1989). *Training and development in organizations.* San Francisco: Jossey-Bass.

Goldstein, I. L., & Gilliam, P. (1990). Training system issues in the year 2000. *American Psychologist, 45,* 134–143.

Gordon, M. M. (1964). *Assimilation in American life.* New York: Oxford University Press.

Gould, K. H. (1988, March–April). Asian and Pacific Islanders: Myth and reality. *Social Work,* pp. 142–147.

Grieco, A. (1987). Scope and nature of sexual harassment in nursing. *Journal of Sex Research, 23*(2), 261–266.

Gruber, J. E., & Bjorn, L. (1982). Blue-collar blues: The sexual harassment of women autoworkers. *Work and Occupations, 9*(3), 271–298.

Gudykunst, W., & Nishida, T. (1986). Attributional confidence in low and high context cultures. *Human Communication Research, 12*(4), 525–549.

Gudykunst. W., & Ting-Toomey, S. (1988). *Culture and interpersonal communication.* Newbury Park, CA: Sage.

Gurney, J. N. (1985). Not one of the guys: The female researcher in a male-dominated setting. *Qualitative Sociology, 8*(1), 42–62.

Gutek, B.A. (1985). *Sex and the workplace.* San Francisco: Jossey-Bass.

Gutek, B. A., Cohen, A. G., & Konrad, A. M. (1990). Predicting social-sexual behavior at work: A contact hypothesis. *Academy of Management Journal, 33*(3), 560–577.

Gutek, B. A., & Morasch, B. (1982). Sex-ratios, sex-role spillover, and sexual harassment of women at work. *Journal of Social Issues, 38*(4), 55–74.

Gutman, H. G. (1977). *Work, culture and society in industrializing America.* New York: Vintage.

Hagen, R. L., & Kahn, A. (1975). Discrimination against competent women. *Journal of Applied Social Psychology, 5,* 363–376.

Hahn, H. (1983). Paternalism and public policy. *Society, 20,* 36–45.

Hall, M. (1986). The lesbian corporate experience. *Journal of Homosexuality, 12*(3/4), 59–75.

Hamilton, D. L. (1982). *Cognitive process in stereotyping and intergroup behavior.* Hillsdale, NJ: Erlbaum.

Hayles, R. (1991, October 1). *Diversity work. Why?* Lecture presented at the conference organized by Personnel Decisions "Assessment: A Changing View," Minneapolis, MN.

Hecht, M. L., & Ribeau, S. (1984). Ethnic communication: A comparative analysis of satisfying communication. *International Journal of Intercultural Relations, 8*(2), 135–151.

Hecht, M. L., Ribeau, S., & Sedano, M. V. (1990). A Mexican American perspective on interethnic communication. *International Journal of Intercultural Relations, 14,* 31–55.

Helson, H. (1964). *Adaptation-level theory.* New York: Harper & Row.

Herskovits, M. J. (1955). *Cultural anthropology.* New York: Knopf.

Hewstone, M. (1989). *Causal attribution: From cognitive processes to collective beliefs.* Oxford: Blackwell.

Hoffman, L. R., Harburg, E., & Maier, N. R. F. (1962). Differences and disagreements as factors in creative group problem-solving. *Journal of Abnormal & Social Psychology, 64,* 206–214.

Hoffman, L. R., & Maier, N. R. F. (1961). Quality and acceptance of problem solutions by members of homogeneous groups and heterogeneous groups. *Journal of Abnormal and Social Psychology, 62,* 401–407.

Hofstede, G. (1980). *Culture's consequences.* Newbury Park, CA: Sage.

Hofstede, G. (1991). *Cultures and organizations.* New York: McGraw-Hill.

Hrop, S., & Rakos, R. F. (1985). The influence of race in the social evaluation of assertion in conflict situations. *Behavior Therapy, 16*(5), 478–493.

Hunsicker, J. F., Jr. (1990, August). Ready or not: The ADA. *Personnel Journal,* 81–86.

Ibarra, H. (1992). Homophily and differential returns: Sex differences in network structure and access in an advertising firm. *Administrative Science Quarterly, 37,* 422–447.

Inkeles, A., & Smith, D. H. (1974). *Becoming modern.* Cambridge, MA: Harvard University Press.

International Center for the Disabled. (1986). *The ICD survey of disabled Americans: Bringing disabled Americans into the mainstream.* New York: Louis Harris & Associates.

Jackson, S. E. (1991a, September 29). *Implications of work force diversity for assessment practices.* Lecture given at the conference organized by Personnel Decisions "Assessment: A Changing View." Minneapolis, MN.

Jackson, S. E. (1991b). Team composition in organizational settings: Issues in managing an increasingly diverse work force. In S. Worchel, W. Wood, & J. Simpson (Eds.), *Group process and productivity* (pp. 138–171). Newbury Park, CA: Sage.

Jackson, S. E., & Alvarez, E. B. (1992). Working through diversity as a strategic imperative. In S. E. Jackson & Associates (Eds.), *Diversity in the workplace: Human resources initiatives* (pp. 13–36). New York: Guilford Press.

Jackson, S. E., & Associates (1992). *Diversity in the workplace: Human resources initiatives.* New York: Guilford Press.

Jackson, S. E., Brett, J. F., Sessa, V. I., Cooper, D. M., Julin, J. A., & Peyronnin, K. (1991). Some differences make a difference: Individual dissimilarity and group heterogeneity as correlates of recruitment, promotions and turnover. *Journal of Applied Psychology. 76,* 675–689.

Jackson, S. E., Stone, V. K., & Alvarez, E. B. (1993). Socialization amidst diversity: Impact of demographics on work team oldtimers and newcomers. In L. L. Cummings & B. M. Staw (Eds.), *Research in organizational behavior* (Vol. 15). Greenwich, CT: JAI Press.

Jago, A. G., & Vroom, V. H. (1982). Sex differences in the incidence and evaluation of participative leader behavior. *Journal of Applied Psychology, 67*(6), 776–783.

James, K., & Khoo, G. (1991). Identity-related influences on the success of minority workers in primarily nonminority organizations. *Hispanic Journal of Behavioral Sciences, 13*(2), 169–192.

Jamieson, D., & O'Mara, J. (1991). *Managing workforce 2000.* San Francisco, CA: Jossey-Bass.

Janis, I. L. (1982). *Groupthink* (2nd ed.). Houghton Mifflin.

Johnson, C. L., & Barer, B. M. (1990). Families and networks among older inner-city blacks. *Gerontologist, 30*(6), 726–733.

Johnson, D. W., & Johnson, R. T. (1983). The socialization and achievement crises: Are cooperative learning experiences the solution? In L. Bickman (Ed.), *Applied social psychology annual* (pp. 119–164). Beverly Hills, CA: Sage.

Johnson, L., & Remus, W. (1985). A comparison of the problems faced by first-year men and women graduate business students. *College Student Journal, 19*(4), 432–437.

Johnston, W. B., & Packer, A. (1987). *Workforce 2000: Work and workers in the 21st century.* Indianapolis: Hudson Institute.

Juni, S., Brannon, R., & Roth, M. M. (1988). Sexual and racial discrimination in service-seeking interactions: A field study in fast food and commercial establishments. *Psychological Reports, 63*(1), 71–76.

Kanter, R. M. (1977a). *Men and women of the corporation.* New York: Basic Books.

Kanter, R. M. (1977b). Some effects of proportion on group life: Skewed sex ratios and responses to token women. *American Journal of Sociology, 5,* 965–990.

Kanter, R. M. (1981). Women and the structure of organizations: Explorations in theory and behavior. In O. Grusky & G. A. Miller (Eds.), *The sociology of organizations* (pp. 395–424). New York: Free Press.

Katz, I., Hass, R. G., & Bailey, J. (1988). Attitudinal ambivalence and behavior toward people with disabilities. In H. E. Yuker (Ed.), *Attitudes toward persons with disabilities* (pp. 47–57). New York: Springer.

Katz, I., Wackenhut, J., & Glass, D. C. (1986). An ambivalence-amplification theory of behavior toward the stigmatized. In S. Worchel & W. G.

Austin (Eds.), *Psychology of intergroup relations* (pp. 103–117). Chicago: Nelson Hall.

Katz, P. A., & Taylor, D. A. (1988). *Eliminating racism.* New York: Plenum Press.

Kavanagh, K. H., & Kennedy, P. H. (1992). *Promoting cultural diversity.* Newbury Park: Sage.

Kinsey, A. C., Pomeroy, W. B., & Martin, C. E. (1948). *Sexual behavior in the human male.* Philadelphia: Saunders.

Kinsey, A. C., Pomeroy, W. B., Martin, C. E., & Gebhart, P. H. (1953). *Sexual behavior in the human female.* Philadelphia: Saunders.

Kirschenman, J., & Neckerman, K. M. (1991). "We'd love to hire them, but ...": The meaning of race for employers. In C. Jencks & P. E. Peterson (Eds.), *The urban underclass* (pp. 203–231). Washington, DC: Brookings Institution.

Kluckhohn, F., & Strodtbeck, F. (1961). *Variations in value orientations.* Evanston, IL: Row-Peterson.

Knouse, S. B. (1991) Racial, ethnic, and gender issues in the military. *International Journal of Intercultural Relations, 15*(4).

Knouse, S., Rosenfeld, P., & Culbertson, A. (Eds.). (1992). *Hispanics in the workplace.* Newbury Park, CA: Sage.

Koenig, A., & Schalock, R. L. (1991). Supported employment: Equal opportunities for severely disabled men and women. *International Labour Review, 130,* 21–37.

Kohl, J. P., & Greenlaw, P. S. (1992, Spring). The Americans with Disabilities Act of 1990: Implications for managers. *Sloan Management Review,* pp. 87–90.

Koontz, E. D. (1981). *A step toward equality: A progress report.* Washington, DC: National Manpower Institute.

Kram, K. E. (1985). *Mentoring at work.* Glenview, IL: Scott, Foresman.

Kronenberger, G. K. (1991, June). Out of the closet. *Personnel Journal,* pp. 40–44.

Lambert, W. E., & Taylor, D. (1990). *Coping with cultural and racial diversity in urban America.* New York: Praeger.

Landis, D., & Brislin, R. W. (Eds.). (1983). *Handbook of intercultural training.* New York: Pergamon Press.

Landis, D., McGrew, P., Day, H., Savage, J., & Saral, T. (1976). Word meanings in black and white. In H. C. Triandis (Ed.), *Variations in black and white perceptions of the social*

environment (pp. 45–80). Urbana: University of Illinois Press.

Landy, F. J., & Farr, J. L. (1980). Performance rating. *Psychological Bulletin, 87,* 72–107.

Langer, E. J. (1983). *The psychology of control.* Beverly Hills, CA: Sage.

Levine, M. P. (1979). Employment discrimination against gay men. *International Review of Modern Sociology, 9*(2), 151–163.

Levitan, S. A., & Taggart, R. (1977). Employment problems of disabled persons. *Monthly Labor Review, 110,* 3–13.

Levitt, E. E., & Klassen, A. D., Jr. (1974). Public attitudes toward homosexuality: Part of the 1970 national survey of the Institute for Sex Research. *Journal of Homosexuality, 1,* 131–139.

Lin, T. R., Dobbins, G. H., & Farh, J. L. (1992). A field study of race and age similarity effects on interview ratings in conventional and situational interviews. *Journal of Applied Psychology, 77,* 363–371.

Linville, P. W., & Jones, E. E. (1980). Polarized appraisals of outgroup members. *Journal of Personality and Social Psychology, 38,* 689–703.

Livneh, H. (1988). A dimensional perspective on the origin of negative attitudes toward persons with disabilities. In H. E. Yuker (Ed.), *Attitudes toward persons with disabilities* (pp. 35–46). New York: Springer.

Lobel, S. A. (1993). Sexuality at work: Where do we go from here? *Journal of Vocational Behavior, 42* (1), 136–152.

Loden, M., & Rosener, J. B. (1991). *Workforce America! Managing employee diversity as a vital resource.* Homewood, IL: Business One Irwin.

Lonner, W. J. (1980). The search for psychological universals. In H. C. Triandis & W. W. Lambert (Eds.), *Handbook of cross-cultural psychology* (Vol. 1, pp. 143–204). Boston: Allyn & Bacon.

Lott, A. J., & Lott, B. E. (1965). Group cohesiveness and interpersonal attraction: A review of relationships with antecedent and consequent variables. *Psychological Bulletin, 64,* 259–302

Maass, A., Salvi, D., Arcuri, L., & Semin, G. (1989). Language use in intergroup contexts: The linguistic intergroup bias. *Journal of Personality and Social Psychology, 57,* 981–993.

MacKinnon, C. A. (1979). *Sexual harassment of working women: A case of sex discrimination.* New Haven: Yale University Press.

Majors, R., & Billson, J. M. (1992). *Cool pose: The dilemmas of black manhood in America.* New York: Lexington Books.

Marin, G., & Marin, B. V. (1991). *Research with Hispanic populations.* Newbury Park, CA: Sage.

Marin, G., & Triandis, H. C. (1985). Allocentrism as an important characteristic of the behavior of Latin Americans and Hispanics. In R. Diaz-Guerrero (Ed.), *Cross-cultural and national studies of social psychology* (pp. 85–104). Amsterdam: North Holland.

Marks, G., & Miller, N. (1987). Ten years of research on the false-consensus effect: An empirical and theoretical review. *Psychological Bulletin, 102,* 72–90.

Markus, H., & Kitayama, S. (1991). Culture and self: Implications for cognition, emotion and motivation. *Psychological Review, 98,* 224–253.

Martin, P. Y., & Shanahan, K. A. (1983). Transcending the effects of sex composition in small groups. *Social Work with Groups, 6,* 19–32.

Martini, M., Behnke, R. R., & King, P. E. (1992). The communication of public speaking anxiety: Perceptions of Asian and American speakers. *Communication Quarterly, 40*(3), 279–288.

McCarthy, H. (1988). Attitudes that affect employment opportunities for persons with disabilities. In H. E. Yuker (Ed.), *Attitudes toward persons with disabilities* (pp. 246–261). New York: Springer.

McCormick, A. E., & Kinloch, G. C. (1986). Interracial contact in the customer-clerk situation. *Journal of Social Psychology, 126*(4), 551–553.

McGrath, J. E. (1984). *Groups: Interaction and performance.* Englewood Cliffs, NJ: Prentice-Hall.

McIlhone, M. (1984). Barriers to advancement: The obstacle course. In R. Ritchie (Chair), *The successful woman manager: how did she get there?* Symposium conducted at 92nd annual meeting of the American Psychological Association.

McKinney, K. (1990). Sexual harassment of university faculty by colleagues and students. *Sex Roles, 23*(7/8), 421–438.

McKirnan, D. J., & Peterson, P. L. (1988). Stress, expectancies, and vulnerability to substance abuse: A test of a model among homosexual men. *Journal of Abnormal Psychology, 97*(4), 461–466.

McLeod, P. L., & Lobel, S. A. (1992, August). The effects of ethnic diversity on idea generation in small groups. *Academy of Management Best Papers Proceedings.*

McNeely, R. L. (1987). Predictors of job satisfaction among three racial/ethnic groups of professional female human service workers. *Journal of Sociology and Social Welfare, 14*(4), 115–136.

Merit Systems Protection Board. (1981). *Sexual harassment in the federal workplace.* Washington, DC: Office of Merit Systems Review and Studies.

Moore, D. P., & Rickel, A. U. (1980). Characteristics of women in traditional and nontraditional managerial roles. *Personnel Psychology, 33,* 317–333.

Mudrick, N. R. (1983). Disabled women. *Society, 20,* 51–55.

Murphy, R. F., Scheer, J., Murphy, Y., & Mack, R. (1988). Physical disability and social liminality: A study in the rituals of adversity. *Social Science and Medicine, 26,* 235–242.

Nahavandi, A., & Malekzadeh, A. R. (1988). Acculturation in mergers and acquisitions. *Academy of Management Review, 13*(1), 79–90.

Nelton, S. (1992, September). Winning with diversity. *Nation's Business,* pp. 18–24.

Newcomb, T. (1956). The prediction of interpersonal attraction. *American Psychologist, 11,* 575–586.

Nieva, V. F., & Gutek, B. A. (1980). Sex effects on evaluation. *Academy of Management Review, 5*(2), 267–276.

Nieva, V. F., & Gutek, B. A. (1981). *Women and work: A psychological perspective.* New York: Praeger.

Nisbett, R. E., & Ross, L. (1980). *Human inference: Strategies and shortcomings of social judgment.* Englewood Cliffs, NJ: Prentice-Hall.

Nkomo, S. M. (1992). The emperor has no clothes: Rewriting "race in organizations." *Academy of Management Review, 17*(3), 487–513.

Noe, R. A. (1988). An investigation of the determinants of successful assigned mentoring relationships. *Personnel Psychology, 41*(3), 457–479.

Oberg, K. (1960). Culture shock: Adjustment to new cultural environments. *Practical Anthropology, 7,* 177–182.

O'Brien, F. P., & Vest, M. J. (1988). A proposed scale to measure beliefs about the consequences of employing homosexuals. *Psychological Reports, 63*(2), 547–551.

Offe, C. (1976). *Industry and inequality: The achievement principle in work and social status.* London: Edward Arnold.

Offermann, L. R., & Gowing, M. K. (1990). Organizations of the future: Changes and challenges. *American Psychologist, 45,* 95–108.

O'Hare, W. (1990). A new look at Asian Americans. *American Demographics, 12*(10), 26–31.

Oliver, M. (1990). *The politics of disablement: A sociological approach.* New York: St. Martin's Press.

O'Reilly, C. A., Caldwell, D. F., & Barnett, W. P. (1989). Work group demography, social integration, and turnover. *Administrative Science Quarterly, 34,* 21–37.

Padgitt, S. C., & Padgitt, J. S. (1986). Cognitive structure of sexual harassment: Implications for university policy. *Journal of College Student Personnel, 27*(1), 34–39.

Paludi, M. (1990). Psychosocial and structural factors related to women's vocational development. *Annals of the New York Academy of Sciences, 602,* 157–168.

Paul, E. A. (1985). Wounded healers: A summary of the Vietnam Nurse Veteran Project. *Military Medicine, 150*(11), 571–576.

Pedersen, P. (1983). Learning about the Chinese culture through the Chinese language. *Communication & Cognition, 16,* 403–412.

Pelto, P. J. (1968, April). The difference between "tight" and "loose" societies. *Transaction,* 37–40.

Pepitone, A., & Triandis, H. C. (1987). On the universality of social psychological theories. *Journal of Cross-Cultural Psychology, 18,* 471–498.

Perdue, C. W., Dovidio, J. F., Gurtman, M. B., & Tyler, R. B. (1990). Us and them: Social categorization and the process of intergroup bias. *Journal of Personality and Social Psychology, 59,* 475–486.

Peters, T. J., & Waterman, R. H., Jr. (1982). *In search of excellence: Lessons from America's best-run companies.* New York: Warner.

Peterson, M. L. (1988). Positive social identity among homosexuals: An intergroup identity approach to minority stress. (Doctoral dissertation, University of Illinois at Chicago). *Dissertation Abstracts International, 49,* 12B, 5573.

Pettigrew, T. F. (1986). The intergroup contact hypothesis reconsidered. In M. Hewstone & R. Brown (Eds.), *Contact and conflict in intergroup encounters.* Oxford, England: Blackwell.

Pettigrew, T. F., & Martin, J. (1987). Shaping the organizational context for Black American inclusion. *Journal of Social Issues, 43*(1), 41–78.

Pettigrew, T. P. (1959). The demography of desegregation. *Journal of Social Issues, 15,* 61–71.

Petty, M. M., & Lee, G. K. (1975). Moderating effects of sex of supervisor and subordinate on relationships between supervisory behavior and subordinate satisfaction. *Journal of Applied Psychology, 60,* 624–628.

Petty, M. M., & Miles, R. H. (1976). Leader sex-role stereotyping in a female-dominated work culture. *Personnel Psychology, 29,* 393–404.

Phelps, R. E., Meara, N. W., Davis, K. L., & Patton, M. J. (1991). Blacks' and whites' perceptions of verbal aggression. *Journal of Counseling and Development, 69,* 345–350.

Popovich, P. M., & Licata, B. J. (1987). A role model approach to sexual harassment. *Journal of Management, 13*(1), 149–161.

Popovich, P. M., Licata, B. J., Nokovich, D., Martelli, T., & Zoloty, S. (1986). Assessing the incidence and perceptions of sexual harassment behaviors among American undergraduates. *Journal of Psychology, 120*(4), 387–396.

Powell, G. N. (1986). Effects of sex role identity and sex on definitions of sexual harassment. *Sex Roles, 14*(1/2), 9–19.

Pryor, J. B., & Day, J. D. (1988). Interpretations of sexual harassment: An attributional analysis. *Sex Roles, 13*(7/8), 405–417.

Quinn, R. E., & Lees, P. L. (1984). Attraction and harassment: Dynamics of sexual politics in the workplace. *Organizational Dynamics, 13*(2), 36–46.

Rabby, R. (1983). Employment of the disabled in large corporations. *International Labour Review, 122,* 23–36.

Ragins, B. R. (1989). Barriers to mentoring: The female manager's dilemma. *Human Relations, 42*(1), 1–22.

Ragins, B. R., & Cotton, J. L. (1991). Easier said than done: Gender differences in perceived barriers to gaining a mentor. *Academy of Management Journal, 34*(4), 939–951.

Ragins, B. R., & McFarlin, D. B. (1990). Perceptions of mentor roles in cross-gender mentoring relationships. *Journal of Vocational Behavior, 37*(3), 321–339.

Ragins, B. R., & Sundstrom, E. (1989). Gender and power in organizations: A longitudinal perspective. *Psychological Bulletin, 105*(1), 51–88.

Reardon, P. T. (1991, October 11). Family support is linked to jobs: Close ties give Mexican immigrants an edge, poverty study says. *Chicago Tribune*, Section 1, p. 3.

Reich, M. H. (1985). Executive views from both sides of mentoring. *Personnel, 62*(3) 42–46.

Reid, P. T., & Comas-Diaz, L. (1990). Gender and ethnicity: Perspectives on dual status. *Sex Roles, 22*(7/8), 397–408.

Ridgeway, C. L. (1982). Status in groups: The importance of motivation. *American Sociology Review, 47*, 76–88.

Roche, G. (1979). Much ado about mentors. *Harvard Business Review, 57*(1), 14–28.

Rogers, E., & Bhowmik, D. K. (1971). Homophily-heterophily: Relational concepts for communication research. In L. Barker & E. Kibler (Eds.), *Speech communication behavior: Perspectives and principles*. New York: McGraw-Hill.

Rohner, R. (1981). Toward a concept of culture for cross-cultural psychology. *Journal of Cross-Cultural Psychology, 15*, 111–138.

Rokeach, M., & Mezei, L. (1966). Race and shared belief as factors in social choice. *Science, 151*, 167–172.

Rosen, B., Miguel, M., & Peirce, E. (1989). Stemming the exodus of women managers. *Human Resource Management, 28*(4), 475–491.

Rosen, B., Templeton, N. C., & Kichline, K. (1981). First few years on the job: Women in management. *Business Horizons, 24*, 26–29.

Rosener, J. B. (1991, November–December). Ways women lead. *Harvard Business Review*, 119–125.

Ross, L. (1977). The intuitive psychologist and his shortcomings. In L. Berkowitz (Ed.), *Advances in experimental social psychology* (Vol. 10, pp. 174–221). New York: Academic Press.

Ross, L., Greene, D., & House, P. (1977). The false consensus effect: An egocentric bias in social perception and attribution processes. *Journal of Experimental Social Psychology, 13*, 279–301.

Ross, L., & Nisbett, R. (1991). *The person and the situation*. New York: McGraw-Hill.

Ross, M. W. (1978). The relationship of perceived social hostility, conformity and psychological adjustment in homosexual males. *Journal of Homosexuality, 4*, 157–168.

Ross, M. W. (1989). Gay youth in four cultures: A comparative study. *Journal of Homosexuality, 17*(3–4), 299–314.

Ross, M. W. (1990). The relationship between life events and mental health in homosexual men. *Journal of Clinical Psychology, 46*, 402–411.

Rowland, D. (1985). *Japanese business etiquette*. New York: Warner Books.

Rubinstein, M. (1988). *The dignity of women at work: A report on the problem of sexual harassment in the member states of the European Communities*. Luxembourg: Office for Official Publications of the European Communities.

Ryan, A. S., & Hendricks, C. O. (1989). Culture and communication: Supervising the Asian and Hispanic social worker. *Clinical Supervisor, 7*(1), 27–40.

Sackett, P. R., DuBois, L. Z., & Noe, A. W. (1991). Tokenism in performance evaluation: The effects of work group representation on male-female and white-black differences in performance ratings. *Journal of Applied Psychology, 76*(2), 263–267.

Safran, C. (1976, November). What men do to women on the job: A shocking look at sexual harassment. *Redbook, 149*, 217–224.

Samovar, L., & Porter, R. (Eds.). (1988). *Intercultural communication: A reader*. Belmont, CA: Wadsworth.

Schein, E. H. (1990). Organizational culture. *American Psychologist, 45*(2), 109–119.

Schein, V. E. (1973). The relationship between sex-role stereotypes and requisite management characteristics. *Journal of Applied Psychology, 57*, 95–100.

Schwartz, S. H. (in press). Universals in the content and structure of values: Theoretical advances and empirical tests in 20 countries. In M. Zanna (Ed.), *Advances in experimental social psychology*. New York: Academic Press.

Segall, M. H., Dasen, P. R., Berry, J. W., & Poortinga, Y. H. (1990). *Human behavior in global perspective*. New York: Pergamon Press.

Shaw, M. E. (1981). *Group dynamics: The psychology of small group behavior.* New York: McGraw-Hill.

Sherif, M., & Sherif, C. W. (1969). *Social psychology* (Rev. ed.). New York: Harper & Row.

Shweder, R., & LeVine, R. A. (1984) *Culture theory.* Cambridge, England: Cambridge University Press.

Simon, H. A., & Daly, E. (1992). Sexual orientation and workplace rights: A potential land mine for employers? *Employee Relations Law Journal, 18*(1), 29–60.

Singer, M. R. (1987). *Intercultural communication: A perceptual approach.* Englewood Cliffs, NJ: Prentice-Hall.

Skinner, B. F. (1981). Selection by consequences. *Science, 213,* 501–504.

Smeltser, L. R., & Leap, T. L. (1988). An analysis of individual reactions to potentially offensive jokes in a work setting. *Human Relations, 41,* 295–304.

Social Security Administration. (1980). *Work disability in the United States: A chartbook* (SSA publication no. 13–11978). Washington, DC: U.S. Government Printing Office.

Solomon, R. (1980). The opponent process theory of acquired motivation. *American Psychologist, 35,* 691–712.

Stead, B. A., & Zinkhan, G. M. (1986). Service priority in department stores: The effects of customer gender and dress. *Sex Roles, 15*(11/12), 601–611.

Steiner, I. D. (1972). *Group process and productivity.* New York: Academic Press.

Stephan, C. W., & Stephan, W. G. (1992). Reducing intercultural anxiety through intercultural contact. *International Journal of Intercultural Relations, 16,* 89–106.

Stephan, W. G. (1985). Intergroup relations. In G. Lindzey & E. Aronson (Eds.), *Handbook of social psychology* (pp. 599–658). New York: Random House.

Stephan, W. G., Ageyev, V., Stephan, C. W., Abalakina, M., Stefanenko, T., & Coates-Shrider, L. (1993). *Measuring sterotypes: A comparision of methods using Russian and American samples.* Manuscript submitted for publication.

Stephan, W. G., & Stephan, C. W. (1984). The role of ignorance in intergroup relations. In N. Miller & M. B. Brewer (Eds.), *Desegregation: Groups in contact* (pp. 229–256). New York: Academic Press.

Stewart, T. A. (1991, December 16). Gay in corporate America. *Fortune,* 42–56.

Storey, B. (1991). History and homogeneity: Effects of perceptions of membership groups on interpersonal communication. *Communication Research, 18*(2), 199–221.

Stroh, L. K., Brett, J. M., & Reilly, A. H. (1992). All the right stuff: A comparison of female and male managers' careers' progression. *Journal of Applied Psychology, 77,* 251–260.

Sue, S., Zane, N. W. S., & Sue, D. (1985). Where are all the Asian American leaders and top executives? *P/AAMHRC Review, 4,* 13–15.

Tajfel, H. (1974). Social identity and intergroup behavior. *Social Science Information, 13,* 65–93.

Tajfel, H., & Turner, J. (1979). An integrative theory of intergroup conflict. In W. G. Austin & S. Worchel (Eds.), *The social psychology of intergroup relations* (pp. 33–47). Monterey: Brooks/Cole.

Tajfel, H., & Turner, J. (1986). The social identity theory of intergroup behavior. In S. Worchel & W. G. Austin (Eds.), *Psychology of intergroup relations* (2nd ed., pp. 7–25). Chicago: Nelson-Hall.

Tangri, S. S., Burt, M. R., & Johnson, L. B. (1982). Sexual harassment at work: Three explanatory models. *Journal of Social Issues, 38*(4), 33–54.

Tannen, D. (1990). *You just don't understand: Women and men in conversation.* New York: Morrow.

Taylor, S. E., Fiske, S. T., Etcoff, N. L,. & Ruderman, A. J. (1978). Categorical and contextual basis of person memory and stereotyping. *Journal of Personality and Social Psychology, 36,* 778–793.

Terborg, J. R., Castore, C., & DeNinno, J. A. (1976). A longitudinal field investigation of the impact of group composition on group performance and cohesion. *Journal of Personality & Social Psychology, 34,* 782–790.

Thernstrom, S. (1980). *Harvard encyclopedia of ethnic diversity and American ethnic groups.* Cambridge, MA: Harvard University.

Thomas, D. A. (1990). The impact of race on managers' experiences of developmental relationships. *Journal of Organizational Behavior, 11*(6), 479–492.

Torrance, E. P. (1957). Group decision making and disagreement. *Social Forces, 35,* 314–318.

Triandis, H. C. (1959). Cognitive similarity and interpersonal communication in industry. *Journal of Applied Psychology, 43,* 321–326.

Triandis, H. C. (1960a). Cognitive similarity and communication in a dyad. *Human Relations, 13,* 175–183.

Triandis, H. C. (1960b). Some determinants of interpersonal communication. *Human Relations, 13,* 279–287.

Triandis, H. C. (1967). Toward an analysis of the components of interpersonal attitudes. In C. Sherif & M. Sherif (Eds.), *Attitudes, ego involvement, and change* (pp. 227–270). New York: Wiley.

Triandis, H. C. (1971). *Attitude and attitude change.* New York: Wiley.

Triandis, H. C. (1972). *The analysis of subjective culture.* New York: Wiley.

Triandis, H. C. (1975). Culture training, cognitive complexity and interpersonal attitudes. In R. Brislin, S. Bochner, & W. Lonner (Eds.), *Cross-cultural perspectives on learning* (pp. 39–77). Beverly Hills, Sage.

Triandis, H. C. (1976a). The future of pluralism. *Journal of Social Issues, 32,* 179–208. Reproduced also in G. K. Verma (Ed.), *Multicultural education* and in P. Katz & D. A. Taylor (Eds.), *Eliminating racism: Profiles in controversy* (pp. 31–50). New York: Plenum.

Triandis, H. C. (1976b). *Variations in black and white perceptions of the social environment.* Urbana: University of Illinois Press.

Triandis, H. C. (1977a). *Interpersonal behavior.* Monterey, CA: Brooks/Cole.

Triandis, H. C. (1977b). Theoretical framework for the evaluation of cross-cultural training effectiveness. *International Journal of Intercultural Relations, 1,* 19–45.

Triandis, H. C. (1988a). Collectivism and individualism: A reconceptualization of a basic concept in cross-cultural psychology. In G. K. Verma & C. Bargley (Eds.)., *Personality, attitudes, and cognitions* (pp. 60–95). London: Macmillan.

Triandis, H. C. (1988b). Cross-cultural contributions to theory in social psychology. In M. Bond (Ed.), *The cross-cultural challenge to social psychology* (pp. 122–140). Newbury Park, CA: Sage.

Triandis, H. C. (1989). The self and social behavior in differing cultural context. *Psychological Review, 96,* 506–520.

Triandis, H. C. (1990). Cross-cultural studies of individualism and collectivism. In J. Berman (Ed.), *Nebraska Symposium on Motivation, 1989* (pp. 44–133). Lincoln: University of Nebraska Press.

Triandis, H. C. (1993). Theoretical and methodological approaches in the study of collectivism and individualism. In U. Kim, H. C. Triandis, & G. Yoon (Eds.), *Individualism and collectivism: Theoretical and methodological issues.* Newbury Park, CA: Sage.

Triandis, H. C., Bontempo, R., Villareal, M., Asai, M., & Lucca, N. (1988). Individualism-collectivism: Cross cultural perspectives on self-ingroup relationships. *Journal of Personality and Social Psychology, 54,* 323–338.

Triandis, H. C., Bontempo, R., et al. (1986). The measurement of etic aspects of individualism and collectivism across cultures. *Australian Journal of Psychology, 38,* 257–267.

Triandis, H. C., Hall, E. R., & Ewen, R. B. (1965). Member heterogeneity and dyadic creativity. *Human Relations, 18,* 33–55.

Triandis, H. C., Hui, C. H., Albert, R. D., Leung, S., Lisansky, J., Diaz-Loving, R., Plascencia, L., Marin, G., Betancourt, H., & Loyola-Cintron, L. (1984). Individual models of social behavior. *Journal of Personality and Social Psychology, 46,* 1389–1404.

Triandis, H. C., Kashima, Y., Shimada, E., & Villareal, M. (1986). Acculturation indicies as a means of confirming cultural differences. *International Journal of Psychology, 21,* 43–70.

Triandis, H. C., Kurowski, L. L., Tecktiel, A., & Chan, K-S. (1993). Extracting the emics of diversity. *International Journal of Intercultural Relations.*

Triandis, H. C., Leung, K., Villareal, M., & Clack, F. L. (1985). Allocentric vs. idiocentric tendencies: Convergent and discriminant validation. *Journal of Research in Personality, 19,* 395–415.

Triandis, H. C., Marin, G., Lisansky, J., & Betancourt, H. (1984). *Simpatia* as a cultural script of Hispanics. *Journal of Personality and Social Psychology, 47,* 1363–1375.

Triandis, H. C., McCusker, C., & Hui, C. H. (1990). Multimethod probes of individualism and collectivism. *Journal of Personality and Social Psychology, 59,* 1006–1020.

Triandis, H. C., & Triandis, L. M. (1960). Race, social class, religion and nationality as determinants of social distance. *Journal of Abnormal and Social Psychology, 61,* 110–118.

Triandis, H. C., & Vassiliou, V. (1967). Frequency of contact and stereotyping. *Journal of Personality and Social Psychology, 7,* 316–328.

Tversky, A., & Kahneman, D. (1981). The framing of decisions and the psychology of choice. *Science, 21,* 453–458.

Vinson, E., & Holloway, M. (1977). The effects of formalization on perceptions of discrimination, effort and performance. *Journal of Vocational Behavior, 10,* 302–315.

Wacquant, L., & Wilson, W. J. (1989, January). The cost of racial and class exclusion in the inner city. *Annals of the American Academy of Political and Social Science, 501,* 8–25.

Ward, C., & Kennedy, A. (1992). Locus of control, mood disturbance, and social difficulty during cross-cultural transitions. *International Journal of Intercultural Relations, 16,* 175–194.

Weinberg, M. S. (1970). Homosexual samples: Differences and similarities. *Journal of Sex Research, 6,* 312–325.

Westie, F. R., & Westie, M. L. (1957). The social distance pyramid: Relationships between caste and class. *American Journal of Sociology, 63,* 190–196.

Whitely, W., Dougherty, T. W., & Dreher, G. F. (1991). Relationship of career mentoring and socioeconomic origin to managers' and professionals' early career progress. *Academy of Management Journal, 34*(2), 331–351.

Whitely, W., Dougherty, T. W., & Dreher, G. F. (1992). Correlates of career-oriented mentoring for early career managers and professionals. *Journal of Organizational Behavior, 13,* 141–154.

Whiting, B., & Whiting, J. W. M. (1975). *Children of six cultures: A psychocultural analysis.* Cambridge, MA: Harvard University Press.

Whorf, B. J. (1952). *Collected papers on metalinguistics.* Washington, DC: Department of State, Foreign Service Institute.

Wickham, J. (1976) Introduction. In C. Offe, *Industry and inequality: The achievement principle in work and social status* (pp. 1–10). London: Edward Arnold.

Willems, E. P., & Clark, R. D., III. (1971). Shift toward risk and heterogeneity of groups. *Journal of Experimental Social Psychology, 7,* 304–312.

Wood, J. T., & Conrad, C. (1983). Paradox in the experiences of professional women. *Western Journal of Speech Communication, 47,* 305–322.

Woolsey, C. (1991a, April 22). Tailor substance abuse care to meet special needs: Experts. *Business Insurance, 24.*

Woolsey, C. (1991b, October 7). Digital pioneers program to fight AIDS, ignorance. *Business Insurance, 80.*

Worchel, S. (1986). The role of cooperation in reducing intergroup conflict. In S. Worchel & W. G. Austin (Eds.), *Psychology of intergroup relations* (pp. 288–304). Chicago: Nelson-Hall.

Yoder, J. D. (1985). An academic woman as a token: A case study. *Journal of Social Issues, 41*(4), 61–72.

Yoder, J. D., Adams, J., Grove, S., & Priest, R. F. (1985). To teach is to learn: Overcoming tokenism with mentors. *Psychology of Women Quarterly, 9*(1), 119–131.

Yuker, H. E. (1988). The effects of contact on attitudes toward disabled persons: Some empirical generalizations. In H. E. Yuker (Ed.), *Attitudes towards persons with disabilities* (pp. 262–274). New York: Springer.

Yukl, G. A. (1981). *Leadership in organizations.* Englewood Cliffs, NJ: Prentice Hall.

Zamarripa, P. O., & Krueger, D. L. (1983). Implicit contracts regulating small group leadership. The influence of culture. *Small Group Behavior, 14,* 187–210.

Zane, N. W. S., Sue, S., Hu, L., & Kwon, J-H. (1991). Asian-American assertion: A social learning analysis of cultural differences. *Journal of Counseling Psychology, 38*(1), 63–70.

Zangwill, I. (1914) *The melting pot: Drama in four acts.* New York: Macmillan.

Zeleny, L. D. (1955). Validity of a sociometric hypothesis—the function of creativity in interpersonal and group relations. *Sociometry, 18,* 439–449.

Name Index

Subject Index